Recommended by **Teachers**
Trusted by **Toppers**

All in One

APPLIED MATHEMATICS
Class 12

EVERYTHING YOU NEED TO SCORE

- Simplified Theory
- Topic & Chapter Exercises
- CBQs; MCQs, A-R, Case Based
- Board Questions Upto 2025
- Sample Question Papers

CBSE Exams 2026

Authors
Laxman Prasad
Brijesh Dwevedi

arihant
SUCCESS AND NOTHING LESS

ARIHANT PRAKASHAN
(School Division Series)

ADMINISTRATIVE & PRODUCTION OFFICES

Regd. Office

'Ramchhaya' 4577/15, Agarwal Road, Darya Ganj, New Delhi -110002
Tele: 011- 47630600, 43518550; Fax: 011- 23280316

Head Office

Kalindi, TP Nagar, Meerut (UP) - 250002, Tel: 0121-7156203, 7156204

SALES & SUPPORT OFFICES

Agra, Ahmedabad, Bengaluru, Bareilly, Chennai, Delhi, Guwahati, Hyderabad, Jaipur, Jhansi, Kolkata, Lucknow, Nagpur & Pune.

PO No : TXT-XX-XXXXXXX-X-XX

Published By Arihant Publications (India) Ltd.

For further information about the books published by Arihant, log on to www.arihantbooks.com or e-mail at info@arihantbooks.com

Follow us on

PRICE ₹475.00

PRODUCTION TEAM

Publishing Managers	Cover Designer	Inner Designer
Mahendra Singh Rawat & Keshav Mohan	Salman Shaikh	Ankit Tyagi
Project Head	**Page Layouting**	**Proof Reader**
Ashwani	Shivam Prajapati	Mukul Khosisk

Index *cum* Study Planner

Latest Course Structure

Grade XII (2025-26)

Number of Paper: 1
Total number of Periods: 240 (35 Minutes Each)
Time: 3 Hours
Max Marks: 80

No.	Units	No. of Periods	Marks
I.	Numbers, Quantification and Numerical Applications	30	11
II.	Algebra	20	10
III.	Calculus	50	15
IV.	Probability Distributions	35	10
V.	Inferential Statistics	10	05
VI.	Time-based data	30	06
VII.	Financial Mathematics	50	15
VIII.	Linear Programming	15	08
	Total	**240**	80
	Internal Assessment		20

Sl.No	Contents	Learning Outcomes: Students will be able to	Notes/Explanation
UNIT-1 NUMBERS, QUANTIFICATION AND NUMERICAL APPLICATIONS			
1.1	Modulo Arithmetic	• Define modulus of an integer • Apply arithmetic operations using modular arithmetic rules	• Definition and meaning • Introduction to modulo operator • Modular addition and subtraction
1.2	Congruence Modulo	• Define congruence modulo • Apply the definition in various problems	• Definition and meaning • Solution using congruence modulo • Equivalence class
1.3	Alligation and Mixture	• Understand the rule of alligation to produce a mixture at a given price • Determine the mean price of a mixture • Apply rule of alligation	• Meaning and Application of rule of alligation • Mean price of a mixture

1.4	Numerical Problems	Solve real life problems mathematically	
	Boats and Streams (upstream and downstream)	• Distinguish between upstream and downstream • Express the problem in the form of an equation	• Problems based on speed of stream and the speed of boat in still water
	Pipes and Cisterns	• Determine the time taken by two or more pipes to fill or empty the tank	• Calculation of the portion of the tank filled or drained by the pipe(s) in unit time
	Races and Games	• Compare the performance of two players w.r.t. time, distance	• Calculation of the time taken/ distance covered / speed of each player
1.5	Numerical Inequalities	• Describe the basic concepts of numerical inequalities • Understand and write numerical inequalities	• Comparison between two statements/situations which can be compared numerically • Application of the techniques of numerical solution of algebraic inequations

UNIT-2 ALGEBRA

2.1	Matrices and types of matrices	• Define matrix • Identify different kinds of matrices • Find the size / order of matrices	• The entries, rows and columns of matrices • Present a set of data in a matrix form
2.2	Equality of matrices, Transpose of a matrix, Symmetric and Skew symmetric matrix	• Determine equality of two matrices • Write transpose of given matrix • Define symmetric and skew symmetric matrix	• Examples of transpose of matrix • A square matrix as a sum of symmetric and skew symmetric matrix • Observe that diagonal elements of skew symmetric matrices are always zero
2.3	Algebra of Matrices	• Perform operations like addition & subtraction on matrices of same order • Perform multiplication of two matrices of appropriate order • Perform multiplication of a scalar with matrix	• Addition and Subtraction of matrices • Multiplication of matrices (It can be shown to the students that matrix multiplication is similar to multiplication of two polynomials) • Multiplication of a matrix with a real number
2.4	Determinants	• Find determinant of a square matrix	• Singular matrix, Non-singular matrix • $\|AB\|=\|A\|\|B\|$ • Simple problems to find determinant value

2.5	Inverse of a matrix	• Define the inverse of a square matrix • Apply properties of inverse of matrices	• Inverse of a matrix using cofactors If A and B are invertible square matrices of same size, (i) $(AB)^{-1} = B^{-1}A^{-1}$ (ii) $(A^{-1})^{-1} = A$ (iii) $(A^T)^{-1} = (A^{-1})^T$
2.6	Solving system of simultaneous equations using matrix method and Cramer's rule	• Solve the system of simultaneous equations using (i) Cramer's Rule (ii) Inverse of coefficient matrix • Formulate real life problems into a system of simultaneous linear equations and solve it using these methods	• Solution of system of simultaneous equations upto three variables only (non- homogeneous equations)

UNIT-3 CALCULUS

Differentiation and its Applications

3.1	Derivative upto second order	• Determine derivatius up to second order • Understand differentiation of parametric functions and implicit functions	• Simple problems based on second order derivatives • Differentiation of parametric functions and implicit functions (upto 2nd order)
3.2	Application of Derivatives	• Determine the rate of change of various quantities	• To find the rate of change of quantities such as area and volume with respect to time or its dimension
3.3	Marginal Cost and Marginal Revenue using derivatives	• Define marginal cost and marginal revenue • Find marginal cost and marginal revenue	• Examples related to marginal cost, marginal revenue, etc.
3.4	Increasing / Decreasing Functions	• Determine whether a function is increasing or decreasing • Determine the conditions for a function to be increasing or decreasing	• Simple problems related to increasing and decreasing behaviour of a function in the given interval

3.5	Maxima and Minima	• Determine critical points of the function • Find the point(s) of local maxima and local minima and corresponding local maximum and local minimum values • Find the absolute maximum and absolute minimum value of a function • Solve applied problems related to optimizations of cost, revenue and profit only.	• A point $x = c$ is called the critical point of f if f is defined at c and $f'(c) = 0$ or f is not differentiable at c • To find local maxima and local minima by: (i) First Derivative Test (ii) Second Derivative Test • Contextualized real life problems

Integration and its Applications

3.6	Integration	• Understand and determine indefinite integrals of simple functions as anti-derivative	• Integration as a reverse process of differentiation • Vocabulary and Notations related to Integration
3.7	Indefinite Integrals as family of curves	• Evaluate indefinite integrals of simple algebraic functions by method of: (i) substitution (ii) partial fraction (iii) by parts	• Simple integrals based on each method (non-trigonometric function)
3.8	Definite Integrals as area under the curve	• Define definite integral as area under the curve • Understand fundamental theorem of Integral calculus and apply it to evaluate the definite integral	• Evaluation of area under simple algebraic curves upto 2nd degree
3.9	Application of Integration	• Identify the region representing C.S. and P.S. graphically • Apply the definite integral to find consumer surplus-producer surplus	Problems based on finding • Total cost when Marginal Cost is given • Total Revenue when Marginal Revenue is given • Equilibrium price and equilibrium quantity and hence consumer and producer surplus

Differential Equations and Modeling

3.10	Differential Equations	• Recognize a differential equation • Find the order and degree of a differential equation	• Definition, order, degree and examples
3.11	Formulating and Solving Differential Equations	• Formulate differential equation • Verify the solution of differential equation • Solve simple differential equation using variable separable method only	• Formation of differential equation by eliminating arbitrary constants • Solution of simple differential equations (direct integration only)

UNIT- 4 PROBABILITY DISTRIBUTIONS

4.1	Probability Distribution	• Understand the concept of Random Variables and its Probability Distributions • Find probability distribution of discrete random variable	• Definition and example of discrete and continuous random variable and their distribution
4.2	Mathematical Expectation	• Apply arithmetic mean of frequency distribution to find the expected value of a random variable	• The expected value of discrete random variable as summation of product of discrete random variable by the probability of its occurrence.
4.3	Variance	• Calculate the Variance and S.D. of a random variable	• Questions based on variance and standard deviation
4.4	Binomial Distribution	• Identify the Bernoulli Trials and apply Binomial Distribution • Evaluate Mean, Variance and S.D of a binomial distribution	• Characteristics of the binomial distribution • Binomial formula: $P(r) = {}^nC_r p^r q^{n-r}$ Where, n = Number of trials P = Probability of success q = Probability of failure Mean $= np$ Variance $= npq$ Standard Deviation $= \sqrt{npq}$
4.5	Poison Distribution	• Understand the Conditions of Poisson Distribution • Evaluate the Mean and Variance of Poisson distribution	• Characteristics of Poisson Probability distribution Poisson formula: $P(x) = \frac{\lambda^x \cdot e^{-\lambda}}{x!}$ • Mean = Variance = λ

4.6	Normal Distribution	• Understand normal distribution is a Continuous distribution • Evaluate value of Standard normal variate • Area relationship between Mean and Standard Deviation	• Characteristics of a normal probability distribution • Total area under the curve = total probability = 1 • Standard Normal Variate $Z = \frac{x-\mu}{\sigma}$, where x = value of the random variable μ = mean σ = S.D.

UNIT-5 INFERENTIAL STATISTICS

5.1	Population and Sample	• Define Population and Sample • Differentiate between population and sample • Define a representative sample from a population • Differentiate between a representative and non-representative sample • Draw a representative sample using simple random sampling • Draw a representative sample using and systematic random sampling	• Population data from census, economic surveys and other contexts from practical life • Examples of drawing more than one sample set from the same population • Examples of representative and non-representative sample • Unbiased and biased sampling • Problems based on random sampling using simple random sampling and systematic random sampling (sample size less than 100)
5.2	Parameter and Statistics and Statistical Interferences	• Define Parameter with reference to Population • Define Statistics with reference to Sample • Explain the relation between Parameter and Statistic • Explain the limitation of Statistic to generalize the estimation for population • Interpret the concept of Statistical Significance and Statistical Inferences • State Central Limit Theorem • Explain the relation between Population-Sampling Distribution-Sample	• Conceptual understanding of Parameter and Statistics • Examples of Parameter and Statistic limited to Mean and Standard deviation only • Examples to highlight limitations of generalizing results from sample to population • Only conceptual understanding of Statistical Significance/Statistical Inferences • Only conceptual understanding of Sampling Distribution through simulation and graphs

5.3	t-Test (one sample t-test and two independent groups t-test)	• Define a hypothesis • Differentiate between Null and Alternate hypothesis • Define and calculate degree of freedom • Test Null hypothesis and make inferences using t-test statistic for one group / two independent groups	• Examples and non-examples of Null and Alternate hypothesis (only non-directional alternate hypothesis) • Framing of Null and Alternate hypothesis • Testing a Null Hypothesis to make Statistical Inferences for small sample size • (for small sample size: *t*- test for one group)

UNIT-6 TIME BASED DATA

6.1	Time Series	• Identify time series as chronological data	• Meaning and Definition
6.2	Components of Time Series	• Distinguish between different components of time series	• Secular trend • Seasonal variation • Cyclical variation • Irregular variation
6.3	Time Series analysis for univariate data	• Solve practical problems based on statistical data and Interpret the result	• Fitting a straight line trend and estimating the value
6.4	Secular Trend	• Understand the long term tendency	• The tendency of the variable to increase or decrease over a long period of time
6.5	Methods of Measuring trend	• Demonstrate the techniques of finding trend by different methods	• Moving Average method • Method of Least Squares

UNIT-7 FINANCIAL MATHEMATICS

7.1	Perpetuity, Sinking Funds	• Explain the concept of perpetuity and sinking fund • Calculate perpetuity • Differentiate between sinking fund and saving account	• Meaning of Perpetuity and Sinking Fund • Real life examples of sinking fund • Advantages of Sinking Fund • Sinking Fund vs. Savings account
7.2	Valuation of Bonds	• Define the concept of valuation of bond and related terms. • Calculate value of bond using present value approach	• Meaning of Bond Valuation • Terms related to valuation of bond : Coupon rate, Maturity rate and Current price • Bond Valuation Method : Present Value Approach
7.3	Calculation of EMI	• Explain the concept of EMI • Calculate EMI using various methods	• Methods to calculate EMI: (i) Flat-Rate Method (ii) Reducing-Balance Method • Real life examples to calculate EMI of various types of loans, purchase of assets, etc.

7.4	Compound Annual Growth Rate	• Understand the concept of Compound Annual Growth Rate • Differentiate between Compound Annual Growth Rate and Annual Growth Rate • Calculate Compound Annual Growth Rate	• Meaning and use of Compound Annual Growth Rate • Formula for Compound Annual Growth Rate
7.5	Linear method of Depreciation	• Define the concept of linear method of Depreciation • Interpret cost, residual value and useful life of an asset from the given information • Calculate depreciation	• Meaning and formula for Linear Method of Depreciation • Advantages and disadvantages of Linear Method

UNIT-8 LINEAR PROGRAMMING

8.1	Introduction and related terminology	• Familiarize with terms related to Linear Programming Problem	• Need for framing linear programming problem • Definition of Decision Variable, Constraints, Objective function, Optimization and Non Negative conditions
8.2	Mathematical formulation of Linear Programming Problem	• Formulate Linear Programming Problem upto 3 non-trival constraints	• Set the problem in terms of decision variables, identify the objective function, identify the set of problem constraints, express the problem in terms of inequations
8.3	Different types of Linear Programming Problems	• Identify and formulate different types of LPP	• Formulate various types of LPP's like Manufacturing Problem, Diet Problem.
8.4	Graphical method of solution for problems in two variables	• Draw the Graph for a system of linear inequalities involving two variables and to find its solution graphically	• Corner Point Method for the Optimal solution of LPP
8.5	Feasible and Infeasible Regions	• Identify feasible, infeasible, bounded and unbounded regions	• Definition and Examples to explain the terms
8.6	Feasible and infeasible solutions, optimal feasible solution	• Understand feasible and infeasible solutions • Find optimal feasible solution	• Problems based on optimization • Examples of finding the solutions by graphical method

CHAPTER **01**

Modulo Arithmetic

In this Chapter...

- Modulo Arithmetic
- Congruence Modulo

Modulo Arithmetic

Modulo Arithmetic considers the remainder when an integer is divided by another integer.

When we divide an integer a by another integer b, we have $a = bq + r$, where $q, r \in I$ and $0 \le r \le |b|$. Hence, a is dividend, b is divisor, q is quotient and r is remainder.

Modulo Arithmetic can be expressed as

$$a \bmod b = r$$

e.g. When 10 is divided by 3, the remainder is 1. Mathematically we write as,

$$10 \bmod 3 = 1$$

Remark When an integer (a) is divided by another positive integer (b), then remainder may be 0, 1, 2, 3, ..., $(b-1)$ i.e. $a \bmod b = \{0, 1, 2, \dots, (b-1)\}$

Properties of Modulo Arithmetic

(i) $(a \bmod n) \bmod n = a \bmod n$

(ii) $n^x \bmod n = 0$ for all positive integer value of x

(iii) $(a + b) \bmod n = [(a \bmod n) + (b \bmod n)] \bmod n$

(iv) $ab \bmod n = [(a \bmod n)\,(b \bmod n)] \bmod n$

(v) $(a \times b + c) \bmod n$

$= [(a \bmod n) \times (b \bmod n) + c \bmod n] \bmod n$

Divisors

Integer $b \ne 0$, is said to be a divisor of integer a, if there exists an integer q such that $a = bq$, we can write $\frac{b}{a}$.

It is noted that if $\frac{a}{m}$ and $\frac{a}{n}$, then

$$\frac{a}{(\lambda m + \mu n)}, \forall\, \lambda, \mu, \in Z$$

Some Properties of Divisors

Let $a, b, c, \dots, \in Z$, then

(i) Every non-zero integer is divisor of integer 0.

(ii) If $\frac{a}{a}, (a \ne 0)$

(iii) If $\frac{a}{b}$ and $\frac{b}{c} \Rightarrow \frac{a}{c}, a \ne 0$

(iv) If $\frac{a}{b} \Rightarrow \frac{-a}{b}, (a \ne 0)$

(v) Two non-zero integers are said to be associate if $\frac{a}{b}$ and $\frac{b}{a}$.

Prime Numbers

An integer $n \ge 2$ is said to be prime number if its only divisors are ± 1 and $\pm n$.

Twin Primes

If the difference of two prime numbers is 2. Then, these prime numbers are called twin primes.

e.g. 17 and 19 are the twin prime numbers.

Coprime Numbers

Two numbers are said to be coprime, if their gcd is 1.

e.g. 2 and 7 are coprime because gcd (2, 7) = 1

EXAMPLE 1. Evaluate the following.

(i) 8 mod 3 (ii) 17mod 5
(iii) −9 mod 2 (iv) −14 mod 7
(v) $(7+13)$ mod 11 (vi) $(57-42)$ mod11
(vii) (9×8) mod 13 (viii) 5 mod 9

Sol. (i) For finding 8 mod 3, we divide, 8 by 3

i.e. 3)8(2
6
2 (remainder)

∴ 8 mod 3 = 2

(ii) For finding 17 mod 5, we divide 17 by 5

i.e. 5)17(3
15
2 (remainder)

∴ 17 mod 5 = 2

(iii) For finding −9 mod 2, we divide −9 by 2

i.e. 2)−9(−5
−10
1 (remainder)

∴ −9 mod 2 = 1

(iv) For finding −14 mod 7, we divide −14 by 7

i.e. 7)−14(−2
− 14
0 (remainder)

∴ −14 mod 7 = 0

(v) For finding $(7+13)$ mod 11 i.e. 20 mod 11, we divide 20 by 11

i.e. 11)20(1
11
9 (remainder)

∴ $(7+13)$ mod 11 = 9

(vi) For finding $(57-42)$ mod 11 i.e. 15 mod 11, we divide 15 by 11

i.e. 11)15(1
11
4 (remainder)

∴ $(57-42)$ mod 11 = 4

(vii) For finding (9×8) mod 13 i.e. 72 mod 13, we divide 72 by 13

i.e. 13)72(5
65
7 (remainder)

∴ (9×8) mod 13 = 7

(viii) For finding 5 mod 9, we divide 5 by 9

i.e. 9)5(0
0
5 (remainder)

∴ 5 mod 9 = 5

Topic Practice 1

1 The product of two prime numbers is always
(a) prime (b) even (c) composite (d) odd

2 If $\frac{b}{a}$ and $\frac{c}{a}$ and $\gcd(b,c)=1$, then
(a) $\frac{a}{bc}$ (b) $\frac{bc}{a}$ (c) $\frac{ac}{b}$ (d) $\frac{c}{ab}$

3 Evaluate the following
(i) 9 mod 4 (ii) 62 mod 11
(iii) −15 mod 8 (iv) −100 mod 25
(v) $(21+15)$ mod 9 (vi) $(65-8)$ mod 21
(vii) (7×4) mod 5 (viii) 11 mod 20

Hints & Solutions

1. (c) The product of two prime numbers is always a composite number.
2. (b) If b divides to a and c divides to a, then bc divides to a.
$\Rightarrow \frac{bc}{a}$
3. (i) Solve as Example 1 (i). **Ans.** 1
(ii) Solve as Example 1 (i). **Ans.** 7
(iii) Solve as Example 1 (iii). **Ans.** 1
(iv) Solve as Example 1 (iii). **Ans.** 0
(v) Solve as Example 1 (v). **Ans.** 0
(vi) Solve as Example 1 (vi). **Ans.** 15
(vii) Solve as Example 1 (vii). **Ans.** 3
(viii) Solve as Example 1 (viii). **Ans.** 11

Congruence Modulo

If a and b are integers and $n > 0$, then $a \equiv b \pmod{n}$ implies when $a - b$ is completely divisible by n.

Hence, $a \equiv b \pmod{n}$ or $a \equiv b$ (modulo n) can be read as a is congruent to b modulo n.

If $a \equiv b \pmod{n}$, then

$\Rightarrow (a - b)$ is divisible by n.

$\Rightarrow \dfrac{(a-b)}{n}$ or $n \mid (a-b)$

$\Rightarrow$ There exists an integer q such that $(a - b) = nq$

$\Rightarrow a = b + nq$

Remark If a is not congruent to b modulo n, then we write

$$a \not\equiv b \pmod{n}$$

EXAMPLE 1. Check, which of the following statements are true?

(i) $19 \equiv 4 \pmod{5}$ (ii) $33 \equiv 6 \pmod{10}$

(iii) $25 \equiv 80 \pmod{9}$ (iv) $-9 \equiv 75 \pmod{12}$

Sol. (i) Given, $19 \equiv 4 \pmod{5}$

$\Rightarrow \dfrac{19-4}{5} = \dfrac{15}{5} = 3,$

which is an integer.

So, given statement is true.

(ii) Given, $33 \equiv 6 \pmod{10}$

$\Rightarrow \dfrac{33-6}{10} = \dfrac{27}{10} = 2.7,$

which is not integer.

So, given statement is not true.

(iii) Given, $25 \equiv 80 \pmod{9}$

$\Rightarrow \dfrac{25-80}{9} = \dfrac{-55}{9} = -6.1,$

which is not an integer.

So, given statement is not true.

(iv) Given, $-9 \equiv 75 \pmod{12}$

$\Rightarrow \dfrac{-9-75}{12} = \dfrac{-84}{12} = -7,$

which is an integer.

So, given statement is true.

EXAMPLE 2. If $140 \equiv 25 \pmod{x}$, then find the value of x.

Sol. Given, $140 \equiv 25 \pmod{x}$

$\Rightarrow 140 - 25$ is divisible by x.

$\Rightarrow 115$ is divisible by x.

$\Rightarrow x$ is a divisor of 115.

$\Rightarrow x = 5, 23, 115$

EXAMPLE 3. If x is an odd integer, prove that

$$x^2 \equiv 1 \pmod{8}.$$

Sol. Given, x is is an odd integer.

$\therefore \quad x = (2n+1)$, for $n \in Z$

$\Rightarrow \quad x^2 = 4n^2 + 1 + 4n$

$\Rightarrow \quad x^2 = 4n(n+1) + 1$

$\Rightarrow \quad x^2 - 1 = 4n(n+1)$ ...(i)

We know that the product of two consecutive integers is always even.

$\therefore \quad n(n+1) = 2\lambda, \lambda \in Z$ ...(ii)

From Eqs. (i) and (ii), we get

$$x^2 - 1 = 4(2\lambda) \Rightarrow x^2 - 1 = 8\lambda$$

$\Rightarrow x^2 - 1$ is divisible by 8.

$\Rightarrow x^2 \equiv 1 \pmod{8}$ **Hence proved.**

EXAMPLE 4. It is currently 10:00 am what time (in am or pm) will be in next 700 h?

Sol. Since, time repeats after every 24 h.

So, we find 700 (mod 24)

Now, $700 = 24 \times 29 + 4$

$\Rightarrow \quad 700 \equiv 4 \pmod{24}$

$\Rightarrow$ 700 h is equivalent to 4 h.

Hence, it will be 2:00 pm.

Properties of Congruences Modulo

Following are some useful properties of congruence modulo which are stated.

1. Let a, b be any two integers and m be a positive integers. Then,

(i) $a \equiv b \pmod{m} \Leftrightarrow a = b + mq, q \in Z$

(ii) $a \equiv b \pmod{m} \Leftrightarrow a$ and b have the same remainder when divided by m.

(iii) $a \equiv b \pmod{m} \Leftrightarrow -a \equiv -b \pmod{m}$

(iv) $a = 0 \bmod m \Leftrightarrow \dfrac{a}{m}$ or $m \mid a$

2. Let a, b, c be any three integers and m be a positive integer. Then,

(i) $a \equiv a \pmod{m}$

i.e. the relation 'Congruence modulo m' is reflexive.

(ii) $a \equiv b \pmod{m} \Rightarrow b \equiv a \pmod{m}$

i.e. the relation 'Congruence modulo m' is symmetric.

(iii) $a \equiv b \pmod m$ and $b \equiv c \pmod m$
$\Rightarrow a \equiv c \pmod m$
i.e. the relation 'Congruence modulo m' is transitive.

3. Properties of addition in congruence modulo
   (i) If $a + b = c$, then
   $$a \pmod m + b \pmod m = c \pmod m$$
   or $$(a+b) \pmod m = a \pmod m + b \pmod m$$
   (ii) If $a \equiv b \pmod m$, then
   $$(a+k) \equiv (b+k) \bmod m,\ \forall\, k \in Z.$$
   (iii) If $a \equiv b \pmod m$ and $c \equiv d \pmod m$, then
   $$(a+c) \equiv (b+d) \pmod m$$
4. Properties of multiplication in Congruence modulo
   (i) If $a \cdot b = c$, then $a \pmod m \cdot b \pmod m = c \pmod m$
   or $a \cdot b \pmod m = a \pmod m \cdot b \pmod m$
   (ii) If $a \equiv b \pmod m$, then
   $ka = kb \pmod m,\ \forall\, k \in Z$
   (iii) If $a \equiv b \pmod m$ and $c \equiv d \pmod m$, then
   $ac \equiv bd \pmod m$
   (iv) If $a \equiv b \pmod m$, then $a^k \equiv b^k \pmod m,\ \forall\, k \in N$.

EXAMPLE 5. Find the remainder when $672 + 541 + 383 + 295 + 101 + 86$ is divided by 3.

Sol. We have to find,

$$\begin{aligned}
&(672 + 541 + 383 + 295 + 101 + 86) \bmod 3\\
&= 672 \pmod 3 + 541 \pmod 3 + 383 \pmod 3\\
&\quad + 295 \pmod 3 + 101 \pmod 3 + 86 \pmod 3\\
&= 0 \pmod 3 + 1 \pmod 3 + 2 \pmod 3\\
&\quad + 1 \pmod 3 + 2 \pmod 3 + 2 \pmod 3\\
&= (0 + 1 + 2 + 1 + 2 + 2) \bmod 3\\
&= 8 \pmod 3\\
&= 2 \pmod 3
\end{aligned}$$

Hence, the remainder when $672 + 541 + 383 + 295 + 101 + 86$ is divided by 3 is 2.

EXAMPLE 6. Find the remainder when $862 \times 783 \times 671 \times 549 \times 411 \times 395 \times 217$ is divided by 8.

Sol. We have to find,

$$\begin{aligned}
&(862 \times 783 \times 671 \times 549 \times 411 \times 395 \times 217) \bmod 8\\
&= 862 \bmod 8 \times 783 \bmod 8 \times 671 \bmod 8\\
&\quad \times 549 \bmod 8 \times 411 \bmod 8 \times 395 \bmod 8\\
&\quad \times 217 \bmod 8\\
&= 6 \pmod 8 \times 7 \pmod 8 \times 7 \pmod 8\\
&\quad \times 5 \pmod 8 \times 3 \pmod 8 \times 3 \pmod 8 \times 1 \pmod 8\\
&= (6 \times 7 \times 7 \times 5 \times 3 \times 3 \times 1) \bmod 8\\
&= (42 \times 35 \times 9) \bmod 8\\
&= 42 \pmod 8 \times 35 \pmod 8 \times 9 \pmod 8\\
&= 2 \pmod 8 \times 3 \pmod 8 \times 1 \pmod 8\\
&= (2 \times 3 \times 1) \bmod 8\\
&= 6 \bmod 8
\end{aligned}$$

Hence, the remainder when $(862 \times 783 \times 671 \times 549 \times 411 \times 395 \times 217)$ is divided by 8 is 6.

EXAMPLE 7. Find the last three-digits of the product 31234×26875.

Sol. To find the last three-digits of the product 31234×26875, we find

$$31234 \times 26875 \pmod{1000}$$

Using the property,

$$a \times b \pmod n = [a \bmod n \times b \bmod n] \bmod n$$

$$\begin{aligned}
&31234 \times 26875 \pmod{1000}\\
&= [31234 \bmod 1000 \times 26875 \bmod 1000] \bmod 1000\\
&= [234 \times 875] \bmod 1000\\
&= [204750] \bmod 1000 = 750
\end{aligned}$$

EXAMPLE 8. Find the value of $6^{12} \pmod 7$.

Sol. We know that

$$a \equiv b \pmod m, \text{ then } a^k \equiv b^k \bmod m$$

Now, $6 \pmod 7 = -1 \pmod 7$

$\Rightarrow\ 6^{12} \pmod 7 \equiv (-1)^{12} \pmod 7$

$\Rightarrow\ 6^{12} \bmod 7 \equiv 1 \bmod 7$

$\therefore\ 6^{12} \bmod 7 \equiv 1$

EXAMPLE 9. Find the remainder when

(i) 2^{150} is divided by 5 (ii) 3^{2100} is divided by 7

(iii) 5^{100} is divided by 9 (iv) 7^{40} is divided by 5

Sol. (i) We know that

$$a \equiv b \pmod m,\ 0 \le b < m$$

b is the remainder when a is divided by m.

Now, $2^1 \equiv 2 \pmod 5$

$\Rightarrow\ 2^2 \equiv 4 \pmod 5$

$\Rightarrow\ 2^2 \equiv -1 \pmod 5$

$\Rightarrow\ 2^3 \equiv -1 \pmod 5$

$\Rightarrow\ (2^3)^{50} \equiv (-1)^{50} \pmod 5$

$\Rightarrow\ 2^{150} \equiv 1 \pmod 5$

Hence, 1 is the remainder when 2^{150} is divided by 5.

(ii) We have, $3^1 \equiv 3 \pmod 7$

$\Rightarrow\ 3^2 \equiv 2 \pmod 7$

$\Rightarrow\ 3^3 \equiv 6 \pmod 7$

$\Rightarrow\ 3^3 \equiv -1 \pmod 7$

$\Rightarrow\ (3^3)^{700} \equiv (-1)^{700} \pmod 7$

$\Rightarrow\ 3^{2100} \equiv 1 \pmod 7$

Hence, 1 is the remainder when 3^{2100} is divided by 7.

(iii) We have, $5^1 \equiv 5 \pmod 9 \Rightarrow 5^2 \equiv 25 \pmod 9$

$\Rightarrow \quad 5^2 \equiv 7 \pmod 9 \Rightarrow 5^3 \equiv 35 \pmod 9$

$\Rightarrow \quad 5^3 \equiv -1 \pmod 9 \Rightarrow (5^3)^{33} \equiv (-1)^{33} \pmod 9$

$\Rightarrow \quad 5^{99} \equiv -1 \pmod 9 \Rightarrow 5^{100} \equiv -5 \pmod 9$

$\Rightarrow \quad 5^{100} \equiv 4 \pmod 9$

Hence, 4 is the remainder when 5^{100} is divided by 9.

(iv) We have, $7^1 \equiv 7 \pmod 5 \Rightarrow 7 \equiv 2 \pmod 5$

$\Rightarrow \quad 7^2 \equiv 14 \pmod 5 \Rightarrow 7^2 \equiv -1 \pmod 5$

$\Rightarrow \quad (7^2)^{20} \equiv (-1)^{20} \pmod 5 \Rightarrow 7^{40} \equiv 1 \pmod 5$

Hence, 1 is the remainder when 7^{40} is divided by 5.

Linear Congruence

A congruence of the form $ax \equiv b \pmod m$, where x is an unknown integer is called a linear congruence in one variable.

Note

(i) Let a, b and m be integer such that $m > 0$ and let $c = (a, m)$.
If c does not divide b, then the congruence $ax \equiv b \pmod m$ has no solution, if $\frac{c}{b}$, then $ax \equiv b \pmod m$ has exactly c incongruent solutions modulo m.

(ii) If $c = (a, m) = 1$, there is a unique solutions modulo m for the equation $ax \equiv b \pmod m$.

EXAMPLE 10. Solve $5x \equiv 4 \pmod 6$.

Sol. We have, $5x \equiv 4 \pmod 6$

$5x - 4$ is an integral multiple of 6.

$$5x - 4 = 6n \Rightarrow x = \frac{6n+4}{5}$$

When $n = 1, 6, 11, 16, \ldots\ldots$, then $6n + 4$ is divisible by 5.

If $n = 1$, $x = \dfrac{6 \times 1 + 4}{5} = 2$

If $n = 6$, $x = \dfrac{6 \times 6 + 4}{5} = 8$

Therefore, the solution are 2, 8, 14, 20, ...

EXAMPLE 11. If x is congruent to 13 modulo 17, then $7x - 3$ is congruent to y modulo 17. Find the value of y.

Sol. $x \equiv 13 \pmod{17}$ ...(i)

$7x - 3 \equiv y \pmod{17}$ ...(ii)

$x - 13$ is a multiple of 17 for some integer n,

$$x - 13 = 17n$$

Therefore, the least positive value of x must be 30, since $30 - 13 = 17$ which is multiple of 17.

So, from Eq. (ii),

$$7 \times 30 - 3 \equiv y \pmod{17}$$

$\Rightarrow \quad 210 - 3 - y = 17n$ for some integer n

$\Rightarrow \quad 207 - y = 17n$

Thus, $207 - y$ is a multiple of 17.

Hence, the least positive value of y must be 3, since $207 - 3 = 204$, which is a multiple of 17.

EXAMPLE 12. Find the last digit of 18^{22}.

Sol. For finding last digit of 18^{22}, we consider $18^{22} \pmod{10}$.

Now, $18 \equiv 8 \pmod{10} \Rightarrow 18 \equiv -2 \pmod{10}$

$\Rightarrow \quad 18^2 \equiv (-2)^2 \pmod{10} \Rightarrow (18)^2 \equiv 4 \pmod{10}$

$\Rightarrow (18^2)^{11} \equiv (4)^{11} \pmod{10} \Rightarrow 18^{22} \equiv 4 \pmod{10}$

Hence, the last digit of 18^{22} is 4.

Topic Practice 2

1 If $100 \equiv x \bmod 7$, then find the least positive value of x.

2 If $150 \equiv 10 \bmod n$, then find the number of values of n.

3 Find the value of x in the set {2, 3, 4, 5, 6} satisfying $92 \equiv -3 \pmod m$.

4 How many solutions has $91x \equiv 42 \pmod{78}$?

5 Find the time 100 h after 7 am.

6 Check which of the following statements are true?

(i) $12 \equiv 2 \pmod 5$ (ii) $37 \equiv 6 \pmod{10}$

(iii) $101 \equiv 5 \pmod 4$ (iv) $-5 \equiv 31 \pmod 6$

(v) $35 \equiv 0 \pmod 7$

7 Find the general solution of $8x \equiv 2 \pmod 9$.

8 If n is odd, then find the solution of $(x-1)(x+2) \equiv (x-2)(x+7) \pmod n$.

9 If $x \equiv 4 \pmod 7$, then find the positive values of x.

10 If x is the least non-negative integer satisfying $218 \equiv x \pmod 7$, then find the value of $x^2 + 1$.

11 Find the last digit of 17^{17}.

12 Find the remainder when

(i) 2^{100} is divided by 5.

(ii) 3^{30} is divided by 11.

(iii) $2^{151} \times 3^{200}$ is divided by 7.

(iv) 5^{121} is divided by 27.

13 It is currently 9 : 00 am what time (in am or pm) will be in next 800 h?

14 Find the last two digits of the product 2345×6789.

Hints & Solutions

1. We have, $100 \equiv x \bmod 7$

Here, $100 - x$ is an integral multiple of 7.

$\Rightarrow 100 - x = 7q$, where $q \in Z$

$\Rightarrow x = 100 - 7q$, where $q \in Z$

Putting $q = \ldots -3, -2, -1, 0, 1, 2, 3 \ldots\ldots$, we get

$x = \ldots\ldots 121, 114, 107, 100, 93, 86, 79, \ldots\ldots$

When put $q = 14$

$x = 100 - 98 = 2$

When put $q = 15$

$x = 100 - 105 = -5$

$\therefore$ Least value of $x = 2$.

2. We have, $150 \equiv 10 \bmod n$

Here, $150 - 10 = 140$ is must be integral multiple of n.

$\therefore n$ is factor of 140.

Factor of 140, is

2, 4, 5, 7, 10, 14, 20, 28, 35, 70, 140

$\therefore$ Value of $n = 2, 4, 5, 7, 10, 14, 20, 28, 35, 70, 140$

Hence, n has 11 values.

3. Given, $92 \equiv -3 (\bmod m)$

$92 + 3 = 95$ is an integral multiple of m.

2, 3, 4 and 6 are not the multiple of 95.

Hence, the value x is 5.

4. As the numbers 91 and 78 are divisible by 13, which is not divisible by 42.

Hence, $91x \equiv 42 (\bmod 78)$ has no solutions.

5. $7 + 100 \equiv x \bmod (12)$

$107 - x$ is a multiple of 12.

$107 - x = 12n$

Therefore, the least positive integer of x must be 11.

Since, $107 - 11 = 96$ is the nearest multiple of 11 less than 107.

So, the time 100 h after 7 O'clock am is 11am.

6. (i) Similar as Example 1 (i). **Ans.** True

(ii) Similar as Example 1 (ii). **Ans.** False

(iii) Similar as Example 1 (i). **Ans.** True

(iv) Similar as Example 1 (iv). **Ans.** True

(v) Similar as Example 1 (i). **Ans.** True

7. We have, $8x \equiv 2 (\bmod 9)$

Here, $a = 8$, $m = 9$

Here, HCF of 8 and 9 is $(8, 9) = 1$.

So, the given equation has only one solution belonging to the set {0, 1, 2, 3, ... 8}, we find that

$8 \times 0 = 0 (\bmod 9)$, $8 \times 1 = 8 (\bmod 9)$,

$8 \times 2 = 7 (\bmod 9)$, $8 \times 3 = 6 (\bmod 9)$,

$8 \times 4 = 5 (\bmod 9)$, $8 \times 6 = 3 (\bmod 9)$,

$8 \times 7 = 2 (\bmod 9)$, $8 \times 8 = 1 (\bmod 9)$

Clearly, $8 \times 7 = 2 (\bmod 9)$

$\Rightarrow$ $x = 7$ is satisfy $8x \equiv 2 (\bmod 9)$

Hence, $x \equiv 7 (\bmod 9)$ is the general solution of the given equation.

8. We have, $(x - 1)(x + 2) \equiv (x - 2)(x + 7) (\bmod n)$

$\Rightarrow \quad x^2 + x - 2 \equiv x^2 + 5x - 14 (\bmod n)$

$\Rightarrow \quad -4x \equiv -12 (\bmod n)$

$\Rightarrow \quad x \equiv 3 (\bmod n)$

9. We have, $x \equiv 4 (\bmod 7)$

$x - 4$ is an integral multiple of 7.

$x - 4 = 7n$

If $n = 0$, $x - 4 = 0 \Rightarrow x = 4$

If $n = 1$, $x - 4 = 7 \Rightarrow x = 11$

If $n = 2$, $x - 4 = 14 \Rightarrow x = 18$

If $n = 3$, $x - 4 = 21 \Rightarrow x = 25$

Hence, the possible value of x is {4, 11, 18, 25, ...}.

10. We have, $218 \equiv x (\bmod 7)$

$218 - x = 7n$

$218 - x$ is an integral multiple of 7.

217 is the multiple of 7.

Hence, $x = 1$

$x^2 + 1 = 1^2 + 1 = 2$

11. Similar as Example 12. **Ans.** 7

12. (i) Similar as Example 9 (i). **Ans.** 1

(ii) Similar as Example 9 (ii) **Ans.** 4

(iii) **Hint** We have, $2^{151} \equiv 2 (\bmod 7)$ ...(i)

and $3^{200} \equiv 2 (\bmod 7)$ ...(ii)

From Eqs. (i) and (ii), we get

$2^{151} \times 3^{200} \equiv 4 (\bmod 7)$

Ans. 4

(iv) Similar as Example 9 (ii). **Ans.** 23

13. Similar as Example 4. **Ans.** 5 pm

14. To find the last two digits of the product ab, we find $ab (\bmod 100)$

$\therefore$ Last two digits of the product 2345×6789,

We find $(2345 \times 6789) \bmod 100$

$= 2345 \bmod 100 \times 6789 \bmod 100$

$= 45 \bmod 100 \times 89 \bmod 100$

$= (45 \times 89) \bmod 100$

$= 4005 \bmod 100$

$= 05 \bmod 100$

Hence, the last two digits of the product 2345×6789 are 05.

Exam Pattern Exercise

Part A - Objective Type Questions

Multiple Choice Type Questions

1 The value of 14 mod 5 is
(a) 4 (b) 2
(c) 3 (d) 1

2 $[(3 \times 7) + 5]$ mod 4 is
(a) 5 (b) 4
(c) 3 (d) 2

3 Today is Tuesday. My uncle will come after 45 days. In which day my uncle will be coming
(a) Monday (b) Friday
(c) Saturday (d) Thursday

4 -41 mod 9 is [CBSE 2025]
(a) 5 (b) 4 (c) 3 (d) 0

5 $(49 + 58)$ mod 51 is
(a) 4 (b) 5 (c) 6 (d) 7

6 $(15 - 73)$ mod 4 is
(a) 1 (b) 4 (c) 0 (d) 2

7 (19×121) mod 6 is
(a) 2 (b) 1 (c) 3 (d) 4

8 The last (unit) digit of $(22)^{12}$ is [CBSE 2023]
(a) 2 (b) 4 (c) 6 (d) 8

9 The least non-negative remainder, when 3^{15} is divided by 7 is [CBSE 2023]
(a) 1 (b) 5 (c) 6 (d) 7

10 What time will it be after 1275 h, if the present time is 9:00 pm? [CBSE 2024]
(a) 11 pm (b) 12 am
(c) 9 pm (d) 9 am

Assertion-Reason Based Questions

Directions (Q. Nos. 11-16) *In the questions given below are two statements labelled as Assertion (A) and Reason (R). In the context of the two statements, which one of the following is correct?*

(a) Both A and R are correct; R is the correct explanation of A
(b) Both A and R are correct; R is not the correct explanation of A
(c) A is correct; R is incorrect
(d) R is correct; A is incorrect

11 **Assertion (A)** 21 mod 2 = 1
Reason (R) Modulo arithmetic is the arithmetic of remainders. So, it can be expressed as $a \bmod b = r$, where a is dividend, b is divisor and r is remainder.

12 **Assertion (A)** It is currently 8:00 am, then it will be 4 : 00 pm in next 500 h.
Reason (R) $a \equiv b (\text{mod} n)$ is that difference of a and b i.e. $(a - b)$ is an integral multiple of n i.e. when $a - b$ is divided by n, remainder is zero.

13 **Assertion (A)** $(486 + 729) (\text{mod } 12) \equiv 3$
Reason (R) $(a + b) (\text{mod } n) \equiv a (\text{mod } n) + b (\text{mod } n)$

14 **Assertion (A)** The remainder when $672 + 541 + 383 + 295 + 101 + 86$ is divided by 3 is 2.
Reason (R) If $a \equiv b (\text{mod } n)$ and $c \equiv d (\text{mod } n)$, then $(a + c) \equiv (b + d) (\text{mod } n)$.

15 **Assertion (A)** $(186 \times 93) (\text{mod } 7) \equiv 2$
Reason (R) $a \cdot b (\text{mod } n) \equiv a (\text{mod } n) \cdot b (\text{mod } n)$.

16 **Assertion (A)** The remainder when $783 \times 657 \times 594 \times 432 \times 346 \times 251$ is divided by 5 is 3.
Reason (R) If $a \equiv b (\text{mod } n)$ and $c \equiv d (\text{mod } n)$, then $ac \equiv bd (\text{mod } n)$.

Part B - Descriptive Questions

Short Answer Type Questions

17 Find the smallest non-negative integer congruent to 2796 (mod 7).

18 Find the value of x in the set $\{0, 1, 2, 3, 4, 5\}$ such that $73583 \equiv x (\text{mod } 6)$.

19 Find the number of value of m satisfying $92 \equiv -3 (\text{mod } m)$.

20 Find the set of values of n satisfying $25 \equiv 4 (\text{mod } m)$.

21 Find the value of x in the set $\{0, 1, 2, 3, ... 10\}$ such that $3 - x \equiv 5 (\text{mod } 11)$.

22 What is time 15 h before 11 pm?

23 Find the last digit of 12^{12}.

24 Solve $(x - 1)(x + 2) \equiv (x - 2)(x + 7) (\text{mod } n)$, if n is odd.

25 Find the number of solutions of $24x \equiv 5 (\text{mod } 4)$.

26 Find the congruence of 3 mod 5.

Case Study Based Questions

27 To enhance the reading skills of class XII student. The school nominates you and your friends to set a class library. There are three sections-Section A, Section B and Section C of class XII. There are 32 students in Section A, 36 students in section B and 40 students in section C.

Based on above information, answer the following questions.

(i) The remainder when total number of student divided by 7 is

(a) 5 (b) 4 (c) 3 (d) 6

(ii) The unit digit of 3^{108} is

(a) 6 (b) 7 (c) 8 (d) 1

(iii) Find the value in set {1, 2, 3, 4} such that number of students in section B and $C \equiv x$ (mod 9).

(a) 1 (b) 3

(c) 2 (d) 4

(iv) If all the students were arranged in 15 rows and each row have equal number of students, then the number of remaining students should be

(a) 3 (b) 4

(c) 5 (d) 6

(v) The remainder when $(32 \times 36 \times 40)$ is divided by 11, is

(a) 2 (b) 10

(c) 1 (d) 9

28 There are 24 h in a day. There are mainly two types of clocks used 12 h clock and 24 h clocks 12 h clock repeat itself twice in a day i.e. 24 h of a day are divided into two periods called am and pm. Each period consists of 12 h numbered 12 (acting as 0), 1, 2, 3, 4, 5, 6, 7, 8, 9, 10, 11. Then, 24 h per day cycle start at 12 mid-night (usually indicated as 12 am) runs through 12 noon (usually indicated as 12 pm) and continues before mid-night at the end of the day.

Based on above information, answer the following questions.

(i) It is currently 6:00 pm in 12 h clock. The time next 375 h will be

(a) 3:00 pm (b) 9:00 am

(c) 9:00 pm (d) 6:00 am

(ii) What time in 24 h clock is equivalent to 5:00 pm in 12 h clocks?

(a) 29:00 (b) 5:00

(c) 17:00 (d) 18:00

(iii) Which of the two times are same in 12 h and 24 h clocks respectively?

(a) 01:00 am, 13:00 (b) 02:00 pm, 02:00

(c) 04:00 am, 16:00 (d) 06:00 pm, 18:00

(iv) If the time after 490 h from now will be 7:00 pm, then current time is

(a) 7:00 am (b) 10:00 am

(c) 9:00 am (d) None of these

(v) What time in 12 h clock is equivalent to 22:00 in 24 h clock?

(a) 10:00 am (b) 8:00 pm

(c) 10:00 pm (d) 2:00 pm

Hints & Solutions

1. (a) 2. (d) 3. (b) 4. (a)
5. (b) 6. (d) 7. (b) 8. (c)
9. (b) 10. (c) 11. (a) 12. (d)
13. (a) 14. (a) 15. (d) 16. (a)

17. **Hint** Let x be a non-negative integer congruent to 2796 (mod 7)

$$x \equiv 2796 \pmod 7$$
$$x = 3 \pmod 7$$

18. We have, $73583 \equiv x \pmod 6$

$$73583 - x = 6n$$

$73583 - x$ is a multiple of 6.

$x \in \{0, 1, 2, 3, 4, 5\}$

If $x = 0$, then $73583 - 0 = 73583$ which is not a multiple of 6.

If $x = 1$, then 73582 is not a multiple of 6.

Similarly, for $x = 2, 3, 4$, $73583 - x$ is not a multiple of 6.

But for $x = 5$, $73583 - 5 = 73578$ is a multiple of 6.

Hence, $x = 5$

19. We have, $92 \equiv -3 \bmod m$

$$92 + 3 = mn, \text{ where } n \in Z$$

95 must be a multiple of m.

Factors of 95 is {1, 5, 19, 95}.

Hence, number of value of m is 4.

20. We have, $25 \equiv 4 \pmod m$

$$25 - 4 = mn$$

21 must be a multiple of m.

Factors of 21 is {1, 3, 7, 21}.

21. We have, $3 - x \equiv 5 \pmod{11}$

$$3 - x - 5 = 11n$$

$-x - 2$ must be completely divisible by 11.

So, by option $x = 9$

$$-9 - 2 \Rightarrow -11$$

[which is completely divisible by 11]

22. $15 \equiv 11 - x \pmod{12}$

$15 - 11 + x = 12n$

$$4 + x = 12n$$

$4 + x$ is a multiple of 12.

Therefore, the least positive value of x must be 8.

Since, $4 + 8 = 12$ is a multiple of 12.

Hence, the time 15 h before 11 pm is 8 pm.

23. To find the last digit of 12^{12}, we find $12^{12} \pmod{10}$

Since, $12 \equiv 2 \pmod{10}$

$\Rightarrow \quad 12^4 = 2^4 \pmod{10} = 16 \pmod{10}$

$\Rightarrow \quad 12^4 = 6 \pmod{10}$

$\Rightarrow (12^4)^3 = (6)^3 \bmod 10$

$\Rightarrow \quad 12^{12} = 216 \bmod 10$

$\Rightarrow \quad 12^{12} = 6 \bmod 10$

Hence, the last digit of 12^{12} is 6.

24. $x \equiv 3 \pmod n$

25. No solution

26. $3, 3 \pm 5, \; 3 \pm 10, \; 3 \pm 15, \ldots$

27. (i) (b) Total number of students $(32 + 36 + 40) = 108$

$(32 + 36 + 40)(\text{mod} 7)$

$= 32 \pmod 7 + 36 \pmod 7 + 40 \pmod 7$

$= (4 + 1 + 5)(\text{mod} 7) = 10 \pmod 7$

$\therefore$ Remainder = 3

(ii) (d) $3^{108} = (3^4)^{27}$

The unit digit of 3^4 is 1.

$\therefore$ The unit digit of 3^{108} = unit digit of $(1)^{27} = 1$

(iii) (d) Number of students in section B and $C = 76$

$$76 \equiv x (\text{mod} 9)$$
$$76 \equiv 4 (\text{mod} 9)$$
$$\therefore \quad x = 4$$

(iv) (a) Total number of students = 108

$$\therefore \quad 108 \equiv x (\text{mod} 15)$$
$$108 \equiv 3 (\text{mod} 15)$$

$\therefore$ 3 students are left out.

(v) (c) To find $(32 \times 36 \times 40) \bmod 11$

$= 32 \pmod{11} \times 36 \pmod{11} \times 40 \pmod{11}$

$= (10 \times 3 \times 7) \bmod 11$

$= 210 \bmod 11 = 1 \bmod 11$

So, remainder = 1

28. (i) (b) $375 = 24 \times 15 + 15$

$\therefore$ 375 h = $(24 \times 15 + 15)$ h

Time = 6 pm + 15 h

= 6 am + 3 h = 9 am

(ii) (c) In 24 h clock 5:00 in 12 h equivalent = 17:00

(iii) (d) 12 h in 6:00 pm = 18:00 in 24 h

(iv) (c) $490 = 24 \times 20 + 10$

The current time = 7:00 pm − 10 h = 9:00 am

(v) (c) 22:00 = 10:00 pm in 12 h clock.

CHAPTER 02

Mixture and Alligation

In this Chapter...

- Mixture and Alligation
- Repeated Dilution

Mixture and Alligation

The new product obtained by mixing two or more ingredients in a certain ratio is called a mixture.

Or

Combination of two or more quantities is known as mixture.

Type of Mixture

There are two types of mixture

(i) Simple mixture (ii) Compound mixture

Simple Mixture

When two different ingredients are mixed together, it is known as simple mixture.

EXAMPLE 1. In a container, milk and water are present in the ratio 7 : 5. If 15 L water is added to this mixture, the ratio of milk and water becomes 7 : 8. Find the quantity of water in the new mixture.

Sol. Let the quantity of milk and water in initial mixture be $7x$ L and $5x$ L.

Then, according to the question,

$$\frac{7x}{5x+15}=\frac{7}{8} \Rightarrow 7x \times 8 = 7(5x+15)$$

$$\Rightarrow \quad 56x = 35x + 105 \Rightarrow 56x - 35x = 105$$

$$\Rightarrow \quad 21x = 105 \Rightarrow x = \frac{105}{21} = 5$$

$\therefore$ Quantity of water in initial mixture $= 5 \times 5 = 25$ L and quantity of water in new mixture $= 25 + 15 = 40$ L

EXAMPLE 2. A vessel contains liquid A and liquid B in the ratio 5 : 7. If 10 L of liquid A is added to the vessel, the new ratio becomes 6 : 7. Find the quantity of liquid A in the original mixture.

Sol. Let the quantity of liquid A and B in the vessel initially be $5x$ and $7x$, respectively.

Then, according to the question,

$$\frac{5x+10}{7x}=\frac{6}{7} \Rightarrow 5x + 10 = 6x \Rightarrow x = 10$$

$\therefore$ Quantity of liquid A in original mixture $= 5 \times 10 = 50$ L

Alligation

Alligation is nothing but a faster technique of solving problems based on the weighted average situation as applied to the case of two groups being mixed together. The word alligation literally means 'linking'.

Mean Price The cost price of a unit quantity of the mixture is called the mean price. It will always be higher than cost price of cheaper quantity and lower than cost price of dearer quantity.

Rule of Mixture or Alligation

It is the rule that enables us to find the ratio in which two or more ingredients at the given price must be mixed to produce a mixture of a desired price.

According to this rule, $\dfrac{n_1}{n_2}=\dfrac{A_2 - A_w}{A_w - A_1}$

where, n_1/n_2 is the ratio, in which two quantities should be mixed, while A_1, A_2 and A_w are the cheaper price, dearer price and mean price, respectively.

The above rule can be represented pictorially as shown below

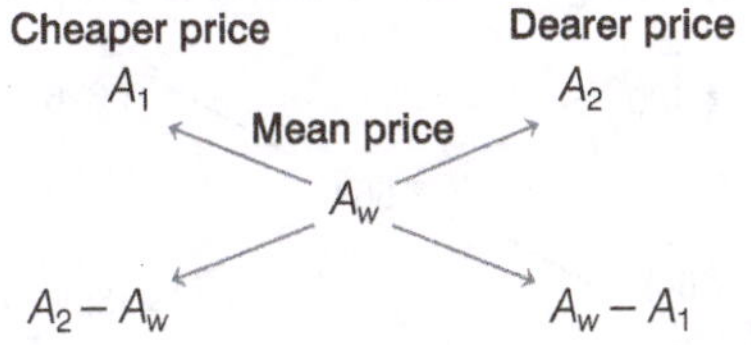

[remember, $A_1 < A_w < A_2$]

Amount of cheaper : Amount of dearer $(n_1 : n_2)$

$$= \frac{A_2 - A_w}{A_w - A_1}$$

Hence, $\dfrac{\text{Amount of cheaper item}}{\text{Amount of dearer item}}$

$$= \frac{\text{Price of dearer} - \text{Mean Price}}{\text{Mean Price} - \text{Price of cheaper}}$$

EXAMPLE 3. A merchant lent out ₹ 6440 in two parts, one at 8% and the other at 12% interest. If the average interest comes out to be 9%. Find the amount lent at 12% interest.

Sol. The alligation grid is as given below

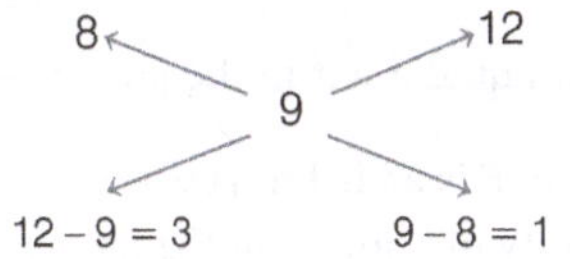

Using alligation law,

$$\frac{\text{Amount lent at 8\%}}{\text{Amount lent at 12\%}} = \frac{3}{1}$$

Thus, ₹ 6440 are divided in two parts in the ratio 3 : 1.

$$\text{Amount lent at 8\%} = \left(\frac{3}{3+1}\right) \times 6440 = \frac{3}{4} \times 6440$$

$$= 3 \times 1610 = ₹\ 4830$$

$$\text{Amount lent at 12\%} = \left(\frac{1}{3+1}\right) \times 6440 = \frac{1}{4} \times 6440 = ₹\ 1610$$

EXAMPLE 4. Three varieties A, B and C of rice are mixed together in the ratio 4 : 1 : 1, respectively. The cost price of rice B is ₹ 82 per kg and that of rice C is ₹ 90 per kg. If the price of the mixture is ₹ 94 per kg, then find the price per kg of rice A.

Sol. Since, B varieties and C varities of rice are added in equal proportion.

So, their average $= \dfrac{82 + 90}{2} = \dfrac{172}{2} = ₹\ 86$ per kg.

Let the price of A varieties of rice be ₹ x per kg.

Variety A and (variety B and variety C) are mixed in the ratio $(4 : 1 + 1) = 4 : 2 = 2 : 1$

Here,

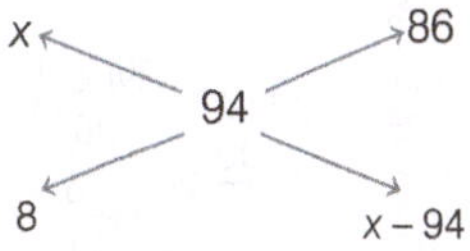

Using alligation law,

$$\frac{8}{x - 94} = \frac{2}{1} \Rightarrow 8 = 2x - 188$$

$$\Rightarrow \quad 2x = 196 \Rightarrow x = ₹\ 98 \text{ per kg}$$

EXAMPLE 5. The cost of Type I sugar is ₹25 per kg and Type II sugar is ₹35 per kg. If both Type I sugar and Type II sugar are mixed in the ratio 3:2, find the price per kg of the mixture. **[CBSE 2025]**

Sol. Given, the cost of Type I sugar = ₹ 25 per kg

and the cost of Type II sugar = ₹ 35 per kg

Let the cost of mixed variety of sugar be ₹ x per kg.

Then, according to the rule of alligation,

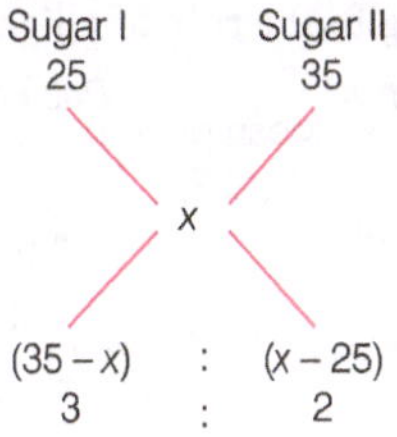

$$\Rightarrow \quad \frac{(35 - x)}{(x - 25)} = \frac{3}{2} \Rightarrow 70 - 2x = 3x - 75 \Rightarrow 5x = 145$$

$$\Rightarrow \quad x = \frac{145}{5} = 29$$

Hence, the price of mixed variety of sugar is 29 per kg.

EXAMPLE 6. In what proportion, must wheat at ₹ 6.20 per kg be mixed with wheat at ₹ 7.20 per kg, so that the mixture be worth ₹ 6.50 per kg?

Sol. Given, cost price of cheaper quantity = ₹ 6.20 per kg

Cost price of dearer quantity = ₹ 7.20 per kg

and mean price = ₹ 6.50 per kg

According to the rule of alligation,

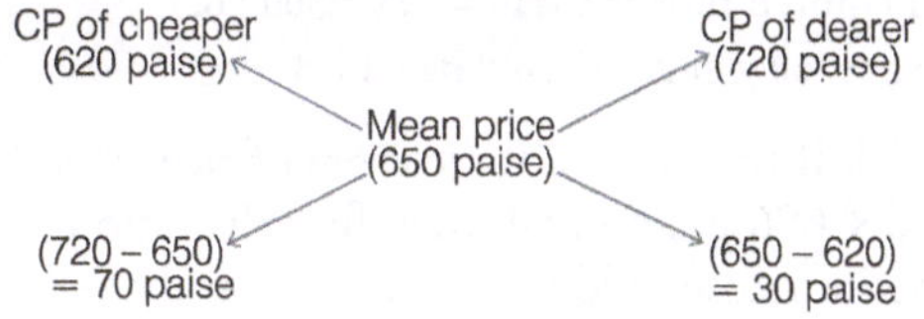

∴ Required ratio = 70 : 30 = 7 : 3

EXAMPLE 7. How many kilograms of tea worth ₹ 25 per kg must be blended with 30 kg of tea worth ₹ 30 per kg, so that by selling the blended variety at ₹ 30 per kg, there should be a gain of 10%?

Sol. Let the quantity of tea worth ₹ 25 per kg be x.

SP = ₹ 30 per kg, gain = 10%

$$\therefore \text{ CP} = \frac{30 \times 100}{110} = ₹\ \frac{300}{11} \text{ per kg}$$

By alligation rule,

Type 1 25 (Mean) $\frac{300}{11}$ Type 2 30

$\frac{30}{11}$ $\frac{25}{11}$

$$\text{Type 1 (₹ 25 per kg) : Type 2 (₹ 30 per kg)} = \frac{30}{11} : \frac{25}{11} = 6:5$$

Using alligation rule, $\frac{6}{5} = \frac{x}{30} \Rightarrow 5x = 180$

$\Rightarrow$ $x = \frac{180}{5} \Rightarrow x = 36\text{ kg}$

EXAMPLE 8. A milkman bought 15 L of milk and mixed 3 L of water in it. If the price per kilogram of the mixture becomes ₹ 22, what is cost price of the milk per litre?

Sol. Let the cost of milk be ₹ x per L and the cost of water is ₹ 0 per L.

Then, according to the rule of alligation,

Price of milk (₹ x) — Mean price (₹ 22) — Price of water (₹ 0)

₹ 22 — ₹ $(x - 22)$

$\therefore$ $22 : (x-22) = 15:3 \Rightarrow \frac{22}{x-22} = \frac{15}{3}$

$\Rightarrow$ $\frac{22}{x-22} = 5 \Rightarrow 22 = 5x - 110 \Rightarrow 5x = 132$

$\therefore$ $x = ₹\ 26.40$

EXAMPLE 9. 300 g of sugar solution has 40% of sugar in it. How much sugar should be added to make it 50% in the solution?

Sol. By alligation rule,

Mixture I (300 g) Sugar 40% — (Mean) 50% — Mixture II Pure sugar 100%

(100 – 50)% = 50% — (50 – 40)% = 10%

$\therefore$ Required ratio = 50 : 10 = 5 : 1 = 300 : 60

Hence, 60 g sugar should be added.

EXAMPLE 10. If the price of three types of rice are ₹ 480, ₹ 576 and ₹ 696 per quintal, then find the ratio in which these types of rice should be mixed, so that the resultant mixture cost ₹ 564 per quintal?

Sol. Let amount of 3 types of rice be x, y and z, respectively.

Using rule of alligation for x and y,

x ₹ 480 — ₹ 564 — y ₹ 576

(576 – 564) = ₹ 12 — (564 – 480) = ₹ 84

$\therefore$ $x : y = 12 : 84 = 1 : 7$

Similarly, using the rule of alligation for x and z,

x ₹ 480 — ₹ 564 — z ₹ 696

(696 – 564) = ₹ 132 — (564 – 480) = ₹ 84

$\therefore$ $x : z = 132 : 84 = 11 : 7 = 1 : \frac{7}{11}$

On combining the two ratios, we get

$$x : y : z = 1 : 7 : \frac{7}{11} = 11 : 77 : 7$$

EXAMPLE 11. A jar contained a mixture of 2 liquids A and B are in the ratio 4 : 1. When 10 L of the mixture was taken out and 10 L of liquid B was poured it to the jar, the ratio becomes 2 : 3. Find the quantity of A and B contained in the jar, initially?

Sol. Let initially the quantity of liquids A and B be $4x$ and x, respectively.

After withdrawing 10 L of mixture,

Quantity of liquid A left in Jar $= 4x - \frac{4}{5} \times 10 = 4x - 8$

Quantity of liquid B left in the jar $= x - \frac{1}{5} \times 10 = x - 2$

10 L of liquid B is added to jar.

Now, quantity of liquid B in the jar $= x - 2 + 10 = x + 8$

According to the question,

$$\frac{4x-8}{x+8} = \frac{2}{3} \Rightarrow 12x - 24 = 2x + 16$$

$\Rightarrow$ $10x = 40 \Rightarrow x = 4$

Hence, initially quantity of A and B are 16 L and 4 L, respectively.

Compound Mixture

When two or more simple mixtures are mixed together to form another mixture, it is known as a compound mixture.

In compound mixture, same mixtures i.e. mixtures of same ingredients are mixed together in different proportion to make a new mixture.

EXAMPLE 12. Vessel A contains milk and water in the ratio 4 : 5. Vessel B contains milk and water in the proportion 5 : 1. In what proportion should quantities be taken from A and B to form a mixture in which milk and water are in the ratio 5 : 4?

Sol. Let us consider the proportion of milk in each mixture be $x : y$.

In vessel A, the proportion of milk $= \frac{4}{(4+5)} = \frac{4}{9}$

and in vessel B, the proportion of milk $= \frac{5}{5+1} = \frac{5}{6}$

Using rule of alligation,

$$\frac{4}{9} \qquad\qquad \frac{5}{6}$$

$$\frac{5}{9}$$

$$\left(\frac{5}{6}-\frac{5}{9}\right)=\frac{5}{18} \qquad\qquad \left(\frac{5}{9}-\frac{4}{9}\right)=\frac{1}{9}$$

Hence, the ratio is $\frac{5}{18}:\frac{1}{9}=5:2$

EXAMPLE 13. Two equal glasses of same type are respectively, $\frac{1}{3}$ and $\frac{1}{4}$ full of milk. They are then filled up with water and contents are mixed in pot. What is the ratio of milk and water in the pot?

Sol. Two ingredients milk and water are in the ratio 1 : 2 and 1 : 3.

In glass first, the proportion of milk $= \frac{1}{3}$

and in glass second the proportion of milk $= \frac{1}{4}$

$\therefore$ In glass first, the proportion of water $= \frac{2}{3}$

and in glass second the proportion of water $= \frac{3}{4}$

$\therefore$ Ratio of milk and water in the pot

$$= \left(\frac{1}{3}+\frac{1}{4}\right):\left(\frac{2}{3}+\frac{3}{4}\right) = \frac{7}{12}:\frac{17}{12} = 7:17$$

Hence, the ratio of milk and water in the pot is 7 : 17.

Topic Practice 1

1 A can contains a mixture of two liquids A and B in the ratio 7 : 5. When 9 L of mixture are drawn off and the can is filled with B, the ratio of A and B becomes 7 : 9. How many litres of liquid A was contained by the can initially?

2 A mixture of 150 L of wine and water contains 20% water. How much more water should be added so that the water becomes 25% of the new mixture?

3 In what proportion must a grocer mix wheat at ₹ 2.04 per kg and ₹ 2.88 per kg, so as to make a mixture of worth ₹ 2.52 per kg?

4 A mixture of certain quantity of milk with 8 L of water is worth 45 paise per L. If pure milk is worth 54 paise per L, how much milk is there in the mixture?

5 A merchant has 2000 kg of rice, one part of which he sells at 36% profit and the rest at 16% profit. He gains 28% on the whole. Find the quantity sold at 16%.

6 A person has ₹ 8400. He lent a part of it at 4% and the remaining at $3\frac{1}{3}$% simple interest. His total annual income was ₹ 294. Find the sum, he lent at 4%.

7 A merchant has 50 kg of pulse. He sells one part at a profit of 10% and other at 5% loss. Overall he had a gain of 7%. Find the quantity of pulses, which he sold at 10% profit and 5% loss.

8 A butler stole wine from a butt of sherry which contained 80% of spirit and he replaced it by wine containing only 32% spirit. Then, the butt was of 48% strength only. How much of the butt did he steal?

9 A trader mixes 14 kg rice of variety A which costs ₹ 60 per kg with 18 kg of quantity of type B rice. He sells the mixture at ₹ 65 per kg and earns a profit of $\frac{100}{3}$%. Then, what was the cost price of type B rice?

10 In what ratio must water be mixed with milk to gain 20% on selling the mixture at cost price?

11 The cost of type I rice is ₹ 15 per kg and type II rice is ₹ 20 per kg. If both types are mixed in the ratio 2 : 3, then what is the price per kilogram of the mixed variety of rice?

12 The ratio of milk and water in a mixture is 5 : 3. How much fraction of the mixture must be drawn off and substituted by water so that the ratio of milk and water in the mixture becomes 1 : 1?

13 In a glass, milk and water are mixed in the ratio 3 : 5 and in another glass they are mixed in the ratio 6 : 1. In what ratio should be content of the two glasses be mixed together so that the new mixture contains milk and water in the ratio 1 : 1?

14 Two types of alloy posses gold and silver in the ratio of 7 : 22 and 21 : 37. In what ratio should these alloys be mixed so as to have a new alloy in which gold and silver would exist in the ratio 25 : 62?

Hints & Solutions

1. Similar as Example 11. **Ans.** 21
2. Similar as Example 9. **Ans.** 10 L
3. Similar as Example 6. **Ans.** 3 : 4
4. As water is available free of cost, so its cost price = ₹ 0

According to the rule of alligation,

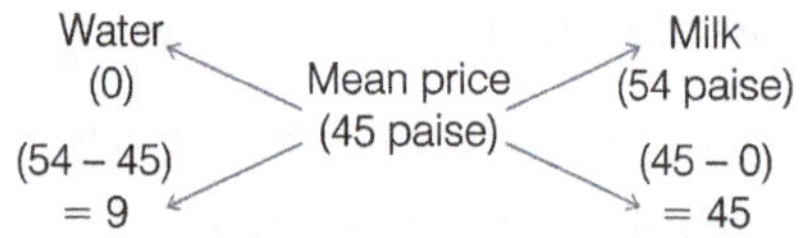

Water : Milk = 9 : 45 = 1 : 5

∴ Quantity of milk = 5 × 8 = 40 L

5. Similar as Example 3. **Ans.** 800 kg
6. SI on ₹ 8400 for 1 yr = ₹ 294

$\therefore$ Rate of interest $= \dfrac{100 \times 294}{8400 \times 1}$

$= \dfrac{7}{2} = 3\dfrac{1}{2}\%$

According to the rule of alligation,

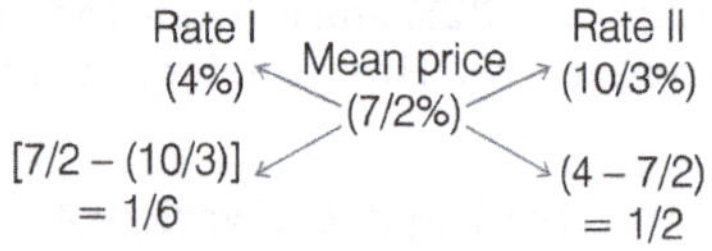

Rate I (4%) : Rate II $\left(\dfrac{10}{3}\%\right) = \dfrac{1}{6} : \dfrac{1}{2} = 1 : 3$

$\therefore$ Money lent at 4% $= \dfrac{1}{4} \times 8400 =$ ₹ 2100

7. According to the rule of alligation,

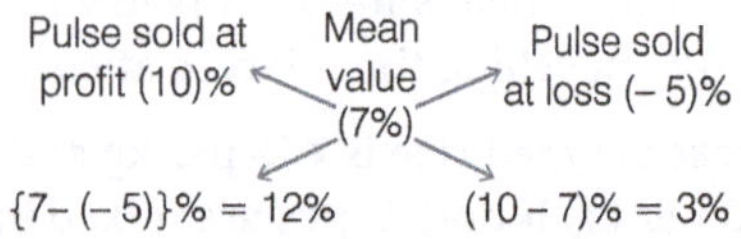

[– ve sign indicates loss]

∴ Ratio of pulses sold at 10% profit and 5% loss

= 12 : 3 = 4 : 1

$\therefore$ Quantity of pulse sold at 10% profit $= \dfrac{4}{4+1} \times 50$

$= \dfrac{4}{5} \times 50 = 40$ kg

and quantity of pulse sold at 5% loss $= \dfrac{1}{4+1} \times 50$

$= \dfrac{1}{5} \times 50 = 10$ kg

8. Similar as Example 3. **Ans.** $\dfrac{2}{3}$
9. Let cost price of mixture be y.

So, $\dfrac{4}{3} y = 65$ $\left[\because \text{Profit} = \dfrac{100}{3}\%\right]$

$\Rightarrow y = 48.75$

From mixture and alligation,

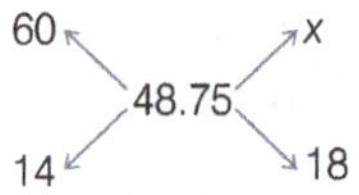

$\dfrac{7}{9} = \dfrac{x - 48.75}{48.75 - 60}$

$\Rightarrow 341.25 - 420 = 9x - 438.75$

$\Rightarrow 360 = 9x$

$\therefore x =$ ₹ 40 per kg

10. Similar as Example 5. **Ans.** 5 : 1
11. Similar as Example 8. **Ans.** 18
12. Let the initial quantity of milk be $5x$ L and initial quantity of water be $3x$ L.

Let y L mixture be taken out.

Quantity of milk left $= 5x - \dfrac{5}{8}y$

Quantity of water left $= 3x - \dfrac{3}{8}y$

After adding y L of water,

Quantity of water in the solution $= 3x - \dfrac{3}{8}y + y$

$= 3x + \dfrac{5}{8}y$

According to the question,

$$\frac{5x - \frac{5}{8}y}{3x + \frac{5}{8}y} = \frac{1}{1}$$

$\Rightarrow 5x - \dfrac{5}{8}y = 3x + \dfrac{5}{8}y$

$\Rightarrow 2x = \dfrac{10}{8}y \Rightarrow 8x = 5y$

Part of mixture taken out $= \dfrac{y}{(5x+3x)} = \dfrac{y}{8x} = \dfrac{y}{5y} = \dfrac{1}{5}$

13. Similar as Example 12. **Ans.** 20 : 7
14. Similar as Example 12. **Ans.** 13 : 8

Repeated Dilution

If A and B are in the ratio $a:b$ in a mixture and some quantity of the mixture is withdrawn, the withdrawn quantity will have A and B in the ratio $a:b$.

If x L is withdrawn, then in these x L quantity of A is $\frac{ax}{a+b}$ and quantity of B is $\frac{bx}{a+b}$.

Suppose a container initially contains a units of some liquid A. From this, b units of liquid A is taken out and replaced by an equal quantity of liquid B.

Then, after first replacement,

Quantity of liquid A in a units of mixture of A and B

$$= (a-b)$$
$$= a\left(1-\frac{b}{a}\right)$$

Quantity of liquid A in '1' unit of mixture of A and B

$$= \left(1-\frac{b}{a}\right)$$

Quantity of liquid A in 'b' units of mixture of A and B

$$= b\left(1-\frac{b}{a}\right)$$

Quantity of liquid A left after taken out 'b' L of mixture of A and $B = a\left(1-\frac{b}{a}\right) - b\left(1-\frac{b}{a}\right)$

$$= (a-b)\left(1-\frac{b}{a}\right) = a\left(1-\frac{b}{a}\right)^2$$

Quantity of liquid A after 2 operations $= a\left(1-\frac{b}{a}\right)^2$

Similarly,

Quantity of liquid A after n operations $= a\left(1-\frac{b}{a}\right)^n$

EXAMPLE 1. A container has 50 L of juice in it. 5 L of juice is taken out and is replaced by 5 L of water. This process is repeated 4 more times. Determine the quantity of juice in the container after final replacement.
[use $(0.9)^5 = 0.59049$] **[CBSE 2024]**

Sol. Given, original quantity of juice, $a = 50$ L

Since, 5 L of juice was taken out and was replaced by 5 L of water, so we have

$$b = 5\text{ L}$$

The process is repeated 5 times.

Quantity of juice in the container after n operations

$$= a\left(1-\frac{b}{a}\right)^n$$

Quantity of juice in the container after 5 operations

$$= 50\left(1-\frac{5}{50}\right)^5 = 5\left(1-\frac{1}{10}\right)^5 = 5(0.9)^5 = 5\times 0.59049$$

[$\because$ Given $(0.9)^5 = 0.59049$]

$$= 2.95245\text{ L}$$

$\therefore$ Quantity of juice in the container after final replacement is 2.95245 L.

EXAMPLE 2. A vessel contains some litres of pure milk. 12 L of milk taken out from it and replaced by water. This process is repeated three times more. The ratio of milk and water in the resultant mixture becomes 16 : 65. Find the initial quantity of milk.

Sol. Using the formula for repeated dilution,

After n operations, the quantity of liquid A in a L of mixture $= a\left(1-\frac{b}{a}\right)^n$

$$\Rightarrow \left(\frac{16}{16+65}\right)\times a = a\left(1-\frac{12}{a}\right)^4 \Rightarrow \left(\frac{2}{3}\right)^4 = \left(1-\frac{12}{a}\right)^4$$

Comparing the base, we get

$$\frac{2}{3} = 1-\frac{12}{a} \Rightarrow \frac{12}{a} = 1-\frac{2}{3}$$

$$\Rightarrow \frac{12}{a} = \frac{1}{3} \Rightarrow a = 36\text{ L}$$

The initial quantity of milk is 36 L.

EXAMPLE 3. A vessel contains 400 L of milk. 20 L of milk taken out from it and replaced by water. Then, again from mixture 40 L are taken out and replaced by water. Then again from mixture 60 L are taken out and replaced by water. Find the ratio of milk and water in the resultant mixture.

Sol. Quantity of milk after repeated dilution

$$= 400\left(1-\frac{20}{400}\right)\left(1-\frac{40}{400}\right)\left(1-\frac{60}{400}\right)$$

$$= 400\times\frac{19}{20}\times\frac{9}{10}\times\frac{17}{20} = 290.7\text{ L}$$

Quantity of water after repeated dilution $= 400 - 290.7$

$$= 109.3\text{ L}$$

Ratio of milk and water $= \frac{290.7}{109.3} = \frac{2907}{1093}$

$$= 2907:1093$$

EXAMPLE 4. A vessel contains a mixture of O_2 and N_2. The quantity of O_2 is 16% of total mixture. Some quantity of mixture taken out from it and replaced by N_2. This process is repeated once more. Now, the quantity of O_2 is 9% of total mixture. If total quantity of mixture was 8 L, then find the quantity of mixture which is taken out.

Sol. Original volume of oxygen = 16% of 8 L

$$= \frac{16}{100} \times 8 = 1.28 \text{ L}$$

Volume of oxygen left after 2 operations = 9% of 8

$$= \frac{9}{100} \times 8$$

$$= 0.72 \text{ L}$$

Suppose, y L of mixture is released each time, then

Volume of oxygen left = Original volume $\left(1 - \frac{y}{8}\right)^2$

$$0.72 = 1.28\left(1 - \frac{y}{8}\right)^2$$

$$\Rightarrow \quad \frac{9}{16} = \left(1 - \frac{y}{8}\right)^2$$

$$\Rightarrow \quad \frac{3}{4} = 1 - \frac{y}{8}$$

$$\Rightarrow \quad \frac{y}{8} = \frac{1}{4} \Rightarrow y = 2$$

Hence, 2 L of mixture is released each time.

Topic Practice 2

1 A container contains 50 L of milk. From this container 10 L of milk was taken out and replaced by water. This process is repeated two more times. How much milk is now left in the container?

2 A container contains 100 L of milk. From this container, 10 L of milk was taken out and replaced by equal amount of water. This process was further repeated twice. How much milk is left in the container?

3 A vessel contains some litres of pure milk. 5 L of milk taken out from it and replaced by water. This process is repeated once more. Then, the ratio of milk and water in the resultant mixture becomes 64 : 17. Find the initial quantity of milk.

4 From a cask full of alcohol 8 L are drawn and then filled with water. This process is repeated three more times. The ratio of the quantity of alcohol left in the cask and that of water is 16 : 65. How many litres of alcohol did the cask hold originally?

5 From a container full of alcohol 6 L of alcohol was drawn out and replaced by water. This process is repeated one more time. The ratio of the quantity of alcohol and water left in the container is 9 : 16. How many litres of alcohol did the container hold originally?

6 A vessel contains 500 L of milk. 50 L of milk taken out from it and replaced by water. Then, again from mixture 100 L are taken out and replaced by water. Then, again from mixture 125 L are taken out and replaced by water. Find the ratio of milk and water in the resultant mixture.

7 A 100 L cylinder contains a mixture of water and sugar, the volume of sugar being 25% of total volume. A few litres of the mixture is released and an equal amount of water is added. This process repeat for one more time. As a result, sugar content becomes 16% of total volume. What is the quantity of mixture released every time?

Hints & Solutions

1. Similar as Example 1. **Ans.** 25.6 L
2. Similar as Example 1. **Ans.** 72.9 L
3. Similar as Example 2. **Ans.** 45 L
4. Similar as Example 2. **Ans.** 24 L
5. Similar as Example 2. **Ans.** 15 L
6. Similar as Example 3. **Ans.** 27 : 23
7. Similar as Example 4. **Ans.** 20

Exam Pattern Exercise

Part A - Objective Type Questions

Multiple Choice Type Questions

1 The ratio in which a grocer mixes two varieties of pulses costing ₹ 85 per kg and ₹ 100 per kg respectively, so as to get a mixture worth ₹ 92 per kg is [CBSE 2023]

(a) 7 : 8 (b) 8 : 7 (c) 5 : 7 (d) 7 : 5

2 A container contains mixture of milk and water in ratio 5 : 3. If 8 L milk is added in it, then ratio of milk to water becomes 11 : 5, then difference between initial quantity of milk and that of water is

(a) 15 L (b) 5 L (c) 30 L (d) 10 L

3 The ratio in which water to be mixed with milk to gain 20% by selling the mixture at cost price, is

(a) 1 :5 (b) 3 : 7 (c) 2 : 5 (d) 3 : 4

4 A milk man mixed some water with milk to gain 25% by selling the mixture at the cost price. The ratio of water and milk is

(a) 2 : 7 (b) 1 : 4 (c) 7 : 2 (d) 2 : 3

5 Find the quantity (in kg) of wheat costing ₹ 84 per kg, must be mixed with 81 kg, of wheat costing ₹ 60 per kg, so that on selling the mixture at ₹ 75.9 per kg, there is a gain of 15%.

(a) 27 (b) 24
(c) 32 (d) 20

6 Gold is 19 times as heavy as water and copper 9 times as heavy as water. In what ratio should these metal be mixed so that the mixture may be 15 times as heavy as water?

(a) 4 : 3 (b) 7 : 5
(c) 3:2 (d) 5: 4

7 Two liquids are mixed in the ratio 3 : 5 and the mixture is sold at ₹ 120 with a profit of 20%. If the first liquid is costlier than the second by ₹ 2 per litre, then the cost of the costlier liquid per litre is

(a) ₹ 110.50 (b) ₹ 104.62
(c) ₹ 95.67 (d) ₹ 101.25

8 In a mixture of milk and water, the proportion of milk by weight is 60%. If from the 80 gm mixture, 20 gm of mixture is taken out and 6 gm of pure water is added to the mixture, then the ratio of milk and water in the new mixture is

(a) 7:6 (b) 4 : 7
(c) 6 : 5 (d) 7 : 4

Assertion-Reason Based Questions

Directions (Q. Nos. 9-10) *In the questions given below are two statements labelled as Assertion (A) and Reason (R). In the context of the two statements, which one of the following is correct?*

(a) Both A and R are correct; R is the correct explanation of A
(b) Both A and R are correct; R is not the correct explanation of A
(c) A is correct; R is incorrect
(d) R is correct; A is incorrect

9 **Assertion (A)** Two varieties of tea costing ₹ 12 per kg and ₹ 15 per kg are mixed together in the ratio 1 : 2, the average price of the resulting mixture is ₹ 14 per kg.

Reason (R) 20 L of a mixture contains milk and water in the ratio 3 : 1. Then, the amount of milk to be added to the mixture so as to have milk and water in ratio 4 : 1 is 10 L.

10 **Assertion (A)** The ratio in which two varieties of pulses costing ₹ 15 and ₹ 20 per kg respectively mixed, so as to get a mixture worth ₹ 16.50 per kg is 7 : 3.

Reason (R) Amit raj mixed 80 kg of sugar worth ₹ 6.75 per kg with 120 kg worth ₹ 8 per kg. The rate at which he sell the mixture to gain 20% is ₹ 9 per kg.

Part B - Descriptive Questions

Very Short Answer Type Questions

11 In what ratio must a shopkeeper mix two types of oranges worth ₹ 30 per kg and ₹ 45 per kg respectively, so as to get a mixture at ₹ 40 per kg?

12 The ratio of milk and water in a mixture is 3 : 5. We added 10 L water to the mixture, then ratio becomes 3 : 7. Find the initial quantity of milk.

13 The ratio of milk and water in a mixture is 3 : 7. We added 10 L water to the mixture, then ratio becomes 1 : 3. Find the initial quantity of milk.

Short Answer Type Questions

14 A merchant lent out ₹ 10000 in two parts, one at 8% and other at 10% interest. The yearly average comes out to be 9.2%. Find the amount lent in two parts.

15 Three varieties A, B and C of tea are mixed together in the ratio 1 : 1 : 3, respectively. The price of tea A is ₹ 127 per kg and that of tea B is ₹ 135 per kg. If the price of the mixture is ₹ 152 per kg, then find the price per kilogram of tea C.

16 In what ratio must a grocer mix two varieties of sugar worth ₹ 40 per kg and ₹ 50 per kg respectively so that by selling the mixture at ₹ 48.40 per kg, he may gain 10%?

17 In what ratio must a grocer mix two varieties of tea worth ₹ 60 per kg and ₹ 65 per kg so that by selling the mixture at ₹ 68.20 per kg may gain 10%?

18 A vessel contains a mixture of two liquids P and Q in the ratio 5 : 7. 12 L of mixture are drawn off from the vessel and 12 L of liquid P is filled vessel. If the ratio of liquids P and Q now becomes 9 : 7, how many litres of liquids P and Q were contained by the vessel initially?

19 Two vessels A and B contain milk and water in the ratio 7 : 5 and 17 : 7, respectively. In what ratio mixtures from two vessels should be mixed to get a new mixture containing milk and water in the ratio 5: 3?

20 Mixture of milk and water has been kept in two separate containers. Ratio of milk to water in one of the containers is 5 : 1 and that in the other container is 7 : 2. In what ratio the mixture of these two containers should be added together, so that the quantity of milk in the new mixture may become 80%?

21 Vijay purchased two different kinds of alcohol. In the first mixture the ratio of alcohol to water is 3 : 4 and in the second mixture it is 5 : 6. If he mixes the two given mixtures and makes a third mixture of 18 L in which the ratio of alcohol to water is 4 : 5, find the quantity of the first mixture (whose ratio is 3 : 4) that is required to make 18 L of the third kind of mixture.

22 Two types of alloy posses gold and silver in the ratio of 7 : 22 and 21 : 31. In what ratio should these alloys be mixed so as to have a new alloy in which gold and silver would exist in the ratio 25 : 62?

23 From a container having pure milk, 20% is replaced by water and the process is repeated thrice. At the end of the third operation, what is the purity of the milk?

24 A 24 L cylinder containing ethylene and acetylene contains 25% ethylene by volume. A few litres of the mixture is released and replaced with equal amount of acetylene. If this process is repeated once, the cylinder is found to contain 16% ethylene by volume. How many litres of the gaseous mixture was released each time?

25 A bottle is full of dettol. One-third of its dettol is taken away and an equal amount of water is poured into the bottle to fill it again. This operation is repeated three times. Find the final ratio of dettol to water in the bottle. **[CBSE 2023]**

26 A container contains 64 L of pure milk. One-fourth of the milk is replaced by water. Again the operation is performed and one-fourth of mixture is replaced by water. Find the final ratio of milk to water in the container.

Case Study Based Questions

27 In first mixture, quantity of milk was 6 L more than that of water. After adding 40 L of second mixture (having ratio of water to milk 3 : 5) in the first mixture ratio of water to milk in the final mixture becomes 9 : 13.

On the basis of above information, answer the following questions.

(i) The quantity of milk in first mixture is

(a) 27 L (b) 24 L (c) 30 L (d) 35 L

(ii) The quantity of water in final mixture is

(a) 45 L (b) 30 L (c) 42 L (d) 36 L

(iii) The quantity of milk in final mixture is

(a) 43 L (b) 39 L (c) 52 L (d) 65 L

28 Two vessels A and B contain spirit and water mixed in the ratio 5:2 and 7:6, respectively. If these mixtures mixed to obtain a new mixture in vessel C containing spirit and water in the ratio 8 : 5. If the cost price of spirit be ₹ 1 per litre.

On the basis of above information, answer the following questions.

(i) Cost price of 1 L mixture in A is

(a) ₹ $\frac{2}{7}$ (b) ₹ $\frac{5}{7}$ (c) ₹ $\frac{7}{13}$ (d) ₹ $\frac{6}{13}$

(ii) Mean price of 1 L mixture in C is

(a) ₹ $\frac{6}{13}$ (b) ₹ $\frac{5}{13}$ (c) ₹ $\frac{8}{13}$ (d) ₹ $\frac{6}{27}$

(iii) The ratio in which these mixtures mixed to obtain new mixture in C is

(a) 7:9 (b) 9 : 7 (c) 9 : 10 (d) 10 : 11

Hints & Solutions

1. (b)	2. (d)	3. (a)	4. (b)
5. (a)	6. (c)	7. (d)	8. (c)
9. (c)	10. (b)	11. 1 : 2	12. 15 L

13. 15 L
14. 6000, 4000
15. ₹ 166 per kg
16. 3 : 2
17. 3 : 2
18. 20 L, 28 L
19. 2 : 1
20. 2 : 3
21. 7 L
22. 13 : 8
23. 51.2%
24. 4.8 L
25. Let the original quantity of dettol be x L and y L be taken out which is replaced by an equal quantity of water.

It is given by that $y = \frac{x}{3} \Rightarrow \frac{y}{x} = \frac{1}{3}$

After 3 operations, the quantity of dettol left $= x\left(1 - \frac{y}{x}\right)^3$

After 3 operations, the quantity of water in bottle

$$= x - x\left(1 - \frac{y}{x}\right)^3$$

∴ Thus, after 3 operations, we get

$$\frac{\text{Quantity of dettol in bottle}}{\text{Quantity of water in bottle}} = \frac{x\left(1-\frac{y}{x}\right)^3}{x - x\left(1-\frac{y}{x}\right)^3}$$

$$= \frac{x\left(1-\frac{x}{3x}\right)^3}{x - x\left(1-\frac{x}{3x}\right)^3}$$

$$= \frac{\left(1-\frac{1}{3}\right)^3}{1-\left(1-\frac{1}{3}\right)^3}$$

$$= \frac{\frac{8}{27}}{1-\frac{8}{27}} = \frac{8}{19}$$

Hence, after 3 operations, ratio of dettol and water is $8:19$.

26. 9 : 7
27. Let quantity of water in first mixture be x L.

∴ Quantity of milk in first mixture $=(x+6)$ L

Quantity of water in second mixture $= \frac{3}{8} \times 40 = 15$ L

Quantity of milk in second mixture $= \frac{5}{8} \times 40 = 25$ L

Now, according to the question,

$$\frac{x+15}{x+6+25} = \frac{8}{13}$$

$$\Rightarrow \quad 13x + 195 = 9x + 279$$

$$\Rightarrow \quad 4x = 84$$

$$\Rightarrow \quad x = 21$$

∴ Quantity of milk in first mixture $= (x+6)$ L $= 27$ L

∴ Quantity of water in final mixture $= x + 15 = 36$ L

∴ Quantity of milk in final mixture $= x + 6 + 25 = 52$ L

Ans. (i) (a), (ii) (d), (iii) (c)

28. Given the cost price of spirit be ₹ 1 per litre.

Spirit in 1 L mixture of $A = \frac{5}{7}$ L

Cost price 1 L mixture in $A = ₹\,\frac{5}{7}$

Spirit in 1 L mixture of $B = \frac{7}{13}$ L

Cost price of 1 L mixture in $B = ₹\,\frac{7}{13}$

Spirit in 1 L mixture of $C = \frac{8}{13}$ L

Mean price $= ₹\,\frac{8}{13}$

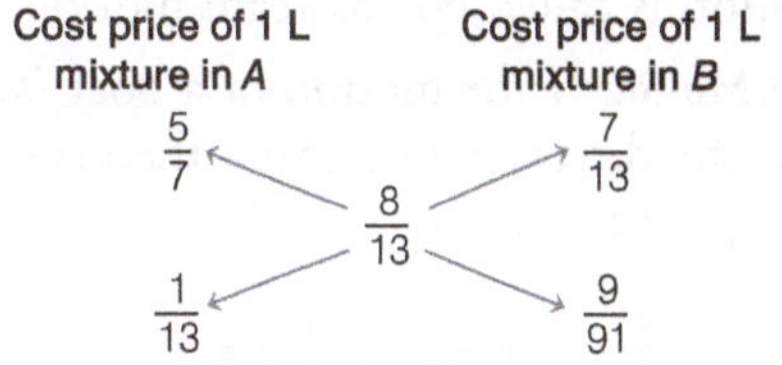

∴ Required ratio $= \frac{1}{13} : \frac{9}{91} = 7:9$

Ans. (i) (b), (ii) (c), (iii) (a)

CHAPTER 03

Boats and Streams

In this Chapter...

- Boats and Streams (Upstream and Downstream)
- Basic Formulae Related to Boats and Streams

Boats and streams are application of concepts of speed, time and distance. Speed of river flowing either aides a swimmer (or boat), while travelling with the direction of river or it opposes when travelling against the direction of river.

Here, we will explain the following concepts

- **Still Water** If the speed of water of a river is zero, then water is considered to be still water.
- **Stream** If the water of a river is moving at a certain speed, then it is called as stream.
- **Speed of Boat** Speed of boat means speed of boat (swimmer) in still water. In other words, if the speed of a boat (swimmer) is given, then that particular speed is the speed in still water.
- **Downstream Motion** If the motion of a boat (swimmer) is along the direction of stream, then such motion is called downstream motion.
- **Upstream Motion** If the motion of a boat (swimmer) is against the direction of stream, then such motion is called upstream motion.

Basic Formulae Related to Boats and Streams

If the speed of a boat in still water is x km/h and speed of the stream is y km/h and speed of downstream is u and speed of upstream is v, then

1. Speed downstream, $u = x + y$ km/h
2. Speed upstream, $v = x - y$ km/h
3. Speed of a boat in still water, $x = \frac{1}{2}(u + v)$
4. Speed of stream, $y = \frac{1}{2}(u - v)$

EXAMPLE 1. A man can row with a speed of 6 km/h in still water. What will be his speed with the stream, if the speed of stream is 2 km/h?

Sol. Given, speed of man in still water $= x = 6$ km/h

and speed of stream $= y = 2$ km/h

$\therefore$ Speed downstream $= x + y = 6 + 2 = 8$ km/h

EXAMPLE 2. If the speed of a boat in still water is 8 km/h and the rate of stream is 4 km/h, then find upstream speed of the boat.

Sol. Given, speed of a boat in still water $= x = 8$ km/h

and speed of stream $= y = 4$ km/h

$\therefore$ Speed upstream $= x - y = 8 - 4 = 4$ km/h

EXAMPLE 3. Shantanu can row upstream at 10 km/h and downstream at 18 km/h. Find the man's rate in still water and the rate of the current.

Sol. Given, speed upstream = 10 km/h

and speed downstream = 18 km/h

According to the formula,

Man's rate in still water

$$= \frac{1}{2}(\text{Speed downstream} + \text{Speed upstream})$$

$$= \frac{1}{2}(18 + 10) = \frac{28}{2} = 14 \text{ km/h}$$

Speed of current

$$= \frac{1}{2}(\text{Speed downstream} - \text{Speed upstream})$$

$$= \frac{1}{2}(18 - 10) = \frac{8}{2} = 4 \text{ km/h}$$

EXAMPLE 4. What time will be taken by a boat to cover a distance of 64 km along the stream, if speed of boat in still water is 12 km/h and speed of stream is 4 km/h?

Sol. Given, distance = 64 km,

speed of boat in still water = $x = 12$ km/h

and speed of stream = $y = 4$ km/h

$\therefore$ Downstream speed of boat = $x + y = 12 + 4 = 16$ km/h

$\therefore$ Required time $= \frac{\text{Distance}}{\text{Speed (downstream)}} = \frac{64}{16} = 4$ h

EXAMPLE 5. A boat takes 8 h to row 48 km downstream and 12 h to row the same distance upstream. Find the boat's rate in still water and rate of current.

Sol. Speed downstream $= \frac{\text{Distance}}{\text{Time}}$

$= \frac{48}{8} = 6$ km/h

Speed upstream $= \frac{48}{12} = 4$ km/h

Now, rate of boat in still water

$= \frac{\text{Speed downstream} + \text{Speed upstream}}{2}$

$= \frac{6+4}{2} = 5$ km/h

and rate of current

$= \frac{\text{Speed downstream} - \text{Speed upstream}}{2}$

$= \frac{6-4}{2} = 1$ km/h

EXAMPLE 6. Rajnish can row 12 km/h in still water. It takes him twice as long to row up as to row down the river. Find the rate of stream.

Sol. Let rate of stream = a km/h

and distance travelled = y km

Given, rate of Rajnish in still water = 12 km/h

Rate of downstream = $(12 + a)$ km/h

Rate of upstream = $(12 - a)$ km/h

According to the question,

Time taken to travel downstream

= 2 × Time taken to travel upstream

$\Rightarrow \frac{12+a}{y} = \frac{2(12-a)}{y}$

$\Rightarrow 12 + a = 2(12 - a)$

$\Rightarrow 12 + a = 24 - 2a$

$\Rightarrow a + 2a = 24 - 12$

$\Rightarrow 3a = 12$

$\Rightarrow a = \frac{12}{3} = 4$ km/h

EXAMPLE 7. Kamal can row a certain distance downstream in 12 h and can return the same distance in 18 h. If the stream flows at the rate of 6 km/h, then find the speed of Kamal in still water.

Sol. Let the speed of Kamal in still water be x km/h.

Then, Kamal's speed downstream = $(x + 6)$ km/h

Kamal's speed upstream = $(x - 6)$ km/h

According to the question,

Distance travelled downstream

= Distance travelled upstream

$\Rightarrow 12(x + 6) = 18(x - 6)$

$\Rightarrow 2x + 12 = 3x - 18$

$\Rightarrow 3x - 2x = 18 + 12$

$\therefore x = 30$ km/h

EXAMPLE 8. A man can row 12 km/h in still water. When the river is running at 2.4 km/h, it takes him 1 h to row to a place and to come back. How far is the place?

Sol. Man's rate downstream = 12 + 2.4 = 14.4 km/h

Man's rate upstream = 12 − 2.4 = 9.6 km/h

Let the required distance be x km.

According to the question,

Total time taken to travel x km upstream and downstream = 1 h

$\Rightarrow \frac{x}{14.4} + \frac{x}{9.6} = 1$

$\Rightarrow 9.6x + 14.4x = 14.4 \times 9.6$

$\Rightarrow 24x = 138.24$

$\therefore x = \frac{138.24}{24}$

$\Rightarrow x = 5.76$ km

EXAMPLE 9. A boat's speed in still water is 10 km/h, while river is flowing with a speed of 2 km/h and time taken to cover a certain distance upstream is 4 h more than time taken to cover the same distance downstream. Find the distance.

Sol. Let distance be x km.

Then, boat's speed downstream = 10 + 2 = 12 km/h

and boat's speed upstream = 10 − 2 = 8 km/h

According to the question,

Difference between the time

= Time taken by boat to travel upstream

− Time taken by boat to travel downstream

$\Rightarrow \frac{x}{8} - \frac{x}{12} = 4$

$\Rightarrow \frac{3x - 2x}{24} = 4$

$\therefore x = 96$ km

Exam Pattern Exercise

Part A - Objective Type Questions

Multiple Choice Type Questions

1 When the speed of a boat in still water is 4 km/h and the rate of stream is 2 km/h, then upstream speed of the boat is

(a) 6 km/h (b) 5 km/h
(c) 2 km/h (d) 7 km/h

2 If the speed of a swimmer in still water is 9 km/h, then downstream speed of the swimmer, when the river is flowing with the speed of 6 km/h is

(a) 15 km/h (b) 18 km/h
(c) 3 km/h (d) 12 km/h

3 A boat goes 48 km downstream in 20 h. It takes 4 h more to cover the same distance against the stream. The speed of the boat in still water is

(a) 2.2 km/h (b) 2 km/h
(c) 4 km/h (d) 4.2 km/h

4 Ravi can row upstream 8 km/h and downstream 16 km/h. The rate of current is

(a) 2 km/h (b) 3 km/h
(c) 4 km/h (d) 5 km/h

5 A person can row with the stream at 8 km/h and against the stream at 6 km/h. The speed of the current is

(a) 1 km/h (b) 2 km/h
(c) 4 km/h (d) 5 km/h

6 A boatman rows 1 km in 5 min along the stream and 6 km in 1 h against the stream. The speed of the stream is

(a) 3 km/h (b) 6 km/h
(c) 10 km/h (d) 12 km/h

7 The speed of a boat in still water is 500% more than the speed of the current. The respective ratio between the speed of the boat downstream and speed of the boat upstream is

(a) 9 : 2 (b) 7 : 3
(c) 7 : 5 (d) 9 : 4

8 Ashutosh can row 24 km/h in still water. It takes him twice as long as to row up as to row down the river. The rate of stream is

(a) 4 km/h (b) 18 km/h
(c) 8 km/h (d) 15 km/h

9 A boat can cover 28 km downstream in 42 min, ratio of speed of boat in still water to speed of stream is 7 : 3, the difference between time taken by boat to cover 60 km downstream and 40 km upstream is

(a) 3 h (b) 4 h (c) 1 h (d) 2 h

10 A man can row $7\frac{1}{2}$ km/h in still water. If in a river running at 1.5 km an hour, it takes him 50 min to row to a place and back, the distance of the place is

(a) 3 km (b) 6 km (c) 4 km (d) 5 km

Assertion-Reason Based Questions

Directions (Q. Nos. 11-13) *In the questions given below are two statements labelled as Assertion (A) and Reason (R). In the context of the two statements, which one of the following is correct?*

(a) Both A and R are correct; R is the correct explanation of A
(b) Both A and R are correct; R is not the correct explanation of A
(c) A is correct; R is incorrect
(d) R is correct; A is incorrect

11 **Assertion (A)** While travelling downstream, a man can row 16 km more in 4 h as compared to travelling upstream, then speed of the stream is 2 km/h.

Reason (R) The speed of a boat when travelling downstream is 32 km/h. Whereas when travelling upstream it is 28 km/h, then the speed of the boat in still water is 30 km/h.

12 **Assertion (A)** The speed of a boat in still water is 15 km/h and the rate of current is 3 km/h. The distance travelled downstream in 12 min is 5 km.

Reason (R) In one hour, a boat goes 11 km along the stream and 5 km against the stream. The speed of the boat in still water is 8 km/h.

13 **Assertion (A)** A boat man rows 1 km in 5 min, along the stream and 6 km in 1 h against the stream, then speed of the stream is 3 km/h.

Reason (R) A man can row upstream at 10 km/h and downstream at 18 km/h, then the man's rate in still water 14 km/h.

Part B - Descriptive Questions

Very Short Answer Type Questions

14 A swimmer's speed downstream is 11 km/h and speed of the stream is 1.5 km/h. Find the upstream speed of swimmer.

15 What time will be taken by a boat to cover a distance of 128 km along the stream, if speed of a boat in still water is 24 km/h and speed of stream is 8 km/h?

16 The time taken by a boat to travel 117 km downstream is 9 h and the same distance upstream is 13 h. The speed of the stream is $\frac{1}{4}$ of the speed of the boat. Then, find the distance travelled by the boat going upstream in 2 h.

17 Keshav can row 60 km downstream and 36 km upstream, taking 10 h each time. What is the velocity of the current?

18 A boat covers a distance of 30 km downstream in 2 h while it takes 6 h to cover the same distance upstream. Then, find the speed (in km/h) of the boat.

19 A man can row 6 km/h in still water. If the speed of the current is 2 km/h, it takes 3 h more in upstream than in the downstream for the same distance. Find the distance.

Short Answer Type Questions

20 The speed of the current is 5 km/h. A motorboat goes 10 km upstream and back again to the starting point in 50 min. Find the speed, (in km/h) of the motorboat in still water.

21 A person can row downstream 20 km in 2 h and upstream 4 km in 2 h. Find the speed of the current.

22 Ramesh rows in still water with a speed of 4.5 km/h to go to a certain place and to come back. Then, find his average speed for the whole journey, if the river is flowing with a speed of 1.5 km/h.

23 A man can row at 10 km/h in still water. If he takes total 5 h to go to a place 24 km away and return, then find the speed of the water current.

24 The speed of the boat in still water is 5 times the speed of the current. It takes 1.1 h to row to point *B* from point *A* downstream. The distance between point *A* and point *B* is 13.2 km. How much distance will it cover in 312 min upstream?

25 A motorboat can travel at 10 km/h in still water. It travelled 91 km downstream in a river and then returned to the same place, taking altogether 20 h. Find the rate of flow of river.

Long Answer Type Questions

26 A man can row against the current three-fourth of a kilometre in 15 min and returns same distance in 10 min, then find ratio of his speed to that of current.

27 The ratio of speed of a motorboat to that of the current of water is 36 : 5. The motorboat goes along with the current in 5 h 10 min. Then, find the time to come back of motorboat.

28 A man rows 12 km in 5 h against the stream, the speed of current being 4 km/h. Then, find the time taken by him to row 15 km with the stream.

29 Speed of the motorboat in still water is 45 km/h. If the motorboat travels 80 km along the stream in 1 h 20 min, then find the time taken by it to cover the same distance against the stream.

30 A boat running upstream takes 528 min to cover a certain distance, while it takes 240 min to cover the same distance running downstream. What is the ratio between the speed of the boat and speed of the water current, respectively?

31 A river is flowing with a steady speed of 4 km/h. One rows his boat downstream in the river and then returns by rowing upstream in the same river. When he returns to the starting point, the total distance covered by him is 42 km. If the return journey takes 2 h more than his outward journey, then find the speed of his rowing in still water.

32 In a river, the ratio of the speed of stream and speed of a boat in still water is 2 : 5. Again, ratio of the speed of the stream and speed of an another boat in still water is 3 : 4. What is the ratio of the speeds of the first boat to the second boat in still water?

33 A motorboat travelling at the some speed, can cover 25 km upstream and 39 km downstream in 8 h. At the same speed, it can travel 35 km upstream and 52 km downstream in 11 h. Find the speed of the stream.

34 *A*, *B* and *C* are situated at the bank of river which is flowing at a constant rate. *B* is at an equal distance with *A* and *C*. A swimmer Avinash takes 10 h to swim from *A* to *B* and *B* to *A*. Also, he takes 4 h to swim from *A* to *C*. What is the ratio of speed of Avinash in still water and speed of the stream?

35 A river is flowing at a speed of 5 km/h in a particular direction. A man, who can swim at a speed of 20 km/h in still water, starts swimming along the direction of flow of the river from point A and reaches another point B which is at a distance of 30 km from the starting point A. On reaching point B, the man turns back and starts swimming against the direction of flow of the river and stops after reaching point A. Find the total time taken by the man to complete his journey.

Case Study Based Questions

36 Shubham is rowing a boat. He takes 8 h to row 48 km upstream whereas he takes 4 h to go the same distance downstream.

Based on the above information, answer the following questions.

(i) His speed of rowing in still water is

(a) 8 km/h (b) 9 km/h
(c) 10 km/h (d) 11 km/h

(ii) The speed of the stream is

(a) 5 km/h (b) 3 km/h
(c) 1 km/h (d) None of these

(iii) His average speed is

(a) 8 km/h (b) 10 km/h
(c) 12 km/h (d) 14 km/h

(iv) The stream is flowing at the speed of 6 km/h. If Shubham rows a certain distance upstream in 4.5 h and return to the same place in 2.5 h, then the speed of Shubham's boat in still water is

(a) 15 km/h (b) 18 km/h
(c) 21 km/h (d) 24 km/h

(v) With reference to part (iv) above, the total distance covered by Shubham is

(a) 132 km (b) 142 km
(c) 152 km (d) 135 km

37 Rishabh goes to school and finds that there is a surprise test today in Maths period. The teacher gives five questions and announce to give a notebook to the students who score full. If you are at Rishabh's place, then try to score full. Five questions are as follows.

Based on the above information, answer the following questions.

(i) A person can row with a speed of 4 km/h in still water. If the speed of the stream is 3 km/h, then the person's speed with the stream is

(a) 7 km/h (b) 8 km/h
(c) 9 km/h (d) 1 km/h

(ii) If the stream's rate is 5 km/h and speed of a boat in still water is 6 km/h, then the upstream speed of the boat is

(a) 11 km/h (b) $\frac{1}{2}$ km/h
(c) 1 km/h (d) 2 km/h

(iii) A boat goes 40 km downstream in 10 h. It takes 5 h more to cover the same distance against the stream. The speed of the boat in still water is

(a) $\frac{8}{3}$ km/h (b) $\frac{10}{3}$ km/h
(c) $\frac{11}{3}$ km/h (d) $\frac{13}{3}$ km/h

(iv) Rishabh can row with the stream at 6 km/h and against the stream at 4 km/h. The speed of the current is

(a) 1 km/h (b) 2 km/h
(c) 3 km/h (d) 4 km/h

(v) A boat man rows 12 km in 2 h along the stream and 6 km in 2 h against the stream. The speed of the stream is

(a) $\frac{7}{2}$ km/h (b) $\frac{5}{2}$ km/h
(c) $\frac{3}{2}$ km/h (d) $\frac{1}{2}$ km/h

Hints & Solutions

1. (c) 2. (a) 3. (a) 4. (c)
5. (a) 6. (a) 7. (c) 8. (c)
9. (c) 10. (a) 11. (b) 12. (d)
13. (b)

14. **Hint** Given, speed of stream = 1.5 km/h

We know that

Speed of stream

$$= \frac{1}{2}(\text{Speed downstream} - \text{Speed upstream})$$

Ans. 8 km/h

15. Given, speed of boat in still water = x = 24 km/h

and speed of stream = y = 8 km/h

$\therefore$ Downstream speed of boat = $x + y = 24 + 8$

= 32 km/h

$$\therefore \text{Required time} = \frac{\text{Distance}}{\text{Speed (downstream)}} = \frac{128}{32} = 4 \text{ km/h}$$

16. $\because$ Distance travelled = 117 km

and time = 13 h

$$\therefore \text{Upstream speed} = \frac{\text{Distance}}{\text{Time}} = \frac{117}{13} = 9 \text{ km/h}$$

Now, distance travelled by boat going upstream in 2 h

= Speed upstream $\times$ 2

= $9 \times 2 = 18$ km

17. $$\text{Speed downstream} = \frac{\text{Distance}}{\text{Time}} = \frac{60}{10} = 6 \text{ km/h}$$

$$\text{Speed upstream} = \frac{\text{Distance}}{\text{Time}} = \frac{36}{10} = 3.6 \text{ km/h}$$

$\therefore$ Velocity of the current

$$= \frac{1}{2}(\text{Speed downstream} - \text{Speed upstream})$$

$$= \frac{1}{2}(6 - 3.6) = \frac{2.4}{2} = 1.2 \text{ km/h}$$

18. Speed of the boat downstream

$$= \frac{\text{Distance covered}}{\text{Time taken}} = \frac{30}{2} = 15 \text{ km/h}$$

Now, speed of the boat upstream

$$= \frac{\text{Distance covered}}{\text{Time taken}} = \frac{30}{6} = 5 \text{ km/h}$$

Now, speed of the boat

$$= \frac{\text{Speed downstream} + \text{Speed upstream}}{2}$$

$$= \frac{15 + 5}{2} = \frac{20}{2} = 10 \text{ km/h}$$

19. **Hint** Let total distance be x km.

According to the question,

$$\frac{x}{6+2} + 3 = \frac{x}{6-2}$$ **Ans.** 24 km

20. 25 km/h

21. Let speed of person be x km/h

and speed of current be y km/h.

Distance = 20 km in downstream and 4 km in upstream

According to the question,

$$\frac{20}{x+y} = 2 \Rightarrow x + y = 10 \quad \text{...(i)}$$

and $$\frac{4}{x-y} = 2 \Rightarrow x - y = 2 \quad \text{...(ii)}$$

From Eqs. (i) and (ii), we get

$x = 6$ and $y = 4$

Hence, the speed of current is 4 km/h.

22. **Hint** Ramesh's speed upstream = 4.5 − 1.5 = 3 km/h

Ramesh's speed downstream = 4.5 + 1.5 = 6 km/h

Let the distance in one direction be x.

Then, time taken in upstream = $\frac{x}{3}$

and time taken in downstream = $\frac{x}{6}$

$$\therefore \text{Average speed} = \frac{\text{Total distance}}{\text{Total time}}$$ **Ans.** 4 km/h

23. **Hint** Let speed of water current be x km/h.

$\therefore$ Speed downstream = $(10 + x)$ km/h

and speed upstream = $(10 - x)$ km/h

According to the question,

$$\frac{24}{10+x} + \frac{24}{10-x} = 5$$ **Ans.** 2 km/h

24. Let the speed of the current be x km/h.

Then, speed of the boat = $5x$ km/h

Total speed in downstream = $x + 5x = 6x$ km/h

Total speed in upstream = $5x - x = 4x$ km/h

According to the question,

$$1.1 \times 6x = 13.2 \Rightarrow x = 2 \text{ km/h}$$

[$\because$ Time $\times$ Speed = Distance]

$\therefore$ Required distance covered in upstream

$$= \text{Time} \times \text{Speed} = \frac{312}{60} \times 4x$$

$$= \frac{312}{60} \times 8 = 5.2 \times 8 = 41.6 \text{ km}$$

25. **Hint** Given, speed of the motorboat = 10 km/h

Let speed of flow of river be x km/h.

$\therefore$ Upstream speed of the motorboat = $(10 - x)$ km/h

and downstream speed of the motorboat = $(10 + x)$ km/h

According to the question,

$$\frac{91}{10-x} + \frac{91}{10+x} = 20$$

Ans. 3 km/h

26. **Hint** Let the speed of a man and the current be x km/h and y km/h, respectively.
upstream speed $= (x - y)$ km/h
and downstream speed $= (x + y)$ km/h
According to the question,

$$\frac{3 \times 60}{4 \times 15} = x - y \Rightarrow x - y = 3 \quad ...(i)$$

and $$\frac{3}{4} \times \frac{60}{10} = x + y \Rightarrow x + y = \frac{9}{2} \quad ...(ii)$$

On solving Eqs. (i) and (ii), we get

$$x = \frac{15}{4}, \ y = \frac{3}{4}$$

Ans. 5 : 1

27. **Hint** Let speed of a motorboat be $36x$ km/h.
and speed of the current $= 5x$ km/h
$\therefore$ Speed downstream $= (36 + 5)x = 41x$ km/h
and speed upstream $= (36 - 5)x = 31x$ km/h
Let the distance be a km.
According to the question,
When motorboat goes along with the current, then
Distance = Time × Speed

$$\Rightarrow \quad a = \left(5 + \frac{10}{60}\right) \times 41x \Rightarrow a = \frac{31}{6} \times 41x \quad ...(i)$$

Again, when motorboat come back

$$a = \text{Time} \times 31x$$

Ans. 6 h 50 min

28. **Hint** Let the speed of the boat be x km/h.
Then, speed of upstream $= (x - 4)$ km/h
According to the question,

$$\frac{12}{x - 4} = 5 \Rightarrow 12 = 5x - 20$$

$$\Rightarrow \quad x = \frac{32}{5} \text{ km/h}$$

$\therefore$ Time taken to row 15 km with the stream $= \dfrac{15}{\frac{32}{5} + 4}$

Ans. 1 h $26\frac{7}{13}$ min

29. **Hint** Let speed of the stream be x km/h.
Given, speed of the motorboat in still water = 45 km/h
$\therefore$ Speed of the motorboat along stream $= (45 + x)$ km/h
According to the question,

$$45 + x = \frac{80}{1\frac{1}{3}} \Rightarrow 45 + x = \frac{80 \times 3}{4}$$

$$\therefore \quad x = 60 - 45 = 15 \text{ km/h}$$

$\therefore$ Speed of the motorboat against stream $= 45 - 15$
$= 30$ km/h

Hence, required time $= \dfrac{\text{Distance}}{\text{Speed}}$ **Ans.** 2 h 40 min

30. **Hint** Let the boat's speed upstream be x km/h and the boat's speed downstream be y km/h.
According to the question,
Distance covered in 528 min
= Distance covered in 240 min
$\Rightarrow$ Distance covered in 8 h 48 min
= Distance covered in 4 h

$$\Rightarrow \quad x \times 8\frac{4}{5} = (y \times 4)$$

$$\Rightarrow \quad \frac{44}{5}x = 4y \Rightarrow y = \frac{11}{5}x$$

$\therefore$ Required ratio $= \left(\dfrac{y + x}{2}\right) : \left(\dfrac{y - x}{2}\right)$ **Ans.** 8 : 3

31. **Hint** Let the speed of rowing in still water be u km/h.
Distance in downstream motion = 21 km
and speed downstream $= (u + 4)$ km/h

$$\therefore \text{ Time} = \frac{21}{u + 4}$$

Distance upstream motion = 21 km
and speed upstream $= (u - 4)$ km

$$\therefore \text{ Time} = \frac{21}{u - 4}$$

According to the question,

$$\frac{21}{u + 4} + 2 = \frac{21}{u - 4}$$ **Ans.** 10 km/h

32. For the first boat,
Speed of the stream : Speed of the boat = 2 : 5
Let speed of the stream $= 2x$ km/h
and speed of the boat $= 5x$ km/h
Similarly, for the second boat
Speed of the stream : Speed of the boat = 3 : 4
Let speed of the stream $= 3y$ km/h
and speed of the boat $= 4y$
In both of the conditions, river is same.

$$\therefore \quad 2x = 3y \Rightarrow x = \frac{3}{2}y$$

Thus, required ratio in speeds of the boats in still water

$$= 5x : 4y = 5 \times \frac{3}{2}y : 4y = 15 : 8$$

33. **Hint** Let the speed of a motorboat and the stream be x km/h and y km/h, respectively.
$\therefore$ Speed of the motorboat along the stream
$= (x + y)$ km/h
and speed of the motorboat against stream
$= (x - y)$ km/h
According to the question,

$$\frac{25}{x - y} + \frac{39}{x + y} = 8 \quad ...(i)$$

and $$\frac{35}{x - y} + \frac{52}{x + y} = 11 \quad ...(ii)$$

On multiplying Eq. (i) by 4 and Eq. (ii) by 3, then subtracting Eq. (ii) from Eq. (i), we get

$$x - y = 5 \quad \text{...(iii)}$$

On substituting the value of $(x - y = 5)$ in Eq. (i), we get

$$x + y = 13 \quad \text{...(iv)}$$

On solving Eqs. (iii) and (iv), we get

$$x = 9 \text{ and } y = 4$$

Ans. Speed of the stream = 4 km/h

34. Let speed of Avinash in still water be a km/h and speed of the stream be b km/h.

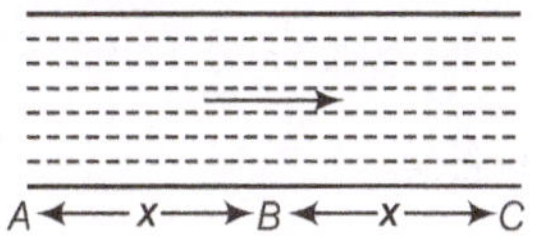

Let $AB = BC = x$ km

From first condition,

$$\frac{x}{a+b} + \frac{x}{a-b} = 10 \quad \text{...(i)}$$

From second condition,

$$\frac{2x}{a+b} = 4$$

$$\Rightarrow \quad \frac{x}{a+b} = 2 \quad \text{...(ii)}$$

Putting the value in Eq. (i), we get

$$2 + \frac{x}{a-b} = 10$$

$$\Rightarrow \quad \frac{x}{a-b} = 8 \quad \text{...(iii)}$$

On dividing Eqs. (iii) by (ii), we get

$$\frac{a+b}{a-b} = \frac{8}{2} = 4$$

$$\Rightarrow \quad a + b = 4a - 4b$$

$$\Rightarrow \quad 3a = 5b$$

$$\therefore \quad a : b = 5 : 3$$

35. Given, speed of the stream = 5 km/h

and speed of the man in still water = 20 km/h

∴ Speed of the man downstream = 20 + 5 = 25 km/h

and speed of the man upstream = 20 − 5 = 15 km/h

∴ Total time taken to complete the whole journey

$$= \frac{30}{25} + \frac{30}{15}$$

$$= 30\left(\frac{3+5}{75}\right) = \frac{30 \times 8}{75}$$

$$= 3 \text{ h } 12 \text{ min}$$

36. **Hint**

(i) (b) Let the speed in still water be x km/h and the speed of the stream be y km/h.

Speed of the boat upstream = $(x - y)$ km/h

Speed of the boat downstream = $(x + y)$ km/h

$$\because \quad \frac{\text{Distance}}{\text{Speed}} = \text{Time}$$

$$\therefore \quad \frac{48}{x-y} = 8 \Rightarrow 6 = x - y \quad \text{...(i)}$$

$$\text{and} \quad \frac{48}{x+y} = 4$$

$$\Rightarrow \quad 12 = x + y \quad \text{...(ii)}$$

On adding Eqs. (i) and (ii), we get

$$18 = 2x \Rightarrow x = 9$$

$$\therefore \quad y = 3 \quad \text{[from Eq. (i)]}$$

Speed of rowing in still water = 9 km/h

(ii) (b) Speed of the stream = 3 km/h

(iii) (a) Total distance covered = 48 + 48 = 96 km

Total time taken = 8 + 4 = 12 h

$$\therefore \text{Average speed} = \frac{\text{Total distance covered}}{\text{Total time taken}}$$

$$= \frac{96}{12} = 8 \text{ km/h}$$

(iv) (c) Speed of the stream = y = 6 km/h

Let distance covered be a km.

and speed of the boat in still water be x km/h.

$$\therefore \quad d = (x - 6)(4.5) \quad \text{...(i)}$$

$$\text{Also,} \quad d = (x + 6)(2.5) \quad \text{...(ii)}$$

On solving Eqs. (i) and (ii), we get

$$x = 21 \text{ km/h}$$

(v) (d) Speed of the boat upstream = (21 − 6) = 15 km/h

Let d km be the distance covered upstream.

Time taken in covering d km upstream = 4.5 h

∴ d = Speed × Time = 15 × 4.5 = 67.5 km

Total distance covered by Shubham

= d km upstream + d km downstream

= $2d$ km = 135 km

37. (i) (a) (ii) (c)

(iii) (b) Speed downstream $= \frac{40}{10} = 4$ km/h

and speed upstream $= \frac{40}{(10+5)} = \frac{8}{3}$ km/h

∴ Speed of the boat in still water

$$= \frac{1}{2}\left(4 + \frac{8}{3}\right) = \frac{20}{2 \times 3} = \frac{10}{3} \text{ km/h}$$

(iv) (a)

(v) (c) Downstream speed $= \frac{12}{2} = 6$ km/h

and upstream speed $= \frac{6}{2} = 3$ km/h

∴ Speed of the stream $= \frac{6-3}{2} = \frac{3}{2}$ km/h

CHAPTER 04

Pipes and Cisterns

In this Chapter...

- Important Facts Related to Pipes and Cisterns
- Some Important Techniques

In this chapter, we will study about pipes and cisterns. Generally, in this chapter, we learn about time taken to fill/empty the tank.

Problems on Pipes and Cisterns are based on the basic concept of time and work. Pipes are connected to a tank or cistern and are used to fill or empty the tank or cistern. In pipe and cistern, the work is done in form of filling or emptying a cistern/tank.

- **Inlet pipe** It fills a tank/cistern/reservoir.
- **Outlet pipe** It empties a tank/cistern/reservoir.

Important Facts Related to Pipes and Cisterns

(i) If a pipe can fill/empty a tank in m h, then the part of tank filled/emptied in 1 h $= \frac{1}{m}$.

e.g. If a pipe can fill the tank in 7 h, then the volume of tank filled in 1 h $= \frac{1}{7}$.

(ii) If a pipe can fill/empty $1/m$ part of a tank in 1 h, then it can fill/empty the whole tank in 'm' h.

e.g. If a pipe can fill 1/5 part of a tank in 1 h, then it can fill the whole tank in 5 h.

(iii) Time taken to fill a tank is taken positive (+ve) and time taken to empty a tank is taken negative (–ve).

(iv) If a pipe fills a tank in m h and another pipe fills in n h. Then, part filled by both pipes in 1 h $= \frac{1}{m} + \frac{1}{n}$.

EXAMPLE 1. An outlet pipe can empty a cistern in 5 h. In what time will the pipe empty $\frac{2}{5}$ part of the cistern?

Sol. $\because$ Time taken to empty full cistern = 5 h

$\therefore$ Time taken to empty $\frac{2}{5}$ part of the cistern $= \frac{2}{5} \times 5 = 2$ h

EXAMPLE 2. Pipe A can fill a tank in 1 hour and Pipe B can fill it in 1½ hours. If both the pipes are opened in the empty tank, how much time will they take to fill the tank? **[CBSE 2025]**

Sol. $\because$ Part filled by A alone in 1 h $= \frac{1}{1} = 1$

and part filled by B alone in 1 h $= \frac{1}{1\frac{1}{2}} = \frac{2}{3}$

$\therefore$ Part filled by $(A+B)$ in 1 h $= 1 + \frac{2}{3} = \frac{5}{3}$

Hence, both the pipes together will fill the tank in $\frac{3}{5}$ h.

EXAMPLE 3. If a pipe can fill a tank in 5 h and another pipe can empty the tank in 10 h, then what part of a tank will be filled by both pipes in 1 h, if both pipes are open simultaneously?

Sol. In 1 h, part filled by 1st pipe $= \frac{1}{m} = \frac{1}{5}$

In 1 h, part emptied by 2nd pipe $= \frac{1}{n} = \frac{1}{10}$

$\therefore$ In 1 h, part filled by both pipes when open simultaneously $= \frac{1}{m} - \frac{1}{n}$

[– ve sign is used, as 2nd pipe empties the tank]

$= \frac{1}{5} - \frac{1}{10} = \frac{2-1}{10} = \frac{1}{10}$ part

Some Important Formulae

A pipe can fill/empty a tank in m h and another pipe can fill/empty the same tank in n h.

(i) If both pipes either fill or empty the tank, then the time taken to fill or empty the tank when both pipes are opened, is $t = \frac{mn}{m+n}$.

(ii) If first pipe fills the tank and second pipe empties the tank, then the time taken to fill the tank when both pipes are opened, is

$$t = \frac{mn}{m-n}, \text{ where } m > n.$$

(iii) If first pipe fills the tank and second pipe empties the tank, then the time taken to empty the tank when both pipes are opened, is

$$t = \frac{mn}{n-m}, \text{ where } n > m.$$

(iv) If three pipes can fill a tank separately in m, n and p h respectively, then part of tank filled in 1 h by all the three pipes is given by $\left(\frac{1}{m}+\frac{1}{n}+\frac{1}{p}\right)$ and total time taken to fill the tank is given by $\frac{mnp}{np+mp+mn}$ h.

Note If any one of the three pipes is used to empty the tank, then time taken by that particular pipe will be negative (–ve). Suppose, third pipe is used to empty the tank. Then, the above formulae takes the form as

$$\left(\frac{1}{m}+\frac{1}{n}-\frac{1}{p}\right) \text{ and } \frac{mnp}{np+mp-mn} \text{ h}$$

EXAMPLE 4. Two pipes A and B can fill a tank in 18 h and 12 h, respectively. If both the pipes are opened simultaneously, then how much time will be taken to fill the tank?

Sol. $\because$ Part filled by A alone in 1 h $= \frac{1}{18}$ and part filled by B alone in 1 h $= \frac{1}{12}$

$\therefore$ Part filled by $(A+B)$ in 1 h $= \frac{1}{18}+\frac{1}{12} = \frac{2+3}{36} = \frac{5}{36}$

Hence, both the pipes together will fill the tank in $\frac{36}{5}$ h, i.e. $7\frac{1}{5}$ h.

EXAMPLE 5. A pipe can fill a tank in 5 h, while another pipe can empty it in 6 h. If both the pipes are opened simultaneously, then how much time will be taken to fill the tank?

Sol. $\because$ Part filled by 1st pipe in 1 h $= \frac{1}{5}$

and part emptied by 2nd pipe in 1 h $= \frac{1}{6}$

$\therefore$ Part filled in 1 h by both pipes $= \frac{1}{5} - \frac{1}{6} = \frac{6-5}{30} = \frac{1}{30}$

Hence, the tank will be filled completely in 30 h.

EXAMPLE 6. A pipe can fill a tank in 10 h. Due to a leak in the bottom, it fills the tank in 20 h. If the tank is full, then how much time will the leak take to empty it?

Sol. Let the leak empties full tank in x h, then part emptied in 1 h by leak $= \frac{1}{x}$

Also, part filled by inlet pipe in 1 h $= \frac{1}{10}$

According to the question,

$$\frac{1}{10} + \frac{1}{x} = \frac{1}{20}$$

$$\Rightarrow \quad \frac{1}{x} = \frac{1}{20} - \frac{1}{10} = \frac{1-2}{20} = -\frac{1}{20}$$

[–ve sign means leak empties the tank]

Hence, leak will empty the full tank in 20 h.

EXAMPLE 7. Two pipes A and B can fill a tank in 3 h and 2 h, respectively. If they are opened on alternate hours and if pipe A is opened first. In how many hours, the tank shall be fill?

Sol. Pipe A and B can fill $\left(\frac{1}{3}+\frac{1}{2}\right)^{\text{th}} = \frac{5}{6}$ part of the tank, if each is open for 1 h alternately.

$\therefore$ Part of the tank filled in 2 h $= \frac{5}{6}$

Now, $\frac{1}{6}$ part of tank remains unfilled and it is filled by A.

Since, A fill the tank in 3 h completely.

Therefore, $\frac{1}{6}$ part fill in $\frac{1}{2}$ h.

Hence, the tank is filled in $2\frac{1}{2}$ h.

EXAMPLE 8. Three pipes m, n and p can fill a tank separately in 4, 5 and 10 h, respectively. Find the time taken by all the three pipes to fill the tank when the pipes are opened together.

Sol. Here, part filled by pipe m in 1 h $= \frac{1}{4}$,

part filled by pipe n in 1 h $= \frac{1}{5}$

and part filled by pipe p in 1 h $= \frac{1}{10}$

$\therefore$ Part filled by $(m+n+p)$ pipes in 1 h $= \frac{1}{4}+\frac{1}{5}+\frac{1}{10}$

$$= \frac{5+4+2}{20} = \frac{11}{20}$$

$\therefore$ Required time to fill the tank $= \frac{20}{11}$ h $= 1\frac{9}{11}$ h

EXAMPLE 9. Pipe A can fill a tank in 20 h while pipe B alone can fill it in 10 h and pipe C can empty the full tank in 30 h. If all the pipes are opened together, then how much time will be needed to make the tank full?

Sol. Part filled by pipe A alone in 1 h $= \frac{1}{20}$,

part filled by pipe B alone in 1 h $= \frac{1}{10}$

and part emptied by pipe C alone in 1 h $= \frac{1}{30}$

Net part filled by $(A+B+C)$ in 1 h $= \left(\frac{1}{20}+\frac{1}{10}-\frac{1}{30}\right)$

$$= \left(\frac{3+6-2}{60}\right) = \frac{7}{60} \text{ h}$$

$\therefore$ Required time to fill the tank $= \frac{60}{7}$ h $= 8\frac{4}{7}$ h

EXAMPLE 10. Two pipes A and B are opened together to fill a tank. Both the pipes fill the tank in time t. If A separately takes 4 min more time than t to fill the tank and B takes 64 min more time than t to fill the tank, then find the value of t.

Sol. Time taken by pipe $A = (4+t)$ min

Time taken by pipe $B = (64+t)$ min

According to the question,

$$\frac{1}{(4+t)}+\frac{1}{(64+t)} = \frac{1}{t}$$

$$\Rightarrow \frac{64+t+4+t}{(4+t)(64+t)} = \frac{1}{t}$$

$$\Rightarrow t(68+2t) = 256+4t+64t+t^2$$

$$\Rightarrow 68t+2t^2 = t^2+68t+256$$

$$\Rightarrow t^2 = 256 \Rightarrow t = 16 \text{ min}$$

EXAMPLE 11. A full tank gets emptied in 6 min due to presence of an orifice in it. On opening a tap which can fill the tank at the rate of 8 L/min, the tank gets emptied in 10 min. Find the capacity of tank.

Sol. Let x be the volume of tank.

Time to be emptied = 6 min

Rate of leak $= \frac{x}{6}$ L/min

Rate of filling = 8 L/min

Then, tank emptied in 10 min.

According to the question,

$$8-\frac{x}{6} = -\frac{x}{10} \Rightarrow \frac{x}{6}-\frac{x}{10} = 8$$

$$\Rightarrow \frac{5x-3x}{30} = 8 \Rightarrow \frac{2x}{30} = 8$$

$$\Rightarrow 2x = 30\times 8 \Rightarrow x = 120 \text{ L}$$

Hence, the capacity of the tank is 120 L.

EXAMPLE 12. Tap A can fill a tank 3 times faster than tap B and takes 28 min less than tap B to fill the tank. If both the taps are opened simultaneously, then find the time taken to fill the tank.

Sol. Let the time taken by tap A to fill the tank be x min.

Then, time taken by tap B to fill the tank be $3x$ min.

Then, according to the question,

$$3x - x = 28 \Rightarrow 2x = 28$$

$$\Rightarrow x = \frac{28}{2} = 14 \text{ min}$$

$\therefore$ Time taken by tap $A = 14$ min,

part filled by tap A in 1 min $= \frac{1}{14}$

Time taken by tap $B = 3\times 14 = 42$ min

Part filled by tap B in 1 min $= \frac{1}{42}$

$\therefore$ Part filled by both taps in 1 min $= \frac{1}{14}+\frac{1}{42} = \frac{3+1}{42}$

$$= \frac{4}{42} = \frac{2}{21}$$

So, time taken by both taps to fill the tank working together $= \frac{21}{2}$ min

EXAMPLE 13. Pipe A is 3 times slower than the pipe B and takes 16 min more time than the pipe B. How much time will pipe B take to fill the tank?

Sol. Let the time taken by pipe A to fill the tank be $3x$ min.

Then, time taken by pipe B to fill the tank be x min.

Then, according to the question,

$$3x - x = 16 \Rightarrow 2x = 16 \Rightarrow x = 8$$

$\therefore$ Time taken by pipe B to fill the tank = 8 min

EXAMPLE 14. Pipe A is 2 times slower than pipe B and takes 9 min more time than the pipe B. How much time will pipe A take to fill the tank?

Sol. Let the time taken by pipe A to fill the tank be $2x$ min.

Then, time taken by pipe B to fill the tank is x min.

Then, according to the question,

$$2x - x = 9$$

$$\Rightarrow x = 9 \text{ min}$$

$\therefore$ Time taken by pipe A to fill the tank $= 2\times 9$

$$= 18 \text{ min}$$

EXAMPLE 15. Two pipes A and B can fill a tank in 24 min and 32 min, respectively. If both the pipes are opened simultaneously, after how much time should B be closed so that the tank is full in 18 min? **[CBSE 2023]**

Sol. Let B be closed after n min. Then, pipe A runs for 18 h and B runs for n min to fill the tank.

$$\therefore \quad \frac{18}{24}+\frac{n}{32}=1$$

$$\Rightarrow \quad \frac{n}{32}=1-\frac{18}{24}=1-\frac{3}{4}=\frac{1}{4}$$

$$\Rightarrow \quad n=\frac{32}{4}=8$$

Hence, pipe B must be closed after 8 h.

EXAMPLE 16. Pipe A can fill a tank in 3 h. There are two outlet pipes B and C from the tank which can empty it in 7 h and 10 h respectively. If all the three pipes are opened simultaneously, how long will it take to fill the tank? **[CBSE 2023]**

Sol. Let the tank be filled in n h it is given that $n_A=3$, $n_B=7$ and $n_C=10$.

$$\therefore \quad \frac{1}{n}=\frac{1}{n_A}-\frac{1}{n_B}-\frac{1}{n_C}$$

$$\Rightarrow \quad \frac{1}{n}=\frac{1}{3}-\frac{1}{7}-\frac{1}{10}=\frac{70-30-21}{210}=\frac{19}{210}$$

$$\Rightarrow \quad n=\frac{210}{19}=11\frac{1}{19}$$

Hence, the tank is filled in $11\frac{1}{19}$ h.

EXAMPLE 17. Three pipes A, B and C can fill a tank together in 9 h. After working at it together for 3 h, B is closed and A and C can fill the remaining part in 12 h. Find the time in which B alone can fill the tank.

Sol. In 1 h, part of the tank filled by A, B and $C=\frac{1}{9}$

$\therefore$ In 3 h, part of the tank filled by A, B and $C=\frac{3}{9}=\frac{1}{3}$

Remaining part $=1-\frac{1}{3}=\frac{2}{3}$

In 12 h, A and C can fill $=\frac{2}{3}$ part of the tank

$\therefore$ In 1 h, A and C can fill $=\frac{2}{3}\times\frac{1}{12}=\frac{1}{18}$ part of the tank

Now, B's 1 hour work $=(A+B+C)$'s 1 hour work $-(A+C)$'s 1 hour work

$$=\frac{1}{9}-\frac{1}{18}=\frac{1}{18}$$

Hence, B alone can fill the tank in 18 h.

EXAMPLE 18. A cistern has three pipes A, B and C. Pipes A and B are inlet pipes whereas pipe C is an outlet pipe. Pipes A and B can fill the cistern separately in 3 h and 4 h respectively, while pipe C can empty the completely filled cistern in 1 h. If the pipes A, B and C are opened in order at 5, 6 and 7 am respectively, at what time will the cistern be empty? **[CBSE 2024]**

Sol. Part of the cistern filled by A in 2 h i.e. till 7 am

$$=\frac{1}{3}\times 2=\frac{2}{3}$$

Part of the cistern filled by B in 1 h i.e. till 7 am $=\frac{1}{4}$

When all the three pipes are opened, the part filled in 1h

$$=\frac{1}{3}+\frac{1}{4}-\frac{1}{1}$$

$$=\frac{4+3-12}{12}=\frac{-5}{12}$$

i.e. $\frac{5}{12}$ part is empted per hour.

$\therefore$ Time taken to empty $\left[\left(\frac{2}{3}+\frac{1}{4}\right)\right]$ part or $\frac{11}{12}$ part

$$=\frac{11}{12}\times\frac{12}{5}=\frac{11}{5}\text{ h}=2\text{ h }12\text{ min}$$

$\therefore$ Required time $=7+2:12=9:12$

Thus, at 9 : 12 am the cistern will be emptied.

EXAMPLE 19. Pipes A and B can fill a tank separately in 20 h and 30 h, respectively. Pipe C can empty the tank in 15 h. If pipes A, B and C are opened successively for one hour each, then how much time to fill the tank?

Sol. In first three hours, part of the tank filled

$$=\frac{1}{20}+\frac{1}{30}-\frac{1}{15}=\frac{1}{60}$$

$\therefore$ Time taken to fill $\left[1-\left(\frac{1}{20}+\frac{1}{30}\right)\right]$

or $\frac{55}{60}$th part of the tank $=3\times 55=165$ min

$\therefore$ Unfilled part of the tank $=1-\frac{55}{60}=\frac{5}{60}=\frac{1}{12}$

Now, its pipe A turn to fill the tank .

Part filled by pipe A in 1 h $=\frac{1}{20}$

Unfilled part left $=\frac{1}{12}-\frac{1}{20}=\frac{1}{30}$

Now, its pipe B turn to fill the tank in one hour, pipe B can fill $\frac{1}{30}$ part of the tank which is same as unfilled part.

Hence, the tank is filled $=3\times 55+1+1=167$ h

i.e. 2 days and 23 h

Exam Pattern Exercise

Part A - Objective Type Questions

Multiple Choice Type Questions

1 Two pipes A and B can fill a tank in 18 h and 12 h, respectively. If both the pipes are opened simultaneously, then the time will be taken to fill the tank is

(a) 6 h (b) $7\frac{1}{5}$ h (c) 7 h (d) $6\frac{1}{5}$ h

2 A pipe can fill a tank in 5 h, while another pipe can empty it in 6 h. If both the pipes are opened simultaneously, then the time will be taken to fill the tank is

(a) 30 h (b) 45 h (c) 17 h (d) 35 h

3 A pipe can fill a cistern in 6 h. Due to a leak in its bottom, it is filled in 7 h. If the cistern is full, then the time will it be emptied by the leak is

(a) 42 h (b) 40 h (c) 43 h (d) 45 h

4 A tank (of capacity 160 L) has one inlet, A and one outlet, B. Inlet A, alone can fill the empty tank in 6 h and outlet B alone can empty the full tank in 24 h. The time taken by inlet A to fill 16 L water in the tank when outlet B is also open is

(a) 1 (b) $\frac{4}{5}$ (c) $\frac{11}{5}$ (d) $1\frac{1}{2}$

5 Pipe A is 4 times faster than pipe B and takes 30 min less than the pipe B to fill the tank. If both pipes are opened together, then the cistern will be fill in

(a) 6 min (b) 8 min
(c) 12 min (d) 9 min

6 Pipe A is 2 times slower than pipe B and takes 9 min more time than the pipe B. How much time will pipe A take to fill the tank?

(a) 18 min (b) 12 min
(c) 10 min (d) 15 min

7 A, B and C are three pipes connected to a tank. A and B together fill the tank in 6 h, B and C together fill the tank in 10 h and A and C together fill the tank in 12 h. The time taken by A, B and C to fill the tank together is

(a) 9 h (b) $5\frac{3}{7}$ h
(c) $5\frac{2}{7}$ h (d) $5\frac{5}{7}$ h

8 Two pipes A and B are opened together to fill a tank. Both the pipes fill the tank in time t. If A separately takes 2 min more time than t to fill the tank and B takes 52 min more time than t to fill the tank, then the value of t is

(a) 14 min (b) 12 min
(c) 10 min (d) 16 min

9 A cistern normally takes 10 h to be filled by a tap but because of one open outlet pipe, it takes 5 h more. In how many hours will the oulet pipe will empty a full cistern?

(a) 30 h (b) 24 h (c) 20 h (d) 15 h

10 Two pipes A and B can separately till a cistern in 60 min and 75 min, respectively. There is a third pipe in the bottom of the cistern to empty it. If all the three pipes are simultaneously opened, then the cistern is full in 50 min. In how much time the third pipe alone can empty the cistern?

(a) 90 min (b) 110 min
(c) 100 min (d) 120 min

Assertion-Reason Based Questions

Directions (Q. Nos. 11-13) *In the questions given below are two statements labelled as Assertion (A) and Reason (R). In the context of the two statements, which one of the following is correct?*

(a) Both A and R are correct; R is the correct explanation of A
(b) Both A and R are correct; R is not the correct explanation of A
(c) A is correct; R is incorrect
(d) R is correct; A is incorrect

11 **Assertion (A)** Two pipes A and B can fill tank in 12 h and 24 h, respectively. If both the pipes are opened simultaneously, then they fill tank in 8 h.

Reason (R) Time taken by both pipes to fill the tank $=\frac{mn}{m+n}$, when m and n are time taken to fill tank by individual pipes.

12 **Assertion (A)** Pipe A can fill a tank in 18 h, while pipe B alone can fill it in 12 h and pipe C can empty the full tank in 24 h. If all the pipes are opened together, then they takes 8 h to make the tank full.

Reason (R) If two pipes can fill a tank separately m and n h, respectively and third pipes empty the tank in p h, then total time taken to fill the tank is given $\frac{mnp}{np+mp-mn}$ h.

13 **Assertion (A)** Pipe A is 2 times slower than pipe B and takes 18 min more time than the pipe B. So, pipe A takes 36 min to fill the tank.

Reason (R) Two pipes A and B can fill a tank in x min and y min, respectively. If both the pipes are opened simultaneously, then the time after which pipe B should be closed, so that tank is full in t min, is $\left(y\left(1-\frac{t}{x}\right)\right)$ min.

Part B - Descriptive Questions

Very Short Answer Type Questions

14 A pipe can fill a cistern in 6 h. Due to a leak in its bottom, it is filled in 7 h. When the cistern is full, in how much time will it be emptied by the leak?

15 There are two tanks A and B to fill up a water tank. The tank can be filled in 40 min, if both taps are on. The same tank can be filled in 60 min, if tap A alone is on. How much time will tap B alone take to fill up the same tank?

16 Through an inlet, a tank takes 8 h to get filled up. Due to a leak in the bottom, it takes 2 h more to get it filled completely. If the tank is full, then how much time will the leak take to empty it?

17 Two pipes A and B can independently fill a tank completely in 20 min and 30 min, respectively. If both the pipes are opened simultaneously, how much time will they take to fill the tank completely?

18 A cistern can be filled up in 4 h by an inlet A. An outlet B can empty the cistern in 8 h. If both A and B are opened simultaneously, then after how much time will the cistern get filled?

19 Pipe A can fill a tank in 30 min, while pipe B can fill the same tank in 10 min and pipe C can empty the full tank in 40 min. If all the pipes are opened together, then how much time will be needed to make the tank full?

20 If tap A can fill a tank 2 times faster than tap B and takes 20 min less than tap B to fill the tank. If both the taps are opened simultaneously, then find the time taken to fill the tank by tap A.

Short Answer Type Questions

21 A tank can be filled by pipe X in 2 h and pipe Y in 6 h. At 10 am, pipe X was opened. At what time will the tank be filled, if pipe Y is opened at 11 am?

22 Two pipes A and B can fill a tank in 1 h and 75 min, respectively. There is also an outlet C. If all the three pipes are opened together, then the tank is full in 50 min. How much time will be taken by C to empty the full tank?

23 A tank is filled in 5 h by three pipes A, B and C. The pipe C is twice as fast as B and B is twice as fast as A. How much time will pipe A alone take to fill the tank?

24 Pipes A and B can fill a tank in 5 and 6 h, respectively. Pipe C can fill it in 30 h. If all the three pipes are opened together, then in how much time the tank will be filled up?

25 Three taps are fitted in a cistern. The empty cistern is filled by the first and the second taps in 3 h and 4 h, respectively. The full cistern is emptied by the third tap in 5 h. If all three taps are opened simultaneously, then how long the empty cistern will be filled up?

26 Three taps A, B and C together can fill an empty cistern in 10 min. The tap A alone can fill it in 30 min and the tap B alone can fill it in 40 min. How long will the tap C alone take to fill it?

27 Two pipes A and B are opened together to fill a tank. Both pipes fill the tank in a certain time. If A separately takes 16 min more than the time taken by $(A+B)$ and B takes 9 min more than the time taken by $(A+B)$. Then, find the time taken by A and B to fill the tank when both the pipes are opened together.

28 A tank has a leak which would empty it in 8 h. A tap is turned on which admits 3 L a min into the tank and it is now emptied in 12 h. How many litres does the tank hold?

29 Two pipes P and Q can fill a cistern in 12 min and 15 min, respectively. If both pipes are opened together and at the end of 3 min, the first is closed, then how much longer will the cistern take to fill?

30 Pipe A alone can fill a tank in 8 h. Pipe B alone can fill the same tank in 10 h. If both the pipes are opened but after 2 h, pipe A is closed, then how long pipe B will fill the tank.

31 Two pipes A and B can fill a tank in 24 min and 32 min, respectively. If both the pipes are opened together, then after how much time pipe B should be closed so that the tank is full in 9 min?

Long Answer Type Questions

32 Two pipes can fill a cistern in 14 h and 16 h, respectively. The pipes are opened simultaneously and it is found that due to leakage in the bottom, it took 92 min more to fill the cistern. When the cistern is full, in what time will the leak empty it?

33 A pipe can fill a cistern in 12 min and another pipe can fill it in 15 min, but a third pipe can empty it in 6 min. The first two pipes are kept open for 5 min in the beginning and then the third pipe is also opened. How long time taken to empty the cistern.

34 A tank can be filled by a tap in 20 min and by another tap in 60 min. Both the taps are kept open for 5 min and then the 1st tap is shut off. After this, how much time the tank will be completely filled?

35 A cistern has three pipes A, B and C. Pipes A and B can fill it in 3 h and 4 h, respectively, while pipe C can empty the completely filled cistern in 1 h. If the pipes are opened in order at 3 : 00 pm, 4 : 00 pm and 5 : 00 pm respectively, then at what time will the cistern be empty?

36 If two pipes function together, then the tank will be filled in 12 h. One pipe fills the tank in 10 h faster than the other. How many hours does the faster pipe take to fill up the tank?

37 A pipe P can fill a tank in 12 min and another pipe R can fill it in 15 min. But, the third pipe M can empty it in 6 min. The first two pipes P and R are kept open for double the 2.5 min in the beginning and then the third pipe is also opened. In what time is the tank emptied?

38 Three pipes A, B and C can fill a tank in 30 min, 20 min and 10 min, respectively. When the tank is empty, all the three pipes are opened. If A, B and C discharge chemical solutions P, Q and R respectively, then find the part of solution R in the liquid in the tank after 3 min.

39 There are three taps of diameters 1 cm, $\frac{4}{3}$ cm and 2 cm, respectively. The ratio of the water flowing through them is equal to the ratio of the square of their diameters. The biggest tap can fill the tank alone in 61 min. If all the taps are opened simultaneously, then how long will the tank take to be filled?

Case Study Based Questions

40 A pipe is connected to a tank or cistern. It is used to fill or empty the cistern. The amount of work done by a pipe is a part of the tank filled or emptied in unit time. Three pipes A, B and C are connected to a tank. A and B fill the tank in 5 h and 9 h, respectively when operated independently. Pipe C empty the full tank in 12 h when opened alone.

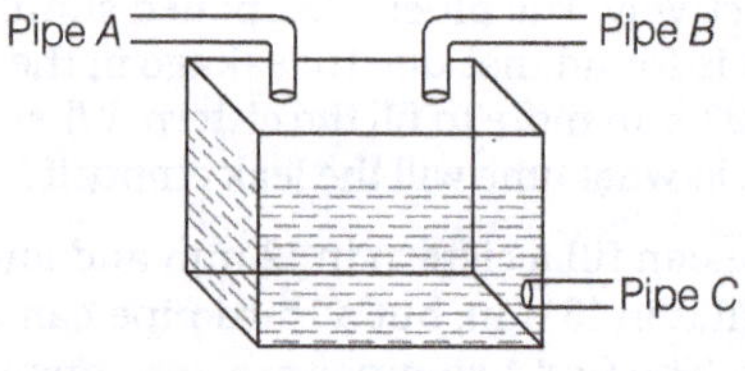

Based on the above information, answer the following questions.

(i) If both pipes A and B are opened together, then the tank can be filled in

(a) $8\frac{4}{7}$ h (b) $3\frac{3}{14}$ h
(c) $\frac{41}{20}$ h (d) None of these

(ii) If pipes A and C are opened together, then the tank can be filled in

(a) $8\frac{4}{7}$ h (b) $3\frac{3}{14}$ h
(c) $\frac{41}{20}$ h (d) None of these

(iii) If pipes B and C are opened together then the tank can be filled in

(a) 30 h (b) 28 h (c) 36 h (d) 40 h

(iv) If all three pipes A, B and C are opened together, then the tank can be filled be

(a) 36 h (b) $\frac{180}{41}$ h (c) 28 h (d) $\frac{56}{41}$ h

(v) If all the pipes are opened, the part of the tank which remains unfilled after 3 h is

(a) $\frac{41}{60}$ (b) $\frac{23}{15}$ (c) $\frac{43}{15}$ (d) $\frac{19}{60}$

41 Three taps A, B and C can fill a tank in 12 h, 15 h and 20 h respectively. If A is open all the time B and C are open for one hour each alternately.
Based on the above information, answer the following questions.

(i) Part of the tank filled after 2 h is

(a) $\frac{23}{60}$ (b) $\frac{17}{60}$
(c) $\frac{18}{60}$ (d) None of these

(ii) Part of the tank filled in 6 h

(a) $\frac{3}{20}$ (b) $\frac{17}{60}$
(c) $\frac{17}{20}$ (d) None of these

(iii) Unfilled part of the tank in 6 h

(a) $\frac{3}{20}$ (b) $\frac{17}{60}$
(c) $\frac{17}{20}$ (d) None of these

(iv) Part of the tank filled by A and B in 1 hour

(a) $\frac{1}{12}$ (b) $\frac{2}{15}$
(c) $\frac{3}{20}$ (d) None of these

(v) The tank will be full in

(a) 6 h (b) 7 h
(c) 3 h (d) None of these

Hints & Solutions

1. (b)	2. (a)	3. (a)	4. (b)
5. (b)	6. (a)	7. (d)	8. (c)
9. (a)	10. (c)	11. (a)	12. (d)
13. (b)	14. 42 h		

15. Part filled by tap A in 1 min $= \frac{1}{60}$

Let tap B fills the tank in x min.

Then, part filled by tap B in 1 min $= \frac{1}{x}$

According to the question,

$$\frac{1}{60} + \frac{1}{x} = \frac{1}{40} \Rightarrow \frac{1}{x} = \frac{1}{40} - \frac{1}{60} \Rightarrow \frac{1}{x} = \frac{3-2}{120} = \frac{1}{120}$$

$\therefore$ Tap B can fill the tank in 120 min.

16. Let the leak takes x h to empty the tank.

Now, part filled by inlet in 1 h $= \frac{1}{8}$

Part filled in 1 h when both tap and leak work together

$$= \frac{1}{8+2} = \frac{1}{10}$$

According to the question,

$$\frac{1}{x} = \frac{1}{8} - \frac{1}{10} = \frac{5-4}{40} = \frac{1}{40} \Rightarrow x = 40 \text{ h}$$

17. 12 min 18. 8 h 19. $9\frac{3}{13}$ h

20. Let the time taken by tap A to fill the tank be x min.
Then, time taken by tap B to fill the tank is $2x$ min.
Then, according to the question,

$$2x - x = 20 \Rightarrow x = 20$$

$\therefore$ Time taken by tap A = 20 min

21. $\because$ Part of tank filled by X in 1 h $= \frac{1}{2}$

and part of tank filled by Y in 1 h $= \frac{1}{6}$

$\therefore$ Part of tank filled by $(X+Y)$ in 1 h $= \frac{1}{2} + \frac{1}{6} = \frac{2}{3}$

During 10 : 00 am to 11 : 00 am, part of tank filled by pipe $X = \frac{1}{2}$

$\therefore$ Remaining part to be filled $= 1 - \frac{1}{2} = \frac{1}{2}$

Time taken by $(X+Y)$ to filled $\frac{1}{2}$ part of tank

$$= \frac{3}{2} \times \frac{1}{2} = \frac{3}{4} \text{ h} = 45 \text{ min}$$

Hence, the tank will be filled at 11 : 45 am.

22. Work done by C in 1 min $= \left(\frac{1}{60} + \frac{1}{75} - \frac{1}{50}\right)$

$$= \frac{5+4-6}{300} = \frac{3}{300} = \frac{1}{100}$$

Hence, C can empty the full tank in 100 min.

23. Let pipe A takes x h to fill the tank.

Then, pipe B takes $\frac{x}{2}$ h to fill the tank

and pipe C takes $\frac{x}{4}$ h to fill the tank.

According to the question,

$$\frac{1}{x} + \frac{2}{x} + \frac{4}{x} = \frac{1}{5} \Rightarrow \frac{7}{x} = \frac{1}{5} \Rightarrow x = 35 \text{ h}$$

24. $2\frac{1}{2}$ h 25. $2\frac{14}{23}$ h

26. Part filled by $(A+B+C)$ in 1 min $= \frac{1}{10}$

Part filled by A in 1 min $= \frac{1}{30}$

Part filled by B in 1 min $= \frac{1}{40}$

Part filled by $(A+B)$ in 1 min $= \frac{1}{30} + \frac{1}{40} = \frac{4+3}{120} = \frac{7}{120}$

$\therefore$ Part filled by C in 1 min $= \frac{1}{10} - \frac{7}{120}$

$$= \frac{12-7}{120} = \frac{5}{120} = \frac{1}{24}$$

Hence, tap C will fill the cistern in 24 min.

27. Here, $a = 16$ and $b = 9$

$\therefore$ Required time $= \sqrt{ab} = \sqrt{16 \times 9} = 4 \times 3 = 12$ min

28. Work done by the inlet in 1 h $= \left(\frac{1}{8} - \frac{1}{12}\right) = \frac{1}{24}$

Work done by the inlet in 1 min $= \frac{1}{24} \times \frac{1}{60} = \frac{1}{1440}$

$\because$ Capacity of $\frac{1}{1440}$ part = 3 L

$\therefore$ Capacity of the whole $= 3 \times 1440 = 4320$ L

29. Part filled by pipe P in 1 min $= \frac{1}{12}$

Part filled by pipe Q in 1 min $= \frac{1}{15}$

Part filled by both pipes in 1 min $= \frac{1}{12} + \frac{1}{15} = \frac{5+4}{60} = \frac{9}{60}$

Now, part filled by both pipes in 3 min $= \frac{3 \times 9}{60} = \frac{27}{60} = \frac{9}{20}$

$\therefore$ Remaining part $= 1 - \frac{9}{20} = \frac{11}{20}$

Let the remaining part be filled by pipe Q in x min.

Then, $x \times \frac{1}{15} = \frac{11}{20} \Rightarrow x = \frac{15 \times 11}{20} = \frac{33}{4} = 8\frac{1}{4}$ min

30. Part of tank filled by pipe A in 1 h $= \frac{1}{8}$

Part of tank filled by pipe B in 1 h $= \frac{1}{10}$

$\therefore$ Part of tank filled by both pipes in 1 h $= \frac{1}{8} + \frac{1}{10}$

$$= \frac{10+8}{80} = \frac{18}{80} = \frac{9}{40}$$

Part of tank filled by both pipes in 2h $= \frac{2 \times 9}{40} = \frac{9}{20}$

Remaining part of tank to be filled $= 1 - \frac{9}{20} = \frac{11}{20}$

$\therefore$ Time taken by pipe B to fill this part $= \frac{11/20}{1/10} = \frac{11}{2}$

$$= 5\frac{1}{2} \text{ h}$$

31. 20 min

32. Part filled by 1st pipe in 1 h $= \frac{1}{14}$

Part filled by 2nd pipe in 1 h $= \frac{1}{16}$

Part filled by the two pipes in 1 h $= \left(\frac{1}{14} + \frac{1}{16}\right)$

$$= \frac{8+7}{112} = \frac{15}{112}$$

$\therefore$ Time taken by these two pipes to fill the cistern

$$= \frac{112}{15} \text{ h} = 7 \text{ h } 28 \text{ min}$$

Due to leakage, the time taken

$$7 \text{ h } 28 \text{ min} + 92 \text{ min} = 9 \text{ h}$$

$\therefore$ Work done by (two pipes + leak) in 1 h $= \frac{1}{9}$

Work done by the leak in 1 h $= \frac{1}{9} - \frac{15}{112}$

$$= \frac{112-135}{1008} = -\frac{23}{1008}$$

$\therefore$ Time taken by leak to empty the full cistern

$$= \frac{1008}{23} = 43\frac{19}{23} \text{ h}$$

33. Let the number of minutes taken to empty the cistern be x min.

According to the question,

$$\frac{x}{6} - \frac{x+5}{12} - \frac{x+5}{15} = 0$$

$$\Rightarrow \frac{x}{6} - \frac{x}{12} - \frac{5}{12} - \frac{x}{15} - \frac{5}{15} = 0$$

$$\Rightarrow \frac{x}{6} - \frac{x}{12} - \frac{x}{15} = \frac{5}{12} + \frac{5}{15}$$

$$\Rightarrow \frac{10x - 5x - 4x}{60} = \frac{25+20}{60} \Rightarrow \frac{x}{60} = \frac{45}{60}$$

$$\Rightarrow x = 45 \text{ min}$$

34. Part of the tank filled by both taps in 5 min

$$= 5 \times \left(\frac{1}{20} + \frac{1}{60}\right) = \frac{5 \times (6+2)}{120} = \frac{8}{24} = \frac{1}{3}$$

$\therefore$ Remaining part $= \left(1 - \frac{1}{3}\right) = \frac{2}{3}$

$\because \frac{1}{60}$ part is now filled in 1 min.

$\therefore \frac{2}{3}$ part is now filled in $60 \times \frac{2}{3} = 40$ min

35. Let the cistern gets emptied in m h after 3:00 pm.

Work done by A in m h, by B in $(m-1)$ h and by C in $(m-2)$ h $= 0$

$$\Rightarrow \frac{m}{3} + \frac{m-1}{4} - (m-2) = 0$$

$$\Rightarrow 4m + 3(m-1) - 12(m-2) = 0$$

$$\Rightarrow 5m = 21 \Rightarrow m = \frac{21}{5}$$

$\therefore$ $m = 4$ h 12 min

$\therefore$ Required time $= 7:12$ pm

36. Let one pipe takes m h to fill the tank.

Then, the other pipe takes $(m-10)$ h.

According to the question,

$$\therefore \frac{1}{m} + \frac{1}{(m-10)} = \frac{1}{12}$$

$$\Rightarrow \frac{m-10+m}{m(m-10)} = \frac{1}{12}$$

$$\Rightarrow 12(m-10+m) = m(m-10)$$

$$\Rightarrow m^2 - 34m + 120 = 0$$

$$\Rightarrow m^2 - 30m - 4m + 120 = 0$$

$$\Rightarrow (m-30)(m-4) = 0$$

$$\therefore m = 30 \text{ or } 4$$

$\therefore$ Faster pipe will take $(30-10)$h $= 20$ h to fill the tank.

37. According to the question,

Double the 2.5 min = 5 min

Now, part filled in 5 min $= 5 \times \left(\frac{1}{12} + \frac{1}{15}\right)$

$$= 5 \times \left(\frac{5+4}{60}\right) = 5 \times \frac{9}{60} = \frac{3}{4}$$

Part emptied in 1 min when P, R and M, all are opened.

$$= \frac{1}{6} - \left(\frac{1}{12} + \frac{1}{15}\right) = \frac{1}{6} - \left(\frac{5+4}{60}\right)$$

$$= \left(\frac{1}{6} - \frac{3}{20}\right) = \frac{1}{60}$$

One-sixtieth part is emptied in 1 min.

$\therefore$ Three-fourth part will be emptied in

$$60 \times \frac{3}{4} = 15 \times 3 = 45 \text{ min}$$

38. Total quantity of solutions P, Q and R from A, B and C respectively, after 3 min $= \frac{3}{30} + \frac{3}{20} + \frac{3}{10} = 3\left(\frac{2+3+6}{60}\right)$

$$= \frac{3 \times 11}{60} = \frac{11}{20}$$

Quantity of solution R in liquid in 3 min $= \frac{3}{10}$

$\therefore$ Part of solution $R = \dfrac{\frac{3}{10}}{\frac{11}{20}} = \dfrac{3 \times 20}{10 \times 11} = \dfrac{6}{11}$

39. Time taken to fill the tank by the tap having 2 cm diameter = 61 min

$\therefore$ Time taken to fill the tank by the tap having 1 cm diameter $= 61 \times \left(\frac{2}{1}\right)^2 = 244$ min

Similarly, time taken to fill the tank by the tap having $\frac{4}{3}$ cm diameter $= 61 \times \left(\frac{2}{4/3}\right)^2 = 61 \times \frac{9}{4} = \frac{549}{4}$ min

$\therefore$ Part of the tank filled by all the three pipes in 1 min

$$= \frac{1}{61} + \frac{1}{244} + \frac{1}{549/4} = \frac{36+9+16}{2196}$$

$$= \frac{61}{2196} = \frac{1}{36}$$

Hence, required time taken = 36 min

40. (i) (b) Part of the tank filled by A in 1 h $= \frac{1}{5}$

Part of the tank filled by B in 1 h $= \frac{1}{9}$

Part of the tank filled by both pipes $= \frac{1}{5} + \frac{1}{9}$

$$= \frac{9+5}{45} = \frac{14}{45}$$

$\therefore$ Time taken to fill the tank $= \frac{45}{14}$ h $= 3\frac{3}{14}$ h

(ii) (a) Part of the tank filled by A in 1 h

$= \frac{1}{5}$ th part of tank

Part of the tank empty by C in 1 h $= \frac{1}{12}$

Part of the tank filled by both pipes $= \frac{1}{5} - \frac{1}{12}$

$$= \frac{12-5}{60} = \frac{7}{60}$$

$\therefore$ Time taken to fill the tank $= \frac{60}{7}$ h $= 8\frac{4}{7}$ h

(iii) (c) Part of the tank filled by B in 1 h $= \frac{1}{9}$

Part of the tank empty by C in 1 h $= \frac{1}{12}$

Part of the tank filled by both pipes $= \frac{1}{9} - \frac{1}{12}$

$$= \frac{4-3}{36} = \frac{1}{36}$$

$\therefore$ Time taken to fill the tank 36 h.

(iv) (b) Part of the tank filled by A in 1 h $= \frac{1}{5}$

Part of the tank filled by B in 1 h $= \frac{1}{9}$

Part of the tank empty by C in 1 h $= \frac{1}{12}$

$\therefore$ Part of the tank filled by pipes A, B and C in 1 h

$$= \frac{1}{5} + \frac{1}{9} - \frac{1}{12}$$

$$= \frac{36+20-15}{180} = \frac{41}{180}$$

Time taken to fill the tank $= \frac{180}{41}$ h

(v) (d) In 1 h, part of the tank filled by all pipes $= \frac{41}{180}$

In 3 h, part of the tank filled by all pipes $= 3 \times \frac{41}{180}$

$= \frac{123}{180} = \frac{41}{60}$ part of the tank

Unfilled part of the tank $= 1 - \frac{41}{60} = \frac{19}{60}$

41. (i) (b) Tap A always remains open and taps B and C are opened alternately for 1 h each.

So, after 2 h, tap A has filled the tank for 2 h, B for 1 h and C for 1 h.

$\therefore$ Part of the tank filled after 2 h $= \left[\frac{2}{12} + \frac{1}{15} + \frac{1}{20}\right]$

$$= \frac{17}{60}$$

(ii) (c) So, after 3 rounds of 2 h each the tank will be partially unfilled and in 4th rounds it overflow.

$$\left[\frac{1}{4} < \frac{17}{60} < \frac{1}{3}\right]$$

Part of the tank filled in 6 h (2×3)h $= 3 \times \frac{17}{60} = \frac{17}{20}$ h

(iii) (a) Remaining part of the tank $= 1 - \frac{17}{20} = \frac{3}{20}$

(iv) (c) Part of the tank filled by A and B in 1 h

$$= \frac{1}{12} + \frac{1}{15} = \frac{3}{20}$$

(v) (b) Part of the tank filled by all the three pipe in 2 h $= \frac{17}{60}$

Part of the tank filled by all the pipe in 6 h $= \frac{51}{60}$

It is A and B turn.

Part of the tank filled in 7 h $= \frac{51}{60} + \frac{3}{20} = 1$

Hence, the time taken by all the three pipes to fill the tank in $(6+1)$h $= 7$ h

CHAPTER 05

Races and Games

In this Chapter...

- Important Terms
- Some Facts about Race

A race or a games of skill includes the contestants in a contest and their skill in the concerned contest/game.

Important Terms

- **Race** A race is a contest of speed in running, driving, riding, sailing or rowing.
- **Race Course** The ground/path on which a contest is organised in a systematic way, is called a race course.
- **Starting Point** The exact point/place from where a race begins, is called starting point.
- **Start** If two persons *A* and *B* are contesting a race and before the start of the race, *A* is at the starting point and *B* is ahead of *A* by 20 m, then it is said that *A* gives *B* a start of 20 m.

  e.g. If *A* and *B* are the contestants for a 100 m race and *A* has to cover 100 m, while *B* has to cover $(100 - 20) = 80$ m.
- **Finishing Point/Winning Point/Goal** The point set to bound a race is called finishing point/winning point or goal.
- **Winner** A person who reaches the finishing point first, is called the winner.
- **Dead Heat Race** A race is said to be a dead heat race, if all the contestants reach the finishing point exactly at the same time.
- **Game** A game of 100 means that the contestant who scores 100 points first, is declared the winner.

  e.g. If in a 100 points game, *A* scores 100 points, while *B* scores 85 points.Then, it is said that *A* can give $(100 - 85) = 15$ points to *B*.

Some Facts about Race

For Two Contestants *A* and *B*

1. If *A* beats *B* by *x* m, then

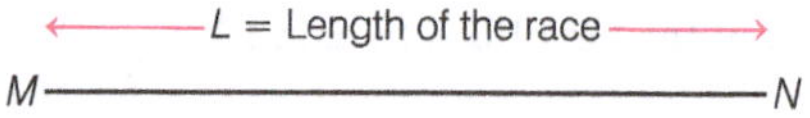

   Distance covered by *A* (winner) $= L$ m

   Distance covered by *B* (loser) $= (L - x)$ m

2. If *B* starts from *x* m ahead of *A* (or *A* gives *B* a start of *x* m), then

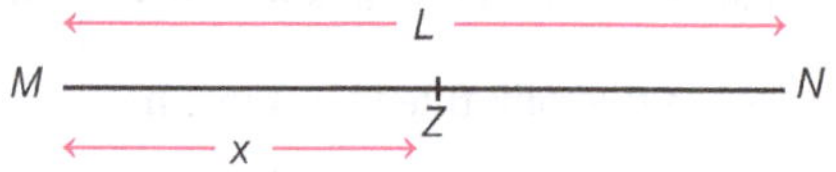

   A starts from *M* and *B* starts from *Z*.

   Distance covered by $B = (L - x)$ m

3. If *A* beats *B* by *T* s, then

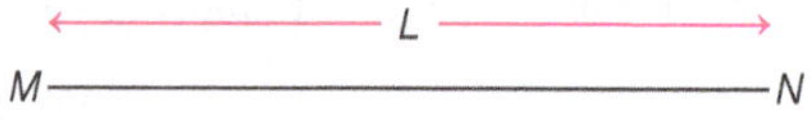

   A and *B* both start from point *M*.

   Time taken by *A* (winner)

   $=$ Time taken by *B* (loser) $- T$

   It means that *A* completes the race in *T* s less time than that of *B*.

4. If *B* starts the race *T* s before the time *A* starts (or if *A* gives *B* a start of *T* s), then

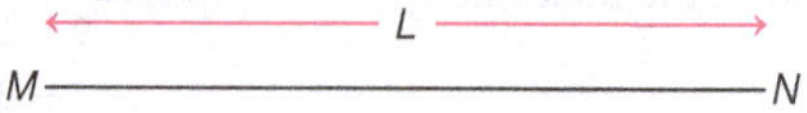

   In such case, we say that *A* starts *T* s after the time *B* starts.

5. If both of the contestants get at the finishing point at the same time, then Difference in time of defeat = 0; Difference in distance of defeat = 0

EXAMPLE 1. In a 100 m race, Ajay runs at the speed of 4 km/h. Ajay gives Brijesh a start of 4 m and still beats him by 15 s. Find the speed of Brijesh.

Sol. Time taken by Ajay to cover 100 m $= \left(\frac{60 \times 60}{4000} \times 100\right)$ s

$= 90$ s

$\therefore$ Brijesh covers $(100 - 4) = 96$ m in $(90 + 15) = 105$ s.

$\therefore$ Brijesh's speed $= \frac{96}{105}$ m/s $= \frac{96}{105} \times \frac{18}{5} = 3.29$ km/h

EXAMPLE 2. P covers 1 km in 4 min 40 s, while Q covers the same distance in 5 min. By what distance does P defeat Q?

Sol. Clearly, P beats Q by 20 s.

Distance covered by Q in 20 s $= \frac{1000}{300} \times 20 = 66\frac{2}{3}$ m

EXAMPLE 3. A can run 1 km in 5 min and B can run the same distance in 6 min. How many metres start, can A give to B in 1 km race, so that the race may end in a dead heat?

Sol. Time taken by A to run 1 km = 300 s

Time taken by B to run 1 km = 360 s

A can give B a start of $(360 - 300) = 60$ s

$\because$ In 360 s, B runs 1000 m.

$\therefore$ In 60 s, B runs $\frac{1000}{360} \times 60$ m $= \frac{1000}{6}$ m $= \frac{500}{3}$ m $= 166\frac{2}{3}$ m

Hence, A can give a start of $166\frac{2}{3}$ m.

EXAMPLE 4. In 1 km race, A beats B by 36 m or 18 s. Find A's time over the course.

Sol. B covers 36 m in 18 s

B covers 1 m in $\frac{18}{36}$ s

B covers 1000 m or 1 km in $\frac{18}{36} \times 1000 = 500$ s

A's time over the course is $(500 - 18) = 482$ s

EXAMPLE 5. In 1 km race, the ratio of the speeds of two contestants L and M is 3 : 4. L has a start of 280 m. Then, L wins by how many metres?

Sol. To reach the winning post, L will have to cover a distance of $(1000 - 280) = 720$ m

When L covers 3 m, then M covers 4 m.

When L covers 720 m, then M covers $\left(\frac{4}{3} \times 720\right) = 960$ m

Thus, when L reaches the winning post, M covers 960 m and therefore, remains 40 m behind.

$\therefore$ L wins by 40 m.

EXAMPLE 6. In a 500 m race, A gives B a start of 6 s and beat him by 20 m. In another race of 500 m, A beats B by $8\frac{1}{7}$ s. Find their speeds.

Sol. In a 500 m race, B takes $8\frac{1}{7}$ s more time than A.

In another 500 m race, B takes 6 s more time and run 20 m less distance than A.

$\therefore$ B can run in $\left(8\frac{1}{7} - 6\right)$ s a distance of 20 m; B can run in 1 s a distance of $\frac{20}{2\frac{1}{7}}$.

$\therefore$ Speed of B is $\frac{28}{3}$ m/s ≈ 9.33 m/s

Let the speed of A be V_A m/s.

Then, according to question,

$$\frac{500}{\text{Speed of } B} - \frac{500}{\text{Speed of } A} = 8\frac{1}{7}$$

$$\Rightarrow \frac{500}{28/3} - \frac{500}{V_A} = \frac{57}{7} \Rightarrow \frac{1500}{28} - \frac{57}{7} = \frac{500}{V_A}$$

$$\therefore V_A \approx 11 \text{ m/s}$$

Hence, speed of A is 11 m/s and speed of B is 9.33 m/s.

EXAMPLE 7. In a race of one kilometer, A gives a start of 100 m and still win by 20 s. But if A gives B a start of 25 s, B wins by 50 m. What is the time taken by A to run one kilometer?

Sol. Let the time taken by A to cover one kilometer be x s

Time taken by B to cover 900 m $= x + 20$

Speed of $A = \frac{1000}{x}$ m/s

Speed of $B = \frac{900}{x + 20}$ m/s

If A gives B a start of 25 s, B wins by 50 m

Time taken by $B = x + 25$

Distance covered by B = Speed $\times$ Time

$= \frac{900}{x + 20} \times (x + 25)$

According to the question,

$$1000 - \left(\frac{900}{x + 20}\right)(x + 25) = 50$$

$$\Rightarrow \frac{900}{(x + 20)}(x + 25) = 950$$

$$\Rightarrow 18x + 450 = 19x + 380$$

$$\Rightarrow x = 70$$

Hence, the time taken by A to cover one km is 70 s.

For Three Contestants A, B and C

Let A, B and C participate in a race of L m.

Let A comes 1st in the race by beating B by x m and C by y m, respectively.

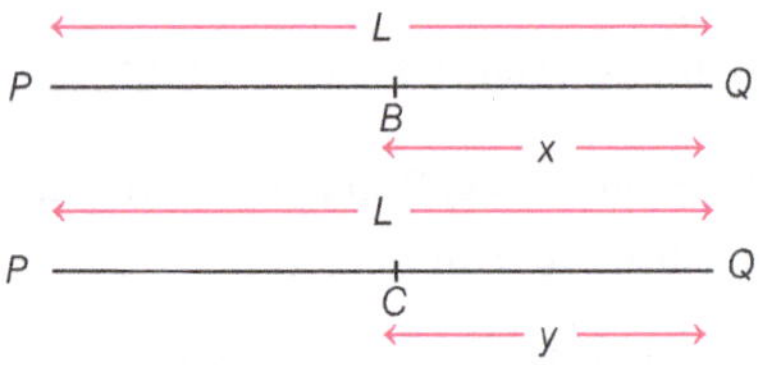

Here, the values of x and y will decide 2nd and 3rd positions. If $x < y$, then B will beat C, i.e. B will get the 2nd position. If $x > y$, then C will beat B, i.e. C will get the 2nd position.

EXAMPLE 8. A, B and C are three contestants in 1 km race. If A can give B a start of 40 m and A can give C a start of 64 m, how many metres start can B give C?

Sol. While A covers 1000 m, B covers $(1000 - 40)$

$= 960$ m and C will cover $(1000 - 64) = 936$ m.

So, when B covers 1000 m, C will cover

$$\left(\frac{936}{960} \times 1000\right) = 975 \text{ m}$$

$\therefore$ B can give C a start of $(1000 - 975)$ m i.e. 25 m.

EXAMPLE 9. A runs 3 times a fast as B. If A gives B a start of 50 m. Find how for must be the finish point on the race course so that A and B's reach the goal at the same time?

Sol. Speed of A and B is 3 : 1

$\Rightarrow$ When A covers 3 m, B covers 1 m a gains $(3 - 1)$ m i.e. 2 m by B in a race of 3 m.

When A gains 2 m by B, the race is of 3 m

When A gains 1 m by B, the race is of $\frac{3}{2}$ m

When A gains 50 m by B, the race is of $\frac{3}{2} \times 50 \text{ m} = 75$ m

Hence, the finishing pont is 7.5 m from the starting point.

EXAMPLE 10. P, Q and R are three contestants in a 2 km race. If P can give Q a start of 100 m and P can give R a start of 138 m, then how many metres start can Q give to R?

Sol. When P covers 2000 m, then Q covers $(2000 - 100)$

$= 1900$ m

and R covers $(2000 - 138) = 1862$ m

When Q covers 1900 m, then R covers 1862 m.

When Q covers 2000 m, then R covers

$$\left(\frac{1862}{1900} \times 2000\right) = 1960 \text{ m}$$

$\therefore$ Q can give R a start of $(2000 - 1960) = 40$ m

EXAMPLE 11. In one-kilometre race, A beats B by 30 sec and B beats C by 15 sec. If A beats C by 180 m, then find the time taken by A to run 1 km. **[CBSE 2023]**

Sol. Let A takes t sec to run 1 km race, then B takes $(t + 30)$ sec and C takes $(t + 30 + 15)$ sec $= (t + 45)$ sec.

A beats C $(30 + 15)$ sec $= 45$ sec and it is given that A beats C by 180 m.

C runs 180 m in 45 sec.

$\because C$ runs 1 km in $\left(\frac{45}{180} \times 1000\right) = 250$ sec $\Rightarrow t + 45 = 250$

$\Rightarrow$ $t = 250 - 45 = 205$

Hence, A takes 205 sec to run 1 km.

EXAMPLE 12. In a race of 1200 m, A can beat B by 120 m while in a race of 500 m, B can beat C by 100 m. By how many metres will A beat C in a race of 800 m?

Sol. If A runs 1200 m, then B runs 1080 m.

If A runs 800 m, then B runs $\left(\frac{1080}{1200} \times 800\right) = 720$ m

When B runs 500 m, then C runs 400 m.

When B runs 720 m, then C runs $\left(\frac{400}{500} \times 720\right) = 576$ m

$\therefore$ A beats C by $(800 - 576)$ m $= 224$ m

EXAMPLE 13. In a mile race, A can be given a start of 100 m by B. If B can give C a start of 40 m in a 160 m dash, then who out of A and C will win a race of three-fourth of a miles and what will be the final lead give by winner to the loser? [one mile is 1600 m]

Sol. In a race of 1600 m, B gives a start of 100 m to A.

Distance covered by A and B are 1500 m and 1600 m, respectively.

Speed of A : Speed of $B = 1500 : 1600 = 15 : 16$

In a race of 160 m, B gives C a start of 40 m.

Distance covered by B and C are 160 m and 120 m

Speed of B : Speed of $C = 4 : 3$

Thus, speed of A : speed $C = 15 : 12$

Total distance covered = Three-fourth of a mile

$= \frac{3}{4} \times 1600 = 1200$ m

Speed of A : Speed of $C = 15 : 12 = 1500 : 1200$

Hence, C wins the race by 300 m.

EXAMPLE 14. In a game of 80 points, A can give 10 points to B and 20 points to C, then how many points can B give C in a games of 70 points.

Sol. In a point of 80 points, A gives 10 points to B and 20 points to C.

This means that when A scores 80 points, B scores $(80 - 10) = 70$ points and C scores $(80 - 20) = 60$ points.

$\Rightarrow$ When B scores 70 points, then C scores 60 points.

Hence, in a game of 70 points, B can give C 10 points.

Exam Pattern Exercise

Part A - Objective Type Questions

Multiple Choice Type Questions

1 In a race of 150 m, A gives B a start of 20 m. Then, distance will be covered by B is
(a) 130 m (b) 170 m
(c) 100 m (d) 150 m

2 In a race, P gives Q a start of 25 m making length of race for Q a distance of 175 m. Then, the total length of race is
(a) 175 m (b) 150 m
(c) 200 m (d) 250 m

3 In a 800 m race, A gives some start to B and this makes the length of race for B 725 m. Then, start does B get from A is
(a) 100 m (b) 75 m
(c) 80 m (d) 1000 m

4 In a game of 100 points, A scores 100 points while B scores only 65 points. In this game, how much points can A give to B?
(a) 35 points (b) 65 points
(c) 100 points (d) 165 points

5 A can run 45 m while B runs 50 m. In a kilometer race, B beats A by
(a) 150 m (b) 120 m
(c) 900 m (d) 100 m

6 A can run 40 m while B runs 50 m. In a kilometer race, B beats A by
(a) 250 m (b) 300 m
(c) 100 m (d) 200 m

7 P is $2\frac{1}{3}$ times as fast as Q. If P gives Q a start of 80 m, how long should the race course be to that both of them reach at the same time?
(a) 150 m (b) 170 m (c) 140 m (d) 160 m

8 In a 400 m race, A gives B a start of 5 s and beats him by 15 m. In another race of 400 m. A beats B by $\frac{50}{7}$ s. Then, there speeds respectively are
(a) 6 m/s, 7 m/s (b) 8 m/s, 7 m/s
(c) 5 m/s, 7 m/s (d) 9 m/s, 5 m/s

9 In a 1 km race, player P beats player Q by 18 metres or 9 seconds. What is P's time to complete the race? [CBSE 2024]
(a) 512 seconds (b) 502 seconds
(c) 491 seconds (d) 481 seconds

10 A runs $\frac{5}{3}$ times as fast as B. If A gives B a start of 80 m, how far must the winning post be so that A and B may reach it at the same time?
(a) 100 m
(b) 200 m
(c) 120 m
(d) 240 m

Assertion-Reason Based Questions

Directions (Q. Nos. 11-13) *In the questions given below are two statements labelled as Assertion (A) and Reason (R). In the context of the two statements, which one of the following is correct?*
(a) Both A and R are correct; R is the correct explanation of A
(b) Both A and R are correct; R is not the correct explanation of A
(c) A is correct; R is incorrect
(d) R is correct; A is incorrect

11 **Assertion (A)** In a kilometers race, if participant A gives participant B a head start of 50 m and participant A gives participant C a head start of 69 m, then participant B can give participant C a head start of 19 m.

Reason (R) The difference between the head starts given by participant A to participant B and C is 19 m, indicating that participant B can give participant C a head start equivalent to this difference in distance.

12 **Assertion (A)** In a 100 m race, if participant A runs at a speed of 6 km/h and gives participant B a head start of 4 m, still beating him by 12 s, then the speed of participant B is $\frac{3}{2}$ m/s.

Reason (R) By analyzing the difference in the times taken by participants A and B to complete the race, along with the distance of the race and the head start given by A to B, the speed of participant B can be determined.

13 **Assertion (A)** In the game where A scores 100 points and B scores only 60 points. A can give B a maximum of 48 points.

Reason (R) The difference between A's score and B's scores is the points, indicating the maximum amount can given to B in the game.

Part B - Descriptive Questions

Very Short Answer Type Questions

14 In a 100 m race, A runs at a speed of $\frac{5}{6}$ m/s. If A gives a start of 4 m to B and still beats him by 12 s, what is the speed of B?

15 In a 400 m race, A runs at a speed of 16 m/s. If A gives B a start of 16 m and still beats him by 40 s. Then, what will be the speed of B?

16 In a 1000 m race, X beats Y by 140 m or 14 s. What will be the X's time over the course?

17 Raman covers 1 km in 8 min while Suman covers the same distance in 10 min. By what distance does Raman beat Suman?

18 Yogesh can run 1 km in 6 min 20 s and Vijay can cover the same distance in 6 min 40 s. By what distance can Yogesh beat Vijay?

19 A runs $1\frac{2}{3}$ times as fast as B. If A gives B a start of 80 m, how far must the winning post from the starting point be so that A and B might reach it at the same time?

20 A runs $1\frac{3}{4}$ times as fast as B. If A gives B a start of 30 m, then how far must the winning post be, so that A and B reach it at the same time?

Short Answer Type Questions

21 In a 200 m race, A can beat B by 50 m and B can beat C by 8 m. In the same race, A can beat C by what distance?

22 A, B and C are three contestants in a 500 m race. If A can give B a start of 20 m and A can give C a start of 32 m, then how many metres start can B give to C?

23 In a race of 600 m, A can beat B by 30 m and in a race of 500 m, B can beat C by 25 m. By how many metres will A beat C in a race of 400 m?

24 A 10 km race is organised at 800 m circular race course. P and Q are the contestants of this race. If the ratio of the speeds of P and Q is 5 : 4, then how many times will the winner overtake the loser?

25 In a game of 200 points, A can give 40 points to B and 56 points to C. How many points can B give to C?

26 A, B and C walk 1 km in 5 min, 8 min and 10 min, respectively. C starts walking from a point at a certain time, B starts from the same point 1 min later and A starts from the same point 2 min later than C. Then, A meet C and B at times.

27 In a race of 1000 m, A beats B by 100 m or 10 s. If they start a race of 1000 m simultaneously from the same point and if B gets injured after running 50 m less than half the race length and due to which his speed gets halved, then by how much time will A beat B?

28 In a game of billiards, A can give B, 20 points in the game of 120 points and he can give C, 30 points in the game of 120 points. How many points can B give C in a game of 90?

29 In a game of 90 points, A can give 15 points to B and 30 points to C. How many points can B give C in a game of 100 points?

30 In a game, A can give 15 points to B, A can give 30 points to C and B an give 20 points to C. How many points make the game?

Long Answer Type Questions

31 In a kilometer race, if A gives B 30 m start, A wins by 20 s but if A gives B 30 s start, B wins by 30 m. What is the speed of B?

32 In a mile race, Akshay can be given a start of 128 m by Bharav. If Bharav can give Chinmay a start of 4 m in a 100 m dash, then who out of Akshay and Chinmay will win a race of one and a half miles and what will be the final lead given by the winner to the loser? [**Hint** One mile is 1600 m]

33 In a kilometre race, If A gives B, a start of 40 m, then B wins by 19 s but if A gives B, a start of 30 s, then B wins by 40 m. Find the time taken by each to run a kilometre.

Case Study Based Questions

34 In a kilometer race between runners A and B various scenarios have been observed based on the start given to B by A.

Scenario 1 B gets a 40 m start. Then, B wins by 19 s.

Scenario 2 B gets 30 s start. Then, B wins by 40 m.

If A and B takes 125 s and 150 s, respectively to run 1 km.

Based on the above information, answer the following questions.

(i) What is the distance covered by B in 19 s?

(ii) What is the difference in time taken by A and B to run a kilometre, when B gets a 40 m start?

(iii) How much distance does A cover in 30 s?

(iv) How much time does B need to cover 40 m at the pace he runs the race?

(v) What is the difference in time taken by A and B to run a kilometre, when B gets a 30 s start?

Hints & Solutions

1. (a)	2. (c)	3. (b)	4. (a)
5. (d)	6. (d)	7. (c)	8. (b)
9. (c)	10. (b)	11. (a)	12. (c)
13. (d)			

14. Let the speed of B be x m/s.

According to the question,

$$\frac{96}{x} - \frac{100}{(5/3)} = 12 \Rightarrow \frac{96}{x} - 60 = 12$$

$$\Rightarrow \quad \frac{96}{x} = 72 \Rightarrow x = \frac{4}{3}$$

Hence, the speed of B is $\frac{4}{3}$ m/s.

15. Time taken by A to cover 400 m $= \frac{\text{Distance}}{\text{Speed}} = \frac{400}{16} = 25$ s

$\therefore$ B covers $(400 - 16) = 384$ m in $(25 + 40) = 65$ s

$\therefore$ B's speed $= \frac{384}{65} = 5.9$ m/s

16. Clearly, Y covers 140 m in 14 s.

$\therefore$ Y's time over the course $= \frac{14}{140} \times 1000 = 100$ s

$\therefore$ X's time over the course $= 100 - 14 = 86$ s

17. Raman covers 1 km in 8 min and Suman cover 1 km in 10 min.

If they starts together, then

distance covered by Suman in 8 min $= \frac{1000}{10} \times 8 = 800$ m

$\therefore$ Raman will beat Suman by $(1000 - 800)$ m $= 200$ m

18. Clearly, Yogesh beats Vijay by 20 s.

Distance covered by Vijay in 400 s $= 1000$ m

[$\because$ 6 min 40 s = 400 s]

Distance covered by Vijay in 20 s $= \left(\frac{1000}{400} \times 20\right)$ m

$= 50$ m

$\therefore$ Yogesh beats Vijay by 50 m.

19. Let the speed of B be x m/s.

$\therefore$ Speed of $A = 1\frac{2}{3}x = \frac{5x}{3}$ m/s

Ratio of speed of A and $B = \frac{5x}{3} : x = 5 : 3$

$\because$ 2 m are gained in a race of 5 m.

$\therefore$ 1 m is gained in a race of $\frac{5}{2}$ m.

So, 80 m are gained in a race of $= \frac{5}{2} \times 80 = 200$ m

20. Since, A is $1\frac{3}{4}$ faster than B.

Then, ratio of the rates of A and $B = 7 : 4$

3 m are gained in a race of 7 m.

30 m are gained in a race of $\frac{7}{3} \times 30 = 70$ m

So, winning post is 70 m away from the starting point.

21. According to the question,

$A : B = 200 : 150$

and $B : C = 200 : 192$

$$\therefore \quad A : C = \left(\frac{A}{B} \times \frac{B}{C}\right)$$

$$= \left(\frac{200}{150} \times \frac{200}{192}\right) = \frac{200}{144}$$

So, A beats C by $(200 - 144)$ m $= 56$ m

22. According to the question,

$A : B = 500 : 480$

and $A : C = 500 : 468$

$$\therefore \quad B:C = \left(\frac{B}{A} \times \frac{A}{C}\right) = \left(\frac{480}{500} \times \frac{500}{468}\right) = \frac{500}{487.5}$$

So, B gives to C a start of $(500 - 487.5)$ m $= 12.5$ m

23. If A runs 600 m, then B runs 570 m.

If A runs 400 m, B then runs

$$\frac{570}{600} \times 400 = 380 \text{ m}$$

When B runs 500 m, then C runs 475 m.

When B runs 380 m, then C runs

$$\frac{475}{500} \times 380 = 361 \text{ m}$$

$\therefore$ A beats C by $(400 - 361)$ m $= 39$ m

24. Speed of P : Speed of $Q = 5 : 4$

Time taken by P to cover 5 rounds

= Time taken by Q to cover 4 rounds

Distance covered by P in 5 rounds $= 5 \times \frac{800}{1000} = 4$ km

Distance covered by Q in 4 rounds $= 4 \times \frac{800}{1000} = \frac{16}{5}$ km

In 5 rounds, P will overtake Q everytime.

It means that after covering 4 km, P will overtake Q one time.

$\therefore$ After covering 10 km P will overtake $Q = \frac{1}{4} \times 10$

$= 2\frac{1}{2}$ times

≈ 2 times

25. $A : B = 200 : 160$, $A : C = 200 : 144$

$$\therefore \quad \frac{B}{C} = \frac{B}{A} \times \frac{A}{C} = \frac{160}{200} \times \frac{200}{144}$$

$$= \frac{160}{144} = \frac{10}{9} = \frac{200}{180}$$

Hence, B can give C 20 points.

26. A walks 1 km in 5 min.

Then, distance covered by A in 1 min $= \frac{1000}{5} = 200$ m

B walks 1 km in 8 min.

Then, distance covered by B in 1 min $= \frac{1000}{8} = 125$ m

C walks 1 km in 10 min.

Then, distance covered by C in 1 min $= \frac{1000}{10} = 100$ m

Let A meets B and C in x and y min, respectively.
Then, according to the question,
Distance covered by C in $(x+2)$ min
= Distance covered by A in x min

$$\Rightarrow 100(x+2) = 200x \Rightarrow 100x + 200 = 200x$$

$$\Rightarrow 200 = 100x \Rightarrow x = \frac{200}{100} = 2 \text{ min}$$

Now, for A and B,
Distance covered by B in $(y+1)$ min
= Distance covered by A in y min

$$\Rightarrow 125(y+1) = 200 \times y \Rightarrow 125y + 125 = 200y$$

$$\Rightarrow 125 = 200y - 125y \Rightarrow 125 = 75y$$

$$\Rightarrow y = \frac{125}{75} = \frac{5}{3} \text{ min}$$

27. Since, either A beats B by 100 m or 10 s. It means that B runs 100 m in 10 s.

$\therefore$ Speed of $B = \frac{100}{10} = 10$ m/s

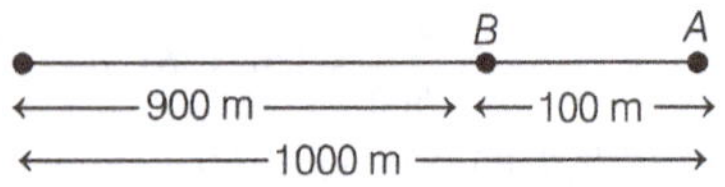

$\because$ B gets injured at a distance of 450 m and his speed gets halved.
So, time taken by B to cover

$$1000 \text{ m} = \frac{450}{10} + \frac{550}{5} = 155 \text{ s}$$

$\because$ Ratio of speed of A and B is equal to ratio of distance covered by A and B.

$$A : B = 1000 : 900 = 10 : 9$$

Now, speed of $A = \frac{10}{9} \times 10 = \frac{100}{9}$ m/s

Time taken by A to cover 1000 m $= \frac{1000}{100} \times 9 = 90$ s

Hence, A beat B by length of time $= (155 - 90)$ s $= 65$ s

28. If A scores 120 points, then B scores 100 points and C scores 90 points.
When B scores 100 points, then C scores 90 points.
When B scores 90 points, then C scores

$$\left(\frac{90}{100} \times 90\right) \text{points} = 81 \text{ points}$$

$\therefore$ B can give C, 9 points in a game of 90.

29. 20 points

30. 60 points

31. Let the time taken by A to cover one km be x sec.
Time taken by B is $x + 20$

Speed of A and B are $\frac{1000}{x}$ and $\frac{970}{x+20}$, respectively.

If A and B a start of 30 s, B wins by 20 m.
Time taken by $B = x + 30$
Distance covered by B = Speed × Time

$$= \frac{970}{x+20} \times (x+30)$$

$$\Rightarrow 1000 - \left(\frac{970}{x+20}\right)(x+30) = 20$$

$$\Rightarrow \frac{970}{(x+20)}(x+30) = 980$$

$$\Rightarrow 97x + 2910 = 98x + 1960$$

$$\Rightarrow x = 950 \text{ sec}$$

$$\Rightarrow \text{Speed of } B = \frac{970}{x+20} = \frac{970}{950+20} \text{ m/s}$$

$$= 1 \text{ m/s}$$

32. Chinmay wins the race by 100 m.

33. 125 s, 150 s.

34. (i) Time taken by B to run 1000 m is 150 s.

So, speed of B, $V_B = \frac{1000}{150} = \frac{20}{3}$ m/s

Now, distance covered by B in 19 s $= \frac{20}{3} \times 19$ m

$$= \frac{380}{3} \text{ m or } 126\frac{2}{3} \text{ m}$$

(ii) When B gets a 40 m start then, B runs 960 m in

$$\frac{150 \times 960}{100} = 144 \text{ s}$$

Hence, distance in time $= 144 - 125 = 19$ s

(iii) Time taken by A is 125 s to run 1000 m

So, speed of A, $V_A = \frac{1000}{125} = 8$ m/s

So, distance cover by A in 30 s $= 30 \times 8 = 240$ m

(iv) Speed of $B = \frac{20}{3}$ m/s

So, to cover 40 m $= \frac{40}{\frac{20}{3}} = 6$ s

(v) Given, speed of $B = \frac{20}{3}$ m/s

Distance covered in 30 s $= 30 \times \frac{20}{3} = 200$ m

Now, B has run 800 m in $\frac{800}{\frac{20}{3}} = 120$ s

and A runs 1000 m in 125 s.

So, difference in time $125 - 120 = 5$ s

CHAPTER 06

Numerical Inequalities

In this Chapter...

- Reasoning Inequalities
- Inequality and Linear Inequalities in One Variable
- System of Inequalities in One Variable
- Applications of Linear Inequalities in One Variable
- Linear Inequalities in Two Variables and Their Graphical Solutions
- Graphical Solutions of System of Linear Inequalities in Two Variables

We have already deal with equations in one variable and two variables. We have also solved some word problems by translating them in the form of equation. But it is not necessary that every word problems translate into equation. It may involve the sign(s) '$<$', '$>$', '$\leq$' and '$\geq$'.

In this chapter, we will study about inequalities, reasoning inequality, linear inequalities in one and two variables and various application involving these inequalities.

Reasoning Inequalities

We have already learning about equality in previous classes. In the chapter we will study about inequalities. Two real numbers or algebraic expressions which are connected by the sign $<$, $>$, $\leq$ or $\geq$ are called inequality.

Numerical Inequalities

Inequalities which involve numerical values or which do not involve variables are called numerical inequalities.

e.g. $3 < 5$, $2 > -1$

Literal Inequalities

Inequalities which involve variables are called literal inequalities.

e.g. $x - 3 > 0$, $2x + 1 \leq 0$, $4x + 5 \geq 3x + 7$,

$x + y - 2 \geq 0$, $x^2 - 3x + 2 \geq 0$, $2x^2 + 3y^2 + 6xy \leq 0$

Note

(i) The inequalities involving $<$, $>$ are called **strict inequalities** e.g. $x - 7 < 0$, $4x + 3 > x - 1$.

(ii) The inequalities involving $\leq$, $\geq$ are called **slack inequalities** e.g. $x + 2 \leq 3$, $x + y \geq 4$.

Properties of Inequalities

Let a, b and c are three real numbers. Then,

1. **Addition property** On adding same real number on both the sides of an inequality the sign of inequality do not changes.
   (i) If $a < c$, then $a + b < c + b$
   (ii) If $a > c$, then $a + b > c + b$
2. **Subtraction property** On subtracting same real number on both the sides of an inequality, the sign of inequality do not changes.
   (i) If $a < c$, then $a - b < c - b$
   (ii) If $a > c$, then $a - b > c - b$
3. **Multiplication property** On multiplying by a same negative real number on the both the sides of an inequality results in sign change, otherwise no change in sign if multiplied by same positive real number.
   (i) If $a < b$, then $ac > bc$ for $c < 0$
   (ii) If $a > b$, then $ac < bc$ for $c < 0$
   (iii) If $a < b$, then $ac < bc$ for $c > 0$
   (iv) If $a > b$, then $ac > bc$ for $c > 0$

4. **Division property** On dividing both the sides of an inequality by non-zero positive real number, the sign of inequality do not changes. While, if we divide by non-zero negative real number on both the sides of an inequality, the sign of inequality changes.
   (i) If $a < b$, then $\frac{a}{c} < \frac{b}{c}$ for $c > 0$
   (ii) If $a > b$, then $\frac{a}{c} > \frac{b}{c}$ for $c > 0$
   (iii) If $a < b$, then $\frac{a}{c} > \frac{b}{c}$ for $c < 0$
   (iv) If $a > b$, then $\frac{a}{c} < \frac{b}{c}$ for $c < 0$
5. **Transitive property** According to this property
   (i) If $a < b$, $b < c$, then $a < c$
   (ii) If $a > b$, $b > c$ then $a > c$
6. **Comparison property** This property states that
   (i) If $a = b + c$ and $c > 0$, then $a > b$
   (ii) If $a = b + c$ and $c < 0$, then $a < b$

Reasoning Inequality

A statement involving some elements with certain coded relationships which are denoted by <, >, =, ≤, ≥ is known as reasoning inequality.

In this we use some symbols. The meaning of some different symbols are as follows

	Symbol	Meaning
(i)	$P < Q$	P is less than Q
(ii)	$P > Q$	P is greater than Q
(iii)	$P = Q$	P is equal to Q
(iv)	$P \neq Q$	P is either less than or greater than Q
(v)	$P \leq Q$	P is less than or equal to Q
(vi)	$P \geq Q$	P is greater than or equal to Q

While solving the problems which involves more than one inequality symbols in one statement, we follow the priority order which is as follows:

1. < or > 2. ≤ or ≥ 3. =

On the basis of above priority order we can conclude some results which as follows

Statement	Conclusion
$A > B > C$	$A > C$
$A > B \geq C$	
$A \geq B > C$	
$A = B > C$	
$A > B = C$	
$A < B < C$	$A < C$
$A < B \leq C$	
$A \leq B < C$	
$A = B < C$	
$A < B = C$	
$A \geq B \geq C$	$A > C$ or $A = C$ i.e. $A \geq C$
$A = B \geq C$	
$A \geq B = C$	
$A \leq B \leq C$	$A < C$ or $A = C$ i.e. $A \leq C$
$A = B \leq C$	
$A \leq B = C$	
$A < B > C$	No conclusion
$A \leq B > C$	
$A < B \geq C$	
$A > B < C$	
$A \geq B \leq C$	
$A > B \leq C$	

Reasoning inequalities are of two types

(i) **Direct Inequality** In this type of inequality, direct symbols <, >, =, ≤, ≥ are used.

(ii) **Coded Inequality** In this type of inequality, coded symbols $, @, #, *, % etc. are used.

EXAMPLE 1. Consider the given statement and conclusion.

Statement : $P < Q < R \geq S = T$

Conclusion I : $R \geq T$

Conclusion II : $P < R$

Which of the following conclusions are true?

Sol. We have, $R \geq S = T \Rightarrow R \geq T$

Again, we have $P < Q < R \Rightarrow P < R$

So, both conclusions are true.

EXAMPLE 2. Consider the statement

$$C = B \geq A \leq D = E$$

Conclusion I : $C = A$

Conclusion II : $C < D$

Which of the following conclusions are true?

Sol. We have, $C = B \geq A \Rightarrow C \geq A$

Again, we have $C = B \geq A \leq D \Rightarrow$ No conclusion

So, both conclusions are false.

EXAMPLE 3. In the following statement, the symbols $, %, #, @, * are used with the following meaning

P $ Q means P > Q; P % Q means P < Q

P # Q means P = Q; P @ Q means P ≥ Q

P * Q means P ≤ Q; Statement : S * P @ Q $ R % T

Conclusion I : Q $ T

Conclusion II : R % P

Which of the above conclusion is true?

Sol. The given statement and conclusions can be write as

Statement : $S \leq P \geq Q > R < T$

Conclusion I : $Q > T$

Conclusion II : $R < P$

Now, we have $Q > R < T$

∴ So no conclusion.

Again, we have $P \geq Q > R \Rightarrow P > R \Rightarrow R < P$

∴ Conclusion II is true.

Topic Practice 1

1 In each of the given questions, one statement and two conclusion are given. Find which of the given conclusion(s) is/are true.

(i) Statement : $Q \geq S < R > T = U \leq P$

Conclusion I : $S > P$

Conclusion II : $R > U$

(ii) Statement : $A > B = C \geq D$

Conclusion I : $C \geq D$

Conclusion II : $A = C$

(iii) Statement : $E = G \geq H = N, C > F \geq M = N$

Conclusion I : $F \geq E$

Conclusion II : $C \geq G$

(iv) Statement : $S > A = N > D > L > E$

Conclusion I : $S > E$

Conclusion II : $A = L$

(v) Statement : $U \leq V < W = X < Y$

Conclusion I : $Y > V$

Conclusion II : $W > U$

2 In the following questions the symbols @, #, $, *, % are used with the following meaning.

'A @ B' means A is less than B

'A # B' means A is greater than B

'A $ B' means A is equal to B

'A * B' means A is less than or equal to B

'A % B' means A is greater than or equal to B.

(i) Statement : L * P % V # D

Conclusion I : L * V

Conclusion II : L $ D

(ii) Statement : L # M # C % Q @ P $ E @ F

Conclusion I : L # Q; Conclusion II : F # C

(iii) Statement : H @ A < T $ G # U % V % B

Conclusion I : T # B; Conclusion II : G # H

(iv) Statement : P @ Q $ R # S @ T * U

Conclusion I : U @ R

Conclusion II : P * S

(v) Statement : A @ B $ C % D * E % F

Conclusion I : C @ E

Conclusion II : A % F

Hints & Solutions

1. (i) We have, $S < R > T = U \leq P \Rightarrow R > U$

So, conclusion II is true.

(ii) We have, $A > B = C \geq D \Rightarrow A > C$ and $C \geq D$

So, conclusion I is true.

(iii) Given statements,

$$E = G \geq H = N$$

and $C > F \geq M = N$

Combining both the statements, we get

$$E = G \geq H = N = M \leq F < C$$

$\Rightarrow F \geq E$ is not true and $C \geq G$ is also not true.

So, both statements are false.

(iv) We have, $S > A = N > D > L > E$

$\Rightarrow$ $S > E$ and $A > L$

So, conclusion I is true.

(v) We have, $U \leq V < W = X < Y$

$\Rightarrow$ $V < Y \Rightarrow Y > V$

and $U < W \Rightarrow W > U$

So, both conclusion are true.

2. (i) We have, L * P % V # D

$\Rightarrow$ $L \leq P \geq V > D$

Thus, we have no conclusion. So both conclusions are false.

(ii) We have, L # M # C % Q @ P $ E @ F

$\Rightarrow$ $L > M > C \geq Q < P = E < F$

Now, $L > M > C \geq Q$

$\Rightarrow$ $L > Q$

and $C \geq Q < P = E < F$

$\Rightarrow$ No conclusion.

So, conclusion I is true.

(iii) Do similar as 2 (ii). **Ans.** Both conclusions are true.

(iv) Do similar as 2 (ii). **Ans.** Both conclusions are false.

(v) Do similar as 2 (ii). **Ans.** Both conclusion are false.

Inequality and Linear Inequalities in One Variable

Inequality

Two real numbers or two algebraic expressions related by the symbols $>$, $<$, $\leq$ or $\geq$ form an inequality or inequation.

In other words, a statement involving the symbols $>$, $<$, $\leq$ or $\geq$ is called an inequality or inequation.

Here, the symbols $<$ (less than), $>$ (greater than), $\leq$ (less than or equal to) and $\geq$ (greater than or equal to) are known as symbol of inequalities.

e.g. $5 < 7$, $x \leq 2$, $x + y \geq 11$

Linear Inequality

An inequality is said to be linear, if the variable (s) occurs in first degree only and there is no term involving the product of the variables. e.g. $ax + b \leq 0$, $ax + by + c > 0$, $ax \leq 4$.

Linear Inequality in One Variable

A linear inequality which has only one variable, is called linear inequality in one variable.

e.g. $ax + b < 0$,

where $a \neq 0$

Linear Inequality in Two Variables

A linear inequality which have only two variables, is called linear inequality in two variables.

e.g. $3x + 11y \leq 0$, $4t + 3y > 0$

Concept of Intervals on a Number Line

On number line or real line, various types of infinite subsets, known as intervals, are defined below:

Closed Interval

If a and b are real numbers, such that $a < b$, then the set of all real numbers x, such that $a \leq x \leq b$, is called a closed interval and is denoted by $[a, b]$.

$\therefore \quad [a, b] = \{x: a \leq x \leq b, x \in R\}$

On the number line, $[a, b]$ may be represented as follows

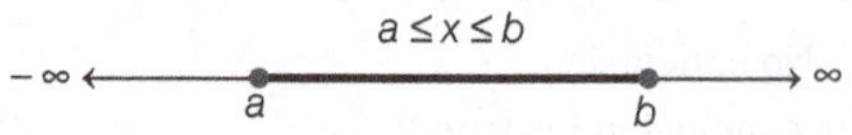

Here, end points of the interval i.e. a and b are included in the interval. So, on number line, draw filled circle (•) at a and b.

Open Interval

If a and b are real numbers, such that $a < b$, then the set of all real numbers x, such that $a < x < b$, is called an open interval and is denoted by (a, b) **or** $]a, b[$.

$\therefore \quad (a, b) = \{x : a < x < b, x \in R\}$

On the number line, (a, b) may be represented as follows

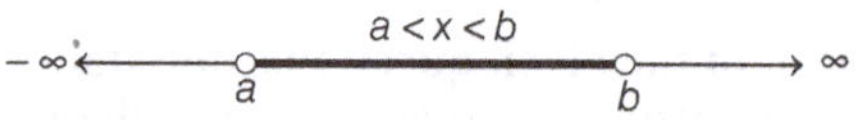

Here, end points of the interval i.e. a and b are not included in the interval. So, on number line, draw open circle (o) at a and b.

Semi-open or Semi-closed Intervals

If a and b are real numbers, such that $a < b$.

Then, $(a, b] = \{x : a < x \leq b, x \in R\}$

and $[a, b) = \{x : a \leq x < b, x \in R\}$

are known as semi-open or semi-closed intervals.

On the number line, these intervals may be represented as follows

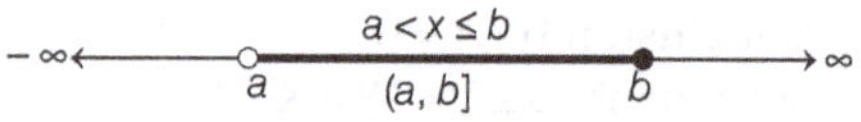

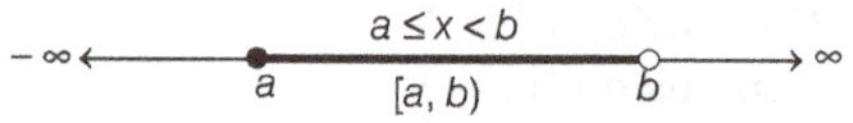

Some properties or rules which are used to solve the inequalities, are given below

Addition or Subtraction

Some number may be added (or subtracted) to (from) both sides of an inequality i.e. if $a > b$, then for any number c,

$$a + c > b + c \text{ or } a - c > b - c$$

e.g. (i) $10 > 5 \Rightarrow 10 + 7 > 5 + 7$ [adding 7 on both sides]

$\Rightarrow 17 > 12$, which is true.

(ii) $-8 > -13 \Rightarrow -8 - 2 > -13 - 2$

[subtracting 2 from both sides]

$\Rightarrow -10 > -15$, which is true.

Multiplication or Division

If both sides of an inequality are multiplied (or divided) by the same positive number, then the sign of inequality remains the same. But when both sides are multiplied (or divided) by the same negative number, then the sign of inequality is reversed.

Let a, b and c be three real numbers, such that $a > b$ and $c \neq 0$.

(i) If $c > 0$, then $\frac{a}{c} > \frac{b}{c}$ and $ac > bc$.

(ii) If $a > b$ and $c < 0$, then $\frac{a}{c} < \frac{b}{c}$ and $ac < bc$.

e.g. (a) $6 > 4 \Rightarrow 6 \times 2 > 4 \times 2$

[multiplying both sides by 2]

$\Rightarrow \quad 12 > 8$, which is true.

(b) $-32 < -24 \Rightarrow \frac{-32}{-8} > \frac{-24}{-8}$

[dividing both sides by -8]

$\Rightarrow 4 > 3$, which is true.

Solution Set

The set of all solutions of an inequality is called the solution set of the inequality.

Algebraic Solution of Linear Inequalities in One Variable

Any solution of a linear inequality in one variable is a value of the variable which makes it a true statement.

e.g. $x = 1$ is the solution of the linear inequality $4x + 7 > 0$.

Method to Solve a Linear Inequality in One Variable

Step I Collect all terms involving the variable (x) on one side and constant terms on other side with the help of above rules and then reduce it in the form $ax < b$ or $ax \leq b$ or $ax > b$ or $ax \geq b$.

Step II Divide this inequality by the coefficient of variable (x). This gives the solution set of given inequality.

Step III Write the solution set.

EXAMPLE 1. Solve $24x < 100$, when

(i) x is a natural number. (ii) x is an integer.

Sol. We have, $24x < 100$

On dividing both sides by 24, we get

$$\frac{24x}{24} < \frac{100}{24} \Rightarrow x < \frac{25}{6}$$

(i) When x is a natural number, then solutions of the inequality $x < \frac{25}{6}$, are all natural numbers, which are less than $\frac{25}{6}$. In this case, the following values of x make the statement true.

$$x = 1, 2, 3, 4$$

Hence, the solution set of inequality is $\{1, 2, 3, 4\}$.

(ii) When x is an integer.

In this case, solutions of given inequality are

$$\ldots, -4, -3, -2, -1, 0, 1, 2, 3, 4$$

Hence, the solution set of inequality is

$$\{\ldots, -4, -3, -2, -1, 0, 1, 2, 3, 4\}$$

EXAMPLE 2. Solve the linear inequality $3x - 5 < x + 7$, when

(i) x is a natural number. (ii) x is a whole number.
(iii) x is an integer. (iv) x is a real number.

Sol. We have, $3x - 5 < x + 7$

$\Rightarrow \quad 3x - 5 + 5 < x + 7 + 5$ [adding 5 on both sides]

$\Rightarrow \quad 3x < x + 12$

$\Rightarrow \quad 3x - x < x + 12 - x$

[subtracting x from both sides]

$\Rightarrow \quad 2x < 12$

$\Rightarrow \quad \frac{2x}{2} < \frac{12}{2}$ [dividing both sides by 2]

$\Rightarrow \quad x < 6$

Now, if

(i) x is natural number, then the solution set is $\{1, 2, 3, 4, 5\}$.

(ii) x is a whole number, then the solution set $\{0, 1, 2, 3, 4, 5\}$.

(iii) x is an integer, then the solution set is $\{\ldots, -3, -2, -1, 0, 1, 2, 3, 4, 5\}$

(iv) x is a real number, then the solution set is $\{x : x \in R \text{ and } x < 6\}$, i.e. any real number less than 6. This can also be written as $(-\infty, 6)$.

TYPE 1 **Solving Equations of the Form**

$$ax + b > cx + d, \; ax + b \geq cx + d,$$
$$ax + b < cx + d, \; ax + b \leq cx + d$$

EXAMPLE 3. Solve the linear inequality $-5x + 25 > 0$.

Sol. We have, $-5x + 25 > 0$

On adding $5x$ to both sides, we get

$$-5x + 25 + 5x > 0 + 5x \Rightarrow 25 > 5x \Rightarrow 5x < 25$$

On dividing both sides by 5, we get

$$\Rightarrow \quad \frac{5x}{5} < \frac{25}{5} \Rightarrow x < 5$$

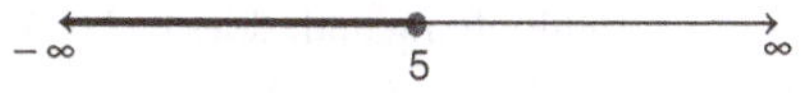

Hence, the required solution set is $(-\infty, 5)$.

EXAMPLE 4. Solve the inequality $\frac{5 - 3x}{3} \leq \frac{x}{6} - 5$.

Sol. We have, $\frac{5 - 3x}{3} \leq \frac{x}{6} - 5 \Rightarrow \frac{5 - 3x}{3} \leq \frac{x - 30}{6}$

$$\Rightarrow \quad \frac{5 - 3x}{3} \times 6 \leq \frac{x - 30}{6} \times 6$$

[multiplying both sides by 6]

$\Rightarrow \quad 2(5-3x) \le x - 30 \Rightarrow 10 - 6x \le x - 30$

$\Rightarrow \quad 10 - 6x - 10 \le x - 30 - 10$ [subtracting 10 from both sides]

$\Rightarrow \quad -6x \le x - 40$

$\Rightarrow \quad -6x - x \le x - 40 - x$ [subtracting x from both sides]

$\Rightarrow \quad -7x \le -40$

$\Rightarrow \quad 7x \ge 40$ [multiplying by -1 on both sides]

$\Rightarrow \quad \frac{7x}{7} \ge \frac{40}{7}$ [dividing by 7 on both sides]

$\Rightarrow \quad x \ge \frac{40}{7}$

i.e. $\quad x \in \left[\frac{40}{7}, \infty\right)$

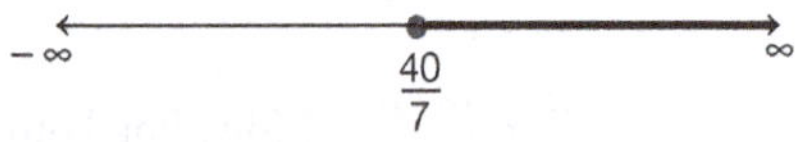

Hence, the required solution set is $\left[\frac{40}{7}, \infty\right)$.

EXAMPLE 5. Solve the following inequality and show the graph of the solution in each case on number line.

(i) $\frac{x}{4} < \frac{5x-2}{3} - \frac{7x-3}{5}$

(ii) $x + \frac{x}{2} + \frac{x}{3} < 11$

(iii) $\frac{1}{2}\left(\frac{3}{5}x + 4\right) \ge \frac{1}{3}(x-6)$

(iv) $\frac{(2x-1)}{3} \le \frac{(3x-2)}{4} - \frac{(2-x)}{5}$

Sol. (i) We have, $\frac{x}{4} < \frac{5x-2}{3} - \frac{7x-3}{5}$

$\Rightarrow \quad \frac{x}{4} < \frac{5(5x-2) - 3(7x-3)}{15}$

$\Rightarrow \quad \frac{x}{4} < \frac{25x - 10 - 21x + 9}{15}$

$\Rightarrow \quad 60\left(\frac{x}{4}\right) < \frac{(4x-1)}{15} \times 60$

[multiplying both sides by LCM (4, 15) = 60]

$\Rightarrow \quad 15x < 4(4x-1)$

$\Rightarrow \quad 15x < 16x - 4$

$\Rightarrow \quad 15x + 4 < 16x - 4 + 4$ [adding 4 on both sides]

$\Rightarrow \quad 15x + 4 < 16x$

$\Rightarrow \quad 15x + 4 - 15x < 16x - 15x$ [subtracting $15x$ from both sides]

$\Rightarrow \quad 4 < x$ or $x > 4$

$\therefore \quad x \in (4, \infty)$

On number line, it can be represented as

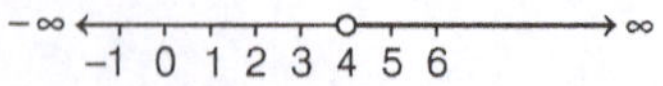

Here, the dark portion on the number line represents the solution of inequality.

(ii) We have, $\quad x + \frac{x}{2} + \frac{x}{3} < 11$

$\Rightarrow \quad \frac{6x + 3x + 2x}{6} < 11 \Rightarrow \frac{11x}{6} < 11$

On multiplying both sides by $\frac{6}{11}$, we get

$\frac{11x}{6} \times \frac{6}{11} < 11 \times \frac{6}{11} \Rightarrow x < 6$

$\therefore \quad x \in (-\infty, 6)$

This can be represented on number line as

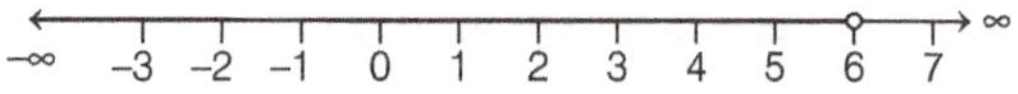

Here, the dark portion on the number line represents the solution of inequality.

(iii) We have, $\frac{1}{2}\left(\frac{3}{5}x + 4\right) \ge \frac{1}{3}(x-6)$

$\Rightarrow \quad \frac{1}{2}\left(\frac{3x+20}{5}\right) \ge \frac{1}{3}(x-6)$

$\Rightarrow \quad \frac{1}{10}(3x+20) \ge \frac{1}{3}(x-6)$

$\Rightarrow \quad \frac{30}{10}(3x+20) \ge \frac{30}{3}(x-6)$

[multiplying both sides by LCM (10, 3) = 30]

$\Rightarrow \quad 3(3x+20) \ge 10(x-6)$

$\Rightarrow \quad 9x + 60 \ge 10x - 60$

$\Rightarrow \quad 9x + 60 - 60 \ge 10x - 60 - 60$ [subtracting 60 from both sides]

$\Rightarrow \quad 9x \ge 10x - 120$

$\Rightarrow \quad 9x - 10x \ge 10x - 120 - 10x$ [subtracting $10x$ from both sides]

$\Rightarrow \quad -x \ge -120 \Rightarrow x \le 120$ [multiplying both sides by -1]

$\therefore \quad x \in (-\infty, 120]$

On number line, it can be represented as

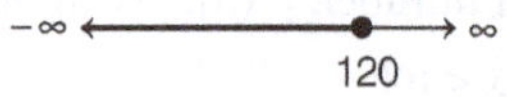

Here, the dark portion on the number line represents the solution of inequality.

(iv) We have, $\frac{2x-1}{3} \le \frac{3x-2}{4} - \frac{2-x}{5}$

On multiplying both sides by LCM of 3, 4 and 5 i.e. 60, we get

$\frac{2x-1}{3} \times 60 \le \frac{3x-2}{4} \times 60 - \frac{2-x}{5} \times 60$

$\Rightarrow \quad 20(2x-1) \le 15(3x-2) - 12(2-x)$

$\Rightarrow \quad 40x - 20 \le 45x - 30 - 24 + 12x$

$\Rightarrow \quad 40x - 20 \le 57x - 54$

$\Rightarrow \quad 40x - 20 + 20 \le 57x - 54 + 20$

[adding 20 on both sides]

$\Rightarrow \quad 40x \le 57x - 34$

$\Rightarrow \quad 40x - 57x \le 57x - 34 - 57x$

[subtracting $57x$ from both sides]

$\Rightarrow \quad -17x \le -34 \Rightarrow \dfrac{-17x}{17} \le \dfrac{-34}{17}$

[dividing both sides by 17]

$\Rightarrow \quad -x \le -2 \Rightarrow x \ge 2$

[multiplying both sides by -1]

Thus, the solution set is $[2, \infty)$.

On number line, it can be represented as

Here, the dark portion on the number line represents the solution of inequality.

EXAMPLE 6. Solve the following inequation.

(i) $\dfrac{1}{x-4} < 0$ (ii) $\dfrac{x+1}{x+3} \ge 1$

Sol. (i) We have, $\dfrac{1}{x-4} < 0$

$\Rightarrow \quad x - 4 < 0 \qquad \left[\because \dfrac{a}{b} < 0 \text{ and } a > 0 \Rightarrow b < 0\right]$

$\Rightarrow \quad x < 4$

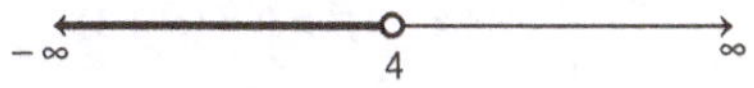

$\therefore \quad x \in (-\infty, 4)$

(ii) We have, $\dfrac{x+1}{x+3} \ge 1$

$\Rightarrow \quad \dfrac{x+1}{x+3} - 1 \ge 1 - 1$ [on subtracting 1 both sides]

$\Rightarrow \quad \dfrac{x+1-x-3}{x+3} \ge 0 \Rightarrow \dfrac{-2}{x+3} \ge 0$

$\Rightarrow \quad \dfrac{2}{x+3} \le 0$ [multiplying both sides by -1]

$\Rightarrow \quad x + 3 < 0 \qquad \left[\because \dfrac{a}{b} < 0 \text{ and } a > 0 \Rightarrow b < 0\right]$

$\Rightarrow \quad x < -3$

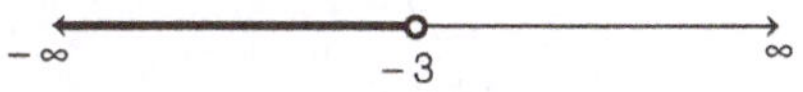

$\therefore \quad x \in (-\infty, -3)$

TYPE 2 When Equality of the Form $\dfrac{ax+b}{cx+d} \gtreqless k$

If the given inequality is of the form

$$\frac{ax+b}{cx+d} > k \text{ or } \frac{ax+b}{cx+d} \ge k$$

or

$$\frac{ax+b}{cx+d} < k \text{ or } \frac{ax+b}{cx+d} \le k,$$

where k is a constant, then we solve these inequalities with the help of following working steps

***Step* I** Collect all terms in the LHS of given inequality to make RHS zero and then reduce it any one of the form

$$\frac{px+q}{cx+d} > 0 \quad \text{or} \quad \frac{px+q}{cx+d} \ge 0$$

$$\text{or} \quad \frac{px+q}{cx+d} < 0 \quad \text{or} \quad \frac{px+q}{cx+d} \le 0$$

***Step* II** Multiply the above inequality by square of denominator to reduce it in the form of product of two expressions, i.e. $(px+q)(cx+d) \gtreqless 0$.

***Step* III** Now, use the result

(i) If product of two terms < 0, then both terms have opposite sign.

(ii) If product of two terms > 0, then both terms have same sign.

***Step* IV** Now, solve both expression separately with suitable inequality sign and get solution sets.

***Step* V** Take the union of above solution sets, which gives the solution of given inequality.

EXAMPLE 7. Solve the inequality $\dfrac{x-2}{x+5} > 2$. Also, represent the solution on the number line.

Sol. We have, $\dfrac{x-2}{x+5} > 2$

On subtracting 2 from both sides, we get

$$\frac{x-2}{x+5} - 2 > 0$$

$\Rightarrow \quad \dfrac{x-2-2(x+5)}{x+5} > 0$

$\Rightarrow \quad \dfrac{x-2-2x-10}{x+5} > 0$

$\Rightarrow \quad \dfrac{-(x+12)}{x+5} > 0$

$\Rightarrow \quad \dfrac{x+12}{x+5} < 0$

[multiplying both sides by -1]

On multiplying both sides by $(x+5)^2$, we get

$$\frac{(x+12)}{(x+5)} \times (x+5)^2 < 0 \times (x+5)^2 \Rightarrow (x+12)(x+5) < 0$$

So, the factors $(x+12)$ and $(x+5)$ have opposite signs.

$\therefore \quad (x+12) > 0 \text{ and } (x+5) < 0$ ...(i)

or $\quad (x+12) < 0 \text{ and } (x+5) > 0$ ...(ii)

From inequality (i), we get

$$x + 12 > 0 \text{ and } x + 5 < 0$$

$\Rightarrow \quad x + 12 - 12 > -12 \text{ and } x + 5 - 5 < 0 - 5$

[subtracting 12 from first inequality and 5 from second]

$\Rightarrow \quad x > -12 \text{ and } x < -5$ ...(iii)

On number line, it can be represented as

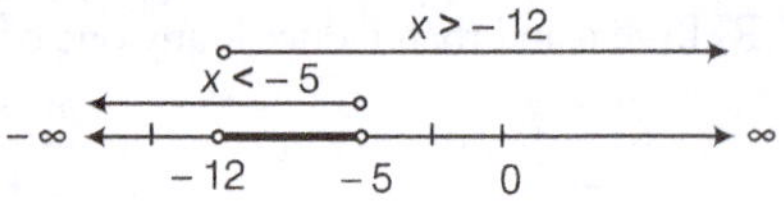

$\therefore$ $$-12 < x < -5 \quad \text{...(iv)}$$

From inequality (ii), we get

$$(x+12) < 0 \text{ and } (x+5) > 0$$

$$x + 12 - 12 < 0 - 12 \text{ and } x + 5 - 5 > -5$$

$\Rightarrow$ $$x < -12 \text{ and } x > -5$$

On number line, it can be represented as

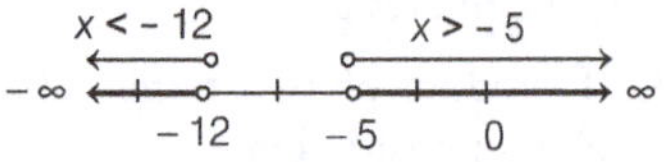

Since, no common point occurs, so it has no solution.

Hence, the solution set of the given inequality is $-12 < x < -5$ i.e. $(-12, -5)$.

EXAMPLE 8. Solve the inequality $\frac{x-4}{x+2} \le 2$. Also, represent the solution on number line.

Sol. We have, $$\frac{x-4}{x+2} \le 2$$

$\Rightarrow$ $$\frac{x-4}{x+2} - 2 \le 2 - 2$$

[subtracting 2 from both sides]

$\Rightarrow$ $$\frac{x-4}{x+2} - 2 \le 0$$

$\Rightarrow$ $$\frac{x-4-2(x+2)}{x+2} \le 0$$

$\Rightarrow$ $$\frac{x-4-2x-4}{x+2} \le 0$$

$\Rightarrow$ $$\frac{-x-8}{x+2} \le 0, \text{ here } x+2 \ne 0; \text{ i.e. } x \ne -2$$

$\Rightarrow$ $$\frac{x+8}{x+2} \ge 0 \quad \text{[multiplying both sides by } -1]$$

$\Rightarrow$ $$\frac{x+8}{x+2} \times (x+2)^2 \ge 0 \times (x+2)^2$$

[multiplying both sides by $(x+2)^2$]

$\Rightarrow$ $(x+8)(x+2) \ge 0$

The factors $(x+8)$ and $(x+2)$ have the same signs.

***Case* I When both are non-negative**

In this case, we have

$x + 8 \ge 0$ and $x + 2 > 0$

[$\because$ $x + 2 \ne 0$ because for $x = -2$, denominator of given inequality becomes 0]

$\Rightarrow$ $x \ge -8$ and $x > -2$

On number line, these can be represented as

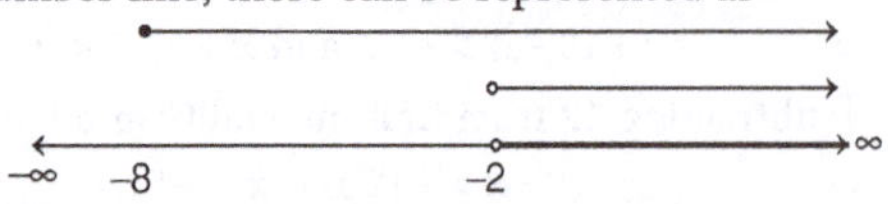

Clearly, the common values of x are lying in the interval $(-2, \infty)$.

$\therefore$ The solution set is $(-2, \infty)$.

***Case* II When both are non-positive**

In this case, we have

$$x + 8 \le 0 \text{ and } x + 2 < 0$$

$\Rightarrow$ $$x \le -8 \text{ and } x < -2$$

On number line, these can be represented as

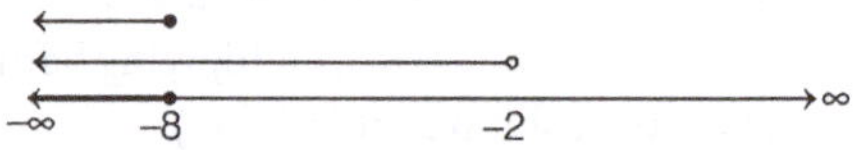

Clearly, the common values of x are lying in the interval $(-\infty, -8]$

$\therefore$ The solution set is $(-\infty, -8]$.

Hence, the required solution set is $(-\infty, -8] \cup (-2, \infty)$ and this can be represented on the number line as

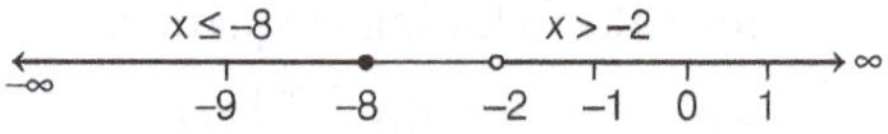

EXAMPLE 9. Solve the inequality $\frac{-3x+10}{x+1} > 0$. Also, represent the solution on the number line.

Sol. We have, $$\frac{-3x+10}{x+1} > 0$$

$\Rightarrow$ $$\frac{-3x+10}{x+1} \times (x+1)^2 > 0 \times (x+1)^2$$

[multiplying both sides by $(x+1)^2$]

$\Rightarrow$ $$(-3x+10)(x+1) > 0$$

$\Rightarrow$ The factors $(-3x+10)$ and $(x+1)$ have the same signs.

***Case* I When both are positive**

In this case, we have

$$-3x + 10 > 0 \text{ and } x + 1 > 0$$

$\Rightarrow$ $$10 > 3x \text{ and } x > -1$$

$\Rightarrow$ $$3x < 10 \text{ and } x > -1$$

$\Rightarrow$ $$x < \frac{10}{3} \text{ and } x > -1$$

$\Rightarrow$ $$-1 < x < \frac{10}{3}$$

$\therefore$ The solution set is $\left(-1, \frac{10}{3}\right)$.

***Case* II When both are negative**

In this case, we have

$$-3x + 10 < 0 \text{ and } x + 1 < 0$$

$\Rightarrow$ $$3x > 10 \text{ and } x < -1$$

$\Rightarrow$ $$x > \frac{10}{3} \text{ and } x < -1, \text{ which is impossible}$$

[$\because$ system of inequalities have no common solution]

Hence, the required solution set is $\left(-1, \frac{10}{3}\right)$ and this can be represented on the number line as

$-1 < x < \frac{10}{3}$

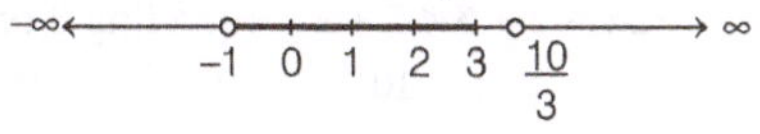

EXAMPLE 10. Solve the inequality $\frac{x+3}{x+4} \geq 1$ and show the solution on the number line. **[NCERT Exemplar]**

Sol. We have, $\frac{x+3}{x+4} \geq 1 \Rightarrow \frac{x+3}{x+4} - 1 \geq 1 - 1$

[subtracting 1 from both sides]

$\Rightarrow \quad \frac{x+3-x-4}{x+4} \geq 0$

$\Rightarrow \quad \frac{-1}{x+4} \geq 0$

$\Rightarrow \quad x+4 \leq 0, x+4 \neq 0$

[multiplying both sides by $-(x+4)^2$]

$\Rightarrow \quad x+4-4 \leq 0-4, x \neq -4$

[subtracting 4 from both sides]

$x \leq -4, x \neq -4$

$\therefore$ The solution set is $(-\infty, -4)$.

On number line, it can be represented as

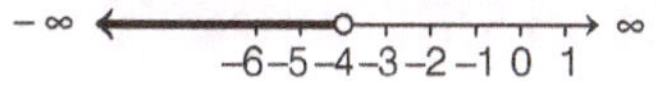

Topic Practice 2

1. Solve $-12x > 30$, when
   (i) x is a natural number. (ii) x is an integer.
2. Solve $3x + 8 > 2$, when
   (i) x is an integer. (ii) x is a real number.
3. Solve the inequality $5x - 3 < 3x + 1$, when x is an integer.
4. Solve the following inequalities
   (i) $4x + 3 < 6x + 7$ (ii) $3(x-1) \leq 2(x-3)$
   (iii) $2(2x+3) - 10 < 6(x-2)$
   (iv) $5x - 1 > 3x + 7$ (v) $\frac{x}{3} > \frac{x}{2} + 1$
   (vi) $37 - (3x+5) \geq 9x - 8(x-3)$
   (vii) $\frac{x}{2} \geq \frac{(5x-2)}{3} - \frac{(7x-3)}{5}$
5. Solve for x : $\frac{x+3}{x-2} \leq 2$. **[CBSE 2023]**
6. Solve the following inequalities
   (i) $\frac{x+8}{x-2} \geq 0$ (ii) $\frac{2x+5}{x-1} > 5$
   (iii) $\frac{7x-5}{8x+3} > 4$ (iv) $\frac{x}{x-5} > \frac{1}{2}$

Hints & Solutions

1. $-12x > 30 \Rightarrow x < -\frac{30}{12}$

Ans. (i) No solution (ii) $\{\ldots, -4, -3\}$

2. Solve as Example 2.

Ans. (i) $\{-1, 0, 1, 2, 3, \ldots\}$ (ii) $(-2, \infty)$

3. Subtracting $(3x-3)$ from both sides of $5x - 3 < 3x + 1$.

Ans. $\{\ldots, -4, -3, -2, -1, 0, 1\}$

4. (i) Subtracting $(4x+7)$ from both sides of $4x + 3 < 6x + 7$. **Ans.** $(-4, \infty)$

(ii) Solve as Example 4. **Ans.** $(-\infty, -3]$

(iii) Solve as Example 4. **Ans.** $(4, \infty)$

(iv) Subtracting $(3x-1)$ from both sides of $5x - 1 > 3x + 7$. **Ans.** $(4, \infty)$

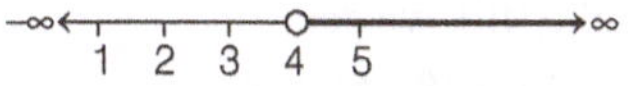

(v) Solve as Example 5, part (ii). **Ans.** $(-\infty, -6)$

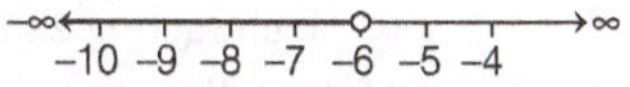

(vi) Solve as Example 5, part (iii). **Ans.** $(-\infty, 2]$

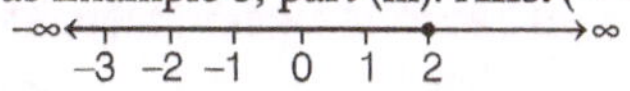

(vii) Solve as Example 5, part (iv). **Ans.** $\left[-\frac{2}{7}, \infty\right)$

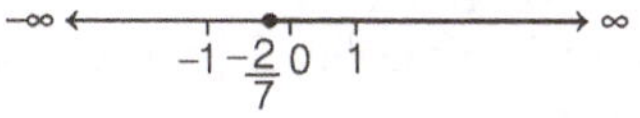

5. Hint We have, $\frac{x+3}{x-2} \leq 2 \Rightarrow x+3 \leq 2(x-2)$

$\Rightarrow \quad x+3 \leq 2x-4 \Rightarrow 3+4 \leq 2x-4 \Rightarrow x \geq 7$

$\therefore \quad x \in [7, \infty)$

6. (i) Solve as Example 9. **Ans.** $(-\infty, -8] \cup (2, \infty)$

(ii) Solve as Example 10. **Ans.** $\left(1, \frac{10}{3}\right)$

(iii) Solve as Example 10. **Ans.** $\left(\frac{-17}{25}, \frac{-3}{8}\right)$

(iv) Solve as Example 10. **Ans.** $(-\infty, -5) \cup (5, \infty)$

System of Inequalities in One Variable

Two or more inequalities taken together comprise a system of inequalities and the solution of the system of inequalities are the solutions common to all the inequalities comprising the system.

e.g. $x = 10$ is the solution of the system of inequalities

$$4x + 3 \leq 91 \text{ and } 2x \geq x + 8$$

Solution of System of Linear Inequalities in One Variable

We know that, the solution set of a linear inequality in one variable is the set of all points on the number line satisfying the given inequality.

Therefore, the solution set of a system of linear inequalities in one variable is defined as the **intersection of the solution set** of the linear inequalities in the system.

e.g. If the solution sets of linear inequalities in the system are $(-\infty, 5]$ and $[5, \infty)$, then the solution of system of linear inequalities in one variable is 5 only. Because, if we represent the solution sets on the number line, we see that the value which are common to both is 5 only.

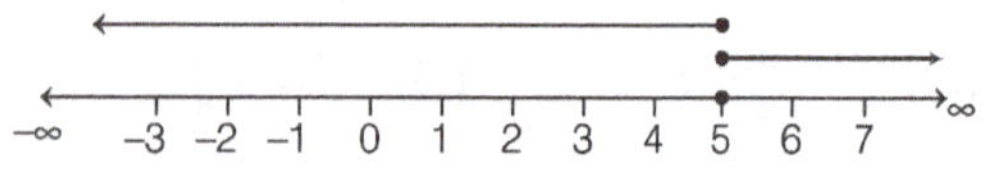

The process of finding solution of system of linear inequalities of different types are given below.

TYPE 1 When Two Separate Linear Inequalities are Given

If the given system of inequalities comprise by two separate linear inequalities, then to solve these we use the following working steps:

Step I Solve each inequality separately and obtain their solution sets.

Step II Represent the solution sets on a number line and then find the values of the variable which are common to them.

Or Find the intersection of the solution sets obtained in Step I.

EXAMPLE 1. Solve the following system of inequalities $2x - 3 < 7$ and $2x > -4$. Also, represent the solution graphically on the number line.

Sol. We have the following inequalities,

$$2x - 3 < 7 \quad \text{...(i)}$$

and $$2x > -4 \quad \text{...(ii)}$$

From inequality (i), we have $2x - 3 < 7$

$\Rightarrow \quad 2x - 3 + 3 < 7 + 3$ [adding 3 on both sides]

$\Rightarrow \quad 2x < 10$

$\Rightarrow \quad \dfrac{2x}{2} < \dfrac{10}{2}$ [dividing both sides by 2]

$\Rightarrow \quad x < 5$

$\therefore$ The solution set is $(-\infty, 5)$.

From inequality (ii), we have

$2x > -4$

$\Rightarrow \quad \dfrac{2x}{2} > \dfrac{-4}{2}$ [dividing both sides by 2]

$\Rightarrow \quad x > -2$

$\therefore$ The solution set is $(-2, \infty)$.

Now, let us draw the graphs of the solutions of both inequalities on number line.

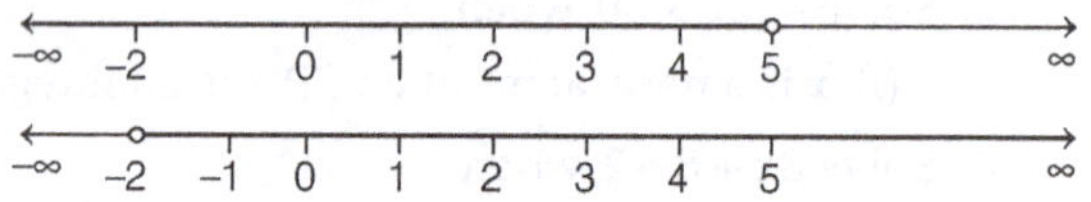

It can be seen that the values of x, which are common to both are lying in the interval $(-2, 5)$.

Hence, the solution set of given system of inequations is $(-2, 5)$ and this can be represented graphically on the number line as

EXAMPLE 2. Solve the following system of inequalities and represent the solution graphically on the number line.

$$5(2x - 7) - 3(2x + 3) \leq 0, \; 2x + 19 \leq 6x + 47$$

Sol. We have the following inequalities

$$5(2x - 7) - 3(2x + 3) \leq 0 \quad \text{...(i)}$$

and $$2x + 19 \leq 6x + 47 \quad \text{...(ii)}$$

From inequality (i), we get

$5(2x - 7) - 3(2x + 3) \leq 0$

$\Rightarrow \quad 10x - 35 - 6x - 9 \leq 0$

$\Rightarrow \quad 4x - 44 \leq 0$

$\Rightarrow \quad 4x - 44 + 44 \leq 44$

[adding 44 on both sides]

$\Rightarrow \quad 4x \leq 44 \Rightarrow x \leq 11$ ...(iii)

[dividing both sides by 4]

$\therefore$ The solution set is $(-\infty, 11]$.

From inequality (ii), we get

$2x + 19 \leq 6x + 47$

$\Rightarrow \quad 2x + 19 - 2x \leq 6x + 47 - 2x$

[subtracting $2x$ from both sides]

$\Rightarrow \quad 19 \leq 4x + 47$

$\Rightarrow \quad 19 - 47 \le 4x + 47 - 47$ [subtracting 47 from both sides]

$\Rightarrow \quad -28 \le 4x$ or $4x \ge -28$

$\Rightarrow \quad \dfrac{4x}{4} \ge \dfrac{-28}{4}$ [dividing both sides by 4]

$\Rightarrow \quad x \ge -7$

$\therefore$ The solution set is $[-7, \infty)$.

Now, let us draw the graphs of the solutions of both inequalities on number line.

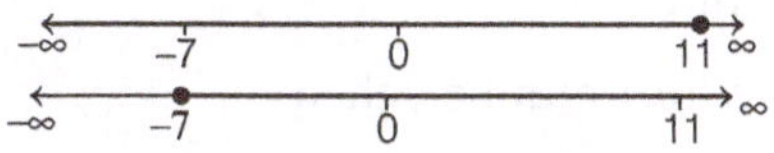

It can be seen that the values of x, which are common to both are lying in the interval $[-7, 11]$.

Hence, the solution set of given system of inequations is $[-7, 11]$ and this can be represented graphically on the number line as

EXAMPLE 3. Solve the following system of linear inequalities and represent the solution graphically on the number line.

$$2(2x+3) - 10 < 6(x-2) \text{ and } \frac{2x-3}{4} + 6 \ge 2 + \frac{4x}{3}$$

Sol. Given system of linear inequalities is

$$2(2x+3) - 10 < 6(x-2) \quad \text{...(i)}$$

and $$\frac{2x-3}{4} + 6 \ge 2 + \frac{4x}{3} \quad \text{...(ii)}$$

From inequality (i), we get

$2(2x+3) - 10 < 6(x-2)$

$\Rightarrow \quad 4x + 6 - 10 < 6x - 12$

$\Rightarrow \quad 4x - 4 < 6x - 12$

$\Rightarrow \quad 4x - 4 + 4 < 6x - 12 + 4$ [adding 4 on both sides]

$\Rightarrow \quad 4x < 6x - 8$

$\Rightarrow \quad 4x - 6x < 6x - 8 - 6x$ [subtracting $6x$ from both sides]

$\Rightarrow \quad -2x < -8$

$\Rightarrow \quad 2x > 8$ [dividing both sides by -1, then inequality sign will also change]

$\Rightarrow \quad \dfrac{2x}{2} > \dfrac{8}{2}$ [dividing both sides by 2]

$\therefore \quad x > 4 \quad \text{...(iii)}$

Thus, any value of x greater than 4 satisfies the inequality.

$\therefore$ The solution set is $(4, \infty)$.

The representation of solution of inequality (i) is

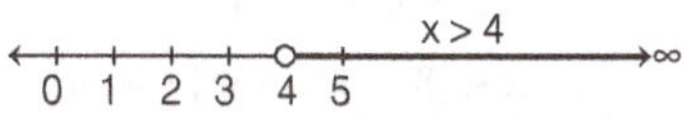

From inequality (ii), we get

$\dfrac{2x-3}{4} + 6 \ge 2 + \dfrac{4x}{3}$

$\Rightarrow \quad \dfrac{2x-3+24}{4} \ge \dfrac{6+4x}{3}$

$\Rightarrow \quad \dfrac{2x+21}{4} \ge \dfrac{6+4x}{3}$

$\Rightarrow \quad 3(2x+21) \ge 4(6+4x)$ [multiplying both sides by LCM $(4, 3) = 12$]

$\Rightarrow \quad 6x + 63 \ge 24 + 16x$

$\Rightarrow \quad 6x + 63 - 63 \ge 24 + 16x - 63$ [subtracting 63 from both sides]

$\Rightarrow \quad 6x \ge 16x - 39$

$\Rightarrow \quad 6x - 16x \ge 16x - 39 - 16x$ [subtracting $16x$ from both sides]

$\Rightarrow \quad -10x \ge -39$

$\Rightarrow \quad 10x \le 39$ [multiplying both sides by -1, the inequality sign will also change]

$\Rightarrow \quad \dfrac{10x}{10} \le \dfrac{39}{10}$ [dividing both sides by 10]

$\Rightarrow \quad x \le 3.9 \quad \text{...(iv)}$

Thus, any value of x less than or equal to 3.9 satisfies the inequality.

$\therefore$ The solution set is $(-\infty, 3.9]$.

Its representation on number line is,

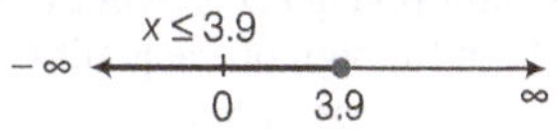

We see that there is no common value of x, which satisfies both inequalites (iii) and (iv).

Hence, the given system of inequalities has no solution set.

TYPE 2 When Inequalities of the form $a \le \dfrac{cx+d}{e} \le b$, where $a, b, c, d \in R$

This type of inequalities will be formed by combining the inequalities

$$a \le \frac{cx+d}{e} \text{ and } \frac{cx+d}{e} \le b.$$

To solve such type of inequalities, make the middle term free from constant (i.e. write the given inequalities as $f \le x \le g$, where f and g are some real numbers by using the rule of addition, subtraction, multiplication, division in each term of given inequalities.

EXAMPLE 4. Solve the inequalities $6 \leq -3(2x-4) < 12$.

Sol. We have, $6 \leq -3(2x-4) < 12$ or $6 \leq -6x + 12 < 12$

On subtracting 12 from each term, we get

$$6 - 12 \leq -6x + 12 - 12 < 12 - 12$$

$$\Rightarrow \quad -6 \leq -6x < 0$$

On dividing each term by -6, we get

$$\frac{-6}{-6} \geq \frac{-6x}{-6} > \frac{0}{-6}$$

[while dividing each term by the same negative number, then sign of inequalities will get change]

$$\Rightarrow \quad 1 \geq x > 0$$

which can be written as $0 < x \leq 1$.

Hence, solution set of given system of inequations is $(0, 1]$.

EXAMPLE 5. Solve the inequalities $-3 \leq 4 - \frac{7x}{2} \leq 18$.

Sol. We have, $-3 \leq 4 - \frac{7x}{2} \leq 18$

On subtracting 4 from each term, we get

$$-3 - 4 \leq 4 - \frac{7x}{2} - 4 \leq 18 - 4 \Rightarrow -7 \leq -\frac{7x}{2} \leq 14$$

On multiplying each term by $\left(\frac{-2}{7}\right)$, we get

$$-7\left(-\frac{2}{7}\right) \geq \frac{-7}{2} x \times \left(\frac{-2}{7}\right) \geq 14 \times \left(\frac{-2}{7}\right)$$

[while multiplying each term by the same negative number, then the sign of inequalities will get change]

$$\Rightarrow \quad 2 \geq x \geq -4$$

or $\quad -4 \leq x \leq 2$

or $\quad x \in [-4, 2]$

Hence, solution set of given system of inequations is $[-4, 2]$.

EXAMPLE 6. Solve the linear inequalities

$$-15 < \frac{3(x-2)}{5} \leq 0.$$

Sol. We have, $-15 < \frac{3(x-2)}{5} \leq 0$

$$\Rightarrow \quad -15 \times 5 < \frac{3(x-2)}{5} \times 5 \leq 0 \times 5$$

[multiplying each term by 5]

$$\Rightarrow \quad -75 < 3(x-2) \leq 0 \Rightarrow \frac{-75}{3} < \frac{3(x-2)}{3} \leq \frac{0}{3}$$

[dividing each term by 3]

$$\Rightarrow \quad -25 < x - 2 \leq 0$$

$$\Rightarrow \quad -25 + 2 < x - 2 + 2 \leq 0 + 2$$

[adding 2 on each term]

$$\Rightarrow \quad -23 < x \leq 2$$

$$\therefore \quad x \in (-23, 2]$$

Hence, solution set of the given system of inequations is $(-23, 2]$.

TYPE 3 When Inequality of the Form $|ax + b| \gtreqless k$, where a, b, k are Real numbers and $a \neq 0$, $k > 0$

If the given inequality is any of the form $|ax + b| < k$ or $|ax + b| > k$ or $|ax + b| \geq k$ or $|ax + b| \leq k$, where $a \neq 0$ and $k > 0$, then we solve the inequality with the help of following results.

If $a > 0$ is any real number, then

(i) $|x| < a \Rightarrow -a < x < a$, $|x| \leq a \Rightarrow -a \leq x \leq a$

(ii) $|x| > a \Rightarrow x > a$ or $x < -a$

$|x| \geq a \Rightarrow x \geq a$ or $x \leq -a$

Expansion of Modulus Function

$$|x - a| = \begin{cases} x - a, & \text{if } x \geq a \\ -(x - a), & \text{if } x < a \end{cases}$$, where a is any real number.

EXAMPLE 7. Solve $|3x - 2| \leq \frac{1}{2}$.

Sol. Given, $|3x - 2| \leq \frac{1}{2}$

$$\therefore \quad \frac{-1}{2} \leq (3x - 2) \leq \frac{1}{2} \quad [\because |x| \leq a \Rightarrow -a \leq x \leq a]$$

$$\Rightarrow \quad -\frac{1}{2} + 2 \leq 3x - 2 + 2 \leq \frac{1}{2} + 2$$

[adding 2 on each term]

$$\Rightarrow \quad \frac{3}{2} \leq 3x \leq \frac{5}{2}$$

$$\Rightarrow \quad \frac{3}{2} \times \frac{1}{3} \leq \frac{3x}{3} \leq \frac{5}{2} \times \frac{1}{3} \quad \text{[dividing each term by 3]}$$

$$\Rightarrow \quad \frac{1}{2} \leq x \leq \frac{5}{6}$$

i.e. $\quad x \in \left[\frac{1}{2}, \frac{5}{6}\right]$

Hence, the required solution set is $\left[\frac{1}{2}, \frac{5}{6}\right]$.

EXAMPLE 8. Solve $|x - 2| \geq 6$.

Sol. We have, $|x - 2| \geq 6$

$$\Rightarrow \quad x - 2 \geq 6 \text{ or } x - 2 \leq -6$$

$[\because |x| \geq a \Rightarrow x \geq a \text{ or } x \leq -a]$

$$\Rightarrow \quad x \geq 8 \text{ or } x \leq -4$$

$$\Rightarrow \quad x \in [8, \infty) \text{ or } x \in (-\infty, 4]$$

$$\Rightarrow \quad x \in [8, \infty) \cup (-\infty, 4]$$

Hence, the required solution set is $(-\infty, 4] \cup [8, \infty)$.

EXAMPLE 9. Solve graphically for $x, |x-1| \le 5, |x| \ge 2$.

Sol. We have the following inequalities

$$|x-1| \le 5 \quad \text{...(i)}$$

and $$|x| \ge 2 \quad \text{...(ii)}$$

From inequality (i), we have

$$-5 \le x-1 \le 5 \quad [\because |x| \le a \Rightarrow -a \le x \le a]$$

$$\Rightarrow \quad -5+1 \le x \le 5+1 \quad [\text{adding 1 on each term}]$$

$$\Rightarrow \quad -4 \le x \le 6 \Rightarrow x \in [-4, 6]$$

$\therefore$ The solution set is $[-4, 6]$.

From inequality (ii), we have

$$|x| \ge 2$$

$$\Rightarrow \quad x \ge 2 \text{ or } x \le -2 \; [\because |x| \ge a \; x \ge a \text{ or } x \le -a]$$

$$\Rightarrow \quad x \in [2, \infty) \text{ or } (-\infty, -2]$$

$$\Rightarrow \quad x \in (-\infty, -2] \cup [2, \infty)$$

$\therefore$ The solution set is $(-\infty, -2] \cup [2, \infty)$.

Now, let us draw the graphs of solutions of both inequality.

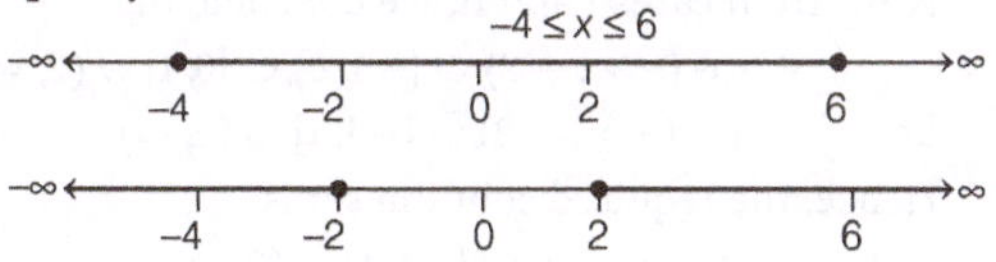

Clearly, the common values of x are lying in the interval $[-4, -2]$ or $[2, 6]$.

Hence, the required solution set is $[-4, -2] \cup [2, 6]$.

TYPE 4 Solution of an Inequality, which contain the Term(s) of the Form $|x \pm a|$ and $|ax \pm b|$

If the given inequality contain the term(s) of the form $|x \pm a|$ or $|ax \pm b|$, then proceed as follows

***Step* I** Put each modulus term equal to zero and find the corresponding value of x. These value of x are called the **critical points.**

e.g. If the given inequality involves the terms

$$|x-a| \text{ and } |x-b| \text{ then put}$$

$$|x-a| = 0 \text{ and } |x-b| = 0$$

$$\Rightarrow \quad x-a=0 \text{ and } x-b=0$$

$$\Rightarrow \quad x=a \text{ and } x=b$$

***Step* II** Divide the whole real line into disjoint intervals with the help of critical points.

e.g. If $x=a$ and $x=b$ are critical points, such that $a<b$, then divide the real line as

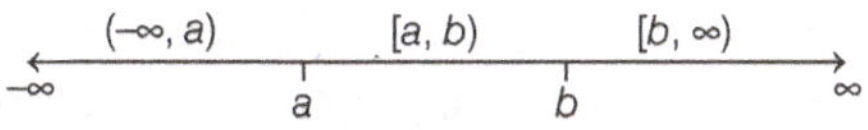

***Step* III** Consider the intervals obtained in Step II and solve the given inequality in each interval.

***Step* IV** Take the union of solution sets, obtained in each case.

This gives the required solution set.

EXAMPLE 10. Solve $|x-1| + |x-2| \ge 4$.

Sol. We have, $|x-1| + |x-2| \ge 4$

Put $$x-1=0 \Rightarrow x=1$$

and $$x-2=0 \Rightarrow x=2$$

Thus, $x=1$ and 2 are critical points, so we will consider three intervals $(-\infty, 1)$, $[1, 2)$ and $[2, \infty)$.

***Case* I** When $-\infty < x < 1$

Then, $|x-1| = -(x-1)$ and $|x-2| = -(x-2)$

$$\left[\because |x-a| = \begin{cases} x-a, & \text{if } x \ge a \\ -(x-a), & \text{if } x < a \end{cases}\right]$$

$$\therefore \quad |x-1| + |x-2| \ge 4$$

$$\Rightarrow \quad -(x-1)-(x-2) \ge 4$$

$$\Rightarrow \quad -x+1-x+2 \ge 4$$

$$\Rightarrow \quad -2x+3 \ge 4$$

$$\Rightarrow \quad -2x \ge 1$$

[subtracting 3 from both sides]

$$\Rightarrow \quad x \le -\frac{1}{2} \quad [\text{dividing both sides by } -2]$$

$\therefore$ Solution set of given inequality in this case is

$$-\infty < x \le -\frac{1}{2} \quad \text{...(i)}$$

***Case* II** When $1 \le x < 2$

Then, $$|x-1| = x-1$$

and $$|x-2| = -(x-2)$$

$$\therefore \quad |x-1| + |x-2| \ge 4$$

$$\Rightarrow \quad x-1-x+2 \ge 4$$

$$\Rightarrow \quad 1 \ge 4, \text{ which is absurd.}$$

So, in this case, given inequality has no solution.

***Case* III** When $2 \le x < \infty$

Then, $|x-1| = x-1$ and $|x-2| = x-2$

$$\therefore \quad |x-1| + |x-2| \ge 4$$

$$\Rightarrow \quad x-1+x-2 \ge 4$$

$$\Rightarrow \quad 2x-3 \ge 4$$

$$\Rightarrow \quad 2x \ge 7 \quad [\text{adding 3 on both sides}]$$

$$\Rightarrow \quad x \ge \frac{7}{2} \quad [\text{dividing both sides by 2}]$$

Here, $2 \le x < \infty$.

$\therefore$ Solution set of given inequality in this case is

$$\frac{7}{2} \le x < \infty \quad \text{...(ii)}$$

On combining inequalities (i) and (ii), we get

$$-\infty < x \le -\frac{1}{2}$$

and $$\frac{7}{2} \le x < \infty$$

i.e. $$x \in \left(-\infty, -\frac{1}{2}\right] \cup \left[\frac{7}{2}, \infty\right)$$

EXAMPLE 11. Solve the inequality $\frac{|x|-1}{|x|-2} \geq 0$, $x \in R$ and $x \neq \pm 2$.

Sol. We have, $\frac{|x|-1}{|x|-2} \geq 0$

Now, put $|x| = 0 \Rightarrow x = 0$

Thus, $x = 0$ is the critical point. So, we will consider two intervals $(-\infty, 0)$ and $[0, \infty)$.

***Case* I** When $x \in (-\infty, 0)$, i.e. $-\infty < x < 0$

In this case, we have

$$\frac{-x-1}{-x-2} \geq 0 \quad \left[\because |x| = \begin{cases} x, & \text{if } x \geq 0 \\ -x, & \text{if } x < 0 \end{cases}\right]$$

$$\Rightarrow \quad \frac{-(x+1)}{-(x+2)} \geq 0$$

$$\Rightarrow \quad \frac{x+1}{x+2} \geq 0$$

Now, multiplying both sides by $(x+2)^2$, we get

$$(x+1)(x+2) \geq 0$$

So, the factors $(x+1)$ and $(x+2)$ have the same sign.

Then, we have

$$x+1 \geq 0 \text{ and } x+2 > 0 \quad \text{...(i)}$$

or $$x+1 \leq 0 \text{ and } x+2 < 0 \quad \text{...(ii)}$$

$[\because x+2 \neq 0$, as $x \neq -2]$

From inequality (i), we get

$$x \geq -1 \text{ and } x > -2$$

$\Rightarrow \quad x \geq -1 \quad$ [common values of x]

Thus, the common values of x are lying in the interval $[-1, 0)$.

[$\because$ we are considering the case, where $-\infty < x < 0$]

$\therefore$ The solution set is $[-1, 0)$.

From inequality (ii), we have

$$x \leq -1 \text{ and } x < -2$$

$\Rightarrow \quad x < -2 \quad$ [common values of x]

Thus, the common values of x are lying in the interval $(-\infty, -2)$.

$\therefore$ The solution set is $(-\infty, -2)$.

Hence, $x \in (-\infty, -2) \cup [-1, 0)$

***Case* II** When $x \in [0, \infty)$, i.e. $0 \leq x < \infty$

In this case, we have

$$\frac{x-1}{x-2} \geq 0 \quad \left[\because |x| = \begin{cases} x, & \text{if } x \geq 0 \\ -x, & \text{if } x < 0 \end{cases}\right]$$

On multiplying both sides by $(x-2)^2$, we get

$$(x-1)(x-2) \geq 0$$

So, the factors $(x-1)$ and $(x-2)$ have the same sign.

Then we have,

$$(x-1) \geq 0 \text{ and } (x-2) > 0 \quad \text{...(iii)}$$

or $$(x-1) \leq 0 \text{ and } (x-2) < 0 \quad \text{...(iv)}$$

$[\because x-2 \neq 0$ as $x \neq 2]$

From inequality (iii), we get

$$x \geq 1 \text{ and } x > 2$$

$\Rightarrow \quad x > 2 \quad$ [common values of x]

$\Rightarrow \quad x \in (2\ \infty)$

$\therefore$ The solution set is $(2, \infty)$.

From inequality (iv), we get

$$x \leq 1 \text{ and } x < 2$$

$\Rightarrow \quad x \leq 1 \quad$ [common values of x]

$\Rightarrow \quad x \in [0, 1]$

[$\because$ we are considering the case, where $0 \leq x < \infty$]

$\therefore$ The solution set is $[0, 1]$

Hence, $x \in [0, 1] \cup (2, \infty)$

Now, from cases I and II, we conclude that

$$x \in (-\infty, -2) \cup [-1, 0) \cup [0, 1] \cup (2, \infty)$$

i.e. $\quad x \in (-\infty, -2) \cup [-1, 1] \cup (2, \infty)$

Hence, the required solution set is

$$(-\infty, -2) \cup [-1, 1] \cup (2, \infty)$$

Alternate Method

We have, $\frac{|x|-1}{|x|-2} \geq 0$

Let $y = |x|$, then we have $\frac{y-1}{y-2} \geq 0$

On multiplying both sides by $(y-2)^2$, we get

$$(y-1)(y-2) \geq 0$$

So, the factors $(y-1)$ and $(y-2)$ have the same signs.

Then, we have, $y-1 \geq 0$ and $y-2 > 0 \quad$ ...(i)

or $\quad y-1 \leq 0$ and $y-2 < 0 \quad$ ...(ii)

$[\because y-2 \neq 0$ as $y = |x| \neq 2]$

From inequality (i), we get

$$y \geq 1 \text{ and } y > 2$$

$\Rightarrow \quad y > 2 \quad$ [common values of y]

From inequality (ii), we get

$$y \leq 1 \text{ and } y < 2$$

$\Rightarrow \quad y \leq 1 \quad$ [common values of y]

Thus, $\quad y \leq 1$ or $y > 2$

$\Rightarrow \quad |x| \leq 1$ or $|x| > 2 \quad [\because y = |x|]$

$\Rightarrow \quad (-1 \leq x \leq 1)$ or $(x > 2$ or $x < -2)$

$\Rightarrow \quad x \in [-1, 1]$ or $x \in (-\infty, -2) \cup (2, \infty)$

$\Rightarrow \quad x \in [-1, 1] \cup (-\infty, -2) \cup (2, \infty)$

Hence, required solution set is

$$(-\infty, -2) \cup [-1, 1] \cup (2, \infty)$$

EXAMPLE 12. Solve for x, $\dfrac{|x+3|+x}{x+2} > 1$. **[NCERT Exemplar]**

Sol. We have, $\dfrac{|x+3|+x}{x+2} > 1 \Rightarrow \dfrac{|x+3|+x}{x+2} - 1 > 0$

$\Rightarrow \dfrac{|x+3|+x-x-2}{x+2} > 0 \Rightarrow \dfrac{|x+3|-2}{x+2} > 0$

Put $x+3=0 \Rightarrow x=-3$

$\therefore$ $x=-3$ is a critical point.

So, here we consider two intervals $(-\infty, -3)$ and $[-3, \infty)$.

***Case* I** When $-3 \le x < \infty$, then $|x+3| = (x+3)$

$\therefore \dfrac{|x+3|-2}{x+2} > 0$

$\Rightarrow \dfrac{x+3-2}{x+2} > 0 \Rightarrow \dfrac{x+1}{x+2} > 0$

$\Rightarrow \dfrac{(x+1)(x+2)^2}{(x+2)} > 0 \times (x+2)^2$

[multiplying both sides by $(x+2)^2$]

$\Rightarrow (x+1)(x+2) > 0$

Product of $(x+1)$ and $(x+2)$ will be positive, if both are of same signs.

$\therefore$ $(x+1) > 0$ and $(x+2) > 0$

or $(x+1) < 0$ and $(x+2) < 0$

$\Rightarrow$ $(x > -1$ and $x > -2)$

or $(x < -1$ and $x < -2)$

Thus, $-1 < x < \infty$ or $-\infty < x < -2$

But, here $-3 \le x < \infty$

$\therefore$ $-1 < x < \infty$ or $-3 \le x < -2$

Hence, solution set in this case is

$x \in [-3, -2) \cup (-1, \infty)$

***Case* II** When $x < -3$, then $|x+3| = -(x+3)$

$\therefore \dfrac{|x+3|-2}{x+2} > 0 \Rightarrow \dfrac{-x-3-2}{x+2} > 0$

$\Rightarrow \dfrac{-(x+5)}{x+2} > 0 \Rightarrow \dfrac{x+5}{x+2} < 0$

$\Rightarrow \dfrac{(x+5)(x+2)^2}{x+2} < 0 \times (x+2)^2$

$\Rightarrow (x+5)(x+2) < 0$

Product of $(x+5)$ and $(x+2)$ will be negative, if both are of opposite sign.

$\therefore$ $(x+5) > 0$ and $(x+2) < 0$

or $(x+5) < 0$ and $(x+2) > 0$

$\Rightarrow$ $x > -5$ and $x < -2$

or $x < -5$ and $x > -2$ [not possible]

Thus, $-5 < x < -2$. i.e. solution set in the case is $(-5, -2)$.

On combining cases I and II, we get the required solution set of given inequality, which is $(-5, -2) \cup (-1, \infty)$.

Topic Practice 3

1 Solve the following system of inequalities

(i) $x+2 > 0$ and $3x-8 < 1$

(ii) $3x-7 > 2(x-6)$ and $6-x > 11-2x$

(iii) $7(2-3x) > 18-19x$ and $5+3x < 5x+6$

(iv) $-2-\dfrac{x}{4} \ge \dfrac{1+x}{3}$ and $3-x < 4(x-3)$

(v) $\dfrac{x}{2x+1} \ge \dfrac{1}{4}$ and $\dfrac{6x}{4x-1} < \dfrac{1}{2}$

2 Solve the following system of inequalities

(i) $2 \le 3x-4 \le 5$

(ii) $-12 < 4-\dfrac{3x}{-5} \le 2$

(iii) $7 \le \dfrac{(3x+11)}{2} \le 11$

(iv) $\dfrac{4}{x+1} \le 3 \le \dfrac{6}{x+1}, x > 0.$

3 Solve the following inequalities

(i) $|x-1| \le 2$

(ii) $|x+3| \ge 10$

(iii) $|3x-7| > 2$

(iv) $|3-4x| \ge 9$

(v) $\dfrac{1}{|x|-3} < 0$

(vi) $1 \le |x-2| \le 3$

(vii) $|x+1| + |x| > 3$

(viii) $\dfrac{|x-2|-1}{|x-2|-2} \le 0$

Hints & Solutions

1. (i) Solve as Example 1. **Ans.** $(-2, 3)$

(ii) Solve as Example 2. **Ans.** $(5, \infty)$

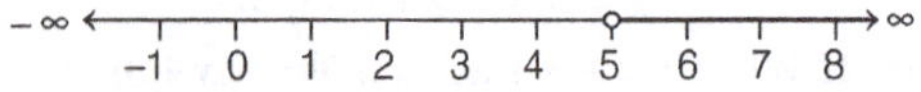

(iii) Solve as Example 2. **Ans.** No solution exists.

(iv) Solve as Example 3. **Ans.** No solution exists.

(v) **Hint** $\dfrac{x}{2x+1} \geq \dfrac{1}{4} \Rightarrow \dfrac{x}{2x+1} - \dfrac{1}{4} \geq 0$

$\Rightarrow \dfrac{2x-1}{4(2x+1)} \geq 0,$

here $2x+1 \neq 0$, i.e. $x \neq -\dfrac{1}{2}$

$\Rightarrow (2x-1)(2x+1) \geq 0$

***Case* I** When both are non-negative

$2x-1 \geq 0$ and $2x+1 > 0$

$\Rightarrow \quad x \geq \dfrac{1}{2}$ and $x > -\dfrac{1}{2}$

$\Rightarrow \quad x \geq \dfrac{1}{2}$

$\therefore \quad x \in \left[\dfrac{1}{2}, \infty\right)$ ...(i)

***Case* II** When both are non-positive

$(2x-1) \leq 0$ and $2x+1 < 0$

$\Rightarrow \quad x \leq \dfrac{1}{2}$ and $x < \dfrac{-1}{2}$

$\therefore \quad x \in \left(-\infty, -\dfrac{1}{2}\right)$ ...(ii)

From Eqs. (i) and (ii), we get

$x \in \left(-\infty, -\dfrac{1}{2}\right) \cup \left[\dfrac{1}{2}, \infty\right)$ ...(iii)

Now, $\dfrac{6x}{4x-1} < \dfrac{1}{2}$

$\Rightarrow \dfrac{6x}{4x-1} - \dfrac{1}{2} < 0$

$\Rightarrow \dfrac{8x+1}{2(4x-1)} < 0 \Rightarrow (8x+1)(4x-1) < 0 \quad \left[\because x \neq \dfrac{1}{4}\right]$

We have, $(8x+1) < 0$ and $(4x-1) > 0$

or $(8x+1) > 0$ and $(4x-1) < 0$

$\Rightarrow \quad \dfrac{-1}{8} < x < \dfrac{1}{4}$ ...(iv)

Now, for the solution set of given system of inequalities take common value of x from Eqs. (iii) and (iv), but there is no common value of x.

Ans. Solution set is a empty set.

2. (i) Solve as Example 4.

Ans. $[2, 3]$

(ii) Solve as Example 5.

Ans. $\left(\dfrac{-80}{3}, \dfrac{-10}{3}\right]$

(iii) Solve as Example 6.

Ans. $\left[1, \dfrac{11}{3}\right]$

(iv) We have, $\dfrac{4}{x+1} \leq 3 \leq \dfrac{6}{x+1}$

$\Rightarrow \quad 4 \leq 3(x+1) \leq 6 \quad [\because x+1 \neq 0 \Rightarrow x \neq -1]$

$\Rightarrow \quad \dfrac{4}{3} \leq x+1 \leq 2$

$\Rightarrow \quad \dfrac{4}{3} - 1 \leq x \leq 2-1$

$\Rightarrow \quad \dfrac{1}{3} \leq x \leq 1$

Ans. $\left[\dfrac{1}{3}, 1\right]$

3. (i) Use $|x| \leq a \Rightarrow -a \leq x \leq a$

and then solved as Example 7.

Ans. $[-1, 3]$

(ii) Use $|x| \geq a \Rightarrow x \geq a$ or $x \leq -a$

and then solved as Example 8.

Ans. $(-\infty, -13] \cup [7, \infty)$

(iii) Use $|x| > a \Rightarrow x > a$ or $x < -a$

and then proceed as Example 8.

Ans. $\left(-\infty, \dfrac{5}{3}\right) \cup (3, \infty)$

(iv) Use $|x| \geq a \Rightarrow x \geq a$ or $x \leq -a$

and then proceed as Example 8.

Ans. $\left(-\infty \dfrac{-3}{2}\right] \cup [3, \infty)$

(v) Let $y = |x|$ and then proceed as Example 11 (alternate method).

Ans. $(-3, 3)$

(vi) Write the given inequalities as $|x-2| \geq 1$ and $|x-2| \leq 3$ Solve each inequality separately and then take the intersection of their solution sets (and then proceed as Example 9).

Ans. $[-1, 1] \cup [3, 5]$

(vii) Firstly, put $x+1=0$ and $x=0 \Rightarrow x=-1$ and $x=0$

$\therefore$ $x=-1$, 0 are critical points. So, we will consider three intervals $(-\infty, -1)$, $[-1, 0)$, $[0, \infty)$ and then proceed as Example 10.

Ans. $(-\infty, -2) \cup (1, \infty)$

(viii) Solve as Example 11.

Ans. $(0, 1] \cup [3, 4)$

Applications of Linear Inequalities in One Variable

In this topic, we shall discuss with various word problems which are based on linear inequalities of one variable. Let us look at the following examples.

TYPE 1 Based on Marks of Students

EXAMPLE 1. Ram needs a minimum of 360 marks in four tests in a Mathematics course to obtain *A* grade. In his first three tests, he scored 88, 96 and 79 marks. What should his score be in the fourth test, so that he can make *A* grade?

Sol. Let Ram scores x marks in the fourth test. Then, the sum of Ram's test scores should be greater than or equal to 360.

i.e. $88 + 96 + 79 + x \geq 360$

$\Rightarrow \quad 263 + x \geq 360$

$\Rightarrow \quad 263 + x - 263 \geq 360 - 263$

[subtracting 263 from both sides]

$\therefore \quad x \geq 97$

Hence, Ram should score 97 or greater than 97 marks in fourth test to obtain *A* grade.

EXAMPLE 2. To receive grade *A* in a course, one must obtain an average of 90 marks or more in five examinations (each of 100 marks). If Sunita's marks in first four examinations are 87, 92, 94 and 95, then find minimum marks that Sunita must obtain in fifth examinations to get grade *A* in the course.

Sol. Let Sunita obtains x marks in her fifth examination.

Then, $\dfrac{87 + 92 + 94 + 95 + x}{5} \geq 90$

$\Rightarrow \quad 368 + x \geq 450$

[multiplying both sides by 5]

$\Rightarrow \quad 368 + x - 368 \geq 450 - 368$

[subtracting 368 from both sides]

$\therefore \quad x \geq 82$

Thus, Sunita must obtain a minimum of 82 marks to get grade A in the course.

EXAMPLE 3. In the first four examinations, each of 100 marks, Mohan got 94, 73, 72 and 84 marks. If a final average greater than or equal to 80 and less than 90 is needed to obtain a final grade *B* in a course, then what range of marks in the fifth (last) examination will result, if Mohan receiving grade *B* in the course?

Sol. Let x be the score obtained by Mohan in the last examination.

Then, $80 \leq \dfrac{94 + 73 + 72 + 84 + x}{5} < 90$

$\Rightarrow \quad 80 \leq \dfrac{323 + x}{5} < 90$

$\Rightarrow \quad 400 \leq 323 + x < 450$

[multiplying both sides by 5]

$\Rightarrow \quad 400 - 323 \leq 323 + x - 323 < 450 - 323$

[subtracting 323 from each term]

$\Rightarrow \quad 77 \leq x < 127$

Since, the upper limit is 100, therefore the required range is $77 \leq x \leq 100$.

TYPE 2 Based on Numbers

EXAMPLE 4. The sum of three consecutive integers must not be more than 12. What are the integers?

Sol. Let the three consecutive integers be $x, (x+1)$ and $(x + 2)$. Since, sum of these integers must not be more than 12, i.e. $x + (x + 1) + (x + 2)$ cannot exceed 12, therefore, we have

$\Rightarrow \quad x + (x + 1) + (x + 2) \leq 12$

$\Rightarrow \quad 3x + 3 \leq 12$

$\Rightarrow \quad 3x + 3 - 3 \leq 12 - 3$

[subtracting 3 from both sides]

$\Rightarrow \quad 3x \leq 9$

$\therefore \quad x \leq 3$ [dividing both sides by 3]

EXAMPLE 5. Find all pairs of consecutive even positive integers, both of which are larger than 5, such that their sum is less than 23.

Sol. Let x be the smaller of the two positive even integers, so that the other one is $x + 2$, then we should have

$x > 5$ ...(i)

$x + 2 > 5$ ...(ii)

and their sum, $x + (x + 2) < 23$ ...(iii)

From inequalities (i) and (ii), we get

$x > 5$ ...(iv)

From inequality (iii), we get

$2x + 2 < 23$

$\Rightarrow \quad 2x + 2 - 2 < 23 - 2$

[subtracting 2 from both sides]

$\Rightarrow \quad 2x < 21$

$\Rightarrow \quad x < 10.5$

[dividing both sides by 2]...(v)

Now, from inequalities (iv) and (v), we get

$5 < x < 10.5$

Since, x is an even number. So x can take the values 6, 8 and 10.

Hence, the required possible pairs will be (6, 8), (8, 10) and (10, 12).

EXAMPLE 6. Find all the pairs of consecutive odd positive integers, both of which are smaller than 10, such that their sum is more than 11.

Sol. Let x be the smaller of two positive odd integers, so that other one is $x + 2$.

We should have $x < 10$ ...(i)

$x + 2 < 10$

$\Rightarrow x < 8$ ...(ii)

and $x + (x + 2) > 11$ ...(iii)

From inequalities (i) and (ii), we get

$x < 8$ ...(iv)

From inequality (iii), we get

$2x + 2 > 11$

$\Rightarrow 2x > 9$

$\Rightarrow x > 4.5$ ...(v)

From inequalities (iv) and (v), we get

$4.5 < x < 8$

Since, x is an odd number, so x can take the values 5 and 7.

Hence the required possible pairs will be (5, 7) and (7, 9).

TYPE 3 Based on Profit, Cost and Revenue

EXAMPLE 7. The cost and revenue functions of a product are given by $C(x) = 20x + 4000$ and $R(x) = 60x + 2000$ respectively, where x is the number of items produced and sold. How many items must be sold to get some profit?

Sol. We know that, Profit = Revenue – Cost

$\therefore$ In order to get some profit, revenue should be greater than the cost.

Thus, we should have $R(x) > C(x)$

$\Rightarrow 60x + 2000 > 20x + 4000$

$\Rightarrow 60x + 2000 - 20x > 20x + 4000 - 20x$

[subtracting $20x$ from both sides]

$\Rightarrow 40x + 2000 > 4000$

$\Rightarrow 40x + 2000 - 2000 > 4000 - 2000$

[subtracting 2000 from both sides]

$\Rightarrow 40x > 2000$

$\Rightarrow \frac{40x}{40} > \frac{2000}{40}$

[dividing both sides by 40]

$\Rightarrow x > 50$

Hence, the manufacturer must sell more than 50 items to get some profit.

TYPE 4 Based on Temperature

EXAMPLE 8. A solution is to be kept between 68°F and 77°F. What is the range of temperature in degree Celsius (C), if the Celsius/Fahrenheit (F) conversion formula is given by $F = \frac{9}{5}C + 32$?

Sol. It is given that, $68 < F < 77$

On putting $F = \frac{9}{5}C + 32$, we get

$$68 < \frac{9}{5}C + 32 < 77$$

$$\Rightarrow 68 - 32 < \frac{9}{5}C < 77 - 32$$

[subtracting 32 from each term]

$$\Rightarrow 36 < \frac{9}{5}C < 45$$

$$\Rightarrow 36 \times \frac{5}{9} < C < 45 \times \frac{5}{9}$$

$\left[\text{multiplying } \frac{5}{9} \text{ in each term}\right]$

$$\Rightarrow 4 \times 5 < C < 5 \times 5$$

$$\Rightarrow 20 < C < 25$$

Hence, the required range of temperature is between 20°C and 25°C.

TYPE 5 Based on Geometry

EXAMPLE 9. The longest side of a triangle is twice the shortest side and the third side is 2 cm longer than the shortest side. If the perimeter of the triangle is more than 166 cm then find the minimum length of the shortest side.

Sol. Let the length of shortest side be x cm.

Then, according to question, we have

Length of longest side = $2x$ cm

and length of third side = $(x + 2)$ cm

Since, the perimeter of the triangle is more than 166 cm.

$\therefore 2x + x + (x + 2) > 166$

$\Rightarrow 4x + 2 > 166$

$\Rightarrow 4x > 164$

[subtracting 2 from both sides]

$\Rightarrow x > 41$ [dividing both sides by 4]

Hence, the length of the shortest side should be greater than 41 cm.

EXAMPLE 10. A man wants to cut three lengths from a single piece of board of length 91 cm, the second length is to be 3 cm longer than the shortest and third length is to be twice as long as the shortest. What are the possible lengths for the shortest board, if third piece is to be atleast 5 cm longer than the second?

Sol. Let the length of the shortest piece be x cm, so that the lengths of second and third piece are $(x + 3)$ cm and $2x$ cm, respectively.

Then, $x + (x + 3) + 2x \le 91$ ...(i)

and $2x \ge (x + 3) + 5$ ...(ii)

From inequality (i), we get

$4x + 3 \le 91$

$\Rightarrow \quad 4x + 3 - 3 \le 91 - 3$ [subtracting 3 from both sides]

$\Rightarrow \quad 4x \le 88$ [dividing both sides by 4]

$\Rightarrow \quad \frac{4x}{4} \le \frac{88}{4}$

$\Rightarrow \quad x \le 22$ ...(iii)

From inequality (ii), we get

$2x \ge x + 8$

$\Rightarrow \quad 2x - x \ge x + 8 - x$ [subtracting x from both sides]

$\Rightarrow \quad x \ge 8$ ...(iv)

From inequalities (iii) and (iv), we get

$8 \le x \le 22$

Hence, the shortest piece must be atleast 8 cm long but not more than 22 cm long.

TYPE 6 Based on Dilution of Acid

EXAMPLE 11. A solution of 8% boric acid is to be diluted by adding a 2% boric acid solution to it. The resulting mixture is to be more than 4% but less than 6% boric acid. If we have 640 litres of the 8% solution, how many litres of the 2% solution will have to be added?

Sol. Let x be the number of litres of 2% boric acid solution.

Then, total mixture = $(640 + x)$ litres

According to the question,

2% of x + 8% of 640 > 4% of $(640 + x)$

$\Rightarrow \quad \frac{2x}{100} + \frac{8}{100} \times 640 > \frac{4}{100}(640 + x)$

$\Rightarrow \quad 2x + 5120 > 2560 + 4x$ [multiplying both sides by 100]

$\Rightarrow \quad 2x + 5120 - 2x > 2560 + 4x - 2x$ [subtracting $2x$ from both sides]

$\Rightarrow \quad 5120 > 2560 + 2x$

$\Rightarrow \quad 5120 - 2560 > 2560 + 2x - 2560$ [subtracting 2560 from both sides]

$\Rightarrow \quad 2560 > 2x$

$\Rightarrow \quad 2x < 2560$

$\Rightarrow \quad x < 1280$ [dividing both sides by 2] ...(i)

Also, 2% of x + 8% of 640 < 6% of $(640 + x)$

$\Rightarrow \quad \frac{2}{100} \times x + \frac{8}{100} \times 640 < \frac{6}{100} \times (640 + x)$

$\Rightarrow \quad 2x + 5120 < 3840 + 6x$ [multiplying both sides by 100]

$\Rightarrow \quad 2x + 5120 - 2x < 3840 + 6x - 2x$ [subtracting $2x$ from both sides]

$\Rightarrow \quad 5120 < 3840 + 4x$

$\Rightarrow \quad 5120 - 3840 < 3840 + 4x - 3840$ [subtracting 3840 from both sides]

$\Rightarrow \quad 1280 < 4x$ or $4x > 1280$

$\Rightarrow \quad \frac{4x}{4} > \frac{1280}{4}$ [dividing both sides by 4]

$\Rightarrow \quad x > 320$ ...(ii)

Now, from inequalities (i) and (ii), we get

$320 < x < 1280$

Thus, the number of litres of the 2% boric acid solution will have to be greater than 320 litres and less than 1280 litres.

EXAMPLE 12. How many litres of water will have to be added to 1125 litres of the 45% solution of acid so that the resulting mixture will contain more than 25% but less than 30% acid content?

Sol. Let x litres of water is required to be added.

Then, total mixture = $(x + 1125)$ litres.

Clearly, the amount of acid in the resulting mixture is 45% of 1125 litres. Since, the resulting mixture contain more than 25% but less than 30% acid content.

Therefore, we have

45% of 1125 > 25% of $(x + 1125)$ ...(i)

and 45% of 1125 < 30% of $(x + 1125)$ ...(ii)

From Eq. (i), we have

$\frac{45}{100} \times 1125 > \frac{25}{100} \times (x + 1125)$

$\Rightarrow \quad 45 \times 1125 > 25 \times (x + 1125)$ [multiplying both sides by 100]

$\Rightarrow \quad 45 \times 1125 > 25x + (25 \times 1125)$

$\Rightarrow \quad 45 \times 1125 - (25 \times 1125) > 25x$ [subtracting 25×1125 from both sides]

$\Rightarrow \quad 25x < 1125(45 - 25)$

$\Rightarrow \quad 25x < 1125 \times 20$

$\Rightarrow \quad x < \frac{1125 \times 20}{25} = 225 \times 4 = 900$ [dividing both sides by 25]

$\Rightarrow \quad x < 900$ ...(iii)

From Eq. (ii), we have

$\frac{45}{100} \times 1125 < \frac{30}{100} \times (x + 1125)$

$45 \times 1125 < 30x + (30 \times 1125)$ [multiplying both sides by 100]

$\Rightarrow \quad 45 \times 1125 - (30 \times 1125) < 30x$ [subtracting 30×1125 from both sides]

$\Rightarrow \quad 30x > 1125(45 - 30)$

$\Rightarrow \quad x > \frac{1125 \times 15}{30} = \frac{1125}{2} = 562.5$

$\Rightarrow \quad x > 562.5$ ...(iv)

From Eqs. (iii) and (iv), we get $562.5 < x < 900$

Thus, the required number of litres of water that is to be added will have to be more than 526.5 but less than 900 litres.

Topic Practice 4

1 Anu needs a minimum of 450 marks in five tests in statistics course to obtain *B* grade. In her first four tests, she scored 90, 94, 96 and 88 marks. What should her score be in the 5th test, so that she can make *B* grade.

2 The marks obtained by a student of class XI in first and second terminal examinations are 62 and 48, respectively. Find the minimum marks he should get in the annual examination to have an average of atleast 60 marks.

3 The sum of four consecutive integers must not be more than 22. What are the integers?

4 Find all the pairs of consecutive positive integers, both of which are larger than 8 such that their sum is less than 28.

5 Find all pairs of consecutive odd natural numbers, both of which are larger than 10, such that their sum is less than 40.

6 IQ (Intelligence Quotient) of a person is given by formula, $\text{IQ} = \frac{\text{MA}}{\text{CA}} \times 100$, where MA stands for the mental age of the person and CA for the chronological age. If $80 \le \text{IQ} \le 140$ for a group of 12 yr children, then find the range of their mental age.

7 A company manufactures cassettes and its cost equation for a week is $C = 300 + 1.5x$ and its revenue equation is $R = 2x$, where x is the number of cassettes sold in a week. How many cassettes must be sold for the company to get a profit?

8 In drilling world's deepest hole it was found that the temperature T in degree celcius x km below the Earth's surface was given by $T(x) = 30 + 25(x - 3)$, where $3 \le x \le 15$. At what depth will the temperature be between 155°C and 205°C?.

9 A solution is to be kept between 86°F and 95°F. What is the range of temperature in degree Celsius, if the Celsius (C)/Fahrenheit (F) conversion formula is given by $\text{F} = \frac{9}{5}\text{C} + 32$.

10 The longest side of a triangle is 3 times the shortest side and the third side is 2 cm shorter than the longest side. If the perimeter of the triangle is atleast 61 cm. Find the minimum length of the shortest side.

11 A solution of 9% acid is to be diluted by adding 3% acid solution to it. The resulting mixture is to be more than 5% but less than 7% acid. If there is 460 litres of the 9% solution. How many litres of 3% solution will have to be added?

Hints & Solutions

1. Solve as Example 1.
   Ans. 82 marks
2. **Hint** Let x marks be obtained by students in the annual examination.
   Then, $\frac{62 + 48 + x}{3} \ge 60$ and then proceed as Example 2.
   Ans. 70
3. Solve as Example 4.
   Ans. Less than or equal to 4.
4. Solve as Example 5.
   Ans. (10, 12), (12, 14)
5. Solve as Example 6.
   Ans. (11, 13), (13, 15), (15, 17), (17, 19)
6. **Hint** Also, $\text{IQ} = \frac{\text{MA}}{\text{CA}} \times 100$
   $\therefore \quad 80 \le \frac{\text{MA}}{\text{CA}} \times 100 \le 140 \Rightarrow 80 \le \frac{\text{MA}}{12} \times 100 \le 140$
   Ans. $9.6 \le \text{MA} \le 16.8$
7. **Hint** Profit = Revenue – Cost
   and in order to get some profit, revenue should be greater than the cost.
   Now, proceed as Example 7.
   Ans. More than 600 cassettes.
8. **Hint** Let at s km below the Earth's surface, the temperature is between 155°C and 205°C.
   $\therefore \quad 155 < T(s) < 205 \Rightarrow 155 < 30 + 25(s - 3) < 205$
   Ans. $8 < s < 10$.
9. Solve as Example 8.
   Ans. Between 30°C and 35°C
10. **Hint** Let the length of shortest side be x cm.
    Then, we have $3x + x + (3x - 2) \ge 61$ and then proceed as Example 9.
    Ans. 9 cm.
11. Solve as Example 12.
    Ans. More than 230 litres but less than 920 litres.

Linear Inequalities in Two Variables and Their Graphical Solutions

An inequality of the form $ax + by + c > 0$ or $ax + by + c < 0$ or $ax + by + c \geq 0$ or $ax + by + c \leq 0$, where $a \neq 0$ and $b \neq 0$, is called a linear inequality in two variables x and y. The region containing all the solutions of an inequality, is called the **solution region.**

Concept of Half Planes

The graph of $ax+by+c=0$ is a straight line which divides the **cartesian plane or XY-plane** into two parts. Each part is known as half plane.

Types of Half Planes

1. **Left and right half planes** A vertical line will divide the XY-plane in two parts, left half plane and right half plane.

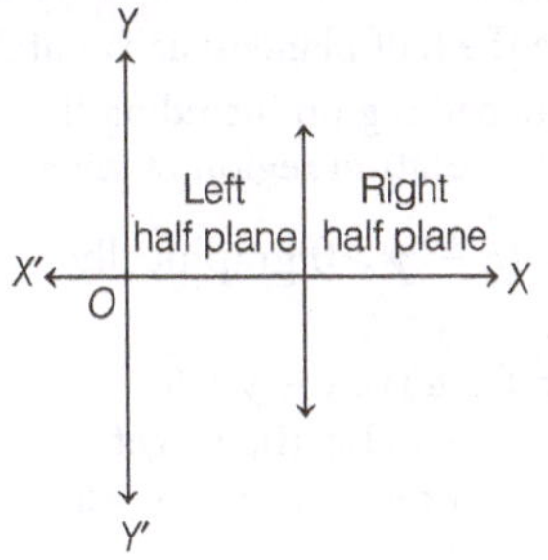

2. **Lower and upper half planes** A non-vertical line will divide the XY-plane into two parts, lower half plane and upper half plane.

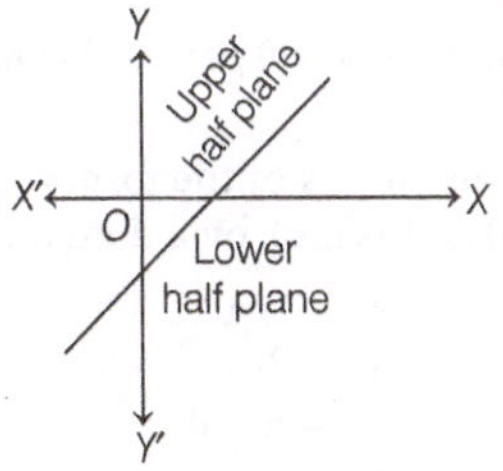

3. **Closed half plane** A half plane in XY-plane is called a closed half plane, if the line separating the plane is also included in the half plane. Therefore, the graph of a linear inequality involving sign $\leq$ or $\geq$ is always closed half plane.
4. **Open half plane** A half plane in XY-plane is called an open half plane, if the line separating the plane is not included in the half plane. Therefore, the graph of a linear inequality involving sign < or > is always an open half plane.

Graph of Linear Inequality in Two Variables

Working rule for drawing the graph of linear inequalities in two variables are discussed below

***Step* I** Consider the equation $ax+by=c$, in place of given inequality $ax+by \leq c$ or $ax+by \geq c$ or $ax+by<c$ or $ax+by>c$, which represents a straight line in XY-plane.

***Step* II** Put $x=0$ in the equation obtained in step I to get the point, where the line meets Y-axis. Similarly, put $y=0$ to obtain a point, where the line meets the X-axis.

***Step* III** Draw a line joining the points obtained in step II. If the inequality is of the form of < or >, then draw dotted line to indicate that the points on the line are excluded. Otherwise, draw a thick or dark line to indicate that the points on this line are included.

***Step* IV** Take any point (preferable origin, i.e. (0, 0)), not lying on the line, and check whether this satisfies the given linear inequality or not.

***Step* V** If the inequality is satisfied, by this point then shade that portion of the plane which contains the chosen point. The shaded region obtained in step V, represents the graph of linear inequality in two variable.

EXAMPLE 1. Draw the graph of the inequality $y+8 \geq 2x$.

Sol. Given inequality is $y+8 \geq 2x$.

In equation form, it can be written as $y+8=2x$ or $2x-y=8$

On putting $y=0$, we get $2x-0=8 \Rightarrow x=4$

$\therefore$ Line $2x-y=8$ cuts the X-axis at $A\ (4, 0)$.

On putting $x=0$, we get $2\times 0-y=8 \Rightarrow y=-8$

$\therefore$ Line $2x-y=8$ cuts the Y-axis at $B(0, -8)$.

On joining the points $A\ (4, 0)$ and $B(0, -8)$ by a dark line, we get the line AB.

[$\because$ given inequality has sign $\geq$, so we draw dark line]

Let us check whether O (0, 0) satisfy the inequality or not and shade the suitable region.

On putting $x=y=0$ in $y+8 \geq 2x$, we get

$$0+8 \geq 2\cdot 0 \Rightarrow 8 \geq 0, \text{ which is true.}$$

So shade the region containing (0, 0) i.e. the region above the line AB.

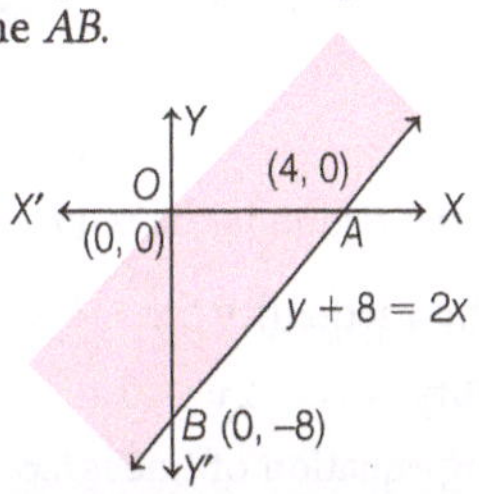

Here, the shaded region including the points on the line represent the graph of the inequality.

EXAMPLE 2. Check whether the half plane $x+2y\geq 4$ contains origin.

Sol. We have, $x+2y\geq 4$

On putting $x=0$ and $y=0$, we get

$$0+2(0)\geq 4 \Rightarrow 0\geq 4$$

This is a false statement.

Therefore, the given half plane does not contain the origin.

EXAMPLE 3. Solve the inequality $2x+y>3$ graphically.

Sol. We have, $2x+y>3$

In equation form, given inequality can be written as

$$2x+y=3 \quad \text{...(i)}$$

On putting $x=0$ in Eq. (i), we get

$$2(0)+y=3 \Rightarrow y=3$$

$\therefore$ Line meets Y-axis at point $A(0, 3)$.

On putting $y=0$ in Eq. (i), we get

$$2x+0=3 \Rightarrow x=\frac{3}{2}$$

$\therefore$ Line meets X-axis at point $B\left(\frac{3}{2}, 0\right)$.

On joining the points $A(0, 3)$ and $B\left(\frac{3}{2}, 0\right)$ by dotted line, we get the line AB. [$\because$ given inequality has sign $>$, so we join the points by a dotted line]

Now, take a point not lying on the line say $(0, 0)$ to check whether it satisfies the given inequality or not.

On putting $x=0$ and $y=0$ in given inequality, we get

$$2(0)+0>3$$

$\Rightarrow$ $0>3$ which is not correct.

So, we shade the portion which does not contain $(0, 0)$ i.e. the region above the dotted line AB.

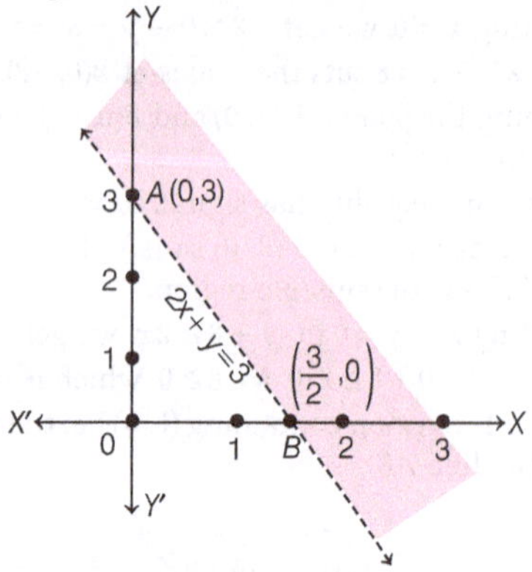

Here, the shaded region is the required solution region.

EXAMPLE 4. Solve the inequality $5x+2y\leq 10$ graphically.

Sol. Given inequality is $5x+2y\leq 10$.

Corresponding equation of line is $5x+2y=10$

On putting $x=0$, we get $5(0)+2y=10 \Rightarrow y=5$

Thus, the line intersect the Y-axis at point $(0, 5)$.

On putting $y=0$, we get $5x+2(0)=10 \Rightarrow x=2$

x	0	2
y	5	0

Thus, the line intersect the X-axis at point $(2, 0)$.

Join the points $A(0, 5)$ and $B(2, 0)$ with a dark line [$\because$ given inequality has sign '$\leq$']

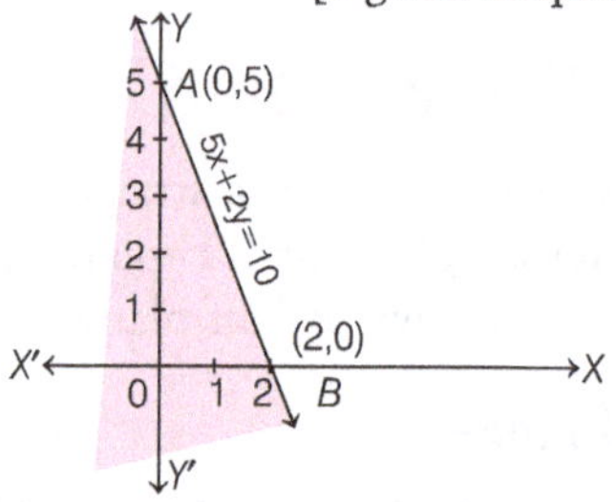

On putting $(0, 0)$ in given inequality, we get

$$5\times 0+2\times 0\leq 10 \Rightarrow 0\leq 10, \text{ which is true.}$$

So, the half plane of $5x+2y\leq 10$ contains origin.

Now, shade the half plane which contain $(0, 0)$.

Here, the shaded region including the points on the line represent the solution region of given inequality.

EXAMPLE 5. Solve $4x-y>0$ graphically.

Sol. We have, $4x-y>0$

Its equation form is $4x-y=0$. ...(i)

On putting $y=0$ in Eq. (i), we get

$$4x-0=0 \Rightarrow x=0$$

On putting $x=1$ in Eq. (i), we get

$$4(1)-y=0 \Rightarrow y=4$$

x	1	0
y	4	0

Thus, the line $4x-y=0$ passes through the points $A(0, 0)$ and $B(1, 4)$

Since, the inequality is of the form $<$, so we join the points $A(0, 0)$ and $B(1, 4)$ by a dotted line.

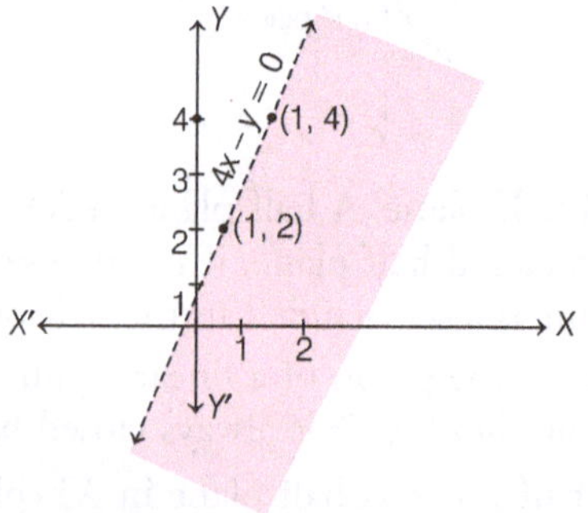

Now, take the point, say $(1, 2)$ not lying on the line, to check whether it satisfies the given linear inequality or not.

At $(1, 2)$, $4(1)-2>0$

$\Rightarrow$ $2>0$, which is true.

∴ (1, 2) satisfies the given inequality, so we shade the region which contains (1, 2). Thus, shaded region (excluding all points on the line) gives the solution region.

EXAMPLE 6. Solve $4x - 6 \geq 0$ graphically in two dimensional plane.

Sol. We have, $4x - 6 \geq 0$

In equation form, it can be written as

$$4x - 6 = 0 \Rightarrow 4x = 6$$

$$\Rightarrow \quad x = \frac{6}{4} = \frac{3}{2}$$

Clearly, it represent a line passes through the point $\left(\frac{3}{2}, 0\right)$ and parallel to Y-axis.

Since, given inequality has the sign $\geq$, so draw a dark line.

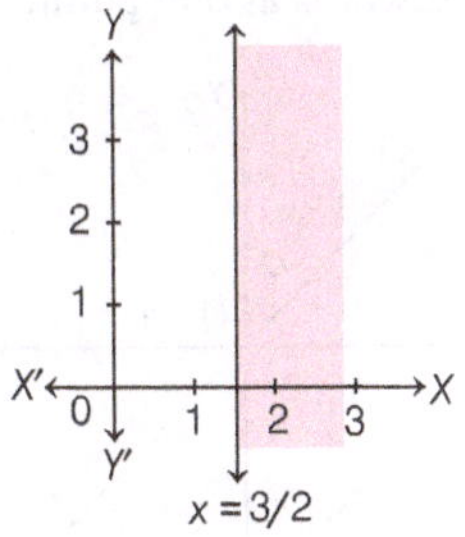

Now, select a point, say (0, 0), not lying on the line and substitute it in given inequality.

On putting $x = y = 0$ in the given inequality, we get

$$4(0) - 6 \geq 0$$

$\Rightarrow \quad -6 \geq 0$, which is false.

So, shade the region which does not contain origin i.e. the region on the right hand side of the line $x = 3/2$.

Here, the shaded region including the points on the line represent the required solution region.

EXAMPLE 7. Solve the inequality $5y - 3 \leq 12$ graphically.

Sol. We have, $\quad 5y - 3 \leq 12$

$\Rightarrow \quad 5y - 3 + 3 \leq 12 + 3 \quad$ [adding 3 on both sides]

$\Rightarrow \quad 5y \leq 15$

$\Rightarrow \quad y \leq 3 \quad$ ...(i)

[dividing both sides by 5]

Clearly, the graph of the line $y = 3$ is the horizontal line passing through (0, 3).

On putting (0, 0) in given inequality (i), we get

$0 \leq 3$, which is true.

∴ Shade the half plane containing origin.

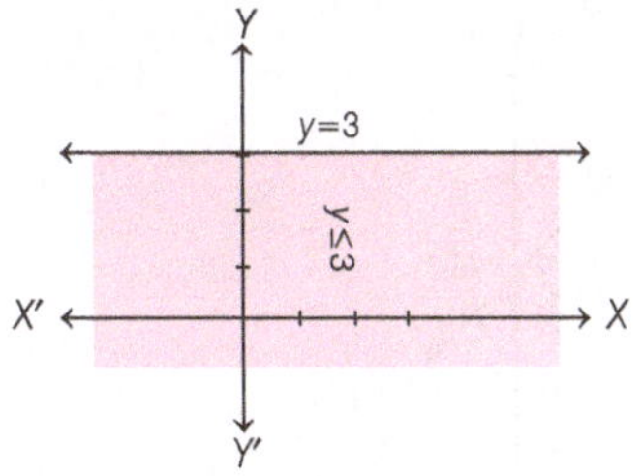

Here, the shaded region including the points on the line represent the solution region of the inequality.

Topic Practice 5

1. Check whether the plane $5x + 2y \leq 5$ contains origin or not.
2. Check whether the given plane $3x - 6y \leq 0$ contains the point (3, 1).
3. Solve the inequality $3y - 5x < 30$ graphically.
4. Solve the inequality $x + y \geq 5$ graphically.
5. Solve the inequality $x > -3$ graphically in two dimensional plane.
6. Solve the inequality $y < -2$ in two dimensional plane.
7. Solve the inequality $-3x + 2y \geq -6$ graphically.
8. Solve the inequality $2x + 3y > 0$ graphically.
9. Solve the inequality $x \leq 8 - 4y$ graphically.
10. Solve the inequality $3x - 2y + 4 \leq x + y - 8$ graphically.

Hints & Solutions

1. Solve as Example 2.
   Ans. Given plane contains origin.
2. **Hint** Put $x = 3$ and $y = 1$ in the given plane and then check whether the statement is true or false.
   Ans. Given plane does not contain the point (3, 1).
3. **Hint** Firstly, consider the given inequation as an equation and then proceed as Example 3.
   Ans.

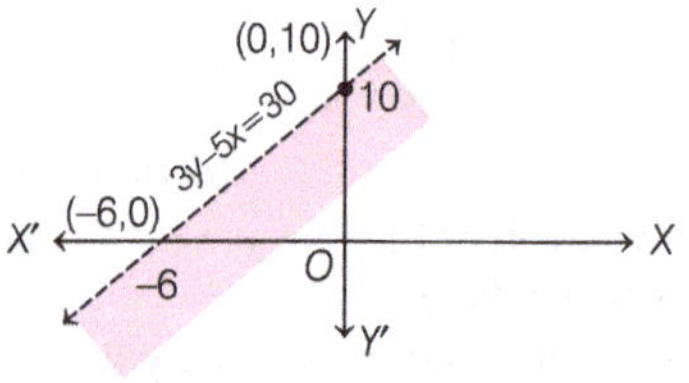

4. **Hint** Firstly, consider the given in equation as an equation and then proceed as Example 3.
   Ans.

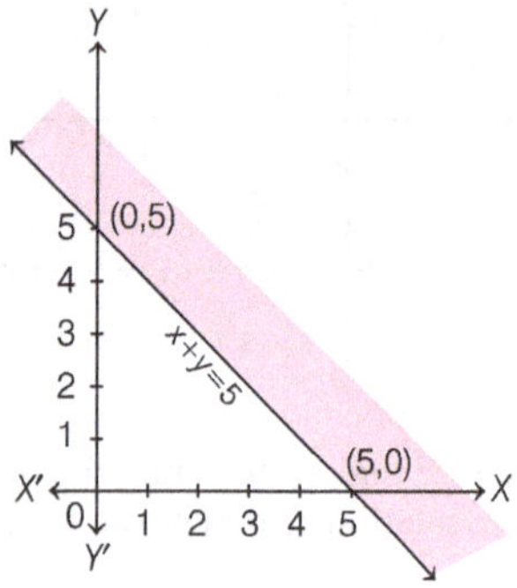

5. Solve as Example 6.
   Ans.

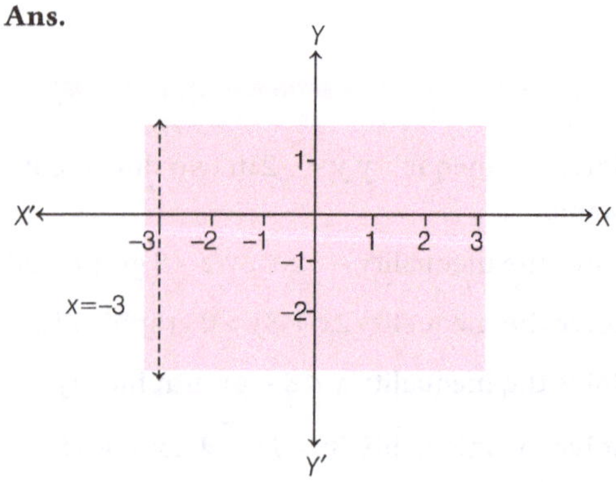

6. Solve as Example 6.
   Ans.

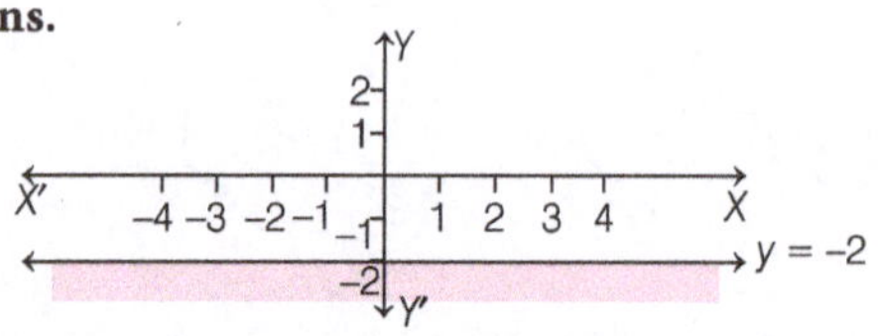

7. **Hint** Write the given inequality as $3x - 2y \leq 6$.
   Solve as Example 4.
   Ans.

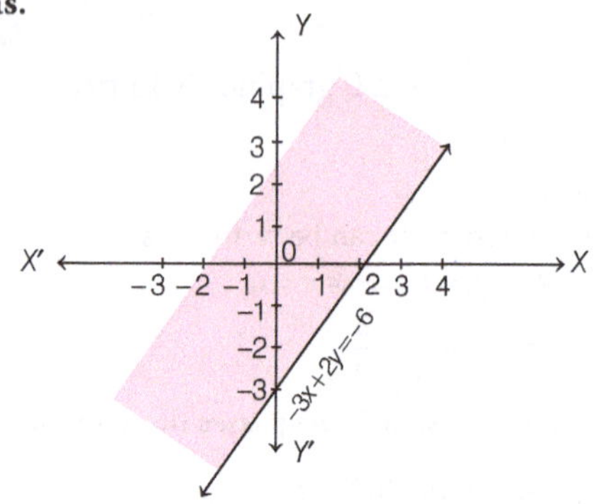

8. **Hint** At point (1, 0), given inequality $2(1) + 3(0) > 0$
   $\Rightarrow 2 > 0$, which in true.
   So, shading is towards at that point.
   Ans.

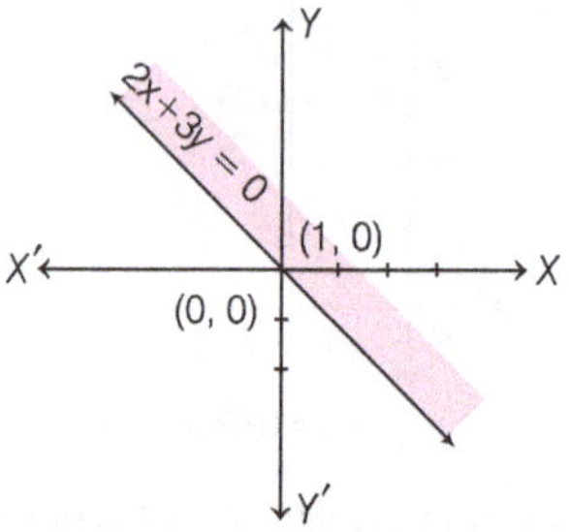

9. Solve as Example 1.
   Ans.

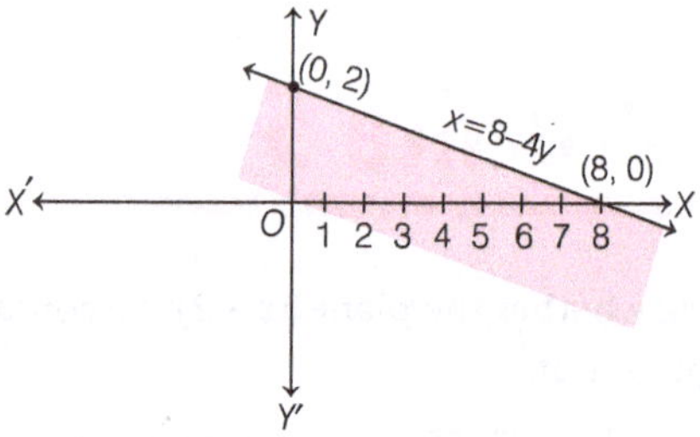

10. **Hint** We have, $3x - 2y + 4 \leq x + y - 8$
    $$\Rightarrow \qquad 2x - 3y \leq -12$$
    Now, consider this inequation as an equation and then proceed as Example 4.
    Ans.

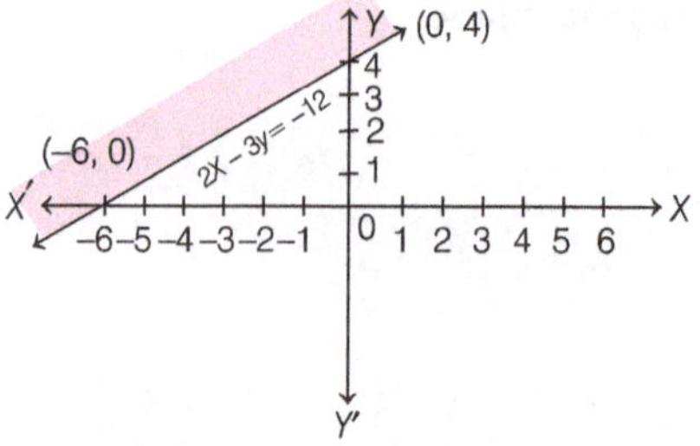

Graphical Solutions of System of Linear Inequalities in Two Variables

A system of linear inequalities in two variables can be solved by graphical method.

For finding the solution, we use the following steps

Step I Draw the graph of all the given inequalities.

Step II Find the common shaded region, which satisfies all the given linear inequalities.

Step III This common region is the required solution region of the system of given inequalities.

If there is no common region, then the system of inequalities has no solution.

EXAMPLE 1. Solve the inequalities $x \geq 3$ and $y \geq 2$ graphically.

Sol. We have the following inequalities

$$x \geq 3 \quad ...(i)$$

and $$y \geq 2 \quad ...(ii)$$

Take inequality (i), $x \geq 3$

In equation form, it can be written as

$$x = 3$$

which represent a vertical line passes through (3, 0).

So, draw a dark line parallel to Y-axis and passes through (3, 0).

On putting (0, 0) in given inequality, we get $0 \geq 3$, which is false.

So, for $x \geq 3$ shade the half plane which does not contain (0, 0)

Take inequality (ii), $y \geq 2$

In equation form, it can be written as $y = 2$, which represent a horizontal line passing through (0, 2).

So, draw a dark line parallel to X-axis and passes through (0, 2).

On putting (0, 0) in given inequality, we get $0 \geq 2$, which is false.

So, for $y \geq 2$, shade the half plane which does not contain (0, 0).

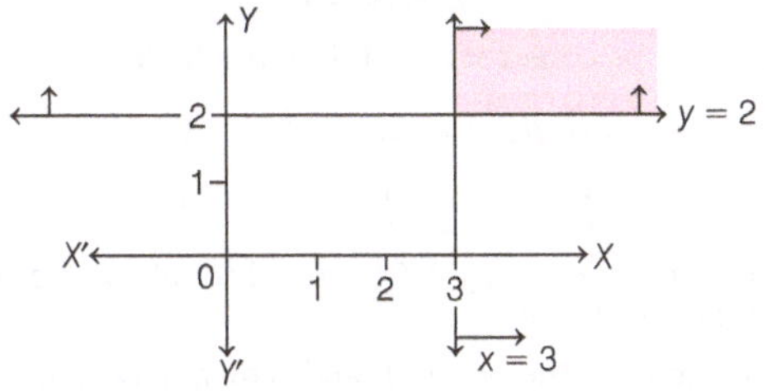

EXAMPLE 2. Solve the system of inequalities graphically.

$$x + y > 6;\ 2x - y < 0$$

Sol. We have, $$x + y > 6 \quad ...(i)$$

and $$2x - y < 0 \quad ...(ii)$$

Take inequality (i), $x + y > 6$

In equation form, it can be written as $x + y = 6$

Now, let us construct the following table

x	0	6
y	6	0

Thus, the line $x + y = 6$ passes through points A (0,6) and B (6, 0).

Now, on joining the points A and B by a dotted line, we get the line AB.

On putting $x = 0$ and $y = 0$ in inequality (i), we get $0 + 0 > 6 \Rightarrow 0 > 6$, which is false.

So, for inequality $x + y > 6$, shade the half plane which does not contain origin.

Take inequality (ii), $2x - y < 0$

In equation form it can be written as $2x - y = 0$

Now, let us construct the following table

x	0	2
y	0	4

Thus, the line $2x - y = 0$ passes through points O (0,0) and C (2, 4).

Now, on joining the points O and C by a dotted line, we get the line OC.

On putting $x = 0$ and $y = 6$ in inequality (ii), we get

$$2(0) - 6 < 0 \Rightarrow -6 < 0, \text{ which is true.}$$

So, for inequality $2x - y < 0$, shade the half plane region which contain (0, 6) excluding all points on line.

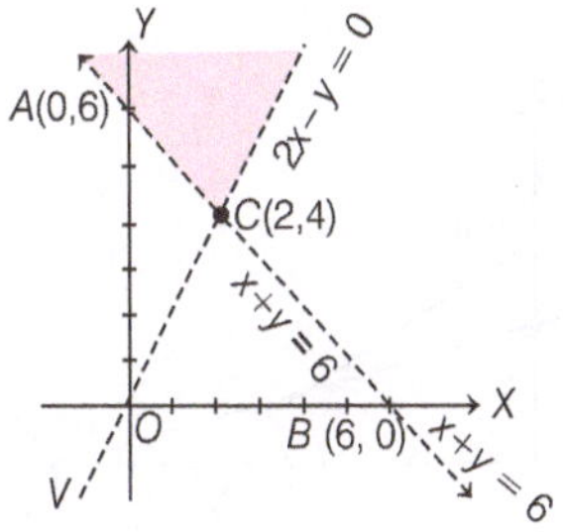

The common shaded region represent the solution region for system of inequality.

EXAMPLE 3. Solve the inequalities graphically $3x + 4y \leq 60$, $x + 3y \leq 30$, $x \geq 0$, $y \geq 0$.

Sol. We have the following inequalities

$$3x + 4y \leq 60 \quad ...(i)$$

$$x + 3y \leq 30 \quad ...(ii)$$

$$x \geq 0 \quad ...(iii)$$

and $$y \geq 0 \quad ...(iv)$$

Take inequality (i),

$$3x + 4y \leq 60$$

In equation form, it can be written as

$$3x + 4y = 60$$

Now, let us construct the following table

x	0	20
y	15	0

Thus, the line intersect X-axis at $A(20, 0)$ and Y-axis at $B(0, 15)$. Now, joining the points A and B by a dark line, we get the line AB.

On putting (0, 0) in the given inequality, we get

$$0 + 0 \le 60 \Rightarrow 0 \le 60, \text{ which is true.}$$

So, for $3x + 4y \le 60$, shade the half plane which contain (0, 0).

Take inequality (ii), $x + 3y \le 30$

In equation form, it can be written as $x + 3y = 30$

Now, let us construct the following table

x	0	30
y	10	0

Thus, the line intersect X-axis at $C(30, 0)$ and Y-axis at $D(0, 10)$.

Now, joining the points C and D by a dark line, we get the line CD.

On putting (0, 0) in the given inequality, we get

$$0 + 0 \le 30 \Rightarrow 0 \le 30, \text{ which is true.}$$

So, for $x + 3y \le 30$, shade the half plane which contain (0, 0).

Take inequalities (iii) and (iv),

$$x \ge 0 \text{ and } y \ge 0$$

These inequalities represent the region of first quadrant including the points on the axes. So, shade the first quadrant.

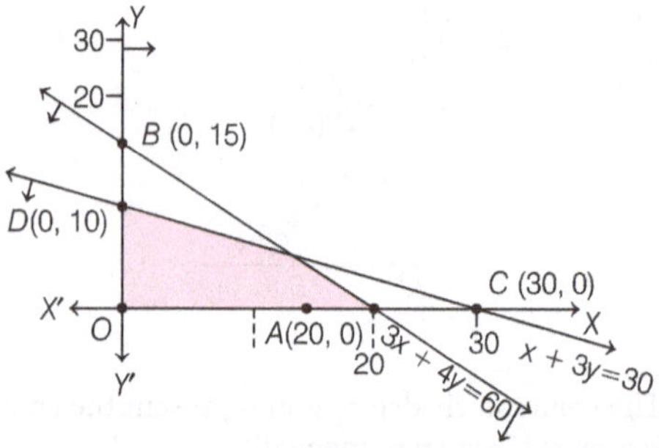

Here, common shaded region represent the solution region for system of inequalities.

Inequality between Coordinate Axes

The inequality $x \ge 0$ consist of Y-axis and the plane on the right side of Y-axis. Also, $y \ge 0$ consist of X-axis and the plane above the X-axis.

$\therefore$ The inequalities $x \ge 0$ and $y \ge 0$, together represent the first quadrant including the point on the axes.

EXAMPLE 4. Solve the system of inequalities graphically.

$$x + y \le 5, 4x + y \ge 4, x + 5y \ge 5, x \le 4 \text{ and } y \le 3$$

Sol. We have,

$$x + y \le 5 \quad ...(i)$$
$$4x + y \ge 4 \quad ...(ii)$$
$$x + 5y \ge 5 \quad ...(iii)$$
$$x \le 4 \quad ...(iv)$$
and
$$y \le 3 \quad ...(v)$$

Take inequality (i), $x + y \le 5$

In equation form, it can be written as $x + y = 5$

Now, let us construct the following table

x	0	5
y	5	0

Thus, the line $x + y = 5$ passes through the points $A(0,5)$ and $B(5, 0)$.

Now, on joining the points A and B by a dark line, we get the line AB.

On putting $x = 0$ and $y = 0$ in inequality (i), we get $0 \le 5$, which is true.

So, for inequality $x + y \le 5$, shade the half plane which contains origin.

Take inequality (ii), $4x + y \ge 4$

In equation form, it can be written as $4x + y = 4$

Now, let us construct the following table

x	0	1
y	4	0

Thus, the line $4x + y = 4$ passes through points $C(0, 4)$ and $D(1, 0)$.

Now, joining the points C and D by a dark line, we get the line CD.

On putting $x = 0$ and $y = 0$ in inequality (ii), we get

$$4(0) + 0 \ge 4 \Rightarrow 0 \ge 4, \text{ which is false.}$$

So, for inequality $4x + y \ge 4$, shade the half plane which does not contain origin.

Take inequality (iii), $x + 5y \ge 5$

In equation form, it can be written as

$$x + 5y = 5$$

Now, let us construct the following table

x	0	5
y	1	0

Thus, the line $x + 5y = 5$ passes through the points $E(0,1)$ and $B(5,0)$.

Now, joining the points E and B by a dark line, we get the line EB.

On putting $x = 0$ and $y = 0$ in inequality (iii), we get

$$0 \ge 5, \text{ which is false.}$$

So, for inequality $x + 5y \ge 5$, shade the half plane which does not contain origin.

Take inequality (iv), $x \leq 4$

Linear equation corresponding to inequality (iv) is $x = 4$. This is a line parallel to Y-axis at a distance 4 units to the right of Y-axis.

For this inequality, shade the half plane which contains origin. [$\because 0 \leq 4$, is true]

Take inequality (v), $y \leq 3$

Linear equation corresponding to inequality (v) is $y = 3$. This is a line parallel to X-axis at a distance of 3 units above the X-axis.

For this inequality, shade the half plane which contains origin. [$\because 0 \leq 3$, is true]

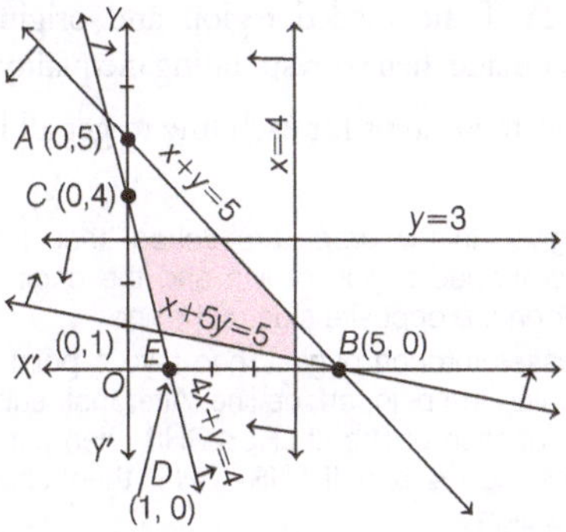

The common shaded region represent the solution region for system of inequalities.

EXAMPLE 5. Solve the following inequalities graphically.
$3x + 2y \leq 12, x + y \geq 8, -x + y \geq 4, 5x \leq 10; x, y \geq 0.$

Sol. We have, inequalities

$$3x + 2y \leq 12 \quad \ldots(i)$$
$$x + y \geq 8 \quad \ldots(ii)$$
$$-x + y \geq 4 \quad \ldots(iii)$$
$$5x \leq 10 \quad \ldots(iv)$$
and $$x, y \geq 0 \quad \ldots(v)$$

Take inequality (i), $3x + 2y \leq 12$

Corresponding equation of line is $3x + 2y = 12$.

Consider the table of values, satisfying the equation $3x + 2y = 12$.

x	0	4
y	6	0

Thus, the line passing through the points $A(0, 6)$ and $B(4, 0)$.

Join the points A and B by a dark line.

On putting (0, 0) in the given inequality (i), we get
$$3(0) + 2(0) \leq 12 \Rightarrow 0 \leq 12, \text{ which is true.}$$

So, half plane corresponding to $3x + 2y \leq 12$ contains the origin.

Take inequality (ii), $x + y \geq 8$

Corresponding equation of line is $x + y = 8$.

Consider the table of values, satisfying the equation $x + y = 8$.

x	0	8
y	8	0

Thus, the line passing through the points $C(0, 8)$ and $D(8, 0)$.

Join the points C and D by a dark line.

On putting (0, 0) in the given inequality (ii), we get
$$0 + 0 \geq 8 \Rightarrow 0 \geq 8, \text{ which is false.}$$

So, half plane corresponding to $x + y \geq 8$ does not contain the origin.

Take inequality (iii), $-x + y \geq 4$

Corresponding equation of line is $-x + y = 4$.

Consider the table of values, satisfying the equation $-x + y = 4$.

x	0	-4
y	4	0

Thus, the line passing through the points $E(0, 4)$ and $F(-4, 0)$.

Join the points E and F by a dark line.

On putting (0, 0) in the given inequality (iii), we get
$$-0 + 0 \geq 4 \Rightarrow 0 \geq 4, \text{ which is false.}$$

So, half plane corresponding to $-x + y \geq 4$ does not contain the origin.

Take inequality (iv), $5x \leq 10$

Corresponding equation of line is $5x = 10 \Rightarrow x = 2$.

This is a line parallel to Y-axis at a distance of 2 units to the right of Y-axis.

On putting (0, 0) in the given inequality (iv), we get
$$5(0) \leq 10 \Rightarrow 0 \leq 10, \text{ which is true.}$$

So, half plane corresponding to $5x \leq 10$ contains the origin.

Take inequality (v), $x, y \geq 0$

These inequalities represent the region of first quadrant including the points on the axes.

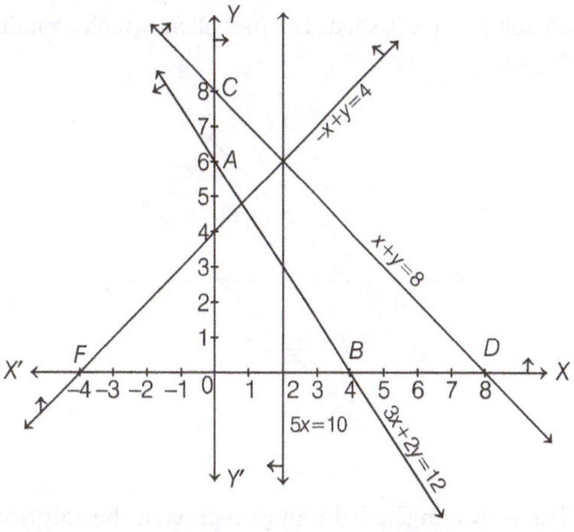

It can be seen that there is no common shaded region, therefore given system of inequalities has no solution.

EXAMPLE 6. Solve the inequalities $|y-x| \leq 3$, graphically.

Sol. We have,

$$|y-x| \leq 3$$

$\Rightarrow \quad -3 \leq y-x \leq 3$

$\Rightarrow \quad y-x \geq -3 \quad \text{...(i)}$

and $\quad y-x \leq 3 \quad \text{...(ii)}$

Take inequality (i), $y-x \geq -3$

In equation form, it can be written as

$$y-x=-3$$

Now, let us construct the table of values, which satisfy the above equation.

x	0	3
y	-3	0

Thus, the line passing through the points $A(3, 0)$ and $B(0, -3)$

Now, join the points A and B by a dark line.

On putting (0, 0) in inequality (i), we get

$0 \geq -3$, which is true.

So, for $y-x \geq -3$, shade the half plane which contain origin.

Take inequality (ii),

$$y-x \leq 3$$

In equation form, it can be written as $y-x=3$

Now, let us construct the table of values, which satisfy the above equation.

x	0	-3
y	3	0

Thus, the line passing through the points $C(-3, 0)$ and $D(0, 3)$. Now, join these points by a dark line.

On putting (0, 0) in inequality (ii), we get

$0 \leq 3$, which is true.

So, for $y-x \leq 3$, shade the half plane which contain origin.

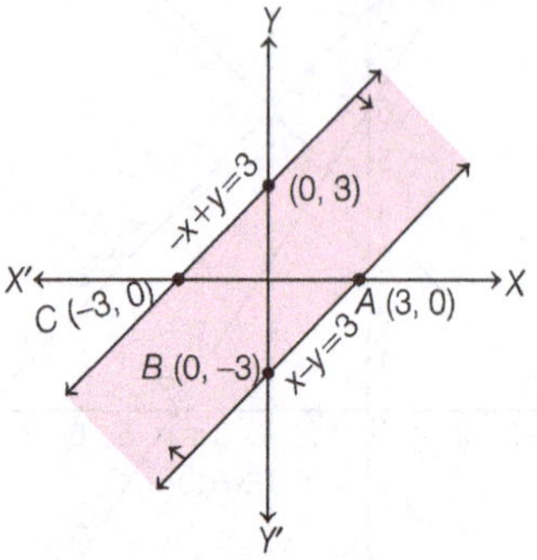

The common shaded region represent the solution region for system of inequalities.

Method of Finding the Linear Inequalities when Their Solution region is Given

When solution region is given, then we can find the linear inequalities with the help of following steps

***Step* I** Choose a line given in graphs.

***Step* II** Check whether the shaded region corresponding to the line and the origin lie on the same side or on the opposite side of the line.

***Step* III** ***Case* I** If the shaded region and origin lie on the same side, then corresponding inequality has sign $\leq$.

***Case* II** If the shaded region and origin lie on the opposite side then corresponding inequality has sign $\geq$.

***Step* IV** Repeat these steps for each line to get all inequalities.

Note

(i) If the lines given in the graph are dotted, then use $<$ or $>$ according as shaded region of line and the origin lie on the same side or on the opposite side of the line.

(ii) If the line passes through origin. Then take a point of solution region, excluding the point on the line. After that, substitute that point in the equation of line. If LHS$\leq$ RHS, then corresponding inequality has sign $\leq$ and if LHS$\geq$ RHS, then corresponding inequality has sign $\geq$.

(iii) (a) If the solution region is above the X-axis, then we may have the inequality $y \geq 0$.

(b) If the solution region is on the right side of Y-axis, then we may have the inequality $x \geq 0$.

EXAMPLE 7. Find the linear inequalities for which the shaded area in figure below is a solution set.

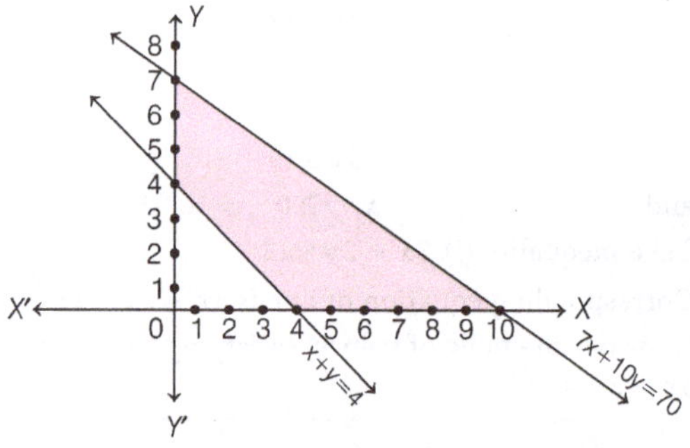

Sol. For the equation $7x+10y=70$, shaded area and origin both lie on the same side of the line, therefore corresponding linear inequality is $7x+10y \leq 70$.

For the equation $x+y=4$, shaded area and origin lie on the opposite side of the line, therefore corresponding linear inequality is $x+y \geq 4$.

Also, the solution region is above the X-axis and on the right side of Y-axis, therefore we have $x \geq 0$ and $y \geq 0$.

Hence, linear inequalities will be

$$7x+10y \leq 70$$
$$x+y \geq 4$$
$$x, y \geq 0$$

EXAMPLE 8. Find the linear inequalities for which the shaded region in the given figure is the solution set.

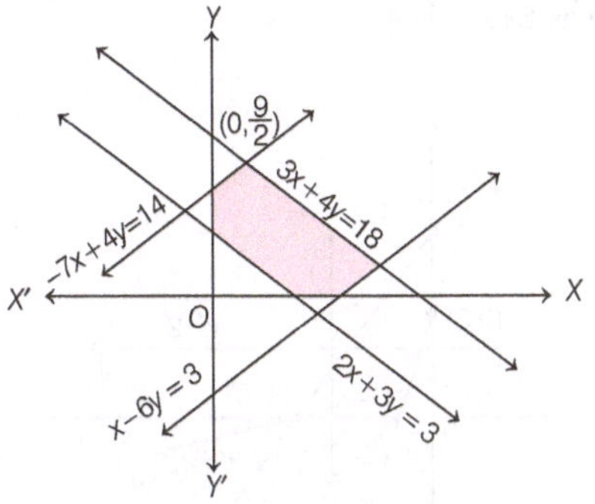

Sol. Consider $2x + 3y = 3$. We observe that, the shaded region and the origin lie on opposite side of this line.
Therefore, $2x + 3y \geq 3$ is the linear inequality corresponding to the line $2x + 3y = 3$.
Consider $3x + 4y = 18$. We observe that, the shaded region and the origin lie on the same side of this line.
Therefore, $3x + 4y \leq 18$ is the linear inequality corresponding to the line $3x + 4y = 18$.
Consider $-7x + 4y = 14$. It is clear from the figure that the shaded region and the origin lie on the same side of this line.
Therefore, $-7x + 4y \leq 14$ is the linear inequality corresponding to the line $-7x + 4y = 14$.
Consider $x - 6y = 3$. It is clear form the figure that the shaded region and origin lie on the same side of this line.
Therefore, $x - 6y \leq 3$ is the linear inequality corresponding to the line $x - 6y = 3$.
Also, the shaded region lies in the first quadrant only. Therefore, $x \geq 0$, $y \geq 0$.
Thus, the linear inequalities corresponding to the given solution set are

$$2x + 3y \geq 3,\ 3x + 4y \leq 18,$$
$$-7x + 4y \leq 14,$$
$$x - 6y \leq 3,\ x \geq 0,\ y \geq 0.$$

Topic Practice 6

1 Solve the following inequalities graphically.
$$y \leq 4, x \geq 1$$

2 Solve graphically $4x + 3y \geq 12$ and $4x - 5y \geq -20$.

3 Solve the following inequalities $2x + y \geq 6$ and $3x + 4y \leq 12$ graphically.

4 Solve the following inequalities $2x + y \geq 4$, $x + y \leq 3$ and $2x - 3y \leq 6$ graphically.

5 Solve the system of inequalities graphically.
$$x + y \leq 4,\ 3x + y \geq 3,$$
$$x + 4y \geq 4,\ \ x \leq 3,\ y \leq 2$$

6 Solve graphically the following system of inequalities.
$$x + 2y \leq 3;\ 3x + 4y \geq 12,$$
$$x \geq 0 \text{ and } y \geq 1$$

7 Solve the following system of inequalities graphically.
$3x + 2y \leq 150$, $x + 4y \leq 80$, $x \leq 15$, $y \geq 0$, $x \geq 0$

8 Find the linear inequalities for which shaded area in figure below is a solution set.

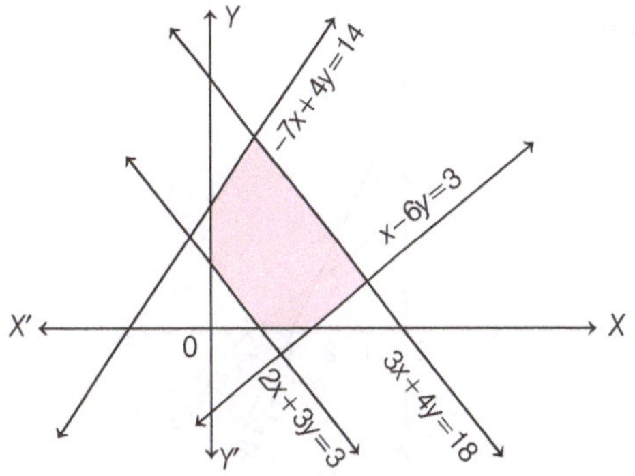

9 Find the linear inequalities for which the shaded region in the given figure is the solution set.

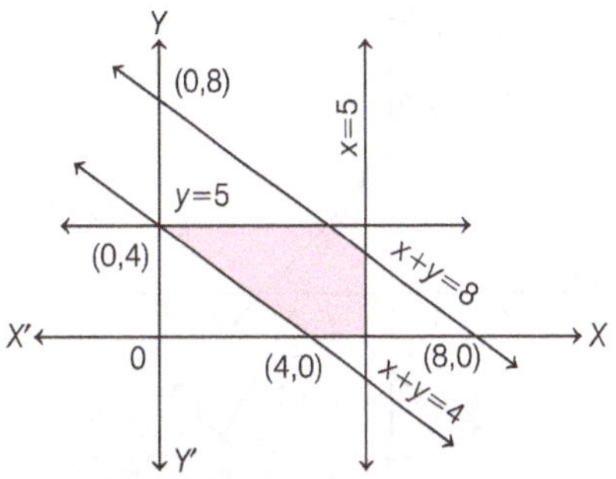

Hints & Solutions

1. Solve as Example 1.

Ans.

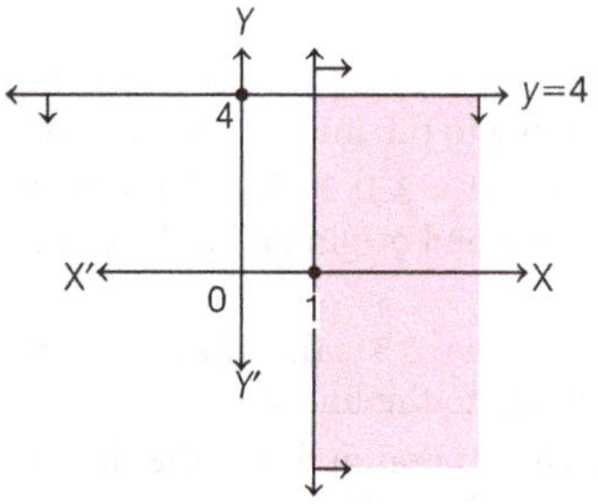

2. Solve as Example 3.

Ans.

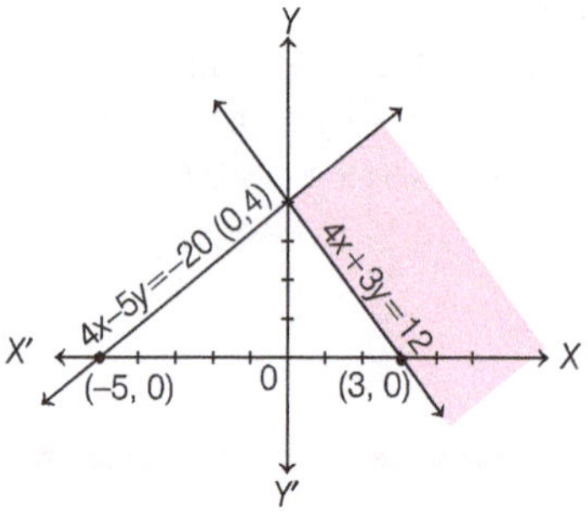

3. Solve as Example 3.

Ans.

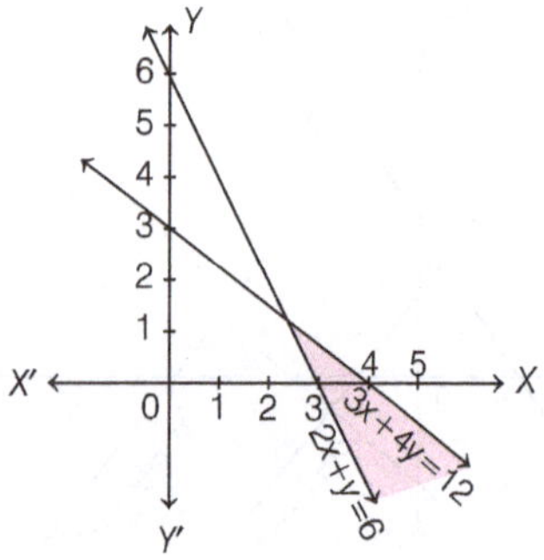

4. Solve as Example 4.

Ans.

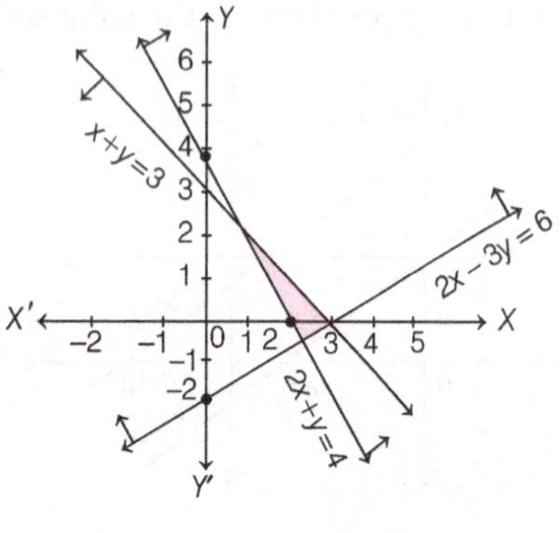

5. Solve as Example 4.

Ans.

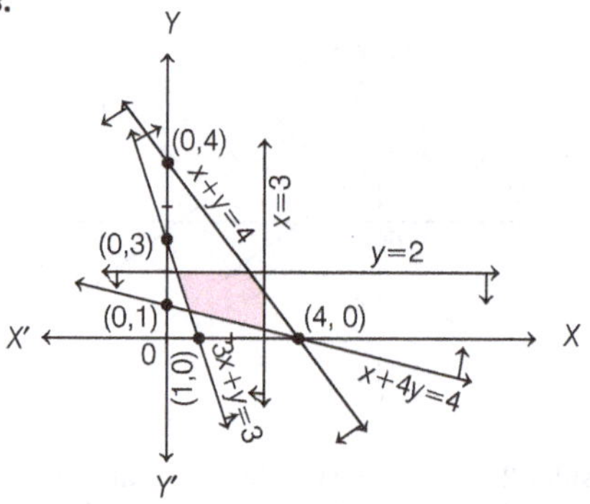

6. Solve as Example 4.

Ans.

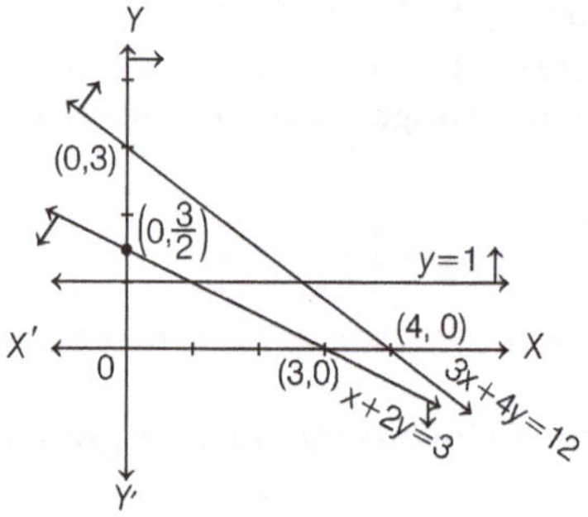

No solution exists.

7. Solve as Example 5.

Ans.

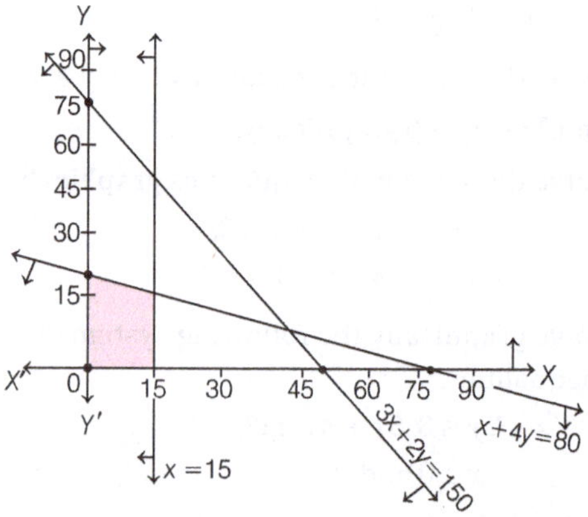

8. Solve as Example 8.

Ans. $3x + 4y \le 18$, $-7x + 4y \le 14$, $2x + 3y \ge 3$, $x - 6y \le 3$, $x \ge 0$, $y \ge 0$

9. Solve as Example 8.

Ans. $x + y \le 8$, $x + y \ge 4$, $x \le 5$, $y \le 5$, $x \ge 0$, $y \ge 0$

Exam Pattern Exercise

Part A - Objective Type Questions

Multiple Choice Type Questions

1 Two real numbers or two algebraic expressions related by the symbol '<', '>', '≤' or '≥' forms an

(a) equation
(b) inequality
(c) set
(d) None of the above

2 Statements : $M \le N < L \ge Q, R > T \ge Q$

Conclusion I : $R \ge L$

Conclusion II : $T \le N$

(a) Only Conclusion I is true
(b) Only Conclusion II is true
(c) Both conclusions are true
(d) Both conclusions are false

3 The graph of the solutions of inequality $\frac{3x-4}{2} \ge \frac{x+1}{4} - 1$ on number line is

(a) 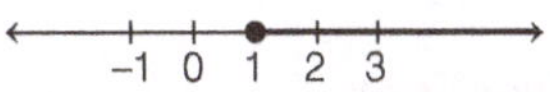

(b) 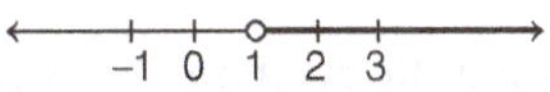

(c) 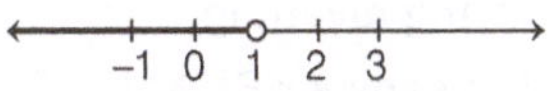

(d) 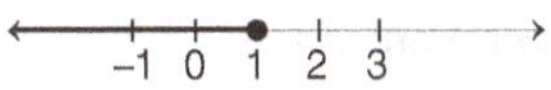

4 If $a>b$ and $c<0$ then which of the following is true? **[CBSE 2025]**

(a) $a+c<b+c$ (b) $a-c<b-c$
(c) $ac>bc$ (d) $a-c>b+c$

5 The solution set of the linear inequalities $-15 < \frac{3(x-2)}{5} \le 0$, is

(a) $(-23, 2]$
(b) $(-20, 4)$
(c) $[-23, 2)$
(d) None of the above

6 If $\frac{|x+1|}{x+1} > 0, x \in R$, then **[CBSE 2023]**

(a) $x \in [-1, \infty)$
(b) $x \in (-1, \infty)$
(c) $x \in (-\infty, -1)$
(d) $x \in (-\infty, -1]$

7 If $x > y$ and $z < 0$, then **[CBSE 2024]**

(a) $xz > yz$ (b) $xz \ge yz$
(c) $\frac{x}{z} > \frac{y}{z}$ (d) $\frac{x}{z} < \frac{y}{z}$

8 The graph of the inequation $2x + 3y > 6$ is the **[CBSE 2024]**

(a) entire *XOY*-plane.
(b) half-plane that contains the origin.
(c) half-plane that neither contains the origin nor the points on the line $2x + 3y = 6$
(d) whole *XOY*-plane excluding the points on the line $2x + 3y = 6$

9 The graph of the inequality $40x + 20y \le 120, x \ge 0, y \ge 0$ is

(a) 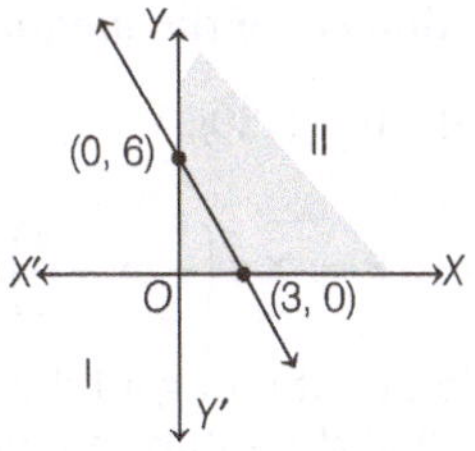

(b) 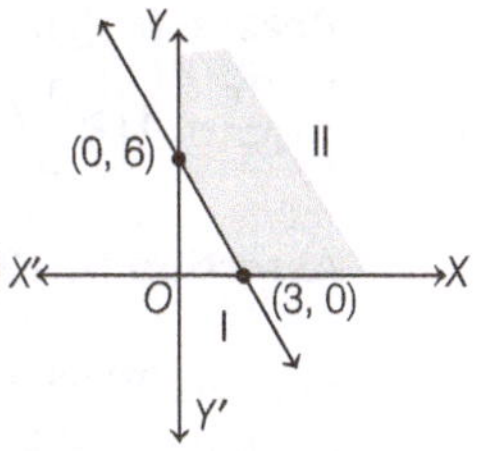

(c) 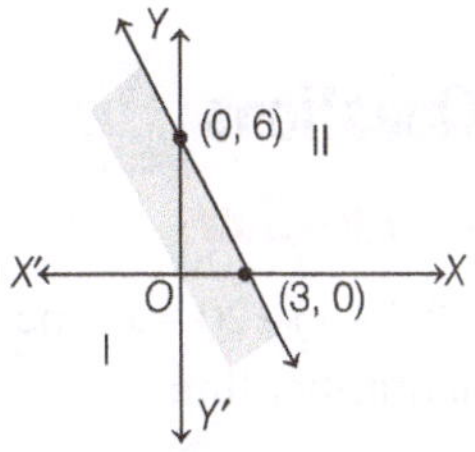

(d) 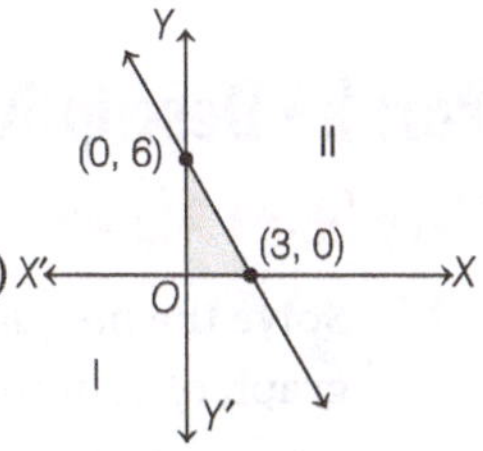

10 The graphical solution of the system of linear inequalities $3x + 4y \ge 12, y \ge 1, x \ge 0$ is

(a) 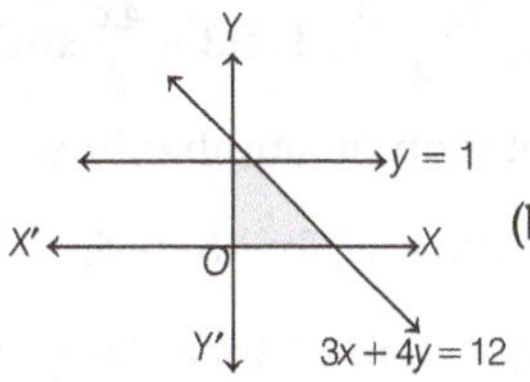

(b) 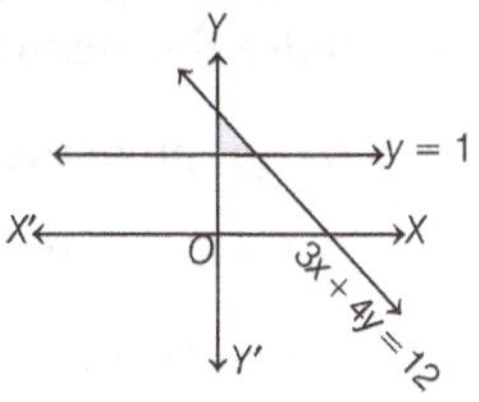

(c) 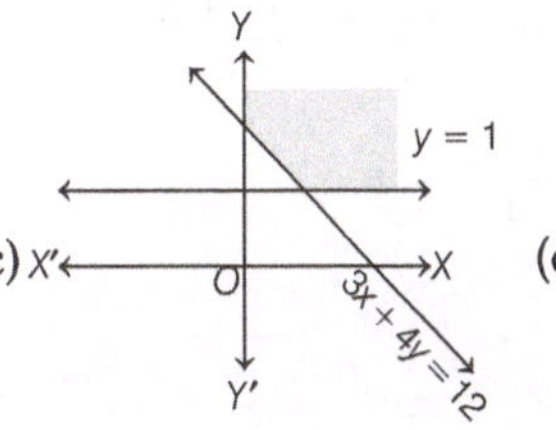

(d) 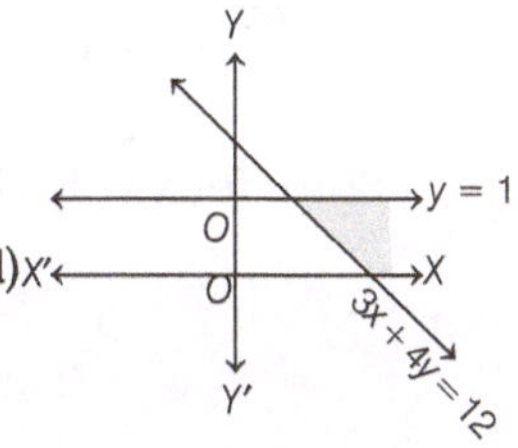

Assertion-Reason Based Questions

Directions (Q. Nos. 11-13) *In the questions given below are two statements labelled as Assertion (A) and Reason (R). In the context of the two statements, which one of the following is correct?*

(a) Both A and R are correct; R is the correct explanation of A

(b) Both A and R are correct; R is not the correct explanation of A

(c) A is correct; R is incorrect

(d) R is correct; A is incorrect

11 **Assertion** (A) If $3x + 8 > 2$, then $x \in \{-1, 0, 1, 2 \ldots\}$, where x is an integer.

Reason (R) The solution set of inequality

$$4x + 3 < 5x + 7 \ \forall\ x \in R \text{ is } [4, \infty).$$

12 **Assertion** (A) The solution set of the inequality

$$\frac{3(x-2)}{5} \le \frac{5(2-x)}{3} \text{ is } (-\infty, 2).$$

Reason (R) The solution set of the inequality

$$\frac{1}{2}\left(\frac{3x}{5} + 4\right) \ge \frac{1}{3}(x-6) \text{ is } (-\infty, 120].$$

13 **Assertion** (A) $|3x - 5| > 9 \Rightarrow x \in \left(-\infty, -\frac{4}{3}\right) \cup \left(\frac{14}{3}, \infty\right)$

Reason (R) The region containing all the solutions of an inequality is called the solution region.

Part B - Descriptive Questions

Very Short Answer Type Questions

14 Solve the inequality $3(2 - x) \ge 2(1 - x)$ and show the graph of solution on number line.

15 Solve $12 + 1\frac{5}{6}x \le 5 + 3x$, when (i) $x \in N$ (ii) $x \in R$.

16 Solve the inequality $\frac{2x-3}{4} + 9 \ge 3 + \frac{4x}{3}$ and show the graph of the solution on number line.

17 Solve for x : $4x + 3 \ge 2x + 17$, $3x - 5 < -2$.

18 Solve the following system of linear inequalities.

$$\frac{4x}{3} - \frac{9}{4} < x + \frac{3}{4} \text{ and } \frac{7x-1}{3} - \frac{7x+2}{6} > x$$

19 Solve for x : $-5 \le \frac{2-3x}{4} \le 9$.

20 Solve $2x - 1 > x + \frac{7-x}{3} > 2, x \in R$.

21 Anshu obtained 73, 67 and 72 marks in the Mathematics test. How many marks should he get in his fourth test, so as to have an average of at least 75?

Short Answer Type Questions

22 Solve for x : $\frac{x-3}{x-5} > 0$.

23 Solve $\frac{5}{x-2} > 3$ and represent the solution set on number line.

24 Solve the following system of inequalities.

$$\frac{2x+1}{7x-1} > 5, \ \frac{x+7}{x-8} > 2$$

25 Solve $|x| < 4$ and represent the solution set on the number line.

26 Solve the inequality $\left|\frac{2}{x-4}\right| > 1; x \ne 4$.

27 Solve $\frac{|x-1|}{x+2} < 1$.

Long Answer Type Questions

28 In the given question the symbols @, *, $, #, % are used with the following meaning

A @ B means A < B

A * B means A > B

A $ B means A = B

A # B means A ≤ B

A % B means A ≥ B

Statement : A $ B # P % D $ Q

Conclusion I : A $ P

Conclusion II : A @ P

Which of the following conclusion is true.

29 Solve the following inequality graphically

$|x - y| \ge 1$

30 A company manufactures cassettes. Its cost and revenue functions are $C(x) = 26000 + 30x$ and $R(x) = 43x$, respectively, where x is the number of cassettes produced and sold in a week. How many cassettes must be sold by the company to realise some profit?

31 The water acidity in a pool is considered normal when the average pH reading of three daily measurements is between 8.2 and 8.5. If the two pH readings are 8.48 and 8.35, find the range of pH value for the third reading that will result in the acidity level being normal.

32 The length of rectangle is three times of the breadth. If the minimum perimeter of the rectangle is 160 cm, then find the shortest value for its breadth.

33 A manufacturer has 600 L of a 12% solution of acid. How many litres of a 30% acid solution must be added to it so that acid content in the resulting mixture will be more than 15% but less than 18%?

34 Check whether the half plane $3x + 6y \geq 0$ contains (1, 1). If so, shade the plane containing (1, 1).

35 Solve the inequalities $3x + 2y \leq 12$, $x \geq 1$ and $y \geq 2$ graphically.

36 Solve the inequalities $x + y \leq 9$, $y > x$ and $x \geq 1$ graphically.

37 Find the linear inequalities for which the shaded region in the given figure is the solution set.

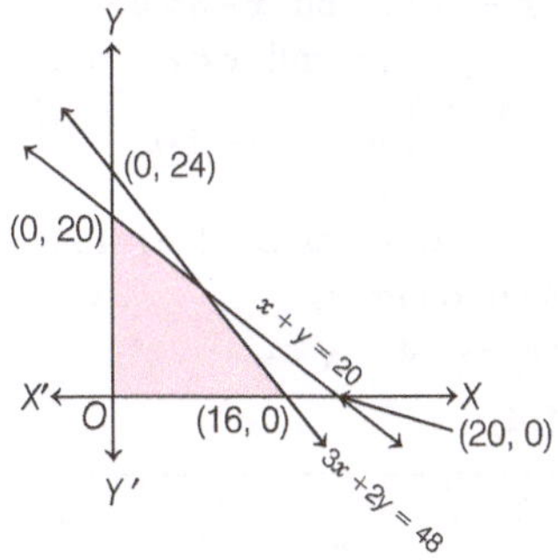

Case Study Based Questions

38 Aman questioned his maths teacher that "if he has more that one linear inequality, then what will be the solution?"

Teacher replies, "The solution set of a system of linear inequations in one variable is the intersection of the solution sets of the linear inequations in the given system."

After that teacher gave Aman some problems to solve.

On the basis of given information, answer the following questions.

(i) The solution of the linear inequality $2(2x+3)-10 < 6(x-2)$ is

(a) $(-\infty, 4)$ (b) $(4, \infty)$
(c) $(-4, 4)$ (d) None of these

(ii) The solution of the linear inequality $\frac{2x-3}{4} + 6 \geq 2 + \frac{4x}{3}$ is

(a) $(-\infty, 3.9]$ (b) $[3.9, \infty)$
(c) $[-3.9, 3.9]$ (d) None of these

(iii) The solution of the linear inequality $\frac{x}{2x+1} \geq \frac{1}{4}$ is

(a) $\left(-\infty, -\frac{1}{2}\right)$ (b) $\left[\frac{1}{2}, \infty\right)$
(c) $\left(-\frac{1}{2}, \frac{1}{2}\right]$ (d) $R - \left[-\frac{1}{2}, \frac{1}{2}\right)$

(iv) The solution of system of linear inequality given by (i) and (ii) is

(a) $[3.9, 4)$ (b) $(-\infty, 3.9]$
(c) ϕ (d) None of these

(v) Solution of system of inequation given by $-11 \leq 4x - 3 \leq 13$ is

(a) $(-2, 4)$ (b) $[-2, 4]$ (c) $(-2, 4]$ (d) $[-2, 4)$

39 The water acidity in a pool is considered normal, when the average pH reading of three daily measurements is between 7.2 and 7.8. The first two pH reading are 7.48 and 7.85, and pH reading of 3rd day is x.

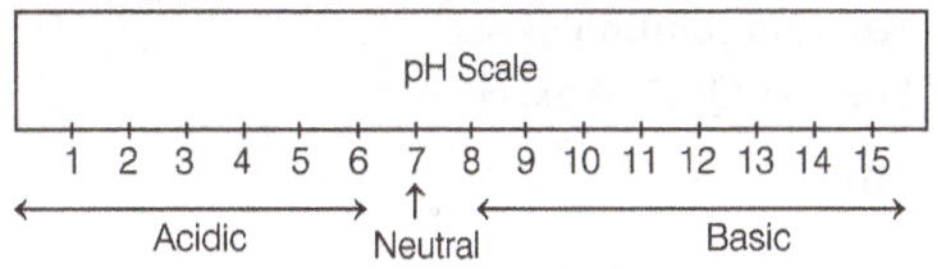

On the basis of above information, answer the following questions.

(i) The average pH of three days is

(a) $5.11 + x$ (b) $5.11 + \frac{x}{3}$
(c) $15.33 + x$ (d) None of these

(ii) The system of linear inequality, which shows the given information is

(a) $7.2 \leq 5.11 + \frac{x}{3} \leq 7.8$ (b) $7.2 < 5.11 + \frac{x}{3} \leq 7.8$
(c) $7.2 \leq 5.11 + \frac{x}{3} < 7.8$ (d) $7.2 < 5.11 + \frac{x}{3} < 7.8$

(iii) The solution of linear inequality $7.2 \leq 5.11 + \frac{x}{3}$ is

(a) $x \geq 6.27$ (b) $x > 6.27$
(c) $x \leq 6.27$ (d) $x < 6.27$

(iv) The solution of linear inequality $5.11 + \frac{x}{3} \leq 7.8$ is

(a) $x \leq 8.07$ (b) $x < 8.07$
(c) $x \geq 8.07$ (d) $x > 8.07$

(v) The value of pH on third day is

(a) $[6.27, 8.07]$ (b) $(6.27, 8.07)$
(c) $(6.27, 8.07]$ (d) $[6.27, 8.07)$

Hints & Solutions

1. (b)	2. (d)	3. (a)	4. (d)
5. (a)	6. (b)	7. (b)	8. (b)
9. (d)	10. (c)	11. (c)	12. (d)

13. (b)

14. **Hint** $3(2-x) \geq 2(1-x)$

$\Rightarrow \quad 6-2 \geq 3x-2x$

$\Rightarrow \quad x \leq 4$

Ans. $(-\infty, 4]$

15. **Hint** $12+\frac{11x}{6} \leq 5+3x$

$\Rightarrow \quad \frac{7x}{6} \geq 7 \Rightarrow x \geq 6$

Ans. (i) $\{6, 7, 8, 9, ...\}$ (ii) $[6, \infty)$

16. Solve as Q. 15. **Ans.** $(-\infty, 6.3]$

17. **Hint** $4x+3 \geq 2x+17$ and $3x-5<-2$

$\Rightarrow \quad 2x \geq 14$ and $3x<3 \Rightarrow x \geq 7$ and $x<1$

Ans. No solution exists.

18. Solve as Q. 17. **Ans.** (4, 9)

19. **Hint** $-5 \leq \frac{2-3x}{4} \leq 9$

$\Rightarrow \quad -20 \leq 2-3x \leq 36$

$\Rightarrow \quad -22 \leq -3x \leq 34 \Rightarrow -34 \leq 3x \leq 22$

Ans. $\left[\frac{-34}{3}, \frac{22}{3}\right]$

20. **Hint** $2x-1>\frac{2x+7}{3}>2$

$\Rightarrow \quad 6x-3>2x+7>6$

$\Rightarrow \quad 6x-3>2x+7$ and $2x+7>6$

$\Rightarrow \quad 4x>10$ and $2x>-1$

$\Rightarrow \quad x>\frac{5}{2}$ and $x>-\frac{1}{2}$ **Ans.** $\left(\frac{5}{2}, \infty\right)$

21. **Hint** $\frac{73+67+72+x}{4} \geq 75$ **Ans.** 88 marks

22. **Hint** $(x-3)(x-5)>0$

***Case* I** When both are positive

$\therefore x>3$ and $x>5 \Rightarrow x>5$

***Case* II** When both are negative

$x-3<0$ and $x-5<0$

$\Rightarrow \quad x<3$ and $x<5 \Rightarrow x<3$

Ans. $(-\infty, 3) \cup (5, \infty)$

23. **Hint** $\frac{5}{x-2}-3>0 \Rightarrow \left(\frac{11-3x}{x-2}\right)>0$

$\Rightarrow \quad 2<x<\frac{11}{3}$ **Ans.** $\left(2, \frac{11}{3}\right)$

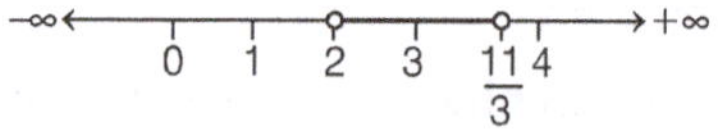

24. **Hint** $\frac{2x+1}{7x-1}-5>0, \frac{x+7}{x-8}-2>0$

$\Rightarrow \quad \frac{-33x+6}{7x-1}>0, \frac{-x+23}{(x-8)}>0$

Now, $\frac{-33x+6}{7x-1}>0 \Rightarrow \frac{11x-2}{7x-1}<0$

$\Rightarrow \quad 11x-2<0$ and $7x-1>0$

$\therefore \quad x>\frac{2}{11}$ and $x<\frac{1}{7}$

Also, $\frac{-x+23}{x-8}>0 \Rightarrow \frac{x-23}{x-8}<0$

$\Rightarrow \quad x-23<0$ and $x-8>0$

$\therefore \quad x>23$ and $x<8$

Thus, $x \in \left(\frac{1}{7}, \frac{2}{11}\right)$ and $x \in (8, 23)$.

Here, there is no common values of x.

Ans. No solution exists

25. **Hint** $|x|<4 \Rightarrow -4<x<4$

Ans. $(-4, 4)$

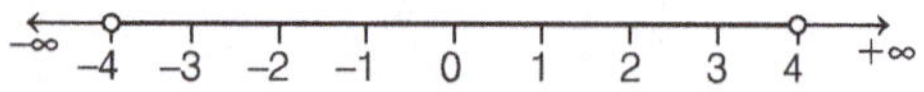

26. **Hint** $\left|\frac{2}{x-4}\right|>1 \Rightarrow \frac{2}{x-4}<-1, \frac{2}{x-4}>1$

$\Rightarrow \frac{2}{x-4}+1<0, \frac{2}{x-4}-1>0 \Rightarrow \frac{-2+x}{x-4}<0, \frac{6-x}{x-4}>0$

$\Rightarrow \quad (-2+x)(x-4)<0$ and $(6-x)(x-4)>0$

Further, solve as Q. 20.

Ans. $(2, 4) \cup (4, 6)$

27. Solve as Q. 26.

Ans. $(-\infty, -2) \cup \left(\frac{-1}{2}, \infty\right)$

28. **Hint** $A=B \leq P \geq D=Q$

Ans. Either Conclusion I is true or Conclusion II is true.

29. **Hint** Solve for $x - y \geq 1$ and $-x + y \geq 1$ by considering both as equation.

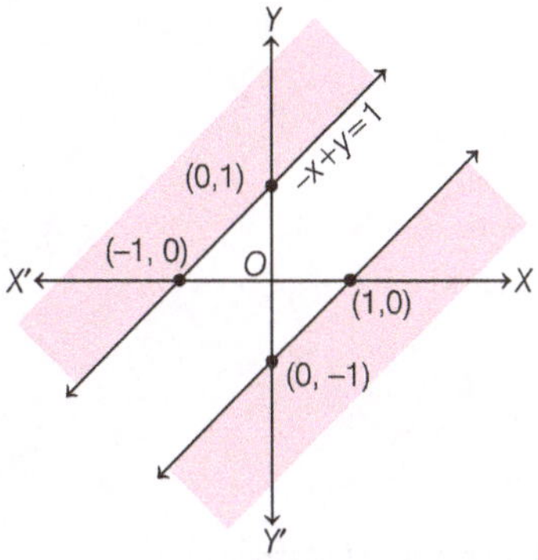

30. **Hint** For profit, $R(x) > C(x)$ **Ans.** More than 2000.

31. **Hint** $8.2 < \dfrac{8.48 + 8.35 + x}{3} < 8.5$

Ans. Between 7.77 and 8.33

32. Let length and breadth of a rectangle be x and y, respectively.

$\because\ x = 3y$

$\therefore\ 2(x + y) \geq 160 \Rightarrow 2(3y + y) \geq 160 \Rightarrow y \geq 20$

Ans. 20 cm

33. Greater than 120 litres and less than 300 litres.

34. **Hint** At point (1, 1), $3(1) + 6(1) \geq 0$

$\Rightarrow\ 9 \geq 0$, which in true.

Ans. Given plane contains (1, 1).

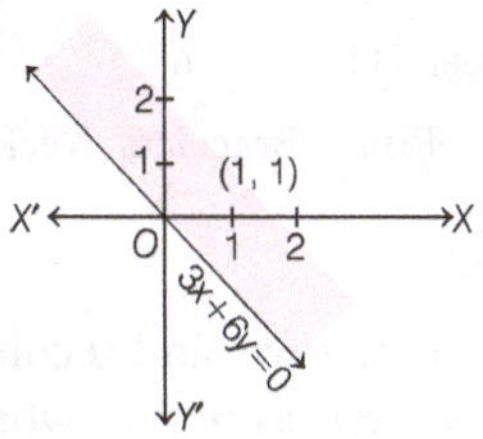

35. **Hint** Firstly, consider the given inequation as an equation and plot the graph of equation.

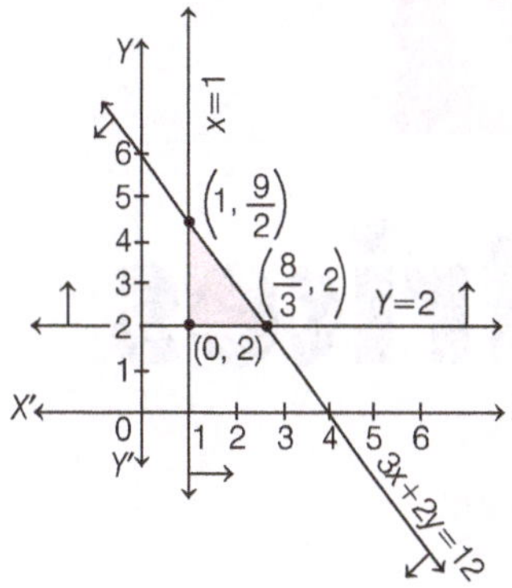

36. **Hint** Firstly, consider the given inequation as an equation and plot the graph of equation.

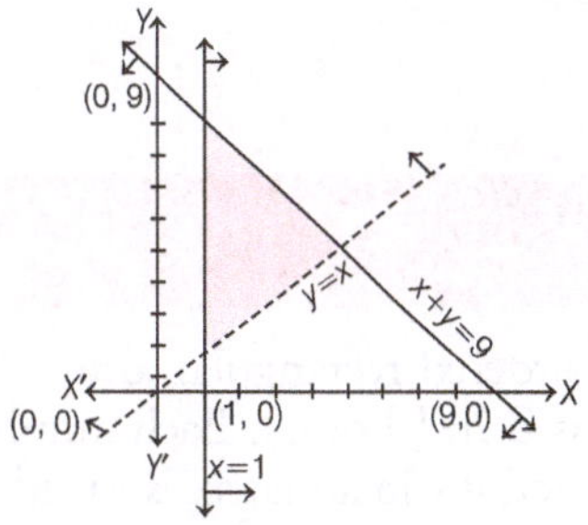

37. **Hint** For the equation $x + y = 20$, the shaded area and origin both lies on the same side of the line, therefore the compounding inequality is $x + y \leq 20$.

Similarly, $3x + 2y \leq 48$

Also, the shaded portion lies in Ist quadrant.

$\therefore\ x \geq 0$ and $y \geq 0$

Ans. $x + y \leq 20, 3x + 2y \leq 48, x \geq 0, y \geq 0$

38. (i) (b), (ii) (a), (iii) (d), (iv) (c), (v) (b)

39. (i) (b), (ii) (d), (iii) (a), (iv) (a), (v) (b)

CHAPTER 07

Matrices

In this Chapter...

- Matrix
- Addition, Subtraction and Scalar Multiplication of Matrices
- Multiplication of Matrices
- Transpose of a Matrix

Matrix

A matrix is an ordered **rectangular array** of numbers or functions enclosed in [ ] or ( ). Each number (real or complex) or functions in a matrix is called an **element** or the **entry** of the matrix.

A matrix is represented by a single **capital letter** like A, B, X, Y, etc., and elements of a matrix are represented by the small letters $a, b, c, \ldots$ etc. In a matrix, horizontal lines are called **rows** and vertical lines are called **columns**.

e.g.

$$A = \begin{bmatrix} 2 & -5 \\ 7 & 0 \\ \sqrt{5} & 3 \end{bmatrix} \begin{matrix} \rightarrow \text{First row } (R_1) \\ \rightarrow \text{Second row } (R_2) \\ \rightarrow \text{Third row } (R_3) \end{matrix}$$

First column (C_1) (C_2) Second column

and

$$B = \begin{bmatrix} 2+3i & 7 & -2/3 \\ 4.2 & -1 & 0 \\ \sqrt{3} & 5 & 5/7 \end{bmatrix} \begin{matrix} \rightarrow R_1 \\ \rightarrow R_2 \\ \rightarrow R_3 \end{matrix}$$

$\downarrow C_1$ $\downarrow C_2$ $\downarrow C_3$

Note In this chapter, we will consider only those matrices whose elements or entries are real numbers or functions taking real values.

EXAMPLE 1. A shopkeeper sells 5 rings, 8 bracelets and 10 necklaces in first week and 11 rings, 6 bracelets and 9 necklaces in next week. Represent this information in a matrix having 2 rows and 3 columns.

Sol. In table form, given information can be written as

	Rings	Bracelets	Necklaces
First week	5	8	10
Next week	11	6	9

Here, we see that table has 2 rows and 3 columns, so given information in a matrix can be written as

$$\begin{matrix} \text{First week} \\ \text{Next week} \end{matrix} \begin{bmatrix} 5 & 8 & 10 \\ 11 & 6 & 9 \end{bmatrix}$$

Rings Bracelets Necklaces

Order of a Matrix

Suppose a matrix has m rows and n columns, then order of matrix is written as $m \times n$, where m represents number of rows and n represents number of columns, and read as m by n matrix.

In general, $m \times n$ matrix has the following rectangular array

$$A = \begin{bmatrix} a_{11} & a_{12} & \cdots & a_{1n} \\ a_{21} & a_{22} & \cdots & a_{2n} \\ \vdots & \vdots & \vdots & \vdots \\ a_{m1} & a_{m2} & \cdots & a_{mn} \end{bmatrix}_{m \times n}$$

In notation form, it can be rewritten as $A = [a_{ij}]_{m \times n}$, where $1 \le i \le m$, $1 \le j \le n$ and $i, j \in N$.

Here, the ith row consists of the elements $a_{i1}, a_{i2}, a_{i3}, \ldots, a_{in}$, while jth column consists of the elements $a_{1j}, a_{2j}, a_{3j}, \ldots, a_{mj}$.

In general, a_{ij} is an element lying in the ith row and jth column. e.g. a_{23} refers to the entry in the second row and third column.

We can also call it as (i, j)th element of matrix A. The number of elements in an $m \times n$ matrix will be equal to mn.

e.g. $$A = \begin{bmatrix} 2 & 0 \\ 4 & -3 \\ -7 & 1 \end{bmatrix}$$

Here, A has 3 rows and 2 columns. So, order of matrix is 3×2 and it has $3 \times 2 = 6$ elements.

EXAMPLE 2. Determine the order of each matrix.

(i) $[2]$ (ii) $[1 \quad -3 \quad 0 \quad 1/2]$

(iii) $\begin{bmatrix} 0 & 0 \\ 0 & 0 \end{bmatrix}$ (iv) $\begin{bmatrix} 5 & 0 \\ 2 & -2 \\ -7 & 4 \end{bmatrix}$

Sol. (i) This matrix has only one row and one column, so the order of matrix is 1×1.

(ii) This matrix has one row and four columns, so the order of the matrix is 1×4.

(iii) This matrix has two rows and two columns, so the order of this matrix is 2×2.

(iv) The matrix has three rows and two columns, so the order of this matrix is 3×2.

EXAMPLE 3. In the matrix

$$A = \begin{bmatrix} 2 & 5 & 19 & -7 \\ 35 & -2 & \frac{5}{2} & 12 \\ \sqrt{3} & 1 & -5 & 17 \end{bmatrix},$$

(i) Write the number of rows in A.
(ii) Write the number of columns in A.
(iii) Write the order of the matrix.
(iv) Write the value of elements a_{13}, a_{21}, a_{23} and a_{33}.

Sol. (i) Here, number of rows in A is 3.

(ii) Here, number of columns in A is 4.

(iii) Here, the matrix A has 3 rows and 4 columns, so the order of the matrix is 3×4.

(iv) Since, a_{ij} represents the element in ith row and jth column.

$\therefore \quad a_{13}$ = element in first row and third column

$\Rightarrow \quad a_{13} = 19$

Similarly, $a_{21} = 35$, $a_{23} = \frac{5}{2}$ and $a_{33} = -5$

Method to Find Order of Matrix When Number of Elements is Given

Suppose number of elements (say P) of a matrix is given, then to find the possible orders of matrix, we use the following steps

I. As matrix of order $m \times n$ has mn elements. So, firstly put mn = number of elements, P.

II. Find all possible factors of P.

III. Now, form all possible ordered pairs with the help of these factors such that the product of elements of each ordered pair is P. These ordered pairs gives the possible orders of given matrix.

EXAMPLE 4. If a matrix has 24 elements, then what are the possible orders it can have? What if it has 13 elements?

Sol. The possible orders of a matrix having 24 elements are 1×24, 24×1, 2×12, 12×2, 3×8, 8×3, 4×6 and 6×4.

The possible orders of a matrix having 13 elements are 1×13 and 13×1.

EXAMPLE 5. What is the total number of possible matrices of order 3×3 with each entry 2 or 0.

Sol. Number of entries in 3×3 matrix is 9. Since, each entry has 2 choices, namely 2 or 0.

Therefore, number of possible matrices

$$= \underbrace{2 \times 2 \times 2 \ldots \times 2}_{9 \text{ times}} = 2^9 = 512$$

Representation of Point(s) in Matrix Form

We can also represent any point (x, y) in a plane by a matrix (column or row) as $\begin{bmatrix} x \\ y \end{bmatrix}$ or $[x\ y]$. e.g. Suppose quadrilateral $ABCD$ has coordinates $A(3, 0)$, $B(-1, 2)$, $C(2, -2)$ and $D(-3, 2)$, we can represent it in matrix form as

$$X = \begin{matrix} A & B & C & D \end{matrix} \\ \begin{bmatrix} 3 & -1 & 2 & -3 \\ 0 & 2 & -2 & 2 \end{bmatrix}_{2\times4} \text{ or } Y = \begin{matrix} A \\ B \\ C \\ D \end{matrix}\begin{bmatrix} 3 & 0 \\ -1 & 2 \\ 2 & -2 \\ -3 & 2 \end{bmatrix}_{4\times2}$$

Thus, matrices can be used as representation of vertices of geometrical figures in a plane.

Formation of a Matrix

Sometimes, a relation between the elements and its position is given to us. Then, to form a matrix, whose elements satisfies this relation, we put different values of i and j according to given order to find all elements and then write the matrix of given order.

EXAMPLE 6. Construct a matrix of order 3×2, whose elements are determined by $a_{ij} = \frac{2i - j}{3}$.

Sol. Let A be a matrix of order 3×2.

Then, $A = [a_{ij}]_{3 \times 2} = \begin{bmatrix} a_{11} & a_{12} \\ a_{21} & a_{22} \\ a_{31} & a_{32} \end{bmatrix}$ ...(i)

Given, $a_{ij} = \frac{2i - j}{3}$

$\therefore \quad a_{11} = \frac{2(1) - 1}{3} = \frac{1}{3}, \; a_{12} = \frac{2(1) - 2}{3} = 0,$

$a_{21} = \frac{2(2) - 1}{3} = 1, \; a_{22} = \frac{2(2) - 2}{3} = \frac{2}{3},$

$a_{31} = \frac{2(3) - 1}{3} = \frac{5}{3}$ and $a_{32} = \frac{2(3) - 2}{3} = \frac{4}{3}$

On putting all above values in Eq. (i), we get

$$A = \begin{bmatrix} 1/3 & 0 \\ 1 & 2/3 \\ 5/3 & 4/3 \end{bmatrix}$$

which is the required 3×2 order matrix.

Types of Matrices

There are various types of matrices, which are given below

(i) **Column Matrix** A matrix having only one column is called a column matrix.

e.g. $B = \begin{bmatrix} 1 \\ 2 \\ 3 \end{bmatrix}_{3 \times 1}$ [one column and three rows]

In general, column matrix $B = [b_{ij}]_{m \times 1}$ where, m is number of rows.

(ii) **Row Matrix** A matrix having only one row is called a row matrix.

e.g. $A = [1 \;\; 2 \;\; 3]_{1 \times 3}$

[one row and three columns]

In general, row matrix $A = [a_{ij}]_{1 \times n}$ where, n is number of columns.

(iii) **Square Matrix** A matrix in which number of rows are equal to number of columns, is called a square matrix.

e.g. $A = \begin{bmatrix} a & b \\ c & d \end{bmatrix}_{2 \times 2}$ [order is 2×2]

In general, square matrix

$$A = [a_{ij}]_{m \times m} \text{ or } [a_{ij}]_{n \times n}$$

where, number of rows = number of columns $= m$ or n.

Note If $A = [a_{ij}]$ is any square matrix of order n, then the elements $a_{11}, a_{22}, a_{33}, \ldots, a_{nn}$ are said to constitute the diagonal of the matrix A. We call these elements as diagonal elements.

e.g. $A = \begin{bmatrix} 1 & -3 & -2 \\ 2 & 7 & -1 \\ 4 & 3 & 8 \end{bmatrix}$,

then the elements of the diagonal of A are 1, 7, 8.

(iv) **Diagonal Matrix** A square matrix $A = [a_{ij}]_{m \times m}$ is said to be a diagonal matrix, if all the elements lying outside the diagonal elements are zero.

e.g. $A = \begin{bmatrix} a & 0 & 0 \\ 0 & b & 0 \\ 0 & 0 & c \end{bmatrix}_{3 \times 3}$ [$a_{ij} = 0$, for $i \neq j$]

In above, A can be written as $A = \text{diag}\,[a, b, c]$.

A diagonal matrix of order $m \times m$ having $a_{11}, a_{22}, \ldots, a_{mm}$ as diagonal elements is denoted by $\text{diag}\,[a_{11}, a_{22}, \ldots, a_{mm}]$.

(v) **Scalar Matrix** A diagonal matrix in which all diagonal elements are equal, is called a scalar matrix.

In other words, a square matrix $A = [a_{ij}]_{m \times m}$ is said to be scalar, if

$$a_{ij} = \begin{cases} 0, & \text{for } i \neq j \\ \text{constant } k, & \text{for } i = j \end{cases}.$$

e.g. $A = \begin{bmatrix} 2 & 0 & 0 \\ 0 & 2 & 0 \\ 0 & 0 & 2 \end{bmatrix}_{3 \times 3}$

[$a_{ij} = 2$, when $i = j$ and $a_{ij} = 0$, when $i \neq j$]

(vi) **Unit or Identity Matrix** A square matrix in which all diagonal elements are 1 and rest are 0, is called an identity matrix.

In other words, a square matrix $A = [a_{ij}]_{n \times n}$ is an identity matrix, if

$$a_{ij} = \begin{cases} 1, & \text{for } i = j \\ 0, & \text{for } i \neq j \end{cases}.$$

Identity matrix of order n is denoted by I_n or simply I (when order is clear from context).

e.g. $A = \begin{bmatrix} 1 & 0 \\ 0 & 1 \end{bmatrix}_{2 \times 2}$

[$a_{ij} = 1$, when $i = j$ and $a_{ij} = 0$, when $i \neq j$]

Note A scalar matrix is an identity matrix, when $k=1$ and every identity matrix is always a scalar matrix.

(vii) **Zero or Null Matrix** If all the elements of a matrix are zero, then it is called a zero or null matrix. It is denoted by letter O.

e.g. $O=\begin{bmatrix}0&0&0\\0&0&0\end{bmatrix}_{2\times 3}$ $[a_{ij}=0, \forall\, i \text{ and } j]$

EXAMPLE 7. Identify the following types of matrices.

(i) $[1\ \ 4\ \ 5]$ (ii) $\begin{bmatrix}1\\2\\-1\end{bmatrix}$ (iii) $\begin{bmatrix}1&2\\4&6\end{bmatrix}$ (iv) $\begin{bmatrix}3&0&0\\0&3&0\\0&0&3\end{bmatrix}$

(v) $\begin{bmatrix}1&0&0\\0&4&0\\0&0&2\end{bmatrix}$ (vi) $\begin{bmatrix}0&0&0\\0&0&0\\0&0&0\end{bmatrix}$ (vii) $\begin{bmatrix}1&0&0\\0&1&0\\0&0&1\end{bmatrix}$

Sol. (i) We have, $[1\ 4\ 5]$. Here, we see that matrix has only one row and three columns, so it is a row matrix.

(ii) We have, $\begin{bmatrix}1\\2\\-1\end{bmatrix}$. Here, we see that matrix has three rows and only one column. So, it is a column matrix.

(iii) We have, $\begin{bmatrix}1&2\\4&6\end{bmatrix}$. Here, we see that matrix has two rows and two columns. So, it is a square matrix.

(iv) We have, $\begin{bmatrix}3&0&0\\0&3&0\\0&0&3\end{bmatrix}$. Here, we see that all diagonal elements of the square matrix are equal but different from one and non-diagonal elements are zero. So, it is a scalar matrix.

(v) We have, $\begin{bmatrix}1&0&0\\0&4&0\\0&0&2\end{bmatrix}$. Here, we see that diagonal elements are not equal and non-diagonal elements are zero. So, it is a diagonal matrix.

(vi) We have, $\begin{bmatrix}0&0&0\\0&0&0\\0&0&0\end{bmatrix}$. Here, we see that all the elements of the matrix are zero. So, it is a zero matrix.

(vii) We have, $\begin{bmatrix}1&0&0\\0&1&0\\0&0&1\end{bmatrix}$. Here, we see that all diagonals elements are 1 and rest are 0. So, it is an identity matrix.

Comparable Matrices

Two matrices are said to be comparable iff each of them contains as many rows and columns as the other.

Equality of Matrices

Two matrices, say $A=[a_{ij}]$ and $B=[b_{ij}]$, are said to be equal, if

(i) their order are same

(ii) their corresponding elements are also equal, i.e. $a_{ij}=b_{ij}, \forall\, i$ and j.

Symbolically, if two matrices A and B are equal, then we write $A=B$.

e.g. $\begin{bmatrix}1&2\\0&4\end{bmatrix}$ and $\begin{bmatrix}1&2\\0&4\end{bmatrix}$ are equal matrices, but $\begin{bmatrix}1&2\\0&4\end{bmatrix}$ and $\begin{bmatrix}2&1\\4&0\end{bmatrix}$ are not equal matrices because corresponding elements are not equal.

EXAMPLE 8. Find the values of a, b and c, when $\begin{bmatrix}a&3\\2&c\end{bmatrix}=\begin{bmatrix}1&b\\2&2\end{bmatrix}$.

Sol. Given, $\begin{bmatrix}a&3\\2&c\end{bmatrix}=\begin{bmatrix}1&b\\2&2\end{bmatrix}$

Here, both matrices are equal, so we equate the corresponding elements.

Now, $a=1$, $3=b$ and $c=2$ i.e. $a=1$, $b=3$ and $c=2$

EXAMPLE 9. If $\begin{bmatrix}x-y&2x+z\\2x-y&3z+w\end{bmatrix}=\begin{bmatrix}-1&5\\0&13\end{bmatrix}$, then find x, y, z and w. **[CBSE 2024]**

Sol. Given, $\begin{bmatrix}x-y&2x+z\\2x-y&3z+w\end{bmatrix}=\begin{bmatrix}-1&5\\0&13\end{bmatrix}$

Here, both matrices are equal, so we equate the corresponding elements

Now, $x-y=-1$ ...(i)

$2x+z=5$ ...(ii)

$2x-y=0$ ...(iii)

and $3z+w=13$ ...(iv)

On solving Eqs. (i) and (iii), we get

$$x=1 \text{ and } y=2$$

On putting the value of x in Eq. (ii), we get

$$2\times1+z=5 \Rightarrow z=5-2=3$$

On putting the value of z in Eq. (iv), we get

$$3\times3+w=13 \Rightarrow w=13-9=4$$

Hence, $x=1$, $y=2$, $z=3$ and $w=4$.

Topic Practice 1

1 Akash, Rashmi and Swati buy magazine and newspaper each week. The tables below show their purchase in three consecutive weeks.

Week 1

	Magazine	Newspaper
Akash	3	1
Rashmi	2	3
Swati	4	4

Week 2

	Magazine	Newspaper
Akash	1	2
Rashmi	4	1
Swati	0	1

Week 3

	Magazine	Newspaper
Akash	4	2
Rashmi	1	0
Swati	1	1

Represent this information in a matrix having 3 rows and 2 columns.

2 Write the order of each of the following matrices.

(i) $\begin{bmatrix} 1 & 2 & 3 \\ 4 & 5 & -1 \end{bmatrix}$ (ii) $[-1]$

(iii) $\begin{bmatrix} -3 & 7 & 15 & 0 \\ 0 & 0 & 3 & 3 \\ 1 & 1 & 6 & 7 \end{bmatrix}$ (iv) $\begin{bmatrix} -7 & 6 & 4 \\ 0 & -5 & 1 \end{bmatrix}$

3 Write the number of all possible matrices of order 2×2 with each entry 1, 2 or 3.

4 If a matrix has 14 elements, then what are the possible orders it can have? What if it has 17 elements?

Directions (Q. Nos. 5-8) *Construct the matrix according to given data in questions.*

5 Write the element a_{23} of a 3×3 matrix $A = [a_{ij}]$, whose elements a_{ij} are given by $a_{ij} = \frac{|i-j|}{2}$.

6 The elements a_{ij} of a 3×3 matrix are given by $a_{ij} = \frac{1}{2}|-3i + j|$. Write the value of element a_{32}.

7 Construct a 3×4 matrix, whose elements are given by $a_{ij} = \frac{1}{2}|-3i + j|$.

8 Construct a matrix of order 2×2, whose elements are given by $a_{ij} = \frac{(i-2j)^2}{2}$.

9 If matrix $A = [a_{ij}]_{2\times 2}$, where $a_{ij} = \begin{cases} 2, & i \neq j \\ 0, & i = j \end{cases}$, then write the matrix A.

10 Find the unknowns in these matrix equations:

(i) $\begin{bmatrix} 2 & 4 & -1 \\ 3 & 1 & k \end{bmatrix} = \begin{bmatrix} 2 & 4 & -1 \\ 3 & 1 & 6 \end{bmatrix}$

(ii) $\begin{bmatrix} 2 & 5 \\ 7 & k \end{bmatrix} = \begin{bmatrix} 2 & 5 \\ 7 & k^2 \end{bmatrix}$ (iii) $\begin{bmatrix} 2 & 1 \\ 3 & 7 \\ 1 & k^2 \end{bmatrix} = \begin{bmatrix} 2 & k \\ 3 & 7 \\ 1 & k \end{bmatrix}$

Directions (Q. Nos. 11-14) *Find the values.*

11 If $\begin{bmatrix} xy & 4 \\ z+6 & x+y \end{bmatrix} = \begin{bmatrix} 8 & w \\ 0 & 6 \end{bmatrix}$, then write the value of $(x + y + z)$.

12 If $\begin{bmatrix} a+4 & 3b \\ 8 & -6 \end{bmatrix} = \begin{bmatrix} 2a+2 & b+2 \\ 8 & a-8b \end{bmatrix}$, then write the value of $a - 2b$.

13 If $\begin{bmatrix} x-y & z \\ 2x-y & w \end{bmatrix} = \begin{bmatrix} -1 & 4 \\ 0 & 5 \end{bmatrix}$, then find the value of $x + y$.

14 Find the values of a, b, c and d from the equation $\begin{bmatrix} 2a+b & a-2b \\ 5c-d & 4c+3d \end{bmatrix} = \begin{bmatrix} 4 & -3 \\ 11 & 24 \end{bmatrix}$.

Directions (Q. Nos. 15-16) *Find the values of x, y and z.*

15 $\begin{bmatrix} x+y+z \\ x+z \\ y+z \end{bmatrix} = \begin{bmatrix} 9 \\ 5 \\ 7 \end{bmatrix}$

16 $\begin{bmatrix} -2x+y \\ x+y+z \\ x+y \end{bmatrix} = \begin{bmatrix} -3 \\ 3 \\ 3 \end{bmatrix}$

Directions (Q. Nos. 17-18) *Find the values of x and y.*

17 $\begin{bmatrix} 2x+1 & 3y \\ 0 & y^2-5y \end{bmatrix} = \begin{bmatrix} x+3 & y^2+2 \\ 0 & -6 \end{bmatrix}$

18 $\begin{bmatrix} x+y & z \\ 5 & xy \end{bmatrix} = \begin{bmatrix} 6 & 2 \\ 5 & 8 \end{bmatrix}$

19 Find the values of a, b, c and d, if $\begin{bmatrix} a+b+c+d \\ a+c-d \\ b-c+d \\ a+d \end{bmatrix} = \begin{bmatrix} 4 \\ 1 \\ 1 \\ 2 \end{bmatrix}$.

Hints & Solutions

1. Similar as Example 1.

Ans. Week 1 Week 2 Week 3

$$\begin{bmatrix} 3 & 1 \\ 2 & 3 \\ 4 & 4 \end{bmatrix} \quad \begin{bmatrix} 1 & 2 \\ 4 & 1 \\ 0 & 1 \end{bmatrix} \quad \begin{bmatrix} 4 & 2 \\ 1 & 0 \\ 1 & 1 \end{bmatrix}$$

2. Similar as Example 2.

Ans. (i) 2×3 (ii) 1×1 (iii) 3×4 (iv) 2×3

3. We know that a matrix of order 2×2 has 4 entries.

Since, each entry has 3 choices, namely 1, 2 or 3, therefore number of required matrices

$$= 3\times3\times3\times3 = 3^4 = 81$$

4. Solve as Example 4.

Ans. 1×14, 14×1, 2×7, 7×2, 1×17, 17×1

5. Given, $a_{ij} = \dfrac{|i-j|}{2}$

$$\therefore \quad a_{23} = \frac{|2-3|}{2} = \frac{|-1|}{2} = \frac{1}{2} \qquad [\text{put } i = 2 \text{ and } j = 3]$$

6. Solve as Question 5. **Ans.** $\dfrac{7}{2}$

7. Let A be a 3×4 matrix.

$$\text{Then, } A = \begin{bmatrix} a_{11} & a_{12} & a_{13} & a_{14} \\ a_{21} & a_{22} & a_{23} & a_{24} \\ a_{31} & a_{32} & a_{33} & a_{34} \end{bmatrix}_{3\times4} \qquad \text{...(i)}$$

Here, $a_{ij} = \dfrac{1}{2}|-3i + j|$

$$\therefore \quad a_{11} = \frac{1}{2}|-3+1| = 1, a_{12} = \frac{1}{2}|-3+2| = \frac{1}{2},$$

$$a_{13} = \frac{1}{2}|-3+3| = 0, a_{14} = \frac{1}{2}|-3+4| = \frac{1}{2},$$

$$a_{21} = \frac{1}{2}|-6+1| = \frac{5}{2}, a_{22} = \frac{1}{2}|-6+2| = 2,$$

$$a_{23} = \frac{1}{2}|-6+3| = \frac{3}{2}, a_{24} = \frac{1}{2}|-6+4| = 1,$$

$$a_{31} = \frac{1}{2}|-9+1| = 4, a_{32} = \frac{1}{2}|-9+2| = \frac{7}{2},$$

$$a_{33} = \frac{1}{2}|-9+3| = 3 \text{ and } a_{34} = \frac{1}{2}|-9+4| = \frac{5}{2}$$

On putting the values in Eq. (i), we get the required

$$\text{matrix, i.e. } A = \begin{bmatrix} 1 & 1/2 & 0 & 1/2 \\ 5/2 & 2 & 3/2 & 1 \\ 4 & 7/2 & 3 & 5/2 \end{bmatrix}_{3\times4}$$

8. Solve as Question 7. **Ans.** $\begin{bmatrix} 1 & 9 \\ \frac{}{2} & \frac{}{2} \\ 0 & 2 \end{bmatrix}$

9. Clearly, $A = \begin{bmatrix} a_{11} & a_{12} \\ a_{21} & a_{22} \end{bmatrix}$

Now, $a_{11} = 0$, $a_{12} = 2$, $a_{21} = 2$ and $a_{22} = 0$

$$\left[\because a_{ij} = \begin{cases} 2, \text{ for } i \neq j \\ 0, \text{ for } i = j \end{cases}\right]$$

$$\therefore \quad A = \begin{bmatrix} 0 & 2 \\ 2 & 0 \end{bmatrix}$$

10. (i) $k = 6$ (ii) $k = 0, 1$ (iii) $k = 1$

11. Given, $\begin{bmatrix} xy & 4 \\ z+6 & x+y \end{bmatrix} = \begin{bmatrix} 8 & w \\ 0 & 6 \end{bmatrix}$

On comparing the corresponding elements, we get

$$xy = 8, 4 = w, \; z+6 = 0 \Rightarrow z = -6 \text{ and } x+y = 6$$

Clearly, $x+y+z = 6+(-6)$ $[\because x+y = 6 \text{ and } z = -6]$

$$= 0$$

12. Similar as Example 9. **Ans.** 0

13. Similar as Example 9. **Ans.** $x + y = 3$

14. Similar as Example 9. **Ans.** $a = 1, b = 2, c = 3$ and $d = 4$

15. Here, two matrices are equal.

Therefore, equating the corresponding elements of two matrices, we get

$$x + y + z = 9 \qquad \text{...(i)}$$

$$x + z = 5 \qquad \text{...(ii)}$$

$$\text{and} \quad y + z = 7 \qquad \text{...(iii)}$$

On solving Eqs. (i) and (ii), we get $y = 9 - 5 = 4$

On putting $y = 4$ in Eq. (iii), we get

$$4 + z = 7 \Rightarrow z = 7 - 4 = 3$$

On putting $z = 3$ in Eq. (ii), we get

$$x + 3 = 5 \Rightarrow x = 5 - 3 = 2$$

Hence, $x = 2$, $y = 4$ and $z = 3$.

16. Solve as Question 15. **Ans.** $x = 2$, $y = 1$ and $z = 0$

17. Consider, $A = B$, then we get

$$\begin{bmatrix} 2x+1 & 3y \\ 0 & y^2-5y \end{bmatrix} = \begin{bmatrix} x+3 & y^2+2 \\ 0 & -6 \end{bmatrix}$$

$$\Rightarrow \quad 2x+1 = x+3 \qquad \text{...(i)}$$

$$3y = y^2 + 2 \qquad \text{...(ii)}$$

$$\text{and} \quad y^2 - 5y = -6 \qquad \text{...(iii)}$$

[$\because$ corresponding elements of two equal matrices are equal]

Now, from Eq. (i), we get

$$2x+1 = x+3 \Rightarrow 2x - x = 3-1 \Rightarrow x = 2$$

Now, from Eq. (ii), we get

$$y^2 - 3y + 2 = 0 \Rightarrow (y-1)(y-2) = 0 \Rightarrow y = 1 \text{ or } y = 2$$

Now, from Eq. (iii), we get

$$y^2 - 5y + 6 = 0 \Rightarrow (y-2)(y-3) = 0 \Rightarrow y = 2 \text{ or } y = 3$$

Hence, $x = 2$ and $y = 2$ $[\because y = 1, 2 \text{ and } y = 2, 3 \Rightarrow y = 2]$

18. **Hint** Use the identity $(x-y)^2 = (x+y)^2 - 4xy$.

Ans. $x = 4, y = 2$ or $x = 2, y = 4$

19. Solve as Question 15. **Ans.** $a = 1, b = 1, c = 1$ and $d = 1$

Addition, Subtraction and Scalar Multiplication of Matrices

Here, we will discuss certain operations on matrices namely, addition of matrices, multiplication of a matrix by a scalar and difference of matrices.

Addition of Matrices

Two or more matrices can be added only if they have same order. The addition matrix of two or more matrix is simply the matrix obtained by adding the corresponding elements of different matrix.

e.g. $A=\begin{bmatrix}2 & 3\\ 0 & -1\end{bmatrix}, B=\begin{bmatrix}6 & 9\\ -4 & 1\end{bmatrix}$,

then $A+B=\begin{bmatrix}2+6 & 3+9\\ 0+(-4) & -1+1\end{bmatrix}=\begin{bmatrix}8 & 12\\ -4 & 0\end{bmatrix}$

In general, let $A=[a_{ij}]$ and $B=[b_{ij}]$ be the two matrices of the same order, say $m\times n$. Then, the sum of two matrices A and B is defined as a matrix $C=[c_{ij}]_{m\times n}$, where $c_{ij}=a_{ij}+b_{ij}$ for all possible values of i and j.

Note If A and B are not of the same order, then $A+B$ is not defined.

EXAMPLE 1. If $A=\begin{bmatrix}3 & 1\\ 2 & 4\end{bmatrix}$ and $B=\begin{bmatrix}3 & 4 & 5\\ 1 & 3 & 2\end{bmatrix}$, then find $A+B$.

Sol. Given, matrices are $A=\begin{bmatrix}3 & 1\\ 2 & 4\end{bmatrix}$ and $B=\begin{bmatrix}3 & 4 & 5\\ 1 & 3 & 2\end{bmatrix}$.

Then, A and B are matrices of order 2×2 and 2×3 respectively.

So, A and B are not comparable.

Hence, $A+B$ is not defined.

EXAMPLE 2. Find the sum of two matrices A and B, if

$A=\begin{bmatrix}1 & \sqrt{2}\\ 3 & 2\end{bmatrix}$ and $B=\begin{bmatrix}3 & -\sqrt{2}\\ 4 & 1\end{bmatrix}$.

Sol. Given, matrices are $A=\begin{bmatrix}1 & \sqrt{2}\\ 3 & 2\end{bmatrix}$ and $B=\begin{bmatrix}3 & -\sqrt{2}\\ 4 & 1\end{bmatrix}$

Here, we see that both matrices are of same order, therefore sum of A and B is defined.

Now, $A+B=\begin{bmatrix}1 & \sqrt{2}\\ 3 & 2\end{bmatrix}+\begin{bmatrix}3 & -\sqrt{2}\\ 4 & 1\end{bmatrix}$

$=\begin{bmatrix}1+3 & \sqrt{2}-\sqrt{2}\\ 3+4 & 2+1\end{bmatrix}$ [$\because$ adding corresponding elements of A and B]

$=\begin{bmatrix}4 & 0\\ 7 & 3\end{bmatrix}$

Multiplication of a Matrix by a Scalar

When a matrix is multiplied by a scalar (a number) then it is called scalar multiplication of matrix. Here, each element of matrix is multiplied by the given scalar.

e.g. If $A=\begin{bmatrix}7 & 18\\ -1 & 3\end{bmatrix}$ and $k=3$.

Then, $kA=3A=3\begin{bmatrix}7 & 18\\ -1 & 3\end{bmatrix}$

$=\begin{bmatrix}3\times 7 & 3\times 18\\ 3\times(-1) & 3\times 3\end{bmatrix}=\begin{bmatrix}21 & 54\\ -3 & 9\end{bmatrix}$

In general, Let $A=[a_{ij}]_{m\times n}$ be a matrix and k be a scalar, then kA is a another matrix which is obtained by multiplying each element of A by the scalar k.

Thus, $kA=k[a_{ij}]_{m\times n}=[k(a_{ij})]_{m\times n}$

i.e. (i, j)th element of kA is ka_{ij} for all possible values of i and j.

EXAMPLE 3. If $A=\begin{bmatrix}1 & 0 & 0\\ 0 & -1 & 0\\ 0 & 0 & 2\end{bmatrix}$ and $B=\begin{bmatrix}2 & 0 & 0\\ 0 & 3 & 0\\ 0 & 0 & -1\end{bmatrix}$, then find $3A+4B$.

Sol. We have, $A=\begin{bmatrix}1 & 0 & 0\\ 0 & -1 & 0\\ 0 & 0 & 2\end{bmatrix}$ and $B=\begin{bmatrix}2 & 0 & 0\\ 0 & 3 & 0\\ 0 & 0 & -1\end{bmatrix}$

Now, $3A+4B=3\begin{bmatrix}1 & 0 & 0\\ 0 & -1 & 0\\ 0 & 0 & 2\end{bmatrix}+4\begin{bmatrix}2 & 0 & 0\\ 0 & 3 & 0\\ 0 & 0 & -1\end{bmatrix}$

$=\begin{bmatrix}3 & 0 & 0\\ 0 & -3 & 0\\ 0 & 0 & 6\end{bmatrix}+\begin{bmatrix}8 & 0 & 0\\ 0 & 12 & 0\\ 0 & 0 & -4\end{bmatrix}$

$=\begin{bmatrix}3+8 & 0 & 0\\ 0 & -3+12 & 0\\ 0 & 0 & 6-4\end{bmatrix}=\begin{bmatrix}11 & 0 & 0\\ 0 & 9 & 0\\ 0 & 0 & 2\end{bmatrix}$

EXAMPLE 4. If $A+B=\begin{bmatrix}1 & 0\\ 1 & 1\end{bmatrix}$ and $A-2B=\begin{bmatrix}-1 & 1\\ 0 & -1\end{bmatrix}$, then find the value of A.

Sol. We have, $A+B=\begin{bmatrix}1 & 0\\ 1 & 1\end{bmatrix}\Rightarrow B=\begin{bmatrix}1 & 0\\ 1 & 1\end{bmatrix}-A$

$\because \quad A-2B=\begin{bmatrix}-1 & 1\\ 0 & -1\end{bmatrix}$

$$\therefore \quad A - 2\left(\begin{bmatrix} 1 & 0 \\ 1 & 1 \end{bmatrix} - A\right) = \begin{bmatrix} -1 & 1 \\ 0 & -1 \end{bmatrix}$$

$$\Rightarrow \quad 3A = \begin{bmatrix} -1 & 1 \\ 0 & -1 \end{bmatrix} + 2\begin{bmatrix} 1 & 0 \\ 1 & 1 \end{bmatrix} = \begin{bmatrix} 1 & 1 \\ 2 & 1 \end{bmatrix}$$

$$\therefore \quad A = \frac{1}{3}\begin{bmatrix} 1 & 1 \\ 2 & 1 \end{bmatrix} = \begin{bmatrix} 1/3 & 1/3 \\ 2/3 & 1/3 \end{bmatrix}$$

EXAMPLE 5. If $2\begin{bmatrix} 1 & 3 \\ 0 & x \end{bmatrix} + \begin{bmatrix} y & 0 \\ 1 & 2 \end{bmatrix} = \begin{bmatrix} 5 & 6 \\ 1 & 8 \end{bmatrix}$, then find the value of $x + y$.

Sol. Given, $2\begin{bmatrix} 1 & 3 \\ 0 & x \end{bmatrix} + \begin{bmatrix} y & 0 \\ 1 & 2 \end{bmatrix} = \begin{bmatrix} 5 & 6 \\ 1 & 8 \end{bmatrix}$

$$\Rightarrow \quad \begin{bmatrix} 2 & 6 \\ 0 & 2x \end{bmatrix} + \begin{bmatrix} y & 0 \\ 1 & 2 \end{bmatrix} = \begin{bmatrix} 5 & 6 \\ 1 & 8 \end{bmatrix}$$

$$\Rightarrow \quad \begin{bmatrix} 2+y & 6+0 \\ 0+1 & 2x+2 \end{bmatrix} = \begin{bmatrix} 5 & 6 \\ 1 & 8 \end{bmatrix}$$

Comparing the corresponding elements, we get

$$2 + y = 5 \text{ and } 2x + 2 = 8$$

$$\Rightarrow \quad y = 5 - 2 = 3 \text{ and } 2x = 8 - 2$$

$$\Rightarrow \quad y = 3 \text{ and } x = \frac{6}{2} = 3$$

$$\therefore \quad x + y = 3 + 3 = 6$$

Negative of a Matrix

The negative of a matrix is represented by $-A$. The negative of a matrix is obtained by multiplying each of its element by -1.

e.g. Let $A = \begin{bmatrix} 1 & 3 \\ -2 & 4 \end{bmatrix}$, then $-A = (-1)A = \begin{bmatrix} -1 & -3 \\ 2 & -4 \end{bmatrix}$

Difference (or Subtraction) of Matrices

Difference of two matrices is simply the matrix whose elements are the difference of the corresponding elements of two matrices.

e.g. $\quad A = \begin{bmatrix} 1 & 2 \\ 3 & 4 \end{bmatrix}, B = \begin{bmatrix} 4 & 3 \\ 2 & 1 \end{bmatrix}$,

then $B - A = \begin{bmatrix} 4-1 & 3-2 \\ 2-3 & 1-4 \end{bmatrix} = \begin{bmatrix} 3 & 1 \\ -1 & -3 \end{bmatrix}$

In general, let $A = [a_{ij}]$ and $B = [b_{ij}]$ be the two matrices of the same order (say $m \times n$), then the difference of these matrices, $A - B$ is defined as a matrix $D = [d_{ij}]$, where $d_{ij} = a_{ij} - b_{ij}$ for all values of i and j.

In other words, $D = A - B = A + (-1)B$

i.e. $D =$ The sum of the matrix A and the matrix $(-B)$.

e.g. Let $A = \begin{bmatrix} a & b \\ c & d \end{bmatrix}$ and $B = \begin{bmatrix} e & f \\ g & h \end{bmatrix}$

Then, $A - B = A + (-1)B = \begin{bmatrix} a & b \\ c & d \end{bmatrix} + (-1)\begin{bmatrix} e & f \\ g & h \end{bmatrix}$

$$= \begin{bmatrix} a & b \\ c & d \end{bmatrix} + \begin{bmatrix} -e & -f \\ -g & -h \end{bmatrix} = \begin{bmatrix} a-e & b-f \\ c-g & d-h \end{bmatrix}$$

EXAMPLE 6. If $A = \begin{bmatrix} 4 & 4 \\ 2 & 7 \end{bmatrix}$, $B = \begin{bmatrix} 1 & 2 \\ -1 & 3 \end{bmatrix}$ and $C = \begin{bmatrix} 1 & 4 \\ 3 & -5 \end{bmatrix}$, then find $A - B - C$.

Sol. Here, A, B and C are the three matrices of same order 2×2.

Now, $A - B - C = A + (-1)B + (-1)C$

$$= \begin{bmatrix} 4 & 4 \\ 2 & 7 \end{bmatrix} + (-1)\begin{bmatrix} 1 & 2 \\ -1 & 3 \end{bmatrix} + (-1)\begin{bmatrix} 1 & 4 \\ 3 & -5 \end{bmatrix}$$

$$= \begin{bmatrix} 4 & 4 \\ 2 & 7 \end{bmatrix} + \begin{bmatrix} -1 & -2 \\ 1 & -3 \end{bmatrix} + \begin{bmatrix} -1 & -4 \\ -3 & 5 \end{bmatrix}$$

$$= \begin{bmatrix} 4-1-1 & 4-2-4 \\ 2+1-3 & 7-3+5 \end{bmatrix} = \begin{bmatrix} 2 & -2 \\ 0 & 9 \end{bmatrix}$$

EXAMPLE 7. Two farmers Ramkishan and Gurucharan Singh cultivate only three varieties of rice namely Basmati, Permal and Navara. The sales (in ₹) of these varieties of rice by both the farmers in the months of September and October are given by the matrices A and B.

September sales (in ₹)

$$A = \begin{array}{c} \begin{matrix} \text{Basmati} & \text{Permal} & \text{Navara} \end{matrix} \\ \begin{bmatrix} 10000 & 20000 & 30000 \\ 50000 & 30000 & 10000 \end{bmatrix} \end{array} \begin{matrix} \text{Ramkishan} \\ \text{Gurucharan Singh} \end{matrix}$$

October sales (in ₹)

$$B = \begin{array}{c} \begin{matrix} \text{Basmati} & \text{Permal} & \text{Navara} \end{matrix} \\ \begin{bmatrix} 5000 & 10000 & 6000 \\ 20000 & 10000 & 10000 \end{bmatrix} \end{array} \begin{matrix} \text{Ramkishan} \\ \text{Gurucharan Singh} \end{matrix}$$

(i) Find the combined sales in September and October for each farmer in each variety.

(ii) Find the decrease in sales from September to October.

(iii) If both farmers receive 2% profit on gross sales, then compute the profit for each farmer and for each variety sold in October.

Sol. (i) Combined sales in September and October for each farmer in each variety is given by

$$A + B = \begin{bmatrix} 10000 & 20000 & 30000 \\ 50000 & 30000 & 10000 \end{bmatrix} + \begin{bmatrix} 5000 & 10000 & 6000 \\ 20000 & 10000 & 10000 \end{bmatrix}$$

$$= \begin{bmatrix} 15000 & 30000 & 36000 \\ 70000 & 40000 & 20000 \end{bmatrix} \begin{matrix} \text{Ramkishan} \\ \text{Gurucharan Singh} \end{matrix}$$
(columns: Basmati, Permal, Navara)

(ii) Changes in sales from September to October is given by

$$A - B = \begin{bmatrix} 10000 & 20000 & 30000 \\ 50000 & 30000 & 10000 \end{bmatrix} - \begin{bmatrix} 5000 & 10000 & 6000 \\ 20000 & 10000 & 10000 \end{bmatrix}$$

$$= \begin{bmatrix} 5000 & 10000 & 24000 \\ 30000 & 20000 & 0 \end{bmatrix} \begin{matrix} \text{Ramkishan} \\ \text{Gurucharan Singh} \end{matrix}$$
(columns: Basmati, Permal, Navara)

(iii) 2% of $B = \frac{2}{100} \times B = 0.02 \times B$

$$= 0.02 \begin{bmatrix} 5000 & 10000 & 6000 \\ 20000 & 10000 & 10000 \end{bmatrix} \begin{matrix} \text{Ramkishan} \\ \text{Gurucharan Singh} \end{matrix}$$
(columns: Basmati, Permal, Navara)

$$= \begin{bmatrix} 100 & 200 & 120 \\ 400 & 200 & 200 \end{bmatrix} \begin{matrix} \text{Ramkishan} \\ \text{Gurucharan Singh} \end{matrix}$$
(columns: Basmati, Permal, Navara)

[multiply each element by 0.02]

Hence, the profits earned by Ramkishan in the sale of each variety of rice are ₹ 100, ₹ 200, ₹ 120 respectively and profits earned by Gurucharan Singh in the sale of each variety of rice are ₹ 400, ₹ 200, ₹ 200 respectively.

Properties of Matrix Addition

Let $A = [a_{ij}]$, $B = [b_{ij}]$ and $C = [c_{ij}]$ be any three matrices of same order $m \times n$. Then, we have the following properties

(i) **Commutative Law** Matrix addition is commutative,

i.e. $A + B = [a_{ij}] + [b_{ij}] = [a_{ij} + b_{ij}] = [b_{ij} + a_{ij}]$
$= [b_{ij}] + [a_{ij}] = B + A$

(ii) **Associative Law** Matrix addition is associative,

i.e. $A + (B + C) = (A + B) + C$

(iii) **Existence of Additive Identity** Let O be a zero matrix of order $m \times n$, then $A + O = O + A = A$.

So, O is the additive identity for matrix addition.

(iv) **Existence of Additive Inverse** Let A be a matrix, then $(-A)$ is another matrix of same order $m \times n$, such that $A + (-A) = O = (-A) + A$.

So, $(-A)$ or negative of A is the additive inverse of A.

EXAMPLE 8. If $A = \begin{bmatrix} 2 & 2 \\ -3 & 1 \\ 4 & 0 \end{bmatrix}$, $B = \begin{bmatrix} 6 & 2 \\ 1 & 3 \\ 0 & 4 \end{bmatrix}$ and $C = \begin{bmatrix} -8 & -4 \\ 2 & -4 \\ -4 & -4 \end{bmatrix}$, then

(i) verify the commutative law with respect to addition, i.e. verify $A + B = B + A$.

(ii) verify the associative law with respect to addition, i.e. verify $A + (B + C) = (A + B) + C$.

(iii) find the additive inverse of matrix A.

Sol. Given, matrices are

$$A = \begin{bmatrix} 2 & 2 \\ -3 & 1 \\ 4 & 0 \end{bmatrix}, B = \begin{bmatrix} 6 & 2 \\ 1 & 3 \\ 0 & 4 \end{bmatrix} \text{ and } C = \begin{bmatrix} -8 & -4 \\ 2 & -4 \\ -4 & -4 \end{bmatrix}.$$

Now,

(i) $A + B = \begin{bmatrix} 2 & 2 \\ -3 & 1 \\ 4 & 0 \end{bmatrix} + \begin{bmatrix} 6 & 2 \\ 1 & 3 \\ 0 & 4 \end{bmatrix} = \begin{bmatrix} 2+6 & 2+2 \\ -3+1 & 1+3 \\ 4+0 & 0+4 \end{bmatrix}$

$$= \begin{bmatrix} 8 & 4 \\ -2 & 4 \\ 4 & 4 \end{bmatrix} \quad \text{...(i)}$$

and $B + A = \begin{bmatrix} 6 & 2 \\ 1 & 3 \\ 0 & 4 \end{bmatrix} + \begin{bmatrix} 2 & 2 \\ -3 & 1 \\ 4 & 0 \end{bmatrix}$

$$= \begin{bmatrix} 6+2 & 2+2 \\ 1-3 & 3+1 \\ 0+4 & 4+0 \end{bmatrix} = \begin{bmatrix} 8 & 4 \\ -2 & 4 \\ 4 & 4 \end{bmatrix}$$

Thus, $A + B = B + A$.

Hence, commutative law verified.

(ii) $A + (B + C) = \begin{bmatrix} 2 & 2 \\ -3 & 1 \\ 4 & 0 \end{bmatrix} + \left(\begin{bmatrix} 6 & 2 \\ 1 & 3 \\ 0 & 4 \end{bmatrix} + \begin{bmatrix} -8 & -4 \\ 2 & -4 \\ -4 & -4 \end{bmatrix} \right)$

$$= \begin{bmatrix} 2 & 2 \\ -3 & 1 \\ 4 & 0 \end{bmatrix} + \begin{bmatrix} 6-8 & 2-4 \\ 1+2 & 3-4 \\ 0-4 & 4-4 \end{bmatrix}$$

$$= \begin{bmatrix} 2 & 2 \\ -3 & 1 \\ 4 & 0 \end{bmatrix} + \begin{bmatrix} -2 & -2 \\ 3 & -1 \\ -4 & 0 \end{bmatrix}$$

$$= \begin{bmatrix} 2-2 & 2-2 \\ -3+3 & 1-1 \\ 4-4 & 0+0 \end{bmatrix} = \begin{bmatrix} 0 & 0 \\ 0 & 0 \\ 0 & 0 \end{bmatrix}$$

$$\text{and } (A+B)+C = \begin{bmatrix} 8 & 4 \\ -2 & 4 \\ 4 & 4 \end{bmatrix} + \begin{bmatrix} -8 & -4 \\ 2 & -4 \\ -4 & -4 \end{bmatrix} \text{ [from Eq. (i)]}$$

$$= \begin{bmatrix} 8-8 & 4-4 \\ -2+2 & 4-4 \\ 4-4 & 4-4 \end{bmatrix} = \begin{bmatrix} 0 & 0 \\ 0 & 0 \\ 0 & 0 \end{bmatrix}$$

Thus, $A+(B+C)=(A+B)+C$.

Hence, associative law verified.

(iii) We know that additive inverse of A is $(-1)A$.

$$\therefore \quad (-1)A = (-1)\begin{bmatrix} 2 & 2 \\ -3 & 1 \\ 4 & 0 \end{bmatrix} = \begin{bmatrix} -2 & -2 \\ 3 & -1 \\ -4 & 0 \end{bmatrix}$$

[multiplying each element by (−1)]

Properties of Scalar Multiplication

Let A and B be the two matrices of same order. Then,

(i) $k(A+B) = kA + kB$, where k is a scalar.

(ii) $(k_1 + k_2)A = k_1 A + k_2 A$, where k_1 and k_2 are scalars.

(iii) $(kl)A = k(lA) = l(kA)$, where l and k are scalars.

EXAMPLE 9. Let A and B be two matrices such that $A = \begin{bmatrix} 2 & 1 \\ -1 & 0 \\ 2 & 5 \end{bmatrix}$ and $B = \begin{bmatrix} -1 & 2 \\ 0 & -1 \\ 3 & 2 \end{bmatrix}$, then verify the following results.

(i) $3(A+B) = 3A+3B$ (ii) $(5+7)A = 5A+7A$

Sol. Given, matrices are $A = \begin{bmatrix} 2 & 1 \\ -1 & 0 \\ 2 & 5 \end{bmatrix}$ and $B = \begin{bmatrix} -1 & 2 \\ 0 & -1 \\ 3 & 2 \end{bmatrix}$

$$\text{(i) LHS} = 3(A+B) = 3\left(\begin{bmatrix} 2 & 1 \\ -1 & 0 \\ 2 & 5 \end{bmatrix} + \begin{bmatrix} -1 & 2 \\ 0 & -1 \\ 3 & 2 \end{bmatrix}\right)$$

$$= 3\begin{bmatrix} 2-1 & 1+2 \\ -1+0 & 0-1 \\ 2+3 & 5+2 \end{bmatrix} = 3\begin{bmatrix} 1 & 3 \\ -1 & -1 \\ 5 & 7 \end{bmatrix} = \begin{bmatrix} 3 & 9 \\ -3 & -3 \\ 15 & 21 \end{bmatrix}$$

[multiplying each element by 3]

and RHS $= 3A + 3B$

$$= 3\begin{bmatrix} 2 & 1 \\ -1 & 0 \\ 2 & 5 \end{bmatrix} + 3\begin{bmatrix} -1 & 2 \\ 0 & -1 \\ 3 & 2 \end{bmatrix} = \begin{bmatrix} 6 & 3 \\ -3 & 0 \\ 6 & 15 \end{bmatrix} + \begin{bmatrix} -3 & 6 \\ 0 & -3 \\ 9 & 6 \end{bmatrix}$$

[multiplying each element by 3]

$$= \begin{bmatrix} 6-3 & 3+6 \\ -3+0 & 0-3 \\ 6+9 & 15+6 \end{bmatrix} = \begin{bmatrix} 3 & 9 \\ -3 & -3 \\ 15 & 21 \end{bmatrix}$$

Thus, LHS = RHS **Hence verified.**

(ii) LHS $= (5+7)A = 12A$

$$= 12\begin{bmatrix} 2 & 1 \\ -1 & 0 \\ 2 & 5 \end{bmatrix} = \begin{bmatrix} 24 & 12 \\ -12 & 0 \\ 24 & 60 \end{bmatrix}$$

[multiplying each element by 12]

and RHS $= 5A + 7A$

$$= 5\begin{bmatrix} 2 & 1 \\ -1 & 0 \\ 2 & 5 \end{bmatrix} + 7\begin{bmatrix} 2 & 1 \\ -1 & 0 \\ 2 & 5 \end{bmatrix} = \begin{bmatrix} 10 & 5 \\ -5 & 0 \\ 10 & 25 \end{bmatrix} + \begin{bmatrix} 14 & 7 \\ -7 & 0 \\ 14 & 35 \end{bmatrix}$$

$$= \begin{bmatrix} 10+14 & 5+7 \\ -5-7 & 0 \\ 10+14 & 25+35 \end{bmatrix} = \begin{bmatrix} 24 & 12 \\ -12 & 0 \\ 24 & 60 \end{bmatrix}$$

Thus, LHS = RHS **Hence verified.**

EXAMPLE 10. If $A = \begin{bmatrix} 8 & 0 \\ 4 & -2 \\ 3 & 6 \end{bmatrix}$ and $B = \begin{bmatrix} 2 & -2 \\ 4 & 2 \\ -5 & 1 \end{bmatrix}$, then find the matrix X, such that $2A + 3X = 5B$.

Sol. Given, $A = \begin{bmatrix} 8 & 0 \\ 4 & -2 \\ 3 & 6 \end{bmatrix}$ and $B = \begin{bmatrix} 2 & -2 \\ 4 & 2 \\ -5 & 1 \end{bmatrix}$

Also given, $2A + 3X = 5B \Rightarrow 3X = 5B - 2A$

$$\Rightarrow X = \frac{1}{3}[5B - 2A] = \frac{1}{3}\left\{5\begin{bmatrix} 2 & -2 \\ 4 & 2 \\ -5 & 1 \end{bmatrix} - 2\begin{bmatrix} 8 & 0 \\ 4 & -2 \\ 3 & 6 \end{bmatrix}\right\}$$

$$= \frac{1}{3}\left\{\begin{bmatrix} 10 & -10 \\ 20 & 10 \\ -25 & 5 \end{bmatrix} + \begin{bmatrix} -16 & 0 \\ -8 & 4 \\ -6 & -12 \end{bmatrix}\right\}$$

$$= \frac{1}{3}\begin{bmatrix} 10-16 & -10+0 \\ 20-8 & 10+4 \\ -25-6 & 5-12 \end{bmatrix}$$

$$= \frac{1}{3}\begin{bmatrix} -6 & -10 \\ 12 & 14 \\ -31 & -7 \end{bmatrix}$$

$$\Rightarrow X = \begin{bmatrix} -2 & -\frac{10}{3} \\ 4 & \frac{14}{3} \\ -\frac{31}{3} & -\frac{7}{3} \end{bmatrix}, \text{ which is the required matrix } X.$$

Topic Practice 2

1 Two matrices are defined as

$$P=\begin{bmatrix}1 & 4\\ -1 & 8\end{bmatrix} \text{ and } Q=\begin{bmatrix}2 & -3\\ -1 & 5\end{bmatrix}$$

Evaluate

(i) $2P$ (ii) $-Q$ (iii) $3Q$

(iv) $2P+Q$ (v) $3P+2Q$ (vi) $Q-4P$

2 If $A=\begin{bmatrix}1 & 1 & 2\\ 0 & -6 & 9\end{bmatrix}$, $B=\begin{bmatrix}1 & 0\\ 2 & 1\\ 0 & -1\end{bmatrix}$, $C=\begin{bmatrix}-3 & -5\\ 0 & 1\\ 3 & 2\end{bmatrix}$,

evaluate, where possible

(i) $-A$ (ii) $-2A$ (iii) $B+C$

(iv) $2B$ (v) $2B-C$ (vi) $3(B+C)$

3 If $X=\begin{bmatrix}1 & 1 & 2\\ 0 & 1 & 4\\ 0 & 2 & 1\end{bmatrix}$, $Y=\begin{bmatrix}-1 & -2 & 3\\ 2 & 0 & 1\\ 2 & 0 & -4\end{bmatrix}$, evaluate

(i) $3X$ (ii) $2Y$ (iii) $X+Y$

(iv) $X-Y$ (v) $3X+2Y$ (vi) $2Y-X$

Directions (Q. Nos. 4-5) *Find the value of $x-y$.*

4 $2\begin{bmatrix}3 & 4\\ 5 & x\end{bmatrix}+\begin{bmatrix}1 & y\\ 0 & 1\end{bmatrix}=\begin{bmatrix}7 & 0\\ 10 & 5\end{bmatrix}$

5 $\begin{bmatrix}1 & 0\\ y & 5\end{bmatrix}+2\begin{bmatrix}x & 0\\ 1 & -2\end{bmatrix}=I$, where I is a 2×2 unit matrix.

Directions (Q. Nos. 6-7) *Find the value of x.*

6 $x\begin{bmatrix}2\\ 3\end{bmatrix}+y\begin{bmatrix}-1\\ 1\end{bmatrix}=\begin{bmatrix}10\\ 5\end{bmatrix}$

7 $3x-y=\begin{bmatrix}5 & 0\\ 1 & 1\end{bmatrix}$ and $y=\begin{bmatrix}4 & 3\\ 2 & 5\end{bmatrix}$.

8 If $A=\text{diag}[2,-1,\ 3]$ and $B=\text{diag}[3,\ 0,-1]$, then find $4A+2B$.

9 If $X=\begin{bmatrix}3 & 1 & -1\\ 5 & -2 & -3\end{bmatrix}$ and $Y=\begin{bmatrix}2 & 1 & -1\\ 7 & 2 & 4\end{bmatrix}$, then find matrix Z, such that $X+Y+Z$ is a zero matrix.

10 Find the values of x and y from the following matrix equation.

$$2\begin{bmatrix}x & 5\\ 7 & y-3\end{bmatrix}+\begin{bmatrix}3 & -4\\ 1 & 2\end{bmatrix}=\begin{bmatrix}7 & 6\\ 15 & 14\end{bmatrix}$$

11 Find x, y, z and t, if $2\begin{bmatrix}x & z\\ y & t\end{bmatrix}+3\begin{bmatrix}1 & -1\\ 0 & 2\end{bmatrix}=3\begin{bmatrix}3 & 5\\ 4 & 6\end{bmatrix}$.

12 Solve the matrix equation $\begin{bmatrix}x^2\\ y^2\end{bmatrix}-3\begin{bmatrix}x\\ 2y\end{bmatrix}=\begin{bmatrix}-2\\ 9\end{bmatrix}$.

13 Find X and Y, if

$$2X+3Y=\begin{bmatrix}2 & 3\\ 4 & 0\end{bmatrix} \text{ and } 3X+2Y=\begin{bmatrix}2 & -2\\ -1 & 5\end{bmatrix}.$$

14 Find X and Y, if $X+Y=\begin{bmatrix}7 & 0\\ 2 & 5\end{bmatrix}$ and $X-Y=\begin{bmatrix}3 & 0\\ 0 & 3\end{bmatrix}$.

15 If $A=\begin{bmatrix}1 & 2 & -3\\ 5 & 0 & 2\\ 1 & -1 & 1\end{bmatrix}$, $B=\begin{bmatrix}3 & -1 & 2\\ 4 & 2 & 5\\ 2 & 0 & 3\end{bmatrix}$ and $C=\begin{bmatrix}4 & 1 & 2\\ 0 & 3 & 2\\ 1 & -2 & 3\end{bmatrix}$,

then compute $(A+B)$ and $(B-C)$.

Also, verify that $A+(B-C)=(A+B)-C$.

Hints & Solutions

1. (i) $\begin{bmatrix}2 & 8\\ -2 & 16\end{bmatrix}$ (ii) $\begin{bmatrix}-2 & 3\\ 1 & -5\end{bmatrix}$ (iii) $\begin{bmatrix}6 & -9\\ -3 & 15\end{bmatrix}$

(iv) $\begin{bmatrix}4 & 5\\ -3 & 21\end{bmatrix}$ (v) $\begin{bmatrix}7 & 6\\ -5 & 34\end{bmatrix}$ (vi) $\begin{bmatrix}-2 & -19\\ 3 & -27\end{bmatrix}$

2. (i) $\begin{bmatrix}-1 & -1 & -2\\ 0 & 6 & -9\end{bmatrix}$ (ii) $\begin{bmatrix}-2 & -2 & -4\\ 0 & 12 & -18\end{bmatrix}$ (iii) $\begin{bmatrix}-2 & -5\\ 2 & 2\\ 3 & 1\end{bmatrix}$

(iv) $\begin{bmatrix}2 & 0\\ 4 & 2\\ 0 & -2\end{bmatrix}$ (v) $\begin{bmatrix}5 & 5\\ 4 & 1\\ -3 & -4\end{bmatrix}$ (vi) $\begin{bmatrix}-6 & -15\\ 6 & 6\\ 9 & 3\end{bmatrix}$

3. (i) $\begin{bmatrix}3 & 3 & 6\\ 0 & 3 & 12\\ 0 & 6 & 3\end{bmatrix}$ (ii) $\begin{bmatrix}-2 & -4 & 6\\ 4 & 0 & 2\\ 4 & 0 & -8\end{bmatrix}$ (iii) $\begin{bmatrix}0 & -1 & 5\\ 2 & 1 & 5\\ 2 & 2 & -3\end{bmatrix}$

(iv) $\begin{bmatrix}2 & 3 & -1\\ -2 & 1 & 3\\ -2 & 2 & 5\end{bmatrix}$ (v) $\begin{bmatrix}1 & -1 & 12\\ 4 & 3 & 14\\ 4 & 6 & -5\end{bmatrix}$ (vi) $\begin{bmatrix}-3 & -5 & 4\\ 4 & -1 & -2\\ 4 & -2 & -9\end{bmatrix}$

4. Given, $2\begin{bmatrix}3 & 4\\ 5 & x\end{bmatrix}+\begin{bmatrix}1 & y\\ 0 & 1\end{bmatrix}=\begin{bmatrix}7 & 0\\ 10 & 5\end{bmatrix}$

$\Rightarrow \begin{bmatrix}6 & 8\\ 10 & 2x\end{bmatrix}+\begin{bmatrix}1 & y\\ 0 & 1\end{bmatrix}=\begin{bmatrix}7 & 0\\ 10 & 5\end{bmatrix}$

$\Rightarrow \begin{bmatrix}7 & 8+y\\ 10 & 2x+1\end{bmatrix}=\begin{bmatrix}7 & 0\\ 10 & 5\end{bmatrix}$

On comparing the corresponding elements, we get

$$8+y=0 \text{ and } 2x+1=5$$

$$\Rightarrow \quad y=-8 \text{ and } x=\frac{5-1}{2}=2$$

$$\therefore \quad x-y=2-(-8)=10$$

5. Solve as Question 4. **Ans.** 2

6. **Hint** Here, $2x-y=10$ ...(i)

and $3x+y=5$ ...(ii)

On adding Eqs. (i) and (ii), we get the required value.

Ans. 3

7. **Hint** $x=\frac{1}{3}\left\{\begin{bmatrix}5 & 0\\1 & 1\end{bmatrix}+y\right\}$

Ans. $x=\begin{bmatrix}3 & 1\\1 & 2\end{bmatrix}$

8. Similar as Example 3.

Hint $A=\begin{bmatrix}2 & 0 & 0\\0 & -1 & 0\\0 & 0 & 3\end{bmatrix}, B=\begin{bmatrix}3 & 0 & 0\\0 & 0 & 0\\0 & 0 & -1\end{bmatrix}$

Ans. $4A+2B=\text{diag}\,[14,-4,10]$

9. **Hint** $X+Y+Z=O \Rightarrow Z=-(X+Y)$

Ans. $\begin{bmatrix}-5 & -2 & 2\\-12 & 0 & -1\end{bmatrix}$

10. Similar as Example 5. **Ans.** $x=2$ and $y=9$

11. Similar as Example 5.

Ans. $x=3$, $y=6$, $z=9$ and $t=6$

12. **Hint** $\begin{bmatrix}x^2-3x\\y^2-6y\end{bmatrix}=\begin{bmatrix}-2\\9\end{bmatrix} \Rightarrow x^2-3x=-2$ and $y^2-6y=9$

Ans. $x=1, 2$ and $y=3\pm3\sqrt{2}$

13. We have, $2X+3Y=\begin{bmatrix}2 & 3\\4 & 0\end{bmatrix}$ ...(i)

and $3X+2Y=\begin{bmatrix}2 & -2\\-1 & 5\end{bmatrix}$ ...(ii)

On multiplying Eq. (i) by 2 and Eq. (ii) by 3, we get

$$4X+6Y=\begin{bmatrix}4 & 6\\8 & 0\end{bmatrix} \quad \text{...(iii)}$$

and $$9X+6Y=\begin{bmatrix}6 & -6\\-3 & 15\end{bmatrix} \quad \text{...(iv)}$$

On subtracting Eq. (iii) from Eq. (iv), we get

$$(9X+6Y)-(4X+6Y)=\begin{bmatrix}6 & -6\\-3 & 15\end{bmatrix}-\begin{bmatrix}4 & 6\\8 & 0\end{bmatrix}$$

$$\Rightarrow 9X+6Y-4X-6Y=\begin{bmatrix}6-4 & -6-6\\-3-8 & 15-0\end{bmatrix}$$

$$=\begin{bmatrix}2 & -12\\-11 & 15\end{bmatrix}$$

$$\Rightarrow X=\frac{1}{5}\begin{bmatrix}2 & -12\\-11 & 15\end{bmatrix}=\begin{bmatrix}\frac{2}{5} & \frac{-12}{5}\\\frac{-11}{5} & 3\end{bmatrix}$$

On substituting the value of X in Eq. (i), we get

$$2\begin{bmatrix}\frac{2}{5} & \frac{-12}{5}\\\frac{-11}{5} & 3\end{bmatrix}+3Y=\begin{bmatrix}2 & 3\\4 & 0\end{bmatrix}$$

$$\Rightarrow \begin{bmatrix}\frac{4}{5} & \frac{-24}{5}\\\frac{-22}{5} & 6\end{bmatrix}+3Y=\begin{bmatrix}2 & 3\\4 & 0\end{bmatrix}$$

$$\Rightarrow 3Y=\begin{bmatrix}2 & 3\\4 & 0\end{bmatrix}-\begin{bmatrix}\frac{4}{5} & \frac{-24}{5}\\\frac{-22}{5} & 6\end{bmatrix}$$

$$\Rightarrow Y=\frac{1}{3}\begin{bmatrix}2-\frac{4}{5} & 3+\frac{24}{5}\\4+\frac{22}{5} & 0-6\end{bmatrix}$$

$$\Rightarrow Y=\frac{1}{3}\begin{bmatrix}\frac{6}{5} & \frac{39}{5}\\\frac{42}{5} & -6\end{bmatrix}=\begin{bmatrix}\frac{2}{5} & \frac{13}{5}\\\frac{14}{5} & -2\end{bmatrix}$$

14. **Hint** Add and subtract the given equations.

Ans. $X=\begin{bmatrix}5 & 0\\1 & 4\end{bmatrix}$ and $Y=\begin{bmatrix}2 & 0\\1 & 1\end{bmatrix}$

15. Similar as Example 8.

Ans. $A+B=\begin{bmatrix}4 & 1 & -1\\9 & 2 & 7\\3 & -1 & 4\end{bmatrix}, B-C=\begin{bmatrix}-1 & -2 & 0\\4 & -1 & 3\\1 & 2 & 0\end{bmatrix}$

Multiplication of Matrices

The product AB of two matrices A and B is defined, if the number of columns of A is equal to the number of rows of B.

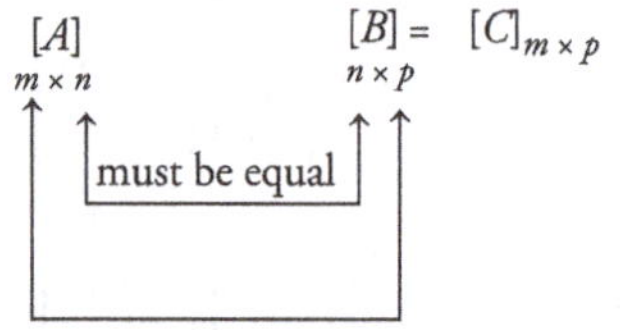

Order of product of matrix

Let $A = [a_{ij}]$ be the $m \times n$ matrix and $B = [b_{jk}]$ be the $n \times p$ matrix. Then, the product AB of the matrices A and B is matrix C of order $m \times p$.

To get the (i, k)th element c_{ik} of the matrix C, we take the ith row of A and kth column of B, multiply them elementwise and take the sum of all these products.

e.g. $[1 \quad 4]\begin{bmatrix} 3 \\ 2 \end{bmatrix} = [(1\times3)+(4\times2)] = [3+8] = [11]$

[multiplying row by column]

Method of Multiplying Two Matrices

Suppose, we have two matrices $A = [a_{ij}]_{m\times n}$ and $B = [b_{jk}]_{n\times p}$, then to multiply them (i.e. for finding AB), we use the following steps

I. First, write the given two matrices (A and B), then find the number of columns of first matrix A and number of rows of second matrix B. If both are same, i.e. equal, then go to next step, otherwise product is not possible.

II. Multiply first row (R_1) of A with first column (C_1) of B elementwise and take the sum of all these products. e.g. If $[a_{11} \quad a_{12} \quad a_{13}]$ is first row of A and $\begin{bmatrix} b_{11} \\ b_{21} \\ b_{31} \end{bmatrix}$ is first column of B, then their multiplication is $a_{11}b_{11} + a_{12}b_{21} + a_{13}b_{31}$.
Similarly, multiply first row (R_1) of A with second column (C_2) of B. Repeat this process to multiply each row of matrix A with each column of B.

III. From Step II, we get the elements of product matrix C, where c_{11} = Sum of products of elements of first row of A with corresponding elements of first column of B.
In general,
$$c_{ik} = a_{i1}b_{1k} + a_{i2}b_{2k} + \ldots + a_{in}b_{nk} = \sum_{j=1}^{n} a_{ij}\, b_{jk}.$$

IV. Now, write the matrix $C = [c_{ik}]_{m\times p}$, whose elements are obtained in Step III.
Thus, we get the required product of A and B.

Note

(i) If AB is defined, then BA need not be defined. Let $A = [a_{ij}]_{2\times3}$ and $B = [b_{jk}]_{3\times3}$, then $AB = [a_{ij}\, b_{jk}]_{2\times3}$ is defined but BA is not defined, since B has 3 rows while A has 2 columns.

(ii) If A is a matrix of order $m \times n$ and B is a matrix of order $k \times l$, then both AB and BA will be defined, if and only if $n = k$ and $l = m$. In particular, if both A and B are square matrices of the same order, then AB and BA both are defined.

EXAMPLE 1. If $A = \begin{bmatrix} 6 & 9 \\ 2 & 3 \end{bmatrix}$ and $B = \begin{bmatrix} 2 & 6 & 0 \\ 7 & 9 & 8 \end{bmatrix}$, then show that AB and BA both exist. Find AB and BA.

Sol. We have, $A = \begin{bmatrix} 6 & 9 \\ 2 & 3 \end{bmatrix}_{2\times2}$ and $B = \begin{bmatrix} 2 & 6 & 0 \\ 7 & 9 & 8 \end{bmatrix}_{2\times3}$

Here, number of columns of A = number of rows of B $= 2$

So, product AB of matrices A and B exists and its order will be 2×3.

Given, $A = \begin{bmatrix} 6 & 9 \\ 2 & 3 \end{bmatrix}$ — Row 1, Row 2 $\quad B = \begin{bmatrix} 2 & 6 & 0 \\ 7 & 9 & 8 \end{bmatrix}$ — Column 1, Column 2, Column 3

In the multiplication of two matrices, elements are multiplied in a row by column manner, i.e. all the elements of the first row of the first matrix and multiplied by the element of first column of the second matrix and added.

Ist row elements, Ist column elements, IInd column elements

$$A \times B = \begin{bmatrix} (6\times2)+(9\times7) & (6\times6)+(9\times9) & (6\times0)+(9\times8) \\ (2\times2)+(3\times7) & (2\times6)+(3\times9) & (2\times0)+(3\times8) \end{bmatrix}$$

IInd row elements, Ist column elements, Ist row elements

$$= \begin{bmatrix} 12+63 & 36+81 & 0+72 \\ 4+21 & 12+27 & 0+24 \end{bmatrix} = \begin{bmatrix} 75 & 117 & 72 \\ 25 & 39 & 24 \end{bmatrix}$$

which is the required product i.e. AB.

Again, B is a 2×3 matrix and A is a 2×2 matrix. So, the number of columns in B is not equal to the number of rows in A. So, BA does not exists.

EXAMPLE 2. If $A=[2 \quad -3 \quad 4]$,

$B=\begin{bmatrix}3\\2\\2\end{bmatrix}$, $X=[1 \quad 2 \quad 3]$ and $Y=\begin{bmatrix}2\\3\\4\end{bmatrix}$, then find $AB+XY$.

Sol. Given, $A=[2 \quad -3 \quad 4]$,

$$B=\begin{bmatrix}3\\2\\2\end{bmatrix},\ X=[1 \quad 2 \quad 3] \text{ and } Y=\begin{bmatrix}2\\3\\4\end{bmatrix}.$$

Now, $AB=[2 \quad -3 \quad 4]\begin{bmatrix}3\\2\\2\end{bmatrix}=[6-6+8]=[8]$

and $XY=[1 \quad 2 \quad 3]\begin{bmatrix}2\\3\\4\end{bmatrix}=[2+6+12]=[20]$

$\therefore \quad AB+XY=[8]+[20]=[28]$

EXAMPLE 3. Compute the product of

$$\begin{bmatrix}2&3&4\\3&4&5\\4&5&6\end{bmatrix} \text{ and } \begin{bmatrix}1&-3&5\\0&2&4\\3&0&5\end{bmatrix}.$$

Sol. Let $A=\begin{bmatrix}2&3&4\\3&4&5\\4&5&6\end{bmatrix}$ and $B=\begin{bmatrix}1&-3&5\\0&2&4\\3&0&5\end{bmatrix}$.

Here, number of columns of $A=$ number of rows of $B=3$, so AB is defined.

Now, $$AB=\begin{bmatrix}2&3&4\\3&4&5\\4&5&6\end{bmatrix}\begin{bmatrix}1&-3&5\\0&2&4\\3&0&5\end{bmatrix}$$

$$=\begin{bmatrix}2+0+12 & -6+6+0 & 10+12+20\\3+0+15 & -9+8+0 & 15+16+25\\4+0+18 & -12+10+0 & 20+20+30\end{bmatrix}$$

$$=\begin{bmatrix}14&0&42\\18&-1&56\\22&-2&70\end{bmatrix}$$

EXAMPLE 4. Find a, if

$$[a \quad -5 \quad -1]\begin{bmatrix}1&0&2\\0&2&1\\2&0&3\end{bmatrix}\begin{bmatrix}a\\4\\1\end{bmatrix}=0$$

Sol. Given that, $$[a \quad -5 \quad -1]\begin{bmatrix}1&0&2\\0&2&1\\2&0&3\end{bmatrix}\begin{bmatrix}a\\4\\1\end{bmatrix}=0$$

$$\Rightarrow \quad [a+0-2 \quad 0-10+0 \quad 2a-5-3]\begin{bmatrix}a\\4\\1\end{bmatrix}=0$$

$$\Rightarrow \quad [a-2 \quad -10 \quad 2a-8]\begin{bmatrix}a\\4\\1\end{bmatrix}=0$$

$$\Rightarrow \quad [(a-2)a+(-10)\times4+(2a-8)\times1]=[0]$$

$$\Rightarrow \quad a^2-2a-40+2a-8=0$$

$$\Rightarrow \quad a^2=48$$

$$\Rightarrow \quad a=\pm4\sqrt{3}$$

EXAMPLE 5. Find the matrix A, for which

$$\begin{bmatrix}5&4\\1&1\end{bmatrix}A=\begin{bmatrix}1&-2\\1&3\end{bmatrix}.$$

Sol. Since, $\begin{bmatrix}5&4\\1&1\end{bmatrix}$ and $\begin{bmatrix}1&-2\\1&3\end{bmatrix}$ are both square matrices of order 2, therefore A must be square matrix of order 2.

Let $A=\begin{bmatrix}a&b\\c&d\end{bmatrix}$, then given matrix equation because

$$\begin{bmatrix}5&4\\1&1\end{bmatrix}\begin{bmatrix}a&b\\c&d\end{bmatrix}=\begin{bmatrix}1&-2\\1&3\end{bmatrix}$$

$$\Rightarrow \quad \begin{bmatrix}5a+4c & 5b+4d\\a+c & b+d\end{bmatrix}=\begin{bmatrix}1&-2\\1&3\end{bmatrix}$$

$\Rightarrow \quad 5a+4c=1 \quad$ ...(i)

$\Rightarrow \quad 5b+4d=-2 \quad$ ...(ii)

$\Rightarrow \quad a+c=1 \quad$ ...(iii)

$\Rightarrow \quad b+d=3 \quad$ ...(iv)

On solving Eqs. (i) and (iii) simultaneously, we obtain

$$a=-3,\ c=4$$

On solving Eqs. (ii) and (iv) simultaneously, we obtain

$$b=-14,\ d=17$$

EXAMPLE 6. Use matrix multiplication to divide ₹30000 in two parts such that the total annual interest at 9% on the first part and 11% on the second part amounts ₹3060.

Sol. Let the two parts be ₹x and ₹$(30000-x)$. Let A be the 1×2 matrix representing these parts and B be the 2×1 matrix representing the annual interest rates on two parts.

i.e. $A=[x \quad 30000-x]$ (Part I, Part II) and $B=\begin{bmatrix}0.09\\0.11\end{bmatrix}$ (Part I, Part II)

Clearly, the total interest is given by the matrix AB,

i.e. $$AB=[x \quad 30000-x]\begin{bmatrix}0.09\\0.11\end{bmatrix}$$

$$=[x\times0.09+(30000-x)\times0.11]$$

$$=[0.09x+3300-0.11x]=[3300-0.02x]$$

Thus, $3300 - 0.02x = 3060$ [$\because$ total interest = ₹3060]

$\Rightarrow \quad 0.02x = 240$

$\Rightarrow \quad x = 12000$

Hence, two parts are ₹12000 and ₹18000, respectively.

Properties of Multiplication of Matrices

Multiplication of matrices have following properties

(i) **Associative Law** Matrix multiplication is associative, i.e. if A, B and C are three matrices, then $A(BC) = (AB)C$, whenever both sides are defined.

(ii) **Distributive Law** Matrix multiplication is distributive over matrix addition, if A, B and C are three matrices, then

$A(B+C) = AB + AC$ or $(A+B)C = AC + BC$, whenever both sides are defined.

(iii) **Existence of Multiplicative Identity** For every square matrix A, there exists an identity matrix I of same order such that $AI = A = IA$. So, I is the multiplicative identity for every square matrix A.

(iv) **Non-commutativity** Generally, matrix multiplication is not commutative, i.e. if A and B are two matrices and AB, BA both exist, then it is not necessary that $AB = BA$.

(v) **Zero Matrix as the Product of Two Non-zero Matrices** If the product of two matrices is a zero matrix, then it is not necessary that one of the matrices is a zero matrix.

e.g. Let $A = \begin{bmatrix} 0 & -1 \\ 0 & 2 \end{bmatrix}$ and $B = \begin{bmatrix} 3 & 5 \\ 0 & 0 \end{bmatrix}$.

Then, $AB = \begin{bmatrix} 0 & -1 \\ 0 & 2 \end{bmatrix} \begin{bmatrix} 3 & 5 \\ 0 & 0 \end{bmatrix} = \begin{bmatrix} 0 & 0 \\ 0 & 0 \end{bmatrix} = O.$

But, here $A \neq O$ and $B \neq O$.

Note Multiplication of diagonal matrices of same order will be commutative.

EXAMPLE 7. If $A = \begin{bmatrix} 1 & -2 & 3 \\ -4 & 2 & 5 \end{bmatrix}$ and $B = \begin{bmatrix} 2 & 3 \\ 4 & 5 \\ 2 & 1 \end{bmatrix}$, then find AB and BA. Show that A and B are not commutative, i.e. $AB \neq BA$.

Sol. Here, order of matrix A is 2×3 and order of matrix B is 3×2.

So, AB will be of order 2×2 and BA will be of order 3×3.

Now, $AB = \begin{bmatrix} 1 & -2 & 3 \\ -4 & 2 & 5 \end{bmatrix} \begin{bmatrix} 2 & 3 \\ 4 & 5 \\ 2 & 1 \end{bmatrix}$

$= \begin{bmatrix} 2-8+6 & 3-10+3 \\ -8+8+10 & -12+10+5 \end{bmatrix}$

[multiplying rows by columns]

$AB = \begin{bmatrix} 0 & -4 \\ 10 & 3 \end{bmatrix}$

and $BA = \begin{bmatrix} 2 & 3 \\ 4 & 5 \\ 2 & 1 \end{bmatrix} \begin{bmatrix} 1 & -2 & 3 \\ -4 & 2 & 5 \end{bmatrix}$

$= \begin{bmatrix} 2-12 & -4+6 & 6+15 \\ 4-20 & -8+10 & 12+25 \\ 2-4 & -4+2 & 6+5 \end{bmatrix}$

[multiplying rows by columns]

$= \begin{bmatrix} -10 & 2 & 21 \\ -16 & 2 & 37 \\ -2 & -2 & 11 \end{bmatrix}$

Clearly, $AB \neq BA$.

EXAMPLE 8. Three matrices A, B and C defined as $A = \begin{bmatrix} 1 & 2 \\ -1 & 3 \end{bmatrix}$, $B = \begin{bmatrix} 4 & 0 \\ 1 & 5 \end{bmatrix}$ and $C = \begin{bmatrix} 2 & 0 \\ 1 & -2 \end{bmatrix}$, then show that matrices A, B and C satisfy

(i) the property of associativity with respect to multiplication, i.e. $A(BC) = (AB)C$.

(ii) the property of distributivity with respect to addition, i.e. $A(B+C) = AB + AC$.

Sol. Given, $A = \begin{bmatrix} 1 & 2 \\ -1 & 3 \end{bmatrix}$, $B = \begin{bmatrix} 4 & 0 \\ 1 & 5 \end{bmatrix}$ and $C = \begin{bmatrix} 2 & 0 \\ 1 & -2 \end{bmatrix}$

(i) Here, $BC = \begin{bmatrix} 4 & 0 \\ 1 & 5 \end{bmatrix} \begin{bmatrix} 2 & 0 \\ 1 & -2 \end{bmatrix} = \begin{bmatrix} 8+0 & 0+0 \\ 2+5 & 0-10 \end{bmatrix}$

[multiplying rows by columns]

$= \begin{bmatrix} 8 & 0 \\ 7 & -10 \end{bmatrix}$ ...(i)

$\therefore$ LHS $= A(BC) = \begin{bmatrix} 1 & 2 \\ -1 & 3 \end{bmatrix} \begin{bmatrix} 8 & 0 \\ 7 & -10 \end{bmatrix}$ [using Eq. (i)]

$= \begin{bmatrix} 8+14 & 0-20 \\ -8+21 & 0-30 \end{bmatrix} = \begin{bmatrix} 22 & -20 \\ 13 & -30 \end{bmatrix}$

[multiplying rows by columns]

and $AB = \begin{bmatrix} 1 & 2 \\ -1 & 3 \end{bmatrix} \begin{bmatrix} 4 & 0 \\ 1 & 5 \end{bmatrix}$

$= \begin{bmatrix} 4+2 & 0+10 \\ -4+3 & 0+15 \end{bmatrix}$

[multiplying rows by columns]

$= \begin{bmatrix} 6 & 10 \\ -1 & 15 \end{bmatrix}$ ...(ii)

$$\therefore \text{RHS} = (AB)C = \begin{bmatrix} 6 & 10 \\ -1 & 15 \end{bmatrix} \begin{bmatrix} 2 & 0 \\ 1 & -2 \end{bmatrix} \quad \text{[using Eq. (ii)]}$$

$$= \begin{bmatrix} 12+10 & 0-20 \\ -2+15 & 0-30 \end{bmatrix}$$

[multiplying rows by columns]

$$= \begin{bmatrix} 22 & -20 \\ 13 & -30 \end{bmatrix}$$

Thus, LHS = RHS

(ii) Here, $B+C = \begin{bmatrix} 4 & 0 \\ 1 & 5 \end{bmatrix} + \begin{bmatrix} 2 & 0 \\ 1 & -2 \end{bmatrix}$

$$= \begin{bmatrix} 4+2 & 0 \\ 1+1 & 5-2 \end{bmatrix} = \begin{bmatrix} 6 & 0 \\ 2 & 3 \end{bmatrix} \quad \text{...(iii)}$$

and $AC = \begin{bmatrix} 1 & 2 \\ -1 & 3 \end{bmatrix} \begin{bmatrix} 2 & 0 \\ 1 & -2 \end{bmatrix} = \begin{bmatrix} 2+2 & 0-4 \\ -2+3 & 0-6 \end{bmatrix}$

$$= \begin{bmatrix} 4 & -4 \\ 1 & -6 \end{bmatrix} \quad \text{...(iv)}$$

[multiplying rows by columns]

$$\text{LHS} = A(B+C) = \begin{bmatrix} 1 & 2 \\ -1 & 3 \end{bmatrix} \begin{bmatrix} 6 & 0 \\ 2 & 3 \end{bmatrix} \quad \text{[using Eq. (iii)]}$$

$$= \begin{bmatrix} 6+4 & 0+6 \\ -6+6 & 0+9 \end{bmatrix} \quad \text{[multiplying rows by columns]}$$

$$= \begin{bmatrix} 10 & 6 \\ 0 & 9 \end{bmatrix}$$

and $\text{RHS} = AB + AC = \begin{bmatrix} 6 & 10 \\ -1 & 15 \end{bmatrix} + \begin{bmatrix} 4 & -4 \\ 1 & -6 \end{bmatrix} = \begin{bmatrix} 10 & 6 \\ 0 & 9 \end{bmatrix}$

[using Eqs. (ii) and (iv)]

Thus, LHS = RHS

Positive Integral Powers of a Square Matrix

If we multiply the square matrix by itself, then it will give the positive integral powers of the square matrix. i.e. For any square matrix, say A, we define $A^1 = A, A^2 = A \cdot A, A^3 = A^2 \cdot A, A^4 = A^3 \cdot A, \ldots,$ $A^n = A^{n-1} \cdot A$, where n is a positive integer.

Note $I^n = I$ for any positive integer n, where I is the identity matrix.

EXAMPLE 9. If $A = \begin{bmatrix} 1 & 0 \\ 1 & 1 \end{bmatrix}$, then find A^3.

Sol. We have, $A = \begin{bmatrix} 1 & 0 \\ 1 & 1 \end{bmatrix}$

Now, $A^2 = A \times A = \begin{bmatrix} 1 & 0 \\ 1 & 1 \end{bmatrix} \begin{bmatrix} 1 & 0 \\ 1 & 1 \end{bmatrix}$

$$A^2 = \begin{bmatrix} 1 & 0 \\ 2 & 1 \end{bmatrix}$$

$$A^3 = A^2 \cdot A = \begin{bmatrix} 1 & 0 \\ 2 & 1 \end{bmatrix} \begin{bmatrix} 1 & 0 \\ 1 & 1 \end{bmatrix} = \begin{bmatrix} 1 & 0 \\ 3 & 1 \end{bmatrix}$$

Method to Solve Problems Based on *n*th Power of a Matrix

In these types of problems, a matrix (say A) is given to us and an equation involving the nth power of A is given to us. We have to show/prove that the given equation is true. For proving/showing such problems, we use the concept of mathematical induction, which is given below.

Suppose there is a statement $P(n)$ involving the natural number n such that

(i) $P(1)$ is true, i.e. statement is true for $n = 1$.

(ii) Truth of $P(k)$ implies the truth of $P(k+1)$, i.e. if the statement is true for $n = k$ (k is positive integer), then statement is also true for $n = k+1$.

Then, by principal of mathematical induction, $P(n)$ is true for all natural numbers n.

Matrix Polynomial

Let $f(x) = a_0 x^n + a_1 x^{n-1} + a_2 x^{n-2} + \ldots + a_{n-1} x + a_n$ be a polynomial and A be a square matrix.

Then, $f(A) = a_0 A^n + a_1 A^{n-1} + a_2 A^{n-2} + \ldots + a_{n-1} A + a_n I$ is called a matrix polynomial, where I is the identity matrix of order of A.

Method to Solve Problems Based on Matrix Polynomial

Sometimes, a square matrix (say A) is given to us and we have to find the value of a polynomial in which the variable is a matrix. (e.g. $A^3 - 23A - 40I$).

For this, firstly we find the value of each term having the power of A by multiplying A by itself as many times as power and then put these values in the given expression to find the required value.

EXAMPLE 10. Let $A = \begin{bmatrix} 0 & 1 \\ 1 & 2 \end{bmatrix}$ and $f(x) = x^2 + x - 1$, then find $f(A)$.

Sol. We have, $A = \begin{bmatrix} 0 & 1 \\ 1 & 2 \end{bmatrix}$

$$\therefore \quad A^2 = A \cdot A = \begin{bmatrix} 0 & 1 \\ 1 & 2 \end{bmatrix} \begin{bmatrix} 0 & 1 \\ 1 & 2 \end{bmatrix} = \begin{bmatrix} 0+1 & 0+2 \\ 0+2 & 1+4 \end{bmatrix} = \begin{bmatrix} 1 & 2 \\ 2 & 5 \end{bmatrix}$$

[multiplying rows by columns]

Now, $f(A) = A^2 + A - I = \begin{bmatrix} 1 & 2 \\ 2 & 5 \end{bmatrix} + \begin{bmatrix} 0 & 1 \\ 1 & 2 \end{bmatrix} - \begin{bmatrix} 1 & 0 \\ 0 & 1 \end{bmatrix}$

$= \begin{bmatrix} 1+0-1 & 2+1-0 \\ 2+1-0 & 5+2-1 \end{bmatrix}$

$= \begin{bmatrix} 0 & 3 \\ 3 & 6 \end{bmatrix}$

EXAMPLE 11. If A is a square matrix such that $A^2 = I$, then find the simplified value of $(A-I)^3 + (A+I)^3 - 7A$.

Sol. Given, $A^2 = I$ ...(i)

Now, $(A-I)^3 + (A+I)^3 - 7A = (A^3 - 3A^2 I + 3AI^2 - I^3)$
$+ (A^3 + 3A^2 I + 3AI^2 + I^3) - 7A$

$= (A^3 - 3A^2 + 3AI - I) + (A^3 + 3A^2 + 3AI + I) - 7A$

[$\because A^2 I = A^2$ and $I^3 = I^2 = I$]

$= 2A^3 + 6AI - 7A = 2A^2 A + 6A - 7A$ [$\because AI = A$]

$= 2\,IA - A$ [from Eq. (i)]

$= 2A - A = A$ [$\because IA = A$]

EXAMPLE 12. If $A = \begin{bmatrix} 2 & 0 & 1 \\ 2 & 1 & 3 \\ 1 & -1 & 0 \end{bmatrix}$, then find $A^2 - 5A + 4I$ and hence find a matrix X, such that $A^2 - 5A + 4I + X = O$.

Sol. We have, $A = \begin{bmatrix} 2 & 0 & 1 \\ 2 & 1 & 3 \\ 1 & -1 & 0 \end{bmatrix}$

$\therefore \quad A^2 = \begin{bmatrix} 2 & 0 & 1 \\ 2 & 1 & 3 \\ 1 & -1 & 0 \end{bmatrix}\begin{bmatrix} 2 & 0 & 1 \\ 2 & 1 & 3 \\ 1 & -1 & 0 \end{bmatrix}$

$= \begin{bmatrix} 4+0+1 & 0+0-1 & 2+0+0 \\ 4+2+3 & 0+1-3 & 2+3+0 \\ 2-2+0 & 0-1+0 & 1-3+0 \end{bmatrix}$

$= \begin{bmatrix} 5 & -1 & 2 \\ 9 & -2 & 5 \\ 0 & -1 & -2 \end{bmatrix}$

[multiplying rows by columns]

Now, consider $A^2 - 5A + 4I$

$= \begin{bmatrix} 5 & -1 & 2 \\ 9 & -2 & 5 \\ 0 & -1 & -2 \end{bmatrix} - 5\begin{bmatrix} 2 & 0 & 1 \\ 2 & 1 & 3 \\ 1 & -1 & 0 \end{bmatrix} + 4\begin{bmatrix} 1 & 0 & 0 \\ 0 & 1 & 0 \\ 0 & 0 & 1 \end{bmatrix}$

$= \begin{bmatrix} 5 & -1 & 2 \\ 9 & -2 & 5 \\ 0 & -1 & -2 \end{bmatrix} - \begin{bmatrix} 10 & 0 & 5 \\ 10 & 5 & 15 \\ 5 & -5 & 0 \end{bmatrix} + \begin{bmatrix} 4 & 0 & 0 \\ 0 & 4 & 0 \\ 0 & 0 & 4 \end{bmatrix}$

$= \begin{bmatrix} -5 & -1 & -3 \\ -1 & -7 & -10 \\ -5 & 4 & -2 \end{bmatrix} + \begin{bmatrix} 4 & 0 & 0 \\ 0 & 4 & 0 \\ 0 & 0 & 4 \end{bmatrix}$

$= \begin{bmatrix} -1 & -1 & -3 \\ -1 & -3 & -10 \\ -5 & 4 & 2 \end{bmatrix}$

Since, $A^2 - 5A + 4I + X = O$

$\therefore \ A^2 - 5A + 4I + X - X = O - X$

[subtracting matrix X from both sides]

$\Rightarrow A^2 - 5A + 4I + O = -X \Rightarrow X = -(A^2 - 5A + 4I)$

$\Rightarrow \quad X = -\begin{bmatrix} -1 & -1 & -3 \\ -1 & -3 & -10 \\ -5 & 4 & 2 \end{bmatrix} = \begin{bmatrix} 1 & 1 & 3 \\ 1 & 3 & 10 \\ 5 & -4 & -2 \end{bmatrix}$

EXAMPLE 13. If $A = \begin{bmatrix} 1 & 0 \\ -1 & 7 \end{bmatrix}$, find the value of k such that $A^2 - 8A + kI = 0$. **[CBSE 2024]**

Sol. Given, $A = \begin{bmatrix} 1 & 0 \\ -1 & 7 \end{bmatrix}$

Now, $A^2 = \begin{bmatrix} 1 & 0 \\ -1 & 7 \end{bmatrix}\begin{bmatrix} 1 & 0 \\ -1 & 7 \end{bmatrix}$

$= \begin{bmatrix} 1+0 & 0+0 \\ -1-7 & 0+49 \end{bmatrix} = \begin{bmatrix} 1 & 0 \\ -8 & 49 \end{bmatrix}$

Since, $A^2 - 8A + kI = 0$

$\therefore \quad \begin{bmatrix} 1 & 0 \\ -8 & 49 \end{bmatrix} - 8\begin{bmatrix} 1 & 0 \\ -1 & 7 \end{bmatrix} + k\begin{bmatrix} 1 & 0 \\ 0 & 1 \end{bmatrix} = \begin{bmatrix} 0 & 0 \\ 0 & 0 \end{bmatrix}$

$\Rightarrow \quad \begin{bmatrix} 1 & 0 \\ -8 & 49 \end{bmatrix} - \begin{bmatrix} 8 & 0 \\ -8 & 56 \end{bmatrix} + \begin{bmatrix} k & 0 \\ 0 & k \end{bmatrix} = \begin{bmatrix} 0 & 0 \\ 0 & 0 \end{bmatrix}$

$\Rightarrow \quad \begin{bmatrix} 1-8+h & 0-0+0 \\ -8+8+0 & 49-56+k \end{bmatrix} = \begin{bmatrix} 0 & 0 \\ 0 & 0 \end{bmatrix}$

$\Rightarrow \quad \begin{bmatrix} -7+k & 0 \\ 0 & -7+k \end{bmatrix} = \begin{bmatrix} 0 & 0 \\ 0 & 0 \end{bmatrix}$

On equating the corresponding elements, we get

$-7 + k = 0$

$\Rightarrow \quad k = 7$

EXAMPLE 14. Find the matrix A such that

$$A\begin{bmatrix}1 & 2 & 3\\ 4 & 5 & 6\end{bmatrix}=\begin{bmatrix}-7 & -8 & -9\\ 2 & 4 & 6\end{bmatrix}.$$

Sol. The right side of the given matrix equation is of order 2×3, so the left side of the given matrix equation should be of order 2×3. It is clear that, the product of A with 2×3 matrix is a 2×3 matrix, therefore A is a 2×2 matrix.

Let $A=\begin{bmatrix}u & v\\ w & x\end{bmatrix}$. Then,

$$\text{LHS}=\begin{bmatrix}u & v\\ w & x\end{bmatrix}\begin{bmatrix}1 & 2 & 3\\ 4 & 5 & 6\end{bmatrix}$$

$$=\begin{bmatrix}u+4v & 2u+5v & 3u+6v\\ w+4x & 2w+5x & 3w+6x\end{bmatrix}$$

$$\therefore \begin{bmatrix}u+4v & 2u+5v & 3u+6v\\ w+4x & 2w+5x & 3w+6x\end{bmatrix}=\begin{bmatrix}-7 & -8 & -9\\ 2 & 4 & 6\end{bmatrix}$$

On comparing the elements from both sides, we get

$$u+4v=-7,\ 2u+5v=-8,\ 3u+6v=-9,$$
$$w+4x=2,\ 2w+5x=4 \text{ and } 3w+6x=6$$

On solving, we get

$$u=1,\ v=-2,\ w=2 \text{ and } x=0$$

$$\therefore \qquad A=\begin{bmatrix}1 & -2\\ 2 & 0\end{bmatrix}$$

Topic Practice 3

1 Let A and B be two matrices of order 3×2 and 2×4 respectively. Write the order of matrix (AB).

2 Evaluate AB and BA, if possible

(i) $A=\begin{bmatrix}2 & 3\\ -1 & 0\end{bmatrix}, B=\begin{bmatrix}-2 & 1\\ 3 & -2\end{bmatrix}$

(ii) $A=[1\ \ -2\ \ 3], B=\begin{bmatrix}1 & 0\\ 2 & -1\\ 1 & 2\end{bmatrix}$

(iii) $A=\begin{bmatrix}2 & -1 & 3\\ -1 & 2 & 1\end{bmatrix}, B=\begin{bmatrix}1 & 3 & 2\\ 2 & -1 & 0\\ 3 & 1 & 2\end{bmatrix}$

(iv) $A=\begin{bmatrix}2 & -2\\ 1 & 5\end{bmatrix}, B=\begin{bmatrix}0 & 1\\ -3 & 5\end{bmatrix}$

(v) $A=\begin{bmatrix}-6 & 5\\ 0 & 3\end{bmatrix}, B=\begin{bmatrix}2 & -2\\ 1 & 1\end{bmatrix}$

(vi) $A=\begin{bmatrix}-2 & 3\\ -5 & 2\end{bmatrix}, B=\begin{bmatrix}0 & 8\\ -5 & 2\end{bmatrix}$

(vii) $A=\begin{bmatrix}4 & -2\\ 0 & -3\end{bmatrix}, B=\begin{bmatrix}2 & -1 & 1\\ -2 & 0 & 1\end{bmatrix}$

(viii) $A=\begin{bmatrix}1 & 2\\ 4 & 7\end{bmatrix}, B=\begin{bmatrix}1/2 & -1/2 & 3\\ 1/3 & 1 & -1/3\end{bmatrix}$

(ix) $A=\begin{bmatrix}2 & 1\\ -3 & 0\end{bmatrix}, B=\begin{bmatrix}1.3 & 1.4 & 1.9\\ -1 & -3.5 & 0\end{bmatrix}$

(x) $A=\begin{bmatrix}1 & -2 & 0\\ -2 & -3 & 1\\ 3 & 0 & 1\end{bmatrix}, B=\begin{bmatrix}1 & -2\\ -5 & 0\\ -2 & -1\end{bmatrix}$

(xi) $A=\begin{bmatrix}1 & 6 & -1\\ 2 & -3 & -9\\ 1 & 2 & 0\end{bmatrix}, B=\begin{bmatrix}6 & 2\\ 0 & 1\\ -1 & 3\end{bmatrix}$

(xii) $A=\begin{bmatrix}1 & 0 & 2\\ 2 & 1 & 0\\ 3 & 0 & 1\end{bmatrix}, B=\begin{bmatrix}6 & 0 & 2\\ 0 & 1 & 0\\ 3 & 3 & 0\end{bmatrix}$

(xiii) $A=\begin{bmatrix}1 & x & x\\ 2 & x & 2x\\ -x & 1 & 2\end{bmatrix}, B=\begin{bmatrix}x & 1\\ x & -x\\ 2x & 0\end{bmatrix}$

(xiv) $A=\begin{bmatrix}a & 2x & -a\\ a & -2a & 0\\ 0 & a & -x\end{bmatrix}, B=\begin{bmatrix}1 & 2 & 3\\ x & 2 & -x\\ a & 0 & 1\end{bmatrix}$

3 For the matrices

$A=\begin{bmatrix}1 & 0\\ 2 & 6\end{bmatrix}, B=\begin{bmatrix}2 & -1 & -1\\ 2 & 0 & -3\end{bmatrix}, C=\begin{bmatrix}2 & -1\\ -3 & 2\\ 1 & 4\end{bmatrix},$

calculate where possible:

(i) AB (ii) BC
(iii) CA (iv) BA
(v) A^2 (vi) ABC

4 Show that if A and B are square matrices such that $AB=BA$, then $(A+B)^2=A^2+2AB+B^2$.

Directions (Q. Nos. 5-8) *Find the value of x.*

5 $A=\begin{bmatrix}2 & -2\\ -2 & 2\end{bmatrix}$ and $A^2=xA$

6 $[2x\ \ 3]\begin{bmatrix}1 & 2\\ -3 & 0\end{bmatrix}\begin{bmatrix}x\\ 8\end{bmatrix}=O$

7 $[x \quad 1]\begin{bmatrix} 1 & 0 \\ -2 & 0 \end{bmatrix} = O.$

8 $[1 \quad x \quad 1]\begin{bmatrix} 1 & 3 & 2 \\ 2 & 5 & 1 \\ 15 & 3 & 2 \end{bmatrix}\begin{bmatrix} 1 \\ 2 \\ x \end{bmatrix} = O$

9 If $X_{m \times 3} Y_{p \times 4} = Z_{2 \times b}$, for three matrices X, Y and Z, then find the values of m, p and b.

10 If $A = \begin{bmatrix} x & 0 \\ 1 & 1 \end{bmatrix}$ and $B = \begin{bmatrix} 1 & 0 \\ 5 & 1 \end{bmatrix}$, then find the value of x for which $A^2 = B$.

11 Find, where possible, the order of the matrix A so that the following equations can be solved.

(i) $\begin{bmatrix} 2 & -1 \\ 1 & 0 \\ -3 & 4 \end{bmatrix} A = \begin{bmatrix} -1 & -8 \\ 1 & -2 \\ 9 & 22 \end{bmatrix}$ (ii) $\begin{bmatrix} a & b \\ c & d \end{bmatrix} A = \begin{bmatrix} x \\ y \end{bmatrix}$

(iii) $A\begin{bmatrix} a & b \\ c & d \end{bmatrix} = \begin{bmatrix} x \\ y \end{bmatrix}$ (iv) $[a \quad b \quad c]A = [x \quad y]$

(v) $[a \quad b \quad c]A = \begin{bmatrix} m & n \\ x & y \\ u & v \end{bmatrix}$ (vi) $A[a \quad b \quad c] = \begin{bmatrix} m & n \\ x & y \\ u & v \end{bmatrix}$

(vii) $\begin{bmatrix} a \\ b \\ c \end{bmatrix} A = \begin{bmatrix} x & y & z \\ k & l & m \\ n & o & p \end{bmatrix}$

12 Let $A = \begin{bmatrix} 2 & -1 \\ 3 & 4 \end{bmatrix}$, $B = \begin{bmatrix} 5 & 2 \\ 7 & 4 \end{bmatrix}$ and $C = \begin{bmatrix} 2 & 5 \\ 3 & 8 \end{bmatrix}$. Find a matrix D such that $CD - AB = O$.

13 If $A = \begin{bmatrix} 1 & -1 \\ 2 & -1 \end{bmatrix}$, $B = \begin{bmatrix} a & 1 \\ b & -1 \end{bmatrix}$ and $(A+B)^2 = A^2 + B^2$, then find the values of a and b.

14 If $A = \begin{bmatrix} 0 & 1 \\ -1 & 0 \end{bmatrix}$, then find the real values x and y such that $(xI + yA)^2 = A$.

15 If A and B are square matrices of the same order such that $AB = BA$, then prove by mathematical induction that $AB^n = B^n A$ for all $n \in N$.

16 If $A = \begin{bmatrix} 1 & 2 & 2 \\ 2 & 1 & 2 \\ 2 & 2 & 1 \end{bmatrix}$, then show that $A^2 - 4A - 5I = O$.

17 If $A = \begin{bmatrix} 1 & 3 & 2 \\ 2 & 0 & -1 \\ 1 & 2 & 3 \end{bmatrix}$, then show that $A^3 - 4A^2 - 3A + 11I = O$.

18 If $A = \begin{bmatrix} 1 & 0 & -2 \\ -2 & -1 & 2 \\ 3 & 4 & 1 \end{bmatrix}$, then show that $A^3 - A^2 - 3A - I_3 = O$.

Hints & Solutions

1. Order of AB is 3×4.

2. (i) $AB = \begin{bmatrix} 5 & -4 \\ 2 & -1 \end{bmatrix}$, $BA = \begin{bmatrix} -5 & -6 \\ 8 & 9 \end{bmatrix}$

(ii) $AB = [0 \quad 8]$, BA cannot be calculated

(iii) $AB = \begin{bmatrix} 9 & 10 & 10 \\ 6 & -4 & 0 \end{bmatrix}$, BA cannot be calculated

(iv) $AB = \begin{bmatrix} 6 & -8 \\ -15 & 26 \end{bmatrix}$, $BA = \begin{bmatrix} 1 & 5 \\ -1 & 31 \end{bmatrix}$

(v) $AB = \begin{bmatrix} -7 & 17 \\ 3 & 3 \end{bmatrix}$, $BA = \begin{bmatrix} -12 & 4 \\ -6 & 8 \end{bmatrix}$

(vi) $AB = \begin{bmatrix} -15 & -10 \\ -10 & -36 \end{bmatrix}$, $BA = \begin{bmatrix} -40 & 16 \\ 0 & -11 \end{bmatrix}$

(vii) $AB = \begin{bmatrix} 12 & -4 & 2 \\ 6 & 0 & -3 \end{bmatrix}$, BA cannot be calculated

(viii) $AB = \begin{bmatrix} \frac{7}{6} & \frac{3}{2} & \frac{7}{3} \\ \frac{13}{3} & 5 & \frac{29}{3} \end{bmatrix}$, BA cannot be calculated

(ix) $AB = \begin{bmatrix} 1.6 & -0.7 & 3.8 \\ -3.9 & -4.2 & -5.7 \end{bmatrix}$, BA cannot be calculated

(x) $AB = \begin{bmatrix} 11 & -2 \\ 11 & 3 \\ 1 & -7 \end{bmatrix}$, BA cannot be calculated

(xi) $AB = \begin{bmatrix} 7 & 5 \\ 21 & -26 \\ 6 & 4 \end{bmatrix}$, BA cannot be calculated

(xii) $AB = \begin{bmatrix} 12 & 6 & 2 \\ 12 & 1 & 4 \\ 21 & 3 & 6 \end{bmatrix}$, $BA = \begin{bmatrix} 12 & 0 & 14 \\ 2 & 1 & 0 \\ 9 & 3 & 6 \end{bmatrix}$

(xiii) $AB = \begin{bmatrix} 3x^2 + x & 1 - x^2 \\ 5x^2 + 2x & 2 - x^2 \\ 5x - x^2 & -2x \end{bmatrix}$, BA cannot be calculated

(xiv) $AB = \begin{bmatrix} a + 2x^2 - a^2 & 2a + 4x & 2a - 2x^2 \\ a - 2ax & -2a & 3a + 2ax \\ 0 & 2a & -ax - x \end{bmatrix}$

and $BA = \begin{bmatrix} 3a & 2x - a & -a - 3x \\ ax + 2a & 2x^2 - 4a - ax & x^2 - ax \\ a^2 & 2ax + a & -a^2 - x \end{bmatrix}$

3. Solve as Example 1.

Ans. (i) $\begin{bmatrix} 2 & -1 & -1 \\ 16 & -2 & -20 \end{bmatrix}$ (ii) $\begin{bmatrix} 6 & -8 \\ 1 & -14 \end{bmatrix}$

(iii) $\begin{bmatrix} 0 & -6 \\ 1 & 12 \\ 9 & 24 \end{bmatrix}$ (iv) cannot be calculated

(v) $\begin{bmatrix} 1 & 0 \\ 14 & 36 \end{bmatrix}$ (vi) $\begin{bmatrix} 6 & -8 \\ 18 & -100 \end{bmatrix}$

4. Given, $AB = BA$

Now, $(A + B)^2 = (A + B)\cdot(A + B)$

$= A\cdot(A+B) + B\cdot(A+B)$

$= A^2 + AB + BA + B^2$

$= A^2 + AB + AB + B^2$ [$\because BA = AB$, given]

$= A^2 + 2AB + B^2$

5. We have, $\begin{bmatrix} 2 & -2 \\ -2 & 2 \end{bmatrix}\begin{bmatrix} 2 & -2 \\ -2 & 2 \end{bmatrix} = x\begin{bmatrix} 2 & -2 \\ -2 & 2 \end{bmatrix}$

$\Rightarrow \begin{bmatrix} 4+4 & -4-4 \\ -4-4 & 4+4 \end{bmatrix} = x\begin{bmatrix} 2 & -2 \\ -2 & 2 \end{bmatrix}$

$\Rightarrow \begin{bmatrix} 8 & -8 \\ -8 & 8 \end{bmatrix} = \begin{bmatrix} 2x & -2x \\ -2x & 2x \end{bmatrix}$

$\Rightarrow 8 = 2x$

$\Rightarrow x = 4$

6. Given matrix equation is

$[2x \;\; 3]\begin{bmatrix} 1 & 2 \\ -3 & 0 \end{bmatrix}\begin{bmatrix} x \\ 8 \end{bmatrix} = O$

$\Rightarrow [2x \;\; 3]\left(\begin{bmatrix} 1 & 2 \\ -3 & 0 \end{bmatrix}\begin{bmatrix} x \\ 8 \end{bmatrix}\right) = O$

[by associative law of multiplication]

$\Rightarrow [2x \;\; 3]\begin{bmatrix} x+16 \\ -3x \end{bmatrix} = O$

$\Rightarrow [2x\,(x+16) - 9x] = [O]$

$\Rightarrow 2x^2 + 32x - 9x = 0$

$\Rightarrow 2x^2 + 23x = 0$

$\Rightarrow x(2x + 23) = 0$

$\Rightarrow x = 0$ and $x = -23/2$

7. Solve as Question 6. **Ans.** 2

8. We have, $[1 \;\; x \;\; 1]\begin{bmatrix} 1 & 3 & 2 \\ 2 & 5 & 1 \\ 15 & 3 & 2 \end{bmatrix}\begin{bmatrix} 1 \\ 2 \\ x \end{bmatrix} = O$

$\Rightarrow [1 \;\; x \;\; 1]\begin{bmatrix} 1 + 6 + 2x \\ 2 + 10 + x \\ 15 + 6 + 2x \end{bmatrix} = O$

$\Rightarrow [1 \;\; x \;\; 1]\begin{bmatrix} 7 + 2x \\ 12 + x \\ 21 + 2x \end{bmatrix} = O$

$\Rightarrow [7 + 2x + x(12 + x) + 21 + 2x] = [0]$

$\Rightarrow x^2 + 16x + 28 = 0$

$\Rightarrow (x + 14)(x + 2) = 0$

$\Rightarrow x = -14$ or $x = -2$

9. Given, $X_{m \times 3}Y_{p \times 4} = Z_{2 \times b}$ ...(i)

XY is defined only, when $p = 3$.

Now, Eq. (i) will be of the form $Z_{m \times 4} = Z_{2 \times b}$, which is possible only, when $m = 2$ and $b = 4$.

$\therefore$ $m = 2$, $p = 3$ and $b = 4$

10. We have, $\begin{bmatrix} x & 0 \\ 1 & 1 \end{bmatrix}\begin{bmatrix} x & 0 \\ 1 & 1 \end{bmatrix} = \begin{bmatrix} 1 & 0 \\ 5 & 1 \end{bmatrix} \Rightarrow \begin{bmatrix} x^2 & 0 \\ x+1 & 1 \end{bmatrix} = \begin{bmatrix} 1 & 0 \\ 5 & 1 \end{bmatrix}$

$\Rightarrow x^2 = 1$ ...(i)

and $x + 1 = 5$ ...(ii)

From Eq. (ii), we get $x = 4$, which does not satisfy Eq. (i). So, no value of x exist.

11. Solve as Example 14.

Ans. (i) 2×2 (ii) 2×1 (iii) not possible (iv) 3×2 (v) not possible (vi) not possible (vii) 1×3

12. Solve as Example 14. **Ans.** $D = \begin{bmatrix} -191 & -110 \\ 77 & 44 \end{bmatrix}$

13. Given, $A = \begin{bmatrix} 1 & -1 \\ 2 & -1 \end{bmatrix}$ and $B = \begin{bmatrix} a & 1 \\ b & -1 \end{bmatrix}$

Clearly, $A + B = \begin{bmatrix} 1 & -1 \\ 2 & -1 \end{bmatrix} + \begin{bmatrix} a & 1 \\ b & -1 \end{bmatrix}$

$= \begin{bmatrix} 1 + a & -1+1 \\ 2 + b & -1-1 \end{bmatrix} = \begin{bmatrix} 1 + a & 0 \\ 2 + b & -2 \end{bmatrix}$

$\Rightarrow (A + B)^2 = \begin{bmatrix} 1 + a & 0 \\ 2 + b & -2 \end{bmatrix}\cdot\begin{bmatrix} 1 + a & 0 \\ 2 + b & -2 \end{bmatrix}$

$= \begin{bmatrix} 1 + a^2 + 2a & 0 \\ 2 + 2a + b + ab - 4 - 2b & 4 \end{bmatrix}$

$= \begin{bmatrix} a^2 + 2a + 1 & 0 \\ 2a - b + ab - 2 & 4 \end{bmatrix}$

Now, $A^2 + B^2 = \begin{bmatrix} 1 & -1 \\ 2 & -1 \end{bmatrix} \cdot \begin{bmatrix} 1 & -1 \\ 2 & -1 \end{bmatrix} + \begin{bmatrix} a & 1 \\ b & -1 \end{bmatrix} \cdot \begin{bmatrix} a & 1 \\ b & -1 \end{bmatrix}$

$$= \begin{bmatrix} -1 & 0 \\ 0 & -1 \end{bmatrix} + \begin{bmatrix} a^2+b & a-1 \\ ab-b & b+1 \end{bmatrix}$$

$$= \begin{bmatrix} a^2+b-1 & a-1 \\ ab-b & b \end{bmatrix}$$

Since, $(A+B)^2 = A^2 + B^2$

$$\therefore \quad \begin{bmatrix} a^2+2a+1 & 0 \\ 2a-b+ab-2 & 4 \end{bmatrix} = \begin{bmatrix} a^2+b-1 & a-1 \\ ab-b & b \end{bmatrix}$$

On equating the corresponding elements, we get

$$a^2 + 2a + 1 = a^2 + b - 1$$

$\Rightarrow \quad 2a - b = -2, \quad$ ...(i)

$a - 1 = 0$

$\Rightarrow \quad a = 1 \quad$ ...(ii)

$2a - b + ab - 2 = ab - b$

$\Rightarrow \quad 2a - 2 = 0$

$\Rightarrow \quad a = 1 \quad$ ...(iii)

and $\quad b = 4 \quad$ ...(iv)

Since, $a = 1, b = 4$ satisfy all four Eqs. (i), (ii), (iii) and (iv), therefore

$$a = 1 \text{ and } b = 4$$

14. We have, $A = \begin{bmatrix} 0 & 1 \\ -1 & 0 \end{bmatrix}$

$\Rightarrow \quad xI + yA = x\begin{bmatrix} 1 & 0 \\ 0 & 1 \end{bmatrix} + y\begin{bmatrix} 0 & 1 \\ -1 & 0 \end{bmatrix}$

$$= \begin{bmatrix} x & 0 \\ 0 & x \end{bmatrix} + \begin{bmatrix} 0 & y \\ -y & 0 \end{bmatrix}$$

$$= \begin{bmatrix} x & y \\ -y & x \end{bmatrix}$$

Now, $(xI + yA)^2 = \begin{bmatrix} x & y \\ -y & x \end{bmatrix}^2 = \begin{bmatrix} x & y \\ -y & x \end{bmatrix}\begin{bmatrix} x & y \\ -y & x \end{bmatrix}$

$$= \begin{bmatrix} x^2-y^2 & 2xy \\ -2xy & x^2-y^2 \end{bmatrix}$$

Since, $(xI + yA)^2 = A$, therefore

$$\begin{bmatrix} x^2-y^2 & 2xy \\ -2xy & x^2-y^2 \end{bmatrix} = \begin{bmatrix} 0 & 1 \\ -1 & 0 \end{bmatrix}$$

$\Rightarrow \quad x^2 - y^2 = 0,\ 2xy = 1,\ -2xy = -1$ and $x^2 - y^2 = 0$

$\Rightarrow \quad x^2 - y^2 = 0$ and $2xy = 1$

$\Rightarrow \quad x = \pm y$ and $2xy = 1$

***Case* I** When $x = y$ and $2xy = 1$.

In this case, $2x^2 = 1$

$\Rightarrow \quad x = \pm\dfrac{1}{\sqrt{2}}$

Thus, $\left(x = \dfrac{1}{\sqrt{2}} \text{ and } y = \dfrac{1}{\sqrt{2}}\right)$ or $\left(x = -\dfrac{1}{\sqrt{2}} \text{ and } y = -\dfrac{1}{\sqrt{2}}\right)$

***Case* II** When $x = -y$ and $2xy = 1$.

In this case, $x^2 = \dfrac{-1}{2} \Rightarrow x = \pm\dfrac{i}{\sqrt{2}}$, which is imaginary.

Hence, only real values of x and y are

$$x = \frac{1}{\sqrt{2}}, y = \frac{1}{\sqrt{2}} \text{ or } x = -\frac{1}{\sqrt{2}}, y = -\frac{1}{\sqrt{2}}$$

15. Given that, $AB = BA \quad$ ...(i)

To prove, $AB^n = B^n A \quad$ ...(ii)

For $n = 1$, Eq. (ii) is obviously true.

Let Eq. (ii) be true for a positive integer $n = m$,

i.e. $\quad AB^m = B^m A \quad$ ...(iii)

Then, for $n = m + 1$, $AB^{m+1} = A(B^m B) = (AB^m)B$

[using associative law of matrix multiplication]

$= (B^m A)B \quad$ [using Eq. (iii)]

$= B^m(AB) = B^m(BA) \quad$ [using Eq. (i)]

$= (B^m B)A = B^{m+1}A$

Hence, by mathematical induction, Eq. (ii) is true for all $n \in N$.

16. Similar as Example 10.

17. **Hint** $A^2 = A \cdot A = \begin{bmatrix} 9 & 7 & 5 \\ 1 & 4 & 1 \\ 8 & 9 & 9 \end{bmatrix}$

and $\quad A^3 = A^2 \cdot A = \begin{bmatrix} 28 & 37 & 26 \\ 10 & 5 & 1 \\ 35 & 42 & 34 \end{bmatrix}$

Now, consider LHS $= A^3 - 4A^2 - 3A + 11I$

$$= \begin{bmatrix} 28 & 37 & 26 \\ 10 & 5 & 1 \\ 35 & 42 & 34 \end{bmatrix} - 4\begin{bmatrix} 9 & 7 & 5 \\ 1 & 4 & 1 \\ 8 & 9 & 9 \end{bmatrix} - 3\begin{bmatrix} 1 & 3 & 2 \\ 2 & 0 & -1 \\ 1 & 2 & 3 \end{bmatrix} + 11\begin{bmatrix} 1 & 0 & 0 \\ 0 & 1 & 0 \\ 0 & 0 & 1 \end{bmatrix}$$

$$= \begin{bmatrix} 0 & 0 & 0 \\ 0 & 0 & 0 \\ 0 & 0 & 0 \end{bmatrix} = 0 = \text{RHS}$$

18. Solve as Question 18.

Transpose of a Matrix

The matrix obtained by interchanging the rows and columns of matrix A is called the transpose of matrix A. The transpose of matrix A is represented by A' or A^c or A^T.

In other words, if $A = [a_{ij}]_{m\times n}$ is a matrix.

Then, $A^T = [a_{ji}]_{n\times m}$.

e.g. Let $A = \begin{bmatrix} 1 & 5 \\ \sqrt{2} & 1 \\ -1/5 & 0 \end{bmatrix}_{3\times 2}$.

Then, $A' = \begin{bmatrix} 1 & \sqrt{2} & -1/5 \\ 5 & 1 & 0 \end{bmatrix}_{2\times 3}$

EXAMPLE 1. Find the transpose of the matrix $\begin{bmatrix} 4 & 3 & 1 \\ 1 & -2 & 3 \\ 4 & 5 & -1 \end{bmatrix}$.

Sol. Let $A = \begin{bmatrix} 4 & 3 & 1 \\ 1 & -2 & 3 \\ 4 & 5 & -1 \end{bmatrix}$.

Then, $A' = \begin{bmatrix} 4 & 3 & 1 \\ 1 & -2 & 3 \\ 4 & 5 & -1 \end{bmatrix}' = \begin{bmatrix} 4 & 1 & 4 \\ 3 & -2 & 5 \\ 1 & 3 & -1 \end{bmatrix}$

[interchanging the elements of rows and columns]

Properties of Transpose of Matrices

For any matrices A and B of suitable orders, we have

(i) $(A')' = A$

(ii) $(kA)' = kA'$, where k is any constant.

(iii) $(A \pm B)' = A' \pm B'$

(iv) $(AB)' = B'A'$ [reversal law]

Note $(A^n)^T = (A^T)^n$, where n is a positive integer.

EXAMPLE 2. If $A = \begin{bmatrix} 3 & \sqrt{3} & 2 \\ 4 & 2 & 0 \end{bmatrix}$ and $B = \begin{bmatrix} 2 & -1 & 2 \\ 1 & 2 & 4 \end{bmatrix}$, then verify that

(i) $(A')' = A$

(ii) $(kB)' = kB'$, where k is any constant.

(iii) $(A + B)' = A' + B'$

Sol. We have, $A = \begin{bmatrix} 3 & \sqrt{3} & 2 \\ 4 & 2 & 0 \end{bmatrix}$ and $B = \begin{bmatrix} 2 & -1 & 2 \\ 1 & 2 & 4 \end{bmatrix}$, then

$A' = \begin{bmatrix} 3 & 4 \\ \sqrt{3} & 2 \\ 2 & 0 \end{bmatrix}$ and $B' = \begin{bmatrix} 2 & 1 \\ -1 & 2 \\ 2 & 4 \end{bmatrix}$

[interchanging the elements of rows and columns]

(i) $(A')' = \begin{bmatrix} 3 & 4 \\ \sqrt{3} & 2 \\ 2 & 0 \end{bmatrix}' = \begin{bmatrix} 3 & \sqrt{3} & 2 \\ 4 & 2 & 0 \end{bmatrix} = A$

[interchanging the elements of rows and columns]

(ii) $kB = k\begin{bmatrix} 2 & -1 & 2 \\ 1 & 2 & 4 \end{bmatrix} = \begin{bmatrix} 2k & -k & 2k \\ k & 2k & 4k \end{bmatrix}$

and $(kB)' = \begin{bmatrix} 2k & -k & 2k \\ k & 2k & 4k \end{bmatrix}' = \begin{bmatrix} 2k & k \\ -k & 2k \\ 2k & 4k \end{bmatrix}$

$= k\begin{bmatrix} 2 & 1 \\ -1 & 2 \\ 2 & 4 \end{bmatrix} = kB'$

Thus, $(kB)' = kB'$

(iii) $A + B = \begin{bmatrix} 3 & \sqrt{3} & 2 \\ 4 & 2 & 0 \end{bmatrix} + \begin{bmatrix} 2 & -1 & 2 \\ 1 & 2 & 4 \end{bmatrix}$

$= \begin{bmatrix} 3+2 & \sqrt{3}-1 & 2+2 \\ 4+1 & 2+2 & 0+4 \end{bmatrix}$

$= \begin{bmatrix} 5 & \sqrt{3}-1 & 4 \\ 5 & 4 & 4 \end{bmatrix}$

$\therefore \quad (A + B)' = \begin{bmatrix} 5 & \sqrt{3}-1 & 4 \\ 5 & 4 & 4 \end{bmatrix}' = \begin{bmatrix} 5 & 5 \\ \sqrt{3}-1 & 4 \\ 4 & 4 \end{bmatrix}$ ...(i)

[interchanging the elements of rows and columns]

and $A' + B' = \begin{bmatrix} 3 & 4 \\ \sqrt{3} & 2 \\ 2 & 0 \end{bmatrix} + \begin{bmatrix} 2 & 1 \\ -1 & 2 \\ 2 & 4 \end{bmatrix}$

$= \begin{bmatrix} 3+2 & 4+1 \\ \sqrt{3}-1 & 2+2 \\ 2+2 & 0+4 \end{bmatrix} = \begin{bmatrix} 5 & 5 \\ \sqrt{3}-1 & 4 \\ 4 & 4 \end{bmatrix}$ ...(ii)

Thus, $(A + B)' = A' + B'$ [from Eqs. (i) and (ii)]

EXAMPLE 3. For the matrices A and B, verify that

$(AB)' = B'A'$, where $A = \begin{bmatrix} 1 \\ -4 \\ 3 \end{bmatrix}$ and $B = [-1 \quad 2 \quad 1]$.

Sol. Given, $A = \begin{bmatrix} 1 \\ -4 \\ 3 \end{bmatrix}_{3\times 1}$ and $B = [-1 \quad 2 \quad 1]_{1\times 3}$

$\therefore \quad A' = [1 \quad -4 \quad 3]_{1\times 3}$

[interchanging the elements of rows and columns]

and $B' = \begin{bmatrix} -1 \\ 2 \\ 1 \end{bmatrix}_{3\times 1}$

[interchanging the elements of rows and columns]

Now, $AB = \begin{bmatrix} 1 \\ -4 \\ 3 \end{bmatrix}_{3\times 1} \begin{bmatrix} -1 & 2 & 1 \end{bmatrix}_{1\times 3}$

Since, number of columns in A is equal to the number of rows in B. So, AB exist.

Thus, $AB = \begin{bmatrix} -1 & 2 & 1 \\ 4 & -8 & -4 \\ -3 & 6 & 3 \end{bmatrix}_{3\times 3}$

[multiplying rows by columns]

$\Rightarrow (AB)' = \begin{bmatrix} -1 & 4 & -3 \\ 2 & -8 & 6 \\ 1 & -4 & 3 \end{bmatrix}_{3\times 3}$ ...(i)

[interchanging the elements of rows and columns]

Now, $B'A' = \begin{bmatrix} -1 \\ 2 \\ 1 \end{bmatrix}_{3\times 1} \begin{bmatrix} 1 & -4 & 3 \end{bmatrix}_{1\times 3} = \begin{bmatrix} -1 & 4 & -3 \\ 2 & -8 & 6 \\ 1 & -4 & 3 \end{bmatrix}_{3\times 3}$

[multiplying rows by columns] ...(ii)

From Eqs. (i) and (ii), we get

$(AB)' = B'A'$ **Hence verified.**

EXAMPLE 4. Find the values of a, b, c if the matrix $A = \begin{bmatrix} 0 & 2b & c \\ a & b & -c \\ a & -b & c \end{bmatrix}$ satisfies the equation $A'A = I_3$.

Sol. Given that, $A = \begin{bmatrix} 0 & 2b & c \\ a & b & -c \\ a & -b & c \end{bmatrix}$

$$\Rightarrow \quad A' = \begin{bmatrix} 0 & a & a \\ 2b & b & -b \\ c & -c & c \end{bmatrix}$$

Now, $A'A = I_3$

$$\Rightarrow \begin{bmatrix} 0 & a & a \\ 2b & b & -b \\ c & -c & c \end{bmatrix} \begin{bmatrix} 0 & 2b & c \\ a & b & -c \\ a & -b & c \end{bmatrix} = \begin{bmatrix} 1 & 0 & 0 \\ 0 & 1 & 0 \\ 0 & 0 & 1 \end{bmatrix}$$

$$\Rightarrow \begin{bmatrix} 2a^2 & 0 & 0 \\ 0 & 6b^2 & 0 \\ 0 & 0 & 3c^2 \end{bmatrix} = \begin{bmatrix} 1 & 0 & 0 \\ 0 & 1 & 0 \\ 0 & 0 & 1 \end{bmatrix}$$

$$\Rightarrow \quad 2a^2 = 1, 6b^2 = 1, 3c^2 = 1$$

$$\Rightarrow \quad a = \pm\frac{1}{\sqrt{2}}, b = \pm\frac{1}{\sqrt{6}}, c = \pm\frac{1}{\sqrt{3}}$$

Symmetric Matrix

A square matrix A is called a symmetric matrix, if the transpose of matrix A is equal to the matrix A, i.e. $A' = A$. In other words, let $A = [a_{ij}]_{n\times n}$, then A is said to be symmetric, if $[a_{ij}] = [a_{ji}]$, for all possible values of i and j.

e.g. $A = \begin{bmatrix} 2 & 1 & 5 \\ 1 & 2 & 7 \\ 5 & 7 & 3 \end{bmatrix}$

Then, $A' = \begin{bmatrix} 2 & 1 & 5 \\ 1 & 2 & 7 \\ 5 & 7 & 3 \end{bmatrix}' = \begin{bmatrix} 2 & 1 & 5 \\ 1 & 2 & 7 \\ 5 & 7 & 3 \end{bmatrix} = A$

[interchanging the elements of rows and columns]

Hence, A is a symmetric matrix. $[\because A' = A]$

EXAMPLE 5. Show that matrix $A = \begin{bmatrix} 3 & -4 & 2 \\ -4 & 0 & 6 \\ 2 & 6 & 1 \end{bmatrix}$ is symmetric matrix.

Sol. Given, $A = \begin{bmatrix} 3 & -4 & 2 \\ -4 & 0 & 6 \\ 2 & 6 & 1 \end{bmatrix}$

Now, $A' = \begin{bmatrix} 3 & -4 & 2 \\ -4 & 0 & 6 \\ 2 & 6 & 1 \end{bmatrix}' = \begin{bmatrix} 3 & -4 & 2 \\ -4 & 0 & 6 \\ 2 & 6 & 1 \end{bmatrix} = A$

[interchanging the elements of rows and columns]

$\therefore A$ is a symmetric matrix.

EXAMPLE 6. Show that all positive integral powers of a symmetric matrix are symmetric.

Sol. Let A be a symmetric matrix and $n \in N$.

Then, $(A^n)^T = [A \cdot A \cdot A \ldots n \text{ times}]^T$

$= [A^T \cdot A^T \ldots n \text{ times}]$ $[\because (AB)^T = B^T A^T]$

$= [A\ A \ldots n \text{ times}] = (A)^n$

$[\because A$ is symmetric, therefore $A^T = A]$

Skew-symmetric Matrix

A square matrix A is said to be skew-symmetric matrix, if the transpose of matrix A is equal to the negative of matrix A. i.e. $A' = -A$.

In other words, let $A = [a_{ij}]_{n\times n}$, then A is said to be skew-symmetric matrix, if $[a_{ji}] = -[a_{ij}]$, for all values of i and j.

e.g. Let $A=\begin{bmatrix}0&1&2\\-1&0&5\\-2&-5&0\end{bmatrix}$. Then, $A'=\begin{bmatrix}0&-1&-2\\1&0&-5\\2&5&0\end{bmatrix}$

[interchanging the elements of rows and columns]

$$=-\begin{bmatrix}0&1&2\\-1&0&5\\-2&-5&0\end{bmatrix}$$

[taking (−1) common from the matrix]

$\Rightarrow \quad A'=-A$

Note

(i) The principal diagonal elements of a skew-symmetric matrix are always zero, because if we put $i=j$ in $a_{ji}=-a_{ij}$, then $a_{ii}=-a_{ii}$.
$\therefore\ 2a_{ii}=0\Rightarrow a_{ii}=0,\ \forall\, i.$

(ii) The only zero matrix is both symmetric and skew-symmetric matrix.

EXAMPLE 7. Show that matrix $B=\begin{bmatrix}0&3&-4\\-3&0&2\\4&-2&0\end{bmatrix}$ is skew-symmetric matrix.

Sol. Given, $B=\begin{bmatrix}0&3&-4\\-3&0&2\\4&-2&0\end{bmatrix}$

Now, $B'=\begin{bmatrix}0&3&-4\\-3&0&2\\4&-2&0\end{bmatrix}'=\begin{bmatrix}0&-3&4\\3&0&-2\\-4&2&0\end{bmatrix}$

[interchanging the elements of rows and columns]

$$=-\begin{bmatrix}0&3&-4\\-3&0&2\\4&-2&0\end{bmatrix}$$

[taking (−1) common from the matrix]

$\therefore \quad B'=-B$

Hence, B is skew-symmetric matrix.

EXAMPLE 8. For what value of x, the matrix $A=\begin{bmatrix}0&1&-2\\-1&0&3\\x&-3&0\end{bmatrix}$ is skew-symmetric matrix?

Sol. Given, $A=\begin{bmatrix}0&1&-2\\-1&0&3\\x&-3&0\end{bmatrix}$.

We know that, if A is a skew-symmetric matrix, then

$$A=-A^T \qquad \text{...(i)}$$

From Eq. (i), we get

$$\begin{bmatrix}0&1&-2\\-1&0&3\\x&-3&0\end{bmatrix}=-\begin{bmatrix}0&-1&x\\1&0&-3\\-2&3&0\end{bmatrix}$$

$$\Rightarrow \begin{bmatrix}0&1&-2\\-1&0&3\\x&-3&0\end{bmatrix}=\begin{bmatrix}0&1&-x\\-1&0&3\\2&-3&0\end{bmatrix}$$

On comparing the corresponding element, we get

$$-2=-x\Rightarrow x=2$$

Some Important Theorems

Theorem 1 For a square matrix A with real number entries, $A+A'$ is a symmetric and $A-A'$ is a skew-symmetric matrix.

Theorem 2 A square matrix A can be expressed as the sum of a symmetric and skew-symmetric matrices.

i.e. $A=\frac{1}{2}(A+A')+\frac{1}{2}(A-A')$, where $\frac{1}{2}(A+A')$ is symmetric and $\frac{1}{2}(A-A')$ is skew-symmetric.

EXAMPLE 9. Prove that the square matrix $\begin{bmatrix}5&2\\3&-6\end{bmatrix}$ can be expressed as a sum of symmetric and skew-symmetric matrices.

Sol. Let $A=\begin{bmatrix}5&2\\3&-6\end{bmatrix}$. Then, $A'=\begin{bmatrix}5&3\\2&-6\end{bmatrix}$

[interchanging the elements of rows and columns]

Now, $A+A'=\begin{bmatrix}5&2\\3&-6\end{bmatrix}+\begin{bmatrix}5&3\\2&-6\end{bmatrix}$

$\Rightarrow \quad A+A'=\begin{bmatrix}5+5&2+3\\3+2&-6-6\end{bmatrix}=\begin{bmatrix}10&5\\5&-12\end{bmatrix}$

$\Rightarrow \quad \frac{1}{2}(A+A')=\frac{1}{2}\begin{bmatrix}10&5\\5&-12\end{bmatrix}$, which is symmetric. ...(i)

Also, $A-A'=\begin{bmatrix}5&2\\3&-6\end{bmatrix}-\begin{bmatrix}5&3\\2&-6\end{bmatrix}$

$$=\begin{bmatrix}5-5&2-3\\3-2&-6+6\end{bmatrix}=\begin{bmatrix}0&-1\\1&0\end{bmatrix}$$

$\Rightarrow \quad \frac{1}{2}(A-A')=\frac{1}{2}\begin{bmatrix}0&-1\\1&0\end{bmatrix}$,

which is skew-symmetric. ...(ii)

On adding Eqs. (i) and (ii), we get

$$\frac{1}{2}(A+A')+\frac{1}{2}(A-A')=\frac{1}{2}\begin{bmatrix}10&5\\5&-12\end{bmatrix}+\frac{1}{2}\begin{bmatrix}0&-1\\1&0\end{bmatrix}$$

$$=\frac{1}{2}\begin{bmatrix}10+0&5-1\\5+1&-12+0\end{bmatrix}$$

$$=\frac{1}{2}\begin{bmatrix}10&4\\6&-12\end{bmatrix}=\begin{bmatrix}5&2\\3&-6\end{bmatrix}=A$$

Hence proved.

EXAMPLE 10. Express the following matrix as a sum of a symmetric and a skew-symmetric matrices $\begin{bmatrix} 3 & -2 & -4 \\ 3 & -2 & -5 \\ -1 & 1 & 2 \end{bmatrix}$.

Sol. Let $A = \begin{bmatrix} 3 & -2 & -4 \\ 3 & -2 & -5 \\ -1 & 1 & 2 \end{bmatrix}$

$$\therefore\ A' = \begin{bmatrix} 3 & 3 & -1 \\ -2 & -2 & 1 \\ -4 & -5 & 2 \end{bmatrix}$$

Now, let $P = \frac{1}{2}(A + A')$

$$= \frac{1}{2}\left\{\begin{bmatrix} 3 & -2 & -4 \\ 3 & -2 & -5 \\ -1 & 1 & 2 \end{bmatrix} + \begin{bmatrix} 3 & 3 & -1 \\ -2 & -2 & 1 \\ -4 & -5 & 2 \end{bmatrix}\right\}$$

$$= \frac{1}{2}\begin{bmatrix} 6 & 1 & -5 \\ 1 & -4 & -4 \\ -5 & -4 & 4 \end{bmatrix} = \begin{bmatrix} 3 & 1/2 & -5/2 \\ 1/2 & -2 & -2 \\ -5/2 & -2 & 2 \end{bmatrix}$$

and $Q = \frac{1}{2}(A - A')$

$$= \frac{1}{2}\left\{\begin{bmatrix} 3 & -2 & -4 \\ 3 & -2 & -5 \\ -1 & 1 & 2 \end{bmatrix} - \begin{bmatrix} 3 & 3 & -1 \\ -2 & -2 & 1 \\ -4 & -5 & 2 \end{bmatrix}\right\}$$

$$= \frac{1}{2}\begin{bmatrix} 0 & -5 & -3 \\ 5 & 0 & -6 \\ 3 & 6 & 0 \end{bmatrix}$$

$$= \begin{bmatrix} 0 & -5/2 & -3/2 \\ 5/2 & 0 & -3 \\ 3/2 & 3 & 0 \end{bmatrix}$$

Clearly, here $P' = \begin{bmatrix} 3 & 1/2 & -5/2 \\ 1/2 & -2 & -2 \\ -5/2 & -2 & 2 \end{bmatrix} = P$

and $Q' = \begin{bmatrix} 0 & 5/2 & 3/2 \\ -5/2 & 0 & 3 \\ -3/2 & -3 & 0 \end{bmatrix} = -Q$

So, P is a symmetric matrix and Q is a skew-symmetric matrix.

Now, $P + Q = \frac{1}{2}(A + A') + \frac{1}{2}(A - A')$

$$= \begin{bmatrix} 3 & 1/2 & -5/2 \\ 1/2 & -2 & -2 \\ -5/2 & -2 & 2 \end{bmatrix} + \begin{bmatrix} 0 & -5/2 & -3/2 \\ 5/2 & 0 & -3 \\ 3/2 & 3 & 0 \end{bmatrix}$$

$$= \begin{bmatrix} 3 & -2 & -4 \\ 3 & -2 & -5 \\ -1 & 1 & 2 \end{bmatrix} = A$$

Thus, given matrix is expressed as the sum of symmetric matrix and skew-symmetric matrix.

Topic Practice 4

1 Find the transpose of the following matrix:

(i) $\begin{bmatrix} -1 & 5 & 6 \\ \sqrt{3} & 5 & 6 \\ 2 & 3 & -1 \end{bmatrix}$ (ii) $\begin{bmatrix} 5 \\ 1/2 \\ -1 \end{bmatrix}$ (iii) $\begin{bmatrix} -4 & 1 & -5 \\ 1 & 2 & 0 \\ 1 & 3 & 1 \end{bmatrix}$

(iv) $\begin{bmatrix} -1 & 2 & 3 \\ 5 & 7 & 9 \\ -2 & 1 & 1 \end{bmatrix}$ (v) $\begin{bmatrix} -1 & 5 & 6 \\ \sqrt{3} & 5 & 6 \\ 2 & 3 & 1 \end{bmatrix}$

2 Verify for the given matrices.

(i) If $A = \begin{bmatrix} -1 & 2 & 3 \\ 5 & 7 & 9 \\ -2 & 1 & 1 \end{bmatrix}$ and $B = \begin{bmatrix} -4 & 1 & -5 \\ 1 & 2 & 0 \\ 1 & 3 & 1 \end{bmatrix}$, then verify that $(A + B)' = A' + B'$.

(ii) If $A' = \begin{bmatrix} 3 & 4 \\ -1 & 2 \\ 0 & 1 \end{bmatrix}$ and $B = \begin{bmatrix} -1 & 2 & 1 \\ 1 & 2 & 3 \end{bmatrix}$, then verify that $(A + B)' = A' + B'$.

(iii) If $A = \begin{bmatrix} 2 & 3 & -5 \\ 0 & -1 & 4 \end{bmatrix}$, then verify that $(3A)' = 3A'$.

(iv) If $A = \begin{bmatrix} 1 & 2 \\ 4 & 1 \\ 5 & 6 \end{bmatrix}$ and $B = \begin{bmatrix} 1 & 2 \\ 6 & 4 \\ 7 & 3 \end{bmatrix}$, then verify that $(2A + B)' = 2A' + B'$.

3 If $A = \begin{bmatrix} 1 & 2 & 2 \\ 2 & 1 & -2 \\ x & 2 & y \end{bmatrix}$ is matrix which statisfies $AA' = 9I_3$, then find the values of x and y.

4 If the matrix $A = \begin{bmatrix} 0 & a & -3 \\ 2 & 0 & -1 \\ b & 1 & 0 \end{bmatrix}$ is skew-symmetric, find the values of 'a' and 'b'.

5 If matrix $\begin{bmatrix} 0 & a & 3 \\ 2 & b & -1 \\ c & 1 & 0 \end{bmatrix}$ is a skew-symmetric matrix, then find the values of a, b and c.

6 Matrix $A = \begin{bmatrix} 0 & 2b & -2 \\ 3 & 1 & 3 \\ 3a & 3 & -1 \end{bmatrix}$ is given to be symmetric, then find the values of a and b.

7 If $A^T = \begin{bmatrix} 3 & 4 \\ -1 & 2 \\ 0 & 1 \end{bmatrix}$ and $B = \begin{bmatrix} -1 & 2 & 1 \\ 1 & 2 & 3 \end{bmatrix}$, then find $A^T - B^T$.

8 Show that matrix $A = \begin{bmatrix} 1 & -1 & 5 \\ -1 & 2 & 1 \\ 5 & 1 & 3 \end{bmatrix}$ is a symmetric matrix.

9 Show that matrix $A = \begin{bmatrix} 0 & 1 & -1 \\ -1 & 0 & 1 \\ 1 & -1 & 0 \end{bmatrix}$ is a skew-symmetric matrix.

Directions (Q. Nos. 10-16) *Verify the statements.*

10 If A is a skew-symmetric matrix, then show that A^2 is a symmetric matrix.

11 Write a 2×2 matrix which is both symmetric and skew-symmetric.

12 Show that $A'A$ and AA' are both symmetric matrices for any matrix A.

13 If A is symmetric, then show that $B'AB$ is a symmetric matrix.

14 Show that all the diagonal elements of a skew-symmetric matrix are zero.

15 If A and B are symmetric matrices, then prove that $AB + BA$ is a symmetric matrix.

16 Show that a matrix which is both symmetric as well as the skew-symmetric matrix is a null matrix.

17 Write a 3×3 skew-symmetric matrix.

18 If $A' = \begin{bmatrix} -2 & 3 \\ 1 & 2 \end{bmatrix}$ and $B = \begin{bmatrix} -1 & 0 \\ 1 & 2 \end{bmatrix}$, then find $(A + 2B)'$.

19 If $A = \begin{bmatrix} 2 & 0 \\ 1 & 4 \end{bmatrix}$ and $B = \begin{bmatrix} -1 & 2 \\ 3 & 0 \end{bmatrix}$, then find $(AB)'$.

20 If $A = \begin{bmatrix} 2 & 4 & 0 \\ 3 & 9 & 6 \end{bmatrix}$ and $B = \begin{bmatrix} 1 & 4 \\ 2 & 8 \\ 1 & 3 \end{bmatrix}$, then verify that $(AB)' = B'A'$.

21 If $A = [a_{ij}]$ is a square matrix such that $a_{ij} = i^2 - j^2$, then check whether A is symmetric or skew-symmetric matrix.

22 For the matrix $A = \begin{bmatrix} 1 & 5 \\ 6 & 7 \end{bmatrix}$, verify that

(i) $(A + A')$ is a symmetric matrix.

(ii) $(A - A')$ is a skew-symmetric matrix.

23 Express the following matrices as a sum of symmetric and skew-symmetric matrices.

(i) $A = \begin{bmatrix} 2 & 3 \\ -1 & 4 \end{bmatrix}$ (ii) $A = \begin{bmatrix} 3 & 5 \\ 1 & -1 \end{bmatrix}$

(iii) $A = \begin{bmatrix} 2 & 4 & -6 \\ 7 & 3 & 5 \\ 1 & -2 & 4 \end{bmatrix}$ (iv) $A = \begin{bmatrix} 2 & 3 & 1 \\ 1 & -1 & 2 \\ 4 & 1 & 2 \end{bmatrix}$

(v) $\begin{bmatrix} 6 & -2 & 2 \\ -2 & 3 & -1 \\ 2 & -1 & 3 \end{bmatrix}$ (vi) $\begin{bmatrix} 3 & 3 & -1 \\ -2 & -2 & 1 \\ -4 & -5 & 2 \end{bmatrix}$

Hints & Solutions

1. Similar as Example 1.

Ans. (i) $\begin{bmatrix} -1 & \sqrt{3} & 2 \\ 5 & 5 & 3 \\ 6 & 6 & -1 \end{bmatrix}$ (ii) $[5 \;\; 1/2 \;\; -1]$

(iii) $\begin{bmatrix} -4 & 1 & 1 \\ 1 & 2 & 3 \\ -5 & 0 & 1 \end{bmatrix}$ (iv) $\begin{bmatrix} -1 & 5 & -2 \\ 2 & 7 & 1 \\ 3 & 9 & 1 \end{bmatrix}$ (v) $\begin{bmatrix} -1 & \sqrt{3} & 2 \\ 5 & 5 & 3 \\ 6 & 6 & 1 \end{bmatrix}$

2. (i) Similar as Example 2 (iii).
(ii) Similar as Example 2 (iii).
(iii) Similar as Example 2 (ii).
(iv) Similar as Example 2 (iii).

3. Similar as Example 8. **Ans.** $x = -2$ and $y = -1$

4. Given, $A = \begin{bmatrix} 0 & a & -3 \\ 2 & 0 & -1 \\ b & 1 & 0 \end{bmatrix}$ is a skew-symmetric matrix.

$\therefore \quad A^T = -A$

$$\Rightarrow \begin{bmatrix} 0 & a & -3 \\ 2 & 0 & -1 \\ b & 1 & 0 \end{bmatrix}^T = -\begin{bmatrix} 0 & a & -3 \\ 2 & 0 & -1 \\ b & 1 & 0 \end{bmatrix}$$

$$\Rightarrow \begin{bmatrix} 0 & 2 & b \\ a & 0 & 1 \\ -3 & -1 & 0 \end{bmatrix} = \begin{bmatrix} 0 & -a & 3 \\ -2 & 0 & 1 \\ -b & -1 & 0 \end{bmatrix}$$

On equating the corresponding elements, we get

$$a = -2 \text{ and } b = 3$$

5. Similar as Question 4. **Ans.** $a=-2, b=0$ and $c=-3$

6. Given, $A=\begin{bmatrix}0 & 2b & -2\\ 3 & 1 & 3\\ 3a & 3 & -1\end{bmatrix}$ is a symmetric matrix.

We know that a matrix A is symmetric, if $A'=A$.

$\therefore$ We have, $\begin{bmatrix}0 & 2b & -2\\ 3 & 1 & 3\\ 3a & 3 & -1\end{bmatrix}'=\begin{bmatrix}0 & 2b & -2\\ 3 & 1 & 3\\ 3a & 3 & -1\end{bmatrix}$

$\Rightarrow \begin{bmatrix}0 & 3 & 3a\\ 2b & 1 & 3\\ -2 & 3 & -1\end{bmatrix}=\begin{bmatrix}0 & 2b & -2\\ 3 & 1 & 3\\ 3a & 3 & -1\end{bmatrix}$

On equating the corresponding elements, we get

$3=2b$ and $3a=-2$

$\therefore \quad b=\frac{3}{2}$ and $a=-\frac{2}{3}$

7. $A^T-B^T=\begin{bmatrix}3 & 4\\ -1 & 2\\ 0 & 1\end{bmatrix}-\begin{bmatrix}-1 & 1\\ 2 & 2\\ 1 & 3\end{bmatrix}=\begin{bmatrix}4 & 3\\ -3 & 0\\ -1 & -2\end{bmatrix}$

8. Similar as Example 5.

9. Similar as Example 7.

10. Now, $(A^2)'=(AA)'$

$=A'A'=(-A)(-A)$ $\quad [\because A'=-A]$

$=A^2$

11. A null or zero matrix of order 2×2 is both symmetric and skew-symmetric.

12. Consider, $(A'A)'=(A)'(A')'$ $\quad [\because (AB)'=B'A']$

$=A'\cdot A$ $\quad [\because (A')'=A]$

Hence, $A'A$ is symmetric matrix for any matrix A.

Now, $(AA')'=(A')'(A)'=A\,A'$ $\quad [\because (AB)'=B'A']$

Hence, $A\,A'$ is also symmetric matrix for any matrix A.

13. Given, A is a symmetric matrix.

$\therefore \quad A'=A$

Now, $(B'A\,B)'=(A\,B)'(B')'$ $\quad [\because (CD)'=D'C']$

$\Rightarrow (B'A\,B)'=B'A'B$ $\quad [\because (B')'=B]$

$\Rightarrow (B'A\,B)'=B'A\,B$ $\quad [\because A'=A]$

Hence, $B'A\,B$ is a symmetric matrix.

14. Let $A=[a_{ij}]$ be a skew-symmetric matrix.

Then, $a_{ij}=-a_{ji}$ for all i,j.

Now, if we put $i=j$, we get

$a_{ii}=-a_{ii}$ for all values of i

$\Rightarrow 2a_{ii}=0$ for all values of i

$\Rightarrow a_{ii}=0$ for all values of i

$\Rightarrow a_{11}=a_{22}=a_{33}=\dots=a_{nn}=0$

$\Rightarrow$ All the diagonal elements of a skew-symmetric matrix are zero.

15. Given, A and B are symmetric matrices.

$\therefore\ A'=A$ and $B'=B$

Now, $(AB+BA)'=(AB)'+(BA)'$

$[\because (A+B)'=A'+B']$

$=B'A'+A'B'$ $\quad [\because (AB)'=B'A']$

$=BA+AB$ $\quad [\because A'=A$ and $B'=B]$

$=AB+BA$

$[\because$ matrix addition is commutative$]$

Hence, $AB+BA$ is a symmetric matrix.

16. Let A be a matrix, which is both symmetric and skew-symmetric.

Then, we have $A^T=A$ $\quad$ [as A is symmetric]...(i)

and $A^T=-A$ $\quad$ [as A is skew-symmetric]...(ii)

From Eqs. (i) and (ii), we get

$A=-A$

$\Rightarrow A+A=O \Rightarrow 2A=O$

$\Rightarrow A=O$

Hence, matrix A, which is both symmetric and skew-symmetric is a null matrix.

17. **Hint** Find the matrix A of order 3×3 such that $A'=-A$.

Ans. $\begin{bmatrix}0 & 2 & -3\\ -2 & 0 & 4\\ 3 & -4 & 0\end{bmatrix}$

18. We have, $A'=\begin{bmatrix}-2 & 3\\ 1 & 2\end{bmatrix}$ and $B=\begin{bmatrix}-1 & 0\\ 1 & 2\end{bmatrix}$

$\therefore \quad A=(A')'=\begin{bmatrix}-2 & 3\\ 1 & 2\end{bmatrix}'=\begin{bmatrix}-2 & 1\\ 3 & 2\end{bmatrix}$

[interchanging the elements of rows and columns]

Now, $A+2B=\begin{bmatrix}-2 & 1\\ 3 & 2\end{bmatrix}+2\begin{bmatrix}-1 & 0\\ 1 & 2\end{bmatrix}$

$=\begin{bmatrix}-2 & 1\\ 3 & 2\end{bmatrix}+\begin{bmatrix}-2 & 0\\ 2 & 4\end{bmatrix}$

$=\begin{bmatrix}-2-2 & 1+0\\ 3+2 & 2+4\end{bmatrix}$

$=\begin{bmatrix}-4 & 1\\ 5 & 6\end{bmatrix}$

$\Rightarrow (A+2B)'=\begin{bmatrix}-4 & 1\\ 5 & 6\end{bmatrix}'=\begin{bmatrix}-4 & 5\\ 1 & 6\end{bmatrix}$

[interchanging the elements of rows and columns]

19. Now, $AB=\begin{bmatrix}2 & 0\\ 1 & 4\end{bmatrix}\begin{bmatrix}-1 & 2\\ 3 & 0\end{bmatrix}$

$=\begin{bmatrix}-2+0 & 4+0\\ -1+12 & 2+0\end{bmatrix}=\begin{bmatrix}-2 & 4\\ 11 & 2\end{bmatrix}$

[multiplying rows by columns]

$\therefore \quad (AB)'=\begin{bmatrix}-2 & 4\\ 11 & 2\end{bmatrix}'=\begin{bmatrix}-2 & 11\\ 4 & 2\end{bmatrix}$

[interchanging the elements of rows and columns]

20. Similar as Example 3.

21. Consider a square matrix of order 2, i.e. $A = [a_{ij}]_{2\times 2}$

Given, $a_{ij} = i^2 - j^2$

$$\therefore \quad a_{11} = 1^2 - 1^2 = 1 - 1 = 0,$$
$$a_{12} = 1^2 - 2^2 = 1 - 4 = -3$$
$$a_{21} = 2^2 - 1^2 = 4 - 1 = 3$$
$$a_{22} = 2^2 - 2^2 = 0$$

Now, $A = \begin{bmatrix} a_{11} & a_{12} \\ a_{21} & a_{22} \end{bmatrix} = \begin{bmatrix} 0 & -3 \\ 3 & 0 \end{bmatrix}$

$$\Rightarrow \quad A' = \begin{bmatrix} 0 & -3 \\ 3 & 0 \end{bmatrix}' = \begin{bmatrix} 0 & 3 \\ -3 & 0 \end{bmatrix}$$

[interchanging the elements of rows and columns]

$$= -\begin{bmatrix} 0 & -3 \\ 3 & 0 \end{bmatrix} = -A$$

[taking (−1) common from the matrix]

Hence, A is skew-symmetric matrix.

22. (i) Here, $A + A' = \begin{bmatrix} 1 & 5 \\ 6 & 7 \end{bmatrix} + \begin{bmatrix} 1 & 5 \\ 6 & 7 \end{bmatrix}'$

$$= \begin{bmatrix} 1 & 5 \\ 6 & 7 \end{bmatrix} + \begin{bmatrix} 1 & 6 \\ 5 & 7 \end{bmatrix}$$

$$= \begin{bmatrix} 2 & 11 \\ 11 & 14 \end{bmatrix}$$

and $(A + A')' = \begin{bmatrix} 2 & 11 \\ 11 & 14 \end{bmatrix} = A + A'$

$\therefore (A + A')$ is a symmetric matrix.

(ii) Here, $A - A' = \begin{bmatrix} 1 & 5 \\ 6 & 7 \end{bmatrix} - \begin{bmatrix} 1 & 5 \\ 6 & 7 \end{bmatrix}'$

$$= \begin{bmatrix} 1 & 5 \\ 6 & 7 \end{bmatrix} - \begin{bmatrix} 1 & 6 \\ 5 & 7 \end{bmatrix} = \begin{bmatrix} 0 & -1 \\ 1 & 0 \end{bmatrix}$$

and $(A - A')' = \begin{bmatrix} 0 & 1 \\ -1 & 0 \end{bmatrix} = -\begin{bmatrix} 0 & -1 \\ 1 & 0 \end{bmatrix} = -(A - A')$

$\therefore (A - A')$ is a skew-symmetric matrix.

23. (i) Similar as Example 10.

Ans. $\begin{bmatrix} 2 & 1 \\ 1 & 4 \end{bmatrix} + \begin{bmatrix} 0 & 2 \\ -2 & 0 \end{bmatrix}$

(ii) Similar as Example 10.

Ans. $\begin{bmatrix} 3 & 3 \\ 3 & -1 \end{bmatrix} + \begin{bmatrix} 0 & 2 \\ -2 & 0 \end{bmatrix}$

(iii) Similar as Example 10.

Ans. $\begin{bmatrix} 2 & \frac{11}{2} & \frac{-5}{2} \\ \frac{11}{2} & 3 & \frac{3}{2} \\ \frac{-5}{2} & \frac{3}{2} & 4 \end{bmatrix} + \begin{bmatrix} 0 & \frac{-3}{2} & \frac{-7}{2} \\ \frac{3}{2} & 0 & \frac{7}{2} \\ \frac{7}{2} & \frac{-7}{2} & 0 \end{bmatrix}$

(iv) Similar as Example 10.

Ans. $\begin{bmatrix} 2 & 2 & \frac{5}{2} \\ 2 & -1 & \frac{3}{2} \\ \frac{5}{2} & \frac{3}{2} & 2 \end{bmatrix} + \begin{bmatrix} 0 & 1 & \frac{-3}{2} \\ -1 & 0 & \frac{1}{2} \\ \frac{3}{2} & \frac{-1}{2} & 0 \end{bmatrix}$

(v) Similar as Example 10.

Ans. $\begin{bmatrix} 6 & -2 & 2 \\ -2 & 3 & -1 \\ 2 & -1 & 3 \end{bmatrix} + \begin{bmatrix} 0 & 0 & 0 \\ 0 & 0 & 0 \\ 0 & 0 & 0 \end{bmatrix}$

(vi) Similar as Example 10.

Ans. $\begin{bmatrix} 3 & \frac{1}{2} & \frac{-5}{2} \\ \frac{1}{2} & -2 & -2 \\ \frac{-5}{2} & -2 & 2 \end{bmatrix} + \begin{bmatrix} 0 & \frac{5}{2} & \frac{3}{2} \\ \frac{-5}{2} & 0 & 3 \\ \frac{-3}{2} & -3 & 0 \end{bmatrix}$

Exam Pattern Exercise

Part A - Objective Type Questions

Multiple Choice Type Questions

1 If $\begin{vmatrix} 2x & 5 \\ 4 & x \end{vmatrix} = \begin{vmatrix} 3 & 5 \\ 4 & 6 \end{vmatrix}$ then the value of x is [CBSE 2025]

(a) $\frac{3}{2}$ (b) 6 (c) 3 (d) ± 3

2 If $\begin{bmatrix} 2x+y & 4x \\ 5x-7 & 4x \end{bmatrix} = \begin{bmatrix} 7 & 7y-13 \\ y & x+6 \end{bmatrix}$, then

(a) $x=3, y=1$ (b) $x=2, y=3$
(c) $x=2, y=4$ (d) $x=3, y=3$

3 If A and B are symmetric matrices of the same order then $(AB'-BA')$ is a [CBSE 2025]

(a) symmetric matrix
(b) null matrix
(c) diagonal matrix
(d) skew-symmetric matrix

4 If $AB=A$ and $BA=B$, then (B^2+B) equals [CBSE 2024]

(a) $2A$ (b) 0
(c) $2I$ (d) $2B$

5 If $A=\begin{bmatrix} 1 & 0 \\ -2 & 1 \end{bmatrix}$ and $B=\begin{bmatrix} -5 & 10 \\ -10 & -5 \end{bmatrix}$, then AB is [CBSE 2023]

(a) $\begin{bmatrix} -5 & 10 \\ 0 & -5 \end{bmatrix}$ (b) $\begin{bmatrix} 0 & -5 \\ 25 & 10 \end{bmatrix}$

(c) $\begin{bmatrix} 10 & -25 \\ -5 & 0 \end{bmatrix}$ (d) $\begin{bmatrix} -5 & 10 \\ 0 & -25 \end{bmatrix}$

6 If $\begin{bmatrix} x+y & x+2 \\ 2x-y & 16 \end{bmatrix} = \begin{bmatrix} 8 & 5 \\ 1 & 3y+1 \end{bmatrix}$, then the values of x and y are [CBSE 2023]

(a) $x=3, y=5$ (b) $x=5, y=3$
(c) $x=2, y=7$ (d) $x=7, y=2$

Assertion-Reason Based Questions

Directions (Q. Nos. 7-9) *In the questions given below are two statements labelled as Assertion (A) and Reason (R). In the context of the two statements, which one of the following is correct?*

(a) Both A and R are correct; R is the correct explanation of A
(b) Both A and R are correct; R is not the correct explanation of A
(c) A is correct; R is incorrect
(d) R is correct; A is incorrect

7 **Assertion (A)** Matrix $\begin{bmatrix} 1 & 0 & 0 \\ 0 & 3 & 0 \\ 0 & 0 & 4 \end{bmatrix}$ is a diagonal matrix.

Reason (R) Identity matrix of order 3 is a diagonal matrix.

8 **Assertion (A)** The product of two matrices $\begin{bmatrix} 1 & 3 & 4 \\ -1 & 2 & 0 \\ 1 & 3 & 2 \end{bmatrix}$ and $\begin{bmatrix} -1 & 2 \\ 3 & 4 \\ -1 & 2 \end{bmatrix}$ is $\begin{bmatrix} 4 & 22 \\ 7 & 6 \\ 6 & 18 \end{bmatrix}$.

Reason (R) The product of two matrices A and B is defined, if the number of columns of A is equal to the number of rows of B.

9 **Assertion (A)** Matrix $A=\begin{bmatrix} 1 & 2 & 4 \\ 2 & 3 & -1 \\ 4 & -1 & 5 \end{bmatrix}$ is symmetric matrix.

Reason (R) Matrix $B=\begin{bmatrix} 0 & 1 & -2 \\ -1 & 0 & 3 \\ 2 & -3 & 0 \end{bmatrix}$ is a skew-symmetric matrix.

Part B - Descriptive Questions

Very Short Answer Type Questions

10 If matrix $A=[a_{ij}]_{2\times 2}$, where $a_{ij}=\begin{cases} 1, & \text{if } i\neq j \\ 0, & \text{if } i=j \end{cases}$, then find value of A^2.

11 Let $A=[a_{ij}]_{n\times n}$ be a diagonal matrix whose diagonal elements are different and $B=[b_{ij}]_{n\times n}$ is some another matrix. If $AB=[c_{ij}]_{n\times n}$, then find c_{ij}.

12 If $\begin{bmatrix} 2x+y & 4x \\ 5x-7 & 4x \end{bmatrix} = \begin{bmatrix} 7 & 7y-13 \\ y & x+6 \end{bmatrix}$, then find the value of x and y.

13 If possible, then find the sum of the matrices A and B, where $A=\begin{bmatrix} \sqrt{3} & 1 \\ 2 & 3 \end{bmatrix}$ and $B=\begin{bmatrix} x & y & z \\ a & b & c \end{bmatrix}$.

14 Find the value of $y-x$ from the following equation.
$2\begin{bmatrix} x & 5 \\ 7 & y-3 \end{bmatrix} + \begin{bmatrix} 3 & -4 \\ 1 & 2 \end{bmatrix} = \begin{bmatrix} 7 & 6 \\ 15 & 14 \end{bmatrix}$

15 Find non-zero values of x satisfying the matrix equation $x\begin{bmatrix} 2x & 2 \\ 3 & x \end{bmatrix} + 2\begin{bmatrix} 8 & 5x \\ 4 & 4x \end{bmatrix} = 2\begin{bmatrix} x^2+8 & 24 \\ 10 & 6x \end{bmatrix}$.

16 If $A=\begin{bmatrix}2 & 4\\ 3 & 2\end{bmatrix}$ and $B=\begin{bmatrix}1 & 3\\ -2 & 5\end{bmatrix}$, then find $A-B$.

17 If $\begin{bmatrix}9 & -1 & 4\\ -2 & 1 & 3\end{bmatrix}=A+\begin{bmatrix}1 & 2 & -1\\ 0 & 4 & 9\end{bmatrix}$, then find the matrix A.

18 If $A=\begin{bmatrix}\alpha & \beta\\ \gamma & -\alpha\end{bmatrix}$ is such that $A^2=I$, then value of $1-\alpha^2-\beta\gamma$.

19 Find x, if $[1 \;\; 2 \;\; 1]\begin{bmatrix}1 & 2 & 0\\ 2 & 0 & 1\\ 1 & 0 & 2\end{bmatrix}\begin{bmatrix}0\\ 2\\ x\end{bmatrix}=0$.

20 Suppose, $A=\begin{bmatrix}5 & 4\\ 2 & 3\end{bmatrix}$ and $B=\begin{bmatrix}3 & 5 & 1\\ 6 & 8 & 4\end{bmatrix}$, then find AB and BA, if they exist.

21 Find x from the matrix equation $\begin{bmatrix}1 & 3\\ 4 & 5\end{bmatrix}\begin{bmatrix}x\\ 2\end{bmatrix}=\begin{bmatrix}5\\ 6\end{bmatrix}$.

22 If $\begin{bmatrix}1 & 0 & 0\\ 0 & y & 0\\ 0 & 0 & 1\end{bmatrix}\begin{bmatrix}x\\ -1\\ z\end{bmatrix}=\begin{bmatrix}1\\ 2\\ 1\end{bmatrix}$, find $x+y+z$.

23 If matrix $A=\begin{bmatrix}1 & -1\\ -1 & 1\end{bmatrix}$ and $A^2=kA$, then write the value of k.

24 If A and B are symmetric matrices of same order, then $(AB'-BA')$ is which type of matrix.

25 If $A=\begin{bmatrix}1 & 2\\ 3 & 4\end{bmatrix}$, then find $A+A'$.

Short Answer Type Questions

26 If $\begin{bmatrix}x+3 & z+4 & 2y-7\\ -6 & a-1 & 0\\ b-3 & -21 & 0\end{bmatrix}=\begin{bmatrix}0 & 6 & 3y-2\\ -6 & -3 & 2c+2\\ 2b+4 & -21 & 0\end{bmatrix}$, then find the values of a, b, c and z.

27 Assume Y, W and P are the matrices of orders $3\times k$, $n\times 3$ and $p\times k$. Find the restrictions on n, k and p, so that $PY+WY$ will be defined.

28 Give one example of skew-symmetric matrix of order 2 and order 3.

29 Find the symmetric and skew-symmetric matrices of matrix $A=\begin{bmatrix}0 & -2 & 4\\ 2 & 0 & -1\\ -4 & 1 & 0\end{bmatrix}$.

30 If A and B are symmetric matrices, then prove that $BA-2AB$ is neither a symmetric matrix nor skew-symmetric matrix.

31 If $A=\begin{bmatrix}3 & -4\\ 1 & 1\\ 2 & 0\end{bmatrix}$ and $B=\begin{bmatrix}2 & 1 & 2\\ 1 & 2 & 4\end{bmatrix}$, then verify that $(BA)^2\neq B^2A^2$.

32 If $A=\begin{bmatrix}0 & 1\\ 1 & 1\end{bmatrix}$ and $B=\begin{bmatrix}0 & -1\\ 1 & 0\end{bmatrix}$, then show that $(A+B)(A-B)\neq A^2-B^2$.

33 Solve the matrix $[x \;\; -5 \;\; -1]\begin{bmatrix}1 & 0 & 2\\ 0 & 2 & 1\\ 2 & 0 & 3\end{bmatrix}\begin{bmatrix}x\\ 4\\ 1\end{bmatrix}=O$.

34 If $[2 \;\; 1 \;\; 3]\begin{bmatrix}-1 & 0 & -1\\ -1 & 1 & 0\\ 0 & 1 & 1\end{bmatrix}\begin{bmatrix}1\\ 0\\ -1\end{bmatrix}=A$, then find the value of A.

35 Find the matrix A satisfying the matrix equation $\begin{bmatrix}2 & 1\\ 3 & 2\end{bmatrix}A\begin{bmatrix}-3 & 2\\ 5 & -3\end{bmatrix}=\begin{bmatrix}1 & 0\\ 0 & 1\end{bmatrix}$.

36 If $A=\begin{bmatrix}2 & 0 & 1\\ 2 & 1 & 3\\ 1 & -1 & 0\end{bmatrix}$, then find A^2-5A+6.

37 If $A=\begin{bmatrix}2 & 3\\ 1 & 2\end{bmatrix}$, then prove that $A^3-4A^2+A=O$.

38 If $A=\begin{bmatrix}1 & 0\\ -1 & 7\end{bmatrix}$, then find k such that $A^2-8A+kI=O$.

39 For the matrix $A=\begin{bmatrix}3 & 1\\ 7 & 5\end{bmatrix}$, find a and b such that $A^2+aI=bA$, where I is a 2×2 identity matrix.

40 If $A=\begin{bmatrix}4 & 0\\ 2k & 5k\end{bmatrix}$ and $B=\begin{bmatrix}k & 0\\ 3 & -1\end{bmatrix}$, such that $AB=BA$. Then, show that $2k^2+17k-12=0$.

41 A manufacturer sells the products x, y and z in two markets. Annual sales are indicated below

Market	Products		
	x	y	z
I	10000	2000	18000
II	6000	20000	8000

(i) If unit sale prices of x, y and z are ₹ 2.50, ₹ 1.50 and ₹ 1.00 respectively, then find the total revenue in each market with the help of matrix algebra.

(ii) If the unit costs of the above three commodities are ₹ 2.00, ₹ 1.00 and 50 paise, respectively. Find the gross profit.
[**Hint** Profit = Revenue − Cost]

42 In a legislative assembly election, a political group hired a public relations firm to promote its candidate in three ways: telephone, house calls and letters. The cost per contact (in paise) is given in matrix A as

$$\text{Cost per contact} \quad A = \begin{bmatrix} 40 \\ 100 \\ 50 \end{bmatrix} \begin{matrix} \text{Telephone} \\ \text{House call} \\ \text{Letter} \end{matrix}$$

The number of contacts of each type made in two cities X and Y is given by

$$\begin{matrix} & \text{Telephone} & \text{House call} & \text{Letter} \end{matrix}$$
$$B = \begin{bmatrix} 1000 & 500 & 5000 \\ 3000 & 1000 & 10000 \end{bmatrix} \begin{matrix} \to X \\ \to Y \end{matrix}$$

Find the total amount spent by the group in the two cities X and Y.

43 If $AB = BA$ for any two square matrices, then prove by mathematical induction that $(AB)^n = A^n B^n$.

44 If $A = \text{diag } [a, b, c]$, then show that $A^n = \text{diag } [a^n, b^n, c^n], \forall\, n \in N$.

45 Prove by mathematical induction that $(A')^n = (A^n)'$, where $n \in N$ for any square matrix A.

46 If $A = \begin{bmatrix} -1 & 2 & 3 \\ 5 & 7 & 9 \\ -2 & 1 & 1 \end{bmatrix}$ and $B = \begin{bmatrix} -4 & 1 & -5 \\ 1 & 2 & 0 \\ 1 & 3 & 1 \end{bmatrix}$, then verify that

(i) $(A + B)' = A' + B'$ (ii) $(A - B)' = A' - B'$

47 Find $\frac{1}{2}(A + A')$ and $\frac{1}{2}(A - A')$, where $A = \begin{bmatrix} 0 & a & b \\ -a & 0 & c \\ -b & -c & 0 \end{bmatrix}$.

48 If $A = \begin{bmatrix} 3 & -4 \\ 1 & -1 \end{bmatrix}$, then show that $(A - A')$ is a skew-symmetric matrix, where A' is the transpose of matrix A.

49 Show that the matrix $B^T AB$ is symmetric or skew-symmetric, according as A is symmetric or skew-symmetric.

Long Answer Type Questions

50 If $A = \begin{bmatrix} 1 & 0 & 2 \\ 0 & 2 & 1 \\ 2 & 0 & 3 \end{bmatrix}$, then prove that A is a root of the polynomial $f(x) = x^3 - 6x^2 + 7x + 2$.
[**Hint** Prove that $f(A) = O$]

51 If $A = \begin{pmatrix} 1 & 0 & 2 \\ 0 & 2 & 1 \\ 2 & 0 & 3 \end{pmatrix}$, prove that $A^3 - 6A^2 + 7A + 2I = O$.

52 Let $A = \begin{bmatrix} 2 & 3 \\ -1 & 2 \end{bmatrix}$ and $f(x) = x^2 - 4x + 7$. Show that $f(A) = O$. Use this result to find A^5.

53 Find matrix A, if $\begin{pmatrix} 2 & -1 \\ 1 & 0 \\ -3 & 4 \end{pmatrix} A = \begin{pmatrix} -1 & -8 & -10 \\ 1 & -2 & -5 \\ 9 & 22 & 15 \end{pmatrix}$.

54 Find matrix X, if $X\begin{pmatrix} 1 & 2 & 3 \\ 4 & 5 & 6 \end{pmatrix} = \begin{pmatrix} -7 & -8 & -9 \\ 2 & 4 & 6 \\ 11 & 10 & 9 \end{pmatrix}$.

Case Study Based Questions

55 In the Jaipur city, there are two factories X and Y. Each factory produces sports clothes for boys and girls. There are three types of clothes produced in both the factories type I, II and III. For boys the numbers of units of types I, II and III respectively are 80, 70 and 65 in factory X and 85, 65 and 72 are in factory Y. For girls, the numbers of units of types I, II and III respectively are 80, 75, 90 in factory X and 50, 55, 80 are in factory Y.

Based on the above information, answer the following questions.

(i) If P represents the matrix of numbers of units of each type produced by factory X for both boys and girls, then P is given by

(a) $\begin{matrix} & \text{Boys} & \text{Girls} \\ \text{I} & 85 & 50 \\ \text{II} & 65 & 55 \\ \text{III} & 72 & 80 \end{matrix}$ (b) $\begin{matrix} & \text{I} & \text{II} & \text{III} \\ \text{Boys} & 50 & 55 & 80 \\ \text{Girls} & 85 & 65 & 72 \end{matrix}$

(c) $\begin{matrix} & \text{I} & \text{II} & \text{III} \\ \text{Boys} & 80 & 75 & 90 \\ \text{Girls} & 80 & 70 & 65 \end{matrix}$ (d) $\begin{matrix} & \text{Boys} & \text{Girls} \\ \text{I} & 80 & 80 \\ \text{II} & 70 & 75 \\ \text{III} & 65 & 90 \end{matrix}$

(ii) If Q represent the matrix of number of units of each type produced by factory Y for both boys and girls, then Q is given by

(a) $\begin{matrix} & \text{Boys} & \text{Girls} \\ \text{I} & 85 & 50 \\ \text{II} & 65 & 55 \\ \text{III} & 72 & 80 \end{matrix}$ (b) $\begin{matrix} & \text{I} & \text{II} & \text{III} \\ \text{Boys} & 50 & 55 & 80 \\ \text{Girls} & 85 & 65 & 72 \end{matrix}$

(c) $\begin{matrix} & \text{I} & \text{II} & \text{III} \\ \text{Boys} & 80 & 75 & 90 \\ \text{Girls} & 80 & 70 & 65 \end{matrix}$ (d) $\begin{matrix} & \text{Boys} & \text{Girls} \\ \text{I} & 80 & 80 \\ \text{II} & 70 & 75 \\ \text{III} & 65 & 90 \end{matrix}$

(iii) The total production of sports clothes of each type for boys is given by the matrix.

(a) $\begin{matrix} I & II & III \\ [165 & 130 & 137] \end{matrix}$ (b) $\begin{matrix} I & II & III \\ [130 & 165 & 137] \end{matrix}$

(c) $\begin{matrix} I & II & III \\ [165 & 135 & 137] \end{matrix}$ (d) $\begin{matrix} I & II & III \\ [137 & 135 & 165] \end{matrix}$

(iv) The total production of sports clothes of each type for girls is given by the matrix

(a) $\begin{matrix} I & II & III \\ [130 & 130 & 170] \end{matrix}$ (b) $\begin{matrix} I & II & III \\ [170 & 130 & 130] \end{matrix}$

(c) $\begin{matrix} I & II & III \\ [130 & 170 & 130] \end{matrix}$ (d) None of these

(v) Let R be a 3×2 matrix that represent the total production of sports clothes of each type of boys and girls, then transpose of R is

(a) $\begin{bmatrix} 165 & 135 & 137 \\ 130 & 130 & 170 \end{bmatrix}$ (b) $\begin{bmatrix} 130 & 130 & 170 \\ 165 & 135 & 138 \end{bmatrix}$

(c) $\begin{bmatrix} 165 & 132 \\ 135 & 130 \\ 137 & 170 \end{bmatrix}$ (d) $\begin{bmatrix} 130 & 168 \\ 130 & 135 \\ 170 & 137 \end{bmatrix}$

56. To promote the making of toilets for women, organisation tried to generate awareness through

(i) house calls
(ii) emails and
(iii) announcements

the cost for each made per attempt is given below

(i) ₹ 50 (ii) ₹ 20 (iii) ₹ 40

The number of attempts made in the villages X, Y and Z are given below

	(i)	(ii)	(iii)
X	400	300	100
Y	300	250	75
Z	500	400	150

Also, the chance of making of toilets corresponding to one attempt of given modes is

(i) 2% (ii) 4% (iii) 20%

Based on the above information, answer the following questions.

(i) The cost incurred by the organisation on village X is
(a) ₹ 10000 (b) ₹ 15000
(c) ₹ 30000 (d) ₹ 20000

(ii) The cost incurred by the organisation on village Y is
(a) ₹ 25000 (b) ₹ 18000
(c) ₹ 23000 (d) ₹ 28000

(iii) The cost incurred by the organisation on village Z is
(a) ₹ 19000 (b) ₹ 39000
(c) ₹ 45000 (d) ₹ 50000

(iv) The total number of toilets that can be expected after the promotion in village X, is
(a) 20 (b) 30
(c) 40 (d) 50

(v) The total number of toilets that can be expected after the promotion in village Z, is
(a) 26 (b) 36
(d) 46 (d) 56

Hints & Solutions

1. (d) **2.** (b) **3.** (a) **4.** (d)
5. (d) **6.** (a) **7.** (b) **8.** (a)
9. (b) **10.** I **11.** $a_{ij} b_{ij}$ **12.** $x = 2, y = 3$
13. Not possible **14.** 7 **15.** $x = 4$

16. $\begin{bmatrix} 1 & 1 \\ 5 & -3 \end{bmatrix}$ **17.** $\begin{bmatrix} 8 & -3 & 5 \\ -2 & -3 & -6 \end{bmatrix}$

18. 0 **19.** $x = -1$

20. $AB = \begin{bmatrix} 39 & 57 & 21 \\ 24 & 34 & 14 \end{bmatrix}$; BA does not exist.

21. $x = -1$ **22.** 0 **23.** $k = 2$

24. $AB' - BA'$ is a skew-symmetric matrix.

25. $\begin{bmatrix} 2 & 5 \\ 5 & 8 \end{bmatrix}$ **26.** $a = -2, b = -7, c = -1$ and $z = 2$

27. $k = 3, p = n$ **28.** $\begin{bmatrix} 0 & 2 \\ -2 & 0 \end{bmatrix}; \begin{bmatrix} 0 & -1 & 3 \\ 1 & 0 & 4 \\ -3 & -4 & 0 \end{bmatrix}$

29. $\begin{bmatrix} 0 & 0 & 0 \\ 0 & 0 & 0 \\ 0 & 0 & 0 \end{bmatrix}; \begin{bmatrix} 0 & -2 & 4 \\ 2 & 0 & -1 \\ -4 & 1 & 0 \end{bmatrix}$

33. $x = \pm 4\sqrt{3}$ **34.** $A = [-4]$

35. $\begin{bmatrix} 1 & 1 \\ 1 & 0 \end{bmatrix}$ **36.** $\begin{bmatrix} 1 & -1 & -3 \\ -1 & -1 & -10 \\ -5 & 4 & 4 \end{bmatrix}$

38. $k = 7$ **39.** $a = 8, b = 8$

41. (i) Total revenue in market I is ₹ 46000 and market II is ₹ 53000.

(ii) Gross profit = ₹ 32000

42. Total amount spent by the group in two cities are ₹ 3400 and ₹ 7200, respectively.

47. $\frac{1}{2}(A + A') = \begin{bmatrix} 0 & 0 & 0 \\ 0 & 0 & 0 \\ 0 & 0 & 0 \end{bmatrix}$ and $\frac{1}{2}(A - A') = \begin{bmatrix} 0 & a & b \\ -a & 0 & c \\ -b & -c & 0 \end{bmatrix}$

52. $A^5 = \begin{bmatrix} -118 & -93 \\ 31 & -118 \end{bmatrix}$

53. $A = \begin{pmatrix} 1 & -2 & -5 \\ 3 & 4 & 0 \end{pmatrix}$

54. $X = \begin{pmatrix} 1 & -2 \\ 2 & 0 \\ -5 & 4 \end{pmatrix}$

55. (i) (d) In factory X, number of units of type I, II and III for boys are 80, 70, 65 respectively and for girls numbers of units of types I, II and III are 80, 75, 90, respectively.

$$\text{So,} \quad \begin{matrix} & \text{Boys} & \text{Girls} \\ \text{I} & 80 & 80 \\ \text{II} & 70 & 75 \\ \text{III} & 65 & 90 \end{matrix}$$

(ii) (a) In factory Y, number of units of type I, II and III for boys are 85, 65, 72 respectively and for girls number of units of types I, II and III are 50, 55, 80 respectively.

$$\text{So,} \quad Q = \begin{matrix} & \text{Boys} & \text{Girls} \\ \text{I} & 85 & 50 \\ \text{II} & 65 & 55 \\ \text{III} & 72 & 80 \end{matrix}$$

(iii) (c) Let A be the matrix that represent that numbers of units of each type produced by factory X for boys and B be the matrix that represent the number of units of each type produced by factory Y for boys.

Then, $A = \overset{\text{I} \quad \text{II} \quad \text{III}}{[80 \quad 70 \quad 65]}$ and $B = \overset{\text{I} \quad \text{II} \quad \text{III}}{[85 \quad 65 \quad 72]}$

Now, required matrix,

$A + B = [80 \quad 70 \quad 65] + [85 \quad 65 \quad 72]$

$= [165 \quad 135 \quad 137]$

(iv) (a) Required matrix

$= [80 \quad 75 \quad 90] + [50 \quad 55 \quad 80]$

$= [130 \quad 130 \quad 170]$

(v) (a) Clearly, $R = P + Q$

$$= \begin{bmatrix} 80 & 80 \\ 70 & 75 \\ 65 & 90 \end{bmatrix} + \begin{bmatrix} 85 & 50 \\ 65 & 55 \\ 72 & 80 \end{bmatrix} = \begin{bmatrix} 165 & 130 \\ 135 & 130 \\ 137 & 170 \end{bmatrix}$$

So, $R' = \begin{bmatrix} 165 & 135 & 137 \\ 130 & 130 & 170 \end{bmatrix}$

56. (i) (c) Let ₹ A, ₹ B and ₹C be the cost incurred by the organisation for villages X, Y and Z respectively, then A, B, C will be given by the following matrix equation.

$$\begin{bmatrix} 400 & 300 & 100 \\ 300 & 250 & 75 \\ 500 & 400 & 150 \end{bmatrix} \begin{bmatrix} 50 \\ 20 \\ 40 \end{bmatrix} = \begin{bmatrix} A \\ B \\ C \end{bmatrix}$$

$$\begin{bmatrix} A \\ B \\ C \end{bmatrix} = \begin{bmatrix} 400 \times 50 + 300 \times 20 + 100 \times 40 \\ 300 \times 50 + 250 \times 20 + 75 \times 40 \\ 500 \times 50 + 400 \times 20 + 150 \times 40 \end{bmatrix} = \begin{bmatrix} 30000 \\ 23000 \\ 39000 \end{bmatrix}$$

(ii) (c)

(iii) (b)

(iv) (c) Total number of toilets that can be expected in each village is given by the following matrix.

$$\begin{matrix} X \\ Y \\ Z \end{matrix} \begin{bmatrix} 400 & 300 & 100 \\ 300 & 250 & 75 \\ 500 & 400 & 150 \end{bmatrix} \begin{bmatrix} 2/100 \\ 4/100 \\ 20/100 \end{bmatrix}$$

$$\Rightarrow \begin{matrix} X \\ Y \\ Z \end{matrix} \begin{bmatrix} 8 + 12 + 20 \\ 6 + 10 + 5 \\ 10 + 16 + 30 \end{bmatrix} = \begin{matrix} X \\ Y \\ Z \end{matrix} \begin{bmatrix} 40 \\ 31 \\ 56 \end{bmatrix}$$

(v) (d)

CHAPTER 08

Determinants

In this Chapter...

- Determinant and Its Elementary Properties
- Minors and Cofactors
- Adjoint of a Matrix
- Solution of Simultaneous Linear Equations

Determinant

Every square matrix can be associated with a number (real or complex), is known as **determinant.**

For a square matrix A, its determinant is denoted by det (A) or $|A|$.

Here, $|A|$ denotes determinant value not modulus of A.

Matrix being an arrangement of numbers has no value, but determinant has a fixed value. Determinants are not defined for non-square matrix.

Determinant of a Matrix of Order 1

Let $A=[a_{11}]$ be a matrix of order 1×1. Then, det A is $|A|=|a_{11}|=a_{11}$.

Determinant of a Matrix of Order 2

Let $A=\begin{bmatrix} a_{11} & a_{12} \\ a_{21} & a_{22} \end{bmatrix}$ be a matrix of order 2×2.

Then, det A is $|A|=\begin{vmatrix} a_{11} & a_{12} \\ a_{21} & a_{22} \end{vmatrix}$

$$= a_{11}a_{22}-a_{21}a_{12}$$

EXAMPLE 1. Evaluate the following determinant.

(i) $|-12|$ (ii) $\begin{vmatrix} 3 & 5 \\ -2 & 4 \end{vmatrix}$

(iii) $\begin{vmatrix} x-1 & 1 \\ x^3 & x^2+x+1 \end{vmatrix}$ (iv) $\begin{vmatrix} 1 & \log_b a \\ \log_a b & 1 \end{vmatrix}$

Sol. (i) Clearly, $|-12|=-12$ $[\because |-a|=-a]$

(ii) We have, $\begin{vmatrix} 3 & 5 \\ -2 & 4 \end{vmatrix}=3\times 4-(-2)\times 5$

$$\left[\because \begin{vmatrix} a_{11} & a_{12} \\ a_{21} & a_{22} \end{vmatrix}=a_{11}a_{22}-a_{21}a_{12}\right]$$

$$=12+10=22$$

(iii) We have, $\begin{vmatrix} x-1 & 1 \\ x^3 & x^2+x+1 \end{vmatrix}=(x-1)(x^2+x+1)-x^3$

$$\left[\because \begin{vmatrix} a_{11} & a_{12} \\ a_{21} & a_{22} \end{vmatrix}=a_{11}a_{22}-a_{21}a_{12}\right]$$

$$=(x^3-1)-x^3$$

$$[\because (a-b)(a^2+ab+b^2)=a^3-b^3]$$

$$=-1$$

(iv) We have, $\begin{vmatrix} 1 & \log_b a \\ \log_a b & 1 \end{vmatrix}=1\times 1-\log_a b\times \log_b a$

$$=1-1=0$$

EXAMPLE 2. If $\begin{vmatrix} 2x & -9 \\ -2 & x \end{vmatrix}=\begin{vmatrix} -4 & 8 \\ 1 & -2 \end{vmatrix}$, then find the value of x.

Sol. We have, $\begin{vmatrix} 2x & -9 \\ -2 & x \end{vmatrix}=\begin{vmatrix} -4 & 8 \\ 1 & -2 \end{vmatrix}$

$$\Rightarrow (2x)(x)-(-2)(-9)=(-4)(-2)-(1)(8)$$

$$\Rightarrow 2x^2-18=8-8$$

$$\Rightarrow 2x^2=18$$

$$\Rightarrow x^2=9$$

$$\Rightarrow x=\pm 3$$

EXAMPLE 3. If $A=\begin{bmatrix}2 & 1\\1 & 3\end{bmatrix}$, then find the determinant of the matrix A^2-2A.

Sol. We have, $A=\begin{bmatrix}2 & 1\\1 & 3\end{bmatrix}$

Now, $A^2=\begin{bmatrix}2 & 1\\1 & 3\end{bmatrix}\begin{bmatrix}2 & 1\\1 & 3\end{bmatrix}=\begin{bmatrix}4+1 & 2+3\\2+3 & 1+9\end{bmatrix}=\begin{bmatrix}5 & 5\\5 & 10\end{bmatrix}$

and $2A=2\begin{bmatrix}2 & 1\\1 & 3\end{bmatrix}=\begin{bmatrix}4 & 2\\2 & 6\end{bmatrix}$

$\therefore\ A^2-2A=\begin{bmatrix}5 & 5\\5 & 10\end{bmatrix}-\begin{bmatrix}4 & 2\\2 & 6\end{bmatrix}=\begin{bmatrix}1 & 3\\3 & 4\end{bmatrix}$

$\therefore |A^2-2A|=\begin{vmatrix}1 & 3\\3 & 4\end{vmatrix}=(1)(4)-(3)(3)$

$=4-9=-5$

EXAMPLE 4. If $A=\begin{bmatrix}1 & 2\\4 & 2\end{bmatrix}$, then show that $|2A|=4|A|$.

Sol. We have, $A=\begin{bmatrix}1 & 2\\4 & 2\end{bmatrix}\Rightarrow 2A=\begin{bmatrix}2 & 4\\8 & 4\end{bmatrix}$

Now, $|A|=\begin{vmatrix}1 & 2\\4 & 2\end{vmatrix}=(1)(2)-(4)(2)=2-8=-6$

and $|2A|=\begin{vmatrix}2 & 4\\8 & 4\end{vmatrix}=(2)(4)-(8)(4)=8-32=-24$

$\therefore\quad |2A|=4|A|$

Determinant of Matrix of Order 3

Determinant of a matrix of order 3 can be determined by expressing it in terms of second order determinants which is known as expansion of a determinant along row or column.

Let $A=\begin{bmatrix}a_{11} & a_{12} & a_{13}\\a_{21} & a_{22} & a_{23}\\a_{31} & a_{32} & a_{33}\end{bmatrix}$

Then, $|A|=\begin{vmatrix}a_{11} & a_{12} & a_{13}\\a_{21} & a_{22} & a_{23}\\a_{31} & a_{32} & a_{33}\end{vmatrix}$

$$=a_{11}\begin{vmatrix}a_{22} & a_{23}\\a_{32} & a_{33}\end{vmatrix}-a_{12}\begin{vmatrix}a_{21} & a_{23}\\a_{31} & a_{33}\end{vmatrix}+a_{13}\begin{vmatrix}a_{21} & a_{22}\\a_{31} & a_{32}\end{vmatrix}$$

[expanding along row R_1]

Similarly, we can determine determinant value by expanding any row or column. Expanding a determinants along any row or column gives same value.

If we expand a determinant by any row or column, we attach following signs for a determinant of order three.

$$\begin{vmatrix}+ & - & +\\- & + & -\\+ & - & +\end{vmatrix}$$

For easier calculations, we should expand determinant along the row or column having maximum number of zeroes.

EXAMPLE 5. Evaluate the determinant of matrix $\begin{bmatrix}3 & -4 & 5\\1 & 1 & -2\\2 & 3 & 1\end{bmatrix}$ by expanding it along.

(i) Row R_1 (ii) column C_2

Sol. Let $A=\begin{bmatrix}3 & -4 & 5\\1 & 1 & -2\\2 & 3 & 1\end{bmatrix}$.

Then, $|A|=\begin{vmatrix}3 & -4 & 5\\1 & 1 & -2\\2 & 3 & 1\end{vmatrix}$

(i) Expanding along R_1

$|A|=3\begin{vmatrix}1 & -2\\3 & 1\end{vmatrix}-(-4)\begin{vmatrix}1 & -2\\2 & 1\end{vmatrix}+5\begin{vmatrix}1 & 1\\2 & 3\end{vmatrix}$

$=3(1+6)+4(1+4)+5(3-2)$

$=21+20+5=46$

(ii) Expanding along C_2

$|A|=-(-4)\begin{vmatrix}1 & -2\\2 & 1\end{vmatrix}+(1)\begin{vmatrix}3 & 5\\2 & 1\end{vmatrix}-3\begin{vmatrix}3 & 5\\1 & -2\end{vmatrix}$

$=4(1+4)+1(3-10)-3(-6-5)$

$=20-7+33$

$=46$

EXAMPLE 6. If $a^2+b^2=5$, then prove that value of $\begin{vmatrix}x & a & b\\-a & -x & 1\\b & 1 & x\end{vmatrix}$ is independent of a and b.

Sol. Let $\Delta=\begin{vmatrix}x & a & b\\-a & -x & 1\\b & 1 & x\end{vmatrix}$

Expanding along R_1, we get

$\Delta=x(-x^2-1)-a(-ax-b)+b(-a+bx)$

$=-x^3-x+a^2x+ab-ab+b^2x$

$=-x^3-x+x(a^2+b^2)$

$=-x^3-x+5x$ $[\because a^2+b^2=5]$

$=-x^3+4x$

Hence, Δ is independent of a and b.

Topic Practice 1

1 Write the value of the following determinants:

(i) $|-91|$ (ii) $\begin{vmatrix} 12 & 1 \\ 4 & 3 \end{vmatrix}$

(iii) $\begin{vmatrix} p & p+1 \\ p-1 & p \end{vmatrix}$ (iv) $\begin{vmatrix} \log_3 512 & \log_4 3 \\ \log_3 8 & \log_4 9 \end{vmatrix}$

(v) $\begin{vmatrix} x^2-x+1 & x-1 \\ x+1 & x+1 \end{vmatrix}$

2 Find the value of x:

(i) $\begin{vmatrix} 2x & 5 \\ 8 & x \end{vmatrix} = \begin{vmatrix} 6 & -2 \\ 7 & 3 \end{vmatrix}$.

(ii) $\begin{vmatrix} 2x & x+3 \\ 2(x+1) & x+1 \end{vmatrix} = \begin{vmatrix} 1 & 5 \\ 3 & 3 \end{vmatrix}$.

3 If $A = \begin{bmatrix} 1 & 2 \\ 3 & -1 \end{bmatrix}$ and $B = \begin{bmatrix} 1 & 3 \\ -1 & 1 \end{bmatrix}$, then write the value of $|AB|$.

4 (i) If $x \in I$ and $\begin{vmatrix} 9 & x \\ 3x & 4 \end{vmatrix} = \begin{vmatrix} 4 & 5 \\ x & 6 \end{vmatrix}$, find the value of x.

(ii) If $x \in N$, and $\begin{vmatrix} x & 1 \\ 4 & x \end{vmatrix} = \begin{vmatrix} 2 & 3 \\ -3 & 6 \end{vmatrix}$, find the value of x.

5 If $A = \begin{bmatrix} 1 & 2 \\ 4 & 2 \end{bmatrix}$, then verify that $|nA| = n^2|A|$.

6 Evaluate $\Delta = \begin{vmatrix} 2 & 3 & -2 \\ 1 & 2 & 3 \\ -2 & 1 & -3 \end{vmatrix}$ by expanding it along.

(i) Second row (ii) Third Column

7 If A is a square matrix satisfying $A^T A = I$, write the value of $|A|$.

8 If A and B are square matrices of the same order 3, such that $|A| = 2$ and $AB = 2I$. Write the value of $|B|$.

9 If one root of $\begin{vmatrix} 7 & 6 & x \\ 2 & x & 2 \\ x & 3 & 7 \end{vmatrix} = 0$ is $-a$, find the other roots.

10 If A is a square matrix of order 3 and $|A| = 4$ and $|2A| = 2^x$, find the value of x.

11 If there are two values of a which makes determinant, $\Delta = \begin{vmatrix} 1 & -2 & 5 \\ 2 & a & -1 \\ 0 & 4 & 2a \end{vmatrix} = 86$, then find the sum of these numbers.

Hints & Solutions

1. (i) Let $\Delta = |-91| = -91$

(ii) Let $\Delta = \begin{vmatrix} 12 & 1 \\ 4 & 3 \end{vmatrix} = 12(3) - (4)(1) = 36 - 4 = 32$

(iii) Let $\Delta = \begin{vmatrix} p & p+1 \\ p-1 & p \end{vmatrix} = p^2 - (p-1)(p+1)$

$= p^2 - (p^2 - 1)$ $[\because (a+b)(a-b) = a^2 - b^2]$

$= p^2 - p^2 + 1 = 1$

(iv) $\begin{vmatrix} \log_3 512 & \log_4 3 \\ \log_3 8 & \log_4 9 \end{vmatrix} = \begin{vmatrix} \log_3 2^9 & \log_{2^2} 3 \\ \log_3 2^3 & \log_{2^2} 3^2 \end{vmatrix}$

$= \begin{vmatrix} 9\log_3 2 & \frac{1}{2}\log_2 3 \\ 3\log_3 2 & \log_2 3 \end{vmatrix}$

$= 9\log_3 2 \times \log_2 3 - \frac{3}{2}\log_3 2 \times \log_2 3$

$= 9 - \frac{3}{2} = \frac{15}{2}$

(v) Let $\Delta = \begin{vmatrix} x^2-x+1 & x-1 \\ x+1 & x+1 \end{vmatrix}$

$= (x+1)(x^2 - x + 1) - (x+1)(x-1)$

$= x^3 + 1 - x^2 + 1 = x^3 - x^2 + 2$

2. (i) Similar as Example 2. **Ans.** $x = \pm 6$

(ii) We have, $\begin{vmatrix} 2x & x+3 \\ 2(x+1) & x+1 \end{vmatrix} = \begin{vmatrix} 1 & 5 \\ 3 & 3 \end{vmatrix}$

$\Rightarrow 2x(x+1) - 2(x+1)(x+3) = 3 - 15$

$\Rightarrow 2x^2 + 2x - 2(x^2 + 3x + x + 3) = -12$

$\Rightarrow 2x^2 + 2x - 2x^2 - 6x - 2x - 6 = -12$

$\Rightarrow -6x - 6 = -12$

$\Rightarrow -6x = -12 + 6 = -6 \Rightarrow x = 1$

3. We have, $A = \begin{bmatrix} 1 & 2 \\ 3 & -1 \end{bmatrix}$ and $B = \begin{bmatrix} 1 & 3 \\ -1 & 1 \end{bmatrix}$

Now, $AB = \begin{bmatrix} 1 & 2 \\ 3 & -1 \end{bmatrix}\begin{bmatrix} 1 & 3 \\ -1 & 1 \end{bmatrix} = \begin{bmatrix} 1-2 & 3+2 \\ 3+1 & 9-1 \end{bmatrix}$

$= \begin{bmatrix} -1 & 5 \\ 4 & 8 \end{bmatrix}$

$\Rightarrow |AB| = \begin{vmatrix} -1 & 5 \\ 4 & 8 \end{vmatrix} = -8 - 20 = -28$

4. (i) $\begin{vmatrix} 9 & x \\ 3x & 4 \end{vmatrix} = \begin{vmatrix} 4 & 5 \\ x & 6 \end{vmatrix}$

$36 - 3x^2 = 24 - 5x \Rightarrow 3x^2 - 5x - 12 = 0$

$3x^2 - 9x + 4x - 12 = 0 \Rightarrow 3x(x-3) + 4(x-3) = 0$

$\Rightarrow x = 3, -\frac{4}{3}$

As $x \in I$, $x = 3$

(ii) $\begin{vmatrix} x & 1 \\ 4 & x \end{vmatrix} = \begin{vmatrix} 2 & 3 \\ -3 & 6 \end{vmatrix}$

$\Rightarrow x^2 - 4 = 12 + 9 \Rightarrow x^2 - 4 = 21$

$\Rightarrow x^2 = 25 \Rightarrow x = \pm 5$

As $x \in N$, $x = 5$

5. Similar as Example 4.
6. Similar as Example 5.

Ans. −37

7. We have, $A^T A = I$

$\Rightarrow |A^T A| = |I|$

$\Rightarrow |A^T||A| = 1$ $\quad [\because |AB| = |A||B|, |I| = 1]$

$\Rightarrow |A|^2 = 1$ $\quad [\because |A^T| = |A|]$

$\Rightarrow |A| = \pm 1$

8. We have,

$AB = 2I$

$\Rightarrow |AB| = |2I|$

$\Rightarrow |A||B| = 2^3 |I|$

$[\because |AB| = |A||B|, |KA| = K^n |A|]$

$\Rightarrow 2|B| = 8$ $\quad [\because |I| = 1]$

$\Rightarrow |B| = 4$

9. Given, $\Delta = \begin{vmatrix} 7 & 6 & x \\ 2 & x & 2 \\ x & 3 & 7 \end{vmatrix} = 0$

Expand along R_1,

$$7\begin{vmatrix} x & 2 \\ 3 & 7 \end{vmatrix} - 6\begin{vmatrix} 2 & 2 \\ x & 7 \end{vmatrix} + x\begin{vmatrix} 2 & x \\ x & 3 \end{vmatrix} = 0$$

$7(7x - 6) - 6(14 - 2x) + x(6 - x^2) = 0$

$49x - 42 - 84 + 12x + 6x - x^3 = 0$

$x^3 - 67x + 126 = 0, -9$ is the root of Δ

$\Rightarrow x + 9$ is the factor of $x^3 - 67x + 126$

$$\begin{array}{r|l} & x^2 - 9x + 14 \\ x+9 & x^3 - 67x + 126 \\ & x^3 + 9x^2 \\ & - \quad - \\ \hline & -9x^2 - 67x + 126 \\ & -9x^2 - 81x \\ & + \quad + \\ \hline & 14x + 126 \\ & 14x + 126 \\ & - \quad - \\ \hline & 0 \end{array}$$

$x^2 - 9x + 14 = 0$

$\Rightarrow x^2 - 7x - 2x + 14 = 0$

$\Rightarrow x(x - 7) - 2(x - 7) = 0$

$\Rightarrow x = 2, 7$

Hence, the other two roots are 2, 7.

10. Given, $|A| = 4$ and $|2A| = 2^x$

$|2A| = 2^3|A| = 2^3 \times 2^2 = 2^5$

Compare it with $|2A| = 2^x$

Here, $x = 5$

11. We have, $\Delta = \begin{vmatrix} 1 & -2 & 5 \\ 2 & a & -1 \\ 0 & 4 & 2a \end{vmatrix} = 86$

$\Rightarrow 1(2a^2 + 4) - 2(-4a - 20) + 0 = 86$

[expanding along C_1]

$\Rightarrow 2a^2 + 4 + 8a + 40 = 86$

$\Rightarrow 2a^2 + 8a + 44 - 86 = 0$

$\Rightarrow a^2 + 4a - 21 = 0$

$\Rightarrow a^2 + 7a - 3a - 21 = 0$

$\Rightarrow (a + 7)(a - 3) = 0$

$\Rightarrow a = -7$ and 3

$\therefore$ Required sum $= -7 + 3 = -4$

Minors and Cofactors

Here, we will study how to write the expansion of a determinant in compact form using minors and cofactors.

Minor

Minor of an element a_{ij} in a determinant $|A|$ is defined as the value of determinant **obtained by deleting *i*th row and *j*th column of $|A|$**. Minor of an element a_{ij} is denoted by M_{ij}.

e.g. If $A = \begin{bmatrix} 3 & -11 \\ -4 & 2 \end{bmatrix}$, then, M_{11} = Minor of $a_{11} = 2$,

M_{12} = Minor of $a_{12} = -4$

M_{21} = Minor of $a_{21} = -11$, M_{22} = Minor of $a_{22} = 3$

Hence, minor of an element a_{ij} of a determinant of order n $(n \geq 2)$ is a determinant of order $(n - 1)$.

Cofactor

If M_{ij} is the minor of an element a_{ij}, then the cofactor of a_{ij} is denoted by C_{ij} or A_{ij} and defined as

$$C_{ij} \text{ or } A_{ij} = (-1)^{i+j} M_{ij}$$

e.g. Let $\Delta = \begin{vmatrix} 2 & 0 & 3 \\ 1 & -3 & 4 \\ 7 & 6 & 5 \end{vmatrix}$.

The minor of $a_{11} (= 2)$ is given by

$$M_{11} = \begin{bmatrix} 2 & 0 & 3 \\ 1 & -3 & 4 \\ 7 & 6 & 5 \end{bmatrix}$$

On removing 1st row and 1st column

$$\begin{vmatrix} -3 & 4 \\ 6 & 5 \end{vmatrix} = -15 - 24 = -39$$

and its cofactor, C_{11} or $A_{11} = (-1)^{1+1} M_{11}$

$$= (-1)^2 (-39) = (+1)(-39) = -39$$

EXAMPLE 1. Find minors and cofactors of all the elements of the determinant $\begin{vmatrix} 2 & -1 \\ 3 & 5 \end{vmatrix}$.

Sol. Minors of elements of determinant $\begin{vmatrix} 2 & -1 \\ 3 & 5 \end{vmatrix}$ are

$M_{11} = 5$ [minor of an element a_{11}]

$M_{12} = 3$ [minor of an element a_{12}]

$M_{21} = -1$ [minor of an element a_{21}]

and $M_{22} = 2$ [minor of an element a_{22}]

Cofactors of elements of determinant $\begin{vmatrix} 2 & -1 \\ 3 & 5 \end{vmatrix}$ are

$C_{11} = (-1)^{1+1} M_{11} = (-1)^2 \times 5 = 5$ [cofactor of element a_{11}]

$C_{12} = (-1)^{1+2} M_{12} = (-1)^3 \times 3 = -3$ [cofactor of element a_{12}]

$C_{21} = (-1)^{2+1} M_{21} = (-1)^3 \times (-1) = 1$ [cofactor of element a_{21}]

$C_{22} = (-1)^{2+2} M_{22} = (-1)^4 \times 2 = 2$ [cofactor of element a_{22}]

EXAMPLE 2. If $A = [a_{ij}]_{3\times 3} = \begin{bmatrix} 5 & 6 & -3 \\ -4 & 3 & 2 \\ -4 & -7 & 3 \end{bmatrix}$, then find the cofactor of a_{12}.

Sol. $M_{12} = \begin{vmatrix} -4 & 2 \\ -4 & 3 \end{vmatrix} = -12 + 8 = -4$

$C_{12} = (-1)^{1+2} M_{12} = -(-4) = 4$

EXAMPLE 3. Find the minors and cofactors of the elements of first row of determinant $\begin{vmatrix} 1 & 2 & 0 \\ 3 & 5 & -1 \\ 4 & 7 & 8 \end{vmatrix}$.

Sol. The minors and cofactors of the elements of first row of the determinant $\begin{vmatrix} 1 & 2 & 0 \\ 3 & 5 & -1 \\ 4 & 7 & 8 \end{vmatrix}$ are given below

$M_{11} = \begin{vmatrix} 5 & -1 \\ 7 & 8 \end{vmatrix} = 40 + 7 = 47$ [minor of an element a_{11}]

$M_{12} = \begin{vmatrix} 3 & -1 \\ 4 & 8 \end{vmatrix} = 24 + 4 = 28$ [minor of an element a_{12}]

$M_{13} = \begin{vmatrix} 3 & 5 \\ 4 & 7 \end{vmatrix} = 21 - 20 = 1$ [minor of an element a_{13}]

$C_{11} = (-1)^{1+1} M_{11} = (-1)^2 \times 47 = 47$ [cofactor of an element a_{11}]

$C_{12} = (-1)^{1+2} M_{12} = (-1)^3 \times 28 = -28$ [cofactor of an element a_{12}]

$C_{13} = (-1)^{1+3} M_{13} = (-1)^4 \times 1 = 1$ [cofactor of an element a_{13}]

EXAMPLE 4. If A_{ij} is the cofactor of the element a_{ij} of the determinant $\begin{vmatrix} 2 & -3 & 5 \\ 6 & 0 & 4 \\ 1 & 5 & -7 \end{vmatrix}$, then write the value of $a_{32} \cdot A_{32}$.

Sol. Let $\Delta = \begin{vmatrix} 2 & -3 & 5 \\ 6 & 0 & 4 \\ 1 & 5 & -7 \end{vmatrix}$

Here, $a_{32} = 5$ [element of third row and second column]

Given, A_{ij} is the cofactor of the element a_{ij}

$= (-1)^{3+2} \begin{vmatrix} 2 & 5 \\ 6 & 4 \end{vmatrix}$ [removing 3rd row and 2nd column]

$= -1(8 - 30) = 22$

$\therefore\ a_{32} \cdot A_{32} = 5 \times 22 = 110$

Value of Determinant in Terms of Cofactors

The value of determinant corresponding to a square matrix is equal to the sum of products of elements in a row (or in a column) with their corresponding cofactors.

e.g. $\Delta = \begin{vmatrix} a_{11} & a_{12} & a_{13} \\ a_{21} & a_{22} & a_{23} \\ a_{31} & a_{32} & a_{33} \end{vmatrix}$

$= a_{11}C_{11} + a_{12}C_{12} + a_{13}C_{13}$

Or

$= a_{11}C_{11} + a_{21}C_{21} + a_{31}C_{31}$

If elements of a row (or column) are multiplied with cofactors of any other row or column, then their sum is zero.

EXAMPLE 5. Using cofactors of first row evaluate

$$\Delta = \begin{vmatrix} 1 & -3 & 2 \\ 4 & -1 & 2 \\ 3 & 5 & 2 \end{vmatrix}.$$

Sol. Given, $\Delta = \begin{vmatrix} 1 & -3 & 2 \\ 4 & -1 & 2 \\ 3 & 5 & 2 \end{vmatrix}$

Using cofactors of elements of first row, we have

$$\Delta = a_{11}C_{11} + a_{12}C_{12} + a_{13}C_{13}$$

$$= (1)(-1)^{1+1}\begin{vmatrix} -1 & 2 \\ 5 & 2 \end{vmatrix} + (-3)(-1)^{1+2}\begin{vmatrix} 4 & 2 \\ 3 & 2 \end{vmatrix} + (2)(-1)^{1+3}\begin{vmatrix} 4 & -1 \\ 3 & 5 \end{vmatrix}$$

$$= 1(-2-10) + 3(8-6) + 2(20+3)$$
$$= -12 + 6 + 46$$
$$= 40$$

EXAMPLE 6. Find minors and cofactors of the elements of the determinant $\begin{vmatrix} 2 & -3 & 5 \\ 6 & 0 & 4 \\ 1 & 5 & -7 \end{vmatrix}$ and verify that $a_{11}C_{31} + a_{12}C_{32} + a_{13}C_{33} = 0$.

Sol. Given, determinant $= \begin{vmatrix} 2 & -3 & 5 \\ 6 & 0 & 4 \\ 1 & 5 & -7 \end{vmatrix}$.

We have, $M_{11} = \begin{vmatrix} 0 & 4 \\ 5 & -7 \end{vmatrix} = 0 - 20 = -20;$

$M_{12} = \begin{vmatrix} 6 & 4 \\ 1 & -7 \end{vmatrix} = -42 - 4 = -46;$

$M_{13} = \begin{vmatrix} 6 & 0 \\ 1 & 5 \end{vmatrix} = 30 - 0 = 30;$

$M_{21} = \begin{vmatrix} -3 & 5 \\ 5 & -7 \end{vmatrix} = 21 - 25 = -4;$

$M_{22} = \begin{vmatrix} 2 & 5 \\ 1 & -7 \end{vmatrix} = -14 - 5 = -19;$

$M_{23} = \begin{vmatrix} 2 & -3 \\ 1 & 5 \end{vmatrix} = 10 + 3 = 13;$

$M_{31} = \begin{vmatrix} -3 & 5 \\ 0 & 4 \end{vmatrix} = -12 - 0 = -12;$

$M_{32} = \begin{vmatrix} 2 & 5 \\ 6 & 4 \end{vmatrix} = 8 - 30 = -22;$

$M_{33} = \begin{vmatrix} 2 & -3 \\ 6 & 0 \end{vmatrix} = 0 + 18 = 18;$

$C_{11} = (-1)^{1+1}M_{11} = (-20) = -20;$

[$\because$ cofactor $C_{ij} = (-1)^{i+j}M_{ij}$]

$C_{12} = (-1)^{1+2}M_{12} = -(-46) = 46;$

$C_{13} = (-1)^{1+3}M_{13} = (30) = 30;$

$C_{21} = (-1)^{2+1}M_{21} = -(-4) = 4;$

$C_{22} = (-1)^{2+2}M_{22} = (-19) = -19$

$C_{23} = (-1)^{2+3}M_{23} = -(13) = -13;$

$C_{31} = (-1)^{3+1}M_{31} = (-12) = -12;$

$C_{32} = (-1)^{3+2}M_{32} = -(-22) = 22;$

$C_{33} = (-1)^{3+3}M_{33} = (18) = 18$

We have, $a_{11} = 2, a_{12} = -3, a_{13} = 5, C_{31} = -12,$
$C_{32} = 22, C_{33} = 18$

$\therefore\ a_{11}C_{31} + a_{12}C_{32} + a_{13}C_{33}$
$= (2)(-12) + (-3)(22) + (5)(18)$
$= -24 - 66 + 90 = -90 + 90 = 0$

Topic Practice 2

1 Write minors and cofactors of elements of following determinants.

(i) $\begin{vmatrix} 2 & -4 \\ 0 & 3 \end{vmatrix}$ (ii) $\begin{vmatrix} a & c \\ b & d \end{vmatrix}$ (iii) $\begin{bmatrix} 2 & -1 & 3 \\ 4 & 2 & 5 \\ 0 & 4 & -1 \end{bmatrix}$

2 If A is a matrix of order 3×3, then find the number of minors in determinant A.

3 Find the minor in the following determinant of indicated row and column.

(i) $\begin{vmatrix} 3 & -2 & 4 \\ 5 & 2 & 1 \\ 1 & 6 & -5 \end{vmatrix}$, second row and third column.

(ii) $\begin{vmatrix} 2 & -1 & 1 \\ -1 & 2 & -1 \\ 1 & -1 & 2 \end{vmatrix}$, third row and first column.

4 Find the minors of the diagonal elements of the determinant $\begin{vmatrix} 1 & i & -i \\ -i & 1 & i \\ 1 & -i & i \end{vmatrix}$.

5 In the following cases, find determinant using cofactors of indicated row or column.

(i) $\begin{vmatrix} 5 & 3 & 8 \\ 2 & 0 & 1 \\ 1 & 2 & 3 \end{vmatrix}$, second row

(ii) $\begin{vmatrix} 0 & 1 & -1 \\ 4 & -3 & 4 \\ 3 & -3 & 4 \end{vmatrix}$, first column

(iii) $\begin{vmatrix} 1 & x & y+z \\ 1 & y & z+x \\ 1 & z & x+y \end{vmatrix}$, third row

(iv) $\begin{vmatrix} 1 & x & yz \\ 1 & y & zx \\ 1 & z & xy \end{vmatrix}$, third column

(v) $\begin{vmatrix} \sqrt{23}+\sqrt{3} & \sqrt{5} & \sqrt{5} \\ \sqrt{15}+\sqrt{46} & 5 & \sqrt{10} \\ 3+\sqrt{115} & \sqrt{15} & 5 \end{vmatrix}$, third row

6 Find the minors and cofactors of the elements of the determinant $\begin{vmatrix} 3 & 4 & 5 \\ -6 & 2 & -3 \\ 8 & 1 & 7 \end{vmatrix}$ and verify that $a_{21}C_{21} + a_{22}C_{22} + a_{23}C_{23} = 0$.

Hints & Solutions

1. Similar as Example 1.

Ans. (i) $M_{11} = 3, M_{12} = 0, M_{21} = -4, M_{22} = 2,$
$C_{11} = 3, \ C_{12} = 0, \ C_{21} = 4$ and $C_{22} = 2$

(ii) $M_{11} = d, M_{12} = b, M_{21} = c$ and $M_{22} = a$
$C_{11} = d, \ C_{12} = -b, C_{21} = -c, C_{22} = a$

(iii) $M_{11} = -22, M_{12} = -4, M_{13} = 16,$
$M_{21} = -11, M_{22} = -2, M_{23} = 8, M_{31} = -11,$
$M_{32} = -2, M_{33} = 8, C_{11} = -22, C_{12} = 4,$
$C_{13} = 16, C_{21} = 11, C_{22} = -2, C_{23} = -8,$
$C_{31} = -11, C_{32} = 2, C_{33} = 8$

2. Since, the matrix have 9 elements, therefore its corresponding determinant have 9 elements. Hence, there are 9 minors in determinant of A.

3. (i) Clearly, M_{23} = determinant obtained after deleting second row and third column

$$= \begin{vmatrix} 3 & -2 \\ 1 & 6 \end{vmatrix} = 18 - (-2) = 18 + 2 = 20$$

(ii) Similar as part (i). **Ans.** -1

4. The minors of the diagonal elements of the determinant $\begin{vmatrix} 1 & i & -i \\ -i & 1 & i \\ 1 & -i & i \end{vmatrix}$ are given below.

$$M_{11} = \begin{vmatrix} 1 & i \\ -i & i \end{vmatrix} = i + i^2 = i - 1 \qquad [\because i^2 = -1]$$

$$M_{22} = \begin{vmatrix} 1 & -i \\ 1 & i \end{vmatrix} = i + i = 2i$$

and $$M_{33} = \begin{vmatrix} 1 & i \\ -i & 1 \end{vmatrix} = 1 + i^2 = 1 - 1 = 0$$

5. (i) Given, $\Delta = \begin{vmatrix} 5 & 3 & 8 \\ 2 & 0 & 1 \\ 1 & 2 & 3 \end{vmatrix}$

Using cofactors of elements of second row, we have

$$\Delta = a_{21}C_{21} + a_{22}C_{22} + a_{23}C_{23}$$
$$= 2\cdot(-1)^{2+1}\begin{vmatrix} 3 & 8 \\ 2 & 3 \end{vmatrix} + 0\cdot(-1)^{2+2}\begin{vmatrix} 5 & 8 \\ 1 & 3 \end{vmatrix} + 1\cdot(-1)^{2+3}\begin{vmatrix} 5 & 3 \\ 1 & 2 \end{vmatrix}$$
$$= -2(9-16) + (-1)(10-3)$$
$$= (-2)(-7) + (-1)(7)$$
$$= 14 - 7 = 7$$

(ii) Similar as part (i).

Ans. -1

(iii) **Hint** Given, $\Delta = \begin{vmatrix} 1 & x & y+z \\ 1 & y & z+x \\ 1 & z & x+y \end{vmatrix}$

Using cofactors of elements of third row, we have

$$\Delta = a_{31}C_{31} + a_{32}C_{32} + a_{33}C_{33}$$
$$= (-1)^{3+1}\cdot 1\begin{vmatrix} x & y+z \\ y & z+x \end{vmatrix} + (-1)^{3+2}\cdot z\begin{vmatrix} 1 & y+z \\ 1 & z+x \end{vmatrix}$$
$$+ (-1)^{3+3}\cdot(x+y)\begin{vmatrix} 1 & x \\ 1 & y \end{vmatrix}$$

$[\because \text{cofactor } A_{ij} = (-1)^{i+j} M_{ij}]$

$$= 1(zx + x^2 - y^2 - yz) - z(z + x - y - z) + (x+y)(y-x)$$
$$= zx + x^2 - y^2 - yz - zx + yz + y^2 - x^2$$ **Ans.** 0

(iv) **Hint** $\Delta = a_{13}C_{13} + a_{23}C_{23} + a_{33}C_{33}$

Ans. $(x-y)(y-z)(z-x)$

(v) Do same as part (iii). **Ans.** 0

6. Do similar as Example 6.

Ans. $M_{11} = 17, M_{12} = -18, M_{13} = -22, M_{21} = 23,$
$M_{22} = -19, M_{23} = -29, M_{31} = -22, M_{32} = 21, M_{33} = 30,$
$A_{11} = 17, A_{12} = 18, A_{13} = -22, A_{21} = -23, A_{22} = -19,$
$A_{23} = 29, A_{31} = -22, A_{32} = -21, A_{33} = 30$

Adjoint of a Matrix

The adjoint of a square matrix $A=[a_{ij}]_{n\times n}$ is defined as the transpose of the matrix formed by corresponding A_{ij} or C_{ij} cofactors of the elements $|A|$ and it is denoted by adj (A).

$$\text{adj } A=[A_{ij} \text{ or } C_{ij}]_{n\times m}$$

Let $A=\begin{bmatrix} a_{11} & a_{12} & a_{13} \\ a_{21} & a_{22} & a_{23} \\ a_{31} & a_{32} & a_{33}\end{bmatrix}$, then adj A

$$=\text{Transpose of}\begin{bmatrix} A_{11} & A_{12} & A_{13} \\ A_{21} & A_{22} & A_{23} \\ A_{31} & A_{32} & A_{33}\end{bmatrix}=\begin{bmatrix} A_{11} & A_{21} & A_{31} \\ A_{12} & A_{22} & A_{32} \\ A_{13} & A_{23} & A_{33}\end{bmatrix}$$

Here, A_{ij} is the corresponding cofactor of a_{ij}.

Note Let A be a square matrix of order 2, then adjoint of A can be calculated by interchanging the elements of main diagonal and change the sign of other diagonal.

Let $A=\begin{bmatrix} a_{11} & a_{12} \\ a_{21} & a_{22}\end{bmatrix}$, then adj $A=\begin{bmatrix} a_{22} & -a_{12} \\ -a_{21} & a_{11}\end{bmatrix}$

EXAMPLE 1. Find the adjoint of the matrix

(i) $\begin{bmatrix} 1 & 2 \\ 3 & 4\end{bmatrix}$. (ii) $\begin{bmatrix} 1 & -1 & 2 \\ 2 & 3 & 5 \\ -2 & 0 & 1\end{bmatrix}$.

Sol. (i) Let $A=\begin{bmatrix} 1 & 2 \\ 3 & 4\end{bmatrix}$, then $|A|=\begin{vmatrix} 1 & 2 \\ 3 & 4\end{vmatrix}$.

Now, cofactors of elements of $|A|$ are

$C_{11}=(-1)^{1+1}4=4,\quad C_{12}=(-1)^{1+2}(3)=-3,$

$C_{21}=(-1)^{2+1}(2)=-2$ and $C_{22}=(-1)^{2+2}(1)=1$

Now, adj $(A)=\begin{bmatrix} C_{11} & C_{12} \\ C_{21} & C_{22}\end{bmatrix}^T=\begin{bmatrix} 4 & -3 \\ -2 & 1\end{bmatrix}^T=\begin{bmatrix} 4 & -2 \\ -3 & 1\end{bmatrix}$

(ii) Let $A=\begin{bmatrix} 1 & -1 & 2 \\ 2 & 3 & 5 \\ -2 & 0 & 1\end{bmatrix}$.

Cofactors of elements of first row of $|A|$ are

$$C_{11}=\begin{vmatrix} 3 & 5 \\ 0 & 1\end{vmatrix}=3-0=3,$$

$$C_{12}=-\begin{vmatrix} 2 & 5 \\ -2 & 1\end{vmatrix}=-(2+10)=-12$$

and $C_{13}=\begin{vmatrix} 2 & 3 \\ -2 & 0\end{vmatrix}=0-(-6)=6$

Cofactors of elements of second row of $|A|$ are

$$C_{21}=-\begin{vmatrix} -1 & 2 \\ 0 & 1\end{vmatrix}=-(-1-0)=1,$$

$$C_{22}=\begin{vmatrix} 1 & 2 \\ -2 & 1\end{vmatrix}=1+4=5$$

and $C_{23}=-\begin{vmatrix} 1 & -1 \\ -2 & 0\end{vmatrix}=-(0-2)=2$

Cofactors of elements of third row of $|A|$ are

$$C_{31}=\begin{vmatrix} -1 & 2 \\ 3 & 5\end{vmatrix}=-5-6=-11,$$

$$C_{32}=-\begin{vmatrix} 1 & 2 \\ 2 & 5\end{vmatrix}=-(5-4)=-1$$

and $C_{33}=\begin{vmatrix} 1 & -1 \\ 2 & 3\end{vmatrix}=3+2=5$

Hence, adj $(A)=\begin{bmatrix} C_{11} & C_{12} & C_{13} \\ C_{21} & C_{22} & C_{23} \\ C_{31} & C_{32} & C_{33}\end{bmatrix}^T$

$$=\begin{bmatrix} 3 & -12 & 6 \\ 1 & 5 & 2 \\ -11 & -1 & 5\end{bmatrix}^T=\begin{bmatrix} 3 & 1 & -11 \\ -12 & 5 & -1 \\ 6 & 2 & 5\end{bmatrix}$$

Important Theorem

If A is any given square matrix of order n, then

$$A(\text{adj } A)=(\text{adj } A)A=|A|\,I_n,$$

where I is the identity matrix of order n.

EXAMPLE 2. Find the adjoint of the matrix

$A=\begin{bmatrix} -1 & -2 & -2 \\ 2 & 1 & -2 \\ 2 & -2 & 1\end{bmatrix}$ and hence verify that

$A(\text{adj } A)=|A|I_3$.

Sol. We have, $A=\begin{bmatrix} -1 & -2 & -2 \\ 2 & 1 & -2 \\ 2 & -2 & 1\end{bmatrix}$.

Let C_{ij} be the cofactor of the element a_{ij} of $|A|$.

Now, cofactors of $|A|$ are

$$C_{11}=(-1)^{1+1}\begin{vmatrix} 1 & -2 \\ -2 & 1\end{vmatrix}=1-4=-3$$

$$C_{12}=(-1)^{1+2}\begin{vmatrix} 2 & -2 \\ 2 & 1\end{vmatrix}=-(2+4)=-6$$

$$C_{13}=(-1)^{1+3}\begin{vmatrix} 2 & 1 \\ 2 & -2\end{vmatrix}=-4-2=-6$$

$$C_{21}=(-1)^{2+1}\begin{vmatrix} -2 & -2 \\ -2 & 1\end{vmatrix}=-(-2-4)=6$$

$$C_{22}=(-1)^{2+2}\begin{vmatrix} -1 & -2 \\ 2 & 1\end{vmatrix}=-1+4=3$$

$$C_{23}=(-1)^{2+3}\begin{vmatrix} -1 & -2 \\ 2 & -2\end{vmatrix}=-(2+4)=-6$$

$$C_{31} = (-1)^{3+1}\begin{vmatrix} -2 & -2 \\ 1 & -2 \end{vmatrix} = 4 + 2 = 6$$

$$C_{32} = (-1)^{3+2}\begin{vmatrix} -1 & -2 \\ 2 & -2 \end{vmatrix} = -(2+4) = -6$$

$$C_{33} = (-1)^{3+3}\begin{vmatrix} -1 & -2 \\ 2 & 1 \end{vmatrix} = -1 + 4 = 3$$

Now, the adjoint of the matrix A is given by

$$\text{adj}(A) = \begin{bmatrix} C_{11} & C_{21} & C_{31} \\ C_{12} & C_{22} & C_{32} \\ C_{13} & C_{23} & C_{33} \end{bmatrix} = \begin{bmatrix} -3 & 6 & 6 \\ -6 & 3 & -6 \\ -6 & -6 & 3 \end{bmatrix}$$

$$\text{Now, } |A| = \begin{vmatrix} -1 & -2 & -2 \\ 2 & 1 & -2 \\ 2 & -2 & 1 \end{vmatrix}$$

$$= -1(1-4) + 2(2+4) - 2(-4-2)$$
$$= -1(-3) + 2(6) - 2(-6) = 3 + 12 + 12 = 27$$

$$\text{and } A\cdot(\text{adj } A) = \begin{bmatrix} -1 & -2 & -2 \\ 2 & 1 & -2 \\ 2 & -2 & 1 \end{bmatrix}\begin{bmatrix} -3 & 6 & 6 \\ -6 & 3 & -6 \\ -6 & -6 & 3 \end{bmatrix}$$

$$= \begin{bmatrix} 3+12+12 & -6-6+12 & -6+12-6 \\ -6-6+12 & 12+3+12 & 12-6-6 \\ -6+12-6 & 12-6-6 & 12+12+3 \end{bmatrix}$$

$$= \begin{bmatrix} 27 & 0 & 0 \\ 0 & 27 & 0 \\ 0 & 0 & 27 \end{bmatrix} = 27\begin{bmatrix} 1 & 0 & 0 \\ 0 & 1 & 0 \\ 0 & 0 & 1 \end{bmatrix}$$

$$= 27 I_3 = |A| I_3$$

Properties of Adjoint of a Matrix

Suppose, A and B are two matrices of same order n. Then,

- $\text{adj}(A^T) = [\text{adj}(A)]^T$
- $\text{adj}(kA) = k^{n-1}(\text{adj } A), k \in R$
- $\text{adj}(AB) = [\text{adj}(B)][\text{adj}(A)]$
- $|\text{adj } A| = |A|^{n-1}$
- $|\text{adj}[\text{adj}(A)]| = |A|^{(n-1)^2}$
- $\text{adj}(\text{adj } A) = |A|^{n-2}\cdot A$

EXAMPLE 3. If $A = \begin{bmatrix} 1 & 2 \\ 3 & 4 \end{bmatrix}$, then verify the following results.

(i) $|\text{adj } A| = |A|$ (ii) $\text{adj}(A^T) = (\text{adj } A)^T$

(iii) $|\text{adj}(\text{adj } A)| = |A|$

Sol. Let $A = \begin{bmatrix} 1 & 2 \\ 3 & 4 \end{bmatrix}$, then $|A| = \begin{vmatrix} 1 & 2 \\ 3 & 4 \end{vmatrix}$.

Now, cofactors of elements of $|A|$ are

$A_{11} = 4, A_{12} = -3, A_{21} = -2$ and $A_{22} = 1$

$$\therefore \text{adj } A = \begin{bmatrix} A_{11} & A_{12} \\ A_{21} & A_{22} \end{bmatrix}^T = \begin{bmatrix} 4 & -3 \\ -2 & 1 \end{bmatrix}^T = \begin{bmatrix} 4 & -2 \\ -3 & 1 \end{bmatrix} \quad \text{...(i)}$$

(i) Now, $|A| = \begin{vmatrix} 1 & 2 \\ 3 & 4 \end{vmatrix} = 4 - 6 = -2$ ...(ii)

and $|\text{adj}(A)| = \begin{vmatrix} 4 & -2 \\ -3 & 1 \end{vmatrix} = 4 - 6 = -2$ ...(iii)

$\therefore$ $|\text{adj}(A)| = |A|$ [from Eqs. (ii) and (iii)]

(ii) We have, $A = \begin{bmatrix} 1 & 2 \\ 3 & 4 \end{bmatrix}$

$\therefore$ $A^T = \begin{bmatrix} 1 & 3 \\ 2 & 4 \end{bmatrix}$ and $|A^T| = \begin{vmatrix} 1 & 3 \\ 2 & 4 \end{vmatrix}$

Now, cofactors of elements of $|A^T|$ are $C_{11} = 4$,

$C_{12} = -2, C_{21} = -3, C_{22} = 1.$

$$\therefore \quad (A^T) = \begin{bmatrix} C_{11} & C_{12} \\ C_{21} & C_{22} \end{bmatrix}^T$$

$$= \begin{bmatrix} 4 & -2 \\ -3 & 1 \end{bmatrix}^T = \begin{bmatrix} 4 & -3 \\ -2 & 1 \end{bmatrix} \quad \text{...(iv)}$$

From Eq. (i), we get

$$(\text{adj } A)^T = \begin{bmatrix} 4 & -2 \\ -3 & 1 \end{bmatrix}^T = \begin{bmatrix} 4 & -3 \\ -2 & 1 \end{bmatrix}$$

$\Rightarrow (\text{adj } A)^T = \text{adj}(A^T)$ [from Eq. (iv)]

(iii) We have, $(\text{adj } A) = \begin{bmatrix} 4 & -2 \\ -3 & 1 \end{bmatrix}$

$\therefore$ $|\text{adj } A| = \begin{vmatrix} 4 & -2 \\ -3 & 1 \end{vmatrix}$

Now, cofactors of elements of $|\text{adj } A|$ are

$C_{11} = 1, C_{12} = 3, C_{21} = 2$ and $C_{22} = 4$.

$$\therefore \quad \text{adj}(\text{adj } A) = \begin{bmatrix} C_{11} & C_{12} \\ C_{21} & C_{22} \end{bmatrix}^T = \begin{bmatrix} 1 & 3 \\ 2 & 4 \end{bmatrix}^T = \begin{bmatrix} 1 & 2 \\ 3 & 4 \end{bmatrix}$$

$$\Rightarrow \quad |\text{adj}(\text{adj } A)| = \begin{vmatrix} 1 & 2 \\ 3 & 4 \end{vmatrix}$$

$= 4 - 6 = -2$

$= |A|$ [from Eq. (ii)]

Hence verified.

EXAMPLE 4. Find $|\text{adj } A|$, if $A = \begin{bmatrix} 5 & 2 \\ 7 & 3 \end{bmatrix}$.

Sol. Given, $A = \begin{bmatrix} 5 & 2 \\ 7 & 3 \end{bmatrix}$

Clearly, $|A| = \begin{vmatrix} 5 & 2 \\ 7 & 3 \end{vmatrix} = 15 - 14 = 1$

We know that,

$|\text{adj } A| = |A|^{n-1}$

$\therefore$ $|\text{adj } A| = |A|^{2-1} = |A| = 1$

Singular and Non-singular Matrices

A square matrix A is said to be a **singular matrix**, if $|A| = 0$ and if $|A| \neq 0$, then matrix A is said to be **non-singular matrix**.

EXAMPLE 5. Check whether the following matrices are singular or non-singular.

(i) $\begin{bmatrix} 2 & 1 \\ 6 & 3 \end{bmatrix}$ (ii) $\begin{bmatrix} 2 & 1 & 3 \\ 4 & -1 & 0 \\ -7 & 2 & 1 \end{bmatrix}$

Sol. (i) Let $A = \begin{bmatrix} 2 & 1 \\ 6 & 3 \end{bmatrix}$.

Now, $|A| = 6 - 6 = 0$

So, the matrix A is a singular matrix.

(ii) Let $B = \begin{bmatrix} 2 & 1 & 3 \\ 4 & -1 & 0 \\ -7 & 2 & 1 \end{bmatrix}$.

Now, $|B| = \begin{vmatrix} 2 & 1 & 3 \\ 4 & -1 & 0 \\ -7 & 2 & 1 \end{vmatrix}$

$$= 2(-1-0) - 1(4-0) + 3(8-7)$$
$$= -2 - 4 + 3 = -6 + 3$$
$$= -3 \neq 0$$

Hence, B is a non-singular matrix.

EXAMPLE 6. For what value of x the matrix

$$A = \begin{bmatrix} 1 & -2 & 3 \\ 1 & 2 & 1 \\ x & 2 & 3 \end{bmatrix} \text{ is singular?}$$

Sol. We know that, A will be singular, iff

$$|A| = 0$$

$$\Rightarrow \begin{vmatrix} 1 & -2 & 3 \\ 1 & 2 & 1 \\ x & 2 & 3 \end{vmatrix} = 0$$

$$\Rightarrow 1[6-2] - (-2)[3-x] + 3[2-2x] = 0$$
$$\Rightarrow 4 + 2(3-x) + 3(2-2x) = 0$$
$$\Rightarrow 4 + 6 - 2x + 6 - 6x = 0$$
$$\Rightarrow 16 - 8x = 0$$
$$\Rightarrow x = 2$$

Some Important Theorem

Theorem 1 If A and B are non-singular matrices of the same order, then AB and BA are also non-singular matrices of the same order.

Theorem 2 The determinant of the product of matrices is equal to the product of their respective determinants

i.e. $|AB| = |A||B|$

where, A and B are square matrices of the same order.

EXAMPLE 7. If for any 2×2 square matrix A, $A(\text{adj } A) = \begin{bmatrix} -7 & 0 \\ 0 & -7 \end{bmatrix}$, then write the value of $|A|$.

Sol. Given, $A(\text{adj } A) = \begin{bmatrix} -7 & 0 \\ 0 & -7 \end{bmatrix}$

$$= 49 - 0 = 49$$

$\Rightarrow |A||\text{adj } A| = 49$ $[\because |AB| = |A||B|]$

$\Rightarrow |A||A|^{2-1} = 49$ $[\because |\text{adj } A| = |A|^{n-1}]$

$\Rightarrow |A||A| = 49$

$\Rightarrow |A| = \pm 7$

EXAMPLE 8. If $A = \begin{bmatrix} 1 & 2 \\ 3 & -1 \end{bmatrix}$ and $B = \begin{bmatrix} 1 & 3 \\ -1 & 1 \end{bmatrix}$, then write the value of $|AB|$.

Sol. We have, $|A| = \begin{vmatrix} 1 & 2 \\ 3 & -1 \end{vmatrix} = -1 - 6 = -7$

and $|B| = \begin{vmatrix} 1 & 3 \\ -1 & 1 \end{vmatrix} = 1 + 3 = 4$

$\therefore$ $|AB| = |A| \cdot |B| = (-7)(4) = -28$

Inverse of a Square Matrix

A non-singular square matrix is said to be invertible if there exist a square matrix B such that $AB = BA = I$ Here, I is identity matrix and matrix B is called the inverse of A. If A is a non-singular matrix (i.e. $|A| \neq 0$), then $A^{-1} = \frac{1}{|A|} \text{adj}(A)$.

e.g. For non-singular matrix $A = \begin{bmatrix} a_{11} & a_{12} & a_{13} \\ a_{21} & a_{22} & a_{23} \\ a_{31} & a_{32} & a_{33} \end{bmatrix}$, the inverse is $A^{-1} = \frac{[A_{ij}]^T}{|A|} = \frac{1}{|A|} \begin{bmatrix} A_{11} & A_{21} & A_{31} \\ A_{12} & A_{22} & A_{32} \\ A_{13} & A_{23} & A_{33} \end{bmatrix}$, where A_{ij} is the cofactor of element a_{ij}.

EXAMPLE 9. Find the inverse of following matrices.

(i) $\begin{bmatrix} -1 & 5 \\ -3 & 2 \end{bmatrix}$ (ii) $\begin{bmatrix} 1 & -1 & 1 \\ 2 & -1 & 0 \\ 1 & 0 & 0 \end{bmatrix}$ **[NCERT]**

Sol. (i) Let $A = \begin{bmatrix} -1 & 5 \\ -3 & 2 \end{bmatrix}$, then $|A| = \begin{vmatrix} -1 & 5 \\ -3 & 2 \end{vmatrix} = -2 + 15 = 13 \neq 0$

So, A is non-singular matrix and therefore A^{-1} exists.

Now, cofactors of each element of $|A|$ are

$$C_{11} = (-1)^{1+1}(2) = 2,$$
$$C_{12} = (-1)^{1+2}(-3) = 3,$$
$$C_{21} = (-1)^{2+1}(5) = -5$$

and $C_{22} = (-1)^{2+2}(-1) = -1$

Thus, matrix of cofactors $= \begin{bmatrix} C_{11} & C_{12} \\ C_{21} & C_{22} \end{bmatrix} = \begin{bmatrix} 2 & 3 \\ -5 & -1 \end{bmatrix}$

and $\text{adj}(A) = \begin{bmatrix} 2 & 3 \\ -5 & -1 \end{bmatrix}^T = \begin{bmatrix} 2 & -5 \\ 3 & -1 \end{bmatrix}$

Now, $A^{-1} = \frac{1}{|A|} \cdot \text{adj} A = \frac{1}{13} \begin{bmatrix} 2 & -5 \\ 3 & -1 \end{bmatrix}$

which is the required inverse of given matrix A.

(ii) Let $A = \begin{bmatrix} 1 & -1 & 1 \\ 2 & -1 & 0 \\ 1 & 0 & 0 \end{bmatrix}$

Then, $|A| = 1\begin{vmatrix} -1 & 0 \\ 0 & 0 \end{vmatrix} - 2\begin{vmatrix} -1 & 1 \\ 0 & 0 \end{vmatrix} + 1\begin{vmatrix} -1 & 1 \\ -1 & 0 \end{vmatrix}$

$= 1(0) - 2(0) + 1(0+1)$ [expanding along C_1]

$= 1 \neq 0$

Thus, A is a non-singular matrix, so A^{-1} exists.

Now, cofactors corresponding to each element of determinant A are

$C_{11} = (-1)^{1+1}\begin{vmatrix} -1 & 0 \\ 0 & 0 \end{vmatrix} = 1(-0-0) = 0$

[$\because C_{ij} = (-1)^{i+j} M_{ij}$]

$C_{12} = (-1)^{1+2}\begin{vmatrix} 2 & 0 \\ 1 & 0 \end{vmatrix} = -1(0-0) = 0$

$C_{13} = (-1)^{1+3}\begin{vmatrix} 2 & -1 \\ 1 & 0 \end{vmatrix} = 1(0+1) = 1$

$C_{21} = (-1)^{2+1}\begin{vmatrix} -1 & 1 \\ 0 & 0 \end{vmatrix} = -1(0-0) = 0$

$C_{22} = (-1)^{2+2}\begin{vmatrix} 1 & 1 \\ 1 & 0 \end{vmatrix} = 1(0-1) = -1$

$C_{23} = (-1)^{2+3}\begin{vmatrix} 1 & -1 \\ 1 & 0 \end{vmatrix} = -1(0+1) = -1$

$C_{31} = (-1)^{3+1}\begin{vmatrix} -1 & 1 \\ -1 & 0 \end{vmatrix} = 1(0+1) = 1$

$C_{32} = (-1)^{3+2}\begin{vmatrix} 1 & 1 \\ 2 & 0 \end{vmatrix} = -1(0-2) = 2$

$C_{33} = (-1)^{3+3}\begin{vmatrix} 1 & -1 \\ 2 & -1 \end{vmatrix} = 1(-1+2) = 1$

Thus, the matrix of cofactors

$$= \begin{bmatrix} C_{11} & C_{12} & C_{13} \\ C_{21} & C_{22} & C_{23} \\ C_{31} & C_{32} & C_{33} \end{bmatrix} = \begin{bmatrix} 0 & 0 & 1 \\ 0 & -1 & -1 \\ 1 & 2 & 1 \end{bmatrix}$$

and $\text{adj}(A) = \begin{bmatrix} 0 & 0 & 1 \\ 0 & -1 & -1 \\ 1 & 2 & 1 \end{bmatrix}^T = \begin{bmatrix} 0 & 0 & 1 \\ 0 & -1 & 2 \\ 1 & -1 & 1 \end{bmatrix}$

[interchange rows and columns]

Now, $A^{-1} = \frac{1}{|A|}\text{adj}(A) = \frac{1}{1}\begin{bmatrix} 0 & 0 & 1 \\ 0 & -1 & 2 \\ 1 & -1 & 1 \end{bmatrix}$

$\Rightarrow \quad A^{-1} = \begin{bmatrix} 0 & 0 & 1 \\ 0 & -1 & 2 \\ 1 & -1 & 1 \end{bmatrix}$

which is the required inverse of given matrix A.

EXAMPLE 10. If $A = \begin{bmatrix} 2 & 3 \\ 5 & -2 \end{bmatrix}$, show that $A^{-1} = \frac{1}{19}A$.

Sol. We have, $|A| = \begin{vmatrix} 2 & 3 \\ 5 & -2 \end{vmatrix}$

$= -4 - 15 = -19 \neq 0$

Thus, A is a non-singular matrix, so A^{-1} exist.

Now, cofactors corresponding to each element of determinant A are

$C_{11} = -2, C_{12} = -5, C_{21} = -3$ and $C_{22} = 2$

$\therefore \quad \text{adj } A = \begin{bmatrix} -2 & -5 \\ -3 & 2 \end{bmatrix}^T = \begin{bmatrix} -2 & -3 \\ -5 & 2 \end{bmatrix}$

Now, $A^{-1} = \frac{1}{|A|}\text{adj } A$

$\Rightarrow \quad A^{-1} = \frac{1}{-19}\begin{bmatrix} -2 & -3 \\ -5 & 2 \end{bmatrix} = \frac{1}{19}\begin{bmatrix} 2 & 3 \\ 5 & -2 \end{bmatrix} = \frac{1}{19}A$

Hence proved.

Properties of Inverse of a Matrix

Let A, B and C be three square invertible matrices of same order. Then,

- $(A^{-1})^{-1} = A$
- $(AB)^{-1} = B^{-1}A^{-1}$ or $(ABC)^{-1} = C^{-1}B^{-1}A^{-1}$ (Reversal Law)
- $(A^T)^{-1} = (A^{-1})^T \quad |A^{-1}| = |A|^{-1}$
- $AA^{-1} = A^{-1}A = I, (kA)^{-1} = \frac{1}{k}A^{-1}, k \neq 0$
- $AB = AC \Rightarrow B = C$ (Left Cancellation Law)
- $BA = CA \Rightarrow B = C$ (Right Cancellation Law)

EXAMPLE 11. If $A = \begin{bmatrix} 2 & 3 \\ 1 & -4 \end{bmatrix}$ and $B = \begin{bmatrix} 1 & -2 \\ -1 & 3 \end{bmatrix}$, then verify that

(i) $AA^{-1} = I$ (ii) $|A^{-1}| = |A|^{-1}$.

(iii) $(AB)^{-1} = B^{-1}A^{-1}$

Sol. (i) Now, $AA^{-1} = \begin{bmatrix} 2 & 3 \\ 1 & -4 \end{bmatrix}\frac{1}{11}\begin{bmatrix} 4 & 3 \\ 1 & -2 \end{bmatrix}$

$= \frac{1}{11}\begin{bmatrix} 2 & 3 \\ 1 & -4 \end{bmatrix}\begin{bmatrix} 4 & 3 \\ 1 & -2 \end{bmatrix} = \frac{1}{11}\begin{bmatrix} 8+3 & 6-6 \\ 4-4 & 3+8 \end{bmatrix}$

$= \frac{1}{11}\begin{bmatrix} 11 & 0 \\ 0 & 11 \end{bmatrix} = \begin{bmatrix} 1 & 0 \\ 0 & 1 \end{bmatrix} = I$ **Hence verified.**

(ii) Now, $|A^{-1}| = \left(\frac{1}{11}\right)^2\begin{vmatrix} 4 & 3 \\ 1 & -2 \end{vmatrix}$

[if A is a matrix of order 2×2, then $|kA| = k^2|A|$]

$= \frac{1}{(11)^2}[-8-3] = \frac{-11}{(11)^2} = -\frac{1}{11}$

and $|A|^{-1} = (-11)^{-1} = -\frac{1}{11}$ **Hence verified.**

(iii) Given, $A = \begin{bmatrix} 2 & 3 \\ 1 & -4 \end{bmatrix}$ and $B = \begin{bmatrix} 1 & -2 \\ -1 & 3 \end{bmatrix}$, then

$$AB = \begin{bmatrix} 2 & 3 \\ 1 & -4 \end{bmatrix}\begin{bmatrix} 1 & -2 \\ -1 & 3 \end{bmatrix}$$

$$= \begin{bmatrix} 2-3 & -4+9 \\ 1+4 & -2-12 \end{bmatrix} = \begin{bmatrix} -1 & 5 \\ 5 & -14 \end{bmatrix}$$

Now, $|A| = \begin{vmatrix} 2 & 3 \\ 1 & -4 \end{vmatrix} = -8-3 = -11 \neq 0$

$$|B| = \begin{vmatrix} 1 & -2 \\ -1 & 3 \end{vmatrix} = 3-2 = 1 \neq 0$$

and $|AB| = \begin{vmatrix} -1 & 5 \\ 5 & -14 \end{vmatrix}$

$$= 14 - 25 = -11 \neq 0$$

Thus A, B and AB are non-singular matrices, so their inverse exists.

Now, $\text{adj}(A) = \begin{bmatrix} -4 & -3 \\ -1 & 2 \end{bmatrix}$, $\left[\because \text{adj}\begin{bmatrix} a & b \\ c & d \end{bmatrix} = \begin{bmatrix} d & -b \\ -c & a \end{bmatrix}\right]$

$\text{adj}(B) = \begin{bmatrix} 3 & 2 \\ 1 & 1 \end{bmatrix}$ and $\text{adj}(AB) = \begin{bmatrix} -14 & -5 \\ -5 & -1 \end{bmatrix}$

$$\therefore (AB)^{-1} = \frac{1}{|AB|}\text{adj}(AB) = \frac{1}{-11}\begin{bmatrix} -14 & -5 \\ -5 & -1 \end{bmatrix} = \frac{1}{11}\begin{bmatrix} 14 & 5 \\ 5 & 1 \end{bmatrix} \quad \text{...(i)}$$

$$A^{-1} = \frac{1}{|A|}\text{adj}(A) = \frac{1}{-11}\begin{bmatrix} -4 & -3 \\ -1 & 2 \end{bmatrix} = \frac{1}{11}\begin{bmatrix} 4 & 3 \\ 1 & -2 \end{bmatrix}$$

and $B^{-1} = \frac{1}{|B|}\text{adj}(B) = \frac{1}{1}\begin{bmatrix} 3 & 2 \\ 1 & 1 \end{bmatrix} = \begin{bmatrix} 3 & 2 \\ 1 & 1 \end{bmatrix}$

Now, $B^{-1}A^{-1} = \begin{bmatrix} 3 & 2 \\ 1 & 1 \end{bmatrix}\frac{1}{11}\begin{bmatrix} 4 & 3 \\ 1 & -2 \end{bmatrix}$

$$= \frac{1}{11}\begin{bmatrix} 3 & 2 \\ 1 & 1 \end{bmatrix}\begin{bmatrix} 4 & 3 \\ 1 & -2 \end{bmatrix}$$

$$= \frac{1}{11}\begin{bmatrix} 12+2 & 9-4 \\ 4+1 & 3-2 \end{bmatrix} = \frac{1}{11}\begin{bmatrix} 14 & 5 \\ 5 & 1 \end{bmatrix} = (AB)^{-1}$$

[from Eq. (i)]

$\therefore \quad (AB)^{-1} = B^{-1}A^{-1}$ **Hence verified.**

EXAMPLE 12. If $A = \begin{bmatrix} 0 & 1 & 3 \\ 1 & 2 & x \\ 2 & 3 & 1 \end{bmatrix}$ and

$$A^{-1} = \begin{bmatrix} \frac{1}{2} & -4 & \frac{5}{2} \\ -\frac{1}{2} & 3 & -\frac{3}{2} \\ \frac{1}{2} & y & \frac{1}{2} \end{bmatrix}$$, then find x and y.

Sol. We know that

$AA^{-1} = I$ [by property of inverse of matrix]

$$\Rightarrow \begin{bmatrix} 0 & 1 & 3 \\ 1 & 2 & x \\ 2 & 3 & 1 \end{bmatrix}\begin{bmatrix} \frac{1}{2} & -4 & \frac{5}{2} \\ -\frac{1}{2} & 3 & -\frac{3}{2} \\ \frac{1}{2} & y & \frac{1}{2} \end{bmatrix} = \begin{bmatrix} 1 & 0 & 0 \\ 0 & 1 & 0 \\ 0 & 0 & 1 \end{bmatrix}$$

$$\Rightarrow \begin{bmatrix} 1 & 3+3y & 0 \\ -\frac{1}{2}+\frac{x}{2} & 2+xy & -\frac{1}{2}+\frac{x}{2} \\ 0 & 1+y & 1 \end{bmatrix} = \begin{bmatrix} 1 & 0 & 0 \\ 0 & 1 & 0 \\ 0 & 0 & 1 \end{bmatrix}$$

$$\Rightarrow 3+3y = 0, -\frac{1}{2}+\frac{x}{2} = 0, 2+xy = 1, 1+y = 0$$

$$\Rightarrow \quad x = 1 \text{ and } y = -1$$

EXAMPLE 13. If $A = \begin{bmatrix} 1 & -1 & 1 \\ 2 & -1 & 0 \\ 1 & 0 & 0 \end{bmatrix}$, then prove that $A^{-1} = A^2$.

Sol. If $AB = I = BA$, then B is the inverse of A.

Here, we have to show that A^2 is the inverse of $A (A.A^2 = I)$

$$A^2 = \begin{bmatrix} 1 & -1 & 1 \\ 2 & -1 & 0 \\ 1 & 0 & 0 \end{bmatrix}\begin{bmatrix} 1 & -1 & 1 \\ 2 & -1 & 0 \\ 1 & 0 & 0 \end{bmatrix} = \begin{bmatrix} 0 & 0 & 1 \\ 0 & -1 & 2 \\ 1 & -1 & 1 \end{bmatrix}$$

Now, $A.A^2 = \begin{bmatrix} 1 & -1 & 1 \\ 2 & -1 & 0 \\ 1 & 0 & 0 \end{bmatrix}\begin{bmatrix} 0 & 0 & 1 \\ 0 & -1 & 2 \\ 1 & -1 & 1 \end{bmatrix} = \begin{bmatrix} 1 & 0 & 0 \\ 0 & 1 & 0 \\ 0 & 0 & 1 \end{bmatrix} = I$

Hence $A^{-1} = A^2$

EXAMPLE 14. If $A = \begin{bmatrix} 2 & -1 \\ -1 & 2 \end{bmatrix}$ and I is the identity matrix of order 2, then show that $A^2 = 4A - 3I$. Hence, find A^{-1}.

Sol. Here, $A = \begin{bmatrix} 2 & -1 \\ -1 & 2 \end{bmatrix}$.

Now, $A^2 = A \cdot A = \begin{bmatrix} 2 & -1 \\ -1 & 2 \end{bmatrix}\begin{bmatrix} 2 & -1 \\ -1 & 2 \end{bmatrix}$

$$= \begin{bmatrix} 4+1 & -2-2 \\ -2-2 & 1+4 \end{bmatrix} = \begin{bmatrix} 5 & -4 \\ -4 & 5 \end{bmatrix}$$

[multiplying row by column]...(i)

Also, $4A - 3I = 4\begin{bmatrix} 2 & -1 \\ -1 & 2 \end{bmatrix} - 3\begin{bmatrix} 1 & 0 \\ 0 & 1 \end{bmatrix}$

$$= \begin{bmatrix} 8 & -4 \\ -4 & 8 \end{bmatrix} - \begin{bmatrix} 3 & 0 \\ 0 & 3 \end{bmatrix} = \begin{bmatrix} 5 & -4 \\ -4 & 5 \end{bmatrix} \quad \text{...(ii)}$$

From Eqs. (i) and (ii), we get

$$A^2 = 4A - 3I \quad \text{...(iii)}$$

Now, $|A| = \begin{vmatrix} 2 & -1 \\ -1 & 2 \end{vmatrix} = 4 - 1 = 3 \neq 0$

$\therefore \quad A^{-1}$ exists.

Now, pre-multiplying both sides of Eq. (iii) by A^{-1}, we get

$$A^{-1}\cdot A^2 = A^{-1}\cdot(4A-3I)$$

$$\Rightarrow \quad (A^{-1}\cdot A)\cdot A = 4A^{-1}\cdot A - 3A^{-1}\cdot I$$

$$\Rightarrow \quad IA = 4I - 3A^{-1}$$

$$[\because A\cdot A^{-1} = I = A^{-1}A \text{ and } A^{-1}\cdot I = A^{-1}]$$

$$\Rightarrow \quad A = 4I - 3A^{-1} \quad [\because IA = A = AI]$$

$$\Rightarrow \quad 3A^{-1} = 4I - A$$

$$\therefore \quad A^{-1} = \frac{1}{3}\left(4\begin{bmatrix}1 & 0\\0 & 1\end{bmatrix} - \begin{bmatrix}2 & -1\\-1 & 2\end{bmatrix}\right)$$

$$= \frac{1}{3}\left(\begin{bmatrix}4 & 0\\0 & 4\end{bmatrix} - \begin{bmatrix}2 & -1\\-1 & 2\end{bmatrix}\right)$$

$$= \frac{1}{3}\begin{bmatrix}2 & 1\\1 & 2\end{bmatrix} = \begin{bmatrix}2/3 & 1/3\\1/3 & 2/3\end{bmatrix}$$

EXAMPLE 15. Show that for the matrix $A = \begin{bmatrix}1 & 1 & 1\\1 & 2 & -3\\2 & -1 & 3\end{bmatrix}$, $A^3 - 6A^2 + 5A + 11I = 0$. Hence, find A^{-1}.

Sol. We have, $A = \begin{bmatrix}1 & 1 & 1\\1 & 2 & -3\\2 & -1 & 3\end{bmatrix}$

$$\therefore \quad A^2 = AA$$

$$= \begin{bmatrix}1 & 1 & 1\\1 & 2 & -3\\2 & -1 & 3\end{bmatrix}\begin{bmatrix}1 & 1 & 1\\1 & 2 & -3\\2 & -1 & 3\end{bmatrix} = \begin{bmatrix}4 & 2 & 1\\-3 & 8 & -14\\7 & -3 & 14\end{bmatrix}$$

and $A^3 = A^2A$

$$= \begin{bmatrix}4 & 2 & 1\\-3 & 8 & -14\\7 & -3 & 14\end{bmatrix}\begin{bmatrix}1 & 1 & 1\\1 & 2 & -3\\2 & -1 & 3\end{bmatrix} = \begin{bmatrix}8 & 7 & 1\\-23 & 27 & -69\\32 & -13 & 58\end{bmatrix}$$

$\therefore\ A^3 - 6A^2 + 5A + 11I_3$

$$= \begin{bmatrix}8 & 7 & 1\\-23 & 27 & -69\\32 & -13 & 58\end{bmatrix} - 6\begin{bmatrix}4 & 2 & 1\\-3 & 8 & -14\\7 & -3 & 14\end{bmatrix} + 5\begin{bmatrix}1 & 1 & 1\\1 & 2 & -3\\2 & -1 & 3\end{bmatrix} + 11\begin{bmatrix}1 & 0 & 0\\0 & 1 & 0\\0 & 0 & 1\end{bmatrix}$$

$$= \begin{bmatrix}8-24+5+11 & 7-12+5+0 & 1-6+5+0\\-23+18+5+0 & 27-48+10+11 & -69+84-15+0\\32-42+10+0 & -13+18-5+0 & 58-84+15+11\end{bmatrix}$$

$$= \begin{bmatrix}0 & 0 & 0\\0 & 0 & 0\\0 & 0 & 0\end{bmatrix} = O$$

$$\Rightarrow \quad A^3 - 6A^2 + 5A + 11I_3 = O$$ **Hence proved.**

Now, pre-multiplying both sides by A^{-1}, we get

$$\Rightarrow A^{-1}(A^3 - 6A^2 + 5A + 11I_3) = A^{-1}O$$

[multiplying both sides by A^{-1}]

$$\Rightarrow \quad A^2 - 6A + 5I + 11A^{-1} = O$$

$$\Rightarrow \quad 11A^{-1} = -A^2 + 6A - 5I$$

$$\Rightarrow \quad 11A^{-1} = -\begin{bmatrix}4 & 2 & 1\\-3 & 8 & -14\\7 & -3 & 14\end{bmatrix} + 6\begin{bmatrix}1 & 1 & 1\\1 & 2 & -3\\2 & -1 & 3\end{bmatrix} - 5\begin{bmatrix}1 & 0 & 0\\0 & 1 & 0\\0 & 0 & 1\end{bmatrix}$$

$$\Rightarrow \quad 11A^{-1} = \begin{bmatrix}-4+6-5 & -2+6+0 & -1+6+0\\3+6+0 & -8+12-5 & 14-18+0\\-7+12+0 & 3-6+0 & -14+18-5\end{bmatrix}$$

$$= \begin{bmatrix}-3 & 4 & 5\\9 & -1 & -4\\5 & -3 & -1\end{bmatrix} \Rightarrow A^{-1} = \frac{1}{11}\begin{bmatrix}-3 & 4 & 5\\9 & -1 & -4\\5 & -3 & -1\end{bmatrix}$$

EXAMPLE 16. Find the matrix A satisfying the matrix equation $\begin{bmatrix}2 & 1\\3 & 2\end{bmatrix}A\begin{bmatrix}-3 & 2\\5 & -3\end{bmatrix} = \begin{bmatrix}1 & 0\\0 & 1\end{bmatrix}$.

Sol. Let $B = \begin{bmatrix}2 & 1\\3 & 2\end{bmatrix}$ and $C = \begin{bmatrix}-3 & 2\\5 & -3\end{bmatrix}$, then the given equation reduces to $BAC = I$ ...(i)

Now, as $|B| = \begin{vmatrix}2 & 1\\3 & 2\end{vmatrix} = 4 - 3 = 1 \neq 0$

and $|C| = \begin{vmatrix}-3 & 2\\5 & -3\end{vmatrix} = 9 - 10 = -1 \neq 0$

$\therefore$ Both B^{-1} and C^{-1} exist.

Now, pre-multiplying both sides of Eq. (i) by B^{-1}, we get

$$B^{-1}(BAC) = B^{-1}\cdot I \quad [\because B^{-1}I = B^{-1}]$$

$$\Rightarrow \quad (B^{-1}B)(AC) = B^{-1} \Rightarrow I(AC) = B^{-1} \quad [\because B^{-1}B = I]$$

$$\Rightarrow \quad AC = B^{-1} \quad \text{...(ii)}$$

Now, post-multiplying both sides of Eq. (ii) by C^{-1}, we get

$$(AC)C^{-1} = B^{-1}C^{-1} \Rightarrow A(CC^{-1}) = B^{-1}C^{-1}$$

$$\Rightarrow \quad A\cdot I = B^{-1}C^{-1} \quad [\because CC^{-1} = I]$$

$$\Rightarrow \quad A = B^{-1}C^{-1} \quad \text{...(iii)}$$

Now, let us find B^{-1} and C^{-1}.

Clearly, $B^{-1} = \dfrac{1}{|B|}\text{adj}(B) = \dfrac{1}{1}\begin{bmatrix}2 & -1\\-3 & 2\end{bmatrix}$

$$\left[\because \text{adj}\begin{bmatrix}a & b\\c & d\end{bmatrix} = \begin{bmatrix}d & -b\\-c & a\end{bmatrix}\right]$$

$$= \begin{bmatrix}2 & -1\\-3 & 2\end{bmatrix}$$

and $C^{-1} = \dfrac{1}{|C|}\text{adj}(C) = \dfrac{1}{-1}\begin{bmatrix}-3 & -2\\-5 & -3\end{bmatrix} = \begin{bmatrix}3 & 2\\5 & 3\end{bmatrix}$

$\therefore$ From Eq. (iii), we get

$$A = \begin{bmatrix}2 & -1\\-3 & 2\end{bmatrix}\begin{bmatrix}3 & 2\\5 & 3\end{bmatrix}$$

$$= \begin{bmatrix}6-5 & 4-3\\-9+10 & -6+6\end{bmatrix} = \begin{bmatrix}1 & 1\\1 & 0\end{bmatrix}$$

Topic Practice 3

1 Find the adjoint of the following matrices.

(i) $\begin{bmatrix} 2 & 3 \\ 1 & 4 \end{bmatrix}$ (ii) $\begin{bmatrix} 3 & -5 \\ -1 & 2 \end{bmatrix}$

(iii) $\begin{bmatrix} 1 & 2 & 5 \\ 2 & 3 & 1 \\ -1 & 1 & 1 \end{bmatrix}$ (iv) $\begin{bmatrix} 4 & 5 & 3 \\ 1 & 0 & 6 \\ 2 & 7 & 9 \end{bmatrix}$

(v) $\begin{bmatrix} 9 & 7 & 3 \\ 5 & -1 & 4 \\ 6 & 8 & 2 \end{bmatrix}$

2 Find the adjoint of the following matrices and verify that $A(\text{adj}A)=|A|I$.

(i) $A=\begin{bmatrix} 1 & 2 \\ 3 & 4 \end{bmatrix}$ (ii) $A=\begin{bmatrix} 1 & 4 & 5 \\ 3 & 2 & 6 \\ 0 & 1 & 0 \end{bmatrix}$

3 If for any 2×2 square matrix A, $A(\text{adj}A)=\begin{bmatrix} 8 & 0 \\ 0 & 8 \end{bmatrix}$, then write the value of $|A|$.

4 If A is matrix of order 3 and $|A|=4$, then find the value of $|\text{adj}(A)|$.

5 If A is a square matrix of order 3 such that $|\text{adj}(A)|=64$, then find $|A|$.

6 Check whether the following matrices are singular or not.

(i) $\begin{bmatrix} 2 & 3 \\ -4 & -6 \end{bmatrix}$ (ii) $\begin{bmatrix} 1 & 2 \\ 3 & 4 \end{bmatrix}$

(iii) $\begin{bmatrix} 1 & 1 & 1 \\ 1 & 2 & -3 \\ 2 & -1 & 3 \end{bmatrix}$ (iv) $\begin{bmatrix} 1 & 2 & 4 \\ 2 & 4 & 8 \\ -3 & 1 & 0 \end{bmatrix}$

7 For what value of λ, the matrix $\begin{bmatrix} 1 & \lambda & 0 \\ 3 & -1 & 2 \\ 4 & 1 & 5 \end{bmatrix}$ is singular?

8 Find $|AB|$, if $A=\begin{bmatrix} 0 & -1 \\ 0 & 2 \end{bmatrix}$ and $B=\begin{bmatrix} 3 & 5 \\ 0 & 0 \end{bmatrix}$.

9 Let A be the non-singular square matrix of order 3×3, then prove that $|\text{adj}(A)|=|A|^2$.

10 Find the inverse of the following matrices, if exists.

(i) $\begin{bmatrix} 2 & -2 \\ 4 & 3 \end{bmatrix}$ (ii) $\begin{bmatrix} 1 & 0 & 0 \\ 3 & 3 & 0 \\ 5 & 2 & -1 \end{bmatrix}$

11 If A is a matrix of order 3×3, then show that $(A^2)^{-1}=(A^{-1})^2$.

12 Given, $A=\begin{bmatrix} 2 & -3 \\ -4 & 7 \end{bmatrix}$, compute A^{-1} and show that $2A^{-1}=9I-A$.

13 If A and B are invertible matrices, then which of the following is incorrect?

(i) $\text{adj}(A)=|A|A^{-1}$

(ii) $(A+B)^{-1}=B^{-1}+A^{-1}$

(iii) $\det(A^{-1})\cdot[\det(A)]=1$

14 Let $A=\begin{bmatrix} 3 & 7 \\ 2 & 5 \end{bmatrix}$ and $B=\begin{bmatrix} 6 & 8 \\ 7 & 9 \end{bmatrix}$, then verify that $(AB)^{-1}=B^{-1}A^{-1}$.

15 If $A=\begin{bmatrix} 1 & -1 & 1 \\ 2 & -1 & 0 \\ 1 & 0 & 0 \end{bmatrix}$, then show that $A^{-1}=A^2$.

16 Find A^{-1}, if $A=\begin{bmatrix} 0 & 1 & 1 \\ 1 & 0 & 1 \\ 1 & 1 & 0 \end{bmatrix}$ and show that $A^{-1}=\dfrac{A^2-3I}{2}$.

17 If $A=\begin{bmatrix} 1 & -2 & 3 \\ 0 & -1 & 4 \\ -2 & 2 & 1 \end{bmatrix}$, then find $(A')^{-1}$.

18 Compute $(AB)^{-1}$, if $A=\begin{bmatrix} 1 & 1 & 2 \\ 0 & 2 & -3 \\ 3 & -2 & 4 \end{bmatrix}$ and $B^{-1}=\begin{bmatrix} 1 & 2 & 0 \\ 0 & 3 & -1 \\ 1 & 0 & 2 \end{bmatrix}$.

19 Show that the matrix $A=\begin{bmatrix} 3 & 1 \\ -1 & 2 \end{bmatrix}$ satisfies the equation $A^2-5A+7I=O$. Hence, find A^{-1}.

20 If $A=\begin{bmatrix} 1 & 2 & 2 \\ 2 & 1 & 2 \\ 2 & 2 & 1 \end{bmatrix}$, then prove that $A^2-4A-5I=O$. Hence, find A^{-1}.

21 For the matrix $A=\begin{bmatrix} 3 & 1 \\ 7 & 5 \end{bmatrix}$, find x and y, so that $A^2+xI=yA$. Hence, find A^{-1}.

22 Suppose a matrix B of order 2×2 such that $B\begin{bmatrix} 1 & -2 \\ 1 & 4 \end{bmatrix}=\begin{bmatrix} 6 & 0 \\ 0 & 6 \end{bmatrix}$. Find matrix B by using the inverse of matrix method.

Hints & Solutions

1. (i) Similar as Example 1 (i). **Ans.** $\begin{bmatrix} 4 & -3 \\ -1 & 2 \end{bmatrix}$

(ii) Similar as Example 1 (i). **Ans.** $\begin{bmatrix} 2 & 5 \\ 1 & 3 \end{bmatrix}$

(iii) Similar as Example 1 (ii). **Ans.** $\begin{bmatrix} 2 & 3 & -13 \\ -3 & 6 & 9 \\ 5 & -3 & -1 \end{bmatrix}$

(iv) Similar as Example 1 (ii). **Ans.** $\begin{bmatrix} -42 & -24 & 30 \\ 3 & 30 & -21 \\ 7 & -18 & -5 \end{bmatrix}$

(v) Similar as Example 1 (ii). **Ans.** $\begin{bmatrix} -34 & 10 & 31 \\ 14 & 0 & -21 \\ 46 & -30 & -44 \end{bmatrix}$

2. (i) We have, $A = \begin{bmatrix} 1 & 2 \\ 3 & 4 \end{bmatrix}$, therefore $|A| = \begin{vmatrix} 1 & 2 \\ 3 & 4 \end{vmatrix}$

Now, cofactors of elements of $|A|$ are

$C_{11} = (-1)^{1+1} \times 4 = 4;\ C_{12} = (-1)^{1+2} \times 3 = -3;$

$C_{21} = (-1)^{2+1} \times 2 = -2$ and $C_{22} = (-1)^{2+2} \times 1 = 1$

$\therefore\ \text{adj}(A) = \begin{bmatrix} C_{11} & C_{12} \\ C_{21} & C_{22} \end{bmatrix}^T$

$= \begin{bmatrix} 4 & -3 \\ -2 & 1 \end{bmatrix}^T = \begin{bmatrix} 4 & -2 \\ -3 & 1 \end{bmatrix}$

Now, $|A| = \begin{vmatrix} 1 & 2 \\ 3 & 4 \end{vmatrix} = 4 - 6 = -2$ ...(i)

and $A\,[\text{adj}(A)] = \begin{bmatrix} 1 & 2 \\ 3 & 4 \end{bmatrix} \begin{bmatrix} 4 & -2 \\ -3 & 1 \end{bmatrix}$

$= \begin{bmatrix} 4-6 & -2+2 \\ 12-12 & -6+4 \end{bmatrix} = \begin{bmatrix} -2 & 0 \\ 0 & -2 \end{bmatrix}$

$= -2\begin{bmatrix} 1 & 0 \\ 0 & 1 \end{bmatrix} = |A|\, I$ [from Eq. (i)]

Hence, $A[\text{adj}(A)] = |A|\, I$.

(ii) Similar as Part (i).

Ans. $\text{adj}(A) = \begin{bmatrix} -6 & 5 & 14 \\ 0 & 0 & 9 \\ 3 & -1 & -10 \end{bmatrix}$

3. **Hint** Use $A(\text{adj}\, A) = |A|\, I$ **Ans.** $|A| = 8$

4. **Hint** Given, $|A| = 4$

$|\text{adj}(A)| = |A|^{3-1} = |A|^2 = 4^2 = 16$

5. **Hint** We know that for a non-singular square matrix of order n, $|\text{adj}(A)| = |A|^{n-1}$.

Here, $n = 3$.

$\therefore\ |\text{adj}(A)| = |A|^{3-1} = |A|^2$

Given, $|\text{adj}\, A| = 64$

$\Rightarrow\ 64 = |A|^2 \Rightarrow (8)^2 = |A|^2$

$\Rightarrow\ |A| = \pm 8$ [taking square root]

6. Similar as Example 5.

Ans. (i) Yes (ii) No (iii) No (iv) Yes

7. Similar as Example 6. **Ans.** $\lambda = -1$

8. Similar as Example 8. **Ans.** 0

9. We know that, $[\text{adj}(A)] \cdot A = |A|\, I$

$= |A| \begin{bmatrix} 1 & 0 & 0 \\ 0 & 1 & 0 \\ 0 & 0 & 1 \end{bmatrix} = \begin{bmatrix} |A| & 0 & 0 \\ 0 & |A| & 0 \\ 0 & 0 & |A| \end{bmatrix}$

On taking determinant both sides, we get

$|(\text{adj}\, A)\cdot(A)| = \begin{vmatrix} |A| & 0 & 0 \\ 0 & |A| & 0 \\ 0 & 0 & |A| \end{vmatrix}$

$\Rightarrow\ |(\text{adj}\, A)A| = |A|^3 \begin{vmatrix} 1 & 0 & 0 \\ 0 & 1 & 0 \\ 0 & 0 & 1 \end{vmatrix}$

$= |A|^3 |I| = |A|^3$ $[\because |I| = 1]$

$\Rightarrow\ |\text{adj}(A)|\,|A| = |A|^3$ $[\because |AB| = |A| \cdot |B|]$

$\therefore\ |\text{adj}(A)| = |A|^2$ $[\because |A| \neq 0]$ **Hence proved.**

10. (i) Similar as Example 9 (i). **Ans.** $\dfrac{1}{14}\begin{bmatrix} 3 & 2 \\ -4 & 2 \end{bmatrix}$

(ii) Similar as Example 9 (ii). **Ans.** $-\dfrac{1}{3}\begin{bmatrix} -3 & 0 & 0 \\ 3 & -1 & 0 \\ -9 & -2 & 3 \end{bmatrix}$

11. $(A^2)^{-1} = (AA)^{-1} = (A^{-1}A^{-1})$ $[\because (AB)^{-1} = B^{-1}A^{-1}]$

$= (A^{-1})^2$

12. We have, $A = \begin{bmatrix} 2 & -3 \\ -4 & 7 \end{bmatrix}$

Here, $|A| = \begin{vmatrix} 2 & -3 \\ -4 & 7 \end{vmatrix} = 14 - 12 = 2 \neq 0$

$\therefore\ A^{-1}$ exists.

Clearly, $\text{adj}(A) = \begin{bmatrix} 7 & 3 \\ 4 & 2 \end{bmatrix}$

$\left[\text{if } A = \begin{bmatrix} a & b \\ c & d \end{bmatrix}, \text{ then adj}(A) = \begin{bmatrix} d & -b \\ -c & a \end{bmatrix}\right]$

$\therefore\ A^{-1} = \dfrac{1}{|A|}\text{adj}(A) = \dfrac{1}{2}\begin{bmatrix} 7 & 3 \\ 4 & 2 \end{bmatrix}$ ...(i)

Now, consider RHS $= 9I - A$

$= 9\begin{bmatrix} 1 & 0 \\ 0 & 1 \end{bmatrix} - \begin{bmatrix} 2 & -3 \\ -4 & 7 \end{bmatrix}$

$= \begin{bmatrix} 9 & 0 \\ 0 & 9 \end{bmatrix} - \begin{bmatrix} 2 & -3 \\ -4 & 7 \end{bmatrix} = \begin{bmatrix} 7 & 3 \\ 4 & 2 \end{bmatrix}$

$= 2A^{-1}$ [using Eq. (i)]

= LHS **Hence proved.**

13. Since, A is an invertible matrix, therefore we have

(i) $A^{-1} = \frac{1}{|A|}\text{adj}(A) \Rightarrow \text{adj}(A) = |A| \cdot A^{-1}$,

which is correct.

(ii) $\because (A+B)^{-1} \neq B^{-1} + A^{-1}$, so given result is incorrect.

(iii) $\because \det(A^{-1}) = (\det(A))^{-1}$

$\Rightarrow \det(A^{-1}) = \frac{1}{\det(A)}$

$\Rightarrow \det(A)\cdot\det(A^{-1}) = 1$, which is correct.

14. Similar as Example 11 (iii).

15. **Hint** Compute A^{-1} and A^2 and prove the result.

16. We have, $A = \begin{bmatrix} 0 & 1 & 1 \\ 1 & 0 & 1 \\ 1 & 1 & 0 \end{bmatrix}$

Now, cofactors of elements of $|A|$ are

$A_{11} = -1, A_{12} = 1, A_{13} = 1, A_{21} = 1, A_{22} = -1,$
$A_{23} = 1, A_{31} = 1, A_{32} = 1$ and $A_{33} = -1$

$\therefore \text{adj}(A) = \begin{bmatrix} -1 & 1 & 1 \\ 1 & -1 & 1 \\ 1 & 1 & -1 \end{bmatrix}^T = \begin{bmatrix} -1 & 1 & 1 \\ 1 & -1 & 1 \\ 1 & 1 & -1 \end{bmatrix}$

Also, $|A| = -1(-1) + 1\cdot 1 = 2$

Now, $A^{-1} = \frac{\text{adj}(A)}{|A|} = \frac{1}{2}\begin{bmatrix} -1 & 1 & 1 \\ 1 & -1 & 1 \\ 1 & 1 & -1 \end{bmatrix}$ ...(i)

and $A^2 = \begin{bmatrix} 0 & 1 & 1 \\ 1 & 0 & 1 \\ 1 & 1 & 0 \end{bmatrix} \cdot \begin{bmatrix} 0 & 1 & 1 \\ 1 & 0 & 1 \\ 1 & 1 & 0 \end{bmatrix} = \begin{bmatrix} 2 & 1 & 1 \\ 1 & 2 & 1 \\ 1 & 1 & 2 \end{bmatrix}$ ...(ii)

$\therefore \frac{A^2 - 3I}{2} = \frac{1}{2}\left\{\begin{bmatrix} 2 & 1 & 1 \\ 1 & 2 & 1 \\ 1 & 1 & 2 \end{bmatrix} - \begin{bmatrix} 3 & 0 & 0 \\ 0 & 3 & 0 \\ 0 & 0 & 3 \end{bmatrix}\right\}$

$= \frac{1}{2}\begin{bmatrix} -1 & 1 & 1 \\ 1 & -1 & 1 \\ 1 & 1 & -1 \end{bmatrix} = A^{-1}$ [using Eq. (i)]

Hence proved.

17. We have, $A = \begin{bmatrix} 1 & -2 & 3 \\ 0 & -1 & 4 \\ -2 & 2 & 1 \end{bmatrix}$.

Now, $|A| = \begin{vmatrix} 1 & -2 & 3 \\ 0 & -1 & 4 \\ -2 & 2 & 1 \end{vmatrix} = 1(-1-8) + 2(0+8) + 3(0-2)$ [expanding along R_1]

$= -9 + 16 - 6$
$= 1 \neq 0$

$\therefore A^{-1}$ exists.

Cofactors of elements of $|A|$ are

$C_{11} = (-1)^{1+1}\begin{vmatrix} -1 & 4 \\ 2 & 1 \end{vmatrix} = (-1-8) = -9$

$C_{12} = (-1)^{1+2}\begin{vmatrix} 0 & 4 \\ -2 & 1 \end{vmatrix} = -(0+8) = -8$

$C_{13} = (-1)^{1+3}\begin{vmatrix} 0 & -1 \\ -2 & 2 \end{vmatrix} = (0-2) = -2$

$C_{21} = (-1)^{2+1}\begin{vmatrix} -2 & 3 \\ 2 & 1 \end{vmatrix} = -(-2-6) = 8$

$C_{22} = (-1)^{2+2}\begin{vmatrix} 1 & 3 \\ -2 & 1 \end{vmatrix} = (1+6) = 7$

$C_{23} = (-1)^{2+3}\begin{vmatrix} 1 & -2 \\ -2 & 2 \end{vmatrix} = -(2-4) = 2$

$C_{31} = (-1)^{3+1}\begin{vmatrix} -2 & 3 \\ -1 & 4 \end{vmatrix} = (-8+3) = -5$

$C_{32} = (-1)^{3+2}\begin{vmatrix} 1 & 3 \\ 0 & 4 \end{vmatrix} = -(4-0) = -4$

$C_{33} = (-1)^{3+3}\begin{vmatrix} 1 & -2 \\ 0 & -1 \end{vmatrix} = (-1-0) = -1$

Thus, $\text{adj}(A) = \begin{bmatrix} C_{11} & C_{12} & C_{13} \\ C_{21} & C_{22} & C_{23} \\ C_{31} & C_{32} & C_{33} \end{bmatrix}^T$

$= \begin{bmatrix} -9 & -8 & -2 \\ 8 & 7 & 2 \\ -5 & -4 & -1 \end{bmatrix}^T$

$\therefore A^{-1} = \frac{1}{|A|}\text{adj}(A) = \frac{1}{1}\begin{bmatrix} -9 & 8 & -5 \\ -8 & 7 & -4 \\ -2 & 2 & -1 \end{bmatrix}$

Now, $(A')^{-1} = (A^{-1})' = \begin{bmatrix} -9 & 8 & -5 \\ -8 & 7 & -4 \\ -2 & 2 & -1 \end{bmatrix}'$

$= \begin{bmatrix} -9 & -8 & -2 \\ 8 & 7 & 2 \\ -5 & -4 & -1 \end{bmatrix}$

18. We have, $A = \begin{bmatrix} 1 & 1 & 2 \\ 0 & 2 & -3 \\ 3 & -2 & 4 \end{bmatrix}$.

Now, $|A| = \begin{vmatrix} 1 & 1 & 2 \\ 0 & 2 & -3 \\ 3 & -2 & 4 \end{vmatrix}$

$= 1(8-6) - 0 + 3(-3-4)$ [expanding along C_1]

$= 2 - 21 = -19 \neq 0$

$\therefore A^{-1}$ exists.

Now, cofactors of elements of $|A|$ are

$C_{11} = (-1)^{1+1}\begin{vmatrix} 2 & -3 \\ -2 & 4 \end{vmatrix} = 8 - 6 = 2$

$C_{12} = (-1)^{1+2}\begin{vmatrix} 0 & -3 \\ 3 & 4 \end{vmatrix} = -(0+9) = -9$

$C_{13} = (-1)^{1+3}\begin{vmatrix} 0 & 2 \\ 3 & -2 \end{vmatrix} = 0 - 6 = -6$

$C_{21} = (-1)^{2+1}\begin{vmatrix} 1 & 2 \\ -2 & 4 \end{vmatrix} = -(4+4) = -8$

$C_{22} = (-1)^{2+2}\begin{vmatrix} 1 & 2 \\ 3 & 4 \end{vmatrix} = 4 - 6 = -2$

$$C_{23} = (-1)^{2+3}\begin{vmatrix} 1 & 1 \\ 3 & -2 \end{vmatrix} = -(-2-3) = 5$$

$$C_{31} = (-1)^{3+1}\begin{vmatrix} 1 & 2 \\ 2 & -3 \end{vmatrix} = -3-4 = -7$$

$$C_{32} = (-1)^{3+2}\begin{vmatrix} 1 & 2 \\ 0 & -3 \end{vmatrix} = -(-3-0) = 3$$

$$C_{33} = (-1)^{3+3}\begin{vmatrix} 1 & 1 \\ 0 & 2 \end{vmatrix} = 2-0 = 2$$

$$\therefore \quad \text{adj}(A) = \begin{bmatrix} C_{11} & C_{12} & C_{13} \\ C_{21} & C_{22} & C_{23} \\ C_{31} & C_{32} & C_{33} \end{bmatrix}^T$$

$$= \begin{bmatrix} 2 & -9 & -6 \\ -8 & -2 & 5 \\ -7 & 3 & 2 \end{bmatrix}^T = \begin{bmatrix} 2 & -8 & -7 \\ -9 & -2 & 3 \\ -6 & 5 & 2 \end{bmatrix}$$

and $$A^{-1} = \frac{1}{|A|}\text{adj}(A)$$

$$= \frac{-1}{19}\begin{bmatrix} 2 & -8 & -7 \\ -9 & -2 & 3 \\ -6 & 5 & 2 \end{bmatrix}$$

Now, $(AB)^{-1} = B^{-1}A^{-1}$

$$= \begin{bmatrix} 1 & 2 & 0 \\ 0 & 3 & -1 \\ 1 & 0 & 2 \end{bmatrix} \cdot \frac{-1}{19}\begin{bmatrix} 2 & -8 & -7 \\ -9 & -2 & 3 \\ -6 & 5 & 2 \end{bmatrix}$$

$[\because (AB)^{-1} = B^{-1}A^{-1}]$

$$= \frac{-1}{19}\begin{bmatrix} 2-18-0 & -8-4+0 & -7+6+0 \\ 0-27+6 & 0-6-5 & 0+9-2 \\ 2+0-12 & -8+0+10 & -7+0+4 \end{bmatrix}$$

[multiplying row by column]

$$= \frac{-1}{19}\begin{bmatrix} -16 & -12 & -1 \\ -21 & -11 & 7 \\ -10 & 2 & -3 \end{bmatrix} = \begin{bmatrix} \frac{16}{19} & \frac{12}{19} & \frac{1}{19} \\ \frac{21}{19} & \frac{11}{19} & \frac{-7}{19} \\ \frac{10}{19} & \frac{-2}{19} & \frac{3}{19} \end{bmatrix}$$

19. Similar as Example 14. **Ans.** $A^{-1} = \frac{1}{7}\begin{bmatrix} 2 & -1 \\ 1 & 3 \end{bmatrix}$

20. Similar as Example 15. **Ans.** $A^{-1} = \frac{1}{5}\begin{bmatrix} -3 & 2 & 2 \\ 2 & -3 & 2 \\ 2 & 2 & -3 \end{bmatrix}$

21. **Hint** (i) First, find A^2.

(ii) Then, put value of A^2 and A in the given equation $A^2 + xI = yA$. Also, solve it to find x and y.

(iii) Now, use the above result to find A^{-1}, as in Example 14.

Ans. $x = 8,\ y = 8,\ A^{-1} = \frac{1}{8}\begin{bmatrix} 5 & -1 \\ -7 & 3 \end{bmatrix}$

22. Solve as Example 16.

Ans. $B = \begin{bmatrix} 4 & 2 \\ -1 & 1 \end{bmatrix}$

Solution of Simultaneous Linear Equations

In solution of system of non-homogeneous equation in two or three variables we always use cramer's rule.

Let $a_1x + b_1y + c_1z = d_1$, $a_2x + b_2y + c_2z = d_2$

$a_3x + b_3y + c_3z = d_3$

is a system of linear equations.

A set of values of variables x, y and z which simultaneously satisfy these three equations is called a solution.

Consistent

If the system of equations has a unique solution or infinite many solution, then the system of equations is known as consistent.

Inconsistent

If the system of equations has no solution, then system of equations is known as inconsitent.

Trival and Non-trival Solution

If the value of all variables of sytem of equations is zero;

i.e. $x = 0$, $y = 0$ and $z = 0$, then solution is known as trival solution.

If system of equations has infinite many solutions, then the solution is known as non-trival solution.

Homogeneous and Non-homogeneous System

If $d_1 = d_2 = d_3 = 0$ in given system of equations, then system of equations is said to be homogeneous otherwise it is said to be non-homogeneous system.

Cramer's Rule

A system of simultaneous linear equations can be solved by Cramer's rule named for the Swiss Mathematician Gabriel Crammer.

The solution of the system of linear equations

$$a_1x+b_1y=c_1 \text{ and } a_2x+b_2y=c_2$$

is given by $x=\frac{D_1}{D}$, $y=\frac{D_2}{D}$,

where $D=\begin{vmatrix} a_1 & b_1 \\ a_2 & b_2 \end{vmatrix}$, $D_1=\begin{vmatrix} c_1 & b_1 \\ c_2 & b_2 \end{vmatrix}$

and $D_2=\begin{vmatrix} a_1 & c_1 \\ a_2 & c_2 \end{vmatrix}$ provided that $D \neq 0$.

Conditions for Consistency of Two Linear Equations

(i) If $D \neq 0$, then the system of equations is consistent and has a unique solution given by

$$x=\frac{D_1}{D} \text{ and } y=\frac{D_2}{D}$$

(ii) If $D=0$ and $D_1=D_2=0$, then the system of equations is consistent with infinitely many solution.

(iii) If $D=0$ and either of D_1 and D_2 is non-zero, then the system of equation is inconsistent.

Note If the given equations represent two straight lines, then there would three possible cases.

(i) If the lines intersect, the given system has unique solution and are consistent.

(ii) If the lines are parallel, the given system has no solution and are inconsistent.

(iii) If the lines coincide, the given system has infinitely many solutions

EXAMPLE 1.

(i) Using Cramer's rule, solve the following system of equations.

$$2x_1+3x_2=5,\ 11x_1-5x_2=6$$ **[CBSE 2024]**

(ii) Solve the following system of equation by Cramer's rule.

$$2x-y=17, 3x+5y=6$$ **[CBSE 2023]**

Sol. (i) $D=\begin{vmatrix} 2 & 3 \\ 11 & -5 \end{vmatrix}=-10-33=-43$

$$D_{x_1}=\begin{vmatrix} 5 & 3 \\ 6 & -5 \end{vmatrix}=-25-18=-43$$

$$D_{x_2}=\begin{vmatrix} 2 & 5 \\ 11 & 6 \end{vmatrix}=12-55=-43$$

$$x_1=\frac{D_{x_1}}{D}=\frac{-43}{-43}=1,$$

$$x_2=\frac{D_{x_2}}{D}=\frac{-43}{43}=1$$

Hence, $x_1=1$ and $x_2=1$

(ii) $D=\begin{vmatrix} 2 & -1 \\ 3 & 5 \end{vmatrix}=10+3=13$

$$D_x=\begin{vmatrix} 17 & -1 \\ 6 & 5 \end{vmatrix}=85+6=91$$

$$D_y=\begin{vmatrix} 2 & 17 \\ 3 & 6 \end{vmatrix}=12-51=-39$$

$$x=\frac{D_x}{D}=\frac{91}{13}=7,\quad y=\frac{D_y}{D}=\frac{-39}{13}=-3$$

Hence, $x=7$ and $y=-3$.

EXAMPLE 2. Find the number of values of K, for which the system of equations

$$(K+1)x+8y=4K$$
$$Kx+(K+3)y=3K-1$$

has no solution ?

Sol. $D=\begin{vmatrix} K+1 & 8 \\ K & K+3 \end{vmatrix}$

$$=(K+1)(K+3)-8K=K^2+4K+3-8K$$
$$=K^2-4K+3=(K-1)(K-3)$$

$$D_1=\begin{vmatrix} 4K & 8 \\ 3K-1 & K+3 \end{vmatrix}=4(K-1)(K-2)$$

$$D_2=\begin{vmatrix} K+1 & 4K \\ K & 3K-1 \end{vmatrix}=-(K-1)^2$$

For inconsistent or no-solution, $D=0$

$$D=(K-1)(K-3)=0 \Rightarrow K=1, 3$$

and at least one of the D_1 and D_2 is non-zero

If $K=1$, $D_1=D_2=0$

If $K=3$, $D_1 \neq 0$ and $D_2 \neq 0$

Hence the system has no solution when $K=3$.

Conditions for Consistency of Three Linear Equations

Let the determinant of coefficient of equations $a_1x+b_1y+c_1z=d_1$, $a_2x+b_2y+c_2z=d_2$ and $a_3x+b_3y+c_3z=d_3$ is D.

$$\therefore \quad D=\begin{vmatrix} a_1 & b_1 & c_1 \\ a_2 & b_2 & c_2 \\ a_3 & b_3 & c_3 \end{vmatrix}$$

The solution of the system of linear equations is given by

$$\frac{x}{D_1}=\frac{y}{D_2}=\frac{z}{D_3}=\frac{1}{D},$$

where $D_1=\begin{vmatrix} d_1 & b_1 & c_1 \\ d_2 & b_2 & c_2 \\ d_3 & b_3 & c_3 \end{vmatrix}$; $D_2=\begin{vmatrix} a_1 & d_1 & c_1 \\ a_2 & d_2 & c_2 \\ a_3 & d_3 & c_3 \end{vmatrix}$

and $D_3=\begin{vmatrix} a_1 & b_1 & d_1 \\ a_2 & b_2 & d_2 \\ a_3 & b_3 & d_3 \end{vmatrix}$

(i) If $D \neq 0$, then the system of equations is consistent and has a unique solution given by

$$x = \frac{D_1}{D},\ y = \frac{D_2}{D} \text{ and } z = \frac{D_3}{D}$$

(ii) If $D = 0$ and $D_1 = D_2 = D_3 = 0$, then the system of equation is consistent with infinitely many solution.

(iii) If $D = 0$ and atleast one of D_1, D_2 and D_3 is non-zero, then the system of equation is inconsistent.

EXAMPLE 3. Solve the following system of linear equations by Crammer's rule $6x + y - 3z = 5$, $x + 3y - 2z = 5$ and $2x + y + 4z = 8$.

Sol. $$D = \begin{vmatrix} 6 & 1 & -3 \\ 1 & 3 & -2 \\ 2 & 1 & 4 \end{vmatrix}$$

$$= 6(12 + 2) - 1(4 + 4) - 3(1 - 6) = 84 - 8 + 15 = 91 \neq 0$$

$$D_1 = \begin{vmatrix} 5 & 1 & -3 \\ 5 & 3 & -2 \\ 8 & 1 & 4 \end{vmatrix}$$

$$= 5(12 + 2) - 1(20 + 16) - 3(5 - 24) = 70 - 36 + 57 = 91$$

$$D_2 = \begin{vmatrix} 6 & 5 & -3 \\ 1 & 5 & -2 \\ 2 & 8 & 4 \end{vmatrix}$$

$$= 6(20 + 16) - 5(4 + 4) - 3(8 - 10) = 216 - 40 + 6 = 182$$

$$D_3 = \begin{vmatrix} 6 & 1 & 5 \\ 1 & 3 & 5 \\ 2 & 1 & 8 \end{vmatrix}$$

$$= 6(24 - 5) - 1(8 - 10) + 5(1 - 6) = 114 + 2 - 25 = 91$$

By Crammer's rule,

$$x = \frac{D_1}{D} = \frac{91}{91} = 1,\ y = \frac{D_2}{D} = \frac{182}{91} = 2,\ z = \frac{D_3}{D} = \frac{91}{91} = 1$$

Hence, the required solution is $x = 1$, $y = 2$, $z = 1$.

EXAMPLE 4. Determine whether the system $x - 3y + 2z = 4$, $2x + y - 3z = -2$, $4x - 5y + z = 5$ is consistent.

Sol. $$D = \begin{vmatrix} 1 & -3 & 2 \\ 2 & 1 & -3 \\ 4 & -5 & 1 \end{vmatrix} = 1(1 - 15) + 3(2 + 12) + 2(-10 - 4)$$

$$= -14 + 42 - 28 = 0$$

$$D_x = \begin{vmatrix} 4 & -3 & 2 \\ -2 & 1 & -3 \\ 5 & -5 & 1 \end{vmatrix} = 4(1 - 15) + 3(-2 + 15) + 2(10 - 5)$$

$$= -56 + 39 + 10 = -7 \neq 0$$

Hence, the system of equation is inconsistent.

EXAMPLE 5. Find the value of a function $f(x)$ using Crammer's rule, where $f(x) = ax^2 + bx + c$, $f(1) = 0$, $f(2) = -2$ and $f(3) = -6$.

Sol. Given, $f(x) = ax^2 + bx + c$ and $f(1) = 0$

$$a + b + c = 0 \quad \text{...(i)}$$

$$\because \quad f(2) = -2$$

$$4a + 2b + c = -2 \quad \text{...(ii)}$$

$$\because \quad f(3) = -6$$

$$9a + 3b + c = -6 \quad \text{...(iii)}$$

The three equations (i), (ii) and (iii) can be determined with the help of Crammer's rule

$$D = \begin{vmatrix} 1 & 1 & 1 \\ 4 & 2 & 1 \\ 9 & 3 & 1 \end{vmatrix}$$

$$= 1(2 - 3) - 1(4 - 9) + 1(12 - 18)$$

$$= -1 + 5 - 6 = -2 \neq 0$$

As $D \neq 0$, there is a unique solution for the system of equation.

$$D_x = \begin{vmatrix} 0 & 1 & 1 \\ -2 & 2 & 1 \\ -6 & 3 & 1 \end{vmatrix}$$

$$= -1(-2 + 6) + 1(-6 + 12) = -4 + 6 = 2$$

$$D_y = \begin{vmatrix} 1 & 0 & 1 \\ 4 & -2 & 1 \\ 9 & -6 & 1 \end{vmatrix}$$

$$= 1(-2 + 6) + 1(-24 + 18) = 4 - 6 = -2$$

$$D_z = \begin{vmatrix} 1 & 1 & 0 \\ 4 & 2 & -2 \\ 9 & 3 & -6 \end{vmatrix}$$

$$= 1(-12 + 6) - 1(-24 + 18) = -6 + 6 = 0$$

$$x = \frac{D_x}{D} = \frac{2}{-2} = -1$$

$$y = \frac{D_y}{D} = \frac{-2}{-2} = 1$$

$$z = \frac{D_z}{D} = \frac{0}{-2} = 0$$

Hence, the function $f(x) = -x^2 + x$.

EXAMPLE 6. Find α and β so that the simultaneous equations $x + y + z = 6$, $x + 2y + 3z = 10$, $x + 2y + \alpha z = \beta$ have

(i) a unique solution

(ii) infinite number of solution

(iii) no solution

Sol. The given system of equation are

$$x + y + z = 6$$
$$x + 2y + 3z = 10$$
$$x + 2y + \alpha z = \beta$$

$$\therefore \quad D = \begin{vmatrix} 1 & 1 & 1 \\ 1 & 2 & 3 \\ 1 & 2 & \alpha \end{vmatrix}$$

$$= 1(2\alpha - 6) - 1(\alpha - 3) + 1(2 - 2) = \alpha - 3$$

$$D_x = \begin{vmatrix} 6 & 1 & 1 \\ 10 & 2 & 3 \\ \beta & 2 & \alpha \end{vmatrix}$$

$$= 6(2\alpha - 6) - 1(10\alpha - 3\beta) + 1(20 - 2\beta)$$
$$= 12\alpha - 36 - 10\alpha + 3\beta + 20 - 2\beta$$
$$= 2\alpha + \beta - 16$$
$$= 2(\alpha - 3) + \beta - 10$$

$$D_y = \begin{vmatrix} 1 & 6 & 1 \\ 1 & 10 & 3 \\ 1 & \beta & \alpha \end{vmatrix}$$

$$= 1(10\alpha - 3\beta) - 6(\alpha - 3) + 1(\beta - 10)$$
$$= 4\alpha - 2\beta + 8 = 4(\alpha - 3) - 2(\beta - 10)$$

$$D_z = \begin{vmatrix} 1 & 1 & 6 \\ 1 & 2 & 10 \\ 1 & 2 & \beta \end{vmatrix}$$

$$= 1(2\beta - 20) - 1(\beta - 10) = \beta - 10$$

(i) For a unique solution,

$$D \neq 0 \Rightarrow \alpha - 3 \neq 0 \Rightarrow \alpha \neq 3$$

Hence, the system of equation must give a unique solution, if $\alpha \neq 3$.

(ii) For infinite number of solutions,

$$D = D_x = D_y = D_z = 0$$
$$\alpha - 3 = 0 \text{ and } \beta - 10 = 0$$
$$\alpha = 3 \text{ and } \beta = 10$$

Hence, the system of equation must give infinite number of solutions, if $\alpha = 3$ and $\beta = 10$.

(iii) For no solution,

$D = 0$ and at least one of D_x, D_y and D_z must be non-zero.

$$D = 0 \Rightarrow \alpha - 3 = 0 \Rightarrow \alpha = 3$$

Atleast one of D_x, D_y and D_z must be non-zero. This can only be possible when $\beta \neq 10$

Hence, the given system of equation must give no solution, if $\alpha = 3$ but $\beta \neq 10$.

Matrix Method

Solution of System of Linear Equations using Inverse of a Matrix

Let the system of linear equations be

$$a_1x + b_1y + c_1z = d_1,$$
$$a_2x + b_2y + c_2z = d_2$$
and $$a_3x + b_3y + c_3z = d_3.$$

Now, let $A = \begin{bmatrix} a_1 & b_1 & c_1 \\ a_2 & b_2 & c_2 \\ a_3 & b_3 & c_3 \end{bmatrix}$, $X = \begin{bmatrix} x \\ y \\ z \end{bmatrix}$ and $B = \begin{bmatrix} d_1 \\ d_2 \\ d_3 \end{bmatrix}$.

Then, the matrix representation of above system of linear equations is

$$AX = B \qquad \text{...(i)}$$

Now following case arises

Case I If A is non-singular matrix, it means its inverse exists, then $X = A^{-1}B$

Above matrix equation will provide the unique solution of the given system of equations as inverse of a matrix is unique.

Case II If A is a singular matrix, i.e. $|A| = 0$

Its inverse does not exist.

In this case, we calculate (adj A)B.

If (adj A)$B \neq O$, here O is zero matrix, then solution does not exist and system of equation is inconsistent.

If (adj A)$B = O$, then system may be consistent or inconsistent, according as the system has infinitely many solution or no solution.

EXAMPLE 7. Examine the consistency of the system of the following equations

(i) $x + 2y = 2$ and $2x + 3y = 3$

(ii) $3x - y = 5$ and $6x - 2y = 3$

Sol. (i) The given system of equations can be written in matrix form as $AX = B$,

where $A = \begin{bmatrix} 1 & 2 \\ 2 & 3 \end{bmatrix}$, $X = \begin{bmatrix} x \\ y \end{bmatrix}$ and $B = \begin{bmatrix} 2 \\ 3 \end{bmatrix}$

Now, $|A| = \begin{vmatrix} 1 & 2 \\ 2 & 3 \end{vmatrix} = 1(3) - 2(2) = 3 - 4 = -1 \neq 0$

Since, A is non-singular, so A^{-1} exists.

Hence, the given system of equations is consistent.

(ii) Given, system of equations is

$$3x - y = 5 \qquad \text{...(i)}$$
and $$6x - 2y = 3 \qquad \text{...(ii)}$$

Given, equations can be written in matrix form as

$$AX = B,$$

where $A = \begin{bmatrix} 3 & -1 \\ 6 & -2 \end{bmatrix}$, $X = \begin{bmatrix} x \\ y \end{bmatrix}$ and $B = \begin{bmatrix} 5 \\ 3 \end{bmatrix}$

Now, $|A| = \begin{vmatrix} 3 & -1 \\ 6 & -2 \end{vmatrix} = -6 + 6 = 0$

$\therefore A^{-1}$ does not exist.

Now, $\text{adj}(A) = \begin{bmatrix} -2 & 1 \\ -6 & 3 \end{bmatrix} \quad \left[\because \text{adj}\begin{bmatrix} a & b \\ c & d \end{bmatrix} = \begin{bmatrix} d & -b \\ -c & a \end{bmatrix}\right]$

$$\therefore \text{adj}(A)B = \begin{bmatrix} -2 & 1 \\ -6 & 3 \end{bmatrix}\begin{bmatrix} 5 \\ 3 \end{bmatrix}$$
$$= \begin{bmatrix} -10 + 3 \\ -30 + 9 \end{bmatrix} = \begin{bmatrix} -7 \\ -21 \end{bmatrix}$$

$\Rightarrow \text{adj}(A)B \neq O$

Hence, the equations are inconsistent and have no solution.

EXAMPLE 8. Show that the following system of equations is consistent.

$$2x - y + 3z = 5, 3x + 2y + z = 7, 4x + 5y - 5z = 9$$

Sol. Given, equations can be written in matrix form as

$$AX = B$$

where, $A = \begin{bmatrix} 2 & -1 & 3 \\ 3 & 2 & 1 \\ 4 & 5 & -5 \end{bmatrix}, X = \begin{bmatrix} x \\ y \\ z \end{bmatrix}$ and $B = \begin{bmatrix} 5 \\ 7 \\ 9 \end{bmatrix}$

Now, $|A| = \begin{vmatrix} 2 & -1 & 3 \\ 3 & 2 & 1 \\ 4 & 5 & -5 \end{vmatrix}$

$= 2(-10-5) + 1(-15-4) + 3(15-8)$

$= -30 - 19 + 21 = -28 \neq 0$

Since, A is non-singular, so A^{-1} exists.

Hence, the given system of equations is consistent.

Hence proved.

EXAMPLE 9. Solve the followig system of linear equations by matrix method.

(i) $4x - 3y = 3$ and $3x - 5y = 7$

(ii) $x - y + z = 4, 2x + y - 3z = 0, x + y + z = 2$

[CBSE 2023]

Sol. (i) The given system of linear equations can be written in matrix form as $AX = B$,

where, $A = \begin{bmatrix} 4 & -3 \\ 3 & -5 \end{bmatrix}, X = \begin{bmatrix} x \\ y \end{bmatrix}$ and $B = \begin{bmatrix} 3 \\ 7 \end{bmatrix}$

Now, $|A| = \begin{vmatrix} 4 & -3 \\ 3 & -5 \end{vmatrix} = -20 + 9 = -11 \neq 0$

So, A^{-1} exists and it is given by

$$A^{-1} = \frac{1}{|A|} \text{adj}(A) = \frac{1}{-11}\begin{bmatrix} -5 & 3 \\ -3 & 4 \end{bmatrix} = \frac{1}{11}\begin{bmatrix} 5 & -3 \\ 3 & -4 \end{bmatrix}$$

$$\left[\because \text{adj}\begin{bmatrix} a & b \\ c & d \end{bmatrix} = \begin{bmatrix} d & -b \\ -c & a \end{bmatrix}\right]$$

$\because \quad X = A^{-1}B$

$\therefore \quad X = \frac{1}{11}\begin{bmatrix} 5 & -3 \\ 3 & -4 \end{bmatrix}\begin{bmatrix} 3 \\ 7 \end{bmatrix}$

$= \frac{1}{11}\begin{bmatrix} 15 - 21 \\ 9 - 28 \end{bmatrix} = \frac{1}{11}\begin{bmatrix} -6 \\ -19 \end{bmatrix}$

$\Rightarrow \begin{bmatrix} x \\ y \end{bmatrix} = \begin{bmatrix} -6/11 \\ -19/11 \end{bmatrix}$

Now, comparing the corresponding elements, we get

$$x = \frac{-6}{11} \text{ and } y = \frac{-19}{11}.$$

(ii) The given system of linear equations can be written in matrix form as

$$AX = B \quad \text{...(i)}$$

where, $A = \begin{bmatrix} 1 & -1 & 1 \\ 2 & 1 & -3 \\ 1 & 1 & 1 \end{bmatrix}, X = \begin{bmatrix} x \\ y \\ z \end{bmatrix}$ and $B = \begin{bmatrix} 4 \\ 0 \\ 2 \end{bmatrix}$

Now, $|A| = \begin{vmatrix} 1 & -1 & 1 \\ 2 & 1 & -3 \\ 1 & 1 & 1 \end{vmatrix}$

$= 1(1+3) + 1(2+3) + 1(2-1)$

[expanding along R_1]

$= 4 + 5 + 1 = 10 \neq 0$

Thus, A is a non-singular matrix.

So, A^{-1} exist. Cofactors of elements of $|A|$ are

$C_{11} = (-1)^{1+1}\begin{vmatrix} 1 & -3 \\ 1 & 1 \end{vmatrix} = (1+3) = 4$

$C_{12} = (-1)^{1+2}\begin{vmatrix} 2 & -3 \\ 1 & 1 \end{vmatrix} = -(2+3) = -5$

$C_{13} = (-1)^{1+3}\begin{vmatrix} 2 & 1 \\ 1 & 1 \end{vmatrix} = (2-1) = 1$

$C_{21} = (-1)^{2+1}\begin{vmatrix} -1 & 1 \\ 1 & 1 \end{vmatrix} = (-1)(-1-1) = 2$

$C_{22} = (-1)^{2+2}\begin{vmatrix} 1 & 1 \\ 1 & 1 \end{vmatrix} = 0$

$C_{23} = (-1)^{2+3}\begin{vmatrix} 1 & -1 \\ 1 & 1 \end{vmatrix} = (-1)(1+1) = 2$

$C_{31} = (-1)^{3+1}\begin{vmatrix} -1 & 1 \\ 1 & -3 \end{vmatrix} = (3-1) = 2$

$C_{32} = (-1)^{3+2}\begin{vmatrix} 1 & 1 \\ 2 & -3 \end{vmatrix} = (-1)(-3-2) = 5$

$C_{33} = (-1)^{3+3}\begin{vmatrix} 1 & -1 \\ 2 & 1 \end{vmatrix} = (1+2) = 3$

Thus, $\text{adj}(A) = \begin{bmatrix} c_{11} & c_{12} & c_{13} \\ c_{21} & c_{22} & c_{23} \\ c_{31} & c_{32} & c_{33} \end{bmatrix}^T = \begin{bmatrix} c_{11} & c_{12} & c_{13} \\ c_{21} & c_{22} & c_{23} \\ c_{31} & c_{32} & c_{33} \end{bmatrix}$

$= \begin{bmatrix} 4 & 2 & 2 \\ -5 & 0 & 5 \\ 1 & -2 & 3 \end{bmatrix}$

Now, $A^{-1} = \frac{1}{|A|}\text{adj}(A) = \frac{1}{10}\begin{bmatrix} 4 & 2 & 2 \\ -5 & 0 & 5 \\ 1 & -2 & 3 \end{bmatrix}$

and the solution of equation (i) is given by $X = A^{-1}B$.

$\therefore \begin{bmatrix} x \\ y \\ z \end{bmatrix} = \frac{1}{10}\begin{bmatrix} 4 & 2 & 2 \\ -5 & 0 & 5 \\ 1 & -2 & 3 \end{bmatrix}\begin{bmatrix} 4 \\ 0 \\ 2 \end{bmatrix}$

$= \frac{1}{10}\begin{bmatrix} 16 + 4 \\ -20 + 10 \\ 4 + 6 \end{bmatrix}$

$= \frac{1}{10}\begin{bmatrix} 20 \\ -10 \\ 10 \end{bmatrix} = \begin{bmatrix} 2 \\ -1 \\ 1 \end{bmatrix}$

On comparing the corresponding elements, we get

$$x = 2, y = -1, z = 1$$

EXAMPLE 10. Using matrix method, solve the following system of equations. $\frac{2}{x}+\frac{3}{y}+\frac{10}{z}=4, \frac{4}{x}-\frac{6}{y}+\frac{5}{z}=1$ and $\frac{6}{x}+\frac{9}{y}-\frac{20}{z}=2$, where x, y and $z \neq 0$.

Sol. The given system of equations is

$$\frac{2}{x}+\frac{3}{y}+\frac{10}{z}=4, \quad \frac{4}{x}-\frac{6}{y}+\frac{5}{z}=1,$$

and $$\frac{6}{x}+\frac{9}{y}-\frac{20}{z}=2; \; x, y, z \neq 0$$

Let $\frac{1}{x}=u, \frac{1}{y}=v$ and $\frac{1}{z}=w$, then system of equations can be written as

$$\left.\begin{aligned} 2u+3v+10w &= 4 \\ 4u-6v+5w &= 1 \\ \text{and} \quad 6u+9v-20w &= 2 \end{aligned}\right\} \quad \text{...(i)}$$

Above system of Eq. (i) can be written in matrix form as $AX=B$, where

$$A=\begin{bmatrix} 2 & 3 & 10 \\ 4 & -6 & 5 \\ 6 & 9 & -20 \end{bmatrix}, B=\begin{bmatrix} 4 \\ 1 \\ 2 \end{bmatrix} \text{ and } X=\begin{bmatrix} u \\ v \\ w \end{bmatrix}.$$

Its solution is given by $X=A^{-1}B$ ...(ii)

Here, $|A| = 2(120-45)-3(-80-30)+10(36+36)$
$= 2(75)-3(-110)+10(72)$
$= 150+330+720=1200$

$\Rightarrow \quad |A|=1200$

Since, $|A| \neq 0$, so unique solution exists.

Now, cofactors of elements of $|A|$ are

$$A_{11}=(-1)^2\begin{vmatrix} -6 & 5 \\ 9 & -20 \end{vmatrix}=1(120-45)=75$$

$$A_{12}=(-1)^3\begin{vmatrix} 4 & 5 \\ 6 & -20 \end{vmatrix}=-1(-80-30)=110$$

$$A_{13}=(-1)^4\begin{vmatrix} 4 & -6 \\ 6 & 9 \end{vmatrix}=1(36+36)=72$$

$$A_{21}=(-1)^3\begin{vmatrix} 3 & 10 \\ 9 & -20 \end{vmatrix}=-1(-60-90)=150$$

$$A_{22}=(-1)^4\begin{vmatrix} 2 & 10 \\ 6 & -20 \end{vmatrix}=1(-40-60)=-100$$

$$A_{23}=(-1)^5\begin{vmatrix} 2 & 3 \\ 6 & 9 \end{vmatrix}=-1(18-18)=0$$

$$A_{31}=(-1)^4\begin{vmatrix} 3 & 10 \\ -6 & 5 \end{vmatrix}=1(15+60)=75$$

$$A_{32}=(-1)^5\begin{vmatrix} 2 & 10 \\ 4 & 5 \end{vmatrix}=-1(10-40)=30$$

$$A_{33}=(-1)^6\begin{vmatrix} 2 & 3 \\ 4 & -6 \end{vmatrix}=1(-12-12)=-24$$

$$\therefore \text{adj}(A)=\begin{bmatrix} A_{11} & A_{12} & A_{13} \\ A_{21} & A_{22} & A_{23} \\ A_{31} & A_{32} & A_{33} \end{bmatrix}^T$$

$$=\begin{bmatrix} 75 & 110 & 72 \\ 150 & -100 & 0 \\ 75 & 30 & -24 \end{bmatrix}^T=\begin{bmatrix} 75 & 150 & 75 \\ 110 & -100 & 30 \\ 72 & 0 & -24 \end{bmatrix}$$

and $$A^{-1}=\frac{\text{adj}(A)}{|A|}=\frac{1}{1200}\begin{bmatrix} 75 & 150 & 75 \\ 110 & -100 & 30 \\ 72 & 0 & -24 \end{bmatrix}$$

On putting the values X, A^{-1} and B in Eq. (ii), we get

$$\begin{bmatrix} u \\ v \\ w \end{bmatrix}=\frac{1}{1200}\begin{bmatrix} 75 & 150 & 75 \\ 110 & -100 & 30 \\ 72 & 0 & -24 \end{bmatrix}\begin{bmatrix} 4 \\ 1 \\ 2 \end{bmatrix}$$

$$=\frac{1}{1200}\begin{bmatrix} 300+150+150 \\ 440-100+60 \\ 288+0-48 \end{bmatrix}$$

$$\Rightarrow \begin{bmatrix} u \\ v \\ w \end{bmatrix}=\frac{1}{1200}\begin{bmatrix} 600 \\ 400 \\ 240 \end{bmatrix}$$

On comparing corresponding elements, we get

$$u=\frac{600}{1200}, \; v=\frac{400}{1200}, \; w=\frac{240}{1200}$$

$\therefore \quad u=\frac{1}{2}, v=\frac{1}{3}$ and $w=\frac{1}{5}$

But $\quad \frac{1}{x}=u, \frac{1}{y}=v$ and $\frac{1}{z}=w$

$\Rightarrow \quad \frac{1}{x}=\frac{1}{2}, \frac{1}{y}=\frac{1}{3}$ and $\frac{1}{z}=\frac{1}{5}$

$\therefore \quad x=2, y=3$ and $z=5$

EXAMPLE 11. Given that $A=\begin{bmatrix} 2 & 3 \\ -5 & 4 \end{bmatrix}$. Find A^{-1} and hence solve the simultaneous equations $2x+3y+4=0$ and $-5x+4y+13=0$.

Sol. Given, $A=\begin{bmatrix} 2 & 3 \\ -5 & 4 \end{bmatrix}$.

Then, $|A|=8+15=23 \neq 0$

Thus, A is a non-singular matrix. So, A^{-1} exists.

Now, cofactors of elements of $|A|$ are

$$C_{11}=(-1)^{1+1}(4)=4; \quad C_{12}=(-1)^{1+2}(-5)=5$$
$$C_{21}=(-1)^{2+1}(3)=-3; \quad C_{22}=(-1)^{2+2}(2)=2$$

Then, $$\text{adj}(A)=\begin{bmatrix} C_{11} & C_{12} \\ C_{21} & C_{22} \end{bmatrix}^T=\begin{bmatrix} 4 & 5 \\ -3 & 2 \end{bmatrix}^T=\begin{bmatrix} 4 & -3 \\ 5 & 2 \end{bmatrix}$$

Now, $$A^{-1}=\frac{1}{|A|}\text{adj}(A)=\frac{1}{23}\begin{bmatrix} 4 & -3 \\ 5 & 2 \end{bmatrix}$$

Given system of linear equations is

$$2x+3y=-4$$
and $$-5x+4y=-13$$

These equations can be written in matrix form as

$$AX=B \quad \text{...(i)}$$

where, $$A=\begin{bmatrix} 2 & 3 \\ -5 & 4 \end{bmatrix}, X=\begin{bmatrix} x \\ y \end{bmatrix} \text{ and } B=\begin{bmatrix} -4 \\ -13 \end{bmatrix}$$

The solution of Eq. (i) is given by

$$X = A^{-1}B \qquad \text{...(ii)}$$

On putting the values of A^{-1} and B in RHS of Eq. (ii), we get

$$X = A^{-1}B = \frac{1}{23}\begin{bmatrix} 4 & -3 \\ 5 & 2 \end{bmatrix}\begin{bmatrix} -4 \\ -13 \end{bmatrix}$$

$$= \frac{1}{23}\begin{bmatrix} -16+39 \\ -20-26 \end{bmatrix} = \frac{1}{23}\begin{bmatrix} 23 \\ -46 \end{bmatrix} = \begin{bmatrix} 1 \\ -2 \end{bmatrix}$$

$$\Rightarrow \quad X = \begin{bmatrix} x \\ y \end{bmatrix} = \begin{bmatrix} 1 \\ -2 \end{bmatrix}$$

$\therefore \quad x = 1$ and $y = -2$.

[comparing corresponding elements]

EXAMPLE 12. If $A = \begin{bmatrix} 2 & -3 & 5 \\ 3 & 2 & -4 \\ 1 & 1 & -2 \end{bmatrix}$, find A^{-1} and hence solve the following system of linear equations.

$2x - 3y + 5z = 11, 3x + 2y - 4z = -5, x + y - 2z = -3$

[CBSE 2025]

Sol. Given, matrix $A = \begin{bmatrix} 2 & -3 & 5 \\ 3 & 2 & -4 \\ 1 & 1 & -2 \end{bmatrix}$

Compute det (A) by expanding along R_1

$$\det(A) = 2(-4+4) + 3(-6+4) + 5(3-2)$$
$$= 2 \times 0 + 3 \times (-2) + 5 = 0 + (-6) + 5 = -1$$

Thus, $\det(A) = -1 \neq 0$, so A is invertible.

Now, cofactors of elements of $|A|$ are

$A_{11} = -4 + 4 = 0, A_{12} = -(-6+4) = 2, A_{13} = 3 - 2 = 1$

$A_{21} = -(6-5) = -1, A_{22} = -4 - 5 = -9, A_{23} = -(2+3) = -5$

$A_{31} = 12 - 10 = 2, A_{32} = -(-8-15) = 23, A_{33} = 4 + 9 = 13$

$$\text{adj } A = \begin{bmatrix} 0 & 2 & 1 \\ -1 & -9 & -5 \\ 2 & 23 & 13 \end{bmatrix}^T = \begin{bmatrix} 0 & -1 & 2 \\ 2 & -9 & 23 \\ 1 & -5 & 13 \end{bmatrix}$$

Now, $\quad A^{-1} = \dfrac{1}{|A|} \text{adj } A$

$$= \frac{1}{-1}\begin{bmatrix} 0 & -1 & 2 \\ 2 & -9 & 23 \\ 1 & -5 & 13 \end{bmatrix} = \begin{bmatrix} 0 & 1 & -2 \\ -2 & 9 & -23 \\ -1 & 5 & -13 \end{bmatrix}$$

Now, the given system of equations can be written in matrix form as

$$\begin{bmatrix} 2 & -3 & 5 \\ 3 & 2 & -4 \\ 1 & 1 & -2 \end{bmatrix}\begin{bmatrix} x \\ y \\ z \end{bmatrix} = \begin{bmatrix} 11 \\ -5 \\ -3 \end{bmatrix}$$

i.e. $\quad AX = B$

$\Rightarrow \quad X = A^{-1}B$

Where, $A = \begin{bmatrix} 2 & -3 & 5 \\ 3 & 2 & -4 \\ 1 & 1 & -2 \end{bmatrix}, B = \begin{bmatrix} 11 \\ -5 \\ -3 \end{bmatrix}, X = \begin{bmatrix} x \\ y \\ z \end{bmatrix}$

Now, $\quad X = A^{-1}B$

$$\Rightarrow \begin{bmatrix} x \\ y \\ z \end{bmatrix} = A^{-1} \cdot B$$

$$\Rightarrow \begin{bmatrix} x \\ y \\ z \end{bmatrix} = \begin{bmatrix} 0 & 1 & -2 \\ -2 & 9 & -23 \\ -1 & 5 & -13 \end{bmatrix}\begin{bmatrix} 11 \\ -5 \\ -3 \end{bmatrix}$$

$$\Rightarrow \begin{bmatrix} x \\ y \\ z \end{bmatrix} = \begin{bmatrix} 0-5+6 \\ -22-45+69 \\ -11-25+39 \end{bmatrix} \Rightarrow \begin{bmatrix} x \\ y \\ z \end{bmatrix} = \begin{bmatrix} 1 \\ 2 \\ 3 \end{bmatrix}$$

On comparing both sides, we get $x = 1$, $y = 2$ and $z = 3$.

EXAMPLE 13. Determine the product of $\begin{bmatrix} -4 & 4 & 4 \\ -7 & 1 & 3 \\ 5 & -3 & -1 \end{bmatrix}\begin{bmatrix} 1 & -1 & 1 \\ 1 & -2 & -2 \\ 2 & 1 & 3 \end{bmatrix}$ and then use it to solve the system of equations $x - y + z = 4$, $x - 2y - 2z = 9$ and $2x + y + 3z = 1$.

Sol. Let $B = \begin{bmatrix} -4 & 4 & 4 \\ -7 & 1 & 3 \\ 5 & -3 & -1 \end{bmatrix}$ and $A = \begin{bmatrix} 1 & -1 & 1 \\ 1 & -2 & -2 \\ 2 & 1 & 3 \end{bmatrix}$

$$\therefore BA = \begin{bmatrix} -4 & 4 & 4 \\ -7 & 1 & 3 \\ 5 & -3 & -1 \end{bmatrix}\begin{bmatrix} 1 & -1 & 1 \\ 1 & -2 & -2 \\ 2 & 1 & 3 \end{bmatrix}$$

$$= \begin{bmatrix} -4+4+8 & 4-8+4 & -4-8+12 \\ -7+1+6 & 7-2+3 & -7-2+9 \\ 5-3-2 & -5+6-1 & 5+6-3 \end{bmatrix}$$

$$= \begin{bmatrix} 8 & 0 & 0 \\ 0 & 8 & 0 \\ 0 & 0 & 8 \end{bmatrix} = 8\begin{bmatrix} 1 & 0 & 0 \\ 0 & 1 & 0 \\ 0 & 0 & 1 \end{bmatrix} = 8I$$

$\Rightarrow BA = 8I \Rightarrow B(AA^{-1}) = 8IA^{-1}$

[post-multiplying both sides by A^{-1}]

$\Rightarrow \quad B = 8A^{-1}$ $\qquad [\because AA^{-1} = I]$

$$\therefore A^{-1} = \frac{1}{8}\begin{bmatrix} -4 & 4 & 4 \\ -7 & 1 & 3 \\ 5 & -3 & -1 \end{bmatrix}$$

Given system of equations can be written in matrix form as

$$AX = C \Rightarrow X = A^{-1}C$$

where, $A = \begin{bmatrix} 1 & -1 & 1 \\ 1 & -2 & -2 \\ 2 & 1 & 3 \end{bmatrix}, C = \begin{bmatrix} 4 \\ 9 \\ 1 \end{bmatrix}$ and $X = \begin{bmatrix} x \\ y \\ z \end{bmatrix}$

$$\therefore \quad X = \frac{1}{8}\begin{bmatrix} -4 & 4 & 4 \\ -7 & 1 & 3 \\ 5 & -3 & -1 \end{bmatrix}\begin{bmatrix} 4 \\ 9 \\ 1 \end{bmatrix}$$

$$\Rightarrow \begin{bmatrix} x \\ y \\ z \end{bmatrix} = \frac{1}{8}\begin{bmatrix} -16+36+4 \\ -28+9+3 \\ 20-27-1 \end{bmatrix} = \frac{1}{8}\begin{bmatrix} 24 \\ -16 \\ -8 \end{bmatrix} = \begin{bmatrix} 3 \\ -2 \\ -1 \end{bmatrix}$$

On comparing corresponding elements, we get

$x = 3$, $y = -2$ and $z = -1$

EXAMPLE 14. Suppose, the demand curve for automobiles over some time period can be written as $x+0.2y=15000$, where x is the price of an automobiles and y is the corresponding quantity. Suppose, the supply curve is $x-0.4y=6000$. Use Crammer's rule to determine the price of an automobile.

Sol. The demand curve is $x+0.2y=15000$

and the supply curve is $x-0.4y=6000$

$$D=\begin{vmatrix}1 & 0.2\\1 & -0.4\end{vmatrix}=-0.4-0.2=-0.6$$

$$D_x=\begin{vmatrix}15000 & 0.2\\6000 & -0.4\end{vmatrix}=-6000-1200=-7200$$

$$D_y=\begin{vmatrix}1 & 15000\\1 & 6000\end{vmatrix}=6000-15000=-9000$$

$\therefore$ $$x=\frac{D_x}{D}=\frac{-7200}{-0.6}=12000$$

$$y=\frac{D_y}{y}=\frac{-9000}{-0.6}=15000$$

Hence, the price of an automobile is ₹ 12000.

EXAMPLE 15. Two schools A and B want to award their selected students on the value of sincerity, truthfulness and helpfulness. The school A wants to award ₹x each, ₹y each and ₹z each for the three respective value of 3, 2 and 1 students, respectively with a total award money of ₹ 1600. School B wants to spend ₹ 2300 to award its 4, 1 and 3 students on the respective values (by giving the same award money to the three values as before). If the total amount of award for one prize on each value is ₹ 900, using matrices, find the award money for each value.

Sol. Let the money awarded to the students on the values of sincerity, truthfulness and helpfulness by ₹x, ₹ y and ₹z, respectively.

According to the question,

$$3x+2y+z=1600,$$
$$4x+y+3z=2300$$

and $$x+y+z=900$$

$\therefore$ $$D=\begin{vmatrix}3 & 2 & 1\\4 & 1 & 3\\1 & 1 & 1\end{vmatrix}=3(1-3)-2(4-3)+1(4-1)$$

$$=-6-2+3=-5\neq 0$$

Since $D\neq 0$, the system is consistent with the unique data.

$$D_x=\begin{vmatrix}1600 & 2 & 1\\2300 & 1 & 3\\900 & 1 & 1\end{vmatrix}$$

$$=1600(1-3)-2300(2-1)+900(6-1)$$
$$=-3200-2300+4500$$
$$=-5500+4500=-1000$$

$$D_y=\begin{vmatrix}3 & 1600 & 1\\4 & 2300 & 3\\1 & 900 & 1\end{vmatrix}$$

$$=-1600(4-3)+2300(3-1)-900(9-4)$$
$$=-1600+4600-4500=-1500$$

[expanding along C_2]

$$D_z=\begin{vmatrix}3 & 2 & 1600\\4 & 1 & 2300\\1 & 1 & 900\end{vmatrix}$$

$$=1600(4-1)-2300(3-2)+900(3-8)$$
$$=4800-2300-4500 \quad \text{[expanding along } C_3]$$
$$=-2000$$

$\therefore$ $$x=\frac{D_x}{D}=\frac{-1000}{-5}=200,$$

$$y=\frac{D_y}{D}=\frac{-1500}{-5}=300$$

and $$z=\frac{D_z}{D}=\frac{-2000}{-5}=400$$

Hence, the award for sincerity is ₹ 200, the award for truthfulness is ₹ 300 and the award for helpfulness is ₹ 400.

EXAMPLE 16. The sum of three numbers is 6. If we multiply third number by 3 and add second number to it, we get 11. By adding first and third numbers, we get double of the second number. Represent it algebraically and find the numbers using matrix method.

Sol. Let first, second and third numbers be denoted by x, y and z, respectively.

Then, according to the question, we get

$$x+y+z=6,\ y+3z=11$$

and $$x+z=2y \Rightarrow x-2y+z=0$$

In matrix form, this system of equations can be written as

$$AX=B \quad \text{...(i)}$$

where, $A=\begin{bmatrix}1 & 1 & 1\\0 & 1 & 3\\1 & -2 & 1\end{bmatrix}, X=\begin{bmatrix}x\\y\\z\end{bmatrix}$ and $B=\begin{bmatrix}6\\11\\0\end{bmatrix}$

Here, $|A|=\begin{vmatrix}1 & 1 & 1\\0 & 1 & 3\\1 & -2 & 1\end{vmatrix}=1(1+6)-1(0-3)+1(0-1)$

[expanding along R_1]

$$=7+3-1=9\neq 0$$

Since, $|A|\neq 0$, so the inverse of A exists.

Now, cofactors corresponding to each element of $|A|$ are

$$C_{11}=(-1)^{1+1}\begin{vmatrix}1 & 3\\-2 & 1\end{vmatrix}=1+6=7$$

$$C_{12}=(-1)^{1+2}\begin{vmatrix}0 & 3\\1 & 1\end{vmatrix}=-(0-3)=3$$

$$C_{13}=(-1)^{1+3}\begin{vmatrix}0 & 1\\1 & -2\end{vmatrix}=0-1=-1$$

$$C_{21}=(-1)^{2+1}\begin{vmatrix}1 & 1\\ -2 & 1\end{vmatrix}=-(1+2)=-3$$

$$C_{22}=(-1)^{2+2}\begin{vmatrix}1 & 1\\ 1 & 1\end{vmatrix}=0$$

$$C_{23}=(-1)^{2+3}\begin{vmatrix}1 & 1\\ 1 & -2\end{vmatrix}=-(-2-1)=3$$

$$C_{31}=(-1)^{3+1}\begin{vmatrix}1 & 1\\ 1 & 3\end{vmatrix}=3-1=2$$

$$C_{32}=(-1)^{3+2}\begin{vmatrix}1 & 1\\ 0 & 3\end{vmatrix}=-(3-0)=-3$$

$$C_{33}=(-1)^{3+3}\begin{vmatrix}1 & 1\\ 0 & 1\end{vmatrix}=1-0=1$$

Then, $\text{adj}(A)=\begin{bmatrix}7 & 3 & -1\\ -3 & 0 & 3\\ 2 & -3 & 1\end{bmatrix}^T=\begin{bmatrix}7 & -3 & 2\\ 3 & 0 & -3\\ -1 & 3 & 1\end{bmatrix}$

Thus, $A^{-1}=\dfrac{1}{|A|}\text{adj}(A)=\dfrac{1}{9}\begin{bmatrix}7 & -3 & 2\\ 3 & 0 & -3\\ -1 & 3 & 1\end{bmatrix}$

Now, the solution of Eq. (i) is given by

$$X=A^{-1}B \quad \text{...(ii)}$$

On putting the values of A^{-1} and B in RHS of Eq. (ii), we get

$$X=\frac{1}{9}\begin{bmatrix}7 & -3 & 2\\ 3 & 0 & -3\\ -1 & 3 & 1\end{bmatrix}\begin{bmatrix}6\\ 11\\ 0\end{bmatrix}$$

$$=\frac{1}{9}\begin{bmatrix}7\times 6-3\times 11+2\times 0\\ 3\times 6+0\times 11-3\times 0\\ -1\times 6+3\times 11+1\times 0\end{bmatrix}$$

$$=\frac{1}{9}\begin{bmatrix}42-33+0\\ 18+0-0\\ -6+33+0\end{bmatrix}$$

$$=\frac{1}{9}\begin{bmatrix}9\\ 18\\ 27\end{bmatrix}=\begin{bmatrix}9/9\\ 18/9\\ 27/9\end{bmatrix}=\begin{bmatrix}1\\ 2\\ 3\end{bmatrix}$$

$$\Rightarrow \begin{bmatrix}x\\ y\\ z\end{bmatrix}=\begin{bmatrix}1\\ 2\\ 3\end{bmatrix}$$

On comparing both sides, we get

$$x=1,\ y=2 \text{ and } z=3$$

which are the required numbers.

Topic Practice 4

1 Solve the following system of linear equation by Cramer's rule.

(i) $4x+3y=-2,\ 8x-2y=12$

(ii) $mx-ny=m^2+n^2,\ x+y=2m$

2 Solve the following system of linear equation by Cramer's rule.

(i) $5x+3y+z=16,\ 2x+y+3z=19,$ $x+2y+4z=25$

(ii) $x+y=5, y+z=3, x+z=4$

3 Examine the consistency of the system of equations.

(i) $2x-y=5, x+y=4$

(ii) $x+3y=5, 2x+6y=8$

(iii) $6x+4y=2, 9x+6y=3$

(iv) $x+y+z=1, 2x+3y+2z=2, bx+by+2bz=4$

(v) $3x-y-2z=2, 2y-z=-1, 3x-5y=3$

(vi) $x+y+z=6, x+2y+3z=14, x+4y+7z=30$

4 Show that the each of the following system of equations has infinite number of solutions and then solve.

(i) $x+2y=10, 4x+8y=40$

(ii) $x-3y+4z=10, x+2y+4z=6,$ $2x-6y+8z=20$

5 Find the values of p,q so that the system of equations $2x+py+6z=8, x+2y+qz=5$ and $x+y+3z=4$ may have

(i) a unique solution

(ii) infinitely many solutions

(iii) no solution

6 Using Crammer's rule, find the quadratic polynomial defined by $f(x)=ax^2+bx+c$, if $f(0)=7, f(1)=9$ and $f(2)=19$

7 Solve the following systems of linear equations using matrix method.

(i) $2x-y=-2$ and $3x+4y=3.$

(ii) $5x+2y=4$ and $7x+3y=5.$

(iii) $x-y+2z=7, 3x+4y-5z=-5$ and $2x-y+3z=12.$

(iv) $x+2y-3z=-4, 2x+3y+2z=2$ and $3x-3y-4z=11.$

(v) $2x+y+z=1, x-2y-z=\dfrac{3}{2}$ and $3y-5z=9.$

(vi) $x+y-z=3, 2x+3y+z=10$ and $3x-y-7z=1$

(vii) $3x+4y+7z=4, 2x-y+3z=-3$ and $x+2y-3z=8$

8 In the following cases, find A^{-1} and hence solve the system of equations.

(i) $A = \begin{bmatrix} 1 & 3 & 4 \\ 2 & 1 & 2 \\ 5 & 1 & 1 \end{bmatrix}$, and system of equations

$x + 3y + 4z = 8,\ 2x + y + 2z = 5, 5x + y + z = 7$

(ii) $A = \begin{bmatrix} 1 & 1 & 1 \\ 1 & 0 & 2 \\ 3 & 1 & 1 \end{bmatrix}$, and system of equations

$x + y + z = 6,\ x + 2z = 7,\ 3x + y + z = 12$

(iii) $A = \begin{bmatrix} 2 & -3 & 5 \\ 3 & 2 & -4 \\ 1 & 1 & -2 \end{bmatrix}$, and system of equations

$2x - 3y + 5z = 11, 3x + 2y - 4z = -5, x + y - 2z = -3$

(iv) If $A = \begin{bmatrix} 1 & 2 & 1 \\ -1 & 1 & 1 \\ 1 & -3 & 1 \end{bmatrix}$, and system of equations

$x + 2y + z = 4, -x + y + z = 0, x - 3y + z = 4$

9 Using matrix method, solve the system of equations.

(i) $\frac{1}{x} - \frac{1}{y} + \frac{1}{z} = 4, \frac{2}{x} + \frac{1}{y} - \frac{3}{z} = 0, \frac{1}{x} + \frac{1}{y} + \frac{1}{z} = 2$

(ii) $\frac{2}{x} - \frac{3}{y} + \frac{3}{z} = 10, \frac{1}{x} + \frac{1}{y} + \frac{1}{z} = 10, \frac{3}{x} - \frac{1}{y} + \frac{2}{z} = 13$

10 If $A = \begin{bmatrix} 2 & 3 & 10 \\ 4 & -6 & 5 \\ 6 & 9 & -20 \end{bmatrix}$, find A^{-1}. Using A^{-1} solve the system of equations

$\frac{2}{x} + \frac{3}{y} + \frac{10}{z} = 2;\ \frac{4}{x} - \frac{6}{y} + \frac{5}{z} = 5;$

and $\frac{6}{x} + \frac{9}{y} - \frac{20}{z} = -4.$

11 Determine the product of matrices in the following cases and use it to solve the system of equations.

(i) Product of matrics $\begin{bmatrix} 1 & -1 & 2 \\ 0 & 2 & -3 \\ 3 & -2 & 4 \end{bmatrix}\begin{bmatrix} -2 & 0 & 1 \\ 9 & 2 & -3 \\ 6 & 1 & -2 \end{bmatrix}$

and system of equations

$x - y + 2z = 1,\ 2y - 3z = 1,\ 3x - 2y + 4z = 2$

(ii) Product of matrics $\begin{bmatrix} 1 & -1 & 0 \\ 2 & 3 & 4 \\ 0 & 1 & 2 \end{bmatrix}\begin{bmatrix} 2 & 2 & -4 \\ -4 & 2 & -4 \\ 2 & -1 & 5 \end{bmatrix}$,

and system of equations

$x - y = 3,\ 2x + 3y + 4z = 17,\ y + 2z = 7$

12 Two schools P and Q want to award their selected students on the values of Tolerance, Kindness and Leadership. The school P wants to award ₹ x each, ₹ y each and ₹ z each for the three respective values to 3, 2 and 1 students respectively with a total award money of ₹ 2200. School Q wants to spend ₹ 3100 to award it 4, 1 and 3 students on the respective values (by giving the same award money to the three values as school P). If the total amount of award for one prize on each values is ₹ 1200, using matrices, find the award money for each value.

13 Two factories decided to award their employees for three values of (a) adaptable to new techniques, (b) careful alert in difficult situations and (c) keeping calm in tense honour, respectively 2, 4 and 3 employees with a total prize money of ₹ 29000. The second factory decided to honour, respectively 5, 2 and 3 employees with the prize money of ₹ 30500. If the three prizes per person together cost ₹ 9500, then

(i) represent the above situation by a matrix equation and form linear equations using matrix multiplication.

(ii) Solve these equations using matrices.

Hints & Solutions

1. (i) Similar as Example 1 (i). **Ans.** $x = 1, y = -2$

(ii) Similar as Example 1 (i). **Ans.** $x = m + n, y = m - n$

2. (i) Similar as Example 3. **Ans.** $x = 1,\ y = 2$ and $z = 5$

(ii) Similar as Example 3. **Ans.** $x = 3,\ y = 2$ and $z = 1$

3. (i) Similar as Example 7 (i). **Ans.** Consistent

(ii) Similar as Example 7 (ii). **Ans.** Inconsistent

(iii) Similar as Example 7 (i). **Ans.** Consistent

(iv) Given system of linear equations is

$x + y + z = 1,\ 2x + 3y + 2z = 2$ and $bx + by + 2bz = 4$

It can be written in matrix form as $AX = B$,

where $A = \begin{bmatrix} 1 & 1 & 1 \\ 2 & 3 & 2 \\ b & b & 2b \end{bmatrix}, X = \begin{bmatrix} x \\ y \\ z \end{bmatrix}$ and $B = \begin{bmatrix} 1 \\ 2 \\ 4 \end{bmatrix}$

Here, $|A| = \begin{vmatrix} 1 & 1 & 1 \\ 2 & 3 & 2 \\ b & b & 2b \end{vmatrix}$

$= 1[6b - 2b] - 1[4b - 2b] + 1[2b - 3b]$

$= 4b - 2b - b = b \neq 0$

Since, A is non-singular. So, A^{-1} exists.

Hence, the given system of equations is consistent.

(v) Similar as Part (iv). **Ans.** Inconsistent

(vi) Similar as Part (iv). **Ans.** Consistent

4. (i) For infinite number of solutions,

$$D = D_x = D_y = 0$$

$$D = \begin{vmatrix} 1 & 2 \\ 4 & 8 \end{vmatrix} = 8 - 8 = 0$$

$$D_x = \begin{vmatrix} 10 & 2 \\ 40 & 8 \end{vmatrix} = 80 - 80 = 0$$

$$D_y = \begin{vmatrix} 1 & 10 \\ 4 & 40 \end{vmatrix} = 40 - 40 = 0$$

Hence, the system of equation has infinite number of solutions. Let $y = K$, then $x = 10 - 2K$.

(ii) For infinite number of solutions,

$$D = D_x = D_y = D_z = 0$$

$$D = \begin{vmatrix} 1 & -3 & 4 \\ 1 & 2 & 4 \\ 2 & -6 & 8 \end{vmatrix}$$

$$= 1(16 + 24) + 3(8 - 8) + 4(-6 - 4)$$

$$40 - 40 = 0$$

$$D_x = \begin{vmatrix} 10 & -3 & 4 \\ 6 & 2 & 4 \\ 20 & -6 & 8 \end{vmatrix}$$

$$= 10[16 + 24] + 3[48 - 80] + 4[-36 - 40]$$

$$= 400 - 96 - 304 = 0$$

$$D_y = \begin{vmatrix} 1 & 10 & 4 \\ 1 & 6 & 4 \\ 2 & 20 & 8 \end{vmatrix}$$

$$= 1(48 - 80) - 10(8 - 8) + 4(20 - 12)$$

$$= -32 + 32 = 0$$

$$D_z = \begin{vmatrix} 1 & -3 & 10 \\ 1 & 2 & 6 \\ 2 & -6 & 20 \end{vmatrix}$$

$$= 1(40 + 36) + 3(20 - 12) + 10(-6 - 4)$$

$$= 76 + 24 - 100 = 0$$

Hence, the given system of equation has infinite number of solution.

Let $z = K$

$$x - 3y = 10 - 4K \text{ and } x + 2y = 6 - 4K$$

Again, use Cramer's rule,

$$D = \begin{vmatrix} 1 & -3 \\ 1 & 2 \end{vmatrix} = 2 + 3 = 5$$

$$D_x = \begin{vmatrix} 10 - 4K & -3 \\ 6 - 4K & 2 \end{vmatrix} = 20 - 8K + 18 - 12K$$

$$= 38 - 20K$$

$$D_y = \begin{vmatrix} 1 & 10 - 4K \\ 1 & 6 - 4K \end{vmatrix} = 6 - 4K - 10 + 4K = -4$$

$$x = \frac{D_x}{D} = \frac{38 - 20K}{5}, \quad y = \frac{D_y}{D} = \frac{-4}{5}$$

5. Similar as Example 6.

Ans. (i) $p \neq 2, q \neq 3$ (ii) $p = 2$ (iii) $p \neq 2, q = 3$

6. Similar as Example 5. **Ans.** $f(x) = 4x^2 - 2x + 7$

7. (i) Similar as Example 9 (i). **Ans.** $x = -\frac{5}{11}, y = \frac{12}{11}$

(ii) Similar as Example 9 (i). Ans. $x = 2, y = -3$

(iii) Similar as Example 9 (ii). **Ans.** $x = 2, y = 1, z = 3$

(iv) Similar as Example 9 (ii). **Ans.** $x = 3, y = -2, z = 1$

(v) Similar as Example 9 (ii). **Ans.** $x = 1, y = \frac{1}{2}, z = -\frac{3}{2}$

(vi) Similar as Example 9 (ii). **Ans.** $x = 3, y = 1, z = 1$

(vii) Similar as Example 9 (ii). **Ans.** $x = 1, y = 2, z = -1$

8. (i) Similar as Example 12.

$$\textbf{Ans. } A^{-1} = \begin{bmatrix} -\frac{1}{11} & \frac{1}{11} & \frac{2}{11} \\ \frac{8}{11} & -\frac{19}{11} & \frac{6}{11} \\ -\frac{3}{11} & \frac{14}{11} & \frac{-5}{11} \end{bmatrix}, x = 1, y = 1 \text{ and } z = 1$$

(ii) Similar as Example 12.

$$\textbf{Ans. } A^{-1} = \frac{1}{4}\begin{bmatrix} -2 & 0 & 2 \\ 5 & -2 & -1 \\ 1 & 2 & -1 \end{bmatrix}, x = 3, y = 1, z = 2$$

(iii) Similar as Example 12.

$$\textbf{Ans. } A^{-1} = \begin{bmatrix} 0 & 1 & -2 \\ -2 & 9 & -23 \\ -1 & 5 & -13 \end{bmatrix} x = 1, y = 2, z = 3$$

(iv) Similar as Example 12.

$$\textbf{Ans. } A^{-1} = \frac{1}{10}\begin{bmatrix} 4 & -5 & 1 \\ 2 & 0 & -2 \\ 2 & 5 & 3 \end{bmatrix}, x = 2, y = 0, z = 2$$

9. Similar as Example 10.

Ans. (i) $x = \frac{1}{2}, y = -1, z = 1$

(ii) $x = \frac{1}{2}, y = \frac{1}{3}, z = \frac{1}{5}$

10. Let $\frac{1}{x} = p, \frac{1}{y} = q$ and $\frac{1}{z} = r$

Then, the given equations becomes

$$2p + 3q + 10r = 2,$$

$$4p - 6q + 5r = 5$$

and $$6p + 9q - 20r = -4$$

This system can be written as $AX = B$, where

$$A = \begin{bmatrix} 2 & 3 & 10 \\ 4 & -6 & 5 \\ 6 & 9 & -20 \end{bmatrix}, X = \begin{bmatrix} p \\ q \\ r \end{bmatrix}, B = \begin{bmatrix} 2 \\ 5 \\ -4 \end{bmatrix}$$

$$\text{Here, } |A| = \begin{vmatrix} 2 & 3 & 10 \\ 4 & -6 & 5 \\ 6 & 9 & -20 \end{vmatrix}$$

$$= 2(120 - 45) - 3(-80 - 30) + 10(36 + 36)$$

$$= 150 + 330 + 720 = 1200 \neq 0$$

Thus, A is non-singular, therefore its inverse exists and the above system has a unique solution given by

$$X = A^{-1}B$$

Cofactors of $|A|$ are

$$A_{11}=75,\quad A_{21}=150,\quad A_{31}=75$$
$$A_{12}=110,\quad A_{22}=-100,\quad A_{32}=30$$
$$A_{13}=72,\quad A_{23}=0,\quad A_{33}=-24$$

$$\text{adj}(A)=\begin{bmatrix}75 & 110 & 72\\ 150 & -100 & 0\\ 75 & 30 & -24\end{bmatrix}'=\begin{bmatrix}75 & 150 & 75\\ 110 & -100 & 30\\ 72 & 0 & -24\end{bmatrix}$$

$$A^{-1}=\frac{1}{|A|}(\text{adj }A)=\frac{1}{1200}\begin{bmatrix}75 & 150 & 75\\ 110 & -100 & 30\\ 72 & 0 & -24\end{bmatrix}$$

Now, $X=A^{-1}B$

$$\Rightarrow \begin{bmatrix}p\\ q\\ r\end{bmatrix}=\frac{1}{1200}\begin{bmatrix}75 & 150 & 75\\ 110 & -100 & 30\\ 72 & 0 & -24\end{bmatrix}\begin{bmatrix}2\\ 5\\ -4\end{bmatrix}$$

$$=\frac{1}{1200}\begin{bmatrix}150+750-300\\ 220-500-120\\ 144+0+96\end{bmatrix}$$

$$=\frac{1}{1200}\begin{bmatrix}900-300\\ 220-620\\ 144+96\end{bmatrix}=\frac{1}{1200}\begin{bmatrix}600\\ -400\\ 240\end{bmatrix}=\begin{bmatrix}1/2\\ -1/3\\ 1/5\end{bmatrix}$$

$$\Rightarrow \quad p=\frac{1}{2},\ q=-\frac{1}{3},\ r=\frac{1}{5}$$

$\therefore \quad x=2,\ y=-3$ and $z=5$

11. (i) Similar as Example 13. **Ans.** $x=0,\ y=5,\ z=3$
    (ii) Similar as Example 13. **Ans.** $x=2,\ y=-1,\ z=4$
12. **Hint** The system of equations is $3x+2y+z=2200$, $4x+y+3z=3100$ and $x+y+z=1200$.
    Then, similar as Example 15.
    Ans. $x=300,\ y=400,\ z=500$
13. (i) **Hint** The system of equations is $2x+4y+3z=29000$, $5x+2y+3z=30500$ and $x+y+z=9500$.
    (ii) **Hint** Solve system of equations obtained in part (i) similar as Example 16.
    Ans. $x=2500,\ y=3000,\ z=4000$

Exam Pattern Exercise

Part A - Objective Type Questions

Multiple Choice Type Questions

1 Which of the following is correct? [NCERT]
(a) Determinant is a square matrix
(b) Determinant is a number associated to a matrix
(c) Determinant is a number associated to a square matrix
(d) None of the above

2 If a, b, c are in AP, then determinant $\begin{vmatrix} x+2 & x+3 & x+2a \\ x+3 & x+4 & x+2b \\ x+4 & x+5 & x+2c \end{vmatrix}$ is
(a) zero (b) 1
(c) x (d) $2x$

3 A square matrix A is said to be singular, if
(a) $|A|=0$ (b) $|A|\neq 0$
(c) $|A|=-1$ (d) $|A|=1$

4 A and B are square matrices each of order 3 such that $|A|=-1$ and $|B|=3$. What is the value of $|3AB|$? [CBSE 2023]
(a) -9 (b) -18
(c) -27 (d) -81

5 If $\begin{vmatrix} 2 & 3 & 2 \\ x & x & x \\ 4 & 9 & 1 \end{vmatrix}+3=0$, then the value of x is [CBSE 2023]
(a) -1 (b) 0
(c) 1 (d) 3

6 If A is a square matrix such that $|A|=2$, then $|AA^T|$ is equal to
(a) 2 (b) 4 (c) 8 (d) 16

7 The inverse of matrix $A=\begin{bmatrix} 4 & -1 \\ 2 & 1 \end{bmatrix}$ is [CBSE 2025]
(a) $\frac{1}{6}\begin{bmatrix} -4 & 2 \\ -1 & -1 \end{bmatrix}$ (b) $\begin{bmatrix} 1/3 & 1/6 \\ 2/3 & -1/6 \end{bmatrix}$
(c) $\begin{bmatrix} 1/6 & 1/6 \\ -1/3 & 2/3 \end{bmatrix}$ (d) $\begin{bmatrix} -2/3 & 1/6 \\ -1/3 & -1/6 \end{bmatrix}$

8 The value of $\Delta=\begin{vmatrix} 42 & 2 & 5 \\ 79 & 7 & 9 \\ 29 & 5 & 3 \end{vmatrix}$ is [CBSE 2024]
(a) 0 (b) 1 (c) -3 (d) -15

9 If $A=\begin{bmatrix} a & 0 & 0 \\ 0 & a & 0 \\ 0 & 0 & a \end{bmatrix}$, then $|\text{adj } A|$ is equal to
(a) a^{27} (b) a^9 (c) a^6 (d) a^2

10 For non-singular square matrix A, B and C of the same order $(AB^{-1}C)^{-1}=$
(a) $A^{-1}BC^{-1}$ (b) $C^{-1}B^{-1}A^{-1}$ (c) CBA^{-1} (d) $C^{-1}BA^{-1}$

Assertion-Reason Based Questions

Directions (Q. Nos. 11-14) *In the questions given below are two statements labelled as Assertion (A) and Reason (R). In the context of the two statements, which one of the following is correct?*
(a) Both A and R are correct; R is the correct explanation of A
(b) Both A and R are correct; R is not the correct explanation of A
(c) A is correct; R is incorrect
(d) R is correct; A is incorrect

11 **Assertion** (A) If Δ_1 the determinant obtained by applying $R_i \to mR_i$ to determinant Δ, then $\Delta=\frac{1}{m}\Delta_1$.
Reason The value of determinant remains unchanged, if the elements of any row (or column) are added k times the corresponding elements of any other row (or column) of the determinant.

12 **Assertion** (A) For matrix $A=\begin{bmatrix} -1 & -2 & -2 \\ 2 & 1 & -2 \\ 2 & -2 & 1 \end{bmatrix}$,
$adj\ A=\begin{bmatrix} -3 & 6 & 6 \\ -6 & -3 & -6 \\ 6 & 6 & -3 \end{bmatrix}$
Reason (R) The adjoint of a square matrix $A=[a_{ij}]_{n\times n}$ is defined as the transpose of the matrix formed by corresponding C_{ij} cofactors of the elements $|A|$.

13 **Assertion** (A) For $\lambda=2$, matrix $\frac{1}{13}\begin{bmatrix} 2 & (1-3\lambda) \\ (2\lambda-1) & -1 \end{bmatrix}$ is the inverse matrix of the matrix $\begin{bmatrix} -1 & 5 \\ -3 & 2 \end{bmatrix}$.
Reason (R) If A is a non-singular matrix (i.e. $|A|\neq 0$), then $A^{-1}=\frac{1}{|A|}\text{adj}(A)$.

14 **Assertion** (A) Equations $3x+6y=15$ and $2x+4y=10$ are consistent with infinitely many solutions.
Reason (R) If $D=0$ and $D_1=D_2=0$, then the system of equations is consistent with infinitely many solutions, where $D=\begin{vmatrix} a_1 & b_1 \\ a_2 & b_2 \end{vmatrix}$, $D_1=\begin{vmatrix} c_1 & b_1 \\ c_2 & b_2 \end{vmatrix}$ and $D_2=\begin{vmatrix} a_1 & c_1 \\ a_2 & c_2 \end{vmatrix}$ for the equations $a_1x+b_1y=c_1$ and $a_2x+b_2y=c_2$.

Part B - Descriptive Questions

Very Short Answer Type Questions

15 If $\begin{vmatrix} 3x & 7 \\ -2 & 4 \end{vmatrix} = \begin{vmatrix} 8 & 7 \\ 6 & 4 \end{vmatrix}$, then find the value of x.

16 If $A = \begin{bmatrix} 1 & 2 \\ 3 & -1 \end{bmatrix}$ and $B = \begin{bmatrix} 1 & 0 \\ -1 & 0 \end{bmatrix}$, then find $|AB|$.

17 If $A = \begin{bmatrix} 1 & 2 \\ 4 & 2 \end{bmatrix}$, then show that $|2A| = 4|A|$.

18 If $x \in N$ and $\begin{vmatrix} x+3 & -2 \\ -3x & 2x \end{vmatrix} = 8$, then find the value of x.

19 If $\begin{vmatrix} 2x & x+3 \\ 2(x+1) & x+1 \end{vmatrix} = \begin{vmatrix} 1 & 5 \\ 3 & 3 \end{vmatrix}$, then write the value of x.

20 If $A = \begin{bmatrix} x & 2 \\ 2 & x \end{bmatrix}$ and $|A^3| = 125$, then find the value(s) of x.

21 If A is a square matrix of order 3 and $|3A| = k|A|$, then find the value of k.

22 If A is an invertible matrix of order 2 and $\det(A) = 4$, then write the value of $\det(A^{-1})$.

23 If A_{ij} is the cofactor of the element a_{ij} of the determinant $\begin{vmatrix} 1 & 3 & -2 \\ 4 & -5 & 6 \\ 3 & 5 & 2 \end{vmatrix}$, then write the value of $a_{32} \cdot A_{32}$.

24 Determine the integral value(s) for x for which the matrix A is singular

$$A = \begin{bmatrix} x+1 & -3 & 4 \\ -5 & x+2 & 2 \\ 4 & 1 & x-6 \end{bmatrix}$$

[CBSE 2023]

25 If A and B are square matrices of order 3 such that $|A| = -1$ and $|B| = 3$, then find $|3AB|$.

26 If A is a square matrix of order 3 such that $|A| = -2$, then find $|3\text{adj}A|$.

Short Answer Type Questions

27 If A is skew-symmetric matrix of order 3, then prove that $\det A = 0$.

28 If $f(x) = \begin{vmatrix} 0 & x-a & x-b \\ x+a & 0 & x-c \\ x+b & x+c & 0 \end{vmatrix}$, then show that $f(0) = 0$.

29 If $A = \begin{bmatrix} x+4, & 2 \\ 3 & 1 \end{bmatrix}$, $B = \begin{bmatrix} x & 2x-1 \\ 2 & 5 \end{bmatrix}$ and $|AB| = 12$, then find the value of x.

30 Prove that the determinant $\begin{vmatrix} x & \sin\theta & \cos\theta \\ -\sin\theta & -x & 1 \\ \cos\theta & 1 & x \end{vmatrix}$ is independent of θ.

31 If the value of a third order determinant is 12, then find the value of the determinant formed by replacing each element by its cofactor.

32 If A is a non-singular symmetric matrix, then write whether A^{-1} is symmetric or skew-symmetric.

33 If $A = \begin{bmatrix} 3 & -5 \\ 4 & 2 \end{bmatrix}$, then find $A(\text{adj}A)$.

34 If $A = \begin{bmatrix} 4 & 5 \\ 2 & 1 \end{bmatrix}$, then show that $A - 3I = 2(I + 3A^{-1})$.

35 If $A = \begin{bmatrix} 3 & -2 \\ 4 & -2 \end{bmatrix}$, then find the value of λ, so that $A^2 = \lambda A - 2I$. Hence, find A^{-1}.

36 Check whether the equation is consistent or inconsistent

$$2x - y = 5,\ 4x - 2y = 7$$

37 Use Cramer's rule to solve the system of equation

$$x + y + z = 1$$
$$ax + by + cz = K$$
$$a^2x + b^2y + c^2z = K^2, \text{ where } a \neq b \neq c$$

38 Solve the following system of linear equations by Crammer's rule

$$6x + y - 3z - 5 = 0$$
$$x + 3y - 2z - 5 = 0$$
$$2x + y + 4z - 8 = 0$$

Long Answer Type Questions

39 If $A = \begin{bmatrix} 1 & 3 & 3 \\ 1 & 4 & 3 \\ 1 & 3 & 4 \end{bmatrix}$, then verify that $A \cdot \text{adj}(A) = |A| I$. Also, find A^{-1}.

40 Find the inverse of the matrix $A = \begin{bmatrix} a & b \\ c & \frac{1+bc}{a} \end{bmatrix}$ and show that $aA^{-1} = (a^2 + bc + 1)I - aA$.

41 Suppose $A = \begin{bmatrix} 2 & 2 & 1 \\ -2 & 1 & 2 \\ 1 & -2 & 2 \end{bmatrix}$ and $B = \begin{bmatrix} 1 & 3 & 2 \\ 1 & 1 & 1 \\ 2 & -3 & 1 \end{bmatrix}$, verify that $(AB)^{-1} = B^{-1}A^{-1}$.

42 Let $A = \begin{bmatrix} 1 & -2 & 1 \\ -2 & 3 & 1 \\ 1 & 1 & 5 \end{bmatrix}$, verify that

$$[\text{adj}\,A]^{-1} = \text{adj}(A^{-1}).$$

43 Using matrices, solve the system of equations $4x + 3y + 2z = 60$, $x + 2y + 3z = 45$ and $6x + 2y + 3z = 70$.

44 If $A=\begin{bmatrix}3 & -4 & 2\\ 2 & 3 & 5\\ 1 & 0 & 1\end{bmatrix}$, then find A^{-1} and hence solve the following system of equations.

$3x-4y+2z=-1, 2x+3y+5z=7$ and $x+z=2$

45 Use product $\begin{bmatrix}1 & -1 & 2\\ 0 & 2 & -3\\ 3 & -2 & 4\end{bmatrix}\begin{bmatrix}-2 & 0 & 1\\ 9 & 2 & -3\\ 6 & 1 & -2\end{bmatrix}$ to solve the system of equations

$x-y+2z=1, 2y-3z=1$ and $3x-2y+4z=2$

46 The cost of 4 kg onion, 3 kg wheat and 2 kg rice is ₹ 60. The cost of 2 kg onion, 4 kg wheat and 6 kg rice is ₹ 90. The cost of 6 kg onion, 2 kg wheat and 3 kg rice is ₹ 70. Find the cost of each item per kg by matrix method.

Case Study Based Questions

47 Two factories decided to award their employees for three values of (a) adaptable to new techniques, (b) careful and alert in difficult situations and (c) keeping calm in tense situations, at the rate of ₹ x, ₹ y and ₹ z per person respectively. The first factory decided to honour respectively 2, 4 and 3 employees with a total prize money of ₹ 29000. The second factory decided to honour respectively 5, 2 and 3 employees with the prize money of ₹ 30500. If the three prizes per person together cost ₹ 9500.

The above situation is expressed by a matrix equation as below

$$AX=B$$

where, A is 3×3 matrix and X and B are 3×1 matrix.

On the basis of above information, answer the following questions.

(i) The matrix A is

(a) $\begin{bmatrix}2 & 4 & 3\\ 5 & 1 & 2\\ 2 & 4 & 1\end{bmatrix}$ (b) $\begin{bmatrix}2 & 4 & 3\\ 5 & 2 & 3\\ 1 & 1 & 1\end{bmatrix}$

(c) $\begin{bmatrix}5 & 2 & 1\\ 4 & 2 & 1\\ 3 & 2 & 4\end{bmatrix}$ (d) None of these

(ii) Inverse of matrix A is

(a) $\begin{bmatrix}1 & 1 & 6\\ 2 & 1 & 9\\ 3 & 2 & 16\end{bmatrix}$ (b) $\begin{bmatrix}1 & 2 & -3\\ 1 & 1 & -2\\ -6 & -9 & 16\end{bmatrix}$

(c) $\begin{bmatrix}1 & 1 & -6\\ 2 & 1 & -9\\ -3 & -2 & 16\end{bmatrix}$ (d) $\begin{bmatrix}1 & 2 & 3\\ 1 & 1 & 2\\ 6 & 9 & 16\end{bmatrix}$

(iii) The value of x is

(a) 2500 (b) 3000

(c) 4000 (d) 4500

(iv) The value of y is

(a) 2500 (b) 3000

(c) 4000 (d) 4500

(v) The value of z is

(a) 2500 (b) 3000

(c) 4000 (d) 4500

48 On her birthday, Prema decides to donate some money to children of an orphanage home.

If there are 8 children less, everyone gets ₹ 10 more. However, if there are 16 children more, everyone gets ₹ 10 less.

Let the number of children in the orphanage home be x and the amount to be donated to each child be ₹ y.

Based on the above information, answer the following questions. [CBSE 2024]

(i) Write the system of linear equations in x and y form of the given situation.

(ii) Write the system of linear equations, obtained in (i) above in matrix form $AX=B$.

(iii) (a) Find the inverse of matrix A.

Or

(b) Determine the values of x and y.

Hints & Solutions

1. (c) 2. (a) 3. (a) 4. (d)
5. (a) 6. (b) 7. (c) 8. (a)
9. (c) 10. (d) 11. (b) 12. (d)
13. (a) 14. (a)

15. **Hint** Given, $\begin{vmatrix} 3x & 7 \\ -2 & 4 \end{vmatrix} = \begin{vmatrix} 8 & 7 \\ 6 & 4 \end{vmatrix}$

$\Rightarrow \quad 3x(4) + 14 = 8(4) - 6(7)$

$\Rightarrow \quad 12x + 14 = -10 \Rightarrow x = -2$ **Ans.** -2

16. **Hint** $AB = \begin{bmatrix} 1 & 2 \\ 3 & -1 \end{bmatrix}\begin{bmatrix} 1 & 0 \\ -1 & 0 \end{bmatrix} = \begin{bmatrix} 1-2 & 0+0 \\ 3+1 & 0+0 \end{bmatrix} = \begin{bmatrix} -1 & 0 \\ 4 & 0 \end{bmatrix}$

$\Rightarrow |AB| = \begin{vmatrix} -1 & 0 \\ 4 & 0 \end{vmatrix} = 0 - 0 = 0$ **Ans.** 0

17. **Hint** We have, $A = \begin{bmatrix} 1 & 2 \\ 4 & 2 \end{bmatrix} \Rightarrow |A| = \begin{vmatrix} 1 & 2 \\ 4 & 2 \end{vmatrix} = 2 - 8 = -6$

$\therefore \quad 4|A| = 4(-6) = -24$ ...(i)

and $|2A| = \begin{vmatrix} 2 & 4 \\ 8 & 4 \end{vmatrix} = 8 - 32 = -24$ ...(ii)

From Eqs. (i) and (ii), we get

$$|2A| = 4|A|$$

18. **Hint** Similar as Question 4 (ii) of Topic practice 1. **Ans.** 2

19. **Hint** Similar as Question 15. **Ans.** 1

20. **Hint** Given, $A = \begin{bmatrix} x & 2 \\ 2 & x \end{bmatrix}$ and $|A^3| = 125$

$\Rightarrow \quad |A|^3 = 5^3 \Rightarrow |A| = 5$

$\therefore \begin{vmatrix} x & 2 \\ 2 & x \end{vmatrix} = 5 \Rightarrow x^2 - 4 = 5 \Rightarrow x = \pm 3$ **Ans.** ± 3

21. **Hint** Given, $|3A| = K|A|$ ...(i)

$\because \quad |3A| = 3 \times 3 \times 3|A|$

$\Rightarrow \quad |3A| = 27|A|$ ...(ii)

From Eqs. (i) and (ii), we get

$K = 27$ **Ans.** 27

22. **Hint** We know, $AA^{-1} = I$

$\therefore \quad |AA^{-1}| = |I| \Rightarrow |A||A^{-1}| = |I|$

$\Rightarrow \quad |A^{-1}| = \dfrac{1}{|A|}$ $[\because |I| = I]$

$\Rightarrow \quad |A^{-1}| = \dfrac{1}{4}$ $[\because |A| = 4 \text{ (given)}]$

Ans. $\dfrac{1}{4}$

23. **Hint** Similar as Example 4 of Topic 2. **Ans.** 70

24. **Hint** Similar as Example 6 of Topic 2. **Ans.** 0

25. **Hint** $\because \quad |3AB| = 3^3|AB| = 27 \times |A| \times |B|$

$\Rightarrow \quad |3AB| = 27 \times (-1) \times (3)$ $[\because |A| = -1, |B| = 3 \text{ (given)}]$

Ans. -81

26. **Hint** Given, $|A| = -2$

$\because \quad |\text{adj } A| = |A|^{n-1} = (-2)^{3-1} = 4$

$\therefore |3\text{adj } A| = 3^3 |\text{adj } A| = 27 \times 4 = 108$

Ans. 108

27. **Hint** Since, A is a skew-symmetric matrix

$\therefore \quad A = -A^T$

$\Rightarrow \quad |A| = -|A^T|$ ...(i)

Also, we know that $|A| = |A^T|$ ...(ii)

From Eqs. (i) and (ii), we get

$$|A| = -|A| \Rightarrow 2|A| = 0 \Rightarrow |A| = 0$$

28. **Hint** $f(0) = \begin{vmatrix} 0 & -a & -b \\ a & 0 & -c \\ b & c & 0 \end{vmatrix} = a(bc) - b(ac) = abc - abc = 0$

29. **Hint** Find product of $|A|$ and $|B|$, then similar as Question 4 (ii) of Topic practice 1. **Ans.** ± 4

30. **Hint** Let $\Delta = \begin{vmatrix} x & \sin\theta & \cos\theta \\ -\sin\theta & -x & 1 \\ \cos\theta & 1 & x \end{vmatrix}$

$\Rightarrow \quad \Delta = x(-x^2 - 1) - \sin\theta(-x\sin\theta - \cos\theta) + \cos\theta(-\sin\theta + x\cos\theta)$ [expanding along R_1]

$\Rightarrow \quad \Delta = -x^3 - x + x(\sin^2\theta + \cos^2\theta)$

$\Rightarrow \quad \Delta = -x^3 - x + x$ $[\because \sin^2\theta + \cos^2\theta = 1]$

$\Rightarrow \quad \Delta = -x^3$

Hence, the given determinant is independent of θ.

31. **Hint** $\because |\text{adj } A| = |A|^{n-1}$

For $n = 3$, $|\text{adj } A| = |A|^{3-1}$

$|adj\ A| = (12)^2$ $[\because |A| = 12]$

$= 144$

32. **Hint** Since, A is a non-singular symmetric matrix.

Then, $|A| \neq 0$ and $A^T = A$

Now, $(A^{-1})^T = (A^T)^{-1} \Rightarrow (A^{-1})^T = A^{-1}$ $[\because A^T = A]$

Hence, A^{-1} is symmetric matrix.

33. **Hint** Similar as Example 1 (i) of Topic 3. **Ans.** $\begin{bmatrix} 26 & 0 \\ 0 & 26 \end{bmatrix}$

34. **Hint** Similar as Exampe 10 of Topic 3.

35. **Hint** Given, $A = \begin{bmatrix} 3 & -2 \\ 4 & -2 \end{bmatrix}$

$\therefore \quad A^2 = \begin{bmatrix} 3 & -2 \\ 4 & -2 \end{bmatrix}\begin{bmatrix} 3 & -2 \\ 4 & -2 \end{bmatrix} = \begin{bmatrix} 1 & -2 \\ 4 & -4 \end{bmatrix}$

Now, $\quad A^2 = \lambda A - 2I \Rightarrow \lambda A = A^2 + 2I$

$\Rightarrow \lambda \begin{bmatrix} 3 & -2 \\ 4 & -2 \end{bmatrix} = \begin{bmatrix} 1 & -2 \\ 4 & -4 \end{bmatrix} + \begin{bmatrix} 2 & 0 \\ 0 & 2 \end{bmatrix}$

$\Rightarrow \begin{bmatrix} 3\lambda & -2\lambda \\ 4\lambda & -2\lambda \end{bmatrix} = \begin{bmatrix} 3 & -2 \\ 4 & -2 \end{bmatrix} \Rightarrow \lambda = 1$

So, $A^2 = A - 2I$

On multiplying by A^{-1} both sides, we get

$$A \cdot A \cdot A^{-1} = A \cdot A^{-1} - 2I\,A^{-1}$$

$$\Rightarrow \quad 2A^{-1} = I - A$$

$$\Rightarrow \quad 2A^{-1} = \begin{bmatrix} 1 & 0 \\ 0 & 1 \end{bmatrix} - \begin{bmatrix} 3 & -2 \\ 4 & -2 \end{bmatrix}$$

Ans. $\lambda = 1,\ A^{-1} = \begin{bmatrix} -1 & 1 \\ -2 & \frac{3}{2} \end{bmatrix}$

36. **Hint** Similar as Example 7 of Topic 4.

Ans. Inconsistent

37. **Hint** Similar as Example 3 of Topic 4.

Ans. $x = \dfrac{(k-b)(c-k)}{(a-b)(c-a)},\ y = \dfrac{(a-k)(c-k)}{(a-b)(b-c)}$

and $z = \dfrac{(b-k)(k-a)}{(b-c)(a-b)}$

38. **Hint** Similar as Example 3 of Topic 4.

Ans. $x = 1,\ y = 2$ and $z = 1$

39. **Hint** We have,

$$A = \begin{bmatrix} 1 & 3 & 3 \\ 1 & 4 & 3 \\ 1 & 3 & 4 \end{bmatrix}$$

$$\therefore \quad |A| = \begin{vmatrix} 1 & 3 & 3 \\ 1 & 4 & 3 \\ 1 & 3 & 4 \end{vmatrix} = 1(7) - 3(1) + 3(-1) = 1$$

$$\therefore \quad \text{adj } A = \begin{bmatrix} 7 & -1 & -1 \\ -3 & 1 & 0 \\ -3 & 0 & 1 \end{bmatrix}^T = \begin{bmatrix} 7 & -3 & -3 \\ -1 & 1 & 0 \\ -1 & 0 & 1 \end{bmatrix}$$

$$\text{Now, } A\,(\text{adj } A) = \begin{bmatrix} 1 & 3 & 3 \\ 1 & 4 & 3 \\ 1 & 3 & 4 \end{bmatrix}\begin{bmatrix} 7 & -3 & -3 \\ -1 & 1 & 0 \\ -1 & 0 & 1 \end{bmatrix} = \begin{bmatrix} 1 & 0 & 0 \\ 0 & 1 & 0 \\ 0 & 0 & 1 \end{bmatrix}$$

$$\because \quad A^{-1} = \frac{1}{|A|}\text{adj } A = \frac{1}{1}\begin{bmatrix} 7 & -3 & -3 \\ -1 & 1 & 0 \\ -1 & 0 & 1 \end{bmatrix}$$

Ans. $\begin{bmatrix} 7 & -3 & -3 \\ -1 & 1 & 0 \\ -1 & 0 & 1 \end{bmatrix}$

40. **Hint** We have, $A = \begin{bmatrix} a & b \\ c & \dfrac{1+bc}{a} \end{bmatrix}$

Here, $|A| = 1 \neq 0$

$\therefore A^{-1}$ exists.

$$\therefore \quad \text{adj } A = \begin{bmatrix} \dfrac{1+bc}{a} & -c \\ -b & a \end{bmatrix}^T = \begin{bmatrix} \dfrac{1+bc}{a} & -b \\ -c & a \end{bmatrix}$$

$$\therefore \quad A^{-1} = \begin{bmatrix} \dfrac{1+bc}{a} & -b \\ -c & a \end{bmatrix} \qquad \left[\because A^{-1} = \frac{1}{|A|}\cdot \text{adj } A\right]$$

$$\text{Now, LHS} = aA^{-1} = a\begin{bmatrix} \dfrac{1+bc}{a} & -b \\ -c & a \end{bmatrix} = \begin{bmatrix} 1+bc & -ba \\ -ac & a^2 \end{bmatrix}$$

$$\text{RHS} = (a^2 + bc + 1)I - aA$$

$$= \begin{bmatrix} (a^2+bc+1) & 0 \\ 0 & (a^2+bc+1) \end{bmatrix} - \begin{bmatrix} a^2 & ba \\ ac & 1+bc \end{bmatrix}$$

$$= \begin{bmatrix} 1+bc & -ba \\ -ac & a^2 \end{bmatrix} = \text{LHS}$$

41. **Hint** First find A^{-1} and B^{-1}, then find product of B^{-1} and A^{-1} i.e., $B^{-1}A^{-1}$.

Now, find product of matrix A and B i.e. AB, then find inverse of matrix AB i.e. $(AB)^{-1}$ and put these in given condition $(AB)^{-1} = B^{-1}A^{-1}$.

42. **Hint** First find adj A, then find A^{-1} by using

$$A^{-1} = \frac{1}{|A|}\text{adj } A.$$

Now, find inverse of adj A by using

$[\text{adj } A]^{-1} = \dfrac{1}{|\text{adj } A|}\cdot \text{adj}\,(\text{adj } A)$ and also find $\text{adj}\,(A^{-1})$.

Put these values in given condition.

43. **Hint** Similar as Example 9 of Topic 4.

Ans. $x = 5,\ y = 8,\ z = 8$

44. **Hint** Similar as Example 12 of Topic 4.

Ans. $A^{-1} = \dfrac{1}{9}\begin{bmatrix} 3 & 4 & -26 \\ 3 & 1 & -11 \\ -3 & -4 & 17 \end{bmatrix};\ x = 3,\ y = 2,\ z = -1$

45. **Hint** Let $A = \begin{bmatrix} 1 & -1 & 2 \\ 0 & 2 & -3 \\ 3 & -2 & 4 \end{bmatrix}$ and $B = \begin{bmatrix} -2 & 0 & 1 \\ 9 & 2 & -3 \\ 6 & 1 & -2 \end{bmatrix}$

$$\therefore \quad AB = \begin{bmatrix} 1 & -1 & 2 \\ 0 & 2 & -3 \\ 3 & -2 & 4 \end{bmatrix}\begin{bmatrix} -2 & 0 & 1 \\ 9 & 2 & -3 \\ 6 & 1 & -2 \end{bmatrix} = \begin{bmatrix} 1 & 0 & 0 \\ 0 & 1 & 0 \\ 0 & 0 & 1 \end{bmatrix}$$

$$\therefore \quad AB = I$$

$$\Rightarrow \quad A^{-1} = B$$

$$\therefore \quad A^{-1} = \begin{bmatrix} -2 & 0 & 1 \\ 9 & 2 & -3 \\ 6 & 1 & -2 \end{bmatrix} \qquad \text{...(i)}$$

Now, the system of equations can be written in the form $AX = C$

$$\Rightarrow \quad X = A^{-1}C$$

$$\Rightarrow \quad \begin{bmatrix} x \\ y \\ z \end{bmatrix} = \begin{bmatrix} -2 & 0 & 1 \\ 9 & 2 & -3 \\ 6 & 1 & -2 \end{bmatrix}\begin{bmatrix} 1 \\ 1 \\ 2 \end{bmatrix}$$

$$\Rightarrow \quad \begin{bmatrix} x \\ y \\ z \end{bmatrix} = \begin{bmatrix} 0 \\ 5 \\ 3 \end{bmatrix}$$

Ans. $x = 0,\ y = 5$ and $z = 3$

46. **Hint** Let the cost of 1 kg onion, 1 kg wheat and 1 kg of rice be ₹ x, ₹ y and ₹ z, respectively.

Then, according to question,

$4x + 3y + 2z = 60$

$2x + 4y + 6z = 90$

$6x + 2y + 3z = 70$

Solve above equations similar as Example 9 of Topic 4.

Ans. Price of onion per kg is ₹5, wheat per kg is ₹8 and rice per kg is ₹8.

47. (i) (b) (ii) (c) (iii) (a) (iv) (b) (v) (c)

48. **Hint**

(i) $(xy) = (x-8)(y+10)$ and $xy = (x+16)(y-10)$

$$5x - 4y = 40 \text{ and } 5x - 8y = -80$$

(ii) $\begin{bmatrix} 5 & -4 \\ 5 & -8 \end{bmatrix} \begin{bmatrix} x \\ y \end{bmatrix} = \begin{bmatrix} 40 \\ -80 \end{bmatrix}$

(iii) (a) $\dfrac{1}{-20} \begin{bmatrix} -8 & 4 \\ -5 & 5 \end{bmatrix}$

Or

(b) $AX = B \Rightarrow X = A^{-1}B$

$$\begin{bmatrix} x \\ y \end{bmatrix} = \frac{1}{-20} \begin{bmatrix} -8 & 4 \\ -5 & 5 \end{bmatrix} \begin{bmatrix} 40 \\ -80 \end{bmatrix} = \frac{1}{-20} \begin{bmatrix} -640 \\ -600 \end{bmatrix}$$

$\Rightarrow \quad x = 32$ and $y = 30$

CHAPTER 09

Differentiation

In this Chapter...

- Differentiation of Implicit Functions
- Differentiation of Parametric Functions
- Second Order Derivative

Differentiation of Implicit Functions

Let $f(x, y) = 0$ be a function in the form of x and y. If it is not possible to express y as a function of x in the form of $y = \phi(x)$, then y is said to be an implicit function of x.

Then, to find $\frac{dy}{dx}$, we first differentiate both sides of equation w.r.t. x and then take all terms involving $\frac{dy}{dx}$ on LHS and remaining terms on RHS to get required value.

EXAMPLE 1. If $xy = 2$, then find $\frac{dy}{dx}$.

Sol. We have, $xy = 2$

On differentiating both sides w.r.t. x, we get

$$x\frac{dy}{dx} + y = 0$$

$$\Rightarrow \quad x\frac{dy}{dx} = -y \Rightarrow \frac{dy}{dx} = -\frac{y}{x}$$

EXAMPLE 2. If $x^2 + xy + y^2 = 1$, then find $\frac{dy}{dx}$.

Sol. We have, $x^2 + xy + y^2 = 1$

On differentiating both sides w.r.t. x, we get

$$2x + x\frac{dy}{dx} + y + 2y\frac{dy}{dx} = 0$$

$$\Rightarrow \quad \frac{dy}{dx}(x + 2y) = -(2x + y)$$

$$\Rightarrow \quad \frac{dy}{dx} = \frac{-(2x + y)}{x + 2y}$$

EXAMPLE 3. If $x^3 + 3xy = y$, then find $\frac{dy}{dx}$.

Sol. We have, $x^3 + 3xy = y$

On differentiating both sides w.r.t. x, we get

$$3x^2 + 3\left(x\frac{dy}{dx} + y\right) = \frac{dy}{dx}$$

$$\Rightarrow \quad 3x^2 + 3x\frac{dy}{dx} + 3y = \frac{dy}{dx}$$

$$\Rightarrow \quad \frac{dy}{dx}(1 - 3x) = 3(x^2 + y)$$

$$\Rightarrow \quad \frac{dy}{dx} = \frac{3(x^2 + y)}{1 - 3x}$$

EXAMPLE 4. If $x + y = t + \frac{1}{t}$ and $x^3 + y^3 = t^3 + \frac{1}{t^3}$, then prove that $\frac{dy}{dx} = -\frac{1}{x^2}$.

Sol. Given, $(x + y) = t + \frac{1}{t}$

On cubing both sides, we get

$$(x + y)^3 = \left(t + \frac{1}{t}\right)^3$$

$$\Rightarrow x^3 + y^3 + 3xy(x + y) = t^3 + \frac{1}{t^3} + 3\left(t + \frac{1}{t}\right)$$

$$[\because (a + b)^3 = a^3 + b^3 + 3ab(a + b)]$$

$$\Rightarrow x^3 + y^3 + 3xy(x + y) = x^3 + y^3 + 3(x + y)$$

$$\Rightarrow \quad 3xy(x + y) = 3(x + y)$$

$$\left[\because x^3 + y^3 = t^3 + \frac{1}{t^3} \text{ and } (x + y) = t + \frac{1}{t}\right]$$

$$\Rightarrow \quad xy = 1 \quad \text{...(i)}$$

On differentiating both sides w.r.t. x, we get

$$x \cdot \frac{dy}{dx} + y \cdot \frac{d}{dx}(x) = \frac{d}{dx} \cdot 1$$

[product rule of derivative]

$$\Rightarrow \quad x \cdot \frac{dy}{dx} + y = 0 \Rightarrow x\frac{dy}{dx} = -y$$

$$\Rightarrow \quad x\frac{dy}{dx} = -\frac{1}{x} \quad \text{[from Eq. (i)]}$$

$$\Rightarrow \quad \frac{dy}{dx} = -\frac{1}{x^2}$$

Hence proved.

EXAMPLE 5. If $x\sqrt{1+y} + y\sqrt{1+x} = 0$ and $x \neq y$, then prove that $\frac{dy}{dx} = -\frac{1}{(x+1)^2}$.

Sol. We have, $x\sqrt{1+y} + y\sqrt{1+x} = 0$

$$\Rightarrow \quad x\sqrt{1+y} = -y\sqrt{1+x}$$

$$\Rightarrow \quad x^2(1+y) = y^2(1+x)$$

$$\Rightarrow \quad x^2 - y^2 = y^2x - x^2y$$

$$\Rightarrow \quad (x+y)(x-y) = -xy(x-y)$$

$$\Rightarrow \quad (x+y) = -xy \Rightarrow x = -y - xy$$

$$\Rightarrow \quad y(1+x) = -x \Rightarrow y = \frac{-x}{1+x}$$

$$\Rightarrow \quad \frac{dy}{dx} = \frac{-1(1+x) - 1(-x)}{(x+1)^2}$$

$$\Rightarrow \quad \frac{dy}{dx} = \frac{-1}{(x+1)^2}$$

EXAMPLE 6. If $ax^2 + 2hxy + by^2 + 2gx + 2fy + c = 0$, then show that $\frac{dy}{dx} \cdot \frac{dx}{dy} = 1$.

Sol. We have, $ax^2 + 2hxy + by^2 + 2gx + 2fy + c = 0$ ...(i)

On differentiating both sides w.r.t. x, we get

$$\frac{d}{dx}(ax^2) + \frac{d}{dx}(2hxy) + \frac{d}{dx}(by^2) + \frac{d}{dx}(2gx) + \frac{d}{dx}(2fy) + \frac{d}{dx}(c) = 0$$

$$\Rightarrow \quad 2ax + 2h\left(x \cdot \frac{dy}{dx} + y \cdot 1\right) + b \cdot 2y\frac{dy}{dx} + 2g + 2f\frac{dy}{dx} + 0 = 0$$

$$\Rightarrow \quad \frac{dy}{dx}[2hx + 2by + 2f] = -2ax - 2hy - 2g$$

$$\Rightarrow \quad \frac{dy}{dx} = \frac{-2(ax+hy+g)}{2(hx+by+f)} = \frac{-(ax+hy+g)}{(hx+by+f)} \quad \text{...(ii)}$$

Now, differentiating both sides of Eq. (i) w.r.t. y, we get

$$\frac{d}{dy}(ax^2) + \frac{d}{dy}(2hxy) + \frac{d}{dy}(by^2) + \frac{d}{dy}(2gx) + \frac{d}{dy}(2fy) + \frac{d}{dy}(c) = 0$$

$$\Rightarrow \quad a \cdot 2x \cdot \frac{dx}{dy} + 2h \cdot \left(x \cdot 1 + y \cdot \frac{d}{dy}x\right) + b \cdot 2y + 2g \cdot \frac{dx}{dy} + 2f + 0 = 0$$

$$\Rightarrow \quad \frac{dx}{dy}[2ax + 2hy + 2g] = -2hx - 2by - 2f$$

$$\Rightarrow \quad \frac{dx}{dy} = \frac{-2(hx+by+f)}{2(ax+hy+g)} = \frac{-(hx+by+f)}{(ax+hy+g)} \quad \text{...(iii)}$$

$$\therefore \text{LHS} = \frac{dy}{dx} \cdot \frac{dx}{dy} = \frac{-(ax+hy+g)}{(hx+by+f)} \cdot \frac{-(hx+by+f)}{(ax+hy+g)}$$

[using Eqs. (ii) and (iii)]

$= 1 = \text{RHS}$

Hence proved.

Topic Practice 1

Directions (Q. Nos. 1-4) *Find $\frac{dy}{dx}$ w.r.t. x in each of the following.*

1. $xy = a^2$
2. $x^2 + y^2 - 4xy = 5$
3. $x^3 + x^2y + xy^2 + y^3 = 81$
4. $(x^2 + y^2)^2 = xy$
5. If $xy^2 = 1$, prove that $2\frac{dy}{dx} + y^3 = 0$.
6. If $xy = 1$, prove that $\frac{dy}{dx} + y^2 = 0$.
7. If $e^x + e^y = e^{x+y}$, prove that $\frac{dy}{dx} = -\frac{e^x(e^y - 1)}{e^y(e^x - 1)}$ or $\frac{dy}{dx} + e^{y-x} = 0$.
8. If $y\sqrt{x^2+1} = \log(\sqrt{x^2+1} - x)$, then show that $(x^2+1)\frac{dy}{dx} + xy + 1 = 0$.
9. If $xy\log(x+y) = 1$, then prove that $\frac{dy}{dx} = \frac{-y(x^2y + x + y)}{x(xy^2 + x + y)}$.

Hints & Solutions

1. Solve as Example 1. **Ans.** $-\frac{y}{x}$

2. Solve as Example 2. **Ans.** $\frac{2y-x}{y-2x}$

3. Solve as Example 2. **Ans.** $\frac{dy}{dx}=\frac{-(3x^2+2xy+y^2)}{x^2+2xy+3y^2}$

4. Solve as Example 2. **Ans.** $\frac{y-4x^3-4xy^2}{4yx^2+4y^3-x}$

5. We have, $xy^2=1 \Rightarrow x=\frac{1}{y^2} \Rightarrow \frac{dx}{dy}=-\frac{2}{y^3}$

$$\Rightarrow \quad \frac{dy}{dx}=-\frac{y^3}{2} \Rightarrow 2\frac{dy}{dx}+y^3=0$$

6. Solve as Q. 5.

7. We have, $e^x+e^y=e^{x+y}$ ...(i)

$\Rightarrow \quad e^{-x}+e^{-y}=1$ ...(ii)

On differentiating both sides of Eq. (ii) w.r.t. x, we get

$$e^{-y}\left(-\frac{dy}{dx}\right)+e^{-x}(-1)=0$$

$$\Rightarrow \quad -e^{-y}\frac{dy}{dx}-e^{-x}=0$$

$$\Rightarrow \quad -e^{-y}\frac{dy}{dx}=e^{-x} \Rightarrow \frac{dy}{dx}=-\frac{e^{-x}}{e^{-y}}$$

$\Rightarrow \quad \frac{dy}{dx}=-e^{(y-x)} \Rightarrow \frac{dy}{dx}+e^{(y-x)}=0$ **Hence proved.**

8. We have, $y\sqrt{x^2+1}=\log(\sqrt{x^2+1}-x)$

On differentiating both sides w.r.t. x, we get

$$\frac{dy}{dx}(\sqrt{x^2+1})+y\cdot\frac{1}{2\sqrt{x^2+1}}\cdot 2x=\frac{1}{\sqrt{x^2+1}-x}\cdot\left\{\frac{1}{2}\cdot\frac{2x}{\sqrt{x^2+1}}-1\right\}$$

$$\Rightarrow \quad (x^2+1)\frac{dy}{dx}+xy=\sqrt{x^2+1}\cdot\left(-\frac{1}{\sqrt{x^2+1}}\right)$$

$\Rightarrow (x^2+1)\frac{dy}{dx}+xy+1=0$ **Hence proved.**

9. Solve as Q. 8.

Differentiation of Parametric Functions

Sometimes, x and y are given as function of one another variable, say $x=\phi(t)$, $y=\psi(t)$, are two functions and t is a variable.

In such a case, x and y are called parametric functions or parametric equations and t is called the parameter.

So, $x=\phi(t)$ and $y=\psi(t)$, then $\frac{dy}{dx}=\frac{dy/dt}{dx/dt}$

EXAMPLE 1. If $x=8t$ and $y=\frac{8}{t}$, then find $\frac{dy}{dx}$.

Sol. We have, $x=8t \Rightarrow \frac{dx}{dt}=8$

and $\quad y=\frac{8}{t} \Rightarrow \frac{dy}{dt}=\frac{-8}{t^2}$

$$\therefore \quad \frac{dy}{dx}=\frac{\left(\frac{dy}{dt}\right)}{\left(\frac{dx}{dt}\right)}=\frac{-8}{t^2 8}=\frac{-1}{t^2}$$

EXAMPLE 2. If $x=2at^2$ and $y=at^4$, then find $\frac{dy}{dx}$.

Sol. We have, $x=2at^2 \Rightarrow \frac{dx}{dt}=4at$

and $\quad y=at^4 \Rightarrow \frac{dy}{dt}=4at^3$

$$\therefore \quad \frac{dy}{dx}=\frac{\left(\frac{dy}{dt}\right)}{\left(\frac{dx}{dt}\right)}=\frac{4at^3}{4at}=t^2$$

EXAMPLE 3. If $x=t^3+t^2$ and $y=t^2+t$, then find $\frac{dy}{dx}$ at $t=1$.

Sol. We have, $x=t^3+t^2 \Rightarrow \frac{dx}{dt}=3t^2+2t$

and $\quad y=t^2+t \Rightarrow \frac{dy}{dt}=2t+1$

$$\therefore \quad \frac{dy}{dx}=\frac{\left(\frac{dy}{dt}\right)}{\left(\frac{dx}{dt}\right)}=\frac{2t+1}{3t^2+2t}$$

Now, $\left(\frac{dy}{dx}\right)_{t=1}=\frac{2+1}{3+2}=\frac{3}{5}$

EXAMPLE 4. If $x=\log(t^2+t+1)$ and $y=2\log t$, then find $\frac{dy}{dx}$ at $t=-1$.

Sol. We have, $x=\log(t^2+t+1)$

$$\Rightarrow \quad \frac{dx}{dt}=\frac{1}{(t^2+t+1)}(2t+1)=\frac{(2t+1)}{(t^2+t+1)}$$

and $\quad y = 2\log t \Rightarrow \dfrac{dy}{dt} = \dfrac{2}{t}$

$\therefore \quad \dfrac{dy}{dx} = \dfrac{\left(\dfrac{dy}{dt}\right)}{\left(\dfrac{dx}{dt}\right)} = \dfrac{2(t^2+t+1)}{t(2t+1)}$

Now, $\left(\dfrac{dy}{dx}\right)_{t=-1} = \dfrac{2(1-1+1)}{(-1)(-2+1)}$

$= \dfrac{2}{(-1)(-1)} = 2$

EXAMPLE 5. If $x = e^t$ and $y = te^t$, then find $\dfrac{dy}{dx}$ at $t = -1$.

Sol. We have, $x = e^t \Rightarrow \dfrac{dx}{dt} = e^t$

and $\quad y = te^t \Rightarrow \dfrac{dy}{dt} = t\,e^t + e^t = e^t(t+1)$

$\therefore \quad \dfrac{dy}{dx} = \dfrac{(dy/dt)}{(dx/dt)} = \dfrac{e^t(t+1)}{e^t} = t+1$

Now, $\left(\dfrac{dy}{dx}\right)_{t=-1} = -1+1 = 0$

EXAMPLE 6. If $x = a\left(t+\dfrac{1}{t}\right)$ and $y = a\left(t-\dfrac{1}{t}\right)$, then prove that $\dfrac{dy}{dx} = \dfrac{x}{y}$.

Sol. We have, $x = a\left(t+\dfrac{1}{t}\right)$ ...(i)

and $\quad y = a\left(t-\dfrac{1}{t}\right)$ ...(ii)

Now, $\quad \dfrac{dx}{dt} = a\left(1-\dfrac{1}{t^2}\right) = a\left(\dfrac{t^2-1}{t^2}\right)$ ...(iii)

and $\quad \dfrac{dy}{dt} = a\left(1+\dfrac{1}{t^2}\right) = a\left(\dfrac{t^2+1}{t^2}\right)$ ...(iv)

$\therefore \quad \dfrac{dy}{dx} = \dfrac{dy/dt}{dx/dt} = \dfrac{a\left(\dfrac{t^2+1}{t^2}\right)}{a\left(\dfrac{t^2-1}{t^2}\right)}$

[using Eqs. (iii) and (iv)]

$= \dfrac{a(t^2+1)}{t^2} \cdot \dfrac{t^2}{a(t^2-1)} = \dfrac{t^2+1}{t^2-1}$ ...(v)

Now, consider $\dfrac{x}{y} = \dfrac{a\left(\dfrac{t^2+1}{t}\right)}{a\left(\dfrac{t^2-1}{t}\right)} = \dfrac{t^2+1}{t^2-1}$ ...(vi)

From Eqs. (v) and (vi), we get

$\dfrac{dy}{dx} = \dfrac{x}{y}$ **Hence proved.**

EXAMPLE 7. If $x = \left(t+\dfrac{1}{t}\right)^a$, $y = a^{t+\frac{1}{t}}$, then find $\dfrac{dy}{dx}$.

Sol. We have, $x = \left(t+\dfrac{1}{t}\right)^a$

Now, differentiating both sides, w.r.t. t, we get

$\dfrac{dx}{dt} = a\left(t+\dfrac{1}{t}\right)^{a-1}\left[1-\dfrac{1}{t^2}\right]$ ...(i)

and $\quad y = a^{t+\frac{1}{t}}$

On differentiating both sides w.r.t. t, we get

$\dfrac{dy}{dt} = a^{\left(t+\frac{1}{t}\right)} \cdot \log a \cdot \left(1-\dfrac{1}{t^2}\right)$ ...(ii)

Now, $\dfrac{dy}{dx} = \dfrac{dy/dt}{dx/dt} = \dfrac{a^{\left(t+\frac{1}{t}\right)} \cdot \log a \cdot \left(1-\dfrac{1}{t^2}\right)}{a\left(t+\dfrac{1}{t}\right)^{a-1}\left[1-\dfrac{1}{t^2}\right]} = \dfrac{a^{\left(t+\frac{1}{t}\right)} \cdot \log a}{a\left(t+\dfrac{1}{t}\right)^{a-1}}$

Topic Practice 2

Directions (Q. Nos. 1-3) *Find* $\dfrac{dy}{dx}$.

1 $x = at^2$ and $y = 2at$

2 $x = \dfrac{1-t^2}{1+t^2}$ and $y = \dfrac{2t}{1+t^2}$

3 $x = e^{\theta}\left(\theta+\dfrac{1}{\theta}\right)$ and $y = e^{-\theta}\left(\theta-\dfrac{1}{\theta}\right)$

4 If $x = \dfrac{1+\log t}{t^2}$, $y = \dfrac{3+2\log t}{t}$, then find $\dfrac{dy}{dx}$.

Hints & Solutions

1. Solve as Example 2. **Ans.** $\frac{1}{t}$

2. Solve as Example 1. **Ans.** $\frac{t^2-1}{2t}$

3. **Hint** $x = e^{\theta}\left(\theta+\frac{1}{\theta}\right)$

$$\frac{dx}{d\theta} = e^{\theta}\frac{d}{d\theta}\left(\theta+\frac{1}{\theta}\right)+\left(\theta+\frac{1}{\theta}\right)\frac{d}{d\theta}(e^{\theta})$$

$$= e^{\theta}\left(1-\frac{1}{\theta^2}\right)+\left(\frac{\theta^2+1}{\theta}\right)e^{\theta} = e^{\theta}\left(1-\frac{1}{\theta^2}+\frac{\theta^2+1}{\theta}\right)$$

$$= e^{\theta}\left(\frac{\theta^3+\theta^2+\theta-1}{\theta^2}\right) \quad \text{...(i)}$$

and $\quad y = e^{-\theta}\left(\theta-\frac{1}{\theta}\right)$

$$\frac{dy}{d\theta} = e^{-\theta}\frac{d}{d\theta}\left(\theta-\frac{1}{\theta}\right)+\left(\theta-\frac{1}{\theta}\right)\frac{d}{d\theta}(e^{-\theta})$$

$$= e^{-\theta}\left(1+\frac{1}{\theta^2}\right)+\left(\theta-\frac{1}{\theta}\right)e^{-\theta}\left\{\frac{d}{d\theta}(-\theta)\right\}$$

$$= e^{-\theta}\left(\frac{-\theta^3+\theta^2+\theta+1}{\theta^2}\right) \quad \text{...(ii)}$$

Now, $\quad \frac{dy}{dx} = \frac{dy/d\theta}{dx/d\theta}$

$$= e^{-\theta}\left(\frac{-\theta^3+\theta^2+\theta+1}{\theta^2}\right)\times\frac{1}{e^{\theta}\left(\frac{\theta^3+\theta^2+\theta-1}{\theta^2}\right)}$$

$$= e^{-2\theta}\left(\frac{-\theta^3+\theta^2+\theta+1}{\theta^3+\theta^2+\theta-1}\right)$$

4. **Hint** $x = \frac{1+\log t}{t^2}$

$$\frac{dx}{dt} = \frac{t^2\left(\frac{1}{t}\right)-(1+\log t)(2t)}{t^4} = \frac{-2\log t-1}{t^3}$$

and $\quad y = \frac{3+2\log t}{t}$

$$\frac{dy}{dt} = \frac{t\left(\frac{2}{t}\right)-(3+2\log t)(1)}{t^2} = \frac{-2\log t-1}{t^2}$$

Now, $\quad \frac{dy}{dx} = \frac{dy/dt}{dx/dt} = \frac{\frac{-2\log t-1}{t^2}}{\frac{-2\log t-1}{t^3}} = t$

Second Order Derivative

Let $y = f(x)$ be a given function, then $\frac{dy}{dx} = f'(x)$ is called the first derivative of y or $f(x)$ and $\frac{d}{dx}\left(\frac{dy}{dx}\right)$ is called the second order derivative of y w.r.t. x and it is denoted by $\frac{d^2y}{dx^2}$ or y'' or y_2 or $f''(x)$ or D^2y.

EXAMPLE 1. Find the second order derivative of x^{20}.

Sol. Let $\quad y = x^{20}$

On differentiating both sides w.r.t. x, we get

$$\frac{dy}{dx} = 20x^{19}$$

Again, differentiating both sides w.r.t. x, we get

$$\frac{d}{dx}\left(\frac{dy}{dx}\right) = (20\times 19)\,x^{18}$$

$$\Rightarrow \quad \frac{d^2y}{dx^2} = 380x^{18}$$

EXAMPLE 2. If $y = e^{ax}$, then find $\frac{d^2y}{dx^2}$.

Sol. We have, $y = e^{ax}$

On differentiating both sides w.r.t. x, we get

$$\frac{dy}{dx} = ae^{ax}$$

Again, differentiating both sides w.r.t. x, we get

$$\frac{d^2y}{dx^2} = a^2e^{ax}$$

EXAMPLE 3. If $y = Ae^{5x} + Be^{-5x}$, then find $\frac{d^2y}{dx^2}$.

Sol. We have, $\quad y = Ae^{5x} + Be^{-5x}$

On differentiating both sides w.r.t. x, we get

$$\frac{dy}{dx} = Ae^{5x}\cdot(5)+Be^{-5x}(-5) = 5Ae^{5x}-5Be^{-5x}$$

$$\Rightarrow \quad \frac{d^2y}{dx^2} = 5Ae^{5x}(5)-5Be^{-5x}(-5) = 25Ae^{5x}+25Be^{-5x}$$

$$\therefore \quad \frac{d^2y}{dx^2} = 25(Ae^{5x}+Be^{-5x}) = 25y$$

$[\because y = Ae^{5x}+Be^{-5x}]$

EXAMPLE 4. If $y=(x^2+x+3)^2$, then find $\frac{d^2y}{dx^2}$ at $x=-1$.

Sol. Given, $y=(x^2+x+3)^2$

$$\therefore \quad \frac{dy}{dx}=2(x^2+x+3)(2x+1)$$

$$=(2x^2+2x+6)(2x+1)$$

$$\frac{dy}{dx}=4x^3+2x^2+4x^2+2x+12x+6$$

$$\frac{dy}{dx}=4x^3+6x^2+14x+6$$

Now, $\frac{d^2y}{dx^2}=12x^2+12x+14$

$$\therefore \quad \left(\frac{d^2y}{dx^2}\right)_{x=-1}=12-12+14=14$$

EXAMPLE 5. Find $\frac{d^2y}{dx^2}$, if $x=t^2$ and $y=2t$.

Sol. We have, $x=t^2$ ...(i)

and $y=2t$ ...(ii)

Here, t is the parameter.

On differentiating Eqs (i) and (ii), respectively w.r.t. t, we get

$$\frac{dx}{dt}=2t \quad \text{...(iii)}$$

and

$$\frac{dy}{dt}=2 \quad \text{...(iv)}$$

On putting the values from Eqs. (iii) and (iv) in the formula $\frac{dy}{dx}=\frac{dy/dt}{dx/dt}$, we get

$$\frac{dy}{dx}=\frac{2}{2t}=\frac{1}{t}$$

Now, differentiating both sides w.r.t. x, we get

$$\frac{d^2y}{dx^2}=\frac{d}{dx}\left(\frac{1}{t}\right)=\frac{d}{dt}\left(\frac{1}{t}\right)\frac{dt}{dx}=-\frac{1}{t^2}\frac{dt}{dx}$$

$$=-\frac{1}{t^2}\frac{1}{2t} \quad \text{[from Eq. (iii)]}$$

$$=-\frac{1}{2t^3}$$

EXAMPLE 6. If $y=x^x$, then prove that

$$\frac{d^2y}{dx^2}-\frac{1}{y}\left(\frac{dy}{dx}\right)^2-\frac{y}{x}=0.$$

Sol. We have, $y=x^x$

Taking log on both sides, we get

$$\log y=\log x^x \Rightarrow \log y=x\log x$$

On differentiating both sides w.r.t. x, we get

$$\frac{1}{y}\frac{dy}{dx}=x\frac{d}{dx}(\log x)+\log x\frac{d}{dx}(x)$$

$$\Rightarrow \frac{1}{y}\frac{dy}{dx}=x\times\frac{1}{x}+\log x \Rightarrow \frac{dy}{dx}=y(1+\log x) \quad \text{...(i)}$$

Again, differentiating both sides of Eq. (i) w.r.t. x, we get

$$\frac{d^2y}{dx^2}=y\frac{d}{dx}(1+\log x)+(1+\log x)\frac{dy}{dx}$$

$$=y\times\frac{1}{x}+(1+\log x)\frac{dy}{dx}$$

$$\Rightarrow \frac{d^2y}{dx^2}=\frac{y}{x}+(1+\log x)\frac{dy}{dx} \quad \text{...(ii)}$$

Now, LHS $=\frac{d^2y}{dx^2}-\frac{1}{y}\left(\frac{dy}{dx}\right)^2-\frac{y}{x}$

On putting the values of $\frac{d^2y}{dx^2}$ and $\frac{dy}{dx}$ from Eqs. (i) and (ii), we get

$$\text{LHS}=\frac{y}{x}+(1+\log x)\,y(1+\log x)-\frac{1}{y}[y^2(1+\log x)^2]-\frac{y}{x}$$

$$=y(1+\log x)^2-y(1+\log x)^2=0=\text{RHS}$$

Hence proved.

EXAMPLE 7. If $y=Pe^{ax}+Qe^{bx}$, then show that

$$\frac{d^2y}{dx^2}-(a+b)\frac{dy}{dx}+aby=0.$$

Sol. We have, $y=Pe^{ax}+Qe^{bx}$ ...(i)

On differentiating both sides w.r.t. x, we get

$$\frac{dy}{dx}=P\frac{d}{dx}(e^{ax})+Q\frac{d}{dx}(e^{bx})$$

$$\Rightarrow \frac{dy}{dx}=Pae^{ax}+Qbe^{bx} \quad \text{...(ii)}$$

Again, differentiating both sides w.r.t. x, we get

$$\frac{d^2y}{dx^2}=Pa\frac{d}{dx}(e^{ax})+bQ\frac{d}{dx}(e^{bx})$$

$$=Pa(ae^{ax})+bQ(be^{bx})=a^2Pe^{ax}+b^2Qe^{bx} \quad \text{...(iii)}$$

Now, LHS $=\frac{d^2y}{dx^2}-(a+b)\frac{dy}{dx}+aby$

On putting the values from Eqs. (i), (ii) and (iii), we get

$$\text{LHS}=a^2Pe^{ax}+b^2Qe^{bx}-(a+b)(aPe^{ax}+bQe^{bx})+ab(Pe^{ax}+Qe^{bx})$$

$$=a^2Pe^{ax}+b^2Qe^{bx}-a^2Pe^{ax}-abQe^{bx}-abPe^{ax}-b^2Qe^{bx}+abPe^{ax}+abQe^{bx}$$

$$=0=\text{RHS}$$

EXAMPLE 8. If $y^3 - y = 2x$, prove that $\frac{d^2y}{dx^2} = -\frac{24y}{(3y^2-1)^3}$.

Sol. We have, $y^3 - y = 2x$

On differentiating both sides w.r.t. y, we obtain

$$(3y^2-1) = 2\frac{dx}{dy} \Rightarrow \frac{dy}{dx} = \frac{2}{3y^2-1}$$

Again, differentiating both sides w.r.t. x, we get

$$\frac{d^2y}{dx^2} = -\frac{2}{(3y^2-1)^2} \cdot \frac{d}{dx}(3y^2-1)$$

$$= -\frac{2}{(3y^2-1)^2} \times 6y \times \frac{dy}{dx} = -\frac{12y}{(3y^2-1)^2} \times \frac{2}{(3y^2-1)}$$

$$\frac{d^2y}{dx^2} = -\frac{24y}{(3y^2-1)^3}$$

Topic Practice 3

1 Find the second order derivative of the following.

(i) $x^3 - x^2 + 2$

(ii) $x^{10} + x^9$

(iii) 2^x

(iv) $\log x$

(v) $x^3 \log x$

(vi) $\log(\log x)$

2 A curve has the equation $y = \frac{x+6}{2x-3}$, when $x \neq \frac{3}{2}$.

(i) Show that the derivative of the curve can be expressed as $\frac{k}{(2x-3)^2}$, where k is a constant.

(ii) Find the value of x for which $\frac{d^2y}{dx^2} = \frac{12}{25}$.

3 If $y = 3e^{2x} + 2e^{3x}$, then prove that $\frac{d^2y}{dx^2} - 5\frac{dy}{dx} + 6y = 0$.

4 If $e^y(x+1) = 1$, then prove that $\frac{d^2y}{dx^2} = \left(\frac{dy}{dx}\right)^2$.

5 If $y = x^3 \log\left(\frac{1}{x}\right)$, then prove that $x\frac{d^2y}{dx^2} - 2\frac{dy}{dx} + 3x^2 = 0$.

6 If $y = x\log\left(\frac{x}{a+bx}\right)$, then prove that $x^3\frac{d^2y}{dx^2} = \left(x\frac{dy}{dx} - y\right)$.

7 If $y = \sqrt{x+1} - \sqrt{x-1}$, then prove that $(x^2-1)\frac{d^2y}{dx^2} + x\frac{dy}{dx} - \frac{1}{4}y = 0$.

8 If $y = 500e^{7x} + 600e^{-7x}$, then prove that $\frac{d^2y}{dx^2} = 49y$.

9 If $y = \log[x + \sqrt{x^2+1}]$, then prove that $(x^2+1)\frac{d^2y}{dx^2} + x\frac{dy}{dx} = 0$.

10 If $y = (x + \sqrt{1+x^2})^n$, then prove that $(1+x^2)\frac{d^2y}{dx^2} + x\frac{dy}{dx} = n^2y$.

11 If $x^m y^n = (x+y)^{m+n}$, then prove that $\frac{d^2y}{dx^2} = 0$.

12 If $(x-a)^2 + (y-b)^2 = c^2$, then prove that $\frac{\left[1+\left(\frac{dy}{dx}\right)^2\right]^{3/2}}{\frac{d^2y}{dx^2}}$ is a constant and independent of a and b.

Hints & Solutions

1. (i) Solve as Example 1. **Ans.** $6x-2$

(ii) Solve as Example 1. **Ans.** $18x^7(5x+4)$

(iii) Let $y = 2^x$

Then, $\frac{dy}{dx} = 2^x \log_e 2$

$\therefore \frac{d^2y}{dx^2} = 2^x (\log 2)^2$

(iv) Let $y = \log x$

Then, $\frac{dy}{dx} = \frac{1}{x} = x^{-1}$

$\therefore \frac{d^2y}{dx^2} = \frac{d}{dx}(x^{-1}) = (-1)x^{-2} = \frac{-1}{x^2}$

(v) **Hint** Let $y = x^3 \log x$

$$\frac{dy}{dx} = \frac{d}{dx}(x^3 \log x) = x^3 \frac{d}{dx}(\log x) + \log x \frac{d}{dx}(x^3)$$

$$= x^3\left(\frac{1}{x}\right) + (\log x)(3x^2) = x^2(1+3\log x)$$

Again, differentiating both sides w.r.t. x, we get

$$\frac{d^2y}{dx^2} = x^2 \frac{d}{dx}(1+3\log x) + \frac{d}{dx}(x^2)\cdot(1+3\log x)$$

$$= x^2\left(0+\frac{3}{x}\right) + (1+3\log x)(2x)$$

$$= 3x + 2x(1+3\log x) = x(5+6\log x)$$

(vi) **Hint** $\frac{dy}{dx} = \frac{1}{\log x}\cdot\frac{1}{x} = (x\cdot\log x)^{-1}$

and $\frac{d^2y}{dx^2} = (-1)(x\log x)^{-2}\cdot\left(x\cdot\frac{1}{x}+\log x\right)$

Ans. $-\frac{1+\log x}{(x\log x)^2}$

2. (i) Given equation of curve is $y = \frac{x+6}{2x-3}$.

On differentiating both sides w.r.t. x, we get

$$\frac{dy}{dx} = \frac{(2x-3)\frac{d}{dx}(x+6) - (x+6)\frac{d}{dx}(2x-3)}{(2x-3)^2}$$

$$= \frac{(2x-3)(1) - (x+6)(2)}{(2x-3)^2}$$

$$\Rightarrow \frac{dy}{dx} = \frac{-15}{(2x-3)^2} \text{ is of the form of } \frac{k}{(2x-3)^2} \quad \text{...(i)}$$

(ii) Again, differentiating both sides of Eq. (i) w.r.t. x, we get

$$\frac{d^2y}{dx^2} = -15\frac{d}{dx}(2x-3)^{-2}$$

$$= -15\times(-2)(2x-3)^{-2-1}\times\frac{d}{dx}(2x-3)$$

$$= 30(2x-3)^{-3}\times 2 = \frac{60}{(2x-3)^3}$$

Also, given $\frac{d^2y}{dx^2} = \frac{12}{25} \Rightarrow \frac{12}{25} = \frac{60}{(2x-3)^3}$

$\Rightarrow (2x-3)^3 = (5)^3$

$\Rightarrow 2x-3 = 5$ [taking cube root]

$\Rightarrow 2x = 8 \Rightarrow x = 4$

3. Solve as Example 8.

4. Given, $e^y(x+1) = 1$

Taking log on both sides, we get

$$\log[e^y(x+1)] = \log 1$$

$\Rightarrow \log e^y + \log(x+1) = \log 1$

$\Rightarrow y + \log(x+1) = \log 1$

On differentiating both sides w.r.t. x, we get

$$\frac{dy}{dx} + \frac{1}{x+1} = 0 \quad \text{...(i)}$$

Again, differentiating both sides w.r.t. x, we get

$$\frac{d^2y}{dx^2} - \frac{1}{(x+1)^2} = 0$$

$\Rightarrow \frac{d^2y}{dx^2} - \left(-\frac{dy}{dx}\right)^2 = 0$ [from Eq. (i)]

$\Rightarrow \frac{d^2y}{dx^2} - \left(\frac{dy}{dx}\right)^2 = 0$

$\Rightarrow \frac{d^2y}{dx^2} = \left(\frac{dy}{dx}\right)^2$ **Hence proved.**

5. **Hint** $y = x^3(\log 1 - \log x) = -x^3\log x$

$\Rightarrow \frac{dy}{dx} = -x^3\cdot\frac{1}{x} + \log x(-3x^2) = -x^2(1+3\log x)$

$\Rightarrow \frac{d^2y}{dx^2} = -x^2\frac{3}{x} + (1+3\log x)(-2x)$

$= -3x - 2x(1+3\log x) = -5x - 6x\log x$

On substituting these values in LHS, we get RHS.

6. **Hint** Find $\frac{dy}{dx}$ and $\frac{d^2y}{dx^2}$ and then putting these values in the given equation, we get LHS = RHS.

7. Given, $y = \sqrt{x+1} - \sqrt{x-1}$

On differentiating both sides w.r.t. x, we get

$$\frac{dy}{dx} = \frac{1}{2\sqrt{x+1}} - \frac{1}{2\sqrt{x-1}} = \frac{1}{2}\left[\frac{\sqrt{x-1}-\sqrt{x+1}}{\sqrt{x^2-1}}\right]$$

$\Rightarrow 2\sqrt{x^2-1}\cdot\frac{dy}{dx} = -y$

Now, squaring both sides, we get

$$4(x^2-1)\left(\frac{dy}{dx}\right)^2 = y^2$$

Again, differentiating both sides w.r.t. x, we get

$$4(x^2-1)\,2\frac{dy}{dx}\cdot\frac{d^2y}{dx^2} + \left(\frac{dy}{dx}\right)^2\cdot 8x = 2y\left(\frac{dy}{dx}\right)$$

On dividing both sides by $2\frac{dy}{dx}$, we get

$$4(x^2-1)\frac{d^2y}{dx^2}+4x\frac{dy}{dx}-y=0$$

$$\therefore \quad (x^2-1)\frac{d^2y}{dx^2}+x\frac{dy}{dx}-\frac{y}{4}=0$$ **Hence proved.**

8. Solve as Example 9.

9. **Hint** $\frac{dy}{dx}=\frac{1}{\sqrt{x^2+1}} \Rightarrow \sqrt{x^2+1}\frac{dy}{dx}=1$ and then again differentiating both sides w.r.t. x. Then, put values of $\frac{d^2y}{dx^2}$ and $\frac{dy}{dx}$ in LHS to get RHS.

10. Given, $y=\left(x+\sqrt{1+x^2}\right)^n$. ...(i)

On differentiating both sides w.r.t. x, we get

$$\Rightarrow \frac{dy}{dx}=n(x+\sqrt{1+x^2})^{n-1}\left(1+\frac{2x}{2\sqrt{1+x^2}}\right)$$ [by chain rule]

$$\Rightarrow \frac{dy}{dx}=n(x+\sqrt{1+x^2})^{n-1}\left(\frac{x+\sqrt{1+x^2}}{\sqrt{1+x^2}}\right)$$

$$\Rightarrow \frac{dy}{dx}=\frac{n(x+\sqrt{1+x^2})^n}{\sqrt{1+x^2}} \Rightarrow \frac{dy}{dx}=\frac{ny}{\sqrt{1+x^2}}$$ [from Eq. (i)]

$$\Rightarrow \sqrt{1+x^2}\frac{dy}{dx}=ny$$

Again, differentiating both sides w.r.t. x, we get

$$\sqrt{1+x^2}\frac{d^2y}{dx^2}+\frac{2x}{2\sqrt{1+x^2}}\cdot\frac{dy}{dx}=n\frac{dy}{dx}$$

$$\Rightarrow (1+x^2)\frac{d^2y}{dx^2}+x\frac{dy}{dx}=n\cdot\sqrt{1+x^2}\frac{dy}{dx}$$ [multiplying both sides by $\sqrt{1+x^2}$]

$$\Rightarrow (1+x^2)\frac{d^2y}{dx^2}+x\frac{dy}{dx}=n\sqrt{1+x^2}\cdot\frac{ny}{\sqrt{1+x^2}}$$

$$\Rightarrow (1+x^2)\frac{d^2y}{dx^2}+x\frac{dy}{dx}=n^2y$$ **Hence proved.**

11. We have, $x^my^n=(x+y)^{m+n}$

On taking log both sides, we get

$$\log(x^my^n)=\log(x+y)^{m+n}$$

$$\Rightarrow \log x^m+\log y^n=\log(x+y)^{m+n}$$

$$\Rightarrow m\log x+n\log y=(m+n)\log(x+y)$$

On differentiating both sides w.r.t. x, we get

$$\frac{m}{x}+\frac{n}{y}\cdot\frac{dy}{dx}=\frac{(m+n)}{x+y}\cdot\left(1+\frac{dy}{dx}\right)$$

$$\Rightarrow \frac{dy}{dx}\left(\frac{n}{y}-\frac{m+n}{x+y}\right)=\frac{m+n}{x+y}-\frac{m}{x}$$

$$\Rightarrow \frac{dy}{dx}\left(\frac{nx+ny-my-ny}{y(x+y)}\right)=\left(\frac{mx+nx-mx-my}{x(x+y)}\right)$$

$$\Rightarrow \frac{dy}{dx}\left(\frac{nx-my}{y(x+y)}\right)=\left(\frac{nx-my}{x(x+y)}\right) \Rightarrow \frac{dy}{dx}=\frac{y}{x}$$ ... (i)

Again, differentiating both sides w.r.t. x, we get

$$\frac{d^2y}{dx^2}=\frac{x\cdot\frac{dy}{dx}-y\cdot 1}{x^2}=\frac{x\left(\frac{y}{x}\right)-y}{x^2}$$ [using Eq. (i)]

$$=\frac{y-y}{x^2}=0$$ **Hence proved.**

12. Given, $(x-a)^2+(y-b)^2=c^2$ ...(i)

On differentiating both sides w.r.t. x, we get

$$2(x-a)+2(y-b)\frac{dy}{dx}=0$$

$$\Rightarrow (x-a)+(y-b)\frac{dy}{dx}=0$$ [dividing both sides by 2]

$$\Rightarrow \frac{dy}{dx}=-\left(\frac{x-a}{y-b}\right)$$ ...(ii)

$$\Rightarrow \frac{d^2y}{dx^2}=-\left[\frac{(y-b)\cdot 1-(x-a)\frac{dy}{dx}}{(y-b)^2}\right]$$ [by quotient rule]

$$\Rightarrow \frac{d^2y}{dx^2}=-\left[\frac{(y-b)+\frac{(x-a)^2}{(y-b)}}{(y-b)^2}\right]$$ [using Eq. (ii)]

$$\Rightarrow \frac{d^2y}{dx^2}=-\left[\frac{(y-b)^2+(x-a)^2}{(y-b)^3}\right]$$

$$\Rightarrow \frac{d^2y}{dx^2}=-\frac{c^2}{(y-b)^3}$$ [using Eq. (i)] ...(iii)

Now, consider $$\frac{\left[1+\left(\frac{dy}{dx}\right)^2\right]^{3/2}}{\frac{d^2y}{dx^2}}=-\frac{\left[1+\frac{(x-a)^2}{(y-b)^2}\right]^{3/2}}{\frac{c^2}{(y-b)^3}}$$

[using Eqs. (ii) and (iii)]

$$=-\frac{\left(\frac{c^2}{(y-b)^2}\right)^{3/2}}{\frac{c^2}{(y-b)^3}}$$ [using Eq. (i)]

$$=-\frac{c^3}{(y-b)^3}\times\frac{(y-b)^3}{c^2}$$

$=-c$, where c is constant and independent of a and b.

Hence proved.

Exam Pattern Exercise

Part A - Objective Type Questions

Multiple Choice Type Questions

1 For the curve $\sqrt{x}+\sqrt{y}=1$, $\frac{dy}{dx}$ at $\left(\frac{1}{4},\frac{1}{4}\right)$ is ....

(a) -2 (b) 0 (c) -1 (d) 2

2 If $xy+xy^2=x$, then $\frac{dy}{dx}$ at $x=1$ and $y=-1$ is equal to

(a) 1 (b) -1 (c) 0 (d) 5

3 If $x=40t$, $y=20t^2$, then $\frac{dy}{dx}$ is equal to

(a) $-t$ (b) t (c) $2t$ (d) $-2t$

4 If $x=2t^2$ and $y=8t^3$, then $\frac{dy}{dx}$ at $t=\frac{1}{6}$ is equal to

(a) 1 (b) 0 (c) 8 (d) -1

5 If $x=t^2+1$ and $y=t+5$, then $\frac{dy}{dx}$ at $t=\frac{1}{2}$ is equal to

(a) -1 (b) 0 (c) 2 (d) 1

6 If $x=e^t$ and $y=8+e^{2t}$, then $\frac{dy}{dx}$ at $t=1$ is equal to

(a) $2e$ (b) e (c) e^{-1} (d) $\frac{e}{2}$

7 If $x=t^2$ and $y=t^3$, then $\frac{d^2y}{dx^2}$ is equal to

(a) $\frac{3}{2t}$ (b) $\frac{3t}{4}$ (c) $\frac{3t}{2}$ (d) $\frac{3}{4t}$

8 If $y=(x+1)^2+(x+2)^2$, then $\frac{d^2y}{dx^2}$ is equal to

(a) 1 (b) 2 (c) 4 (d) 5

9 If $y=e^x+e^{-x}$ and $y=k\frac{d^2y}{dx^2}$, then k is equal to

(a) 1 (b) 3 (c) 4 (d) 2

10 If $y=e^{-2x}$, then $\frac{d^2y}{dx^2}$ is equal to

(a) $2e^{-2x}$ (b) e^{-4x} (c) $4e^{-4x}$ (d) $-4e^{-2x}$

Assertion-Reason Based Questions

Directions (Q. Nos. 11-13) *In the questions given below are two statements labelled as Assertion (A) and Reason (R). In the context of the two statements, which one of the following is correct?*

(a) Both A and R are correct; R is the correct explanation of A

(b) Both A and R are correct; R is not the correct explanation of A

(c) A is correct; R is incorrect

(d) R is correct; A is incorrect

11 **Assertion (A)** If $e^{xy}+\log(xy)+\cos(xy)+4=0$, then $\frac{dy}{dx}=-\frac{y}{x}$.

Reason (R) $\frac{d}{dx}(xy)=0 \Rightarrow \frac{dy}{dx}=-\frac{y}{x}$

12 **Assertion (A)** If $\sin(x+y)=\log_e(x+y)$, then $\frac{dy}{dx}=-1$.

Reason (R) The derivative of an odd function is always an even function.

13 **Assertion (A)** If $x=at^2$ and $y=2at$, then $\left.\frac{d^2y}{dx^2}\right|_{t=2}=-\frac{1}{16a}$.

Reason (R) $\frac{d^2y}{dx^2}=\left(\frac{dy}{dx}\right)^2\times\left(\frac{dt}{dx}\right)^2$.

Part B - Descriptive Questions

Very Short Answer Type Questions

14 If $x^a y^b=(x+y)^{(a+b)}$, then find $\frac{dy}{dx}$.

15 If $x^y=e^{x-y}$, then find $\frac{dy}{dx}$.

16 If $x=a\left(\frac{1+t^2}{1-t^2}\right)$ and $y=\frac{2t}{1-t^2}$, then find $\frac{dy}{dx}$.

Short Answer Type Questions

17 If $5x+3y=\log(5x-3y)$, then find $\frac{dy}{dx}$.

18 Differentiate $x^{1/x}$ with respect to x,.

19 If $y=x^{\log x}+(\log x)^x$, then find $\frac{dy}{dx}$.

20 If $x^{16}y^9=(x^2+y)^{17}$, then prove that $x\frac{dy}{dx}=2y$.

21 If $x=\frac{3at}{1+t^2}$ and $y=\frac{3at^2}{1+t^2}$, then find $\frac{dy}{dx}$.

22 If $y=\frac{\log x}{x}$, then find $\frac{d^2y}{dx^2}$.

Long Answer Type Questions

23 Find $\frac{dy}{dx}$, if $y^x + x^y + x^x = a^b$.

24 If $\log(\sqrt{1+x^2} - x) = y(\sqrt{1+x^2})$, then prove that $(1+x^2)\frac{dy}{dx} + xy + 1 = 0$.

25 If $(x-y)e^{x/x-y} = a$, then prove that $y\frac{dy}{dx} + x = 2y$.

26 If $y = ae^{2x} + be^{-x}$, then showthat $\frac{d^2y}{dx^2} - \frac{dy}{dx} - 2y = 0$.

27 If $y = a\{x + \sqrt{x^2+1}\}^n + b\{x - \sqrt{x^2-1}\}^{-n}$, then prove that $(x^2-1)\frac{d^2y}{dx^2} + x\frac{dy}{dx} - x^2y = 0$.

Case Study Based Questions

28 Let $f(x, y) = 0$ be a function in the form of x and y. If it is not possible to express y as a function of x in the form of $y = \phi(x)$, then y is said to be an implicit function of x.

e.g. $x^2 + y^2 = xy$

Following steps are used to find $\frac{dy}{dx}$ of implicit functions.

I. Write the given equation in x and y and then differentiate both sides of the given equation w.r.t. x.

II. Take all terms involving $\frac{dy}{dx}$ on LHS and transfer the remaining terms on RHS to get equation in the form of $\frac{dy}{dx} f(x, y) = g(x, y)$.

III. Now, find $\frac{dy}{dx}$, i.e. $\frac{dy}{dx} = \frac{g(x, y)}{f(x, y)}$.

On the basis of above information answer the following questions.

(i) If $y = 5x^2 - 9e^y$, then $\frac{dy}{dx}$ is equal to

(a) $\frac{10x}{1+9e^y}$ (b) $\frac{-10x}{1+9e^y}$

(c) $\frac{10x}{1+e^y}$ (d) $\frac{-10x}{1+e^y}$

(ii) If $x^4 + y^3 - 3x^2y = 0$, then $\frac{dy}{dx}$ is equal to

(a) $\frac{6xy - 4x^3}{3x^2 - 3y^2}$ (b) $\frac{6xy - 4x^3}{3y^2 - 3x^2}$

(c) $\frac{6xy + 4x^3}{3y^2 - 3x^2}$ (d) None of these

(iii) If $y = x^2 + 3y^2 + xy$, then $\frac{dy}{dx}$ is equal to

(a) $\frac{2x+y}{1-x-6y}$ (b) $\frac{2x-y}{1-x-6y}$

(c) $\frac{x+y}{1-x-6y}$ (d) None of these

(iv) If $3x^2 + y^3 = 6$, then $\frac{dy}{dx}$ is equal to

(a) $\frac{-2x}{y^3}$ (b) $\frac{2x}{y^2}$

(c) $-\frac{2x}{y^2}$ (d) $\frac{x}{y}$

(v) If $xy + y = 5$, then $\frac{dy}{dx}$ is equal to

(a) $\frac{y}{(1+x)}$ (b) $\frac{x}{(1+y)}$

(c) $\frac{-x}{(1+y)}$ (d) $\frac{-y}{(1+x)}$

29 Second order derivative of a function is the derivative of the first order derivative of the function.

Let $y = f(x)$ ...(i)

Then, $\frac{dy}{dx} = f'(x)$ is called the first derivative of y or $f(x)$. It can also be written as y' or y_1.

If $f'(x)$ is differentiable, then derivative of dy/dx exists.

Again, differentiating Eq. (i) both sides w.r.t. x, we get

$$\frac{d}{dx}\left(\frac{dy}{dx}\right) = \frac{d}{dx}[f'(x)] \Rightarrow \frac{d^2y}{dx^2} = f''(x)$$

where, $\frac{d}{dx}\left(\frac{dy}{dx}\right)$ is called the **second order**

On the basis of above information answer the following questions.

(i) If $x = at^2$ and $y = at$, then $\frac{d^2y}{dx^2}$ is equal to

(a) $\frac{-1}{4at^3}$ (b) $\frac{1}{4at^3}$ (c) $\frac{-1}{at^3}$ (d) $\frac{1}{at^3}$

(ii) If $y = x^2e^{mx}$, where m is a constant, then $\frac{d^2y}{dx^2}$ is equal to

(a) $e^{mx}(m^2x^2 + 4mx + 2)$

(b) $(2m^3xe^{mx})$

(c) $me^{mx}(m^2x^2 + 2mx + 2)$

(d) None of the above

(iii) If $y = t^{10} + 1$ and $x = t^8 + 1$, then $\frac{d^2y}{dx^2}$ is equal to

(a) $\frac{5}{2}t$

(b) $20t^8$

(c) $\frac{5}{16t^6}$

(d) None of the above

(iv) If $y = x^5$, then $\frac{d^2y}{dx^2}$ is equal to

(a) $6x^2$ (b) $50x^2$

(c) $20x^3$ (d) $60x$

(v) If $y = 2x^2 + 3x + 4$, then $\frac{d^2y}{dx^2}$ is equal to

(a) 1 (b) 2

(c) 12 (d) 4

Hints & Solutions

1. (c) 2. (b) 3. (b) 4. (a)
5. (d) 6. (a) 7. (d) 8. (c)
9. (a) 10. (d) 11. (a) 12. (b)
13. (c)

14. **Hint** Take log and differentiate both sides w.r.t. x.

Ans. $\frac{y}{x}$

15. **Hint** Take log and differentiate both sides w.r.t. x.

Ans. $\frac{\log x}{(1+\log x)^2}$

16. **Hint** Differentiate both x and y w.r.t. t. **Ans.** $\frac{1+t^2}{2at}$

17. **Hint** We have, $5x + 3y = \log(5x - 3y)$

On differentiating both sides w.r.t. x, we get

$$\frac{d}{dx}(5x) + \frac{d}{dx}(3y) = \frac{d}{dx}\{\log(5x-3y)\}$$

$$\Rightarrow \quad 5 + 3\frac{dy}{dx} = \frac{1}{(5x-3y)} \cdot \left(5 - 3\frac{dy}{dx}\right)$$

$$\Rightarrow \quad 3\frac{dy}{dx} + \frac{3}{(5x-3y)}\frac{dy}{dx} = \frac{5}{5x-3y} - 5$$

Ans. $\frac{dy}{dx} = \frac{5}{3}\left(\frac{1-5x+3y}{5x-3y+1}\right)$

18. **Hint** Let $y = x^{1/x}$

On taking log both sides, we get

$$\log y = \frac{1}{x}\log x$$

On differentiating both sides w.r.t. x, we get

Ans. $x^{1/x}\left(\frac{1-\log x}{x^2}\right)$

19. We have, $y = x^{\log x} + (\log x)^x$

$$\Rightarrow \quad y = e^{\log (x^{\log x})} + e^{\log (\log x)^x}$$

$$\Rightarrow \quad y = e^{\log x \log x} + e^{x \log (\log x)}$$

$$\Rightarrow \quad y = e^{(\log x)^2} + e^{x \log (\log x)}$$

$$\Rightarrow \quad \frac{dy}{dx} = e^{(\log x)^2}\frac{d}{dx}(\log x)^2 + e^{x\log(\log x)}\frac{d}{dx}\{x\log(\log x)\}$$

$$= (x)^{\log x}\left(2\log x \times \frac{1}{x}\right) + (\log x)^x\left\{\log(\log x) + \frac{x}{\log x} \times \frac{1}{x}\right\}$$

$$= \frac{2x^{\log x}}{x}\log x + (\log x)^x\left\{\log(\log x) + \frac{1}{\log x}\right\}$$

21. **Hint** Differentiate both x and y w.r.t. t.

Ans. $\frac{2t}{1-t^2}$

22. **Hint** We have, $y = \frac{\log x}{x}$

Let $u = \log x$ and $v = \frac{1}{x}$

$$\frac{d}{dx}(uv) = u\frac{dv}{dx} + v\frac{du}{dx}$$

$$\frac{d}{dx}\left(\frac{\log x}{x}\right) = \log x \cdot \frac{d}{dx}\left(\frac{1}{x}\right) + \frac{1}{x} \cdot \frac{d}{dx}(\log x)$$

Ans. $\frac{2\log x - 3}{x^3}$

23. **Hint** Apply product rule and quotient rule.

Ans. $-\frac{[y^x \log y + y \cdot x^{y-1} + x^x(1+\log x)]}{x \cdot y^{x-1} + x^y \log x}$

24. Given, $\log(\sqrt{1+x^2} - x) = y\sqrt{1+x^2}$

On differentiating both sides w.r.t. x, we get

$$\frac{1}{\sqrt{1+x^2} - x}\frac{d}{dx}(\sqrt{1+x^2} - x)$$

$$= y\frac{d}{dx}\sqrt{1+x^2} + \sqrt{1+x^2}\frac{dy}{dx}$$

$$\Rightarrow \frac{1}{\sqrt{1+x^2}-x}\left[\frac{1}{2\sqrt{1+x^2}}\frac{d}{dx}(1+x^2)-1\right]$$

$$= \frac{y}{2\sqrt{1+x^2}}\frac{d}{dx}(1+x^2)+\sqrt{1+x^2}\frac{dy}{dx}$$

$$\Rightarrow \frac{1}{\sqrt{1+x^2}-x}\left[\frac{2x}{2\sqrt{1+x^2}}-1\right]$$

$$= y\times\frac{2x}{2\sqrt{1+x^2}}+\sqrt{1+x^2}\frac{dy}{dx}$$

$$\Rightarrow \frac{1}{\sqrt{1+x^2}-x}\left[\frac{x-\sqrt{1+x^2}}{\sqrt{1+x^2}}\right]=\frac{xy}{\sqrt{1+x^2}}+\sqrt{1+x^2}\frac{dy}{dx}$$

$$\Rightarrow \frac{-1}{\sqrt{1+x^2}}=\frac{xy+(1+x^2)\frac{dy}{dx}}{\sqrt{1+x^2}} \Rightarrow -1 = xy+(1+x^2)\frac{dy}{dx}$$

$$\Rightarrow (1+x^2)\frac{dy}{dx}+xy+1=0$$

26. **Hint** Putting $\frac{d^2y}{dx^2}$, $\frac{dy}{dx}$ and y in the given equation, we get LHS = RHS.

28. (i) (a) Given, $y = 5x^2 - 9e^y$

$$\therefore \frac{dy}{dx} = 10x - 9e^y\frac{dy}{dx} \Rightarrow \frac{dy}{dx}(1+9e^y)=10x$$

$$\therefore \frac{dy}{dx}=\frac{10x}{1+9e^y}$$

(ii) (b) Given, $x^4 + y^3 - 3x^2y = 0$

$$\therefore 4x^3+3y^2\frac{dy}{dx}-3\left(x^2\frac{dy}{dx}+2xy\right)=0$$

$$\therefore \frac{dy}{dx}(3y^2-3x^2)=6xy-4x^3 \Rightarrow \frac{dy}{dx}=\frac{6xy-4x^3}{3y^2-3x^2}$$

(iii) (a) Given, $y = x^2 + 3y^2 + xy$

$$\therefore \frac{dy}{dx}=2x+6y\frac{dy}{dx}+x\frac{dy}{dx}+y$$

$$\Rightarrow \frac{dy}{dx}(1-x-6y)=2x+y$$

$$\Rightarrow \frac{dy}{dx}=\frac{2x+y}{1-x-6y}$$

(iv) (c) Given, $3x^2 + y^3 = 6$

$$\therefore 6x+3y^2\frac{dy}{dx}=0$$

$$\Rightarrow \frac{dy}{dx}=-\frac{2x}{y^2}$$

(v) (d) Given, $xy + y = 5$

$$\therefore x\frac{dy}{dx}+y+\frac{dy}{dx}=0$$

$$\frac{dy}{dx}(1+x)=-y \Rightarrow \frac{dy}{dx}=\frac{-y}{(1+x)}$$

29. (i) (a) Given, $x = at^2 \Rightarrow \frac{dx}{dt}=2at$; $y = at \Rightarrow \frac{dy}{dt}=a$

$$\therefore \frac{dy}{dx}=\frac{\left(\frac{dy}{dt}\right)}{\left(\frac{dx}{dt}\right)}=\frac{a}{2at}=\frac{1}{2t}$$

$$\therefore \frac{d^2y}{dx^2}=\frac{d}{dx}\left(\frac{dy}{dx}\right)=\frac{d}{dx}\left(\frac{1}{2t}\right)=\frac{d}{dt}\left(\frac{1}{2t}\right)\frac{dt}{dx}$$

$$=\frac{-1}{2t^2(2at)}=\frac{-1}{4at^3}$$

(ii) (a) We have, $y = x^2e^{mx}$

$$\therefore \frac{dy}{dx}=2xe^{mx}+mx^2e^{mx}$$

Again, $\frac{d^2y}{dx^2}=2(e^{mx}+mxe^{mx})+m(2xe^{mx}+x^2me^{mx})$

$$=e^{mx}(m^2x^2+4mx+2)$$

(iii) (c) Here, $y = t^{10}+1$ and $x = t^8+1$

So, $t^8=(x-1) \Rightarrow t^2=(x-1)^{1/4}$

$$\Rightarrow y=(x-1)^{5/4}+1$$

$$\Rightarrow \frac{dy}{dx}=\frac{5}{4}(x-1)^{1/4} \Rightarrow \frac{d^2y}{dx^2}=\frac{5}{16}(x-1)^{-3/4}$$

$$\Rightarrow \frac{d^2y}{dx^2}=\frac{5}{16(x-1)^{3/4}}=\frac{5}{16(t^2)^3}=\frac{5}{16t^6}$$

(iv) (c) Given, $y = x^5$

$$\therefore \frac{dy}{dx}=5x^4 \Rightarrow \frac{d^2y}{dx^2}=20x^3$$

(v) (d) Given, $y = 2x^2+3x+4$

$$\therefore \frac{dy}{dx}=4x+3$$

$$\Rightarrow \frac{d^2y}{dx^2}=4$$

CHAPTER 10

Application of Derivatives

In this Chapter...

- Rate of Change of Quantities
- Increasing and Decreasing Functions
- Maxima and Minima

In this chapter, we will study the use of derivatives

(i) determine rate of change of quantities.

(ii) find interval on which a given function is increasing or decreasing.

(iii) find the equation of tangents and normal to a curve at a point.

(iv) find turning points on the graph of a function which in turn will help us to locate points at which largest or smallest value of a function occurs.

(v) find maximum and minimum values of a function.

Rate of Change of Quantities

Let $y = f(x)$ be a function of x. Then, $\frac{dy}{dx}$ represents the rate of change of y with respect to x.

Also, $\left(\frac{dy}{dx}\right)_{\text{at } x=x_0}$ represents the rate of change of y with respect to x at $x = x_0$.

- Suppose two variables are varying with respect to another variable t, i.e. $y = f(t)$ and $x = g(t)$. Then, rate of change of y with respect to x is given by $\frac{dy}{dx} = \frac{dy}{dt} \cdot \frac{dt}{dx}$. [by chain rule of derivative]
- $\frac{dy}{dx}$ is positive, if y increases as x increases. $\frac{dy}{dx}$ is negative, if y decreases as x increases.

EXAMPLE 1. The radius of a circle increases at a rate of 0.2 cm/s. Calculate the rate of the increase of the area, when the radius is 5 cm.

Sol. Here, we have to calculate rate of change of area with respect to radius.

So, let x be the radius and y be the area of circle. Then,

$$y = \pi x^2 \quad \text{...(i)}$$

Also, rate of change of radius with respect to time is 0.2 cm/s.

$$\therefore \quad \frac{dx}{dt} = 0.2 \quad \text{...(ii)}$$

[∵ radius changing with time, so area depends on time]

Now, differentiating both sides of Eq. (i) w.r.t. t, we get

$$\frac{dy}{dt} = \pi \cdot 2x \cdot \frac{dx}{dt} \quad \text{[by chain rule]}$$

$$= 2\pi x\,(0.2) = 0.4\pi x \quad \text{[using Eq. (ii)]}$$

When radius $x = 5$ cm, then

$$\left(\frac{dy}{dt}\right) = 0.4\,\pi \times 5$$

$$= 2\pi \text{ cm}^2/\text{s}$$

Hence, the required rate of increase of the area is 2π cm^2/s.

EXAMPLE 2. A balloon which always remains spherical has a variable radius, find the rate at which its volume is increasing with respect to its radius, when the radius is 7 cm.

Sol. Here, we have to find rate of change of volume with respect to radius, so volume is dependent quantity and radius is independent quantity.

Let r be the radius and V be the volume of spherical balloon, then $V = \frac{4}{3}\pi r^3$.

On differentiating both sides w.r.t. r, we get

$$\frac{dV}{dr} = \frac{4}{3}\pi(3r^2) = 4\pi r^2 \quad ...(i)$$

Now, we have to find rate of change of volume, when radius is 7 cm. So, putting $r = 7$ in Eq. (i), we get

$$\left(\frac{dV}{dr}\right)_{r=7} = 4\pi(7)^2 = 4\pi(49) = 196\pi \text{ cm}^3/\text{cm}$$

Hence, the volume is increasing with respect to its radius at the rate of 196π cm^3/cm, when the radius is 7 cm.

EXAMPLE 3. The volume of a cube is increasing at the rate of 8 cm^3/s. How fast is the surface area increasing when the length of its edge is 12 cm?

Sol. Let x be the length of an edge of the cube, V be the volume and S be the surface area at any time t.

Then, $V = x^3$ and $S = 6x^2$.

It is given that, $\frac{dV}{dt} = 8$ cm^3/sec

$$\Rightarrow \quad \frac{d}{dt}(x^3) = 8$$

$$\Rightarrow \quad 3x^2\frac{dx}{dt} = 8 \Rightarrow \frac{dx}{dt} = \frac{8}{3x^2}$$

Now, $S = 6x^2$

$$\Rightarrow \quad \frac{dS}{dt} = 12x\frac{dx}{dt} \Rightarrow \frac{dS}{dt} = 12x \times \frac{8}{3x^2}$$

$$\Rightarrow \quad \frac{dS}{dt} = \frac{32}{x}$$

$$\Rightarrow \quad \left(\frac{dS}{dt}\right)_{x=12} = \frac{32}{12}\text{ cm}^2/\text{sec} = \frac{8}{3}\text{ cm}^2/\text{sec}$$

EXAMPLE 4. The length x of a rectangle is decreasing at the rate of 6 cm/min and the width y is increasing at the rate of 5 cm/min. Find the rate of change of the perimeter and the area of the rectangle when $x = 10$ cm and $y = 8$ cm.

Sol. Given that $\frac{dx}{dt} = -6$ cm/min and $\frac{dy}{dt} = 5$ cm/min

Let P and A be the perimeter and area of rectangle.

Then, $P = 2(x + y)$

On differentiating w.r.t. t, we get

$$\frac{dP}{dt} = 2\left(\frac{dx}{dt} + \frac{dy}{dt}\right) = 2(-6+5) = -2 \text{ cm/min}$$

And $\quad A = xy$

On differentiating w.r.t. t, we get

$$\frac{dA}{dt} = \frac{dx}{dt}y + x\cdot\frac{dy}{dt}$$

$$= [-6 \times 8 + 10 \times 5] = -48 + 50 = 2 \text{ cm}^2/\text{min}$$

Hence, perimeter of a rectangle is decreasing at the rate of 2 cm/min and area of rectangle is increasing at the rate of 2 cm^2/min.

EXAMPLE 5. Find the point on the curve $y^2 = 8x$ for which the abscissa and ordinate change at the same rate.

Sol. Let the required point be (x, y).

Given, $\quad \frac{dy}{dt} = \frac{dx}{dt} \quad ...(i)$

and $\quad y^2 = 8x \quad ...(ii)$

On differentiating both sides of Eq. (ii) w.r.t. t, we get

$$2y\frac{dy}{dt} = 8\cdot\frac{dx}{dt} \Rightarrow 2y = 8 \quad \text{[from Eq. (i)]}$$

$$\Rightarrow \quad y = 4$$

On putting $y = 4$ in Eq. (ii), we get

$$8x = 16 \Rightarrow x = 2$$

Hence, the required point is (2, 4).

EXAMPLE 6. The radius r of a right circular cone is decreasing at the rate of 3 cm/min and the height h is increasing at the rate of 2 cm/min. When $r = 9$ cm and $h = 6$ cm, find the rate of change of its volume.

Sol. We have, $\quad \frac{dr}{dt} = -3$ cm/min $\quad ...(i)$

and $\quad \frac{dh}{dt} = 2$ cm/min $\quad ...(ii)$

Let V be the volume of a cone.

Then, $\quad V = \frac{1}{3}\pi r^2 h$

$$\Rightarrow \quad \frac{dV}{dt} = \frac{1}{3}\pi\left(r^2\cdot\frac{dh}{dt} + h\cdot 2r\frac{dr}{dt}\right)$$

$$\Rightarrow \quad \frac{dV}{dt} = \frac{1}{3}\pi\,[2r^2 + 2rh(-3)]$$

[using Eqs. (i) and (ii)]

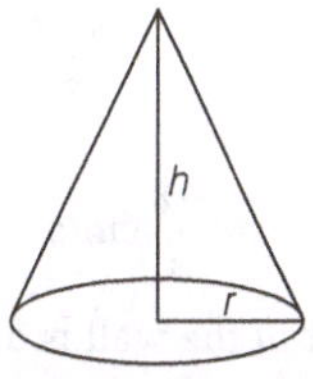

Now, $\frac{dV}{dt}$ when $r = 9$ and $h = 6$, is given by

$$\left(\frac{dV}{dt}\right)_{\text{at } r=9,\, h=6} = \frac{1}{3}\pi[2(9)^2 - 6(9)(6)] = \frac{1}{3}\pi(162 - 324)$$

$$= \frac{1}{3}\pi(-162) = -54\pi \text{ cm}^3/\text{min}$$

Thus, the volume is decreasing at the rate 54π cm^3/min.

EXAMPLE 7. A ladder 5 m long is leaning against a wall. The bottom of the ladder is pulled along the ground away from the wall at the rate of 2 cm/s. How fast is its height on the wall decreasing, when the foot of the ladder is 4 m away from the wall?

Sol. Let $AC = 5$m be the length of ladder and AB be the distance of the ladder from the wall at any time t, such that $AB = x$ and $BC = y$ (BC be the wall)

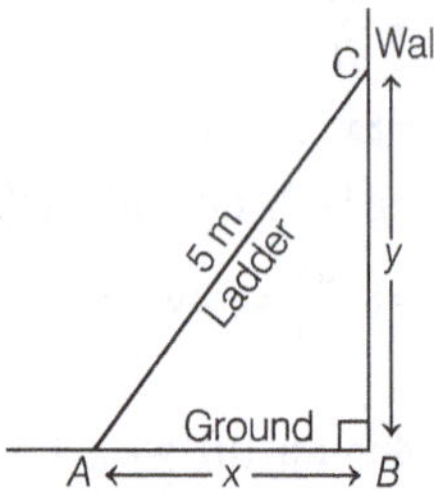

Given, $x = 4$ m, $\frac{dx}{dt} = 2$ cm/s $= 0.02$ m/s

In right angled ΔABC, we get

$$AB^2 + BC^2 = AC^2 \quad \text{[by Pythagoras theorem]}$$

$$\therefore \quad x^2 + y^2 = (5)^2$$

$$\Rightarrow \quad x^2 + y^2 = 25 \quad \text{...(i)}$$

When $x = 4$, then $16 + y^2 = 25$

$$\Rightarrow \quad y = \sqrt{25 - 16} = \sqrt{9} = 3$$

On differentiating both sides of Eq. (i) w.r.t. t, we get

$$2x\frac{dx}{dt} + 2y\frac{dy}{dt} = 0 \Rightarrow x\frac{dx}{dt} + y\frac{dy}{dt} = 0$$

$$\Rightarrow 4 \times 0.02 + 3 \times \frac{dy}{dt} = 0$$

$$\Rightarrow \quad 3\frac{dy}{dt} = -0.08$$

$$\Rightarrow \quad \frac{dy}{dt} = \frac{-0.08}{3} \text{ m/s}$$

$$= \frac{-0.08 \times 100}{3} \text{ cm/s} \quad [\because 1 \text{ m} = 100 \text{ cm}]$$

$$= \frac{-8}{3} \text{ cm/s}$$

Hence, the height of the wall is decreasing at the rate of $\frac{8}{3}$ cm/s, when the ladder is 4 m away from the wall.

EXAMPLE 8. Water is leaking from a conical funnel at the rate of 5 cm^3/s. If the radius of the base of funnel is 5 cm and height is 10 cm, then find the rate at which the water level is dropping when it is 2.5 cm from the top.

Sol. Let r be the radius of base, h be the height at any stage and V be the volume of water in conical funnel.

Here, the radius of base of the conical funnel is 5 cm and height of the conical funnel is 10 cm.

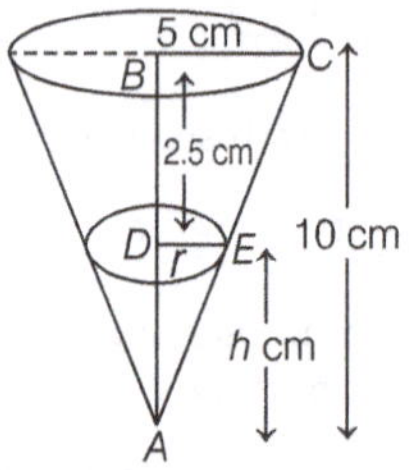

$$\therefore \quad \frac{dV}{dt} = -5 \text{ cm}^3/\text{s}$$

[here, negative (−) sign taken for leaking of water]

and $\quad h = 10 - 2.5 = 7.5$ cm

Since, $\Delta ABC \sim \Delta ADE$

$$\therefore \quad \frac{AB}{AD} = \frac{BC}{DE} \quad \text{[by property of similar triangles]}$$

$$\Rightarrow \quad \frac{10}{h} = \frac{5}{r} \Rightarrow 10r = 5h \Rightarrow r = h/2$$

Now, we know that

Volume of cone $= \frac{1}{3}\pi r^2 h$

$\therefore$ Volume of water in conical funnel

$$V = \frac{1}{3}\pi\left(\frac{h}{2}\right)^2 \cdot h = \frac{\pi}{12}h^3$$

On differentiating both sides w.r.t. t, we get

$$\frac{dV}{dt} = \frac{\pi}{12} \times 3h^2 \times \frac{dh}{dt} = \frac{\pi}{4}h^2\frac{dh}{dt}$$

$$\Rightarrow \quad -5 = \frac{\pi}{4} \times (7.5)^2 \frac{dh}{dt}$$

$$\Rightarrow \quad \frac{dh}{dt} = -5 \times \frac{4}{\pi} \times \frac{1}{56.25}$$

$$\Rightarrow \quad \frac{dh}{dt} = \frac{-20 \times 100}{\pi \times 5625} = \frac{-20 \times 4}{\pi \times 225} = \frac{-16}{45\pi} \text{ cm/s}$$

Hence, the rate at which the water level dropping is $\frac{16}{45\pi}$ cm/s.

Marginal Cost

If $C(x)$ represents the cost function for x units produced, then marginal cost denoted by MC, is given by

$$\text{MC} = \frac{d}{dx}\{C(x)\}.$$

EXAMPLE 9. The total cost $C(x)$ of producing x items in a firm is given by

$$C(x) = 0.005x^3 - 0.02\,x^2 + 30x + 6000.$$

Find the marginal cost when 4 units are produced.

Sol. We have, $C(x) = 0.005\,x^3 - 0.02x^2 + 30x + 6000$

$\therefore$ Marginal cost,

$$MC = \frac{dC}{dx} = 0.005 \times 3x^2 - 0.02 \times 2x + 30$$

$$\Rightarrow \; [MC]_{x=4} = (0.005 \times 3 \times 16) - (0.02 \times 2 \times 4) + 30$$
$$= 0.24 - 0.16 + 30$$
$$= 30.08$$

Hence, the required marginal cost is ₹ 30.08.

Marginal Revenue

If $R(x)$ represents the revenue function for x units sold, then marginal revenue denoted by MR, is given by

$$MR = \frac{d}{dx}\{R(x)\}.$$

If fixed cost and variable cost of a commodity is given, then total cost can be determined by the relation.

Total cost = Fixed cost + Variable cost

i.e. $C(x) = f(c) + v(x)$.

EXAMPLE 10. The total revenue (in ₹) received from the sale of x units of a product is given by $R(x) = 3x^2 + 6x + 5$. Find the marginal revenue, when $x = 5$.

Sol. Given, $R(x) = 3x^2 + 6x + 5$.

We know that marginal revenue is the rate of change of total revenue with respect to the number of units sold.

$\therefore$ Marginal Revenue, $MR = \dfrac{dR}{dx} = 6x + 6$

When $x = 5$, then $MR = 6(5) + 6 = 36$.

Hence, the required marginal revenue is ₹ 36.

Topic Practice 1

1 The radius of a circle is increasing at the rate of 0.7 cm/s. What is the rate of increase of its circumference?

2 The radius of an air bubble is increasing at the rate of $\frac{1}{2}$ cm/s. At what rate is the volume of bubble increasing, when the radius is 1 cm?

3 A balloon which always remains spherical on inflation is being inflated by pumping in 900 cu cm of gas per second. Find the rate at which the radius of the balloon increases, when the radius is 15 cm.

4 The sides of an equilateral triangle are increasing at the rate of 2 cm/s. Find the rate at which the area increases, when the side is 10 cm.

5 The volume of a cube is increasing at a rate of 9 cm^3/s. How fast is the surface area increasing when the length of an edge is 10 cm?

6 The volume of a cube increases at a constant rate. Prove that the increase in its surface area varies inversely as the length of the side.

7 If the area of a circle increase at a uniform rate, then prove that perimeter varies inversely as the radius.

8 The length x of a rectangle is decreasing at the rate of 5 cm/min and the width y is increasing at the rate of 4 cm/min. When $x = 8$ cm and $y = 6$ cm, find the rate of change of
(i) the perimeter.
(ii) the area of the rectangle.

9 Find the point on the curve $x^2 = 4y$, in which abscissa and ordinate change at the same rate.

10 The radius r of a right circular cylinder is increasing at the rate of 5 cm/min and its height h, is decreasing at the rate of 4 cm/min. Find the rate of change of volume when its $r = 8$ cm and $h = 6$ cm.

11 A balloon which always remains spherical has a variable diameter $\frac{3}{2}(2x+1)$. Then, find the rate of change of its volume with respect to x.

12 For the curve $y = 5x - 2x^3$, if x increase at the rate of 2 units/s, then find the rate of change of the slope of curve changing when $x = 3$.

13 A particle moves along the curve $6y = x^3 + 2$. Find the points on the curve at which the y-coordinate is changing 2 times as fast as the x-coordinate.

14 A spherical ball of salt is dissolving in water in such a manner that the rate of decreasing of the volume at any instant is proportional to the surface. Prove that the radius is decreasing at a constant rate.

15 A man 2 m tall, walks at a uniform speed of 6 km/h away from a lamp post 6 m high. Find the rate at which the length of his shadow increases.

16 A car starts from a point P at time $t=0$ s and stops at Q. The distance x (in metres), covered by it in t seconds is given by $x=t^2\left(2-\frac{t}{3}\right)$. Find the time taken by it to reach Q and also the distance P and Q.

17 A swimming pool is to be drained for cleaning. If L represents the number of litres of water in the pool t seconds after the pool has been plugged off to drain and $L=200(10-t)^2$. How fast is the water running out at the end of 5 s and what is the average rate at which the water flows out during the first 5 s?

18 A kite is moving horizontally at a height of 151.5 m. If the speed of kite is 10 m/s, then how fast is the string being let out, when the kite is 250 m away from the boy who is flying the kite, if the height of boy is 1.5m?

19 Sand is pouring from a pipe at the rate of 12 cm^3/s. The falling sand form a cone on the ground in such a way that the height of the cone is always one-sixth of the radius of the base. How fast is the height of the sand cone increasing when the height is 4 cm?

20 An Airforce plane is ascending vertically at the rate of 100 km/h. If the radius of the Earth is r km, then how fast is the area of the Earth visible from the plane increasing at 3 min after it started ascending? Given that the visible area A at height h is given by $A=2\pi r^2\frac{h}{r+h}$.

21 Water is running into a conical vessel, 15 cm deep and 5 cm in radius at the rate of 0.1 cm^3/s, when the water is 6 cm deep. Find at what rate is
(i) the water level rising?
(ii) the water surface area increasing?
(iii) the wetted surface of the vessel increasing?

22 If the total cost $C(x)$ (in ₹) associated with the production of x units of an item is given by $C(x)=0.007x^3-0.003x^2+15x+4000$, then find the marginal cost when 17 units are produced.

23 The total cost $C(x)$ in rupees, associated with the production of x units of an item is given by $C(x)=0.005x^3-0.02x^2+30x+5000$. Find the marginal cost when 3 units are produced, whereby marginal cost, we mean the instantaneous rate of change of total cost at any level of output.

24 The total revenue in rupees received from the sale of x units of a product is given by $R(x)=13x^2+26x+15$. Find the marginal revenue, when $x=7$.

Hints & Solutions

1. Let r be the radius and C be the circumference of circle.

Given, $\frac{dr}{dt}=0.7$ cm/s

Now, circumference of a circle, $C=2\pi r$

On differentiating both sides w.r.t. t, we get

$$\frac{dC}{dt}=2\pi\frac{dr}{dt} \Rightarrow \frac{dC}{dt}=2\pi\times 0.7=1.4\pi \text{ cm/s}$$

Hence, the rate of increase of circumference is 1.4π cm/s.

2. Similar as Example 2.

Ans. The volume of bubble is increasing at the rate of 2π cm^3/s.

3. Similar as Example 2. **Ans.** $\frac{1}{\pi}$ cm/s

4. Let the side of triangle be a.

Given, $\frac{da}{dt}=2$ cm/s

Now, area of equilateral triangle having side a is given by

$$A=\frac{\sqrt{3}a^2}{4}$$

On differentiating both sides w.r.t. t, we get

$$\frac{dA}{dt}=\frac{\sqrt{3}}{4}\cdot(2a)\frac{da}{dt}$$

On putting $\frac{da}{dt}=2$ cm/s and $a=10$ cm, we get

$$\frac{dA}{dt}=\frac{\sqrt{3}}{4}\times 2\times 10\times 2=10\sqrt{3}\ cm^2/s$$

5. Similar as Example 3. **Ans.** 3.6 cm^2/s

6. Hint $\frac{dV}{dt}=k$ (constant) $\Rightarrow 3a^2\frac{da}{dt}=k \Rightarrow \frac{da}{dt}=\frac{k}{3a^2}$

Now, $\frac{dS}{dt}=\frac{d}{dt}(6a^2)=12a\frac{da}{dt}=12a\cdot\frac{k}{3a^2}=4\frac{k}{a}$

$\Rightarrow \frac{dS}{dt}\propto\frac{1}{a}$

7. Let r be the radius, A be the area and P be the perimeter.

Then, we have $\frac{dA}{dt}=$ constant $=k$ (say)

$$\Rightarrow \frac{d}{dt}(\pi r^2)=k \Rightarrow 2\pi r\frac{dr}{dt}=k \Rightarrow \frac{dr}{dt}=\frac{k}{2\pi r} \quad \text{...(i)}$$

Now, $\frac{dp}{dt}=\frac{d}{dt}(2\pi r)=2\pi\frac{dr}{dt}$

$=2\pi\times\frac{k}{2\pi r}=\frac{k}{r}$ [from Eq. (i)]

Thus, $\frac{dp}{dt}\propto\frac{1}{r}$ **Hence proved.**

8. Similar as Example 4.
Ans. (i) Perimeter decreases at the rate of 2 cm/min.
(ii) Area increases at the rate of 2 cm^2/min.

9. Similar as Example 5. **Ans.** $(x = 2, y = 1)$

10. Similar as Example 6. **Ans.** $224\pi\, cm^3/s$

11. Given, diameter of the balloon $= \frac{3}{2}(2x+1)$

$\therefore$ Radius of the balloon $= \frac{\text{Diameter}}{2}$

$$= \frac{1}{2}\left[\frac{3}{2}(2x+1)\right] = \frac{3}{4}(2x+1)$$

For the balloon, the volume V is given by

$$V = \frac{4}{3}\pi(\text{radius})^3 = \frac{4}{3}\pi\left[\frac{3}{4}(2x+1)\right]^3 = \frac{9\pi}{16}(2x+1)^3$$

For the rate of change of volume, differentiate w.r.t. x, we get

$$\frac{dV}{dx} = \frac{9\pi}{16} \times 3(2x+1)^2 \times 2 = \frac{27\pi}{8}(2x+1)^2$$

Thus, the rate of change of volume is $\frac{27\pi}{8}(2x+1)^2$.

12. Given, curve is $y = 5x - 2x^3$ and $\frac{dx}{dt} = 2$ units/s ...(i)

Now, slope of the curve $\frac{dy}{dx} = 5 - 6x^2 = M$ (say)

Rate of change of the slope,

$$\frac{dM}{dt} = -6\frac{d}{dt}(x^2) \Rightarrow \frac{dM}{dt} = -12x\frac{dx}{dt}$$

When $x = 3$, then $\frac{dM}{dt} = -12 \times 3 \times 2 = -72$ unit/s

Thus, the slope of the curve is decreasing at a rate of 72 units/s.

13. Hint Given, $6y = x^3 + 2 \Rightarrow y = \frac{x^3+2}{6}$

Let the coordinates on the curve be (x, y).

According to question,

$$\frac{dy}{dx} = 2 \Rightarrow \frac{d}{dx}\left(\frac{x^3+2}{6}\right) = 2 \Rightarrow x^2 = 4 \Rightarrow x = \pm 2$$

When $x = 2$, $y = \frac{(x^3+2)}{6} = \frac{8+2}{6} = \frac{5}{3}$

When $x = -2$, $y = \frac{x^3+2}{6} = \frac{-8+2}{6} = -1$

Therefore, required points are $\left(2, \frac{5}{3}\right)$ and $(-2, -1)$.

Ans. $(-2, -1)$ and $\left(2, \frac{5}{3}\right)$

14. Let the radius of spherical ball of the salt be r.

$\therefore$ Volume of the ball, $V = \frac{4}{3}\pi r^3$ and surface area, $S = 4\pi r^2$

$$\therefore \quad \frac{dV}{dt} = \frac{d}{dt}\left(\frac{4}{3}\pi r^3\right) = -\frac{4}{3}\pi \cdot 3r^2\frac{dr}{dt} = -4\pi r^2\frac{dr}{dt}$$

[here, we take negative sign because salt is dissolving]

According to the given condition,

$\frac{dV}{dt} \propto S \Rightarrow \frac{dV}{dt} = kS$, where k is proportionality constant.

$$\Rightarrow \quad -4\pi r^2\frac{dr}{dt} = k \cdot 4\pi r^2 \Rightarrow \frac{dr}{dt} = -k$$

Hence, the radius of ball is decreasing at constant rate.

15. Let AB be the lamp post and a man CD be at a distance x from the lamp post and let $CE = y$ be his shadow.

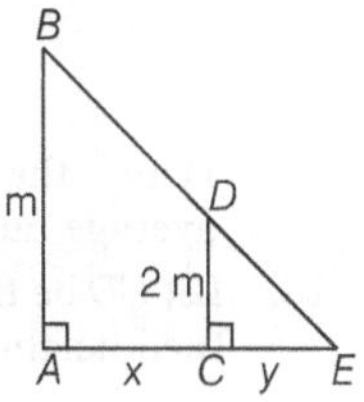

Given that, $\frac{dx}{dt} = 6$ km / h,

$AB = 6\text{ m} = \frac{6}{1000}$ km

and $CD = 2\text{ m} = \frac{2}{1000}$ km [$\because$ 1 km = 1000 m]

Here, $\Delta BAE \sim \Delta DCE$

$$\therefore \quad \frac{AB}{CD} = \frac{AE}{CE} \quad \text{[by property of similar triangles]}$$

$$\Rightarrow \quad \frac{\frac{6}{1000}}{\frac{2}{1000}} = \frac{x+y}{y} \Rightarrow 3 = \frac{x+y}{y}$$

$$\Rightarrow \quad 3y = x + y \Rightarrow 3y - y = x \Rightarrow 2y = x$$

On differentiating both sides w.r.t. t, we get

$$2\frac{dy}{dt} = \frac{dx}{dt} \Rightarrow 2\frac{dy}{dt} = 6 \quad \left[\because \frac{dx}{dt} = 6\right]$$

$$\Rightarrow \quad \frac{dy}{dt} = \frac{6}{2} = 3 \text{ km/h}$$

Hence, the shadow increases at the rate of 3 km/h.

16. We have, $x = t^2\left(2 - \frac{t}{3}\right) = 2t^2 - \frac{t^3}{3}$

Let v be the velocity of car.

Then, $v = \frac{dx}{dt} = 4t - t^2$

Now, $v = 0 \Rightarrow \frac{dx}{dt} = 0 \Rightarrow 4t - t^2 = 0 \Rightarrow t(4-t) = 0$

$\Rightarrow \quad t = 0$ or $t = 4$

Thus, the car takes 4 s to reach at Q.

Hence, the distance between P and Q is the value of x at $t = 4$, which is $\frac{32}{3}$ m.

$$\left[\because x = 2(4)^2 - \frac{(4)^3}{3} = 32 - \frac{64}{3} = \frac{32}{3}\right]$$

17. Given that L represents the number of litres of water in the pool, t seconds after the pool has been plugged off to drain, then

$$L = 200(10-t)^2$$

$\therefore$ Rate at which the water is running out,

$$\frac{dL}{dt} = -200 \cdot 2(10-t) \cdot (-1) = 400(10-t)$$

[here, we take negative sign, because the water is decreasing]

Rate at which the water is running out at the end of 5 s

$= 400(10-5) = 2000$ L /s = Final rate

Initial rate (at $t = 0$) $= \left(\dfrac{dL}{dt}\right)_{t=0} = 4000$ L/s

$\therefore$ Average rate during 5 s $= \dfrac{\text{Initial rate} + \text{Final rate}}{2}$

$= \dfrac{4000 + 2000}{2} = 3000$ L/s

Hence, the water flows out during the first 5 s with average rate of 3000 L /s.

18. Let CD be the height of kite and AB be the height of boy, then height of kite $CD = h = 151.5$ m.

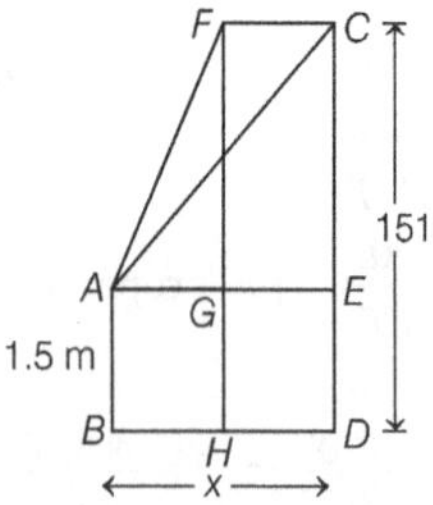

Let $DB = x$ m $= EA$

Since, the kite is 250 m away from the boy. So,

$AC = y = 250$ m

Speed of the kite, $v = \dfrac{dx}{dt} = 10$ m/s

From the figure, we get

$EC = 151.5 - 1.5 = 150$ m

In right angled ΔCEA, we get

$AE^2 + EC^2 = AC^2$ [by Pythagoras theorem]

$\Rightarrow \quad x^2 + (150)^2 = y^2 \quad$ ...(i)

$\Rightarrow \quad x^2 + (150)^2 = (250)^2 \Rightarrow x^2 = (250)^2 - (150)^2$

$\Rightarrow \quad x^2 = (250+150)(250-150) = 400 \times 100$

$\Rightarrow \quad x = 20 \times 10 = 200$

On differentiating both sides of Eq. (i) w.r.t. t, we get

$2x \cdot \dfrac{dx}{dt} + 0 = 2y \dfrac{dy}{dt} \Rightarrow 2y \cdot \dfrac{dy}{dt} = 2x \dfrac{dx}{dt}$

$\Rightarrow \dfrac{dy}{dt} = \dfrac{x}{y} \cdot \dfrac{dx}{dt} = \dfrac{200}{250} \cdot 10 = 8$ m/s $\quad \left[\because \dfrac{dx}{dt} = 10 \text{ m/s}\right]$

Hence, the required rate at which the string is being let out is 8 m/s.

19. Let r be the radius, h be the height and V be the volume of the sand cone.

Also given that, $\dfrac{dV}{dt} = 12$ cm^3/s, $h = \dfrac{1}{6} r$

$\Rightarrow \quad r = 6h$ and $h = 4$ cm

Volume of sand cone, $V = \dfrac{1}{3} \pi r^2 h \Rightarrow V = \dfrac{1}{3} \pi (6h)^2 h \quad [\because r = 6h]$

$\Rightarrow \quad V = \dfrac{1}{3} \pi \times 36\, h^2 \times h = 12\, \pi h^3$

On differentiating both sides w.r.t. t, we get

$\dfrac{dV}{dt} = 12\, \pi \times 3h^2 \dfrac{dh}{dt} = 36\, \pi h^2 \dfrac{dh}{dt}$

$\Rightarrow \quad 12 = 36\pi (4)^2 \dfrac{dh}{dt} \Rightarrow \dfrac{dh}{dt} = \dfrac{12}{36\pi \times 16} = \dfrac{1}{48\pi}$ cm/s

Hence, the height of the sand cone is increasing at the rate of $\dfrac{1}{48\pi}$ cm/s, when the height is 4 cm.

20. Hint Given, $\dfrac{dh}{dt} = 100$ km/h, then find $\dfrac{dA}{dt}$.

Height of the plane after 3 min $= 100 \times \dfrac{3}{60} = 5$ km.

Ans. $\dfrac{200\, \pi\, r^3}{(r+5)^2}$

21. Hint $\because \dfrac{dV}{dt} = 0.1$ cm^3/s

(i) To find $\dfrac{dh}{dt}$, where $h = 6$ cm

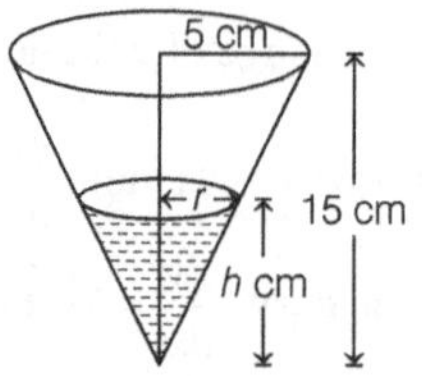

Ans. $\dfrac{1}{40\pi}$ cm/s

(ii) Water surface area (A) at any time $t = \pi r^2$

$= \pi \dfrac{h^2}{9} \quad \left[\text{from part (i), } \dfrac{5}{r} = \dfrac{15}{h} \Rightarrow r = \dfrac{h}{3}\right]$

$\Rightarrow \quad \dfrac{dA}{dt} = \dfrac{2\pi}{9} h \dfrac{dh}{dt}$

Now, $\left(\dfrac{dA}{dt}\right)_{h=6} = \dfrac{2\pi}{9} \times 6 \times \dfrac{1}{40\pi}$

$\left[\because \dfrac{dh}{dt} = \dfrac{1}{40\pi}, \text{ from part (i)}\right]$

Ans. $\dfrac{1+\sqrt{10}}{30}$ cm^2/ s

(iii) Wetted surface area (S) of the vessel at any time $t = \pi r l$

$= \pi \dfrac{h}{3} \sqrt{r^2 + h^2} = \pi \dfrac{h}{3} \sqrt{\dfrac{h^2}{9} + h^2} = \pi \cdot \dfrac{h}{3} \cdot \dfrac{\sqrt{10}h}{3} = \dfrac{\pi}{9} \sqrt{10} h^2$

Now, $\dfrac{dS}{dt} = \dfrac{2\pi\sqrt{10}}{9} h \dfrac{dh}{dt} \Rightarrow \left(\dfrac{dS}{dt}\right)_{\text{at } h=6} = \dfrac{2\pi\sqrt{10}}{9} \times 6 \times \dfrac{1}{40\pi}$

Ans. $\dfrac{\sqrt{10}}{30}$ cm^2/s

22. Similar as Example 9. **Ans.** ₹ 20.967

23. Similar as Example 9. **Ans.** ₹ 30.015

24. Similar as Example 10. **Ans.** ₹ 208

Increasing and Decreasing Functions

In this topic, we shall learn about the monotonicity of functions.

A function $f(x)$ is said to be a monotonically increasing function in the interval $[a, b]$, if

(i) the value of $f(x)$ increases with the increase in x.

or

(ii) the value of $f(x)$ decrease with the decrease in x.

And a function $f(x)$ is said to be a monotonically decreasing function in the interval $[a, b]$, if

(i) the value of $f(x)$ decreases with the increase in x.

or

(ii) the value of $f(x)$ increase with the decrease in x

The monotonicity of the functions in $[a, b]$ is related to its derivative in $[a, b]$.

Hence, to find out the intervals we need to solve the inequations $f'_{(x)} > 0$. But before this we shall learn about the procedure of solving some ration algebraic inequations.

Solving the Rational Algebraic Inequations

In this, we shall discuss the following rational algebraic inequations if $P(x)$ and $Q(x)$ are polynomials.

(i) $\dfrac{P(x)}{Q(x)} > 0$ (ii) $\dfrac{P(x)}{Q(x)} < 0$

(iii) $\dfrac{P(x)}{Q(x)} \geq 0$ (iv) $\dfrac{P(x)}{Q(x)} \leq 0$

Algorithm

(i) First factorise $P(x)$ and $Q(x)$ into linear factors.

(ii) Now, make coefficient of x positive in all factors.

(iii) Equate all the factors to zero and find the corresponding values of x which are know as critical point.

(iv) Write down the critical points on the number line. Note n critical points will give $(n+1)$ intervals on the number line.

(v) In the right most region, the expression will be positive and in the remaining region it will be alternatively negative and positive. So, mark the sign accordingly.

(vi) Get the solution set of the given inequation by selecting appropriate region in step (v).

Following examples will illustrate the above algorithm.

EXAMPLE 1. Solve $2x^3 - 16x^2 + 38x - 24 > 0$.

Sol. We have,

$$2x^3 - 16x^2 + 38x - 24 > 0$$

$$\Rightarrow \quad 2(x^3 - 8x^2 + 19x - 12) > 0$$

$$\Rightarrow \quad x^3 - 8x^2 + 19x - 12 > 0 \quad [\because 2 > 0]$$

$$\Rightarrow \quad (x-1)(x^2 - 7x + 12) > 0$$

$$\Rightarrow \quad (x-1)(x-3)(x-4) > 0$$

On equating all the factors to zero, we get $x = 1, 3, 4$ as critical points. Let us plot them on number line.

As per the algorithm, we shall mark the positive/negative sign in the regions of the number line.

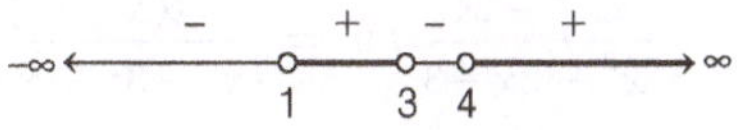

$$(x-1)(x-3)(x-4) > 0$$

$$\Rightarrow \quad x \in (1, 3) \cup (4, \infty)$$

Hence, the solution set is $(1, 3) \cup (4, \infty)$.

EXAMPLE 2. Solve $\dfrac{1}{(x+2)} - \dfrac{8}{(x+4)^2} > 0, x \neq = -2, -4$.

Sol. We have, $\dfrac{1}{(x+2)} - \dfrac{8}{(x+4)^2} > 0$

$$\Rightarrow \quad \frac{(x+4)^2 - 8(x+2)}{(x+2)(x+4)^2} > 0$$

$$\Rightarrow \quad \frac{x^2 + 8x + 16 - 8x - 16}{(x+2)(x+4)^2} > 0 \Rightarrow \frac{x^2}{(x+2)(x+4)^2} > 0$$

$$\Rightarrow \quad \frac{1}{(x+2)} \cdot \left(\frac{x}{x+4}\right)^2 > 0 \Rightarrow \frac{1}{x+2} > 0 \text{ and } x \neq 0$$

$$\left[\because \left(\frac{x}{x+4}\right)^2 > 0, \text{ if } a > 0, ab > 0 \Rightarrow b > 0\right]$$

$$\Rightarrow \quad x + 2 > 0 \text{ and } x \neq 0 \quad \left[\because \frac{a}{b} > 0 \text{ and } a > 0 \Rightarrow b > 0\right]$$

$$\Rightarrow \quad x > -2 \text{ and } x \neq 0$$

$$x \in (-2, 0) \cup (0, \infty)$$

Hence, the solution set is $(-2, 0) \cup (0, \infty)$.

EXAMPLE 3. Solve $\dfrac{3x-15}{x} \leq 5 - x$.

Sol. We have, $\dfrac{3x-15}{x} \leq 5 - x \Rightarrow \dfrac{3x-15}{x} + x \leq 5 - x + x$

$$\Rightarrow \quad \frac{3x-15}{x} + x \leq 5 \Rightarrow \frac{3x-15}{x} + x - 5 \leq 5 - 5$$

$$\Rightarrow \quad \frac{3x-15}{x} + x - 5 \leq 0 \Rightarrow \frac{3x - 15 + x^2 - 5x}{x} \leq 0$$

$$\Rightarrow \frac{x^2-2x-15}{x} \le 0 \Rightarrow \frac{(x+3)(x-5)}{x} \le 0$$

On equating all factors to zero, we get critical points, $x = -3, 5$ and also 0.

[Zero is critical point because at $x = 0$ in equation is not defined]

Now, we shall mark the positive negative sign in the region of the number line.

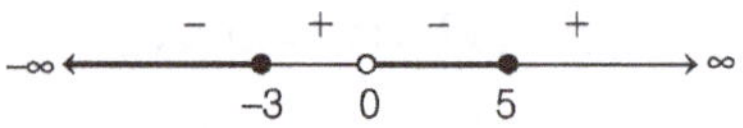

$$\frac{(x+3)(x-5)}{x} \le 0 \Rightarrow x \in (-\infty, -3] \cup (0, 5]$$

Hence, solution set is $(-\infty, -3] \cup (0, 5]$.

EXAMPLE 4. Solve $\dfrac{6x^2-24}{x^2-2x-3} < 0$

Sol. We have, $\dfrac{6x^2-24}{x^2-2x-3} < 0 \Rightarrow \dfrac{6(x^2-4)}{x^2-3x+x-3} < 0$

$$\Rightarrow \frac{x^2-2^2}{x(x-3)+1(x-3)} < 0 \quad [\because 6 > 0]$$

$$\Rightarrow \frac{(x-2)(x+2)}{(x-3)(x+1)} < 0 \quad [\because a^2-b^2 = (a-b)(a+b)]$$

Equating all the factors to zero, we get $x = -2, -1, 2$ and 3 as critical points.

Now, we shall mark the positive or negative sign in the region of the number line.

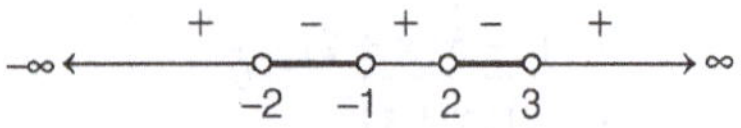

$$\frac{(x-2)(x+2)}{(x-3)(x+1)} < 0 \Rightarrow x \in (-2, -1) \cup (2, 3)$$

Hence, the solution set is $(-2, -1) \cup (2, 3)$.

EXAMPLE 5. Solve $\dfrac{x^2-5x+12}{x^2-4x+5} > 3$.

Sol. We have, $\dfrac{x^2-5x+12}{x^2-4x+5} > 3$

$$\Rightarrow \frac{x^2-5x+12}{x^2-4x+5} - 3 > 0$$

$$\Rightarrow \frac{x^2-5x+12-3(x^2-4x+5)}{x^2-4x+5} > 0$$

$$\Rightarrow \frac{x^2-5x+12-3x^2+12x-15}{x^2-4x+5} > 0$$

$$\Rightarrow \frac{-2x^2+7x-3}{x^2-4x+5} > 0$$

$$\Rightarrow \frac{-(2x^2-7x+3)}{x^2-4x+5} > 0$$

$$\Rightarrow \frac{2x^2-7x+3}{x^2-4x+5} < 0$$

$$\Rightarrow \frac{(x-3)(2x-1)}{(x-2)^2+1} < 0$$

$$\Rightarrow (x-3)(2x-1) < 0 \quad [\because 1+(x-2)^2 > 0]$$

Equating all the factors to zero, we get $x = \frac{1}{2}, 3$ as the critical points.

Now, we shall mark the positive or negative sign in the region of the number line.

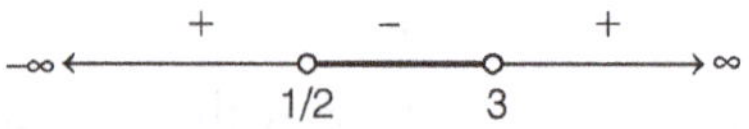

$$(x-3)(2x-1) < 0 \Rightarrow x \in \left(\frac{1}{2}, 3\right)$$

Hence, the solution is $\left(\frac{1}{2}, 3\right)$.

EXAMPLE 6. Solve $\dfrac{2(x-3)}{(x-1)(x-10)} \ge \dfrac{1}{x-2}$.

Sol. We have, $\dfrac{2(x-3)}{(x-1)(x-10)} \ge \dfrac{1}{x-2}$

$$\Rightarrow \frac{2(x-3)}{(x-1)(x-10)} - \frac{1}{(x-2)} \ge 0$$

$$\Rightarrow \frac{2(x-3)(x-2)-(x-1)(x-10)}{(x-1)(x-10)(x-2)} \ge 0$$

$$\Rightarrow \frac{2(x^2-5x+6)-(x^2-11x+10)}{(x-1)(x-2)(x-10)} \ge 0$$

$$\Rightarrow \frac{x^2+x+2}{(x-1)(x-2)(x-10)} \ge 0$$

$$\Rightarrow \frac{\left(x+\frac{1}{2}\right)^2+\left(\frac{\sqrt{7}}{2}\right)^2}{(x-1)(x-2)(x-10)} \ge 0$$

$$\Rightarrow \frac{1}{(x-1)(x-2)(x-10)} \ge 0$$

$$\left[\because \left(x+\frac{1}{2}\right)^2+\left(\frac{\sqrt{7}}{2}\right)^2 > 0\right]$$

$$\Rightarrow (x-1)(x-2)(x-10) > 0$$

$$\left[\text{if } \frac{a}{b} \ge 0 \text{ and } a > 0, \text{ then } b > 0\right]$$

Equating all the factors to zero, we get $x = 1, 2, 10$ as critical points.

Now, we shall mark the positive or negative sign in the region of the number line.

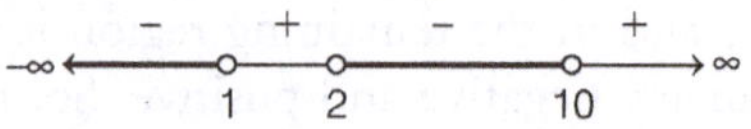

$$((x-1)(x-2)(x-10) > 0$$

$$\Rightarrow x \in (-\infty, 1) \cup (2, 10)$$

Hence, the solution set is $(-\infty, 1) \cup (2, 10)$.

Now we comes to the increasing and decreasing functions.

Increasing Function

A function f is called a increasing function in an open internal (a, b) I, if $x_1 < x_2 \Rightarrow f(x_1) \le f(x_2)$ for all $x_1, x_2 \in I(a, b)$.

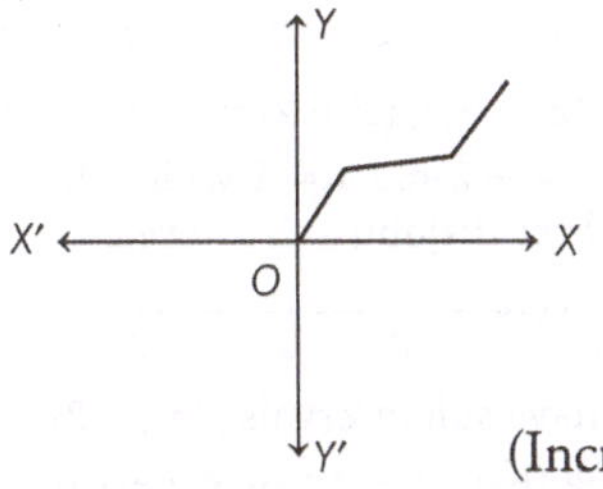

(Increasing Curve)

Strictly Increasing Function

A function f is called a strictly increasing function in an open internal (a, b) I, if $x_1 < x_2 \Rightarrow f(x_1) < f(x_2)$ for all $x_1, x_2 \in I(a, b)$.

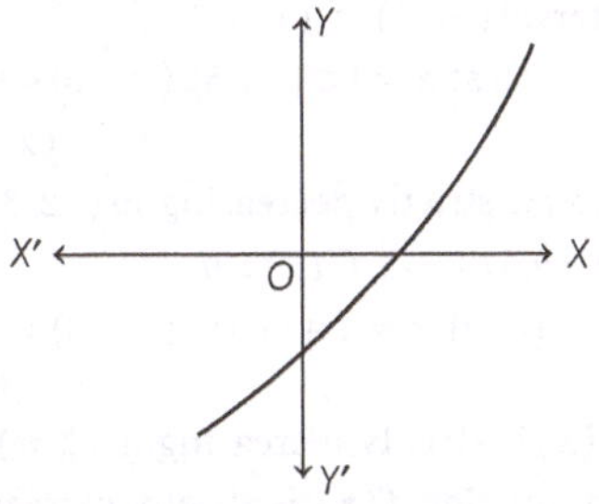

(Strictly Increasing Curve)

EXAMPLE 7. Show that the following functions is a strictly increasing function on R.

(i) $f(x) = 3x + 5$ (ii) $g(x) = e^{3x}$

Sol. (i) We have, $f(x) = 3x + 5$

Let $x_1, x_2 \in R$, such that $x_1 < x_2$.

Then, $x_1 < x_2$

$\Rightarrow$ $3x_1 < 3x_2$ [multiplying both sides by 3]

$\Rightarrow$ $3x_1 + 5 < 3x_2 + 5$ [adding 5 on both sides]

$\Rightarrow$ $f(x_1) < f(x_2)$

Thus, $x_1 < x_2$

$\Rightarrow$ $f(x_1) < f(x_2), \forall x_1, x_2 \in R$

Hence, $f(x)$ is strictly increasing on R.

(ii) We have, $f(x) = e^{3x}$

Let $x_1, x_2 \in R$ such that

$x_1 < x_2 \Rightarrow 3x_1 < 3x_2 \Rightarrow e^{3x_1} < e^{3x_2}$

$[\because e > 1 \text{ and } x_2 > x_1 \Rightarrow e^{x_2} > e^{x_1}]$

Thus, $x_1 < x_2 \Rightarrow e^{3x_1} < e^{3x_2}$

Hence, $g(x)$ is strictly decreasing function on R.

Decreasing Function

A function f is called a decreasing function in an open internal (a, b) I, if $x_1 < x_2 \Rightarrow f(x_1) \ge f(x_2)$ for all $x_1, x_2 \in I(a, b)$.

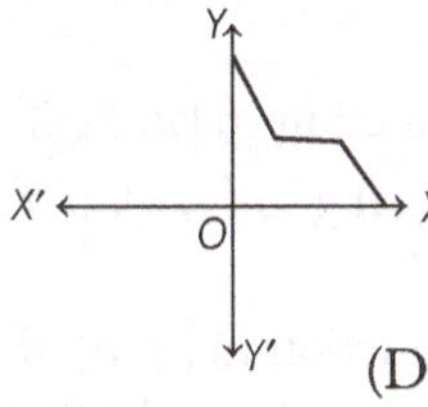

(Decreasing function)

Strictly Decreasing Function

A function f is called a strictly decreasing function in an open internal $]a, b[$ I, if $x_1 < x_2 \Rightarrow f(x_1) > f(x_2)$ for all $x_1, x_2 \in I\ ]a, b[$.

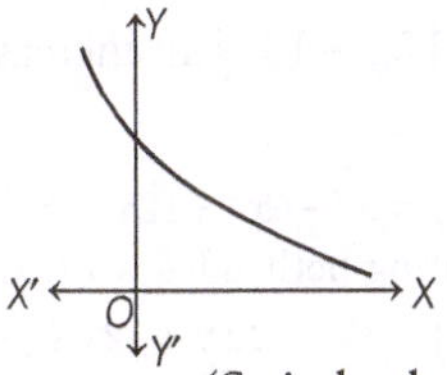

(Strictly decreasing function)

Hence, a strictly decreasing function is an decreasing function but a decreasing function may or may not be strictly decreasing (same is true for increasing function).

EXAMPLE 8. Show that the following functions are strictly decreasing on R.

(i) $f(x) = -5x + 8$ (ii) $f(x) = a^x, 0 < a < 1$

Sol. (i) We have, $f(x) = -5x + 8$

Let $x_1, x_2 \in R$ such that $x_1 < x_2$.

Then, $x_1 < x_2 \Rightarrow -5x_1 > -5x_2$

$\Rightarrow -5x_1 + 8 > -5x_2 + 8$

Thus, $x_1 < x_2 \Rightarrow f(x_1) > f(x_2)$ for all $x_1, x_2 \in R$

Hence, $f(x)$ is strictly decreasing on R.

(ii) We have, $f(x) = a^x, 0 < a < 1$

Let $x_1, x_2 \in R$ such that $x_1 < x_2$.

Then, $x_1 < x_2 \Rightarrow a^{x_1} > a^{x_2}$

$[\because 0 < a < 1, \text{ when } x_1 < x_2, \text{ then } a^{x_1} > a^{x_2}]$

$\Rightarrow$ $f(x_1) > f(x_2), \forall x_1, x_2 \in R$

Hence, $f(x)$ is strictly decreasing on R.

Theorem First Derivative Test

Let f be continuous on $[a, b]$ and differentiable on the open interval (a, b). Then,

(i) f is increasing in $[a, b]$, if $f'(x) > 0$ for each $x \in (a, b)$.

(ii) f is decreasing in $[a, b]$, if $f'(x) < 0$ for each $x \in (a, b)$.

(iii) f is a constant function in $[a, b]$, if $f'(x) = 0$ for each $x \in (a, b)$.

Conclusion

- f is increasing function in $[a, b]$, if $f'(x) \geq 0$.
- f is strictly increasing in (a, b), if $f'(x) > 0$ for each $x \in (a, b)$.
- f is decreasing function in $[a, b]$, if $f'(x) \leq 0$.
- f is strictly decreasing in (a, b), if $f'(x) < 0$ for each $x \in (a, b)$.
- A function will be increasing (decreasing) in R, if it is so as even interval of R.

EXAMPLE 9. Show that the function $f(x) = x^3 - 6x^2 + 12x - 18$ is an increasing function on R.

Sol. We have, $f(x) = x^3 - 6x^2 + 12x - 18$

On differentiating both sides w.r.t. x, we get

$$f'(x) = 3x^2 - 12x + 12 = 3(x^2 - 4x + 4)$$
$$= 3(x - 2)^2 \geq 0, \forall x \in R$$

Thus, $f'(x) \geq 0, \forall x \in R$

Hence, $f(x)$ is an increasing function on R.

EXAMPLE 10. Show that the function f defined by $f(x) = (x - 1)e^x + 1$ is an increasing function for all $x > 0$.

Sol. We have, $f(x) = (x - 1)e^x + 1$

On differentiating w.r.t. x, we get

$$f'(x) = (x - 1)e^x + e^x \Rightarrow f'(x) = xe^x \ \forall \ x > 0$$

$\Rightarrow \quad f'(x) > 0.$

$\therefore$ $f(x)$ is an increasing for all $x > 0$.

EXAMPLE 11. Show that the function $f(x) = (3x^2 - x + 1)$ is neither increasing nor decreasing on $(0, 1)$.

Sol. We have, $f(x) = 3x^2 - x + 1$

On differentiating w.r.t. x, we get

$$f'(x) = 6x - 1$$

Put $f'(x) = 0 \Rightarrow 6x - 1 = 0 \Rightarrow x = \frac{1}{6}$

Here, $f'(x) < 0$ when $x \in \left(0, \frac{1}{6}\right)$

and $f'(x) > 0$ when $x \in \left(\frac{1}{6}, 1\right)$

Thus, $f(x)$ is decreasing in $\left(0, \frac{1}{6}\right)$ and increasing in $\left(\frac{1}{6}, 1\right)$.

Hence, the given function is neither increasing nor decreasing on $(0, 1)$.

EXAMPLE 12. Find the intervals in which the function f given by $f(x) = 4x^3 - 6x^2 - 72x + 30$ is strictly increasing and strictly decreasing. Also, check on whole real line.

Sol. Given, $f(x) = 4x^3 - 6x^2 - 72x + 30, \forall x \in R$

On differentiating both sides w.r.t. x, we get

$$f'(x) = 12x^2 - 12x - 72$$

On putting $f'(x) = 0$, we get

$$12x^2 - 12x - 72 = 0 \Rightarrow 12(x^2 - x - 6) = 0$$

$$\Rightarrow \quad 12(x - 3)(x + 2) = 0 \Rightarrow x = 3, -2$$

We have, $x = -2$ and $x = 3$, which divides the number line into three disjoint sub intervals.

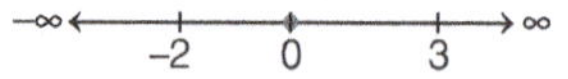

Thus, we have sub intervals $(-\infty, -2)$, $(-2, 3)$ and $(3, \infty)$.

Now, check that $f'(x) > 0$ or $f'(x) < 0$.

In the interval $(-\infty, -2)$, $f'(x) > 0$

$\left[\text{as at } x = -4 \in (-\infty, -2), (x - 3) < 0, (x + 2) < 0, \text{ so } (x - 3)(x + 2) > 0\right]$

$\Rightarrow \quad f(x)$ is strictly increasing in $(-\infty, -2)$.

In the interval $(-2, 3)$, $f'(x) < 0$

[as at $x = 1 \in (-2, 3)$, $(x - 3) < 0$, $(x + 2) > 0$ so, $(x - 3)(x + 2) < 0$]

$\Rightarrow \quad f(x)$ is strictly decreasing in $(-2, 3)$.

In the interval $(3, \infty)$, $f'(x) > 0$

[as at $x = 4 \in (3, \infty)$, $(x - 3) > 0$, $(x + 2) > 0$ so, $(x - 3)(x + 2) > 0$]

$\Rightarrow \quad f(x)$ is strictly increasing in $(3, \infty)$.

Since, the function $f(x)$ is strictly increasing in $(-\infty, -2)$ and $(3, \infty)$ and strictly decreasing in $(-2, 3)$, so f is neither increasing nor decreasing in R.

EXAMPLE 13. Find the intervals on which the function $f(x) = (x - 1)^3 (x - 2)^2$ is

(a) strictly increasing (b) strictly decreasing.

Sol. Given function is $f(x) = (x - 1)^3(x - 2)^2$.

On differentiating w.r.t. x, we get

$$f'(x) = 3(x - 1)^2(x - 2)^2 + 2(x - 2)(x - 1)^3$$
$$= (x - 1)^2(x - 2)[3(x - 2) + 2(x - 1)]$$
$$= (x - 1)^2(x - 2)[5x - 8]$$

sign scheme of $f'(x)$

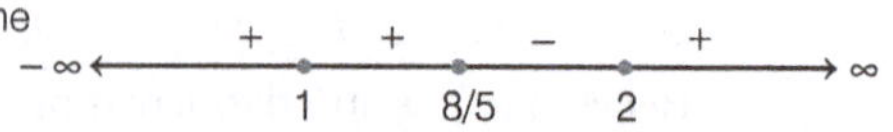

For strictly increasing $f'(x) > 0$.

We get positive $f'(x)$ in the interval $\left(-\infty, \frac{8}{5}\right) \cup (2, \infty)$.

And for strictly decreasing $f'(x) < 0$, we get negative $f'(x)$ in the interval $\left(\frac{8}{5}, 2\right)$.

Topic Practice 2

1 Show that the following functions are strictly increasing without use of derivative

(i) $f(x)=7x-3$.

(ii) $f(x)=ax+b$, where a and b are constants and $a>0$.

(iii) $g(x)=e^{3x+5}$.

2 Show that the following functions are strictly decreasing without use of derivative.

(i) $f(x)=-8x+7$

(ii) $g(x)=5^{3x}$

3 Prove that $f(x)=\frac{3}{x}+7$ is strictly decreasing for $x \in R, (x \neq 0)$.

4 Show that $f(x)=x^2$ is strictly decreasing in $(-\infty, 0)$.

5 Show that the function $f(x)=4x^3-18x^2+27x-7$ is always increasing on R.

6 Show that the function $f(x)=\frac{x}{3}+\frac{3}{x}$ decreases in the intervals $(-3, 0) \cup (0, 3)$.

7 Let I be an interval disjoint from $(-1, 1)$. Prove that the function $f(x)=\left(x+\frac{1}{x}\right)$ is strictly increasing on I.

8 Find the intervals in which the following functions is strictly increasing or strictly decreasing.

(i) $f(x)=-2x^3-9x^2-12x+1$

(ii) $f(x)=20-9x+6x^2-x^3$ **[CBSE 2024]**

(iii) $f(x)=\frac{3}{10}x^4-\frac{4}{5}x^3-3x^2+\frac{36x}{5}+11$

(iv) $f(x)=3x^4-4x^3-12x^2+5$

9 Find the intervals in which the following functions is increasing or decreasing.

(i) $x^2+2x-15$

(ii) $f(x)=x^4-\frac{4x^3}{3}$

(iii) $f(x)=x^3+\frac{1}{x^3}, x \neq 0$

(iv) $f(x)=x^x, x>0$

(v) $f(x)=x^4-8x^3+22x^2-24x+21$

(vi) $f(x)=(x-1)^3(x-2)^2$

(vii) $f(x)=2x^3+9x^2+12x+20$

(viii) $f(x)=2x^3-9x^2+12x-15$

(ix) $f(x)=x^4-2x^2$

(x) $f(x)=2\log(x-2)-x^2+4x+1$

(xi) $f(x)=\frac{x}{\log x}$

(xii) $f(x)=2x^3+9x^2+12x-1$

10 Show that the function $f(x)=(4x^2-3x+5)$ is neither increasing nor decreasing on $(0, 1)$.

11 Find the value(s) of x for which $y=[x(x-2)]^2$ is an increasing function.

12 Find the interval in which $y=x^2e^{-x}$ is increasing.

13 Find the intervals in which the function $f(x)=\frac{x^4}{4}-x^3-5x^2+24x+12$ is

(a) strictly increasing (b) strictly decreasing.

14 Prove that the function f defined by $f(x)=x^2-x+1$ is neither increasing nor decreasing in $(-1, 1)$. Hence find the interval in which $f(x)$, is

(i) strictly increasing. (ii) strictly decreasing.

15 Prove that $\frac{x}{1+x}<\log(1+x)<x$ for $x>0$.

Hints & Solutions

1. (i) Similar as Example 7 (i). (ii) Similar as Example 7 (i).
(iii) Similar as Example 7 (ii).

2. (i) Similar as Example 8 (i). (ii) Similar as Example 8 (ii).

3. Given function is $f(x)=\frac{3}{x}+7, x \neq 0 \Rightarrow f(x)=3x^{-1}+7$

On differentiating both sides w.r.t. x, we get

$$f'(x)=3(-1)x^{-2}+0=\frac{-3}{x^2}<0, \forall x \in R-\{0\}$$

$\therefore$ $f(x)$ is strictly decreasing for $x \in R, (x \neq 0)$.

Hence proved.

4. Here, $f'(x)=2x<0, \forall x \in (-\infty, 0)$

$\therefore f$ is strictly decreasing function in $(-\infty, 0)$.

5. Similar as Example 9.

6. Given, $f(x)=\frac{x}{3}+\frac{3}{x}$

$$\Rightarrow \quad f'(x)=\frac{1}{3}-\frac{3}{x^2} \Rightarrow f'(x)=\frac{x^2-9}{3x^2}$$

When $x \in (-3, 0) \cup (0, 3)$, $f'(x)<0$

$\therefore$ $f(x)$ is decreasing function in $(-3, 0) \cup (0, 3)$.

7. We have, $f(x) = x + \frac{1}{x}$ and $I = R - (-1, 1)$

$$= (-\infty, -1] \cup [1, \infty).$$

Clearly, $f'(x) = 1 - \frac{1}{x^2} = \frac{x^2 - 1}{x^2} > 0, \forall x \in I$

$$[\because x^2 > 1, \forall x \in I \text{ and } x^2 - 1 > 0, \forall x \in I]$$

Hence, $f(x)$ is strictly increasing on I.

8. (i) Similar as Example 12.

Ans. $f(x)$ is strictly increasing in the interval $(-2, -1)$ and $f(x)$ is strictly decreasing in the interval $(-\infty, -2) \cup (-1, \infty)$.

(ii) Similar as Example 12.

Ans. Strictly increasing in $(1, 3)$ and strictly decreasing in $(-\infty, 1) \cup (3, \infty)$.

(iii) Given, $f(x) = \frac{3}{10}x^4 - \frac{4}{5}x^3 - 3x^2 + \frac{36x}{5} + 11$

On differentiating both sides w.r.t. x, we get

$$f'(x) = \frac{12x^3}{10} - \frac{12x^2}{5} - 6x + \frac{36}{5} + 0$$

Put $f'(x) = 0$

$$\Rightarrow \frac{12x^3}{10} - \frac{12x^2}{5} - 6x + \frac{36}{5} = 0$$

$$\Rightarrow \frac{6x^3 - 12x^2 - 30x + 36}{5} = 0$$

$$\Rightarrow x^3 - 2x^2 - 5x + 6 = 0 \quad \left[\text{divide by } \frac{6}{5}\right]$$

$$\Rightarrow (x-1)(x^2 - x - 6) = 0$$

$$\Rightarrow (x-1)(x+2)(x-3) = 0$$

$$\Rightarrow x - 1 = 0$$

or $x + 2 = 0$ or $x - 3 = 0$

$\therefore x = -2, 1, 3$

Now, we find the intervals in which $f(x)$ is strictly increasing or strictly decreasing.

Interval	Sign of $f'(x)$ $f'(x) = (x-1)(x+2)(x-3)$	Nature of function
$(-\infty, -2]$	$(-)(-)(-) = (-) < 0$	Strictly decreasing
$[-2, 1]$	$(-)(+)(-) = (+) > 0$	Strictly increasing
$[1, 3]$	$(+)(+)(-) = (-) < 0$	Strictly decreasing
$[3, \infty)$	$(+)(+)(+) = (+) > 0$	Strictly increasing

(a) $f(x)$ is strictly increasing in the interval $(-2, 1) \cup (3, \infty)$.

(b) $f(x)$ is strictly decreasing in the interval $(-\infty, -2) \cup (1, 3)$.

(iv) Similar as part (iii).

Ans. Strictly increasing $(-1, 0) \cup (2, \infty)$ and strictly decreasing $(-\infty, -1) \cup (0, 2)$

9. (i) **Hint** For increasing, put $f'(x) > 0$

and for decreasing, put $f'(x) < 0$

Ans. Increasing in $(-1, \infty)$, decreasing in $(-\infty, -1)$.

(ii) Similar as Example 13.

Ans. Increasing in $[1, \infty)$, decreasing in $(-\infty, 1]$

(iii) Similar as Example 13.

Ans. Increasing in $x \le -1$ or $x \ge 1$, decreasing in $-1 \le x \le 1$

(iv) **Hint** Let $y = x^x$, $\log y = x \log x$

$$\Rightarrow \frac{dy}{dx} = x^x(1 + \log x) = 0$$

$$\Rightarrow x = \frac{1}{e}$$

Ans. Increasing in $\left[\frac{1}{e}, \infty\right)$, decreasing in $\left(0, \frac{1}{e}\right]$

(v) Similar as Example 13.

Ans. Increasing in $[1, 2] \cup [3, \infty)$ and decreasing in $(-\infty, 1] \cup [2, 3]$.

(vi) Similar as Example 13.

Ans. Increasing in $(-\infty, 1] \cup \left[1, \frac{8}{5}\right] \cup [2, \infty)$, decreasing in $\left[\frac{8}{5}, 2\right]$.

(vii) Similar as Example 13.

Ans. Increasing in $(-\infty, 2] \cup [-1, \infty)$, decreasing in $[-2, -1]$.

(viii) Similar as Example 13.

Ans. Increasing in $(-\infty, 1] \cup [2, \infty)$, decreasing in $[1, 2]$

(ix) Similar as Example 13.

Ans. $f(x)$ is increasing in $[-1, 0] \cup [1, \infty]$, $f(x)$ is decreasing in $[-\infty, -1] \cup [0, 1]$.

(x) Similar as Example 13.

Ans. $f(x)$ is increasing in $(2, 3]$, $f(x)$ is decreasing in $[3, \infty)$.

(xi) **Hint** $f(x) = \frac{x}{\log x}$

$$\therefore f'(x) = \frac{\log x - 1}{(\log x)^2}, x \ne 1$$

Now, $f'(x) \ge 0$, $x \ge e$ and $f'(x) \le 0$, $x \in (0, e] - \{1\}$

Ans. $f(x)$ is increasing in $[e, \infty)$, $f(x)$ is decreasing in $(0, e] - \{1\}$.

(xii) We have, $f(x) = 2x^3 + 9x^2 + 12x - 1$

$$\therefore f'(x) = 6x^2 + 18x + 12$$

$$= 6(x^2 + 3x + 2) = 6(x+2)(x+1)$$

So, $f'(x) \le 0$, for decreasing.

On drawing number lines as below

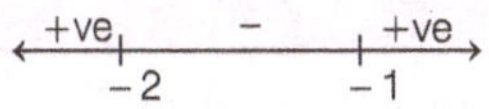

We see that $f'(x)$ is decreasing in $[-2, -1]$.

$f'(x) > 0$, for increasing

$$x \in (-\infty, -2) \cup (-1, \infty)$$

10. Similar as Example 11.

11. Given, $y = [x(x-2)]^2 = [x^2 - 2x]^2$

On differentiating both sides w.r.t. x, we get

$$\frac{dy}{dx} = 2(x^2 - 2x) \cdot \frac{d}{dx}(x^2 - 2x)$$
$$= 2(x^2 - 2x)(2x - 2)$$
$$= 2[2x^3 - 6x^2 + 4x]$$
$$= 4x[x^2 - 3x + 2]$$
$$= 4x(x-2)(x-1)$$

On putting $\frac{dy}{dx} = 0$, we get

$$4x(x-2)(x-1) = 0$$
$$\Rightarrow \quad x = 0, 1 \text{ and } 2$$

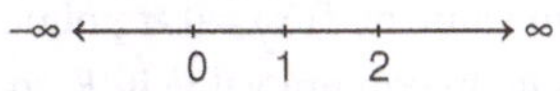

These values divide the real line into four disjoint intervals $(-\infty, 0)$, $(0, 1)$, $(1, 2)$ and $(2, \infty)$.

In each interval, nature of $y(x)$ is given below

Interval	Sign of $f(x)$	Nature of $y(x)$
$(-\infty, 0)$	$(-)(-)(-) = -$ve	Strictly decreasing
$(0, 1)$	$(+)(-)(-) = +$ ve	Strictly increasing
$(1, 2)$	$(+)(-)(+) = -$ ve	Strictly decreasing
$(2, \infty]$	$(+)(+)(+) = +$ve	Strictly increasing

Therefore, $y(x)$ is increasing in $(0, 1)$ and $(2, \infty)$.

$\Rightarrow \quad 0 < x < 1$ and $x > 2$.

12. **Hint** $\frac{dy}{dx} = -e^{-x}\, x(x-2)$. Solve $\frac{dy}{dx} \geq 0$.

Ans. $[0, 2]$

13. We have, $f(x) = \frac{x^4}{4} - x^3 - 5x^2 + 24x + 12$

On differentiating both sides w.r.t. x, we get

$$f'(x) = x^3 - 3x^2 - 10x + 24$$
$$= (x-2)(x^2 - x - 12)$$
$$= (x-2)(x^2 - 4x + 3x - 12)$$
$$= (x-2)(x(x-4) + 3(x-4))$$
$$= (x-2)(x-4)(x+3)$$

Now, put $f'(x) = 0$, which gives $x = 2, 4$ and -3.

The points $x = -3$, $x = 2$ and $x = 4$ divides the whole real line into four disjoint intervals namely, $(-\infty, -3)$, $(-3, 2)$, $(2, 4)$, $(4, \infty)$

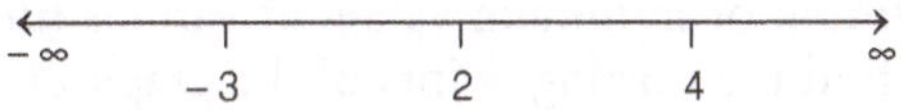

Note that, for $x \in (-\infty, -3)$, $f'(x) < 0$

for $x \in (-3, 2)$, $f'(x) > 0$

for $x \in (2, 4)$, $f'(x) < 0$

and for $x \in (4, \infty)$, $f'(x) > 0$

$\therefore f(x)$ is strictly increasing in the intervals $(-3, 2)$ and $(4, \infty)$, and strictly decreasing in the intervals $(-\infty, -3)$ and $(2, 4)$.

14. **Hint** $f'(x) = 2x - 1$, which is both positive and negative in $(-1, 1)$.

Hence, $f(x)$ is neither increasing nor decreasing, further proceed as Example 12.

Ans. (i) $\left(\frac{1}{2}, 1\right)$ (ii) $\left(-1, \frac{1}{2}\right)$

15. Let $f(x) = \log(1+x) - \frac{x}{1+x}$.

Then, $f'(x) = \frac{1}{1+x} - \frac{1}{(1+x)^2} = \frac{x}{(1+x)^2} > 0$ for $x > 0$

Since, $f'(x) > 0$, $\forall x > 0$ and $f'(0) = 0$, it follows that $f(x)$ is increasing on $(0, \infty)$.

Now, $x > 0 \Rightarrow f(x) > f(0) \Rightarrow f(x) > 0 \quad [\because f(0) = 0]$

$$\Rightarrow \quad \left[\log(1+x) - \frac{x}{1+x}\right] > 0$$
$$\Rightarrow \quad \log(1+x) > \frac{x}{1+x} \quad \text{...(i)}$$

Again, let $g(x) = x - \log(1+x)$,

then $g'(x) = \left[1 - \frac{1}{1+x}\right] = \frac{x}{1+x} > 0$ for $x > 0$

Now, $g'(x) > 0$, $\forall x > 0$ and $g'(0) = 0$

$\therefore g(x)$ is strictly increasing on $(0, \infty)$.

Also, $g(0) = 0$

Now, $x > 0 \Rightarrow g(x) > g(0)$

$\Rightarrow \quad g(x) > 0 \quad [\because g(0) = 0]$

$\Rightarrow \quad [x - \log(1+x)] > 0$

$$x > \log(1+x) \quad \text{...(ii)}$$

From Eqs. (i) and (ii), we get

$$\frac{x}{1+x} < \log(1+x) < x \text{ for } x > 0$$

Maxima and Minima

Here, we will use the concept of derivatives to calculate the maximum or minimum values of various functions. We will find the turning points of the graph of a function and then find points at which the graph reaches its highest (or lowest) locally, algorithm, we will find the absolute maximum and absolute minimum of a function.

Maximum and Minimum Values in an Interval

Let f be a function defined on interval I (i.e. I is the domain of f). Then,

(i) A function $f(x)$ is said to have a **maximum value** in I, if there exists a point c in interval I, such that $f(c) > f(x)\ \forall\ x \in I$.

Here, the number $f(c)$ is called the maximum value of f in I and point c is called a **point of maximum value** of f in I.

(ii) A function $f(x)$ is said to have a **minimum value** in I, if there exists a point c in interval I, such that

$$f(c) < f(x)\ \forall\ x \text{ in } I$$

Here, the number $f(c)$ is called the minimum value of f in I and the point c is called a **point of minimum value** of f in I.

(iii) f is said to have an **extreme value** in I, if there exists a point c in I such that $f(c)$ is either a maximum value or a minimum value of f in I. The number $f(c)$ is called an extreme value of f in I and the point c is called an **extreme point.**

Important Results

(i) Graphs of certain particular functions help us to find maximum value and minimum value at a point. From graph, we can also find maximum/minimum value of a function at a point at which it is not even differentiable.

(ii) Every monotonic function, i.e. either increasing or decreasing function assumes its maximum/minimum value at the end points of the domain of the function.

(iii) Every continuous function on a closed interval has a maximum and a minimum value.

e.g. Let $f(x) = x, x \in (0, 1)$. In $(0, 1)$, $f(x)$ has neither the maximum value nor the minimum value. If we include the points 0 and 1 in the domain, i.e. if domain is $[0,1]$, then $f(x) = x$ has minimum value 0 at $x = 0$ and maximum value 1 at $x = 1$.

EXAMPLE 1. Find the maximum and minimum values of the following function

$$f(x) = |x|, x \in R$$

Sol. We have, $f(x) = |x|$

Its graph is given below

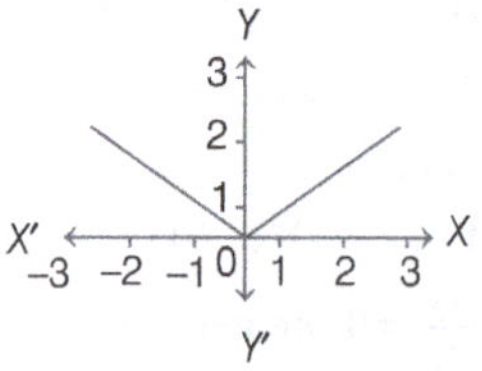

Here, $f(x) \geq 0,\ \forall x \in R$

and $f(x) = 0$, if $x = 0$.

$\therefore$ Minimum value of $f(x) = 0$ at point $x = 0$.

Also, f has no maximum value in R, so no point of maximum value in R.

Local Maxima and Local Minima

Let f be a real valued function and c be an interior point in the domain of f, then

- c is called a point of **local maxima**, if there is an $h > 0$ such that
$$f(c) > f(x)\ \forall\ x \text{ in } (c-h, c+h)$$
Here, value $f(c)$ is called the **local maximum value** (or relative maximum value) of f.
- c is called a point of **local minima**, if there is an $h > 0$ such that
$$f(c) < f(x)\ \forall\ x \text{ in } (c-h, c+h)$$
Here, value $f(c)$ is called the **local minimum value** (or relative minimum value) of f.

Geometrically, the graph of local maximum and local minimum are shown below

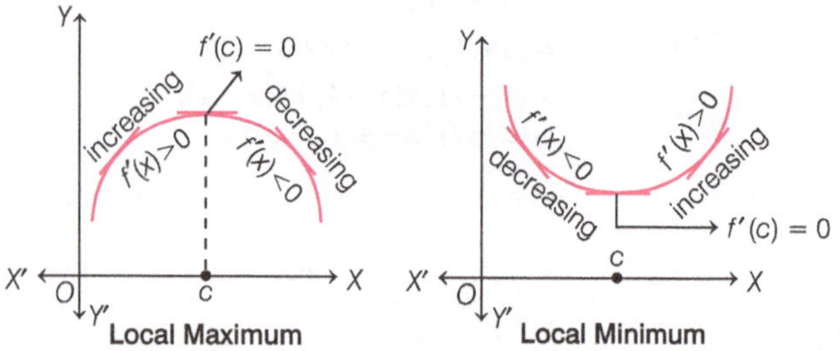

Local Maximum　　Local Minimum

Some Important Theorems

Theorem 1

Let f be a function defined on an open interval I. Suppose $c \in I$ be any point. If f has a local maxima or a local minima at $x = c$, then either $f'(c) = 0$ or f is not differentiable at c.

The converse of above theorem need not be true.
e.g. If $f(x) = x^3$, then $f'(x) = 3x^2$ and so $f'(0) = 0$. But 0 is neither a point of local maxima nor a point of local minima.

Theorem 2 **(First Derivative Test)**

Let f be a function defined on an open interval I and f be continuous at a critical point c in I.

(i) If $f'(x)$ changes sign from positive to negative as x increases through point c, i.e. (i.e. $f'(x) > 0$ when $x \in (c - h, h)$ and $f'(x) < 0$ when $x \in (c, c + h)$), then c is a point of **local maxima.**

(ii) If $f'(x)$ changes sign from negative to positive as x increases through point c, (i.e. $f'(x) < 0$, when $x \in (c - h, h)$ and $f'(x) > 0$, when $x \in (c, c + h)$), then c is a point of **local minima.**

(iii) If $f'(x)$ does not change sign as x increases through c, then c is neither a point of local maxima nor a point of local minima. Infact, such a point is called **point of inflection.**

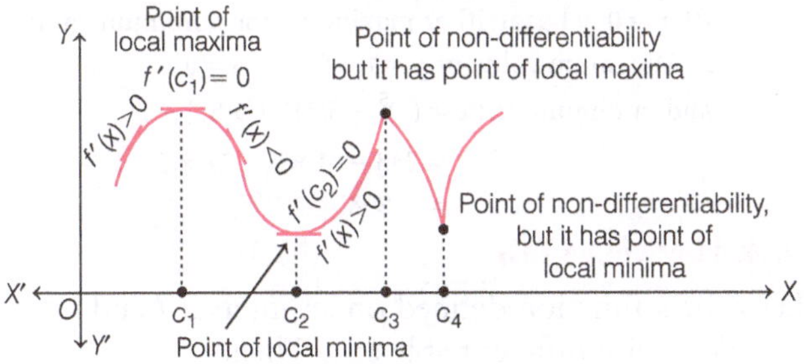

Critical Point A point c in the domain of a function f at which either $f'(c) = 0$ or f is not differentiable, is called a critical (stationary or turning) point of f.

Working Rule to Find Local Maxima/ Minima by First Derivative Test

Suppose $f(x)$ be the given function, then to find local maxima and local minima of $f(x)$ by first derivative test, we use the following steps

I. Firstly, write the given function $f(x)$ and differentiate it w.r.t. x, i.e. find $f'(x)$.

II. Put $f'(x) = 0$ and solve it to find critical points (say a and b) which could possibly be the points of local maxima or local minima of f.

III. Take these points one-by-one and check that it is a point of local maxima/minima, i.e. check the following.

Values of x		Sign of $f'(x)$	Nature of point
Close to a	to the right of a and to the left of a	> 0 < 0	Local minima
Close to b	to the right of b and to the left of b	< 0 > 0	Local maxima

IV. Now, find the local maximum or minimum value of function by putting corresponding point in given function in place of x.

EXAMPLE 2. Find the local maxima or local minima, if any of the function $f(x) = \dfrac{1}{x^2 + 5}$.

Sol. We have, $f(x) = \dfrac{1}{x^2+5} \Rightarrow f'(x) = \dfrac{-2x}{(x^2+5)^2}$

For a local maxima or local minima,

put $f'(x) = 0 \Rightarrow -\dfrac{2x}{(x^2+5)^2} = 0 \Rightarrow x = 0$

Now, when x is slightly less than 0, i.e. when x is negative, then $f'(x) = -\dfrac{2x}{(x^2+5)^2}$ is positive.

When x is slightly greater than 0, then

$f'(x) = -\dfrac{2x}{(x^2+5)^2}$ is negative.

Thus, $f'(x)$ changes sign from positive to negative.

So, $x = 0$ is a point of local maxima and local maximum value is $f(0) = \dfrac{1}{0+5} = \dfrac{1}{5}$.

EXAMPLE 3. Find the points of local maxima and local minima of the function $f(x) = (x - 1)^3 (x + 1)^2$.

Sol. We have, $f(x) = (x-1)^3 (x+1)^2$

$\therefore \; f'(x) = 3(x-1)^2 (x+1)^2 + (x-1)^3 \, 2(x+1)$

$= (x-1)^2 (x+1)[3(x+1) + 2(x-1)]$

$= (x-1)^2 (x+1)(5x+1)$

For local maxima or local minima, put $f'(x) = 0$,

$\Rightarrow (x-1)^2 (x+1)(5x+1) = 0 \Rightarrow x = -\dfrac{1}{5}, -1, 1$

For $x = -1$, $f'(x) > 0$ to the left of $x = -1$ and $f'(x) < 0$ to the right of $x = -1$.

$\therefore \; x = -1$ is a point of local maxima.

For $x = -\frac{1}{5}$, $f'(x) < 0$ to the left of $x = -\frac{1}{5}$ and $f'(x) > 0$ to the right of $x = -\frac{1}{5}$.

$\therefore \quad x = -\frac{1}{5}$ is a point of local minima.

For $x = 1$, $f'(x) > 0$ to the left of $x = 1$ and $f'(x) > 0$ to the right of $x = 1$.

Sign of $f'(x)$

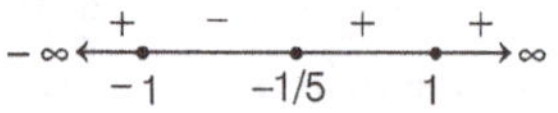

$\therefore \; x = 1$ is neither a point of local maxima nor local minima. Thus, we have the following table

Value of x		Sign of $f'(x)$	Nature of point
Close to -1	to the right of -1	< 0	Local maxima
	and to the left of -1	> 0	
Close to $\frac{-1}{5}$	to the right of $\frac{-1}{5}$	> 0	Local minima
	and to the left of $\frac{-1}{5}$	< 0	
Close to 1	to the right of 1	> 0	Neither local maxima nor local minima
	and to the left of 1	> 0	

At $x = \frac{-1}{5}$,

$$f\left(-\frac{1}{5}\right) = \left(-\frac{1}{5} - 1\right)^3 \left(-\frac{1}{5} + 1\right)^2 = \left(\frac{-6}{5}\right)^3 \left(\frac{4}{5}\right)^2 = -\frac{3456}{3125}$$

At $x = -1$, $f(-1) = (-1-1)^3 (-1+1)^2 = 0$

Hence, the point of local maxima is -1 and the local maximum value $= 0$ and the point of local minima is $-\frac{1}{5}$ and the local minimum value $= \frac{-3456}{3125}$.

Also, point $x = 1$ is the point of inflection.

EXAMPLE 4. Find all the points of local maxima and minima of the function $f(x) = x^3 - 6x^2 + 9x - 8$. **[CBSE 2023]**

Sol. We have, $f(x) = x^3 - 6x^2 + 9x - 8$

On differentiating both sides w.r.t. x, we get

$$f'(x) = 3x^2 - 12x + 9$$

Put $f'(x) = 0$

$\Rightarrow \quad 3x^2 - 12x + 9 = 0$

$\Rightarrow \quad 3(x^2 - 4x + 3) = 0$

$\Rightarrow \quad 3(x-1)(x-3) = 0 \qquad$ ...(i)

$\Rightarrow \quad x = 1, 3$

These are the critical points.

Now, for values close to 1 and to the right of 1, $f'(x) < 0$ and for values close to 1 and to the left of 1, $f'(x) > 0$.

$\therefore \; x = 1$ is a point of local maxima.

For values close to 3 and to the right of 3, $f'(x) > 0$ and for values close to 3 and to the left of 3, $f'(x) < 0$.

$\therefore \; x = 3$ is a point of local minima.

Hence, $x = 1$ is a point of local maxima and $x = 3$ is a point of local minima for given function.

EXAMPLE 5. For what values of x, function $f(x) = x^5 - 5x^4 + 5x^3 - 1$ is maximum or minimum? Also, show that function is neither maximum nor minimum at $x = 0$.

Sol. Given that, $f(x) = x^5 - 5x^4 + 5x^3 - 1$

On differentiating w.r.t. x, we get

$$f'(x) = 5x^4 - 20x^3 + 15x^2$$

For maxima or minima, $f'(x) = 0$

$\Rightarrow \quad 5x^4 - 20x^3 + 15x^2 = 0$

$\Rightarrow \quad 5x^2(x^2 - 4x + 3) = 0$

$\Rightarrow \quad 5x^2(x^2 - 3x - x + 3) = 0$

$\Rightarrow \quad 5x^2[x(x-3) - 1(x-3)] = 0$

$\Rightarrow \quad 5x^2[(x-1)(x-3)] = 0$

$\therefore \quad x = 0, 1, 3$

Sign scheme for $\frac{dy}{dx} = 5x^2(x-1)(x-3)$

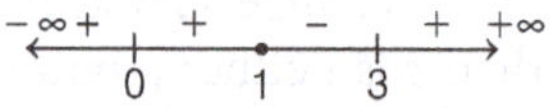

So, y has maximum value at $x = 1$ and minimum value at $x = 3$.

At $x = 0$, y has neither maximum nor minimum value.

$\therefore$ Maximum value of $y = 1 - 5 + 5 - 1 = 0$

and minimum value $= (3)^5 - 5(3)^4 + 5(3)^3 - 1$

$= 243 - 81 \times 5 - 27 \times 5 - 1$

$= -298$

Second Derivative Test

Let f be a function defined on an interval I and $c \in I$ and f be twice differentiable at c. Then,

- $x = c$ is a point of local maxima, if $f'(c) = 0$ and $f''(c) < 0$

  The value $f(c)$ is **local maximum value of f.**
- $x = c$ is a point of local minima, if $f'(c) = 0$ and $f''(c) > 0$.

  The value $f(c)$ is **local minimum value of f.**
- The test fails, if $f'(c) = 0$ and $f''(c) = 0$.

  In this case, we go back to the first derivative test and find whether c is a point of local maxima, local minima or a point of inflection.

Working Rule

To Find Local Maxima/ Minima by Second Derivative Test

Suppose $f(x)$ be the given function. Then, to find local maxima and local minima by second derivative test, we use the following steps

***Step* I** First, write the given function and differentiate it w.r.t. x, i.e. find first derivative.

***Step* II** Put first derivative, i.e. $f'(x)=0$ and find the critical points which could be possibly the points of local maxima or local minima.

***Step* III** Find second derivative of $f(x)$, i.e. again differentiate $f'(x)$ w.r.t. x to get $f''(x)$.

***Step* IV** Check the sign of $f''(x)$ at each critical point obtained in step II to get local maxima/minima, i.e. Suppose $x=a$ is a critical point, then if at $x=a$,

(i) $f''(a)<0$, then a is point of local maxima.

(ii) $f''(a)>0$, then a is point of local minima.

(iii) $f''(a)=0$, then test fails.

***Step* V** Now, find the local maximum or minimum value of function by putting corresponding point in the given function in place of x.

Properties of Maxima and Minima

(i) If $f(x)$ is continuous function in its domain, then atleast one maximum or one minimum must lie between two equal values of $f(x)$.

(ii) Maxima and minima occur alternately, i.e. between two maxima there is one minimum and *vice-versa.*

(iii) If $f(x)\to\infty$ as $x\to a$ or b and $f'(x)=0$. Only for one value of x (say c) between a and b, then $f(c)$ is necessarily the minimum and the least value.

If $f(x)\to-\infty$ as $x\to a$ or b, then $f(c)$ is necessarily the maximum and the greatest value.

EXAMPLE 6. Find the local maxima and local minima and the corresponding local maximum and local minimum values of the following functions.

(i) $f(x)=\dfrac{2}{x}+\dfrac{x}{2}, x>0$

(ii) $f(x)=x\sqrt{1-x}$, where $x\le 1$

(iii) $f(x)=\dfrac{x}{(x-1)(x-4)}$, where $1<x<4$.

Sol. (i) Given $f(x)=\dfrac{2}{x}+\dfrac{x}{2}$

On differentiating twice w.r.t. x, we get

$$f'(x)=-\frac{2}{x^2}+\frac{1}{2} \text{ and } f''(x)=\frac{4}{x^3}+0$$

For local maxima and local minima, put $f'(x)=0$

$$\Rightarrow\quad -\frac{2}{x^2}+\frac{1}{2}=0\Rightarrow x^2=4\Rightarrow x=\pm 2$$

Since it is given $x>0$, so we consider $x=2$ only.

Now $f''(2)=\dfrac{4}{2^3}=\dfrac{4}{8}=\dfrac{1}{2}>0,$

Thus, $f(x)$ is local minima at $x=2$

So, local minimum value of $f(x)$ at $x=2$ is

$$f(2)=\frac{2}{2}+\frac{2}{2}=1+1=2.$$

(ii) Given, $f(x)=x\sqrt{1-x}$

On differentiating twice w.r.t. x, we get

$$f'(x)=\frac{-x}{2\sqrt{1-x}}+\sqrt{1-x}=\frac{(2-3x)}{2\sqrt{1-x}}$$

$$\text{and}\quad f''(x)=\frac{1}{2}\left[\frac{\sqrt{1-x}\,(0-3)-(2-3x)\times\dfrac{-1}{2\sqrt{1-x}}}{(\sqrt{1-x})^2}\right]$$

$$=\frac{(3x-4)}{4(1-x)^{3/2}}$$

For local maxima and local minima, put $f'(x)=0$

$$\Rightarrow\quad (2-3x)=0\Rightarrow x=\frac{2}{3}$$

$$\text{and}\quad f''\left(\frac{2}{3}\right)=\frac{\left(3\times\dfrac{2}{3}-4\right)}{4\left(1-\dfrac{2}{3}\right)^{3/2}}=\frac{-3^{3/2}}{2}<0$$

$\therefore\quad x=\dfrac{2}{3}$ is a point of local maxima.

Hence, local maximum value $=f\left(\dfrac{2}{3}\right)=\dfrac{2}{3\sqrt{3}}.$

(iii) Given, $f(x)=\dfrac{x}{(x-1)(x-4)}=\dfrac{x}{(x^2-5x+4)}$

On differentiating twice w.r.t. x, we get

$$f'(x)=\frac{(x^2-5x+4)1-x(2x-5)}{(x^2-5x+4)^2}=\frac{4-x^2}{(x^2-5x+4)^2}$$

$$\text{and}\quad f''(x)=\frac{\left[\begin{array}{r}(x^2-5x+4)^2(-2x)-(4-x^2)2\\(x^2-5x+4)(2x-5)\end{array}\right]}{(x^2-5x+4)^4}$$

$$\Rightarrow\quad f''(x)=\frac{2[(x^2-5x+4)(-x)-(4-x^2)(2x-5)]}{(x^2-5x+4)^3}$$

$$=\frac{2[-x^3+5x^2-4x-(8x-20-2x^3+5x^2)]}{(x^2-5x+4)^3}$$

$$=\frac{2[x^3-12x+20]}{(x^2-5x+4)^3}$$

For local maxima and local minima, put

$$f'(x)=0 \Rightarrow (4-x^2)=0 \Rightarrow x=\pm 2$$

But $1<x<4 \Rightarrow x=2$ $\quad [\because x=-2 \notin (1,4)]$

$$\text{Now, } f''(2)=\frac{2[2^3-(12\times 2)+20]}{(2^2-(5\times 2)+4)^3}=\frac{2(4)}{(-2)^3}=-1<0.$$

$\therefore$ $x=2$ is a point of local maxima.

Thus, local maximum value $= f(2)$

$$=\frac{2}{(2-1)(2-4)}$$

$$=\frac{2}{-2}=-1$$

EXAMPLE 7. Find the local maximum and local minimum value of the following function.

(i) $f(x)=e^{x+2}$ (ii) $f_{(x)}=\log(x+5)$

Sol. (i) We have, $f(x)=e^{x+2}$

On differentiating both sides w.r.t. x, we get

$$f'(x)=e^{x+2}$$

For local maximum and local minimum,

put $f'(x)=0 \Rightarrow e^{x+2}=0 \Rightarrow$ No value of x exist.

Hence, no local maximum and no local minimum value can be determined.

(ii) We have, $f(x)=\log(x+5)$

On differentiating both sides w.r.t. x, we get

$$f'(x)=\frac{1}{x+5}$$

For local maximum and local minimum, put $f'(x)=0$

$$\Rightarrow \frac{1}{x+5}=0 \Rightarrow \text{No value of } x \text{ exist}$$

Hence, no local maximum and no local minimum value can be determined.

EXAMPLE 8. Find the minimum value of $(ax+by)$, where $xy=c^2$.

Sol. Let $f(x)=ax+by$, whose minimum value is required.

Then, $f(x)=ax+\dfrac{bc^2}{x}$ $\quad \left[\because xy=c^2 \Rightarrow y=\dfrac{c^2}{x}\right]$

On differentiating both sides w.r.t. x, we get

$$f'(x)=a-\frac{bc^2}{x^2}$$

For maximum or minimum value of $f(x)$, put $f'(x)=0$

$$\Rightarrow a-\frac{bc^2}{x^2}=0 \Rightarrow a=\frac{bc^2}{x^2}$$

$$\Rightarrow x^2=\frac{bc^2}{a} \Rightarrow x=\pm\sqrt{\frac{b}{a}}\,c$$

$$\text{Now, } f''(x)=0+\frac{2bc^2}{x^3}$$

$$\text{At } x=+\sqrt{\frac{b}{a}}c,\ f''(x)=\frac{2bc^2}{\left(\sqrt{\frac{b}{a}}c\right)^3}=+\text{ve}$$

Hence, $f(x)$ has minimum value at $x=\sqrt{\dfrac{b}{a}}\,c$.

$$\text{At } x=-\sqrt{\frac{b}{a}}c,\ f''(x)=\frac{2bc^2}{\left(-\sqrt{\frac{b}{a}}c\right)^3}=-\text{ve}$$

Hence, $f(x)$ has maximum value at $x=-\sqrt{\dfrac{b}{a}}\,c$.

$$\text{When } x=\sqrt{\frac{b}{a}}c, \text{ then } y=\frac{c^2}{x}=\frac{c^2}{\left(\sqrt{\frac{b}{a}}c\right)}=\sqrt{\frac{a}{b}}\,c$$

$$\therefore \text{ Minimum value of } f(x)=a\sqrt{\frac{b}{a}}\cdot c+b\sqrt{\frac{a}{b}}\cdot c$$

$$=\sqrt{ab}\cdot c+\sqrt{ab}\cdot c=2\sqrt{ab}\cdot c$$

EXAMPLE 9. The cost function of a product is given by $C(x)=\dfrac{x^3}{3}-45x^2-900x+39$, where x is the number of units produced. In order to minimise the marginal cost how many units of the product must be produced?

Sol. Given the cost function $C(x)=\dfrac{x^3}{3}-45x^2-900x+39$

$$\therefore \text{Marginal cost} = MC=\frac{d}{dx}(C(x))$$

$$\Rightarrow MC=\frac{1}{3}\cdot 3x^2-45\cdot 2x-900\cdot 1+0$$

$$\Rightarrow MC=x^2-90x-900$$

$\because$ MC is minimum

$$\therefore \frac{d}{dx}(MC)=0 \text{ and } \frac{d^2}{dx^2}(MC)>0$$

$$\text{Now, } \frac{d}{dx}(MC)=2x-90 \text{ and } \frac{d^2}{dx^2}(MC)=2$$

$$\frac{d}{dx}(MC)=0 \Rightarrow 2x-90=0 \Rightarrow x=45$$

$$\text{When } x=45,\ \frac{d^2}{dx^2}(MC)=2>0$$

Hence, marginal cost (MC) is minimum when $x=45$.

EXAMPLE 10. The cost of manufacturing of certain items consists of ₹ 1600 as overheads, ₹ 20 per item as the cost of material and the labour cost $\dfrac{x^2}{100}$ for x items produced. How many items must be produced to have a minimum average cost?

Sol. The cost of material for producing x items = ₹ $20x$

Overhead cost = ₹ 1600 and labour cost of producing x items = ₹ $\dfrac{x^2}{100}$.

$\therefore$ Total cost of producing x items,

$$C(x) = ₹\left(1600 + 20x + \frac{x^2}{100}\right).$$

$\therefore$ Average cost, $AC = \frac{C(x)}{x}$

$$= ₹\left(\frac{1600}{x} + 20 + \frac{x}{100}\right).$$

$\because$ AC is minimum.

$\therefore$ $\frac{d}{dx}(AC) = 0$ and $\frac{d^2}{dx^2}(AC) > 0.$

Now, $\frac{d}{dx}(AC) = -\frac{1600}{x^2} + 0 + \frac{1}{100}$ and

$$\frac{d^2}{dx^2}(AC) = -1600(-2)x^{-3} + 0 = \frac{3200}{x^3}.$$

$$\frac{d}{dx}(AC) = 0 \Rightarrow -\frac{1600}{x^2} + \frac{1}{100} = 0 \Rightarrow x^2 = 160000$$

$\Rightarrow$ $x = 400, -400$ but $x > 0$

$\Rightarrow$ $x = 400$

When $x = 400$, $\frac{d^2}{dx^2}(AC) = \frac{3200}{(4000)^3} > 0.$

Hence, the average cost is minimum when $x = 400$.

EXAMPLE 11. The demand function is $y = \frac{24 - 2p}{3}$, where y is the number of units demanded and p is the price per unit. Find

(i) the revenue function R in terms of p.

(ii) the price and the number of units demanded for which the revenue is maximum.

Sol. Given, the demand function is $y = \frac{24 - 2p}{3}$.

(i) Revenue function $R = py = p \times \frac{24 - 2p}{3}$

$\Rightarrow$ $R = 8p - \frac{2}{3}p^2$

(ii) To find value of p for which R is maximum, we should find value(s) of p where $\frac{dR}{dp} = 0$ and $\frac{d^2R}{dp^2} < 0.$

Now, $\frac{dR}{dp} = 8 \cdot 1 - \frac{2}{3} \cdot 2p = 8 - \frac{4}{3}p$

and $\frac{d^2R}{dp^2} = 0 - \frac{4}{3} \cdot 1 = -\frac{4}{3}.$

$$\frac{dR}{dp} = 0 \Rightarrow 8 - \frac{4}{3}p = 0 \Rightarrow p = 6.$$

When $p = 6$, $\frac{d^2R}{dp^2} = -\frac{4}{3} < 0.$

$\therefore$ The revenue is maximum when $p = 6$
i.e. the price per unit is ₹ 6.

The number of units demanded is given by

$$y = \frac{24 - 2 \times 6}{3} = 4.$$

Hence, the revenue is maximum when 4 units are demanded and the price per unit ₹ 6.

EXAMPLE 12. A steel plant is capable of producing x tonnes per day of low-grade steel and y tonnes per day of a high-grade steel, where $y = \frac{32 - 5x}{10 - x}$. If the fixed price of low-grade steel is half that of high-grade steel, find the quantity of low-grade steel that should be produced per day for maximum receipts.

Sol. Let ₹ p per tonne be the fixed market price of low-grade steel then ₹ $2p$ per tonne is the fixed market price of high-grade steel. Let ₹ R be the total revenue then

$$R = px + 2py = px + 2p \cdot \frac{32 - 5x}{10 - x} = p \cdot \frac{-x^2 + 64}{10 - x}.$$

$$\therefore \quad \frac{dR}{dx} = p \cdot \frac{(10 - x)(-2x) - (-x^2 + 64)(-1)}{(10 - x)^2}$$

$$= p \cdot \frac{x^2 - 20x + 64}{(10 - x)^2}$$

For R to be maximum, $\frac{dR}{dx} = 0$

$\Rightarrow x^2 - 20x + 64 = 0 \Rightarrow (x - 4)(x - 16) = 0 \Rightarrow x = 4, 16$

Now, $\frac{dR}{dx} = p \cdot \frac{x^2 - 20x + 64}{(10 - x)^2} = p \cdot \frac{(10 - x)^2 - 36}{(10 - x)^2}$

$$= p\left(1 - \frac{36}{(10 - x)^2}\right)$$

$$\Rightarrow \quad \frac{d^2R}{dx^2} = p(0 - 36 \cdot (-2)(10 - x)^{-3}(-1)).$$

$$= -\frac{72p}{(10 - x)^3}$$

$$\therefore \quad \left.\frac{d^2R}{dx^2}\right|_{x=4} = -\frac{72p}{6^3} = -\frac{p}{3} < 0; \left.\frac{d^2R}{dx^2}\right|_{x=16} = -\frac{72p}{(-6)^3} = \frac{p}{3} > 0.$$

$\therefore$ R is maximum when $x = 4$.

Hence, the receipts are maximum when the steel plant produces 4 tonnes of low-grade steel per day.

EXAMPLE 13. The total cost function is given by $C(x) = \frac{1}{3}x^3 - 5x^2 + 30x - 20$ and the selling price per unit is ₹ 6. Find for what value of x will the profit be maximum.

Sol. Since, the selling price per unit is ₹ 6.

$\therefore$ Revenue function $R(x) = 6x$.

Given, total cost function $C(x) = \frac{1}{3}x^3 - 5x^2 + 30x - 20.$

Profit function $P(x) = \text{Revenue} - \text{Cost} = R(x) - C(x)$

$$\Rightarrow \quad P(x) = 6x - \left(\frac{1}{3}x^3 - 5x^2 + 30x - 20\right)$$

$$= -\frac{1}{3}x^3 + 5x^2 - 24x + 20$$

To find the value(s) of x when $P(x)$ is maximum,

we should find value(s) of x when $\frac{dP}{dx} = 0$ and $\frac{d^2P}{dx^2} < 0.$

Now, $\frac{dP}{dx} = -\frac{1}{3}\cdot 3x^2 + 5\cdot 2x - 24\cdot 1 + 0 = -x^2 + 10x - 24$

and $\frac{d^2P}{dx^2} = -2x + 10.$

$$\frac{dP}{dx} = 0 \Rightarrow -x^2 + 10x - 24 = 0$$

$$\Rightarrow \quad x^2 - 10x + 24 = 0$$

$$\Rightarrow \quad (x-4)(x-6) = 0 \Rightarrow x = 4, 6$$

At $x = 4$, $\frac{d^2P}{dx^2} = -2\times 4 + 10 = 2 > 0$ and

at $x = 6$, $\frac{d^2P}{dx^2} = -2\times 6 + 10 = -2 < 0.$

Hence, the profit is maximum when $x = 6$.

Maximum and Minimum Values of a Function in a Closed Interval

Theorem 1

Let f be a continuous function on an interval $I = [a, b]$. Then, f has the absolute maximum value and f attains it atleast once in I. Also, f has the absolute minimum value and attains it atleast once in I.

Theorem 2

Let f be a differentiable function on a closed interval I and c be any interior point of I. Then,

- $f'(c) = 0$, if f attains its absolute maximum value at c.
- $f'(c) = 0$, if f attains its absolute minimum value at c.

Method to Find Absolute Maximum or Absolute Minimum Values in an Interval $[a, b]$

Suppose $f(x)$ be the given function. Then, to find absolute maximum and absolute minimum values in the given interval, we use the following steps

I. Find all critical points of f in the interval, i.e. find points at which either $f'(x) = 0$ or f is not differentiable.

II. Take the end points of the interval, i.e. $f(a)$ and $f(b)$.

III. At all these points listed in steps I and II, calculate the values of f.

IV. Identify the maximum and minimum values of f out of the values calculated in step III. This maximum value will be the absolute maximum (greatest) value of f and the minimum value will be the absolute minimum (least) value of f.

EXAMPLE 14. Find absolute maximum and minimum values of a function f given by

$$f(x) = 12x^{4/3} - 6x^{1/3}, x \in [-1, 1].$$

Sol. We have, $f(x) = 12x^{4/3} - 6x^{1/3}$

On differentiating both sides w.r.t. x, we get

$$f'(x) = 12\times\frac{4}{3}x^{1/3} - 6\times\frac{1}{3}x^{-2/3}$$

$$= 16x^{1/3} - \frac{2}{x^{2/3}} = \frac{2(8x-1)}{x^{2/3}}$$

For critical points, put $f'(x) = 0$

$$\Rightarrow \quad \frac{2(8x-1)}{x^{2/3}} = 0 \Rightarrow 8x - 1 = 0 \Rightarrow x = \frac{1}{8}$$

Also, $f'(x)$ is not defined at $x = 0$, so critical points are $x = 0$ and $x = \frac{1}{8}$ and end points of interval are -1 and 1.

Now, $f(-1) = 12(-1)^{4/3} - 6(-1)^{1/3} = 12 + 6 = 18$

$$f(0) = 12(0) - 6(0) = 0$$

$$f\left(\frac{1}{8}\right) = 12\left(\frac{1}{8}\right)^{4/3} - 6\left(\frac{1}{8}\right)^{1/3} = 12\left(\frac{1}{16}\right) - 6\left(\frac{1}{2}\right) = \frac{-9}{4}$$

and $f(1) = 12(1)^{4/3} - 6(1)^{1/3} = 6$

Hence, absolute maximum value of function f is 18 at $x = -1$ and absolute minimum value of function f is $\frac{-9}{4}$ at $x = \frac{1}{8}$.

Topic Practice 4

1 Find the maximum and minimum values, if any of the following functions without using derivatives

(i) $h(x) = x + 1, x \in (-1, 1)$

(ii) $f(x) = |x + 2| - 1$

(iii) $g(x) = -|x + 1| + 3$

(iv) $f(x) = \frac{(x-1)(x-6)}{x-10}, x \neq 0$

2 Find the stationary (critical) point of the function $f(x) = x^x$.

3 Find all the points of local maxima and local minima of the following functions.

(i) $f(x) = \frac{1}{x^2 - 7}$ (ii) $f(x) = (x-5)^4$

(iii) $g(x) = (x-1)(x+2)^2$

(iv) $f(x) = -\frac{3}{4}x^4 - 8x^3 - \frac{45}{2}x^2 + 105$ [CBSE 2024]

4 Find the points at which the function f given by $f(x) = (x-4)^4 (x+1)^3$ has

(i) local maxima. (ii) local minima.

(iii) point of inflection.

5 Find the local maxima and local minima also determine the correspond local maximum and local minimum values of each of the following function.

(i) $g(x) = \frac{3}{x} + \frac{x}{3}, x > 0$

(ii) $g(x) = x + \sqrt{1-x}, x \leq 1$

(iii) $g(x) = x\sqrt{32 - x^2}, -5 \leq x \leq 5$

(iv) $\frac{(x-1)(x-6)}{x-10}, x \neq 10$

(v) $f(x) = e^{3x+5}$

(vi) $f(x) = \log(3x + 8)$

6 It is given that at $x = 1$, the function $x^4 - 62x^2 + ax + 9$ attains maximum value on the interval (0, 2). Find the value of a.

7 Find the maximum slope of curve $y = -x^3 + 3x^2 + 9x - 27$.

8 Prove that the maximum value of $\left(\frac{1}{x}\right)^x$ is $e^{1/e}$.

9 Find the least value of $f(x) = e^x + e^{-x}$.

10 Find the points of local maxima, local minima and the points of inflection of the function $f(x) = x^5 - 5x^4 + 5x^3 - 1$. Also, find the corresponding local maximum and local minimum values.

11 Find the point P on the curve $y^2 = 4ax$, which is nearest to the point $(11a, 0)$.

12 Let AP and BQ be two vertical poles at points A and B, respectively. If $AP = 16$ m, $BQ = 22$ m and $AB = 20$ m, then find the distance of a point R on AB from the point A such that $RP^2 + RQ^2$ is minimum.

13 A firm has the cost function $C = \frac{x^3}{3} - 7x^2 + 11x + 25$ and demand function $x = 100 - p$.

(i) Write the total revenue function in terms of x.

(ii) Formulate the total profit function P in terms of x.

(iii) Find the profit maximising level of output x.

(iv) What is the maximum profit?

14 For a monopolist's product, the demand function is $p = \frac{50}{\sqrt{x}}$ and average cost function $AC = 0.5 + \frac{200}{x}$. Find the profit maximising level of output. At this level, show that the marginal revenue and marginal cost are equal.

15 Find the absolute maximum and minimum values of $f(x) = 2x^3 - 24x + 57$ in the interval [1, 3].

16 Find the maximum and minimum values of $g(x) = 3x^4 - 8x^3 + 12x^2 - 48x + 25$ on [0, 3].

Hints & Solutions

1. Similar as Example 6.

Ans.

(i) Neither minimum nor maximum value.

(ii) Minimum value = –1, no maximum value

(iii) Maximum value = 3, no minimum value

(iv) Let $y = \frac{(x-1)(x-6)}{x-10} = \frac{x^2 - 7x + 6}{x-10}$

On differentiating both sides w.r.t. x, we get

$$\frac{dy}{dx} = \frac{(x-10)(2x-7) - (x^2 - 7x + 6)\cdot 1}{(x-10)^2}$$

[using quotient rule of derivative]

$$= \frac{2x^2 - 7x - 20x + 70 - x^2 + 7x - 6}{(x-10)^2}$$

$$= \frac{x^2 - 20x + 64}{(x-10)^2} = \frac{(x-4)(x-16)}{(x-10)^2}$$

For local maxima and local minima, put $dy/dx = 0$

$$\Rightarrow \quad \frac{(x-4)(x-16)}{(x-10)^2} = 0 \Rightarrow (x-4)(x-16) = 0$$

$$\therefore \quad x = 4, 16$$

For $x = 4$,

When x is slightly < 4, then $\frac{dy}{dx} = \frac{(-)(-)}{(+)}$ = Positive

When x is slightly > 4, then $\frac{dy}{dx} = \frac{(+)(-)}{(+)}$ = Negative

Thus, $\frac{dy}{dx}$ changes sign from positive to negative.

So, y is local maxima at $x = 4$.

$\therefore$ Local maximum value at $x = 4$ is

$$y = \frac{(4-1)(4-6)}{4-10} = \frac{3 \times -2}{-6} = 1$$

For $x = 16$,

When x is slightly < 16, then $\frac{dy}{dx} = \frac{(+)(-)}{(+)}$ = Negative

When x is slightly > 16, then $\frac{dy}{dx} = \frac{(+)(+)}{(+)}$ = Positive

Thus, $\frac{dy}{dx}$ changes sign from negative to positive.

So, y is local minima at $x = 16$.

$\therefore$ Local minimum value at $x = 16$ is

$$y = \frac{(16-1)(16-6)}{16-10} = \frac{15 \times 10}{6} = 25$$

2. Hint We have, $f(x) = x^x$

Let $y = x^x$ and $\log y = x \log x$

$$\therefore \quad \frac{1}{y}\cdot\frac{dy}{dx} = x \cdot \frac{1}{x} + \log x \cdot 1 \Rightarrow \frac{dy}{dx} = (1 + \log x)\cdot x^x$$

$$\therefore \quad \frac{dy}{dx} = 0 \Rightarrow (1 + \log x)\cdot x^x = 0$$

$$\Rightarrow \log x = -1 \Rightarrow \log x = \log e^{-1}$$

$$\Rightarrow \quad x = e^{-1} \Rightarrow x = \frac{1}{e}$$

Ans. $f(x)$ has a stationary point at $x = \frac{1}{e}$.

3. (i) Similar as Example 2. **Ans.** Local maxima at $x = 0$

(ii) Similar as Example 3. **Ans.** Local maxima at $x = 5$

(iii) Similar as Example 3.

Ans. Local maxima at $x = -2$ and local minima at $x = 0$

(iv) Similar as Example 4.

Ans. Local maxima at $x = 0, -5$;

Local minima at $x = -3$

4. Similar as Example 3.

Ans. (i) Local maxima at $x = 8/7$.

(ii) Local minima at $x = 4$.

(iii) Point of inflection at $x = -1$.

5. (i) Similar as Example 6 (i).

Ans. Local minima at $x = 3$ and local minimum value is 2.

(ii) Similar as Example 6 (ii).

Ans. Local maxima at $x = \frac{3}{4}$ and local maximum value is $\frac{5}{4}$.

(iii) Similar as Example 6 (ii).

Ans. Local minima at $x = -4$ and its value is -16

Local maxima at $x = 4$ and its value is 16.

(iv) Similar as Example 6 (iii).

Ans. Local maxima at $x = 4$ and $f(4) = 1$

Local minima at $x = 16$, $f(16) = 25$

(v) Similar as Example 7 (i).

Ans. No local maximum and local minimum value exist.

(vi) Similar as Example 7 (ii).

Ans. No local maximum and local minimum value exist.

6. Hint $f'(x) = 4x^3 - 124x + a$, put $f'(1) = 0$

Ans. $a = 120$

7. We have, $y = -x^3 + 3x^2 + 9x - 27$

$$\therefore \quad \frac{dy}{dx} = -3x^2 + 6x + 9 = \text{Slope of the curve}$$

$$\text{and} \quad \frac{d^2y}{dx^2} = -6x + 6 = -6(x-1)$$

$$\therefore \quad \frac{d^2y}{dx^2} = 0 \Rightarrow -6(x-1) = 0 \Rightarrow x = 1 > 0$$

Now, $\frac{d^3y}{dx^3} = -6 < 0$

So, the maximum slope of given curve is at $x = 1$.

$\therefore \quad \left(\frac{dy}{dx}\right)_{(x=1)} = -3\cdot1^2 + 6\cdot1 + 9 = 12$

8. **Hint** Let $y = x^{-x} \Rightarrow \frac{dy}{dx} = -x^{-x}(1 + \log x)$

$\Rightarrow \quad \frac{dy}{dx} = 0 \Rightarrow x = \frac{1}{e}$

9. **Hint** $\frac{dy}{dx} = e^x - e^{-x} = 0 \Rightarrow e^{2x} = 1 \Rightarrow x = 0$. **Ans.** 2

10. **Ans.** $x = 1$ is point of local maxima,
$x = 3$ is point of local minima, $x = 0$ is point of inflection,
Local maximum value = 0,
Local minimum value = − 28

11. Similar as Example 10. **Ans.** $(9a, 6a)$.

12. **Hint** Let $AR = x$, then $BR = 20 - x$

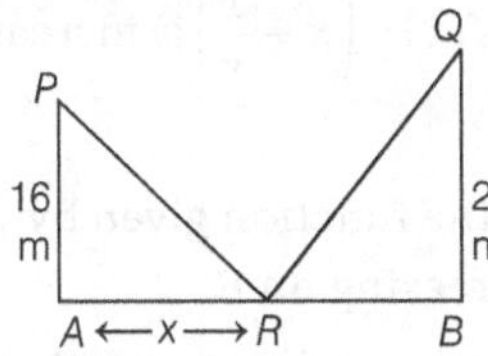

$\because \quad RP^2 + RQ^2 = x^2 + (20 - x)^2 + 740$ **Ans.** 10m

13. (i) Demand function is $x = 100 - p \Rightarrow p = 100 - x$

$\therefore$ Revenue function, $R(x) = p \cdot x$

$= x(100 - x) = 100x - x^2$.

(ii) Profit function, $P(x)$ = Revenue − Cost = $R(x) - C(x)$.

$\Rightarrow \quad P(x) = (100x - x^2) - \left(\frac{x^3}{3} - 7x^2 + 11x + 25\right)$

$= -\frac{x^3}{3} + 6x^2 - 11x - 25 \quad$ ....(i)

(iii) To find values of x so that $P(x)$ is maximum, we should find value(s) of x, where $\frac{dP}{dx} = 0$ and $\frac{d^2P}{dx^2} < 0$.

Now, $\frac{dP}{dx} = 0 \Rightarrow -x^2 + 12x - 11 = 0$

$\Rightarrow \quad x^2 - 12x + 11 = 0$

$\Rightarrow \quad (x - 1)(x - 11) = 0 \Rightarrow x = 1, 11.$

$\frac{d^2P}{dx^2} = \frac{d}{dx}(-x^2 + 12x - 11) = -2x + 12.$

At $x = 1$, $\frac{d^2P}{dx^2} = -2\times1 + 12 = 10 > 0$ and

at $x = 11$, $\frac{d^2P}{dx^2} = -2\times11 + 12 = -10 < 0.$

Hence, the profit maximising level is at $x = 11$.

(iv) Putting $x = 11$ in Eq. (i), we get

$P(11) = -\frac{(11)^3}{3} + 6\times(11)^2 - 11\times11 - 50$

$= -\frac{1331}{3} + 726 - 121 - 25$

$= -\frac{1331}{3} + 580 = 136.33$

Hence, maximum profit = ₹ 136.33

14. Let $R(x)$, $C(x)$ and $P(x)$ be the revenue function, cost function and profit function at the output level of x items.

Given, $p = \frac{50}{\sqrt{x}}$ and $AC = 0.5 + \frac{2000}{x}$.

$\therefore \quad R(x) = px = \frac{50}{\sqrt{x}} \times x = 50\sqrt{x} \quad$ ...(i)

and $C(x) = (AC) \times x = \left(0.5 + \frac{2000}{x}\right)x$

$C(x) = 0.5x + 2000 \quad$ ...(ii)

$\therefore \quad P(x) = R(x) - C(x) = 50\sqrt{x} - (0.5x + 2000)$

$\therefore \frac{d}{dx}(P(x)) = 50\cdot\frac{1}{2\sqrt{x}} - 0.5 = \frac{25}{\sqrt{x}} - \frac{1}{2}$ and

$\frac{d^2}{dx^2}(P(x)) = 25\cdot\left(-\frac{1}{2}\right)x^{-3/2} = -\frac{25}{2x^{3/2}}.$

For maximum profit, $\frac{d}{dx}(P(x)) = 0$

$\Rightarrow \quad \frac{25}{\sqrt{x}} - \frac{1}{2} = 0 \Rightarrow \sqrt{x} = 50 \Rightarrow x = 2500.$

$\left.\frac{d^2}{dx^2}(P(x))\right|_{x=2500} = -\frac{25}{2(2500)^{3/2}} < 0$

$\therefore \ P(x)$ is maximum when $x = 2500$.

Putting $x = 2500$ in $p = \frac{50}{\sqrt{x}}$, we get $p = \frac{50}{\sqrt{2500}} = 1.$

Thus, profit is maximum when $x = 2500$ i.e. when 2500 items are produced and sold at ₹ 1 per item.

$MR = \frac{d}{dx}(R(x)) = \frac{d}{dx}(50\sqrt{x}) = \frac{25}{\sqrt{x}}$ and

$MC = \frac{d}{dx}(C(x)) = \frac{d}{dx}(0.5x + 2000) = 0.5$

When $x = 2500$, $MR = \frac{25}{\sqrt{2500}} = \frac{1}{2}$ and $MC = 0.5 = \frac{1}{2}$.

$\therefore MR = MC$ when $x = 2500$.

15. Similar as Example 14.

Ans. Maximum value is 39 at $x = 3$, minimum value is 25 at $x = 2$

16. **Hint** $f'(x) = 12x^3 - 24x^2 + 24x - 48 = 0$

$\Rightarrow \quad 12(x^3 - 2x^2 + 2x - 4) = 0$

$\Rightarrow \quad 12(x - 2)(x^2 + 2) = 0$

$\Rightarrow \quad x = 2 \quad [\because x^2 + 2 \neq 0]$

So, $f(0) = 25$, $f(2) = -39$, $f(3) = 16$

Hence, minimum value of $f(x)$ is −39 at $x = 2$.

and maximum value of $f(x)$ is 25 at $x = 0$.

Exam Pattern Exercise

Part A - Objective Type Questions

Multiple Choice Type Questions

1 The function $f(x) = x^2 - x + 1$ is [CBSE 2024]

(a) increasing in $(0, 1)$
(b) decreasing in $(0, 1)$
(c) increasing in $\left(0, \frac{1}{2}\right)$ and decreasing in $\left(\frac{1}{2}, 1\right)$
(d) increasing in $\left(\frac{1}{2}, 1\right)$ and decreasing in $\left(0, \frac{1}{2}\right)$

2 The interval in which the function $f(x) = 6 - 9x - x^2$ is increasing is

(a) $(-\infty, \infty)$ (b) $\left(-\infty, -\frac{9}{2}\right]$
(c) $\left[-\frac{9}{2}, \infty\right)$ (d) None of these

3 If the function f is given by $f(x) = x^3 - 3x + 3$, then

(a) $x = \pm 2$ are the only critical points for local maxima or local minima
(b) $x = 3$ is a point of local minima
(c) Local minimum value is 2
(d) Local maximum value is 5

4 The local minima of $f(x) = xe^x$ is at $x =$ ....

(a) -1 (b) 1 (c) 0 (d) -5

5 The smallest value of polynomial $x^3 - 18x^2 + 96x$ in [0, 9] is

(a) 126 (b) 0 (c) 135 (d) 160

6 The least value of the function $f(x) = ax + \frac{b}{x}$ $(a > 0, b > 0, x > 0)$ is

(a) $\sqrt{ab}$ (b) $2\sqrt{ab}$ (c) $3\sqrt{ab}$ (d) $4\sqrt{ab}$

Assertion-Reason Based Questions

Directions (Q. Nos. 11-13) *In the questions given below are two statements labelled as Assertion (A) and Reason (R). In the context of the two statements, which one of the following is correct?*

(a) Both A and R are correct; R is the correct explanation of A
(b) Both A and R are correct; R is not the correct explanation of A
(c) A is correct; R is incorrect
(d) R is correct; A is incorrect

7 **Assertion (A)** The function $f(x) = x^2 - x + 1$ is strictly increasing on $(-1, 1)$.

Reason (R) If $f(x)$ is continuous on $[a, b]$ and derivable on (a, b), then $f(x)$ is strictly increasing on $[a, b]$ if $f'(x) > 0$ for all $x \in (a, b)$. [CBSE 2024]

Part B - Descriptive Questions

Very Short Answer Type Questions

8 The total revenue received from the sale of x units of a product is given by $R(x) = 3x^2 + 36x + 5$. Find the marginal revenue when $x = 5$, where by marginal revenue, we mean the rate of change of total revenue with respect to the number of items sold at an instant.

9 Show that $f(x) = \left(x - \frac{1}{x}\right)$ is increasing for all $x \in R$, $x \neq 0$.

10 Show that the function given by $f(x) = e^{2x}$ is strictly increasing on R.

11 Show that $f(x) = e^{1/x}$ is a strictly decreasing function for all $x > 0$.

12 Show that the function $f(x) = x^3 - 3x^2 + 6x - 100$ is increasing on R.

13 Find the values of k for which $f(x) = kx^3 - 9kx^2 + 9x + 3$ is increasing on R.

Short Answer Type Questions

14 Determine the interval in which the function $f(x) = 2x^3 - 15x^2 + 36x + 1$ is strictly increasing and strictly decreasing.

Directions (Q. Nos. 15-16) *Find the interval(s) in which the following functions are increasing and decreasing.*

15 $f(x) = (x + 2)\, e^{-x}$

16 $f(x) = \log(1 + x) - \frac{x}{1 + x}, x \neq -1$

17 Find the maximum profit that a company can make, if the profit function is given by $P(x) = 41 + 24x - 18x^2$.

18 A telephone company in a town has 500 subscribers on its list and collect fixed charges of ₹ 300 per subscriber per year. The company proposes to increase the annual subscription and it is believed that for every increase of ₹ 1 per one subscriber will discontinue the service. Find what increase will bring maximum profit?

Long Answer Type Questions

19 Find the point on the curve $y = \frac{x}{1+x^2}$, where the tangent to the curve has the greatest slope.

20 Find the point on the curve $y^2 = 2x$, which is at a minimum distance from point (1, 4).

21 The demand function of an output is $x = 106 - 2p$, where x is the number of units and p be the price per unit and the average cost per unit is $5 + \frac{x}{50}$. If the total revenue is px, then determine the number of units for maximum profit.

Case Study Based Questions

22 The shape of a toy is given as $f(x) = 6(2x^4 - x^2)$. To make the toy beautiful 2 sticks which are perpendicular to each other were placed at a point (2, 3).

Answer the following questions using the above information.

(i) Which value from the following may be abscissa of critical point?

(a) $\pm\frac{1}{4}$ (b) $\pm\frac{1}{2}$

(c) ± 1 (d) None of these

(ii) Find the second order derivative of the function at $x = 5$.

(a) 598 (b) 1176

(c) 3588 (d) 3312

(iii) At which of the following intervals will $f(x)$ be increasing?

(a) $(-\infty, -1/2) \cup (1/2, \infty)$

(b) $(-1/2, 0) \cup (1/2, \infty)$

(c) $(0, 1/2) \cup (1/2, \infty)$

(d) $(-\infty, -1/2) \cup (0, 1/2)$

23 A company wants to form a poster for advertisement purpose. The top and bottom margins of poster should be 12 cm and the side margins should be 8 cm. Also, the area for printing the advertisement should be 1064 cm^2.

Based on the above information, answer the following questions.

(i) If w cm be the width and h cm be the height of poster, then the area of poster, expressed in terms of w and h, is given by

(a) $680 - 24w - 16h$

(b) $864 + 24w + 16h$

(c) $680 + 24w + 16h$

(d) None of the above

(ii) The relation between w and h is given by

(a) $w = \frac{680 + 16h}{h - 24}$ (b) $w = \frac{680 + h}{16h - 24}$

(c) $h = \frac{680 - 16w}{w - 24}$ (d) None of these

(iii) Area of poster in terms of h is given by

(a) $\frac{680 + 16h^2}{h + 24}$ (b) $\frac{680h + 16h^2}{h - 24}$

(c) $\frac{680 + 16h^2}{h - 24}$ (d) None of these

(iv) The value of h, so that area of the poster is minimised, is

(a) 54 (b) 36

(c) 63.94 (d) 16

(v) The value of w, so that area of the poster is minimised, is

(a) 124 (b) 136

(c) 42.63 (d) 122

24 Vihan's father wants to construct a rectangular field using a brick wall on one side of the garden and wire fencing for the other three sides as shown in figure. He has 400 ft of wire fencing.

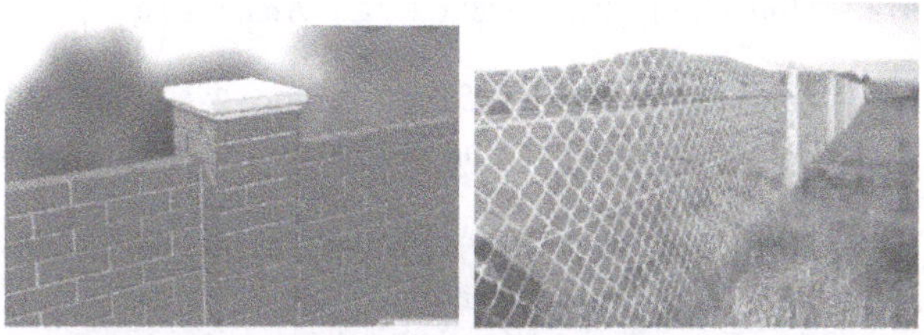

Based on the above information, answer the following questions.

(i) To construct a field using 400 ft of fencing, we need to maximise its

(a) volume (b) area

(c) perimeter (d) length of the side

(ii) If a denotes the length of side field perpendicular to brick wall and b denotes the length of side field parallel to brick wall, then find the relation representing total amount of fencing wire.

(a) $a + 2b = 150$

(b) $a + 2b = 500$

(c) $b + 2a = 400$

(d) $b + 2a = 100$

(iii) Area of the field as a function of a say $A(a)$ can be represented as

(a) $400 + 2a^2$

(b) $a - 2a^2$

(c) $400a - 2a^2$

(d) $400 - a^2$

(iv) Maximum value of $A(a)$ occurs at a equals

(a) 100 ft (b) 50 ft

(c) 26 ft (d) 31 ft

(v) Maximum area of field will be

(a) 2500 sq ft (b) 4000 sq ft

(c) 20000 sq ft (d) 6000 sq ft

25 A cable network provider in a small town has 500 subscribers and he used to collect ₹ 300 per month from each subscriber. He proposes to increase the monthly charges and it is believed from past experience that for every increase of ₹1, one subscriber will discontinue the service.

Based on the above information, answer the following questions

(i) If ₹ x is the monthly increase in subscription amount then find the number of subscribers.

(ii) What is the total revenue R?

(iii) Find the number of subscribers which gives the maximum revenue.

(iv) What is increase in charges per subscriber that yields maximum revenue?

Or

Find the maximum revenue generated

Hints & Solutions

1. (d) 2. (b) 3. (d) 4. (a)

5. (b) 6. (b) 7. (d)

8. Solve as Example 10 of Topic 1. **Ans.** ₹ 66

9. **Hint** $f'(x) = 1 + \frac{1}{x^2} \Rightarrow f'(x) > 0 \; \forall \; x \in R$ and $x \neq 0$

10. Solve as Example 7 (ii) of Topic 2.

11. **Hint** $f(x) = e^{\frac{1}{x}}\left(\frac{-1}{x^2}\right) < 0$

12. Solve as Example 9 of Topic 2.

13. **Hint** $f'(x) = 3kx^2 - 18kx + 9 \geq 0$ **Ans.** $k \in \left(0, \frac{1}{3}\right)$

14. Solve as Qusetion 13 of Topic Practice 2.
Ans. Strictly increasing in $(-\infty, 2) \cup (3, \infty)$ and strictly decreasing in $(2, 3)$.

15. **Hint** $f'(x) = -e^{-x}(1 + x)$, solve $f'(x) \geq 0$ for increasing and $f'(x) \leq 0$ for decreasing.
Ans. Increasing in $(-\infty, -1]$ and decreasing in $[-1, \infty)$.

16. **Hint** $f'(x) = \frac{x}{(1+x)^2}$, Solve $f'(x) \geq 0$ for increasing and $f'(x) \leq 0$ for decreasing.
Ans. Increasing in $[0, \infty)$ and decreasing in $(-\infty, -1) \cup (-1, 0)$.

17. **Hint** $P'(x) = 24 - 36x$ and $P''(x) = -36$

$P(x)$ is maxima at $x = \frac{2}{3}$

$$P\left(\frac{2}{3}\right) = 49 \quad \textbf{Ans. } ₹\ 49$$

18. **Hint** Total revenue of company after increment is given by

$$R(x) = (500 - x)(300 + x)$$

$\Rightarrow$ $R'(x) = -2x + 200$

$\Rightarrow$ $R''(x) = -2 < 0$

S, $R(x)$ is maximum when $x = 100$.

Ans. Company should increase subscription fee by ₹ 100 so that it has maximum profit.

19. **Hint** $\dfrac{dy}{dx} = \dfrac{(1+x^2)\dfrac{d}{dx}(x) - x \times \dfrac{d}{dx}(1+x^2)}{(1+x^2)^2}$

$$= \frac{(1+x^2) - x(2x)}{(1+x^2)^2}$$

$$\Rightarrow \quad m = \frac{1-x^2}{(1+x^2)^2}$$

$$\Rightarrow \frac{dm}{dx} = \frac{(1+x^2)^2\dfrac{d}{dx}(1-x^2) - (1-x^2)\dfrac{d}{dx}(1+x^2)^2}{[(1+x^2)^2]^2}$$

$$= \frac{(1+x^2)^2(-2x) - (1-x^2) \times 2(1+x^2) \times 2x}{(1+x^2)^4}$$

$$= \frac{2x(1+x^2)[(1+x^2)(-1) - 2(1-x^2)]}{(1+x^2)^4}$$

$$= \frac{2x[x^2-3]}{(1+x^2)^3}$$

For maxima or minima, put $\dfrac{dm}{dx} = 0$

$$\Rightarrow \frac{2x(x^2-3)}{(1+x^2)^3} = 0 \Rightarrow x = 0, \pm\sqrt{3}$$

Ans. (0, 0)

20. Solve as Example 10 of Topic 4. **Ans.** (2, 2)

21. **Hint** Revenue, $R = Px = \dfrac{1}{2}(106 - x)\,x$

$$\text{Cost } C = (AC)\,x = \left(5 + \frac{x}{50}\right)x$$

Profit (P) = Revenue − Cost

$$\frac{dP}{dx} = 0 \Rightarrow x = \frac{600}{13}$$

Ans. $\dfrac{600}{13}$

22. (i) (b), (ii) (d), (iii) (b), (iv) (c), (v) (b)

23. (i) (c), (ii) (a), (iii) (b), (iv) (c), (v) (c)

24. (i) (b), (ii) (a), (iii) (c)

25. (i) Since, with increase of ₹ 1 in subscription, one subscriber discontinues the service and there is an increase of ₹ x in subscription, so the number of subscribers left = $500 - x$.

(ii) New monthly subscription charge (in ₹) = $300 + x$

$\Rightarrow$ Total revenue (in ₹) $R = (300 + x)(500 - x)$

(iii) $\dfrac{dR}{dx} = (500 - x) \times 1 + (-1)(300 + x) = 200 - 2x$

and $\dfrac{d^2R}{dx^2} = -2.$

Now, $\dfrac{dR}{dx} = 0 \Rightarrow 200 - 2x = 0 \Rightarrow x = 100.$

At $x = 100$, $\dfrac{d^2R}{dx^2} = -2 < 0 \Rightarrow R$ is maximum.

Thus, the revenue is maximum when the subscription is increased by ₹ 100.

The number of subscribers left = 500 − 100 = 400.

(iv) Increase in charges per month = ₹ 100

Or

New charges per subscriber = ₹ (300 + 100) = ₹ 400 and the number of subscribers left = 400.

Maximum revenue generated = ₹ (400 × 400)

= ₹ 160000.

CHAPTER 11

Indefinite Integrals

In this Chapter...

- Integration and Its Properties
- Integration by Substitution
- Some Special Integrals
- Integration by Partial Fractions
- Integration by Parts

Integration and Its Properties

Integration is reverse process of differentiation. If the derivative of $F(x)$ is $f(x)$, then we say that the integral (anti-derivative or primitive) of $f(x)$ is $F(x)$ and we write

$$\int f(x)\, dx = F(x) + C$$

Where, C is an arbitrary constant known as **constant of integration**. Here, $f(x)$ is called the integrand and x is called the variable of integration.

Integration of some standard functions are given below:

	Functions	Integration
1.	$\int x^n\, dx$	$\dfrac{x^{n+1}}{n+1} + C, n \neq -1$ [This is called power rule]
2.	$\int dx$	$x + C$
3.	$\int \frac{1}{x}\, dx$	$\log\lvert x\rvert + C$
4.	$\int e^x\, dx$	$e^x + C$
5.	$\int a^x\, dx$	$\dfrac{a^x}{\log a} + C, a > 0, a \neq 1$

Remarks

1. The derivative of a function (if exists) will be unique but the integral of a function is not so. The integral of a function differ by a real constant (number).
2. The derivative of a function is determined at a point but the integral of a function is not determined at a point. Instead, we find it in an interval.

EXAMPLE 1. Evaluate the following integrals.

(i) $\int x^6 dx$ (ii) $\int \frac{1}{x^{3/4}} dx$

(iii) $\int \frac{1}{\sqrt[3]{x^5}} dx$ (iv) $\int a^{3 \log_a x}\, dx$

(v) $\int \frac{e^{7\log x} - e^{6\log x}}{e^{5\log x} - e^{4\log x}}\, dx$ (vi) $\int 5^x\, dx$

Sol. (i) Let $I = \int x^6 dx$

$$= \frac{x^{6+1}}{6+1} + C \qquad \left[\because \int x^n dx = \frac{x^{n+1}}{n+1} + C, n \neq -1\right]$$

$$= \frac{x^7}{7} + C$$

(ii) Let $I = \int \left[\frac{1}{x^{3/4}}\right] dx = \int x^{-3/4}\, dx$

$$= \frac{x^{-\frac{3}{4}+1}}{-\frac{3}{4}+1} + C \qquad \left[\because \int x^n dx = \frac{x^{n+1}}{n+1}, n \neq -1\right]$$

$$= \frac{x^{1/4}}{1/4} + C = 4x^{1/4} + C$$

(iii) Let $I = \int \frac{1}{\sqrt[3]{x^5}} dx = \int \frac{1}{(x^{5/3})} dx$

$$= \int x^{-5/3} dx = \frac{x^{-\frac{5}{3}+1}}{\frac{-5}{3}+1} + C$$

$$= \frac{x^{-2/3}}{\frac{-2}{3}} + C = -\frac{3}{2}x^{-2/3} + C$$

(iv) Let $I = \int a^{3\log_a x} dx = \int a^{\log_a x^3} dx$ $[\because m\log n = \log n^m]$

$$= \int x^3 dx \qquad [\because a^{\log_a f(x)} = f(x)]$$

$$= \frac{x^4}{4} + C \qquad \left[\because \int x^n dx = \frac{x^{n+1}}{n+1} + C, n \neq -1\right]$$

(v) Let $I = \int \frac{e^{7\log x} - e^{6\log x}}{e^{5\log x} - e^{4\log x}} dx$

$$= \int \frac{e^{\log x^7} - e^{\log x^6}}{e^{\log x^5} - e^{\log x^4}}$$

$$= \int \frac{x^7 - x^6}{x^5 - x^4} dx$$

$$= \int \frac{x^6(x-1)}{x^5(x-1)} dx = \int x\, dx = \frac{x^2}{2} + C$$

(vi) Let $I = \int 5^x dx = \frac{5^x}{\log 5} + C \qquad \left[\because \int a^x dx = \frac{a^x}{\log a}\right]$

Properties of Indefinite Integrals

(i) $\frac{d}{dx}(\int f(x)\, dx) = f(x)$

(ii) $\int \{f(x) \pm g(x)\}\, dx = \int f(x)\, dx \pm \int g(x)\, dx$

(iii) $\int k \cdot f(x)\, dx = k \cdot \int f(x)\, dx$, where k is any non-zero real number.

(iv) In general, if $f_1, f_2, \ldots, f_n$ are functions and $k_1, k_2, \ldots, k_n$ are non-zero real numbers, then

$$\int [k_1 f_1(x) + k_2 f_2(x) + \ldots + k_n f_n(x)]\, dx$$

$$= k_1 \int f_1(x) dx + k_2 \int f_2(x)\, dx + \ldots + k_n \int f_n(x) dx$$

EXAMPLE 2. Evaluate the following.

(i) $\int \left(x^4 + 5x^3 + 3 - \frac{7}{x} + \frac{1}{\sqrt{x}}\right) dx$

(ii) $\int \left(\frac{x^4 + x^2 + 1}{x^2 - x + 1}\right) dx$

Sol. (i) Let $I = \int \left(x^4 + 5x^3 + 3 - \frac{7}{x} + \frac{1}{\sqrt{x}}\right) dx$

$$= \int x^4 dx + 5\int x^3 dx + \int 3dx - 7\int \frac{1}{x} dx + \int \frac{1}{\sqrt{x}} dx$$

[by property (ii) and (iii)]

$$= \frac{x^5}{5} + \frac{5x^4}{4} + 3x - 7\log x + 2\sqrt{x} + C$$

(ii) Let $I = \int \left(\frac{x^4 + x^2 + 1}{x^2 - x + 1}\right) dx$

$$= \int \frac{(x^2 - x + 1)(x^2 + x + 1)}{x^2 - x + 1} dx$$

$$= \int (x^2 + x + 1)\, dx = \int x^2 dx + \int x\, dx + \int 1 dx$$

[by property (ii) and (iii)]

$$= \frac{x^3}{3} + \frac{x^2}{2} + x + C$$

EXAMPLE 3. Evaluate $\int \frac{(1+x)^2}{\sqrt{x}} dx.$

Sol. Let $I = \int \frac{(1+x)^2}{\sqrt{x}} dx = \int \frac{(1 + x^2 + 2x)}{\sqrt{x}} dx$

$$= \int \frac{1}{\sqrt{x}} dx + \int \frac{x^2}{\sqrt{x}} dx + 2\int \frac{x}{\sqrt{x}} dx$$

[by property (ii) and (iii)]

$$= \int x^{-\frac{1}{2}} dx + \int x^{2-\frac{1}{2}} dx + 2\int x^{1-\frac{1}{2}} dx$$

$$= \int x^{-1/2} dx + \int x^{3/2} dx + 2\int x^{1/2} dx$$

$$= \frac{x^{-\frac{1}{2}+1}}{-\frac{1}{2}+1} + \frac{x^{\frac{3}{2}+1}}{\frac{3}{2}+1} + \frac{2x^{\frac{1}{2}+1}}{\frac{1}{2}+1} + C \qquad \left[\because \int x^n dx = \frac{x^{n+1}}{n+1}\right]$$

$$= \frac{x^{1/2}}{1/2} + \frac{x^{5/2}}{5/2} + \frac{2x^{3/2}}{3/2} + C$$

$$= 2x^{1/2} + \frac{2}{5}x^{5/2} + \frac{4}{3}x^{3/2} + C$$

$$= 2\sqrt{x} + \frac{2}{5}x^{5/2} + \frac{4}{3}x^{3/2} + C$$

EXAMPLE 4. Evaluate $\int \frac{(2^x + 3^x)^2}{6^x} dx.$

Sol. Let $I = \int \frac{(2^x + 3^x)^2}{6^x} dx = \int \frac{(2^x)^2 + (3^x)^2 + 2 \cdot 2^x \cdot 3^x}{6^x} dx$

$$= \int \frac{4^x + 9^x + 2 \cdot 6^x}{6^x} dx = \int \left(\frac{4^x}{6^x} + \frac{9^x}{6^x} + 2\right) dx$$

$$= \int \left[\left(\frac{2}{3}\right)^x + \left(\frac{3}{2}\right)^x + 2\right] dx$$

$$= \int \left(\frac{2}{3}\right)^x dx + \int \left(\frac{3}{2}\right)^x dx + 2\int dx$$

[by property (ii) and (iii)]

$$= \frac{\left(\frac{2}{3}\right)^x}{\log\left(\frac{2}{3}\right)} + \frac{\left(\frac{3}{2}\right)^x}{\log\left(\frac{3}{2}\right)} + 2x + C$$

EXAMPLE 5. Evaluate $\int (e^x a^x + 2^{\log_e x})\, dx$.

Sol. Let $I = \int (e^x a^x + 2^{\log_e x}) dx$

$$= \int [(ea)^x + x^{\log_e 2}] dx \qquad [\because x^{\log_e y} = y^{\log_e x}]$$

$$= \int (ea)^x dx + \int x^{\log_e 2} dx$$

$$= \frac{(ea)^x}{\log(ea)} + \frac{x^{\log_e 2+1}}{\log_e 2+1} + C$$

$$= \frac{(ea)^x}{\log(ea)} + \frac{x^{\log(2e)}}{\log(2e)} + C$$

EXAMPLE 6. Evaluate

(i) $\int \frac{x^6+1}{x^2+1} dx$ (ii) $\int \frac{x^3-8}{x^2+2x+4} dx$

Sol. (i) Let $I = \int \frac{x^6+1}{x^2+1} dx = \int \frac{(x^2)^3 + 1^3}{x^2+1} dx$

$$= \int \frac{(x^2+1)((x^2)^2 + 1^2 - (x^2)(1))}{x^2+1} dx$$

$$[\because a^3 + b^3 = (a+b)(a^2+b^2) - ab)]$$

$$= \int (x^4 + 1 - x^2)\, dx$$

$$= \int x^4 \cdot dx + \int 1 \cdot dx - \int x^2 dx$$

$$= \frac{x^5}{5} + x - \frac{x^3}{3} + C = \frac{x^5}{5} - \frac{x^3}{3} + x + C$$

(ii) Let $I = \int \frac{x^3-8}{x^2+2x+4} dx = \int \frac{(x)^3 - (2)^3}{x^2+2x+4} dx$

$$= \int \frac{(x-2)(x^2+2^2+x.2)}{x^2+2x+4} dx$$

$$[\because a^3 - b^3 = (a-b)(a^2+b^2+ab)]$$

$$= \int \frac{(x-2)(x^2+2x+4)}{(x^2+2x+4)} dx = \int (x-2)\, dx$$

$$= \int x\, dx - 2\int dx = \frac{x^2}{2} - 2x + C$$

Topic Practice 1

1 Evaluate the following integrals.

(i) $\int \frac{1}{x^5} dx$ (ii) $\int \frac{1}{x^{3/2}} dx$

(iii) $\int \frac{1}{\sqrt[3]{x^2}} dx$ (iv) $\int 3^{2\log_3 x} dx$

(v) $\int \frac{e^{6\log x} - e^{5\log x}}{e^{4\log x} - e^{3\log x}} dx$ (vi) $\int 3^x\, dx$

(vii) $\int \log_x x\, dx$

2. Evaluate the following integrals.

(i) $\int \left(6x^5 - \frac{2}{x^4} - 7x + \frac{3}{x} - 5 + 4e^x + 7^x\right) dx$

(ii) $\int \left(\frac{x}{a} + \frac{a}{x} + x^a + a^x + a + x + ax\right) dx$

(iii) $\int \sqrt{x}\,(ax^2 + bx + c)\, dx$

(iv) $\int \left(x^2 - \frac{1}{x^2}\right)^3 dx$ (v) $\int \frac{(1+2x)^3}{x^4} dx$

(vi) $\int \frac{(a^x + b^x)^2}{a^x b^x} dx$ (vii) $\int \frac{x^3 - x^2 + x - 1}{x-1} dx$

(viii) $\int (e^{x\log a} + e^{a\log x} + e^{a\log a}) dx$

(ix) $\int \frac{x^4}{x^2+1} dx$

(x) $\int \frac{(x^3+8)(x-1)}{x^2-2x+4} dx$

(xi) $\int (1-x)(2+3x)(5-4x) dx$

3 Evaluate the following integrals.

(i) $\int (1-x)(2\sqrt{x})\, dx$ (ii) $\int \frac{(2+5y)(3-y^2)}{\sqrt{y}} dy$

(iii) $\int \left(\sqrt{x} + \frac{1}{x^2}\right)^2 dx$ (iv) $\int \frac{(x+n)^2}{\sqrt{x}} dx$

4 Find the anti-derivative F of f defined by $f(x) = 4x^5 - 6x$, where $F(0) = 2$.

5 If $\frac{d}{dx} f(x) = 4x^3 - \frac{3}{x^4}$ such that $f(2) = 0$. Then, find $f(x)$.

6 Find an anti-derivative (or integral) of the following functions by the method of inspection.

(i) $3x^2 + 4x^3$ (ii) e^{2x}

(iii) $(ax + b)^2$

Hints & Solutions

1. Do similar as Example 1.

Ans. (i) $-\frac{1}{4x^4}+C$ (ii) $-\frac{2}{\sqrt{x}}+C$ (iii) $3(x)^{1/3}+C$

(iv) $\frac{x^3}{3}+C$ (v) $\frac{x^3}{3}+C$ (vi) $\frac{3^x}{\log 3}+C$

(vii) Let $I=\int \log_x x\,dx=\int 1\,dx=x+C$ $[\because \log_a a=1]$

2. (i) Do similar as Example 2 (i).

Ans. $x^6+\frac{2}{3x^3}-\frac{7x^2}{2}+3\log(x)-5x+4e^x+\frac{7^x}{\log 7}+C$

(ii) Do similar as Example 2 (i).

Ans. $\frac{x^2}{2a}+a\log|x|+\frac{x^{a+1}}{a+1}+\frac{a^x}{\log a}+ax+\frac{x^2}{2}+\frac{ax^2}{2}+C$

(iii) Do similar as Example 3.

Ans. $\frac{2ax^{7/2}}{7}+\frac{2bx^{5/2}}{5}+\frac{2cx^{3/2}}{3}+C$

(iv) Let $I=\int\left(x^2-\frac{1}{x^2}\right)^3 dx=\int\left(x^6-3x^2+\frac{3}{x^2}-\frac{1}{x^6}\right)dx$

$$=\frac{x^7}{7}-x^3-\frac{3}{x}+\frac{1}{5x^5}+C$$

(v) Do similar as Example 3.

Ans. $\frac{-1}{3x^3}+8\log|x|-\frac{3}{x^2}-\frac{12}{x}+C$

(vi) Do similar as Example 4.

Ans. $\frac{\left(\frac{a}{b}\right)^x}{\log\left(\frac{a}{b}\right)}+\frac{\left(\frac{a}{b}\right)^x}{\log\left(\frac{b}{a}\right)}+2x+C$

(vii) Let $I=\int\frac{x^3-x^2+x-1}{x-1}dx$

$$=\int\frac{x^2(x-1)+1(x-1)}{(x-1)}dx=\int\frac{(x-1)(x^2+1)}{(x-1)}dx$$

$$=\int(x^2+1)\,dx=\frac{x^3}{3}+x+C$$

(viii) Let $I=\int(e^{x\log a}+e^{a\log x}+e^{a\log a})\,dx$

$$=\int(e^{\log a^x}+e^{\log x^a}+e^{\log a^a})\,dx$$

$$=\int(a^x+x^a+a^a)\,dx=\frac{a^x}{\log a}+\frac{x^{a+1}}{a+1}+a^a x+C$$

(ix) Let $I=\int\frac{x^4}{x^2+1}dx=\int\frac{x^4-1+1}{x^2+1}dx$

$$=\int\frac{x^4-1}{x^2+1}dx+\int\frac{1}{x^2+1}dx$$

$$=\int\left(\frac{(x^2-1)(x^2+1)}{x^2+1}+\frac{1}{x^2+1}\right)dx$$

$[\because a^4-b^4=(a^2-b^2)(a^2+b^2)]$

$$=\int(x^2-1)dx+\int\frac{1}{x^2+1}dx$$

$$=\int x^2dx-\int dx+\int\frac{dx}{x^2+1}$$

$$=\frac{x^3}{3}-x+\tan^{-1}x+C \quad \left[\because \int\frac{dx}{x^2+1}=\tan^{-1}x\right]$$

(x) Let $I=\int\frac{(x^3+8)(x-1)}{x^2-2x+4}dx$

$$=\int\frac{(x+2)(x^2+2^2-2x)(x-1)}{(x^2-2x+4)}dx$$

$$=\int(x+2)(x-1)\,dx$$

$$=\int(x^2+x-2)\,dx=\frac{x^3}{3}+\frac{x^2}{2}-2x+C$$

(xi) Let $I=\int(1-x)(2+3x)(5-4x)dx$

$$=\int(10-3x-19x^2+12x^3)dx$$

$$=10\int dx-3\int x\,dx-19\int x^2\,dx+12\int x^3dx$$

$$=10x-\frac{3x^2}{2}-\frac{19x^3}{3}+3x^4+C$$

3. (i) Let $I=\int(1-x)(2\sqrt{x})dx=2\int(1-x)\sqrt{x}\,.\,dx$

$$=2\int(\sqrt{x}-x\sqrt{x})\,dx=2\int x^{1/2}\cdot dx-2\int x^{3/2}\,dx$$

$$=2.\frac{x^{3/2}}{\left(\frac{3}{2}\right)}-2\cdot\frac{x^{5/2}}{\left(\frac{5}{2}\right)}+C=\frac{4}{3}x^{3/2}-\frac{4}{5}x^{5/2}+C$$

(ii) Let $I=\int\frac{(2+5y)(3-y^2)}{\sqrt{y}}dy$

$$=\int\frac{6+15y-2y^2-5y^3}{\sqrt{y}}$$

$$=\int\left(\frac{6}{\sqrt{y}}+15\sqrt{y}-2y^{3/2}-5y^{5/2}\right)dy$$

$$=6\int y^{-1/2}dy+15\int y^{1/2}dy$$

$$-2\int y^{3/2}dy-5\int y^{5/2}dy$$

$$=6.\frac{y^{1/2}}{1/2}+15\frac{y^{3/2}}{3/2}-2\frac{y^{5/2}}{5/2}-5\frac{y^{7/2}}{7/2}+C$$

$$=12\sqrt{y}+10y^{3/2}-\frac{4}{5}y^{5/2}-\frac{10}{7}y^{7/2}+C$$

(iii) Let $I = \int \left(\sqrt{x} + \frac{1}{x^2}\right)^2 dx = \int \left(x + \frac{1}{x^4} + 2\cdot\sqrt{x}\cdot\frac{1}{x^2}\right) dx$

$= \int (x + x^{-4} + 2x^{-3/2})\, dx$

$= \int x\, dx + \int x^{-4} dx + 2\int x^{-3/2} dx$

$= \frac{x^2}{2} + \frac{x^{-3}}{-3} + 2.\frac{x^{-1/2}}{(-1/2)} + C$

$= \frac{x^2}{2} - \frac{1}{3x^3} - \frac{4}{\sqrt{x}} + C = \frac{x^2}{2} - \frac{1}{3x^3} - \frac{4\sqrt{x}}{x} + C$

(iv) Let $I = \int \frac{(x+n)^2}{\sqrt{x}} dx = \int \frac{(x^2 + n^2 + 2nx)}{\sqrt{x}} dx$

$= \int (x^{3/2} + n^2 x^{-1/2} + 2nx^{1/2}) dx$

$= \int x^{3/2} dx + n^2 \int x^{-1/2} dx + 2n \int x^{1/2} dx$

$= \frac{x^{5/2}}{5/2} + n^2 \frac{x^{1/2}}{1/2} + 2n\frac{x^{3/2}}{3/2} + dx$

$= \frac{2}{5}x^{5/2} + \frac{4n}{3}x^{3/2} + 2n^2\sqrt{x} + C$

4. Given, $f(x) = 4x^5 - 6x$

On integrating both sides, we get

$\int f(x)\, dx = \int (4x^5 - 6x)\, dx$

$\Rightarrow \quad F(x) = \frac{4x^{5+1}}{5+1} - \frac{6x^2}{2} + C \quad \left[\because \int x^n\, dx = \frac{x^{n+1}}{n+1}\right]$

$\Rightarrow \quad F(x) = \frac{4}{6}x^6 - \frac{6}{2}x^2 + C$

$\Rightarrow \quad F(x) = \frac{2}{3}x^6 - 3x^2 + C \quad$ ...(i)

Also, given $F(0) = 2$, therefore putting $x = 0$ in Eq. (i), we get

$F(0) = \frac{2}{3}(0) - 3(0) + C$

$\Rightarrow \quad 2 = 0 - 0 + C$

$\Rightarrow \quad C = 2$

Now, putting $C = 2$ in Eq. (i), we get

$F(x) = \frac{2x^6}{3} - 3x^2 + 2$

5. Solve as Question 4.

Ans. $x^4 + \frac{1}{x^3} - \frac{129}{8}$

6. (i) Let us look for a function whose derivative is $3x^2 + 4x^3$.

Note that, $\frac{d}{dx}(x^3 + x^4) = 3x^2 + 4x^3$

$\therefore$ An anti-derivative of $3x^2 + 4x^3$ is $x^3 + x^4$.

(ii) $\int e^{2x}\, dx = \frac{1}{2}e^{2x} + C$

$\left[\because \frac{d}{dx}\frac{1}{2}e^{2x} + C = \frac{1}{2}e^{2x}\cdot 2 = e^{2x}\right]$

(iii) $\int (ax+b)^2 dx = \frac{1}{3a}(ax+b)^3 + C$

$\left[\because \frac{d}{dx}\left(\frac{1}{3a}(ax+b)^3 + C\right) = \frac{1}{3a}3(ax+b)^2\cdot a = (ax+b)^2\right]$

Integration by Substitution

We have the following methods of integration:

(i) Integration by substitution

(ii) Integration by partial fractions

(iii) Integration by parts

Here, we will discuss integration by substitution.

The method of reducing a given integral into one of the standard integrals by a proper substitution is called method of substitution.

Suppose, in the integral $I = \int f(x)\, dx$, $f(x)$ is not in any standard form.

Now, $\int f(x)\, dx$ can be transformed to another form by changing the independent variable x to other variable t by substituting $x = g(t)$.

$\therefore \quad \frac{dx}{dt} = g'(t) \quad$ or $\quad dx = g'(t)\, dt$

Now, putting the value of dx in the above integral, we get

$$\int f(x)\, dx = \int g'(t)\, dt$$

EXAMPLE 1. Evaluate

(i) $\int (2x+3)^6 dx$ (ii) $\int (4-3x)^7 dx$

(iii) $\int \frac{1}{5x-4}\cdot dx$ (iv) $\int e^{2x+5} dx$

(v) $\int a^{3x-5}\cdot dx$

Sol. (i) Let $I = \int (2x+3)^6 dx$

Put $(2x+3) = t \Rightarrow 2\, dx = dt \Rightarrow dx = \frac{1}{2}dt$

$\therefore \quad I = \frac{1}{2}\int t^6 dt = \frac{1}{2}\cdot\frac{t^7}{7} + C$

$= \frac{1}{14}(2x+3)^7 + C$

(ii) Let $I = \int (4-3x)^7 dx$

Put $4 - 3x = t \Rightarrow -3dx = dt \Rightarrow dx = -\frac{1}{3}dt$

$\therefore \quad I = -\frac{1}{3}\int t^7 dt$

$= -\frac{1}{3}\cdot\frac{t^8}{8} + C = -\frac{1}{24}(4-3x)^8 + C$

(iii) Let $I = \int \frac{1}{5x-4}\,.\,dx$

Put $5x - 4 = t \Rightarrow 5dx = dt$

$\Rightarrow \quad dx = \frac{dt}{5}$

$\therefore \quad I = \frac{1}{5}\int \frac{1}{t}\cdot dt = \frac{1}{5}\log_e t + C$

$= \frac{\log(5x-4)}{5} + C$

(iv) Let $I = \int e^{2x+5} dx$

Put $2x + 5 = t \Rightarrow 2\,dx = dt \Rightarrow dx = \frac{1}{2}dt$

$\therefore \quad I = \frac{1}{2}\int e^t dt = \frac{1}{2}e^t + C = \frac{1}{2}e^{2x+5} + C$

(v) Let $I = \int a^{3x-5}\,.\,dx$

Put $3x - 5 = t \Rightarrow dx = \frac{dt}{3}$

$\therefore \quad I = \frac{1}{3}\int a^t dt = \frac{1}{3}\frac{a^t}{\log a} + C = \frac{a^{3x-5}}{3\log a} + C$

Some Important Results using Substitutions

(i) $\int (ax+b)^n dx = \frac{(ax+b)^{n+1}}{a(n+1)} + C,\ n \neq -1$ and n is a rational number.

(ii) $\int \frac{1}{ax+b}dx = \frac{1}{a}\log|ax+b| + C$

(iii) $\int e^{(ax+b)} dx = \frac{e^{(ax+b)}}{a} + C$

(iv) $\int a^{mx+b} dx = \frac{a^{mx+b}}{m\log_e a} + C$

Note Above integral can be derived by substituting $ax + b = t$ and $dx = \frac{1}{a}dt$.

EXAMPLE 2. Evaluate

(i) $\int \sqrt{ax+b}\,dx$ (ii) $\int \frac{1}{8x+3}dx$

(iii) $\int e^{-x+1}\cdot dx$ (iv) $\int a^{3x+2} dx$

(v) $\int \frac{dx}{\sqrt{x+a}+\sqrt{x+b}}$

(vi) $\int \left[(2x-5)^5 + \frac{1}{(7x-5)^3} + \frac{1}{\sqrt{5x-4}} + \frac{1}{2-3x} + \sqrt{3x+2}\right]dx$

Sol. (i) Let $I = \int \sqrt{ax+b}\,dx = \int (ax+b)^{1/2} dx$

$= \frac{(ax+b)^{(1/2)+1}}{((1/2)+1)\cdot a} + C$

$= \frac{2}{3}\frac{(ax+b)^{3/2}}{a} + C$

$= \frac{2}{3a}(ax+b)^{3/2} + C$

(ii) Let $I = \int \frac{1}{8x+3}dx = \frac{1}{8}\log|8x+3| + C$

(iii) Let $I = \int e^{-x+1}\cdot dx = \frac{e^{-x+1}}{(-1)} + C = -e^{-x+1} + C$

(iv) Let $I = \int a^{3x+2} dx = \frac{1}{3\log a}a^{3x+2} + C$

(v) Let $I = \int \frac{dx}{\sqrt{x+a}+\sqrt{x+b}}$

$= \int \frac{(\sqrt{x+a}-\sqrt{x+b})}{(\sqrt{x+a}+\sqrt{x+b})(\sqrt{x+a}-\sqrt{x+b})}dx$

[rationalising denominator]

$= \int \frac{\sqrt{x+a}-\sqrt{x+b}}{(\sqrt{x+a})^2-(\sqrt{x+b})^2}dx$

$= \int \frac{(\sqrt{x+a}-\sqrt{x+b})}{(x+a)-(x+b)}dx$

$= \frac{1}{a-b}\int [(x+a)^{1/2} - (x+b)^{1/2}]dx$

$= \frac{1}{a-b}\left[\frac{2}{3}(x+a)^{3/2} - \frac{2}{3}(x+b)^{3/2}\right] + C$

$= \frac{2}{3(a-b)}[(x+a)^{3/2} - (x+b)^{3/2}] + C$

(vi) Let $I = \int \left[(2x-5)^5 + \frac{1}{(7x-5)^3} + \frac{1}{\sqrt{5x-4}} + \frac{1}{2-3x} + \sqrt{3x+2}\right]dx$

$= \int (2x-5)^5 dx + \int (7x-5)^{-3} dx + \int (5x-4)^{-1/2} dx + \int \frac{1}{2-3x}dx + \int (3x+2)^{1/2} dx$

$$= \frac{(2x-5)^6}{2\times 6} + \frac{(7x-5)^{-2}}{7\times(-2)} + \frac{(5x-4)^{1/2}}{5\times\frac{1}{2}} + \frac{1}{-3}\log|2-3x| + \frac{(3x+2)^{3/2}}{3\times\frac{3}{2}} + C$$

$$= \frac{1}{12}(2x-5)^6 - \frac{1}{14}(7x-5)^{-2} + \frac{2}{5}\sqrt{5x-4} - \frac{1}{3}\log|2-3x| + \frac{2}{9}(3x+2)^{3/2} + C$$

Integral of Type $\int \frac{P(x)}{(ax+b)^n}\,dx,\ n \in N, z$ where $P(x)$ is a Polynomial

First express $\frac{P(x)}{(ax+b)^n}$ as proper fraction, i.e. degree of $P(x) < n$. Then, put $ax+b=t$ and integrate.

EXAMPLE 3. Evaluate

(i) $\int \frac{x^3}{(x+2)^4}\,dx$ (ii) $\int \frac{x^2+1}{(x+1)^2}\,dx$

Sol. (i) Let $I = \int \frac{x^3}{(x+2)^4}\,dx$

Put $x+2=t \Rightarrow dx = dt$ and $x = t-2$

$$\therefore \quad I = \int \frac{(t-2)^3}{t^4}\,dt = \int \frac{t^3-6t^2+12t-8}{t^4}\,dt$$

$$= \int\left(\frac{1}{t} - \frac{6}{t^2} + \frac{12}{t^3} - \frac{8}{t^4}\right)dt$$

$$= \log t + \frac{6}{t} - \frac{6}{t^2} + \frac{8}{3t^3} + C$$

$$= \log|x+2| + \frac{6}{x+2} - \frac{6}{(x+2)^2} + \frac{8}{3(x+2)^3} + C$$

(ii) Let $I = \int \frac{x^2+1}{(x+1)^2}\,dx$

$$= \int \frac{x^2+1+2x-2x}{(x+1)^2}\,dx \qquad [\because P(x) \ge n]$$

$$= \int \frac{(x+1)^2-2x}{(x+1)^2}\,dx$$

$$= \int 1 - \frac{2x}{(x+1)^2}\,dx = \int 1\cdot dx - 2\int \frac{x}{(x+1)^2}\,dx$$

$$= x - 2I_1,$$

where $I_1 = \int \frac{x}{(x+1)^2}\,dx$

Now, $I_1 = \int \frac{x}{(x+1)^2}\,dx$

Put $x+1=t \Rightarrow dx = dt$ and $x = t-1$

$$\therefore \ I_1 = \int \frac{t-1}{t^2}\,dt = \int\left(\frac{1}{t} - \frac{1}{t^2}\right)dt$$

$$= \log|t| + \frac{1}{t} + C = \log|x+1| + \frac{1}{x+1} + C$$

$$\therefore \ I = x - 2\log|x+1| - \frac{2}{x+1} + C$$

Note In a rational function, if the degree of the numerator of the integrand is equal to or greater than that of the denominator, divide the numerator by the denominator until the degree of the remainder is less than that of the denominator.

So, $\frac{\text{Numerator}}{\text{Denominator}} = \text{Quotient} + \frac{\text{Remainder}}{\text{Denominator}}$

Integral of Type $\int (ax+b)\sqrt{cx+d}\,dx$ and $\int \frac{ax+b}{\sqrt{cx+d}}\,dx$

In this type of integral, put $cx+d=t$ and then integrate.

EXAMPLE 4. Evaluate

(i) $\int (7x-2)\sqrt{3x+2}\,dx$ (ii) $\int \frac{x+1}{\sqrt{2x+1}}\,dx$

Sol. (i) Let $I = \int (7x-2)\sqrt{3x+2}\,dx$

Put $3x+2=t \Rightarrow 3\,dx = dt$

$\Rightarrow dx = \frac{1}{3}dt$ and $x = \frac{t-2}{3}$

$$\therefore \quad I = \frac{1}{3}\int\left[7\left(\frac{t-2}{3}\right) - 2\right]\sqrt{t}\,dt = \frac{1}{9}\int (7t-20)\sqrt{t}\,dt$$

$$= \frac{7}{9}\int t^{3/2}\,dt - \frac{20}{9}\int t^{1/2}\,dt$$

$$= \frac{7}{9}\cdot\frac{t^{5/2}}{\left(\frac{5}{2}\right)} - \frac{20}{9}\frac{t^{3/2}}{\left(\frac{3}{2}\right)} + C$$

$$= \frac{14}{45}(3x+2)^{5/2} - \frac{40}{27}(3x+2)^{3/2} + C$$

(ii) Let $I = \int \frac{x+1}{\sqrt{2x+1}}\,dx$

Put $2x+1=t \Rightarrow 2dx = dt \Rightarrow dx = \frac{1}{2}dt$ and $x = \frac{t-1}{2}$

$$\therefore \quad I = \frac{1}{2}\int \frac{\frac{t-1}{2}+1}{\sqrt{t}}\,dt = \frac{1}{4}\int \frac{t+1}{\sqrt{t}}\,dt$$

$$= \frac{1}{4}\int (t^{1/2} + t^{-1/2})\,dt = \frac{1}{4}\left[\frac{t^{3/2}}{(3/2)} + \frac{t^{1/2}}{(1/2)}\right] + C$$

$$= \frac{1}{6}(2x+1)^{3/2} + \frac{1}{2}(2x+1)^{1/2} + C$$

Integral of The Form $\int \frac{f'(x)}{f(x)}\,dx$

In this type of integral, let $I = \int \frac{f'(x)}{f(x)}\,dx$

Put $f(x) = t \Rightarrow f'(x)\,dx = dt$

$\therefore \quad I = \int \frac{dt}{t} = \log t + C = \log|f(x)| + C.$

EXAMPLE 5. Evaluate

(i) $\int \frac{2x+3}{x^2+3x-7}\,dx$ (ii) $\int \frac{1}{x(6+\log x)}\,dx$

(iii) $\int \frac{e^x - e^{-x}}{e^x + e^{-x}}\,dx$ (iv) $\int \frac{dx}{1+a^{-x}}$

Sol. (i) Let $I = \int \frac{2x+3}{x^2+3x-7}\,dx$

Put $x^2+3x-7 = t \Rightarrow (2x+3)\,dx = dt$

$\therefore \; I = \int \frac{dt}{t} = \log|t| + C = \log|x^2+3x-7| + C$

(ii) Let $I = \int \frac{1}{x(6+\log x)}\,dx$

Put $6 + \log x = t \Rightarrow \frac{1}{x}dx = dt$

$\therefore \; I = \int \frac{1}{t}.dt = \log t + C = \log(6+\log x) + C$

(iii) Let $I = \int \frac{e^x - e^{-x}}{e^x + e^{-x}}\,dx$

Put $e^x + e^{-x} = t \Rightarrow (e^x - e^{-x})\,dx = dt$

$\therefore \; I = \int \frac{dt}{t} = \log|t| + C = \log|e^x + e^{-x}| + C$

(iv) Let $I = \int \frac{dx}{1+a^{-x}} = \int \frac{a^x}{a^x+1}\,dx$

Put $a^x + 1 = x \Rightarrow a^x \log a\,dx + dt \Rightarrow a^x dx = \frac{dt}{\log a}$

$\therefore \; I = \frac{1}{\log a}\int \frac{1}{t}dt = \frac{1}{\log a}\log t + C$

$= \frac{1}{\log a}\log(a^x+1) + C$

Integral of The Form $\int (f(x))^n f'(x)\,dx$

In this type of integral, let $I = \int (f(x))^n f'(x)\,dx$

Put $f(x) = t \Rightarrow f'(x)\,dx = dt$

$\therefore \; I = \int t^n\,dt = \frac{t^{n+1}}{n+1} + C = \frac{(f(x))^{n+1}}{n+1} + C$

EXAMPLE 6. Evaluate

(i) $\int \frac{(\log x)^3}{x}\,dx$ (ii) $\int \frac{(8-\log x)^4}{x}\,dx$

(iii) $\int \frac{3x+1}{(3x^2+2x+1)^3}\,dx$ (iv) $\int \frac{(x^4-x)^{1/4}}{x^5}\,dx$

Sol. (i) Let $I = \int \frac{(\log x)^3}{x}\,dx$

Put $\log x = t$

$\Rightarrow \frac{1}{x}\,dx = dt$

$\therefore \quad I = \int t^3 dt = \frac{t^4}{4} + C$

$= \frac{(\log x)^4}{4} + C$

(ii) Let $I = \int \frac{(8-\log x)^4}{x}\,dx$

Put $8 - \log x = t \Rightarrow -\frac{1}{x}dx = dt \Rightarrow \frac{1}{x}dx = -dt$

$\therefore \; I = -\int t^4 dt = -\frac{t^5}{5} + C = -\frac{(8-\log x)^5}{5} + C$

(iii) Let $I = \int \frac{3x+1}{(3x^2+2x+1)^3}\,dx$

Put $3x^2 + 2x + 1 = t$

$\Rightarrow \; (6x+2)\,dx = dt$

$\Rightarrow \; (3x+1)\,dx = \frac{1}{2}dt$

$\therefore \quad I = \frac{1}{2}\int \frac{dt}{t^3} = \frac{1}{2}\int t^{-3}dt$

$= \frac{1}{2}\frac{t^{-2}}{(-2)} + C = \frac{-1}{4t^2} + C$

$= \frac{-1}{4(3x^2+2x+1)^2} + C$

(iv) Let $I = \int \frac{(x^4-x)^{1/4}}{x^5}\,dx$

$= \int \frac{x\left(1-\frac{1}{x^3}\right)^{1/4}}{x^5}\,dx = \int \left(1-\frac{1}{x^3}\right)^{1/4}\frac{dx}{x^4}$

Put $\left(1-\frac{1}{x^3}\right) = t \Rightarrow -(-3)x^{-4}dx = dt$

$\Rightarrow \quad \frac{3}{x^4}dx = dt \Rightarrow \frac{dx}{x^4} = \frac{dt}{3}$

$\therefore \quad I = \frac{1}{3}\int t^{1/4}dt = \frac{1}{3}.\frac{t^{5/4}}{(5/4)} + C$

$= \frac{4}{15}\left(1-\frac{1}{x^3}\right)^{5/4} + C$

Topic Practice 2

1 Evaluate the following

(i) $\int (3x+5)^7 dx$ (ii) $(5-7x)^3 dx$

2 Evaluate the following

(i) $\int \frac{1}{\sqrt{3x+4}-\sqrt{3x+1}} dx$

(ii) $\int \left(\frac{1}{(7x-5)^3} + (2x-3)^5 + \sqrt{3x+2} + \frac{1}{\sqrt{5x-4}} \right) dx$

3 Evaluate the following

(i) $\int \frac{2x-1}{(x-1)^2} dx$ (ii) $\int \frac{x+2}{(x+1)^2} dx$

(iii) $\int \frac{x^7}{x+1} dx$ (iv) $\int \frac{x^3}{x+2} dx$

4 Evaluate the following

(i) $\int (x+2)\sqrt{3x+5}\, dx$

(ii) $\int \frac{x}{\sqrt{x+4}} dx$

5 Evaluate $\int 2^{2^{2^x}} 2^{2^x} 2^x dx$.

6 Evaluate the following

(i) $\int \frac{1}{x \log x \log(\log x)} \cdot dx$

(ii) $\int (e^x-1)^2 e^x dx$ (iii) $\int \left(e^x + \frac{1}{e^x}\right)^2 dx$

(iv) $\int \frac{1}{e^x+1} dx$ (v) $\int \frac{8^{1+x}+4^{1-x}}{2^x} \cdot dx$

Hints & Solutions

1. (i) Do same as Example 1 (i). **Ans.** $\frac{1}{24}(3x+5)^8 + C$

(ii) Do same as Example 1 (i). **Ans.** $-\frac{1}{28}(5-7x)^4 + C$

2. (i) Do same as Example 2 (v).

Ans. $\frac{2(3x+4)^{3/2}}{27} + \frac{2(3x+1)^{3/2}}{27} + C$

(ii) Do same as Example 2 (vi).

Ans. $\frac{-1}{14(7x-5)^2} + \frac{(2x-3)^6}{12} + \frac{2(3x+2)^{3/2}}{9} + \frac{2}{5}\sqrt{5x-4} + C$

3. (i) Do same as Example 3 (i).

Ans. $-\frac{1}{x-1} + 2\log|x-1| + C$

(ii) Do same as Example 3 (i). **Ans.** $\log|x+1| - \frac{1}{x+1} + C$

(iii) **Hint** On dividing, we get

Ans. $\frac{x^7}{7} - \frac{x^6}{6} + \frac{x^5}{5} - \frac{x^4}{4} + \frac{x^3}{3} - \frac{x^2}{2} + x - \log|x+1| + C$

(iv) Do same as Example 3 (ii).

Ans. $\frac{x^3}{3} - x^2 + 4x - 8\log|x+2| + C$

4. (i) Do same as Example 4 (i).

Ans. $\frac{2}{135}(9x+20)(3x+5)^{3/2} + C$

(ii) Do same as Example 4 (ii). **Ans.** $\frac{2}{3}(x-8)\sqrt{x+4} + C$

5. **Hint** Put $2^{2^{2^x}} = t$ **Ans.** $\frac{2^{2^{2^x}}}{(\log 2)^3} + C$

6. (i) Let $I = \int \frac{1}{x \log x \log(\log x)} \cdot dx$

Put $\log(\log x) = t$

$\Rightarrow \frac{1}{\log x} \cdot \frac{1}{x} . dx = dt \Rightarrow \frac{1}{x \log x} dx = dt$

$\therefore\ I = \int \frac{1}{t} dt = \log t + c = \log(\log(\log x)) + C$

(ii) **Hint** Put $e^x - 1 = t$ **Ans.** $\frac{1}{3}(e^x-1)^3 + C$

(iii) **Hint** Expand the whole square.

Ans. $\frac{1}{2}e^{2x} + 2x - \frac{1}{2}e^{-2x} + C$

(iv) Let $I = \int \frac{1}{e^x+1} dx = \int \frac{e^{-x}}{1+e^{-x}} dx$

Put $1 + e^{-x} = t \Rightarrow -e^{-x}dx = dt \Rightarrow e^{-x}dx = -dt$

$\therefore\ I = -\int \frac{dt}{t} = -\log|t| + C = -\log|1+e^{-x}| + C$

(v) Let $I = \int \frac{8^{1+x}+4^{1-x}}{2^x} dx = \int \frac{(2^3)^{1+x}+(2^2)^{1-x}}{2^x} dx$

$= \int \frac{2^{3x+3}}{2^x} + \frac{2^{2-2x}}{2^x} dx = \int 2^{2x+3} + 2^{2-3x} dx$

$= \frac{2^{2x+3}}{2\log 2} + \frac{2^{2-3x}}{(-3)\log 2} + C = \frac{2^{2x+2}}{\log 2} - \frac{2^{2-3x}}{3\log 2} + C$

Some Special Integrals

In this topic, we discuss some standard formulae with their proof and the methods to solve some other standard integrals with the help of these formulae.

(i) $\int \frac{dx}{x^2 - a^2} = \frac{1}{2a} \log \left| \frac{x-a}{x+a} \right| + C$

(ii) $\int \frac{dx}{a^2 - x^2} = \frac{1}{2a} \log \left| \frac{a+x}{a-x} \right| + C$

(iii) $\int \frac{dx}{\sqrt{x^2 - a^2}} = \log |x + \sqrt{x^2 - a^2}| + C$

(iv) $\int \frac{dx}{\sqrt{x^2 + a^2}} = \log |x + \sqrt{x^2 + a^2}| + C$

EXAMPLE 1. Find the following integrals.

(i) $\int \frac{dx}{x^2 - 16}$ (ii) $\int \frac{dx}{\sqrt{9 + 25x^2}}$

(iii) $\int \frac{1}{36 - x^2} dx$ (iv) $\int \frac{1}{\sqrt{9x^2 - 16}} dx$

Sol. (i) Let $I = \int \frac{dx}{x^2 - 16} = \int \frac{dx}{x^2 - 4^2}$

$= \frac{1}{2(4)} \log \left| \frac{x-4}{x+4} \right| + C = \frac{1}{8} \log \left| \frac{x-4}{x+4} \right| + C$

(ii) Let $I = \int \frac{dx}{\sqrt{9 + 25x^2}}$

$= \int \frac{dx}{\sqrt{25\left(\frac{9}{25} + x^2\right)}} = \frac{1}{5} \int \frac{dx}{\sqrt{\left(\frac{3}{5}\right)^2 + x^2}}$

$= \frac{1}{5} \log \left[x + \sqrt{\left(\frac{3}{5}\right)^2 + x^2} \right] + C$

$= \frac{1}{5} \log \left[\frac{5x + \sqrt{9 + 25x^2}}{5} \right] + C$

$= \frac{1}{5} \log [5x + \sqrt{9 + 25x^2}] - \frac{1}{5} \log 5 + C$

$= \frac{1}{5} \log [5x + \sqrt{9 + 25x^2}] + C_1$

where $C_1 = -\frac{1}{5} \log 5 + C$

(iii) Let $I = \int \frac{1}{36 - x^2} dx = \int \frac{1}{(6)^2 - x^2} dx$

$= \frac{1}{2 \times 6} \log \left| \frac{6+x}{6-x} \right| + C = \frac{1}{12} \log \left| \frac{6+x}{6-x} \right| + C$

(iv) Let $I = \int \frac{1}{\sqrt{9x^2 - 16}} dx = \int \frac{1}{\sqrt{9\left(x^2 - \frac{16}{9}\right)}} . dx$

$= \frac{1}{3} \int \frac{1}{\sqrt{x^2 - \left(\frac{4}{3}\right)^2}} dx$

$= \frac{1}{3} \log \left[x + \sqrt{x^2 - \frac{16}{9}} \right] + C$

$= \frac{1}{3} \log \left[\frac{3x + \sqrt{9x^2 - 16}}{3} \right] + C$

$= \frac{1}{3} \log [3x + \sqrt{9x^2 - 16}] - \frac{1}{3} \log 3 + C$

$= \frac{1}{3} \log [3x + \sqrt{9x^2 - 16}] + C_1$

where $C_1 = -\frac{1}{3} \log 3 + C$

Integral of the Type $\int \frac{dx}{ax^2 + bx + c}$

To evaluate such integrals, we use the following steps :

I. First, take a common from denominator to make coefficient of x^2 unity, i.e. $I = \int \frac{dx}{a\left(x^2 + \frac{b}{a}x + \frac{c}{a}\right)}$

II. Add and subtract $(b/2a)^2$ from denominator and try to write denominator in the form $X^2 - k^2$ or $k^2 - X^2$,

where, $X^2 = \left(x \pm \frac{b}{2a}\right)^2$ and $k^2 = \left(\frac{c}{a} \mp \frac{b^2}{4a^2}\right)$.

III. Substitute $x \pm \frac{b}{2a} = t$ and reduce the integral obtained in step II into one of the form

$\frac{1}{a} \int \frac{dt}{t^2 - k^2}$ or $\frac{1}{a} \int \frac{dt}{k^2 - t^2}$.

EXAMPLE 2. Evaluate $\int \frac{1}{9x^2 + 6x - 5} dx$.

Sol. Let $I = \int \frac{1}{9x^2 + 6x - 5} dx = \frac{1}{9} \int \frac{1}{x^2 + \frac{2}{3}x - \frac{5}{9}} dx$

[take 9 common from denominator]

$$=\frac{1}{9}\int\frac{1}{x^2+2\cdot\frac{1}{3}\cdot x+\left(\frac{1}{3}\right)^2-\frac{5}{9}-\left(\frac{1}{3}\right)^2}dx$$

[here $a=9$ and $b=6$, adding and subtracting $\left(\frac{b}{2a}\right)^2=\left(\frac{6}{2\times 9}\right)^2=\left(\frac{1}{3}\right)^2$ from denominator]

$$=\frac{1}{9}\int\frac{1}{x^2+\frac{2}{3}x+\left(\frac{1}{3}\right)^2-\frac{5}{9}-\frac{1}{9}}dx$$

$$=\frac{1}{9}\int\frac{1}{\left(x+\frac{1}{3}\right)^2-\left(\frac{\sqrt{6}}{3}\right)^2}dx$$

$$=\frac{1}{9}\times\frac{1}{2\times\frac{\sqrt{6}}{3}}\log\left|\frac{x+\frac{1}{3}-\frac{\sqrt{6}}{3}}{x+\frac{1}{3}+\frac{\sqrt{6}}{3}}\right|+C$$

$$=\frac{1}{6\sqrt{6}}\log\left|\frac{3x+1-\sqrt{6}}{3x+1+\sqrt{6}}\right|+C$$

EXAMPLE 3. Evaluate $\int\frac{e^x}{e^{2x}+6e^x+5}dx.$

Sol. Let $I=\int\frac{e^x}{e^{2x}+6e^x+5}dx=\int\frac{e^x}{(e^x)^2+6(e^x)+5}dx$

Put $e^x=t\Rightarrow e^x\,dx=dt$

$$\therefore\quad I=\int\frac{dt}{t^2+6t+5}=\int\frac{dt}{(t+3)^2-(2)^2}$$

$$=\frac{1}{2\times 2}\log\left|\frac{t+3-2}{t+3+2}\right|+C=\frac{1}{4}\log\left|\frac{e^x+1}{e^x+5}\right|+C$$

EXAMPLE 4. Evaluate $\int\frac{1}{x(x^n+1)}dx.$

Sol. Let $I=\int\frac{1}{x(x^n+1)}dx=\int\frac{x^{n-1}}{x^n(x^n+1)}dx$

Put $x^n=t\Rightarrow nx^{n-1}dx=dt\Rightarrow x^{n-1}dx=\frac{1}{n}dt$

$$\therefore\quad I=\frac{1}{n}\int\frac{dt}{t(t+1)}=\frac{1}{n}\int\frac{dt}{t^2+t}=\frac{1}{n}\int\frac{dt}{\left(t+\frac{1}{2}\right)^2-\left(\frac{1}{2}\right)^2}$$

$$=\frac{1}{n}\cdot\frac{1}{2\times\left(\frac{1}{2}\right)}\log\left|\frac{t+\frac{1}{2}-\frac{1}{2}}{t+\frac{1}{2}+\frac{1}{2}}\right|+C$$

$$=\frac{1}{n}\log\left|\frac{t}{t+1}\right|+C=\frac{1}{n}\log\left|\frac{x^n}{x^n+1}\right|+C$$

Integral of the Type $\int\frac{dx}{\sqrt{ax^2+bx+c}}$

To evaluate such integrals, we do same steps as previous integral. The only difference is that, here reduced integral (obtained after step II) will be of the form $\frac{1}{a}\int\frac{dt}{\sqrt{t^2\pm k^2}}$, which can be integrated by using suitable formulae.

EXAMPLE 5. Evaluate $\int\frac{dx}{\sqrt{3-x+x^2}}.$

Sol. Let $I=\int\frac{dx}{\sqrt{3-x+x^2}}=\int\frac{dx}{\sqrt{x^2-x+3}}$

$$=\int\frac{dx}{\sqrt{x^2-2\times x\times\frac{1}{2}+\left(\frac{1}{2}\right)^2-\left(\frac{1}{2}\right)^2+3}}$$

[here $a=1, b=-1$, adding and subtracting $\left(\frac{b}{2a}\right)^2=\left(\frac{-1}{2}\right)^2=\left(\frac{1}{2}\right)^2$ from denominator]

$$=\int\frac{dx}{\sqrt{\left(x-\frac{1}{2}\right)^2+3-\frac{1}{4}}}=\int\frac{dx}{\sqrt{\left(x-\frac{1}{2}\right)^2+\frac{11}{4}}}$$

Now, put $x-\frac{1}{2}=t\ \Rightarrow\ dx=dt$

$$\therefore\quad I=\int\frac{dt}{\sqrt{t^2+\left(\frac{\sqrt{11}}{2}\right)^2}}=\log\left|t+\sqrt{t^2+\left(\frac{\sqrt{11}}{2}\right)^2}\right|+C$$

$$\left[\because\int\frac{dx}{\sqrt{x^2+a^2}}=\log|x+\sqrt{x^2+a^2}|\right]$$

$$=\log\left|\left(x-\frac{1}{2}\right)+\sqrt{\left(x-\frac{1}{2}\right)^2+\left(\frac{\sqrt{11}}{2}\right)^2}\right|+C$$

$$\left[\because t=x-\frac{1}{2}\right]$$

Hence, $I=\log\left|\left(x-\frac{1}{2}\right)+\sqrt{3-x+x^2}\right|+C.$

EXAMPLE 6. Evaluate $\int\frac{1}{\sqrt{2x^2-3x-2}}dx.$

Sol. Let $I=\int\frac{1}{\sqrt{2x^2-3x-2}}dx$

$$=\frac{1}{\sqrt{2}}\int\frac{1}{\sqrt{x^2-\frac{3}{2}x-1}}dx=\frac{1}{\sqrt{2}}\int\frac{1}{\sqrt{\left(x-\frac{3}{4}\right)^2-\frac{9}{16}-1}}dx$$

$$= \frac{1}{\sqrt{2}} \int \frac{1}{\sqrt{\left(x - \frac{3}{4}\right)^2 - \left(\frac{5}{4}\right)^2}} dx$$

Now, put $x - \frac{3}{4} = t \Rightarrow dx = dt$

$$\therefore \quad I = \frac{1}{\sqrt{2}} \int \frac{1}{\sqrt{t^2 - \left(\frac{5}{4}\right)^2}} dt = \frac{1}{\sqrt{2}} \log \left| t + \sqrt{t^2 - \left(\frac{5}{4}\right)^2} \right| + C$$

$$= \frac{1}{\sqrt{2}} \log \left| \left(x - \frac{3}{4}\right) + \sqrt{\left(x - \frac{3}{4}\right)^2 - \frac{25}{16}} \right| + C$$

$$= \frac{1}{\sqrt{2}} \log \left| \left(x - \frac{3}{4}\right) + \sqrt{x^2 - \frac{3}{2}x + \frac{9}{16} - \frac{25}{16}} \right| + C$$

$$= \frac{1}{\sqrt{2}} \log \left| \left(x - \frac{3}{4}\right) + \sqrt{x^2 - \frac{3}{2}x - 1} \right| + C$$

EXAMPLE 7. Evaluate $\dfrac{2x}{\sqrt{1 - x^2 + x^4}} dx$

Sol. Let $I = \int \dfrac{2x}{\sqrt{1 - x^2 + x^4}} dx = \dfrac{2x}{\sqrt{1 - x^2 + (x^2)^2}} dx$

Now, let $x^2 = t \Rightarrow 2x\, dx = dt \Rightarrow dx = \dfrac{dt}{2x}$

$$\therefore I = \frac{1}{\sqrt{1 - t + t^2}} dt = \int \frac{1}{\sqrt{(t^2 - t + 1)}} dt$$

$$= \int \frac{1}{\sqrt{\left(t^2 - t + \frac{1}{4} - \frac{1}{4} + 1\right)}} dt$$

$$= \int \frac{1}{\sqrt{\left(t - \frac{1}{2}\right)^2 + \frac{3}{4}}} dt = \int \frac{1}{\sqrt{\left(t - \frac{1}{2}\right)^2 + \left(\frac{\sqrt{3}}{2}\right)^2}} dt$$

$$= \log \left| \left(t - \frac{1}{2}\right) + \sqrt{t^2 - t + 1} \right|$$

$$= \log \left| \left(x^2 - \frac{1}{2}\right) + \sqrt{x^4 - x^2 + 1} \right| + C$$

Integral of the Types $\int \dfrac{px + q}{ax^2 + bx + c} dx$ and $\int \dfrac{px + q}{\sqrt{ax^2 + bx + c}} dx$

To evaluate such integrals, we firstly write the numerator as

$$px + q = A\left\{\frac{d}{dx}(ax^2 + bx + c)\right\} + B$$

$$= A(2ax + b) + B$$

Then, find A and B by comparing the coefficients of like powers of x from both sides.

Now, put the resultant value of $(px + q)$ in given integral and then given integral is reduced to one of the known forms which can be integrate easily.

EXAMPLE 8. Evaluate $\int \dfrac{4x + 1}{x^2 + 3x + 2} dx$.

Sol. Let $(4x + 1) = A\dfrac{d}{dx}(x^2 + 3x + 2) + B$

$\Rightarrow \quad 4x + 1 = A(2x + 3) + B \quad$ ...(i)

$\Rightarrow \quad 4x + 1 = 2Ax + (3A + B)$

On equating the coefficients of x and constant term from both sides, we get

$$4 = 2A \text{ and } 1 = 3A + B$$

$\Rightarrow \quad A = 2$ and $1 = 3 \times 2 + B$

$\Rightarrow \quad A = 2$ and $B = -5$

From Eq. (i), we get

$$4x + 1 = 2(2x + 3) - 5$$

$$\therefore \quad I = \int \frac{4x + 1}{x^2 + 3x + 2} dx = \int \frac{2(2x + 3) - 5}{x^2 + 3x + 2} dx$$

$$= 2\int \frac{2x + 3}{x^2 + 3x + 2} dx - 5 \int \frac{1}{x^2 + 3x + 2} dx$$

$$= 2I_1 - 5I_2 \quad \text{...(ii)}$$

where, $I_1 = \int \dfrac{2x + 3}{x^2 + 3x + 2} dx$ and $I_2 = \int \dfrac{1}{x^2 + 3x + 2} dx$

Now, $\quad I_1 = \int \dfrac{2x + 3}{x^2 + 3x + 2} dx$

Put $x^2 + 3x + 2 = t \Rightarrow (2x + 3)dx = dt$

$$\therefore \quad I_1 = \int \frac{dt}{t} = \log|t| + C_1 = \log|x^2 + 3x + 2| + C_1$$

and $I_2 = \int \dfrac{dx}{x^2 + 3x + 2}$

$$= \int \frac{dx}{\left(x + \frac{3}{2}\right)^2 + 2 - \frac{9}{4}} = \int \frac{dx}{\left(x + \frac{3}{2}\right)^2 - \left(\frac{1}{2}\right)^2}$$

$$= \frac{1}{2 \times \frac{1}{2}} \log \left| \frac{x + \frac{3}{2} - \frac{1}{2}}{x + \frac{3}{2} + \frac{1}{2}} \right| + C_2 = \log \left| \frac{x + 1}{x + 2} \right| + C_2$$

$$\therefore \quad I = 2\log|x^2 + 3x + 2| - 5\log\left|\frac{x + 1}{x + 2}\right| + C,$$

where $C = 2C_1 - 5C_2$

EXAMPLE 9. Evaluate $\int \dfrac{2x + 3}{\sqrt{x^2 + 4x + 1}} dx$.

Sol. Let $2x + 3 = A\dfrac{d}{dx}(x^2 + 4x + 1) + B$

$\Rightarrow \quad 2x + 3 = A(2x + 4) + B \quad$ ...(i)

$\Rightarrow \quad 2x + 3 = 2Ax + (4A + B)$

On equating the coefficients of x and constants term from both sides, we get

$$2 = 2A \text{ and } 3 = 4A + B$$

$\Rightarrow \quad A = 1$ and $3 = 4 + B \Rightarrow A = 1$ and $B = -1$

From Eq. (i), we get

$$2x + 3 = (2x + 4) - 1$$

$$\therefore \quad I = \int \frac{2x+4}{\sqrt{x^2+4x+1}}dx - \int \frac{1}{\sqrt{x^2+4x+1}}dx$$

$$= I_1 - I_2,$$

where $I_1 = \int \frac{2x+4}{\sqrt{x^2+4x+1}}dx$, $I_2 = \int \frac{1}{\sqrt{x^2+4x+1}}dx$ ...(ii)

Now, $I_1 = \int \frac{2x+4}{\sqrt{x^2+4x+1}}dx$

Put $x^2 + 4x + 1 = t \Rightarrow (2x+4)dx = dt$

$$\therefore \quad I_1 = \int \frac{dt}{\sqrt{t}} = 2\sqrt{t} + C_1 = 2\sqrt{x^2+4x+1} + C_1$$

and $I_2 = \int \frac{1}{\sqrt{x^2+4x+1}}dx = \int \frac{dx}{\sqrt{(x+2)^2+1-4}}$

$$= \int \frac{dx}{\sqrt{(x-2)^2-(\sqrt{3})^2}}$$

$$= \log|(x+2) - \sqrt{x^2+4x+1}| + C_2$$

$$\therefore \quad I = I_1 - I_2$$

$$= 2\sqrt{x^2+4x+1} - \log|(x+2) - \sqrt{x^2+4x+1}| + C, \text{ where } C_1 - C_2 = C$$

EXAMPLE 10. Evaluate $\int \frac{x^2+5x+4}{x^2+3x+2}dx$.

Sol. Let $I = \int \frac{x^2+5x+4}{x^2+3x+2}dx$

$$\Rightarrow I = \int \left(1 + \frac{2x+2}{x^2+3x+2}\right)dx$$

$$\Rightarrow I = \int 1dx + \int \frac{2x+3-1}{x^2+3x+2}dx$$

$$\Rightarrow I = \int 1dx + \int \frac{2x+3}{x^2+3x+2}dx - \int \frac{1}{x^2+3x+2}dx$$

$$\Rightarrow I = x + \log|x^2+3x+2| - \int \frac{1}{\left(x+\frac{3}{2}\right)^2 - \left(\frac{1}{2}\right)^2}$$

$$\Rightarrow I = x + \log|x^2+3x+2| - \frac{1}{2\left(\frac{1}{2}\right)}\log\left|\frac{x+\frac{3}{2}-\frac{1}{2}}{x+\frac{3}{2}+\frac{1}{2}}\right| + C$$

$$\Rightarrow I = x + \log|x^2+3x+2| - \log\left|\frac{x+1}{x+2}\right| + C$$

Topic Practice 3

1 Evaluate the following

(i) $\int \frac{1}{9x^2-4}dx$ (ii) $\int \frac{1}{3-x^2}dx$

(iii) $\int \frac{1}{\sqrt{16x^2+25}}dx$ (iv) $\int \frac{1}{\sqrt{(2-x)^2+1}}dx$

(v) $\int \frac{1}{\sqrt{4x^2-9}}dx$

2 Evaluate the following

(i) $\int \frac{dx}{5-8x-x^2}$ (ii) $\int \frac{dx}{2x^2+x-1}$

(iii) $\int \frac{dx}{3x^2+13x-10}$ (iv) $\int \frac{dx}{6x-x^2}$

3 Evaluate the following

(i) $\int \frac{dx}{x(x^3+8)}$

(ii) $\int \frac{1}{x\{6(\log x)^2+7\log x+2\}}dx$

(iii) $\int \frac{x}{\sqrt{x^4-a^4}}dx$

4 Evaluate the following

(i) $\int \frac{1}{\sqrt{x^2-4x}}dx$ (ii) $\int \frac{1}{x\sqrt{4+(\log x)^2}}dx$

5 Evaluate the following

(i) $\int \frac{2x-3}{\sqrt{x^2+4}}dx$ (ii) $\int \frac{x+3}{x^2-2x-5}dx$

(iii) $\int \frac{x+2}{\sqrt{x^2+5x+6}}dx$ (iv) $\int \frac{x}{x^2+x-1}dx$

(v) $\int \frac{x+2}{\sqrt{x^2+2x-1}}dx$

Hints & Solutions

1. (i) Do same as Example 1 (i). **Ans.** $\frac{1}{12}\log\left|\frac{3x-2}{3x+2}\right|+C$

(ii) Do same as Example 1 (iii). **Ans.** $\frac{1}{2\sqrt{3}}\log\left|\frac{\sqrt{3}+x}{\sqrt{3}-x}\right|+C$

(iii) Do same as Example 1 (ii).

Ans. $\frac{1}{4}\log\left[4x+\sqrt{16x^2+25}\right]+C$

(iv) **Hint** Put $2-x=t$

Ans. $-\log\left[(2-x)+\sqrt{(2-x)^2+1}\right]+C$

(v) **Hint** Put $2x=t$ **Ans.** $\frac{1}{2}\log\left|2x+\sqrt{4x^2-9}\right|+C$

2. (i) Let $I=\int\frac{dx}{5-8x-x^2}=\int\frac{dx}{5-2\cdot4\cdot x-x^2-(4)^2+(4)^2}$

$$=\int\frac{dx}{5+16-[x^2+(4)^2+2\cdot4\cdot x]}$$

$$=\int\frac{dx}{21-(x+4)^2}=\int\frac{dx}{(\sqrt{21})^2-(x+4)^2}$$

$$=\frac{1}{2\sqrt{21}}\log\left|\frac{\sqrt{21}+x+4}{\sqrt{21}-x-4}\right|+C$$

$$\left[\because\int\frac{dx}{a^2-x^2}=\frac{1}{2a}\log\left|\frac{a+x}{a-x}\right|+C\right]$$

(ii) Solve as Example 2. **Ans.** $\frac{1}{3}\log\left|\frac{2x-1}{2(x+1)}\right|+C$

(iii) Solve as Example 2. **Ans.** $\frac{1}{17}\left\{\log\frac{1}{3}+\log\left|\frac{3x-2}{x+5}\right|\right\}+C$

(iv) Similar as part (i). **Ans.** $\frac{1}{6}\log\left|\frac{x}{6-x}\right|+C$

3. (i) Let $I=\int\frac{dx}{x(x^3+8)}=\int\frac{x^2}{x^3(x^3+8)}dx$

[multiply numerator and denominator by x^2]

Now, put $x^3+8=t \Rightarrow 3x^2\,dx=dt \Rightarrow x^2\,dx=\frac{dt}{3}$

$$\therefore\quad I=\frac{1}{3}\int\frac{dt}{(t-8)\,t}=\frac{1}{3}\int\frac{dt}{t^2-8t}$$

$$=\frac{1}{3}\int\frac{dt}{t^2-8t+(4)^2-(4)^2}$$

[adding and subtracting by $(4)^2$ from denominator]

$$=\frac{1}{3}\int\frac{dt}{(t-4)^2-(4)^2}$$

$$=\frac{1}{3}\times\frac{1}{2\times4}\log\left|\frac{t-4-4}{t-4+4}\right|+C$$

$$=\frac{1}{24}\log\left|\frac{t-8}{t}\right|+C=\frac{1}{24}\log\left|\frac{x^3}{x^3+8}\right|+C$$

$[\because t=x^3+8]$

(ii) **Hint** Put $\log x=t$ **Ans.** $\log\left|\frac{2\log x+1}{3\log x+2}\right|+C$

(iii) Let $I=\int\frac{x}{\sqrt{x^4-a^4}}dx=\int\frac{x}{\sqrt{(x^2)^2-(a^2)^2}}dx$

Put $x^2=t \Rightarrow 2x\,dx=dt \Rightarrow x\,dx=\frac{dt}{2}$

$$\therefore\quad I=\frac{1}{2}\int\frac{dt}{\sqrt{t^2-(a^2)^2}}=\frac{1}{2}\log\left|t+\sqrt{t^2-(a^2)^2}\right|+C$$

$$=\frac{1}{2}\log\left|x^2+\sqrt{x^4-a^4}\right|+C$$

4. (i) Let $I=\int\frac{dx}{\sqrt{x^2-4x}}=\int\frac{dx}{\sqrt{x^2-2\cdot2\cdot x+2^2-2^2}}$

$$=\int\frac{dx}{\sqrt{(x-2)^2-2^2}}$$

$$=\log\left|(x-2)+\sqrt{(x-2)^2-2^2}\right|+C$$

$$=\log\left|(x-2)+\sqrt{x^2-4x}\right|+C$$

(ii) Let $I=\int\frac{1}{x\sqrt{4+(\log x)^2}}dx$

Put $\log x=t \Rightarrow \frac{1}{x}dx=dt$

$$\therefore\ I=\int\frac{1}{\sqrt{2^2+t^2}}dt=\log\left|t+\sqrt{2^2+t^2}\right|+C$$

$$=\log\left|\log x+\sqrt{4+(\log x)^2}\right|+C$$

5. (i) Let $I=\int\frac{2x-3}{\sqrt{x^2+4}}dx=\int\frac{2x}{\sqrt{x^2+4}}-\int\frac{3}{\sqrt{x^2+4}}dx$

In first part, put $x^2+4=t \Rightarrow 2x\,dx=dt$

$$\therefore\ I=\int\frac{dt}{\sqrt{t}}-3\int\frac{1}{\sqrt{x^2+2^2}}dx$$

$$=2\sqrt{t}-3\log\left|x+\sqrt{x^2+2^2}\right|+C$$

$$=2\sqrt{x^2+4}-3\log\left|x+\sqrt{x^2+4}\right|+C$$

(ii) Similar as Example 8.

Ans. $\frac{1}{2}\log\left|x^2-2x-5\right|+\frac{2}{\sqrt{6}}\log\left|\frac{x-1-\sqrt{6}}{x-1+\sqrt{6}}\right|+C$

(iii) Similar as Example 9.

Ans. $\sqrt{x^2+5x+6}-\frac{1}{2}\log\left|\left(x+\frac{5}{2}\right)+\sqrt{x^2+5x+6}\right|+C$

(iv) Similar as Example 7.

Ans. $\frac{1}{2}\log\left|x^2+x-1\right|-\frac{1}{2\sqrt{5}}\log\left|\frac{2x+1-\sqrt{5}}{2x+1+\sqrt{5}}\right|+C$

(v) Similar as Example 9.

Ans. $\sqrt{x^2+2x-1}+\log\left|x+1+\sqrt{x^2+2x-1}\right|+C$

Integration by Partial Fractions

Here, we will learn to integrate rational functions, which are not in simple form.

Rational Functions

If $f(x)$ and $g(x)$ are polynomial functions such that $g(x) \neq 0$, then $\frac{f(x)}{g(x)}$ is known as **rational function.**

- If degree of $f(x) < g(x)$, then we called $\frac{f(x)}{g(x)}$ as **proper rational function.**
- If degree of $f(x) \geq g(x)$, then we called $\frac{f(x)}{g(x)}$ as **improper rational function.**

So, if $\frac{f(x)}{g(x)}$ is an improper rational function, then first we divide $f(x)$ by $g(x)$ and express $\frac{f(x)}{g(x)}$ as the sum of a polynomial and a proper rational function.

$$\frac{f(x)}{g(x)} = P(x) + \frac{f_1(x)}{g(x)}$$

Here, $P(x)$ is a polynomial in (x) and $\frac{f_1(x)}{g(x)}$ is a proper rational function.

Partial Fraction Decomposition

To express a rational function which is not in simple form as the sum of simpler rational function, is called partial function decomposition.

Here, each simple rational function is called **partial function.**

Now, integration of rational function is obtained by integrating each simple rational function separately.

To convert the given rational function into partial function, its denominator is to be resolved into simplest factors, which may be of the following types:

(i) Linear non-repeated

(ii) Linear repeated

(iii) Quadratic non-repeated

On the basis of factors of denominator, corresponding partial fractions are obtained.

Table given below shows the types of partial functions associated with different types of rational functions.

Form of the rational function	Form of the partial fraction
$\frac{px+q}{(x-a)(x-b)}, a \neq b$	$\frac{A}{x-a} + \frac{B}{x-b}$
$\frac{px+q}{(x-a)^2}$	$\frac{A}{(x-a)} + \frac{B}{(x-a)^2}$
$\frac{px^2+qx+r}{(x-a)(x-b)(x-c)}$	$\frac{A}{(x-a)} + \frac{B}{(x-b)} + \frac{C}{(x-c)}$
$\frac{px^2+qx+r}{(x-a)^2(x-b)}$	$\frac{A}{(x-a)} + \frac{B}{(x-a)^2} + \frac{C}{(x-b)}$
$\frac{px^2+qx+r}{(x-a)(x^2+bx+c)}$	$\frac{A}{x-a} + \frac{Bx+C}{x^2+bx+c}$

where x^2+bx+c cannot be factorised.

The values of $A, B, C, \ldots$ can be find as given below example:

EXAMPLE 1. Resolve $\frac{x^3-6x^2+10x-2}{x^2-5x+6}$ into partial fractions.

Sol. Here, degree of numerator > degree of denominator.

So, it is an improper fraction.

Now, divide numerator by denominator, we get

$$\frac{x^3-6x^2+10x-2}{x^2-5x+6} = (x-1) + \frac{(-x+4)}{x^2-5x+6} \quad \text{...(i)}$$

Now, $$\frac{-x+4}{x^2-5x+6} = \frac{-x+4}{(x-2)(x-3)}$$

$[\because x^2-5x+6 = x^2-2x-3x+6 = (x-2)(x-3)]$

So, let $$\frac{-x+4}{x^2-5x+6} = \frac{A}{x-2} + \frac{B}{x-3} \quad \text{...(ii)}$$

[from fraction table, it is of the form 1]

$$\Rightarrow -x+4 = A(x-3) + B(x-2) \quad \text{...(iii)}$$

[multiply both sides by x^2-5x+6]

On putting $x-3=0$, i.e. $x=3$ in Eq. (iii), we get

$$-3+4 = A(0) + B(3-2) \Rightarrow B = 1$$

Again, putting $x-2=0$, i.e. $x=2$ in Eq. (iii), we get

$$-2+4 = A(2-3) + B(0) \Rightarrow A = -2$$

Now, putting the values of A and B in Eq. (ii), we get

$$\frac{-x+4}{x^2-5x+6} = \frac{-2}{x-2} + \frac{1}{x-3}$$

Hence, $$\frac{x^3-6x^2+10x-2}{x^2-5x+6} = x-1-\frac{2}{x-2}+\frac{1}{x-3}$$

[from Eq. (i)]

EXAMPLE 2. Resolve $\dfrac{2x-3}{(x+1)(x^2+2)}$ into partial fractions.

Sol. Let $\dfrac{2x-3}{(x+1)(x^2+2)}=\dfrac{A}{(x+1)}+\dfrac{Bx+C}{x^2+2}$.

Then, $\dfrac{2x-3}{(x+1)(x^2+2)}=\dfrac{A(x^2+2)+(Bx+C)(x+1)}{(x+1)(x^2+2)}$

$$\Rightarrow \quad 2x-3=A(x^2+2)+(Bx+C)(x+1) \quad \text{...(i)}$$

Putting $x+1=0$ or $x=-1$ in Eq. (i), we get

$$-5=A(3)$$

$$\therefore \quad A=-\frac{5}{3}$$

Comparing coefficients of like powers of x on both sides of Eq. (i), we get

$$A+B=0,\ C+2A=-3 \text{ and } B+C=2$$

$$\therefore -\frac{5}{3}+B=0,\ C+2\left(-\frac{5}{3}\right)=-3 \qquad \left[\text{putting } A=-\frac{5}{3}\right]$$

$$\Rightarrow \quad B=\frac{5}{3},\ C=-3+\frac{10}{3},\ C=\frac{-9+10}{3}$$

$$\Rightarrow \quad B=\frac{5}{3},\ C=\frac{1}{3}$$

$$\therefore \frac{2x-3}{(x+1)(x^2+2)}=-\frac{5}{3(x+1)}+\frac{\frac{5}{3}x+\frac{1}{3}}{(x^2+2)}$$

EXAMPLE 3. Evaluate $\displaystyle\int \frac{2x}{(x^2+1)(x^2+2)}\,dx$.

Sol. Let $I=\displaystyle\int \frac{2x}{(x^2+1)(x^2+2)}\,dx$

Putting $x^2=t$ and $2x\,dx=dt$, we get

$$I=\int \frac{dt}{(t+1)(t+2)}$$

Let $\dfrac{1}{(t+1)(t+2)}=\dfrac{A}{t+1}+\dfrac{B}{t+2}$ ...(i)

$$\Rightarrow \quad 1=A(t+2)+B(t+1)$$

$$\Rightarrow \quad 1=(A+B)t+(2A+B) \quad \text{...(ii)}$$

On comparing the coefficients of t and constant term on both sides of Eq. (ii), we get

$$A+B=0,\ 2A+B=1$$

$$\Rightarrow \quad A=1,\ B=-1$$

Substituting the values of A and B in Eq. (i), we get

$$\frac{1}{(t+1)(t+2)}=\frac{1}{t+1}-\frac{1}{t+2}$$

$$\therefore \quad I=\int \frac{1}{(t+1)(t+2)}\,dt=\int\left(\frac{1}{t+1}-\frac{1}{t+2}\right)dt$$

$$=\log|t+1|-\log|t+2|+C$$

$$=\log\left|\frac{t+1}{t+2}\right|+C=\log\left|\frac{x^2+1}{x^2+2}\right|+C$$

EXAMPLE 4. Evaluate $\displaystyle\int \frac{2x-1}{(x-1)(x+2)(x-3)}\,dx$.

Sol. Let $\dfrac{2x-1}{(x-1)(x+2)(x-3)}=\dfrac{A}{x-1}+\dfrac{B}{x+2}+\dfrac{C}{x-3}$ ...(i)

$$2x-1=A(x+2)(x-3)+B(x-1)(x-3)+C(x-1)(x+2) \quad \text{...(ii)}$$

$$2x-1=(A+B+C)x^2+(-A-4B+C)x+(-6A+3B-2C)$$

On comparing the coefficients of x^2, x and constant term on both sides of Eq. (ii), we get

$$A+B+C=0,\ -A-4B+C=2 \text{ and } -6A+3B-2C=-1$$

$$\Rightarrow A=-\frac{1}{6},\ B=-\frac{1}{3} \text{ and } C=\frac{1}{2}$$

On substituting the values of A, B and C in Eq. (i), we get

$$\frac{2x-1}{(x-1)(x+2)(x-3)}=-\frac{1}{6}\cdot\frac{1}{x-1}-\frac{1}{3}\cdot\frac{1}{x+2}+\frac{1}{2}\cdot\frac{1}{x-3}$$

$$\therefore\ I=\int\frac{2x-1}{(x-1)(x+2)(x-3)}\,dx$$

$$\Rightarrow I=-\frac{1}{6}\int\frac{1}{x-1}\,dx-\frac{1}{3}\int\frac{1}{x+2}\,dx+\frac{1}{2}\int\frac{1}{x-3}\,dx$$

$$\Rightarrow I=-\frac{1}{6}\log|x-1|-\frac{1}{3}\log|x+2|+\frac{1}{2}\log|x-3|+C$$

EXAMPLE 5. Evaluate $\displaystyle\int \frac{x}{(x-1)^2(x+2)}\,dx$.

Sol. Let $I=\displaystyle\int\frac{x}{(x-1)^2(x+2)}\,dx$

Here, integrand is a proper rational function.
So, by using the form of partial fraction, we write

$$\frac{x}{(x-1)^2(x+2)}=\frac{A}{(x-1)}+\frac{B}{(x-1)^2}+\frac{C}{(x+2)} \quad \text{...(i)}$$

$$\Rightarrow \frac{x}{(x-1)^2(x+2)}=\frac{A(x-1)(x+2)+B(x+2)+C(x-1)^2}{(x-1)^2(x+2)}$$

$$\Rightarrow \quad x=A(x-1)(x+2)+B(x+2)+C(x-1)^2 \quad \text{...(ii)}$$

On putting $x=1$ in Eq. (ii), we get

$$1=A(1-1)(1+2)+B(1+2)+C(1-1)^2$$

$$\Rightarrow \quad 1=3B \ \Rightarrow\ B=1/3$$

On putting $x=-2$ in Eq. (ii), we get

$$-2=A(-2-1)(-2+2)+B(-2+2)+C(-2-1)^2$$

$$\Rightarrow \quad -2=0+0+9C \ \Rightarrow\ C=\frac{-2}{9}$$

On putting $x=0$ in Eq. (ii), we get

$$0=A(0-1)(0+2)+B(0+2)+C(0-1)^2$$

$$\Rightarrow \quad 0=-2A+2B+C$$

$$\Rightarrow \quad 0=-2A+2\cdot\frac{1}{3}-\frac{2}{9} \qquad \left[\because B=\frac{1}{3},\ C=-\frac{2}{9}\right]$$

$$\Rightarrow \quad 0=-2A+\frac{2}{3}-\frac{2}{9}\ \Rightarrow\ 0=-2A+\frac{6-2}{9}$$

$$\Rightarrow\ 2A=4/9\ \Rightarrow\ A=2/9$$

Now, putting the values of A, B and C in Eq. (i), we get

$$\frac{x}{(x-1)^2(x+2)}=\frac{2/9}{(x-1)}+\frac{1/3}{(x-1)^2}+\frac{-2/9}{(x+2)}$$

$$\therefore I=\int\frac{x}{(x-1)^2(x+2)}dx$$

$$=\frac{2}{9}\int\frac{dx}{x-1}+\frac{1}{3}\int\frac{dx}{(x-1)^2}-\frac{2}{9}\int\frac{dx}{x+2}$$

$$=\frac{2}{9}\log|x-1|+\frac{1}{3}\int(x-1)^{-2}dx-\frac{2}{9}\log|x+2|+C$$

$$=\frac{2}{9}\log|x-1|+\frac{1}{3}\cdot\frac{(x-1)^{-1}}{(-1)}-\frac{2}{9}\log|x+2|+C$$

$$=\frac{2}{9}\log|x-1|-\frac{1}{3(x-1)}-\frac{2}{9}\log|x+2|+C$$

$$=\frac{2}{9}\log\left|\frac{x-1}{x+2}\right|-\frac{1}{3(x-1)}+C\quad\left[\because \log m-\log n=\log\frac{m}{n}\right]$$

Topic Practice 4

Evaluate the following

1 $\int\frac{x}{(x-1)(x-2)}dx$

2 $\int\frac{2x-3}{(x^2-1)(2x+3)}dx$

3 $\int\frac{2x}{(x^2+1)(x^2+3)}dx$

4 $\int\frac{e^x}{(e^x-1)^2(e^x+2)}dx$

5 $\int\frac{x^2+x+1}{(x-1)^3}dx$

6 $\int\frac{x^2+6x-8}{x^3-4x}dx$

7 $\int\frac{1}{x\log x(3+\log x)}dx$

8 $\int\frac{x^3}{(x-1)(x-2)(x-3)}dx$

9 $\int\frac{x^2+1}{(2x+1)(x^2-1)}dx$

10 $\int\frac{x^2+1}{x(x^2-1)}dx$

11 $\int\frac{2x^2+7x-3}{x^2(2x+1)}dx$

Hints & Solutions

1. Let $\frac{x}{(x-1)(x-2)}=\frac{A}{(x-1)}+\frac{B}{(x-2)}$

$\Rightarrow\quad x=A(x-2)+B(x-1)$

Putting $x=1$, we get $A=-1$

and putting $x=2$, we get $B=2$

Thus, $\int\frac{x}{(x-1)(x-2)}=\int\frac{-1}{x-1}dx+2\int\frac{dx}{x-2}$

$$=-\log|x-1|+2\log|x-2|+C=\log\left|\frac{(x-2)^2}{x-1}\right|+C$$

2. Do similar as Example 4.

Ans. $\frac{5}{2}\log|x+1|-\frac{1}{10}\log|x-1|-\frac{12}{5}\log|2x+3|+C$

3. Hint Firstly, put $x^2=t\Rightarrow 2x\,dx=dt$ and then

$$I=\int\frac{dt}{(t+1)(t+3)}.$$

Ans. $\frac{1}{2}\log\left|\frac{x^2+1}{x^2+3}\right|+C$

4. Let $I=\int\frac{e^x dx}{(e^x-1)^2(e^x+2)}$

Put $e^x=t\quad\Rightarrow\quad e^x dx=dt$

$$\therefore\quad I=\int\frac{dt}{(t-1)^2(t+2)}$$

Now, let $\frac{1}{(t-1)^2(t+2)}=\frac{A}{(t-1)}+\frac{B}{(t-1)^2}+\frac{C}{(t+2)}$

$\Rightarrow\quad 1=A(t-1)(t+2)+B(t+2)+C(t-1)^2$

$\Rightarrow\quad 1=A(t^2+t-2)+B(t+2)+C(t^2-2t+1)$

$\Rightarrow\quad 1=t^2(A+C)+t(A+B-2C)-2A+2B+C$

On comparing the coefficient of t^2, t and the constant term from the both sides, we get

$A+C=0$, $A+B-2C=0$ and $-2A+2B+C=1$

$\Rightarrow\quad A=-C,$ ...(i)

$A+B=2C$ ...(ii)

and $\quad -2A+2B+C=1$ ...(iii)

On substituting $A=-C$ in Eqs. (ii) and (iii), we get

$-C+B=2C\Rightarrow B=3C$ ...(iv)

and $\quad 2C+2B+C=1$

$\Rightarrow\quad 2C+2(3C)+C=1$ [from Eq. (iv)]

$\Rightarrow\quad 9C=1$

$\Rightarrow\quad C=\frac{1}{9}$

Now, from Eqs. (i) and (iv), we get

$$A=\frac{-1}{9},\ B=\frac{1}{3}$$

Now, $I=\int\left[-\frac{1}{9}\frac{1}{(t-1)}+\frac{1}{3}\frac{1}{(t-1)^2}+\frac{1}{9}\frac{1}{(t+2)}\right]dt$

$$=-\frac{1}{9}\int\frac{dt}{t-1}+\frac{1}{3}\int\frac{dt}{(t-1)^2}+\frac{1}{9}\int\frac{dt}{t+2}$$

$$=-\frac{1}{9}\log|t-1|+\frac{1}{3}\cdot\frac{(t-1)^{-2+1}}{(-2+1)}+\frac{1}{9}\log|t+2|+C$$

$$= \frac{1}{9}\log\left|\frac{t+2}{t-1}\right| - \frac{1}{3}\cdot\frac{1}{(t-1)} + C$$

$$= \frac{1}{9}\log\left|\frac{e^x+2}{e^x-1}\right| - \frac{1}{3(e^x-1)} + C \qquad [\because t = e^x]$$

5. Let $I = \int \frac{x^2+x+1}{(x-1)^3}.dx$

The above integral can be solved by putting $x-1=t$ and $dx = dt$ also but using partial fraction this integral can be solved in the following way.

Write, $\frac{x^2+x+1}{(x-1)^3} = \frac{A}{(x-1)} + \frac{B}{(x-1)^2} + \frac{C}{(x-1)^3}$ ...(i)

$\Rightarrow \quad x^2+x+1 = A(x-1)^2 + B(x-1) + C$

$\Rightarrow \quad x^2+x+1 = A(x^2+1-2x) + Bx - B + C$

$\Rightarrow \quad x^2+x+1 = Ax^2 + (-2A+B)x + (A-B+C)$

On comparing the coefficient of x^2, x and constant term from the both sides, we get

$A = 1, -2A + B = 1$ and $A - B + C = 1$

Put $A = 1$ into $-2A + B = 1$, we get

$\Rightarrow \quad -2(1) + B = 1 \Rightarrow B = 1 + 2 = 3$

Put $A = 1$ and $B = 3$ into $A - B + C = 1$, we get

$\Rightarrow \quad 1 - 3 + C = 1 \Rightarrow C = 1 + 2 = 3$

Now, from Eq. (i),

$$\frac{x^2+x+1}{(x-1)^3} = \frac{1}{(x-1)} + \frac{3}{(x-1)^2} + \frac{3}{(x-1)^3}$$

$$\Rightarrow \int \frac{x^2+x+1}{(x-1)^3}dx = \int\left[\frac{1}{(x-1)} + \frac{3}{(x-1)^2} + \frac{3}{(x-1)^3}\right]dx$$

$$I = \int \frac{1}{(x-1)}dx + \int \frac{3}{(x-1)^2}dx + \int \frac{3}{(x-1)^3}.dx$$

$$= \int \frac{1}{(x-1)}dx + 3\int (x-1)^{-2}dx + 3\int (x-1)^{-3}dx$$

$$= \log(x-1) + \frac{3(x-1)^{-1}}{(-1)} + 3\frac{(x-1)^{-2}}{(-2)} + C$$

$$= \log(x-1) - \frac{3}{(x-1)} - \frac{3}{2}\cdot\frac{1}{(x-1)^2} + C$$

6. Let $I = \int \frac{x^2+6x-8}{x^3-4x}dx = \int \frac{x^2+6x-8}{x(x^2-4)}.dx$

$$I = \int \frac{x^2+6x-8}{x(x+2)(x-2)}dx$$

Write, $\frac{x^2+6x-8}{x(x+2)(x-2)} = \frac{A}{x} + \frac{B}{(x+2)} + \frac{C}{(x-2)}$ ...(i)

$\Rightarrow \quad x^2+6x-8 = A(x+2)(x-2) + Bx(x-2) + Cx(x+2)$

Put $x = 0 \Rightarrow 0 + 0 - 8 = A(2)(-2) + 0 + 0$

$\Rightarrow \quad -8 = -4A \Rightarrow A = 2$

Put $x = 2 \Rightarrow 4 + 12 - 8 = A(4)(0) + B(2)(0) + C(2)(4)$

$\Rightarrow \quad 8 = 8C \Rightarrow C = 1$

Put $x = -2 \Rightarrow 4 - 12 - 8 = A(0)(-4) + B(-2)(-4) + C(-2)(0)$

$\Rightarrow -16 = 8B \Rightarrow B = -2$

Now, from Eq. (i),

$$\frac{x^2+6x-8}{x(x+2)(x-2)} = \frac{2}{x} + \frac{-2}{(x+2)} + \frac{1}{(x-2)}$$

$$\int \frac{x^2+6x-8}{x(x+2)(x-2)}dx = \int\left[\frac{2}{x} - \frac{2}{(x+2)} + \frac{1}{(x-2)}\right]dx$$

$$I = 2\int \frac{1}{x}dx - 2\int \frac{1}{x+2}dx + \int \frac{1}{x-2}.dx$$

$$= 2\log x - 2\log(x+2) + \log(x-2) + C$$

$$= \log x^2 - \log(x+2)^2 + \log(x-2) + C$$

$$= \log\left|\frac{x^2(x-2)}{(x+2)^2}\right| + C$$

7. Let $I = \int \frac{1}{x\log x(3+\log x)}dx$

Put $\log x = t \Rightarrow \frac{1}{x}dx = dt$

$$I = \int \frac{1}{t(3+t)}dt$$

Write $\frac{1}{t(3+t)} = \frac{A}{t} + \frac{B}{(3+t)}$ ...(i)

$\Rightarrow \quad 1 = A(3+t) + Bt$

Put $t = 0 \Rightarrow 1 = A(3+0) + B(0) \Rightarrow 1 = 3A \Rightarrow A = \frac{1}{3}$

Put $t = -3 \Rightarrow 1 = A(3-3) + B(-3)$

$\Rightarrow 1 = 0 - 3B \Rightarrow B = -\frac{1}{3}$

Now, from Eq. (i), $\frac{1}{t(3+t)} = \frac{1/3}{t} + \frac{-1/3}{(3+t)}$

$$\int \frac{1}{t(3+t)}.dt = \frac{1}{3}\int\frac{1}{t}dt - \frac{1}{3}\int\frac{1}{(3+t)}dt$$

$$I = \frac{1}{3}\log t - \frac{1}{3}\log(3+t) + C$$

$$= \frac{1}{3}\log\frac{t}{3+t} + C = \frac{1}{3}\log\frac{\log x}{3+\log x} + C$$

8. Solve as Example 4.

Ans. $x + \frac{1}{2}\log|x-1| - 8\log|x-2| + \frac{27}{2}\log|x-3| + C$

9. Do similar as Example 4.

Ans. $-\frac{5}{6}\log|2x+1| + \frac{1}{3}\log|x-1| + \log|x+1| + C$

10. Do similar as Example 4. **Ans.** $\log\left|\frac{x^2-1}{x}\right| + C$

11. Do similar as Example 5.

Ans. $\frac{3}{x} + 13\log|x| - 12\log|2x+1| + C$

Integration by Parts

Let u and v be two differentiable functions of x.

Then, $\int \underset{\text{I}}{u} \cdot \underset{\text{II}}{v}\, dx = u\int v\, dx - \int\left(\frac{d}{dx}(u)\int v\, dx\right) dx$

i.e. the integral of the product of these two functions

= Ist function × Integral of the IInd function

−Integral of [Derivatives of Ist function

× Integral of the IInd function]

Here, we can choose first function according to its position in ILATE, where

I : Inverse trigonometric function. e.g. $\sin^{-1} x$

L : Logarithmic function. e.g. $\log x$

A : Algebraic function. e.g. $1, x, x^2$

T : Trigonometric function. e.g. $\sin x, \cos x$

E : Exponential function. e.g. e^x

The function which comes first in ILATE should taken as first function and other as second function.

Note

(i) If the integrand contains a logarithmic or an inverse trigonometric function and the second function is not given, we take second function as 1. e.g. In the integral of $\int \sin^{-1} x\, dx$, we take second function as unity (i.e. 1).

(ii) Integration by parts is not applicable in all cases. For instance, the method does not work for $\int \sqrt{x} \sin x\, dx$.

The reason is that there does not exist any function whose derivative is $\sqrt{x} \sin x$.

EXAMPLE 1. Evaluate $\int x \log x\, dx$.

Sol. Let $I = \int \underset{\text{II}}{x} \underset{\text{I}}{\log x}\, dx$

$$= \log x\int x\, dx - \int\left\{\frac{d}{dx}(\log x) \times \int x\, dx\right\} dx$$

$$= (\log x).\frac{x^2}{2} - \int \frac{1}{x} \times \frac{x^2}{2}\, dx = \frac{1}{2}x^2 \log x - \frac{1}{2}\int x\, dx$$

$$= \frac{1}{2}x^2 \log x - \frac{1}{2}\left(\frac{x^2}{2}\right) + C = \frac{1}{2}x^2 \log x - \frac{x^2}{4} + C$$

EXAMPLE 2. Evaluate $\int x^2 e^x\, dx$.

Sol. Let $I = \int \underset{\text{I}}{x^2} \underset{\text{II}}{e^x}\, dx$

$$= x^2\int e^x dx - \int\left\{\frac{d}{dx}(x^2)\int e^x dx\right\} dx$$

$$= x^2 e^x - \int 2x e^x dx$$

$$= x^2 e^x - 2\int \underset{\text{I}}{x} \underset{\text{II}}{e^x} dx$$

$$= x^2 e^x - 2\left[x\int e^x dx - \int\left\{\frac{d}{dx}(x)\int e^x dx\right\} dx\right]$$

$$= x^2 e^x - 2[xe^x - \int e^x dx]$$

$$= x^2 e^x - 2xe^x + 2e^x + C$$

EXAMPLE 3. Evaluate

(i) $\int \log x\, dx$ (ii) $\int (\log x)^2\, dx$

(iii) $\int \frac{\log x}{x^2}\, dx$ (iv) $\int x \log(1+x) dx$

(v) $\int x^3 \log 2x\, dx$ (vi) $\int \log(x^2 - 1)\, dx$

Sol. (i) Let $I = \int \log x\, dx = \int \underset{\text{I}}{\log x} \cdot \underset{\text{II}}{1} dx$

$$= \log x\int 1 dx - \int\left\{\frac{d}{dx}(\log x) \cdot \int 1 dx\right\} dx$$

$$= (\log x)\, x - \int \frac{1}{x} \cdot x\, dx = x \log x - \int 1 \cdot dx$$

$$= x \log x - x + C$$

(ii) Let $I = \int (\log x)^2 dx = \int \underset{\text{I}}{(\log x)^2} \cdot \underset{\text{II}}{1} dx$

$$= (\log x)^2 \int 1 dx - \int\left\{\frac{d}{dx}(\log x)^2 \int 1 \cdot dx\right\} dx$$

$$= (\log x)^2 \cdot x - \int 2\log x.\frac{1}{x}.x\, dx = x(\log x)^2 - 2$$

$$\left[\log x \cdot \int 1 dx - \int\left\{\frac{d}{dx}(\log x) \cdot \int 1 dx\right\} dx\right]$$

$$= x(\log x)^2 - 2\left[(\log x)x - \int \frac{1}{x} \cdot x\, dx\right]$$

$$= x(\log x)^2 - 2x \log x + 2x + C$$

(iii) Let $I = \int \frac{\log x}{x^2}\, dx = \int \underset{\text{I}}{\log x} \cdot \underset{\text{II}}{\frac{1}{x^2}}\, dx$

$$= \log x\int \frac{1}{x^2} dx - \int\left\{\frac{d}{dx}(\log x)\int \frac{1}{x^2} dx\right\} dx$$

$$= \log x\left(-\frac{1}{x}\right) - \int \frac{1}{x}\left(-\frac{1}{x}\right) dx$$

$$= -\frac{\log x}{x} + \int \frac{1}{x^2} dx$$

$$= \frac{-\log x}{x} - \frac{1}{x} + C$$

$$= -\frac{1}{x}(1 + \log x) + C$$

(iv) Let $I = \int \underset{\text{II}}{x} \underset{\text{I}}{\log(1+x)}\, dx$

$$= \log(1+x)\int x\,dx - \int\left\{\frac{d}{dx}\log(1+x)\cdot \int x\,dx\right\}dx$$

$$= \log(1+x).\frac{x^2}{2} - \int \frac{1}{1+x}.\frac{x^2}{2}\,dx$$

$$= \frac{1}{2}x^2\log(1+x) - \frac{1}{2}\int \frac{x^2}{1+x}\,dx$$

$$= \frac{1}{2}x^2\log(1+x) - \frac{1}{2}\int\left(x-1+\frac{1}{1+x}\right)dx$$

$$= \frac{1}{2}x^2\log(1+x) - \frac{1}{2}\left[\frac{x^2}{2} - x + \log(1+x)\right] + C$$

$$= \frac{1}{2}x^2\log(1+x) - \frac{1}{4}x^2 + \frac{1}{2}x - \frac{1}{2}\log(1+x) + C$$

(v) Let $I = \int \underset{\text{II}}{x^3} \underset{\text{I}}{\log 2x}\, dx$

$$= \log 2x\int x^3dx - \int\left\{\frac{d}{dx}(\log 2x)\int x^3dx\right\}dx$$

$$= \log 2x.\frac{x^4}{4} - \int \frac{1}{2x}.2.\frac{x^4}{4}dx$$

$$= \frac{1}{4}x^4\log 2x - \frac{1}{4}\int x^3dx$$

$$= \frac{1}{4}x^4\log 2x - \frac{1}{16}x^4 + C$$

(vi) Let $I = \int \log(x^2-1)dx = \int \underset{\text{II}}{1}\cdot \underset{\text{I}}{\log(x^2-1)}dx$

$$= \log(x^2-1)\int 1dx - \int\left[\frac{d}{dx}\log(x^2-1).\int 1.dx\right]dx$$

$$= \log(x^2-1)\cdot x - \int \frac{1}{(x^2-1)} \times 2x\cdot x\cdot dx$$

$$= x\cdot\log(x^2-1) - 2\int \frac{x^2}{x^2-1}\,dx$$

$$= x\log(x^2-1) - 2\int \frac{x^2-1+1}{x^2-1}\,dx$$

$$= x\log(x^2-1) - 2\int 1 + \frac{1}{x^2-1}\,dx$$

$$= x\log(x^2-1) - 2\left\{x + \frac{1}{2}\log\left|\frac{x-1}{x+1}\right|\right\} + C$$

$$= x\log(x^2-1) - 2x - \log\left|\frac{x-1}{x+1}\right| + C$$

EXAMPLE 4. Evaluate $\int \frac{\log x}{(x+1)^2}\,dx.$

Sol. Let $I = \int \frac{\log x}{(x+1)^2}\,dx = \int \underset{\text{I}}{\log x}\cdot \underset{\text{II}}{\frac{1}{(x+1)^2}}\,dx$

On applying integration by parts, we get

$$I = \log x\cdot\int\frac{dx}{(x+1)^2} - \int \frac{d}{dx}(\log x)\cdot\left(\int\frac{dx}{(x+1)^2}\right)dx$$

$$\left[\because \int \underset{\text{I}}{u}\cdot \underset{\text{II}}{v}\,dx = u\int v\,dx - \int\left(\frac{d}{dx}(u)\int v\,dx\right)dx\right]$$

$$= \log x\cdot\frac{(-1)}{x+1} + \int\frac{1}{x(x+1)}\,dx$$

$$\left[\because \int\frac{1}{(x+1)^2}\,dx = -\frac{1}{(x+1)}\right]$$

$$= \frac{-\log x}{x+1} + I_1,$$

where $I_1 = \int \frac{dx}{x(x+1)}$ (say) ...(i)

Now, using partial fraction method, consider

$$\frac{1}{x(x+1)} = \frac{A}{x} + \frac{B}{x+1}$$

$\Rightarrow \quad 1 = A(x+1) + Bx$

On putting $x = 0$, we get $A = 1$

Again, putting $x = -1$, we get $B = -1$

$\therefore \quad I_1 = \int\left(\frac{1}{x} - \frac{1}{x+1}\right)dx = \int\frac{1}{x}\,dx - \int\frac{dx}{x+1}$

$= \log|x| - \log|x+1| + C$ ...(ii)

Now, from Eqs. (i) and (ii), we get

$$I = \frac{-\log x}{x+1} + \log|x| - \log|x+1| + C$$

$$= \frac{-\log x}{x+1} + \log\left|\frac{x}{x+1}\right| + C \quad \left[\because \log m - \log n = \log\frac{m}{n}\right]$$

EXAMPLE 5. Evaluate $\int \frac{\sqrt{x^2+1}\,\{\log(x^2+1) - 2\log x\}}{x^4}\,dx.$

Sol. Let $I = \int \frac{\sqrt{x^2+1}\,\{\log(x^2+1) - 2\log x\}}{x^4}\,dx$

$$\Rightarrow I = \int \frac{\sqrt{x^2+1}}{x^4}\{\log(x^2+1) - \log x^2\}\,dx$$

$$\Rightarrow I = \int \sqrt{1+\frac{1}{x^2}}\log\left(1+\frac{1}{x^2}\right)\frac{1}{x^3}\,dx$$

Let $1 + \frac{1}{x^2} = t.$

Then, $d\left(1+\frac{1}{x^2}\right) = dt$

$$\Rightarrow \quad -\frac{2}{x^3}dx = dt$$

$$\Rightarrow \quad \frac{1}{x^3}dx = -\frac{1}{2}dt$$

$$\therefore \quad I = -\frac{1}{2}\int \underset{\text{II}}{\sqrt{t}}\ \underset{\text{I}}{\log t}\,dt$$

$$\Rightarrow \quad I = -\frac{1}{2}\left\{\frac{2}{3}(\log t)t^{3/2} - \frac{2}{3}\int \frac{1}{t} \times t^{3/2} dt\right\}$$

$$= -\frac{1}{2}\left\{\frac{2}{3}(\log t)t^{3/2} - \frac{4}{9}t^{3/2}\right\} + C$$

$$\Rightarrow \quad I = -\frac{1}{3}t^{3/2}\left\{\log t - \frac{2}{3}\right\} + C$$

$$= -\frac{1}{3}\left(1 + \frac{1}{x^2}\right)^{3/2}\left\{\log\left(1 + \frac{1}{x^2}\right) - \frac{2}{3}\right\} + C$$

EXAMPLE 6. Evaluate $\int e^{\sqrt{x}} . dx$

Sol. Let $I = \int e^{\sqrt{x}}\, dx$

Put $x = t^2 \Rightarrow dx = 2t\, dt$

$$\therefore \quad I = \int e^{\sqrt{t^2}} .2t\, dt$$

$$\Rightarrow \quad I = 2\int e^t \cdot t \cdot dt = 2\left[t\int e^t dt - \int\left\{\frac{d}{dx}t\int e^t dt\right\} dt\right] + C$$

$$= 2\,[t e^t - \int 1 \cdot e^t \cdot dt] + C = 2\,[te^t - e^t] + C$$

$$= 2e^t(t-1) + C = 2e^{\sqrt{x}}(\sqrt{x} - 1) + C$$

EXAMPLE 7. Evaluate $\int\left(\frac{1-x}{1+x^2}\right)^2 e^x\, dx.$

Sol. Let $I = \int\left(\frac{1-x}{1+x^2}\right)^2 \cdot e^x dx$

$$= \int \frac{(1+x^2) - 2x}{(1+x^2)^2} \cdot e^x dx$$

$$= \int \frac{1}{(1+x^2)} \cdot e^x dx - \int \frac{2x}{(1+x^2)^2} \cdot e^x dx$$

[Integrating the first integral by parts, taking $\frac{1}{1+x^2}$ as first function]

$$= \frac{1}{(1+x^2)}e^x - \int -\frac{1}{(1+x^2)} \cdot 2x \cdot e^x dx - \int \frac{2x}{(1+x^2)^2} e^x \cdot dx + C$$

$$= \frac{e^x}{(1+x^2)} + \int \frac{2x}{(1+x^2)^2} \cdot e^x dx - \int \frac{2x}{(1+x^2)^2} e^x \cdot dx + C$$

$$= \frac{e^x}{(1+x^2)} + C$$

EXAMPLE 8. Evaluate $\int\left(\log(\log x) + \frac{1}{\log x}\right) \cdot dx.$

Sol. Let $I = \int\left(\log(\log x) + \frac{1}{\log x}\right). dx$

Put $\log x = t \Rightarrow x = e^t \Rightarrow dx = e^t dt$

$$\therefore \quad I = \int\left(\log t + \frac{1}{t}\right) e^t dt = \int \log t . e^t dt + \int \frac{1}{t} \cdot e^t dt$$

[Integrating first integral by parts, taking $\log t$ as first function]

$$= \log t \int e^t dt - \int\left\{\frac{d}{dt}\log t \int e^t dt\right\} dt + \int \frac{1}{t} \cdot e^t dt + C$$

$$= \log t . e^t - \int \frac{1}{t} \cdot e^t dt + \int \frac{1}{t} \cdot e^t dt + C$$

$$= \log t \cdot e^t + C$$

$$= \log(\log x) \cdot e^{\log x} + C$$

$$= \log(\log x) \cdot x + C$$

$$= x \log(\log x) + C$$

Integral of the Type $\int e^x[f(x) + f'(x)]\, dx$

In this type of integral, integrand is the product of two functions. One is in exponential form and second function is the sum of two functions in which one is derivative of other function. Then, to evaluate such integrals, we directly use the following formula

$$\int e^x\, [f(x) + f'(x)]\, dx = e^x\, f(x) + C$$

EXAMPLE 9. Evaluate the following

(i) $\int e^x\left(\frac{1}{x} - \frac{1}{x^2}\right) dx$ (ii) $\int e^x \frac{x}{(x+1)^2} dx$

(iii) $\int e^x \frac{x-3}{(x-1)^3} dx$ (iv) $\int\left(\log\left(\log x + \frac{1}{(\log x)^2}\right)\right) dx$

(v) $\int e^x \frac{x+1}{(x+4)^4} dx$

Sol. (i) Let $I = \int e^x\left(\frac{1}{x} - \frac{1}{x^2}\right) dx = \int e^x\left(\frac{1}{x} + \frac{(-1)}{x^2}\right) dx$

Here, $f(x) = \frac{1}{x}$ and $f'(x) = \frac{-1}{x^2}$ so the given integral is of the form $I = \int e^x[f(x) + f'(x)] \cdot dx$

We know that,

$$\int e^x[f(x) + f'(x)]. dx = e^x f(x) + C$$

$$\therefore \quad I = e^x \cdot \frac{1}{x} + C = \frac{e^x}{x} + C$$

(ii) Let $I = \int e^x \frac{x}{(x+1)^2} dx = \int e^x \frac{x+1-1}{(x+1)^2} dx$

$$= \int e^x\left\{\frac{1}{x+1} + \frac{-1}{(x+1)^2}\right\} dx \quad \text{...(i)}$$

Now, let $f(x) = \frac{1}{x+1} \Rightarrow f'(x) = \frac{-1}{(x+1)^2}$

Then Eq. (i) becomes of the form

$$I = \int e^x [f(x) + f'(x)]dx$$

Also, we know that,

$$\int e^x [f(x) + f'(x)]\,dx = e^x f(x) + C$$

Hence, $I = \dfrac{e^x}{x+1} + C$

(iii) Let $I = \int \dfrac{x-3}{(x-1)^3} e^x\,dx$

$$= \int \frac{x-1-2}{(x-1)^3} e^x\,dx$$

$$= \int e^x \left(\frac{x-1}{(x-1)^3} - \frac{2}{(x-1)^3}\right) dx$$

$$= \int e^x \left(\frac{1}{(x-1)^2} - \frac{2}{(x-1)^3}\right) dx \qquad \text{...(i)}$$

Now, let $f(x) = \dfrac{1}{(x-1)^2}$

$\Rightarrow \qquad f'(x) = \dfrac{-2}{(x-1)^3}$

Then, Eq. (i) becomes of the form

$$I = \int e^x [f(x) + f'(x)]\,dx$$

Also, we know that,

$$\int e^x [f(x) + f'(x)]\,dx = e^x f(x) + C$$

Hence, $I = \dfrac{e^x}{(x-1)^2} + C.$

(iv) Let $I = \int \left(\log(\log x) + \dfrac{1}{(\log x)^2}\right) dx$

Put $\log x = t \Rightarrow x = e^t \Rightarrow dx = e^t\,dt$

$\therefore \quad I = \int \left(\log t + \dfrac{1}{t^2}\right) e^t\,dt$

$$= \int \left(\log t + \frac{1}{t} - \frac{1}{t} + \frac{1}{t^2}\right) e^t\,dt$$

Now, let $f(t) = \log t - \dfrac{1}{t}$

$\Rightarrow \qquad f'(t) = \dfrac{1}{t} + \dfrac{1}{t^2}$

Then, Eq. (i) becomes of the form

$$I = \int e^x [f(x) + f'(x)]dx$$

Also we know that,

$$\int e^x [f(x) + f'(x)]dx = e^x f(x) + C$$

Hence, $I = e^t \left(\log t - \dfrac{1}{t}\right) + C$

$$= x\left(\log(\log x) - \frac{1}{\log x}\right) + C$$

(v) Let $I = \int e^x \dfrac{x+1}{(x+4)^4} \cdot dx$

$$= \int e^x \frac{(x+4-3)}{(x+4)^4} \cdot dx$$

$$= \int e^x \left(\frac{1}{(x+4)^4} - \frac{3}{(x+4)^4}\right) \cdot dx \qquad \text{...(i)}$$

Now, let $f(x) = \dfrac{1}{(x+4)^3}$

$\Rightarrow \qquad f'_{(x)} = -\dfrac{3}{(x+4)^4}$

Then, equation (i) becomes of the form

$$I = \int e^x [f(x) + f'(x)]\,.\,dx$$

Also we know that,

$$\int e^x [f(x) + f'(x)]\,dx = e^x f(x) + C$$

Hence, $I = \dfrac{e^x}{(x+4)^3} + C$

Some more Special Types of Integrals

Here, we will discuss some more special types of integrals, which can be proved by using integration by parts and directly used to evaluate the given integrals.

(i) $\int \sqrt{x^2 - a^2}\,dx = \dfrac{x}{2}\sqrt{x^2 - a^2} - \dfrac{a^2}{2}\log|x + \sqrt{x^2 - a^2}| + C$

(ii) $\int \sqrt{x^2 + a^2}\,dx = \dfrac{x}{2}\sqrt{x^2 + a^2} + \dfrac{a^2}{2}\log|x + \sqrt{x^2 + a^2}| + C$

EXAMPLE 10. Evaluate $\sqrt{1 + \dfrac{x^2}{9}}$.

Sol. Let $I = \int \sqrt{1 + \dfrac{x^2}{9}}\,dx = \int \dfrac{\sqrt{9 + x^2}}{3}\,dx = \dfrac{1}{3}\int \sqrt{3^2 + x^2}\,dx$

$$= \frac{1}{3}\left[\frac{x}{2}\sqrt{3^2 + x^2} + \frac{3^2}{2}\log|x + \sqrt{3^2 + x^2}|\right] + C$$

$$\left[\because \int \sqrt{a^2 + x^2} = \frac{x}{2}\sqrt{a^2 + x^2} + \frac{a^2}{2}\log|x + \sqrt{x^2 + a^2}| + C\right]$$

$$= \frac{x}{6}\sqrt{9 + x^2} + \frac{3}{2}\log|x + \sqrt{9 + x^2}| + C$$

EXAMPLE 11. Evaluate $\int \sqrt{2x^2 - 32} \cdot dx$.

Sol. Let $I = \int \sqrt{2x^2 - 32}\, dx$

$$= \int \sqrt{2(x^2 - 16)}\, dx = \sqrt{2} \int \sqrt{x^2 - 4^2}\, dx$$

$$= \sqrt{2}\left[\frac{x}{2}\sqrt{x^2 - 4^2} - \frac{4^2}{2}\log|x + \sqrt{x^2 - 4^2}| + C\right.$$

$$= \sqrt{2}\left[\frac{x}{2}\sqrt{x^2 - 16} - 8\log|x + \sqrt{x^2 - 16}| + C\right.$$

Integrals of Type $\int \sqrt{ax^2 + bx + c}\, dx$

To evaluate this type of integral, we use following steps:

I. Firstly, take a common from integrand to make coefficient of x^2 unity,

i.e. $I = \int \sqrt{a\left(x^2 + \frac{b}{a}x + \frac{c}{a}\right)}\, dx$

II. Add and subtract $\left(\frac{b}{2a}\right)^2$ from integrand inside the square root and convert it in the form $\sqrt{X^2 \pm k^2}$,

where $X^2 = \left(x \pm \frac{b}{2a}\right)^2$ and $k^2 = \left(\frac{c}{a} \mp \frac{b^2}{4a^2}\right)$.

III. Substitute $x \pm \frac{b}{2a} = t$ and reduce the integral obtained from step II into one of the form $\int \sqrt{t^2 \pm k^2}\, dt$.

Then, apply suitable formula to integrate.

EXAMPLE 12. Evaluate the following.

(i) $\int \sqrt{x^2 - 8x + 7}\, dx$ (ii) $\int \sqrt{2x^2 + 8x + 12}\, dx$

Sol. (i) Let $I = \int \sqrt{x^2 - 8x + 7}\, dx$

Here, the coefficient of x^2 is unity.

$\therefore I = \int \sqrt{x^2 - 8x + 7}\, dx$

$$= \int \sqrt{x^2 - 8x + 7 + 4^2 - (4)^2}\, dx$$

[here $a = 1$ and $b = -8$, adding and subtracting $\left(\frac{b}{2a}\right)^2 = \left(\frac{-8}{2}\right)^2 = (4)^2$, under the square root]

$$= \int \sqrt{(x-4)^2 + 7 - 16}\, dx = \int \sqrt{(x-4)^2 - (3)^2}\, dx$$

Now, put $x - 4 = t \Rightarrow dx = dt$

$\therefore I = \int \sqrt{t^2 - 3^2}\, dt$

$$= \frac{t}{2}\sqrt{t^2 - 3^2} - \frac{(3)^2}{2}\log\left|t + \sqrt{t^2 - 3^2}\right| + C$$

$\left[\because \int \sqrt{x^2 - a^2}\, dx = \frac{x}{2}\sqrt{x^2 - a^2} - \frac{a^2}{2}\log|x + \sqrt{x^2 - a^2}|\right]$

$$= \frac{(x-4)}{2}\sqrt{(x-4)^2 - (3)^2} - \frac{(3)^2}{2}\log|x - 4 + \sqrt{(x-4)^2 - (3)^2}| + C$$

$$= \frac{x-4}{2}\sqrt{x^2 - 8x + 7} - \frac{9}{2}\log|(x-4) + \sqrt{x^2 - 8x + 7}| + C$$

(ii) Let $I = \int \sqrt{2x^2 + 8x + 12}\, dx$

Here, the coefficient of x^2 is unity.

$\therefore\ I = \sqrt{2}\int \sqrt{x^2 + 4x + 2^2 + 6 - 4}\, dx$

$\left[\text{adding and subtracting } \left(\frac{b}{2a}\right)^2 = 2^2\right]$

$$= \sqrt{2}\int \sqrt{(x+2)^2 + (\sqrt{2})^2}\, dx$$

$$= \sqrt{2}\frac{(x+2)}{2}\sqrt{x^2 + 4x + 6} + \frac{2\sqrt{2}}{2}\log|(x+2) + \sqrt{x^2 + 4x + 6}| + C$$

$\left[\because \int \sqrt{x^2 + a^2}\, dx = \frac{x}{2}\sqrt{x^2 + a^2} + \frac{a^2}{2}\log|x + \sqrt{x^2 + a^2}|\right]$

$$\Rightarrow I = \frac{\sqrt{2}(x+2)}{2}\sqrt{x^2 + 4x + 6} + \sqrt{2}\log|(x+2) + \sqrt{x^2 + 4x + 6}| + C$$

Integrals of Type $\int (px+q)\sqrt{ax^2 + bx + c}\, dx$

To evaluate such integrals, we firstly write $(px + q)$ as

$$px + q = A\frac{d}{dx}(ax^2 + bx + c) + B$$

$$= A(2ax + b) + B.$$

Then, find A and B by comparing the coefficient of like powers of x from both sides.

Now, put this value of $(px + q)$ in the given integral and then given integral is reduce to one of the known forms which can be integrated easily.

EXAMPLE 13. Evaluate $\int (x-3)\sqrt{x^2+3x-18}\,dx$.

Sol. Let $I = \int (x-3)\sqrt{x^2+3x-18}\,dx$

Now, let $x - 3 = A\dfrac{d}{dx}(x^2+3x-18) + B$

$\Rightarrow \quad x - 3 = A(2x+3) + B$

On equating the coefficients of x and constant term from both sides, we get

$$2A = 1 \text{ and } 3A + B = -3 \Rightarrow A = \frac{1}{2}$$

and $3 \times \dfrac{1}{2} + B = -3 \Rightarrow B = -\dfrac{9}{2}$

Thus, the given integral reduces in the following form

$$I = \int \left\{\frac{1}{2}(2x+3) - \frac{9}{2}\right\}\sqrt{x^2+3x-18}\,dx$$

$$\Rightarrow \quad I = \frac{1}{2}\int (2x+3)\sqrt{x^2+3x-18}\,dx - \frac{9}{2}\int \sqrt{x^2+3x-18}\,dx$$

$$= \frac{1}{2}I_1 - \frac{9}{2}I_2 \quad \text{...(i)}$$

where, $I_1 = \int (2x+3)\sqrt{x^2+3x-18}\,dx$

Now, put $x^2+3x-18 = t \Rightarrow (2x+3)\,dx = dt$

$$\therefore \quad I_1 = \int t^{1/2}\,dt = \frac{2}{3}t^{3/2} + C_1$$

$$= \frac{2}{3}(x^2+3x-18)^{3/2} + C_1 \quad [\because t = x^2+3x-18]$$

and $I_2 = \int \sqrt{x^2+3x-18}\,dx = \int \sqrt{\left(x+\dfrac{3}{2}\right)^2 - 18 - \dfrac{9}{4}}\,dx$

$$= \int \sqrt{\left(x+\frac{3}{2}\right)^2 - 18 - \left(\frac{3}{2}\right)^2}\,dx$$

$$= \int \sqrt{\left(x+\frac{3}{2}\right)^2 - \left(\frac{9}{2}\right)^2}$$

$$= \frac{\left(x+\frac{3}{2}\right)}{2}\sqrt{x^2+3x-18} - \frac{81}{8}\log\left|\left(x+\frac{3}{2}\right) + \sqrt{x^2+3x-18}\right| + C_2$$

$$\left[\because \int \sqrt{x^2-a^2}\,dx = \frac{x}{2}\sqrt{x^2-a^2} - \frac{a^2}{2}\log|x+\sqrt{x^2-a^2}|\right]$$

$$= \frac{2x+3}{4}\sqrt{x^2+3x-18} - \frac{81}{8}\log\left|\frac{2x+3}{2} + \sqrt{x^2+3x-18}\right| + C_2$$

On putting the values of I_1 and I_2 in Eq. (i), we get

$$I = \frac{1}{2}\left[\frac{2}{3}(x^2+3x-18)^{3/2} + C_1\right] - \frac{9}{2}\left[\frac{2x+3}{4}\sqrt{x^2+3x-18} - \frac{81}{8}\log\left|\frac{2x+3}{2} + \sqrt{x^2+3x-18}\right| + C_2\right]$$

$$\Rightarrow \quad I = \frac{1}{3}(x^2+3x-18)^{3/2} - \frac{9}{8}(2x+3)\sqrt{x^2+3x-18} + \frac{729}{16}\log\left|\frac{2x+3}{2} + \sqrt{x^2+3x-18}\right| + C,$$

where $C = \dfrac{C_1}{2} - \dfrac{9C_2}{2}$

EXAMPLE 14. Evaluate $\int (2x-1)\sqrt{x^2+4x+6}$.

Sol. Let $I = \int (2x-1)\sqrt{x^2+4x+6}\,.\,dx$

Let $2x - 1 = A\dfrac{d}{dx}(x^2+4x+6) + B = A(2x+4) + B$

On equating the coefficient of x and constant term from both sides, we get

$$2 = 2A \Rightarrow A = 1$$

$$-1 = 4A + B$$

$$\Rightarrow \quad -1 = 4 \times 1 + B$$

$$\Rightarrow \quad B = -5$$

Thus, the given integral reduces in the following form

$$I = \int (1.(2x+4) - 5)\sqrt{x^2+4x+6}\,dx$$

$$= \int (2x+4)\sqrt{x^2+4x+6}\,dx - 5\int \sqrt{x^2+4x+6}\,dx$$

$$= I_1 - 5I_2 \quad \text{...(i)}$$

where, $I_1 = \int (2x+4)\sqrt{x^2+4x+6}\,dx$

Put $x^2+4x+6 = t \Rightarrow (2x+4)dx = dt$

$$\therefore \quad I_1 = \int \sqrt{t}\,dt$$

$$= \int t^{1/2}dt = \frac{t^{3/2}}{3/2} + C_1$$

$$= \frac{2}{3}t^{3/2} + C_1$$

$$I_1 = \frac{2}{3}(x^2+4x+6)^{3/2} + C_1$$

and $I_1 = \int \sqrt{x^2+4x+6}\,dx = \int \sqrt{(x+2)^2 + (\sqrt{2})^2}\,dx$

$$= \frac{(x+2)}{2}\sqrt{(x+2)^2 + (\sqrt{2})^2} + \frac{(\sqrt{2})^2}{2}\log|(x+2) + \sqrt{(x+2)^2 + (\sqrt{2})^2}| + C_2$$

$$= \frac{(x+2)}{2}\sqrt{x^2+4x+6} + \log|x+2+\sqrt{x^2+4x+6}| + C_2$$

On putting the value of I_1 and I_2 into eq. (i), we get

$$I = \frac{2}{3}(x^2+4x+6)^{3/2} - \frac{5}{2}(x+2)\sqrt{x^2+4x+6} - 5\log|x+2+\sqrt{x^2+4x+6}| + C,$$

where $C = C_1 - 5C_2$

Topic Practice 5

1 Evaluate the following.

(i) $\int x^3 \cdot e^x dx$ (ii) $\int (x^2+1)\log x \, dx$

(iii) $\int \frac{\log(x+1)}{(x+1)^2} dx$ (iv) $\int (\log x)^2 x \cdot dx$

2 Evaluate the following.

(i) $\int \frac{x^2+1}{(x+1)^2} e^x dx$ (ii) $\int \frac{2x-5}{(2x-3)^3} e^{2x} dx$

(iii) $\int \left(\frac{1}{\log x} - \frac{1}{(\log x)^2}\right) dx$

(iv) $\int \frac{e^x}{x}\{x(\log x)^2 + 2\log x\}\, dx$

3 Evaluate the following.

(i) $\int \sqrt{x^2-2x}\, dx$ (ii) $\int \sqrt{5-2x+x^2}\, dx$

(iii) $\int (3x-2)(\sqrt{x^2+x+1})\, dx$

Hints & Solutions

1. (i) Solve as Example 2.

Ans. $x^3e^x - 3(x^2e^x - 2xe^x + 2e^x) + C$

(ii) **Hint** Let $I = \int \underset{\text{II}}{(x^2+1)} \underset{\text{I}}{\log x}\, dx$

Ans. $\left(\frac{x^3}{3} + x\right)\log x - \frac{x^3}{9} - x + C$

(iii) Let $I = \int \frac{\log(x+1)}{(x+1)^2} dx = \int \underset{\text{I}}{\log(x+1)} \cdot \underset{\text{II}}{\frac{1}{(x+1)^2}} dx$

$$= \log(x+1)\left(\frac{-1}{x+1}\right) - \int \left(\frac{1}{x+1}\right)\left(\frac{-1}{x+1}\right) dx$$

$$= -\frac{\log(x+1)}{x+1} + \int \frac{1}{(x+1)^2} dx$$

$$= \frac{-\log(x+1)}{x+1} - \frac{1}{(x+1)} + C$$

(iv) Let $I = \int \underset{\text{I}}{(\log x)^2} \cdot \underset{\text{II}}{x}\, dx$

$$I = (\log x)^2 \int x\, dx - \int \left\{\frac{d}{dx}(\log x)^2 \int x\, dx\right\} dx + C$$

$$= (\log x)^2 \cdot \frac{x^2}{2} - \int 2(\log x) \cdot \frac{1}{x} \cdot \frac{x^2}{2} dx + C$$

$$= \frac{x^2(\log x)^2}{2} - \int (\log x) \cdot x \cdot dx + C$$

$$= \frac{(x\log x)^2}{2} - \left[\log x \int x\, dx - \int \left\{\frac{d}{dx}\log x \int x\, dx\right\} dx\right] + C$$

$$= \frac{(x\log x)^2}{2} - \left[\log x \cdot \frac{x^2}{2} - \int \frac{1}{x} \cdot \frac{x^2}{2} dx\right] + C$$

$$= \frac{(x\log x)^2}{2} - \frac{x^2\log x}{2} - \frac{1}{2} \cdot \frac{x^2}{2} + C$$

$$= \frac{(x\log x)^2}{2} - \frac{x^2\log x}{2} - \frac{x^2}{4} + C$$

2. (i) Let $I = \int e^x \frac{x^2+1}{(x+1)^2} dx$

$$\Rightarrow I = \int e^x \left(1 - \frac{2x}{(x+1)^2}\right) dx$$

$$= \int e^x\, dx - 2\int e^x \frac{x}{(x+1)^2} dx$$

$$\Rightarrow I = e^x - 2\int e^x \frac{x+1-1}{(x+1)^2} dx$$

$$\Rightarrow I = e^x - 2\int e^x \left\{\frac{1}{x+1} + \frac{-1}{(x+1)^2}\right\} dx$$

$$\Rightarrow I = e^x - 2\left\{\int \underset{\text{II}}{e^x} \underset{\text{I}}{\frac{1}{x+1}} dx - \int e^x \frac{1}{(x+1)^2} dx\right\}$$

$$\Rightarrow I = e^x - 2\left\{\frac{1}{x+1}e^x - \int -\frac{1}{(x+1)^2} e^x dx - \int e^x \frac{1}{(x+1)^2} dx\right\}$$

[using integration by part]

$$\Rightarrow I = e^x - 2\left\{\frac{1}{x+1}e^x + \int e^x \frac{1\, dx}{(x+1)^2} - \int e^x \frac{1}{(x+1)^2} dx\right\} + C$$

$$\Rightarrow I = e^x - 2\frac{e^x}{x+1} + C$$

(ii) Let $I = \int \frac{(2x-5)e^{2x}}{(2x-3)^3} dx = \int \frac{(2x-3-2)e^{2x}}{(2x-3)^3} dx$

$$= \int \frac{e^{2x}}{(2x-3)^2} dx - 2\int \frac{e^{2x}}{(2x-3)^3} dx$$

$$= \int \underset{\text{II}}{e^{2x}} \underset{\text{I}}{(2x-3)^{-2}}\, dx - 2\int e^{2x}(2x-3)^{-3}\, dx$$

$$= \left[\begin{array}{l}(2x-3)^{-2}\int e^{2x}dx \\ -\int\left\{\dfrac{d}{dx}(2x-3)^{-2}\int e^{2x}\,dx\right\}dx\end{array}\right] - 2\int e^{2x}(2x-3)^{-3}\,dx$$

[using integration by parts]

$$= (2x-3)^{-2}\frac{e^{2x}}{2} - \int -2(2x-3)^{-3} \times 2 \times \frac{e^{2x}}{2}\,dx - 2\int e^{2x}(2x-3)^{-3}\,dx$$

$$= \frac{e^{2x}(2x-3)^{-2}}{2} + 2\int e^{2x}(2x-3)^{-3}\,dx - 2\int e^{2x}(2x-3)^{-3}\,dx$$

$$= \frac{e^{2x}(2x-3)^{-2}}{2} + C$$

(iii) Let $I = \int\left(\dfrac{1}{\log x} - \dfrac{1}{(\log x)^2}\right)dx$

Put $\log x = t \Rightarrow x = e^t \Rightarrow dx = e^t\,dt$

$$\therefore \quad I = \int e^t\left(\frac{1}{t} - \frac{1}{t^2}\right)dt$$

$$= \int e^t\left(\frac{1}{t} + \frac{-1}{t^2}\right)dt = \int e^t \cdot \frac{1}{t}dt + \int e^t\left(\frac{-1}{t^2}\right)dt$$

$$= \frac{1}{t}e^t - \int e^t\left(-\frac{1}{t^2}\right)dt + \int e^t\left(-\frac{1}{t^2}\right)dt$$

$$= \frac{e^t}{t} + C = \frac{x}{\log x} + C$$

(iv) Let $I = \int \dfrac{e^x}{x}\{x(\log x)^2 + 2\log x\}\,dx$

$$= \int e^x\left((\log x)^2 + \frac{2\log x}{x}\right)dx$$

$$= \int \underset{\text{II}}{e^x}\underset{\text{I}}{(\log x)^2}dx + \int e^x\left(\frac{2\log x}{x}\right)dx$$

$$= (\log x)^2 e^x - \int e^x\left(\frac{2\log x}{x}\right)dx + \int e^x\left(\frac{2\log x}{x^2}\right)dx$$

$$= e^x(\log x)^2 + C$$

3. (i) Let $I = \int\sqrt{x^2 - 2x}\,dx$

$$= \int\sqrt{(x^2 - 2x + 1) - 1}\,dx$$

$$= \int\sqrt{(x-1)^2 - 1^2}\,dx$$

$$= \frac{(x-1)}{2}\sqrt{x^2 - 2x} - \frac{1}{2}\log|(x-1) + \sqrt{x^2 - 2x}| + C$$

(ii) Similar as Example 12 (i).

Ans. $\dfrac{(x-1)}{2}\sqrt{5 - 2x + x^2} + 2\log|(x-1) + \sqrt{5 - 2x + x^2}| + C$

(iii) Similar as Example 13.

Ans. $(x^2 + x + 1)^{3/2} - \dfrac{7}{4}\left(x + \dfrac{1}{2}\right)\sqrt{x^2 + x + 1} - \dfrac{21}{16}\log\left|\left(x + \dfrac{1}{2}\right) + \sqrt{x^2 + x + 1}\right| + C$

Exam Pattern Exercise

Part A - Objective Type Questions

Multiple Choice Type Questions

1 $\int |x|^5 dx$ is equal to

(a) $-\frac{x^5}{5}+C$ (b) $\frac{x^5}{5}+C$

(c) $\frac{|x|^5}{5}+C$ (d) None of these

2 The value of the integral $\int \frac{(x+1)(x+\log x)^2}{x}dx$

(a) $\frac{(x+\log x)^3}{3}+C$ (b) $\frac{(x+\log x)^2}{3}+C$

(c) $\frac{(x+\log x)}{3}+C$ (d) $\frac{(x+\log x)^3}{2}+C$

3 The value of the integral $\int \frac{1}{x+x\log x}.dx$

(a) $\log|1+\log x|+C$ (b) $\log|1-\log x|+C$

(c) $-\log|1+\log x|+C$ (d) $-\log|1-\log x|+C$

4 The value of the integral $\int \frac{x}{\sqrt{1+x^2}}dx$

(a) $-x\sqrt{1+x^2}+C$ (b) $x\sqrt{1+x^2}+C$

(c) $\sqrt{1+x^2}+C$ (d) $-\sqrt{1+x^2}+C$

5 If $\int \frac{2^{1/x}}{x^2}dx = A2^{1/x}+C$, then A is equal to

(a) $-\frac{1}{\log 2}$ (b) $\log 2$ (c) -1 (d) 2

6 The anti derivative of the function $\int \frac{x^9}{(4x^2+1)^6}.dx$

(a) $\frac{1}{5}\left(4+\frac{1}{x^2}\right)^{-5}+C$ (b) $\frac{1}{10}\left(4+\frac{1}{x^2}\right)^{-5}+C$

(c) $\frac{1}{5x}\left(4+\frac{1}{x^2}\right)^{-5}+C$ (d) $\frac{1}{10x}\left(4+\frac{1}{x^2}\right)^{-5}+C$

7 $\int \frac{x}{x^4-1}dx$ is equal to

(a) $\frac{1}{4}\log\left|\frac{x^4-1}{x^4+1}\right|+C$ (b) $\frac{1}{4}\log\left|\frac{x^2+1}{x^2-1}\right|+C$

(c) $\frac{1}{4}\log\left|\frac{x^2-1}{x^2+1}\right|+C$ (d) None of these

8 $\int \frac{x^2}{(1+x^3)(2+x^3)}dx$ is equal to

(a) $\frac{1}{3}\log\left|\frac{1+x^3}{2+x^3}\right|+C$ (b) $-\frac{1}{3}\log\left|\frac{1+x^3}{2+x^3}\right|+C$

(c) $\frac{1}{6}\log\left|\frac{1+x^3}{2+x^3}\right|+C$ (d) $\frac{1}{6}\log\left|\frac{2+x^3}{1+x^3}\right|+C$

9 $\int (x-1)e^{-x}dx$ is equal to [CBSE 2023]

(a) $(x-2)e^{-x}+C$

(b) $xe^{-x}+C$

(c) $-xe^{-x}+C$

(d) $(x+1)e^{-x}+C$

10 The value of the integral $\int e^x\left(\frac{x+2}{(x+7)^6}\right).dx$

(a) $e^x.\frac{1}{(x+7)^7}+C$

(b) $e^x.\frac{1}{(x+7)^6}+C$

(c) $e^x.\frac{1}{(x+7)^5}+C$

(d) $e^x.\frac{1}{(x+7)^4}+C$

Assertion-Reason Based Questions

Directions (Q. Nos. 11-13) *In the questions given below are two statements labelled as Assertion (A) and Reason (R). In the context of the two statements, which one of the following is correct?*

(a) Both A and R are correct; R is the correct explanation of A

(b) Both A and R are correct; R is not the correct explanation of A

(c) A is correct; R is incorrect

(d) R is correct; A is incorrect

11 **Assertion (A)** $\int \frac{X^{9/2}}{\sqrt{1+X^{11}}}dx = \frac{2}{11}\log|X^{11/2}+\sqrt{1+X^{11}}|+C$

Reason (R) $\int \frac{dX}{\sqrt{1+X^2}} = \log|X+\sqrt{1+X^2}|+C$

12 **Assertion (A)** $\int \frac{x^2-1}{x^2}\frac{e^{x^2+1}}{x}dx = \frac{e^{x^2+1}}{2x^2}+C$

Reason (R) $\int f'(x)e^{f(x)}dx = f(x)+C$

13 **Assertion (A)** The integral of $x\sin(x)$ equals $-x\cos(x)+\sin(x)+C$, where C is the constant of integration.

Reason (R) This result is obtained by applying integration by parts, where $u=x$ and $du=\sin(x)\,dx$. Integrating du gives $u=-\cos(x)$, and differentiating u gives $du=dx$. Applying the integration by parts formula yields the expression $-x\cos(x)+\sin(x)+C$, where C is the constant of integration.

Part B - Descriptive Questions

Very Short Answer Type Questions

Directions (Q. Nos. 14-18) *Evaluate the following integrals.*

14 $\int (1-x)\sqrt{x}\, dx$

15 $\int e^x \left(\frac{1-x}{1+x^2}\right)^2 dx$

16 $\int \frac{1}{1+e^x} dx$

17 $\int e^{3\log x}(x^4+1)^{-1} dx$

18 $\int x\sqrt{x^4-1}\, dx$

Short Answer Type Questions

Directions (Q. Nos. 19-24) *Evaluate the following integrals.*

19 $\int \frac{x+2}{\sqrt{x^2+2x+3}} dx$

20 $\int \frac{dx}{x(x^5+3)}$

21 $\sqrt{\frac{1+x}{x}}\, dx$

22 $\int \frac{(3x+1)}{(x+1)^2\,(x+3)} dx$

23 $\int \frac{\log x}{(1+\log x)^2} dx$

24 $\int \frac{\sqrt{x}}{x+1} dx$

Long Answer Type Questions

Directions (Q. Nos. 25-28) *Evaluate the following integrals.*

25 $\int x(\log x)^2 dx$

26 $\int \frac{3x+5}{x^3-x^2-x+1} dx$

27 $\int \frac{x^2+1}{(x-1)^2(x+3)} dx$

28 $\int \left(4x-\frac{1}{2}\right)\sqrt{x^2-x-2}$

Case Study Based Questions

29 Mr. Mahesh Padra of Pride and Honour School is teaching the partial integration to his student in the classroom.

Let $f(x)$ and $g(x)$ be the,differential function, then

$$\int f(x)\cdot g(x)\cdot dx$$
$$= f(x)\int g(x)dx - \int\left[\frac{d}{dx} f(x)\cdot \int g(x)\cdot dx\right] dx$$

if $f(x) = 4$ and $g(x) = v$, then

$$\int uv = dx = 4\int v dx - \int\left[\frac{du}{dx}\int v dx\right] dx$$

On the basis of the above information, the following question given to the student to solve them.

(i) Evaluate $\int \left(1+x-\frac{1}{x}\right)e^{x+\frac{1}{x}}\cdot dx$

(ii) Find $\int \log_{10} x\, dx$.

(iii) Find $\int \frac{\log x}{x^n} dx$.

(iv) Find $\int (x+1)e^x \log(xe^x) dx$

30 Let $f(x)$ be a function and $f'(x)$ be its derivative. Now, teacher ask Raju, can you answer my question. Raju says, "What is you question?"

Teacher wrote question on blackboard.

After reading the question, Raju gave the answer as $e^x f(x)+C$.

On the basis of above information, answer the following questions.

(i) If $\int e^x\left(\frac{1}{x^2}-\frac{2}{x^3}\right)dx = e^x f(x)+C$, then $f(x)$ is equal to

(a) x^2 (b) $\frac{1}{x^2}$ (c) x^3 (d) $\frac{1}{x^3}$

(ii) $\int e^x\left(\log x+\frac{1}{x}\right)dx$ is equal to

(a) $\frac{e^x}{x}+C$ (b) $e^x \log x + C$

(c) $\frac{e^x}{x^2}+C$ (d) $e^x(\log x)^2 + C$

(iii) $\int \frac{e^x}{x}\{x(\log x)^2 + 2\log x\} dx$ is equal to

(a) $e^x \log x + C$ (b) $e^x(\log x)^2 + C$

(c) $\frac{e^x \log x}{x}+C$ (d) $\frac{e^x}{x}+C$

(iv) $\int \frac{xe^x}{(1+x)^2} dx$ is equal to

(a) $\frac{e^x}{(1+x)^2}+C$ (b) $\frac{e^x}{(1+x)^3}+C$

(c) $\frac{e^x}{1+x}+C$ (d) None of these

Hints & Solutions

1. (d) 2. (a) 3. (a) 4. (c)
5. (a) 6. (b) 7. (c) 8. (a)
9. (c) 10. (c) 11. (a) 12. (c)
13. (a)

14. **Hint** $\int(\sqrt{x}-x\sqrt{x})dx=\int(x^{1/2}-x^{3/2})dx$

Ans. $\frac{2}{3}x^{3/2}-\frac{2}{5}5^{5/2}+C$

15. **Hint** Use $\int e^x(f(x)+f'(x))dx$

Ans. $\frac{e^x}{(1+x^2)^2}+C$

16. **Hint** Divide numerator and denominator both by e^x.

Ans. $-\log(1+e^{-x})+C$

17. **Hint** $I=\int\frac{x^3}{(x^4+1)}dx$ s

Ans. $\frac{1}{4}\log(x^4+1)+C$

18. **Hint** Put $x^2=t$

Ans. $\frac{1}{2}\left[\frac{x^2\sqrt{x^4-1}}{2}-\frac{1}{2}\log\left|x^2+\sqrt{x^4-1}\right|\right]+C$

19. **Hint** Write given integral as

$$\int\frac{(x+1)}{\sqrt{x^2+2x+3}}dx+\int\frac{1}{\sqrt{x^2+2x+3}}dx]$$

Ans. $\sqrt{x^2+2x+3}+\log\left|(x+1)+\sqrt{x^2+2x+3}\right|+C$

20. **Hint** Multiply numerator and denominator by x^4.

Ans. $\frac{1}{15}\log\left|\frac{x^5}{x^5+3}\right|+C$

21. **Hint** $\int\sqrt{\frac{1+x}{x}}dx=\int\sqrt{\frac{1+x}{x}}.\sqrt{\frac{1+x}{1+x}}dx$

$$=\int\frac{1+x}{\sqrt{x^2+x}}dx$$

Ans. $\sqrt{x^2+x}+\frac{1}{2}\log\left|\left(x+\frac{1}{2}\right)+\sqrt{x^2+x}\right|+C$

22. $2\log\left|\frac{x+1}{x+3}\right|+\frac{1}{(x+1)}+C$

23. **Hint** Put $\log x=t\Rightarrow x=e^t\Rightarrow dx=e^t\,dt$,

so $I=\int\frac{e^t t\,dt}{(1+t)^2}$

Ans. $\frac{x}{(\log x+1)}+C$

24. **Hint** $\int\frac{\sqrt{x}}{x+1}dx=\int\frac{x\,dx}{\sqrt{x}(x+1)}$

Ans. $2[\sqrt{x}-\tan^{-1}\sqrt{x}]+C$

25. **Hint** Use integration by parts.

Ans. $\frac{x^2}{2}(\log x)^2-\frac{x^2}{2}\log x+\frac{x^2}{4}+C$

26. **Hint** Use the partial fractions

Ans. $\frac{1}{2}\log\left|\frac{x+1}{x-1}\right|-\frac{4}{(x-1)}+C$

27. $\frac{3}{8}\log|x-1|-\frac{1}{2(x-1)}+\frac{5}{8}\log|x+3|+C$

28. $\frac{4}{3}(x^2-x-2)^{3/2}+\frac{3}{4}(2x-1)\sqrt{x^2-x-2}$

$$-\frac{27}{8}\log\left|\left(x-\frac{1}{2}\right)+\sqrt{x^2-x-2}\right|+C$$

29. (i) $xe^{x+\frac{1}{x}}+C$

(ii) $\frac{1}{\log 10}\{x(\log x-1)\}+C$

(iii) $\frac{x^{1-n}}{1-n}\log x-\frac{x^{1-n}}{(1-n)^2}+C$

(iv) $xe^x\{\log(xe^x)-1\}+C$

30. (i) (b) **Hint** $\frac{d}{dx}.\left(\frac{1}{x^2}\right)=-\frac{2}{x^3}$

(ii) (b) **Hint** $f(x)=\log x$

(iii) (b) **Hint** $f(x)=x(\log x)^2$

(iv) (c) **Hint** $\int\frac{e^x x}{(1+x)^2}dx=\int e^x\left(\frac{1}{1+x}-\frac{1}{(1+x)^2}\right)dx$

CHAPTER 12

Definite Integrals

In this Chapter...

- Fundamental Theorem of Definite Integrals
- Definite Integral by Substitution Method
- Area of a Curve Between Two Ordinates

A definite integral is denoted by $\int_a^b f(x)\,dx$, where a is called the **lower limit** of the integral and b is called the **upper limit** of the integral. The definite integral has a unique value.

Also, we define $\int_a^b f(x)\,dx$ as the area of the region bounded by the curve $y = f(x), a \le x \le b$, the X-axis and the ordinates $x = a$ and $x = b$.

Fundamental Theorem of Definite Integrals

1. **First Fundamental Theorem of Integral Calculus** Let the area function be defined by
$A(x) = \int_a^x f(x)\,dx$ for all $x \ge a$, where function f is assumed to be continuous on $[a, b]$, then
$A'(x) = f(x)$ for all $x \in [a, b]$.
2. **Second Fundamental Theorem of Integral Calculus** Let f be a continuous function of x defined on the closed interval $[a, b]$ and F is another function, such that $\frac{d}{dx}F(x) = f(x)$ for all x in the domain of f, then
$\int_a^b f(x)\,dx = [F(x)+C]_a^b = F(b) - F(a).$
This is called definite integral of f over the range $[a, b]$.

Note In $\int_a^b f(x)\,dx$, the function f needs to be well-defined and continuous in $[a, b]$. For instance, the consideration of definite integral $\int_{-2}^3 x(x^2-1)^{1/2}dx$ is erroneous, since the function f expressed by $f(x) = x(x^2-1)^{1/2}$ is not defined in a portion $-1 < x < 1$ of the closed interval $[-2, 3]$.

EXAMPLE 1. Evaluate the following

(i) $\int_2^4 x\,dx$ (ii) $\int_{-4}^{-2} \frac{1}{x}\,dx$

(iii) $\int_0^2 \frac{1}{\sqrt{x}+\sqrt{1+x}}\,dx$ (iv) $\int_{-1}^1 2^x\,dx$

(v) $\int_0^1 \frac{e^{2x}+e^{4x}}{e^{3x}}\,dx$

Sol. (i) Let $I = \int_2^4 x\,dx = \left[\frac{x^2}{2}\right]_2^4$

$$= \frac{4^2}{2} - \frac{2^2}{2} = 8 - 2 = 6$$

(ii) Let $I = \int_{-4}^{-2}\frac{1}{x}dx = [\log|x|]_{-4}^{-2}$

$$= \log|-2| - \log|-4|$$
$$= \log 2 - \log 4$$
$$= \log 2 - 2\log 2 = -\log 2$$

(iii) Let $I = \int_0^2 \frac{1}{\sqrt{x}+\sqrt{1+x}}\,dx$

$$= \int_0^2 \frac{\sqrt{1+x}-\sqrt{x}}{(\sqrt{1+x}+\sqrt{x})(\sqrt{1+x}-\sqrt{x})}\,dx$$

$$= \int_0^2 (\sqrt{1+x} - \sqrt{x})\, dx$$

$$= \left[\frac{2}{3}(1+x)^{3/2} - \frac{2}{3}x^{3/2}\right]_0^2$$

$$= \frac{2}{3}(3^{3/2} - 1) - \frac{2}{3}(2)^{3/2}$$

$$= \frac{2}{3} \times 3\sqrt{3} - \frac{2}{3} - \frac{2}{3} \times 2\sqrt{2}$$

$$= 2\sqrt{3} - \frac{2}{3} - \frac{4}{3}\sqrt{2}$$

(iv) $\int_{-1}^{1} 2^x\, dx = \left[\frac{2^x}{\log 2}\right]_{-1}^{1}$ $\left[\because \int a^x\, dx = \frac{a^x}{\log a}\right]$

$$= \frac{1}{\log 2}(2^1 - 2^{-1}) = \frac{1}{\log 2}\left(2 - \frac{1}{2}\right) = \frac{3}{2\log 2}$$

(v) $\int_0^1 \frac{e^{2x} + e^{4x}}{e^{3x}}\, dx = \int_0^1 \left(\frac{e^{2x}}{e^{3x}} + \frac{e^{4x}}{e^{3x}}\right) dx$

$$= \int_0^1 (e^{-x} + e^x)\, dx = [-e^{-x} + e^x]_0^1$$

$$= [(-e^{-1} + e) - (-e^{-0} + e^0)]$$

$$= \left(-\frac{1}{e} + e\right) - (-1+1) \quad [\because e^0 = e^{-0} = 1]$$

$$= e - \frac{1}{e} = \frac{e^2 - 1}{e}$$

EXAMPLE 2. Evaluate $\int_1^2 (4x^3 - 5x^2 + 6x + 9)\, dx$.

Sol. Let $I = \int_1^2 (4x^3 - 5x^2 + 6x + 9)\, dx$

$$= \left[\frac{4x^4}{4} - \frac{5x^3}{3} + \frac{6x^2}{2} + 9x\right]_1^2 = \left[x^4 - \frac{5}{3}x^3 + 3x^2 + 9x\right]_1^2$$

$$= \left[(2)^4 - \frac{5}{3}(2)^3 + 3(2)^2 + 9(2)\right] - \left[1 - \frac{5}{3}(1)^3 + 3(1)^2 + 9(1)\right]$$

$$= \left[16 - \frac{40}{3} + 12 + 18\right] - \left[1 - \frac{5}{3} + 3 + 9\right]$$

$$= \left[46 - \frac{40}{3}\right] - \left[13 - \frac{5}{3}\right] = \left[\frac{138 - 40}{3}\right] - \left[\frac{39 - 5}{3}\right]$$

$$= \frac{98}{3} - \frac{34}{3} = \frac{64}{3}$$

EXAMPLE 3. If $\int_a^b x^3\, dx = 0$ and if $\int_a^b x\, dx = \frac{128}{3}$, find a and b.

Sol. We have, $\int_a^b x^3\, dx = 0 \Rightarrow \left[\frac{x^4}{4}\right]_a^b = 0$

$$\Rightarrow \quad \frac{1}{4}(b^4 - a^4) = 0 \Rightarrow b^4 - a^4 = 0$$

$$\Rightarrow (b^2 + a^2)(b^2 - a^2) = 0 \Rightarrow b^2 - a^2 = 0$$

$$\Rightarrow \quad b^2 = a^2 \Rightarrow b = -a \quad [\because b \neq a]$$

Now, $\int_a^b x^2 dx = \frac{128}{3} \Rightarrow \left[\frac{x^3}{3}\right]_a^b = \frac{128}{3}$

$$\Rightarrow \quad \frac{1}{3}(b^3 - a^3) = \frac{128}{3} \Rightarrow b^3 - a^3 = 128$$

$$\Rightarrow \quad (-a)^3 - a^3 = 128 \Rightarrow -2a^3 = 128$$

$$\Rightarrow \quad a^3 = -64 \Rightarrow a = -4$$

$$\therefore \quad b = -a \Rightarrow b = 4$$

Hence, $a = -4$ and $b = 4$

EXAMPLE 4. Evaluate $\int_0^2 \frac{1}{4 + x - x^2}\, dx$.

Sol. Let $I = \int_0^2 \frac{1}{4 + x - x^2}\, dx = -\int_0^2 \frac{1}{x^2 - x - 4}\, dx$

$$= -\int_0^2 \frac{1}{\left(x - \frac{1}{2}\right)^2 - \left(\frac{\sqrt{17}}{2}\right)^2}\, dx$$

$$= \int_0^2 \frac{1}{\left(\frac{\sqrt{17}}{2}\right)^2 - \left(x - \frac{1}{2}\right)^2}\, dx$$

$$= \frac{1}{2 \times \left(\frac{\sqrt{17}}{2}\right)}\left[\log\left|\frac{\frac{\sqrt{17}}{2} + \left(x - \frac{1}{2}\right)}{\frac{\sqrt{17}}{2} - \left(x - \frac{1}{2}\right)}\right|\right]_0^2$$

$$= \frac{1}{\sqrt{17}}\left[\log\left|\frac{\sqrt{17} + 2x - 1}{\sqrt{17} - 2x + 1}\right|\right]_0^2$$

$$= \frac{1}{\sqrt{17}}\left[\log\left|\frac{\sqrt{17} + 3}{\sqrt{17} - 3}\right| - \log\left|\frac{\sqrt{17} - 1}{\sqrt{17} + 1}\right|\right]$$

$$= \frac{1}{\sqrt{17}}\left[\log\left|\frac{(\sqrt{17} + 3)^2}{17 - 9}\right| - \log\left|\frac{(\sqrt{17} - 1)^2}{17 - 1}\right|\right]$$

$$= \frac{1}{\sqrt{17}}\left[\log\left|\frac{(\sqrt{17} + 3)^2}{8}\right| - \log\left|\frac{(\sqrt{17} - 1)^2}{16}\right|\right]$$

$$= \frac{1}{\sqrt{17}} \log\left[2\left(\frac{\sqrt{17} + 3}{\sqrt{17} - 1}\right)^2\right]$$

$$= \frac{1}{\sqrt{17}} \log\left[2\left(\frac{17 + 9 + 6\sqrt{17}}{17 + 1 - 2\sqrt{17}}\right)\right]$$

$$= \frac{1}{\sqrt{17}} \log\left[2\left(\frac{26 + 6\sqrt{17}}{18 - 2\sqrt{17}}\right)\right]$$

$$= \frac{1}{\sqrt{17}} \log\left[\left(\frac{52 + 12\sqrt{17}}{18 - 2\sqrt{17}} \times \frac{18 + 2\sqrt{17}}{18 + 2\sqrt{17}}\right)\right]$$

$$= \frac{1}{\sqrt{17}} \log\left[\frac{1344 + 320\sqrt{17}}{256}\right] = \frac{1}{\sqrt{17}} \log\left[\frac{21 + 5\sqrt{17}}{4}\right]$$

EXAMPLE 5. Evaluate the following

(i) $\int_0^1 xe^{2x}\,dx$ (ii) $\int_0^1 x\log(1+x)\,dx$

(iii) $\int_1^2 e^{2x}\left(\frac{1}{x}-\frac{1}{2x^2}\right)dx$

Sol. (i) Let $I=\int_0^1 \underset{\text{I}}{x}\,\underset{\text{II}}{e^{2x}}dx=\left[x\frac{e^{2x}}{2}\right]_0^1-\int_0^1 1\cdot\frac{e^{2x}}{2}dx$

$$=\frac{1}{2}[xe^{2x}]_0^1-\frac{1}{4}[e^{2x}]_0^1$$

$$=\frac{1}{2}[e^2-0]-\frac{1}{4}[e^2-1]=\frac{1}{4}e^2+\frac{1}{4}=\frac{1}{4}(e^2+1)$$

(ii) Let $I=\int_0^1 \underset{\text{II}}{x}\,\underset{\text{I}}{\log(1+x)}dx$

$$=\left[\log(1+x)\cdot\frac{x^2}{2}\right]_0^1-\int_0^1\frac{1}{x+1}\cdot\frac{x^2}{2}dx$$

$$=\frac{1}{2}[x^2\log(1+x)]_0^1-\frac{1}{2}\int_0^1\frac{x^2}{x+1}dx$$

$$=\frac{1}{2}[x^2\log(1+x)]_0^1-\frac{1}{2}\int_0^1\left(x-1+\frac{1}{x+1}\right)dx$$

$$=\frac{1}{2}[x^2\log(1+x)]_0^1-\frac{1}{2}\left[\frac{x^2}{2}-x+\log(1+x)\right]_0^1$$

$$=\frac{1}{2}[\log 2-0]-\frac{1}{2}\left[\frac{1}{2}-1+\log 2-(0-0+0)\right]$$

$$=\frac{1}{2}\log 2+\frac{1}{4}-\frac{1}{2}\log 2=\frac{1}{4}$$

(iii) Let $I=\int_1^2 e^{2x}\left(\frac{1}{x}-\frac{1}{2x^2}\right)$

$$I=\int_1^2 e^{2x}\cdot\frac{1}{x}\,dx-\int_1^2 e^{2x}\cdot\frac{1}{2x^2}\,dx$$

$$=\left[\frac{1}{x}\cdot\frac{e^{2x}}{2}\right]_1^2+\int_1^2\frac{1}{x^2}\cdot\frac{e^{2x}}{2}\,dx-\int_1^2 e^{2x}\cdot\frac{1}{2x^2}dx$$

$$=\left(\frac{1}{4}e^4-\frac{1}{2}e^2\right)=\frac{e^4-2e^2}{4}$$

EXAMPLE 6. Evaluate

(i) $\int_1^2\frac{1}{(x+1)(x+2)}dx$ (ii) $\int_1^3\frac{1}{x^2(x+1)}dx$

(iii) $\int_1^2\frac{1}{4x^2-1}\cdot dx$

Sol. (i) Let $\frac{1}{(x+1)(x+2)}=\frac{A}{x+1}+\frac{B}{x+2}$ ...(i)

$\therefore\ 1=A(x+2)+B(x+1)$ ...(ii)

On putting $x+2=0$ or $x=-2$ in Eq. (ii), we get

$$B=-1$$

and on putting $x+1=0$ or $x=-1$ in Eq. (ii), we get

$$A=1$$

$$\therefore\quad\frac{1}{(x+1)(x+2)}=\frac{1}{x+1}-\frac{1}{x+2}$$

$$\therefore\quad I=\int_1^2\frac{1}{(x+1)(x+2)}dx=\int_1^2\left(\frac{1}{x+1}-\frac{1}{x+2}\right)dx$$

$$=[\log|x+1|-\log|x+2|]_1^2=\left[\log\left|\frac{x+1}{x+2}\right|\right]_1^2$$

$$=\log\left|\frac{2+1}{2+2}\right|-\log\left|\frac{1+1}{1+2}\right|=\log\frac{3}{4}-\log\frac{2}{3}=\log\left(\frac{9}{8}\right)$$

(ii) Let $\frac{1}{x^2(x+1)}=\frac{A}{x}+\frac{B}{x^2}+\frac{C}{x+1}$

$$\Rightarrow\quad 1=Ax(x+1)+B(x+1)+Cx^2$$

$$\Rightarrow\quad 1=(A+C)x^2+(A+B)x+B$$

On comparing, we get

$$A+C=0$$
$$A+B=0$$
$$B=1$$

On solving above equations, we get

$$A=-1,B=1,C=1$$

$$\therefore\quad\frac{1}{x^2(x+1)}=\frac{-1}{x}+\frac{1}{x^2}+\frac{1}{x+1}$$

$$\therefore\quad I=\int_1^3\frac{1}{x^2(x+1)}dx=\int_1^3\left(-\frac{1}{x}+\frac{1}{x^2}+\frac{1}{x+1}\right)dx$$

$$=\left[-\log x-\frac{1}{x}+\log|x+1|\right]_1^3$$

$$=\left[(-\log 3+\log 1)-\left(\frac{1}{3}-1\right)+\log 4-\log 2\right]$$

$$=(\log 4-\log 3-\log 2)+\frac{2}{3}$$

$$=\log\left(\frac{4}{3\times 2}\right)+\frac{2}{3}=\log\left(\frac{2}{3}\right)+\frac{2}{3}$$

(iii) Let $I=\int_1^2\frac{1}{4x^2-1}dx=\frac{1}{4}\int_1^2\frac{1}{x^2-\left(\frac{1}{2}\right)^2}dx$

$$=\frac{1}{4}\cdot\frac{1}{2\times\frac{1}{2}}\left[\log\left|\frac{x-\frac{1}{2}}{x+\frac{1}{2}}\right|\right]_1^2$$

$$=\frac{1}{4}\left[\log\left|\frac{2x-1}{2x+1}\right|\right]_1^2$$

$$=\frac{1}{4}\left(\log\frac{3}{5}-\log\frac{1}{3}\right)=\frac{1}{4}\log\left(\frac{3}{5}\times\frac{3}{1}\right)=\frac{1}{4}\log\frac{9}{5}$$

Topic Practice 1

1 Evaluate the following.

(i) $\int_2^3 3^x dx$ (ii) $\int_4^9 \frac{1}{\sqrt{x}} dx$

(iii) $\int_{-2}^3 \frac{1}{x+7} dx$ (iv) $\int_0^\infty e^{-x} dx$

(v) $\int_0^1 \frac{1-x}{1+x} dx$ (vi) $\int_0^1 \frac{dx}{\sqrt{1+x}-\sqrt{x}}$

2 Evaluate $\int_0^4 (5x^2 - 3x + 8)\, dx$.

3 Evaluate the following.

(i) $\int_1^2 \log x\, dx$ (ii) $\int_1^e \frac{e^x}{x}(1 + x\log x)\, dx$

4 Evaluate the following.

(i) $\int_1^2 \frac{x}{(x+1)(x+2)} dx$ (ii) $\int_2^3 \frac{x^3+1}{x(x-1)} dx$

5 If $\int_1^k (3x^2 + 2x + 1)\, dx = 11$, find k.

Hints & Solutions

1. (i) $\int_2^3 3^x dx = \left(\frac{3^x}{\log 3}\right)_2^3 = \frac{1}{\log 3}(3^x)_2^3 = \frac{1}{\log 3}(3^3 - 3^2)$

$= \frac{1}{\log 3}(27 - 9) = \frac{18}{\log 3}$

(ii) $\int_4^9 \frac{1}{\sqrt{x}} dx = [2\sqrt{x}]_4^9 = 2[\sqrt{9} - \sqrt{4}] = 2[3 - 2] = 2$

(iii) $\int_{-2}^3 \frac{1}{x+7} dx = [\log|x+7|]_{-2}^3 = \log 10 - \log 5 = \log 2$

(iv) $\int_0^\infty e^{-x} dx = [-e^{-x}]_0^\infty = -[e^{-\infty} - e^{-0}] = -[0-1] = 1$

(v) $\int_0^1 \frac{1-x}{1+x} dx = \int_0^1 \left(\frac{2}{1+x} - 1\right) dx = [2\log|1+x| - x]_0^1$

$= (2\log 2 - 1) - (2\log 1 - 0) = 2\log 2 - 1$

$= \log 4 - \log e = \log(4e)$

(vi) **Hint** Rationalise the denominator i.e. multiply numerator and denominator by $\sqrt{1+x} + \sqrt{x}$. **Ans.** $\frac{4\sqrt{2}}{3}$

2. Do same as Example 2. **Ans.** $\frac{344}{3}$

3. (i) $\int_1^2 \underset{\text{II}}{1}\underset{\text{I}}{\log x}\, dx = [x\log x]_1^2 - \int_1^2 x \cdot \frac{1}{x} dx$

$= [2\log 2 - \log 1] - [x]_1^2$

$= 2\log 2 - [2 - 1] = 2\log 2 - 1$

(ii) $\int_1^e \frac{e^x}{x}(1 + x\log x)\, dx = \int_1^e e^x\left(\frac{1}{x} + \log x\right) dx$

$= \int_1^e \underset{\text{II}}{e^x}\, \underset{\text{I}}{\log x}\, dx + \int_1^e \frac{e^x}{x} dx$

$= [\log x\, e^x]_1^e - \int_1^e e^x \cdot \frac{1}{x} dx + \int_1^e e^x \cdot \frac{1}{x} dx$

$= [\log x \cdot e^x]_1^e = \log e \cdot e^e - \log 1 \cdot e^1 = e^e$

4. (i) Do same as Example 6 (i). **Ans.** $\log \frac{32}{27}$

(ii) Let $I = \int_2^3 \frac{x^3+1}{x(x-1)} \cdot dx$

$I = \int_2^3 \left(x + 1 + \frac{x+1}{x(x-1)}\right) dx$ [by division]

Let $\frac{x+1}{x(x-1)} = \frac{A}{x} + \frac{B}{x-1}$

$\Rightarrow x + 1 = A(x-1) + Bx$

On comparing the coefficient of x and constant term on both sides, we get

$A + B = 1$ and $-A = 1$

$\Rightarrow$ $A = -1$ and $B = 2$

$\therefore \int_2^3 \frac{x^3+1}{x(x-1)} dx = \int_2^3 \left(x + 1 - \frac{1}{x} + \frac{2}{x-1}\right) dx$

$= \left[\frac{x^2}{2} + x - \log|x| + 2\log|x-1|\right]_2^3$

$= \left(\frac{9}{2} + 3 - \log 3 + 2\log 2\right)$

$-(2 + 2 - \log 2 + 2\log 1)$

$= \frac{15}{2} - \log 3 + 2\log 2 - 4 + \log 2 + 2.0$

$= \frac{7}{2} + 3\log 2 - \log 3$

5. We have, $\int_1^k (3x^2 + 2x + 1)\, dx = 11$

$\Rightarrow [x^3 + x^2 + x]_1^k = 11$

$\Rightarrow (k^3 + k^2 + k) - (1 + 1 + 1) = 11$

$\Rightarrow k^3 + k^2 + k - 3 - 11 = 0$

$\Rightarrow k^3 + k^2 + k - 14 = 0$

$\Rightarrow (k-2)(k^2 + 3k + 7) = 0$

$\Rightarrow k = 2$

$[\because k^2 + 3k + 7 \neq 0, \forall\, k \in R]$

Definite Integral by Substitution Method

Consider the integral $\int_a^b f(g(x))g'(x)\, dx$.

Let $g(x) = t$, then $g'(x)dx = dt$.

Also, when $x = a$, $t = g(a)$ and $t = g(b)$ for $x = b$.

$$\therefore \int_a^b f(g(x))g'(x)\, dx = \int_{g(a)}^{g(b)} f(t)\, dt$$

To find the definite integral by substitution is similar to be the substitution method that we learnt in indefinite integral. To evaluate the definite integral, say $\int_a^b f(x)\, dx$ by substitution method, following steps are used.

I. Consider the integral without limits and substitute, $y = f(x)$ or $x = g(y)$ to reduce the given integral to a known form.

II. Integrate the new integrand with respect to the new variable without mentioning the constant of integration.

III. If the limits of the integral is not changed, resubstitute for the new variable and write the answer in terms of the original variable. If the limits of the integral is changed then there is no need to resubstitution i.e. no need to write the answer in terms of the original variable.

IV. Find the values of answers obtained in step III at the given limits of integral and find the difference of the values at the upper and lower limits.

EXAMPLE 1. Find the value of $\int_0^1 \frac{x}{(1+x^2)^{1/2}}\, dx$.

Sol. Let $I = \int_0^1 \frac{x}{(1+x^2)^{1/2}}\, dx$ ...(i)

Put $1 + x^2 = t \Rightarrow 2x\, dx = dt \Rightarrow x\, dx = \frac{dt}{2}$

Lower limit When $x = 0$, then $t = 1 + (0)^2 = 1$

Upper limit When $x = 1$, then $t = 1 + (1)^2 = 2$

$$\therefore \quad I = \int_1^2 \frac{dt}{2} \cdot \frac{1}{t^{1/2}} = \frac{1}{2}\int_1^2 t^{-1/2}\, dt = \frac{1}{2}\left[\frac{t^{\frac{-1}{2}+1}}{-\frac{1}{2}+1}\right]_1^2$$

$$= \frac{1}{2}\left[\frac{t^{1/2}}{1/2}\right]_1^2 = \frac{1}{2} \times 2\, [t^{1/2}]_1^2$$

$$= 1\,(2^{1/2} - 1) = \sqrt{2} - 1$$

EXAMPLE 2. Evaluate $\int_1^3 \frac{1}{x(1+\log x)}\, dx$.

Sol. Let $I = \int_1^3 \frac{dx}{x(1+\log x)}$

Now, putting $\log x = t \Rightarrow \frac{1}{x}dx = dt$

Lower limit When $x = 1$, then $t = \log 1 \Rightarrow t = 0$

Upper limit When $x = 3$, then $t = \log 3$

Now, $I = \int_0^{\log 3} \frac{dt}{(1+t)} = [\log|1+t|]_0^{\log 3}$

$= \log|1+\log 3| - \log|1+0|$

$= \log|1+\log 3| - \log 1$

$= \log|1+\log 3| - 0$ $\quad [\because \log 1 = 0]$

$= \log|1+\log 3|$

EXAMPLE 3. Evaluate $\int_0^4 \frac{1}{x+\sqrt{x}}\, dx$.

Sol. Let $I = \int_0^4 \frac{1}{x+\sqrt{x}}\, dx = \int_0^4 \frac{1}{\sqrt{x}(\sqrt{x}+1)}\, dx$

Let $\sqrt{x} + 1 = t \Rightarrow \frac{1}{2\sqrt{x}}\, dx = dt \Rightarrow \frac{1}{\sqrt{x}} dx = 2dt$

when $x = 0 \Rightarrow t = 0 + 1 = 1 \Rightarrow x = 4 \Rightarrow t = 2 + 1 = 3$

$\therefore \quad I = \int_1^3 \frac{1}{t}.(2dt) = 2[\ln|t|]_1^3 = 2[\log 3 - \log 1] = 2\log 3$

EXAMPLE 4. Evaluate $\int_1^3 x\sqrt{x+3}\, dx$.

Sol. Let $I = \int_0^3 x\sqrt{x+3}\, dx$

Let $x + 3 = t^2 \Rightarrow x\, dx = 2t\, dt$

[here, $x = t^2 - 3$ and $t = (x+3)^{1/2}$]

$\therefore I = \int_0^3 (t^2 - 3)\cdot t \cdot 2t\, dt = \int_0^3 2t^2(t^2-3)\cdot dt$

$= \int_0^3 2t^4 - 6t^2 \cdot dt = 2\left[\frac{t^5}{5}\right]_0^3 - 6\left[\frac{t^3}{3}\right]_0^3$

$= \frac{2}{5}[t^5]_0^3 - 2[t^3]_0^3 = \frac{2}{5}[(x+3)^{5/2}]_0^3 - 2[(x+3)^{3/2}]_0^3$

$= \frac{2}{5}[6^{5/2} - 3^{5/2}] - 2\,[6^{3/2} - 3^{3/2}]$

$= \frac{2}{5}[36\sqrt{6} - 9\sqrt{3}] - 2[6\sqrt{6} - 3\sqrt{3}]$

$= \frac{72\sqrt{6}}{5} - \frac{18\sqrt{3}}{5} - 12\sqrt{6} + 6\sqrt{3}$

$= \sqrt{6}\left(\frac{72}{5} - 12\right) + \sqrt{3}\left(6 - \frac{18}{5}\right)$

$= \frac{12\sqrt{6}}{5} + \frac{12\sqrt{3}}{5} = \frac{12}{5}(\sqrt{3} + \sqrt{6})$

EXAMPLE 5. Evaluate : $\int_0^1 \frac{e^{-x}}{1+e^x} dx$ [CBSE 2024]

Sol. Let $I = \int_0^1 \frac{e^{-x}}{1+e^x} dx$

Let $e^x = t \Rightarrow e^x dx = dt \Rightarrow dx = \frac{dt}{e^x} = \frac{dt}{t}$

When $x = 0 \Rightarrow t = 1$

When $x = 1 \Rightarrow t = e$

$\therefore I = \int_1^e \frac{dt}{t^2(1+t)} = \int_1^e \left(\frac{1}{1+t} - \frac{t-1}{t^2}\right) dt$

$= \int_1^e \left(\frac{1}{1+t} - \frac{1}{t} + \frac{1}{t^2}\right) dt = \left[\log(1+t) - \log t - \frac{1}{t}\right]_1^e$

$= \left(\log(1+e) - \log e - \frac{1}{e}\right) - (\log 2 - \log 1 - 1)$

$= \log(e+1) - \log e - \frac{1}{e} - \log 2 + \log 1 + 1$

$= \log(e+1) - 1 - \frac{1}{e} - \log 2 + 0 + 1$

$= \log(e+1) - \frac{1}{e} - \log 2 = \log\left(\frac{e+1}{2}\right) - \frac{1}{e}$

Topic Practice 2

Evaluate the following.

1. $\int_e^{e^2} \frac{dx}{x \log x}$
2. $\int_2^4 \frac{x}{x^2+1} dx$
3. $\int_0^1 x e^{x^2} dx$
4. $\int_0^1 \frac{x}{\sqrt{1+x^2}} dx$
5. $\int_0^1 \frac{dx}{e^x + e^{-x}}$
6. $\int_4^{12} x(x-4)^{1/3} \cdot dx$
7. $\int_{-1}^1 5x^4 \sqrt{x^5+1} \cdot dx$
8. $\int_0^a \frac{x}{\sqrt{a^2+x^2}} \cdot dx$

Hints & Solutions

1. Let $I = \int_e^{e^2} \frac{dx}{x \log x}$

Now, put $\log x = t \Rightarrow \frac{1}{x} dx = dt$

Lower limit When $x = e$, then $t = \log e = 1$

Upper limit When $x = e^2$, then $t = \log e^2 = 2 \log e = 2$

Now, $I = \int_1^2 \frac{dt}{t} = [\log t]_1^2 = \log 2 - \log 1 = \log 2$

$[\because \log 1 = 0]$

2. **Hint** On putting $1 + x^2 = t$, given integral reduces to $\frac{1}{2}\int_5^{17} \frac{dt}{t}$.

Ans. $\frac{1}{2} \log\left(\frac{17}{5}\right)$

3. Let $I = \int_0^1 x e^{x^2} dx$

Now, put $x^2 = t \Rightarrow 2x\, dx = dt$

Upper limit when $x = 1$, then $t = 1^2 = 1$

Lower limit When $x = 0$, $t = 0$

$\therefore \quad I = \int_0^1 e^t \frac{dt}{2}$

$= \frac{1}{2}[e^t]_0^1$

$= \frac{1}{2}[e^1 - e^0] = \frac{1}{2}(e-1)$

4. **Hint** On putting $1 + x^2 = t$, given integral reduces to $\frac{1}{2}\int_1^2 \frac{dt}{\sqrt{t}}$.

Ans. $\sqrt{2} - 1$

5. Let $I = \int_0^1 \frac{dx}{e^x + e^{-x}} = \int_0^1 \frac{e^x}{e^{2x}+1} dx$

Now, put $e^x = t \Rightarrow e^x dx = dt$

Upper limit When $x = 1$, then $t = e^1 = e$

Lower limit When $x = 0$, then $t = e^0 = 1$

$\therefore \quad I = \int_1^e \frac{dt}{t^2+1} = [\tan^{-1} t]_1^e$

$= \tan^{-1} e - \tan^{-1} 1$

$= \tan^{-1} e - \frac{\pi}{4}$

6. In this, put $x - 4 = t^3$ and solve as Example 4.

Ans. $\frac{720}{7}$

7. Solve as Example 4.

Ans. $\frac{4\sqrt{2}}{3}$

8. Solve as Example 1.

Ans. $a(\sqrt{2} - 1)$

Area of a Curve Between Two Ordinates

- The area bounded by the curve $y = f(x)$, the X-axis and the ordinates $x = a$ and $x = b$ is calculated as

$$\text{Area} = \int_a^b y\, dx$$
$$= \int_a^b f(x)\, dx$$

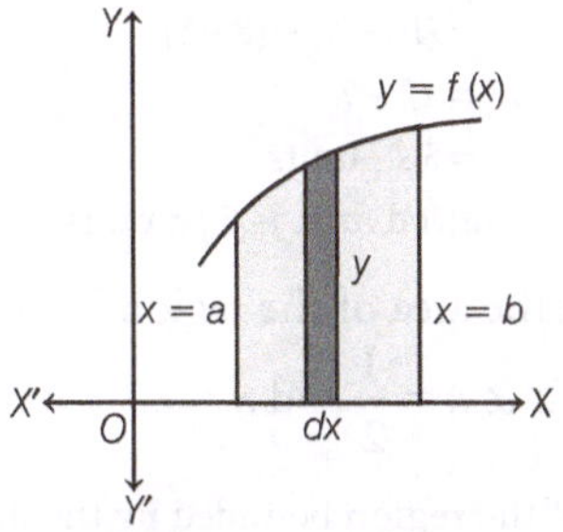

- If curve lies below X-axis, then its area is negative. In such case, we take its absolute value because the area of region is always positive.

$$\text{Area} = \left|\int_a^b y\, dx\right| = \left|\int_a^b f(x)\, dx\right|$$

Area of a Curve Between Two Abscissae

- The area bounded by the curve $x = f(y)$, the Y-axis and the lines $y = c$ and $y = d$ is calculated as

$$\text{Area} = \int_c^d x\, dy$$
$$= \int_c^d f(y)\, dy$$

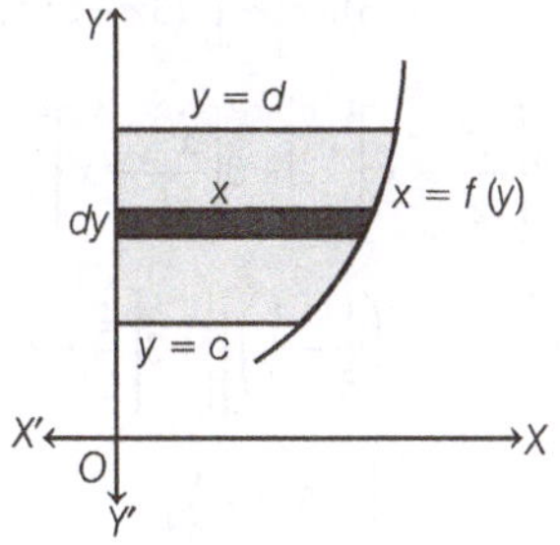

- If curve lies to the left of Y-axis, then its area is negative. In such case, we take its absolute value because the area of region is always positive.

$$\text{Area} = \left|\int_a^b x\, dy\right|$$
$$= \left|\int_a^b f(y)\, dy\right|$$

EXAMPLE 1. Find the area of the region bounded by the parabola $y^2 = 4ax$, its axis and two ordinates $x = 4$ and $x = 9$ in first quadrant.

Sol. Given equation of parabola is $y^2 = 4ax$, its axis is $Y = 0$ and vertex is (0, 0).

Also, given ordinates $x = 4$ and $x = 9$.

The bounded region in I quadrant is $ABCDA$.

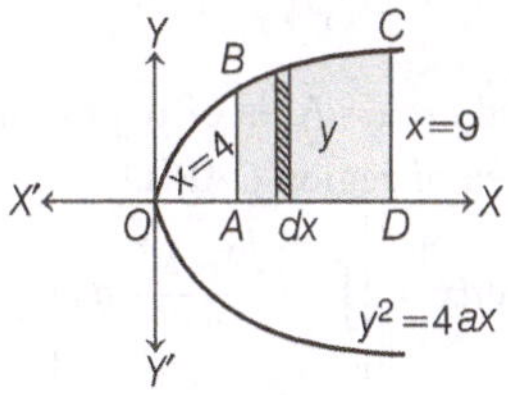

$$\therefore \text{ Required area} = \int_4^9 y\, dx$$
$$= \int_4^9 \sqrt{4ax}\, dx$$

$[\because y^2 = 4ax \Rightarrow y = \sqrt{4ax}$, as y is in I quadrant$]$

$$= 2\sqrt{a}\int_4^9 \sqrt{x}\, dx$$
$$= 2\sqrt{a}\left[\frac{x^{3/2}}{3/2}\right]_4^9$$
$$= 2\sqrt{a} \times \frac{2}{3}[(9)^{3/2} - (4)^{3/2}]$$
$$= \frac{4}{3}\sqrt{a}\,[(3^2)^{3/2} - (2^2)^{3/2}]$$
$$= \frac{4}{3}\sqrt{a}\,[27 - 8]$$
$$= \frac{4}{3}\sqrt{a}\,(19)$$
$$= \frac{76}{3}\sqrt{a} \text{ sq units}$$

Hence, the required area is $\frac{76\sqrt{a}}{3}$ sq units.

EXAMPLE 2. Find the area of the region bounded by the ellipse $\frac{x^2}{9} + \frac{y^2}{4} = 1$ in fourth quadrant.

Sol. Given equation of ellipse is

$$\frac{x^2}{9} + \frac{y^2}{4} = 1 \quad \text{...(i)}$$

We know that the standard equation of ellipse is

$$\frac{x^2}{a^2} + \frac{y^2}{b^2} = 1 \quad \text{...(ii)}$$

On comparing Eqs. (i) and (ii), we get

$$a^2 = 9 \text{ and } b^2 = 4 \Rightarrow a = 3 \text{ and } b = 2$$

Here, we see that $a > b$, so the horizontal ellipse will be formed.

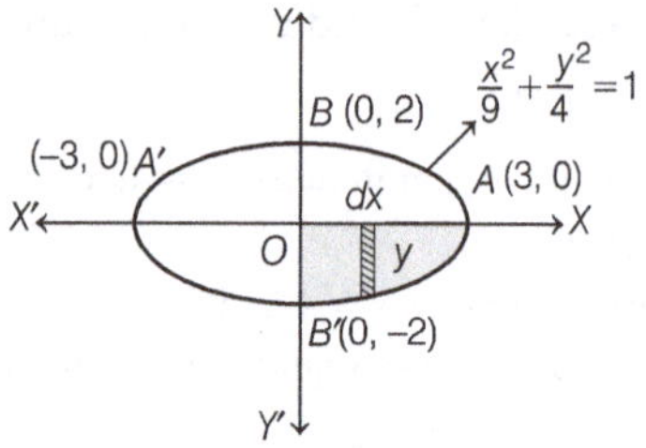

Now, required area = Area of region in IV quadrant

= Area of region $OAB'O$

$$= \left|\int_0^3 y\,dx\right| = \left|\int_0^3 \frac{2\sqrt{9-x^2}}{3}\,dx\right|$$

$$\left[\because \frac{y^2}{4} = 1 - \frac{x^2}{9} \Rightarrow y = \frac{2\sqrt{9-x^2}}{3}\right]$$

$$= \frac{2}{3}\left|\left[\frac{x}{2}\sqrt{9-x^2} + \frac{9}{2}\sin^{-1}\left(\frac{x}{3}\right)\right]_0^3\right|$$

$$\left[\because \int\sqrt{a^2-x^2}\,dx = \frac{x}{2}\sqrt{a^2-x^2} + \frac{a^2}{2}\sin^{-1}\left(\frac{x}{a}\right)\right]$$

$$= \frac{2}{3}\left|\left[\frac{3}{2}\sqrt{9-9} + \frac{9}{2}\sin^{-1}\frac{3}{3} - 0 - \frac{9}{2}\sin^{-1}(0)\right]\right|$$

$$= \frac{2}{3}\left|\left[0 + \frac{9}{2}\times\frac{\pi}{2} - 0\right]\right|$$

$$= \frac{2}{3}\times\frac{9\pi}{4} = \frac{3\pi}{2} \text{ sq units}$$

Hence, the required area is $\frac{3\pi}{2}$ sq units.

EXAMPLE 3. Using integration, find the area of region bounded by the line $2x + y = 8$, the Y-axis and the lines $y = 2$ and $y = 4$.

Sol. The given line AB is

$$2x + y = 8 \Rightarrow x = 4 - \frac{1}{2}y$$

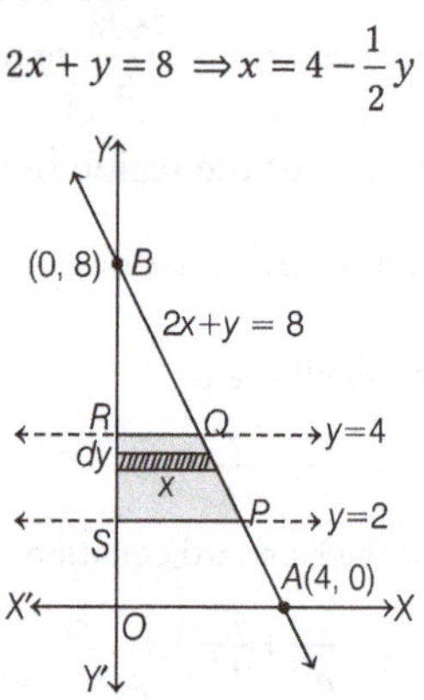

Required area = Area of region $PQRSP$

= Area between the line $x = 4 - \frac{1}{2}y$, the Y-axis and the lines $y = 2$ and $y = 4$

$$= \int_2^4 x\,dy = \int_2^4 \left(4 - \frac{1}{2}y\right)dy$$

$$= \left[4y - \frac{y^2}{4}\right]_2^4$$

$$= (16-4) - (8-1)$$

$$= 12 - 7$$

$$= 5 \text{ sq units}$$

Hence, the required area is 5 sq units.

EXAMPLE 4. Find the area of the region bounded by the line $3x - y = 3$ and lines $x = \frac{1}{2}$ and $x = 2$.

Sol. The area of the region bounded by the line $3x - y = 3$ and lines $x = \frac{1}{2}$ and $x = 2$ is given by

$$\text{Area} = \left|\int_{1/2}^1 y\,dx\right| + \int_1^2 y\,dx$$

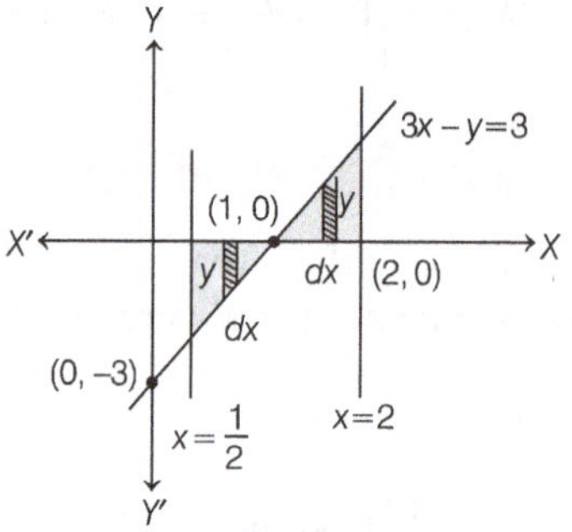

$$= \left|\int_{1/2}^1 (3x-3)\,dx\right| + \int_1^2 (3x-3)\,dx$$

$$= \left|3\left[\frac{x^2}{2} - x\right]_{1/2}^1\right| + 3\left[\frac{x^2}{2} - x\right]_1^2$$

$$= 3\left|\left[\frac{1}{2} - 1 - \left(\frac{1}{8} - \frac{1}{2}\right)\right]\right| + 3\left[\frac{4}{2} - 2 - \left(\frac{1}{2} - 1\right)\right]$$

$$= 3\left|\left[-\frac{1}{2} + \frac{3}{8}\right]\right| + 3\left[0 + \frac{1}{2}\right]$$

$$= 3\left|-\frac{1}{8}\right| + \frac{3}{2}$$

$$= \frac{3}{8} + \frac{3}{2}$$

$$= \frac{3+12}{8}$$

$$= \frac{15}{8} \text{ sq units}$$

EXAMPLE 5. Find the area bounded by the curve $y = \sin x$ between $x = 0$ and $x = 2\pi$.

Sol. The graph of $y = \sin x$ is shown in the figure below.

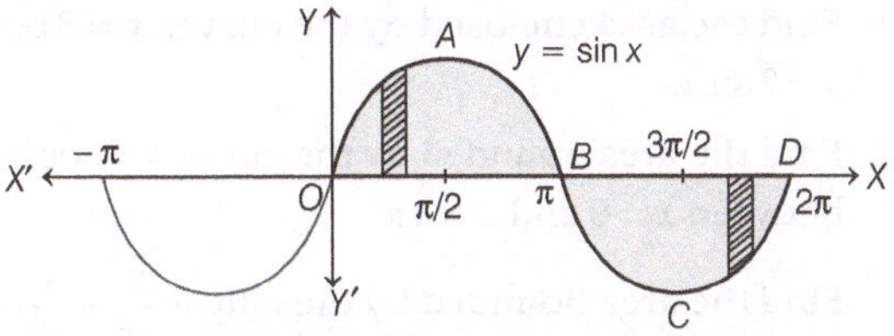

Clearly, required region is bounded by $y = \sin x$, X-axis and lines $x = 0$ and $x = 2\pi$, which is represented by shaded region.

$\therefore$ Required area = Area of region $OABO$ + Area of region $BCDB$

$$= \int_0^{\pi} \sin x \, dx + \left| \int_{\pi}^{2\pi} \sin x \, dx \right|$$

[since, in region $BCDB$, the graph is below the X-axis, so its area comes out to be negative, therefore we take the absolute value]

$$= [-\cos x]_0^{\pi} + \left| [-\cos x]_{\pi}^{2\pi} \right|$$
$$= (-\cos \pi + \cos 0) + |-\cos 2\pi + \cos \pi|$$
$$= (1 + 1) + |-1 - 1| = 2 + |-2|$$
$$= 2 + 2 = 4 \text{ sq units}$$

Hence, the required area is 4 sq units.

Area of Symmetrical Region

Sometimes, the bounded region, for which we have to calculate area, is symmetrical about X-axis (i.e. symmetric in I and IV or in II and III quadrants) or Y-axis (i.e. symmetric in I and II or in III and IV quadrants) or both X-axis and Y-axis (i.e. symmetric in all quadrants) or origin (i.e. symmetric in I and III or in II and IV quadrants). Then, firstly we calculate the area of bounded region in one quadrant and then multiply this area by number of quadrants in which region is symmetrical.

EXAMPLE 6. Sketch the region $\{(x, y) : y = \sqrt{4 - x^2}\}$ and X-axis. Find the area of the region using integration.

Sol. Given region is $\{(x, y) : y = \sqrt{4 - x^2}\}$ and X-axis.

We have, $y = \sqrt{4 - x^2}$

$\Rightarrow \quad y^2 = 4 - x^2 \Rightarrow x^2 + y^2 = 4$

This represent the equation of circle having centre (0, 0) and radius 2 units.

But, original equation is $y = \sqrt{4 - x^2}$, so y is positive.

It means that we have to take a curve above the X-axis.

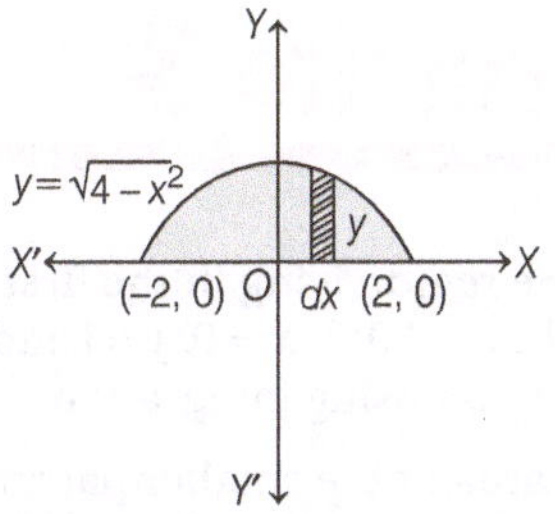

Thus, only semi-circle is formed above the X-axis.

Since, the region is symmetrical about Y-axis.

$\therefore$ Area of shaded region,

$$A = 2\int_0^2 y \, dx$$
$$= 2\int_0^2 \sqrt{4 - x^2} \, dx = 2\int_0^2 \sqrt{2^2 - x^2} \, dx$$
$$= 2\left[\frac{x}{2}\sqrt{2^2 - x^2} + \frac{2^2}{2} \cdot \sin^{-1}\frac{x}{2}\right]_0^2$$
$$= 2\left[\frac{2}{2} \cdot 0 + 2 \cdot \frac{\pi}{2} - \frac{0}{2} \cdot 2 - 2\sin^{-1} 0\right]$$
$$= 2\left[2 \cdot \frac{\pi}{2} + 0\right] = 2\pi \text{ sq units}$$

EXAMPLE 7. Using integration, find the area enclosed by the circle $x^2 + y^2 = a^2$.

Sol. Given equation of circle is $x^2 + y^2 = a^2$, its centre is (0, 0) and radius is a. It cuts the X-axis at $A(a, 0)$ and Y-axis at $B(0, a)$. Also, it is symmetrical about X and Y-axes both.

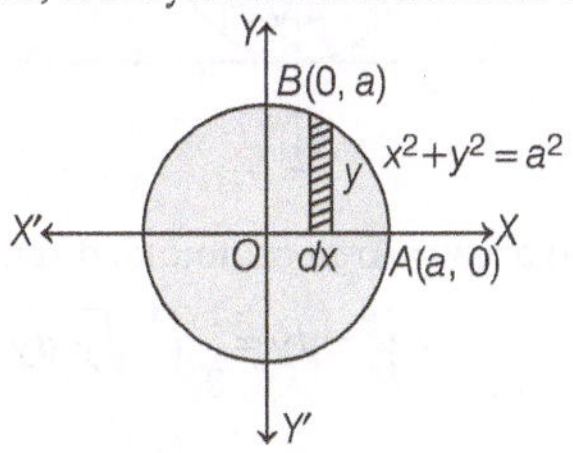

Clearly, area of region in I quadrant

$$= \int_0^a y \, dx = \int_0^a \sqrt{a^2 - x^2} \, dx \quad \text{[consider vertical strip]}$$

$[\because x^2 + y^2 = a^2 \Rightarrow y = \sqrt{a^2 - x^2}$, as y is in I quadrant$]$

$$= \left[\frac{x}{2}\sqrt{a^2 - x^2} + \frac{a^2}{2}\sin^{-1}\frac{x}{a}\right]_0^a$$
$$= \left[\left(\frac{a}{2} \times 0 + \frac{a^2}{2}\sin^{-1} 1\right) - 0\right]$$
$$= \frac{a^2}{2} \cdot \frac{\pi}{2} = \frac{\pi a^2}{4} \qquad \left[\because \sin^{-1} 1 = \frac{\pi}{2}\right]$$

Now, required area = 4 × Area of region in I quadrant

$$= 4 \times \frac{\pi a^2}{4} = \pi a^2 \text{ sq units}$$

[since, region is symmetrical in all quadrants]

Topic Practice 3

1 Sketch the region lying in the first quadrant and bounded by $y = 9x^2$, $x = 0$, $y = 1$ and $y = 4$. Find the area of region using integration.

2 Find the area of the smaller part of the circle $x^2 + y^2 = a^2$ cut-off by the line $x = \frac{a}{\sqrt{2}}$.

3 Find the area of the region bounded by the curve $y = x^2$ and the line $y = 4$.

4 Find the area of the region bounded by the curves $x = at^2$ and $y = 2at$ between the ordinates corresponding to $t = 1$ and $t = 2$.

5 Find the area enclosed by the curves $x = 3\cos t$ and $y = 2\sin t$.

6 Find the area bounded by the curve $y = \cos x$ between $x = 0$ and $x = 2\pi$.

7 Find the area bounded by the ellipse $\frac{x^2}{a^2} + \frac{y^2}{b^2} = 1$ and the coordinates $x = 0$ and $x = ae$, where $b^2 = a^2(1 - e^2)$ and $e < 1$.

Hints & Solutions

1. Hint Given curve is $y = 9x^2$

$$\Rightarrow \quad x^2 = \frac{1}{9}y \quad \text{...(i)}$$

It is a parabolic curve, which open upwards, symmetrical about Y-axis and passes through the origin.

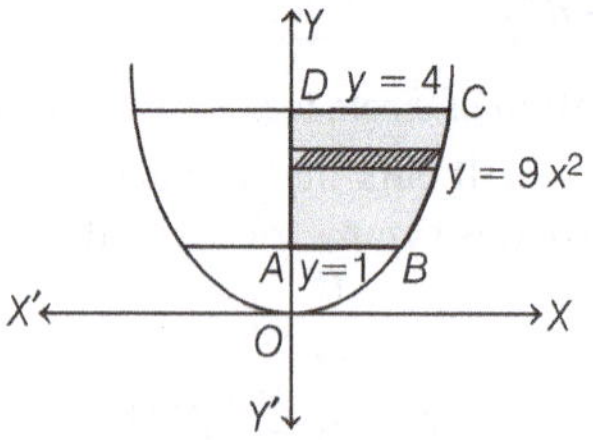

$\therefore$ Required area = Area of bounded region $ABCDA$

$$= \int_1^4 x\,dy = \frac{1}{3}\int_1^4 \sqrt{y}\,dy$$

Ans. $\frac{14}{9}$ sq units

2. Hint Given equations of circle and line are

$$x^2 + y^2 = a^2 \quad \text{...(i)}$$

and $$x = \frac{a}{\sqrt{2}} \quad \text{...(ii)}$$

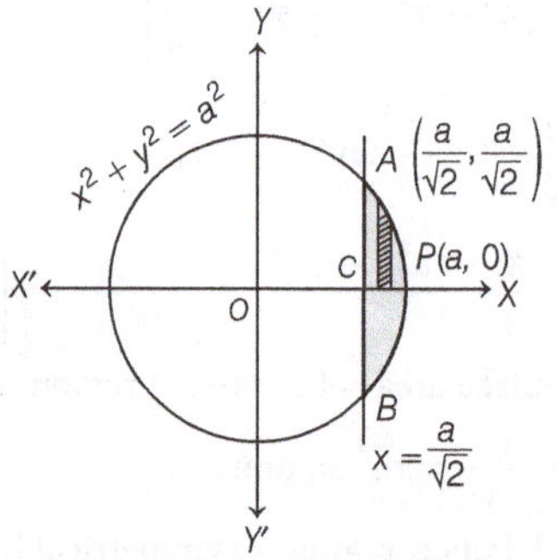

Clearly, required region is $APBCA$, which is symmetrical about X-axis and the x-coordinate of point of intersection of curve and line is $\frac{a}{\sqrt{2}}$.

Now, required area = Area of region $APBCA$

$$= 2\,(\text{Area of region } APCA)$$

$$= 2\int_{a/\sqrt{2}}^{a} y\,dx$$

$$= 2\int_{a/\sqrt{2}}^{a} \sqrt{a^2 - x^2}\,dx$$

Ans. $\frac{a^2(\pi - 2)}{4}$ sq units

3. Hint Required area = 2 (Area of region $OABO$)

$$= 2\int_0^4 x\,dy$$

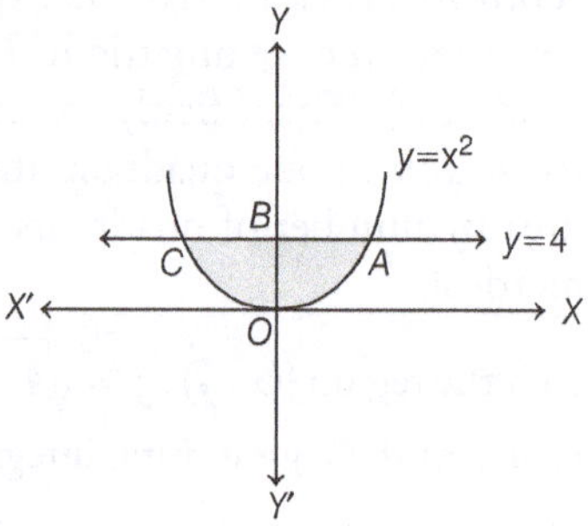

Ans. $\frac{32}{3}$ sq units

4. Hint Given equations of curves are

$$x = at^2 \quad \text{...(i)}$$

and $$y = 2at \quad \text{...(ii)}$$

Now, for converting the equation in cartesian form, put the value of t from Eq. (ii) in Eq. (i).

i.e. $x = a\left(\dfrac{y}{2a}\right)^2$

$\Rightarrow \quad x = a \cdot \dfrac{y^2}{4a^2}$

$\Rightarrow \quad y^2 = 4ax$ ...(iii)

On putting $t = 1$ and $t = 2$ in Eq. (i), we get

$x = a$ and $x = 4a$, respectively.

Now, the region bounded by the curve $y^2 = 4ax$ between $x = a$ and $x = 4a$ is given below

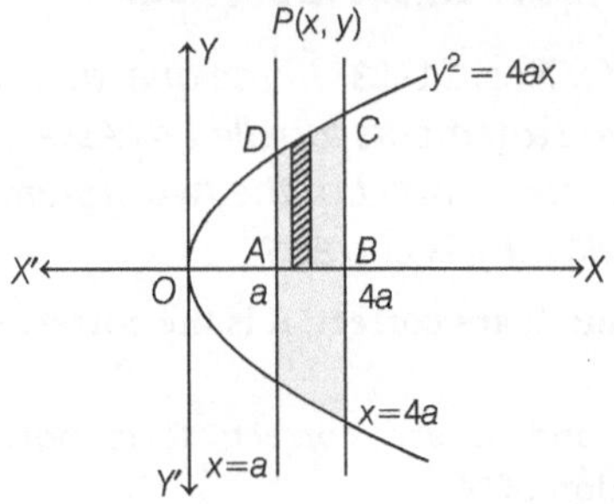

Now, required area = Area of shaded region

$= 2$ (Area of region $ABCDA$)

$= 2\int_a^{4a} y\,dx$

$= 2\int_a^{4a} \sqrt{4ax}\,dx$

Ans. $\dfrac{56a^2}{3}$ sq units

5. **Hint** Given curves are $x = 3\cos t$ and $y = 2\sin t$.
On squaring both sides, we get

$$x^2 = 9\cos^2 t \text{ and } y^2 = 4\sin^2 t$$

$$\Rightarrow \frac{x^2}{9} = \cos^2 t \text{ and } \frac{y^2}{4} = \sin^2 t$$

$$\therefore \frac{x^2}{9} + \frac{y^2}{4} = \cos^2 t + \sin^2 t$$

$$\Rightarrow \frac{x^2}{9} + \frac{y^2}{4} = 1$$

This is the equation of ellipse having centre (0, 0), vertices $(\pm 3, 0)$ and major axis along X-axis.

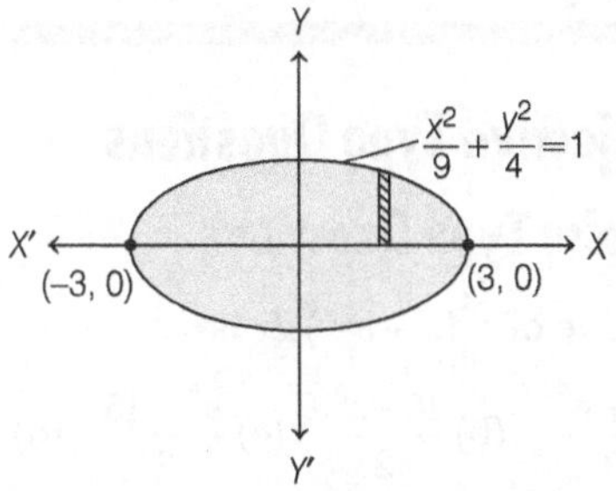

$\therefore$ Required area = Area of shaded region

$= 4$ (Area of I quadrant)

$= 4\int_0^3 y\,dx$

$= 4\int_0^3 2\sqrt{\dfrac{9 - x^2}{9}}\,dx$

$= 8\int_0^3 \dfrac{\sqrt{9 - x^2}}{3}\,dx$

Ans. 6π sq units

6. Similar as Example 5.

Ans. 4 sq units

7. **Hint**

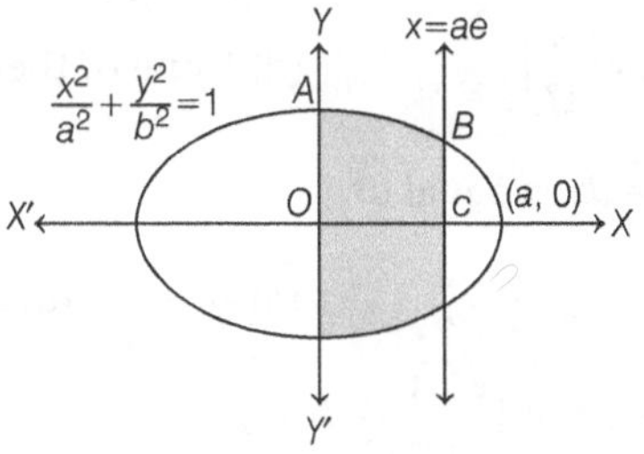

Therefore, shaded area = $2 \times$ Area ($OABCO$)

$= 2\int_0^{ae} \dfrac{b}{a}\sqrt{a^2 - x^2}\,dx$

$= ab[e\sqrt{1 - e^2} + \sin^{-1} e]$ sq units

Exam Pattern Exercise

Part A - Objective Type Questions

Multiple Choice Type Questions

1 The value of $\int_0^4 (x + e^{2x})\, dx$ is

(a) $\frac{15+e^8}{2}$ (b) $\frac{15-e^8}{2}$ (c) $\frac{e^8-15}{2}$ (d) $\frac{-e^8-15}{2}$

2 If $\int_1^a 2x\, dx = 8$, then the value of a is

(a) −3 (b) 3
(c) Both (a) and (b) (d) None of these

3 The value of $\int_1^2 \frac{3x}{9x^2-1}\, dx$ is

(a) $\frac{1}{6}(\log(35/8))$ (b) $6\log(35/8)$
(c) $\log(8/35)$ (d) $6\log(8/35)$

4 $\int_2^4 \frac{x}{x^2+1}\, dx$ is equal to

(a) $\frac{1}{4}\log\left(\frac{5}{17}\right)$ (b) $\frac{1}{2}\log\left(\frac{17}{5}\right)$
(c) $\frac{1}{2}\log\left(\frac{5}{17}\right)$ (d) None of these

5 $\int_1^e \frac{\log x}{x}\, dx$ is equal to

(a) 1 (b) $\frac{1}{2}$ (c) $\frac{1}{4}$ (d) zero

6 The value of $\int_2^3 \frac{1}{\log x^x}\, dx$ is

(a) $\log 3/\log 2$ (b) $\log^2/\log 3$
(c) $\log(\log 3/\log 2)$ (d) $\log(\log 2/\log 3)$

7 The area of the region bounded by the curve $y = \sin x$ between the ordinates $x = 0$, $x = \frac{\pi}{2}$ and the X-axis is

(a) 2 sq units (b) 4 sq units
(c) 3 sq units (d) 1 sq unit

8 The area of the region bounded by the circle $x^2 + y^2 = 1$ is

(a) $2\pi^2$ sq units (b) π sq unit
(c) $\frac{\pi}{2}$ sq unit (d) π^2 sq units

9 Area of the region bounded by the parabola $y^2 = 4ax$ and its latusrectum is

(a) $\frac{8a^2}{3}$ sq unit (b) $8a^2$ sq units
(c) $\frac{8}{5}a$ sq unit (d) $8a$ sq units

10 If a curve $y = a\sqrt{x} + bx$ passes through the point (1, 2) and the area bounded by the curve, line $x = 4$ and X-axis is 8 sq units, then

(a) $a = 3, b = -1$ (b) $a = 3, b = 1$
(c) $a = -3, b = 1$ (d) $a = -3, b = -1$

Assertion-Reason Based Questions

Directions (Q. Nos. 11-13) *In the questions given below are two statements labelled as Assertion (A) and Reason (R). In the context of the two statements, which one of the following is correct?*

(a) Both A and R are correct; R is the correct explanation of A
(b) Both A and R are correct; R is not the correct explanation of A
(c) A is correct; R is incorrect
(d) R is correct; A is incorrect

11 **Assertion (A)** The area bounded by $y^2 = 4x$ and $y = x$ is $\frac{8}{3}$ sq units.

Reason (R) The area bounded by $y^2 = 4ax$ and $y = mx$ is $\frac{8a^2}{3m^3}$ sq units.

12 **Assertion (A)** The area bounded by the curve $y = \sin x$ between $x = 0$ and $x = 4\pi$ is 4 sq units.

Reason (R) $\int_0^{\pi/2} \sin x\, dx = 1$.

13 **Assertion (A)** The area of the region bounded by the line $y-1=x$, the X-axis and the ordinates $x=-1$ and $x=1$ is 2 square units.

Reason (R) The area of the region bounded by the curve $y=f(x)$, the x-axis and the ordinates $x=a$ and $x=b$ is given by $\int_a^b f(x)\, dx$. **[CBSE 2025]**

Part B - Descriptive Questions

Very Short Answer Type Questions

Directions (Q. Nos. 14-15) *Evaluate the following integrals.*

14 $\int_0^1 \frac{dx}{4-x^2}$.

15 $\int_0^1 \frac{dx}{x^2-9}$

Short Answer Type Questions

Directions (Q. Nos. 16-17) *Evaluate the following integrals.*

16 Find the area of the region bounded by $y=-1$, $y=2$, $x=y^3$ and $x=0$.

17 $\int_0^2 x\sqrt{x+2}\,dx$

Long Answer Type Questions

Directions (Q. Nos. 18-22) *Evaluate the following integrals.*

18 $\int_1^2 \frac{5x^2}{x^2+4x+3}\,dx$

19 $\int_1^3 \left(\frac{1}{x}-\frac{1}{2x^2}\right)e^{2x}dx$

20 $\int_{1/3}^1 \frac{(x-x^3)^{1/3}}{x^4}\,dx$

21 $\int_2^4 \frac{(x^2+x)}{\sqrt{2x+1}}\,dx$

22 Find the area of the region bounded by the line $y=3x+2$, the X-axis and the ordinates $x=-1$ and $x=1$.

Case Study Based Questions

23 Let $f(x)$ be a function and $f'(x)$ be its derivative. Now, teacher ask Raju, can you answer my question. Raju says, 'What is your question?' Teacher wrote question on blackboard.

On the basis of above information, answer the following questions.

(i) $\int_0^{\pi/4} \tan x\,dx$ is equal to

(a) $\log 2$ (b) $\log\sqrt{2}$ (c) $\log 3$ (d) $\log\sqrt{3}$

(ii) $\int_0^{\pi/4} \sqrt{1+\sin 2x}\,dx$ is equal to

(a) 2 (b) 3 (c) 0 (d) 1

(iii) $\int_0^{\sqrt{2}} \sqrt{2-x^2}\,dx$ is equal to

(a) π (b) 2π (c) $\frac{\pi}{2}$ (d) $\frac{3\pi}{2}$

(iv) $\int_1^2 \log x\,dx$ is equal to

(a) $2\log 2-1$ (b) $\log 2$

(c) $\log 2+1$ (d) 0

Hints & Solutions

1. (a)	*2.* (c)	*3.* (a)	*4.* (b)
5. (b)	*6.* (c)	*7.* (d)	*8.* (b)
9. (a)	*10.* (a)	*11.* (a)	*12.* (d)

13. (a) **Assertion** Given line is $y-1=x$

$$\Rightarrow \quad y=x+1$$

$\therefore$ The area of the region bounded by the line $y=x+1$, the X-axis and ordinates $x=a$ and $x=b$ is given by

$$\int_{-1}^1 (x+1)dx = \left[\frac{x^2}{2}+x\right]_{-1}^1$$

$$=\frac{1}{2}+1-\frac{1}{2}+1=2$$

Reason provides the general formula for calculating the area under a curve.

So, Assertion and Reason both are true and Reason is the correct explanation of Assertion.

14. Solve as Example 6 (iii) of Topic 1. **Ans.** $\frac{1}{4}\log 3$

15. Solve as Example 6 (iii) of Topic 1. **Ans.** $-\frac{1}{6}\log 2$

16. **Hint** Required area $= \int_0^2 y^3 dy + \left|\int_{-1}^0 y^3 dy\right|$

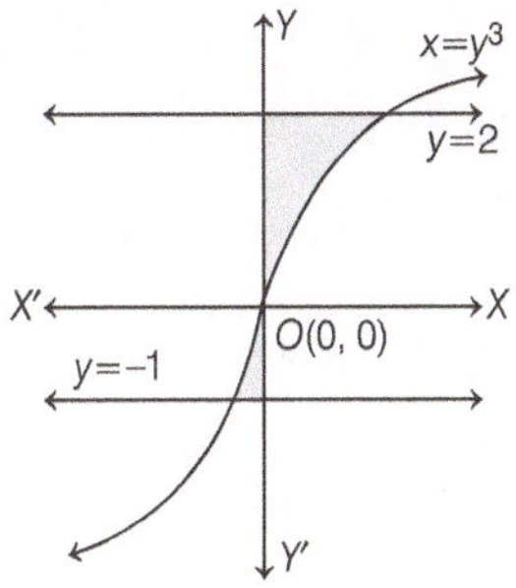

Ans. $\frac{17}{4}$ sq units

17. **Hint** Put $x+2=t^2$ **Ans.** $\frac{16\sqrt{2}}{15}(\sqrt{2}+1)$

18. **Hint** $\int \frac{5x^2}{x^2+4x+3}dx = \int\left(5-\frac{20x+15}{x^2+4x+3}\right)dx$

and $\frac{20x+15}{x^2+4x+3} = \frac{\frac{45}{2}}{x+3} - \frac{\frac{5}{2}}{x+1}$

Ans. $5 - \frac{45}{2}\log\frac{5}{4} + \frac{5}{2}\log\frac{3}{2}$

19. Solve as Example 5 (iii) of Topic 1.

Ans. $\frac{e^2(e^4-3)}{6}$

20. **Hint** $\frac{(x-x^3)^{1/3}}{x^4} = \frac{\left[x^3\left(\frac{1}{x^2}-1\right)\right]^{1/3}}{x^4}$

$$= \frac{(x^3)^{1/3}\left(\frac{1}{x^2}-1\right)^{1/3}}{x^4}$$

$$= \frac{\left(\frac{1}{x^2}-1\right)^{1/3}}{x^3}.$$

Now, put $\frac{1}{x^2}-1=t$ **Ans.** 6

21. **Hint** Integrate by parts by taking (x^2+x) as Ist function and $\frac{1}{\sqrt{2x+1}}$ as IInd function.

Ans. $\sqrt{\frac{57-5\sqrt{5}}{5}}$

22. **Hint** Given lines are

$$y = 3x + 2 \quad \text{...(i)}$$

$$y = 0 \quad \text{[X-axis] ...(ii)}$$

$$x = -1 \quad \text{...(iii)}$$

and $$x = 1 \quad \text{...(iv)}$$

Table for $y = 3x + 2$ is

x	0	$-2/3$
y	2	0

The region bounded by $y = 3x + 2$, X-axis and the ordinates $x = -1$ and $x = 1$ is represented by the shaded portion.

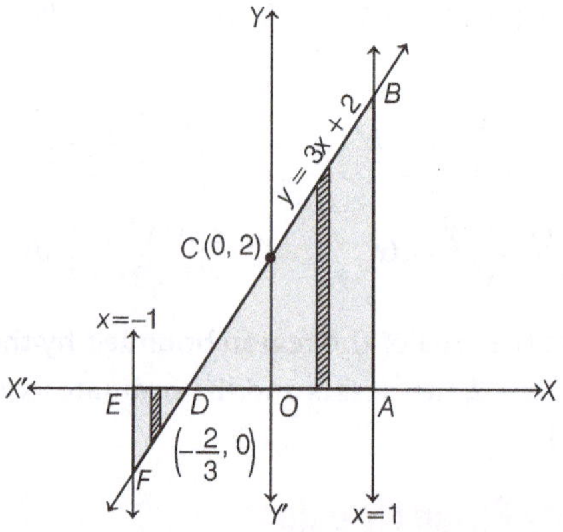

∴ Required area

= Area of region $EFDE$ + Area of region $ABDA$

$$= \left|\int_{-1}^{-2/3} y\,dx\right| + \int_{-2/3}^{1} y\,dx$$

Ans. $\frac{13}{3}$ sq units

23. (i) (b), (ii) (d), (iii) (c), (iv) (a)

CHAPTER 13

Application of Integration

In this Chapter...

- Determination of Cost Function
- Consumer Surplus
- Producer Surplus

The area of bounded regions under curves using integration has application to investigate the economic surplus refers to two related quantities as consumer surplus and producer surplus.

Determination of Cost Function

The integration method is employed to drive the total cost function when the Marginal Cost (MC) is given and to determine the total revenue function when Marginal Revenues (MR) is given, let C represents the total cost and since $\text{MC} = \frac{dc}{dx}$ is marginal cost; then

$$C = C(x) = \int (\text{MC})\,dx + k.$$

Here, k denotes the constant of integration, k, being the constant, is the fixed cost.

Average Cost

Average cost is the total cost per unit of output. It is calculated by dividing the total cost by the quantity produced $AC = \frac{C}{Q}$.

Here, C denotes total cost and Q denotes quantity.

EXAMPLE 1. The marginal cost function of producing x units of a product is given by $mc = \frac{x}{\sqrt{x^2 + 2500}}$. Find the total cost function, if the fixed cost is ₹ 1000.

Sol. We have, $mc = \frac{x}{\sqrt{x^2 + 2500}}$

$$\therefore \quad c(x) = \int \frac{x}{\sqrt{x^2 + 2500}}\,dx + k$$

On putting $x^2 + 2500 = t^2 \Rightarrow xdx = tdt$

So, $c(x) = \int \frac{tdt}{t} + k$

$$\Rightarrow c(x) = \int dt + k = t + k \Rightarrow c(x) = \sqrt{x^2 + 2500} + k$$

Given that, when $x = 0$, $c(x) =$ ₹ 1000

$$\therefore \quad 1000 = \sqrt{2500} + k$$

$$\Rightarrow \quad 1000 = 50 + k$$

$$\Rightarrow \quad k = 1000 - 50 = 950$$

Total cost function, $c(x) = \sqrt{x^2 + 2500} + 950$

EXAMPLE 2. The marginal cost function of a firm is $mc = (\log x)^2$. Find the total cost function when the cost of production one unit is ₹ 50.

Sol. We have, $mc(x) = (\log x)^2$

$$\therefore c(x) = \int (\log x)^2 dx + k$$

$$= (\log x)^2 \int dx - \int \left(\frac{d}{dx} (\log x)^2 \int dx \right) dx + k$$

$$= (\log x)^2 \cdot x - \int \frac{2 \log x}{x} \cdot x\,dx + k$$

$$= x(\log x)^2 - 2(x \log x - x) + k$$

$$= x(\log x)^2 - 2x \log x + 2x + k \quad \text{... (i)}$$

when, $x = 1$, then $c = 50$

From Eq. (i), we get $50 = 2 + k \Rightarrow k = 48$

$\therefore$ Total cost, $c(x) = x(\log x)^2 - 2x \log x + 2x + 48$

Determination of Total Revenue Function

Let $R(x)$ denotes the total revenue function and $\text{MR} = \frac{d}{dx}[R(x)]$ represents the marginal revenue function.

$\therefore \quad R(x) = \int (\text{MR})\, dx + k,$

where k is the constant of integration.

EXAMPLE 3. The marginal revenue function of a commodity is given as $\text{MR} = 12 - 3x^2 + 4x$. Find the total revenue from the rate of 4 units.

Sol. We have, $\text{MR}(x) = 12 - 3x^2 + 4x$

$$\therefore \quad R(x) = \int \text{MR}\, dx + k$$
$$= \int (12 - 3x^2 + 4x)\, dx + k$$
$$= 12x - x^3 + 2x^2 + k$$

We know that when $x = 0$ then, $R = 0$

$\therefore \quad k = 0$

Thus, $R(x) = 12x - x^3 + 2x^2$

Now, the total revenue from the safe of 4 units is given by

$$R(4) = 48 - 64 + 32 = 16$$

EXAMPLE 4. A firm has a marginal revenue function given by $\text{MR} = \frac{a}{x+b} - c$, where x is the output and a, b and c are constants. Then, prove that the demand function is given by $p = \frac{a}{x}\log\left(\frac{x+b}{b}\right) - c$, where p is the price per unit when x units are sold.

Sol. We have, $\text{MR}(x) = \frac{a}{x+b} - c$

$$\therefore \quad R(x) = \int \text{MR}(x) dx + k = \int \left(\frac{a}{x+b} - c\right) dx + k$$
$$= a\int \frac{1}{x+b} dx - c\int dx + k$$

$$\Rightarrow \quad R(x) = a\log(x+b) - cx + k \quad \ldots\text{(i)}$$

We know that when $x = 0$, then $R = 0$

$\therefore$ From Eq. (i), we get

$$0 = a\log(0+b) - c \times 0 + k$$
$$\Rightarrow \quad k = -a\log b$$

$\therefore$ Total revenue function,

$$R(x) = a\log(x+b) - cx - a\log b$$
$$= a\log\left(\frac{x+b}{b}\right) - cx$$

If p is the price per unit when x units are sold.

Then, the demand function is given by

$$p = \frac{R}{x} = \frac{a}{x}\log\left(\frac{x+b}{b}\right) - c$$

Law of Demand

Demand tells us the price that consumers would be willing to pay for each different quantity. According to the law of demand, when the price increases, the demand decreases and conversely, as the prices decreases, the demand increases. A demand curve represents the relationship between the quantity demanded of a good and its price. The point where the demand curve intersects the vertical axis determines the price at which the consumers are unwilling to buy the good at all.

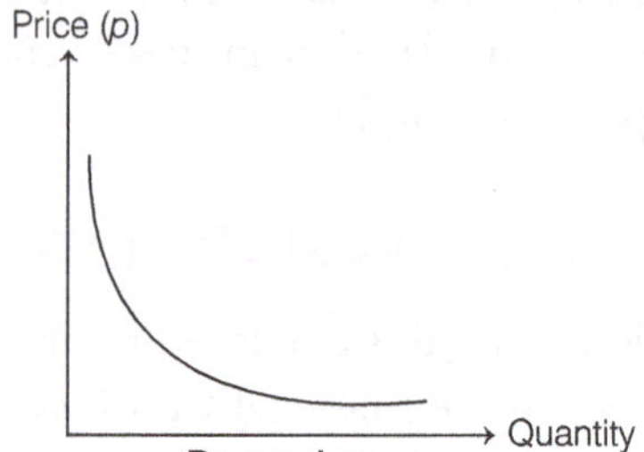

Demand curve

Law of Supply

Supply tells us the price that producers would be willing to accept in order to sell different quantities. The law of supply asserts that as the price of a good rises, the quantity supplied rises, and conversely, as the price of a good falls, the quantity supplied falls. The supply curve represents the relationship between the quantity supplied of a good and the price of good. The point where the supply curve intersects the vertical axis determines the price at which the producers are not willing to sell the commodity at all.

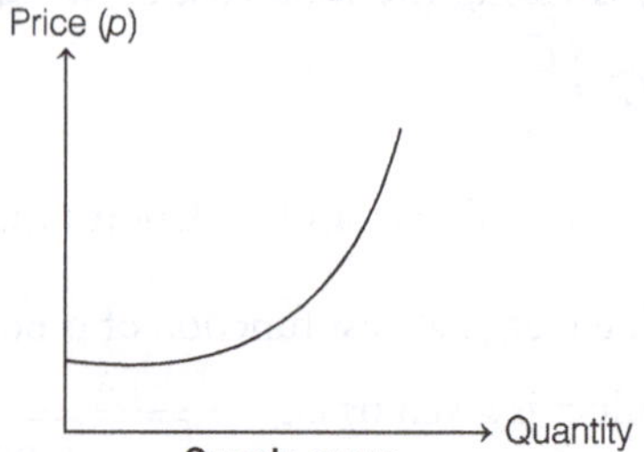

Supply curve

Intersection of Demand and Supply Line

The demand and supply curve intersects at the equilibrium point (x_0, p_0), where p_0 is the equilibrium prices and x_0 is the equilibrium quantity.

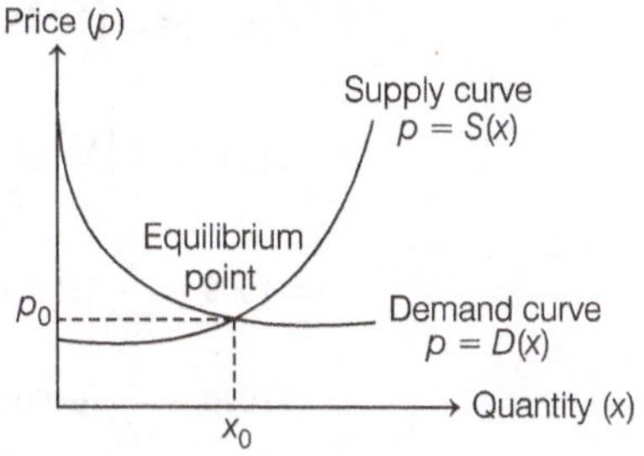

Two essential applications of the demand and supply curves in economics are the consumer surplus and producer surplus.

Consumer Surplus

Consumer surplus is the economic gain accruing to a consumer when engaging in trade. Representing for a difference between the price, they are willing to pay and the actual price.

At the equilibrium point, the consumer surplus is the difference between what consumers are willing to pay and their actual expenditure.

The area of the region between the demand curve $p = D(x)$ and the line $p = p_0$ represents the consumer surplus.

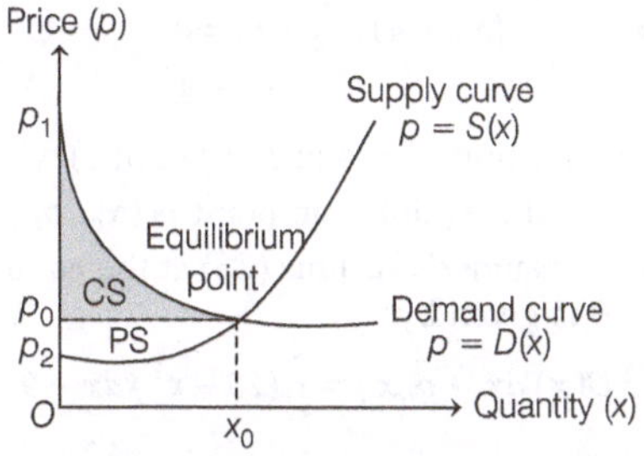

Let the price per unit of a product is p_0; and the market demand is x_0 units. Consumers benefit by paying the equilibrium price p_0.

$\because$ The total benefit of consumers is knows as consumer surplus.

$\therefore$ Consumer Surplus (CS) $= \int_0^{x_0} D(x)\,dx - p_0x_0$

Producer Surplus

The producer surplus measures the supplier's gain from trade, represents the total amount gained by producers when selling at the current price instead of the price they would have been willing to accept. A producer might be willing to sell at a price lower than p_0 to stay in business.

The area between the line $p = p_0$ and the supply curve $p = S(x)$ represents the producer surplus as follows.

$$\text{Producer Surplus (PS)} = p_0x_0 - \int_0^{x_0} S(x)dx$$

If x_0 units of goods are sold at a price of p_0 per unit, suppliers benefit by selling at equilibrium price p_0.

The total benefit of suppliers is known as producers surplus.

EXAMPLE 5. If demand for a consumer is given by the function $p = 27 - 3x - x^2$ (where x = quantity demand, p = price).Find the consumer surplus at $x_0 = 3$.

Sol. We have, demand function $p = 27 - 3x - x^2$

At $x_0 = 3$, $p_0 = 27 - 3\times 3 - (3)^2 = 27 - 9 - 9 = 9$

$\therefore$ Consumer surplus,

$$CS = \int_0^{x_0} D(x)dx - p_0x_0$$
$$= \int_0^3 (27 - 3x - x^2)\,dx - 9\times 3$$
$$= \left(27x - \frac{3x^2}{2} - \frac{x^3}{3}\right)_0^3 - 27$$
$$= \left(27\times 3 - \frac{3}{2}(3)^2 - \frac{(3)^3}{3}\right) - 27$$
$$= 81 - \frac{27}{2} - 9 - 27 = 81 - 49.5 = 31.5$$

EXAMPLE 6. The demand function for a commodity is given by $p = 20 - 2x - x^2$. Find the consumer's surplus when $p_0 = 5$.

Sol. We have, demand function

$$p = 20 - 2x - x^2$$

At $p_0 = 5$, we obtain

$$5 = 20 - 2x_0 - x_0^2$$
$$\Rightarrow \quad x_0^2 + 2x_0 - 15 = 0$$
$$\Rightarrow \quad x_0^2 + 5x_0 - 3x_0 - 15 = 0$$
$$\Rightarrow \quad x_0(x_0 + 5) - 3(x_0 + 5) = 0$$
$$\Rightarrow \quad (x_0 + 5)(x_0 - 3) = 0$$
$$\Rightarrow \quad x_0 - 3 = 0 \qquad [\because x_0 + 5 \neq 0]$$
$$\Rightarrow \quad x_0 = 3$$

$\therefore$ Consumer's Surplus (CS)

$$= \int_0^{x_0} p\,dx - p_0x_0$$
$$= \int_0^3 (20 - 2x - x^2)dx - 5\times 3$$

$$= \left[20x - 2.\frac{x^2}{2} - \frac{x^3}{3}\right]_0^3 - 15$$

$$= \left(20 \times 3 - (3)^2 - \frac{(3)^3}{3}\right) - 15$$

$$= 60 - 9 - 9 - 15 = 60 - 33 = 27$$

EXAMPLE 7. The demand function of a product is $p = 10e^{-x}$. Find the consumer's surplus when the market price $p = 1$. (given $\log_{10} e = 0.4343$)

Sol. Given, the demand function is $p = 10e^{-x}$ and $p_0 = 1$

$$\therefore \quad 1 = 10e^{-x_0}$$

$$\Rightarrow \quad e^{-x_0} = \frac{1}{10} \Rightarrow e^{x_0} = 10$$

$$\Rightarrow \quad x_0 \log_e e = \log_e 10 \Rightarrow x_0 = \log_e 10$$

$$\Rightarrow \quad x_0 = \frac{1}{\log_{10} e} \Rightarrow x_0 = \frac{1}{0.4343} = 2.30$$

$$\therefore \text{ Consumer's surplus (CS)} = \int_0^{x_0} 10e^{-x} dx - 1 \times 2.30$$

$$= -10[e^{-x}]_0^{x_0} - 2.30$$

$$= -10[e^{-x_0} - e^0] - 2.30$$

$$= -10\left[\frac{1}{10} - 1\right] - 2.30$$

$$= -10 \times (-0.9) - 2.30$$

$$= 9.0 - 2.30 = 6.70$$

EXAMPLE 8. The supply function for a commodity is $p = 13 + x$. Determine producer's surplus, if 22 units of the goods are sold.

Sol. Given, the supply function is $p = 13 + x$

at $x_0 = 22$, we obtain

$$p_0 = 13 + 22 = 35$$

$$\therefore \text{ Producer's surplus (PS)} = p_0 x_0 - \int_0^{x_0} S(x)\, dx$$

$$= 35 \times 22 - \int_0^{22} (13 + x)\, dx$$

$$= 770 - \left[13x + \frac{x^2}{2}\right]_0^{22}$$

$$= 770 - \left(13 \times 22 + \frac{(22)^2}{2}\right)$$

$$= 770 - (286 + 242)$$

$$= 770 - 528 = 242$$

EXAMPLE 9. Supply function of a producer is given by $40p = (x + 15)^2$. Find the producer's surplus when the market price is ₹ 40.

Sol. Given, the supply function is $40p = (x + 15)^2$ at $p_0 = 40$, we obtain

$$40 \times 40 = (x_0 + 15)^2 \Rightarrow 1600 = (x_0 + 15)^2$$

$$\Rightarrow (x_0 + 15) = 40 \Rightarrow x_0 = 25$$

$$\therefore \text{ Producer's surplus (PS)} = p_0 x_0 - \int_0^{x_0} S(x)\, dx$$

$$= 40 \times 25 - \int_0^{25} \frac{(x_0 + 15)^2}{40} dx$$

$$= 1000 - \frac{1}{40}\left[\frac{(x_0 + 15)^3}{3}\right]_0^{25}$$

$$= 1000 - \frac{1}{120}[(25 + 15)^3 - (15)^3]$$

$$= 1000 - \frac{1}{120}[64000 - 3375]$$

$$= 1000 - \frac{1}{120}[60625]$$

$$= 1000 - 505.21 = 494.79$$

EXAMPLE 10. The demand and supply functions are $p = 25 - x^2$ and $p = 2x + 1$, respectively. Find each of the following

(i) The equilibrium point.

(ii) The consumer's surplus at the equilibrium point.

(iii) The producer's surplus at the equilibrium point.

Sol. Given, the demand and supply functions are $p = D(x) = 25 - x^2$ and $p = S(x) = 2x + 1$

(i) At equilibrium point $D(x) = S(x)$

$$\Rightarrow \quad 25 - x_0^2 = 2x_0 + 1$$

$$\Rightarrow \quad x_0^2 + 2x_0 - 24 = 0$$

$$\Rightarrow \quad (x_0 - 4)(x_0 + 6) = 0$$

$$\Rightarrow \quad x_0 = 4 \quad [\because x_0 + 6 \neq 0]$$

Now, putting $x_0 = 4$ in $D(x)$ or $S(x)$ we get $p_0 = 9$

Hence, the equilibrium point is (x_0, p_0), i.e. (4, 9)

(ii) The consumer's surplus (CS) at the equilibrium point (4, 9) is given by

$$\int_0^{x_0} D(x)\, dx - p_0 x_0 = \int_0^4 (25 - x^2)\, dx - 9 \times 4$$

$$= \left[25x - \frac{x^3}{3}\right]_0^4 - 36$$

$$= \left[25 \times 4 - \frac{(4)^3}{3}\right] - 36$$

$$= 100 - \frac{64}{3} - 36 = \frac{128}{3}$$

(iii) The producer's surplus (PS) at the equilibrium point (4, 9) is given by $p_0 x_0 - \int_0^{x_0} S(x) dx$.

$$= 9 \times 4 - \int_0^4 (2x + 1)\, dx$$

$$= 36 - \left[\frac{2x^2}{2} + x\right]_0^4 = 36 - [(4)^2 + 4] = 16$$

Exam Pattern Exercise

Part A - Objective Type Questions

Multiple Choice Type Questions

1 Law of demand shows a relation between the
(a) Income and price of a commodity
(b) Quantity demand and quantity supply of a commodity
(c) Income and quantity demand of a commodity
(d) Price and quantity of a commodity

2 The total cost function is given by $C(x) = x^2 + 30x + 1500$. The marginal cost when 10 units are produced is
(a) ₹ 20 (b) ₹ 70
(c) ₹ 30 (d) ₹ 50

3 The marginal cost of production of the commodity is $20 + 2x$, it is known that fixed cost is ₹ 300. Find the total cost.
(a) $x^2 + 20x + 300$ (b) $x^2 + 20x + 200$
(c) $x^2 - 20x + 300$ (d) $x^2 - 20x - 300$

4 If the cost function of a firm is given by $C(x) = 2x^2 - 4x + 5$, then average cost, when $x = 2$ is
(a) 1 (b) 2
(c) 2.5 (d) 1.5

5 The marginal revenue for a commodity is $MR = e^x + x + x^2$. Find the revenue function.
(a) $e^x + \frac{x^2}{2} + \frac{x^3}{3} - 1$ (b) $e^x + \frac{x^2}{2} + \frac{x^3}{3} + 1$
(c) $e^{-x} - \frac{x^2}{2} + \frac{x^3}{3} - 1$ (d) $e^{-x} + \frac{x^2}{2} - \frac{x^3}{3} + 1$

6 A company has determined that marginal cost function for x product of a particular commodity is given by $MC = 25 + 10x - x^2$, where C is the cost of producing X units of the commodity if the fixed cost is ₹ 250. What is the cost of producing 15 units?
(a) 627 (b) 620
(c) 623 (d) 625

7 The marginal revenue function of a commodity is $MR = 12 + 4x - 3x^2$, find the revenue function.
(a) $12x + x^2 + x^3$ (b) $12x + 2x^2 - x^3$
(c) $12x - 2x^2 + x^3$ (d) $12x + 2x^2 + x^3$

8 Find the value of x if demand function $P_d = 25 - 3x$ and supply function $P_s = 5 + 2x$.
(a) 4 (b) 3 (c) –3 (d) 2

9 The demand function for a commodity is given by $P = 50 - 45x$. Find the consumer's surplus at equilibrium price $P_0 = 2$.
(a) 27.5 (b) 24.6 (c) 25.6 (d) 28.5

10 The relation between marginal and average cost of producing 'x' units of a product is **[CBSE 2023]**
(a) $\frac{d(AC)}{dx} = x(MC - AC)$
(b) $\frac{d(AC)}{dx} = x(AC - MC)$
(c) $\frac{d(AC)}{dx} = \frac{1}{x}(AC - MC)$
(d) $\frac{d(AC)}{dx} = \frac{1}{x}(MC - AC)$

Assertion-Reason Based Questions

Directions (Q. Nos. 11-13) *In the questions given below are two statements labelled as Assertion (A) and Reason (R). In the context of the two statements, which one of the following is correct?*
(a) Both A and R are correct; R is the correct explanation of A
(b) Both A and R are correct; R is not the correct explanation of A
(c) A is correct; R is incorrect
(d) R is correct; A is incorrect

11 **Assertion (A)** When the price of a product increases, people prefer to buy less of that product.
Reason (R) The law of demand states that the demand for a product is inversely related to its price.

12 **Assertion (A)** Surplus is an amount of something left over when requirements have been met.
Reason (R) Surplus is an excess of production or supply.

13 **Assertion (A)** Total revenue is at its maximum point when marginal revenue is zero.
Reason (R) When every additional unit is sold at the same price, marginal revenue = Average

Part B - Descriptive Questions

Very Short Answer Type Questions

14 The marginal cost function of a product is given by $MC = \frac{500}{\sqrt{2x+25}}$. If C is in rupees determine the cost involved to decreases production from 100 units to 300 units.

15 If the marginal revenue function for output x is given by $MR = \frac{6}{(x+2)^2} + 5$, find the total revenue function and the demand function.

16 If marginal cost function of manufacturing x units of a product is $5 + 16x - 3x^2$ and total cost of production of 5 items is ₹ 500, then find the total cost function.

17 The marginal cost function MC for a product is given by $MC = \frac{2}{\sqrt{2x+9}}$ and the fixed cost ₹ 14. Find the average cost for 8 units of output.

18 Find the total revenue from the sale of 2000 pens, if the marginal revenue function $R(x)$ is given by $MR(x) = \frac{x}{2000} + 3.50$, where x denotes the number of units sold.

Short Answer Type Questions

19 The cost function of a form is given by $C = 2x^2 + x - 5$. Find
(i) the average cost.
(ii) the marginal cost, when $x = 4$.

20 The marginal revenue function of a commodity is given by $MR = 9 - 2x + 4x^2$. Find the total revenue function.

21 The marginal revenue function of a form is given by $MR = \frac{ab}{(x-b)^2} - c$. Prove that the total revenue function is given by $R(x) = \frac{ab}{b-x} - cx - a$.

22 The demand function for a commodity is $P = 35 - 2x - x^2$. Find the consumer's surplus at equilibrium price $P_0 = 20$.

23 The supply function for a commodity is $P = 4 + x$. Determine producer's surplus of 12 units of goods are sold.

Long Answer Type Questions

24 Find the consumer's surplus for the demand function
(i) $(x-5)^2$, when $x = 3$.
(ii) $4 - x^2$, when $x = 1$.

25 The demand function for goods is given by $P = 100 - 8x$. Find the consumer's surplus corresponding to the market price $P_0 = 4$.

26 The demand and supply functions under pure competition are $P = 16 - x^2$ and $P = 2x^2 + 4$ respectively. Find the consumer's surplus and producer's surplus.

27 In each of the following (i) to (ii) $P(d)$ is the price in rupees per unit that the consumers are willing to pay for x units of an item, and $P(s)$ is the price in rupees per unit that producers are willing to accept for x units.
(i) $P(d) = -3x + 7$, $P(s) = 2x + 2$
(ii) $P(d) = 18 - 2x - x^2$, $P(s) = 2x - 3$

28 The supply function for a commodity is $100P = (x + 20)^2$. Find the producer's surplus when the market price is ₹ 25.

Case Study Based Questions

29 The marginal cost (MC) of producing x units of a commodity in a day is given as $MC = 14x - 1720$. The selling price is fixed at ₹ 11 per unit and the fixed cost ₹ 1900 per day.

(i) Cost function is
(a) $7x^2 - 1720x + 1900$
(b) $13x^2 - 1000x + 1800$
(c) $13x^2 - 1000x + 1300$
(d) $9x^2 - 1000x + 1700$

(ii) When $x = 1$, the value of cost function is
(a) 311 (b) 187 (c) 410 (d) 176

(iii) The revenue function (R) is
(a) $11x$ (b) $9x$ (c) $17x$ (d) $20x$

(iv) The profit function is
(a) $-5x^2 + 1731x - 1900$
(b) $-6x^2 + 1530x - 1300$
(c) $-7x^2 + 1731x - 1900$
(d) $-5x^2 + 1530x + 1200$

(v) When $x = 2$, the profit (in ₹) is
(a) 1600 (b) 1534 (c) 1320 (d) 1420

30 Consumer surplus and producer surplus

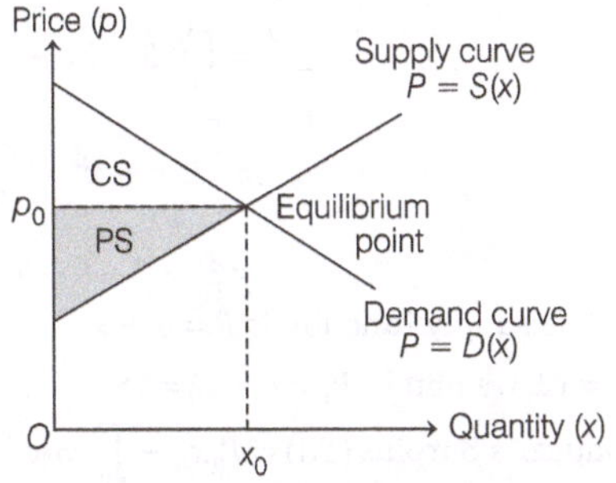

The above graph showing the demand and supply curves of tyre manufacturer company are linear. '*ABC*' tyre manufacturer sold 25 units every month when the price of a tyre was ₹ 20000 per units and '*ABC*' tyre manufacturer sold 125 units every month when the price dropped to ₹ 15000 per unit. When the price was ₹ 25000 per unit, 180 tyres were available per month for sale and when the price was only ₹ 15000 per unit, 80 tyres remained.

Answer the following questions based on the above information.

(i) The demand function $D(x)$ is

(a) $-40x + 21000$ (b) $-50x + 21250$
(c) $-60x + 20000$ (d) $-65x + 20000$

(ii) The supply function $S(x)$ is

(a) $100x + 7000$ (b) $110x + 6500$
(c) $105x + 8000$ (d) $90x + 6500$

(iii) The equilibrium point is

(a) (95, 16500) (b) (92, 16000)
(c) (90, 17000) (d) (97, 17200)

(iv) The consumer surplus is

(a) ₹ 210720 (b) ₹ 227065
(c) ₹ 225625 (d) ₹ 2152729

(v) The producer surplus is

(a) ₹ 467230 (b) ₹ 451250
(c) ₹ 441623 (d) ₹ 468564

Hints & Solutions

1. (d)	2. (d)	3. (a)	4. (c)
5. (a)	6. (d)	7. (b)	8. (a)
9. (c)	10. (d)	11. (a)	12. (b)
13. (a)			

14. Given, $\text{MC} = \dfrac{500}{\sqrt{2x+25}}$

$\therefore$ Required cost $= C(300) - C(100)$

$$= \int_{100}^{300} \frac{500}{\sqrt{2x+25}}\,dx$$

$$= 500\,[\sqrt{2x+25}]_{100}^{300}$$

$$= 5000$$

15. We have, $\text{MR}(x) = \dfrac{6}{(x+2)^2} + 5$

$$R(x) = \int \text{MR}\,dx + k$$

$$R(x) = \int\left(\frac{6}{(x+2)^2} + 5\right)dx + k$$

$$R(x) = -\frac{6}{x+2} + 5x + k$$

We know that when $x = 0$, then

$$R = 0,\ k = 3$$

$$\therefore \quad R(x) = \frac{3x}{x+2} + 5x$$

and the demand function $= P = \dfrac{R(x)}{x} = \dfrac{3}{x+2} + 5$

16. $C(x) = \int \text{MC}(x)\,dx + k$

$$= \int (5 + 16x - 3x^2)dx + k$$

$$C(x) = 5x + 8x^2 - x^3 + k$$

Since, $C(x) = 500$, when $x = 5$

$$k = 400$$

$$C(x) = 5x + 8x^2 - x^3 + 400$$

17. $C(x) = \int \dfrac{2dx}{\sqrt{2x+9}} + k \Rightarrow C = 2\sqrt{2x+9} + k$

When $x = 0$, $C = 14$

$\therefore k = 8$

$\therefore C(x) = 2\sqrt{2x+9} + 8$

$\therefore \quad \text{AC} = \dfrac{C}{x} = \dfrac{2}{x}\sqrt{2x+9} + \dfrac{8}{x}$

When $x = 8$, then $C = \dfrac{9}{4}$

18. Total revenue from the sale of 2000 pens $= \int_0^{2000} (\text{MR})dx$

$$= \int_0^{2000}\left(\frac{x}{2000} + 3.5\right)dx = ₹\ 8000$$

19. We have, $C(x) = 2x^2 + x - 5$

(i) Average Cost, (AC) $= \dfrac{C(x)}{x}$

$$= \frac{2x^2 + x - 5}{x} = 2x + 1 - \frac{5}{x}$$

(ii) Marginal Cost (MC) $= \frac{d}{dx}(C(x))$

$$= \frac{d}{dx}(2x^2 + x - 5) = 4x + 1$$

When $x = 4$, then MC $= 16 + 1 = 17$

20. We have, $MR(x) = 9 - 2x + 4x^2$

$$R(x) = \int MR(x)\,dx + k$$

$$R(x) = \int (9 - 2x + 4x^2)\,dx + k$$

$$R(x) = 9x - 2x^2 + \frac{4x^3}{3} + k$$

We know that when $x = 0$, then $R = 0$

$$k = 0$$

Thus, $R(x) = 9x - x^2 + \frac{4x^3}{3}$

21. We have, $MR(x) = \frac{ab}{(x-b)^2} - c$

$$R(x) = \int MR(x)\,dx + k$$

$$R(x) = \int \left(\frac{ab}{(x-b)^2} - c\right) dx + k$$

$$R(x) = \int \frac{ab}{(x-b)^2}\,dx - c\int dx + k$$

Let $(x - b) = t \Rightarrow dx = dt$

$$R(x) = ab\int \frac{dt}{t^2} - cx + k$$

$$R(x) = ab\left(-\frac{1}{t}\right) - cx + k$$

$$R(x) = \frac{ab}{(b-x)} - cx + k$$

We know that when $x = 0$, then $R = 0$

$$0 = \frac{ab}{(b-0)} - c(0) + k$$

$$0 = \frac{ab}{b} + k$$

$$k = -a$$

$\therefore$ Total revenue function, $R(x) = \frac{ab}{b-x} - cx - a$

22. We have, demand function, $P = 35 - 2x - x^2$

At $P_0 = 20$, we obtain

$$20 = 35 - 2x_0 - x_0^2$$

$$0 = 35 - 2x_0 - x_0^2 - 20$$

$$x_0^2 + 2x_0 - 15 = 0$$

$$x_0^2 + 5x_0 - 3x_0 - 15 = 0$$

$$x_0(x_0 + 5) - 3(x_0 + 5) = 0$$

$$(x_0 - 3)(x_0 + 5) = 0$$

$$x_0 - 3 = 0 \qquad [\because x_0 + 5 \neq 0]$$

$$x_0 = 3$$

$\therefore$ Consumer's Surplus (CS) $= \int_0^{x_0} P\,dx - P_0 x_0$

$$= \int_0^3 (35 - 2x - x^2)\,dx - 60$$

$$= \left[35x - x^2 - \frac{x^3}{3}\right]_0^3 - 60$$

$$= 35 \times 3 - 9 - 9 - 60 = 27$$

23. Given, the supply function is $P = 4 + x$

At $x_0 = 12$, we obtain $P_0 = 4 + 12 = 16$

$\therefore$ Producer's Surplus (PS) $= P_0 x_0 - \int_0^{x_0} S(x)\,dx$

$$= 16 \times 12 - \int_0^{12} (4 + x)\,dx$$

$$= 192 - \left[4x + \frac{x^2}{2}\right]_0^{12}$$

$$= 192 - \left[48 + \frac{144}{2}\right] = 72$$

24. (i) We have, demand function, $P = (x - 5)^2$

At $x_0 = 3$, $P_0 = (3-5)^2 = (-2)^2 = 4$

$\therefore$ Consumer surplus, (CS) $= \int_0^{x_0} P(x)\,dx - P_0 x_0$

$$= \int_0^3 (x - 5)^2\,dx - 12$$

$$= \int_0^3 (x^2 + 25 - 10x)\,dx - 12$$

$$= \left[\frac{x^3}{3} + 25x - 5x^2\right]_0^3 - 12$$

$$= 9 + 25 \times 3 - 45 - 12 = 27$$

(ii) We have, demand function, $P = 4 - x^2$

At $x_0 = 1$, $P_0 = 4 - 1 = 3$

$\therefore$ Consumer surplus, (CS) $= \int_0^{x_0} P(x)\,dx - P_0 x_0$

$$= \int_0^1 (4 - x^2)\,dx - 3$$

$$= \left[4x - \frac{x^3}{3}\right]_0^1 - 3$$

$$= 4 - \frac{1}{3} - 3$$

$$= \frac{12 - 1 - 9}{3} = \frac{2}{3}$$

25. We have, demand function, $P = 100 - 8x$

At $P_0 = 4$, we obtain $4 = 100 - 8x \Rightarrow 96 = 8x$

$$x = 12$$

$\therefore$ Consumer's surplus (CS) $= \int_0^{x_0} P\,dx - P_0 x_0$

$$= \int_0^{12} (100 - 8x)\,dx - 12 \times 4$$

$$= (100x - 4x^2)_0^{12} - 48$$

$$= 1200 - 576 - 48 = 576$$

26. Given, the demand function and supply are

$$P = D(x) = 16 - x^2 \text{ and } P = S(x) = 2x^2 + 4$$

At equilibrium point $D(x) = S(x)$

$$16 - x^2 = 2x^2 + 4$$

$\Rightarrow$ $16 - 4 = 3x^2$

$\Rightarrow$ $12 = 3x^2$

$\Rightarrow$ $4 = x^2$

$\Rightarrow$ $x = \pm 2$

$\Rightarrow$ $x_0 = 2$

Now, putting $x_0 = 2$ in $D(x)$ or $S(x)$ we get $P_0 = 12$.

Hence, the equilibrium point is (x_0, P_0) i.e. (2, 12).

The consumer's surplus (CS) at the equilibrium point (2, 12) is given by

$$\int_0^{x_0} D(x)\,dx - P_0x_0 = \int_0^2 (16 - x^2)\,dx - 12 \times 2$$

$$= \left[16x - \frac{x^3}{3}\right]_0^2 - 24$$

$$= \left[32 - \frac{8}{3} - 24\right]$$

$$= \frac{96 - 8 - 72}{3} = \frac{16}{3}$$

The producer's surplus (PS) at the equilibrium point (2, 12) is given by

$$P_0x_0 - \int_0^{x_0} S(x)\,dx = 24 - \int_0^2 (2x^2 + 4)\,dx$$

$$= 24 - \left[\frac{2x^3}{3} + 4x\right]_0^2$$

$$= 24 - \frac{16}{3} - 8$$

$$= \frac{72 - 16 - 24}{3} = \frac{32}{3}$$

27. (i) $P(d) = -3x + 7,\ P(s) = 2x + 2$

Given, the demand function and supply are

$P = D(x) = -3x + 7$ and $P = S(x) = 2x + 2$

At equilibrium point $D(x) = S(x)$

$$-3x + 7 = 2x + 2$$

$\Rightarrow$ $-3x - 2x = -5 \Rightarrow -x_0 = -1 \Rightarrow x_0 = 1$

Now, putting $x_0 = 1$ in $D(x)$ or $S(x)$, we get

$$P_0 = 4$$

Hence, the equilibrium point is (x_0, P_0) i.e. (1, 4).

The consumer's surplus (CS) at the equilibrium point (1, 4) is given by

$$\int_0^{x_0} D(x)dx - P_0x_0 = \int_0^1 (-3x + 7)dx - 4$$

$$= \left[\frac{-3x^2}{2} + 7x\right]_0^1 - 4$$

$$= \frac{-3}{2} + 7 - 4 = \frac{-3 + 14 - 8}{2} = \frac{3}{2}$$

The producer's surplus (PS) at the equilibrium point (1, 4) is given by

$$P_0x_0 - \int_0^{x_0} S(x)\,dx = 4 - \int_0^1 (2x + 2)dx$$

$$= 4 - \left[\frac{2x^2}{2} + 2x\right]_0^1$$

$$= 4 - 1 - 2 = 1$$

(ii) $P(d) = 18 - 2x - x^2,\ P(S) = 2x - 3$

Given, the demand function and supply are

$P = D(x) = 18 - 2x - x^2$ and $P = S(x) = 2x - 3$

At equilibrium point $D(x) = S(x)$

$$18 - 2x - x^2 = 2x - 3$$

$\Rightarrow$ $x^2 + 4x - 21 = 0$

$\Rightarrow$ $(x - 3)(x + 7) = 0$

$\Rightarrow$ $x - 3 = 0$ $[\because x + 7 \neq 0]$

$\Rightarrow$ $x = 3$

Now, putting $x_0 = 3$ in $D(x)$ or $S(x)$ we get $P_0 = 3$.

Hence, the equilibrium point is (x_0, P_0) i.e. (3, 3).

The consumer's surplus (CS) at the equilibrium point (3, 3) is given by

$$\int_0^{x_0} D(x)\,dx - P_0x_0 = \int_0^3 (18 - 2x - x^2)\,dx - 9$$

$$= \left[18x - x^2 - \frac{x^3}{3}\right]_0^3 - 9$$

$$= 54 - 9 - 9 - 9 = 27$$

The producer's surplus (PS) at the equilibrium point (3, 3) is given by

$$P_0x_0 - \int_0^{x_0} S(x)dx = 9 - \int_0^3 (2x - 3)\,dx$$

$$= 9 - [x^2 - 3x]_0^3 = 9$$

28. Given, the supply function is $100P = (x + 20)^2$

At $P_0 =$ ₹ 25 , we obtain

$$100P_0 = (x_0 + 20)^2$$

$\Rightarrow$ $100 \times 25 = (x_0 + 20)^2$

$\Rightarrow$ $50 = x_0 + 20 \Rightarrow x_0 = 30$

$\therefore$ Producer's Surplus (PS) $= P_0x_0 - \int_0^{x_0} S(x)\,dx$

$$= 25 \times 30 - \int_0^{30} \frac{(x + 20)^2}{100}\,dx$$

$$= 25 \times 30 - \int_0^{30} \frac{(x^2 + 400 + 40x)}{100}\,dx$$

$$= 750 - \frac{1}{100}\left[\frac{x^3}{3} + 400x + 20x^2\right]_0^{30}$$

$$= 750 - \frac{1}{100}[9000 + 12000 + 18000]$$

$$= 360$$

29. Marginal cost (MC) $= 14x - 1720$

(i) (a) Cost function $C(x) = \int (\text{MC})\, dx$

$$C(x) = \int (14x - 1720)dx$$

$$C(x) = 7x^2 - 1720x + k$$

When $x = 0$, then $C(x) = 1900$

$\therefore$ Cost function, $1900 = 7(0) - 1720(0) + k$

$$k = 1900$$

$$C(x) = 7x^2 - 1720x + 1900$$

(ii) (b) When $x = 1$, then

$$C = 7 \times 1 - 1720 \times 1 + 1900$$

$$C = 187$$

(iii) (a) The selling price is fixed at ₹ 11 per unit. So, that revenue function R is given by

$$R = 11x$$

(iv) (c) The profit function P is given by

$$P = R - C$$

$$P = 11x - (7x^2 - 1720x + 1900)$$

$$P = -7x^2 + 1731x - 1900$$

(v) (b) When $x = 2$, then

$$P = -7(2)^2 + 1731(2) - 1900 = 1534$$

30. (i) (b) Let the demand function be

$$D(x) = ax + b \quad \text{... (i)}$$

When $x = 25$, then $P = 20000$

From Eq. (i), we have

$$20000 = 25a + b \quad \text{... (ii)}$$

and when $x = 125$, then $P = 15000$

From Eq. (i), we have

$$15000 = 125a + b \quad \text{... (iii)}$$

On solving Eqs. (i) and (ii), we get

$$a = -50 \text{ and } b = 21250$$

$\therefore$ Demand function $D(x) = -50x + 21250$

(ii) (a) Let the supply function be

$$S(x) = cx + d \quad \text{... (i)}$$

When $x = 180$, then

$$P = 25000$$

From Eq. (i), we have

$$25000 = 180c + d \quad \text{... (ii)}$$

and when, $x = 80$, then

$$P = 15000$$

From Eq. (i), we have

$$15000 = 80c + d \quad \text{... (iii)}$$

On solving Eqs. (ii) and (iii), we get

$$c = 100 \text{ and } d = 7000$$

$\therefore$ Supply function $S(x) = 100x + 7000$

(iii) (a) For equilibrium point $D(x) = S(x)$

$\Rightarrow \quad -50x_0 + 21250 = 100x_0 + 7000$

$\Rightarrow \quad -150x_0 = -14250$

$\Rightarrow \quad x_0 = 95$

On putting the value of x_0 in demand function on supply function, we get $p_0 = 16500$.

(iv) (c) Consumer surplus (CS) $= \int_0^{x_0} D(x)\, dx - P_0 x_0$

$$= \int_0^{95} (-50x + 21250)dx - 16500 \times 95$$

$$= \left[\frac{-50x^2}{2} + 21250x\right]_0^{95} - 1567500$$

$$= 1793125 - 1567500$$

$$= ₹\ 225625$$

(v) (b) The producer surplus (PS) $= P_0 x_0 - \int_0^{x_0} S(x)\, dx$

$$= 16500 \times 95 - \int_0^{95} (100x + 7000)\, dx$$

$$= 1567500 - [50x^2 + 7000x]_0^{95}$$

$$= 1567500 - 1116250$$

$$= ₹\ 451250$$

CHAPTER 14

Differential Equations

In this Chapter...

- Order and Degree of Differential Equations
- Solution of a Differential Equation
- Formation of a Differential Equation
- Methods of Solving First Order and First Degree of Differential Equations
- Application of Differential Equation

Order and Degree of Differential Equations

An equation involving independent variable (variables), dependent variable and derivative or derivatives of dependent variable with respect to one (or more) independent variable is called a **differential equation**.

e.g. $2x\frac{dy}{dx} - 3y = 5$ and $4\frac{d^2y}{dx^2} + \left(\frac{dy}{dx}\right)^3 = 0$ are differential equations, but $2x - 3y = 0$ is not a differential equation as derivatives of dependent variable (y) with respect to independent variable (x) is not present.

If a differential equation contains only one independent variable and derivatives w.r.t. to that independent variable is, called an ordinary differential equation.

Order of a Differential Equation

The order of the highest derivative involved in a differential equation, is called order of differential equation.

e.g. (i) $\frac{dy}{dx} - 5x = 0$

(ii) $\frac{d^3y}{dx^3} + x^2\left(\frac{d^2y}{dx^2}\right) = 0$

Here, in e.g. (i), equation has the highest derivative of first order and in e.g. (ii), equation has the highest derivative of third order. Hence, orders of the differential equations in e.g. (i) and (ii) are 1 and 3, respectively.

Degree of a Differential Equation

The highest power (positive integral index) of the highest order derivative involved in a differential equation, when it is written as a polynomial in derivatives, is called the degree of a differential equation.

e.g. $\left(\frac{d^3y}{dx^3}\right)^2 + x\left(\frac{d^3y}{dx^3}\right) + 3y\left(\frac{dy}{dx}\right) = 0$

In above differential equation, highest order derivative is $\left(\frac{d^3y}{dx^3}\right)$, whose highest power is 2. So, degree of differential equation is 2.

Important Note

In case of differential equations involving one or more terms of the form $e^{(dy/dx)}$, $\log\left(\frac{dy}{dx}\right)$, etc. the degree is not defined.

However, the degree of the differential equation containing terms like e^x, e^y, $\log x$, $\log y$, etc. is defined as usual.

EXAMPLE 1. Find the order and degree (if defined) of each of the following differential equation.

(i) $\frac{dy}{dx} - x = 0$ (ii) $y''' + y^2 + e^{y'} = 0$

(iii) $y = x\frac{dy}{dx} + \sqrt{1 + \left(\frac{dy}{dx}\right)^2}$ (iv) $\left(\frac{d^3y}{dx^3}\right)^3 + 2\frac{d^2y}{dx^2} = \log\frac{dy}{dx}$

(v) $\frac{d^2y}{dx^2} = \sqrt{y + \left(\frac{dy}{dx}\right)^2}$

Sol. (i) Given differential equation is $\frac{dy}{dx} - x = 0.$

The highest order derivative occurring in the differential equation is $\frac{dy}{dx}$, so its order is 1.

It is a polynomial in $\frac{dy}{dx}$ and highest power raised to $\frac{dy}{dx}$ is 1. So, its degree is 1.

(ii) Given differential equation is $y''' + y^2 + e^{y'} = 0$

The highest order derivative occurring in the differential equation is y''', so its order is 3.

The given differential equation is not a polynomial equation in derivatives of y, so its degree is not defined.

(iii) Given differential equation is $y = x\frac{dy}{dx} + \sqrt{1 + \left(\frac{dy}{dx}\right)^2}$.

It has radical sign in power, i.e. not have positive integer powers, so we first convert it into differential equation having positive integer powers.

We can rewrite the given differential equations as

$$y - x\frac{dy}{dx} = \sqrt{1 + \left(\frac{dy}{dx}\right)^2}$$

$$\Rightarrow \quad y^2 + x^2\left(\frac{dy}{dx}\right)^2 - 2xy\frac{dy}{dx} = 1 + \left(\frac{dy}{dx}\right)^2$$

[squaring both sides]

$$\Rightarrow (x^2 - 1)\left(\frac{dy}{dx}\right)^2 - 2xy\frac{dy}{dx} + y^2 - 1 = 0$$

which represents a quadratic polynomial in $\frac{dy}{dx}$.

Since, highest order derivative is $\frac{dy}{dx}$.

So, order of the differential equation is 1 and degree of the differential equation is 2.

(iv) Given differential equation is

$$\left(\frac{d^3y}{dx^3}\right)^3 + 2\frac{d^2y}{dx^2} = \log\left(\frac{dy}{dx}\right)$$

The highest order derivative which occurs in the given differential equation is $\frac{d^3y}{dx^3}$, so its order is 3.

The given differential equation is not a polynomial equation in derivatives of y, so its degree is not defined.

(v) Given differential equation is $\frac{d^2y}{dx^2} = \sqrt{y + \left(\frac{dy}{dx}\right)^2}$

On squaring both sides, we get

$$\left(\frac{d^2y}{dx^2}\right)^2 = y + \left(\frac{dy}{dx}\right)^2 \Rightarrow \left(\frac{d^2y}{dx^2}\right)^2 - y - \left(\frac{dy}{dx}\right)^2 = 0$$

Here, highest order derivative $= \frac{d^2y}{dx^2}$

$\therefore$ Order of differential equation = 2

and degree of differential equation

= power of highest order derivative = 2

EXAMPLE 2. Find the order and degree of differential equation $y = px + \sqrt{a^2p^2 + b^2}$, where $p = dy/dx$.

Sol. Given differential equation is $y = px + \sqrt{a^2p^2 + b^2}$

where, $p = \frac{dy}{dx}$.

$$\Rightarrow \quad y - px = \sqrt{a^2p^2 + b^2}$$

$$\Rightarrow \quad (y - px)^2 = a^2p^2 + b^2$$

$$\Rightarrow \quad y^2 + p^2x^2 - 2xpy = a^2p^2 + b^2$$

$$\Rightarrow \quad (x^2 - a^2)p^2 - 2xyp + (y^2 - b^2) = 0$$

$$\Rightarrow \quad (x^2 - a^2)\left(\frac{dy}{dx}\right)^2 - 2xy\left(\frac{dy}{dx}\right) + (y^2 - b^2) = 0$$

Clearly, order = 1 and degree = 2.

EXAMPLE 3. Write the sum of the order and degree of the differential equation $\frac{d}{dx}\left\{\left(\frac{dy}{dx}\right)^3\right\} = 0.$

Sol. Given equation is $\frac{d}{dx}\left\{\left(\frac{dy}{dx}\right)^3\right\} = 0 \Rightarrow 3\left(\frac{dy}{dx}\right)^2\frac{d^2y}{dx^2} = 0$

Clearly, the highest order derivative occurring in the differential equation is d^2y/dx^2.

So, its order is 2. Also, it is a polynomial equation in derivatives and highest power raised to d^2y/dx^2 is 1, so its degree is 1.

Hence, the sum of the order and degree of the above differential equation is $2 + 1 = 3$.

Topic Practice 1

1 Find the order and degree of each of the following differential equations.

(i) $x\left(\frac{d^3y}{dx^3}\right)^2 + \left(\frac{dy}{dx}\right)^4 + y^2 = e^{-x}$

(ii) $\left(\frac{ds}{dt}\right)^4 + 3s\frac{d^2s}{dt^2} = 0$

(iii) $x\sqrt{1-y^2}dx + y\sqrt{1-x^2}dy = 0$

(iv) $y + \frac{dy}{dx} = \frac{1}{4}\int y\,dx$

(v) $\left(\frac{d^2y}{dx^2}\right)^3 + \left(\frac{dy}{dx}\right)^2 + \log\left(\frac{dy}{dx}\right) + 1 = 0$

(vi) $\left(\frac{d^2y}{dx^2}\right) + \log\left(\frac{dy}{dx}\right) = 0$

(vii) $\left[1+\left(\frac{dy}{dx}\right)^2\right]^{3/2} = \frac{d^2y}{dx^2}$

(viii) $x - \log\left(\frac{dy}{dx}\right) = 0$

(ix) $\log_e\left(1+\frac{d^2y}{dx^2}\right) = x$

2 Write the sum of order and degree of differential equation $1+\left(\frac{dy}{dx}\right)^4 = 7\left(\frac{d^2y}{dx^2}\right)^3$.

Hints & Solutions

1. (i) Given differential equation is

$$x\left(\frac{d^3y}{dx^3}\right)^2 + \left(\frac{dy}{dx}\right)^4 + y^2 = e^{-x}$$

Since, the highest order derivative is $\frac{d^3y}{dx^3}$. So, its order is 3.

It is a polynomial equation in $\frac{dy}{dx}, \frac{d^3y}{dx^3}$ and the highest power of $\frac{d^3y}{dx^3}$ is 2. So, its degree is 2.

(ii) Solve as Part (i). **Ans.** Order = 2, Degree = 1

(iii) The given equation can be rewritten as

$$x\sqrt{1-y^2}dx = -y\sqrt{1-x^2}dy \Rightarrow \frac{dy}{dx} = \frac{-x\sqrt{1-y^2}}{y\sqrt{1-x^2}}$$

Since, the highest order derivative is $\frac{dy}{dx}$.

So, its order is 1.

It is a polynomial equation in $\frac{dy}{dx}$ and highest power of $\frac{dy}{dx}$ is 1. So, its degree is 1.

(iv) Given differential equation is

$$y + \frac{dy}{dx} = \frac{1}{4}\int y\,dx \quad \text{...(i)}$$

Let us first remove the integral sign by differentiating it w.r.t. x.

On differentiating Eq. (i) w.r.t. x, we get

$$\frac{dy}{dx} + \frac{d^2y}{dx^2} = \frac{1}{4}y$$

Since, the highest order derivative is $\frac{d^2y}{dx^2}$.

So, its order is 2.

Also, it is a polynomial equation in $\frac{d^2y}{dx^2}$ and $\frac{dy}{dx}$, where highest power of $\frac{d^2y}{dx^2}$ is 1.

So, its degree is 1.

(v) Given differential equation is

$$\left(\frac{d^2y}{dx^2}\right)^3 + \left(\frac{dy}{dx}\right)^2 + \log\left(\frac{dy}{dx}\right) + 1 = 0$$

Since, the highest order derivative is $\frac{d^2y}{dx^2}$.

So, its order is 2.

Degree is not defined as it is not a polynomial in derivatives.

(vi) Solve as Part (v).
Ans. Order = 2, Degree = not defined

(vii) Given differential equation is $\left[1+\left(\frac{dy}{dx}\right)^2\right]^{3/2} = \frac{d^2y}{dx^2}$.

On squaring both sides, we get

$$\left[1+\left(\frac{dy}{dx}\right)^2\right]^3 = \left(\frac{d^2y}{dx^2}\right)^2$$

Here, highest order derivative is $\frac{d^2y}{dx^2}$, whose highest power is 2.

So, order of differential equation is 2 and degree is also 2.

(viii) Given differential equation is $x - \log\left(\frac{dy}{dx}\right) = 0.$

Since, the highest order derivative is $\frac{dy}{dx}$.

So, its order is 1.

Now, if possible, then convert the given differential equation into polynomial equation of derivatives.

Consider, $x - \log\left(\frac{dy}{dx}\right) = 0$

$\Rightarrow \quad \log\left(\frac{dy}{dx}\right) = x \Rightarrow \frac{dy}{dx} = e^x,$

which is a polynomial in $\frac{dy}{dx}$.

Also, highest power of $\frac{dy}{dx}$ is 1. So, its degree is 1.

(ix) Given differential equation is $\log_e\left(1 + \frac{d^2y}{dx^2}\right) = x,$

which can be rewritten as $1 + \frac{d^2y}{dx^2} = e^x$

Clearly, the order of differential equation is 2 and its degree is 1.

2. Given differential equation is $1 + \left(\frac{dy}{dx}\right)^4 = 7\left(\frac{d^2y}{dx^2}\right)^3.$

Here, highest order derivative is $\frac{d^2y}{dx^2}$, whose highest power is 3.

So, order = 2 and degree = 3

Sum of order and degree = $2 + 3 = 5$

Solution of a Differential Equation

A function of independent variable that satisfies the given differential equation will be a solution of differential equation.

General Solution of a Differential Equation

If the solution of a differential equation of order *n*, contains *n* arbitrary constants, then it is called a general solution.

The general solution is also called complete primitive or complete solution of differential equation.

The general solution of an ordinary differential equation of *n*th order contains *n* independent arbitrary constants. Thus, the general solution of an ordinary differential equation of order one contains one arbitrary constants and so on.

Particular Solution of a Differential Equation

The solution of a differential equation obtained by giving particular values to the arbitrary constants in the general solution, is called the particular solution.

In other words, the solution free from arbitrary constant is called particular solution (or particular primitive).

EXAMPLE 1. Verify that the function $y = e^{-3x}$ is a solution of the differential equation $\frac{d^2y}{dx^2} + \frac{dy}{dx} - 6y = 0.$

Sol. Given differential equation is

$$\frac{d^2y}{dx^2} + \frac{dy}{dx} - 6y = 0 \quad \text{...(i)}$$

and given function is $y = e^{-3x}$. ...(ii)

Here, order of the given differential equation is 2.

So, we differentiate Eq. (ii) two times.

On differentiating Eq. (ii), w.r.t. *x* two times, we get

$$\frac{dy}{dx} = -3e^{-3x} \quad \text{and} \quad \frac{d^2y}{dx^2} = 9e^{-3x}$$

On putting the values of y, $\frac{dy}{dx}$ and $\frac{d^2y}{dx^2}$ in LHS of Eq. (i), we get

$$\text{LHS} = 9e^{-3x} + (-3e^{-3x}) - 6e^{-3x}$$

$$= 9e^{-3x} - 3e^{-3x} - 6e^{-3x} = 0 = \text{RHS}$$

Hence, the given function is a solution of given differential equation.

EXAMPLE 2. Verify that the function $y = Ax + \frac{B}{x}, x \neq 0$ is a solution of the differential equation $x^2\frac{d^2y}{dx^2} + x\frac{dy}{dx} - y = 0.$

Sol. Given, $y = Ax + \frac{B}{x}, x \neq 0$ ...(i)

Differentiating w.r.t. *x*, we get

$$\frac{dy}{dx} = A - \frac{B}{x^2} \quad \text{...(ii)}$$

Differentiating w.r.t. *x*, we get

$$\frac{d^2y}{dx^2} = \frac{2B}{x^3} \quad \text{...(iii)}$$

Substituting the value of y, $\frac{dy}{dx}$ and $\frac{d^2y}{dx^2}$ in $\frac{x^2d^2y}{dx^2} + x\frac{dy}{dx} - y = 0$, we get

$$\text{LHS} = x^2\left(\frac{2B}{x^3}\right) + x\left(A - \frac{B}{x^2}\right) - \left(Ax + \frac{B}{x}\right)$$

$$= \frac{2B}{x} + Ax - \frac{B}{x} - Ax - \frac{B}{x} = 0 = \text{RHS}$$

Thus, the function $y = Ax + \frac{B}{x}$ satisfies the given differential equation.

Hence, $y = Ax + \frac{B}{x}$ is a solution of the given differential equation.

EXAMPLE 3. Verify that the function $y = \frac{a}{x+a}$ is a solution of the differential equation $xy_1 + y = y^2$.

Sol. Given, $y = \frac{a}{x+a} \Rightarrow y(x+a) = a$ ...(i)

Differentiating w.r.t. x, we get

$$y \cdot 1 + (x+a)y_1 = 0, \text{ where } y_1 = \frac{dy}{dx}$$

$$\Rightarrow \quad x + a = -\frac{y}{y_1} \quad \text{...(ii)}$$

$$\Rightarrow \quad a = -x - \frac{y}{y_1} \quad \text{...(iii)}$$

Substituting the values of $x + a$ and a into Eq. (i), we get

$$y\left(-\frac{y}{y_1}\right) = -x - \frac{y}{y_1} \Rightarrow y^2 = xy_1 + y$$

Hence, $y = \frac{a}{x+a}$ is a solution of the given differential equation.

EXAMPLE 4. Show that the function $y = ax + 2a^2$ is a solution of the differential equation

$$2\left(\frac{dy}{dx}\right)^2 + x\left(\frac{dy}{dx}\right) - y = 0.$$

Sol. Given function is $y = ax + 2a^2$ ...(i)

Here, order of differential equation is 1.

So, we differentiate Eq. (i) one time.

On differentiating Eq. (i), w.r.t. x, we get

$$\frac{dy}{dx} = a$$

Substituting the value of a in Eq. (i), we get

$$y = x\left(\frac{dy}{dx}\right) + 2\left(\frac{dy}{dx}\right)^2$$

$$\Rightarrow \quad 2\left(\frac{dy}{dx}\right)^2 + x\left(\frac{dy}{dx}\right) - y = 0$$

Hence, $y = ax + 2a^2$ is a solution of differential equation

$$2\left(\frac{dy}{dx}\right)^2 + x\left(\frac{dy}{dx}\right) - y = 0$$

EXAMPLE 5. Show that $y = x^2 + 2x + 1$ is the solution of the initial value problem

$$\frac{d^3y}{dx^3} = 0, \; y(0) = 1, \; y'(0) = 2, \; y''(0) = 2.$$

Sol. Given function is $y = x^2 + 2x + 1$ ...(i)

Here, order of the given differential equation is 3. So, we differentiate Eq. (i) three times.

On differentiating Eq. (i) w.r.t. x three times, we get

$$\frac{dy}{dx} = 2x + 2 \quad \text{...(ii)}$$

$$\frac{d^2y}{dx^2} = 2 \quad \text{...(iii)}$$

$$\frac{d^3y}{dx^3} = 0,$$

which is the given differential equation.

So, $y = x^2 + 2x + 1$ is the solution of given differential equation.

Now, $y(0) = (0)^2 + 2(0) + 1 = 1$ [using Eq. (i)]

$$y'(0) = \left(\frac{dy}{dx}\right)_{\text{at } x=0} = 2(0) + 2 = 2 \quad \text{[using Eq. (ii)]}$$

and $\left(\frac{d^2y}{dx^2}\right)_{\text{at } x=0} = 2$ [using Eq. (iii)]

Hence, $y = x^2 + 2x + 1$ is the solution of initial value problem.

Topic Practice 2

Directions (Q. Nos. 1-5) *Verify that the given function (explicit or implicit) is a solution of the corresponding equation.*

1 $y = nx : x\frac{dy}{dx} = y.$

2 $y = cx + \frac{a}{c} : y = xy_1 + \frac{a}{y_1}$

3 $y = \log x : xy'' + y' = 0.$

4 $y = cx^3 + x^2 + a : y''' = 6c.$

5 $y^2 = 4ax : y = x\frac{dy}{dx} + a\frac{dx}{dy}$

6 Verify that the function $y = \sqrt{a^2 - x^2}, x \in (-a, a)$ is a solution of differential equation

$$x + y\frac{dy}{dx} = 0 \; (y \neq 0).$$

7 Verify that $y = e^{-x} + Ax + B$ is a solution of the differential equation $e^x\left(\frac{d^2y}{dx^2}\right) = 1$.

8 Verify that the function $x^2 = 2y^2 \log y$ is a solution of the differential equation $(x^2 + y^2)\frac{dy}{dx} - xy = 0$.

9 Show that the function $xy = \log y + C$ is a solution of the differential equation $y' = \frac{y^2}{1-xy}, (xy \neq 1)$.

10 Show that $y = Ae^{mx} + Be^{nx}$ is a solution of the differential equation $\frac{d^2y}{dx^2} - (m+n)\frac{dy}{dx} + mny = 0$.

11 Prove that $(x^2 - y^2) = c(x^2 + y^2)^2$ is the general solution of the differential equation

$$(x^3 - 3xy^2)\,dx = (y^3 - 3x^2y)\,dy,$$

where c is a parameter.

Hints & Solutions

1. **Hint** Find $\frac{dy}{dx}$ and put it into the differential equation.
2. **Hint** Put $\frac{dy}{dx} = c$ into the given differential equation.
3. Solve as Example 2.
4. Solve as Example 5.
5. **Hint** Find $\frac{dy}{dx}$ and put it into the differential equation.
6. **Hint** $\frac{dy}{dx} = \frac{-x}{\sqrt{a^2 - x^2}} \Rightarrow \frac{dy}{dx} = \frac{-x}{y} \Rightarrow x + y\frac{dy}{dx} = 0$
7. **Hint** $\frac{dy}{dx} = e^{-x}(-1) + A;\ \frac{d^2y}{dx^2} = e^{-x}$
8. **Hint** $\frac{dy}{dx} = \frac{x}{y(1 + 2\log y)}$

   Now, substitute the value of x^2 from the given equation and $\frac{dy}{dx}$ in LHS.

9. Given, $xy = \log y + C$

   On differentiating both sides w.r.t. x, we get

   $$xy' + y \cdot 1 = \frac{1}{y} \cdot y' + 0$$

   [using product rule of derivative]

   $$\Rightarrow \quad xy' + y = \frac{y'}{y} \Rightarrow xy \cdot y' + y^2 = y'$$

   $$\Rightarrow \quad y^2 = y' - xy \cdot y' \Rightarrow y^2 = y'(1 - xy)$$

   $$\Rightarrow \quad y' = \frac{y^2}{1-xy}, \quad xy \neq 1$$

   Hence proved.

10. Given, $y = Ae^{mx} + Be^{nx}$ ...(i)

    On differentiating both sides of Eq. (i) w.r.t. x, we get

    $$\frac{dy}{dx} = A \cdot e^{mx} \cdot m + Be^{nx} \cdot n \quad \text{...(ii)}$$

    Again, on differentiating both sides of Eq. (ii) w.r.t. x, we get

    $$\frac{d^2y}{dx^2} = m \cdot Ae^{mx} \cdot m + n \cdot Be^{nx} \cdot n$$

    $$\Rightarrow \quad \frac{d^2y}{dx^2} = m^2Ae^{mx} + n^2Be^{nx}$$

    Now, consider LHS $= \frac{d^2y}{dx^2} - (m+n)\frac{dy}{dx} + mny$

    $$= m^2Ae^{mx} + n^2Be^{nx} - (m+n)(mAe^{mx} + nBe^{nx}) + mn(Ae^{mx} + Be^{nx})$$

    $$= m^2Ae^{mx} + n^2Be^{nx} - m^2Ae^{mx} - mnBe^{nx} - nmAe^{mx} - n^2Be^{nx} + mnAe^{mx} + mnBe^{nx}$$

    $= 0 =$ RHS

    Thus, LHS = RHS

    Hence, $y = Ae^{mx} + Be^{nx}$ is a solution of given differential equation. **Hence proved.**

11. The given differential equation is

    $$(x^3 - 3xy^2)\,dx = (y^3 - 3x^2y)\,dy \quad \text{...(i)}$$

    and the given function is

    $$(x^2 - y^2) = c(x^2 + y^2)^2 \quad \text{...(ii)}$$

    On differentiating Eq. (ii) w.r.t. x, we get

    $$2x - 2y\frac{dy}{dx} = 2c(x^2 + y^2)\left(2x + 2y\frac{dy}{dx}\right)$$

    $$\Rightarrow \quad \left(x - y\frac{dy}{dx}\right) = 2c(x^2 + y^2)\left(x + y\frac{dy}{dx}\right) \quad \text{...(iii)}$$

    $$\Rightarrow \quad \left(x - y\frac{dy}{dx}\right) = \frac{2(x^2 - y^2)}{(x^2 + y^2)^2}(x^2 + y^2)\left(x + y\frac{dy}{dx}\right)$$

    [using Eq. (ii)]

    $$\Rightarrow (x^2 + y^2)\left(x - y\frac{dy}{dx}\right) = 2(x^2 - y^2)\left(x + y\frac{dy}{dx}\right)$$

    $$\Rightarrow (x^2 + y^2)x - (x^2 + y^2)y\frac{dy}{dx} = 2(x^2 - y^2)x + 2(x^2 - y^2)y\frac{dy}{dx}$$

    $$\Rightarrow \{x(x^2 + y^2) - 2x(x^2 - y^2)\} = \{2y(x^2 - y^2) + y(x^2 + y^2)\}\frac{dy}{dx}$$

    $$\Rightarrow \quad (3xy^2 - x^3) = (3x^2y - y^3)\frac{dy}{dx}$$

    $$\Rightarrow \quad (x^3 - 3xy^2)\,dx = (y^3 - 3x^2y)\,dy$$

    which is the given differential equation.

    Hence, the given function is the solution of the given differential equation.

Formation of a Differential Equation

Sometimes, a general solution or a equation of family of curves (containing n arbitrary constants or parameters) is given to us and we need to find the differential equation representing this solution or family of curves. For finding such differential equation, we use the following procedure

Formation of Differential Equation for a Curve Having One Arbitrary Constant

Suppose, given equation is $f(x, y, a) = 0$ ...(i)

i.e. the function of x, y and a,

where, a is an arbitrary constant or parameter.

On differentiating Eq. (i) w.r.t. x, we get an equation involving y', y, x and a,

i.e. $g(x, y, y', a) = 0$ ...(ii)

Now, eliminate a from Eqs. (i) and (ii) to get required differential equation of the form $F(x, y, y') = 0$.

EXAMPLE 1. Find the differential equation of the family of curve $y = mx$, where m is an arbitrary constant.

Sol. Given, family of curve is $y = mx$ ...(i)

On differentiating Eq. (i) w.r.t. x, we get

$$\frac{dy}{dx} = m$$

On putting the value of m in Eq. (i), we get

$$y = \frac{dy}{dx} \cdot x$$

$$\Rightarrow \quad x\frac{dy}{dx} - y = 0 \quad \text{[which is free from } m\text{]}$$

which is the required differential equation.

EXAMPLE 2. Find the differential equation of the family of curves $x^2 + y^2 = a^2$, where a is a parameter.

Sol. Given equation of family of curve is

$$x^2 + y^2 = a^2 \quad \text{...(i)}$$

Here, number of parameters = 1.

So, we differentiate Eq. (i) only one time.

On differentiating both sides of Eq. (i) w.r.t. x, we get

$$2x + 2y\frac{dy}{dx} = 0 \Rightarrow x + y\frac{dy}{dx} = 0$$

Now, as no arbitrary constant is present in the above equation, so $x + y\frac{dy}{dx} = 0$ is the required differential equation.

EXAMPLE 3. Form the differential equation representing the family of parabolas having vertex at origin and axis along positive direction of X-axis.

Sol. Let the coordinates of focus of parabola be $(a, 0)$.

Then, equation of family of parabolas is

$$y^2 = 4ax \quad \text{...(i)}$$

where, a is an arbitrary constant.

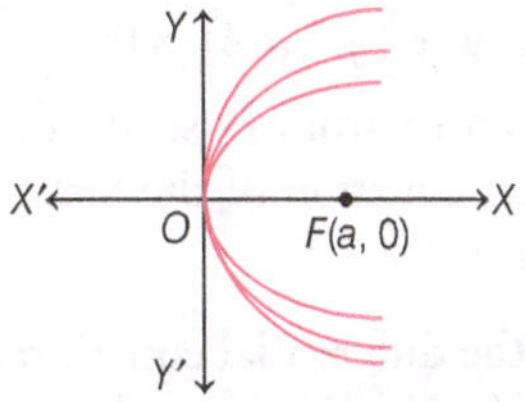

On differentiating both sides of Eq. (i) w.r.t. x, we get

$$2y\frac{dy}{dx} = 4a \Rightarrow a = \frac{\left(y\frac{dy}{dx}\right)}{2}$$

On putting the value of a in Eq. (i), we get

$$y^2 = 4\left[\frac{y(dy/dx)}{2}\right] \cdot x$$

$$\Rightarrow \quad y^2 = 2xy\frac{dy}{dx} \Rightarrow 2xy\frac{dy}{dx} - y^2 = 0$$

EXAMPLE 4. Find the differential equation of system of concentric circles with centre (1, 2).

Sol. The family of concentric circles with centre (1, 2) and radius a is given by

$$(x-1)^2 + (y-2)^2 = a^2$$

$$\Rightarrow \quad x^2 + 1 - 2x + y^2 + 4 - 4y = a^2$$

$$\Rightarrow \quad x^2 + y^2 - 2x - 4y + 5 = a^2 \quad \text{...(i)}$$

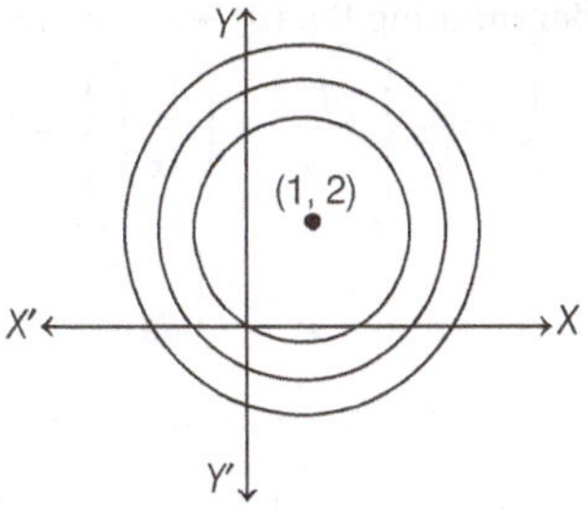

On differentiating Eq. (i) w.r.t. x, we get

$$2x + 2y\frac{dy}{dx} - 2 - 4\frac{dy}{dx} = 0$$

$$\Rightarrow \quad (2y - 4)\frac{dy}{dx} + 2x - 2 = 0$$

$$\Rightarrow \quad (y - 2)\frac{dy}{dx} + (x - 1) = 0$$

Formation of Differential Equation of a Curve Having Two Arbitrary Constants

Suppose, given equation is $f(x, y, a, b) = 0$ ...(i)

where, a and b are arbitrary constants or parameters.

On differentiating Eq. (i) w.r.t. x, we get an equation involving y', x, y, a and b,

i.e. $g(x, y, y', a, b) = 0$ ...(ii)

Again, differentiating Eq. (ii) w.r.t. x, we get an equation of the form

$$h(x, y, y', y'', a, b) = 0 \quad ...(iii)$$

Now, eliminate a and b from Eqs. (i), (ii) and (iii) to get required differential equation of the form $F(x, y, y', y'') = 0$.

EXAMPLE 5. Form the differential equation of the family of hyperbolas having foci on X-axis and centre at the origin.

Sol. Clearly, the equation of family of a hyperbolas having foci on the X-axis and centre at the origin, is

$$\frac{x^2}{a^2} - \frac{y^2}{b^2} = 1 \quad ...(i)$$

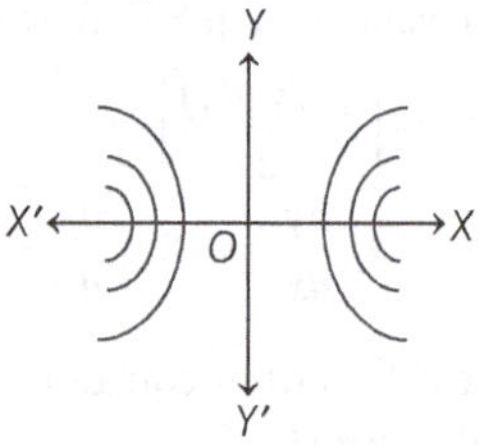

Here, the equation of family of hyperbolas contains two arbitrary constants, therefore we differentiate it two times w.r.t. x.

On differentiating Eq. (i) w.r.t. x, we get

$$\frac{2x}{a^2} - \frac{2y}{b^2}\cdot\frac{dy}{dx} = 0 \Rightarrow \frac{x}{a^2} - \frac{y}{b^2}\cdot\frac{dy}{dx} = 0 \quad ...(ii)$$

Again, differentiating Eq. (ii) w.r.t. x, we get

$$\frac{1}{a^2} - \frac{1}{b^2}\left\{y\frac{d^2y}{dx^2} + \left(\frac{dy}{dx}\right)^2\right\} = 0$$

$$\Rightarrow \quad \frac{1}{a^2} = \frac{1}{b^2}\left\{y\frac{d^2y}{dx^2} + \left(\frac{dy}{dx}\right)^2\right\}$$

On putting the value of $\frac{1}{a^2}$ in Eq. (ii), we get

$$\frac{x}{b^2}\left\{y\frac{d^2y}{dx^2} + \left(\frac{dy}{dx}\right)^2\right\} - \frac{y}{b^2}\cdot\frac{dy}{dx} = 0$$

$$\Rightarrow \quad \frac{1}{b^2}\left\{xy\frac{d^2y}{dx^2} + x\left(\frac{dy}{dx}\right)^2 - y\frac{dy}{dx}\right\} = 0$$

$$\Rightarrow \quad xy\frac{d^2y}{dx^2} + x\left(\frac{dy}{dx}\right)^2 - y\frac{dy}{dx} = 0$$

which is the required differential equation.

EXAMPLE 6. Find the differential equation of the family of curves $y = Ax - \frac{B}{x}$, where A and B are arbitrary constants.

Sol. Given equation of family of curve has two arbitrary constants so we will differentiate it two times and then eliminate A and B.

Given equation of family of curve is $y = Ax - \frac{B}{x}$ ...(i)

Here, number of arbitrary constant = 2.

So, we differentiate Eq. (i) two times.

On differentiating Eq. (i) w.r.t. x two times, we get

$$\frac{dy}{dx} = A - \frac{B}{x^2} \quad ...(ii)$$

and $$\frac{d^2y}{dx^2} = -2\frac{B}{x^3} \Rightarrow B = -\frac{x^3}{2}\cdot\frac{d^2y}{dx^2}$$

On putting this value in Eq. (ii), we get

$$\frac{dy}{dx} = A - \frac{1}{x^2}\left(-\frac{x^3}{2}\cdot\frac{d^2y}{dx^2}\right)$$

$$\Rightarrow \quad \frac{dy}{dx} = A - \frac{x}{2}\cdot\frac{d^2y}{dx^2} \Rightarrow A = \frac{dy}{dx} + \frac{x}{2}\cdot\frac{d^2y}{dx^2}$$

On putting the values of A and B in Eq. (i), we get

$$y = x\left(\frac{dy}{dx} + \frac{x}{2}\frac{d^2y}{dx^2}\right) + \frac{x^2}{2}\cdot\frac{d^2y}{dx^2} \Rightarrow x^2\frac{d^2y}{dx^2} + x\frac{dy}{dx} = y$$

which is the required differential equation.

EXAMPLE 7. Find the differential equation of all straight lines, which are at a unit distance from origin.

Sol. Let the family of straight line be

$$ax + by = 1 \quad ...(i)$$

$\because$ Eq. (i) is at unit distance from origin.

$$\therefore \quad \frac{|a\times 0 + b\times 0 - 1|}{\sqrt{a^2+b^2}} = 1 \Rightarrow \frac{1}{\sqrt{a^2+b^2}} = 1$$

$$\Rightarrow \quad a^2 + b^2 = 1 \quad ...(ii)$$

On differentiating Eq. (i) w.r.t. x, we get

$$a + b\frac{dy}{dx} = 0 \Rightarrow a = -b\frac{dy}{dx} \quad ...(iii)$$

From Eqs. (ii) and (iii), we get

$$b^2\left\{1 + \left(\frac{dy}{dx}\right)^2\right\} = 1 \quad ...(iv)$$

Now, equating the value of a from Eqs. (i) and (iii), we get

$$\frac{1-by}{x} = -b\frac{dy}{dx} \Rightarrow b\left(y - x\frac{dy}{dx}\right) = 1 \Rightarrow b = \frac{1}{y - x\frac{dy}{dx}}$$

On putting the value of b in Eq. (iv), we get

$$1 + \left(\frac{dy}{dx}\right)^2 = \left(x\frac{dy}{dx} - y\right)^2$$

which is the required differential equation.

Topic Practice 3

1 Find the differential equation of the family of curves given by $x^2 + y^2 = 2ax$.

2 Form the differential equation of the family of circles touching X-axis at the origin.

Or Form the differential equation of all circles which pass through the origin and whose centre lies on Y-axis.

3 Form the differential equation of the family of circles touching the Y-axis at the origin.

4 Find the differential equation of system of concentric circles with centre (1, 2).

5 Form the differential equation of the family of all circles in first quadrant and touching the coordinate axes. **[CBSE 2024]**

6 Form the differential equation of the family of circles in the second quadrant and touching the coordinates axes.

7 Form the differential equation of the family of parabolas having vertex at origin and axis along positive Y-axis.

8 Find the differential equation representing the family of curves $V = \frac{A}{r} + B$, where A and B are arbitrary constants.

9 Find the differential equation representing the family of curves $y = ae^{bx+5}$, where a and b are arbitrary constants.

10 Form the differential equation for the family of curves $ay^2 = (x - c)^3$, where c is a parameter.

11 Form the differential equation for the family of the curves $y^2 = a(b - x)(b + x)$, where a and b are arbitrary constants.

12 Form the differential equation of the family of all circles of radius r.

13 Form the differential equation of the family of ellipses having foci on Y-axis and centre at origin.

14 Form the differential equation representing the family of ellipses having foci on X-axis and centre at the origin.

15 Find the differential equation of all the parabolas with latusrectum '$4a$' and whose axes are parallel to positive X-axis.

Hints & Solutions

1. Given curve is $x^2 + y^2 = 2ax$ ... (i)

On differentiating both sides of Eq. (i) w.r.t. x, we get

$$2x + 2y\frac{dy}{dx} = 2a \Rightarrow x + y\frac{dy}{dx} = a \Rightarrow a = x + y\frac{dy}{dx}$$

On putting the value of a in Eq. (i), we get

$$x^2 + y^2 = 2\left(x + y\frac{dy}{dx}\right)x$$

$$\Rightarrow \quad x^2 + y^2 = 2x^2 + 2xy\frac{dy}{dx}$$

$$\therefore \quad 2xy\frac{dy}{dx} + x^2 - y^2 = 0$$

2. Hint Let a be the radius of family of circles. Then, family of circles touching X-axis at the origin is $x^2 + (y - a)^2 = a^2$ or $x^2 + y^2 - 2ay = 0$.

Further, solve as Question 1. **Ans.** $\frac{dy}{dx} = \frac{2xy}{x^2 - y^2}$

3. Hint Equation of family of circles touching Y-axis at origin is

$$(x - a)^2 + y^2 = a^2 \Rightarrow x^2 + y^2 - 2ax = 0$$

where a is radius of circle. Further, solve as Question 1.
Ans. $2xyy' + x^2 = y^2$

4. Hint Equation of system of concentric circles with centre (1, 2) is $(x - 1)^2 + (y - 2)^2 = a^2$,

where a is radius of circle.

Ans. $(x - 1) + (y - 2)\frac{dy}{dx} = 0$

5. Clearly, equation of family of all circles lying in first quadrant and touching the coordinate axes is

$$(x - a)^2 + (y - a)^2 = a^2, \quad \text{...(i)}$$

where a is a parameter.

Since, this equation contains one arbitrary constant, so we will differentiate it only once.

On differentiating Eq. (i) w.r.t. x, we get

$$2(x - a) + 2(y - a)\frac{dy}{dx} = 0$$

$$\Rightarrow \quad (x - a) + (y - a)\frac{dy}{dx} = 0$$

$$\Rightarrow \quad (x - a) + (y - a)p = 0, \text{ where } \frac{dy}{dx} = p$$

$$\Rightarrow \quad x + yp = a(1 + p)$$

$$\Rightarrow \quad a = \frac{(x + yp)}{(1 + p)} \quad \text{... (ii)}$$

On substituting the value of a from Eq. (ii) in Eq. (i), we get

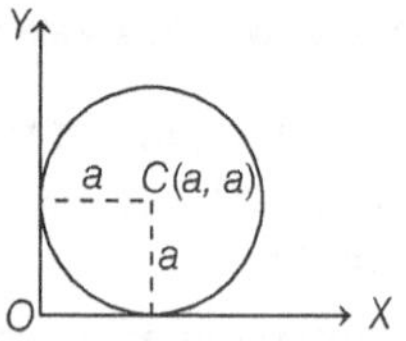

$$\left(x - \frac{x+yp}{1+p}\right)^2 + \left(y - \frac{x+yp}{1+p}\right)^2 = \left(\frac{x+yp}{1+p}\right)^2$$

$$\Rightarrow \quad (xp - yp)^2 + (y-x)^2 = (x+yp)^2$$

$$\Rightarrow \quad (x-y)^2 p^2 + (x-y)^2 = (x+yp)^2$$

$$\Rightarrow \quad (x-y)^2 (p^2+1) = (x+yp)^2$$

$$\Rightarrow \quad (x-y)^2 \left\{\left(\frac{dy}{dx}\right)^2 + 1\right\} = \left(x + y\frac{dy}{dx}\right)^2 \quad \left[\text{where, } \frac{dy}{dx} = p\right]$$

which is the required differential equation.

6. **Hint** Equation of circle will be

$$(x+a)^2 + (y-a)^2 = a^2$$

Ans. $(x+y)^2 [(y')^2 + 1] = (x + yy')^2$

7. **Hint** Equation of family of parabolas having vertex at origin and axis along positive Y-axis is $x^2 = 4ay$.

Ans. $xy' - 2y = 0$

8. We have, equation of family of curves

$V = \frac{A}{r} + B$, where A and B are arbitrary constants.

On differentiating both sides w.r.t. r, we get

$$\frac{dV}{dr} = \frac{-A}{r^2} + 0 = -\frac{A}{r^2} \Rightarrow \frac{dV}{dr} = \frac{-A}{r^2} \quad \text{...(i)}$$

Now, again differentiating Eq. (i) w.r.t. r, we get

$$\frac{d^2V}{dr^2} = \frac{2A}{r^3}$$

$$\Rightarrow \quad \frac{d^2V}{dr^2} = \frac{2}{r^3} \times \left(-r^2 \frac{dV}{dr}\right) \quad \text{[from Eq. (i)]}$$

$$\Rightarrow \quad \frac{d^2V}{dr^2} = -\frac{2}{r}\frac{dV}{dr}$$

Thus, the required differential equation is

$$\frac{d^2V}{dr^2} + \frac{2}{r}\frac{dV}{dr} = 0$$

9. We have, $\quad y = ae^{bx+5} \quad$ ...(i)

On differentiating both sides w.r.t. x, we get

$$\frac{dy}{dx} = a\,e^{bx+5} \cdot b$$

$$\Rightarrow \quad \frac{dy}{dx} = by \quad \text{[using Eq. (i)] ...(ii)}$$

Again, on differentiating both sides w.r.t. x, we get

$$\frac{d^2y}{dx^2} = b\frac{dy}{dx}$$

$$\Rightarrow \quad \frac{d^2y}{dx^2} = \left(\frac{1}{y}\cdot\frac{dy}{dx}\right)\left(\frac{dy}{dx}\right) \quad \text{[using Eq. (ii)]}$$

$$\Rightarrow \quad \frac{d^2y}{dx^2} = \frac{1}{y}\left(\frac{dy}{dx}\right)^2 \Rightarrow y\frac{d^2y}{dx^2} - \left(\frac{dy}{dx}\right)^2 = 0,$$

which is the required differential equation.

10. Here, given equation of family of curves is

$$ay^2 = (x-c)^3 \quad \text{...(i)}$$

where, c is a parameter.

Since, the given equation has only one parameter, therefore we shall differentiate it only once.

On differentiating Eq. (i), w.r.t. x, we get

$$2ayy_1 = 3(x-c)^2 \quad \text{...(ii)}$$

On dividing Eq. (i) by Eq. (ii), we get

$$\frac{ay^2}{2ayy_1} = \frac{(x-c)^3}{3(x-c)^2}$$

$$\Rightarrow \quad \frac{y}{2y_1} = \frac{x-c}{3} \Rightarrow x - c = \frac{3y}{2y_1}$$

On putting the value of $(x-c)$ in Eq. (i), we get

$$ay^2 = \left(\frac{3y}{2y_1}\right)^3 \Rightarrow ay^2 = \frac{27y^3}{8y_1^3}$$

$$\Rightarrow \quad 8ay_1^3 = 27y \Rightarrow 8ay_1^3 - 27y = 0,$$

which is the required differential equation.

11. Given equation of family of curves is

$$y^2 = a(b-x)(b+x),$$

which can be rewritten as

$$y^2 = a(b^2 - x^2) \Rightarrow y^2 = ab^2 - ax^2 \quad \text{...(i)}$$

Since, the given equation has two parameters, therefore we shall differentiate it two times.

On differentiating Eq. (i) w.r.t. x, we get

$$2yy_1 = -2ax \Rightarrow yy_1 = -ax \quad \text{...(ii)}$$

Again, differentiating Eq. (ii) w.r.t. x, we get

$$yy_2 + (y_1)^2 = -a$$

On putting the value of $(-a)$ in Eq. (ii), we get

$$yy_1 = [yy_2 + (y_1)^2]\,x$$

$$\Rightarrow \quad yy_1 = xyy_2 + x(y_1)^2$$

$$\Rightarrow \quad xy\frac{d^2y}{dx^2} + x\left(\frac{dy}{dx}\right)^2 - y\left(\frac{dy}{dx}\right) = 0,$$

which is the required differential equation.

12. Clearly, the equation of the family of all circles of radius r is

$$(x-a)^2 + (y-b)^2 = r^2 \quad \text{...(i)}$$

where, a and b are parameters.

Since, the equation of family of circles contains two arbitrary constants, therefore we shall differentiate it two times.

On differentiating Eq. (i) w.r.t. x, we get

$$2(x-a) + 2(y-b)\,y_1 = 0$$

$$\Rightarrow \quad (x-a) + (y-b)y_1 = 0 \quad \text{...(ii)}$$

Again, on differentiating Eq. (ii) w.r.t. x, we get

$$1+(y-b)y_2+(y_1)^2=0 \Rightarrow (y-b)y_2=-[1+(y_1)^2]$$

$$\Rightarrow \quad (y-b)=-\frac{[1+(y_1)^2]}{y_2} \quad ...(iii)$$

On putting the value of $(y-b)$ in Eq. (ii), we get

$$(x-a)+\left[\frac{-[1+(y_1)^2]}{y_2}\right]y_1=0$$

$$\Rightarrow \quad (x-a)=\frac{(1+(y_1)^2)y_1}{y_2} \quad ...(iv)$$

Now, by using Eqs. (iii) and (iv) in Eq. (i), we get

$$\left[\frac{\{1+(y_1)^2\}y_1}{y_2}\right]^2+\left[\frac{-\{1+(y_1)^2\}}{y_2}\right]^2=r^2$$

$$\Rightarrow \quad \frac{y_1^2(1+y_1^2)^2}{y_2^2}+\frac{(1+y_1^2)^2}{y_2^2}=r^2$$

$$\Rightarrow \quad y_1^2(1+y_1^2)^2+(1+y_1^2)^2=y_2^2r^2$$

$$\Rightarrow \quad (1+y_1^2)^2(y_1^2+1)=y_2^2r^2$$

$$\Rightarrow \quad (1+y_1^2)^3=y_2^2r^2$$

which is the required differential equation.

13. Equation of family of ellipses is of the form

$$\frac{x^2}{b^2}+\frac{y^2}{a^2}=1, [a>b] \quad ...(i)$$

[since, foci is on Y-axis, so we draw a vertical ellipse]

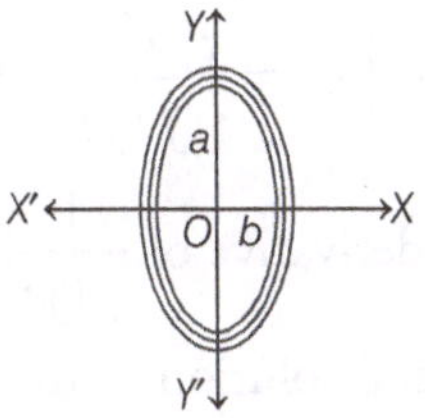

On differentiating both sides of Eq. (i) w.r.t. x, we get

$$\frac{1}{b^2}\cdot 2x+\frac{1}{a^2}\cdot 2yy'=0$$

$$\Rightarrow \quad \frac{yy'}{x}=-\frac{a^2}{b^2} \quad ...(ii)$$

Again, on differentiating both sides of Eq. (ii) w.r.t. x, we get

$$\frac{x\frac{d}{dx}(yy')-yy'\frac{d}{dx}(x)}{x^2}=0$$

$$\left[\text{using quotient rule of derivative, } \frac{d}{dx}\left(\frac{u}{v}\right)=\frac{v\frac{d}{dx}(u)-u\frac{d}{dx}(v)}{v^2}\right]$$

$$\Rightarrow \quad \frac{x[yy''+(y')^2]-yy'\cdot 1}{x^2}=0$$

$$\left[\text{using product rule of derivative, } \frac{d}{dx}(u\cdot v)=\left(u\frac{d}{dx}(v)+v\frac{d}{dx}(u)\right)\right]$$

$$\Rightarrow \quad xyy''+x(y')^2-yy'=0,$$

which is the required differential equation.

14. **Hint** Let the equation of ellipses be $\frac{x^2}{a^2}+\frac{y^2}{b^2}=1, a>b$

Further, solve as Question 13.

Ans. $xyy''+x(y')^2-yy'=0$

15. **Hint** Equation of family of parabolas with latusrectum $4a$ and having axes parallel to positive X-axis is $(y-k)^2=4a(x-h)$, where h and k are arbitrary constants. **Ans.** $2ay_2+y_1^3=0$

Methods of Solving First Order and First Degree Differential Equations

In this topic, we will learn various types of techniques of obtaining solutions of various types of differential equations.

Differential Equations of the Type $\frac{dy}{dx}=f(x)$

In this types of differential equations, we integrate both sides to obtain general solutions.

Let $$\frac{dy}{dx}=f(x)$$

$$\Rightarrow \quad dy=f(x)\,dx$$

Integrating both sides, we obtain

$$\int dy=\int f(x)\,dx+C \Rightarrow y=F(x)+C,$$

where $F(x)$ is the anti-derivative of $f(x)$. And the final solution is the general solution of the differential equation.

EXAMPLE 1. Solve the following differential equation

(i) $(e^x+e^{-x})\frac{dy}{dx}=(e^x-e^{-x})$ (ii) $\frac{dy}{dx}=x\log x$

(iii) $(x+3)\frac{dy}{dx}=x^2+6x-9,\ x\neq -3$

Sol. (i) We have, $(e^x + e^{-x})\dfrac{dy}{dx} = (e^x - e^{-x})$

$$\Rightarrow \frac{dy}{dx} = \frac{e^x - e^{-x}}{e^x + e^{-x}} \Rightarrow dy = \frac{e^x - e^{-x}}{e^x + e^{-x}}\,dx$$

Integrating both sides, we get

$$\int dy = \int \frac{e^x - e^{-x}}{e^x + e^{-x}}\,dx$$

Let $e^x + e^{-x} = t \Rightarrow (e^x - e^{-x})dx = dt$

$$\Rightarrow \int dy = \int \frac{dt}{t} \Rightarrow y = \log|t| + C$$

$$\Rightarrow y = \log|e^x + e^{-x}| + C$$

Which is required solution.

(ii) We have, $\dfrac{dy}{dx} = x\log x \Rightarrow dy = x\log x\,dx$

Integrating both sides, we get

$$\int dy = \int \underset{\text{II}}{x}\underset{\text{I}}{\log x}\,dx$$

$$\Rightarrow y = \log x\left(\frac{x^2}{2}\right) - \int\left(\frac{x^2}{2}\cdot\frac{1}{x}\right)dx + C$$

$$= \frac{x^2(2\ln x - 1)}{4} + C$$

(iii) We have, $(x+3)\dfrac{dy}{dx} = x^2 + 6x - 9$

$$\Rightarrow \frac{dy}{dx} = \frac{x^2 + 6x - 9}{x+3}$$

$$\Rightarrow dy = \frac{x^2 + 6x + 9 - 18}{x+3}\,dx$$

$$\Rightarrow dy = \frac{(x+3)^2 - 18}{(x+3)}\,dx$$

$$\Rightarrow dy = \left\{x + 3 - \frac{18}{x+3}\right\}dx$$

Integrating both sides, we get

$$\int dy = \int\left(x + 3 - \frac{18}{x+3}\right)dx$$

$$\Rightarrow y = \frac{x^2}{2} + 3x - 18\log_e|x+3| + C$$

Here $x \neq -3$

Hence, $y = \dfrac{x^2}{2} + 3x - 18\log_e|x+3| + C, x \in R - \{3\}$ is the solution of the given differential equation.

EXAMPLE 2. Solve the differential equation

$$e^{dy/dx} = x + 1;\quad y(0) = 5.$$

Sol. We have, $e^{dy/dx} = x + 1$

$$\Rightarrow \frac{dy}{dx} = \log(x+1) \Rightarrow dy = \log(x+1)\,dx$$

On integrating both sides, we get

$$\int dy = \int \log(x+1)\,dx$$

$$\Rightarrow y = \int \underset{\text{I}}{\log(x+1)}\,.\,\underset{\text{II}}{1}\,dx$$

$$\Rightarrow y = x.\log(x+1) - \int \frac{x}{x+1}\,dx$$

$$\Rightarrow y = x\log(x+1) - \int \frac{x+1-1}{x+1}\,dx$$

$$\Rightarrow y = x\log(x+1) - \int\left(1 - \frac{1}{x+1}\right)dx$$

$$\Rightarrow y = x\log(x+1) - x + \log(x+1) + C \quad \text{...(i)}$$

Now, it is given that $y(0) = 5$ i.e. when $x = 0$, we have

$$y = 5$$

$$\therefore \quad 5 = \log 1 + C \Rightarrow C = 5 \quad \text{...(ii)}$$

From Eqs. (i) and (ii), we have

$$y = x\log(x+1) - x + \log(x+1) + 5$$

Differential Equations of the Type $\dfrac{dy}{dx} = f(y)$

In this type of differential equation, we integrate both sides to obtain general solutions.

Let $\dfrac{dy}{dx} = f(y) \Rightarrow \dfrac{dy}{f(y)} = dx$

Integrating both sides, we obtain

$$\int \frac{dy}{f(y)} = \int dx \Rightarrow \int dx = \int \frac{dy}{f(y)} \Rightarrow x = F(y) + C,$$

where $F(y)$ is anti-derivative of $\dfrac{1}{f(y)}$. And the final solution is the general solution of the differential equation.

EXAMPLE 3. Solve the following differential equation

(i) $\dfrac{dy}{dx} = \dfrac{1+y^2}{y^3}$ (ii) $\dfrac{dy}{dx} + 2y^2 = 0$

Sol. (i) We have, $\dfrac{dy}{dx} = \dfrac{1+y^2}{y^3}$

$$\Rightarrow \frac{dx}{dy} = \frac{y^3}{1+y^2} \Rightarrow dx = \frac{y^3}{1+y^2}\,dy$$

Integrating both the sides, we get

$$\int dx = \int \frac{y^3}{1+y^2}\,dy \Rightarrow x = \int\left(y - \frac{y}{1+y^2}\right)dy$$

$$\Rightarrow x = \frac{y^2}{2} - \frac{1}{2}\log(1+y^2) + C$$

Which is the required solution.

(ii) We have, $\frac{dy}{dx} + 2y^2 = 0 \Rightarrow \frac{dy}{dx} = -2y^2$

$$\Rightarrow \quad \frac{dy}{-2y^2} = dx \Rightarrow dx = -\frac{1}{2}\frac{dy}{y^2}$$

Integrating both sides w.r.t. y, we get

$$\int dx = -\frac{1}{2}\int \frac{dy}{y^2}$$

$$\Rightarrow \quad x = -\frac{1}{2} \cdot \frac{y^{-1}}{(-1)} + C$$

$$\Rightarrow \quad x = \frac{1}{2y} + C,$$

which is the required solution.

Differential Equation with Variables Separable

A first order and first degree differential equation $\frac{dy}{dx} = F(x, y)$ is in the form of variable separable, if the function F can be expressed as the product of the functions of x and the functions of y.

i.e. $$\frac{dy}{dx} = h(y) \cdot g(x) \quad \text{..(i)}$$

If $h(y) \neq 0$, then separate the variables, i.e. write Eq. (i) as

$$\frac{1}{h(y)} dy = g(x) dx$$

On integrating both sides, we get

$$\int \frac{1}{h(y)} dy = \int g(x) dx \quad \text{or} \quad H(y) = G(x) + C$$

which is the required solution of given differential equation, where $H(y)$, $G(x)$ are the anti-derivatives of $\frac{1}{h(y)}$, $g(x)$ respectively and C is the arbitrary constant.

EXAMPLE 4. Solve the differential equation $x\frac{dy}{dx} + y = 1$.

Sol. Given differential equation is $x\frac{dy}{dx} + y = 1$

$$\Rightarrow \quad x\frac{dy}{dx} = 1 - y \Rightarrow \frac{dy}{(1-y)} = \frac{dx}{x}$$

Integrating both sides, we get

$$\int \frac{dy}{(1-y)} = \int \frac{dx}{x} \Rightarrow -\log|1-y| = \log|x| - \log|c|$$

$$\Rightarrow \quad \log|x| = \log|c| - \log|1-y|$$

$$\Rightarrow \quad \log|x| = \log\left|\frac{c}{1-y}\right| \Rightarrow x = \frac{c}{1-y},$$

which is the required solution.

EXAMPLE 5. Find the general solution of the differential equation $(x+2)\frac{dy}{dx} = x^2 + 5x$, $x \neq -2$.

Sol. Given differential equation is $(x+2)\frac{dy}{dx} = x^2 + 5x$

$$\Rightarrow \quad dy = \frac{x^2 + 5x}{(x+2)} dx \quad \text{[separating the variables]}$$

On integrating both sides, we get

$$\int dy = \int \frac{x^2 + 5x}{(x+2)} dx \Rightarrow y = \int \left\{(x+3) - \frac{6}{(x+2)}\right\} dx$$

[dividing $(x^2 + 5x)$ by $(x + 2)$]

$$\Rightarrow \quad y = \frac{x^2}{2} + 3x - 6\log|x+2| + C,$$

which is the required general solution.

EXAMPLE 6. Solve the differential equation

$$\frac{dy}{dx} = e^{x-y} + x^2 e^{-y}.$$

Sol. Given differential equation is

$$\frac{dy}{dx} = e^{x-y} + x^2 e^{-y} \Rightarrow \frac{dy}{dx} = e^{-y}(e^x + x^2)$$

$$\Rightarrow \quad \frac{1}{e^{-y}} dy = (e^x + x^2)\, dx \quad \text{[separating the variables]}$$

$$\Rightarrow \quad e^y dy = (e^x + x^2) dx$$

On integrating both sides, we get

$$\int e^y dy = \int (e^x + x^2)\, dx$$

$$\Rightarrow \quad e^y = e^x + \frac{x^3}{3} + C$$

$$\left[\because \int e^x\, dx = e^x \text{ and } \int x^n\, dx = \frac{x^{n+1}}{n+1}\right]$$

which is the required solution.

EXAMPLE 7. Solve the differential equation

$$\log\left(\frac{dy}{dx}\right) = ax + by.$$

Sol. Given differential equation is $\log\left(\frac{dy}{dx}\right) = ax + by$

$$\Rightarrow \quad \frac{dy}{dx} = e^{ax+by}$$

$$\Rightarrow \quad \frac{dy}{dx} = e^{ax} \cdot e^{by}$$

$$\Rightarrow \quad e^{-by} dy = e^{ax}\, dx$$

$$\Rightarrow \quad \int e^{-by} dy = \int e^{ax} dx$$

$$\Rightarrow \quad -\frac{1}{b}e^{-by} = \frac{1}{a}e^{ax} + C$$

This is the required solution.

EXAMPLE 8. Solve the differential equation
$$\frac{dy}{dx} = xy + x + y + 1.$$

Sol. Given differential equation is $\frac{dy}{dx} = xy + x + y + 1$

$$\frac{dy}{dx} = x(y+1) + 1(y+1) = (x+1)(y+1)$$

On separating the variables, we get
$$\frac{dy}{(y+1)} = (x+1)\,dx \quad \text{...(i)}$$

On integrating Eq. (i), we get
$$\int \frac{dy}{(y+1)} = \int (x+1)\,dx$$
$$\Rightarrow \quad \log|y+1| = \frac{x^2}{2} + x + C,$$
which is the required solution of the given differential equation.

EXAMPLE 9. Solve the differential equation
$$(1-x)\,dy - (3+y)\,dx = 0.$$

Sol. Given differential equation is
$$(1-x)\,dy - (3+y)\,dx = 0$$
$$\Rightarrow \quad (1-x)dy = (3+y)dx$$

On separating the variables, we get
$$\frac{dy}{3+y} = \frac{dx}{1-x}$$

On integrating both sides, we get
$$\int \frac{dy}{3+y} = \int \frac{dx}{1-x}$$
$$\Rightarrow \quad \log|3+y| = -\log|1-x| + \log C$$
$$\Rightarrow \quad \log|1-x| + \log|3+y| = \log C$$
$$\Rightarrow \quad \log|(1-x)(3+y)| = \log C$$
$$[\because \log m + \log n = \log mn]$$
$$\Rightarrow \quad (1-x)(3+y) = C$$
which is the required solution of the given differential equation.

EXAMPLE 10. Find the particular solution of the differential equation $x\sqrt{1+y^2}\,dx + y\sqrt{1+x^2}\,dy = 0$ given that $y = \sqrt{3}$, when $x = 0$.

Sol. Given differential equation is
$$x\sqrt{1+y^2}\,dx + y\sqrt{1+x^2}\,dy = 0$$
$$\Rightarrow \quad y\sqrt{1+x^2}\,dy = -x\sqrt{1+y^2}\,dx$$
$$\Rightarrow \quad \frac{y\,dy}{\sqrt{1+y^2}} = -\frac{x\,dx}{\sqrt{1+x^2}}$$

On integrating both sides, we get
$$\Rightarrow \quad \int \frac{y}{\sqrt{1+y^2}}\cdot dy = -\int \frac{x}{\sqrt{1+x^2}}\cdot dx$$
$$\Rightarrow \quad \frac{1}{2}\int (1+y^2)^{-1/2}(2y)dy = -\frac{1}{2}\int (1+x^2)^{-1/2}\cdot(2x)dx$$
$$\Rightarrow \quad \frac{1}{2}\cdot\frac{(1+y^2)^{1/2}}{\frac{1}{2}} = -\frac{1}{2}\cdot\frac{(1+x^2)^{1/2}}{\frac{1}{2}} + C$$
$$\Rightarrow \quad \sqrt{1+y^2} = -\sqrt{1+x^2} + C$$
$$\Rightarrow \quad \sqrt{1+x^2} + \sqrt{1+y^2} = C \quad \text{...(i)}$$
$$\because \quad y = \sqrt{3}, \text{ when } x = 0$$
$$\Rightarrow \quad 1 + \sqrt{4} = c \Rightarrow c = 3$$

Put $c = 3$ into Eq. (i), we get
$$\sqrt{1+x^2} + \sqrt{1+y^2} = 3,$$
which is a particular solution of given differential equation.

EXAMPLE 11. Find the particular solution of differential equation $\frac{dy}{dx} = -4xy^2$, given that $y = 1$, when $x = 0$.

Sol. Given differential equation is
$$\frac{dy}{dx} = -4xy^2 \quad \text{...(i)}$$
$$\Rightarrow \quad \frac{dy}{y^2} = -4x\,dx \quad \text{[separating the variables]}$$

On integrating both sides, we get
$$\int \frac{dy}{y^2} = -\int 4x\,dx \Rightarrow -\frac{1}{y} = -2x^2 + C$$
$$\Rightarrow \quad y = \frac{1}{2x^2 - C} \quad \text{...(ii)}$$
which is a general solution of the given differential equation.

Also, given $y = 1$, when $x = 0$

On putting $x = 0$ and $y = 1$ in Eq. (ii), we get
$$1 = \frac{1}{2(0)^2 - C} \Rightarrow C = -1$$

On putting the value of C in Eq. (ii), we get
$$y = \frac{1}{2x^2 - (-1)} \Rightarrow y = \frac{1}{2x^2 + 1}$$
which is a particular solution of given differential equation.

EXAMPLE 12. For the differential equation given below, find a particular solution satisfying the given condition
$(x+1)\frac{dy}{dx} = 2e^{-y} + 1;\ y = 0$ when $x = 0$.

Sol. Given differential equation is
$$(x+1)\frac{dy}{dx} = 2e^{-y} + 1 \Rightarrow (x+1)\frac{dy}{dx} = \frac{2+e^y}{e^y}$$
$$\Rightarrow \quad \frac{e^y}{e^y + 2}dy = \frac{dx}{x+1}$$

On integrating both sides, we get

$$\int \frac{e^y}{e^y+2}dy = \int \frac{dx}{x+1}$$

$\Rightarrow$ $\log(e^y+2) = \log(x+1) + \log C$

$\Rightarrow$ $\log(e^y+2) = \log C(x+1)$

$\Rightarrow$ $e^y + 2 = C(x+1)$ ...(i)

Also given $y = 0$, when $x = 0$

On putting $x = 0$ and $y = 0$ in Eq. (i), we get

$$e^0 + 2 = C(0+1)$$

$\Rightarrow$ $C = 1 + 2 = 3$

On putting C in Eq. (i), we get

$$e^y + 2 = 3(x+1)$$

$\Rightarrow$ $e^y = 3x + 3 - 2$

$\Rightarrow$ $e^y = 3x + 1 \Rightarrow y = \log(3x+1)$

Topic Practice 4

1 Solve the following differential equation
$$\frac{dy}{dx} - \frac{x}{x^2+1} = 0$$

2 Solve the following differential equation
$x(x^2-1)\frac{dy}{dx} = 1$, $y = 0$, when $x = 2$

3 Given that $\frac{dy}{dx} = e^{-2y}$ and $y = 0$, when $x = 5$. Find the value of x, when $y = 3$.

4 Solve the following differential equations.

(i) $\frac{dy}{dx} = x^3 e^{-2y}$

(ii) $(x+1)\frac{dy}{dx} = 2xy$

(iii) $\frac{dy}{dx} = \frac{xy+y}{xy+x}$

(iv) $xy\frac{dy}{dx} = (x+2)(y+2)$

(v) $\frac{dy}{dx} = 1 - x + y - xy$

(vi) $y\log y\,dx - x\,dy = 0$

(vii) $\log\left(\frac{dy}{dx}\right) = 3x + 4y$

(viii) $(x-1)\frac{dy}{dx} = 2x^3 y$

5 Find the particular solution of the differential equation $e^x\sqrt{1-y^2}dx + \frac{y}{x}dy = 0$, given that $y = 1$, when $x = 0$.

6 Find the particular solution of the differential equation $\frac{dy}{dx} = 1 + x + y + xy$, given that $y = 0$, when $x = 1$.

7 Find the particular solution of the differential equation $x(1+y^2)\,dx - y(1+x^2)\,dy = 0$, given that $y = 1$, when $x = 0$.

8 Find the particular solution of the differential equation $(1-y^2)(1+\log|x|)\,dx + 2xy\,dy = 0$, given that $y = 0$ when $x = 1$.

9 Find a particular solution of the differential equation $(x-y)(dx+dy) = dx - dy$, given that $y = -1$, when $x = 0$.

10 Find the general solution of the following differential equation $\left(y - x\frac{dy}{dx}\right) = a\left(y^2 + \frac{dy}{dx}\right)$.

11 Find the equation of a curve passing through the point $(0, -2)$, given that at any point (x, y) on the curve, the product of the slope of its tangent and y-coordinate of the point is equal to the x-coordinate of the point.

12 At any point (x, y) of a curve, the slope of the tangent is twice the slope of the line segment joining the point of contact to the point $(-4, -3)$. Find the equation of the curve given that it passes through $(-2, 1)$.

13 Find the equation of a curve whose tangent at any point on it, different from origin, has slope $y + \frac{y}{x}$.

14 Find the equation of a curve passing through the point $(1, 1)$, if the tangent drawn at any point $P(x, y)$ on the curve meets the coordinate axes at A and B such that P is the mid-point of AB.

15 Find the equation of the curve passes through the point $(1, 0)$, if the slope of the tangent to the curve at any point (x, y) is $\frac{y-1}{x^2+x}$.

Hints & Solutions

1. Given differential equation is

$$\frac{dy}{dx} - \frac{x}{x^2+1} = 0 \Rightarrow \frac{dy}{dx} = \frac{x}{x^2+1}$$

On separating the variables, we get

$$dy = \frac{x}{x^2+1}\,dx$$

On integrating both sides, we get

$$\int dy = \int \frac{x}{x^2+1}dx \Rightarrow \int dy = \frac{1}{2}\int \frac{2x}{x^2+1}\,dx$$

$$\left[\begin{aligned} &\text{put } x^2+1 = t \Rightarrow 2x\,dx = dt \\ &\therefore \int \frac{2x}{x^2+1}dx = \int \frac{1}{t}\,dt = \log|t| + C \\ &\qquad = \log|x^2+1| + C \end{aligned}\right]$$

$$\therefore \quad y = \frac{1}{2}\log|x^2+1| + C$$

which is the required solution.

2. Hint $x(x^2-1)\frac{dy}{dx} = 1 \Rightarrow \frac{dy}{dx} = \frac{1}{x(x^2-1)}$

$$\Rightarrow \quad \frac{dy}{dx} = \frac{1}{x(x-1)(x+1)}$$

$$[\because a^2 - b^2 = (a-b)(a+b)]$$

$$\Rightarrow \quad dy = \frac{dx}{x(x-1)(x+1)}$$

$$\Rightarrow \quad \int dy = \int \frac{dx}{x(x-1)(x+1)} + C$$

$$\Rightarrow \quad y = I + C \quad \text{...(i)}$$

where $I = \int \frac{dx}{x(x-1)(x+1)}$

Let $\frac{1}{x(x-1)(x+1)} = \frac{A}{x} + \frac{B}{x-1} + \frac{C}{x+1}$

$\Rightarrow 1 = A(x-1)(x+1) + Bx(x+1) + Cx(x-1)$

On comparing coefficients of x^2, x and constant terms from both sides, we get

$$A + B + C = 0 \quad \text{...(ii)}$$

$$B - C = 0 \quad \text{...(iii)}$$

and $\quad -A = 1 \Rightarrow A = -1$

On putting $A = -1$ in Eq. (ii), we get

$$B + C = 1 \quad \text{...(iv)}$$

Now, adding Eqs. (iii) and (iv), we get

$$2B = 1 \Rightarrow B = \frac{1}{2}$$

On putting $B = \frac{1}{2}$ in Eq. (iii), we get

$$\frac{1}{2} - C = 0 \Rightarrow C = \frac{1}{2}$$

$$\therefore \quad A = -1,\ B = \frac{1}{2} \text{ and } C = \frac{1}{2}$$

Thus, $\frac{1}{x(x-1)(x+1)} = \frac{-1}{x} + \frac{1/2}{x-1} + \frac{1/2}{x+1}$

On integrating both sides w.r.t. x, we get

$$I = \int \frac{1}{x(x-1)(x+1)}\,dx$$

$$= \int \frac{-1}{x}\,dx + \frac{1}{2}\int \frac{dx}{x-1} + \frac{1}{2}\int \frac{dx}{x+1}$$

$$\Rightarrow \quad I = -\log|x| + \frac{1}{2}\log|x-1| + \frac{1}{2}\log|x+1|$$

On putting the value of I in Eq. (i), we get

$$y = -\log|x| + \frac{1}{2}\log|x-1| + \frac{1}{2}\log|x+1| + C \quad \text{...(v)}$$

Also, given that $y = 0$, when $x = 2$

On putting $y = 0$ and $x = 2$ in Eq. (v), we get

$$0 = -\log 2 + \frac{1}{2}\log 1 + \frac{1}{2}\log 3 + C$$

$$\Rightarrow \quad C = \log 2 - \frac{1}{2}\log 1 - \frac{1}{2}\log 3$$

$$\Rightarrow \quad C = \log 2 - \log\sqrt{3} \quad [\because \log 1 = 0]$$

$$\Rightarrow \quad C = \log\frac{2}{\sqrt{3}}$$

Ans. $y = -\log|x| + \frac{1}{2}\log|x-1| + \frac{1}{2}\log|x+1| + \log\frac{2}{\sqrt{3}}$

3. Hint $\int e^{2y}dy = \int 1dx$

Put $y = 3$, to get the required value of x.

Ans. $\frac{e^6+9}{2}$

4. (i) **Hint** Write the given equation as $e^{2y}dy = x^3dx$ and solve it. **Ans.** $\frac{e^{2y}}{2} = \frac{x^4}{4} + C$

(ii) **Hint** $(x+1)\frac{dy}{dx} = 2xy \Rightarrow \frac{dy}{y} = \frac{2x}{x+1}dx$

$$\Rightarrow \quad \int \frac{dy}{y} = 2\int \frac{x}{x+1}\,dx$$

$$\Rightarrow \quad \int \frac{dy}{y} = 2\int \frac{(x+1)-1}{(x+1)}\,dx$$

$$\Rightarrow \quad \int \frac{dy}{y} = 2\left[\int dx - \int \frac{1}{(x+1)}\,dx\right]$$

$$\Rightarrow \quad \log|y| = 2\int dx - 2\int \frac{1}{x+1}\,dx$$

$$\Rightarrow \quad \log|y| = 2x - 2\log|x+1| + C$$

Ans. $\log|y| = 2(x - \log|x+1|) + C$

(iii) **Hint** Write the given equation as

$$\left(\frac{y+1}{y}\right)dy=\left(\frac{x+1}{x}\right)dx \text{ and solve it.}$$

Ans. $y = C\,x\,e^{(x-y)}$

(iv) **Hint** $xy\dfrac{dy}{dx}=(x+2)(y+2)$ ...(i)

$$\Rightarrow \quad \frac{y}{y+2}dy=\frac{x+2}{x}dx$$

$$\Rightarrow \quad \int\frac{y}{y+2}dy=\int\frac{x+2}{x}dx$$

$$\Rightarrow \quad \int\left(\frac{y+2-2}{y+2}\right)dy=\int\frac{x+2}{x}dx$$

$$\Rightarrow \int\frac{y+2}{y+2}dy-\int\frac{2}{y+2}dy=\int\frac{x}{x}dx+\int\frac{2}{x}dx$$

$$\Rightarrow \quad \int dy-2\int\frac{1}{y+2}dy=\int dx+2\int\frac{1}{x}dx$$

Ans. $y-2\log|y+2|=x+2\log|x|+C$

(v) **Hint** Write the given equation as $\dfrac{dy}{dx}=(1-x)(1+y)$ and solve it. **Ans.** $\log|1+y|=x-\dfrac{x^2}{2}+C$

(vi) **Hint** Write the given equation as $\dfrac{dy}{y\log y}=\dfrac{1}{x}dx$ and solve it. **Ans.** $y=e^{cx}$

(vii) Given differential equation is $\log\left(\dfrac{dy}{dx}\right)=3x+4y$

$$\Rightarrow \quad \frac{dy}{dx}=e^{3x+4y} \Rightarrow \frac{dy}{dx}=e^{3x}e^{4y}$$

On separating the variables, we get

$$\frac{1}{e^{4y}}dy=e^{3x}dx$$

On integrating both sides, we get

$$\int e^{-4y}dy=\int e^{3x}dx \Rightarrow \frac{e^{-4y}}{-4}=\frac{e^{3x}}{3}+C \quad ...(i)$$

which is the required general solution of given differential equation.

(viii) **Hint** $(x-1)\dfrac{dy}{dx}=2x^3y \Rightarrow \dfrac{dy}{y}=\dfrac{2x^3}{(x-1)}dx$

$$\Rightarrow \quad \frac{dy}{y}=2\left(\frac{x^3}{x-1}\right)dx$$

$$\Rightarrow \quad \frac{dy}{y}=2\left[\frac{(x^3-1)+1}{x-1}\right]dx$$

$$=2\left[\frac{(x-1)(x^2+x+1)}{(x-1)}+\frac{1}{(x-1)}\right]dx$$

$$[\because a^3-b^3=(a-b)(a^2+ab+b^2)]$$

$$\Rightarrow \quad \frac{dy}{y}=2\left(x^2+x+1+\frac{1}{x-1}\right)dx$$

$$\int\frac{dy}{y}=2\int\left(x^2+x+1+\frac{1}{x-1}\right)dx$$

Ans. $\log|y|=2\left(\dfrac{x^3}{3}+\dfrac{x^2}{2}+x+\log|x-1|\right)+C$

5. Hint $e^x\sqrt{1-y^2}\,dx+\dfrac{y}{x}dy=0$

$$\Rightarrow \quad e^x\sqrt{1-y^2}\,dx=\frac{-y}{x}dy$$

$$\Rightarrow \quad \frac{-y}{\sqrt{1-y^2}}dy=xe^x dx$$

$$\Rightarrow \quad \int\frac{-y}{\sqrt{1-y^2}}dy=\int xe^x dx$$

On putting $1-y^2=t$, then $-y\,dy=\dfrac{dt}{2}$ in LHS, we get

$$\int\frac{1}{2\sqrt{t}}dt=\int xe^x dx$$

$$\Rightarrow \quad \frac{1}{2}[2\sqrt{t}]=x\int e^x dx-\int\left[\frac{d}{dx}(x)\int e^x dx\right]dx$$

$$\Rightarrow \quad \sqrt{1-y^2}=xe^x-\int e^x dx \quad [\text{put } t=1-y^2]$$

$$\Rightarrow \quad \sqrt{1-y^2}=xe^x-e^x+C \quad ...(i)$$

On putting $y=1$ and $x=0$ in Eq. (i), we get

$$\sqrt{1-1}=0-e^0+C$$

$$\Rightarrow \quad C=1 \quad [\because e^0=1]$$

Now, substituting the value of C in Eq. (i).

Ans. $\sqrt{1-y^2}=xe^x-e^x+1$

6. Given, $\dfrac{dy}{dx}=1+x+y+xy \Rightarrow \dfrac{dy}{dx}=1(1+x)+y(1+x)$

$$\Rightarrow \quad \frac{dy}{dx}=(1+x)(1+y) \quad ...(i)$$

On separating the variables, we get

$$\frac{1}{(1+y)}dy=(1+x)dx \quad ...(ii)$$

On integrating both sides of Eq. (ii), we get

$$\int\frac{1}{1+y}dy=\int(1+x)dx$$

$$\Rightarrow \quad \log|1+y|=x+\frac{x^2}{2}+C \quad ...(iii)$$

On substituting $x=1$, $y=0$ in Eq. (iii), we get

$$\log|1+0|=1+\frac{1}{2}+C \Rightarrow C=-\frac{3}{2} \quad [\because \log 1=0]$$

Now, substituting the value of C in Eq. (iii), we get

$$\log|1+y|=x+\frac{x^2}{2}-\frac{3}{2}$$

which is the required particular solution of differential equation.

7. **Hint** Write the given equation as

$$\frac{x}{1+x^2}dx = \frac{y}{1+y^2}dy \text{ and solve it.}$$

Use $x = 0$ and $y = 1$ to find the value of C.

Ans. $y^2 - 2x^2 - 1 = 0$

8. **Hint** $(1 - y^2)(1 + \log|x|)\,dx + 2xy\,dy = 0$

$$\frac{(1+\log|x|)}{x}dx + \frac{2y}{1-y^2}dy = 0$$

$$\int\left(\frac{1}{x} + \frac{\log|x|}{x}\right)dx + \int\frac{2y}{1-y^2}dy = 0$$

$$\Rightarrow \quad \log|x| + \frac{(\log|x|)^2}{2} - \log|1-y^2| = \log C \quad \text{...(i)}$$

Also, given $y = 0$ and $x = 1$

$$\therefore \quad \log 1 + \frac{(\log 1)^2}{2} - \log|1-0| = \log C$$

$$\Rightarrow \quad 0 + 0 - 0 = \log C \Rightarrow \log C = 0$$

Now, put $\log C = 0$ in Eq. (i).

Ans. $\log|x| + \dfrac{(\log|x|)^2}{2} - \log|1-y^2| = 0$

9. **Hint** $(x - y)(dx + dy) = dx - dy$

$$\Rightarrow \quad dx + dy = \frac{dx-dy}{x-y}$$

$$\Rightarrow \quad \int(dx+dy) = \int\frac{dx-dy}{x-y} \quad \text{...(i)}$$

Put $x - y = t$, then $dx - dy = dt$

From Eq. (i), we get

$$x + y = \int\frac{dt}{t} = \log|t| + C$$

$$\Rightarrow \quad x + y = \log|x-y| + C \quad [\text{put } t = x - y] \text{...(ii)}$$

It is given that, when $x = 0$, then $y = -1$

$$\therefore \quad 0 + (-1) = \log|0+1| + C$$

$$\Rightarrow \quad C = -1 \quad [\because \log 1 = 0]$$

Now, substituting the value of C in Eq. (ii).

$$x + y = \log|x-y| - 1$$

Ans. $\log|x-y| = x + y + 1$

10. **Hint** $\dfrac{dy}{y(1-ay)} = \dfrac{dx}{(x+a)}$

$$\Rightarrow \quad \int\left[\frac{1}{y} + \frac{a}{(1-ay)}\right]dy = \int\frac{dx}{x+a}$$

Ans. $y = C(x+a)(1-ay)$

11. Let x and y be the x and y-coordinates of the point on the curve, respectively.

We know that the slope of a tangent to the curve is given by $\dfrac{dy}{dx}$.

According to the question, product of the slope of tangent with y-coordinate = x-coordinate

i.e. $$y \cdot \frac{dy}{dx} = x$$

Now, separating the variables, we get

$$y\,dy = x\,dx$$

On integrating both sides, we get

$$\int y\,dy = \int x\,dx \Rightarrow \frac{y^2}{2} = \frac{x^2}{2} + C \quad \text{...(i)}$$

Since, the curve passes through the point $(0, -2)$, therefore we have

$$\frac{(-2)^2}{2} = 0 + C \Rightarrow C = \frac{4}{2} = 2$$

On putting the value of C in Eq. (i), we get

$$\frac{y^2}{2} = \frac{x^2}{2} + 2 \Rightarrow x^2 - y^2 + 4 = 0$$

which is the required equation of the curve.

12. It is given that (x, y) is the point of contact of tangent to the curve.

The slope of the line segment joining the points $(x_2, y_2) \equiv (x, y)$ and $(x_1, y_1) \equiv (-4, -3)$

$$= \frac{y-(-3)}{x-(-4)} = \frac{y+3}{x+4} \quad \left[\because \text{slope of tangent} = \frac{y_2 - y_1}{x_2 - x_1}\right]$$

According to the question, slope of tangent is twice the slope of the line segment.

$$\therefore \quad \frac{dy}{dx} = 2\left(\frac{y+3}{x+4}\right)$$

Now, separating the variables, we get

$$\frac{dy}{y+3} = \left(\frac{2}{x+4}\right)dx$$

On integrating both sides, we get

$$\int\frac{dy}{y+3} = \int\left(\frac{2}{x+4}\right)dx$$

$$\Rightarrow \quad \log|y+3| = 2\log|x+4| + \log|C|$$

$$\Rightarrow \quad \log|y+3| = \log|x+4|^2 + \log|C|$$

$$\Rightarrow \quad \log\frac{|y+3|}{|x+4|^2} = \log|C| \quad \left[\because \log m - \log n = \log\frac{m}{n}\right]$$

$$\Rightarrow \quad \frac{(y+3)}{(x+4)^2} = C \quad \text{...(i)}$$

Since, the curve passes through the point $(-2, 1)$, therefore we have

$$\frac{(1+3)}{(-2+4)^2} = C \Rightarrow C = 1$$

On putting $C = 1$ in Eq. (i), we get

$$\frac{(y+3)}{(x+4)^2} = 1$$

$$\Rightarrow \quad y + 3 = (x+4)^2$$

which is the required equation of curve.

13. **Hint** $\dfrac{dy}{dx} = y + \dfrac{y}{x}$

Ans. $y = Kxe^x$

14. The figure obtained by the given information is given below

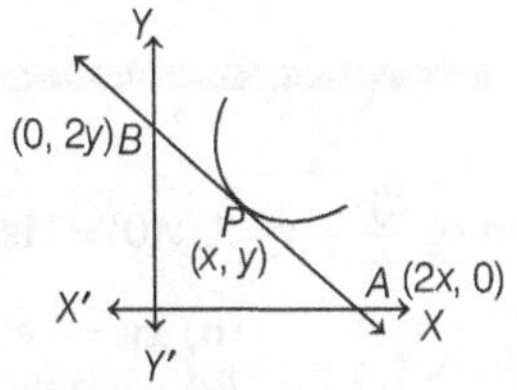

Let the coordinate of the point P be (x, y). It is given that, P is mid-point of AB. So, the coordinates of points A and B are $(2x, 0)$ and $(0, 2y)$, respectively.

Now, slope of $AB = \frac{0-2y}{2x-0} = -\frac{y}{x}$

Since, the segment AB is a tangent to the curve at P.

$$\therefore \quad \frac{dy}{dx} = -\frac{y}{x}$$

$$\Rightarrow \quad \frac{dy}{y} = -\frac{dx}{x}$$

On integrating both sides, we get

$$\log|y| = -\log|x| + \log|C|$$

$$\Rightarrow \quad \log|yx| = \log|C| \Rightarrow yx = C \quad \text{...(i)}$$

Since, the given curve passes through the point (1, 1).

$$\therefore \quad 1\cdot 1 = C \Rightarrow C = 1$$

On putting $C = 1$ in Eq. (i), we get

$$xy = 1$$

15. It is given that, slope of tangent to the curve at any point (x, y) is $\frac{y-1}{x^2+x}$.

$$\therefore \quad \left(\frac{dy}{dx}\right)_{(x,\,y)} = \frac{y-1}{x^2+x} \Rightarrow \frac{dy}{dx} = \frac{y-1}{x^2+x}$$

$$\Rightarrow \quad \frac{dy}{y-1} = \frac{dx}{x^2+x}$$

On integrating both sides, we get

$$\int\frac{dy}{y-1} = \int\frac{dx}{x^2+x} \Rightarrow \int\frac{dy}{y-1} = \int\frac{dx}{x(x+1)}$$

$$\Rightarrow \quad \int\frac{dy}{y-1} = \int\left(\frac{1}{x} - \frac{1}{x+1}\right)dx$$

$$\Rightarrow \quad \log|y-1| = \log|x| - \log|x+1| + \log|C|$$

$$\Rightarrow \quad \log|y-1| = \log\left|\frac{xC}{x+1}\right| \Rightarrow y-1 = \frac{xC}{(x+1)}$$

Since, the given curve passes through the point (1, 0).

$$\therefore \quad 0-1 = \frac{1\cdot C}{1+1} \Rightarrow C = -2$$

The particular solution is $y-1 = \frac{-2x}{x+1}$

$$\Rightarrow \quad (y-1)(x+1) = -2x$$

$$\Rightarrow \quad (y-1)(x+1) + 2x = 0$$

Exam Pattern Exercise

Part A - Objective Type Questions

Multiple Choice Type Questions

1 The order and the degree of the differential equation $y\,dx + x\log\left(\frac{y}{x}\right)dy - 2x\,dy = 0$ are respectively [CBSE 2024]

(a) 1, 1 (b) 1, 2
(c) 2, 1 (d) 1, not defined

2 The order of the differential equation satisfying $\sqrt{1-x^2}+\sqrt{1-y^2} = a(x-y)$ is

(a) 1 (b) 2
(c) 3 (d) None of these

3 The sum of order and degree of differential equation $\frac{dy}{dx}+y=\frac{1+y}{x}$ is

(a) 1 (b) 2
(c) 3 (d) 0

4 Let F be the family of ellipses whose centre is the origin and major axis is the Y-axis. Then the differential equation of family F is

(a) $\frac{d^2y}{dx^2}+\frac{dy}{dx}\left(x\frac{dy}{dx}-y\right)=0$

(b) $xy\frac{d^2y}{dx^2}-\frac{dy}{dx}\left(x\frac{dy}{dx}-y\right)=0$

(c) $xy\frac{d^2y}{dx^2}+\frac{dy}{dx}\left(x\frac{dy}{dx}-y\right)=0$

(d) $\frac{d^2y}{dx^2}-\frac{dy}{dx}\left(x\frac{dy}{dx}-y\right)=0$

5 The solution of the differential equation $\frac{dx}{x}+\frac{dy}{y}=0$ is [CBSE 2023]

(a) $\frac{1}{x}+\frac{1}{y}=C$ (b) $xy=C$
(c) $\log x \log y = C$ (d) $x+y=C$

6 The solution of $\frac{dy}{dx}=\frac{x}{x^2+1}$ is $y=$...... .

(a) $\frac{1}{2}\log|x^2+1|+C$
(b) $\log|x^2+1|$
(c) $2\log|x^2+1|$
(d) None of the above

7 The solution of $\frac{dy}{dx}-y=1$, $y(0)=1$ is given by

(a) $xy=-e^{x}$ (b) $xy=-e^{-x}$
(c) $xy=-1$ (d) $y=2e^{x}-1$

8 The differential equation $y\frac{dy}{dx}+x=C$ represents

(a) family of hyperbolas
(b) family of parabolas
(c) family of ellipses
(d) family of circles

9 The solution of differential equation $\frac{dy}{dx}=2x^2$ at $x=0$, $y=0$ is

(a) $y=x^3+2$ (b) $y=\frac{2}{3}x^3$
(c) $y=2x^3$ (d) $y=\frac{2}{3}x^2$

10 The solution of $\frac{dy}{dx}=e^{-x}$, $y(0)=0$ is

(a) $y=e^{x}(x-1)$ (b) $y=-e^{-x}+1$
(c) $y=xe^{-x}+1$ (d) $y=(x+1)e^{-x}$

Assertion-Reason Based Questions

Directions (Q. Nos. 11-13) *In the questions given below are two statements labelled as Assertion (A) and Reason (R). In the context of the two statements, which one of the following is correct?*

(a) Both A and R are correct; R is the correct explanation of A
(b) Both A and R are correct; R is not the correct explanation of A
(c) A is correct; R is incorrect
(d) R is correct; A is incorrect

11 **Assertion (A)** Order of the differential equation whose solution is $y=c_1e^{x+c_3}+c_2e^{-x+c_4}$ is 4.

Reason (R) Order of the differential equation is equal to the number of independent arbitrary constant mentioned in the solution of differential equation.

12 **Assertion (A)** The degree of the differential equation $\frac{d^2y}{dx^2}+2\left(\frac{dy}{dx}\right)^2=x^3\ln\left(\frac{d^2y}{dx^2}\right)$ is not defined.

Reason (R) If the differential equation is a polynomial in term of its derivatives, then its degree is defined.

13 **Assertion (A)** The differential equation representing the family of parabolas $y^2 = 4ax$, where 'a' is a parameter, is $x\frac{dy}{dx} - 2y = 0$.

Reason (R) If the given family of curves has n parameters, then it is to be differentiated n times to eliminate the parameter and obtain the nth order differential equation. **[CBSE 2023]**

Part B - Descriptive Questions

Very Short Answer Type Questions

Directions (Q. Nos. 14-17) *Find the order and degree of the following differential equations.*

14 $x + \log\left(\frac{d^3y}{dx^3}\right) = 1$

15 $\frac{d^2y}{dx^2} = \sqrt{1 + \left(\frac{dy}{dx}\right)^2}$

16 $x\frac{dy}{dx} + \frac{2}{(dy/dx)} = y^2$

17 $x^3\left(\frac{d^2y}{dx^2}\right)^2 + x\left(\frac{dy}{dx}\right)^4 = 0$

18 Write the differential equation representing the family of curves $y = mx$, where m is an arbitrary constant.

Directions (Q. Nos. 19-22) *Solve the following differential equations.*

19 $\frac{dy}{dx} + y = 1,\ y \neq 1$

20 $\frac{dy}{dx} - \frac{y\,(x+1)}{x} = 0$

21 $\frac{dy}{dx} = 2^{y-x}$

22 $\sqrt{a+x}\,\frac{dy}{dx} + x = 0$

23 Write the general solution of differential equation $\frac{dy}{dx} = \frac{y}{x}$.

24 State whether $y = e^{-x}(x+a)$ is a solution of differential equation $\frac{dy}{dx} + y = e^{-x}$.

25 Find the differential equation of the family of curves $y^2 = 4ax$.

26 Show that $y = Cx + \frac{a}{C}$ is a solution of differential equation $y = x\frac{dy}{dx} + \frac{a}{\left(\frac{dy}{dx}\right)}$, where C is a parameter.

27 Show that the function $y = (A + Bx)\,e^{3x}$ is a solution of the equation $\frac{d^2y}{dx^2} - 6\frac{dy}{dx} + 9y = 0$.

28 Find the differential equation of the family of curves $y = Ae^x + Be^{-x}$, where A and B are constants.

29 Form the differential equation by eliminating A and B in $Ax^2 + By^2 = 1$.

Short Answer Type Questions

30 Prove that $xy = ae^x + be^{-x} + x^2$ is the general solution of the differential equation

$$x\frac{d^2y}{dx^2} + 2\frac{dy}{dx} - xy + x^2 - 2 = 0.$$

31 Find the differential equation of all non-horizontal lines in a plane.

32 If $\frac{dy}{dx} = ye^x$ and $x = 0$, $y = e$, then find the value of y, when $x = 1$.

33 Solve $2(y+3) - xy\frac{dy}{dx} = 0$, given that $y(1) = -2$.

34 Solve the initial value problem

$$dy = e^{2x+y}\,dx,\ y(0) = 0.$$

Long Answer Type Questions

35 Find the particular solution of the differential equation $\frac{dy}{dx} = \frac{x(2\log x + 1)}{\sin y + y\cos y}$, given that $y = \frac{\pi}{2}$, when $x = 1$.

36 Show that the general solution of the differential equation $\frac{dy}{dx} + \frac{y^2 + y + 1}{x^2 + x + 1} = 0$ is given by $(x + y + 1) = A(1 - x - y - 2xy)$, where A is a parameter.

Case Study Based Questions

37 The order of a differential equation is the order of the highest order derivative appearing in the equation and the power of the highest order derivative is a degree.

On the basis of the above information, solve the following questions.

(i) The order of the differential equation $\left(\frac{d^3y}{dx^3}\right)^3 + 5\left(\frac{d^2y}{dx^2}\right)^5 - 8y = 0$ is

(a) 4 (b) 3 (c) 2 (d) 1

(ii) The degree of the differential equation

$$y = \sqrt{1 + \left(\frac{dy}{dx}\right)^2} \text{ is}$$

(a) 2 (b) 3
(c) 1 (d) does not exist

(iii) The degree of the differential equation

$$\left(\frac{d^2y}{dx^2}\right)^2 + \left(\frac{dy}{dx}\right)^3 = \log\left(\frac{dy}{dx}\right) \text{ is}$$

(a) 0 (b) 1
(c) 2 (d) Can't determined

(iv) The sum of the order and degree of a differential equation $4\sqrt{\dfrac{d^2y}{dx^2}} = \sqrt{3\dfrac{dy}{dx}}$ is

(a) 4 (b) 2
(c) 3 (d) 6

(v) The solution of the differential equation $\dfrac{dy}{dx} = x^2y^2$ is

(a) $3x^3 + y + c = 0$ (b) $\dfrac{x^3}{3} + \dfrac{1}{y} + c = 0$

(c) $3x^3 - y + c = 0$ (d) $\dfrac{x^3}{3} - \dfrac{1}{y} + c = 0$

Hints & Solutions

1. (d) 2. (a) 3. (b) 4. (c) 5. (b)
6. (a) 7. (d) 8. (d) 9. (b) 10. (b)
11. (d) 12. (a) 13. (d)

14. Order = 3, degree = not defined

15. Order = 2, degree = 2

16. Order = 1, degree = 2

17. Order = 2, degree = 2

18. $x\,dy - y\,dx = 0$

19. $x + \log|1 - y| = C$

20. $y = Cx\,e^x$

21. $2^{-x} - 2^{-y} = k$

22. **Hint** Put $a + x = t$

Ans. $y = -\dfrac{2}{3}(a+x)^{3/2} + 2a\sqrt{a+x} + C$

23. $y = Cx$

24. **Hint** Find y', then put y and y' in given differential equation LHS. **Ans.** Yes

25. $2xy\dfrac{dy}{dx} - y^2 = 0$

28. **Hint** Find y', y'', then eliminate A and B.

Ans. $\dfrac{d^2y}{dx^2} - y = 0$

29. $xy\,y'' + x(y')^2 - yy' = 0$

31. **Hint** Consider, $ax + by = c$, where $a \neq 0$.

Differentiate above equation w.r.t. y **Ans.** $\dfrac{d^2x}{dy^2} = 0$

32. **Hint** Use variable separable. **Ans.** $y = e^e$

33. $x^2(y+3)^3 = e^{y+2}$

34. **Hint** $dy = e^{2x} \cdot e^y dx$

$$\int \frac{dy}{e^y} = \int e^{2x} dx$$

$$\int e^{-y} dy = \int e^{2x} dx$$

Ans. $y = \log\left|\dfrac{2}{3 - e^{2x}}\right|$

35. $y\sin y = x^2 \log x + \dfrac{\pi}{2}$

36. $x + y + 1 = A(1 - x - y - 2xy)$

where, $A = \dfrac{1}{\sqrt{3}} \tan k$ is an arbitrary constant.

37. (i) (b) (ii) (a) (iii) (d) (iv) (c) (v) (b)

CHAPTER 15

Probability Distribution

In this Chapter...

- Random Variable
- Bernoulli Trials
- Poisson Distribution
- Probability Distribution of a Continuous Random Variable

Random Variable

A random variable is a real valued function, whose domain is the sample space of a random experiment. Generally, it is denoted by capital letter X. Also, more than one random variables can be defined on the same sample space.

e.g. Let a coin be tossed twice.

Then, sample space, $S = \{HT, TH, HH, TT\}$

If X denotes the number of heads in two tosses, then X is a random variable and for each outcome, its value is

$$X(TT) = 0,\ X(HT) = 1,\ X(TH) = 1 \text{ and } X(HH) = 2$$

Clearly, values of X are 0, 1and 2.

Let Y denotes the number of heads minus the number of tails for each outcome of the above sample space S and for each outcome, its value is

$$Y(HH) = 2-0=2,$$
$$Y(HT) = 1-1=0,$$
$$Y(TH) = 1-1=0$$

and $$Y(TT) = 0-2=-2$$

Thus, X and Y are two different random variables defined on the same sample space S.

EXAMPLE 1. A bag contains 2 black and 1 green balls. One ball is drawn at random and then put back in the box after noting its colour. The process repeated again. Let X denotes the number of green balls recorded in the two draws, describe X.

Sol. Given, a bag contains 2 black and 1 green balls. Black balls are denoted by b_1, b_2 and green ball is denoted by g_1, then the sample space for two draws is

$S = \{b_1b_1, b_1b_2, b_2b_1, b_2b_2, b_1g_1, b_2g_1, g_1b_1, g_1b_2, g_1g_1\}$

Now, X denotes the number of green balls. Then,

$$X(b_1b_1) = X(b_1b_2) = X(b_2b_1) = X(b_2b_2) = 0,$$
$$X(b_1g_1) = X(b_2g_1) = X(g_1b_1) = X(g_1b_2) = 1$$

and $X(g_1g_1) = 2$

Hence, X is a random variable whose range is {0, 1, 2}.

Probability Distribution of a Random Variable

The system in which the values of a random variable are given along with their corresponding probability, is called probability distribution.

If X is a random variable and takes the values of $x_1, x_2, x_3, \ldots, x_n$ with respective probabilities $p_1, p_2, p_3, \ldots, p_n$.

Then, the probability distribution of X is represented by

X	x_1	x_2	x_3	...	x_n
$P(X)$	p_1	p_2	p_3	...	p_n

where, $p_i > 0$ and $\sum_{i=1}^{n} p_i = 1; i = 1, 2, 3, \ldots, n$

Note If x_i is one of the possible values of a random variable X, then statement $X = x_i$ is true only at some point(s) of the sample space. Hence, the probability that X takes value x_i, is always non-zero, i.e. $P(X = x_i) \neq 0$.

EXAMPLE 2. Let X be a discrete random variable whose probability distribution is defined as

$$P(X=x)=\begin{cases} k(x+1), & \text{for } x=1,2,3,4 \\ 2kx, & \text{for } x=5,6,7 \\ 0, & \text{otherwise} \end{cases}$$

where, k is a constant. Determine

(i) k (ii) $P(X<4)$

(iii) $P(X\geq 5)$ (iv) $P(2<X<7)$

Sol. (i) We know that $\sum_{i=1}^{n} pi = 1$

$$\Rightarrow k(1+1)+k(2+1)+k(3+1)+k(4+1) + 2k(5)+2k(6)+2k(7)+0=1$$

$$\Rightarrow 2k+3k+4k+5k+10k+12k+14k+0=1$$

$$\Rightarrow 50k=1$$

$$\Rightarrow k=\frac{1}{50}$$

(ii) $P(X<4)=P(1)+P(2)+P(3)$

$$= k(1+1)+k(2+1)+k(3+1)$$

$$= 2k+3k+4k=9k=9\left(\frac{1}{50}\right)=\frac{9}{50}$$

(iii) $P(X\geq 5)=P(5)+P(6)+P(7)+0$

$$=2k(5)+2k(6)+2k(7)$$

$$=10k+12k+14k=36k$$

$$=36\left(\frac{1}{50}\right)=\frac{18}{25}$$

(iv) $P(2<X<7)=P(3)+P(4)+P(5)+P(6)$

$$=k(3+1)+k(4+1)+2k(5)+2k(6)$$

$$=4k+5k+10k+12k=31k=\frac{31}{50}$$

EXAMPLE 3. Let X be a random variable which assumes values x_1, x_2, x_3, x_4 such that

$$3P(X=x_1)=2P(X=x_2)=4P(X=x_3)=5P(X=x_4)$$

Find the probability distribution of X.

Sol. We have,

$$3P(X=x_1)=2P(X=x_2)=4P(X=x_3)=5P(X=x_4)=k \quad \text{(let)}$$

$$\Rightarrow P(X=x_1)=\frac{k}{3}, P(X=x_2)=\frac{k}{2}$$

$$P(X=x_3)=\frac{k}{4} \text{ and } P(X=x_4)=\frac{k}{5}$$

Since, $\Sigma P(X=x_i)=1$

$$\Rightarrow \frac{k}{3}+\frac{k}{2}+\frac{k}{4}+\frac{k}{5}=1$$

$$\Rightarrow \frac{20k+30k+15k+12k}{60}=1$$

$$\Rightarrow \frac{77k}{60}=1 \Rightarrow k=\frac{60}{77}$$

$$\therefore P(X=x_1)=\frac{k}{3}=\frac{20}{77}, P(X=x_2)=\frac{k}{2}=\frac{30}{77},$$

$$P(X=x_3)=\frac{k}{4}=\frac{15}{77} \text{ and } P(X=x_4)=\frac{k}{5}=\frac{12}{77}$$

$\therefore$ Required probability distribution of X.

X	x_1	x_2	x_3	x_4
$P(X)$	$\frac{20}{77}$	$\frac{30}{77}$	$\frac{15}{77}$	$\frac{12}{77}$

EXAMPLE 4. Two cards are drawn successively with replacement from a well-shuffled deck of 52 cards. Find the probability distribution of the number of aces.

Sol. Let the number of aces is a random variable denoted by X. Here, two cards are drawn.

Let A denotes an ace card and B denotes a non-ace card, then sample space for two cards is

$$S=\{AB, BA, AA, BB\}$$

Then, $X(AB)=1$, $X(BA)=1$, $X(AA)=2$ and $X(BB)=0$.

So, X takes the values 0, 1 or 2.

Since, the draws are done with replacement, two draws form independent experiments.

$$\therefore P(X=0)=P(BB)=P(B)\times P(B)=\frac{48}{52}\times\frac{48}{52}$$

[$\because$ in 52 cards, 4 aces and remaining 48 are non-ace cards]

$$=\frac{144}{169}$$

$$P(X=1)=P(AB \text{ or } BA)=P(AB)+P(BA)$$

$$=P(A)\cdot P(B)+P(B)\cdot P(A)$$

$$=\frac{4}{52}\times\frac{48}{52}+\frac{48}{52}\times\frac{4}{52}=\frac{12}{169}+\frac{12}{169}=\frac{24}{169}$$

and $P(X=2)=P(AA)=P(A)\cdot P(A)=\frac{4}{52}\times\frac{4}{52}=\frac{1}{169}$

Hence, the required probability distribution is

X	0	1	2
$P(X)$	$\frac{144}{169}$	$\frac{24}{169}$	$\frac{1}{169}$

Verification Sum of probabilities,

$$\sum_{i=1}^{n} p_i=\frac{144}{169}+\frac{24}{169}+\frac{1}{169}=\frac{144+24+1}{169}=\frac{169}{169}=1$$

EXAMPLE 5. From a lot of 15 bulbs which include 5 defectives, a sample of 2 bulbs is drawn at random (without replacement). Find the probability distribution of the number of defective bulbs.

Sol. Total number of bulbs = 15

Number of defective bulbs = 5

$\therefore$ Good bulbs $=15-5=10$

Let X be the random variable of number of defective bulbs.

$\therefore$ $X = 0, 1, 2$

$$P(X=0)=\frac{10}{15}\times\frac{9}{14}=\frac{9}{21}$$

$$P(X=1)=\frac{10}{15}\times\frac{5}{14}+\frac{5}{15}\times\frac{10}{14}=\frac{10}{21}$$

and $$P(X=2)=\frac{5}{15}\times\frac{4}{14}=\frac{2}{21}$$

$\therefore$ Required probability distribution table is

X	0	1	2
P (X)	$\frac{9}{21}$	$\frac{10}{21}$	$\frac{2}{21}$

Mean of a Random Variable

Let X be a random variable taking values $x_1, x_2, x_3, \ldots, x_n$ with probabilities $p_1, p_2, p_3, \ldots, p_n$, respectively. Then, mean of X denoted by μ, is the number $\sum_{i=1}^{n} x_i p_i$, i.e. the mean of X is the weighted average of the possible values of X, each value being weighted by its probability with which it occurs. It is also called the expectation of X, denoted by $E(X)$.

Then, $E(X)=\mu=\sum_{i=1}^{n} x_i p_i = x_1 p_1 + x_2 p_2 + \ldots + x_n p_n$

Thus, in other words we can say that the mean or expectation of a random variable X is the sum of the products of all possible values of X by their respective probabilities.

EXAMPLE 6. Let X denotes the number of hours a Class 12 student studies during a randomly selected school day. The probability that X can take the values x_i, for an unknown constant 'k'.

$$P(X=k)=\begin{cases} 0.1 & \text{if } x_i = 0 \\ kx_i & \text{if } x_i = 1 \text{ or } 2 \\ k(5-x_i) & \text{if } x_i = 3 \text{ or } 4 \end{cases}$$

(i) Find the value of k.

(ii) Determine the probability that the student studied for atleast 2 h.

(iii) Determine the probability that the student studied for atmost 2 h. **[CBSE 2024]**

Sol. Tabular format

X	0	1	2	3	4
P(X)	0.1	k	$2k$	$2k$	k

(i) Since, X is a random variable $\sum_{0}^{4} P(X) = 1$

$\Rightarrow P(X=0)+P(X=1)+P(X=2)$
$+P(X=3)+P(X=4)=1$

$\Rightarrow$ $0.1+k+2k+2k+k=1$

$\Rightarrow$ $6k = 1-0.1$

$\Rightarrow$ $6k = 0.9$

$\Rightarrow$ $k=\frac{0.9}{6}=0.15$

(ii) P(student studied for atleast two hours)

$=P(X\geq 2)=P(X=2)+P(X=3)+P(X=4)$

$=2k+2k+k=5k$

$=5\times 0.15$ $[\because k = 0.15]$

$=0.75$

(iii) P(student studied for atmost 2 hours) $=P(X\leq 2)$

$=P(X=0)+P(X=1)+P(X=2)$

$=0.1+k+2k=0.1+3k$

$=0.1+3\times 0.15$ $[\because k=0.15]$

$=0.1+0.45=0.55$

EXAMPLE 7. In a game, a man wins ₹ 5 for getting a number greater than 4 and loses ₹ 1 otherwise, when a fair die is thrown. The man decided to throw a die thrice but to quit as and when he gets a number greater than 4. Find the expected value of the amount he wins/loses.

Sol Let X be a random variable that denotes the amount received by the man. Then, X can take values 5, 4, 3 and -3.

Now, $P(X=5)=P$ (getting a number greater than 4 in the first throw)

$$=\frac{2}{6}=\frac{1}{3}$$

$P(X=4)=P$ (getting a number less than or equal to 4 in the first throw and getting a number greater than 4 in the second throw)

$$=\frac{4}{6}\times\frac{2}{6}=\frac{2}{9}$$

$P(X=3)=P$ (getting a number less than or equal to 4 in first two throws and getting a number greater than 4 in the third throw)

$$=\frac{4}{6}\times\frac{4}{6}\times\frac{2}{6}=\frac{4}{27}$$

and $P(X=-3)=P$ (getting a number less than or equal to 4 in all three throws)

$$=\frac{4}{6}\times\frac{4}{6}\times\frac{4}{6}=\frac{8}{27}$$

Thus, the probability distribution of X is

X	5	4	3	-3
$P(X=x)$	$\frac{1}{3}$	$\frac{2}{9}$	$\frac{4}{27}$	$\frac{8}{27}$

Now, expected value of the amount $=E(X)=\Sigma x_i p_i$

$$=5\cdot\frac{1}{3}+4\cdot\frac{2}{9}+3\cdot\frac{4}{27}-3\cdot\frac{8}{27}$$

$$=\frac{45+24+12-24}{27}=\frac{57}{27}=\frac{19}{9}$$

Variance of a Random Variable

Let X be a random variable whose possible values $x_1, x_2, \ldots, x_n$ occur with probabilities $p(x_1), p(x_2), \ldots, p(x_n)$, respectively.

The variance of X, denoted by Var (x) or σ_x^2 is defined as

$$\sigma^2 = \text{Var}(X) = \sum_{i=1}^{n}(x_i - \mu)^2 p(x_i) \text{ or } \sigma_x^2 = E(X-\mu)^2$$

where, $\mu = E(X) =$ Mean of X

Another Formula to Find the Variance of a Random Variable

The variance of a random variable can also find by using the formula given below

$$\text{Var}(X) = E(X^2) - [E(X)]^2$$

where, $E(X^2) = \sum_{i=1}^{n} x_i^2 \; p(x_i)$

or $\quad \text{Var}(X) = \sum_{i=1}^{n} x_i^2 \; p(x_i) - \left(\sum_{i=1}^{n} x_i \; p(x_i)\right)^2$

Proof We know that, $\text{Var}(X) = \sum_{i=1}^{n}(x_i - \mu)^2 p(x_i)$

$$= \sum_{i=1}^{n}(x_i^2 + \mu^2 - 2\mu x_i) p(x_i)$$

$$= \sum_{i=1}^{n} x_i^2 p(x_i) + \sum_{i=1}^{n} \mu^2 p(x_i) - \sum_{i=1}^{n} 2\mu x_i p(x_i)$$

$$= \sum_{i=1}^{n} x_i^2 p(x_i) + \mu^2 \sum_{i=1}^{n} p(x_i) - 2\mu \sum_{i=1}^{n} x_i p(x_i)$$

$$= \sum_{i=1}^{n} x_i^2 p(x_i) + \mu^2 - 2\mu^2$$

$$\left[\because \sum_{i=1}^{n} p(x_i) = 1 \text{ and } \mu = \sum_{i=1}^{n} x_i p(x_i)\right]$$

$$= \sum_{i=1}^{n} x_i^2 p(x_i) - \mu^2$$

$\Rightarrow \quad \text{Var}(X) = \sum_{i=1}^{n} x_i^2 p(x_i) - \left(\sum_{i=1}^{n} x_i p(x_i)\right)^2$

or $\quad \textbf{Var}(X) = E(X^2) - [E(X)]^2$

Where, $\quad E(X^2) = \sum_{i=1}^{n} x_i^2 \; p(x_i)$

Note The variability or spread in the values of a random variable may be measured by variance.

Standard Deviation

Standard deviation of the probability distribution is the square root of variance, which is represented by σ and it is given by

$$\sigma = \sqrt{\text{Variance}} = \sqrt{\sum_{i=1}^{n}(x_i - \mu)^2 p(x_i)} \text{ or } \sqrt{E(X-\mu)^2}$$

EXAMPLE 8. Two cards are drawn simultaneously (without replacement) from a well-shuffled deck of 52 cards. Find the mean and variance of number of red cards.

Sol. Here, we have to drawn two cards simultaneously from a deck.

Let X denotes the number of red cards (since mean and variance of red card to be calculated here), then X can take values 0 (no red card), 1 (one red card) and 2 (both red cards).

For $X = 0$, $P(X=0) = P(\text{getting no red card}) = \dfrac{^{26}C_2}{^{52}C_2}$

[$\because$ there are 26 red and 26 black cards in a deck]

$$= \frac{\frac{26 \times 25}{2 \times 1}}{\frac{52 \times 51}{2 \times 1}} = \frac{1}{2} \times \frac{25}{51} = \frac{25}{102}$$

For $X = 1$, $P(X=1)$

$= P(\text{getting one red and other black card})$

$$= \frac{^{26}C_1 \times {}^{26}C_1}{^{52}C_2} = \frac{26 \times 26 \times 2}{52 \times 51} = \frac{26}{51}$$

For $X = 2$, $P(X=2) = \dfrac{^{26}C_2}{^{52}C_2} = \dfrac{\frac{26 \times 25}{2 \times 1}}{\frac{52 \times 51}{2 \times 1}} = \dfrac{25}{102}$

The required probability distribution is

X	0	1	2
$P(X)$	$\frac{25}{102}$	$\frac{26}{51}$	$\frac{25}{102}$

We know that mean,

$$\overline{X} = \sum_{i=1}^{n} x_i \; p(x_i)$$

$$\therefore \quad \overline{X} = \left(0 \times \frac{25}{102}\right) + \left(1 \times \frac{26}{51}\right) + \left(2 \times \frac{25}{102}\right)$$

$$= 0 + \frac{26}{51} + \frac{50}{102}$$

$$= \frac{26}{51} + \frac{25}{51} = \frac{51}{51} = 1$$

Hence, mean = 1

We know that,

$$\text{Var}(X) = \sum_{i=1}^{n} x_i^2 \; p(x_i) - (\text{Mean})^2 \quad \ldots(\text{i})$$

Here, $\sum_{i=1}^{n} x_i^2\, p(x_i) = (0)^2 \times \frac{25}{102} + (1)^2 \times \frac{26}{51} + (2)^2 \times \frac{25}{102}$

$$= \frac{26}{51} + \frac{100}{102} = \frac{26}{51} + \frac{50}{51} = \frac{76}{51}$$

Then, from Eq. (i), we have

$$\text{Var}(X) = \frac{76}{51} - (1)^2 = \frac{76-51}{51} = \frac{25}{51}$$

EXAMPLE 9. Two numbers are selected at random (without replacement) from positive integers 2, 3, 4, 5, 6 and 7. Let X denotes the larger of the two numbers obtained. Find the mean and variance of the probability distribution of X.

Sol. The total number of pairs will be formed by taking two numbers at a time $= {}^6C_1 \times {}^5C_1 = 30$.

Let X denotes larger of the two numbers be obtained.

Obviously, X may have values 3, 4, 5, 6 and 7.

Now, $P(X = 3) = P$[getting (2,3), (3,2) out of 30 pairs]

$$= \frac{2}{30} = \frac{1}{15}$$

$P(X = 4) = P$ [getting (2,4), (3,4), (4,2), (4,3) out of 30 pairs]

$$= \frac{4}{30} = \frac{2}{15}$$

$P(X = 5) = P$ [getting (2,5), (5,2), (3,5), (5,3), (4,5),(5,4) out of 30 pairs]

$$= \frac{6}{30} = \frac{3}{15}$$

$P(X = 6) = P$ [getting (2,6), (6,2), (3,6), (6,3), (4,6),(6,4), (5,6), (6,5) out of 30 pairs]

$$= \frac{8}{30} = \frac{4}{15}$$

$P(X = 7) = P$ [getting (2,7), (7,2), (3,7), (7,3), (4,7), (7,4), (5,7), (7,5), (6,7), (7,6) out of 30 pairs]

$$= \frac{10}{30} = \frac{5}{15}$$

Therefore, required probability distribution is

X	3	4	5	6	7
$P(X)$	1/15	2/15	3/15	4/15	5/15

$\therefore$ Required mean $= \mu = \Sigma x_i p_i$

$$= 3 \times \frac{1}{15} + 4 \times \frac{2}{15} + 5 \times \frac{3}{15} + 6 \times \frac{4}{15} + 7 \times \frac{5}{15}$$

$$= \frac{3}{15} + \frac{8}{15} + \frac{15}{15} + \frac{24}{15} + \frac{35}{15} = \frac{85}{15} = \frac{17}{3}$$

Variance $= \Sigma x_i^2 p_i - \mu^2$, where μ = mean

$$= \left(9 \times \frac{1}{15} + 16 \times \frac{2}{15} + 25 \times \frac{3}{15} + 36 \times \frac{4}{15} + 49 \times \frac{5}{15}\right) - \left(\frac{17}{3}\right)^2$$

$$= \left(\frac{9}{15} + \frac{32}{15} + \frac{75}{15} + \frac{144}{15} + \frac{245}{15}\right) - \frac{289}{9}$$

$$= \frac{505}{15} - \frac{289}{9} = \frac{101}{3} - \frac{289}{9} = \frac{303-289}{9} = \frac{14}{9}$$

EXAMPLE 10. An urn contains 4 white and 3 red balls. Let X be the number of red balls in a random draw of 3 balls. Find the mean and variance of X.

Sol. When 3 balls are drawn at random, there may be no red ball, 1 red ball, 2 red balls or 3 red balls.

Let X denotes the random variable showing the number of red balls in a draw of 3 balls.

Then, X can take the values 0, 1, 2 or 3.

$P(X = 0) = P$ (getting no red ball)

$= P$ (getting 3 white balls)

$$= \frac{{}^4C_3}{{}^7C_3} = \left(\frac{4 \times 3 \times 2}{3 \times 2 \times 1} \times \frac{3 \times 2 \times 1}{7 \times 6 \times 5}\right) = \frac{4}{35}$$

$P(X = 1) = P$ (getting 1 red and 2 white balls)

$$= \frac{{}^3C_1 \times {}^4C_2}{{}^7C_3} = \left(\frac{3 \times 4 \times 3}{2} \times \frac{3 \times 2 \times 1}{7 \times 6 \times 5}\right) = \frac{18}{35}$$

$P(X = 2) = P$ (getting 2 red and 1 white balls)

$$= \frac{{}^3C_2 \times {}^4C_1}{{}^7C_3}$$

$$= \left(\frac{3 \times 2}{2 \times 1} \times 4 \times \frac{3 \times 2 \times 1}{7 \times 6 \times 5}\right) = \frac{12}{35}$$

$P(X = 3) = P$ (getting 3 red balls)

$$= \frac{{}^3C_3}{{}^7C_3} = \frac{3 \times 2 \times 1}{7 \times 6 \times 5} = \frac{1}{35}$$

Thus, the probability distribution of X is given below

$X = x_i$	0	1	2	3
p_i	$\frac{4}{35}$	$\frac{18}{35}$	$\frac{12}{35}$	$\frac{1}{35}$

$\therefore$ Mean, $\mu = \Sigma x_i p_i$

$$= 0 \times \frac{4}{35} + 1 \times \frac{18}{35} + 2 \times \frac{12}{35} + 3 \times \frac{1}{35}$$

$$= \frac{45}{35} = \frac{9}{7}$$

Variance, $\sigma^2 = \Sigma x_i^2 p_i - \mu^2$

$$= 0 \times \frac{4}{35} + 1 \times \frac{18}{35} + 4 \times \frac{12}{35} + 9 \times \frac{1}{35} - \frac{81}{49}$$

$$= \left(\frac{15}{7} - \frac{81}{49}\right)$$

$$= \frac{105-81}{49} = \frac{24}{49}$$

Topic Practice 1

1 An urn contains 6 red and 3 black balls. Two balls are randomly drawn. Let X represents the number of black balls. What are the possible values of X?

2 State whether the following distribution is a probability distribution of a random variable or not.

X	3	2	1	0	-1
$P(X)$	0.3	0.2	0.4	0.1	0.05

3 The probability distribution of a discrete random variable X is given below

X	2	3	4	5
$P(X)$	$5/k$	$7/k$	$9/k$	$11/k$

Find the value of k.

4 An unbiased die is thrown again and again until three sixes are obtained. Find the probability of obtaining a third six in the sixth throw of the die. [CBSE 2023]

5 Find the probability distribution of number of tails in the simultaneously tosses of three coins.

6 A biased die is such that $P(4)=\frac{1}{10}$ and other scores being equally likely. The die is tossed twice. If X is the 'number of four seen', then find the variance of the random variable X.

7 3 defective bulbs are mixed up with 7 good ones. 3 bulbs are drawn at random. Find the probability distribution of defective bulbs.

8 Suppose that, two cards are drawn at random from a deck of cards. Let X be the number of aces obtained. What is the value of $E(X)$?

9 Three cards are drawn at random (without replacement) from a well-shuffled pack of 52 playing cards. Find the probability distribution of number of red cards and also find the mean of the distribution.

10 Three cards are drawn successively with replacement from a well-shuffled pack of 52 cards. Find the probability distribution of the number of spades. Also, find the mean of the distribution.

11 From a lot of 30 bulbs, which includes 6 defectives, 3 bulbs are drawn one-by-one at random with replacement. Find the probability distribution of number of defective bulbs. Hence, find the mean and variance of the distribution.

12 In a meeting, 70% of the members favour a certain proposal, 30% being opposite. A member is selected at random and let $X=0$, if he opposed and $X=1$, if he is in favour. Find $E(X)$ and $V(X)$.

13 Suppose, 10000 tickets are sold in a lottery each for ₹ 1. First prize is of ₹ 3000 and the second prize is of ₹ 2000. There is third prizes of ₹ 500 each. If you buy one ticket, then what is your expectation?

14 There are 4 cards numbered 1, 3, 5 and 7, one number on one card. Two cards are drawn at random without replacement. Let X denote the sum of the numbers on the two drawn cards. Find the mean and variance of X.

15 The probability distribution of a random variable X is given as under

$$P(X=x)=\begin{cases} kx^2, & x=1,2,3 \\ 2kx, & x=4,5,6 \\ 0, & \text{otherwise} \end{cases},$$

where k is a constant. Calculate

(i) $E(X)$ (ii) $E(X^2)$ (iii) $P(X \geq 4)$

16 A random variable X has following probability distribution.

X	0	1	2	3	4	5	6	7
$P(X)$	0	k	$2k$	$2k$	$3k$	k^2	$2k^2$	$7k^2+k$

Find

(i) k (ii) $P(X<3)$
(iii) $P(X>6)$ (iv) $P(0<X<3)$.

17 Let X denotes the sum of the numbers obtained, when two fair dice are rolled. Find the variance and standard deviation of X.

18 There are 5 cards numbered 1 to 5, one number on one card. Two cards are drawn at random without replacement. Let X denotes the sum of the numbers on two cards drawn. Find the mean and variance of X.

19 A coin is biased so that the head is 4 times as likely to occur as tail. If the coin is tossed thrice, find the probability distribution of number of tails. Hence, find the mean and variance of the distribution.

20 An urn contains 3 white and 6 red balls. Four balls are drawn one-by-one with replacement from the urn. Find the probability distribution of the number of red balls drawn. Also, find mean and variance of the distribution.

21 Two numbers are selected at random (without replacement) from the first six positive integers. Let X denotes the larger of the two numbers obtained. Find the probability distribution of the random variable X and also find the mean of the distribution.

22 Three numbers are selected at random (without replacement) from first six positive integers. Let X denotes the largest of the three numbers obtained. Find the probability distribution of X. Also, find the mean and variance of the distribution.

Hints & Solutions

1. Here, two balls are drawn, so possible values of X are 0, 1 and 2.

2. **Hint** $\sum_{i=1}^{n} p_i = 1.05$ **Ans.** No

3. **Hint** $\Sigma P(X) = 1 \Rightarrow \frac{32}{k} = 1$ **Ans.** $k = 32$

4. Let p be the probability of obtaining a 'six' in a single throw of die, then

$$p = \frac{1}{6}$$

and $$q = 1 - p = 1 - \frac{1}{6} = \frac{5}{6}$$

Obtaining 3rd six in the sixth throw of the die that is first five throw there are 2 sixes and the third six is obtained in sixth throw.

$$\therefore \text{ Required probability} = {}^5C_2 \left(\frac{1}{6}\right)^2 \left(\frac{5}{6}\right)^3 \times \frac{1}{6}$$

$$= 10 \times \frac{125}{6^6}$$

$$= \frac{625}{23328}$$

5. Solve as Question 4.

Ans.

X	0	1	2	3
$P(X)$	1/8	3/8	3/8	1/8

6. Since, X = Number of four seen

On tossing two dice, $X = 0, 1, 2$

Also, $P(4) = \frac{1}{10}$ and $P(\text{not } 4) = \frac{9}{10}$

So, $P(X = 0) = P(\text{not } 4) \cdot P(\text{not } 4)$

$$= \frac{9}{10} \cdot \frac{9}{10} = \frac{81}{100}$$

$$P(X = 1) = P(\text{not } 4) \cdot P(4) + P(4) \cdot P(\text{not } 4)$$

$$= \frac{9}{10} \cdot \frac{1}{10} + \frac{1}{10} \cdot \frac{9}{10}$$

$$= \frac{18}{100}$$

$$P(X = 2) = P(4) \cdot P(4) = \frac{1}{10} \cdot \frac{1}{10} = \frac{1}{100}$$

Thus, we get the following table

X	0	1	2
$P(X)$	81/100	18/100	1/100
$XP(X)$	0	18/100	2/100
$X^2P(X)$	0	18/100	4/100

$$\therefore \text{Var}(X) = E(X^2) - [E(X)]^2$$

$$= \Sigma X^2 P(X) - [\Sigma X P(X)]^2$$

$$= \left(0 + \frac{18}{100} + \frac{4}{100}\right) - \left(0 + \frac{18}{100} + \frac{2}{100}\right)^2$$

$$= \frac{22}{100} - \left(\frac{20}{100}\right)^2$$

$$= \frac{11}{50} - \frac{1}{25}$$

$$= \frac{11 - 2}{50} = \frac{9}{50}$$

$$= \frac{18}{100} = 0.18$$

7. Given, defective bulbs = 3 and good bulbs = 7

Here, total number of bulbs = 3 + 7 = 10

Let X denotes the number of defective bulbs.

Then, X takes the values 0, 1, 2 and 3.

Now, $P(X = 0) = P$ (getting 0 defective bulb)

$$= \frac{({}^3C_0 \times {}^7C_3)}{{}^{10}C_3} = \frac{\left(1 \times \frac{7 \times 6 \times 5}{3 \times 2 \times 1}\right)}{\left(\frac{10 \times 9 \times 8}{3 \times 2 \times 1}\right)}$$

$$= \frac{7 \times 6 \times 5}{10 \times 9 \times 8} = \frac{7}{24}$$

$P(X = 1) = P$ (getting 1 defective bulb)

$$= \frac{({}^3C_1 \times {}^7C_2)}{{}^{10}C_3} = \frac{\left(3 \times \frac{7 \times 6}{2 \times 1}\right)}{\left(\frac{10 \times 9 \times 8}{3 \times 2 \times 1}\right)}$$

$$= \frac{3 \times 7 \times 6 \times 3}{10 \times 9 \times 8} = \frac{21}{40}$$

$P(X=2) = P$ (getting 2 defective bulbs)

$$= \frac{({}^3C_2 \times {}^7C_1)}{{}^{10}C_3} = \frac{\left(\frac{3\times 2}{2\times 1}\times 7\right)}{\left(\frac{10\times 9\times 8}{3\times 2\times 1}\right)}$$

$$= \frac{3\times 2\times 7\times 3}{10\times 9\times 8}$$

$$= \frac{7}{40}$$

$P(X=3) = P$ (getting 3 defective bulbs)

$$= \frac{({}^3C_3 \times {}^7C_0)}{{}^{10}C_3}$$

$$= \frac{1\times 1}{\left(\frac{10\times 9\times 8}{3\times 2\times 1}\right)}$$

$$= \frac{3\times 2\times 1}{10\times 9\times 8} = \frac{1}{120}$$

∴ Required probability distribution as follows

X	0	1	2	3
$P(X)$	7/24	21/40	7/40	1/120

8. Similar as Example 4. **Ans.** $\frac{2}{13}$

9. Similar as Example 8.

Ans.

X	0	1	2	3
$P(X)$	2/17	13/34	13/34	2/17

, Mean = 1.5

10. Let X be a random variable that denotes the number of spades in a draw of three cards.

So, X can takes values 0, 1, 2 and 3.

Now, $P(X=0) = P$ (no spade)

$$= \frac{39}{52}\times\frac{39}{52}\times\frac{39}{52}$$

$$= \frac{3}{4}\times\frac{3}{4}\times\frac{3}{4} = \frac{27}{64}$$

[∵ cards are drawn with replacement]

$P(X=1) = P$ (one spade and two non-spade)

$= P$ (Ist card is spade, IInd and IIIrd cards are non-spade) + P (Ist card is non-spade, IInd card is spade and IIIrd is non-spade) + P (Ist and IInd cards are non-spade and IIIrd card is spade)

$$= \frac{13}{52}\times\frac{39}{52}\times\frac{39}{52} + \frac{39}{52}\times\frac{13}{52}\times\frac{39}{52} + \frac{39}{52}\times\frac{39}{52}\times\frac{13}{52}$$

$$= 3\left(\frac{1}{4}\times\frac{3}{4}\times\frac{3}{4}\right) = \frac{27}{64}$$

$P(X=2) = P$ (two spade and one non-spade)

$$= \frac{13}{52}\times\frac{13}{52}\times\frac{39}{52} + \frac{13}{52}\times\frac{39}{52}\times\frac{13}{52} + \frac{39}{52}\times\frac{13}{52}\times\frac{13}{52}$$

$$= 3\left(\frac{1}{4}\times\frac{1}{4}\times\frac{3}{4}\right)$$

$$= \frac{9}{64}$$

∴ $P(X=3) = P$ (all are spade cards)

$$= \frac{13}{52}\times\frac{13}{52}\times\frac{13}{52}$$

$$= \frac{1}{4}\times\frac{1}{4}\times\frac{1}{4} = \frac{1}{64}$$

Thus, the required probability distribution is as follows

X	0	1	2	3
$P(X)$	27/64	27/64	9/64	1/64

Now, mean of above distribution is given by

$$E(X) = \sum_{x=0}^{3} x\cdot P(X=x)$$

$$= 0\cdot P(X=0) + 1\cdot P(X=1) + 2\cdot P(X=2) + 3\cdot P(X=3)$$

$$= 0\cdot\frac{27}{64} + 1\cdot\frac{27}{64} + 2\cdot\frac{9}{64} + 3\cdot\frac{1}{64}$$

$$= \frac{27+18+3}{64}$$

$$= \frac{48}{64} = \frac{3}{4}$$

11. **Hint** Let X denotes the number of defective bulbs drawn.

Then, P (getting defective bulbs) $= \frac{1}{5}$,

P (non-getting defective bulbs) $= \frac{4}{5}$

and $X = 0, 1, 2, 3$

Now, $P(X=0) = \frac{4}{5}\times\frac{4}{5}\times\frac{4}{5} = \frac{64}{125}$

$$P(X=1) = 3\times\frac{4}{5}\times\frac{4}{5}\times\frac{1}{5} = \frac{48}{125}$$

$$P(X=2) = 3\times\frac{4}{5}\times\frac{1}{5}\times\frac{1}{5} = \frac{12}{125}$$

$$P(X=3) = \frac{1}{5}\times\frac{1}{5}\times\frac{1}{5} = \frac{1}{125}$$

∴ $\text{Mean} = \frac{48}{125} + \frac{24}{125} + \frac{3}{125}$

and $\text{variance} = \left(\frac{48}{125} + \frac{48}{125} + \frac{9}{125}\right) - \left(\frac{3}{5}\right)^2$

Ans. Mean $= \frac{3}{5}$, variance $= \frac{12}{25}$

12. Hint

X	0	1
$P(X)$	3/10	7/10

Ans. $E(X) = \frac{7}{10}$, $\text{Var}(X) = \frac{21}{100}$

13. Hint

X	0	500	2000	3000
$P(X)$	$\frac{9995}{10000}$	$\frac{3}{10000}$	$\frac{1}{10000}$	$\frac{1}{10000}$
P_iX_i	0	$\frac{1500}{10000}$	$\frac{2000}{10000}$	$\frac{3000}{10000}$

$\because E(X) = \Sigma XP(X)$ **Ans.** 0.65

14. Here, $S = \{(1, 3), (1, 5), (1, 7), (3, 1)(3, 5), (3, 7), (5, 1), (5, 3), (5, 7), (7, 1), (7, 3), (7, 5)\}$

$\Rightarrow n(S) = 12$

Let random variable X denotes the sum of the numbers on two cards drawn. So, the random variables X may have values 4, 6, 8, 10 and 12.

At $X = 4$, $P(X) = \frac{2}{12} = \frac{1}{6}$,

At $X = 6$, $P(X) = \frac{2}{12} = \frac{1}{6}$

At $X = 8$, $P(X) = \frac{4}{12} = \frac{1}{3}$,

At $X = 10$, $P(X) = \frac{2}{12} = \frac{1}{6}$

At $X = 12$, $P(X) = \frac{2}{12} = \frac{1}{6}$

Therefore, the required probability distribution is as follows

X	4	6	8	10	12
$P(X)$	1/6	1/6	1/3	1/6	1/6

$\therefore$ Mean, $E(X) = \Sigma X\,P(X)$

$$= 4 \times \frac{1}{6} + 6 \times \frac{1}{6} + 8 \times \frac{1}{3} + 10 \times \frac{1}{6} + 12 \times \frac{1}{6}$$

$$= \frac{2}{3} + 1 + \frac{8}{3} + \frac{5}{3} + 2$$

$$= \frac{2 + 8 + 5}{3} + 3$$

$$= \frac{15}{3} + 3 = 5 + 3 = 8$$

Also, $\Sigma X^2P(X) = 16 \times \frac{1}{6} + 36 \times \frac{1}{6} + 64 \times \frac{1}{3} + 100 \times \frac{1}{6} + 144 \times \frac{1}{6}$

$$= \frac{8}{3} + 6 + \frac{64}{3} + \frac{50}{3} + 24$$

$$= \frac{8 + 64 + 50}{3} + 30$$

$$= \frac{122}{3} + 30$$

$$= \frac{122 + 90}{3}$$

$$= \frac{212}{3}$$

$\therefore$ Variance $(X) = \Sigma X^2P(X) - [\Sigma X\,P(X)]^2$

$$= \frac{212}{3} - (8)^2 = \frac{212}{3} - 64$$

$$= \frac{212 - 192}{3} = \frac{20}{3}$$

15. The probability distribution table for given function is

X	1	2	3	4	5	6	otherwise
$P(X)$	k	$4k$	$9k$	$8k$	$10k$	$12k$	0

We know that, $\Sigma P_i = 1$

$\therefore \quad k + 4k + 9k + 8k + 10k + 12k + 0 = 1$

$\Rightarrow \quad 44k = 1$

$\Rightarrow \quad k = \frac{1}{44}$

(i) $E(X) = \Sigma X \cdot P(X)$

$$= 1 \times k + 2 \times 4k + 3 \times 9k + 4 \times 8k + 5 \times 10k + 6 \times 12k + 0$$

$$= k + 8k + 27k + 32k + 50k + 72k$$

$$= 190k = 190 \times \frac{1}{44} \qquad \left[\because k = \frac{1}{44}\right]$$

$$= \frac{95}{22}$$

(ii) $E(X^2) = \Sigma X^2P(X)$

$$= (1)^2 \times k + (2)^2 \times 4k + (3)^2 \times 9k + (4)^2 \times 8k + (5)^2 \times 10k + (6)^2 \times 12k$$

$$= k + 16k + 81k + 128k + 250k + 432k$$

$$= 908k = 908 \times \frac{1}{44}$$

$$= 20.64 \text{ (approx.)}$$

(iii) $P(X \geq 4) = P(X = 4) + P(X = 5) + P(X = 6)$

$$= 30k = 30 \times \frac{1}{44} = 0.68$$

16. Hint Use $\Sigma P(X) = 1$

Ans. (i) 1/10 (ii) 3/10 (iii) 17/100 (iv) 3/10

17. Let X denotes the sum of the numbers obtained when two fair dice are rolled. So, X may have values 2, 3, 4, 5, 6, 7, 8, 9, 10, 11 or 12.

[as 1 cannot be the sum of two numbers on fair dice]

$P(X=2)=P\{(1,1)\}=\frac{1}{36}$,

$P(X=3)=P\{(1,2),(2,1)\}=\frac{2}{36}$,

$P(X=4)=P\{(1,3),(2,2),(3,1)\}=\frac{3}{36}$,

$P(X=5)=P\{(1,4),(2,3),(3,2),(4,1)\}=\frac{4}{36}$,

$P(X=6)=P\{(1,5),(2,4),(3,3),(4,2),(5,1)\}=\frac{5}{36}$,

$P(X=7)=P\{(1,6),(2,5),(3,4),(4,3),(5,2),(6,1)\}=\frac{6}{36}$,

$P(X=8)=P\{(2,6),(3,5),(4,4),(5,3),(6,2)\}=\frac{5}{36}$,

$P(X=9)=P\{(3,6),(4,5),(5,4),(6,3)\}=\frac{4}{36}$,

$P(X=10)=P\{(4,6),(5,5),(6,4)\}=\frac{3}{36}$,

$P(X=11)=P\{(5,6),(6,5)\}=\frac{2}{36}$ and

$P(X=12)=P\{(6,6)\}=\frac{1}{36}$

The probability distribution of X is represented by

X	2	3	4	5	6	7	8	9	10	11	12
$P(X)$	$\frac{1}{36}$	$\frac{2}{36}$	$\frac{3}{36}$	$\frac{4}{36}$	$\frac{5}{36}$	$\frac{6}{36}$	$\frac{5}{36}$	$\frac{4}{36}$	$\frac{3}{36}$	$\frac{2}{36}$	$\frac{1}{36}$

Mean, $X=\Sigma X\,P(X)$

$$=\frac{\begin{bmatrix}2\times1+3\times2+4\times3+5\times4+6\times5+7\times6\\+8\times5+9\times4+10\times3+11\times2+12\times1\end{bmatrix}}{36}$$

$$=\frac{[2+6+12+20+30+42+40+36+30+22+12]}{36}$$

$$=\frac{252}{36}=7$$

$\therefore \text{Var}(X)=\Sigma X^2\,P(X)-(\text{Mean})^2$

$$=\frac{\begin{bmatrix}2^2\times1+3^2\times2+4^2\times3+5^2\times4+6^2\times5+7^2\times6\\+8^2\times5+9^2\times4+10^2\times3+11^2\times2+12^2\times1\end{bmatrix}}{36}-7^2$$

$$=\frac{1}{36}\times(4+18+48+100+180+294+320+324+300+242+144)-49$$

$$=\frac{1974}{36}-49=\frac{1974-1764}{36}=\frac{210}{36}=\frac{35}{6}$$

$\therefore$ Standard deviation $=\sqrt{\text{Var}(X)}=\sqrt{\frac{35}{6}}$

$=\sqrt{5.83}=2.415$

18. Here, $S=\begin{Bmatrix}(1,2),(2,1),(1,3),(3,1),(2,3),(3,2),\\(1,4),(4,1),(1,5),(5,1),(2,4),(4,2),(2,5),\\(5,2),(3,4),(4,3),(3,5),(5,3),(5,4),(4,5)\end{Bmatrix}$

$\Rightarrow n(S)=20$

Let random variable X denotes the sum of the numbers on two cards drawn.

So, the random variables X may have values 3, 4, 5, 6, 7, 8 and 9.

At $X=3$, $P(X)=\frac{2}{20}=\frac{1}{10}$,

At $X=4$, $P(X)=\frac{2}{20}=\frac{1}{10}$,

At $X=5$, $P(X)=\frac{4}{20}=\frac{1}{5}$,

At $X=6$, $P(X)=\frac{4}{20}=\frac{1}{5}$,

At $X=7$, $P(X)=\frac{4}{20}=\frac{1}{5}$,

At $X=8$, $P(X)=\frac{2}{20}=\frac{1}{10}$,

At $X=9$, $P(X)=\frac{2}{20}=\frac{1}{10}$

Therefore, the required probability distribution is as follows

X	3	4	5	6	7	8	9
$P(X)$	$\frac{1}{10}$	$\frac{1}{10}$	$\frac{1}{5}$	$\frac{1}{5}$	$\frac{1}{5}$	$\frac{1}{10}$	$\frac{1}{10}$

$\therefore$ Mean, $E(X)=\Sigma X\,P(X)$

$$=3\times\frac{1}{10}+4\times\frac{1}{10}+5\times\frac{1}{5}+6\times\frac{1}{5}+7\times\frac{1}{5}+8\times\frac{1}{10}+9\times\frac{1}{10}$$

$$=\frac{3}{10}+\frac{4}{10}+\frac{5}{5}+\frac{6}{5}+\frac{7}{5}+\frac{8}{10}+\frac{9}{10}$$

$$=\frac{3+4+10+12+14+8+9}{10}$$

$$=\frac{60}{10}=6$$

Also, $\Sigma X^2P(X)=\frac{9}{10}+\frac{16}{10}+\frac{25}{5}+\frac{36}{5}+\frac{49}{5}+\frac{64}{10}+\frac{81}{10}$

$$=\frac{9+16+50+72+98+64+81}{10}$$

$$=\frac{390}{10}=39$$

$\therefore \text{Var}(X)=\Sigma X^2P(X)-[\Sigma X\,P(X)]^2$

$=39-(6)^2$

$=39-36$

$=3$

19. **Hint** P (head) = $4P$ (tail) $\Rightarrow P(H) = \frac{4}{5}, P(T) = \frac{1}{5}$

X (Number of tails)	0	1	2	3
P(X)	$\frac{64}{125}$	$\frac{48}{125}$	$\frac{12}{125}$	$\frac{1}{125}$
XP(X)	0	$\frac{48}{125}$	$\frac{24}{125}$	$\frac{3}{125}$
$X^2P(X)$	0	$\frac{48}{125}$	$\frac{48}{125}$	$\frac{9}{125}$

$\therefore$ Mean $= \Sigma XP(X) = \frac{75}{125}$

Variance $= \Sigma X^2P(X) - [\Sigma XP(X)]^2 = \frac{105}{125} - \frac{9}{25}$

Ans. Mean $= \frac{3}{5}$, variance $= \frac{12}{25}$

20. Consider p = Probability of getting a red ball $= \frac{6}{9} = \frac{2}{3}$

and q = Probability of getting a white ball $= \frac{3}{9} = \frac{1}{3}$

Let X denotes the number of red balls in four draws.
Then, X can take values 0, 1, 2, 3 and 4.
Now, $P(X = 0) = P$ (no red balls) $= P$ (all white balls)

$$= \frac{1}{3} \times \frac{1}{3} \times \frac{1}{3} \times \frac{1}{3} = \frac{1}{81}$$

$P(X = 1) = P$ (one red and three white balls)

$$= \frac{2}{3} \times \frac{1}{3} \times \frac{1}{3} \times \frac{1}{3} + \frac{1}{3} \times \frac{2}{3} \times \frac{1}{3} \times \frac{1}{3} + \frac{1}{3} \times \frac{1}{3} \times \frac{2}{3} \times \frac{1}{3} + \frac{1}{3} \times \frac{1}{3} \times \frac{1}{3} \times \frac{2}{3} = 4 \times \frac{2}{81} = \frac{8}{81}$$

$P(X = 2) = P$ (two red and two white balls)

$$= 6 \times \frac{4}{81} = \frac{24}{81}$$

$P(X = 3) = P$ (three red and one white ball)

$$= 4 \times \frac{8}{81} = \frac{32}{81}$$

$P(X = 4) = P$ (all red balls) $= 1 \times \frac{16}{81} = \frac{16}{81}$

Hence, the probability distribution is shown below

X	0	1	2	3	4
P(X)	$\frac{1}{81}$	$\frac{8}{81}$	$\frac{24}{81}$	$\frac{32}{81}$	$\frac{16}{81}$

Now, mean of distribution, $E(X) = \Sigma X \cdot P(X)$

$$= 0 \cdot \frac{1}{81} + 1 \cdot \frac{8}{81} + 2 \cdot \frac{24}{81} + 3 \cdot \frac{32}{81} + 4 \cdot \frac{16}{81}$$

$$= \frac{1}{81}[0 + 8 + 48 + 96 + 64]$$

$$= \frac{216}{81} = \frac{8}{3}$$

and variance of distribution $= E(X)^2 - [E(X)]^2$

$$= \Sigma X^2 P(X) - \left(\frac{8}{3}\right)^2$$

$$= \left(0^2 \cdot \frac{1}{81} + 1^2 \cdot \frac{8}{81} + 2^2 \cdot \frac{24}{81} + 3^2 \cdot \frac{32}{81} + 4^2 \cdot \frac{16}{81}\right) - \frac{64}{9}$$

$$= \frac{1}{81}(0 + 8 + 96 + 288 + 256) - \frac{64}{9}$$

$$= \frac{648}{81} - \frac{64}{9} = \frac{648 - 576}{81} = \frac{72}{81} = \frac{8}{9}$$

21. Similar as Example 9.

Ans.

X	2	3	4	5	6
P(X)	$\frac{1}{15}$	$\frac{2}{15}$	$\frac{3}{15}$	$\frac{4}{15}$	$\frac{5}{15}$

22. Given, X denotes the largest of the three positive integers.

So, the random variable X may have values 3, 4, 5 or 6.

$P(X = 3) = P$ (getting 3 and two numbers less than 3)

$$= \frac{{}^1C_1 \times {}^2C_2}{{}^6C_3} = \frac{1}{20}$$

$P(X = 4) = P$ (getting 4 and two numbers less than 4)

$$= \frac{{}^1C_1 \times {}^3C_2}{{}^6C_3} = \frac{3}{20}$$

$P(X = 5) = P$ (getting 5 and two numbers less than 5)

$$= \frac{{}^1C_1 \times {}^4C_2}{{}^6C_3} = \frac{6}{20}$$

$P(X = 6) = P$ (getting 6 and two numbers less than 6)

$$= \frac{{}^1C_1 \times {}^5C_2}{{}^6C_3} = \frac{10}{20}$$

$\therefore$ Probability distribution is shown below

X	3	4	5	6
P(X)	$\frac{1}{20}$	$\frac{3}{20}$	$\frac{6}{20}$	$\frac{10}{20}$

Now, mean of distribution, $E(X) = \Sigma X \cdot P(X)$

$$= 3 \times \frac{1}{20} + 4 \times \frac{3}{20} + 5 \times \frac{6}{20} + 6 \times \frac{10}{20}$$

$$= \frac{3 + 12 + 30 + 60}{20} = \frac{105}{20} = \frac{21}{4}$$

and variance of distribution $= E(X^2) - [E(X)]^2$

$$= \Sigma X^2 P(X) - [E(X)]^2$$

$$= 3^2 \times \frac{1}{20} + 4^2 \times \frac{3}{20} + 5^2 \times \frac{6}{20} + 6^2 \times \frac{10}{20} - \left(\frac{21}{4}\right)^2$$

$$= \frac{9}{20} + \frac{48}{20} + \frac{150}{20} + \frac{360}{20} - \frac{441}{16}$$

$$= \frac{567}{20} - \frac{441}{16} = \frac{63}{80}$$

Bernoulli Trials

There are many experiments which have only two outcomes as a tossed coin shows a head or tail, the response to a question might be yes or no, etc. In such examples, we call one of the outcomes as 'success' and the other 'not success or failure'. The outcome of any trial is independent of the outcome of any other trial. In each of such trials, the probability of success or failure remains constant. Such independent trials which have only two outcomes are called **Bernoulli trials.**

Definition Trials of a random experiment are called Bernoulli trials if they satisfy the following conditions

(i) there should be a finite number of trials.

(ii) the trials should be independent.

(iii) each trial has exactly two outcomes, success or failure.

(iv) the probability of success remains the same in each trial.

EXAMPLE 1. Five balls are drawn successively from a bag containing 8 black and 9 blue balls. Tell whether or not the trials of drawing balls are Bernoulli trials when after each draw the ball drawn is

(i) replaced. (ii) not replaced in bag.

Sol. Given, a bag contains 8 black and 9 blue balls and five balls are drawn.

(i) When the balls are drawn with replacement.

Then, probability of success (say black ball), $p = \frac{8}{17}$.

It is same for all five trials, so trial of drawing ball with replacement are Bernoulli trials.

(ii) When the balls are drawn without replacement. Then,probability of success (say black ball) in first trial $= \frac{8}{17}$

In second trial $= \frac{7}{16}$ (if first ball drawn is black) and $\frac{8}{16}$ (if first ball drawn is blue) and so on.

Thus, probability of success is not same for all trials. Hence, trial of drawing ball without replacement are not Bernoulli trials.

Binomial Distribution

The probability distribution of number of successes X in an experiment consisting n Bernoulli trials can be obtained by the binomial expansion $(p+q)^n$, as shown below

X	0	1	2	$\dots r \dots$	n
$P(X)$	${}^nC_0\, p^0\, q^n$	${}^nC_1 p^1\, q^{n-1}$	${}^nC_2\, p^2\, q^{n-2}$	${}^nC_r\, p^r\, q^{n-r}$	${}^nC_n\, p^n$

This probability distribution is known as binomial distribution with parameters n and p, because for given values of n and p, we can find the complete probability distribution.

Here, $P(X = r) = {}^nC_r p^r q^{n-r}$ is called the **probability function** of the binomial distribution.

Where p = Probability of success, q = Probability of failure, n = Number of trials and also $p+q=1$.

A binomial distribution with n Bernoulli trials and probability of success in each trial as p is denoted by $B(n, p)$.

Mean and variance of binomial distribution

Mean (μ)	$\sum_{i=1}^{n} x_i p_i = np$
Variance (σ^2)	$\sum_{i=1}^{n} x_i^2 p_i - \mu^2 = npq$
Standard deviation (σ)	$\sqrt{\sum_{i=1}^{n} x_i^2 p_i - \mu^2} = \sqrt{npq}$

Note In a binomial distribution, an outcome having highest probability is called most likely outcome.

EXAMPLE 2. A factory produces bulbs. The probability that any one bulb is defective is $\frac{1}{50}$ and they are packed in boxes of 10. From a single box, find the probability that

(i) none of the bulbs is defective.

(ii) exactly two bulbs are defective.

(iii) more than 8 bulbs work properly.

Sol. Let X be the random variable, which denotes the number of defective bulbs.

Also, $n = 10$, $p = \frac{1}{50}$, $q = \frac{49}{50}$ and $P(X = r) = {}^nC_r\, p^r q^{n-r}$

(i) None of the bulbs is defective, i.e. $r = 0$.

$$\therefore\ P(X=0) = P(0) = {}^{10}C_0\left(\frac{1}{50}\right)^0\left(\frac{49}{50}\right)^{10-0} = \left(\frac{49}{50}\right)^{10}$$

(ii) Exactly two bulbs are defective, i.e. $r = 2$.

$$\therefore\ P(X=2) = P(2) = {}^{10}C_2\left(\frac{1}{50}\right)^2\left(\frac{49}{50}\right)^8$$

$$= \frac{10!}{8!2!}\left(\frac{1}{50}\right)^2 \cdot \left(\frac{49}{50}\right)^8 = 45 \times \left(\frac{1}{50}\right)^{10} \times (49)^8$$

(iii) More than 8 bulbs work properly, i.e. there is less than 2 bulbs which are defective.

So, $r < 2 \Rightarrow r = 0, 1$

$$\therefore\ P(X=r) = P(X<2) = P(0) + P(1)$$

$$= {}^{10}C_0\left(\frac{1}{50}\right)^0\left(\frac{49}{50}\right)^{10-0} + {}^{10}C_1\left(\frac{1}{50}\right)^1\left(\frac{49}{50}\right)^{10-1}$$

$$= \left(\frac{49}{50}\right)^{10} + \frac{10!}{1!9!}\cdot\frac{1}{50}\cdot\left(\frac{49}{50}\right)^9 = \left(\frac{49}{50}\right)^{10} + \frac{1}{5}\cdot\left(\frac{49}{50}\right)^9$$

$$= \left(\frac{49}{50}\right)^9\left(\frac{49}{50}+\frac{1}{5}\right) = \left(\frac{49}{50}\right)^9\left(\frac{59}{50}\right) = \frac{59(49)^9}{(50)^{10}}$$

EXAMPLE 3. If a fair coin is tossed 10 times, then find the probability of

(i) exactly 6 heads. (ii) at least 6 heads.

(iii) at most 6 heads.

Sol. Here, a fair coin is tossed 10 times and in each trial, we get either head or tail. Repeated tosses of a coin are Bernoulli trials.

Let X denotes the number of heads in an experiment of 10 trials. X has the binomial distribution with

$$n = 10 \text{ and } p = \frac{1}{2}.$$

(i) $P(\text{exactly 6 heads}) = P(X=6)$

$$= {}^{10}C_6\left(\frac{1}{2}\right)^6\left(\frac{1}{2}\right)^{10-6} = {}^{10}C_6\left(\frac{1}{2}\right)^{10}$$

$$[\because P(X=r) = {}^nC_r p^r q^{n-r}]$$

$$= \frac{10!}{6!4!} \times \frac{1}{2^{10}} = \frac{105}{512}$$

(ii) $P(\text{at least 6 heads}) = P(X \geq 6)$

$$= P(X=6) + P(X=7) + P(X=8) + P(X=9) + P(X=10)$$

$$= {}^{10}C_6\left(\frac{1}{2}\right)^6\left(\frac{1}{2}\right)^{10-6} + {}^{10}C_7\left(\frac{1}{2}\right)^7\left(\frac{1}{2}\right)^{10-7} + {}^{10}C_8\left(\frac{1}{2}\right)^8\left(\frac{1}{2}\right)^{10-8} + {}^{10}C_9\left(\frac{1}{2}\right)^9\left(\frac{1}{2}\right)^{10-9} + {}^{10}C_{10}\left(\frac{1}{2}\right)^{10}\left(\frac{1}{2}\right)^{10-10}$$

$$= {}^{10}C_6\left(\frac{1}{2}\right)^{10} + {}^{10}C_7\left(\frac{1}{2}\right)^{10} + {}^{10}C_8\left(\frac{1}{2}\right)^{10} + {}^{10}C_9\left(\frac{1}{2}\right)^{10} + {}^{10}C_{10}\left(\frac{1}{2}\right)^{10}$$

$$= \left(\frac{1}{2}\right)^{10}({}^{10}C_6 + {}^{10}C_7 + {}^{10}C_8 + {}^{10}C_9 + {}^{10}C_{10})$$

$$= \left(\frac{1}{2}\right)^{10}\left(\frac{10!}{6!\times 4!} + \frac{10!}{7!\times 3!} + \frac{10!}{8!\times 2!} + \frac{10!}{9!\times 1!} + \frac{10!}{10!}\right)$$

$$= \frac{(210+120+45+10+1)}{2^{10}} = \frac{386}{1024} = \frac{193}{512}$$

(iii) Here, we have to find probability of at most six heads.

$$\therefore\ P(X \leq 6) = P(X=0) + P(X=1) + P(X=2) + P(X=3) + P(X=4) + P(X=5) + P(X=6)$$

$$= {}^{10}C_0\left(\frac{1}{2}\right)^0\left(\frac{1}{2}\right)^{10-0} + {}^{10}C_1\left(\frac{1}{2}\right)^1\left(\frac{1}{2}\right)^{10-1} + {}^{10}C_2\left(\frac{1}{2}\right)^2\left(\frac{1}{2}\right)^{10-2} + {}^{10}C_3\left(\frac{1}{2}\right)^3\left(\frac{1}{2}\right)^{10-3} + {}^{10}C_4\left(\frac{1}{2}\right)^4\left(\frac{1}{2}\right)^{10-4} + {}^{10}C_5\left(\frac{1}{2}\right)^5\left(\frac{1}{2}\right)^{10-5} + {}^{10}C_6\left(\frac{1}{2}\right)^6\left(\frac{1}{2}\right)^{10-6}$$

$$= {}^{10}C_0\left(\frac{1}{2}\right)^{10} + {}^{10}C_1\left(\frac{1}{2}\right)^{10} + {}^{10}C_2\left(\frac{1}{2}\right)^{10} + {}^{10}C_3\left(\frac{1}{2}\right)^{10} + {}^{10}C_4\left(\frac{1}{2}\right)^{10} + {}^{10}C_5\left(\frac{1}{2}\right)^{10} + {}^{10}C_6\left(\frac{1}{2}\right)^{10}$$

$$= \left(\frac{1}{2^{10}}\right)({}^{10}C_0 + {}^{10}C_1 + {}^{10}C_2 + {}^{10}C_3 + {}^{10}C_4 + {}^{10}C_5 + {}^{10}C_6)$$

$$= \frac{1}{2^{10}}\left(1 + 10 + \frac{10!}{8!2!} + \frac{10!}{7!3!} + \frac{10!}{6!4!} + \frac{10!}{5!5!} + \frac{10!}{4!6!}\right)$$

$$= \frac{1}{2^{10}}(1+10+45+120+210+252+210)$$

$$= \frac{848}{1024} = \frac{53}{64}$$

EXAMPLE 4. Four cards are drawn successively with replacement from a well-shuffled deck of 52 cards. What is the probability that

(i) all the four cards are spades?

(ii) only 2 cards are spades?

Sol. This is a case of Bernoulli trials with $n = 4$.

$$P = P\text{ (a success)}$$

$$= P\text{ (a spade in a single draw)} = \frac{13}{52} = \frac{1}{4}$$

and $q = 1 - p = 1 - \frac{1}{4} = \frac{3}{4}$

(i) P (all the four cards are spades) $= P(X=4)$

$$= {}^4C_4\, p^4 q^0 = 1\cdot\left(\frac{1}{4}\right)^4 = \frac{1}{256}$$

(ii) P (only 2 spades) $= P(X=2) = {}^4C_2 p^2 q^2$

$$= \frac{4\cdot 3}{2\cdot 1}\left(\frac{1}{4}\right)^2\left(\frac{3}{4}\right)^2 = 6 \times \frac{1}{16} \times \frac{9}{16} = \frac{27}{128}$$

EXAMPLE 5. For 6 trials of an experiment, let X be a Binomial variable which satisfies the relation $9P(X=4)=P(X=2)$. Find the probability of success.

Sol. Let $p=$ Probability of success, $q=$ Probability of failure and X be a random variable that denote the number of success in 6 trials.

As X follows binomial distribution with parameters, $n=6$ and p.

$\therefore \quad P(X=x)={}^6C_x p^x q^{6-x}$

where $x=0, 1, 2, 3, 4, 5$ and 6 and $p+q=1$

Also, $\quad 9P(X=4)=P(X=2)$ [given]

$\therefore \quad 9\times({}^6C_4 p^4 q^2)={}^6C_2 p^2 q^4$

$\Rightarrow \quad 9p^2=q^2$ $\quad [\because {}^6C_4={}^6C_2]$

$\Rightarrow \quad 9p^2=(1-p)^2$ $\quad [\because p+q=1]$

$\Rightarrow \quad 9p^2=1+p^2-2p$

$\Rightarrow \quad 8p^2+2p-1=0$

$\Rightarrow \quad 8p^2+4p-2p-1=0$

$\Rightarrow \quad 4p(2p+1)-1(2p+1)=0$

$\Rightarrow \quad (2p+1)(4p-1)=0$

$\therefore \quad p=\frac{-1}{2}$ or $p=\frac{1}{4}$

Thus, $p=\frac{1}{4}$. $\quad$ [$\because$ probability cannot be negative]

EXAMPLE 6. The probability of a man hitting a target is $\frac{1}{2}$. How many times must be fire so that the probability of hitting the target atleast once is more than 90%?

Sol. Let X denotes the number of times he hits the target in n trials.

$\therefore \quad P(X=r)={}^nC_r\left(\frac{1}{2}\right)^r\left(\frac{1}{2}\right)^{n-r}$

$={}^nC_r\left(\frac{1}{2}\right)^n, r=0, 1, 2, \ldots, n$

Now, $P(X\geq 1)>\frac{90}{100} \Rightarrow 1-P(X=0)>\frac{90}{100}$

$\Rightarrow \quad P(X=0)<1-\frac{90}{100}$

$\Rightarrow \quad {}^nC_0\left(\frac{1}{2}\right)^n<\frac{1}{10} \Rightarrow \left(\frac{1}{2}\right)^n<\frac{1}{10}$

$\therefore \quad \left(\frac{1}{2}\right)^n<\frac{1}{10}$

$\Rightarrow n=4, 5, 6, \ldots$

$\Rightarrow$ Thus, he must fire atleast 4 times.

EXAMPLE 7. A die is thrown thrice getting an even number is considered a success. What is the mean and variance of the binomial distribution?

Sol. We have, $n=3$

Let $p=$ probability of getting an even number in a single throw

Then, $p=\frac{3}{6}=\frac{1}{2}$ and $q=1-p=1-\frac{1}{2}=\frac{1}{2}$

$\because$ Mean $=np=3\times\frac{1}{2}=\frac{3}{2}$

$\because$ Variance $=npq=3\times\frac{1}{2}\times\frac{1}{2}=\frac{3}{4}$

EXAMPLE 8. If X follows a binomial distribution with mean 4 and variance 2, then find $P(X\geq 7)$.

Sol. We know that, mean $=np$ and variance $=npq$

$\therefore np=4$ and $npq=2$

$\frac{npq}{np}=\frac{2}{4} \Rightarrow q=\frac{1}{2} \Rightarrow p=1-q=1-\frac{1}{2}=\frac{1}{2}$

Now, $np=4 \Rightarrow n\times\frac{1}{2}=4 \Rightarrow n=8$

So, binomial distribution is given by

$P(X=r)={}^nC_r p^r q^{n-r}={}^8C_r\left(\frac{1}{2}\right)^r\left(\frac{1}{2}\right)^{8-r}={}^8C_r\left(\frac{1}{2}\right)^8$

$\therefore \quad P(X\geq 7)=P(X=7)+P(X=8)$

$={}^8C_7\left(\frac{1}{2}\right)^8+{}^8C_8\left(\frac{1}{2}\right)^8$

$=\frac{1}{2^8}(8+1)=\frac{9}{2^8}=\frac{9}{256}$

Topic Practice 2

1. A die is thrown 6 times. If getting an odd number is a success, then what is the probability of 5 success?
2. If the probability that a person is not a swimmer is 0.3, then find the probability that out of 5 persons 4 are swimmer.
3. An experiment succeeds thrice as often as it fails. Find the probability that in the next five trials, there will be atleast 3 successes.
4. Suppose, X has a binomial distribution $B\left(6, \frac{1}{2}\right)$. Show that $X=3$ is the most likely outcome.
5. Find the probability that in 10 throws of a fair die, a score which is a multiple of 3 will be obtained in atleast 8 of the throws.
6. How many times must a man toss a fair coin, so that the probability of having atleast one head is more than 80%?

7 It is known that 10% of certain articles manufactured are defective, what is the probability that in a random sample of 12 such articles 9 are defective?

8 The probability that a bulb produced by a factory will fuse after 150 days of used is 0.05. Find the probability that out of 5 such bulbs
(i) none is fuse.
(ii) not more than one bulb is fuse.
(iii) more than one bulb is fuse.
(iv) at least one will fuse after 150 days of use.

9 Five cards are drawn one-by-one with replacement from a well-shuffled deck of 52 cards. Find the probability that
(i) all the five cards are diamonds.
(ii) only 3 cards are diamonds.
(iii) none is a diamond.

10 On a multiple choice examination with three possible options for each of the five questions, what is the probability that a candidate would get four or more correct answers just by guessing?

11 A person buys a lottery ticket in 50 lotteries in each of which his chance of winning a prize is $\frac{1}{100}$.
What is the probability that he will win a prize
(i) at least once? (ii) exactly once?
(iii) at least twice?

12 For a binomial distribution, the mean is 6 and the standard deviation is $\sqrt{2}$. Find the probability of getting 5 successes.

13 Find the binomial distribution, whose mean is 5 and variance is 2.5.

14 An unbiased coin is tossed 4 times. Find the mean and variance of the number of heads obtained.

15 The mean and variance of binomial distribution are 4 and $\frac{4}{3}$, respectively. Find $P(X \geq 1)$.

16 If two dice are rolled 12 times, obtain the mean and the variance of the distribution of successes, if getting a total greater than 4 is considered a success.

17 The sum and the product of the mean and variance of a binomial distribution are 24 and 128, respectively. Find the distribution.

18 If X follows binomial distribution with mean 4 and variance 2. Find $P(|x-4| \leq 2)$.

19 The difference between mean and variance of a binomial distribution is 1 and the difference of their squares is 11. Find the distribution.

20 In a binomial distribution, the sum of its mean and variance is 1.8. Find the probability of two success, if the event was conducted 5 times.

Hints & Solutions

1. **Hint** Given, $n = 6$

and $p = \dfrac{\text{Number of odd number in one die}}{\text{Total number in one die}} = \dfrac{3}{6} = \dfrac{1}{2}$

$\therefore \quad q = 1 - p = 1 - \frac{1}{2} = \frac{1}{2}$

So, P (getting a 5 success in six trials)

$= P(X = 5) = {}^6C_5\, p^5 q^1$ **Ans.** $\frac{3}{32}$

2. **Hint** $q = 0.3$, $p = 1 - 0.3 = 0.7$ and $n = 5$

Ans. ${}^5C_4 (0.7)^4 (0.3)$

3. **Hint** Let p denotes the probability of getting success in the experiment and q denotes the probability of getting failure in the experiment.

According to the question,

$$p = 3q \Rightarrow p = 3(1-p) \qquad [\because p + q = 1]$$

$$\Rightarrow \quad p = 3 - 3p \Rightarrow p + 3p = 3$$

$$\Rightarrow \quad 4p = 3 \Rightarrow p = \frac{3}{4}$$

and then $q = 1 - p \Rightarrow q = 1 - \frac{3}{4} = \frac{1}{4}$

Let X denotes the number of successes in 5 trials. Then, X follows binomial distribution with $n = 5$, $p = \frac{3}{4}$ and $q = \frac{1}{4}$ such that

$$P(X = r) = {}^5C_r \left(\frac{3}{4}\right)^r \left(\frac{1}{4}\right)^{5-r} \quad ; r = 0, 1, 2, \ldots, 5$$

$\therefore$ Required probability,

$$P(X \geq 3) = P(X = 3) + P(X = 4) + P(X = 5)$$

$$= {}^5C_3 \left(\frac{3}{4}\right)^3 \left(\frac{1}{4}\right)^2 + {}^5C_4 \left(\frac{3}{4}\right)^4 \left(\frac{1}{4}\right)^1 + {}^5C_5 \left(\frac{3}{4}\right)^5 \left(\frac{1}{4}\right)^0$$

Ans. $\frac{459}{512}$

4. **Hint** X is the random variable whose binomial distribution is $B\left(6, \frac{1}{2}\right)$.

Therefore, $n = 6$, $p = \frac{1}{2}$ and $q = 1 - p = 1 - \frac{1}{2} = \frac{1}{2}$

Then, $P(X = r) = {}^6C_r \left(\frac{1}{2}\right)^r \left(\frac{1}{2}\right)^{6-r}$

Here,

$P(X=0)={}^6C_0\,p^0q^6=\dfrac{1}{64},\ P(X=1)={}^6C_1\,p^1\,q^5=\dfrac{6}{64}$

$P(X=2)={}^6C_2\,p^2\,q^4=\dfrac{15}{64},\ P(X=3)={}^6C_3\,p^3\,q^3=\dfrac{20}{64}$

$P(X=4)={}^6C_4\,p^4\,q^2=\dfrac{15}{64},\ P(X=5)={}^6C_5\,p^5\,q^1=\dfrac{6}{64}$

and $P(X=6)={}^6C_6\,p^6\,q^0=\dfrac{1}{64}$

It is clear that $\dfrac{20}{64}$ is maximum of all the above values.

It means that, $X=3$ is the most likely outcome.

5. **Hint** $n=10,\ p=\dfrac{2}{6}=\dfrac{1}{3}$ and $q=\dfrac{2}{3}$

Required probability $=\sum_{r=8}^{10}{}^{10}C_r\left(\dfrac{1}{3}\right)^r\left(\dfrac{2}{3}\right)^{10-r}$

Ans. $\dfrac{201}{3^{10}}$

6. Let man tosses the coin n times.

Now, given that P (having atleast one head) > 80%

i.e. $\quad P(X\ge 1)>\dfrac{80}{100}$

Where, X is the number of heads.

$\therefore\quad 1-P(X=0)>\dfrac{80}{100}\ \Rightarrow\ 1-{}^nC_0p^0q^n>\dfrac{80}{100}$

$\Rightarrow\ 1-{}^nC_0\left(\dfrac{1}{2}\right)^0\left(\dfrac{1}{2}\right)^n>\dfrac{8}{10}\ \Rightarrow 1-\dfrac{1}{2^n}>\dfrac{4}{5}$

$\Rightarrow\quad \dfrac{1}{2^n}<1-\dfrac{4}{5}$

$\Rightarrow\quad \dfrac{1}{2^n}<\dfrac{1}{5}\Rightarrow 2^n>5$ ...(i)

Inequality (i) is satisfied for $n\ge 3$.

Hence, coin must be tossed 3 or more times.

7. **Hint** $n=12,\ p=\dfrac{1}{10}$ and $q=\dfrac{9}{10}$

Now, find $P(X=9)$. **Ans.** $\dfrac{22\times 9^3}{10^{11}}$

8. **Hint** $n=5,\ p=0.05$ and $q=0.95$

(i) $P(X=0)$ (ii) $P(X\le 1)$

(iii) $P(X\ge 2)$ (iv) $P(X\ge 1)$

Ans. (i) $(0.95)^5$ (ii) $1.2\times(0.95)^4$

(iii) $1-\{1.2\times(0.95)^4\}$ (iv) $1-(0.95)^5$

9. **Hint** $n=5,\ p=\dfrac{1}{4}$ and $q=\dfrac{3}{4}$

(i) $P(X=5)$ (ii) $P(X=3)$ (iii) $P(X=0)$

Ans. (i) $\dfrac{1}{1024}$ (ii) $\dfrac{45}{512}$ (iii) $\dfrac{243}{1024}$

10. **Hint** $n=5,\ p=\dfrac{1}{3}$ and $q=\dfrac{2}{3}$

$P(X\ge 4)=P(X=4)+P(X=5)$

Ans. $\dfrac{11}{243}$

11. **Hint** $n=50,\ p=\dfrac{1}{100}$ and $q=\dfrac{99}{100}$

(i) $P(X\ge 1)=1-P(X=0)$

(ii) $P(X=1)$

(iii) $P(X\ge 2)=1-[P(X=0)+P(X=1)]$

Ans. (i) $1-\left(\dfrac{99}{100}\right)^{50}$ (ii) $\dfrac{1}{2}\left(\dfrac{99}{100}\right)^{49}$ (iii) $1-\dfrac{149}{100}\left(\dfrac{99}{100}\right)^{49}$

12. **Hint** $np=6,\ npq=2$

and required probability $=P(X=5)$ **Ans.** ${}^9C_5\left(\dfrac{2}{3}\right)^5\left(\dfrac{1}{3}\right)^4$

13. **Hint** $np=5,\ npq=2.5=\dfrac{5}{2}$

Ans. $P(X=r)={}^{10}C_r\left(\dfrac{1}{2}\right)^r\left(\dfrac{1}{2}\right)^{10-r},\ r=0,1,2,\dots,10$

14. **Hint** $n=4,\ p=\dfrac{1}{2},\ q=\dfrac{1}{2}$

Mean $=np=4\times\dfrac{1}{2}=2$, Variance $=npq=4\times\dfrac{1}{2}\times\dfrac{1}{2}=1$

15. **Hint** $np=4,\ npq=\dfrac{4}{3},\ p(X\ge 1)=1-p(X=0)$

Ans. $p(X\ge 1)=\dfrac{728}{729}$

16. **Hint** $p=\dfrac{5}{6},\ q=\dfrac{1}{6}$

Ans. Mean $=10$, Variance $=\dfrac{5}{3}$

17. **Hint** $np+npq=24,\ n^2p^2q=128$

Ans. $P(X=r)={}^{32}C_r\left(\dfrac{1}{2}\right)^{32-r}\left(\dfrac{1}{2}\right)^r;\ r=0,1,2,\dots 32$

18. **Hint** $np=4,\ npq=2$

$p(|X-4|\le 2)=p(-2\le X-4\le 2)$

$p(2\le X\le 6)$

$\Rightarrow p(|X-4|\le 2)=p(X=2)+p(X=3)$
$+p(X=4)+p(X=5)+p(X=6)$

Ans. $\dfrac{119}{128}$

19. **Hint** $np-npq=1,\ (np)^2-(npq)^2=11$

Ans. $P(X=r)={}^{36}C_r\left(\dfrac{1}{6}\right)^r\left(\dfrac{5}{6}\right)^{36-r}$

20. **Hint** $np+npq=1.8,\ n=5$

Ans. $P(X=2)=0.2048$

Poisson Distribution

The Poisson distribution is a theoretical discrete probability distribution that is very useful in situations where the discrete events occurs in continuous manner.

Poisson Distribution as a Limiting Form of Binomial Distribution

Poisson experiment is a statistical experiment that classifies the experiment into two categories, such as success or failure. Poisson distribution is a limiting process of the binomial distribution. A poisson random variable 'x' defines the number of success in the experiment. This distribution occurs when there are events that do not occur as the outcomes. Poisson distribution is under certain condition. They are

(i) the number of trials n is indefinitely large. i.e. n tends to infinity or $n \to \infty$.

(ii) probability of success p for each trial is indefinitely small, i.e. $p \to 0$.

(iii) $np = \lambda$ (say) is finite.

Let X be a binomial variate with parameters n and p. Then,

$$P(r) = P(X = r) = {}^nC_r p^r q^{n-r} \quad (\text{for } r = 0, 1, 2, \ldots, n)$$

$$= \frac{n(n-1)(n-2)\ldots(n-r+1)}{r!} \cdot \frac{\lambda^r}{n^r}\left(1 - \frac{\lambda}{n}\right)^{n-r}$$

$$\left[\text{putting } p = \frac{\lambda}{n}, q = 1 - p = 1 - \frac{\lambda}{n}\right]$$

$$= \frac{\lambda^r}{r!}\left(1 - \frac{1}{n}\right)\left(1 - \frac{2}{n}\right)\ldots\left(1 - \frac{r-1}{n}\right) \cdot \frac{\left(1 - \frac{\lambda}{n}\right)^n}{\left(1 - \frac{\lambda}{n}\right)^r} \quad \ldots(i)$$

When $n \to \infty$, each of the factors $1 - \frac{1}{n}, 1 - \frac{2}{n}, \ldots 1 - \frac{r-1}{n}$ tends to 1, $\left(1 - \frac{\lambda}{n}\right)^r$ also tends to 1 as λ and r are finite, and

$$\underset{n \to \infty}{\text{Lt}}\left(1 - \frac{\lambda}{n}\right)^n = \underset{\frac{n}{\lambda} \to \infty}{\text{Lt}}\left[\left(1 - \frac{\lambda}{n}\right)^{-\frac{n}{\lambda}}\right]^{-\lambda} = e^{-\lambda}$$

Hence, from Eq. (i), we get

$$\underset{n \to \infty}{\text{Lt}} P(r) = \frac{\lambda^r}{r!} e^{-\lambda}$$

Hence, in the limiting case, when $n \to \infty$, $p \to 0$, such that $np = \lambda = a$ finite number, the binomial distribution reduces to the poisson distribution with probability function $P(r)$ defined by

$$P(r) = P(x = r) = \frac{e^{-\lambda}\lambda^r}{r!}, \; r = 0, 1, 2, \ldots \text{ to } \infty$$

Let us assure ourselves that this limiting function is indeed a probability function

$$\sum_{r=0}^{\infty} P(r) = e^{-\lambda} + \frac{\lambda e^{-\lambda}}{1!} + \frac{\lambda^2 e^{-\lambda}}{2!} + \frac{\lambda^3 e^{-\lambda}}{3!} + \ldots \text{ to } \infty$$

$$= e^{-\lambda}\left(1 + \frac{\lambda}{1!} + \frac{\lambda^2}{2!} + \frac{\lambda^3}{3!} + \ldots \text{ to } \infty\right)$$

$$= e^{-\lambda} . e^{\lambda} = 1$$

Note that binomial distribution has two parameters n and p, but poisson distribution has only one parameter λ. Tables are available to find the values of $e^{-\lambda}$, so calculations are easy.

Recurrence Formula for Probabilities of Poisson Distribution

$$P(r) = \frac{e^{-\lambda}\lambda^r}{r!} \text{ and } P(r+1) = \frac{e^{-\lambda}.\lambda^{r+1}}{(r+1)!}$$

$$\frac{P(r+1)}{P(r)} = \frac{e^{-\lambda}.\lambda^{r+1}}{(r+1)!} \cdot \frac{r!}{e^{-\lambda}\lambda^r} = \frac{\lambda}{r+1}$$

Thus, $P(r+1) = \frac{\lambda}{r+1} P(r)$, for $r = 0, 1, 2, 3, \ldots$

Hence, to find successive probabilities, we calculate $P(0) = e^{-\lambda}$, and then use

$$P(1) = \lambda P(0), P(2) = \frac{\lambda}{2} P(1), P(3) = \frac{\lambda}{3} P(2), \ldots$$

Mean And Variance of Poisson Distribution

For the poisson distribution, we have

$$P(r) = \frac{e^{-\lambda}\lambda^r}{r!} \text{ for } r = 0, 1, 2, \ldots$$

$$\therefore \; E(X) = \mu = \sum_{r=0}^{\infty} r P(r) = \sum_{r=0}^{\infty} r \frac{e^{-\lambda}\lambda^r}{r!}$$

$$= 0 + 1.\lambda e^{-\lambda} + 2\frac{\lambda^2 e^{-\lambda}}{2!} + 3\frac{\lambda^3 e^{-\lambda}}{3!} + \ldots \text{ to } \infty$$

$$= \lambda e^{-\lambda}\left(1 + \frac{\lambda}{1!} + \frac{\lambda^2}{2!} + \ldots \text{ to } \infty\right) = \lambda e^{-\lambda}.e^{\lambda} = \lambda$$

Thus, the mean of the poisson distribution is equal to the parameter λ.

The variance σ^2 is given by

$$\sigma^2 = \sum_{r=0}^{\infty} r^2 P(r) - \mu^2 = \sum_{r=0}^{\infty} r^2 \frac{e^{-\lambda}\lambda^r}{r!} - \lambda^2$$

$$= e^{-\lambda}\left[1^2 \cdot \frac{\lambda}{1!} + 2^2 \cdot \frac{\lambda^2}{2!} + 3^2 \cdot \frac{\lambda^3}{3!} + 4^2 \cdot \frac{\lambda^4}{4!} \ldots \text{to } \infty\right] - \lambda^2$$

$$= \lambda e^{-\lambda}\left[1 + \frac{2\lambda}{1!} + \frac{3\lambda^2}{2!} + \frac{4\lambda^3}{3!} + \ldots \text{to } \infty\right] - \lambda^2$$

$$= \lambda e^{-\lambda}\left[1 + \frac{(1+1)\lambda}{1!} + \frac{(1+2)\lambda^2}{2!} + \frac{(1+3)\lambda^3}{3!} + \ldots \text{to } \infty\right] - \lambda^2$$

$$= \lambda e^{-\lambda}\left[\left(1 + \frac{\lambda}{1!} + \frac{\lambda^2}{2!} + \frac{\lambda^3}{3!} + \ldots \text{to } \infty\right) + \lambda\left(1 + \frac{\lambda}{1!} + \frac{\lambda^2}{2!} + \ldots \text{to } \infty\right)\right] - \lambda^2$$

$$= \lambda e^{-\lambda}(e^{\lambda} + \lambda e^{\lambda}) - \lambda^2 = \lambda + \lambda^2 - \lambda^2 = \lambda$$

Hence, the variance of the poisson distribution is also λ and standard deviation is $\sqrt{\lambda}$.

EXAMPLE 1. For the Poisson distribution. Find

(i) $P(3)$, given $\lambda = 2$ (ii) $P(2)$, given $\lambda = 0.02$

Sol. For a poisson distribution, $P(X = r) = \dfrac{\lambda^r e^{-\lambda}}{r!}$

(i) $P(x=3) = P(3) = \dfrac{\lambda^3 e^{-\lambda}}{3!} = \dfrac{(2)^3 e^{-2}}{3!} = \dfrac{8e^{-2}}{6} = \dfrac{4}{3}e^{-2}$

(ii) $P(X=2) = P(2) = \dfrac{\lambda^2 e^{-\lambda}}{2!} = \dfrac{(0.02)^2 e^{-0.02}}{2}$

$= \dfrac{e^{-0.02} \times 0.0004}{2}$

$= 0.0002e^{-0.02}$

EXAMPLE 2. Suppose, 2% of the items made by a factory are defective. Find the probability that there are 3 defective items in a sample of 100 items.
(given $e^{-2} = 0.135$) **[CBSE 2023]**

Sol. Let P be the probability that an item is defective.

Then, $P = \dfrac{2}{100} = 0.02$

We have, $n = 100$

$\therefore \lambda = np = 100 \times \dfrac{2}{100} = 2$

Let X denotes the number of defective items.

Now, required probability

$P(X=3) = \dfrac{\lambda^3 e^{-\lambda}}{3!} = \dfrac{2^3 e^{-2}}{6} = \dfrac{4}{3}e^{-2}$

$= \dfrac{4}{3}(0.135)$ $\quad [\because e^{-2} = 0.135]$

$= 0.180$

EXAMPLE 3. The probability that an individual suffers from reaction by an injection is $\dfrac{1}{1000}$. Find the probability that out of 5000 individuals given that injections

(i) exactly 5 will suffer from reaction

(ii) no one will suffer from reaction.
(given $e^{-5} = 0.00672$)

Sol. We have, P = Probability that an individual suffers from reaction by an injection $= \dfrac{1}{1000}$, $n = 5000$

$\therefore \lambda = np = 5000 \times \dfrac{1}{1000} = 5$

(i) We have, $P(X=5) = \dfrac{\lambda^5 e^{-\lambda}}{5!}$

$= \dfrac{5^5 e^{-5}}{120} = \dfrac{3125}{120}(0.00672) = 0.175$

(ii) We have, $P(X=0) = \dfrac{\lambda^0 e^{-\lambda}}{0!} = \dfrac{5^0 e^{-5}}{1} = e^{-5} = 0.00672$

EXAMPLE 4. A telephone exchange receives on an average 4 calls per minute. Find the probability on the basis of the poisson distribution of

(i) 2 or less calls per minutes

(ii) up to 4 calls per minutes

(iii) more than 4 calls per minutes. (given $e^{-4} = 0.0183$)

Sol. It is given that $\lambda = 4$

(i) We have,

$P(X \le 2) = P(X=0) + P(X=1) + P(X=2)$

$= \dfrac{4^0 e^{-4}}{0!} + \dfrac{4^1 e^{-4}}{1!} + \dfrac{4^2 e^{-4}}{2!} = e^{-4}(1+4+8)$

$= 0.0183 \times 13 = 0.2379$

(ii) We have,

$P(X \le 4) = P(X=0) + P(X=1) + P(X=2) + P(X=3) + P(X=4)$

$= \dfrac{4^0 e^{-4}}{0!} + \dfrac{4^1 e^{-4}}{1!} + \dfrac{4^2 e^{-4}}{2!} + \dfrac{4^3 e^{-4}}{3!} + \dfrac{4^4 e^{-4}}{4!}$

$= e^{-4}\left(1 + 4 + 8 + \dfrac{32}{3} + \dfrac{32}{3}\right) = 0.6283$

(iii) We have,

$P(X > 4) = 1 - P(X \le 4) = 1 - 0.6283 = 0.3717$

EXAMPLE 5. The probability that a man aged 35 yr will die before reaching the age of 40 yr may be taken as 0.018. Out of a group of 400 men, now aged 35 yr, what is the approximate probability that 2 men will die with in next 5 yr? (given, $e^{-7.2} = 0.000747$)

Sol. Let P denote the probability that a man aged 35 yr will die before reaching the age of 40 yr. Then, $P = 0.018$

We have, $n = 400$

$\therefore \lambda = np = 400 \times 0.018 = 7.2$

Now, required probability $= P(X=2) = \dfrac{\lambda^2 e^{-\lambda}}{2!}$

$$= \frac{(7.2)^2 e^{-7.2}}{2} = 51.84 \times 0.000747$$

$$= 0.01936$$

EXAMPLE 6. For a poisson distribution, $3P(X=2) = P(X=4)$. Find $P(X=3)$. (given, $e^{-6} = 0.00248$)

Sol. Given, $3P(X=2) = P(X=4)$

$$\Rightarrow \frac{3\lambda^2 e^{-\lambda}}{2!} = \frac{\lambda^4 e^{-\lambda}}{4!}$$

$$\Rightarrow \frac{3}{2}\lambda^2 = \frac{\lambda^4}{24}$$

$$\Rightarrow \lambda^2 = \frac{3 \times 24}{2} = 36$$

$$\Rightarrow \lambda = 6 \quad [\lambda > 0]$$

Hence, $P(X=3) = \dfrac{\lambda^3 e^{-\lambda}}{3!} = \dfrac{6^3 e^{-6}}{6} = 36 \times 0.00248 = 0.08928$

EXAMPLE 7. If the variance of the poisson distribution is 2. Find the distribution for $r = 1, 2, 3, 4$ and 5 from the recurrence relation of the distribution. (given, $e^{-2} = 0.1353$)

Sol. It is given that variance, $\lambda = 2$

$$P(X=0) = \frac{\lambda^0 e^{-\lambda}}{0!} = e^{-2} = 0.1353$$

Now, we use the recurrence relation of the poisson distribution

$$P(r+1) = \frac{\lambda}{r+1} P(r)$$

$$P(1) = \frac{2}{1} P(0) = 2 \times 0.1353 = 0.2706$$

$$P(2) = \frac{2}{2} P(1) = 1 \times 0.2706 = 0.2706$$

$$P(3) = \frac{2}{3} P(2) = \frac{2}{3} \times 0.2706 = 0.1804$$

$$P(4) = \frac{2}{4} P(3) = \frac{1}{2} \times 0.1804 = 0.0902$$

and $P(5) = \dfrac{2}{5} P(4) = \dfrac{2}{5} \times 0.0902 = 0.0361$

EXAMPLE 8. If a random variable X follows Poisson's distributions such that $P(X=2) = 9P(X=4) + 90P(X=6)$. Find the mean and variance of X.

Sol. We have, $P(X=2) = 9P(X=4) + 90P(X=6)$

$$\frac{\lambda^2 e^{-\lambda}}{2!} = \frac{9\lambda^4 e^{-\lambda}}{4!} + \frac{90\lambda^6 e^{-\lambda}}{6!}$$

$$\Rightarrow \frac{\lambda^2}{2} = \frac{9\lambda^4}{24} + \frac{90\lambda^6}{720}$$

$$\Rightarrow 1 = \frac{3}{4}\lambda^2 + \frac{1}{4}\lambda^4$$

$$\Rightarrow \lambda^4 + 3\lambda^2 - 4 = 0 \Rightarrow (\lambda^2+4)(\lambda^2-1) = 0$$

$$\Rightarrow \lambda^2 \neq -4,\ \lambda^2 = 1,\ \lambda = 1 \quad [\because \lambda > 0]$$

$\therefore$ Mean = Variance = λ

Hence, mean and variance of X is 1.

Topic Practice 3

1 For the poisson distribution. Find

(i) $P(2)$, given $\lambda = 0.3$ (ii) $P(4)$, given $\lambda = 2$

2 If a random variable X has a poisson distribution such that $P(X=1) = 2P(X=2)$. Find $P(X=0)$.

3 If 2% of the books bound at a certain workshop have defective binding. Find the probability that 3 books out of 100 books will have defective binding.

4 In a certain factory turning razor blades. There is a small chance $\frac{1}{500}$ for any blade to be defective. The blacks are in packet of 10. Use poisson's distribution to calculate the approximate number of packets containing no defectives, one defective and two defectives blades, respectively in a consignment of 10000 packets. (Use $e^{-0.02} = 0.9802$)

5 A manufacturer of screws known that 4% of his product is defective. If he sells the screws in boxes of 50 and guaranteed that not more than 2 screws will be defective. What is the probability that a box will fail to meet the quality? (Use $e^{-2} = 0.1353$)

6 In an automatic telephone exchange the probability that any one call is wrongly connected is 0.001. What is the minimum number of independent calls required to ensure a probability of 0.09 that of least one call is wrongly connected? (Use $e^{-4.6} = 0.01$)

7 Suppose, a book of 585 pages contains 43 typographical errors. If these errors are randomly distributed throughout the book. What is the probability that 10 pages, selected at random will be free from errors?
(Use $e^{-0.735} = 0.4795$)

8 A river near a small town floods and overflows twice in every 10 years on an average. Assuming that the Poisson distribution is appropriate, what is the mean expectation? Also, calculate the probability of 3 or less overflows and floods in a 10-year interval.
[Given, $e^{-2} = 0.13534$] **[CBSE 2024]**

9 The probability that a man aged 50 yr will die within a year is 0.01125. What is the probability that out of 12 such men atleast 11 will reach their fifty first birthday? (Use $e^{-0.135} = 0.87371$)

10 Assuming that the chance of a traffic accident in a day on a road of Delhi is 0.001, on how many days out of a total of 1000 days can we except.
No accident, more than three accidents, if there are 1000 such roads in the whole city.

11 A box contains 200 tickets, each bearing one of the numbers from1 to 200. 20 tickets are drawn, successively with replacement from the box. Find the probability that atmost 4 tickets bear numbers divisible by 20.

12 If X is a poisson variate such that $3P(X=2) = 2P(X=1)$. Find $P(X=0)$ and $P(X=3)$.

13 If X has a poisson distribution such that $P(X=1) = P(X=2)$. Find $P(X=4)$. Also find mean and variance.

Hints & Solutions

1. (i) $0.045e^{-0.3}$ (ii) $\frac{2}{3}e^{-2}$

2. **Hint** $\lambda e^{-\lambda} = \frac{2\lambda^2 e^{-\lambda}}{2!} \Rightarrow \lambda = 1$ **Ans.** $P(X=0) = e^{-1}$

3. **Hint** $n = 100$, $P = \frac{2}{100}$, $\lambda = 2$

Ans. $P(X=3) = \frac{2^3}{3!}e^{-2} = \frac{4}{3}e^{-2}$

4. Here, $N = 10000$, $n = 10$, $P = \frac{1}{500}$

$\Rightarrow \quad \lambda = np = 10 \times \frac{1}{500} = 0.02$

$$P(X=0) = \frac{e^{-0.02}.(0.02)^0}{0!} = e^{-0.02} = 0.9802$$

$\therefore$ The approximate number of packet containing no defective blade $= 10000 \times 0.9802 = 9802$

$$P(X=1) = \frac{e^{-0.02}(0.02)}{1} = 0.9802 \times 0.02 = 0.0196$$

$\therefore$ The approximate number of packets containing one defective blade $= 10000 \times 0.0196 = 196$

$$P(X=2) = \frac{e^{-0.02}(0.02)^2}{2!} = \frac{0.9802 \times 0.0004}{2} = 0.000196$$

$\therefore$ The approximate number of packets containing two defective blads $= 10000 \times 0.000196 = 1.96 = 2$

5. **Hint** $n = 50$, $p = \frac{4}{100}$, $\lambda = 2$

$[P(X > 2) = 1 - [P(X=0) + P(X=1) + P(X=2)]$

Ans. 0.3235

6. **Hint** $P = 0.001 = \frac{1}{1000}$, $\lambda = np$, $n = 1000\lambda$

$P(X \geq 1) = 1 - P(X=0)$

$0.09 = 1 - e^{-\lambda} \Rightarrow e^{-\lambda} = 1 - 0.09 = 0.01$

$e^{-\lambda} = e^{-4.6} \Rightarrow \lambda = 4.6$

$n = 1000 \times 4.6 = 4600$

7. **Hint** $P = \frac{43}{585} = 0.0735$, $n = 10$, $\lambda = 0.735$ **Ans.** 0.4795

8. We have, $\lambda = 2 =$ Mean expectation

Now, P (3 or less overflows) $= P(X \leq 3)$

$= P(X=0) + P(X=1) + P(X=2) + P(X=3)$

$$= \frac{\lambda^0 e^{-2}}{0!} + \frac{\lambda^1 e^{-2}}{1!} + \frac{\lambda^2 e^{-2}}{2!} + \frac{\lambda^3 e^{-2}}{3!}$$

$$= e^{-2}\left(1 + \lambda + \frac{\lambda^2}{2!} + \frac{\lambda^3}{3!}\right) = e^{-2}\left(1 + 2 + \frac{(2)^2}{2!} + \frac{(2)^3}{3!}\right)$$

$$= e^{-2}\left(1 + 2 + 2 + \frac{8}{6}\right) = e^{-2} \times \frac{19}{3}$$

$$= 0.13534 \times \frac{19}{3} \qquad [\because e^{-2} = 0.13534]$$

$$= \frac{2.57146}{3} = 0.8572$$

9. **Hint** $n = 12$, $p = 0.01125$, $\lambda = np = 0.135$

Required probability $P(X \leq 1) = P(X=0) + P(X=1)$

Ans. 0.996

10. No accidents = 369. More than 3 accidents = 984

11. 0.996

12. $P(X=0) = e^{-4/3}$, $P(X=3) = \frac{32}{81}e^{-4/3}$

13. $P(X=4) = \frac{2}{3}e^{-2}$, Mean = Variance = 2

Probability Distribution of a Continuous Random Variable

A continuous distribution has a range of values that are infinite, and therefore uncountable.

e.g. time is infinite, you could count from 0 seconds to a billion seconds, a trillion seconds, height and weight of people, scientific instruments etc. The probability distribution of a continuous random variable is called continuous probability distribution.

Probability Density Function

Let X be a continuous random variable the function $f(x)$ is called as probability density function of X, if it satisfies.

(i) $f(x) \geq 0, \forall\, x \in R$

(ii) $\int_{-\infty}^{\infty} f(x) dx = 1$

(iii) $P(a \leq X < b) = \int_a^b f(x) dx$

Distribution Function

Let X be a continuous random variable with probability density function $f(x)$. The cumulative distribution function $f(x)$ of X is defined for every real number x_i by

$$F(x_i) = P[X \leq x_i] = \int_{-\infty}^{x_i} f(x)\, dx$$

EXAMPLE 1. If the probability density function of a random variable X, if $f(x) = \frac{x}{2}$ in $0 \leq x \leq 2$. Find $P(X > 1)$.

Sol. We have, $f(x) = \frac{x}{2}, x \in [0, 2]$

We know, $P(a \leq X \leq b) = \int_a^b f(x)\, dx$

$$\therefore P(X > 1) = \int_1^2 f(x)\, dx$$

$$= \int_1^2 \frac{x}{2} dx$$

$$= \left[\frac{x^2}{4}\right]_1^2 = \frac{2^2}{4} - \frac{1}{4}$$

$$= 1 - \frac{1}{4} = \frac{3}{4}$$

EXAMPLE 2. The probability density function $f(x)$ of a continuous random variable X is given by

$f(x) = \lambda x^2, 0 \leq x \leq 1.$

Find (i) λ (ii) $P(X < 0.3)$

Sol. We have, $f(x) = \lambda x^2, 0 \leq x \leq 1$

(i) Since, $f(x)$ is the probability density function of random variable X.

$$\therefore \quad \int_0^1 f(x)\, dx = 1$$

$$\Rightarrow \quad \int_0^1 \lambda x^2\, dx = 1$$

$$\Rightarrow \quad \left[\frac{\lambda x^3}{3}\right]_0^1 = 1$$

$$\Rightarrow \quad \frac{\lambda}{3} = 1$$

$$\Rightarrow \quad \lambda = 3$$

(ii) $P(X < 0.3) = \int_0^{0.3} f(x)\, dx$

$$= \int_0^{0.3} 3x^2 dx = \left[\frac{3x^3}{3}\right]_0^{0.3}$$

$$= (0.3)^3 - 0 = 0.027$$

Normal Distribution

The normal distribution is probably most important distribution in all probability and statistics many population have distribution that can be fit very closely by an appropriate normal or gaussian curve.

e.g. height, weight and other physical characteristics, scores on various tests, etc.

Definition A random variable X, is said to be normal distribution with parameters μ (mean) and σ^2 (variance). If its probability distribution function is given by

$$f(x) = \frac{1}{\sigma\sqrt{2\pi}} e^{-\frac{(x-\mu)^2}{2\sigma^2}}, -\infty < x < \infty$$

$$-\infty < \mu < \infty, \sigma > 0,$$

where, $\sqrt{2\pi} = 2.5066$ and $e = 2.7183$

The statement that X is normally distributed with parameters μ and σ^2 is often abbreviated $X \sim N(\mu, \sigma^2)$ clearly $f(x; \mu, \sigma) \geq 0$, but a some what complicated calculus argument must be used to verify that

$$\int_{-\infty}^{\infty} f(x; \mu, \sigma)\, dx = 1$$

Figure below present graphs of $f(x; \mu, \sigma)$ for several different (μ, σ) pairs

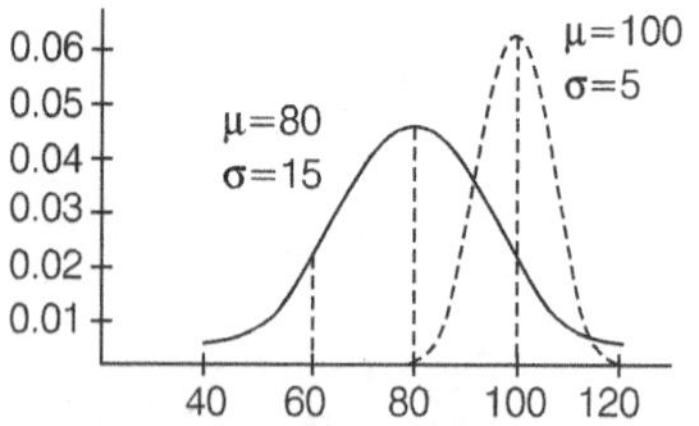

Two different normal density curve

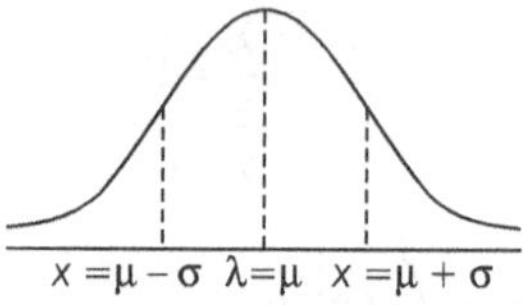

Visualizing μ and σ for a normal distribution

Properties of Normal Distribution

The probability distribution function of a normal variate with mean μ and variance σ^2 is given by

$$f(x) = \frac{1}{\sigma\sqrt{2\pi}} e^{-\frac{(x-\mu)^2}{2\sigma^2}}, \quad -\infty < x < \infty$$

The curve $y = f(x)$ is known as the normal probability curve and it has the following properties:

(i) The curve is bell shaped, so the distribution is symmetric about the mean-half the values fall below the mean and half above the mean.

(ii) The mean, median and mode are exactly the same.

(iii) The distribution can be described by the two values the mean (μ) and the standard deviation (σ). The mean is the location parameter while the standard deviation is the scale parameter.

(iv) The mean determines the peak of the curve is central, increasing the mean moves the curve right, while decreasing it moves the curve left.

(v) X-axis is an asymptote to the curve i.e. it touches the curve at $x = \pm\infty$.

(vi) The area bounded by the curve $y = f(x)$ is one unit i.e. $\int_{-\infty}^{\infty} f(x)\, dx = 1$.

Standard Normal Distribution

A random variable has a normal distribution with means $\mu = 0$ and standard deviation $\sigma = 1$ is called standard normal probability distribution.

The random variable in case of standard normal distribution is represented by Z.

So, the density function of the standard normal variable Z is given by

$$f(Z) = \frac{1}{\sqrt{2\pi}} e^{-\frac{Z^2}{2}}, \quad -\infty < Z < \infty$$

Area Under Standard Normal Curve

The area under the standard normal curve also represents the probability.

We need to three types of probability

(i) $P(Z < z)$

(ii) $P(z_1 < Z < z_2)$

(iii) $P(Z > z)$

To calculate the probability, we define a cumulative distribution function $F(Z)$ for any $Z \in (-\infty, \infty)$, we define

$$F(Z) = \int_{-\infty}^{Z} \frac{1}{\sqrt{2\pi}} e^{-Z^2/2} dz$$

(i) The function $F(Z)$ represent the entire area under standard normal curve which is on the left of the line $Z = z$.

So, $P(Z < z) = F(z)$

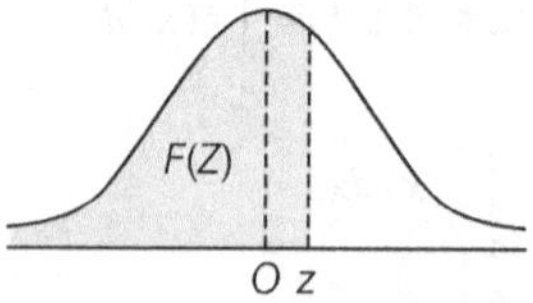

(ii) $P(z_1 < Z < z_2)$ is the area under the standard normal curve from z_1 and z_2 shown in figure.

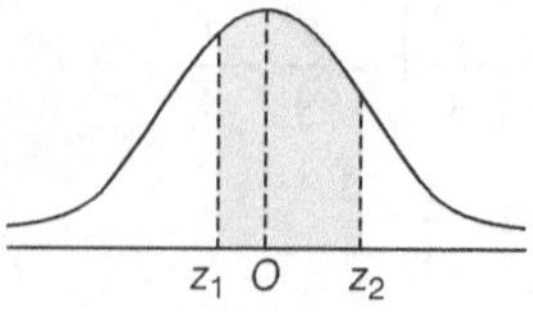

$\therefore P(z_1 < Z < z_2) = F(z_2) - F(z_1)$

(iii) $P(Z > z)$ is the area under the standard normal curve which is right of line $Z = z$ as shown in figure.

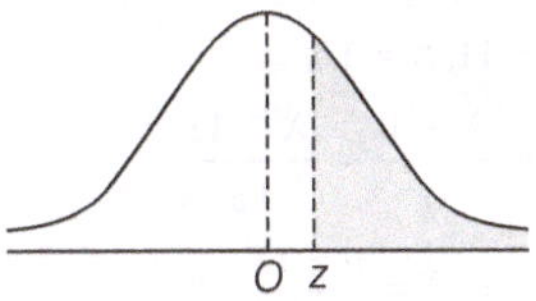

$\therefore P(Z > z) = 1 - P(Z \le z)$

$P(Z > z) = 1 - F(z)$

Properties of $F(Z)$

(i) $F(\infty) = \dfrac{1}{\sqrt{2\pi}} \displaystyle\int_{-\infty}^{\infty} e^{\frac{-Z^2}{2}} dz = 1$

(ii) $F(0) = \dfrac{1}{\sqrt{2\pi}} \displaystyle\int_{-\infty}^{0} e^{-\frac{Z^2}{2}} dz = 0.5$

(iii) $F(-z) = 1 - F(z)$

EXAMPLE 3. If Z is a standard normal variable. Find each of the following probabilities.

(i) $P(0 \le Z \le 1.5)$ (ii) $P(Z \ge 1.13)$
(iii) $P(Z < -1.05)$ (iv) $P(-0.46 \le Z \le 2.21)$
(v) $P(-2-38 < Z < -1.45)$

Sol. (i) $P(0 \le Z \le 1.5) = F(1.5) - F(0)$ [$\because P(z_1 < Z < z_2) = F(z_2) - F(z_1)$]

$= 0.9332 - 0.5000$ [using table]

$= 0.4332$

(ii) $P(Z \ge 1.13) = 1 - F(1.13)$ [$\because P(Z \ge Z) = 1 - F(Z)$]

$= 1 - 0.8708$ [using table]

$= 0.1292$

(iii) $P(Z < -1.05) = F(-1.05)$ [$\because P(Z < z) = F(Z)$]

$= 1 - F(1.05)$ [$\because F(-Z) = 1 - F(Z)$]

$= 1 - 0.8531$ [using table]

$= 0.1469$

(iv) $P(-0.46 \le Z \le 2.21) = F(2.21) - F(-0.46)$

$= F(2.21) - (1 - F(0.46))$

$= 0.9864 - (1 - 0.6772)$ [using table]

$= 0.9864 - 0.3228$

$= 0.6636$

(v) $P(-2.38 < Z < -1.45) = F(-1.45) - F(-2.38)$

$= 1 - F(1.45) - 1 + F(2.38)$

$= F(2.38) - F(1.45)$

$= 0.9913 - 0.9265$ [using table]

$= 0.0648$

EXAMPLE 4. If X is a normal distribution random variable with mean $\mu = 10$ and standard deviation $\sigma = 2$, find each of the following probabilities

(i) $P(X > 16)$ (ii) $P(X < 13)$
(iii) $P(12 < X < 14.5)$

Sol. Given, $\mu = 10, \sigma = 2$

$\therefore Z = \dfrac{X - \mu}{\sigma} \Rightarrow Z = \dfrac{X - 10}{2}$

(i) When $X = 16$,

$Z = \dfrac{16 - 10}{2} = 3$

$\therefore P(X > 16) = P(Z > 3) = 1 - P(Z \le 3)$

$= 1 - F(3)$

$= 1 - 0.9986$ [using table]

$= 0.0014$

(ii) When $X = 13$,

$Z = \dfrac{13 - 10}{2} = 1.5$

$\therefore P(X < 13) = P(Z < 1.5)$

$= F(1.5)$

$= 0.9332$ [using table)

(iii) For $X = 12$, $Z = \dfrac{12 - 10}{2} = 1$

For $X = 14.5$ $Z = \dfrac{14.5 - 10}{2} = 2.25$

$\therefore P(12 < X < 14.5) = P(1 < Z < 2.25)$

$= F(2.25) - F(1)$

$= 0.9878 - 0.8413$

$= 0.1465$

EXAMPLE 5. If the height of 1000 students are normally distributed with mean 173 cm and standard deviation 7.5 cm, how many students have heights

(i) greater than 183 cm?
(ii) less than 162.5 cm?
(iii) between 165 cm and 180 cm?

Sol. Let X denotes the height of the students

We have, mean $(\mu) = 173$

and standard deviation $(\sigma) = 7.5$

Then, $Z = \dfrac{X - \mu}{\sigma} = \dfrac{X - 173}{7.5}$

(i) $P(X > 183) = P\left(Z > \dfrac{183 - 173}{7.5}\right) = P(Z > 1.33)$

$= 1 - P(Z \le 1.33) = 1 - F(1.33)$

$= 1 - 0.9082$

$= 0.0918$

$\therefore$ Number of students height greater than 183 cm

$= 1000 \times 0.0918 = 91.8 = 92$

(ii) $P(X < 162.5) = P\left(z < \frac{162.5 - 173}{7.5}\right)$

$= P(Z < -1.4) = F(-1.4) = 1 - F(1.4)$

$= 1 - 0.9192 = 0.0808$

∴ Number of students height less than 162.5 cm

$= 1000 \times 0.0808 = 80.8 = 81$

(iii) $P(165 < X < 180) = P\left(\frac{165 - 173}{7.5} < Z < \frac{180 - 173}{7.5}\right)$

$= P(-1.07 < Z < 0.93)$

$= F(0.93) - F(-1.07)$

$= F(0.93) - [1 - F(1.07)]$

$= 0.8238 - (1 - 0.8577)$

$= 0.8238 - 0.1423 = 0.6815$

∴ Number of students whose height between 165 and 180 cm $= 1000 \times 0.6815 = 681$

EXAMPLE 6. In a distribution exactly normal, 7% of the items are under 35 and 89% are under 63. Find the mean and standard deviation of the distribution.

Sol. Let X be the normal variate represent the given distribution. Let μ and σ be mean and standard deviation, respectively.

We have, $P(X \le 35) = 7\% = 0.07$

and $P(X \le 63) = 89\% = 0.89$

$$Z = \frac{X - \mu}{\sigma} = \frac{35 - \mu}{\sigma} \quad \text{[when } X = 35]$$

$$P(X \le 35) = P\left(z \le \frac{35 - \mu}{\sigma}\right) = 0.07$$

$$\frac{F(35 - \mu)}{\sigma} = 0.07 = F\left(\frac{35 - \mu}{\sigma}\right) = F(-1.48)$$

$$= \frac{35 - \mu}{\sigma} = -1.48$$

$\Rightarrow \mu - 1.48\sigma = 35$ ...(i)

And $P(X \le 63) = P\left(Z \le \frac{63 - \mu}{\sigma}\right) = 0.89$

$\Rightarrow F\left(\frac{63 - \mu}{\sigma}\right) = 0.89$

$\Rightarrow F\left(\frac{63 - \mu}{\sigma}\right) = F(1.23) = \frac{63 - \mu}{\sigma} = 1.23$

$\Rightarrow \mu + 1.23\sigma = 63$ ...(ii)

Solving Eq. (i) and (ii), we get

$\mu = 50 \cdot 3$ and $\sigma = 10.33$

Hence, the mean of distribution = 50.3

and standard deviation = 10.33

EXAMPLE 7. If X is a normal variate with mean 11 and standard deviation 1.5. Find the number 'a' such that $P(X > a) = 0.09$

Sol. We have, $\mu = 11, \sigma = 1.5$

$$Z = \frac{X - \mu}{\sigma} = \frac{X - 11}{1.5}$$

When $X = a \Rightarrow Z = \frac{a - 11}{1.5}$

$$P(X > a) = P\left(Z > \frac{a - 11}{1.5}\right) = 0.09$$

$\Rightarrow 1 - P\left(Z \le \frac{a - 11}{1.5}\right) = 0.09$

$\Rightarrow 1 - F\left(\frac{a - 11}{1.5}\right) = 0.09$

$\Rightarrow F\left(\frac{a - 11}{1.5}\right) = 1 - 0.09 = 0.91$

$\Rightarrow F\left(\frac{a - 11}{1.5}\right) = F(1.34)$ [using table $F(1.34) = 0.91$]

$\Rightarrow \frac{a - 11}{1.5} = 1.34$

$\Rightarrow a - 11 = 1.5 \times 1.34 = 2.01$

$\Rightarrow a = 11 + 2.01 = 13.01$

EXAMPLE 8. The monthly salaries of the worker in a certain factory are normally distributed with mean ₹ 5000 and standard deviation ₹ 500. There are 14 workers getting more that ₹ 6500 per month. Find the number of workers in the factory.

Sol. Let the total number of workers infactory be n.

We have, $\mu = 5000, \sigma = 500$, then

$$Z = \frac{X - 5000}{500}$$

$$P(X > 6500) = P\left(Z > \frac{6500 - 5000}{500}\right) = P(Z > 3)$$

$= 1 - P(Z \le 3) = 1 - F(3)$

$= 1 - 0.9986 = 0.0014$

According to question,

$n \times 0.0014 = 14$

$\Rightarrow n = \frac{14}{0.0014} = 10000$

Hence, total number of workers = 10000

Topic Practice 4

1 If Z is a standard normal variable. Find each of the following probability.
   (i) $P(Z < 0.73)$
   (ii) $P(Z > -1.64)$
   (iii) $P(0 < Z < 1.45)$
   (iv) $P(-1.3 < Z < 2.4)$
   (v) $P(-1.96 < Z < 1.96)$

2 If X is a normal distribution random variable with mean 12 and standard deviation 4. Find
   (i) $P(X \geq 20)$
   (ii) $P(X \leq 20)$
   (iii) $P(0 \leq X \leq 12)$

3 Given, Z is a standard normal random variable. Find Z for each of the following.
   (i) The area to the left of Z is 0.9332
   (ii) The area between 0 and Z is 0.4222
   (iii) The area to the right of Z is 0.3300
   (iv) The area between $-Z$ to Z is 0.9030

4 In an intelligence test administrated to 1000 children, the average score is 42 and standard deviation is 24. Find how many children have score
   (i) more than 60
   (ii) between 20 and 40

5 Suppose the temperature during june is normally distributed with mean 20°C and standard deviation 3.33°C. Find the probability that the temperature between 2.11°C and 26.66°C.

6 Given that the scores of a set of candidates on an IQ test are normally distributed. If the IQ test has a mean of 100 and a standard deviation of 10, determine the probability that a candidate who takes the test will score between 90 and 110.
[Given, $P(Z < 1) = 0.8413$ and $P(Z < -1) = 0.1587$)
[CBSE 2024]

7 In a distribution exactly normal, 10.03% of the items are under 25 kg weight and 89.97% of the items are under 70 kg weight. What are the mean and standard deviation of the distribution.

8 The income distribution of workers in a certain factory was found to be normal with mean ₹ 500 and standard deviation equal ₹ 50. There were 228 persons getting above ₹ 600. How many workers were there in all? [Area under the standard normal curve between height at 0 and 2 is 0.4772]

9 The monthly salaries of workers in a certain factory are normally distributed. The mean salary is ₹ 4000 and standard deviation is ₹ 450. If 668 workers are getting salary less than ₹ 3325. Find the total number of workers in factory.

10 If X is normally distributed with mean 10 and standard deviation 1.5. Find x such that $P(X > x) = 0.0038$.

Hints & Solutions

1. (i) 0.7673 (ii) 0.9495 (iii) 0.4265 (iii) 0.895 (v) 0.95
2. (i) 0.0228 (ii) 0.9772 (iii) 0.4986
3. (i) 1.5 (ii) 1.42 (iii) 0.44 (iv) 1.66
4. (i) 227 (ii) 289
5. 0.3479
6. Given, $\mu = 100, \sigma = 10$

   Then, $Z = \dfrac{X-\mu}{\sigma} = \dfrac{X-100}{10}$

   When $X = 90$, $Z = \dfrac{90-100}{10} = -1$

   When $X = 110$, $Z = \dfrac{110-100}{10} = 1$

   Now, $P(-1 < Z < 1) = P(Z < 1) - P(Z < -1)$
   $= 0.8413 - 0.1587$
   $= 0.6826$
7. $\mu = 47.5$, $\sigma = 17.58$
8. 10000
9. 10000
10. 14

Exam Pattern Exercise

Part A - Objective Type Questions

Multiple Choice Type Questions

1 A random variable 'X' has the following distribution:

X	0	1	2	3	4	5	6	7
$P(X)$	k	k	$2k$	$3k$	k^2	$2k^2$	$7k^2$	$2k$

The value of k is

(a) -1 (b) $-\frac{1}{10}$ (c) 1 (d) $\frac{1}{10}$

2 If X is a Poisson variable such that $P(X=1)=2P(X=2)$, then $P(X=0)$ is [CBSE 2023]

(a) e (b) $\frac{1}{e}$ (c) 1 (d) e^2

3 A fair coin is tossed twice and outcomes are noted. If the random variable X represents the number of heads that appeared in the experiment, then the mathematical expectation of X is [CBSE 2024]

(a) 1 (b) $\frac{1}{2}$ (c) $\frac{1}{4}$ (d) $1\frac{1}{2}$

4 If for a Poisson variate X,

$$P(X=k)=P(X=k+1),$$

then the variance of X is [CBSE 2024]

(a) $k-1$ (b) k (c) $k+1$ (d) $k+2$

5 A book contains 100 bulbs, out of which 10 are defective. A sample of 5 bulbs is drawn. The probability that none is defective, is

(a) $\frac{9}{10}$ (b) $\left(\frac{1}{10}\right)^5$ (c) $\left(\frac{9}{10}\right)^5$ (d) $\left(\frac{1}{2}\right)^5$

6 A bag contains 2 white and 4 black balls. A ball is drawn 5 times with replacement the probability that atleast 4 of the balls drawn are white is

(a) $\frac{8}{243}$ (b) $\frac{10}{243}$ (c) $\frac{11}{243}$ (d) $\frac{32}{243}$

7 An experiment succeeds twice as often as it fails. The probability that in 4 trials there will be atleast three successes, is

(a) $\frac{4}{27}$ (b) $\frac{8}{27}$ (c) $\frac{16}{27}$ (d) $\frac{24}{27}$

8 If X is a binomial variate with the range $\{0, 1, 2, 3, 4, 5, 6\}$ and $P(X=2)=4P(X=4)$, then the parameter p of X is

(a) $\frac{1}{3}$ (b) $\frac{1}{2}$ (c) $\frac{2}{3}$ (d) $\frac{3}{4}$

9 If the mean and variance of a binomial variate X are 8 and 4 respectively, then $P(X<3)$ equals

(a) $\frac{265}{2^{15}}$ (b) $\frac{137}{2^{14}}$ (c) $\frac{137}{2^{16}}$ (d) $\frac{265}{2^{16}}$

10 In a book of 500 pages, it is found that there are 250 typing errors. Assume that Poisson law holds for the number of errors per page. Then, the probability that a random sample of 2 pages will contain no error, is

(a) $e^{-0.3}$ (b) $e^{-0.5}$ (c) e^{-1} (d) e^{-2}

11 If the probability density function of a random variable X, if $f(x)=\frac{x}{2}$ in $0\le x\le 2$, then $P\left(\frac{X>1.5}{X>1}\right)$ is equal to

(a) $\frac{7}{16}$ (b) $\frac{3}{4}$ (c) $\frac{7}{12}$ (d) $\frac{21}{64}$

12 If X is normally distributed with mean 12 and standard deviation 3, then standard normal variable Z corresponding $X=9$ is

(a) 1 (b) -1
(c) 0 (d) 2

Assertion-Reason Based Questions

Directions (Q. Nos. 13-15) *In the questions given below are two statements labelled as Assertion (A) and Reason (R). In the context of the two statements, which one of the following is correct?*

(a) Both A and R are correct; R is the correct explanation of A
(b) Both A and R are correct; R is not the correct explanation of A
(c) A is correct; R is incorrect
(d) R is correct; A is incorrect

13 **Assertion (A)** If $\lambda=1$ in Poisson distribution, then the value of $P(5)$ is 0.00307.

Reason (R) An urn contains 6 red and 3 black balls. Two balls are randomly drawn. Let X represents the number of black balls. The possible values of X are 0, 1, 2.

14 In a binomial distribution, $n=200$ and $p=0.04$. Taking Poisson distribution as an approximation to the binomial distribution.

Assertion (A) Mean of Poisson distribution $=8$

Reason (R) $P(X=4)=\frac{512}{3e^8}$. [CBSE 2024]

15 **Assertion (A)** In an examination, 10% of the candidate score more than 75 marks and 30% of the candidate score less than 40 marks. If the distribution of marks is normal, then the standard deviation is 19.44.

Reason (R) Suppose 2% of the bolts manufactured by the factory are defective. The probability of 5 defective bolts from a sample of 200 bolts is 0.642. [use $e^{-4} = 0.0183$]

Part B - Descriptive Questions

Very Short Answer Type Questions

16 Two cards are drawn successively with replacement from a well shuffled pack of 52 cards, find the probability distributions of number of kings.

17 A fair die is tossed twice. If the number appearing on the top is less than 3, it is a success. Find the probability distribution of number of success.

18 A descrete random variable X has the probability distribution given below

X	0.5	1	1.5	2
$P(X)$	K	K^2	$2K^2$	K

(i) Find the value of K.
(ii) Find the mean of the distribution.

19 The probability of a man hitting of target is $\frac{1}{4}$. If he fires 7 times. What is the probability of his hitting the target at least twice?

20 Suppose that 90% of people are right handed. What is the probability that at most 6 of a random sample of 10 people are right handed.

21 If X follows binomial distribution with mean 4 and variance 2. Find $P(X \geq 5)$.

22 Records show that the probability is 0.00002 that a car will have a flat tyre while during over a certain bridge. Use the poisson's distribution to determine the probability that among 20000 cars driven over bridge, not more than one will have a flat tyre. (given, $e^{-0.4} = 0.670$)

23 The probability of getting no misprint in a page of a book is e^{-4}. What is the probability that a page contains more than 2 misprints?

24 If X is a poisson variate such that $P(X = 1) = 2P(X = 2)$. Find (i) mean (ii) variance.

25 If X is a normal variate with mean 30 and standard deviation 5. Find $P(26 \leq X \leq 40)$.

Short Answer Type Questions

26 An urn contains 5 red and 2 black balls. Two balls are randomly drawn without replacement. Find the probability distribution of the black balls drawn. Also, find the mean and variance of the black balls drawn.

27 The random variable X has probability distribution $P(X)$ of the following form, where K is some number.

$$P(X = x) = \begin{cases} K, & \text{if } x = 0 \\ 2K, & \text{if } x = 1 \\ 3K, & \text{if } x = 2 \\ 0, & \text{otherwise} \end{cases}$$

(i) Determine the value of K.
(ii) Find $P(X < 2)$; $P(X \geq 2)$.

28 How many times must a man toss a fair coins that the probability of having atleast one head is more than 80%?

29 A man take a step forward with probability 0.4 and backward with probability 0.6. Find the probability that at the end of eleven steps he is one step away from the starting point.

30 If the mean and the variance of binomial distribution are 4 and 3 respectively, find the probability of six success.

31 There are 50 telephone lines in an exchange. The probability that any one of them will be busy is 0.1. Find the probability that all the lines are busy.

32 If X is normally distributed with mean 10 and standard deviation 4, then probability of X between 10 and x is 0.4772, find the value of x.

33 In a certain factory turning razor blades. There is a small chance $\frac{1}{200}$ for any blade to be defective. The blades are in packets of 4. Find the approximate number of packets containing no defective blade in a consignment of 30000 packet. (use $e^{-0.02} = 0.9802$)

Long Answer Type Questions

34 The random variable X can take values, 0, 1, 2, 3 given that $P(X = 0) = P(X = 1) = P$ and $P(X = 2) = P(X = 3)$ such that $E(X^2) = 2E(X)$. Find the value of P.

35 The sum of mean and variance of a binomial distribution is 15 and the sum of their square is 117. Find the distribution.

36 If the sum and the product of the mean and variance of binomial distribution are 1.8 and 0.8, respectively. Find the probability distribution and the probability of at least one success.

37 There are 500 boxes, each containing 1000 ballot papers for elections. The chance that a ballot paper is defective is 0.002. Assuming poisson distribution. Find the number of boxes containing at most two defective ballot papers.
(use $e^{-2} = 0.1353$)

38 Eight percent of the bolts produced in a certain factory turn out to be defective. Find the probability that in a sample of 25 bolts chosen at random.

(i) exactly 3 bolts will defective
(ii) more than 3 bulbs defective.
(use $e^{-2} = 0.135$)

39 In a examination 15% of the candidate got first class (60% marked or above) while 40% failed (securing below 40%). Assuming that the marks be normally distributed. Find the mean and standard deviation.

40 Students of a class were given a mechanical aptitude test. Their marks were found to be normally distributed with mean 60 and standard deviation 5. What percent of student scored

(i) more than 60 marks?
(ii) between 45 and 65 marks?

Case Study Based Questions

41 A factory produces bulbs, of which 6% are defective bulbs in a large bulk of bulbs.

Based on the above information, answer the following questions.

(i) Find the probability that in a sample of 100 bulbs selected at random, none of the bulbs is defective.
(Use $e^{-6} = 0.0024$)
(ii) Find the probability that the sample of 100 bulbs has exactly two defective bulbs.
(iii) Find the probability that the sample of 100 bulbs will include not more than one defective bulb.

Or Find the mean and the variance of the distribution of number of defective bulbs in a sample of 100 bulbs.

42 The marks obtained in an intelligence test, which is conducted on 1000 students, follow normal distribution with the average score 42 and standard deviation 24.

Based on the above information, answer the following questions.

(i) Number of students getting more than 50 marks are
(a) 352 (b) 371 (c) 338 (d) 382
(ii) Number of students getting marks between 30 and 54 are
(a) 312 (b) 354 (c) 328 (d) 383
(iii) Value of score obtained by top 100 students is
(a) 72 (b) 79 (c) 68 (d) 73
(iv) Number of successful students, if the minimum pass marks are 40 are
(a) 511 (b) 532 (c) 564 (d) 555
(v) Number of student getting Ist division (more than 60 marks) are
(a) 215 (b) 205 (c) 227 (d) 240

Hints & Solutions

1. (d) 2. (b) 3. (a) 4. (c)
5. (c) 6. (c) 7. (c) 8. (a)
9. (c) 10. (c) 11. (c) 12. (b)
13. (b) 14. (b) 15. (c)

16.

X	0	1	2
P(X)	$\frac{144}{169}$	$\frac{24}{169}$	$\frac{1}{169}$

17.

X	0	1	2
P(X)	4/9	4/9	1/9

18. (i) $\frac{1}{3}$ (ii) $\frac{23}{18}$ 19. $\frac{4547}{8192}$

20. $1 - \sum_{r=7}^{10} {}^{10}C_r (0.9)^r (0.1)^{10-r}$

21. **Hint** $np = 4, npq = 2$ **Ans.** $\frac{93}{256}$

22. **Hint** $n = 20000, P = 0.00002$
$\lambda = np = 0.4$
$P(X \le 1) = P(X = 0) + P(X = 1)$ **Ans.** 0.938

23. **Hint** $P(X = 0) = e^{-4}$
Ans. $P(X \le 2) = 8e^{-4}$

24. (i) $\mu = 1$ (ii) $\sigma^2 = 1$

25. **Hint** $\mu = 30, \sigma = 5$
$P(26 \le X \le 40)$
$= P\left(\frac{26-30}{5} \le Z \le \frac{40-30}{5}\right) = P\left(-\frac{4}{5} \le Z \le 2\right)$
$= F(2) - F(-0.8) = F(2) - (1 - F(0.8))$
Ans. 0.7563

26.

X	0	1	2
$P(X)$	$\frac{10}{21}$	$\frac{10}{21}$	$\frac{1}{21}$

Mean $(\mu) = \frac{4}{7}, \sigma^2 = \frac{50}{147}$

27. (i) $K = \frac{1}{6}$ (ii) $P(X < 2) = \frac{1}{2}$; $P(X \geq 2) = \frac{1}{2}$

28. **Hint** $P(X \geq 1) > 80\% \Rightarrow 1 - P(X = 0) \geq \frac{4}{5} \Rightarrow 1 - \left(\frac{1}{2}\right)^n > \frac{4}{5}$

Ans. $n \geq 3$

29. The man is one step away from starting point in two cases :

(i) He takes 6 steps forward and 5 steps backward.
(ii) He takes 5 steps forward and 6 steps backward.

$\therefore$ Required probability

$$= {}^{11}C_6(0.4)^6(0.6)^5 + {}^{11}C_5(0.4)^5(0.6)^6 = 0.37$$

30. Given, $\mu = 4, \sigma^2 = 3, \mu = np$ and $\sigma^2 = npq$

$\therefore \quad np = 4 \quad$ ...(i)

$npq = 3 \quad$ ...(ii)

From Eqs. (i) and (ii), we get

$$q = \frac{3}{4}, p = 1 - q = 1 - \frac{3}{4} = \frac{1}{4}, \; n = \frac{4}{p} = \frac{4}{\frac{1}{4}} = 16$$

Required probability, $P(X = 6) = {}^{16}C_6\left(\frac{1}{4}\right)^6\left(\frac{3}{4}\right)^{10}$

31. Here $n = 50$, $p = 0.1$

$\therefore \quad \lambda = np = 50 \times 0.1 = 5$

Required probability : $P(X = 50) = \frac{e^{-5}5^{50}}{50!}$

32. $P(10 < X < x) = 0.4772$

$$\Rightarrow P\left(\frac{10-10}{4} < Z < \frac{x-10}{4}\right) = 0.4772$$

$$\Rightarrow P\left(0 < Z < \frac{x-10}{4}\right) = 0.4772$$

$$\Rightarrow F\left(\frac{x-10}{4}\right) - F(0) = 0.4772$$

$$\Rightarrow F\left(\frac{x-10}{4}\right) = 0.4772 + F(0)$$

$$\Rightarrow F\left(\frac{x-10}{4}\right) = 0.4772 + 0.5$$

$$\Rightarrow F\left(\frac{x-10}{4}\right) = 0.9772$$

$$\Rightarrow \frac{x-10}{4} = 2$$

$$\Rightarrow x - 10 = 8 \Rightarrow x = 18$$

33. **Hint** $n = 4$, $P = \frac{1}{200}$, $\lambda = np = 0.02$

$$P(X = 0) = \frac{\lambda^0 e^{-\lambda}}{0!} = e^{-0.02} = 0.9802$$

Total number of blades in 30000 packet $= 30000 \times 0.9802$

Ans. 29406

34. **Hint** Let $P(X = 2) = P(X = 3) = x$

$\because P(X = 0) + P(X = 1) + P(X = 3) = 1$

$\Rightarrow P + P + x + x = 1 \Rightarrow x = \frac{1 - 2P}{2}$

X	0	1	2	3
$P(X)$	P	P	$\frac{1-2P}{2}$	$\frac{1-2P}{2}$

Put the values in $E(X^2) = 2E(X)$ **Ans.** $P = \frac{3}{8}$

35. **Hint** $np + npq = 15$ and $(np)^2 + (npq)^2 = 117$

Solve, we get $n = 27$, $p = \frac{1}{3}, q = \frac{2}{3}$

Ans. $P(X = r) = {}^{27}C_r\left(\frac{1}{3}\right)^r\left(\frac{2}{3}\right)^{27-r}$

36. **Hint** $np + npq = 1.8$ and $n^2p^2q = 0.8$

On solving, we get $n = 5$, $p = \frac{1}{5}, q = \frac{4}{5}$

Ans. $P(X \geq 1) = \frac{2101}{3125}$

37. **Hint** $n = 1000$ $P = 0.002$, $\lambda = np = 2$ **Ans.** 338

38. (i) 0.18 (ii) 0.325

39. Standard deviation $(\sigma) = 15.5$, Mean $(\mu) = 43.87$

40. (i) 50% (ii) 83.99%

41. Let X be number of defective bulbs. Then, X has a Poisson variate.

Here, $n = 100$ and $p = 6\% = \frac{6}{100}$

$$\lambda = np = 100 \times \frac{6}{100} = 6$$

(i) $P(\text{no defective bulb}) = P(X = 0)$

$$= \frac{e^{-6} \times (6)^0}{0!} = e^{-6} = 0.0024$$

(ii) $P(\text{two defective bulbs}) = P(X = 2)$

$$= \frac{e^{-6}6^2}{2!} = \frac{36 \times 0.0024}{2} = 18 \times 0.0024 = 0.0432$$

(iii) $P(\text{not more than defective bulb}) = P(X \leq 1)$

$$P(X = 0) + P(X = 1) = \frac{e^{-6}6^0}{0!} + \frac{e^{-6}6^1}{1!}$$

$$= e^{-6}(1 + 6) = 7e^{-6} = 7 \times 0.0024 = 0.0168$$

Or

Mean $(= \lambda) = np = 100 \times \frac{6}{100} = 6$

and variance $= np = 100 \times \frac{6}{100} = 6$

42. (i) (b), (ii) (d), (iii) (d), (iv) (b), (v) (c)

CHAPTER 16

Inferential Statistics

In this Chapter...

- Sampling and Statistical Inference
- Hypothesis Testing and Degree of Freedom

Statisticians are after concerned in studying some characteristics of a larger whole of which every member cannot be observed for some particle reasons. Sampling theory is a study of relationships existing between a population and samples drawn from the population sampling theory is applicable only two random samples. The population or a universe may be defined as a aggregate of items possessing common trait or traits.

Sampling and Statistical Inference

Population

In statistics, the term population refers to group of objects, creatures, experiments and observations etc. under study.

e.g. Height of all females aged below 40 yr in Delhi and all students of class-XIIth in India etc.

According to number of objects in population, it may be of two types

(i) **Finite population** If number of objects in population is countable, then it is finite population.

(ii) **Infinite population** If number of objects in population is uncountable, then it is infinite population.

Sample

A finite subset (smaller group) of objects (individuals) in a population is called a sample. Process of selecting samples from a population is called sampling and the number of objects in a sample is called the sample size.

Sampling are of two types

(i) **Probability Sampling** When selection of objects from the population is random, so objects of the population has an equal chance of selection.

(ii) **Non-probability sampling** When selection of objects from the population is non-random, so object of the population has not equal chance of selection.

Simple Random Sampling

In simple random sampling each and every object of the population has an equal chance of being included in the sample.

e.g. If we want to take sample of 20 persons out of a population of 200, write the names of all the 200 persons on separate slips of paper, fold these slips, mix them thoroughly and then make a blindfold selection of 20 slips.

Systematic Sampling

Systematic sampling is relatively a simple technique and may be more efficient than simple random, provided the lists are arranged wholly as random.

e.g. If a complete list of 1500 students of a university is available and, if we want to draw a sample of 500 students by using this method, select every *k*th item ($k = 3$) from the list, where *k* refers to the sample interval. The first item between one and three will be selected at random.

Purpose of Sampling

Sampling is only a tool which helps us to know the characteristics of the population by examining only a small part of it.

Representative Sample from a Population

A representative sample is defined as a small quantity or a subset of something larger. It contains the same charcteristics and proportions like that of a larger population.

e.g. A group of citizen representing the whole country is designated as a nationally representative example.

Difference between Representative and Non-representative Samples

Representative and non-representative sampling are techniques that used to help ensure data is free of bias.

A statistics is representative if it represent the attributes of a known parameter is the population. When the statistic does not represent the population parameter, it is called non-representative.

Sampling Unit

The ultimate unit sampled from the population and observed is called a sampling unit.

Sampling Frame

It is the complete list of population unit from which the sample is drawn. The list of all street addresses, the list of all farmers, census report etc.

Parameter and Statistics

Parameter

The values (measurable characteristics) obtained from the study of population such as the population mean (μ), population variance (σ^2), population standard deviation (σ) etc. are called parameters. Parameter is used to describe the entire population.

Statistics

The values (measurable characteristics) of a sample is called statistics. Such as sample mean ($\bar{x}$), sample variance (S^2), sample standard deviation (S) etc. are called statistics.

Sample Errors

Sampling errors arise due to the fact that samples are used and to the particular method used in selecting the items from the population. There are mainly two types of sampling errors.

(i) Biased (ii) Unbiased

Sampling Distribution

If $S_1, S_2, S_3, \ldots\ldots, S_n$ are values of statistics S (like mean, variance, etc.) obtained from n independent random samples of a definite size selected from a given population, then $S_1, S_2, S_3, \ldots, S_n$ form a sampling distribution of statistics.

Then, Mean $(\bar{S}) = \frac{1}{n}\sum_{i=1}^{n} S_i$ and $\text{Var}(S) = \frac{1}{n}\sum_{i=1}^{n}(S_i - \bar{S})^2$

Statistical Inference

The process through which inference about the population are drawn which is based on population parameter is called statistical inference.

There are mainly three types of statistical inferences

(i) Point Estimation

(ii) Interval Estimation

(iii) Hypothesis testing

Point Estimation

It is used in sample data to calculate a single value of unknown population parameter. This single value of sample data is known as point of estimation.

e.g. Sample mean $\bar{x}$ is a point estimate of population mean μ. sample standard deviation S, is a point estimate of population standard deviation σ.

Let us consider, a sample consists of n objects and the population consists of N objects and every possible samples of n objects are equally likely to occur.

Then, sample mean $\bar{x} = \frac{\Sigma x_i}{n}$

Sample proportion (probability), $\bar{p} = \frac{x}{n}$

Sample standard deviation $S = \sqrt{\frac{\Sigma(x_i - \bar{x})^2}{n-1}}$

Interval Estimation

The interval estimation of a population parameter is given
by two numbers between which the parameter may be considered to lie.

The sample distribution of sample mean is normally distributed with μ and standard deviation $\frac{\sigma}{\sqrt{n}}$.

The sampling distribution of $\bar{x}$ can be transformed into the standard normal distribution by

$$Z = \frac{\bar{x} - \mu}{\sigma / \sqrt{n}}.$$

Interval Estimation of Population Proportion

Consider $\bar{p}$ is sample proportion and p is population proportion, then the interval estimation of population proportion is $p = \bar{p} \pm$ margin of error

and margin of error $= Z_{\alpha/2}\sqrt{\frac{\bar{p}(1-\bar{p})}{n}}$, where $Z_{\alpha/2}$ is the Z value providing an area of $\frac{\alpha}{2}$ in the upper tail of the standard normal probability distribution.

Central Limit Theorem

The central limit theorem states that, if you have population with mean μ and standard deviation σ and take sufficiently large random samples from the population with replacement. Then, the distribution of the sample means will be approximately normally distributed. This will hold true regardless of whether the source population in normal or skewed, provided the sample size is sufficiently large.

The values of $Z_{\alpha/2}$ for most commonly used confidence levels is given below

Confidence level	α	$\frac{\alpha}{2}$	$Z_{\alpha/2}$
90%	0.10	0.05	1.645
95%	0.05	0.025	1.960
99%	0.01	0.005	2.576

EXAMPLE 1. A student wants to estimate the mean grade point average (GPA) for the students staying in his dormitory. Instead of obtaining a list of all students in the dormitory and conducting an SRS,he observes that the dormitory consists of 100 rooms, each with four students. He chooses 5 rooms randomly out of 100 rooms and asks every students of the selected 5 rooms what his GPA is. The results are as follows

Student No.	Rooms 1	2	3	4	5
1	3.08	2.36	2.00	3.00	2.68
2	2.60	3.04	2.56	2.88	1.92
3	3.44	3.28	2.52	3.44	3.28
4	3.04	2.68	1.88	3.64	3.20
Total	12.16	11.36	8.96	12.96	11.08

Estimate the population mean GPA.

Sol. Given, $M = 100$, $m = 5$, $n_i = 4$.

The number of units in each cluster is same,

i.e. $n_1 = n_2 = n_3 = n_4 = n_5 = 4$,

Thus, $\sum_{i=1}^{5} n_i = 20$.

Estimate of population mean of GPA

$$= \frac{(12.16 + 11.36 + 8.96 + 2.96 + 11.08)}{20} = 2.826$$

EXAMPLE 2. A population consists of 4 units 3, 5, 7, 5. Find point estimate for

(i) Population mean (μ)

(ii) Population variance (σ^2)

(iii) Population standard deviation (σ)

Sol. (i) $\bar{x} = \frac{3+5+7+5}{4} = 5$

Hence, point estimate for population mean (μ) is 4.

(ii) $S^2 = \frac{1}{n-1}\sum_i (x_i - \bar{x})^2$

$$= \frac{1}{(4-1)}[(3-5)^2 + (5-5)^2 + (7-5)^2 + (5-5)^2]$$

$$= \frac{1}{3} \times 8 = \frac{8}{3} = 2.66$$

$\therefore$ Point estimate for population variance (σ^2) is 2.66.

(iii) Point estimate for population standard deviation is S, i.e. $\sqrt{2.66} = 1.63$.

EXAMPLE 3. A random sample of size 16 has 53 mean. The sum of the squares of the deviations taken from mean is 150. Compute the value of the test statistics such that the population mean is 56.

Sol. Given, $n = 16, \overline{X} = 53, \mu = 56$

and $\sum_{i=1}^{16}(x_i - \bar{x})^2 = 150$

$$\therefore \quad S^2 = \frac{1}{n-1}\sum_{i=1}^{16}(x_i - \bar{x})^2$$

$$= \frac{1}{(16-1)} \times 150 = 10$$

$$\therefore \text{ Test statistics, } t = \frac{\overline{X} - \mu}{S/\sqrt{n}}$$

$$= \frac{53-56}{\sqrt{\frac{10}{16}}} = \frac{-3\times 4}{\sqrt{10}} = \frac{-12}{\sqrt{10}}$$

$$= -3.794$$

EXAMPLE 4. The mean and variance of a random sample of 81 observations were computed as 200 and 144 respectively. Compute the 95% confidence limits for population mean.

Sol. Given, $n = 81, \bar{x} = 200$ and $\sigma^2 = 144 \Rightarrow \sigma = 12$

$\therefore$ Confidence limits (95%) are

$$\bar{x} \pm 1.96\left(\frac{\sigma}{\sqrt{n}}\right) = \bar{x} \pm 1.96\left(\frac{12}{\sqrt{81}}\right)$$

$$= \left[200 - 1.96\left(\frac{12}{9}\right), 200 + 1.96\left(\frac{12}{9}\right)\right]$$

$$= [200 - 2.61, 200 + 2.61]$$

$$= [197.39, 202.61]$$

EXAMPLE 5. Suppose a student measuring the boiling temperature of a certain liquid observes the reading (in degree celsius) 102.5, 101.7, 103.1, 100.9, 100.5 and 102.2 on 6 different samples of the liquid. If he knows that the standard deviation for this procedure is 1.2°C, what is the interval estimation for the population mean at a 95% confidence level?

Sol. We have, $n = 6$ and $\sigma = 1.2$

Now, Sample mean ($\bar{x}$)

$$= \frac{102.5 + 101.7 + 103.1 + 100.9 + 100.5 + 102.2}{6}$$

$$= \frac{610.9}{6} = 101.82$$

Given, confidence level = 95%

$$\Rightarrow \quad (1-\alpha) = 0.95$$

$$\Rightarrow \quad \alpha = 1 - 0.95 = 0.05$$

$$\Rightarrow \quad \frac{\alpha}{2} = 0.025$$

$$\therefore \quad Z_{\alpha/2} = Z_{0.025}$$

Now, margin of error $= Z_{\alpha/2} \cdot \dfrac{\sigma}{\sqrt{n}}$

$$= Z_{0.025} \times \frac{1.2}{\sqrt{6}}$$

$$= 1.96 \times \frac{1.2}{2.45}$$

$$= 0.96$$

$\therefore$ Interval estimation for the population mean,

$$\mu = \bar{x} \pm \text{margin of error}$$

$$= 101.82 \pm 0.96$$

$$= (101.82 - 0.96, 101.82 + 0.96)$$

$$= (100.86, 102.78)$$

Thus, confidence interval = (100.86, 102.78)

EXAMPLE 6. A 95% confidence interval for a population mean was reported to be 152 to 160. If $\sigma = 15$, what sample size was used in this study?

Sol. We have, $\sigma = 15$

confidence level = 95%

and confidence interval (152, 160)

Now, let sample mean be $\bar{x}$ and margin of error be E.

$$\therefore \quad \bar{x} - E = 152 \quad \text{...(i)}$$

$$\text{and} \quad \bar{x} + E = 160 \quad \text{...(ii)}$$

On solving Eqs. (i) and (ii), we get

$$\bar{x} = 156 \text{ and } E = 4$$

Also, $1 - \alpha = 0.95$

$$\Rightarrow \quad \alpha = 0.05 \Rightarrow \frac{\alpha}{2} = 0.025$$

$$\therefore \quad z_{\alpha/2} = z_{0.025} = 1.96$$

$\therefore$ Margin of error $= z_{\alpha/2} \cdot \dfrac{\sigma}{\sqrt{n}}$

$$\Rightarrow \quad 4 = 1.96 \times \frac{15}{\sqrt{n}}$$

$$\Rightarrow \quad 4\sqrt{n} = 1.96 \times 15$$

$$\Rightarrow \quad \sqrt{n} = \frac{1.96 \times 15}{4} = 0.49 \times 5$$

$$\Rightarrow \quad n = (0.49 \times 15)^2$$

$$\Rightarrow \quad n = 54.0225$$

$$\Rightarrow \quad n = 54$$

$\therefore$ Sample size = 54

Topic Practice 1

1 The following data : 6, 7, 9, 12, 16, 10 form a random sample. What is the point estimate of population standard deviation?

2 In a survey question for a sample of 500 individuals, 180 persons gave response 'Yes' 230 gave response 'No' and 90 gave no response. What is the point estimate of the proportion in the population who respond 'No'?

3 Consider two independent populations with 5 units each as follows

Population I : 3, 3, 2, 6, 1

Population II : 1, 2, 3, 2, 2

Find the point estimates for the population mean (for both I and II), Also find standard error of the difference of two independent simple means say $\bar{x}_1$ and $\bar{x}_2$.

4 A sample random sample of 60 items resulted in a sample mean of 80. The population standard deviation is $\sigma = 15$.

(i) Complete the 95% confidence interval for the population mean.

(ii) Assume that same sample mean was obtained from a sample of 120 items. Provide a 95% confidence interval for the population mean.

5 A research worker wishes to estimate the mean of population by using sufficiently large sample. The probability is 0.95 that the sample mean will not differ by true mean by more than 95% of the standard deviation. How large a sample should be taken?

6 If a coin is tossed 20 times and the coin coil falls on head after any toss. It is success. suppose the probability of success is 0.5. What is the probability that the number of success is less than or equal to 12?

7 A diameter of a component produced on a semi-automatic machine is known to be distributed normally with a mean of 10 mm and a standard deviation of 0.1 mm. If we pick up a random sample of size 5, what is the probability that the sample mean be between 9.95 mm and 10.05 mm?

8 The average height of a random sample of 400 adult makes of a city is 175 cm. It is know that population standard deviation is 40.

(i) Determine the 90% confidence interval for the population mean.

(ii) Determine the 95% confidence interval for the population mean.

9 In a survey, the sample proportion for the population proportion is $\bar{p} = 0.35$. How large a sample should be taken to provide a 95% confidence level with a margin of error of 0.05?

10 In a large consignment of DVD's the store manager of an electronic store wants to have an idea about the proportion of defectives for making decision about accepting or returning the lot.

(i) If he examined 100 DVD's and found 7 defectives, then construct a 95% confidence interval for proportion of defectives in the consignment.

(ii) How many DVD's should be sampled and checked in order to estimate the proportion of defectives within 0.05 (more or less) with 95% confidence?

Hints & Solutions

1. Here, mean $(\bar{x}) = \dfrac{\Sigma x_i}{n}$

$$= \frac{6+7+9+12+16+10}{6} = \frac{60}{6} = 10$$

Now, $\Sigma(x_i - \bar{x})^2 = (6-10)^2 + (7-10)^2 + (9-10)^2 + (12-10)^2 + (16-10)^2 + (10-10)^2$

$$= 16 + 9 + 1 + 4 + 36 = 66$$

The point estimate of population standard deviation,

$$S = \sqrt{\frac{\Sigma(x_i - \bar{x})^2}{n-1}} = \sqrt{\frac{66}{6-1}} = \sqrt{\frac{66}{5}} = \sqrt{13.2} = 3.63$$

2. The point estimate of the proportion in the population who respond 'No'

$$\bar{p} = \frac{x_{\text{No}}}{n} = \frac{230}{500} = 0.46$$

3. $\bar{x}_1 = \dfrac{3+3+2+6+1}{5} = 3$, $\bar{x}_2 = \dfrac{1+2+3+2+2}{5} = 2$

$\therefore$ Point estimate of population mean (μ_1) is 3 and for population mean (μ_2) is 2.

$$S_1^2 = \frac{1}{n-1}\Sigma(x_i - \bar{x})^2 = \frac{1}{4}(0^2 + 0^2 + (-1)^2 + (3)^2 + (-2)^2)$$

$$= \frac{1}{4} \times 14 = \frac{7}{2}$$

and $S_2^2 = \frac{1}{4}[(-1)^2 + 0^2 + 1^2 + 0^2 + 0^2] = \frac{1}{2}$

∴ Standard error of the difference of two independent samples

i.e. $SE(\bar{x}_1 - \bar{x}_2) = \sqrt{\frac{\sigma_1^2}{n_1} + \frac{\sigma_2^2}{n_2}}$

$= \sqrt{\left(\frac{7/2}{5}\right) + \left(\frac{1/2}{5}\right)}$

$= \sqrt{\frac{7}{10} + \frac{1}{10}} = \sqrt{\frac{8}{10}}$

$= \sqrt{0.8} = 0.8944$

4. (i) (76.2, 83.8) (ii) (77.32, 82.68)

5. According to the question,

We Considering 95% confidence interval

∴ $1.96 \times \frac{\sigma}{\sqrt{n}} = \frac{\sigma}{2}$

⇒ $\sqrt{n} = 1.96 \times 2$

⇒ $n = (1.96 \times 2)^2 = 15.36$

6. We have, $\mu = np = 20 \times 0.5 = 10$

$\sigma = \sqrt{npq} = \sqrt{20 \times 0.5 \times 0.5}$

$= \sqrt{5} = 2.24$

∴ $z = \frac{X - \mu}{\sigma} = \frac{X - np}{\sqrt{npq}}$

$= \frac{12 - 10}{2.24} = 0.89$

The corresponding value of $z = 0.89$ is 0.8133 (for table)

∴ The probability that the number of successes is less than or equal to 12 is 0.8133.

7. We have, $\mu = 10$, $\sigma = 0.1$ and $n = 5$

$z_1 = \frac{\bar{X} - \mu}{\sigma/\sqrt{n}} = \frac{10.05 - 10}{01/\sqrt{5}}$

$= \frac{0.05}{0.0447} = 1.12$

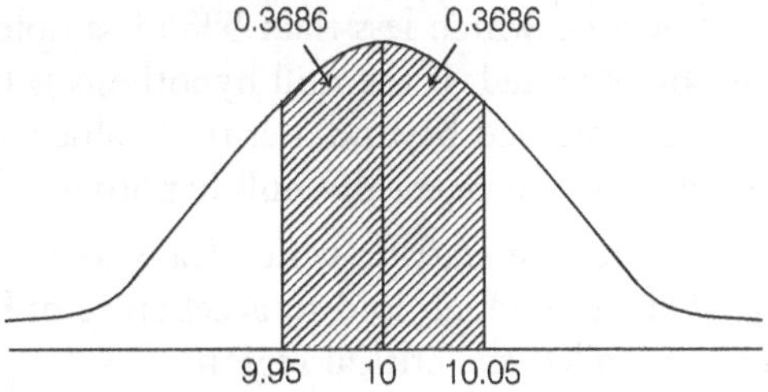

$z_2 = \frac{9.95 - 10}{01/\sqrt{5}} = \frac{-0.05}{0.0447} = -1.12$

The area corresponding to $Z = 1.12$ is 3.686.

Hence, the required probability is 0.3686 + 0.3686 = 0.7372

8. We have, $n = 400$, $\bar{x} = 175$, $\sigma = 40$

(i) Confidence level = 90%

⇒ $1 - \alpha = 0.9$

⇒ $\alpha = 01$

⇒ $\frac{\alpha}{2} = \frac{01}{2} = 0.05$

∴ $z_{\alpha/2} = 1.645$

Now, margin of error $= Z_{\alpha/2} \frac{\sigma}{\sqrt{n}}$

$= 1.645 . \frac{40}{\sqrt{400}}$

$= 1.645 \times 2 = 3.29$

∴ $\mu = \bar{x} \pm$ margin of error

$= 175 \pm 3.29$

$= (175 - 3.29, 175 + 3.29)$

$= (171.71, 178.29)$

(ii) (171.08, 178.92)

9. Given, margin of error = 0.05, $\bar{p} = 0.35$

Confidence level = 95%

∴ Marginal of error $= z_{\alpha/2}\sqrt{\frac{\bar{p}(1-\bar{p})}{n}}$

⇒ $0.05 = 1.96\sqrt{\frac{0.35 \times (1 - 0.35)}{n}}$

⇒ $n = 350$

∴ Sample size = 35

10. (i) Here, $p = \frac{7}{100} = 0.07$, $z_{0.025} = 1.96$

Thus, a 95% confidence interval for p, the proportion of defectives in the consignment is

$0.07 \mp 1.96\sqrt{\frac{0.07 \times 0.93}{100}}$

or, 0.07 ∓ 0.05, i.e., (0.02, 0.12)

Thus, with 95% confidence he can make decision that the proportion of defectives in the consignment is between 0.02 and 0.12, i.e., 2% and 12%.

(ii) Here, $n = \left(\frac{1.96}{0.05}\right)^2 \times 0.07 \times 0.93 = 100.03$

The required sample size is 100.

Hypothesis Testing and Degree of Freedom

Hypothesis Testing

Hypothesis is an assumption about the population parameter to be tested based on sample information, assumptions, which may or may not be true are called statistical hypothesis.

In hypothesis testing, hypothesis are normally referred to as

(i) H_0 : null hypothesis

(ii) H_1 : alternative hypothesis

Here, null hypothesis asserts that there is no true difference in sample statistics and population parameter under consideration i.e. there is no difference between assumed and actual value of the parameter and the hypothesis that is different from the null hypothesis is alternative hypothesis. The rejection of the null hypothesis (H_0) indicates that there is enough evidence to show that alternate hypothesis (H_1) is true.

Not rejection of the null hypothesis (H_0) indicates that there is not enough evidence to show that alternate hypothesis (H_1) is true.

Hypothesis Test for Population Mean

There are three types of possibilities

$$H_0 : \mu \geq \mu_0, \ H_0 : \mu \leq \mu_0, \ H_0 : \mu = \mu_0$$
$$H_1 : \mu < \mu_0, \ H_1 : \mu > \mu_0, \ H_1 : \mu \neq \mu_0$$

Where μ_0 denote the hypothesized value of population mean μ and it may be noted that the equality sign (=) should always appear in the null hypothesis.

Level of Significance

The confidence with which an experimenter rejects or retains null hypothesis depends on the significance level adopted and it is usually denoted by "α". It is generally specified before any sample is drawn.

For hypothesis test about a population mean (σ), a test statistic is standard normal random variable Z and value of test statistic Z is given by

$$Z = \frac{\bar{x} - \mu_0}{\sigma / \sqrt{n}},$$

where $\bar{x}$: sample mean

μ_0 : hypothesized value of population mean

σ : population standard deviation

n : number of sample points

e.g. If we take $\sigma = 5\%$ level of significance, then there are about 5 chance out of 100 that we would reject the null hypothesis when it should be accepted means that 95% confident that we have made the right decision.

If $\alpha = 0.5$, the test result is said to be 'significant' and when the null hypothesis is rejected at $\alpha = 0.01$, the test result is said to be highly significant.

There are two approaches for making a decision regarding rejection or non-rejection of H_0

(i) p-value approach

(ii) critical value approach

p-Value Approach

It is based on probability that a test statistics will take the value as extreme as or more extreme than the actually observed,when H_0 is true. It is also know as observed level of significance. If p-value is less than or equal to α, then the null hypothesis is rejected in favour of the alternative hypothesis. And, if the p-value is greater than α, then the null hypothesis is not rejected.

Determination of Test Statistics

To determine a suitable test statistics, generally test statistics will encounter in the following form

Test statistics

$$= \frac{\text{Sample statistics} - \text{Hypothesized population parameter}}{\text{Standard error of the sample statistics}}$$

Critical Value and Critical Region

Critical value is a cut off value that define the boundaries beyond which less than 5% of sample means can be obtained, if the null hypothesis is true sample means obtained beyond a critical value will result in a decision to reject the null hypothesis.

The values of the test statistic which leads to a rejection of H_0 and which lead to acceptance of H_0. The former is called the critical region.

Type I and Type II Errors

If we reject a hypothesis when it should be accepted, then we say that it is a Type I error and, if we accept a hypothesis when it should be rejected, then we say that it is a Type II error.

There are two types of errors that can be made in the hypothesis testing.

Decision	H_0 true	H_0 False
Accept H_0	Correct conclusion	Type II error
Reject H_0	Type I error	Correct conclusion

In most cases of hypothesis testing Type-I error can be controlled.

One-Tailed and Two-Tailed Test

Mainly, there are two types of problems of test of hypothesis

1. One-tailed Test

A one-tailed test is a statistical hypothesis test set up to show that the sample mean would be higher or lower than the population mean, but not both i.e. hypothesis about population mean is rejected only for value of falling into one of the tails of the sampling distribution.

Right-tailed test

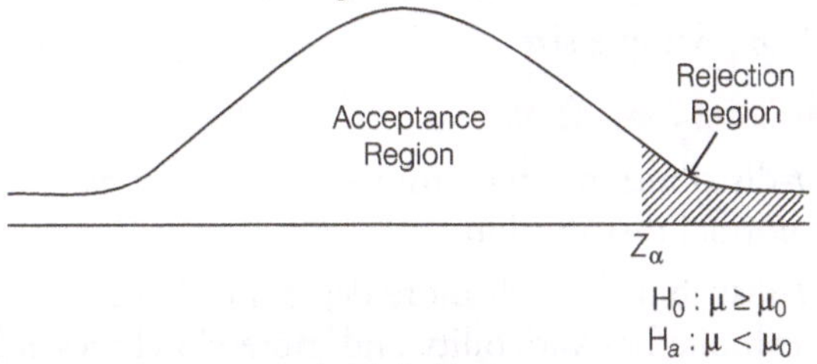

Left-tailed test

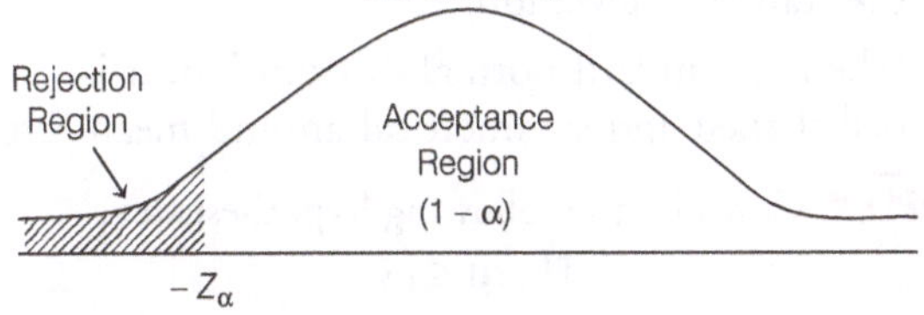

2. Two-Tailed Test

In two-tailed test the critical area of a distribution is two sided and tests whether a sample is greater or less than a range of values i.e. the hypothesis about the population mean is rejected for values falling into either tail of the sampling distribution.

EXAMPLE 1. Consider the following hypothesis test

$$H_0 : \mu \leq 30;\ H_a : \mu > 30$$

A sample of 50 provides a sample mean of 32.6 and the population standard deviation is 8. Compute the value of the test statistic.

Sol. Given, $\mu_0 = 30, n = 50, \bar{x} = 32.6$ and $\sigma = 8$

$$\therefore \text{Test statistic, } Z = \frac{\bar{x} - \mu_0}{\sigma/\sqrt{n}} = \frac{32.6 - 30}{8/\sqrt{50}}$$

$$= \frac{2.6 \times \sqrt{50}}{8} = \frac{18.38}{8} = 2.3$$

EXAMPLE 2. Consider the following hypothesis test

$$H_0 : \mu = 15$$
$$H_a : \mu \neq 15$$

A sample of 50 provided a sample mean of 14.15, the population standard deviation is 3, if $\alpha = 0.05$, then what is the p-value?

Sol. Given, $\bar{x} = 14.15, n = 50, \sigma = 3$ and $\mu_0 = 15$

$$\text{Now, } Z = \frac{\bar{x} - \mu_0}{\sigma/\sqrt{n}} = \frac{14.15 - 15}{3/\sqrt{50}}$$

$$= \frac{(-0.85) \times \sqrt{50}}{3}$$

$$= -2.003$$

$$\therefore \quad Z = -2$$

$\therefore$ p-value = 2 (Area under the standard normal curve to the left of Z)

$$= 2 \times (0.0228) = 0.0456$$

$\therefore$ p-value = 0.0456

EXAMPLE 3. Consider the following hypothesis

$$H_0 : \mu = 295$$
$$H_a : \mu \neq 295$$

A sample of 50 provided a sample mean of 297.6. The population standard deviation is 12 and level of significance, $\alpha = 0.05$. Check the hypothesis test given above using interval estimation.

Sol. We have, $\mu_0 = 295, \bar{x} = 297.6, \sigma = 12, \alpha = 0.05$ and $n = 50$

$$\text{Now, } Z_{\alpha/2} = Z_{0.025} = 1.96$$

$$\therefore \text{Confidence interval} = \bar{x} \pm Z_{\alpha/2} \frac{\sigma}{n}$$

$$= 297.6 \pm 1.96 \times \frac{12}{\sqrt{50}}$$

$$= 297.6 \pm 3.3$$

$$= (297.6 - 3.3,\ 297.6 + 3.3)$$

$$= (294.3,\ 300.9)$$

Since, the hypothesized value of population $\mu_0 = 295$ lies in the confidence interval (294.3, 300.9). Therefore, H_0 cannot be rejected.

t-Test

t-test is a statistical test that is used to compare the means of two groups. It is often used in hypothesis testing to determine whether two groups are different from one another.

The t-test assumes, data are

(i) independent
(ii) approximately normally distributed.
(iii) have a similar amount of variance within each group being compared.

There are mainly three types of t-tests

(i) **One sample t-Test** If the groups comes from a single population (e.g. measuring before and after an experimental treatment), perform one sample t-test. If there is one group being compared against a standard value (e.g. comparing the acidity of a liquid with neutral pH of 7), perform a one-sample t-test.
(ii) **Two sample t-Test** If the groups come from two different populations (e.g. two different species or people from two separate cities), perform a two-sample t-Test (or independent t-test).
(iii) **Pair t-Test** If the group come from a single population (e.g. measuring before and after an experimental treatment) perform a paired t-test.

Degrees of Freedom

The maximum number of logically independent values, which are values that have the freedom to vary, in the sample.

The number of degrees of freedom

= Total number of observation (n)
− number of independent constraints imposed on the observation (k)

e.g. If $\Sigma x_i = x_1 + x_2 + x_3$, has 3 degrees of freedom. Since, if we assign values to any three of these we get value of the fourth observation automatically determined.

t-distribution

It is type of normal distribution used for smaller sample sizes, (say 30 or less) where the variance in the data is unknown. The t-distribution also known as student's t-distribution is a way of describing data that follow a bell curve when plotted on a graph, with the maximum number of observation close to the mean and fewer observation in the tails.

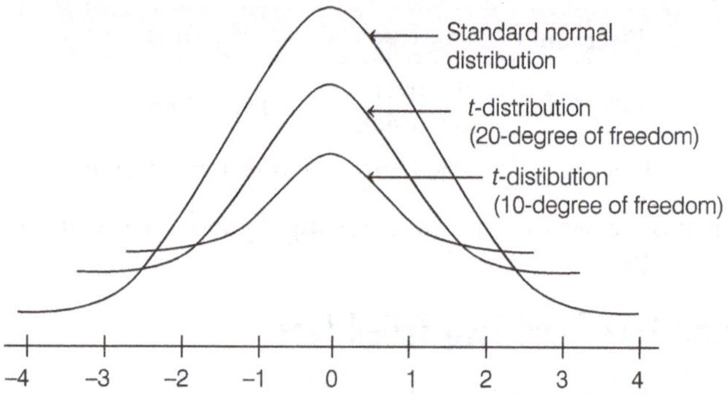

Consider $x_1, x_2, x_3, \ldots. x_n$ be random sample of size n from a normal population with mean μ and variance σ^2.

Then, t-distribution is defined by the statistics,

$$t = \frac{\bar{x} - \mu_0}{S / \sqrt{n}}$$

where, $\bar{x}$: Sample mean

μ_0 : Hypothesized value of population mean

S : Sample standard deviation

n : Sample size

Properties of t-distribution

(i) t-distribution range from $-\infty$ to ∞ just as does a normal distribution.
(ii) t-distribution with more degrees of freedom exhibits less variability and more closely resembles the standard deviation.
(iii) Like the standard normal distribution, it is bell-shaped and symmetrical around mean zero.

EXAMPLE 4. Consider the following hypothesis test

$$H_0 : \mu \le 18$$
$$H_a : \mu > 18$$

A sample of 28 provided a sample mean, $\bar{x} = 20$ and a sample standard deviation, $S = 5.68$, use the t-distribution table to compute a range for the p-value.

Sol. We have, $n = 28$, $\bar{x} = 20$, $S = 5.68$ and $\mu_0 = 18$

$\therefore$ Test statistics, $t = \dfrac{\bar{x} - \mu_0}{S / \sqrt{n}}$

$$= \frac{20 - 18}{5.68 / \sqrt{28}} = \frac{2 \times \sqrt{28}}{5.68} = 1.86$$

$\therefore$ $t = 1.86$

and degree of freedom = 28 − 1 = 27

$\because$ $t = 1.86$

$\Rightarrow$ p-values of 1.86 = Area under the t-distribution curve to the right of t.

From the distribution table, $t = 1.86$ lies between 1.703 and 2.052 for which area lies between 0.025 and 0.05, therefore p-value lies between 0.025 and 0.05.

EXAMPLE 5. Consider the following hypothesis test.

$$H_0 : \mu = 25$$
$$H_a : \mu \neq 25$$

A sample of 72 provided a sample mean of 22.15. The population standard deviation is 8.

(i) Compute the value of the test statistic.

(ii) What is the p-value?

(iii) At $\alpha = 0.05$, what is your conclusion?

(iv) What is the rejection rule using the critical value? What is your conclusion?

Sol. We have, $\mu_0 = 25,\ n = 72,\ \bar{x} = 22.15$ and $S = 8$

(i) $t = \dfrac{\bar{x} - \mu_0}{S/\sqrt{n}} = \dfrac{22.15 - 25}{8/\sqrt{72}}$

$= \dfrac{-2.85 \times \sqrt{72}}{8} = -3.03$

$\therefore t = -3.03$

(ii) Since, $t = -3.03$

So, p-value = 2 (area under the standard normal curve to the left of t)

$= 2 \times 0.0012 = 0.0024$

(iii) Since, p-value < 0.05

So, reject H_0.

(iv) We know that if $t \leq -t_{\alpha/2}$, then reject H_0.

Since, $-t_{\alpha/2} = -t_{0.025} = -1.96$

Here, $-3.03 < -1.96$

$\Rightarrow$ Reject H_0

EXAMPLE 6. The mean weekly sales of 4-wheeler was 50 units per agency in 20 agencies. After an advertising campaign, the mean weekly sales increased to 55 units per agency with standard deviation of 10 units. Test whether the advertising campaign was successful.

[Given $\sqrt{5} = 2.24,\ t_{19}(0.05) = 1.729$ J] **[CBSE 2024]**

Sol. Given, $n = 20,\ \bar{x} = 55,\ S = 10,\ \mu = 50$

Null Hypothesis : The advertising campaign is not successful

i.e. $H_0 : \mu = 50$ (There is no significant difference between the mean weekly sales of units in agencies before and after advertising campaign).

Alternate Hypothesis, $H_1 : \mu > 50$. The advertising campaign was successful.

Test statistics, $t = \dfrac{\bar{x} - \mu}{\dfrac{S}{\sqrt{n-1}}} = \dfrac{55 - 50}{\dfrac{10}{\sqrt{20-1}}}$

$= \dfrac{5 \times \sqrt{20-1}}{10} = \dfrac{5 \times \sqrt{19}}{10}$

$= \dfrac{5 \times 4.358}{10} = \dfrac{21.794}{10}$

$= 2.179$

$t > t_{0.05} = 1.729$

Since, the computed value of $t = 2.179$ is greater than the critical value of $t = 1.729$.

So, reject our null hypothesis.

Therefore, the advertising campaign was successful.

EXAMPLE 7. Two types of batteries are tested for their length of life and the following results are obtained.

Battery	Sample Size	Mean (hours)	Standard deviation (hours)
ABC	100	1000	10
XYZ	120	1050	11

Conclude that the two types of batteries are having the same mean life?

Sol. Given, $\bar{X}_1 = 1000,\ \bar{X}_2 = 1050$,

$S_1 = 10,\ S_2 = 11,\ n_1 = 100$

and $n_2 = 120$

Let there is no significant difference in the mean life of the two types of batteries i.e. consider the null hypothesis.

$\therefore\ H_0 : \mu_1 = \mu_2$

Test statistics, $Z = \dfrac{\bar{X}_1 - \bar{X}_2}{\sqrt{\dfrac{S_1^2}{n_1} + \dfrac{S_2^2}{n_2}}}$

$= \dfrac{1000 - 1050}{\sqrt{\dfrac{(10)^2}{100} + \dfrac{(11)^2}{120}}}$

$= \dfrac{-50}{\sqrt{\dfrac{100}{100} + \dfrac{121}{120}}}$

$= \dfrac{-50}{\sqrt{1 + 1.0083}}$

$= \dfrac{-50}{\sqrt{2.0083}}$

$= \dfrac{-50}{1.42} = -35.21$

Since, the computed value of $Z = 35.21$ is greater than the critical value of $Z = 1.96$ (5% level of significance).

So, reject our null hypothesis, therefore, we conclude that the two types of batteries are having different mean life.

Topic Practice 2

1 Define t-distribution?

2 Give at least two important application of t-distribution?

3 What is paired t-test?

4 What is the two-sample t-test?

5 If the critical region is evenly distributed, then the test is referred as?

6 The assumed hypothesis which is tested for rejection considering it to be true is called?

7 Consider the following hypothesis test

$$H_0 : \mu \geq 45$$
$$H_a : \mu < 45$$

A sample of 36 provided a sample mean, $\bar{x} = 44$ and a sample standard deviation, $S = 5.2$. If $\alpha = 0.01$, then what is your conclusion?

8 Two batches of the same product are tested for their mean life. Assuming that, the lives of the product follow a normal distribution with an unknown variance, test the hypothesis that the mean life is the same for both the branches, given the following information.

Batch	Sampl e size	Mean life (in hours)	Standard deviation (in ₹)
Batch I	10	750	12
Batch II	8	820	14

[given, $t_{16}(0.05) = 2.2120$]

9 The Educational Testing Service conducted a study to investigate difference between the scores of male and female students on the Scholastic Aptitude Test. The study identified a random sample of 562 female and 852 male students, who had achieved the same high score on the mathematics portion of the test. That is, female and male students were viewed as having similarly high abilities in mathematics. The verbal scores for the two samples are as given

Female students, $\bar{x}_1 = 557$ and $S_1 = 83$

Male students, $\bar{x}_2 = 545$ and $S_2 = 78$

Do the data support the conclusion that given a population of female students and a population of male students with similarly high mathematics abilities, the female students will have a significantly higher verbal ability? Test at a 5% level of significance. What is your conclusion?

10 A random sample of 12 families in one city showed an average weekly food expenditure of ₹ 1380 with a standard deviation of ₹ 100 and a random sample of 15 families in another city showed an average weekly food expenditure of ₹ 1320 with a standard deviation of ₹ 120. Test, whether the difference between the two means is significant at a level of significance of 0.01.

11 Samples of sales in similar shops in towns A and B regarding a new product yielded the following information.

For town A	$\bar{x}_1 = 3.45$	$\Sigma x_i = 38$	$\Sigma x_i^2 = 228$	$n_1 = 11$
For town B	$\bar{x}_2 = 4.44$	$\Sigma y_i = 40$	$\Sigma y_i^2 = 222$	$n_2 = 9$

Is there any evidence of difference in sales in the two towns? [given $t_{18}(0.05) = 2.10$]

12 Samples of two different types of bulbs were tested for length of life and the following data were obtained

	Type I	Type II
Sample size	8	7
Sample mean	1234 h	1136 h
Sample SD	36 h	40 h

Is the difference in mean life of two types of bulbs significant?

13 From the following data obtained from a sample of 1000 persons, calculate the standard error of mean.

Weekly earnings (₹ in hundred)	Number of persons
0-10	50
10-20	100
20-30	150
30-40	200
40-50	200
50-60	100
60-70	100
70-80	100

Is it likely that the sample has come from the population with an average weekly earnings of ₹ 4200.

14 Consider the following hypothesis test.

$H_0 : \mu \le 30$

$H_a : \mu > 30$

A sample of 45 provided a sample mean of 32.4. The population standard deviation is 6.

(i) Compute the value of the test statistic.

(ii) What is the p-value?

(iii) At $\alpha = 0.01$, what is your conclusion?

15 You are given the following data about the life of two brands of bulbs.

	Mean life	Standard deviation	Sample size
Brand *A* (in hours)	2100	250	12
Brand *B* (in hours)	2180	300	15

Do you think, there is a significant difference in the quality of the two brands of bulbs? [the table value of t for 25 degree of freedom at 5% level of significance is 1.708].

Hints & Solutions

1. The t-distribution is a probability distribution method where in the hypothesis of the mean of a small sample is tested, which is drawn from the systematic population whose standard deviation is unknown. It is a statistical measure used to compare the observed data with data expected to be obtained from a specific hypothesis.
2. In statistics, the t-distribution is most often used to
   (i) Find the critical values for a confidence interval when the data is approximately normally distribute
   (ii) Test of hypothesis about the population mean.
   (iii) Test of hypothesis about coefficient of correlation.
3. If two groups come from a single population, performed paired t-test. The paired t-test is also known as the dependent sample t-test.
4. The two-sample t-test (also known as the independent sample t-test) is a method used to test whether the unknown population means of two groups are equal or not.
5. In two-tailed test the critical region is evenly distributed. One region contains the area where null hypothesis is accepted and another contains the area where it is rejected.
6. Null hypothesis asserts that there is no true difference in sample statistics and population parameter under consideration.
7. Given, $n = 36$, $\bar{x} = 44$, $S = 5.2$ and $\mu_0 = 45$,

$$\therefore \quad t = \frac{\bar{x} - \mu_0}{S/\sqrt{n}} = \frac{44 - 45}{5.2/\sqrt{36}}$$

$$= \frac{-1 \times 6}{5.2} = -1.15 < 0$$

and degree of freedom $= 36 - 1 = 35$

$\therefore p$-value $= 2$ (Area under the standard normal curve to the left of Z)

$= 2 \times$ Area under the t-distribution curve to the right of t.

From the t-distribution table, we find the $t = 1.15$ lies between 1.306 and 1.690 for which area lies between 0.05 and 0.10.

So, p-value lies between 2×0.05 and 2×0.10 i.e. between 0.10 and 0.20.

So, $0.10 < p\text{-value} < 0.20$

Since, p-value > 0.01

So, we do not reject H_0.

8. Given, $n_1 = 10$, $n_2 = 8$, $\bar{x}_1 = 750$, $\bar{x}_2 = 820$, $S_1 =$ ₹ 12 and $S_2 =$ ₹ 14

Consider, Null hypothesis H_0 : Mean life is same for both the batches.

Alternate hypothesis H_1 : Two batches have different mean lives.

Test statistics,

$$t = \frac{\bar{x}_1 - \bar{x}_2}{S} \times \sqrt{\frac{n_1 n_2}{n_1 + n_2}},$$

where $$S = \sqrt{\frac{n_1 S_1^2 + n_2 S_2^2}{n_1 + n_2 - 2}}$$

$$\Rightarrow \quad S = \sqrt{\frac{10 \times 144 + 8 \times 196}{10 + 8 - 2}} = \sqrt{\frac{3008}{16}} = 13.71$$

$$\therefore \quad t = \frac{750 - 820}{13.71} \times \sqrt{\frac{10 \times 8}{10 + 8}} = \frac{-70}{13.71} \times \sqrt{\frac{80}{18}}$$

$$= \frac{-70}{13.711} \times 2.1081 = -10.763$$

Since, calculated value $|t| = 10.763 >$ tabulated value $t_{16}(0.05) = 2.2120$

So, rejected the null hypothesis at 5% level of significance.

Hence, the mean life for both the batches is not the same.

9. We have, $\bar{x}_1 = 557$, $\bar{x}_2 = 545$, $S_1 = 83$, $S_2 = 78$, $n_1 = 562$ and $n_2 = 852$

Consider, the null hypothesis be that there is no significant difference between male and female verbal ability,

$$H_0 : \mu_1 - \mu_2 \ge 0 \text{ and } H_1 : \mu_1 - \mu_2 < 0$$

Test statistics,

$$Z = \frac{\bar{x}_1 - \bar{x}_2}{\sqrt{\frac{S_1^2}{n_1} + \frac{S_2^2}{n_2}}} = \frac{557 - 545}{\sqrt{\frac{(83)^2}{562} + \frac{(78)^2}{852}}}$$

$$= \frac{12}{\sqrt{\frac{6889}{562} + \frac{6084}{852}}} = \frac{12}{\sqrt{12.2580 + 7.1408}}$$

$$= \frac{12}{\sqrt{19.3988}} = \frac{12}{4.4044} = 2.725$$

Here, the computed value of Z is greater than the table value of Z i.e. 1.96. So, reject the null hypothesis. Hence, there is a significant difference between the male and female verbal ability or female students have higher verbal ability.

10. Given, $n_1 = 12$, $n_2 = 15$, $\bar{x}_1 = 1380$, $\bar{x}_2 = 1320$, $S_1 = ₹\,100$ and $S_2 = ₹\,120$

Consider, the null hypothesis that there is no significant difference in the mean expenditure of the families in the two cities.

We know that, test statistics

$$t = \frac{\bar{x}_1 - \bar{x}_2}{S}\sqrt{\frac{n_1 n_2}{n_1 + n_2}}$$

$$S = \sqrt{\frac{(n_1 - 1)S_1^2 + (n_2 - 1)S_2^2}{n_1 + n_2 - 2}}$$

$$= \sqrt{\frac{(12-1)(100)^2 + (15-1)(120)^2}{12 + 15 - 2}}$$

$$= \sqrt{\frac{11 \times 10000 + 14 \times 14400}{25}}$$

$$= \sqrt{\frac{110000 + 201600}{25}}$$

$$= \sqrt{\frac{311600}{25}} = \sqrt{12464} = 111.64$$

$$\Rightarrow \quad t = \frac{1380 - 1320}{111.64}\sqrt{\frac{12 \times 15}{12 + 15}} = \frac{60 \times 2.582}{111.64} = 1.39$$

Here, degree of freedom $v = 12 + 15 - 2 = 25$

From $v = 25$, test statistics, $t_{0.01} = 2.485$.

Here, the calculated value t is less than the table value. Therefore, the null hypothesis is accepted. Hence, the difference between the two means is not significant.

11. Consider, null hypothesis H_0 : There is no significant difference in sales in similar shops in towns A and B, and alternate hypothesis H_1 : Sales in similar shops in towns A and B are not same.

Test statistics

$$t = \frac{\bar{x}_1 - \bar{x}_2}{S} \times \sqrt{\frac{n_1 n_2}{n_1 + n_2}},$$

where $\quad S = \dfrac{n_1 S_1^2 + n_2 S_2^2}{n_1 + n_2 - 2}$

Given, $n_1 = 11$, $\bar{x}_1 = 3.45$, $\Sigma x_i = 38$, $\Sigma x_i^2 = 228$

$n_2 = 9$, $\bar{x}_2 = 4.44$, $\Sigma y_i = 40$ and $\Sigma y_i^2 = 222$

Now, $\quad S^2 = \dfrac{\Sigma(x_i - \bar{x}_1)^2 + \Sigma(y_i - \bar{x}_2)^2}{n_1 + n_2 - 2}$

$$\Rightarrow \quad S^2 = \frac{\Sigma x_i^2 - n_1\bar{x}_1^2 + \Sigma y_i^2 - n_2\bar{x}_2^2}{n_1 + n_2 - 2}$$

$$\Rightarrow \quad S^2 = \frac{228 - 11 \times (3.45)^2 + 222 - 9 \times (4.44)^2}{11 + 9 - 2}$$

$$\Rightarrow \quad S^2 = \frac{228 - 11 \times 11.9025 + 222 - 9 \times 19.7136}{18}$$

$$\Rightarrow \quad S^2 = \frac{450 - 130.93 - 177.42}{18} = \frac{141.65}{18} = 7.869$$

$$\Rightarrow \quad SS = \sqrt{7.869} = 2.805$$

$$\therefore \quad t = \frac{\bar{x}_1 - \bar{x}_2}{S} \times \sqrt{\frac{n_1 n_2}{n_1 + n_2}}$$

$$\Rightarrow \quad t = \frac{3.45 - 4.44}{2.805} \times \sqrt{\frac{11 \times 9}{11 + 9}}$$

$$= -0.353 \times 2.22$$

$$= -0.784$$

Here, degree of freedom,

$$v = n_1 + n_2 - 2 = 11 + 9 - 2 = 18$$

Since, calculated value of $t(-0.784)$ is less than tabulated value of $t[t_{18}(0.05) = 2.10]$, therefore the null hypothesis is accepted a 5% level of significance. Hence, there is no difference is sales in two towns.

12. Given, $n_1 = 8$, $n_2 = 7$, $S_1 = 36$, $S_2 = 40$, $\bar{x}_1 = 1234$ and $\bar{x}_2 = 1136$

Let us take the null hypothesis that there is no significant difference in the mean life of the two types of bulbs.

Test statistics,

$$t = \frac{\bar{x}_1 - \bar{x}_2}{S}\sqrt{\frac{n_1 n_2}{n_1 + n_2}}$$

$$S = \sqrt{\frac{(n_1 - 1)S_1^2 + (n_2 - 1)S_2^2}{n_1 + n_2 - 2}}$$

$$= \sqrt{\frac{(8-1)(36)^2 + (7-1)(40)^2}{8 + 7 - 2}}$$

$$= \sqrt{\frac{7 \times 1296 + 6 \times 1600}{13}}$$

$$= \sqrt{\frac{9072 + 9600}{13}}$$

$$= \frac{18672}{13} = \sqrt{1436.31} = 37.9$$

Then, $\quad t = \dfrac{1234 - 1136}{37.9}\sqrt{\dfrac{8 \times 7}{8 + 7}}$

$$= \frac{98}{37.9} \times 1.932 = 5$$

From table with $v = 8 + 7 - 2 = 13$, test statistics $t_{0.05} = 2.16$.

Since, the calculated value of t is greater than the tabulated value.

Therefore, the null hypothesis is rejected.

Hence, there is a significant difference in the mean life of two types of bulbs.

13. Table for Mean and Standard Deviation

Weekly earnings (₹ in hundred)	x	f	$\frac{(x-45)}{10}$ (d)	fd	fd^2
0-10	5	50	−4	−200	800
10-20	15	100	−3	−300	900
20-30	25	150	−2	−300	600
30-40	35	200	−1	−200	200
40-50	45	200	0	0	0
50-60	55	100	+1	+100	100
60-70	65	100	+2	+200	400
70-80	75	100	+3	+300	900
		$n = 1000$		$\Sigma fd = -400$	$\Sigma fd^2 = 3900$

We know that,

$$\bar{x} = A + \frac{\Sigma fd}{n} \times i = 45 - \frac{400}{1000} \times 10 = 41$$

and
$$S = \sqrt{\frac{\Sigma fd^2}{n} - \left(\frac{\Sigma fd}{n}\right)^2} \times i$$

$$= \sqrt{\frac{3900}{1000} - \left(\frac{-400}{1000}\right)^2} \times 10$$

$$= \sqrt{3.9 - 0.16} \times 10$$

$$= \sqrt{3.74} \times 10$$

$$= 1.934 \times 10 = 19.34$$

$$\sigma_{\bar{x}} = \frac{S}{\sqrt{n}} = \frac{19.34}{\sqrt{1000}} = \frac{19.34}{31.62} = 0.612$$

Because standard error of mean is 0.612.

Now, $\bar{x} = 41, \mu = 42$ and $\sigma_{\bar{x}} = 0.612$

$$\therefore \quad Z = \frac{\bar{x} - \mu}{\sigma_{\bar{x}}} = \frac{41 - 42}{0.612} = -1.634$$

Here, we find that the computed value of Z is less than the critical value of $Z = \pm 1.96$, so there is no significant difference between the sample average. Hence, the population average weekly earnings and the difference could have arisen due to fluctuations of sampling.

14. Given, $\mu_0 = 30, n = 45, \bar{x} = 32.4, \sigma = 6$ and $\alpha = 0.01$.

(i) Test statistics, $Z = \dfrac{\bar{x} - \mu_0}{\frac{\sigma}{\sqrt{n}}} = \dfrac{32.4 - 30}{\frac{6}{\sqrt{45}}}$

$$= \frac{2.4 \times \sqrt{45}}{6} = 2.68$$

$$\therefore \quad Z = 2.68$$

(ii) $\because Z = 2.68 > 0$

So, p-value of 2.68 = Area under the standard normal curve to the right of Z

= 1 − 0.9963 (using table)

= 0.0037

$\therefore$ p-value = 0.0037

(iii) $\because$ p-value < 0.01

So, reject H_0.

15. Given, $\bar{x}_1 = 2100, S_1 = 250$ and $n_1 = 12$,

$\bar{x}_2 = 2180, S_2 = 300$ and $n_2 = 15$

Consider, null hypothesis : There is no significant difference in the quality of the two brands of bulbs.

$$t = \frac{\bar{x}_1 - \bar{x}_2}{S}\sqrt{\frac{n_1 n_2}{n_1 + n_2}}$$

where, $S = \sqrt{\dfrac{(n_1 - 1)S_1^2 + (n_2 - 1)S_2^2}{n_1 + n_2 - 2}}$

$$= \sqrt{\frac{11(250)^2 + 14(300)^2}{12 + 15 - 2}}$$

$$= \sqrt{\frac{11(62500) + 14(90000)}{25}}$$

$$= \sqrt{\frac{687500 + 1260000}{25}}$$

$$= \sqrt{\frac{1947500}{25}}$$

$$= \sqrt{77900} = 279.11$$

$$t = \frac{2100 - 2180}{279.11}\sqrt{\frac{12 \times 15}{12 + 15}} = \frac{-80}{279.11}\sqrt{\frac{180}{27}}$$

$$= \frac{-80}{279.11}\sqrt{6.6667}$$

$$= \frac{-80 \times 2.58}{279.11}$$

$$= \frac{-206.4}{279.11}$$

$$= -0.739$$

Since, the computed value of $t = 0.739$ is less than the table value of $t = 1.708$ [at 5% for 25 degree of freedom], we accept the null hypothesis.

Exam Pattern Exercise

Part A - Objective Type Questions

Multiple Choice Type Questions

1 The process of using sample data to estimate the values of unknown population parameters is called
(a) estimation (b) population
(c) sampling (d) interval estimation

2 The process of making estimates about the population parameter from a sample is called statistical
(a) decision (b) inference
(c) hypothesis (d) independence

3 A member of the population is called
(a) data (b) element
(c) family (d) group

4 Random sampling is useful as it is
(a) reasonably more accurate as compared to other methods
(b) economical in nature
(c) free from personal biases of the investigator
(d) All of the above

5 A statement made about a population for testing purpose is called
(a) testing statistics
(b) level of significance
(c) statistics
(d) hypothesis

6 If the calculated value of $|t| < t_v(\alpha)$, then the null hypothesis is **[CBSE 2023, 2024]**
(a) rejected
(b) accepted
(c) cannot be determined
(d) neither accepted nor rejected

7 Population value is called
(a) variable (b) parameters
(c) data (d) statistics

8 For testing the significance of difference between the means of two independent samples, the degree of freedom (v) is taken as **[CBSE 2023, 2024]**
(a) $n_1 - n_2 + 2$ (b) $n_1 - n_2 - 2$
(c) $n_1 + n_2 - 2$ (d) $n_1 + n_2 - 1$

9 A hypothesis which defines the population distribution is called
(a) statistical hypothesis
(b) null hypothesis
(c) composite hypothesis
(d) simple hypothesis

10 The probability of Type I error is referred as
(a) β (b) $1-\alpha$
(c) α (d) $1-\beta$

11 The point estimate of the population mean from a simple random sample 3, 6, 8, 10, 12, 15 is
(a) 6 (b) 9 (c) 4 (d) 12

12 In a statistical hypothesis test, then hypothesis is true but our test rejects it, it is
(a) Type II error
(b) Type I error
(c) Both Type I and II error
(d) None of the above

13 If 700 throws of six-faced die, odd points appeared 400 times, the die is fair at 6% level of significance, then hypothesis is
(a) rejected (b) accept
(c) error (d) None of these

14 Consider the following hypothesis test

$$H_0 : \mu \le 20$$
$$H_a : \mu > 20$$

A sample of 40 provided a sample mean of 24.3 and population standard deviation is 5. The value of the test statistics is
(a) 4.24 (b) 5.63 (c) 6.84 (d) 2.36

Assertion-Reason Based Questions

Directions (Q. Nos. 15-17) *In the questions given below are two statements labelled as Assertion (A) and Reason (R). In the context of the two statements, which one of the following is correct?*
(a) Both A and R are correct; R is the correct explanation of A
(b) Both A and R are correct; R is not the correct explanation of A
(c) A is correct; R is incorrect
(d) R is correct; A is incorrect

15 **Assertion (A)** The t-distribution depends on a parameter known as degree of freedom.
Reason (R) A sample of size 9 from a normal population $\bar{x} = 15.8$ and $s^2 = 10.3$. The 99% confidence interval for population mean is [39.902, 43.098]. [use t_8 (0.01) = 3.335]

16 **Assertion (A)** A population consists of four observation 1, 3, 5, 7, then the variance is 11.

Reason (R) In a sample of 100 customers of a departmental store 43 used master card. In another sample of 100 customers, 58 used a visa card, then the proportions of customers using two credit cards are different. [consider $\alpha = 0.05$]

17 **Assertion (A)** A random sample of size 25 from a normal population has the mean 47.5 and standard deviation 8.4, this information refute the claim that the mean of the population is 42%. [given t_{24} (0.05) = 2.06]

Reason (R) A p-value is a probability that provides a measure of the evidence against the null hypothesis.

Part B - Descriptive Questions

Very Short Answer Type Questions

18 What is one of the distinct difference between a population parameter and a sample statistics?

19 What is sampling Distribution?

20 What is systematic random sampling?

21 Describe probability sampling.

22 What is the significance level?

23 How do you know, if a p-value is statistically significant?

Short Answer Type Questions

24 A population consisting of 6 units 1, 2, 3, 4, 5 and 9. Find 95% confidence interval for estimating the population mean.

25 A random sample of size 16 has 53 as mean. The sum of squares of deviations from mean is 150. Can this sample be regard as taken from the population having 56 as mean? Level of significance is 5%. [given $t_{15}(0.05) = 1.753$]

26 A random sample of 36 workers is drawn from a factory to test, if their average monthly wages is ₹ 1500 or not. The population wages distribution is assumed to be normal with standard deviation of ₹ 300. The average monthly wages based on the 36 observations comes out to be ₹ 1800. Perform a test at 5% level of significance. Calculate test statistics.

27 Consider, a hypothetical population comprising only four values 4, 6, 8 and 10. Find point estimation of population variance (σ^2). Also, find standard error of sample variance (S^2).

Long Answer Type Questions

28 Ten oil tins are taken at random from an automatic filling machine. The mean weight of the tins is 17.2 kg and standard deviation is 0.62 kg. Does the sample mean differ significantly from the intended weight of 18 kg? [given, $t_9(0.05) = 2.26$]

29 Consider the following hypothesis

$$H_0 : \mu = 315 \text{ and } H_a : \mu \neq 315$$

A sample of 60 provided a sample mean of 324.6. The population standard is 14 and level of significance $\alpha = 0.05$. Check the hypothesis test given above, using interval estimation.

30 The average nicotine content of a particular brand of cigarette is supposed to be 2.2 mg per cigarette. A smoker of this brand wants to see, if it is really 2.2 mg or more. With this purpose the nicotine contents of 50 cigarettes are measured. The sample mean based on 50 cigarettes is 2.95 mg per cigarette. The population standard deviation is 0.8 mg. Do the data provide enough evidence that the average nicotine content exceeds 2.2 mg? Test at 5% level using p-value approach and critical value approach. [given, $Z_{0.05} = 1.645$]

31 The daily yield at a chemical plant, recorded for 50 days, possesses a sample mean of 884 tons. The population standard deviation is know to be 42 tons. Do the data provide enough evidence to indicate that the average daily yield of the chemical plant is 900 tons per day? Test at 1% level of significance, carry out the test using p-value approach and critical value approach.

Case Study Based Questions

32 A company producing electric bulbs may be interested in the average life of bulbs produced by them during a shift for this consider the following hypothesis test

$$H_0 : \mu \leq 36$$
$$H_a : \mu > 36$$

A sample of 60 provided a sample mean of 38.6. The population standard deviation is 7.

On the basis of above information, answer the following questions.

(i) The value of Σx_i is

(a) 2310 (b) 2316 (c) 2325 (d) 2340

(ii) The value of the test statistics is

(a) 2.88 (b) 3.10 (c) 3.05 (d) 2.67

(iii) What is the p-value?

(a) 0.642 (b) 0.012 (c) 0.002 (d) 0.50

(iv) What is your conclusion, when $\alpha = 0.01$?
(a) do not reject H_0 (b) reject H_0
(c) can not say (d) None of these

(v) What is the rejection rule using critical value?
(a) reject H_0
(b) do not reject H_0
(c) reject H_a
(d) do not reject H_a

33 A company is interested in knowing investor sentiment survey every month to determine the number of investors, who are Bullish, Bearish or Neutral on the stock market for next few months.

The results for the month ending October 2021 are as follows:

Bullish 208, Bearish 150, Neutral 142.

Based on above information, answer the following questions.

(i) The point estimate of the population proportion who are Bullish, is
(a) 0.519 (b) 0.416
(c) 0.369 (d) 0.345

(ii) The point estimate of the population proportion who are Bearish, is
(a) 0.2 (b) 0.8 (c) 0.3 (d) 0.4

(iii) The point estimate of the population proportion who are Neutral, is
(a) 0.193 (b) 0.284 (c) 0.43 (d) 0.431

(iv) A 95% confidence interval for the population proportion, who are Bullish, is
(a) (0.373, 0.459) (b) (0.628, 0.741)
(c) (0.291, 0.429) (d) (0.282, 0.362)

(v) A 95% confidence interval for the population proportion who are Bearish, is
(a) (0.41, 0.57) (b) (0.42, 0.56)
(c) (0.34, 0.43) (d) (0.26, 0.34)

Hints & Solutions

1. (a) 2. (b) 3. (b) 4. (d)
5. (d) 6. (b) 7. (b) 8. (c)
9. (d) 10. (b) 11. (b) 12. (b)
13. (a) 14. (a) 15. (b) 16. (d)
17. (b)

18. The measurable characteristics of population is called parameter and measurable characteristics of sample is called statistics. Population parameter is a constant that is not generally known and needed to be estimated from statistics. The sample value are subjected to change, as it depends upon sample value which are chosen at random, hence statistics are not constant.

19. If $S_1, S_2, S_3, \ldots, S_n$ are values of statistics S (like mean, variance etc.) obtained from n independent random samples. If a definite size selected from a given population, then $S_1, S_2, S_3, \ldots, S_n$ form a sampling distribution of statistics.

Then, Mean $(\bar{S}) = \frac{1}{n}\sum_{i=1}^{n} S_i$ and $\text{Var}(S) = \frac{1}{n}\sum_{i=1}^{n}(S_i - \bar{S})^2$

20. Systematic sampling is relatively a simple technique and may be more efficient than simple random sampling, provided the lists are arranged wholly as random. If populations are sufficient large, systematic sampling can often be expected to yield result that are similar to those obtained by proportional stratified sampling.

21. When selection of objects from the population is random so objects of the population has an equal chance of selection. Probability sampling is more complex, more time consuming and usually more costly than non-probability sampling.

22. The significance level, also known as α, is a measure of the strength of the evidence that must be present in your sample before you will reject the null hypothesis and conclude that the effect is statistically significant, the statistian determines the significance level before conducting the experiment. The significance level is the probability of rejecting the null hypothesis.

23. A p-value or probability value, is a number describing how likely it is that your data would have occurred by random change. The level of statistical is often expressed as p-value between 0 and 1. The smaller the p-value, the stronger the evidence that you should reject the null hypothesis.

24. Mean, $\bar{x} = \frac{24}{6} = 4$

Now, $S^2 = \frac{1}{n-1}\Sigma(x_i - \bar{x})^2$

$$= \frac{1}{5}[(-3)^2 + (-2)^2 + (-1)^2 + 0^2 + (1)^2 + (5)^2]$$

$$= \frac{1}{5}[9 + 4 + 1 + 1 + 25]$$

$$= \frac{1}{5} \times 40 = 8$$

$\therefore$ $S = \sqrt{8} = 2\sqrt{2}$

$\therefore$ Point estimate for σ is $2\sqrt{2}$.

$\therefore$ 95% confidence interval is

$$= \left[4 - 1.96\left(\frac{2\sqrt{2}}{\sqrt{6}}\right), 4 + 1.96\left(\frac{2\sqrt{2}}{\sqrt{6}}\right)\right]$$

$$\left[\because \bar{x} - 1.96\left(\frac{\sigma}{\sqrt{6}}\right) \text{and } \bar{x} + 1.96\left(\frac{\sigma}{\sqrt{6}}\right)\right]$$

$$= \left[4 - 1.96\left(\sqrt{\frac{4}{3}}\right), 4 + 1.96\left(\sqrt{\frac{4}{3}}\right)\right] = [1.74, 6.26]$$

25. Consider $H_0 : \mu = 56$

$H_a : \mu > 56$

Here, $n = 16$, $\bar{x} = 53$

and $\Sigma(x_i - \bar{x})^2 = 150$

$$\therefore \quad S^2 = \frac{1}{n-1}\Sigma(x_i - \bar{x})^2 = \frac{150}{15} = 10$$

$$\Rightarrow \quad S = \sqrt{10} = 3.1622$$

Test statistics, $t = \dfrac{\bar{x} - \mu}{(S/\sqrt{n})} = \dfrac{53 - 56}{3.1622/\sqrt{16}}$

$$= \frac{(-3) \times 4}{3.1622} = -3.795$$

Since, calculated value of $|t| = 3.795$ is greater than tabulated value, so H_0 can be rejected.

26. Consider, $H_0 : \mu = 1500$

$H_1 : \mu \neq 1500$

$\bar{x} = 1800, \mu_0 = 1500$

$\sigma = 300$ and $n = 36$

$\therefore$ Test statistics, $Z = \dfrac{\bar{x} - \mu_0}{\sigma/\sqrt{n}}$

$$= \frac{1800 - 1500}{300/\sqrt{36}}$$

$$= \frac{300 \times 6}{300} = 6$$

27. Here, $\bar{x} = \dfrac{4 + 6 + 8 + 10}{4} = 7$

$$\Sigma(x_i - \bar{x})^2 = (4-7)^2 + (6-7)^2 + (8-7)^2 + (10-7)^2$$

$$= 9 + 1 + 1 + 9 = 20$$

$$\therefore \quad S^2 = \frac{1}{n-1}\Sigma(x_i - \bar{x})^2$$

$$= \frac{1}{(4-1)} \times 20 = \frac{20}{3}$$

$\therefore$ Point estimate of population variance

$$(\sigma^2) = \frac{20}{3}$$

The standard error of the sample variance (S^2)

$$= \sigma^2\sqrt{\frac{2}{n}} = \frac{20}{3}\sqrt{\frac{2}{4}}$$

$$= \frac{20}{3} \times \frac{1}{\sqrt{2}} = 4.71$$

28. Given, $n = 10$, $\bar{x} = 17.2, \mu = 18$ and $S = 0.62$

Consider, $H_0 : \mu = 18$

$H_1 : \mu \neq 18$

$\therefore$ Test statistics,

$$t = \frac{\bar{x} - \mu}{S/\sqrt{n}} = \frac{17.2 - 18}{0.62/\sqrt{10}} = -\frac{0.8 \times \sqrt{10}}{0.62} = -4.08$$

Since, calculated value of $|t|$ is greater than the tabulated value of t. So, H_0 is not accepted. Thus, the difference between sample mean weight and the intended weight is not insignificant.

29. Given, $\mu_0 = 315$, $n = 60$, $\bar{x} = 324.6$

$\sigma = 14$ and $\alpha = 0.05$

$\therefore$ Confidence interval $= \bar{x} \pm Z_{\alpha/2}\dfrac{\sigma}{\sqrt{n}}$

$$= 324.6 \pm 1.96 \times \frac{14}{\sqrt{60}}$$

$$[\because Z_{\alpha/2} = Z_{0.025} = 1.96]$$

$\therefore$ Confidence interval $= 324.6 \pm 1.96 \times 1.81$

$= 324.6 \pm 3.54$

$= (324.6 - 3.54, 324.6 + 3.54)$

$= (321.06, 328.14)$

Since, the hypothesis value of population mean $\mu_0 = 315$ does not lies in confidence interval, so H_0 rejected.

30. Consider $H_0 : \mu = 2.2$

$H_a : \mu > 2.2$

$\bar{x} = 2.95, \mu_0 = 2.2$, $n = 50$ and $\sigma = 0.8$

$\therefore$ Test statistics, $t = \dfrac{\bar{x} - \mu_0}{\sigma/\sqrt{n}} = \dfrac{2.95 - 2.2}{0.8/\sqrt{50}}$

$$= \frac{0.75 \times \sqrt{50}}{0.8} = \frac{0.75 \times 7.07}{0.8}$$

$$= 6.628$$

Since, $|t| > Z_{0.05}$

So, reject H_0 at 5% level.

Means provide sufficient evidence to conclude that average nicotine content exceeds 1.5 mg per cigarette.

31. Let μ be the mean daily yield of the chemical plant, sample size $n = 50$,

sample mean $\bar{x}$=884 tons

and population standard deviation $(\sigma) = 42$ tons.

Now, $H_0 : \mu = 900$

$H_a : \mu \neq 900$ at level $\alpha = 0.01$

$\therefore$ Test statistic, $z_0 = \dfrac{\bar{x} - \mu_0}{\sigma/\sqrt{n}} = \dfrac{884 - 900}{42/\sqrt{50}} = -2.69$

$\therefore$ p-value $= 2P(z > |z_0|)$

$= 2P(z > 2.69)$

$= 2 \times 0.0036$

$= 0.0072$,

which is less than 0.01, then pressigned level of significance.

Since, p -value is less than 0.01, H_0 should be rejected at 1% level which show the enough evidence to conclude that the mean daily yield differs from 900 tons.

By using critical value approach,

$$z_{\alpha/2} = z_{0.005} = 2.575$$

Since, $|z_0| = 2.69 > 2.575 = z_{0.005}$, the critical value, reject H_0 at 1%.

32. Given, $\mu_0 = 36, n = 60, \bar{x} = 38.6, \sigma = 7$ and $\alpha = 0.01$

(i) (b) We know that,

$$\bar{x} = \frac{\Sigma x_i}{n} \Rightarrow \Sigma x_i = \bar{x} \cdot n = 38.6 \times 60 = 2316$$

(ii) (a) $\therefore Z = \dfrac{\bar{x} - \mu_0}{\sigma/\sqrt{n}} = \dfrac{38.6 - 36}{\frac{7}{\sqrt{60}}} = \dfrac{2.6 \times \sqrt{60}}{7} = 2.88$

(iii) (c) Since, $Z > 2.88 > 0$

So, p-value of 2.88 = Area under the standard normal curve to the right of $Z = 1 - 0.9980 = 0.002$

(iv) (a) Since, p-value > 0.01

So, we do not reject H_0.

(v) (b) We know that, Reject H_0, if $Z \geq Z_\alpha$

$\Rightarrow \quad Z \geq Z_{0.01} \Rightarrow Z \geq 2.326$

$\Rightarrow \quad 2.88 \geq 2.33$, which is true.

So, we do not reject H_0.

33. Given, total number of investors $= 208 + 150 + 142 = 500$

(i) (b) The point estimate of the proportion in the population who are Bullish $= \dfrac{208}{500} = 0.416$

(ii) (c) The point estimate of the proportion in the population who are Bearish $= \dfrac{150}{500} = 0.3$

(iii) (b) The point estimate of the population proportion who are Neutral $= \dfrac{142}{500} = 0.284$

(iv) (a) We have, $1 - \alpha = 0.95 \Rightarrow \dfrac{\alpha}{2} = 0.025$

$$Z_{\alpha/2} = Z_{0.025} = 1.96$$

$\therefore$ Margin of error $= Z_{\alpha/2}\sqrt{\dfrac{\bar{p}(1-\bar{p})}{n}}$

$= 1.96\sqrt{\dfrac{0.416(1 - 0.416)}{500}}$

$= 1.96\dfrac{\sqrt{0.416 \times 0.584}}{\sqrt{500}}$

$= \dfrac{1.96 \times 0.493}{\sqrt{500}} = \dfrac{0.966}{\sqrt{500}}$

$= 0.043$

$\therefore p = \bar{p} \pm$ margin of error $= 0.416 \pm 0.043$

$= (0.416 - 0.043, 0.416 + 0.043)$

$= (0.373, 0.459)$

(v) (d) For 95% confidence interval for the population proportion who are Bearish.

Margin of error $= Z_{\alpha/2}\sqrt{\dfrac{\bar{p}(1-\bar{p})}{n}}$

$= 1.96\sqrt{\dfrac{0.3(1 - 0.3)}{500}} = 1.96\sqrt{\dfrac{0.3 \times 0.7}{500}}$

$= \dfrac{1.96 \times 0.46}{\sqrt{500}} = 0.04$

$\therefore p = \bar{p} \pm$ margin error

$= 0.3 \pm 0.04 = (0.3 - 0.04, 0.3 + 0.04)$

$= (0.26, 0.34)$

CHAPTER 17

Time Based Data

In this Chapter...

- Time Series and Moving Average
- Method of Least Squares

Time Series and Moving Average

Time Series

A time series is a sequence of observations which are ordered in time (space). If observation are made on some phenomenon throughout time it is most sensible to display the date in the order in which they arose, particularly, since successive observations will properly be dependent.

Component (Variations) of Time Series

The various reasons or the forces that affect the values of an observation in a time series are called the components of a time series. There are four categories of components of a time series as follows

Trend Variation

A trend exists when there is a long-term increase or decrease in the data. It does not have to be linear.

Sometimes we will refer to a trend as "changing direction" when it might go from an increasing trend to a decreasing trend.

e.g. A new apartment construction is going on, and someone has opened a shop of hardware materials, so until all the apartments get constructed, people will make purchases from that store. This will result in the trend of the sales revenue increasing.

Seasonal Variation

This type of variation depends on weather and other natural forces or social conditions. Like the sale of ice-creams increase in the summer season.

Cyclical Variation

Many industrial or financial sectors face ups and downs (booms or slumps) over a regular period of time. It is a very short period of variation and they do not affect the trend such periodic variations are known as cyclical variation.

Irregular Variation

- Irregular/random variation constitutes one of four components of a time series.
- Irregular variations do not follow a particular model and are not predictable.

Time Series Analysis

Time series analysis is a statistical technique that deals with time series data or trend analysis. Time series data means that data is in a series of particular time periods or intervals.

The data is considered in three types

(i) **Time series data** A set of observations on the values that a variable takes at different times.

(ii) **Cross-sectional data** Data of one or more variables, are collected at the same point in time.

(iii) **Pooled data** A combination of time series data and cross-sectional data.

Model of Time Series Analysis

There are two models which are generally used for the decomposition of time series into its four components.

(i) **Additive Model** In this model, we represent a particular observation in a time series as, if O represents the original data, T represents the trend, S represents the seasonal variations, C represents the cyclical variations and I represents the irregular variations.

Then, $O = T + S + C + I$

(ii) **Multiplicative Model** In this model, four components have a multiplicative relationship. We represent a particular observation in a time series as the product of these four components.

i.e. $O = T \times S \times C \times I,$

where O, T, S, C and I represents the terms as in additive model.

Trend Analysis

A trend is a recurring pattern and trend analysis is the practice of collecting data in an attempt to spot that pattern. When the user needs and behaviour are changing rapidly. Trend analysis is a method that can act as a window into the future demands of users.

Methods of Measuring Trend

Trend is measured using by the following methods

(i) Graphical method

(ii) Semi-averages method

(iii) Moving averages method

(iv) Method of least squares.

Here, we discuss (iii) moving averages methods and (iv) method of least squares.

Purpose of Moving Averages

The following points are main purpose of moving averages

- It helps in technical traders like tract the trend of financial assets by smoothing out the day-to-day price fluctuations.
- By identifying trend, moving averages allow traders, to make these trends work in their favour and increases the number of winning trades. It helps in trading strategies.

Period of Cycles

The time-interval covering the number of years is called the period of the cycles.

Note Cycles always found in series.

Calculation of Moving Average

Procedure for calculating the moving average in two cases

Case I

(Period of moving average is an odd number i.e. 3, 5, 7, ...).

For 3-yearly moving average

Year	Value	3-yearly moving average
1st	x_1	
2nd	x_2	$\frac{x_1 + x_2 + x_3}{3} = m_1$
3rd	x_3	$\frac{x_2 + x_3 + x_4}{3} = m_2$
4th	x_4	$\frac{x_3 + x_4 + x_5}{3} = m_3$
5th	x_5	$\frac{x_4 + x_5 + x_6}{3} = m_4$
6th	x_6	$\frac{x_5 + x_6 + x_7}{3} = m_5$
7th	x_7	

Note $m_1, m_2, \ldots, m_5$ are moving average points (mean point).

Case II

(Period of moving average is an even number i.e. 4, 6, 8, ...). For 4-yearly moving average

Year	Value	4-yearly moving average	4-yearly moving average centered
1st	x_1		
2nd	x_2	$\frac{x_1+x_2+x_3+x_4}{4}=m_1$	
3rd	x_3	$\frac{x_2+x_3+x_4+x_5}{4}=m_2$	$\frac{m_1+m_2}{2}=A$
4th	x_4	$\frac{x_3+x_4+x_5+x_6}{4}=m_3$	$\frac{m_2+m_3}{2}=B$
5th	x_5	$\frac{x_4+x_5+x_6+x_7}{4}=m_4$	$\frac{m_3+m_4}{2}=C$
6th	x_6		
7th	x_7		

Note A, B and C are centered points m_1, m_2 and m_3 are moving average points.

EXAMPLE 1. Consider the following data

Dates in the month of April	12	13	14	15	16	17	18	19	20	21	22	23	24	25
Number of units sold	2	5	0	12	13	25	45	13	31	18	11	2	3	1

Calculate three days moving average and display these and the original figures on the same graph.

Sol. Given table is shown below:

Dates in April	12	13	14	15	16	17	18	19	20	21	22	23	24	25
Number of units sold	2	5	0	12	13	25	45	13	31	18	11	2	3	1

Let the moving average for three days be m.

$$m_1 = \frac{2+5+0}{3} = \frac{7}{3} = 2.33 \quad \text{[say } A\text{]}$$

$$m_2 = \frac{5+0+12}{3} = \frac{17}{3} = 5.66 \quad \text{[say } B\text{]}$$

$$m_3 = \frac{0+12+13}{3} = \frac{25}{3} = 8.33 \quad \text{[say } C\text{]}$$

$$m_4 = \frac{12+13+25}{3} = \frac{50}{3} = 16.66 \quad \text{[say } D\text{]}$$

$$m_5 = \frac{13+25+45}{3} = \frac{83}{3} = 27.66 \quad \text{[say } E\text{]}$$

$$m_6 = \frac{25+45+13}{3} = \frac{83}{3} = 27.66 \quad \text{[say } F\text{]}$$

$$m_7 = \frac{45+13+31}{3} = \frac{89}{3} = 29.67 \quad \text{[say } G\text{]}$$

$$m_8 = \frac{13+31+18}{3} = \frac{62}{3} = 20.67 \quad \text{[say } H\text{]}$$

$$m_9 = \frac{31+18+11}{3} = \frac{60}{3} = 20 \quad \text{[say } I\text{]}$$

$$m_{10} = \frac{18+11+2}{3} = \frac{31}{3} = 10.33 \quad \text{[say } J\text{]}$$

$$m_{11} = \frac{11+2+3}{3} = \frac{16}{3} = 5.33 \quad \text{[say } K\text{]}$$

$$m_{12} = \frac{2+3+1}{3} = \frac{6}{3} = 2 \quad \text{[say } L\text{]}$$

On the basis of above data we can draw the following graph

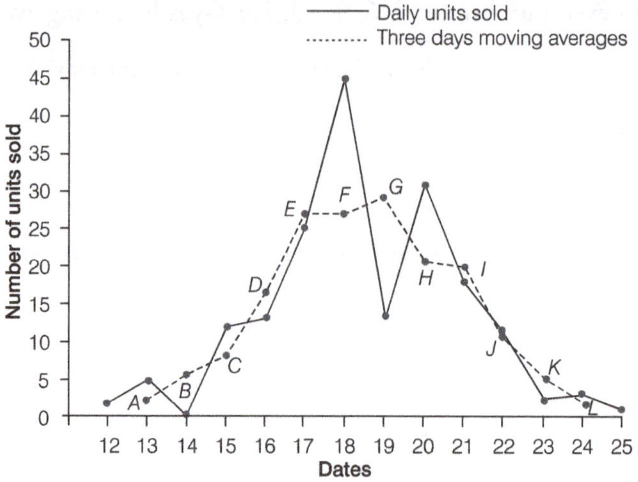

EXAMPLE 2. The production of a soft drink company in thousand of litres during each month of a year is as follows

Jan	Feb	Mar	Apr	May	Jun	Jul	Aug	Sep	Oct	Nov	Dec
1.2	0.8	1.4	1.6	1.8	2.4	2.6	3.0	3.6	2.8	1.9	3.4

Calculate the five monthly moving average and show these moving averages on a graph.

Sol. Given table is shown below:

Months	Jan	Feb	Mar	Apr	May	Jun	Jul	Aug	Sep	Oct	Nov	Dec
Production (in thousand litre)	1.2	0.8	1.4	1.6	1.8	2.4	2.6	3.0	3.6	2.8	1.9	3.4

Let the moving average production for five months be m.

So,

$$m_1 = \frac{1.2 + 0.8 + 1.4 + 1.6 + 1.8}{5} = \frac{6.8}{5} = 1.36 \quad \text{[say } A\text{]}$$

$$m_2 = \frac{0.8 + 1.4 + 1.6 + 1.8 + 2.4}{5} = \frac{8}{5} = 1.6 \quad \text{[say } B\text{]}$$

$$m_3 = \frac{1.4 + 1.6 + 1.8 + 2.4 + 2.6}{5} = \frac{9.8}{5} = 1.96 \quad \text{[say } C\text{]}$$

$$m_4 = \frac{1.6 + 1.8 + 2.4 + 2.6 + 3.0}{5} = \frac{11.4}{5} = 2.28 \quad \text{[say } D\text{]}$$

$$m_5 = \frac{1.8 + 2.4 + 2.6 + 3.0 + 3.6}{5} = \frac{13.4}{5} = 2.68 \quad \text{[say } E\text{]}$$

$$m_6 = \frac{2.4 + 2.6 + 3.0 + 3.6 + 2.8}{5} = \frac{14.4}{5} = 2.88 \quad \text{[say } F\text{]}$$

$$m_7 = \frac{2.6 + 3.0 + 3.6 + 2.8 + 1.9}{5} = \frac{13.9}{5} = 2.78 \quad \text{[say } G\text{]}$$

$$m_8 = \frac{3.0 + 3.6 + 2.8 + 1.9 + 3.4}{5} = \frac{14.7}{5} = 2.94 \quad \text{[say } H\text{]}$$

On the basis of above data we can draw the following graph

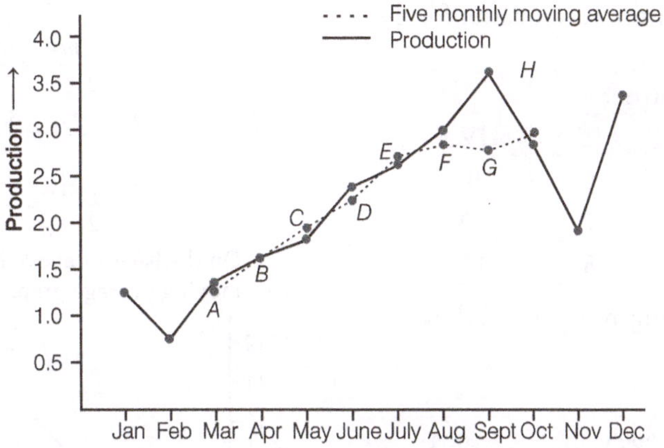

EXAMPLE 3. The table given below shows the daily attendance in thousand at a certain exhibition over a period of two weeks

Week 1	52	48	64	68	52	70	72
Week 2	55	47	61	65	58	75	81

Calculate seven day moving averages and illustrate these and original information on the same graph using the same scales.

Sol. According to the question,

Week	1							2						
Days	Sun	Mon	Tue	Wed	Thu	Fri	Sat	Sun	Mon	Tue	Wed	Thu	Fri	Sat
Attendance (in thousand)	52	48	64	68	52	70	72	55	47	61	65	58	75	81

Let the days moving average for seven days be m.

So, $m_1 = \dfrac{52+48+64+68+52+70+72}{7} = 60.85$, $m_2 = \dfrac{48+64+68+52+70+72+55}{7} = 61.28$

$m_3 = \dfrac{64+68+52+70+72+55+47}{7} = 61.14$, $m_4 = \dfrac{68+52+70+72+55+47+61}{7} = 60.71$

$m_5 = \dfrac{52+70+72+55+47+61+65}{7} = 60.28$, $m_6 = \dfrac{70+72+55+47+61+65+58}{7} = 61.14$

$m_7 = \dfrac{72+55+47+61+65+58+75}{7} = 61.85$, $m_8 = \dfrac{55+47+61+65+58+75+81}{7} = 63.14$

On the basis of above data we can draw the following moving average graph

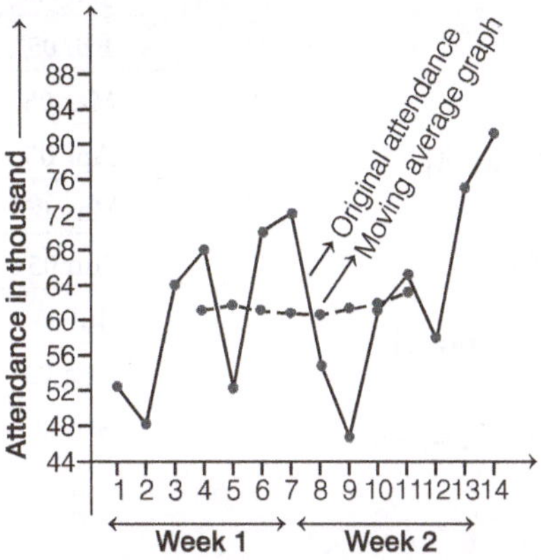

EXAMPLE 4. The table below gives details of the electricity generated in million kilowatt hours in each quarter for the years

Year	Quarter			
	I	II	III	IV
2002	8	7	6	9
2003	10	7	7	10
2004	11	7	8	10

Calculate the four quarterly moving averages and show these moving averages on a graph.

Sol. Given table is shown below:

Years	2002				2003				2004			
Quarters	I	II	III	IV	I	II	III	IV	I	II	III	IV
Number of electricity (in kilowatt)	8	7	6	9	10	7	7	10	11	7	8	10

Let the moving average of four months be m.

Now, $m_1 = \dfrac{8+7+6+9}{4} = \dfrac{30}{4} = 7.5,$

$$m_2 = \frac{7+6+9+10}{4} = \frac{32}{4} = 8,$$

$$m_3 = \frac{6+9+10+7}{4} = \frac{32}{4} = 8,$$

$$m_4 = \frac{9+10+7+7}{4} = \frac{33}{4} = 8.25,$$

$$m_5 = \frac{10+7+7+10}{4} = \frac{34}{4} = 8.5,$$

$$m_6 = \frac{7+7+10+11}{4} = \frac{35}{4} = 8.75,$$

$$m_7 = \frac{7+10+11+7}{4} = \frac{35}{4} = 8.75,$$

$$m_8 = \frac{10+11+7+8}{4} = \frac{36}{4} = 9,$$

$$m_9 = \frac{11+7+8+10}{4} = \frac{36}{4} = 9$$

Centred moving averages are

$$\frac{m_1+m_2}{2} = \frac{7.5+8}{2} = \frac{15.5}{2} = 7.75 \text{ [say } A]$$

$$\frac{m_2+m_3}{2} = \frac{8+8}{2} = \frac{16}{2} = 8 \text{ [say } B]$$

$$\frac{m_3+m_4}{2} = \frac{8+8.25}{2} = \frac{16.25}{2} = 8.125 \text{ [say } C]$$

$$\frac{m_4+m_5}{2} = \frac{8.25+8.5}{2} = \frac{16.75}{2} = 8.375 \text{ [say } D]$$

$$\frac{m_5+m_6}{2} = \frac{8.5+8.75}{2} = \frac{17.25}{2} = 8.625 \text{ [say } E]$$

$$\frac{m_6+m_7}{2} = \frac{8.75+8.75}{2} = \frac{17.50}{2} = 8.75 \text{ [say } F]$$

$$\frac{m_7+m_8}{2} = \frac{8.75+9}{2} = \frac{17.75}{2} = 8.875 \text{ [say } G]$$

$$\frac{m_8+m_9}{2} = \frac{9+9}{2} = \frac{18}{2} = 9 \text{ [say } H]$$

On the basis of above data we can draw the following moving average graph

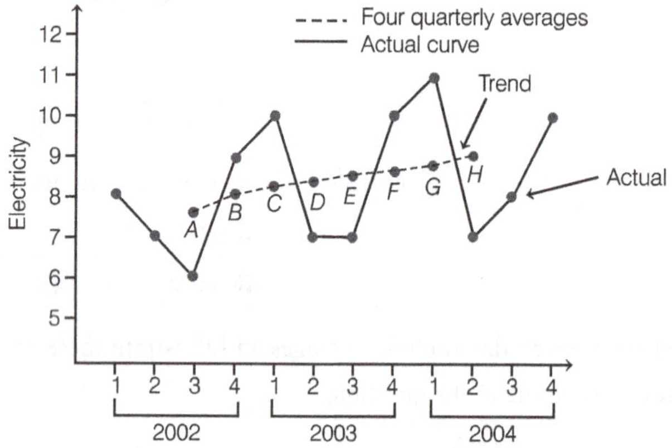

EXAMPLE 5. Coded monthly sales figures of a particular brand of TV for 18 months commencing January 2005 are as follows :

Year	Jan	Feb	Mar	Apr	May	Jun	Jul	Aug	Sep	Oct	Nov	Dec
2005	18	16	23	27	28	19	31	29	35	27	28	24
2006	24	28	29	30	29	22						

Calculate six monthly moving averages and display these and the original figures on the same graph using the same axis for both.

Sol. Given table is shown below:

Months	Sales	Months	Sales
Jan 05	18	Oct 05	27
Feb 05	16	Nov 05	28
Mar 05	23	Dec 05	24
Apr 05	27	Jan 06	24
May 05	28	Feb 06	28
Jun 05	19	Mar 06	29
Jul 05	31	Apr 06	30
Aug 05	29	May 06	29
Sep 05	35	Jun 06	22

Let the moving average for six months be m,

So, $m_1 = \frac{18 + 16 + 23 + 27 + 28 + 19}{6} = \frac{131}{6} = 21.83$, $m_2 = \frac{16 + 23 + 27 + 28 + 19 + 31}{6} = \frac{144}{6} = 24.00$

$m_3 = \frac{23 + 27 + 28 + 19 + 31 + 29}{6} = \frac{157}{6} = 26.2$, $m_4 = \frac{27 + 28 + 19 + 31 + 29 + 35}{6} = \frac{169}{6} \approx 28.2$

$m_5 = \frac{28 + 19 + 31 + 29 + 35 + 27}{6} = \frac{169}{6} \approx 28.2$, $m_6 = \frac{19 + 31 + 29 + 35 + 27 + 28}{6} = \frac{169}{6} \approx 28.20$

$m_7 = \frac{31 + 29 + 35 + 27 + 28 + 24}{6} = \frac{174}{6} = 29.00$, $m_8 = \frac{29 + 35 + 27 + 28 + 24 + 24}{6} = \frac{167}{6} = 27.83$

$m_9 = \frac{35 + 27 + 28 + 24 + 24 + 28}{6} = \frac{166}{6} = 27.66$, $m_{10} = \frac{27 + 28 + 24 + 24 + 28 + 29}{6} = \frac{160}{6} = 26.66$

$m_{11} = \frac{28 + 24 + 24 + 28 + 29 + 30}{6} = \frac{163}{6} = 27.16$, $m_{12} = \frac{24 + 24 + 28 + 29 + 30 + 29}{6} = \frac{164}{6} = 27.33$

$m_{13} = \frac{24 + 28 + 29 + 30 + 29 + 22}{6} = \frac{162}{6} = 27.00$

For centred moving average,

$\frac{m_1 + m_2}{2} = \frac{21.83 + 24.00}{2} = 22.91$ [say A], $\frac{m_2 + m_3}{2} = \frac{24.00 + 26.2}{2} = 25.1$ [say B],

$\frac{m_3 + m_4}{2} = \frac{26.2 + 28.2}{2} = 27.2$ [say C], $\frac{m_4 + m_5}{2} = \frac{28.2 + 28.2}{2} = 28.2$ [say D],

$\frac{m_5 + m_6}{2} = \frac{28.2 + 28.2}{2} = 28.2$ [say E], $\frac{m_6 + m_7}{2} = \frac{28.2 + 29.00}{2} = 28.6$ [say F],

$\frac{m_7 + m_8}{2} = \frac{29.00 + 27.83}{2} = 28.415$ [say G], $\frac{m_8 + m_9}{2} = \frac{27.83 + 27.66}{2} = 27.745$ [say H],

$\frac{m_9 + m_{10}}{2} = \frac{27.66 + 26.66}{2} = 27.16$ [say I], $\frac{m_{10} + m_{11}}{2} = \frac{26.66 + 27.16}{2} = 26.91$ [say J],

$\frac{m_{11} + m_{12}}{2} = \frac{27.16 + 27.33}{2} = 27.245$ [say K]. $\frac{m_{12} + m_{13}}{2} = \frac{27.33 + 27}{2} = 27.165$ [say L]

On the basis of above data we can draw the following graph

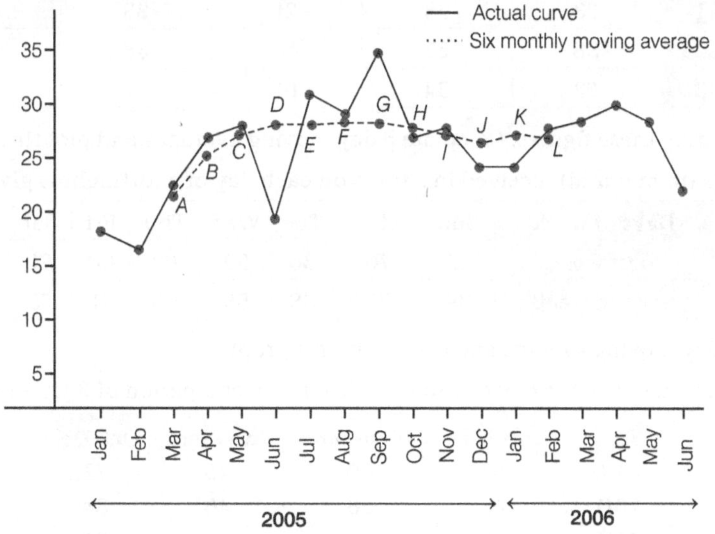

Topic Practice 1

1 What is a Time Series?

2 Write the components for time series.

3 Define linear and non-linear trend.

4 Describe the purpose of moving averages.

5 The average number (in lakh) of working days lost in strikes during each year of the period 1981-90 was

1981	1982	1983	1984	1985	1986	1987	1988	1989	1990
1.5	1.8	1.9	2.2	2.6	3.7	2.2	6.4	3.6	5.4

Calculate the three yearly moving averages and draw the moving averages graph.

6 Calculate 3-yearly moving averages for the following data

Year	2005	2006	2007	2008	2009	2010	2011	2012
Annual sales (in 0000 ₹)	3.6	4.3	4.3	3.4	4.4	5.4	3.4	2.4

7 In an influenza epidemic the number of cases diagnosed were

Date (March)	1	2	3	4	5	6	7	8	9	10	11	12	13	14
Numbers	2	0	5	12	20	27	46	30	31	18	11	5	0	1

Calculate 3-day moving averages and display them and the original figures on the same graph.

8 Calculate the 5 yearly moving average of the number of students in a college from the following data and plot them on a graph paper.

Year	1981	1982	1983	1984	1985	1986	1987	1988	1989	1990
Number	332	317	357	392	402	405	510	427	405	438

9 Daily absence from a school during 3 weeks is recorded as follows:

	Monday	Tuesday	Wednesday	Thursday	Friday
Week 1	23	28	21	33	40
Week 2	38	52	43	58	63
Week 3	52	54	61	51	51

Draw a graph, illustrating these figures. Calculate 5 day moving averages and plot them on the same graph.

10 The number of letters (in hundred) received in a town on each day of a fortnight is given below:

Days of week	Sun	Mon	Tue	Wed	Thu	Fri	Sat
First week	35	70	36	59	62	60	71
Second week	39	72	38	56	63	71	75

Calculate the seven day moving average and display it on a graph.

11 The number of road accidents in the city due to rash driving, over a period of 3 yr, is given in the following table

Year	Jan-Mar	April-June	July-Sept	Oct-Dec
2010	70	60	45	72
2011	79	56	46	84
2012	90	64	45	82

Calculate four quarterly moving average and illustrate them with original figures on one graph using the same for both.

12 The table below gives details on the electricity generated in million kilowatt hours in each quarter for the year 2017 to 2019.

Year	Quarter			
	Ist	2nd	3rd	4th
2017	8	7	6	9
2018	10	7	7	10
2019	11	7	8	10

Calculate the four quarterly moving averages and show these moving averages on a graph. Comment on the general ternd.

13 The profit of a soft drink firm (in ₹ thousand) during each month of the year is a given below

Months	Jan	Feb	Mar	Apr	May	Jun	Jul	Aug	Sep	Oct	Nov	Dec
Profit (in ₹ thousands)	3.6	4.3	4.3	3.4	4.4	5.4	3.4	2.4	3.4	1.8	0.8	1.2

Calculate the four monthly moving averages and plot these and the original data on a graph sheet.

14 Using the following data, find out the trend by using quarterly moving average and plot them on the graph

Year/Quarter	Q_1	Q_2	Q_3	Q_4
2010	29	37	43	35
2011	40	42	55	43
2012	41	51	63	53

15 Consider the following data

Year	1983	1984	1985	1986	1987	1988	1989	1990	1991	1992	1993	1994
Production	137	140	134	137	151	121	124	159	157	169	172	150

Calculate a suitable moving average, and show on a graph against the original data.

Hints & Solutions

1. Time series is simply a series of data points ordered in time. In a time series, time is often the independent variable and the goal is usually to make a forecast for the future.
2. The four categories of the components of time series are
   (i) Trend
   (ii) Seasonal variations
   (iii) Cyclic variations
   (iv) Random or Irregular variations
3. If we plot the time series value on a graph in accordance with time t. The pattern of the data clustering shows the type of trend. If the set of data clusters is more or less around a straight line, then the trend is linear otherwise it is non-linear.
4. The following points are main purpose of moving average
   (i) It helps in technical trading by tracking the trend of financial assets by smoothing out the day-to-day price fluctuations.
   (ii) By identifying trend, moving averages allow traders, to make these trends work in their favour and increases the number of wining trades. It is helps in trading strategies.
5. Similar as Example 1.
   Ans. 1.73, 1.96, 2.23, 2.83, 2.83, 4.1, 4.06, 5.13.

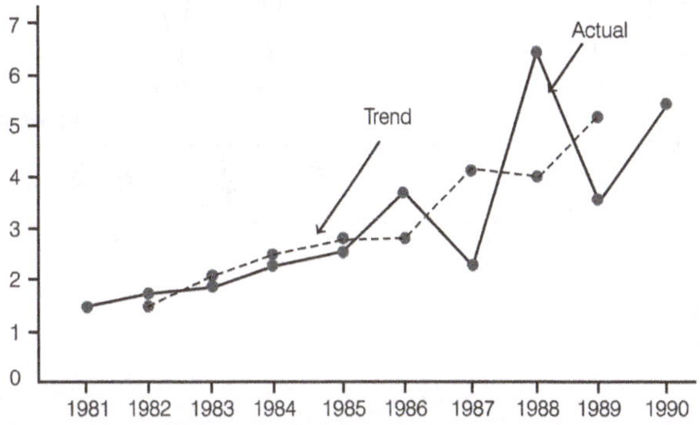

6. Similar as Example 1.
Ans. 4.067, 4, 4.04, 4.40, 4.40, 3.73

7. Similar as Example 1.
Ans. The 3-day moving averages are
2.3, 5.6, 12.3, 19.6, 31.0, 34.3, 35.67, 26.33, 20.0, 11.3, 5.3, 2.0.
This shows a steady increase (arrival of fresh cases every day) and then decrease (control over epidemic).

8. Similar as Example 2.
Ans. 360, 374.6, 413.2, 427.2, 429.8, 437.

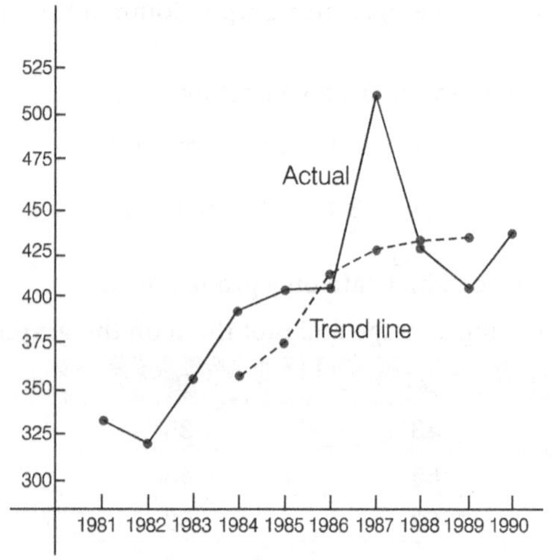

9. Similar as Example 3.
Ans. 5-day moving averages are
29, 32, 36.8, 41.2, 46.2, 50.8, 53.6, 54, 57.6, 56.2, 53.8

10. Similar as Example 3.
Ans. Seven days moving average.
56.14, 56.71, 57.00, 57.28, 56.86, 57.00, 58.57, 59.14.

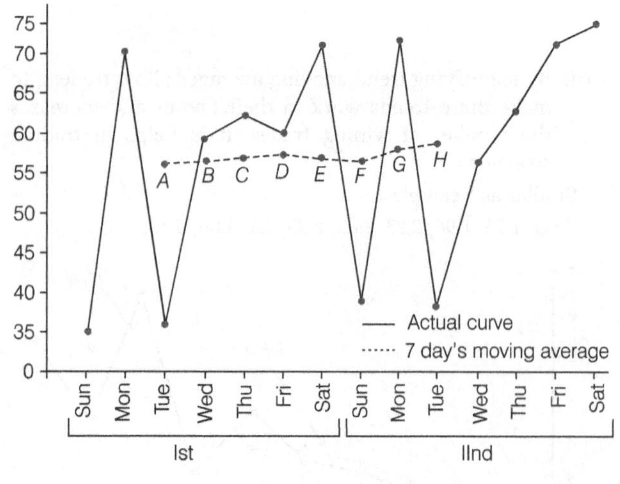

11. Similar as Example 4
Ans. Four quarterly moving average.
61.75, 64, 63, 63.25, 66.25, 69, 71, 70.75, 70.25

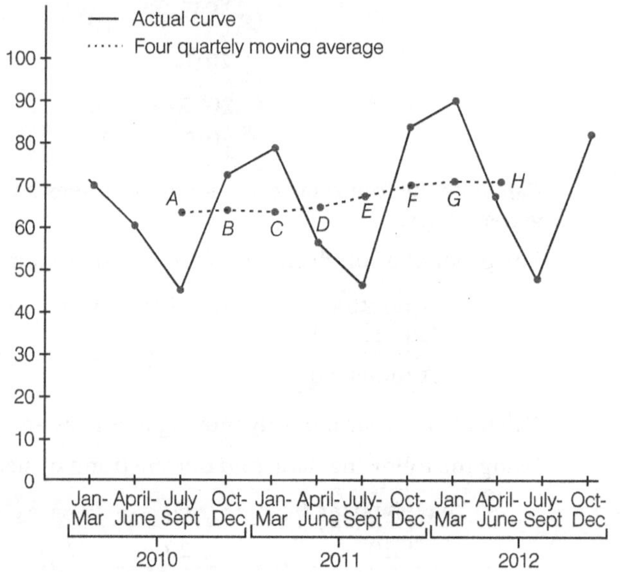

12. Similar as Example 4.
Ans. Quarterly moving averages
7.5, 8, 8, 8.25, 8.5, 8.75, 8.75, 9, 9

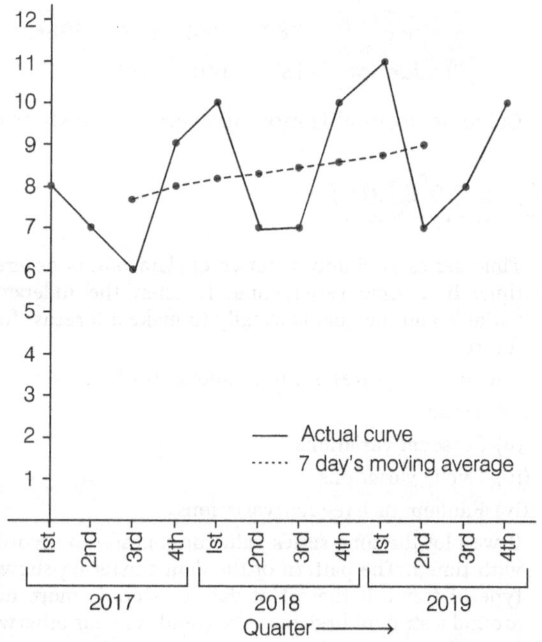

13. Similar as Example 4

Ans. Monthly moving average are 3.9, 4.1, 4.38, 4.15, 3.9, 3.65, 2.75, 2.1, 1.8

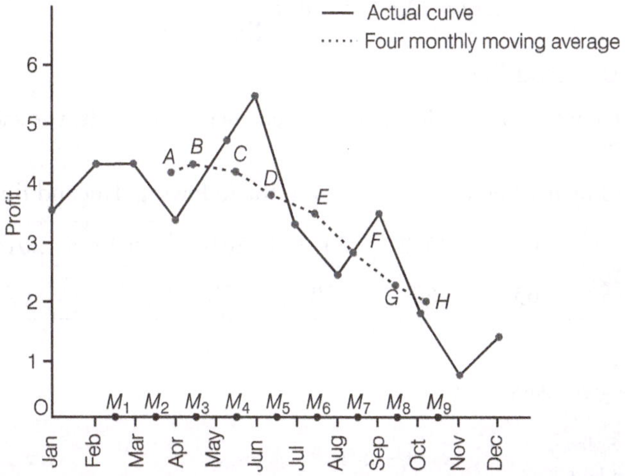

14. Similar as Example 4.

Ans. Quarterly moving averages (centered) as 35.75, 38.5, 39.75, 42.75, 45, 45.25, 47.5, 49.5, 52

This shows long term steady increase

15. Similar as Example 1.

Ans. 3 years moving average are 137.00, 137.00, 140.67, 136.33, 132.00, 134.67, 146.67, 161.67, 166.00, 163.67

Method of Least Squares

The least square method is the method of determining the least-fitting curve or line for the processing data. This method provides a visual demonstration of the relation between the data points which determines the trend line for the given time series. This trend line is known as the best fitting line.

Hence, the least square method is the process of finding the least fitting line for data points through reduction of the sum of squares of the offsets points from the curve.

Let us assume that $(t_1, y_1), (t_2, y_2), (t_3, y_3) \ldots (t_n, y_n)$ denotes the time series, where t's are the independent values and y's are the dependent variable.

(i) The sum of deviations of y from their corresponding trend value is zero.

i.e. $\Sigma(y - y_t) = 0$

(ii) The sum of the squares of deviations of y must be minimal.

i.e. $\Sigma(y - y_t)^2$ is minimal.

Equation of the Trend Line

The equation of the trend line can be written as

$$y_t = a + bx \quad \ldots\text{(i)}$$

where, y_t is the trend value of y, x is the deviation of time t from origin, a and b are constants.

Now, $\Sigma y_t = \Sigma a + b\Sigma x$ and $\Sigma y = na + b\Sigma x \quad \ldots\text{(ii)}$

where, n be the number of years given in the data.

Eq. (i) can be written as

$$xy_t = ax + bx^2 \text{ and } \Sigma xy = a\Sigma x + b\Sigma x^2 \quad \ldots\text{(iii)}$$

Eqs. (ii) and (iii) are called normal equations from where we get the value of a and b.

Assume the mid-point of time is taken as origin, then $\Sigma x = 0$.

$\therefore$ From Eq. (ii), we get

$$\Sigma y = na$$

$$\Rightarrow \quad a = \frac{\Sigma y}{n}$$

Here, a represents the mean of y and from Eq. (iii), we get

$$\Sigma xy = b\Sigma x^2 \Rightarrow b = \frac{\Sigma xy}{\Sigma x^2}$$

Here, b represents the slope of the trend line.

Note If n is odd, then we take middle year as the origin and if n is even, then there will be two middle years, then we take mean of the two middle years as origin.

EXAMPLE 1. Fit a straight line trend by method of least squares to the following data and find the trend values. **[CBSE 2023]**

Year	2010	2012	2013	2014	2015	2016	2019
Sales (in lakh ₹)	65	68	70	72	75	67	73

Sol. Let assumed mean be 2014.

Let us make the table for the given data.

Year (t_i)	Sales y (in lakh ₹ y)	$x = t_i - 2014$	x^2	xy	Trend value $y_t = a + bx$
2010	65	−4	16	−260	61.56
2012	68	−2	4	−136	65.78
2013	70	−1	1	−70	67.89
2014	72	0	0	0	70
2015	75	1	1	75	72.11
2016	67	2	4	134	74.22
2019	73	5	25	365	80.55
Total	$\Sigma y = 490$	$\Sigma x = 1$	$\Sigma x^2 = 51$	$\Sigma xy = 108$	

Now, $a = \frac{\Sigma y}{n} = \frac{490}{7} = 70$ and $b = \frac{\Sigma xy}{\Sigma x^2} = \frac{108}{51} \Rightarrow b = 2.11$

So, the required equation of the straight line trend is

$$y_t = a + bx \Rightarrow y_t = 70 + 2.11x$$

So, trend value for year 2010, at $x = -4$

$\therefore \quad y_t = 70 + 2.11 \times (-4) = 70 - 8.44 = 61.56$

For year 2012, at $x = -2$ $\quad y_t = 70 - 2.11 \times 2 = 70 - 4.22 = 65.78$

For year 2013, at $x = -1$ $\quad y_t = 70 - 2.11 = 67.89$

For year 2014, at $x = 0$ $\quad y_t = 70 + 0 = 70$

For year 2015, at $x = 1$ $\quad y_t = 70 + 2.11 = 72.11$

For year 2016, at $x = 2$ $\quad y_t = 70 + 2.11 \times 2 = 70 + 4.22 = 74.22$

For year 2019 at $x = 5$ $\quad y_t = 70 + 2.11 \times 5 = 70 + 10.55 = 80.55$

EXAMPLE 2. Fit a straight line trend, equation by the method of least squares and estimate the trend value.

Year	1991	1992	1993	1994	1995	1996	1997	1998
Values	80	90	92	83	94	99	92	104

Sol. Here, $n = 8$ (even). So, origin is mean of two middle years. i.e. $\frac{1994 + 1995}{2} = 1994.5$

Year (t)	Values (y)	$x = t_i - 1994.5$	x^2	xy	$y_t = a + bx$
1991	80	− 3.5	12.25	− 280	83
1992	90	− 2.5	6.25	− 225	85.5
1993	92	− 1.5	2.25	− 138	87.5
1994	83	− 0.5	0.25	− 41.5	90.5
1995	94	0.5	0.25	47	90.5
1996	99	1.5	2.25	148.5	92.5
1997	92	2.5	6.25	230	97.5
1998	104	3.5	12.25	364	100
	$\Sigma y = 734$	$\Sigma x = 0$	$\Sigma x^2 = 42$	$\Sigma xy = 105$	

Here, $a = \frac{\Sigma y}{n} = \frac{734}{8} = 91.75$ and $b = \frac{\Sigma xy}{\Sigma x^2} = \frac{105}{42} = 2.5$

$\therefore$ The required equation of the trend line $y_t = 91.75 + 2.5x$

So, trend values

For year 1991, $x = -3.5$: $y_t = 91.75 + 2.5 \times (-3.5) = 83$;

For year 1992, $x = -2.5$: $y_t = 91.75 + 2.5 \times (-2.5) = 85.5$;

For year 1993, $x = -1.5$: $y_t = 91.75 + 2.5 \times (-1.5) = 88$;

For year 1994, $x = -0.5$: $y_t = 91.75 + 2.5 \times (-0.5) = 90.5$;

For year 1995, $x = 0.5$: $y_t = 91.75 + 2.5 \times (0.5) = 93$;

For year 1996, $x = 1.5$: $y_t = 91.75 + 2.5 \times (1.5) = 95.5$;

For year 1997, $x = 2.5$: $y_t = 91.75 + 2.5 \times 2.5 = 98$;

For year 1998, $x = 3.5$: $y_t = 91.75 + 2.5 \times 3.5 = 100.5$

Topic Practice 2

Fit a straight line trend on the following data using the least squares method.

1

Period (year)	1996	1997	1998	1999	2000	2001	2002	2003	2004
y	4	7	7	8	9	11	13	14	17

2

Year	2000	2001	2002	2003	2004	2005	2006
Production (in tonnes)	40	45	46	42	47	50	46

3

Year	1950	1951	1952	1953	1954	1955	1956	1957
Value	346	411	392	512	626	640	611	796

4

Year	1980	1981	1982	1983	1984	1985	1986	1987
Production ('000 quintals)	346	411	392	512	626	640	611	796

5 Fit a straight line trend by the method of least squares and tabulate the trend values from the following data

Year	1995	1996	1997	1998	1999	2000	2001	2002
Sales (in ₹ crores)	6.7	5.3	4.3	6.1	5.6	7.9	5.8	6.1

Hints & Solutions

1. Similar as Example 1. **Ans.** $y = 10 + 1.47x$

Year	1996	1997	1998	1999	2000	20001	20002	20003	2004
Trend Values	4.12	5.59	7.06	8.53	10	11.47	12.94	14.41	15.88

2. Similar as Example 1. **Ans.** $y = 45.143 + 1.036x$

Year	2000	2001	2002	2003	2004	2005	2006
Trend Values	42.03	43.07	44.11	45.14	46.18	47.21	48.25

3. Similar as Example 1. **Ans.** $y = 541.75 + 59.60x$

Year	1950	1951	1952	1953	1954	1955	1956	1957
Trend Values	333.15	392.75	452.35	511.95	571.55	631.15	690.75	750.35

4. Similar as Example 2. **Ans.** $y = 541.75 + 59.62x$

Year	1980	1981	1982	1983	1984	1985	1986	1987
Trend Values	333.08	392.7	452.32	511.94	571.56	631.18	690.8	750.42

5. Similar as Example 2. **Ans.** $y = 5.975 + 0.102x$

Year	1995	1996	1997	1998	1999	2000	2001	2002
Trend Values	5.62	5.72	5.82	5.92	6.03	6.13	6.23	6.33

Exam Pattern Exercise

Part A - Objective Type Questions

Multiple Choice Type Questions

1 An orderly set of data arranged in accordance with their time of occurrence is
(a) time series (b) arithmetic series
(c) geometric series (d) harmonic series

2 Which of the following is an example of time series model?
(a) Moving average
(b) Native approach
(c) Exponential smoothing
(d) All of the above

3 Which of the following can not be component for a time series?
(a) Seasonality (b) Cyclical
(c) Noise (d) None of these

4 The time series analysis helps
(a) to make predictions
(b) to compare the two or more series
(c) to know the behaviour of business
(d) All of the above

5 In a time series values of the variables y(say) depend on time t represented as $y = F(t)$, has
(a) four components (b) two components
(c) three components (d) five components

6 The component of a time series attached to long-term variations is termed as
(a) seasonal variations
(b) irregular variations
(c) secular trend variations
(d) cyclic variations

7 Prosperity, recession and depression in a business is an example of
(a) seasonal trend (b) cyclical trend
(c) irregular trend (d) secular trend

8 A fire in a factor delaying production for some weeks is
(a) secular trend (b) irregular trend
(c) cyclical trend (d) seasonal trend

9 Seasonal variations are
(a) long term variation
(b) sudden variation
(c) short term variation
(d) None of the above

10 In the time series, shortage of certain consumer goods before the annual budget is due to
(a) irregular variation (b) cyclical variation
(c) seasonal variation (d) secular trend

11 Additive model for time series O is equal to
(a) $T + S + C + I$ (b) $T - S + C - I$
(c) $T + S - C - I$ (d) $-T + S - C + I$

12 Multiplicative model for time series O is equal to
(a) $T + S \times C \times I$ (b) $T \times S \times C + I$
(c) $T \times S \times C \times I$ (d) $TS + S \times I$

13 For the given values 23, 32, 40, 47, 58, 33, 42; the 5-yearly moving average are **[CBSE 2024]**
(a) 38, 40, 42 (n) 40, 42, 44
(c) 40, 42, 46 (d) 42, 44, 46

14 If $x_1, x_2, x_3, \ldots, x_n$ is the given annual time series, then 3-yearly moving average are
(a) $\frac{x_1 + x_2 + x_3}{3}, \frac{x_2 + x_3 + x_4}{3}, \frac{x_3 + x_4 + x_5}{3}, \ldots$, which are placed against years 2, 3, 4, ... respectively
(b) $\frac{x_1 + x_2 + x_3}{3}, \frac{x_2 + x_3 + x_4}{3}, \frac{x_2 + x_4 + x_5}{3}$, which are against 1, 2, 4, ... respectively.
(c) $\frac{x_1 + x_3 + x_5}{3}, \frac{x_2 + x_4 + x_5}{3}, \frac{x_1 + x_2 + x_4}{3}$, ...which are against ... respectively.
(d) None of the above

15 The general pattern of increases or decreases in economics or social phenomena is known by
(a) irregular trend (b) secular trend
(c) seasonal trend (d) cyclical trend

16 Method of moving average is used to find the
(a) cyclical variation (b) irregular variation
(c) seasonal variation (d) secular trend

17 The best fitting trend is one which the sum of squares of residuals is
(a) maximum (b) zero
(c) minimal (d) None of these

18 Moving average method is used for measurement of trend when
(a) trend is non linear (b) trend is linear
(c) trend is curvilinear (d) trend is parabolic

19 In the trend line equation $y = a + bx$, b is the
(a) slope (b) mean
(c) x-intercept (d) y-intercept

20 The straight line trend is represented by the equation [CBSE 2023]
(a) $y_c = a + bx$ (b) $y_c = a - bx$ (c) $y_c = na + b\Sigma x$ (d) $y_c = na - b\Sigma x$

21 In a trend line equation $y = a + bx$, where a is the
(a) mean of x (b) mean of y (c) Slope (d) None of these

22 The actual sales of a product in different months of a particular year are given below

Sep	Oct	Nov	Dec	Jan	Feb
180	280	250	190	240	?

Using the 4 month moving average method forecast of the sale, for the month of February is
(a) 350 (b) 240 (c) 300 (d) 280

23 The demand of a product over 6 weeks is 90, 110, 105, 130, 85 and 102. If 3 month moving averages is x and 5 month moving average is y, then $(x + y)$ is
(a) 202.70 (b) 105.67 (c) 212.07 (d) 180.67

Part B - Descriptive Questions

Very Short Answer Type Questions

24 What is non-linear trend?

25 Write any two limitations of moving average.

26 Write a trend line equation to the following time series data.

Year	2008	2009	2010	2011	2012
Sale of sugar (in tonnes)	80	90	92	83	94

Short Answer Type Questions

27 Consider the following data

Year	1983	1984	1985	1986	1987	1988	1989	1990	1991	1992	1993	1994
Production	137	140	134	137	151	121	124	159	157	169	172	150

Calculate a suitable moving average.

28 Construct 3-yearly, moving averages from the following data

Year	2012	2013	2014	2015	2016	2017	2018
Imported cotton consumption in India (in thousand bales)	132	135	108	85	97	88	96

29 Work out the centered 4-yearly moving average for the following data

Year	Tonnage of cargo cleared	year	Tonnage of cargo cleared
2001	1102	2007	1452
2002	1250	2008	1549
2003	1180	2009	1586
2004	1340	2010	1476
2005	1212	2011	1624
2006	1317	2012	1586

30 Given the numbers 3, 7, 4, 9, 2, 6, 1, write down the weighted moving average of period 3, the weights being 1, 4, 1.

31 Construct 5-yearly moving average from the following data

Year	2000	2001	2002	2003	2004	2005	2006	2007	2008	2009	2010	2011	2012
Production	103	109	107	110	111	113	115	119	121	127	129	135	136

Long Answer Type Questions

32 Fit a straight line trend for the following data and find the trend values. Estimate the sales for 2020.

Year	2006	2007	2008	2009	2010	2011	2012
Sales (₹ in lakh)	33	35	60	67	68	82	90

33 Fit a straight line trend by the method of least squares. Estimate the sales for 1995.

Year	1995	1996	1997	1998	1999	2000	2001	2002
Sales (₹ in crores)	6.7	5.3	4.3	6.1	5.6	7.9	5.8	6.1

Case Study Based Questions

34 When observed over a long period of time, a time series data can predict trends that can forecast increase or decrease or stagnation of a variable under consideration. Such analytical studies can benefit a business for forecasting or prediction of future estimated sales or production.
The table below shows the sale of an item in a district during 1996-2001:

Year	1996	1997	1998	1999	2000	2001
Sales (in lakh ₹)	6.5	5.3	4.3	6.1	5.6	7.8

Based on the above information, answer the following questions:

(i) Determine the equation of the straight line trend.

(ii) (a) Tabulate the trend values of the years and also compute expected sales trends for the year 2002.

Or (b) Fit a straight-line trend by the method of least squares for the following data:

Year	2004	2005	2006	2007	2008	2009	2010
Profit (₹ 000)	114	130	126	144	138	156	164

[CBSE 2024]

35 Fit a straight line trend by using the method of least square for the following data

Year	1962	1963	1964	1965	1966	1967	1968	1969	1970	1971	1972
Production (in tonnes)	2	4	3	4	4	2	4	9	7	10	8

If the equation of the trend line can be written as

$$y_t = a + bx \quad \text{...(i)}$$

Based on the above information, answer the following questions.

(i) The value of constant a in Eq. (i), is

(a) 5.12 (b) 6.2 (c) 5.18 (d) 3.69

(ii) The value of constant b in Eq. (i), is

(a) 0.74 (b) 0.69 (c) 0.52 (d) 0.48

(iii) The equation of the trend line is

(a) $y_t = 5.18 + 0.69x$ (b) $y_t = 3.12 + 0.54x$ (c) $y_t = 1.45 + 0.52x$ (d) $y_t = 2.42 + 0.72x$

(iv) The trend value for year 1962 is

(a) 0.52 (b) 0.39 (c) 2.14 (d) 1.73

(v) The trend value for year 1970 is

(a) 7.25 (b) 4.2 (c) 3.92 (d) 5.1

Hints & Solutions

1. (a)	2. (d)	3. (d)	4. (d)
5. (a)	6. (c)	7. (b)	8. (b)
9. (c)	10. (c)	11. (a)	12. (c)
13. (b)	14. (a)	15. (b)	16. (d)
17. (c)	18. (b)	19. (a)	20. (a)
21. (b)	22. (b)	23. (c)	

24. A time series may have faster or slower increase at early stage and have a slower or faster increase at more rescent time. In such case, better description of the time series is given by a non-linear curve rather than straight line.

25. (i) The effect of averaging is to give a smoother curve, lessening the influence of the fluctuations.

(ii) The moving average method is most commonly applied data, which are characterised by cyclical movements.

26.

Year	Sales (y)	x	xy	x^2
2008	80	−2	−160	4
2009	90	−1	−90	1
2010	92	0	0	0
2011	83	1	83	1
2012	94	2	188	4
$n = 5$	$\Sigma y = 439$	$\Sigma x = 0$	$\Sigma xy = 21$	$\Sigma x^2 = 10$

Here, $a = \frac{\Sigma y}{n} = \frac{439}{5} = 87.8$ and $b = \frac{\Sigma xy}{\Sigma x^2} = \frac{21}{10} = 2.1$

$\therefore$ Trend line equation, $y_t = a + bx = 87.8 + 2.1x$

27. Here, we have to estimate the length of the cycle of the above data. Concentrate on the second row of data. We find the pattern (137, 140, 134); (137, 151, 121); (124, 159, 157); (169, 172, 150).

Thus, we have cycle length of 3.

Calculation of 3-yearly moving average

Year	Production	3-yearly total	3-yearly moving average
1983	137	–	–
1984	140	411	137.00
1985	134	411	137.00
1986	137	422	140.67
1987	151	409	136.33
1988	121	396	132.00
1989	124	404	134.67
1990	159	440	146.67
1991	157	485	161.67
1992	169	498	166.00
1993	172	491	163.67
1994	150	–	–

28. Construction of 3-yearly moving average

Year	Imported cotton consumption in India (in thousand bales)	3-yearly moving totals	3-yearly moving averages
2012	132	--	--
2013	135	375	125
2014	108	328	109.33
2015	85	290	96.67
2016	97	270	90.00
2017	88	281	93.67
2018	96	--	--

29. Table for centered 4-yearly moving average

Year	Tonnage of cargo cleared	4-yearly moving totals	4-yearly moving average	4-yearly centered moving average
2001	1102			
2002	1250			
		4872	1218.00	
2003	1180			1231.75
		4982	1245.50	
2004	1340			1253.87
		5049	1262.25	
2005	1212			1296.25
		5321	1330.25	
2006	1317			1356.37
		5530	1382.50	
2007	1452			1429.25
		5904	1476.00	
2008	1549			1495.87
		6063	1515.75	
2009	1586			1537.25
		6235	1558.75	
2010	1476			1563.37
		6272	1568.00	
2011	1624			
2012	1586			

30. The weighted moving average is obtained on dividing the weighted moving totals by the sum of the weights viz; $1 + 4 + 1 = 6$.

Weighted MA $= \frac{\Sigma wx}{\Sigma w} = \frac{\Sigma wx}{6}$.

Computation of Weighted MA of Period 3

Values (X)	Weighted moving totals of period 3	MA of periods Weighted
3	--	--
7	$1 \times 3 + 4 \times 7 + 1 \times 4 = 35$	$35 \div 6 = 5.8$
4	$1 \times 7 + 4 \times 4 + 1 \times 9 = 32$	$32 \div 6 = 5.3$
9	$1 \times 4 + 4 \times 9 + 1 \times 2 = 42$	$42 \div 6 = 7$
2	$1 \times 9 + 4 \times 2 + 1 \times 6 = 23$	$23 \div 6 = 3.8$
6	$1 \times 2 + 4 \times 6 + 1 \times 1 = 27$	$27 \div 6 = 4.5$
1		

31. Calculation of moving averages

Year	Production Y	5-yearly totals	5-yearly moving averages
2000	103	--	--
2001	109	--	--
2002	107	540	108
2003	110	550	110
2004	111	556	111.2
2005	113	568	113.6
2006	115	579	115.8
2007	119	595	119
2008	121	611	122.2
2009	127	631	126.2
2010	129	648	129.6
2011	135	--	--
2012	136	--	--

32. Here, $n = 7$ (odd)

So, middle year 2009 in taken as origin.

Table for fitting straight line trend

Year	Sales (y)	x	xy	x^2	y
2006	33	-3	-99	9	32.893
2007	35	-2	-70	4	42.643
2008	60	-1	-60	1	52.393
2009	67	0	0	0	62.143
2010	68	$+1$	$+68$	1	71.893
2011	82	$+2$	$+164$	4	81.643
2012	90	$+3$	$+270$	9	91.393
$n = 7$	$\Sigma y = 435$	$\Sigma x = 0$	$\Sigma xy = 273$	$\Sigma x^2 = 28$	$\Sigma y = 435$

The equation of the straight line trend is $y_t = a + bx$.

Here, $a = \frac{\Sigma y}{n} = \frac{435}{7} = 62.143$, $b = \frac{\Sigma xy}{\Sigma x^2} = \frac{273}{28} = 9.75$

$y_t = 62.143 + 9.75x$

Hence, $y_{2006} = 62.143 + 9.75(-3) = 62.143 - 29.25 = 32.893$

$y_{2007} = 62.143 + 9.75(-2) = 42.643$, etc

For 2020, x shall be $+11$;

$y_{2020} = 62.143 + 9.75(11) = 62.143 + 107.25 = 169.393$

The estimated sales for the year 2020 is ₹ 169.393 lakh.

33. Here, $n = 8$ (even)

So, origin is mean of two middle years

$\therefore \quad \frac{1998 + 1999}{2} = 1998.5$

Construct the table as under

Year (t)	Sales (y)	$x = t_i - 1998.5$	x^2	xy
1995	6.7	-3.5	12.25	-23.45
1996	5.3	-2.5	6.25	-13.25
1997	4.3	-1.5	2.25	-6.45
1998	6.1	-0.5	0.25	-3.05
1999	5.6	0.5	0.25	2.8
2000	7.9	1.5	2.25	11.85
2001	5.8	2.5	6.25	14.5
2002	6.1	3.5	12.25	21.35
	$\Sigma y = 47.8$	$\Sigma x = 0$	$\Sigma x^2 = 42$	$\Sigma xy = 4.3$

Now, $a = \frac{\Sigma y}{n} = \frac{47.8}{8} \Rightarrow a = 5.975$

and $b = \frac{\Sigma xy}{\Sigma x^2} = \frac{4.3}{42} \Rightarrow b = 0.102$

$\therefore$ The required equation of the straight line trend is

$y_t = 5.975 + 0.102x$

So, trend values for year 1995, $x = -3.5$

$\therefore \quad y_t = 5.975 + 0.102 \times (-3.5) = 5.62$

34. (i) Here, $n = 6$ (even). So, origin is mean of two middle years i.e. $\frac{1998 + 1999}{2} = 1998.5$

Year (t)	Values (y)	$x = t_i - 1998.5$	x^2	xy
1996	6.5	-2.5	6.25	-16.25
1997	5.3	-1.5	2.25	-7.95
1998	4.3	-0.5	0.25	-2.15
1999	6.1	0.5	0.25	3.05
2000	5.6	1.5	2.25	8.4
2001	7.8	2.5	6.25	19.5
	$\Sigma y = 35.6$	$\Sigma x = 0$	$\Sigma x^2 = 17.5$	$\Sigma xy = 4.6$

Here, $a = \frac{\Sigma y}{n} = \frac{35.6}{6} = 5.94$ and $b = \frac{\Sigma xy}{\Sigma x^2} = \frac{4.6}{17.5} = 0.263$

$\therefore$ The required equation of the trend line

$y_t = 5.94 + 0.263x$

(ii) (a)

Year	1996	1997	1998	1999	2000	2001
Trend values	5.28	5.54	5.80	6.07	6.33	6.59

For 2002, x shall be + 3.5;

$$y_{2022} = 5.94 + 0.263(3.5)$$
$$= 5.94 + 0.9205 = 6.86$$

Or

(b) Here, $n = 7$ (odd)

Let assumed mean be 2007.

Year (t)	Values (y)	$x = t_i - 2007$	x^2	xy	$y_t = a + bx$
2004	114	−3	9	−342	115.93
2005	130	−2	4	−260	123.57
2006	126	−1	1	−126	131.21
2007	144	0	0	0	138.85
2008	138	1	1	138	146.49
2009	156	2	4	312	154.13
2010	164	3	9	492	161.77
	$\Sigma y = 972$	$\Sigma x = 0$	$\Sigma x^2 = 28$	$\Sigma xy = 214$	

Here, $a = \frac{\Sigma y}{n} = \frac{972}{7} = 138.85$

and $b = \frac{\Sigma xy}{\Sigma x^2} = \frac{214}{28} = 7.64$

∴ The required equation of the trend line

$$y_t = 138.85 + 7.64x$$

35. Here, $n = 11$ (odd number)

Year (t)	Production (y) (in tonnes)	$x = t_i - 1967$	x^2	xy	$y_t = a + bx$
1962	2	−5	25	−10	1.73
1963	4	−4	16	−16	2.42
1964	3	−3	9	−9	3.11
1965	4	−2	4	−8	3.8
1966	4	−1	1	−4	4.99
1967	2	0	0	0	5.18
1968	4	1	1	4	5.87
1969	9	2	4	18	6.56
1970	7	3	9	21	7.25
1971	10	4	16	40	7.94
1972	8	5	25	40	8.63
	$\Sigma y = 57$	$\Sigma x = 0$	$\Sigma x^2 = 110$	$\Sigma xy = 76$	

Here, $a = \frac{\Sigma y}{n} = \frac{57}{11} = 5.18$ and $b = \frac{\Sigma xy}{\Sigma x^2} = \frac{76}{110} = 0.69$

∴ The required equation of the trend line

$y_t = 5.18 + 0.69x$

(i) (c) 5.18

(ii) (b) 0.69

(iii) (a) $y_t = 5.18 + 0.69x$

(iv) (d) For year 1962, $x = -5$

$$y_t = 5.18 + 0.69 \times (-5) = 5.18 - 3.45 = 1.73$$

(v) (a) For year 1970, $x = 3$

$$y_t = 5.18 + 0.69 \times 3 = 5.18 + 2.07 = 7.25$$

CHAPTER 18

Perpetuity, Sinking Funds, Valuation of Bonds and EMI

In this Chapter...

- Perpetuity and Sinking Funds
- Equated Monthly Installment (EMI)

Perpetuity

A **perpetuity** is an annuity in which the periodic payments begin on a fixed date and continue indefinitely.

In other words, a perpetuity is an ordinary annuity without any end.

e.g.

(i) if a buyer obtains a property and then choose to rent it out. He/she recieves an infinite cash flow as long as the property continues to exists.

(ii) A person get pension after retirement from government will continue to exists forever.

There are two types of Perpetuities.

(i) Perpetuity payable at the end of each payment period.

(ii) Perpetuity payable at the begining of each payment period.

Present Value of a Perpetuity Payable at the end of Each Payment Period

Let a perpetuity of ₹ R payable at the end of each period, the first payment due one period.

Hence, the money be worth i per period. The present value of this perpetuity is defined to be that sum of money which, invested now at the rate i per period, will yield ₹ R at the end of each period forever.

The present value of the perpetuity is the sum of the present value of all payments,

0 1 2 3

$$R \quad R \quad R$$

$$\downarrow \quad \downarrow \quad \downarrow$$

$$\frac{R}{(1+i)} \quad \frac{R}{(1+i)^2} \quad \frac{R}{(1+i)^3}$$

The present value of the first payment, $P_1 = \dfrac{R}{1+i}$

The present value of the second payment, $P_2 = \dfrac{R}{(1+i)^2}$

The present value of the third payment, $P_3 = \dfrac{R}{(1+i)^3}$

and so on.

So, the present value of the perpetuity P is given by

$$P = P_1 + P_2 + P_3 + P_4 + ...$$

$$P = \frac{R}{1+i} + \frac{R}{(1+i)^2} + \frac{R}{(1+i)^3} + ...$$

$$P = \frac{R}{1+i}\left[1 + \frac{1}{1+i} + \frac{1}{(1+i)^2} + ...\right]$$

$$P = \frac{R}{1+i}\left[\frac{1}{1-\frac{1}{1+i}}\right]$$

$$P = \frac{R}{1+i}\left[\frac{1+i}{1+i-1}\right] \Rightarrow P = \frac{R}{i}$$

Hence, the present value of ₹R payable at the end of each payment period when money is worth i per period is $\frac{R}{i}$.

Thus, R is the cash equivalent of an unlimited number of periodic payment of ₹R each, the first being due one period hence.

EXAMPLE 1. Find the present value of a perpetuity of ₹ 900 payable at the end of each year. If money worth 5% per annum.

Sol. Let P be the present value of the perpetuity

Here, $R =$ ₹900

$$i = 5\% = \frac{5}{100} = 0.05 \quad \therefore P = \frac{R}{i} = \frac{900}{0.05} = 18000$$

Hence, the present value is ₹ 18000.

EXAMPLE 2. At what rate of interest will the present value of a perpetuity of ₹ 300 payable at the end of each quarter be ₹ 24000?

Sol. Let the rate of interest be $r\%$ per annum.

Now, r is quarterly.

$$\therefore \quad i = \frac{r}{400}$$

Here, $R =$ ₹300 $P =$ ₹ 24000

$$\therefore \quad P = \frac{R}{i} \Rightarrow i = \frac{R}{P} = \frac{300}{24000} \Rightarrow r = \frac{400 \times 300}{24000} = 5$$

Hence, rate of interest = 5% per annum.

Present Value of a Perpetuity Payable at the Begining of Each Payment Period

Let a perpetuity of ₹ R payable at the begining of each payment period. The first payment due now. Let the money be worth i per period.

Present value of first payment $P_1 = R$

Present value of second payment $P_2 = \frac{R}{1+i}$

Present value of third payment $P_3 = \frac{R}{(1+i)^2}$

Present value of fourth payment $P_4 = \frac{R}{(1+i)^3}$

and so on.

So, the present value P of the perpetuity is given by

$$P = P_1 + P_2 + P_3 + P_4 + ...$$

$$P = R + \frac{R}{1+i} + \frac{R}{(1+i)^2} + \frac{R}{(1+i)^3} + ...$$

$$P = R\left(1 + \frac{1}{1+i} + \frac{1}{(1+i)^2} + ...\right)$$

$$P = R\left(\frac{1}{1-\frac{1}{1+i}}\right)$$

$$P = \frac{R(1+i)}{i} = \frac{R}{i} + R = R + \frac{R}{i}$$

Hence, if money is worth i per period, then the present value of a perpetuity of ₹R payable at the begining each period is $R + \frac{R}{i}$.

EXAMPLE 3. What sum of money is needed to invest now, so as to get ₹ 6000 at the beginning of every month forever, if the money is worth 9% per annum compounded monthly?

Sol. Given, $R =$ ₹ 6000, $r = \frac{9}{12}\% = 0.75$ per month

and $\quad i = \frac{0.75}{100} = 0.0075$

$$\therefore \quad P = R + \frac{R}{i} = 6000 + \frac{6000}{0.0075}$$

$$= 6000 + 800000 = ₹\ 806000$$

Thus, ₹ 806000 are needed to invest to get ₹ 6000 at the beginning of every month forever.

Sinking Fund

A sinking fund is like a special purpose saving account. Company deposits money with an intention to repay a debt/replace an asset to acquisition in the future. The money in fund is but regularly and one uses only for the predifined purpose.

Or

A sinking fund is a fund created to accumulate money over the years to discharge a future obligation like replacing an old machine by a new machine, renovation of house, etc.

Amount of Sinking Fund

An annuity whose periodic payment is ₹R payable at the end of each payment period of n period, interest beings r% per period or $i = \frac{r}{100}$.

Then, the amount of obligation which can be discharged

$$S = \frac{R[(1+i)^n - 1]}{i}$$

Sinking Fund Payment

The periodic payment of ₹ R required to accumulate a sum of ₹ S over n periods with interest charged at the rate of i per period is given by

$$R = \frac{i \times S}{(1+i)^n - 1}$$

EXAMPLE 4. A company intends to create a sinking fund to replace at the end of 20th year assets costing ₹ 500000. Calculate the amount to be retained out of profits every year, if the interest rate is 5% per annum.
[given $(1.05)^{20} = 2.6532$]

Sol. Given, $S =$ ₹ 500000 and $i = \frac{5}{100} = 0.05$ and $n = 20$ yr

We know that

$$R = \frac{i \times S}{(1+i)^n - 1} = \frac{(0.05)(500000)}{(1+0.05)^{20} - 1} = \frac{(0.05)(500000)}{(1.05)^{20} - 1}$$

$$= \frac{25000}{2.6532 - 1} = \frac{25000}{1.6532} = ₹\ 15122.18$$

Thus, ₹ 15122.18 are retained out of profits every year for 20 yr to accumulate ₹ 500000.

EXAMPLE 5. A firm sets aside a sum of ₹ 10000 annually for 15 yr to pay off a debenture issue of ₹ 220000. If the fund accumulates at 6% per annum, find the surplus after the fall redemption of the debenture issue.
[given $(1.06)^{15} = 2.3966$]

Sol. Given, $R =$ ₹ 10000, $n = 15$, $i = 6\% = 0.06$

$$\therefore S = R\left[\frac{(1+i)^n - 1}{i}\right] = 10000\left[\frac{(1+0.06)^{15} - 1}{0.06}\right]$$

$$= 10000\left[\frac{(1.06)^{15} - 1}{0.06}\right] = 10000\left(\frac{2.3966 - 1}{0.06}\right) = ₹\ 232766.67$$

Amount required to redeem the debenture = ₹ 220000

∴ The surplus = ₹ 232766 − 220000 = ₹ 12766

Bonds

Bonds are debt instruments and represent a loan mode to the issuer. Bonds allow individual investors to take on the role of lender. Governments and corporations commonly used bonds to borrow money for roads, schools, dams or other infrastructure.

Corporations often borrow to grow their business, purchase property and equipment, undertake profitable projects, fund research and development, or hire employees.

Face Value

The face value of a bond is the price at which the bond is sold to buyers at the time of issue.

Note It is also the price at which the bond is redeemed at maturity.

Maturity Rate

The maturity rate refers to the time period until a financial instrument, such as a bond or loan, reaches its full value or becomes due for repayment. It indicates when the principal and any accrued interest is paid back to the investor or lender.

Coupon Rate

The bond coupon rate represents the annual interest rate paid by the bond issuer to the bond holder.

Current Price

The current price of a bond is the agreed upon open market value between a buyer and investor.

Valuation of Bonds

The valuation of bonds refers to the process of determining the current worth or price of a bond in the market.

The fundamental principle of bond valuation is that its current price is equal to the sum of present values of its expected cash flows also. This valuation is influenced by factors such as the bond's coupon rate and the time to maturity.

The value of bond can be calculated by discounting its future cash flows (coupon payments and the principal repayment) back to the present using an appropriate discount rate, often based on current market interest rates. This allows investors to assess the bond's current price compared to its market value.

Present Vale Approach

In the present value approach, we first calculate the present value of each expected cash flow and then we add all the individual present values to obtain the value or fair value of purchase price of a bond.

Let there be a bond with the

Face value $= F$

Redemption price or, Maturity value $=C$

Yield rate or market interest rate per period $=i$

Number of periodic payments or Number of cash flows $=n$

Periodic interest (dividend) payment or Coupon payment $=R$

Value of bond or Purchase price of bond or Market price of bond $= V$

Then,

Bond value = Present value of first periodic payment + Present value of second periodic payment + ... + Present value of nth periodic payment + Present value of Maturity value or, Redemption price

$$\Rightarrow \text{Bond value} = \frac{R}{1+i} + \frac{R}{(1+i)^2} + \dots + \frac{R}{(1+i)^n} + \frac{C}{(1+i)^n}$$

$$\Rightarrow \text{Bond value} = \frac{R}{1+i} \frac{\left\{1 - \left(\frac{1}{1+i}\right)^n\right\}}{\left(1 - \frac{1}{1+i}\right)} + \frac{C}{(1+i)^n}$$

$$\Rightarrow \text{Bond value} = R\left\{\frac{1-(1+i)^{-n}}{i}\right\} + C(1+i)^{-n}$$

$$\therefore \text{Bond value} = R\left\{\frac{1-(1+i)^{-n}}{i}\right\} + F(1+i)^{-n}.$$

[$\because$ *a* bond is redeemed at part then $C = F$]

EXAMPLE 6. A company *XYZ* Ltd has issued a bond having a face value of ₹ 10000 paying annual dividends at 10%. The bond will be redeemed at par at the end of 10 years. Find the purchase price of this bond if the investor wishes a yield rate of 8% (Given $(1.08)^{-10} = 0.46319349$).

Sol. Given, F = Face value of the bond = ₹ 10000

n = Number of periodic dividend payments = Period of redemption = 10

i = Annual yield rate $= \frac{8}{100} = 0.08$

R = Annual dividend = 10 % of face value

$= ₹\left(\frac{10}{100} \times 10000\right) = ₹\ 1000$

The bond is redeemed at par.

$\therefore C$ = Redemption price or Maturity value

= Face value = ₹ 10000.

Let V be the purchase price of the bond.

Then, $V = R\left\{\frac{1-(1+i)^{-n}}{i}\right\} + C(1+i)^{-n}$

$$\Rightarrow \quad V = ₹\left[1000\left\{\frac{1-(1+0.08)^{-10}}{0.08}\right\} + 10000\,(1+0.08)^{-10}\right]$$

$$\Rightarrow \quad V = ₹\left[\frac{100000}{8}\{1-(1.08)^{-10}\} + 10000\,(1+1.08)^{-10}\right]$$

$$\Rightarrow \quad V = ₹\ \{12500\,(1-0.46319349) + 10000 \times 0.46319349\}$$

$$\Rightarrow \quad V = ₹\ (12500 \times 0.53680651 + 10000 + 0.46319349)$$

$$\Rightarrow \quad V = ₹\ (6710.08 + 4631.93) = ₹\ 11342.01$$

Hence, the purchase price of the bond is ₹ 11342.01.

EXAMPLE 7. An organisation has issued a bond having face value of ₹ 100000, carrying an annual divided rate of 7% and maturing in 10 years. If the prevailing market rate of interest is 9%, and the bond is redeemed at par, find the bond value. Given $(1.09)^{-10} = 0.4224108$

Sol. Given, F = Face value of the bond = ₹ 100000

n = Period of redemption = Number of annual dividends = 10

i = Annual yield rate $= \frac{9}{100} = 0.09$

R = Annual dividend = 7% of face value

$= ₹\ \frac{7}{100} \times 100000 = ₹\ 7000$

The bond is redeemed at par.

$\therefore C$ = Redemption price or Maturity value

= Face value = ₹ 100000.

Let V be the bond value.

Then, $V = R\left\{\frac{1-(1+i)^{-n}}{i}\right\} + C(1+i)^{-n}$

$$\Rightarrow \quad V = ₹\left[7000\left\{\frac{1-(1+0.09)^{-10}}{0.09}\right\} + 100000(1+0.09)^{-10}\right]$$

$$\Rightarrow V = ₹\left[\frac{700000}{9}\{1-(1.09)^{-10}\} + 100000(1.09)^{-10}\right]$$

$$\Rightarrow V = ₹\left[\frac{700000}{9}(1-0.4224108) + 100000 \times 0.4224108\right]$$

$$\Rightarrow V = ₹\left(\frac{700000}{9} \times 0.5775892 + 42,241.08\right)$$

$= ₹\ 44923.604 + 42241.08$

$= ₹\ 87164.684$

Hence, the bond value is ₹ 87164.684.

Topic Practice 1

1 Find the present value of a perpetuity of ₹ 9600 at the end of each year. If money is 6% per annum,

2 At 6% per annum, compounded quarterly, find the present value of a perpetuity of ₹ 600 payable at the end of each quarter. [CBSE 2024]

3 Find the present value of a sequence of payment of ₹ 1400 made at the end of each 6 months and continuity forever, if money is worth 7% converted semi-annually.

4 If the cash equivalent of a perpetuity of ₹ 1200 payable at the end of each quarter is ₹ 96000. Find the rate of interest convertible quarterly.

5 At what rate of interest will the present value of ₹ 600 payable at the end of every 6 months be ₹ 10000?

6 What sum of money is needed to invest now, so as to get ₹ 5000 at the beginning of every month forever. If the money is 6% per annum compounded monthly.

7 Vikram wants to retire from his job and get hold of ₹ 30000 per month. He wants the money to go the future generation after his death.He will earn interest get of 8% compounded annually. What is the total amount he will need to achieved the perpetuity goal.

8 How much money is needed to ensure monthly pension of ₹ 96000 at the begining of each month forever. If the money is worth 8% per annum compounded monthy.

9 The present value of a perpetual income of ₹ R at the end of each 6 months is ₹ 36000. Find the value of R if money is worth 6% compounded semi-annually.

10 At what rate converted semi-annually will present value of a perpetuity of ₹ 1500 payable at the end of 6 months be ₹ 40,000?

11 A person has set up a sinking fund in order to have ₹ 100000 after 10 yr for his children's college education. How much amount should be set aside bi-annually into an account paying 5% per annum compounded half-yearly? [given $(1.025)^{20} = 1.6386$]

12 A company intends to create a sinking fund to replace at the end of 20th year assets costing ₹ 50000. Calculate the amount to be retained out of profit every year, if the interest rate is 5% [given $(1.05)^{20} = 2.6532$]

13 A company establish a sinking fund to provide for payment of ₹ 250000 debt, maturing in 4 yr. Contributions to the fund are made at the end of every year. Find the amount of each annual deposit, if the interest is 18% per annum. [given $(1.18)^4 = 1.9387$]

14 A sinking fund is created for redemption of debentures of ₹ 2500000 at the end of 20 years. How much money should be provided out of the profits of each year for the sinking fund if the investment can earn interest at 8% per annum.

15 A company *PQR* has issued a bond having the face value of ₹ 100000 carrying a coupon rate of 5% to be paid semi-annually and maturing in 5 years. If the prevailing market rate of interest is 7%, find the bond value. (Given $(1.035)^{-10} = 0.70891881$).

16 A bond has a face value of ₹ 10000 and matures in 15 years at part. The nominal interest is 10%. What is the price of the bond that will yield an effective interest of 8%? (Given $(1.08)^{-15} = 0.31524170$).

Hints & Solutions

1. **Hint** Here, $R =$ ₹ 9600 $i = 6\% = 0.06$

$$P = \frac{R}{i} = \frac{9600}{0.06} = \frac{960000}{6}$$ **Ans.** ₹ 160000

2. **Hint** Here, $R = 600$, rate of interest is quarterly

$$\therefore\ i = \frac{r}{4} = \frac{6}{4}\% = \frac{3}{200} = 0.015$$

$$P = \frac{R}{i} = \frac{600}{0.015} = \frac{600000}{15}$$ **Ans.** ₹ 40000

3. **Hint** Here, $R = 1400$, $i = \frac{7}{2}\% = \frac{7}{200}$

$$\therefore P = \frac{R}{i} = \frac{1400 \times 200}{7}$$ **Ans.** ₹ 40000

4. **Hint** Here, $R = 1200$, $P = 96000$, $i = \frac{r}{400}$

$$i = \frac{R}{P} \Rightarrow \frac{r}{400} = \frac{1200}{96000} \Rightarrow r = \frac{1200 \times 400}{96000}$$ **Ans.** 5%

5. **Hint** Here, $R = 600$, $P = 10000$, $i = \frac{r}{200}$

$$i = \frac{R}{P} \Rightarrow \frac{r}{200} = \frac{600}{10000}$$ **Ans.** 12%

6. **Hint** Here, $R = 5000$, $i = \frac{6}{1200}$

$$P = R + \frac{R}{i} = 5000 + \frac{5000 \times 1200}{6}$$

$$= 5000 + 1000000$$ **Ans.** ₹ 1005000

7. ₹ 4497750

8. **Hint** Use $P = R + \frac{R}{i}$ **Ans.** ₹ 14496000

9. **Hint** Use $R = P_i$ **Ans.** ₹ 1080

10. **Hint** Use $i = \frac{R}{P}$ **Ans.** 7.5%

11. **Hint** Use $= R = \frac{Si}{(1+i)^n - 1}$ **Ans.** ₹ 3914.81

12. **Hint** Use $= R = \frac{Si}{(1+i)^n - 1}$ **Ans.** ₹ 1512.218

13. **Hint** Use $R = \frac{Si}{(1+i)^n - 1}$ **Ans.** ₹ 47938.64

14. **Hint** Use $R = \frac{Si}{(1+i)^n - 1}$ **Ans.** ₹ 54630.52

15. **Hint** $V = R\left\{\frac{1-(1+i)^{-n}}{i}\right\} + C(1+i)^{-n}$ **Ans.** 91683.394

16. **Hint** $V = R\left\{\frac{1-(1+i)^{-n}}{i}\right\} + C(1+i)^{-n}$ **Ans.** 11711.895

Equated Monthly Installment (EMI)

An equated monthly installment (EMI) is a fixed payment amount made by a borrower to a lender at a specified date each calender month. Equated monthly installments are applied to both interest and principal each month so that over a specified number of years. The loan is paid off in full. In the most common types of loans, such as real estate monet gages, auto loans, student loans the borrower makes fixed periodic payments to the lender over several years to retire the loan.

An equated monthly installment (EMI) is the fixed amount paid by a borrower every month to clear off the loan taken from a lender.

EMI depends on the following factors:

(i) Principal amount (ii) The loan tenure

(iii) The interest rate

EMI can be calculated by two methods:

Flat Rate Method

In flat rate method the principal amount remains same throughout the tenure and the interest is charged on it at a constant rate throughout the loan tenure.

Suppose an amount of ₹ P is borrowed at flat rate of r per rupee per month for a period of n months. Then,

$$\text{Interest} = P \times i \times n, \text{ where } i = \frac{r}{100}$$

$$\therefore \quad \text{EMI} = \frac{\text{Principal} + \text{Interest}}{n}$$

$$\Rightarrow \quad \text{EMI} = \frac{P + P \times i \times n}{n} = P\left(i + \frac{1}{n}\right)$$

Note The flat-rate method results in a higher effective interest rate.

EXAMPLE 1. Sudha takes a loan of ₹ 500000 at a interest of 15% compounded annually for a period of 4 years. Find her EMI using flat rate method.

Sol. We have, Principal (P) = ₹ 500000

i = Rate of interest per month $= \frac{15}{1200} = 0.0125$

n = Number of instalment $= 4 \times 12 = 48$

$$\text{EMI} = P\left(i + \frac{1}{n}\right) = ₹\, 500000\left(0.0125 + \frac{1}{48}\right)$$

$$= ₹\, 500000\,(0.0125 + 0.0208)$$

$$= ₹\, 500000(0.0333) = ₹\, 16650$$

Hence, Sudha's EMI = ₹ 16650

Reducing Balance Method

In reducing balance method principal paid back gets deducted from the outstanding loan amount and the interest for the subsequent year is charged on the remaining deducted balance and not on the entire loan amount unlike the flat rate method.

Let the amount P is borrowed on which interest is payable at the rate of r% per installment period. This amount is to be paid back along with the interest in n equal installments of ₹E. Each installment comprises some part of the principal P that is paid back the rest is the interest on the amount the was outstanding for that installment period.

Let P_n denote the principal amount left at the end of the nth month.

First month, we have

Principal = P, Installment paid = E,

Interest accrued = P_i

Outstanding mount $= (P + Pi) - E = P(1 + i) - E$

$$\Rightarrow \quad P_1 = P(1 + i) - E$$

Second month, we have

Principal = P_1, Installment paid = E

Interest accrued = $P_1 i$

$$\text{Outstanding amount} = (P_1 + P_1 i) - E = P_1(1+i) - E$$
$$= (P(1+i) - E)(1+i) - E \quad [\because P_1 = P(1+i)]$$
$$= P(1+i)^2 - E(1+i+1)$$
$$\Rightarrow \quad P_2 = P(1+i)^2 - E(1+i+1)$$

Similarly, $P_3 = P(1+i)^3 - E\{(1+i)^2 + (1+i) + 1\}$

and $P_n = P(1+i)^n - E[(1+i)^{n-1} + (1+i)^{n-2} + \ldots (1+i) + 1]$

As the loan is fully paid in n months

∴ Outstanding at the end of nth months is zero

i.e. $P_n = 0$

$$\Rightarrow P(1+i)^n - E[(1+i)^{n-1} + \ldots (1+i) +] = 0$$
$$\Rightarrow E[1 + (1+i) + (1+i)^2 + \ldots (1+i)^{n-1}] = P(1+i)^n$$
$$\Rightarrow E\left[\frac{(1+i)^n - 1}{(1+i) - 1}\right] = P(1+i)^n$$
$$\Rightarrow E = \frac{Pi(1+i)^n}{(1+i)^n - 1} = \frac{Pi}{1-(1+i)^{-n}}$$
$$\therefore \text{EMI} = \frac{Pi}{1-(1+i)^{-n}} \text{ or } \frac{P(1+i)^n \cdot i}{(1+i)^n - 1}$$

where P = Principal borrowed

i = Rate of interest per month

n = Number of payments

EXAMPLE 2. Amrita bought a car worth ₹ 1250000 and makes a down payment of ₹ 300000. The balance amount is to be paid in 4 yr by equal monthly instalments at an interest rate of 15% p.a. Find the EMI that Amrita has to pay for the car. [Given $(1.0125)^{-48} = 0.5508565$]

Sol. Cost of car = ₹ 1250000

Down payment = ₹ 300000

∴ Balance amount = 1250000 − 300000 = ₹ 950000

So, P = ₹ 950000, $i = \frac{15}{12 \times 100} = 0.0125$ and $n = 12 \times 4 = 48$

$$\therefore \text{EMI} = \frac{P \times i}{(1+i)^{-n} - 1}$$
$$\text{EMI} = \frac{950000 \times 0.0125}{1-(1+0.0125)^{-48}} = \frac{11875}{1-(1.0125)^{-48}}$$
$$= \frac{11875}{1-0.5508565} \quad [\because (1.0125)^{-48} = 0.5508565]$$
$$= \frac{11875}{0.4491435} = 26439.211$$

Hence, EMI is ₹ 26439.21.

EXAMPLE 3. Mrs. Sood took a housing loan of ₹ 800000 to be paid in 10 years by equal monthly installments. The interest charged in 10.5% compounded monthly. Find her monthly installment.
[given $(1.00875)^{-120} = 0.3515$]

Sol. We have, P = ₹ 800000, $i = \frac{10.5}{1200} = 0.00875$

and $n = 10 \times 12 = 120$

$$\therefore \quad \text{EMI} = \frac{Pi}{1-(1+i)^{-n}} = ₹\frac{800000(0.00875)}{1-(1+0.00875)^{-120}}$$
$$\text{EMI} = ₹\frac{7000}{1-(1.00875)^{-120}} = ₹\frac{7000}{1-0.3515} = ₹\frac{7000}{0.6485}$$
$$\text{EMI} = ₹\ 10794.14$$

Hence, monthly installment of Mrs Sood is ₹ 10794.14.

EXAMPLE 4. A person buys a house for which he agrees to pay ₹ 5000 at the end of each month for 8 yr. If money is worth 12% converted monthly. What is the cash price of house? [given $(1.01)^{-96} = 0.3847$]

Sol. We have EMI = ₹ 5000

n = Number of installment = $8 \times 12 = 96$

$$i = \frac{12}{1200} = 0.01$$

Let P the cash price of the house

$$\therefore \quad \text{EMI} = \frac{P \times i}{1-(1+i)^{-n}} \Rightarrow 5000 = \frac{P(0.01)}{1-(1.01)^{-96}}$$
$$\Rightarrow \quad P = \frac{5000(1-0.3847)}{0.01} = 500000 \times 0.6153$$
$$= ₹\ 307650$$

Hence, the cash price of house is ₹ 307650.

Amortization of Loans

Amortization refers to the process of paying off a loan through a scheduled, pre-determined sequence of equal payments that includes

(i) interest on the outstanding loan and

(ii) repayment of part of the loan i.e. principal.

A loan is said to be amortized if each installment is used to pay interest and the part of the principal.

Amortization Formulas

While amortizing a loan, one should know the principal outstanding at the beginning of any period, interest and principal amounts in any EMI, total interest paid etc. The formulas for the same are given below.

Principal outstanding at beginning of kth period

$$= \frac{\text{EMI } [(1+i)^{n-k+1} - 1]}{i(1+i)^{n-k+1}} \text{ or } \frac{\text{EMI}(1-(1+i)^{k-(n+1)})}{i}$$

Interest paid in kth payment

$$= \frac{\text{EMI}[(1+i)^{n-k+1} - 1]}{(1+i)^{n-k+1}} \quad \text{or} \quad \text{EMI}\,(1-(1+i)^{k-(n+1)})$$

Principal paid in kth payment

$$= \text{EMI} - \text{Interest paid in } k\text{th period}$$

Total interest paid $= n \times \text{EMI} - P$

EXAMPLE 5. A loan of ₹ 400000 at the interest rate of 6.75% per annum compounded monthly is to be amortized by equal payment at the end of each month for 10 yr, find

(i) the size of each monthly payment

(ii) the principal outstanding at the beginning of 61st month.

[given $(1.005625)^{120} = 1.9603$ and $(1.005625)^{60} = 1.4001$]

Sol. Given, $P =$ ₹ 400000, $n = 12 \times 10 = 120$

and $i = \frac{6.75}{1200} = 0.005625$

(i) Size of monthly payment

$$\text{EMI} = \frac{P \times i(1+i)^n}{(1+i)^n - 1}$$

$$= \frac{400000 \times 0.005625\,(1+0.005625)^{120}}{(1+0.005625)^{120} - 1}$$

$$= \frac{2250 \times 1.9603}{1.9603 - 1} = \frac{4410.675}{0.9603} = ₹\ 4593$$

$\therefore$ Monthly payment = ₹ 4593

(ii) We know that

Principal outstanding at beginning of kth period

$$= \frac{\text{EMI}[(1+i)^{n-k+1} - 1]}{i(1+i)^{n-k+1}}$$

So, principal outstanding at beginning of 61st month

$$= \frac{\text{EMI}\,((1+i)^{120-61+1} - 1)}{i(1+i)^{120-61+1}} = \frac{\text{EMI}\,((1+i)^{60} - 1)}{i(1+i)^{60}}$$

$$= \frac{4593\,((1.005625)^{60} - 1)}{0.005625(1.005625)^{60}} = \frac{4593\,(1.4001 - 1)}{0.005625(1.4001)}$$

$$= \frac{4593 \times 0.4001}{0.005625 \times 1.4001} = ₹\ 233336.89$$

Principal outstanding at beginning of 61st month is ₹ 233336.89.

Topic Practice 2

1 Mahima takes a loan of ₹ 500,000 from a bank at an interest rate of 6% per annum for 10 years. She wants to pay back the loan in equated monthly installments. Find the EMI by using flat rate method.

2 Ramesh bought a car in 2020 worth ₹ 500000. He decided to repay by monthly installment in 5 years. The interest charged is 8% compounded monthly. How much monthly installment Ramesh will pay? [given $(1.0067)^{60} = 1.4928$]

3 A person buys a house for which he agrees to pay ₹ 25000 at the end of each month for 8 yr. If money is worth 12% converted monthly, what is the cash price of house? [given $(1.01)^{-96} = 0.3847$]

4 Amrita buys a car for which she makes a down payment of ₹ 250000 and the balance is to be paid in 2 years by monthly instalments of ₹ 25448 each. If the financers charges interest at the rate of 20% p.a., find the actual price of the car.

$\left[\text{given} \left(\frac{61}{60}\right)^{-24} = 0.67253\right]$ **[CBSE 2024]**

5 A person amortizes a loan of ₹ 250,000 for a new home by obtaining a 8 years mortgage at rate of 9% compounded monthly payment. Find (i) EMI (ii) the total interest paid.

[given $(1.0075)^{96} = 2.0489$]

6 Neha Suman purchased a house from a company for ₹ 600000 and made a down payment of ₹ 200000. She repays the balance in 20 yr by monthly installments at 12% compounded monthly. [given $(1.01)^{-240} = 0.092$]

(i) What are monthly payments?

(ii) What is the total interest payment?

7 A loan of ₹ 250000 at the interest rate of 6% per annum compounded monthly is to be amortized bye qual payments at the end of each month for 5 years. Find

(i) the size of each monthly payment

(ii) the principal outstanding at begining of 40th month.

[given $(1.005)^{60} = 1.3489, (1.005)^{21} = 1.1104$]

Hints & Solutions

1. **Hint** Use EMI $= P\left(i + \frac{1}{n}\right)$

   Ans. ₹ 6666.67

2. **Hint** Use EMI $= \frac{Pi(1+i)^n}{(1+i)^n - 1}$

   Ans. ₹ 10147.89

3. **Hint** Use $P = \frac{\text{EMI}(1-(1+i)^{-n})}{i}$

   Ans. ₹ 1538250

4. **Hint** Price of car = 250000 + P

   $$P = \frac{\text{EMI}\,(1-(1+i)^{-n})}{i}$$

   Ans. ₹ 750007.39

5. (i) **Hint** Use EMI $= \frac{Pi(1+i)^n}{(1+i)^n - 1}$

   Ans. ₹ 3662.58

   (ii) **Hint** Total interest paid $= n \times \text{EMI} - P$

   Ans. 101607.68

6. (i) ₹ 4405.29

   (ii) ₹ 657269.60

7. Given, $P =$ ₹ 250000, $i = \frac{6}{1200} = 0.005$ and $n = 5 \times 12 = 60$

   (i) Monthly payment $= \frac{250000 \times 0.005 \times (1.005)^{60}}{(1.005)^{60} - 1}$

   $= \frac{250000 \times 0.005 \times 1.3489}{0.3489} =$ ₹ 4832.69

   (ii) Principal outstanding at begining of 40th month

   $= \frac{\text{EMI}\,[(1+i)^{60-40+1} - 1]}{i(1+i)^{60-40+1}}$

   $= \frac{4832.69 \times [(1.005)^{21} - 1]}{0.005 \times (1.005)^{21}}$

   $= \frac{4832.69 \times (1.1104 - 1)}{0.005 \times 1.1104}$

   $= \frac{4832.69 \times 0.1104}{0.005 \times 1.1104}$

   $=$ ₹ 96096.72

Exam Pattern Exercise

Part A - Objective Type Questions

Multiple Choice Type Questions

1 The present value of a perpetuity of ₹ 4000 payable at the end of each year.If money is worth 5% compounded annually is
(a) ₹ 40000 (b) ₹ 80000
(c) ₹ 10000 (d) ₹ 60000

2 Ashwani holds a perpetual bond that generates an annual of ₹ 50000 each year. He believes that the borrower is credit worthy and that an 8% interest rate will be suitable for this bond. Then, present value of this perpetuity is
(a) ₹ 625000 (b) ₹ 400000
(c) ₹ 600000 (d) ₹ 62500

3 The present value of a perpetuity of ₹R payable at the end of each payment period, when the money is worth i per period, is given by **[CBSE 2023]**
(a) Ri (b) $R+\frac{R}{i}$ (c) $\frac{R}{i}$ (d) $R-Ri$

4 What sum of money should be deposited at the end of every 6 months to accumulate ₹ 50000 in 8 years, if money is worth 6% p.a. compounded semi-annually? [given $(1.03)^{16}=1.6047$] **[CBSE 2024]**
(a) ₹ 3432.53 (b) ₹ 2783.08
(c) ₹ 2480.57 (d) ₹ 2149.93

5 Simran purchased a number of stocks of Amazon. At the end of first year, she received a payment of ₹ 8000, which grows at a rate of 3% per year and continues forever. If the discount rate is 7%. Then, the present value of Simran's investment is
(a) ₹ 32000 (b) ₹ 20000
(c) ₹ 200000 (d) ₹ 40000

6 A machine costing ₹ 200000 has effective life of 7 yr and its scrap value is ₹ 30000. What amount should the company put into a sinking fund earning 5% per annum, so that it can replace the machine after its useful life? Assume that a new machine will cost ₹ 300000 after 7 yr [given $(1.05)^7=1.4071$]
(a) ₹ 22169.53 (b) ₹ 21878.38
(c) ₹ 20879.39 (d) ₹ 21888.39

7 A fund which is created to accumulated money over the years to discharge a future obligation is called
(a) perpetuity (b) bonds
(c) EMI (d) sinking fund

8 Using flat rate method, the EMI to repay a loan of ₹ 20000 in $2\frac{1}{2}$ years at an interest rate of 8% p.a. is **[CBSE 2024]**
(a) ₹ 700 (b) ₹ 800 (c) ₹ 900 (d) ₹ 100

9 Mr. Malik borrowed ₹ 500000 from a bank to purchase a house and decided to repay the loan by equal monthly payment in 10 yr. If bank charges interest at 7.5% per annum compounded monthly, then EMI is [given $(1.00625)^{120}=2.1121$]
(a) ₹ 5935 (b) ₹ 6380 (c) ₹ 7340 (d) ₹ 8520

Assertion-Reason Based Questions

Directions (Q. Nos. 10-13) *In the questions given below are two statements labelled as Assertion (A) and Reason (R). In the context of the two statements, which one of the following is correct?*
(a) Both A and R are correct; R is the correct explanation of A
(b) Both A and R are correct; R is not the correct explanation of A
(c) A is correct; R is incorrect
(d) R is correct; A is incorrect

10 **Assertion (A)** The present value of a sequence of payments of ₹800 made at the end of each 3 months continuing forever, if money is worth 9% converted quarterly, is ₹35555.56.

Reason (R) The present value of an immediate perpetuity of ₹R at r per annum compounded continuously is given by $P=\frac{R}{i}$.

11 **Assertion (A)** A sum of ₹54000 invested at r% compounded quarterly will provide payments of ₹600 each at the end of every 3 months, the value of r is 6%.

Reason (R) If the first payment is made at the beginning of the first period and the subsequent payments at equal intervals forever the annuity is called perpetuity due.

12 **Assertion (A)** Dr. Kumar creates an endowment fund of ₹50000 to provide a prize at the starting of every year. This fund earns interest at 8% per annum compounded annually, then prize amount is ₹3703.70.

Reason (R) The present value of a perpetuity due of ₹R payable at the beginning of every period at a rate of i per period is given by $P=R+\frac{R}{i}$.

13 **Assertion (A)** Mr. Parth borrows a sum of ₹125000 at an interest rate of 10% (flat) for a tenure of 4 years, then his EMI is ₹5216.25.

Reason (R) EMI payments are made every month, generally on a fixed date, for the entire tenure of the loan, till the outstanding amount has been completely repaid.

Part-B Descriptive Questions

Very Short Answer Type Questions

14 Find the present value of a perpetuity of ₹ 1200 payable at the end of each year. If money is worth 8% per annum.

15 Find the present value of a perpetuity of ₹ 300 payable at the begining of every 6 months, if money is worth 6% per annum.

16 What amount is received at the end of every 6 months forever, if ₹ 72000 kept in a bank earn 12% per annum compounded half yearly.

17 At what rate of interest will the present value of a perpetuity at ₹ 500 payable at the end of each quarter is ₹ 40000?

18 Aarushi purchased a number of stocks of Tata Motors. At the end of first year. She received a payment of ₹ 6000, which grows at a rate of 4% per year and continues forever. If the discount rate is 10%. Find the present value of Aarushi's investment.

19 Rajni takes a loan of ₹ 300000 at a interest of 5% compounded annually for a period of 2 years. Find her EMI using flat rate method.

Short Answer Type Questions

20 A sinking fund is created for the redemption of debentures of ₹ 100,000 at the end of 25 years. How much money should be provided out of profits each year for the sinking fund. If the investment can even interest 4% per annum? [given $(1.04)^{25} = 2.6658$]

21 To save for a child education, a family decides to invest ₹ 3000 at the end of each six month period in a fund paying 8% per year compounded semi-annually. Find the amount of the investment at the end of 18 years. [given $(1.04)^{36} = 4.1039$]

22 A firm anticipates a capital expenditure of ₹ 80000 for a new equipment in 5 yr. How much should be deposited quarterly in sinking fund carrying 12% per annum compounded quarterly to provide for the purchase? [given $(1.03)^{20} = 1.8061$]

23 A company sets a side a sum of ₹ 1000 at the end of each year in a sinking fund so that at the end of 10 years. If would amount to a balance sufficient to replace the machinery. Assuming that the cost of machineary remains constant at the end of 10 years and that money earns 5% per annum compound interest. Find the cost of machinery.

24 Find the purchase price of a ₹ 20000 bond, redeemable at the end of 10 years at 110, and paying annual dividends at 5% if the yield rate is to be 5% effective. (Given $(1.05)^{-10} = 0.61391325$).

25 Mr. Taneja wishes to purchases a flat for ₹ 6000000 with a down payment of ₹ 1000000 and balance in equal monthly payment for 20 years. If bank charges 7.5% per annum compounded monthly. Calculate the EMI [given $(1.00625)^{240} = 4.4608$]

26 Mr. Kailash has taken a personal loan of ₹ 200000 for 2 yr at an interest rate of 20% per annum, which is to be paid back in equal monthly installments. How much monthly installment Mr. Kailash will pay? $\left[\text{given } \left(\frac{61}{60}\right)^{-24} = 0.6725\right]$

27 Darshan buys a car for which he makes down payment of ₹ 90,000 and the balance is to be paid in 4 years by monthly installment of ₹ 12500. If the financer charges interest at the rate of 15% per annum. Find the actual price of car. [given $(1.0125)^{-48} = 0.5508$]

Long Answer Type Questions

28 A machine is bought for ₹ 320000. Its effective life is 8 yr, after which its salvage value would be ₹ 25000. It is decided to create a sinking fund to replace this machine at the end of its effective life by making half yearly payments that will earn an interest of 8% per annum compounded half yearly. If it is known that the cost of machine increases by 5% per annum. Calculate the amount of each payment to the sinking fund. [given $(1.04)^{16} = 1.8730$ and $(1.05)^{8} = 1.4774$]

29 Find the purchase price of a ₹ 50000, 6% bond, dividends payable semi-annually redeemable at par in 10 years, if the yield rate is to be 5% compounded semi-annually. (Given $(1.025)^{-20} = 0.61027094$).

30 Rajesh purchased a house from a company for ₹ 2500000 and made a down payment of ₹ 500000. He repays the balance in 25 yr by monthly installments at the rate of 9% per annum compounded monthly

(i) What are the monthly payment?
(ii) What is the total interest payment?
[given $(1.0075)^{-300} = 0.1062$]

31 A machine costs a company of ₹ 52000 and its effective life is estimated to be 12 years. A sinking fund is created for replacing the machine by a new model at the end of its life time. When its scrap realizes a sum of ₹ 5000 only. The price of new model is estimated to be 25% higher than the price of the present one. Find what amount should be aside of the end of each year. Out o profit for the sinking fund. If it accumulates at 10% effective. [given $(1.1)^{12} = 3.1384$]

32 In year 2020, Mr. Jain amortizes a loan of ₹ 1500000 for renovation of his house by 8 years mortgage at the rate of 12% per annum compounded monthly. Find
(i) The size of each monthly payment
(ii) The principal outstanding at the begining of 50th month.
[given $(1.01)^{-96} = 0.3847$ and $(1.01)^{-47} = 0.6265$]

Case Study Based Questions

33 Aryan bought a car in 2020 worth ₹5.95 lakh. He made a down payment of ₹1.5 lakh and took an auto loan for the rest of amount at the rate 12% per annum for four years [given $(1.01)^{48} = 1.6122$]
(i) Find the rate of interest per month.
(ii) What is the principle for calculating EMI?
(iii) Calculate EMI.

34. Ramesh borrowed a home loan amount of ₹ 7,00,000 from a bank at an interest of 12% per annum for 30 years, to be paid in monthly installments.

Based on the above information, answer the following questions
(i) Write the formula for calculating EMI by reducing balance method.
(ii) Write the values of P, i and n respectively.
(iii) Find the EMI. [use $(1.01)^{-360} = 0.02781668$]
Or If the loan is to be returned in 20 years, find EMI. [use $(1.01)^{-240} = 0.09180584$] **[CBSE 2025]**

Hints & Solutions

1. (b)	2. (a)	3. (c)	4. (c)
5. (c)	6. (c)	7. (d)	8. (b)
9. (a)	10. (a)	11. (d)	12. (a)
13. (d)	14. ₹ 15000	15. ₹ 10300	16. ₹ 4320
17. 5%	18. ₹ 100000	19. ₹ 13750	20. ₹ 2401.25
21. ₹ 232792.50	22. ₹ 2977.29	23. ₹ 12580	

24. Given, n = Number of periods = 10,

$$i = \text{Yield rate} = \frac{5}{100} = 0.05$$

$$R = \text{Annual dividend} = 4\% \text{ of face value}$$

$$= ₹\left(\frac{5}{100} \times 20,000\right) = ₹\ 1000$$

$$C = \text{Redemption price} = ₹\left(20,000 \times \frac{110}{100}\right) = ₹\ 22,000$$

$$V = R\left[\frac{1-(1+i)^{-n}}{i}\right] + C(1+i)^{-n}$$

$$\Rightarrow V = ₹\left[1000\left\{\frac{1-(1+0.05)^{-10}}{0.05}\right\} + 22,000(1+0.05)^{-10}\right]$$

$$\Rightarrow V = ₹\ [20,000\,\{1-(1.05)^{-10}\} + 20,000(1.05)^{-10}]$$

$$\Rightarrow V = ₹\ [20,000\,(1-0.61391325) + 22,000 \times 0.61391325]$$

$$\Rightarrow V = ₹\ (20,000 \times 0.38608675 + 22,000 \times 0.61391325)$$

$$\Rightarrow V = ₹\ (7721.735 + 13506.0915) = ₹\ 21227.8265$$

25. ₹ 40279.70 **26.** ₹ 10178 **27.** ₹ 539200

28. Let each semi-annually deposit in the sinking fund of ₹ R. Since, the cost of new machine is increases by 5% per annum the cost of present.

Cost of machine at present = ₹ 320000

Cost of machine after increasing 5% per annum after

$$8 \text{ yr} = 320000\left(1+\frac{5}{100}\right)^8$$

$$= 32000\,(1.05)^8 = 320000 \times 1.4774$$

$$= ₹\ 472768$$

Salvage value of present machine = ₹ 25000

So, net amount required at the end of 8 yr to purchase the new model is ₹ (472768 − 25000) = ₹ 447768

We know that $R = \dfrac{i \times S}{(1+i)^n - 1}$

Here, S = ₹ 447768, $n = 8 \times 2 = 16$ yr and $i = \dfrac{8}{200} = 0.04$

$$\therefore \quad R = \frac{(0.04)\times(447768)}{(1+0.04)^{16} - 1}$$

$$= \frac{17910.72}{(1.04)^{16} - 1} = \frac{17910.72}{1.8730 - 1}$$

$$= \frac{17910.72}{0.8730} = ₹\ 20516.28$$

Thus, ₹ 20516.28 deposited half yearly out of the profit to purchase the new model of the machine.

29. Given, F = Face value of bond = ₹ 50000,

$$i = \text{Yield rate} = \frac{5}{200} = 0.025$$

$$R = \text{Semi-annual dividend} = ₹\left(\frac{5}{200} \times 50000\right) = ₹\ 1250$$

n = Number of periodic payments = $2 \times 10 = 20$

The bond is redeemable at par.

Therefore, C = Redemption price = ₹ 50000

Let V be the purchase price of the bond.

$$\text{Then, } V = R\left\{\frac{1-(1+i)^{-n}}{i}\right\} + C(1+i)^{-n}$$

$$\Rightarrow V = ₹\left[1250\left\{\frac{1-(1+0.025)^{-20}}{0.025}\right\} + 50000(1+0.025)^{-20}\right]$$

$$\Rightarrow V = ₹\ [50000\ \{1-(1.025)^{-20}\} + 50000\ (1.025)^{-20}]$$

$$\Rightarrow V = ₹\ [50000\ (1-0.61027094) + 50000 + 0.61027094]$$

$$\Rightarrow V = ₹\ (50000 + 0.38972906 + 50000 \times 0.61027094)$$

$$= ₹\ (19486.453 + 30513.547) = ₹\ 50000$$

30. Cost of house = ₹ 2500000

Down payment = ₹ 500000

∴ Principal amount = ₹ (2500000 − 500000) = ₹ 2000000

$$n = 25 \times 12 = 300 \text{ and } i = \frac{9}{1200} = 0.0075$$

(i) We know that

$$\text{EMI} = \frac{P \times i}{1-(1+i)^{-n}} = \frac{2000000 \times 0.0075}{1-(1+0.0075)^{-300}}$$

$$= \frac{15000}{1-(1.0075)^{-300}} = \frac{15000}{1-(0.1062)}$$

$$= \frac{15000}{0.8938} = ₹\ 16782.27$$

∴ Monthly payment = ₹ 16782.27

(ii) We have, EMI = ₹ 16782.27, $n = 300$ and $P = 2000000$

∴ Total interest = $n \times \text{EMI} - P$

$$= 300 \times 16782.27 - 2000000$$

$$= 5034681 - 2000000 = ₹\ 3034681$$

∴ Total interest = ₹ 3034681

31. Hint Let ₹ R be the amount set aside each year.

∵ Cost of new machine = ₹ 52000

∴ Cost of machine after increasing the 25% of cost of machine

$$\text{i.e. } 52000 + 25\% \text{ of } 52000 = 52000 \times \frac{5}{4} = ₹\ 65000$$

Now, scrap value of present machine = ₹ 5000

∴ Net amount = ₹ (65000 − 5000) = ₹ 60000

Here, S = ₹ 60000, n = 12 yr and $i = \frac{10}{100} = 0.1$

Now, put all the values in $R = \dfrac{i \times S}{(1+i)^n - 1}$

Ans. 2805.84

32. (i) ₹ 24378.35 (ii) ₹ 910531

33. (i) We have, r = 12% p.a = 1% p.a. = 0.01 p.a.

$$n = 4 \times 12 = 48 \text{ months}$$

(ii) P = ₹595000 − ₹150000 = ₹445000

(iii) $$\text{EMI} = 445000 \times 0.01 \times \left[\frac{(1+0.01)^{48}}{(1+0.01)^{48}-1}\right]$$

$$= 4450 \times \frac{(1+0.01)^{48}}{(1.01)^{48}-1}$$

$$= 4450\left(\frac{1.6122}{0.6122}\right)$$

$$= 11718.86$$

∴ EMI under reducing balance = ₹ 11718.86

34. (i) The formula for equated monthly installment (EMI) using the reducing balance method is

$$\text{EMI} = \frac{PX_i \times (1+i)^n}{(1+i)^n - 1}$$

(ii) The values of P = ₹ 700000

Interest Rate, $i = 12\% \div 12 = 0.01$

and loan duration, $n = 30 \times 12$ [∵ 1 year = 12 months]

$$= 360 \text{ months}$$

(iii) EMI for 30 years,

$$\text{EMI} = \frac{700000 \times 0.01 \times (1.01)^{360}}{(1.01)^{360} - 1}$$

$$= \frac{700000 \times 0.01 \times 35.949}{35.949 - 1}$$

$$\left[\because \frac{1}{0.02781668} = 35.949\right]$$

$$= \frac{251643}{34.949}$$

$$\approx ₹\ 7200.29$$

Or

Now, EMI for 20 years,

Loan duration = 20 × 12 = 240 months

$$\therefore \quad \text{EMI} = \frac{700000 \times 0.01 \times (1.01)^{240}}{(1.01)^{240} - 1}$$

$$\Rightarrow \quad (1.01)^{240} = \frac{1}{0.091805}$$

$$= 10.893$$

$$\Rightarrow \quad \text{EMI} = \frac{700000 \times 0.01 \times 10.893}{10.893 - 1}$$

$$= \frac{7000 \times 10.893}{9.893}$$

$$= \frac{76251}{9.893}$$

$$\approx ₹\ 7707.57$$

CHAPTER 19

Compound Growth Rate and Depreciation

In this Chapter...

- Compound Annual Growth Rate
- Depreciation

Compound Annual Growth Rate

The Compound Annual Growth Rate (CAGR) is the rate of return that would be required for an investment to grow from its beginning balance to its ending balance, assuming the profits were re-invested at the end of each period of the investments life span.

Formula and Calculation of the Compound Annual Growth Rate (CAGR)

$$\text{CAGR} = \left(\frac{\text{EV}}{\text{BV}}\right)^{\frac{1}{n}} - 1$$

where, EV = Ending value

BV = Beginning value

n = number of years

EXAMPLE 1. Assume an investment's starting value is ₹ 20000 and it grows to ₹ 50000 in 3 years. Calculate CAGR (Compounded Annual Growth Rate).

[use $(2.5)^{1/3} = 1.355$] **[CBSE 2024]**

Sol. Given, beginning value of investment = ₹ 20000

Ending value of an investment = ₹ 50000

Number of years, $n = 3$

$$\therefore \quad \text{CAGR} = \left(\frac{EV}{BV}\right)^{\frac{1}{n}} - 1$$

$$= \left(\frac{50000}{20000}\right)^{\frac{1}{3}} - 1$$

$$= (2.5)^{\frac{1}{3}} - 1 = 1.355 - 1 = 0.355$$

Hence, CAGR is $(0.355 \times 100)\% = 35.5\%$

EXAMPLE 2. Mr. Ahmed invested ₹ 10000 in a company's fund. His yearly investment values are shown in the table given below

Year	0	1	2	3
Amount (in ₹)	10000	14000	14700	22056

Calculate CAGR of his investment.

(given $(2.205)^{1/3} = 1.3016$)

Sol. Given, beginning value of an investment (BV) = ₹ 10000

Ending value of an investment (EV) = ₹ 22050

Number of years (n) = 3

$$\text{So,} \quad \text{CAGR} = \left(\frac{\text{EV}}{\text{BV}}\right)^{\frac{1}{3}} - 1 \quad \left[\because \text{CAGR} = \left(\frac{\text{EV}}{\text{BV}}\right)^{\frac{1}{n}} - 1\right]$$

$$= \left(\frac{22050}{10000}\right)^{1/3} - 1$$

$$= (2.205)^{1/3} - 1 = 1.3016 - 1 = 0.3016$$

$$\Rightarrow \quad \text{CAGR} = (0.3016 \times 100)\% = 30.16\%$$

Hence, CAGR is 30.16%.

Depreciation

Depreciation is defined as the reduction of original cost of fixed asset such as buildings, furniture, machinery, vehicles, etc over a period of time due to wear and tear. Original cost is the total price at which the asset was purchased.

- **Useful life** The useful life of an asset is an accounting estimate of the number of years it is likely to remain in service for the purpose of cost effective revenue generation.
- **Scrap value/Salvage value** The value of a depreciable asset at the end of its useful life is called its scrap value.
- **Total Depreciation** The difference between the original value of an asset and the scrap value is the total depreciation.
- **Book value** The book value of an asset on a given data is the original value of the asset minus the accumulated depreciation at time.

Methods of Computing Depreciation

There are several methods of computing depreciations. Following are some commonly used methods.

(i) Straight line method or linear method of depreciation.
(ii) Reducing balance method
(iii) Sum of the years digits method
(iv) Double declining balance method
(v) Units of production method.

Linear or Straight Line Method

The linear or straight line depreciation method is the simplest and most widely used method. In this method, the value of an asset is reduced uniformly over each period until it reaches to its Scrap or Salvage value. The formula of calculating annual depreciation by linear method is given below

Annual depreciation

$$= \frac{\text{Original cost of an asset} - \text{Scrap value}}{\text{Useful life of asset in years}}$$

EXAMPLE 3. An asset costing ₹ 80000 has a useful life of 8 yr, if annual depreciation is ₹ 9000, then find the scrap value of asset.

Sol. Here, original cost = ₹ 80000
Annual depreciation = ₹ 9000
Useful life = 8 yr

$$\therefore \text{ Annual depreciation} = \frac{\text{Original cost} - \text{Scrap value}}{\text{Useful life of asset in year}}$$

$$\Rightarrow \quad 9000 = \frac{80000 - \text{Scrap value}}{8}$$

$$\Rightarrow \quad \text{Scrap value} = 80000 - 72000 = ₹\ 8000$$

EXAMPLE 4. A machine costing ₹ 50000 has a useful life of 4 yr. The estimated scrap value is ₹ 10000. Find the rate of depreciation per annum.

Sol. $$\text{Annual depreciation} = \frac{\text{Original value} - \text{Scrap value}}{\text{Useful life of asset}}$$

$$= \frac{50000 - 10000}{4} = ₹\ 10000$$

Original cost of machine – Salvage value of machine
= ₹ (50000 – 10000) = ₹ 40000

∴ Depreciation rate percent

$$= \left(\frac{\text{Annual Depreciation}}{\text{Original Cost of Machine} - \text{Scrap Value of Machine}}\right)$$

$$= \left(\frac{10000}{40000} \times 100\right)\% = 25\%$$

EXAMPLE 5. The annual depreciation of a car is ₹ 30000, if the scrap value of the car after 15 yr is ₹ 50000, then find the original cost of the car, when depreciation is linear.

Sol. (a) Here, Annual depreciation = ₹ 30000
Scrap value of car = ₹ 50000
Useful life of car = 15 yr
Let the original cost of car is ₹ x.

$$\therefore \text{ Annual depreciation} = \frac{\text{Original cost} - \text{Scrap value}}{\text{Useful life of car in year}}$$

$$30000 = \frac{x - 50000}{15}$$

$$\Rightarrow \quad x = 450000 + 50000 = 500000$$

Hence, the original cost of car was ₹ 500000.

EXAMPLE 6. A Lenevo computer, whose cost is ₹ 600000 will depreciate to a scrap value of ₹ 60000 in 5 yr. Using linear method of depreciation, find the book value of the computer at the end of third year.

Sol. We know, C = Original cost of computer = ₹ 600000
S = Scrap value of computer = ₹ 60000
n = useful life of computer = 5 yr

∴ Annual depreciation

$$= \frac{\text{Original cost of computer} - \text{Scrap value}}{\text{Useful life of computer in years}}$$

$$= \frac{600000 - 60000}{5} = \frac{540000}{5} = ₹\ 108000$$

The book value at the end of third year

$$= 600000 - 3 \times 108000 = ₹\ 276000$$

EXAMPLE 7. An asset costing ₹ 150000 is expected to have a useful life of 5 yr and scrap value of ₹ 30000. Find the annual depreciation charge and the depreciation rate by using the linear depreciation method.

Sol. Given, original cost of an assets = ₹ 150000

Scrap value of an assets = ₹ 30000

Useful life = 5 yr

∴ Annual depreciation

$$= \frac{\text{Original cost of an asset} - \text{Scrap value}}{\text{Useful life of asset in years}}$$

$$= \frac{150000 - 30000}{5} = \frac{120000}{5} = 24000$$

Hence, annual depreciation is ₹ 24000.

∴ Depreciation rate percent

$$= \left[\left(\frac{\text{Annual depreciation}}{\text{Original value} - \text{Scrap value}}\right) \times 100\right]\%$$

$$= \left[\left(\frac{24000}{120000}\right) \times 100\right]\%$$

$$= 20\%$$

EXAMPLE 8. An asset costs ₹ 450000 with an estimated useful life of 5 yr and a scrap value of ₹ 100000. Using linear depreciation method, find the annual depreciation of the asset and construct a yearly depreciation schedule.

[CBSE 2023]

Sol. We have, C = Original value = ₹ 450000

S = Salvage value = ₹ 100000

and n = Useful life = 5 yr

The annual depreciation D is given by

$$D = \frac{C - S}{n} = ₹\left(\frac{450000 - 100000}{5}\right) = ₹\ 70000$$

At the first year the accumulated depreciation is ₹ 70000. Hence, the depreciation charge for the first year is ₹ 70000.

The book value at the end of first year or in the beginning of second year is ₹ (450000 − 70000)

= ₹ 380000

Depreciation Schedule

Year	Book value (Beginning of year)	Depreciation	Book value (End of year)
1	₹ 450000	₹ 70000	₹ 380000
2	₹ 380000	₹ 70000	₹ 310000
3	₹ 310000	₹ 70000	₹ 240000
4	₹ 240000	₹ 70000	₹ 170000
5	₹ 170000	₹ 70000	₹ 100000

Exam Pattern Exercise

Part A - Objective Type Questions

Multiple Choice Type Questions

1 The formula for calculating CAGR is

(a) CAGR $=\left(\frac{PV}{FV}\right)^{n}-1$ (b) CAGR $=\left(\frac{FV}{PV}\right)^{n}-1$

(c) CAGR $=\left(\frac{FV}{PV}-1\right)^{\frac{1}{n}}$ (d) CAGR $=\left(\frac{FV}{PV}\right)^{\frac{1}{n}}-1$

2 Sarita invested ₹ 180000 in a mutual fund in year 2020. If the value of mutual fund increased to ₹ 225000 in year 2024, then compound annual growth rate of his investment is

[use $(1.25)^{1/4}=1.057$]

(a) 5.7% (b) 6.57%
(c) 3.57% (d) None of these

3 Deepa invested ₹ 30000 in a mutual fund in 2015. The value of mutual fund increased to ₹ 48000 in year 2020. Calculate the compound annual growth rate of his investment. [given $(1.6)^{1/5}=1.099$]

(a) 9.5% (b) 8.5%
(c) 8.9% (d) 9.9%

4 A machine costing ₹ C would reduce to ₹ 10000 in 7 yr, if annual depreciation charge is ₹ 10000, then the value of C is

(a) ₹ 80000 (b) ₹ 70000
(c) ₹ 60000 (d) ₹ 75000

5 A machine costing ₹ 125000 has scrap value of ₹ 25000. If annual depreciation charge is ₹ 12500, then useful life of the vehicle is

(a) 5 years (b) 12 years
(c) 8 years (d) 4 years

6 A mobile phone costs ₹ 12000 and its scrap value after a useful life of 3 years is ₹ 3000. Then, the book value of the mobile phone at the end of 2 years is [CBSE 2024]

(a) ₹ 3000 (b) ₹ 6000
(c) ₹ 5000 (d) ₹ 7000

Assertion-Reason Based Questions

Directions (Q. Nos. 7-9) *In the questions given below are two statements labelled as Assertion (A) and Reason (R). In the context of the two statements, which one of the following is correct?*

(a) Both A and R are correct; R is the correct explanation of A
(b) Both A and R are correct; R is not the correct explanation of A
(c) A is correct; R is incorrect
(d) R is correct; A is incorrect

7 **Assertion (A)** Ms. Rachna has invested ₹ 6 lakhs in a financial plan and differ the completion of 4 yr, she received a sum of ₹ 10 lakhs, then the Compound Annual Growth Rate (CAGR) is 10%.

Reason (R) Compound Annual Growth Rate

$$(\text{CAGR})=\left[\left(\frac{\text{Final value}}{\text{Present value}}\right)^{\frac{1}{n}}-1\right]\times 100$$

8 **Assertion (A)** A machine costing ₹45000 has a useful life of 4 yr and the machine has a no scrap value at the end of its life, then annual depreciation is ₹ 11250.

Reason (R) Annual depreciation

$$=\frac{\text{Original cost}-\text{Scrap value}}{\text{Useful life of asset in year}}$$

9 **Assertion (A)** A machine costing ₹ 40000 (originally) has a final scrap value of ₹ 10000. If the annual depreciation is ₹ 5000, then the estimated useful life of the machine is 6.

Reason (R) The value of depreciable assets at the end of its useful life is called the scrap value.

Part B - Descriptive Questions

Very Short Answer Type Questions

10 Mrs Vandana invested ₹ 35000 in a shares of company and reinvested the earnings every year in byuying the shares of the same company. At the end of 5 years, the value of shares increased to ₹ 56000. Calculate the compound annual growth rate of her investment.

11 An asset costing ₹ 15000 is expected to have a useful life of 5 years. If scrap value of the asset is ₹ 3000, then find annual depreciation charge.

12 A machine costing ₹ x would reduce to ₹ 10000 in 7 years. If annual depreciation charge is ₹ 10000, then find the value of x.

Short Answer Type Questions

13 A mainframe computer whose cost is ₹ 500000 will depreciate to a scrap value of ₹ 50000 in 5 yr. Using linear method of depreciation, find the book value of the computer at the end of third year.

14 Saurab invested ₹ 35000 in a annual fund in 2016. The value of mutual fund increased to ₹ 45000 in year 2021. Calculate the compounded annual growth rate of his investment.

[given, $(1.28)^{1/5} = 1.0506$]

15 Vishal invested ₹ 32000 in a mutual fund in year 2015. The value of mutual fund increased to ₹ 57600 in year 2021. Calculate the compound growth rate of his investment.
[given, $(1.8)^{1/6} = 1.1029$]

16 A machine costing ₹ 150000 has scrap value of ₹ 22500. If annual depreciation charge is ₹ 8500, then find useful life of the machine.

17 A machine costing ₹ 30000 has a scrap value of ₹ 4000, if annual depreciation charge is ₹ 2000. Find its useful life in years.

18 Mrs. Jyothsha invested ₹ 35000 in a mutual fund. In 2015, the value of mutual fund increased to ₹ 56000. In 2020, find the CAGR.

19 Mr. Rahim invested ₹ 20000 in company's fund. His yearly investment values are shown below.

Year	0	1	2	3
Amount (₹)	20000	22000	22400	23100

Calculate CAGR of above investment.

[given, $(1.155)^{1/3} = 1.0492$]

20 The value of a bike depriciate 15% every year. By what percentage will the value of the car decreases after 3 yr.

21 Define Compound Annual Growth Rate (CAGR) and give the formula for calculating CAGR. Using the formula, calculate CAGR of Vikas's investment given below:

Vikas invested ₹10000 in a stock of a company for 6 yr. The value of his investment at the end of each year is given below:

Year 1	Year 2	Year 3	Year 4	Year 5	Year 6
₹11000	₹11500	₹11650	₹11800	₹12200	₹14000

[Use $(1.4)^{1/6} = 1.058$] [CBSE 2023]

Long Answer Type Questions

22 Neha invested ₹ 20000 in a mutual fund in year 2010. The value of mutual fund increased to ₹ 32000 in year 2015. Calculate the compound annual growth rate of her investment.

23 Mr Chandan Mishra invested ₹ 5000 in a fund at the beginning of year 2018 and by the end of year 2018 his investment was worth ₹ 9000. Next year market crashed and he lost ₹ 3000 and ending up with ₹ 6000 at the end of year 2019. Next year i.e. 2020 he gained ₹ 4500 and ending up with ₹ 10500 at the end of the year. Find CAGR of his investment.

24 Mr Rakesh invested ₹ 10000 in a company's fund. His yearly investment values are shown in the table given below

Year	0	1	2	3
Amount (in ₹)	10000	13000	11000	9400

Calculate CAGR of his investment.

Case Study Based Questions

25 A recent accounting graduate opened a new business and installed a computer system that costs ₹ 45200. The computer system will be depreciated linearly over 3 years and will have a scrap value of ₹ 0.

(i) What is the rate of depreciation?

(ii) Give a linear equation that describes the computer system's book value at the end of tth year, where $0 \le t \le 3$.

(iii) What will be the computer system's book value at the end of the first year and a half?

26 Suppose there is a business and its profit figures (yearly basis) are as below.

Year	1	2	3	4	5	6
Profit (in lakhs ₹)	5	10	16	18	22	25

[given, $(5)^{1/5} = 1.38$]

Answer the following questions.

(i) Find the absolute return.

(ii) Find the simple annual growth rate.

(iii) Find the compound annual growth rate.

Hints & Solutions

1. (d) 2. (a) 3. (d) 4. (a)
5. (c) 6. (a) 7. (d) 8. (a)
9. (b) 10. 9.8% 11. ₹ 2400 12. 8000

13. We have, C = Original cost of computer = ₹ 500000
S = Scrap value of computer = ₹ 50000
n = Useful life of computer = 5 yr
Let D be the annual depreciation.

Then, $D = \frac{C - S}{n} \Rightarrow D = \frac{(500000 - 50000)}{5} = 90000$

Hence, annual depreciation is ₹ 90000.
∴ The value at the end of the third year
= ₹ (500000 − 3 × 90000)
= ₹ (500000 − 270000) = ₹ 230000

14. 5.06% 15. 10.29%

16. Here, original cost of machine = ₹ 150000
Scrap value of machine = ₹ 22500
Annual depreciation = ₹ 8500

$\therefore$ Annual depreciation $= \frac{\text{Original cost} - \text{Scrap value}}{\text{Useful life of machine in year}}$

Useful life of machine $= \frac{150000 - 22500}{8500} = \frac{127500}{8500} = 15$ yr

17. Given, original cost of machine = ₹ 30000
Annual depreciation = ₹ 2000
Scrap value of machine = ₹ 4000
Let useful life of machine is n yr.

$\therefore$ Annual depreciation $= \frac{\text{Original Cost} - \text{Scrap value}}{\text{Useful life of machine in years}}$

$\Rightarrow \quad 2000 = \frac{30000 - 4000}{n} \Rightarrow n = \frac{26000}{2000} = 13$

Hence, useful life is 13 yr.

18. Here, begining value of the investment (BV) = ₹ 35000
Ending value of investment (EV) = ₹ 56000
Number of years (n) = 5

So, CAGR $= \left(\frac{\text{EV}}{\text{BV}}\right)^{\frac{1}{n}} = \left(\frac{56000}{35000}\right)^{\frac{1}{5}} - 1$

$= (1.6)^{1/5} - 1 = 1.098 - 1 = 0.098$

Hence, CAGR = (0.098 × 100)% = 9.8%

19. 4.92% 20. 38.59

21. Given, present value = ₹ 10000
Final value = ₹ 14000 and $n = 6$ yr

So, CAGR $= \left(\frac{\text{Final value}}{\text{Present value}}\right)^{\frac{1}{n}} - 1 = \left(\frac{14000}{10000}\right)^{\frac{1}{6}} - 1$

$= (1.4)^{\frac{1}{6}} - 1 = 1.058 - 1 \qquad [\because (1.4)^{\frac{1}{6}} = 1.058]$

$= 0.058$

Hence, CAGR = (0.058 × 100)% = 5.8%

22. Given beginning value of the investment = ₹ 20000
Final value of the investment = ₹ 32000
Number of years = 5

So, CAGR $= \left(\frac{FV}{PV}\right)^{\frac{1}{n}} - 1 = \left(\frac{32000}{20000}\right)^{\frac{1}{5}} - 1 = (1.6)^{\frac{1}{5}} - 1$

Let $x = (1.6)^{\frac{1}{5}}$

$\Rightarrow \log x = \frac{1}{5}\log 1.6 = \frac{1}{5} \times 0.2041 = 0.04082$

$\Rightarrow \quad x = \text{antilog } 0.04082 = 1.098$

So, CAGR = 1.098 − 1 = 0.098
Hence, CAGR = 0.098 × 100% = 9.8%

23. 28% 24. 2.05%

25. Original cost = ₹ 45200
Scrap value = ₹ 0
Useful life span = 3 yr

(i) Rate of depreciation $= \frac{\text{Original cost} + \text{Scrap value}}{\text{Useful life span}}$

$= \frac{0 - 45200}{3} = \frac{-45200}{3}$

(ii) The linear equation is given as

$$y(t) = \frac{-45200}{3}t + 45200$$

(iii) $y\left(1\frac{1}{2}\right) = y(1.5) = \frac{-45200}{3}(1.5) + 45200$

$= -22600 + 45200 = ₹\ 22600$

26. Given, present value = 5
Final value = 25

(i) Absolute return $= \frac{\text{Final value} - \text{Present value}}{\text{Present value}} \times 100\%$

$= \frac{25 - 5}{5} \times 100$ ss$= \frac{20}{5} \times 100 = 400\%$

(ii) Simple annual growth rate $= \frac{\text{Absolute return}}{n}$

$= \frac{400\%}{5} = 80\%$

(iii) The compound annual growth rate

$= \left[\left(\frac{\text{Final value}}{\text{Present value}}\right)^{\frac{1}{n}} - 1\right] \times 100\%$

$= \left[\left(\frac{25}{5}\right)^{\frac{1}{5}} - 1\right] \times 100\%$

$= [(5)^{\frac{1}{5}} - 1] \times 100\%$

$= (1.38 - 1) \times 100\% = 38\%$

CHAPTER 20

Linear Programming

In this Chapter...

- Linear Programming Problem (LPP)
- Mathematical Formulation and Different Types of LPP

The term 'programming' means 'planning' and it refers to a particular plan of action from amongst several alternatives for maximising or minimising a function under given restrictions such as maximising profit or minimising cost, etc. The term 'linear' means that 'all inequations' or 'equations used' and the function to be maximised or minimised are linear. Thus, linear programming is a technique for resource utilisation.

Linear Programming Problem (LPP)

Linear programming is a mathematical method for maximising and minimising a linear function of several variables subject to the constraints on the variables that satisfy the linear inequation.

Here, linear function is known as objective function and constraints are linear inequalities.

Mathematical Form of LPP

The mathematical form of a linear programming problem is as follows

Objective function, $Z = c_1x + c_2y$,

Subject to constraints are $a_1x + b_1y \le d_1$, $a_2x + b_2y \le d_2$, etc., and $x \ge 0$, $y \ge 0$.

Important Terms Related to LPP

- **Constraints** The linear inequations or inequalities or restrictions on the variables of a linear programming problem are called constraints.

  The conditions $x \ge 0$, $y \ge 0$ are called **non-negative restrictions.**
- **Optimisation Problem** A problem which need to maximise or minimise a linear function subject to certain constraints as determined by a set of linear inequalities is called an optimisation problem. Linear programming problems are special type of optimisation problems.
- **Objective Function** A linear function of two or more variables which has to be maximised or minimised under the given restrictions is called an objective function. The variables used in the objective function are called **decision variables.**
- **Optimal Value** The maximum or minimum value of an objective function is known as the optimal value of LPP.
- **Feasible and Infeasible Region** The common region determined by all the constraints including non-negative constraints $x, y \ge 0$ of a linear programming problem is called the feasible region or solution region. The region other than feasible region is called an infeasible region.
- **Bounded and Unbounded Region** A feasible region of a system of linear inequalities is said to be bounded, if it can be enclosed within lines. Otherwise, it is said to be unbounded region, i.e. the feasible region does extend infinitely in any direction.
- **Feasible and Infeasible Solution** Points within and on the boundary of the feasible region, represents feasible solution of the constraints. Any point outside the feasible region is called an infeasible solution.

- **Optimal Feasible Solution** A feasible solution at which the objective function has optimal value (maximum or minimum), is called the optimal solution or optimal feasible solution of the linear programming problem.
- **Optimisation Technique** The process of obtaining the optimal solution of the linear programming problem is called optimisation technique.
- **Corner Point** A corner point of a feasible region is a point of intersection of two boundary lines in the region.

Some Important Theorems

Theorem 1 Let R be the feasible region (convex polygon) for a linear programming problem and $Z = ax + by$ be the objective function. When Z has an optimal value (maximum or minimum), where the variables x and y are subject to constraints described by linear inequalities, this optimal value must occur at a corner point (vertex) of the feasible region.

Theorem 2 Let R be the feasible region for a linear programming problem and $Z = ax + by$ be the objective function.

If R is **bounded**, then the objective function Z has both a maximum and minimum value on R and each of these occurs at a corner point (vertex) of R. If R is **unbounded**, then a maximum or minimum value of the objective function may not exist. However, if it exists, it must occur at a corner point of R.

Graphical Method for Solving Linear Programming Problem

This method of solving linear programming problem is referred as **corner point method.** The process of this method is as follows

I. Draw the graph of each linear equation.

II. Find the feasible region of the LPP and determine its corner points (vertices).

III. Determine the value of objective function $Z = ax + by$ at each corner point.

(a) When the feasible region is **bounded**, then find maximum (M) and minimum (m) values of Z.

(b) When the feasible region is **unbounded**, then

(i) The maximum (M) value of Z exist, if the open half plane determined by $ax + by > M$ has no point in common with the feasible region. Otherwise, Z has no maximum value.

(ii) The minimum (m) value of Z exist, if the open half plane determined by $ax + by < m$ has no point in common with the feasible region. Otherwise, Z has no minimum value.

(c) It two corner points of the feasible region are both optimal solution of the same type, i.e. both produce the same maximum or minimum, then any point on the line segment joining these two points is also an optimal solution of the same type.

EXAMPLE 1. Find the minimum and maximum value of function $Z = 3x + 4y$ subject to constraints are $x \geq 0$, $y \geq 0$, $x + 2y \leq 10$ and $2x + y \leq 14$.

Sol. Given objective function is $Z = 3x + 4y$.

Subject to constraints are

$$x + 2y \leq 10;\ 2x + y \leq 14;\ x \geq 0,\ y \geq 0$$

Given constraints can be written in equation form as

$$x + 2y = 10 \quad \text{...(i)}$$

$$2x + y = 14 \quad \text{...(ii)}$$

and $x = 0,\ y = 0$

Table for line $x + 2y = 10$

x	0	10
y	5	0

$\therefore$ Line $x + 2y = 10$ passes through the points (0, 5) and (10, 0). On putting (0, 0) in inequality $x + 2y \leq 10$, we get $0 \leq 10$ [true]

So, the half plane is towards the origin.

Table for line $2x + y = 14$

x	0	7
y	14	0

$\therefore$ Line $2x + y = 14$ passes through the points (0, 14) and (7, 0).

On putting (0, 0) in inequality $2x + y \leq 14$, we get

$0 \leq 14$ [true]

So, the half plane lies towards the origin.

Intersection point of Eqs. (i) and (ii) is B (6, 2).

On plotting the graph and shading the common region, we get the feasible region $OABC$.

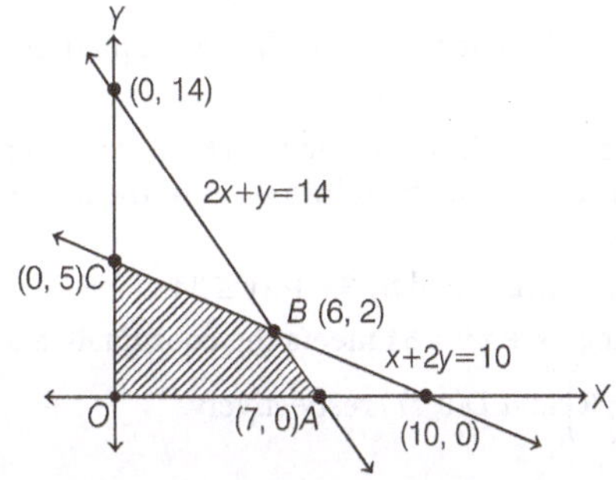

The value of Z at corner points are given below

Corner points	$Z = 3x + 4y$
$O(0, 0)$	$Z = 0 + 0 = 0$ (minimum)
$A(7, 0)$	$Z = 3 \times 7 + 0 = 21$
$B(6, 2)$	$Z = 3 \times 6 + 4 \times 2 = 26$ (maximum)
$C(0, 5)$	$Z = 0 + 4 \times 5 = 20$

Hence, the minimum value of Z is 0 at (0, 0) and maximum value of Z is 26 at (6, 2).

EXAMPLE 2. Solve the following linear programming problem graphically

Maximise $Z = 50x + 30y$

Subject to $2x + y \leq 18, 3x + 2y \leq 34, x, y \geq 0$ **[CBSE 2025]**

Sol.

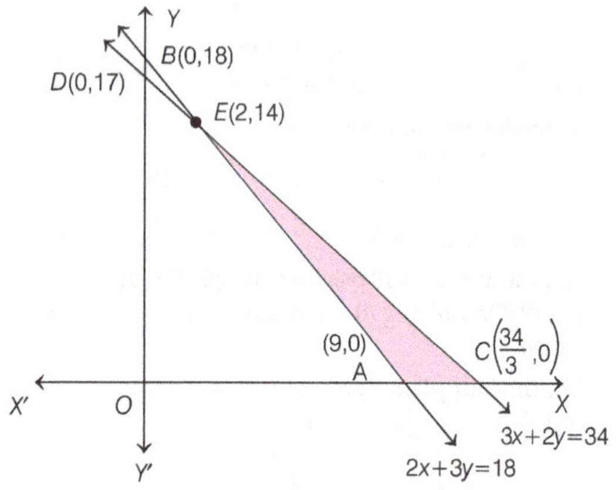

First, we will convert the given inequation into equations, we obtain the following equation are

$$2x + y = 18,$$
$$3x + 2y = 34,$$
$$x = 0 \text{ and } y = 0$$

Region represented by $2x + y \geq 18$.

The line $2x + y = 18$ meets the coordinate axes at $A(9, 0)$ and $B(0, 18)$, respectively.

By joining these points we obtain the line

$$2x + y = 18$$

Clearly, (0, 0) does not satisfy the inequation

$$2x + y \geq 18$$

So, the region in XY-plane which does not contain the origin represents the solution set of the inequation $2x + y \geq 18$.

Region represented by $3x + 2y \leq 34$.

The line $3x + 2y = 34$ meets the coordinate axes at $C\left(\frac{34}{3}, 0\right)$ and $D(0, 17)$ respectively.

By joining these points we obtain the line $3x + 2y = 34$. Clearly, (0, 0) satisfies the inequation $3x + 2y \leq 34$. So, region containing the origin represents the solution set of the inequation $3x + 2y \leq 34$.

The corner points of the feasible region are

$$A(9, 0), C\left(\frac{34}{3}, 0\right) \text{ and } E(2, 14).$$

Corner point	$Z = 50x + 30y$
$A(9, 0)$	$50 \times 9 + 3 \times 0 = 450$
$C\left(\frac{34}{3}, 0\right)$	$50 \times \frac{34}{3} + 30 \times 0 = \frac{1700}{3}$
$E(2, 14)$	$50 + 2 + 30 \times 14 = 520$

$\therefore$ The maximum value of Z is $\frac{1700}{3}$ at the point $\left(\frac{34}{3}, 0\right)$.

EXAMPLE 3. Solve the following problem graphically.

Minimise and maximise $Z = 3x + 9y$, subject to constraints $x + 3y \leq 60, x + y \geq 10, x \leq y; x \geq 0, y \geq 0$

Sol. Given objective function is maximise and minimise $Z = 3x + 9y$. Subject to constraints,

$$x + 3y \leq 60 \quad \text{...(i)}$$
$$x + y \geq 10 \quad \text{...(ii)}$$
$$x \leq y \quad \text{...(iii)}$$
and $$x \geq 0, y \geq 0 \quad \text{...(iv)}$$

Table for line $x + 3y = 60$ is

x	60	0
y	0	20

So, the line $x + 3y = 60$ is passing through (60, 0) and (0, 20).

On putting (0, 0) in the inequality $x + 3y \leq 60$, we get

$$0 + 0 \leq 60, \text{ which is true.}$$

So, the half plane is towards the origin.

Table for line $x + y = 10$ is

x	10	0
y	0	10

So, the line $x + y = 10$ is passing through (10, 0) and (0, 10).

On putting (0, 0) in the inequality $x + y \geq 10$, we get

$$0 + 0 \geq 10, \text{ which is not true.}$$

So, the half plane is away from the origin.

Table for line $x = y$ is

x	0	5
y	0	5

So, the line $x = y$ is passing through (0, 0) and (5, 5).

On putting (0, 4) is the inequality $x \leq y$, we get

$$0 \leq 4, \text{ which is true.}$$

So, the half plane is towards the Y-axis.

Also, $x \geq 0$ and $y \geq 0$, so the region lies in the I quadrant. On drawing these lines on graph paper, we get the following graph

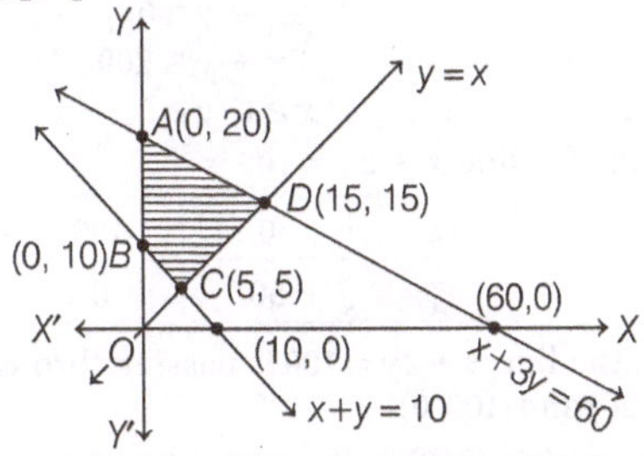

The intersection point of lines corresponding to Eqs. (i) and (iii) is D (15, 15) corresponding to Eqs. (ii) and (iii) is C(5, 5).

Now, shading the common region, we get the feasible region $ABCDA$.

Hence, the region is bounded and corner points of feasible region are A(0, 20), B(0, 10), C(5, 5) and D(15, 15).

The values of Z at corner points are given below

Corner points	$Z = 3x + 9y$
A(0, 20)	$Z = 3(0) + 9(20) = 180$
B(0, 10)	$Z = 3(0) + 9(10) = 90$
C(5, 5)	$Z = 3(5) + 9(5) = 60$
D(15, 15)	$Z = 3(15) + 9(15) = 180$

Here, minimum value of Z is 60 which occur at point C(5, 5) and maximum value of Z is 180 which occur at two points A(0, 20) and D(15, 15). So, each point on the line segment AD will give the maximum value of Z.

EXAMPLE 4. Solve the following LPP graphically. Minimise $Z = 5x + 10y$, subject to the constraints $x + 2y \leq 120$, $x + y \geq 60$, $x - 2y \geq 0$ and $x, y \geq 0$.

Sol. Our problem is to minimise

$$Z = 5x + 10y \quad \text{...(i)}$$

Subject to constraints

$$x + 2y \leq 120 \quad \text{...(ii)}$$

$$x + y \geq 60 \quad \text{...(iii)}$$

$$x - 2y \geq 0 \quad \text{...(iv)}$$

and $\quad x \geq 0,\ y \geq 0$

Firstly, draw the graph of the line $x + 2y = 120$.

x	0	120
y	60	0

Put (0, 0) in the inequality $x + 2y \leq 120$, we get

$$0 + 2 \times 0 \leq 120 \Rightarrow 0 \leq 120, \text{ which is true.}$$

So, the half plane is towards the origin. Secondly, draw the graph of the line $x + y = 60$.

x	0	60
y	60	0

Put (0, 0) in the inequality $x + y \geq 60$, we get

$$0 + 0 \geq 60 \Rightarrow 0 \geq 60, \text{ which is false.}$$

So, the half plane is away from the origin.

Thirdly, draw the graph of the line $x - 2y = 0$.

x	0	10
y	0	5

Put (5, 0) in the inequality $x - 2y \geq 0$, we get

$$5 - 2 \times 0 \geq 0 = 5 \geq 0, \text{ which is true.}$$

So, the half plane is towards the X-axis. Since, $x, y \geq 0$ the feasible region lies in the first quadrant.

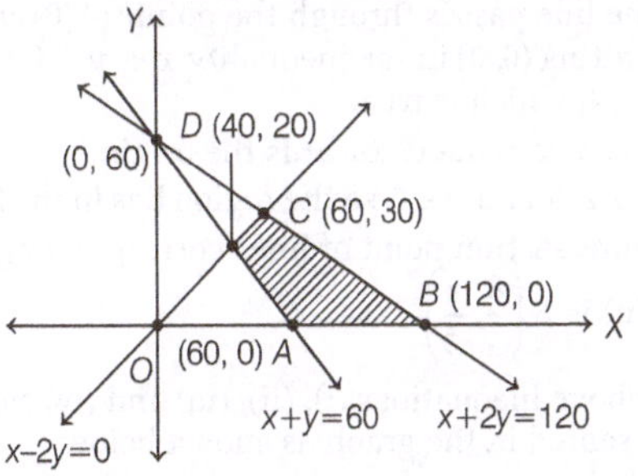

On solving equations $x - 2y = 0$ and $x + y = 60$, we get D(40, 20) and solving equations $x - 2y = 0$ and $x + 2y = 120$, we get C (60, 30).

So, the feasible region is $ABCDA$. The corner points of the feasible region are A (60, 0), B (120, 0), C (60, 30) and D (40, 20). The values of Z at these points are as follows

Corner points	$Z = 5x + 10y$
A (60, 0)	300 (minimum)
B (120, 0)	600
C (60, 30)	600
D (40, 20)	400

So, the minimum value of Z is 300 at the point (60, 0).

EXAMPLE 5. Find graphically, the maximum value of $Z = 2x + 5y$, subject to constraints are $2x + 4y \leq 8$, $3x + y \leq 6$, $x + y \leq 4$, $x \geq 0$, $y \geq 0$.

Sol. We have the following LPP

Maximise $Z = 2x + 5y$

Subject to constraints,

$$2x + 4y \leq 8 \text{ or } x + 2y \leq 4 \quad \text{...(i)}$$

$$3x + y \leq 6 \quad \text{...(ii)}$$

$$x + y \leq 4 \quad \text{...(iii)}$$

and $\quad x \geq 0,\ y \geq 0 \quad$ ...(iv)

Table for line $x + 2y = 4$ is

x	4	0
y	0	2

So, the line passes through the points (4, 0) and (0, 2).

On putting (0, 0) in the inequality $x + 2y \leq 4$, we get

$$0 + 0 \leq 4, \text{ which is true.}$$

So, the half plane is towards the origin.

Table for line $3x + y = 6$ is

x	2	0
y	0	6

So, the line passes through the points (2, 0) and (0, 6).
On putting (0, 0) in the inequality $3x + y \le 6$, we get

$0 + 0 \le 6$, which is true.

So, the half plane is towards the origin.
Table for line $x + y = 4$ is

x	4	0
y	0	4

So, the line passes through the points (4, 0) and (0, 4).
On putting (0, 0) in the inequality $x + y \le 4$, we get
$0 + 0 \le 4$, which is true.

So, the half plane is towards the origin.

Also, $x \ge 0$ and $y \ge 0$, so the region lies in the I quadrant.

The intersection point of lines corresponding to Eqs. (i) and (ii) is $B\left(\frac{8}{5}, \frac{6}{5}\right)$.

The above inequations (i), (ii), (iii) and (iv) can be represented in the graph as shown below

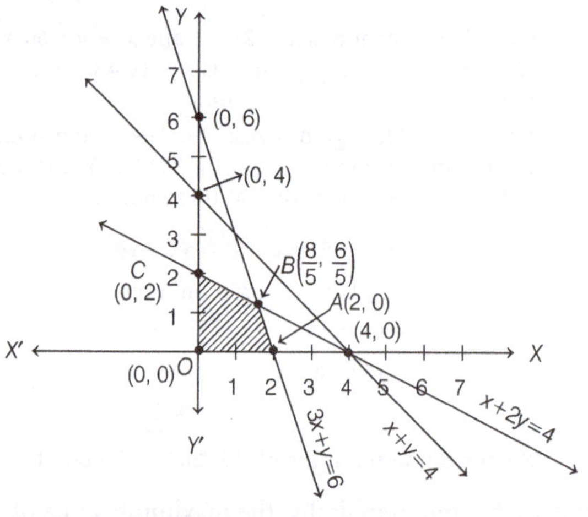

Clearly, the feasible region is $OABCO$, where corner points are $O(0, 0)$, $A(2, 0)$, $B\left(\frac{8}{5}, \frac{6}{5}\right)$ and $C(0, 2)$.

The values of Z at corner points are given below

Corner points	$Z = 2x + 5y$
$O(0, 0)$	$Z = 2 \times 0 + 5 \times 0 = 0$
$A(2, 0)$	$Z = 2 \times 2 + 5 \times 0 = 4$
$B\left(\frac{8}{5}, \frac{6}{5}\right)$	$Z = 2 \times \frac{8}{5} + 5 \times \frac{6}{5} = \frac{46}{5} = 9.2$
$C(0, 2)$	$Z = 2 \times 0 + 5 \times 2 = 10$

Hence, the maximum value of Z is 10 at $C(0, 2)$.

EXAMPLE 6. Maximise and minimise $Z = x + 2y$, subject to the constraints are $x + 2y \ge 100$, $2x - y \le 0$, $2x + y \le 200$ and $x, y \ge 0$. Solve the LPP graphically.

Sol. Our problem is to minimise and maximise

$$Z = x + 2y \quad \text{...(i)}$$

Subject to constraints, $x + 2y \ge 100$ ...(ii)

$2x - y \le 0$ ...(iii)

$2x + y \le 200$ ...(iv)

and $x \ge 0, y \ge 0$ ...(v)

Table for line $x + 2y = 100$ is

x	0	100
y	50	0

So, the line $x + 2y = 100$ is passing through the points (0, 50) and (100, 0).

On putting (0, 0) in the inequality $x + 2y \ge 100$, we get

$0 + 2 \times 0 \ge 100 \Rightarrow 0 \ge 100$, which is not true.

So, the half plane is away from the origin.

Table for line $2x - y = 0$ is

x	0	10
y	0	20

So, the line $2x - y = 0$ is passing through the points (0, 0) and (10, 20).

On putting (5, 0) in the inequality $2x - y \le 0$, we get

$2 \times 5 - 0 \le 0 \Rightarrow 10 \le 0$, which is not true.

So, the half plane is towards Y-axis.

Table for line $2x + y = 200$ is

x	0	100
y	200	0

So, the line $2x + y = 200$ is passing through the points (0, 200) and (100, 0).

On putting (0, 0) in the inequality $2x + y \le 200$, we get

$2 \times 0 + 0 \le 200 \Rightarrow 0 \le 200$, which is true.

So, the half plane is towards the origin. Also, $x, y \ge 0$.

So, the region lies in the I quadrant.

On solving equations $2x - y = 0$ and $x + 2y = 100$, we get $B(20, 40)$.

Again, solving the equations $2x - y = 0$ and $2x + y = 200$, we get $C(50, 100)$.

Clearly, the feasible region is $ABCDA$.

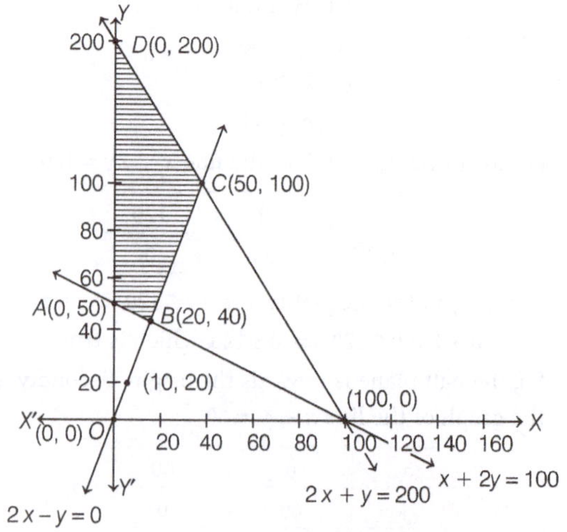

The corner points of the feasible region are $A(0, 50)$, $B(20, 40)$, $C(50, 100)$ and $D(0, 200)$.

The values of Z at corner points are given below

Corner points	$Z = x + 2y$
$A(0, 50)$	$Z = 0 + 2 \times 50 = 100$
$B(20, 40)$	$Z = 20 + 2 \times 40 = 100$
$C(50, 100)$	$Z = 50 + 2 \times 100 = 250$
$D(0, 200)$	$Z = 0 + 2 \times 200 = 400$

The maximum value of Z is 400 at $D(0, 200)$ and the minimum value of Z is 100 at all the points on the line segment joining $A(0, 50)$ and $B(20, 40)$.

EXAMPLE 7. Determine graphically the minimum value of the objective function $Z = -50x + 20y$, subject to constraints are $2x - y \geq -5$, $3x + y \geq 3$, $2x - 3y \leq 12$ and $x \geq 0$, $y \geq 0$.

Sol. Given objective function is

Minimise $Z = -50x + 20y$

subject to constraints, $2x - y \geq -5$ ...(i)

$3x + y \geq 3$ ...(ii)

$2x - 3y \leq 12$ ...(iii)

and $x \geq 0, y \geq 0$ ...(iv)

Table for line $2x - y = -5$ is

x	$-5/2$	0
y	0	5

So, the line passes through the points $\left(\frac{-5}{2}, 0\right)$ and $(0, 5)$.

On putting $(0, 0)$ in the inequality $2x - y \geq -5$, we get

$0 - 0 \geq -5 \Rightarrow 0 \geq -5$, which is true.

So, the half plane is towards the origin.

Table for line $3x + y = 3$ is

x	0	1
y	3	0

So, the line passes through the points $(0, 3)$ and $(1, 0)$.

On putting $(0, 0)$ in the inequality $3x + y \geq 3$, we get

$0 + 0 \geq 3 \Rightarrow 0 \geq 3$, which is not true.

So, the half plane is away from the origin.

Table for line $2x - 3y = 12$ is

x	0	6
y	-4	0

On putting $(0, 0)$ in the inequality $2x - 3y \leq 12$, we get

$0 - 0 \leq 12 \Rightarrow 0 \leq 12$, which is true.

So, the half plane is towards the origin.

Also, $x \geq 0$ and $y \geq 0$, so the region lies in the I quadrant.

On drawing the graph of each linear equation, we get the following graph. In first quadrant, these equations has no intersection point.

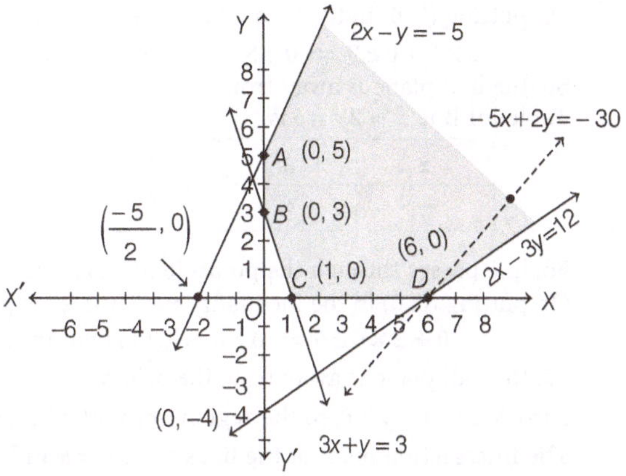

Thus, we get the common shaded region $ABCD$, which gives the feasible region and it is unbounded.

The corner points of feasible region are $A(0, 5)$, $B(0, 3)$, $C(1, 0)$ and $D(6, 0)$.

The value of Z at corner points are given below

Corner points	$Z = -50x + 20y$
$A(0, 5)$	$Z = -50(0) + 20(5) = 100$
$B(0, 3)$	$Z = -50(0) + 20(3) = 60$
$C(1, 0)$	$Z = -50(1) + 20(0) = -50$
$D(6, 0)$	$Z = -50(6) + 20(0) = -300$

Here, feasible region is unbounded so the minimum and maximum value may or may not be exist.

Now, we draw a dotted line of inequation

$-50x + 20y < -300$ or $-5x + 2y < -30$

Here, we see that half plane determined by $-5x + 2y < -30$ has a point in common with the feasible region.

Hence, no minimum value exists.

EXAMPLE 8. Minimise $Z = x + 2y$, subject to constraints are $2x + y \geq 3$, $x + 2y \geq 6$ and $x, y \geq 0$.

(i) Show that the minimum of Z occurs at more than two points.

(ii) Also, check whether the point $P(5, 2)$ lies inside the shaded portion, if it lies inside the shaded region, then find the distance between the origin and point.

Sol. Our problem is to minimise, $Z = x + 2y$ ...(i)

subject to constraints,

$2x + y \geq 3$ ...(ii)

$x + 2y \geq 6$ ...(iii)

and $x \geq 0, y \geq 0$ ...(iv)

Table for line $2x + y = 3$ is

x	0	3/2
y	3	0

So, line passes through the points $(0, 3)$ and $\left(\frac{3}{2}, 0\right)$.

On putting (0, 0) in the inequality $2x + y \geq 3$, we get

$2 \times 0 + 0 \geq 3 \Rightarrow 0 \geq 3$, which is not true.

So, the half plane is away from the origin.

Table for line $x + 2y = 6$ is

x	0	6
y	3	0

So, line passes through the points (0, 3) and (6, 0).

On putting (0, 0) in the inequality $x + 2y \geq 6$, we get

$0 + 2 \times 0 \geq 6 \Rightarrow 0 \geq 6$, which is not true.

So, the half plane is away from the origin.

Also, $x \geq 0$ and $y \geq 0$, so the region lies in the I quadrant.

The intersection point of the lines $x + 2y = 6$ and $2x + y = 3$ is $B(0, 3)$.

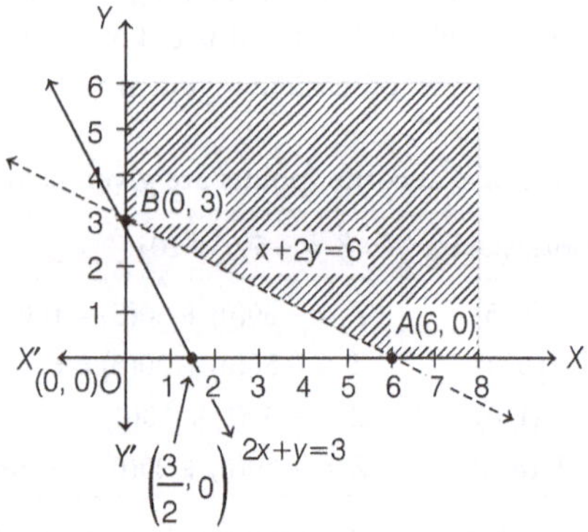

The corner points of the feasible region are $A(6, 0)$ and $B(0, 3)$.

The values of Z at the corner points are given below

Corner points	$Z = x + 2y$
$A(6, 0)$	$Z = 6 + 2 \times 0 = 6$
$B(0, 3)$	$Z = 0 + 2 \times 3 = 6$

As the feasible region is unbounded, therefore 6 may or may not be the minimum value of Z.

For this we draw a dotted graph of the inequality $x + 2y < 6$ and check whether the resulting half plane has points in common with a feasible region or not.

It can be seen that the feasible region has no common point with $x + 2y < 6$.

Therefore, the minimum value of Z is 6.

Thus, the minimum value of Z occurs at more than 2 points. [the value of Z is minimum at every point on the line segment AB]

Let $f(x, y) = x + 2y - 6$

At point $P(5, 2)$, $f(5, 2) = 5 + 2 \times 2 - 6 = 3 > 0$

Hence, point lies inside the shaded region.

Now, distance between O and $P = \sqrt{(5-0)^2 + (2-0)^2}$

$= \sqrt{25 + 4}$

$= \sqrt{29}$

$= 5.39$

Topic Practice 1

1 In the given figure, the feasible region for a LPP is shown. Determine the maximum and minimum value of $Z = x + 2y$.

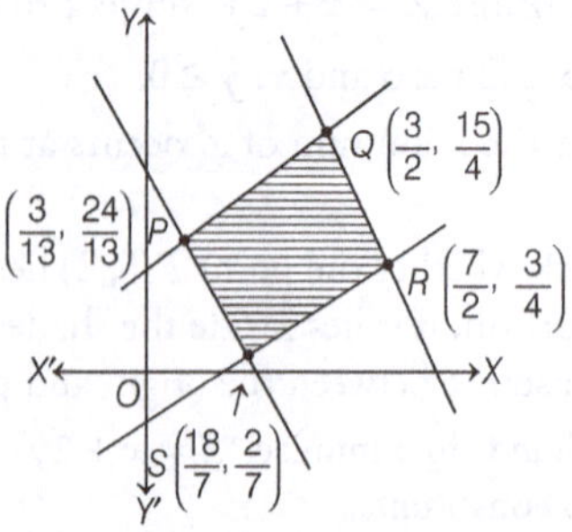

2 The corner points of the feasible region determined by the system of linear constraints are (0, 3), (1, 1) and (3, 0). Let $Z = px + qy$, where $p, q > 0$. Find the condition in p and q, so that the minimum of Z occurs at (3, 0) and (1, 1).

3 Maximise the following linear programming problems graphically.

(i) $Z = 2x + 3y$

subject to constraints

$x + 2y \leq 10, 2x + y \leq 14$ and $x \geq 0, \ y \geq 0$

(ii) $Z = 300x + 190y$

subject to constraints

$x + y \leq 24, 2x + y \leq 32, x \geq 0, y \geq 0$ **[CBSE 2023]**

(iii) $Z = 6x + 11y$

subject to constraints

$2x + y \leq 104, x + 2y \leq 76$ and $x \geq 0, y \geq 0$

(iv) $Z = x + y$

subject to constraints

$x - y \leq -1, -x + y \leq 0$ and $x, y \geq 0$ **[CBSE 2024]**

(v) $Z = -x + 2y$,

subject to constraints are

$x \geq 3, x + y \geq 5, x + 2y \geq 6$ and $x, y \geq 0$.

(vi) $Z = 105x + 90y$ under the following constraints. $x + y \leq 50, 2x + y \leq 80, x \geq 20$ and $x \geq 0, y \geq 0$

(vii) $Z = 4x + y$

subject to the constraints

$x + y \leq 50, 3x + y \leq 90, x \geq 10; x, y \geq 0.$

(viii) $Z = 20x + 10y$

subject to the constraints

$x + 2y \le 28, 3x + y \le 24, x \ge 2; x, y \ge 0$

(ix) $Z = 7x + 10y$

subject to the constraints

$4x + 6y \le 240, 6x + 3y \le 240, x \ge 10$

and $x \ge 0, y \ge 0$

4 Minimise the following linear programming problems graphically.

(i) $Z = 2x + 3y$

Subject to constraints

$2x + 5y \ge 100, 8x + 5y \le 200; x, y \ge 0$

(ii) Minimise $Z = 3x + 5y$

Subject to constraints

$x + 3y \ge 3, x + y \ge 2$ and $x, y \ge 0.$

(iii) Minimise $Z = x + y$

Subject to constraints

$3x + 2y \ge 12, x + 3y \ge 11$ and $x \ge 0, y \ge 0$

(iv) $Z = 18x + 10y$

Subject to the constraints

$4x + y \ge 20, 2x + 3y \ge 30$ and $x, y \ge 0$

(v) $Z = 6x + 3y$

Subject to the constraints

$4x + y \ge 80, x + 5y \ge 115, 3x + 2y \le 150,$

$x \ge 0, y \ge 0.$

5 Solve the following LPP graphically $Z = 3x + 2y$

Subject to constraints are

$x + 2y \le 10, 3x + y \le 15$ and $x \ge 0, y \ge 0.$

Also, determine the area of the feasible region.

Hints & Solutions

1. Hint From the given figure, corner points of feasible region are

$P\left(\frac{3}{13}, \frac{24}{13}\right), Q\left(\frac{3}{2}, \frac{15}{4}\right), R\left(\frac{7}{2}, \frac{3}{4}\right)$ and $S\left(\frac{18}{7}, \frac{2}{7}\right)$

The value of objective function at corner points are given below

Corner points	$Z = x + 2y$
$P\left(\frac{3}{13}, \frac{24}{13}\right)$	$Z = \frac{3}{13} + 2 \times \frac{24}{13} = \frac{51}{13} = 3.92$
$Q\left(\frac{3}{2}, \frac{15}{4}\right)$	$Z = \frac{3}{2} + 2 \times \frac{15}{4} = \frac{6+30}{4} = \frac{36}{4} = 9$
$R\left(\frac{7}{2}, \frac{3}{4}\right)$	$Z = \frac{7}{2} + 2 \times \frac{3}{4} = \frac{10}{2} = 5$
$S\left(\frac{18}{7}, \frac{2}{7}\right)$	$Z = \frac{18}{7} + 2 \times \frac{2}{7} = \frac{22}{7} = 3.14$

Ans. Maximum and minimum values of Z are 9 and 3.14.

2. Given corner points of feasible region are (0,3), (1,1) and (3,0). The value of objective function at these corner points are given below

Corner points	$Z = px + qy$
(0, 3)	$Z = p \times 0 + q \times 3 = 3q$
(1, 1)	$Z = p \times 1 + q \times 1 = p + q$
(3, 0)	$Z = p \times 3 + q \times 0 = 3p$

Also, given that the minimum of Z occurs at (3, 0) and (1, 1).

$\therefore \quad 3p = p + q \Rightarrow 2p = q$

3. (i) Similar as Example 1.

Hint

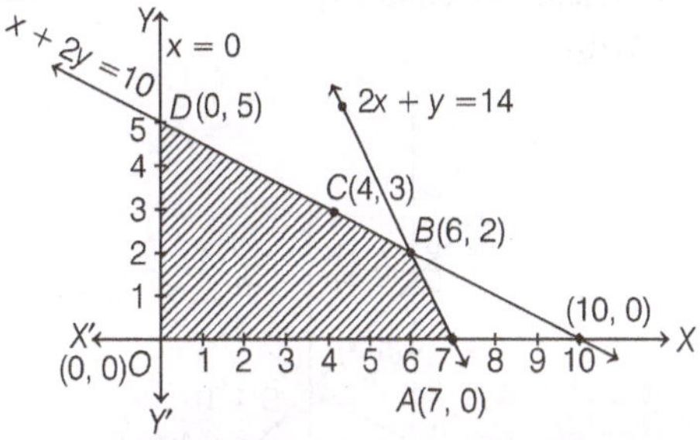

The values of Z at corner points are given below

Corner points	$Z = 2x + 3y$
$O(0, 0)$	$Z = 2 \times 0 + 3 \times 0 = 0$
$A(7, 0)$	$Z = 2 \times 7 + 3 \times 0 = 14$
$B(6, 2)$	$Z = 2 \times 6 + 3 \times 2 = 18$
$D(0, 5)$	$Z = 2 \times 0 + 3 \times 5 = 15$

Ans. The maximum value of Z is 18 at the point $B(6, 2)$.

(ii) Similar as Example 1.

Maximise $Z = 300x + 190y$, subject to constraints

$x + y \le 24, 2x + y \le 32, x \ge 0, y \ge 0$

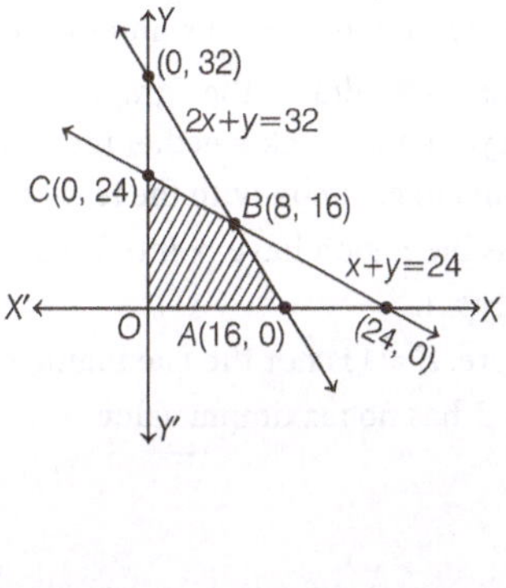

We draw the line $x + y = 24$, $2x + y = 32$ and shade the region satisfied the given inequalities.

The coordinates of the corner points O, A, B, C are (0, 0), (16, 0), (8, 16) and (0, 24) respectively.

Ans. The maximum value of Z is 5440 at $B(8, 16)$.

(iii) Similar as Example 1.

Ans. Maximum $Z = 440$ at (44, 16)

(iv) **Hint**

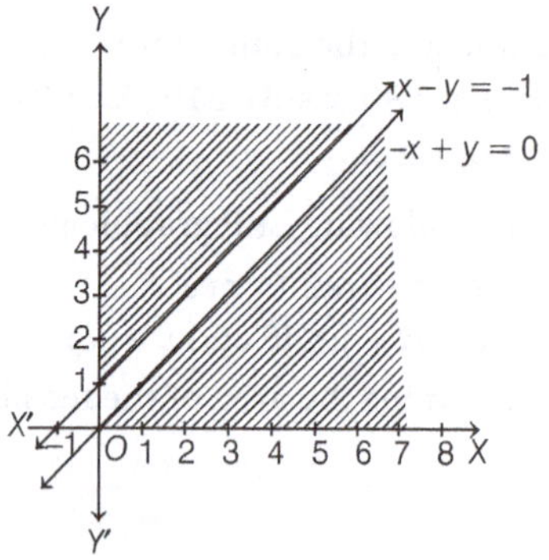

Ans. Hence, there is no feasible region and thus Z has no maximum value.

(v) Similar as Example 7.

Hint

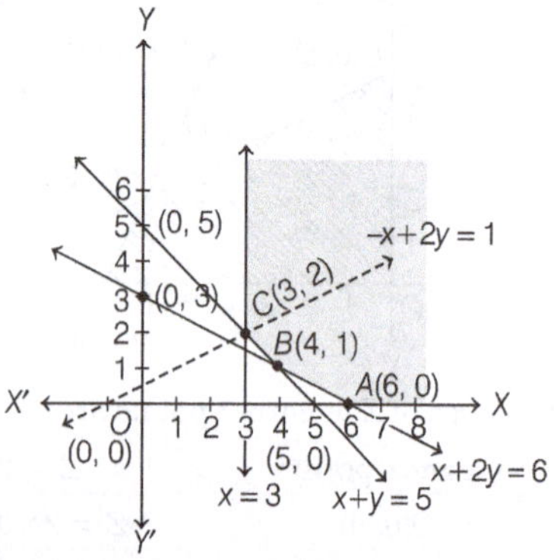

Corner points	$Z = -x + 2y$
$A(6, 0)$	$Z = -6 + 2 \times 0 = -6$
$B(4, 1)$	$Z = -4 + 2 \times 1 = -2$
$C(3, 2)$	$Z = -3 + 2 \times 2 = 1$

As the feasible region is unbounded, therefore $Z = 1$ may or may not be the maximum value.

For this, we draw the graph of the inequality $-x + 2y > 1$ and check whether the resulting half plane has points in common with the feasible region or not.

The feasible region have points in common with the $-x + 2y > 1$.

Therefore, $Z = 1$ is not the maximum value.

Hence, Z has no maximum value.

(vi) **Hint**

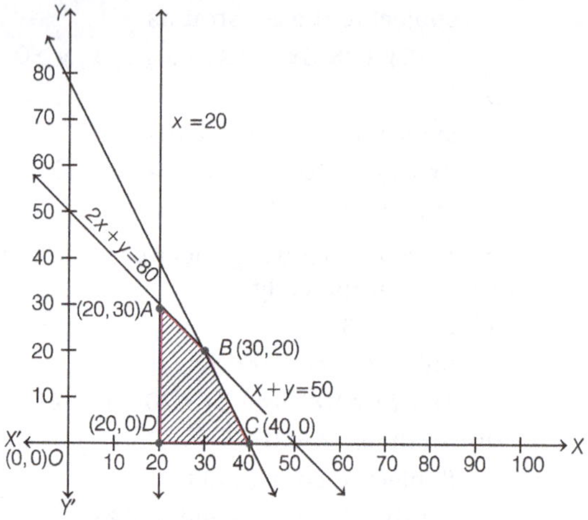

Corner points	Value of Z
$D(20, 0)$	2100
$C(40, 0)$	4200
$B(30, 20)$	4950 (max)
$A(20, 30)$	4800

Ans. Maximum value of Z is 4950, when $x = 30$, $y = 20$.

(vii) Similar as part (vi).

Ans. Maximum $Z = 120$ at (30, 0)

(viii) Maximum $Z = 200$ at (4, 12)

(ix) Maximum $Z = 410$ at (30, 20)

4. (i) Similar as Example 2.

Hint

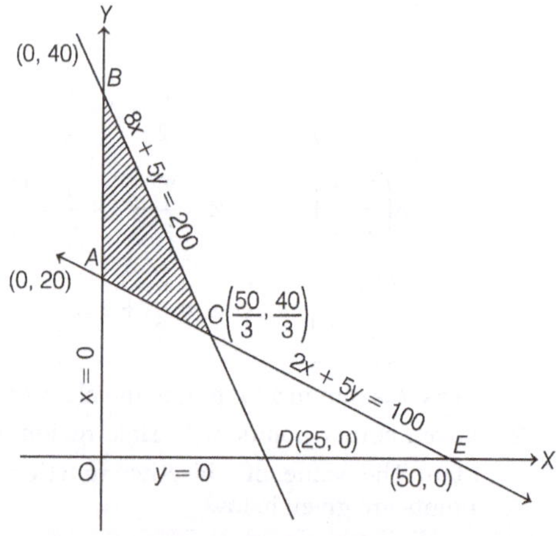

Corner points	$Z = 2x + 3y$
$A(0, 20)$	$Z = 2 \times 0 + 3 \times 20 = 60$
$B(0, 40)$	$Z = 2 \times 0 + 3 \times 40 = 120$
$C\left(\frac{50}{3}, \frac{40}{3}\right)$	$Z = 2 \times \frac{50}{3} + 3 \times \frac{40}{3} = 73.33$

The minimum value of Z is 60 at point $A(0, 20)$.

(ii) Similar as Example 8.

Ans. Minimum $Z = 7$ at $\left(\frac{3}{2}, \frac{1}{2}\right)$

(iii)

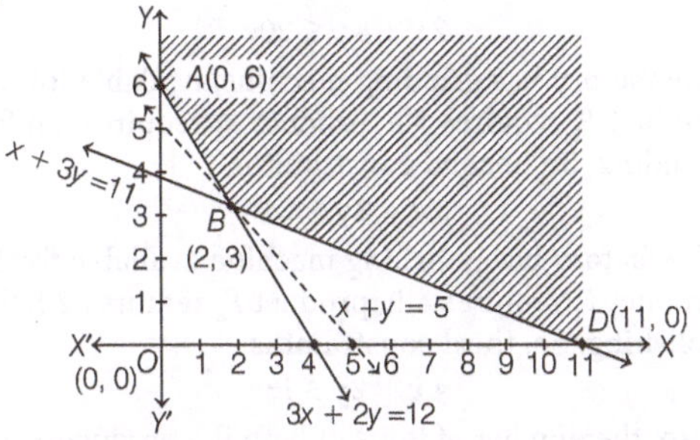

The values of Z at corner points are given below

Corner points	$Z = x + y$
$A(0, 6)$	$Z = 0 + 6 = 6$
$B(2, 3)$	$Z = 2 + 3 = 5$
$D(11, 0)$	$Z = 11 + 0 = 11$

Thus, the minimum value of Z is 5 at the point $B(2, 3)$.

As the feasible region is unbounded, therefore 5 may or may not be the minimum value of Z. For this, we draw a dotted graph of the inequality $x + y < 5$ and check whether the resulting half plane has points in common with a feasible region or not. It can be seen that the feasible region has no common point with $x + y < 5$.

Therefore, the minimum value of Z is 5 at $B(2, 3)$.

(iv) Similar as Example 8.

Ans. Minimum value of Z is 134 at point $(3, 8)$.

(v) **Hint**

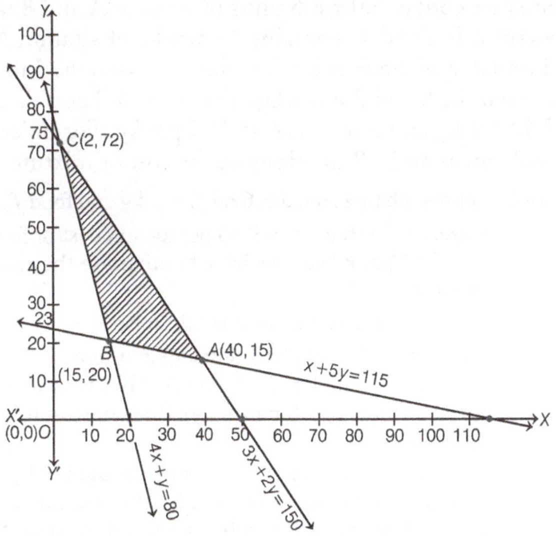

Corner points	Value of Z
$A(40, 15)$	285
$B(15, 20)$	150 (min)
$C(2, 72)$	228

Ans. Minimum $Z = 150$,

when $x = 15$, $y = 20$.

5. Hint

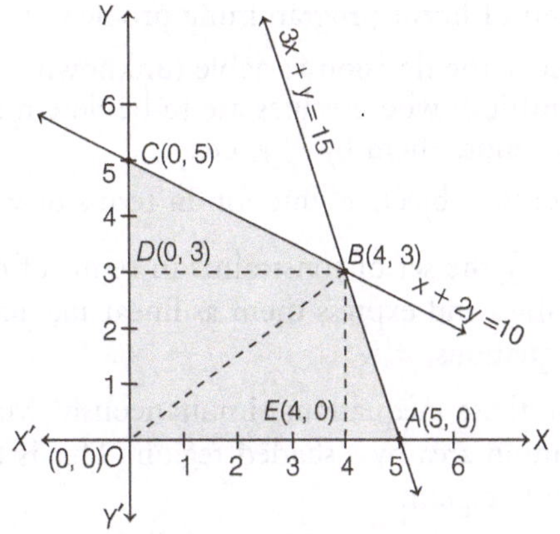

The corner points of the feasible region are

$O(0, 0)$, $A(5, 0)$, $B(4, 3)$ and $C(0, 5)$.

The values of Z at the corner points are given below

Corner points	$Z = 3x + 2y$
$O(0, 0)$	$Z = 3 \times 0 + 2 \times 0 = 0$
$A(5, 0)$	$Z = 3 \times 5 + 2 \times 0 = 15$
$B(4, 3)$	$Z = 3 \times 4 + 2 \times 3 = 18$
$C(0, 5)$	$Z = 3 \times 0 + 2 \times 5 = 10$

Therefore, the maximum value of Z is 18 at the point $B(4, 3)$.

$\therefore$ Area of feasible region

$= \text{Area of } \Delta BOC + \text{Area of } \Delta OAB$

$= \frac{1}{2} \times OC \times BD + \frac{1}{2} \times OA \times BE$

$= \frac{1}{2} \times 5 \times 4 + \frac{1}{2} \times 5 \times 3$

$= 10 + \frac{15}{2}$

$= 10 + 7.5$

$= 17.5$ sq units

Mathematical Formulation and Different Types of LPP

Mathematical Formulation of LPP

Formulation of the problem is the process of transforming the verbal description of a decision problem into a mathematical form. There is no particular method to formulate linear programming problem but following steps will be helpful in the formulation of linear programming problems.

I. Identify the decision variable (unknown quantities), whose values are to be determined and denote them by x, y, etc.

II. Write the objective function in terms of x and y.

III. Identify the set of constraints in terms of decision variables and express them as linear inequations or equations.

IV. Solve these inequations simultaneously. Mark the common area by a shaded region. This is the feasible region.

V. Determine the coordinates of all the vertices of the feasible region.

VI. Determine the value of the objective function at each vertex of the feasible region.

VII. Determine the value of x and y for which the objective function has maximum or minimum value.

EXAMPLE 1. A factory produces two products P_1 and P_2. Each of the product P_1 requires 2 h for moulding, 3 h for grinding and 4 h for polishing and each of the product P_2 requires 4 h for moulding, 2 h for grinding and 2 h for polishing. The factory has moulding machine available for 20 h, grinding machine for 24 h and polishing machine for 13 h. The profit is ₹ 5 per unit of P_1 and ₹ 3 per unit of P_2 and the factory can sell all that it produces.
Formulate the problem as a linear programming problem to maximise the profit.

Sol. Here, two unknown quantities are number of units of products P_1 and P_2. So, let decision variables be x and y, where x represents units of product P_1 and y represents units of product P_2 which are produced.

Now, the profit is ₹ 5 per unit of P_1 and ₹ 3 per unit of P_2 and we have to maximise the profit.

$\therefore$ Objective function is maximise, $Z = 5x + 3y$

The factory has moulding machine available for 20 h and product P_1 requires 2 h, product P_2 requires 4 h for moulding.

So, first constraint is

$$2x + 4y \le 20$$

The factory has grinding machine available for 24 h and product P_1 requires 3 h, product P_2 requires 2 h for grinding. So, second constraint is

$$3x + 2y \le 24$$

The factory has polishing machine available for 13 h and product P_1 requires 4 h, product P_2 requires 2 h for polishing. So, third constraint is

$$4x + 2y \le 13$$

Also, the number of units of both the products cannot be negative. So, non-negative restrictions or constraints are

$$x \ge 0,\ y \ge 0$$

Hence, the linear programming problem for the given problem is as follows:

Maximise $Z = 5x + 3y$

Subject to constraints, $2x + 4y \le 20$, $3x + 2y \le 24$
$4x + 2y \le 13$ and $x \ge 0$, $y \ge 0$

Different Types of LPP

1. Diet Problems

In these problems, we have to find out the amount of different kinds of constituents/nutrients included in a diet, so as to minimise the cost of the desired diet such that it contains a certain minimum amount of each constituent/nutrient.

EXAMPLE 2. A dietician wishes to mix two types of foods f_1 and f_2 in such a way that the vitamin contents of the mixture contain atleast 6 units of vitamin A and 8 units of vitamin B. Food f_1 contains 2 units/kg of vitamin A and 3 units/kg of vitamin B while food f_2 contains 3 units/kg of vitamin A and 2 units/kg of vitamin B. Food f_1 costs ₹ 50 per kg and food f_2 costs ₹ 75 per kg. Formulate the problem as an LPP to minimise the cost of mixture.

Sol. Let the mixture contains food $f_1 = x$ kg and food $f_2 = y$ kg.

Here, cost of food f_1 = ₹ 50 per kg and cost of food f_2 = ₹ 75 per kg and we have to minimise the cost of mixture.

So, the objective function is Minimise $Z = 50x + 75y$

Here, food f_1 contains 2 units/kg and food f_2 contains 3 units/kg of vitamin A. Also, mixture contains atleast 6 units of vitamin A. So, first constraint is $2x + 3y \ge 6$.

Similarly, food f_1 contains 3 units/kg and food f_2 contains 2 units/kg of vitamin B. Also, mixture contains atleast 8 units of vitamin B. So, second constraint is $3x + 2y \ge 8$.

Also, foods f_1 and f_2 cannot be negative, so $x \ge 0$, $y \ge 0$.
Thus, linear constraints are $2x + 3y \ge 6$, $3x + 2y \ge 8$ and $x, y \ge 0$.

Consider, the constraints as linear equations

$$2x + 3y = 6 \quad \text{...(i)}$$
$$3x + 2y = 8 \quad \text{...(ii)}$$
and $$x = 0, y = 0 \quad \text{...(iii)}$$

Table for line $2x + 3y = 6$ is

x	0	3
y	2	0

So, line passes through the points (0, 2) and (3, 0).

On putting (0, 0) in the inequality $2x + 3y \geq 6$, we get

$2(0) + 3(0) \geq 6 \Rightarrow 0 \geq 6$, which is not true.

So, the half plane is away from the origin.

Table for line $3x + 2y = 8$ is

x	0	8/3
y	4	0

So, line passes through the points (0, 4) and $\left(\frac{8}{3}, 0\right)$.

On putting (0, 0) in the inequality $3x + 2y \geq 8$, we get

$3(0) + 2(0) \geq 8 \Rightarrow 0 \geq 8$, which is not true.

So, the half plane is away from the origin.

Also, $x \geq 0$, $y \geq 0$, so the region lies in I quadrant.

On plotting these lines, we get the following graph.

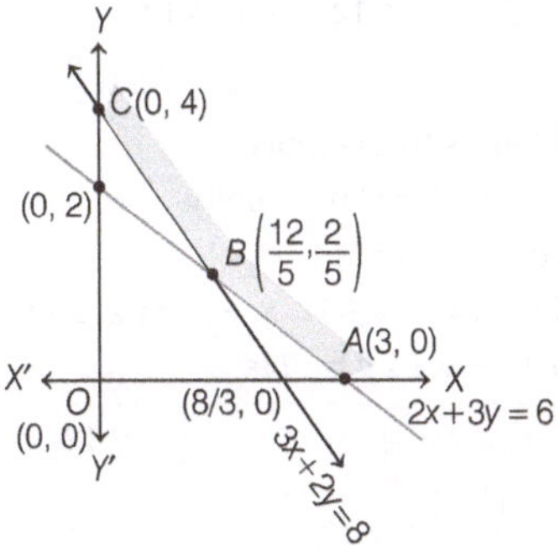

The intersection point of lines (i) and (ii) is $B\left(\frac{12}{5}, \frac{2}{5}\right)$.

Hence, the shaded region is a feasible region, which is unbounded.

Now, the corner points are A (3, 0), $B\left(\frac{12}{5}, \frac{2}{5}\right)$ and C (0, 4).

The values of Z at the corner points are given below

Corner points	$Z = 50x + 75y$
$A(3, 0)$	$Z = 50(3) + 75(0) = 150$
$B\left(\frac{12}{5}, \frac{2}{5}\right)$	$Z = 50\left(\frac{12}{5}\right) + 75\left(\frac{2}{5}\right) = 150$
$C(0, 4)$	$Z = 50(0) + 75(4) = 300$

As the feasible region is unbounded, therefore 150 may or may not be the minimum value of Z.

For this, we draw a graph of inequality $50x + 75y < 150$ or $2x + 3y < 6$ and check whether the resulting half plane has points in common with the feasible region or not. It can be seen that the feasible region has no common point with $2x + 3y < 6$.

Hence, minimum cost of the mixture will be ₹ 150 at each point of the line segment joining the points $A(3, 0)$ and $B\left(\frac{12}{5}, \frac{2}{5}\right)$.

2. Manufacturing Problems

In these problems, we have to find out the number of units of different products which should be produced and sold by a firm, when each product requires a fixed manpower, machine hours, labour hour per unit of product, etc, in order to make maximum profit.

EXAMPLE 3. A company manufactures two types of novelty souvenirs made of plywood. Souvenirs of type A requires 5 minutes each for cutting and 10 minutes each for assembling. Souvenirs of type B require 8 minutes each for cutting and 8 minutes each for assembling. Given that total time for cutting is 3 hours 20 minutes and for assembling 4 hours. The profit for type A souvenir is ₹ 100 each and for type B souvenir, profit is ₹ 120 each. How many souvenirs of each type should the company manufacture in order to maximize the profit? Formulate the problem as an LPP and solve it graphically.

Sol. Let x be the number of souvenirs of type A and y be the number of souvenirs of type B.

Then, we have the following table from the given data.

Machine	Number of souvenirs		Availability
	$A(x)$	$B(y)$	
Cutting machine	5 min	8 min	200 min
Assembling machine	10 min	8 min	240 min

Now, the mathematical model of the given problem is

Maximise, $Z = 100x + 120y$

Subject to constraints,

$5x + 8y \leq 200$ and $10x + 8y \leq 240$

or $5x + 4y \leq 120$ and $x, y \geq 0$.

Table for line $5x + 8y = 200$ is

x	0	40
y	25	0

So, the line passes through the points (0, 25) and (40, 0).

On putting (0,0) is the inequality $5x + 8y \leq 200$, we get $0 + 0 \leq 200$ or $0 \leq 200$ which is true.

So, the half plane is towards the origin.
Table for line $5x + 4y = 120$ is

x	0	24
y	30	0

So, the line passes through the points (0, 30) and (24, 0).
On putting (0, 0) in the inequality $5x + 4y \le 120$, we get $0 + 0 \le 120$ or $0 \le 120$, which is true.
So, the half plane is towards the origin.
Also, $x, y \ge 0$, so the region lies in the I quadrant.
The point of intersection of lines $5x + 8y = 200$ and $5x + 4y = 120$ is $B(8, 20)$.

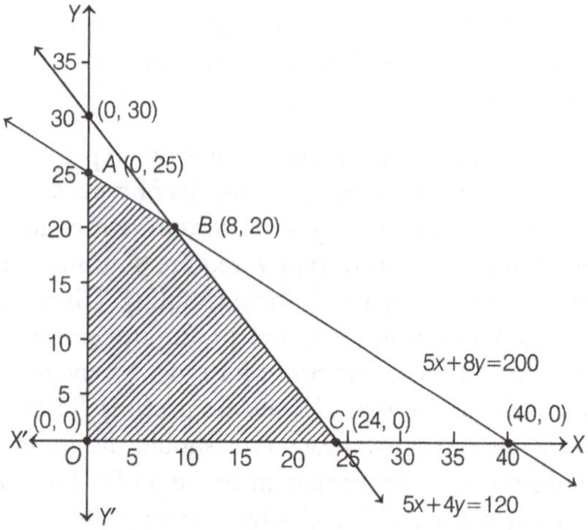

Therefore, the feasible region is $OABC$.
The corner points of the feasible region are $O(0, 0)$, $A(0, 25)$ and $B(8, 20)$ and $C(24, 0)$.
The value of Z at the corner points are

Corner points	$Z = 100x + 120y$
$O(0, 0)$	$Z = 100 \times 0 + 120 \times 0 = 0$
$A(0, 25)$	$Z = 100 \times 0 + 120 \times 25 = 3000$
$B(8, 20)$	$Z = 100 \times 8 + 120 \times 20 = 3200$ (maximum)
$C(24, 0)$	$Z = 100 \times 24 + 120 \times 0 = 2400$

The maximum value of Z is 3200 at point $B(8, 20)$.
Hence, the manufacturer should produce 8 novelty souvenirs of type A and 20 novely souvenirs of type B.

EXAMPLE 4. A manufacturer has three machines I, II and III Installed in his factory. Machine I and II are capable operated for at most 12 hours whereas machine III must be operated for at least 5 hours a day. He produces only two items M and N each requiring the use of all the three machines.
The number of hours required for producing 1 unit of M and N on three machines are given in the following table.

Items	Number of hours required on machines		
	I	II	III
M	1	2	1
N	2	1	1.25

He makes a profit of ₹ 600 and ₹ 400 on one unit of items M and N respectively. How many units of each item should he produce so as to maximize his profit assuming that he can sell all the items that he produced. What will be the maximum profit?

Sol. Let the manufacturer maker M type of item be x and N type of item be y.

Now, we construct the following table

Items	Number of items	Time of Machine I (in h)	Time of Machine II (in h)	Time of Machine III (in h)	Profit
M	x	x	$2x$	x	$600x$
N	y	$2y$	y	$1.25y$	$400y$
Total	$x + y$	$x + 2y$	$2x + y$	$x + 1.25y$	$600x + 400y$
Maximum time requires		≤ 12	≤ 12	≥ 5	

Our problem is to maximise

$$Z = 600x + 400y$$

Subject to constraints

$x + 2y \le 12$, $2x + y \le 12$, $x + 1.25y \ge 5$ and $x \ge 0$, $y \ge 0$

Table for line $x + 2y = 12$ is

x	0	12
y	6	0

So, the line passes through the points (0, 6) and (12, 0).
On putting (0, 0) in the inequality $x + 2y \le 12$, we get $0 + 0 \le 12$ or $0 \le 12$, which is true.
So, the half plane is towards the origin.
Table for line $2x + y = 12$ is

x	0	6
y	12	0

So, the line passes through the points (0, 12) and (6, 0).
On putting (0, 0) in the inequality $2x + y \le 12$, we get $0 + 0 \le 12$ or $0 \le 12$ which is true.
So, the half plane is towards the origin.
Table for line $x + 1.25y = 5$ is

x	0	5
y	4	0

So, the line passes through the points (0, 4) and (5, 0).

On putting (0, 0) in the inequality, we get

$$0+0 \geq 5 \text{ which is not true.}$$

So, the half plane is away from the origin.

Also, $x, y \geq 0$, so the region lies in the I quadrant.

The point of intersection of lines $x+2y=12$ and $2x+y=12$ is $C(4, 4)$.

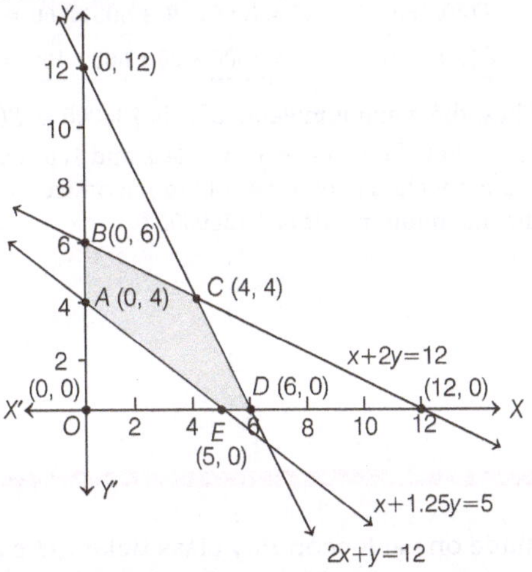

Therefore, the feasible region is $ABCDE$.

The corner points of the feasible region are A (0, 4), B (0, 6), C (4, 4), D (6, 0) and E (5, 0)

The value of Z at the corner points are

Corner points	$Z=600x+400y$
A (0, 4)	$Z=600\times 0+400\times 4=1600$
B (0, 6)	$Z=600\times 0+400\times 6=2400$
C (4, 4)	$Z=600\times 4+400\times 4=4000$ (Maximum)
D (6, 0)	$Z=600\times 6+0=3600$
E (5, 0)	$Z=600\times 5+0=3000$

Thus, the maximum value of Z is at C (4, 4).

Hence, the manufacturer should manufacture 4 items of type M and 4 items of type N.

EXAMPLE 5. An aeroplane can carry a maximum of 200 passengers. A profit of ₹ m is made on each executive class ticket and a profit of ₹ n is made on each economy class ticket, where m and n are obtained on multiplying first term and common ratio by 100 of the geometric series 10,60,360,... times. The airline reserves atleast 20 seats for executive class. However, atleast 4 times as many passengers prefer to travel by economy class than by the executive class. Determine, how many tickets of each type must be sold in order to maximise the profit for the airline. What is the maximum profit?

Sol. Given geometric series is 10, 60, 360, ...

Here, first term $(a)=10$ and common ratio $(r)=\frac{60}{10}=6$

According to the given condition,

$$m=a\times 100 \text{ and } n=r\times 100$$

$\therefore \quad m=10\times 100$ and $n=6\times 100$

$\Rightarrow \quad m=1000$ and $n=600$

Let x passengers travel by executive class and y passengers travel by economy class.

We construct the following table

Class	Number of tickets	Profit (in ₹)
Executive	x	$1000x$
Economy	y	$600y$
Total	$x+y$	$1000x+600y$

So, our problem is to maximise

$$Z=1000x+600y \quad \text{...(i)}$$

subject to constraints

$$x+y \leq 200 \quad \text{...(ii)}$$

$$x \geq 20 \quad \text{...(iii)}$$

$$y-4x \geq 0 \text{ or } y \geq 4x \quad \text{...(iv)}$$

and $\quad x \geq 0, y \geq 0 \quad$ ...(v)

Table for line $x+y=200$ is

x	0	200
y	200	0

So, line passes through the points (0, 200) and (200, 0).

On putting (0, 0) in the inequality $x+y \leq 200$, we get

$$0+0 \leq 200$$

$\Rightarrow \quad 0 \leq 200$, which is true.

So, the half plane is towards the origin.

Table for line $y=4x$ is

x	0	20
y	0	80

So, line passes through the points (0, 0) and (20, 80).

On putting (10, 0) in the inequality $y \geq 4x$, we get

$$0 \geq 4\times 10$$

$\Rightarrow \quad 0 \geq 40$, which is not true.

So, the half plane is towards Y-axis.

Now, draw the graph of the line $x=20$.

On putting (0, 0) in the inequality $x \geq 20$, we get

$$0 \geq 20, \text{ which is not true.}$$

So, the half plane is away from the origin.

Also, $x, y \geq 0$, so the region lies in the I quadrant.

On solving Eqs. (ii), (iii) and (iv), we get $A(20, 80)$, $B(40, 160)$ and $C(20, 180)$.

∴ Feasible region is $ABCA$.

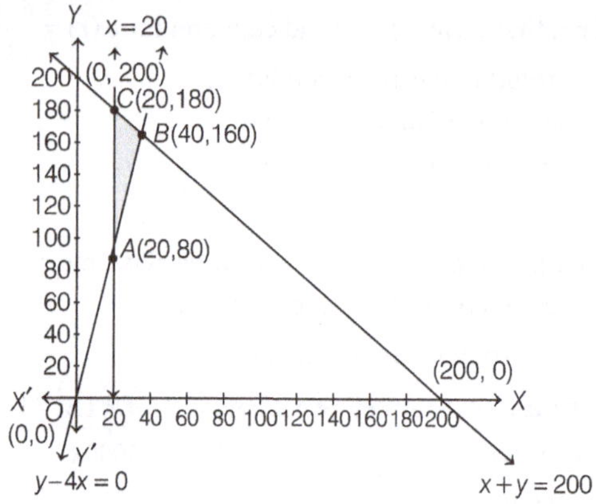

The corner points of the feasible region are $A(20, 80)$, $B(40, 160)$ and $C(20, 180)$.

The value of Z at the corner points are given below

Corner points	$Z = 1000x + 600y$
$A(20, 80)$	$Z = 1000 \times 20 + 600 \times 80 = 68000$
$B(40, 160)$	$Z = 1000 \times 40 + 600 \times 160 = 136000$
$C(20, 180)$	$Z = 1000 \times 20 + 600 \times 180 = 128000$

Thus, the maximum value of Z is 136000 at $B(40, 160)$.

Thus, 40 tickets of executive class and 160 tickets of economy class should be sold to maximise the profit and the maximum profit is ₹ 136000.

Topic Practice 2

1. Two tailors A and B earn ₹ 300 and ₹ 400 per day, respectively. A can stitch 6 shirts and 4 pairs of trousers while B can stitch 10 shirts and 4 pairs of trousers per day. To find how many days should each of them work and if it is desired to produce at least 60 shirts and 32 pairs of trousers at a minimum labour cost, formulate this as an LPP.

2. A small firm manufactures necklaces and bracelets. The total number of necklaces and bracelets that it can handle per day is at most 24. It takes one hour to make a bracelet and half an hour to make a necklace. The maximum number of hours available per day is 16. If the profit on a necklace is ₹ 100 and that on a bracelet is ₹300. Formulate linear programming problem for finding how many, each should be produced daily to maximise the profit, if it is being given that atleast one of each must be produced?

3. A firm has to transport atleast 1200 packages daily using large vans which carry 200 packages each and small vans which can take 80 packages each. The cost for engaging each large van is ₹ 400 and each small van is ₹ 200. Not more than ₹ 3000 is to be spent daily on the job and the number of large vans cannot exceed the number of small vans. Formulate this problem as an LPP given that the objective is to minimise cost.

4. An aeroplane can carry a maximum of 250 passengers. A profit of ₹ 1500 is made on each executive class ticket and a profit of ₹ 1000 is made on each economy class ticket. The airline reserves atleast 25 seats for executive class. However, atleast 3 times as many passengers prefer to travel by economy class than by executive class. Frame the linear programming problem to determine how many tickets of each type must be sold in order to maximise the profit for the airline?

5. A dietician wishes to mix two types of foods in such a way that the vitamin contents of the mixture contains atleast 8 units of vitamin A and 10 units of vitamin C. Food I contains 2 units per kg of vitamin A and 1 unit per kg of vitamin C. Food II contains 1 unit per kg of vitamin A and 2 units per kg of vitamin C. It costs ₹ 50 per kg to purchase food I and ₹ 70 per kg to purchase food II. Formulate the problem as a linear programming problem to minimise the cost of such mixture and find the minimise cost graphically.

6. A diet for a sick person must contain at least 4000 units of vitamins, 50 units of minerals and 1400 calories. Two foods, A and B, are available at a cost of ₹ 4 and ₹ 3 per unit respectively. If one unit of A contains 200 units of vitamins, 1 unit of minerals and 40 calories, and 1 unit of B contains 100 units of vitamins, 2 units of minerals and 40 calories, find what combination of foods should be used to have the least cost.

7 Suppose every gram of wheat provides 0.1 g of proteins and 0.25 g of carbohydrates, and the corresponding values for rice are 0.05 g and 0.5 g respectively. Wheat costs ₹ 5 and rice ₹ 20 per kilogram. The minimum daily requirements of proteins and carbohydrates for an average man are 50 g and 200 g respectively. In what quantities should wheat and rice be mixed in the daily diet to provide the minimum daily requirements of proteins and carbohydrates at minimum cost, assuming that both wheat and rice are to be taken in the diet?

8 A new cereal formed of a mixture of bran and rice contains atleast 88 g of protein and atleast 36 mg of iron. Knowing that bran contains 80 g of protein and 40 mg of iron per kilogram and the rice contains, 100 g of protein and 30 mg of iron per kilogram, then find the minimum cost of producing a kilogram of this new cereal, if bran costs ₹ 28 per kg and rice costs ₹ 25 per kg.

9 A factory manufactures two types of screws *A* and *B*, each type requiring the use of two machines, an automatic and a hand-operated. It takes 4 min on the automatic and 6 min on the hand-operated machines to manufacture a packet of screw '*A*' while it takes 6 min on the automatic and 3 min on the hand-operated machine to manufacture a packet of screw '*B*'. Each machine is available for atmost 4 h on any day. The manufacturer can sell a packet of screw '*A*' at a profit of 70 paise and screw '*B*' at a profit of ₹1.

Assuming that he can sell all the screws he manufactures, how many packets of each type should the factory owner produce in a day in order to maximize his profit? Formulate the above LPP and solve it graphically and find the maximum profit.

10 A company produces two types of goods, *A* and *B*, that require gold and silver. Each unit of type *A* requires 3 g of silver and 1 g of gold while that of type *B* requires 1 g of silver and 2 g of gold. The company can use at the most 9 g of silver and 8 g of gold. If each unit of type *A* brings a profit of ₹ 40 and that of type *B* ₹ 50, find the number of units of each type that the company should produce to maximize profit. Formulate the above LPP and solve it graphically and also find the maximum profit.

11 A manufacturer has employed 5 skilled men and 10 semi-skilled men and makes two models *A* and *B* of an article. The making of one item of model *A* requires 2 h work by a skilled man and 2 h work by a semi-skilled man. One item of model *B* requires 1 h by a skilled man and 3 h by a semi-skilled man. No man is expected to work more than 8 h per day. The manufacturer profit on an item of model *A* is ₹ 15 and on an items of model *B* is ₹ 10. How many of items of each models should be made per day in order to maximize daily profit? Formulate the above LPP and solve it graphically and find the maximum profit.

12 A manufacturing company makes two types of teaching aids *A* and *B* of Mathematics for Class XII. Each type of *A* requires 9 labour hours of fabricating and 1 labour hour for finishing. Each type of *B* requires 12 labour hours for fabricating and 3 labour hours for finishing. For fabricating and finishing, the maximum labour hours available per week are 180 and 30, respectively. The company makes a profit of ₹ 80 on each piece of type *A* and ₹ 120 on each piece of type *B*. How many pieces of type *A* and type *B* should be manufactured per week to get a maximum profit? Make it as an LPP and solve it graphically. What is the maximum profit per week?

13 A company manufactures three kinds of calculators: *A*, *B* and *C* in its two factories I and II. The company has got an order for manufacturing atleast 6400 calculators of kind *A*, 4000 of kind *B* and 4800 of kind *C*. The daily output of factory I is of 50 calculators of kind *A*, 50 calculators of kind *B* and 30 calculators of kind *C*. The daily output of factory II is 40 calculators of kind *A*, 20 of kind *B* and 40 of kind *C*. The cost per day to run factory I is ₹ 12000 and of factory II is ₹ 15000. How many days do the two factories have to be in operation to produce the order with the minimum cost? Formulate this problem as an LPP and solve it graphically.

14 A manufacturer makes two types of toys *A* and *B*. Three machines are needed for this purpose and the time (in min) required for each toy on the machines is given below

Types	Machines		
	I	II	III
A	12	18	6
B	6	0	9

Each machine is available for a maximum of 6 h per day. If the profit on each toy of type *A* is ₹ 7.50 and that the each toy of type *B* is ₹ 5, then show that 15 toys of type *A* and 30 of type *B* should be manufactured in a day to get maximum profit.

15 A factory makes tennis rackets and cricket bats. A tennis racket takes 1.5 h of machine time and 3 h of craftman's time in its making, while a cricket bat takes 3 h of machine time and 1 h of craftman's time. In a day, the factory has the availability of not more than 42 h of machine time and 24 h of craftman's time.

If the profits on a racket and a bat are ₹ 20 and ₹ 10 respectively, then find the number of tennis rackets and cricket bats that the factory must manufacture to earn the maximum profit. Make it as an LPP and solve it graphically.

16 A man owns a field of area 1000 m^2. He wants to plant fruit trees in it. He has a sum of ₹ 1400 to purchase young trees. He has the choice of two types of trees. Type *A* requires 10 m^2 of ground per tree and costs ₹ 20 per tree, and type *B* requires 20 m^2 of ground per tree and costs ₹ 25 per tree. When full grown, a type-*A* tree produces an average of 20 kg of fruit which can be sold at a profit of ₹ 2 per kg and a type-*B* tree produces an average of 40 kg of fruit which can be sold at a profit of ₹ 1.50 per kg. How many of each type should be planted to achieve maximum profit when trees are fully grown? What is the maximum profit?

17 A publisher sells a hardcover edition of a book for ₹ 72 and a paperback edition of the same for ₹ 40. Costs to the publisher are ₹ 56 and ₹ 28 respectively in addition to weekly costs of ₹ 9600. Both types require 5 minutes of printing time although the hardcover edition requires 10 minutes of binding time and the paperback edition requires only 2 minutes. Both the printing and binding operations have 4800 minutes available each week. How many of each type of books should be produced in order to maximize the profit? Also, find the maximum profit per week.

18 A cottage industry manufactures pedestal lamps and wooden shades, each requiring the use of a grinding/cutting machine and a sprayer. It takes 2 h on the grinding/cutting machine and 3 h on the sprayer to manufacture a pedestal lamp. It takes 1 h on the grinding/cutting machine and 2 h on the sprayer to manufacture a shade. On any day, the sprayer is available for the atmost 20 h and the grinding/cutting machine for the atmost 12 h. The profit from the sale of a lamp is ₹ 5 and that from a shade is ₹ 3. Assuming that the manufacturer can sell all the lamps and shades that he produces, how should he schedule his daily production in order to maximise his profit? Formulate the above as a LPP and solve it graphically.

19 A dealer in rural area wishes to purchase a number of sewing machines. He has only ₹ 5760 to invest and has space for atmost 20 items for storage. An electronic sewing machine cost him ₹ 360 and a manually operated sewing machine ₹ 240. He can sell an electronic sewing machine at a profit of ₹ 22 and a manually operated sewing machine at a profit of ₹ 18. Assuming that he can sell all the items that he can buy, how should he invest his money in order to maximise his profit? Make it as an LPP and solve it graphically.

20 A gardener has a supply of fertilizers of the type I which consists of 10% nitrogen and 6% phosphoric acid, and of the type II which consists of 5% nitrogen and 10% phosphoric acid. After testing the soil conditions, he finds that he needs at least 14 kg of nitrogen and 14 kg of phosphoric acid for his crop. If the type-I fertilizer costs 60 paise per kg and the type-II fertilizer costs 40 paise per kg, determine how mnay kilograms of each type of fertilizer should be used so that the nutrient requirements are met at a minimum cost. What is the minimum cost?

21 A fruit grower can use two types of fertiliser in his garden, brand *P* and brand *Q*. The amounts (in kg) of nitrogen, phosphoric acid, potash and chlorine in a bag of each brand are given in the table. Tests indicate that the garden needs atleast 240 kg of phosphoric acid, atleast 270 kg of potash and atmost 310 kg of chlorine. If the grower wants to maximise the amount of nitrogen added to the garden, then how many bags of each brand should be added? What is the maximum amount of nitrogen added?

Fruit grower	Brand *P*	Brand *Q*
Nitrogen	3	3.5
Phosphoric acid	1	2
Potash	3	1.5
Chlorine	1.5	2

Hints & Solutions

1. **Hint** Suppose tailor A work for x days and tailor B work for y days. The given data can be written in the tabular form as follows

Tailor	Number of shirts	Number of trousers	Cost/day
A	6	4	₹ 300
B	10	4	₹ 400
Minimum requirement	60	32	

Required linear programming problem is

Min $(Z) = 300x + 400y$

subject to constraints

$6x + 10y \geq 60,\ 4x + 4y \geq 32$ and $x \geq 0,\ y \geq 0$

2. **Hint** Let x necklaces and y bracelets manufactured by small firm.

Item	Number	Manufactures times (in hours)	Profit (in ₹)
Necklaces	x	$x/2$	$100x$
Bracelets	y	y	$300y$
Total	$x + y$	$\frac{x}{2} + y$	$100x + 300y$
Availability	24	16	

Our problem is to maximise $Z = 100x + 300y$ subject to constraints are

$$x + y \leq 24,\ \frac{x}{2} + y \leq 16 \text{ and } x \geq 1,\ y \geq 1$$

3. **Hint** Let the number of large vans $= x$

and number of small vans $= y$

Minimise cost $Z = 400x + 200y$

subject to constraints

$200x + 80y \geq 1200$ or $5x + 2y \geq 30$,

$400x + 200y \leq 3000$ or $2x + y \leq 15$,

$x < y$ and $x \geq 0,\ y \geq 0$

4. **Hint** Let the number of executive class tickets be x and economy class tickets be y.

$\therefore$ LPP is maximise profit $P = 1500x + 1000y$ subject to constraints

$x + y \leq 250,\ x \geq 25,\ y \geq 3x$ and $x,\ y \geq 0$.

5. **Hint** Minimise $Z = 50x + 70y$

subject to constraints are

$2x + y \geq 8,\ x + 2y \geq 10$ and $x, y \geq 0$

Ans. Minimum cost is ₹ 380 at (2, 4)

6. **Hint** $Z = 4x + 3y$

Subject to constraints are

$200x + 100y \geq 4000,\ x + 2y \geq 50,\ 40x + 40y \geq 1400$

Ans. 5 units of A and 30 units of B.

7. **Hint** $Z = \frac{x}{200} + \frac{y}{50}$

Subject to constraints are

$2x + y \geq 1000,\ x + 2y \geq 800$ and $x,\ y \geq 0$.

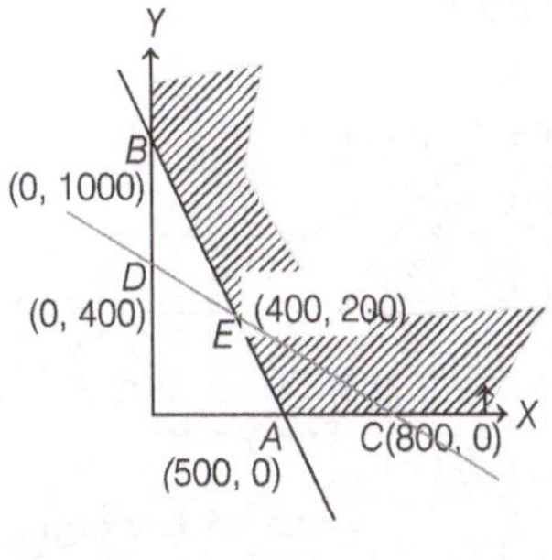

Ans. 400 g of wheat and 200 g of rice.

8. **Hint** Minimise $Z = 28x + 25y$

Subject to constraints are

$80x + 100y \geq 88,\ 40x + 30y \geq 36,\ x + y = 1$ and $x, y \geq 0$

Ans. Bran = 0.6 kg, rice = 0.4 kg; Minimum cost is ₹ 26.8

9. **Hint** Maximize $Z = 0.7x + y$

Subject to the constraints,

$4x + 6y \leq 240$ or $2x + 3y \leq 120$ ...(i)

$6x + 3y \leq 240$ or $2x + y \leq 80$ ...(ii)

and $x, y \geq 0$ ...(iii)

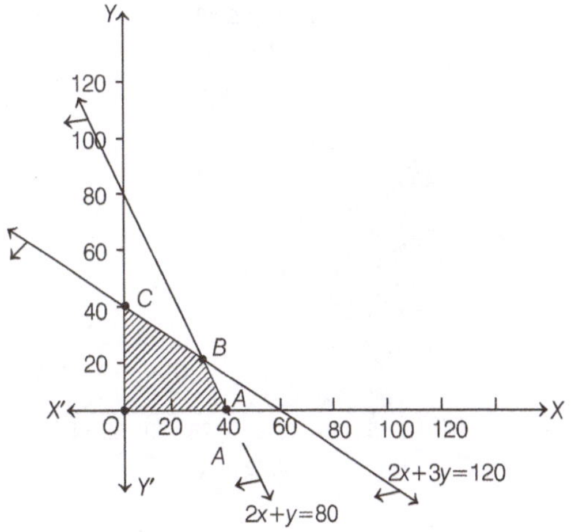

Corner points	Value of $Z = 0.7x + y$
O (0, 0)	0
A (40,0)	28
B (30, 20)	41 ← maximum
C (0, 40)	40

We find that maximum value of Z is 41 at B (30, 20).

Ans. The manufacturer should produce 30 packets of screw A and 20 packets of screw B to get a maximum profit of ₹ 41.

10. Hint Now, the given LPP is to maximise profit :

$$P = 40x + 50y$$

Subject to following constraints

$3x + y \le 9,\ x + 2y \le 8$ and $x \ge 0,\ y \ge 0$

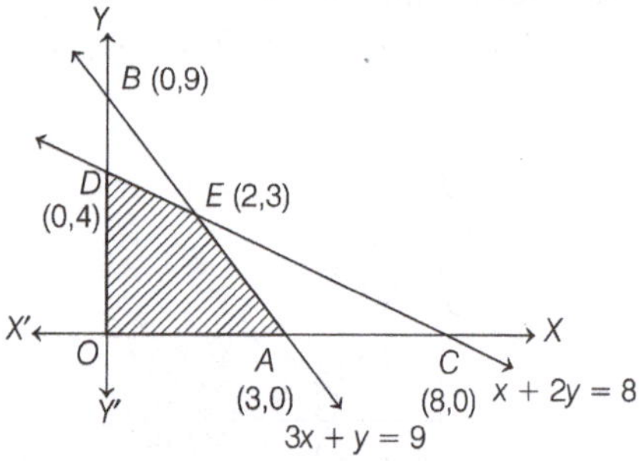

Points (x, y)	Value of the objective function $P = 40x + 50y$
$O(0, 0)$	$P = 40 \times 0 + 50 \times 0 = 0$
$A\ (3, 0)$	$P = 40 \times 3 + 50 \times 0 =$ ₹ 120
$E\ (2, 3)$	$P = 40 \times 2 + 50 \times 3 =$ ₹ 230
$D\ (0, 4)$	$P = 40 \times 0 + 50 \times 4 =$ ₹ 200

Clearly, P is maximum at $x = 2$ and $y = 3$

Ans. The maximum value of P is ₹ 230.

11. Hint Maximize profit is $P = 15x + 10y$

Subject to the constraints

$$2x + y \le 40 \quad \text{...(i)}$$

$$2x + 3y \le 80 \quad \text{...(ii)}$$

Also, $x \ge 0$ and $y \ge 0$

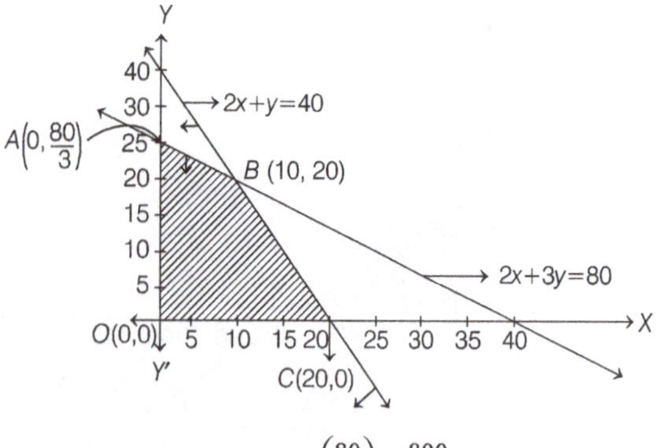

At point $A : Z = 15(0) + 10\left(\frac{80}{3}\right) = \frac{800}{3}$

At point $B : Z = 15(10) + 10(20) = 350$

At point $C : Z = 15(20) + 10(0) = 300$

At point $O : Z = 15(0) + 10(0) = 0$

Thus, the maxima lies at point B having coordinates $x = 10$ and $y = 20$ and the maximum profit = ₹ 350.

Ans. The manufacturer should makes 10 items of A model and 20 items of B model for maximum profit of ₹ 350.

12. Hint $Z = 80x + 120y$ ...(i)

subject to constraints,

$$9x + 12y \le 180 \text{ or } 3x + 4y \le 60 \quad \text{...(ii)}$$

$$x + 3y \le 30 \quad \text{...(iii)}$$

and $x \ge 0,\ y \ge 0$ ...(iv)

The graphical representation of the lines is given below

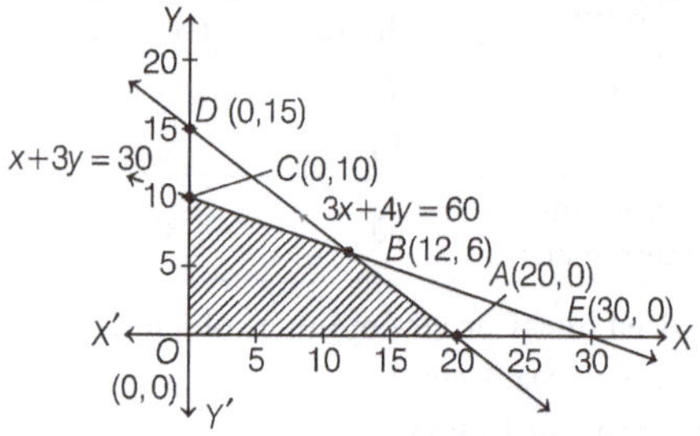

Corner points	$Z = 80x + 120y$
$O(0, 0)$	$Z = 80(0) + 120(0) = 0$
$A(20, 0)$	$Z = 80(20) + 120(0) = 1600$
$B(12, 6)$	$Z = 80(12) + 120(6) = 1680$
$C(0, 10)$	$Z = 80(0) + 120(10) = 1200$

Hence, the maximum value of Z is ₹ 1680.

The manufacturer should produce 12 pieces of type A and 6 pieces of type B to earn maximum profit of ₹ 1680.

13. Hint Then, minimise $Z = 12000x + 15000y$,

subject to constraints are

$$50x + 40y \ge 6400 \text{ or } 5x + 4y \ge 640 \quad \text{...(i)}$$

$$50x + 20y \ge 4000 \text{ or } 5x + 2y \ge 400 \quad \text{...(ii)}$$

$$30x + 40y \ge 4800 \text{ or } 3x + 4y \ge 480 \quad \text{...(iii)}$$

and $x \ge 0,\ y \ge 0$ ...(iv)

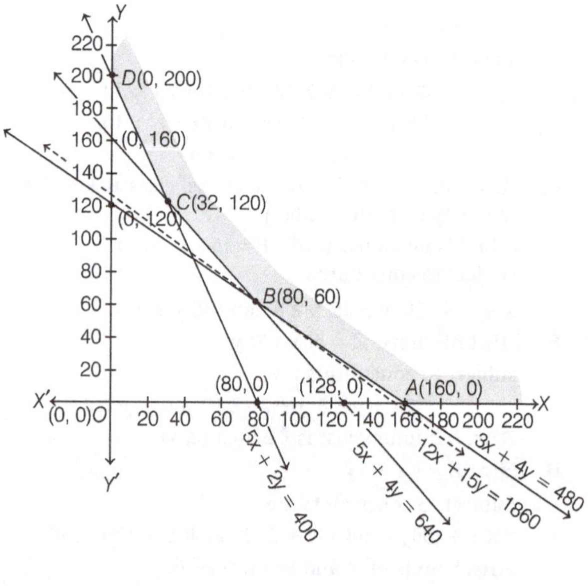

Corner points	$Z = 12000x + 15000y$
$A(160, 0)$	$Z = 12000 \times 160 + 15000 \times 0 = 1920000$
$B(80, 60)$	$Z = 12000 \times 80 + 15000 \times 60 = 1860000$
$C(32, 120)$	$Z = 12000 \times 32 + 15000 \times 120 = 2184000$
$D(0, 200)$	$Z = 12000 \times 0 + 15000 \times 200 = 3000000$

In the above table, we find that minimum value of Z is 1860000 occur at the point $B(80, 60)$.

But we cannot say that it is a minimum value of Z as region is unbounded.

Therefore, we have to draw the graph of the inequality

$12000x + 15000y < 1860000$

or $\quad 12x + 15y < 1860$ or $\dfrac{x}{155} + \dfrac{y}{124} < 1$

Now, check whether the resulting open half plane has any point common with feasible region. From figure, we see that it has no point in common.

Thus, the minimum value of Z is ₹ 1860000 attained at the point $B(80, 60)$.

Ans. Factory I should run for 80 days and factory II should run for 60 days.

14. Hint $\quad Z = 7.50x + 5y$ ...(i)

Subject to constraints,

$12x + 6y \le 360 \Rightarrow 2x + y \le 60$ ...(ii)

$18x \le 360 \Rightarrow x \le 20$ ... (iii)

$6x + 9y \le 360$

$\Rightarrow \quad 2x + 3y \le 120$ ...(iv)

and $\quad x \ge 0, \quad y \ge 0$ ... (v)

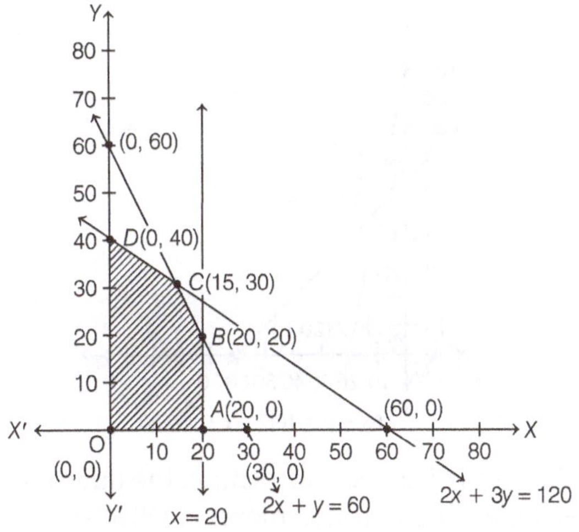

Corner points	$Z = 7.50x + 5y$
$O(0, 0)$	$Z = 7.50(0) + 5(0) = 0$
$A(20, 0)$	$Z = 7.50(20) + 5(0) = 150$
$B(20, 20)$	$Z = 7.50(20) + 5(20) = 250$
$C(15, 30)$	$Z = 7.50(15) + 5(30) = 262.5$
$D(0, 40)$	$Z = 7.50(0) + 5(40) = 200$

Thus, the maximum value of Z is at $C(15, 30)$.

Hence, the manufacturer should manufacture 15 toys of type A and 30 toys of type B to maximise the profit.

15. Hint Maximise $Z = 20x + 10y$,

Subject to constraints are

$1.5x + 3y \le 42, \; 3x + y \le 24$ and $x, y \ge 0$

Ans. For maximum profit of ₹ 200, 4 tennis rackets and 12 cricket bats must be produced.

16. Hint Let x plants tree of type A and y plants tree of type B be planted.

Then, maximum profit, $Z = 2 \times 20x + \dfrac{3}{2} \times 40y$

$= 40x + 60y$

Subject to the constraints are

$20x + 25y \le 1400, 10x + 20y \le 1000, x, \; y \ge 0$

Ans. Type A = 20 plants, Type B = 40 plants

Maximum profit = ₹ 3200

17. Hint Let x and y copies of hardcover edition and paperback edition be prepared respectively.

Then, maximum profit, $Z = (16x + 12y) - 9600$

Subject to the constraints are

$5x + 5y \le 4800$

or $\quad 10x + 2y \le 4800$

and $\quad x, \; y \ge 0$

Ans. Maximum profit, Z = ₹ 3360 at $x = 360$ and $y = 600$

18. Hint Maximise $Z = 5x + 3y$

Subject to constraints are $2x + y \le 12$,

$3x + 2y \le 20$ and $x, y \ge 0$

Ans. The manufacturer should produce 4 pedestal lamps and 4 wooden shades daily to maximum his profit.

19. Hint Maximise profit $Z = 22x + 18y$

Subject to constraints are

$360x + 240y \le 5760, \; x + y \le 20$ and $x, y \ge 0$

Ans. Dealer should purchase electronic sewing machine = 8 and manually operated sewing machine = 12;

Maximum profit = ₹ 392

20. Hint Let x and y kg of type I fertilizer and type II fertilizer be used.

Then, minimum cost function, $Z = \dfrac{60}{100}x + \dfrac{40}{100}y$

$= \dfrac{3}{5}x + \dfrac{2}{5}y$

Subject to the constraints are

$\dfrac{10}{100}x + \dfrac{5}{100}y \ge 14, \dfrac{6}{100}x + \dfrac{10}{100}y \ge 14, \; x, \; y \ge 0$

Ans. Minimum cost = ₹ 92 for producing 100 kg of Type I fertilizer and 80 kg of Type II fertilizer.

21. Hint Maximise $Z = 3x + 3.5y$

Subject to constraints are

$x + 2y \ge 240, 3x + 1.5y \ge 270, \; 1.5x + 2y \le 310$ and $x, y \ge 0$

Ans. 140 bags of brand P and 50 bags of brand Q;

Maximum amount of nitrogen = 595 kg

Exam Pattern Exercise

Part A - Objective Type Questions

Multiple Choice Type Questions

1 The graph of the inequality $2x + 3y > 6$ is
(a) half plane that contains the origin
(b) half plane that neither contains the origin nor the points of the line $2x + 3y = 6$
(c) whole XOY – plane excluding the points on the line $2x + 3y = 6$
(d) entire XOY plane

2 Which of the term is not used in a linear programming problem?
(a) Optimal solution (b) Feasible solution
(c) Concave region (d) Objective function

3 The linear inequalities or equations or restrictions on the variables of a linear programming problem are called
(a) linear relations (b) constraints
(c) functions (d) objective functions

4 The objective function of an LPP is
(a) a constraint
(b) a function to be optimised
(c) a relation between the variables
(d) None of the above

5 The corner points of the feasible region determined by the system of linear constraints are (0, 10), (5, 5), (15, 15), (0, 20). Let $Z = px + qy$, where $p, q > 0$. Then, the condition on p and q, so that the maximum of Z occurs at both the points (15, 15) and (0, 20) is
(a) $p = q$ (b) $p = 2q$
(c) $q = 2p$ (d) $q = 3p$

6 In an LPP, if the objective function has $Z = ax + by$ has the same maximum value on two corner points of the feasible region, then the number of points at which Z_{max} occurs is **[CBSE 2024]**
(a) 0 (b) 2 (c) finite (d) infinite

7 The feasible region for the following constraints $L_1 \le 0, L_2 \ge 0, L_3 = 0, x \ge 0, y \ge 0$ in the diagram shown is

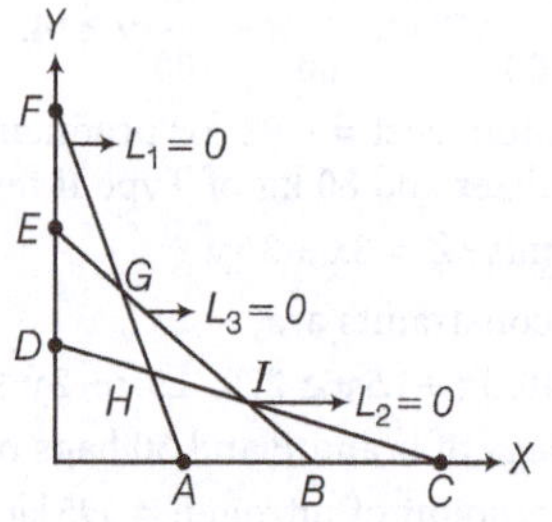

(a) area DHF (b) area AHC
(c) line segment EG (d) line segment GI

8 A wholesale merchant wants to start the business of cereal with ₹24000. Wheat is ₹400 per quintal and rice is ₹600 per quintal. He has capacity to store 200 quintal cereal. He earns the profit ₹25 per quintal on wheat and ₹40 per quintal on rice. If he stores x quintal rice and y quintal wheat, then maximum profit of the objective function is
(a) $25x + 40y$
(b) $40x + 25y$
(c) $400x + 600y$
(d) $\frac{400}{40}x + \frac{600}{25}y$

Assertion-Reason Based Questions

Directions (Q. Nos. 9-11) *Consider the graph of constraints stated as linear inequalities as below*

$$5x + y \le 100 \quad \text{...(i)}$$
$$x + y \le 60 \quad \text{...(ii)}$$
$$x \ge 0 \quad \text{...(iii)}$$
$$y \ge 0 \quad \text{...(iv)}$$

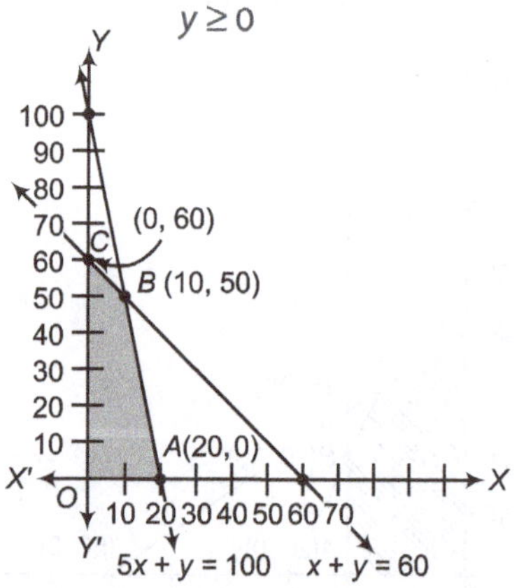

On the basis of above information, the questions given below has two statements labelled as Assertion (A) and Reason (R). In the context of the two statements, which one of the following is correct?
(a) Both A and R are correct; R is the correct explanation of A
(b) Both A and R are correct; R is not the correct explanation of A
(c) A is correct; R is incorrect
(d) R is correct; A is incorrect

9 **Assertion (A)** The points (10, 50), (0, 60) or (20, 0) are feasible solutions.

Reason (R) Points within and on the boundary of the feasible region represent feasible solutions of the constraints.

10 **Assertion (A)** The objective function

$Z = -50x + 20y$

Subject to the constraints

$2x - y \geq -5, 3x + y \geq 3, 2x - 3y \leq 12, x \geq 0, y \geq 0$

in the feasible region has no minimum value.

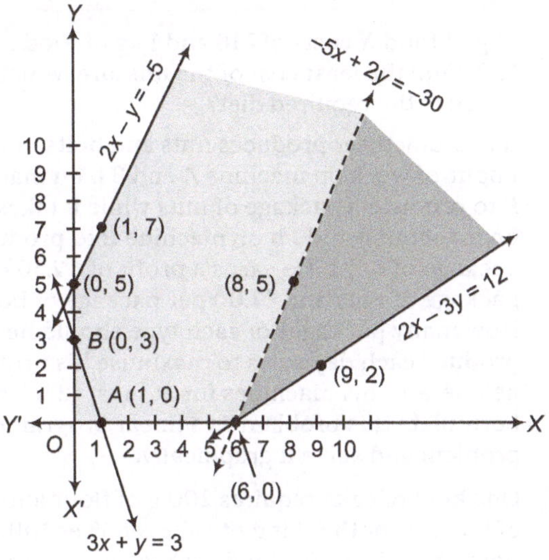

Reason (R) If the open half plane determined by $ax + by < m$, where m is the minimum value of Z, has a point in common with feasible region, then Z has no minimum value.

11 **Assertion (A)** The maximum value of $Z = 11x + 7y$.

Subject to the constraints

$2x + y \leq 6, x \leq 2, x \geq 0, y \geq 0$

in the feasible region occurs at the corner point (0, 6).

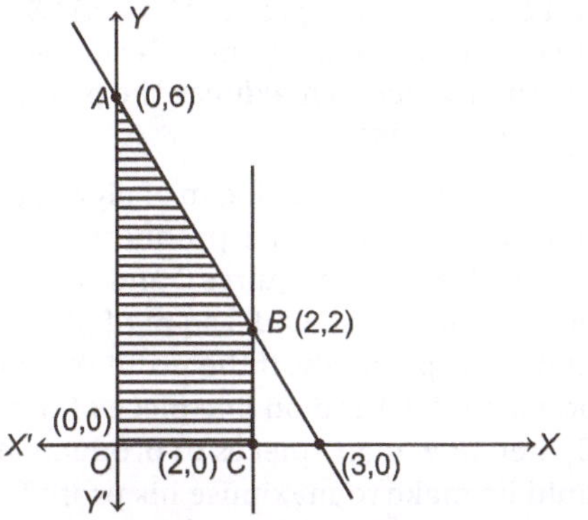

Reason (R) If the feasible region of the given LPP is bounded, then the maximum and minimum value of the objective function occurs at corner points.

Part B - Descriptive Questions

Very Short Answer Type Questions

12 Write the linear inequation represented by the shaded region.

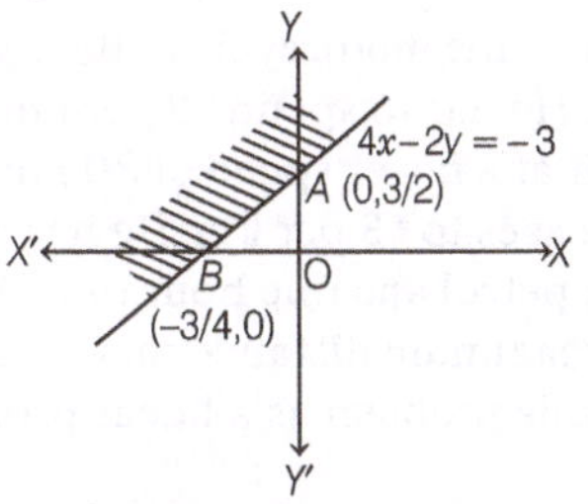

13 The corner points of the feasible region determined by the system of linear constraints are (0, 10), (5, 5), (15, 15), (0, 20). Let $Z = px + qy$, where $p, q > 0$. Then, find the condition on p and q, so that the maximum of Z occurs at both the points (15, 15) and (0, 10).

14 The feasible region for an LPP is shown in the following figure.

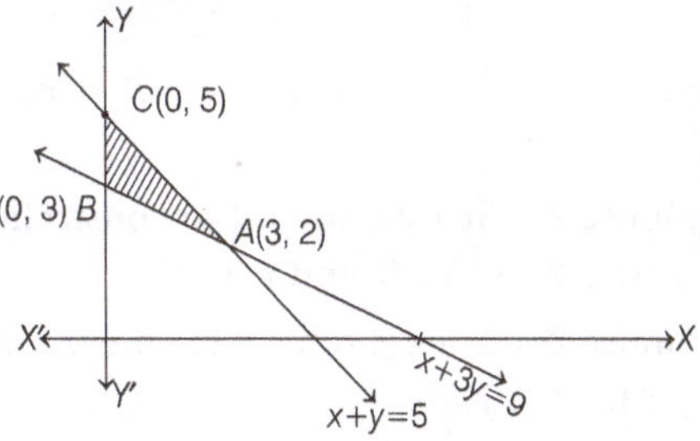

Then, find the minimum value of $Z = 11x + 7y$.

15 Find the maximum value of $Z = 4x + 3y$, if the feasible region for an LPP is as shown below.

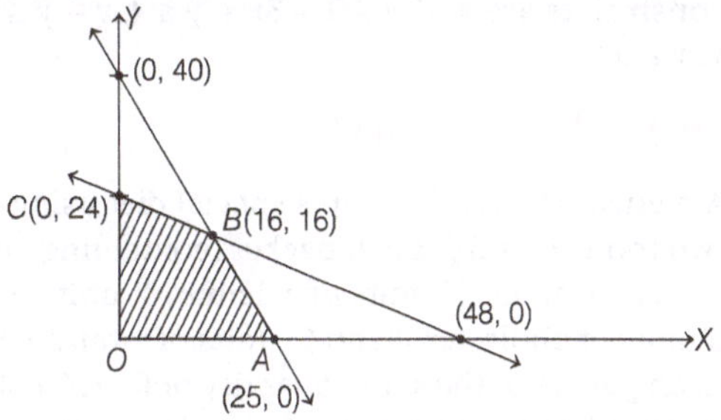

16 The corner points of the feasible region for the LPP are $A(15, 0)$, $B(40, 0)$, $C(6, 12)$ and $D(4, 18)$ of the objective function of LPP is $Z = 20x + 10y$, then find the minimize value of Z.

Short Answer Type Questions

17 A diet for a sick person must contain atleast 4000 units of vitamins, 50 units of minerals and 1400 calories. Two foods A and B are available at a cost of ₹ 4 and ₹ 3 per unit, respectively. Food A contains 200 units of vitamins, 1 unit of minerals and 40 calories. Food B contains 100 units of vitamins, 2 units of minerals and 40 calories. Express this problem as a linear programming problem.

18 A man rides his motorcycle at the speed of 50 km/h. He has to spend ₹ 2 per km on petrol. If he rides it at a faster speed of 80 km/h, the petrol cost increases to ₹ 3 per km. He has atmost ₹ 120 to spend on petrol and one hour time. He wishes to find the maximum distance that he can travel. Express this problem as a linear programming problem.

19 Feasible region (shaded) for an LPP is shown in the following figure, Maximise $Z = 5x + 7y$.

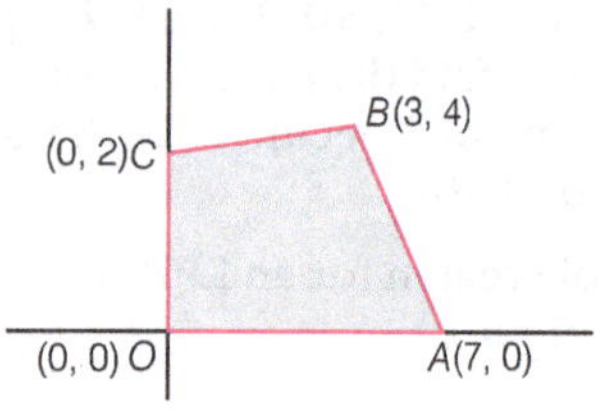

Directions (Q. Nos. 20-23) *Solve the following LPP graphically.*

20 Maximise $Z = 3x + 2y$, subject to constraints are $x + y \geq 8$, $3x + 5y \leq 15$ and $x, y \geq 0$.

21 Maximise $Z = 3x + 4y$, subject to constraints are $x + y \leq 1$; $x \geq 0$, $y \geq 0$.

22 Minimise $Z = 2x + 4y$, subject to constraints are $x + y \geq 8$, $x + 4y \geq 12$, $x \geq 3$, $y \geq 2$ and $x, y \geq 0$.

23 Maximise and minimise $Z = 3x - 4y$, subject to constraints are $x - 2y \leq 0$, $-3x + y \leq 4$, $x - y \leq 6$ and $x, y \geq 0$.

Long Answer Type Questions

24 A dietician has to develop a special diet using two foods P and Q. Each packet (containing 30 g) of food P contains 12 units of calcium, 4 units of iron, 6 units of cholesterol and 6 units of vitamin A. Each packet of the same quantity of food Q contains 3 units of calcium, 20 units of iron, 4 units of cholesterol and 3 units of vitamin A. The diet requires atleast 240 units of calcium, atleast 460 units of iron and atmost 300 units of cholesterol. How many packets of each food should be used to minimise the amount of vitamin A in the diet? What is the minimum amount of vitamin A?

25 A dietician wishes to mix together two kinds of foods X and Y in such a way that the mixture contains atleast 10 units of vitamin A, 12 units of vitamin B and 8 units of vitamin C.

The vitamin contents of 1 kg food is given below

Food	Vitamin A	Vitamin B	Vitamin C
X	1	2	3
Y	2	2	1

1 kg of food X costs of ₹ 16 and 1 kg of food Y costs ₹ 20. Find the least cost of the mixture, which will produce the required diet?

26 A manufacturer produces nuts and bolts. It takes 1 hour of work on machine A and 3 h on machine B to produce a package of nuts while it takes 3 h on machine A and 1 h on machine B to produce a package of bolts. He earns a profit of ₹ 2.50 per package of nuts and ₹ 1.00 per package of bolts. How many packages of each type should he produce each day so as to maximise his profit, if he operates his machines for at most 12 h a day? Formulate this problem as a linear programming problem and solve it graphically.

27 One kind of cake requires 200 g of flour and 25 g of fat and another kind of cake requires 100 g of flour and 50 g of fat. Find the maximum number of cakes which can be made from 5 kg of flour and 1 kg of fat assuming that there is no shortage of other ingredients used in making the cakes. Formulate the above as a linear programming problem and solve it graphically.

28 A firm deals with two kinds of fruit juice. These are mixed and two mixtures are sold as soft drink A and B. 1 tin of A requires 4 of pineapple and 1 of orange juice. 1 tin of B requires 2 of pineapple and 3 of orange juice. The firm has only 46 of pineapple juice and 24 of orange juice. Each tin of A and B are sold at a profit of ₹ 4 and ₹ 3, respectively. How many tins of each type should the firm produce to maximise the profit? Solve the problem graphically.

29 A carpenter has 20 and 15 sq m of plywood and sunmica, respectively. He produces products A and B. Product A requires 2 and 1 sq m and product B requires 1 and 3 sq m of plywood and sunmica, respectively. If the profit on one piece of product A is ₹ 30 and on one piece of product B is ₹ 20, then how many pieces of products A and B should he make to maximise his profit?

30 A small firm manufactures gold rings and chains. The total number of rings and chains manufactured per day is atmost 24. It takes 1h to make a ring and 30 min to make a chain. The maximum number of hours available per day is 16. If the profit on a ring is ₹ 300 and that on a chain is ₹ 190, then find the number of rings and chains that should be manufactured per day, so as to earn the maximum profit, make it as an LPP and solve it graphically.

31 A manufacturer of patient medicines is preparing plan on medicines A and B. There are sufficient raw materials available to make 20000 bottles of A and 40000 bottles of B, but there are only 45000 bottles into which either of the medicines can be put. Further, it takes 3 h to prepare enough material to fill 1000 bottles of A, it takes 1 h to prepare enough material to fill 1000 bottles of B and there are 66 h available for this operation. The profit is ₹ 8 per bottle for A and ₹ 7 per bottle for B. How should the manufacturer schedule his production in order to maximise his profit?

32 A company manufactures two types of screws A and B. All the screws have to pass through a threading machine and a slotting machine. A box of type A screw require 2 min on the threading machine and 3 min on the slotting machine. A box of type B screws requires 8 min on the threading machine and 2 min on the slotting machine. In a week, each machine is available for 60 h.

On selling these screws, the company gets a profits of ₹ 100 per box on type A screws and ₹ 170 per box on type B screws. Formulate this problem as an LPP given that the objective is to maximise profit. Solve the linear programming problem and determine the maximum profit to the manufacturer.

33 A manufacturer produces two products A and B. Both the products are processed on two different machines. The available capacity of first machine is 12 h and that of second machine is 9 h per day. Each unit of product A requires 3 h on both machines and each unit of product B requires 2 h on first machine and 1 h on second machine. Each unit of product A is sold at a profit of ₹ 7 and B at a profit of ₹ 4. Find the production level per day for maximum profit graphically.

34 A farmer mixes two brands P and Q of cattle feed. Brand P, costing ₹ 250 per bag, contains 3 units of nutritional element A, 2.5 units of elements B and 2 units of element C.

Brand Q, costing ₹ 200 per bag, contains 1.5 units of nutritional element A, 11.25 units of element B and 3 units of element C. The minimum requirements of nutrients A, B and C are 18 units, 45 units and 24 units, respectively. Determine the number of bags of each brand which should be mixed in order to produce a mixture having a minimum cost per bag? What is the minimum cost of the mixture per bag?

35 A merchant plans to sell two types of personal computers, a desktop model and a portable model that will cost ₹ 25000 and ₹ 40000, respectively. He estimates that the total monthly demand of computers will not exceed 250 units. Determine the number of units of each type of computers which the merchant should stock to get maximum profit, if he does not want to invest more than ₹ 70 lakh and his profit on the desktop model is ₹ 4500 and on the portable model is ₹ 5000. Make it as an LPP and solve it graphically.

36 A manufacturer makes two types A and B of tea cups. Three machines are needed for this purpose and the time (in minutes) required for each cup on the machine is given below

Type	Machines		
	I	II	III
A	4	6	2
B	2	0	3

Each machine is available for a maximum of 2 h per day. The profit on each cup of type A is ₹ 6 and that on each cup of type B is ₹ 5. Show that 15 tea cups of type A and 30 of type B should be manufactured in a day to get the maximum profit.

37 A library has to accommodate two different types of books on a shelf. The books are 6 cm and 4 cm thick and weight 1 kg and $1\frac{1}{2}$ kg each, respectively. The shelf is 96 cm long and atmost can support a weight of 21 kg. How should the shelf be filled with the books of two types in order to include the greatest number of books? Make it as an LPP and solve it graphically.

38 A retired person wants to invest an amount of ₹ 50000. His broker recommends investing in two type of bonds 'A' and 'B' yielding 10% and 9% return respectively on the invested amount.

He decides to invest atleast ₹ 20000 in bond 'A' and atleast ₹ 10000 in bond 'B'. He also wants to invest atleast as much in bond 'A' as in bond 'B'. Solve this linear programming problem graphically to maximise his returns.

Case Study Based Questions

39 In number theory, it is often important to find factors of an integer N. The number N has two trivial factors, namely 1 and N. Any other factor, if exists, is called non-trivial factor of N. Naresh has plotted a graph of some constraints (linear inequations) with points $A(0, 50)$, $B(20, 40)$, $C(50, 100)$, $D(0, 200)$ and $E(100, 0)$. This graph is constructed using three non-trivial constraints and two trivial constraints. One of the non-trivial constraints is $x + 2y \geq 100$.

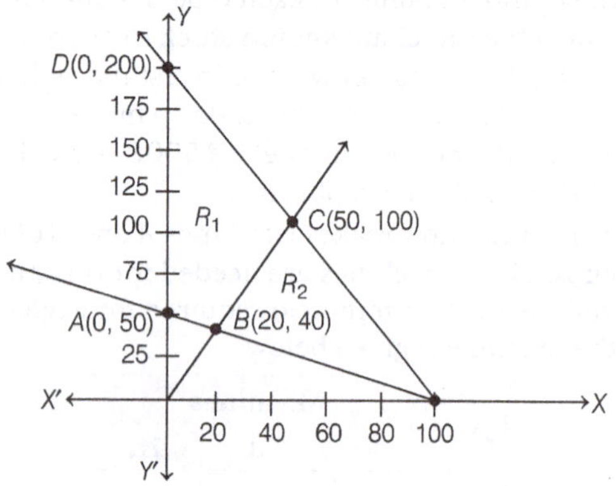

Based on the above information, answer the following questions.

(i) What are the two trivial constraints?

(ii) (a) If R_1 is the feasible region, then what are the other two non-trivial constraints?

Or

(b) If R_2 is the feasible region, then what are the other two non-trivial constraints?

(iii) If R_1 is the feasible region, then find the maximum value of objective function $Z = 5x + 2y$. **[CBSE 2024]**

40 A factory manufactures tennis rackets and cricket bats. A tennis racket takes $1\frac{1}{2}$ h of machine time and 3 h of craftsmanship in its making, while a cricket bat takes 3 h of machine time and 1 h of craftsmanship. In a day, the factory has availability of not more than 42 h of machine time and 24 h of craftsmanship. Profit on a racket and on a bat are ₹20 and ₹10 respectively.

Based on the above information, answer the following questions.

(i) If x and y are the numbers of bats and rackets manufactured by the factory, then write the expression of total profit.

(ii) Write the constraint that relates the number of craftsmanship hours.

(iii) Determine the maximum profit (in ₹) earned by the factory.

Or

How many bats and rackets respectively, are manufactured to earn maximum profit? **[CBSE 2023]**

Hints & Solutions

1. (b) The inequality $2x+3y>6$ represent half plane that neither contains the origin nor the points of the line $2x+3y=6$

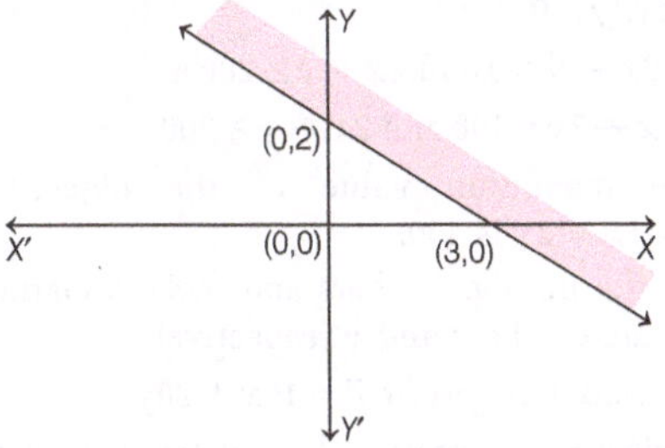

2. (c)	3. (b)	4. (b)	5. (d)
6. (d)	7. (c)	8. (c)	9. (a)
10. (a)	11. (a)		

12. $4x-2y\leq -3$
13. $q=-3p$
14. 21
15. 1112
16. 240
17. **Hint** Min $Z=4x+3y$, subject to constraints
    $200x+100y\geq 4000$, $x+2y\geq 50$, $40x+40y\geq 1400$ and $x\geq 0$, $y\geq 0$.
18. **Hint** Max $Z=x+y$, subject to constraints are
    $2x+3y\leq 120$, $8x+5y\leq 400$ and $x\geq 0$, $y\geq 0$.
19. **Hint** Find $Z=5x+7$ at O, A, B and C

    Ans. $Z=43$ at $B(3,4)$
20. **Hint** Draw the graph of inequality $x+y\geq 8, 3x+5y\leq 15$ and $x, y\geq 0$

    Ans. There is no feasible region, so no maximum value exist.
21. **Hint**

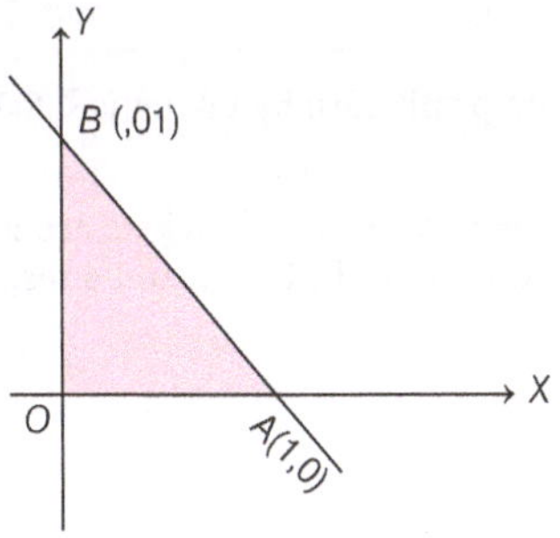

Ans. Maximum value of Z is 4 at (0, 1).

22. **Hint**

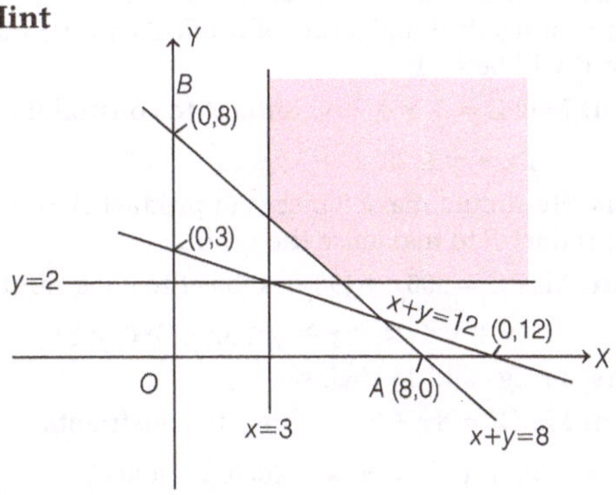

Ans. Unbounded solution

23. **Hint**

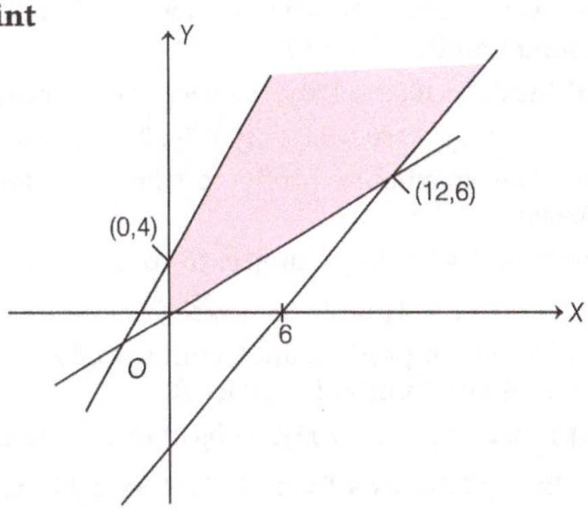

Ans. Maximum value = 12 and no minimum value exist.

24. **Hint** Min $Z=6x+3y$, subject to constraints
    $4x+y\geq 80$, $x+3y\geq 115$, $3x+2y\leq 150$, $x\geq 0, y\geq 0$

    Ans. 15 packets of food P and 20 packets of food Q should be used to minimise the amount of vitamin A. The minimum amount of vitamin A is 150 units.
25. **Hint** Min $Z=16x+20y$, subject to constraints
    $x+2y\geq 10$, $x+y\geq 6$, $3x+y\geq 8$, $x, y\geq 0$

    Ans. Mixture contains 2 kg of food X and 4 kg of food Y, Minimum cost = ₹ 112.
26. **Hint** Max $Z=2.50x+y$, subject to constraints
    $x+3y\leq 12$, $3x+y\leq 12$, $x, y\geq 0$

    Ans. The manufacturer should produce 3 packages of nuts and 3 packages of bolts each day for maximum profit = ₹ 10.5.
27. **Hint** Max $Z=x+y$, subject to constraints
    $2x+y\leq 50$, $x+2y\leq 40$, $x\geq 0, y\geq 0$

    Ans. Number of first kind cake = 20, number of second kind cake = 10, maximum number of cakes = 30.

28. **Hint** Max $Z = 4x + 3y$, subject to constraints

$$2x + y \le 23,\ x + 3y \le 24,\ x, y \ge 0$$

Ans. For maximise the profit, the firm should produce 9 tins of drink A and 5 tins of drink B and the maximum profit will be ₹ 51.

29. **Hint** Max $Z = 30x + 20y$, subject to constraints

$$2x + y \le 20,\ x + 3y \le 15,\ x, y \ge 0$$

Ans. He should make 9 pieces of product A and 2 pieces of product B to maximise the profit.

30. **Hint** Max $Z = 300x + 190y$, subject to constraints

$$x + y \le 24,\ 2x + y \le 32,\ x \ge 0,\ y \ge 0$$

Ans. 8 rings and 16 chains

31. **Hint** Max $Z = 8x + 7y$, subject to constraints

$$3x + y \le 66000,\ x \le 2000,\ y \le 40000,$$
$$x + y \le 45000,\ x, y \ge 0$$

Ans. 10500 bottles of type A, 34500 bottles of type B; maximum profit = ₹ 325500

32. **Hint** Max $Z = 100x + 170y$, subject to constraints

$$x + 4y \le 1800,\ 3x + 2y \le 3600,\ x, y \ge 0$$

Ans. The maximum profit to the manufacturer is ₹ 138600.

33. **Hint** Max $Z = 7x + 4y$, subject to constraints

$$3x + 2y \le 12,\ 3x + y \le 9,\ x, y \ge 0$$

Ans. Maximum profit, manufacturer produce 2 units of product A and 3 units of product B.

34. **Hint** Min $Z = 250x + 200y$, subject to constraints

$$2x + y \ge 12,\ 2x + 9y \ge 36,\ 2x + 3y \ge 24,\ x, y \ge 0$$

Ans. 3 bags of brand P and 6 bags of brand Q should be used in the mixture of minimise the cost to ₹ 1950.

35. **Hint** Max $Z = 4500x + 5000y$,

subject to constraints

$$x + y \le 250,\ 5x + 8y \le 1400,\ x, y \ge 0$$

Ans. The profit is maximum, i.e. ₹ 1150000, when 200 desktop computers and 50 portable computers are stocked.

36. **Hint** Max, $Z = 6x + 5y$,

subject to constraints

$$4x + 2y \le 120,\ 6x + 0y \le 120,\ 2x + 3y \le 120 \text{ and } x, y \ge 0$$

37. **Hint** Max $Z = x + y$, subject to constraints

$$3x + 2y \le 48,\ 2x + 3y \le 42,\ x, y \ge 0$$

Ans. 12 and 6

38. **Hint** Max $Z = \frac{x}{10} + \frac{9y}{100}$, subject to constraints

$$x \ge 20000,\ y \ge 10000,\ x \ge y \text{ and } x + y \le 50000$$

Ans. To get maximum returns he invest ₹ 40000 in Bond A and ₹ 10000 in Bond B.

39. (i) $x \ge 0,\ y \ge 0$

(ii) (a) $2x - y \le 0$ and $2x + y \ge 200$

(b) $x + 2y \le 100$ and $2x + y \ge 200$

(iii) The maximum value of the objective function $Z = 5x + 2y$ is 450.

40. (i) Let the number of bats and rackets manufactured by the factory be x and y respectively.

∴ Maximise profit $Z = 10x + 20y$

(ii) Subject to constraints that relates to craftsman hours

$$3x + 1.5y \le 42,\ x + 3y \le 24 \text{ and } x \ge 0,\ y \ge 0$$

(iii) Graph of linear inequality are

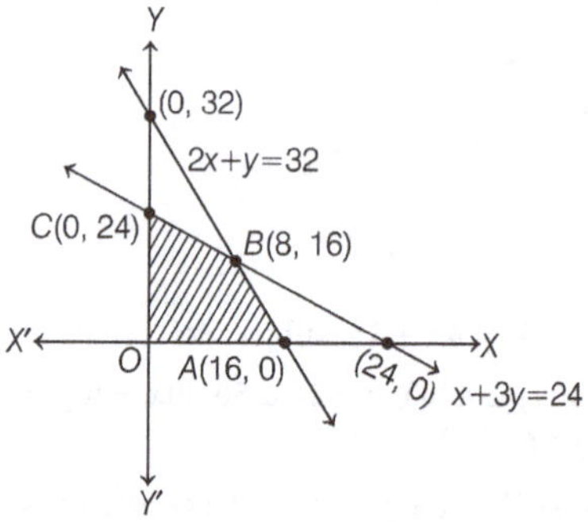

The corner points of the feasible region are $O(0, 0)$, $A(14, 0)$, $B(12, 4)$ and $C(0, 8)$.

Corner points	$Z = 10x + 20y$
$O(0, 0)$	0
$A(14, 0)$	140
$B(12, 4)$	200 (Maximum)
$C(0, 8)$	160

Maximum profit earn by taking is ₹200 at $B(12, 4)$.

Or

The numbers of bats and rackets are manufactured to earn maximum profit is ₹ 12 and 4 respectively.

CBSE EXAMINATION PAPER 2025
APPLIED MATHEMATICS

Time 3 Hours **Max. Marks 80**

General Instructions

Read the following instructions very carefully and strictly follow them.

(i) This question paper contains 38 questions. All questions are compulsory.

(ii) This question paper is divided into five Sections - Section A, B, C, D, and E.

(iii) In Section - A, Questions Number 1 to 18 are Multiple Choice Questions (MCQs) and questions Number 19 and 20 are Assertion-Reason based questions of 1 mark each.

(iv) In Section - B, Questions Number 21 to 25 are Very Short Answer (VSA) type questions, carrying 2 marks each.

(v) In Section-C, Questions Number 26 to 31 are Short Answer (SA) type questions, carrying 3 marks each.

(vi) In Section-D, Questions Number 32 to 35 are Long Answer (LA) type questions, carrying 5 marks each.

(vii) In Section-E, Questions Number 36 to 38 are case study based questions, carrying 4 marks each.

(viii) There is no overall choice. However, an internal choice has been provided in 2 questions in Section-B, 2 questions in Section-C, 2 questions in Section-D and 3 questions in Section-E.

(ix) Use of calculators is Not allowed.

SECTION A

Multiple Choice Questions

Each question carries 1 mark

Directions (Q. Nos. 1-18) *All questions are compulsory. No Internal Choice is provided in this section.*

1. $-41 \bmod 9$ is

(a) 5 (b) 4

(c) 3 (d) 0

2. If $a>b$ and $c<0$ then which of the following is true?

(a) $a+c<b+c$

(b) $a-c<b-c$

(c) $ac>bc$

(d) $a-c>b+c$

3. If A and B are symmetric matrices of the same order then $(AB'-BA')$ is a

(a) symmetric matrix

(b) null matrix

(c) diagonal matrix

(d) skew-symmetric matrix

4. The inverse of matrix $A=\begin{bmatrix}4 & -1\\ 2 & 1\end{bmatrix}$ is

(a) $\frac{1}{6}\begin{bmatrix}-4 & 2\\ -1 & -1\end{bmatrix}$ (b) $\begin{bmatrix}1/3 & 1/6\\ 2/3 & -1/6\end{bmatrix}$

(c) $\begin{bmatrix}1/6 & 1/6\\ -1/3 & 2/3\end{bmatrix}$ (d) $\begin{bmatrix}-2/3 & 1/6\\ -1/3 & -1/6\end{bmatrix}$

5. If $\begin{vmatrix}2x & 5\\ 4 & x\end{vmatrix}=\begin{vmatrix}3 & 5\\ 4 & 6\end{vmatrix}$ then the value of x is

(a) $\frac{3}{2}$ (b) 6 (c) 3 (d) ± 3

6. The slope of the normal to the curve $y=\frac{x-3}{x-4}$ at $x=6$ is

(a) 4 (b) $-\frac{1}{4}$ (c) -4 (d) $\frac{1}{4}$

7. The rate of change of population $P(t)$ with respect to time (t), where α and β are the constant birth and death rates, respectively is

(a) $\frac{dP}{dt}=(\alpha+\beta)P$ (b) $\frac{dP}{dt}=(\alpha-\beta)P$

(c) $\frac{dP}{dt}=\frac{\alpha+\beta}{P}$ (d) $\frac{dP}{dt}=\frac{\alpha-\beta}{P}$

* *Out of syllabus*

8. A pair of dice is thrown two times. If X represents the number of doublets obtained then the expectation of X is

(a) $\frac{1}{6}$ (b) 1 (c) $\frac{1}{3}$ (d) $\frac{11}{36}$

9. The mean of t-distribution is

(a) 0 (b) 1

(c) 2 (d) Not defined

10. The variations which occur due to change in climate, festivals or weather conditions are known as

(a) secular variations (b) cyclic variations

(c) seasonal variations (d) irregular variations

11. In a LPP, the maximum value of $Z=3x+4y$ subject to the constraints $x+y\le 40$, $x+2y\le 60$, $x, y\ge 0$ is

(a) 120 (b) 140 (c) 150 (d) 130

12. The present value of a sequence of payments of ₹100 made at the end of every year and continuing forever if the money is worth 5% compounded annually, is

(a) ₹ 2,000 (b) ₹ 20,000

(c) ₹ 5, 000 (d) ₹ 12,000

13. The demand function of a monopolist is given by $p=30+5x-3x^2$, where x is the number of units demanded and p is the price per unit. The marginal revenue when 2 units are sold, is

(a) ₹ 28 (b) ₹ 23 (c) ₹ 1 (d) ₹ 14

14. If the cost function and revenue function of x items are respectively given as $C(x)=100+0.015x^2$, $R(x)=3x$ then the value of x for maximum profit is

(a) 50 (b) 100 (c) 150 (d) 200

15. If a random variable X has the probability distribution $P(X=x)=\begin{cases} k, & \text{if} \quad x=0 \\ 2k, & \text{if} \quad x=1 \text{ or } 2 \\ 0, & \text{otherwise} \end{cases}$

then the value of k is

(a) $\frac{1}{3}$ (b) $\frac{1}{5}$ (c) $\frac{1}{6}$ (d) $\frac{1}{4}$

16. The test statistics t for testing the significance of differences between the means of two independent samples is given by

(a) $t=\frac{\bar{x}-\bar{y}}{\sqrt{s}}$ (b) $t=\frac{\bar{x}-\bar{y}}{s\sqrt{\frac{1}{n_1}+\frac{1}{n_2}}}$

(c) $t=\frac{\bar{x}-\bar{y}}{\frac{s}{\sqrt{n-1}}}$ (d) $t=\frac{\bar{x}+\bar{y}}{s\sqrt{\frac{1}{n_1}-\frac{1}{n_2}}}$

17. The effective rate of interest equivalent to a nominal rate of 4% compounded semi-annually, is

(a) 4.12% (b) 4.04% (c) 4.08% (d) 4.14%

18. The CAGR of an investment, whose starting value is ₹5,000 and it grows to ₹25,000 in 4 years, is [given $(5)^{0.25}=1.4953$]

(a) 49.53% (b) 14.95% (c) 495.3% (d) 1.49%

Directions (Q. Nos. 19 and 20) are Assertion-Reason based questions of 1 mark each. Two statements are given-one labelled Assertion (A) and other labelled Reason (R). Select the correct answer to these questions from the codes (A), (B), (C) and (D) as given below

(A) Both Assertion and Reason are true and Reason is correct explanation of Assertion.

(B) Both Assertion and Reason are true but Reason is not correct explanation of Assertion.

(C) Assertion is true but Reason is false.

(D) Assertion is false but Reason is true.

19. **Assertion** (A) The area of the region bounded by the line $y-1=x$, the X-axis and the ordinates $x=-1$ and $x=1$ is 2 square units.

Reason (R) The area of the region bounded by the curve $y=f(x)$, the x-axis and the ordinates $x=a$ and $x=b$ is given by $\int_a^b f(x)\,dx$.

20. **Assertion** (A) The differential equation representing the family of curves $y=mx$, m being an arbitrary constant, is $x\frac{dy}{dx}-y=0$.

Reason (R) For a family of curves, the differential equation is obtained by differentiating the equation of family of curves with respect to x and then eliminating the arbitrary constant if any.

SECTION B

Directions (Q. Nos. 21-25) are Very Short Answer (VSA) type questions of 2 marks each.

21. (a) The cost of Type I sugar is ₹25 per kg and Type II sugar is ₹35 per kg. If both Type I sugar and Type II sugar are mixed in the ratio 3:2, find the price per kg of the mixture.

OR

(b) Pipe A can fill a tank in 1 hour and Pipe B can fill it in 1½ hours. If both the pipes are opened in the empty tank, how much time will they take to fill the tank?

22. A boat goes 3.5km upstream and then returns. Total time taken is 1 hour and 12 minutes. If the speed of the current is 1km/h then find the speed of the boat in still water.

23. A runs $\frac{3}{2}$ times as fast as B. If A gives B a start of 40m, how far must the winning post from the starting point be, so that A and B reach at the same time?

24. Given, $A=\begin{bmatrix} 2 & 0 & 1 \\ 3 & 4 & 5 \\ 0 & 2 & 3 \end{bmatrix}$ and $B=\begin{bmatrix} 1 & 1 & -5 \\ -5 & 1 & -5 \\ 1 & -2 & 4 \end{bmatrix}$, find BA.

25. (a) If a fair coin is tossed 6 times, find the probability of getting atleast 4 heads.

OR

(b) Given that mean of a normal variate X is 9 and standard deviation is 3 then find
(i) the Z-score the data point 15.
(ii) the data point if its Z-score is 4.

SECTION C

Directions (Q. Nos. 26-31) are Short Answer (SA) type questions of 3 marks each.

26. Find the units digit in 7^{295}.

27. Two numbers are selected at random (without replacement) from first six positive integers. Let X denote the smaller of the two numbers obtained. Calculate the mathematical expectation of X.

28. (a) If the mean and variance of a binomial distribution are $\frac{4}{3}$ and $\frac{8}{9}$, respectively then find $P(x=1)$.

OR

(b) The mortality rate for a certain disease is 0.007. Using Poisson distribution, calculate the probability for 2 deaths in a group of 400 people. [use $e^{-2.8}=0.0608$]

29. (a) There are two types of fertilizers F_1 and F_2. F_1 consists of 10% nitrogen and 6% phosphoric acid. F_2 consists of 5% nitrogen and 10% phosphoric acid. After testing the soil conditions, a farmer finds that he needs atleast 14 kg of nitrogen and 14 kg of phosphoric acid for his crop. If F_1 costs ₹6 per kg and F_2 costs ₹5 per kg, how much of each type of fertilizer should be used, so that the cost is minimum. Formulate a linear programming problem.

OR (b) Solve the following linear programming problem graphically

Maximise $Z=50x+30y$

Subject to $2x+y\le 18$, $3x+2y\le 34$, $x, y\ge 0$

30. A machinist is making engine parts with axle diameter of 0.7cm. A random sample of 10 parts shows means diameter 0.742 cm with a standard deviation of 0.04 cm. On the basis of this sample, find if you would say that the work is inferior.

[given $t_9(0.05)=2.262$]

31. Calculate EMI under Flat-Rate System for a loan of ₹5,00,000 with 7.5% annual interest rate for 5 years.

SECTION D

Directions (Q. Nos. 32-35) are Long Answer (LA) type questions of 5 marks each.

32. (a) If $A=\begin{bmatrix} 2 & -3 & 5 \\ 3 & 2 & -4 \\ 1 & 1 & -2 \end{bmatrix}$, find A^{-1} and hence solve the following system of linear equations.

$2x-3y+5z=11$, $3x+2y-4z=-5$,
$x+y-2z=-3$

OR

*(b) Using properties of determinants, prove that

$$\Delta=\begin{vmatrix} (b+c)^2 & a^2 & a^2 \\ b^2 & (c+a)^2 & b^2 \\ c^2 & c^2 & (a+b)^2 \end{vmatrix}=2abc(a+b+c)^3$$

33. If the supply function is $P_s=4-5x+x^2$ then find the producer's surplus when price is 18.

34. (a) Compute the seasonal indices by 4-year moving averages from the given data of production of paper (in thousand tons)

Year 2001 2002 2003 2004 2005 2006 2007 2008 2009 2010

Index number 2450 1470 2150 1800 1210 1950 2300 2500 2480 2680

OR (b) Fit a straight-line trend by method of least squares for the following data

Year 2011 2012 2013 2014 2015 2016

Production (in tons) 210 225 275 220 240 235

35. A machine costs ₹1,00,000 and its effective life is estimated to be 12 years. A sinking fund is created for replacing the machine by a new model at the end of its life time when its scrap realizes a sum of ₹5,000 only. Find what amount should be set aside at the end of each year, out of the profits for the sinking fund if it accumulates at 5% effective.

[use $(1.05)^{12}=1.7958$]

SECTION E

Directions (Q. Nos. 36-38) are case-study based questions of 4 marks each.

36. A man has an expensive square shaped piece of golden board of side 36 cm. He wants to turn it into a box without top by cutting a square from each corner and folding the flaps. Let x cm be the side of square which is cut from each corner.

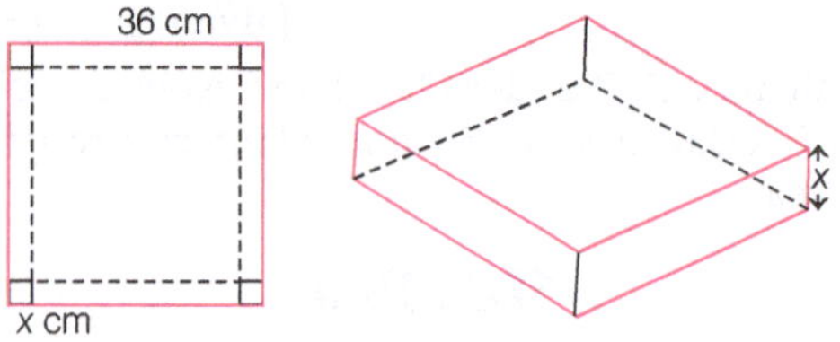

Based on the above information, answer the following questions

(i) Find the expression for the volume (V) of open box in terms of x.

(ii) Find $\frac{dV}{dx}$.

*(iii) Find the value of x for which the volume (V) is maximum.

OR

*Find the maximum volume of the open box.

37. There are two factories located one at P and the other at Q. From these locations, a certain commodity is to be delivered to each of the three depots situated at A, B and C. The weekly requirements of the depots are respectively 4, 4 and 6 units of the commodity while the production capacity of the factories at P and Q are 9 and 5 units, respectively. The cost of transportation per unit is given as

From / To	Cost (in ₹)		
	A	B	C
P	160	100	150
Q	100	120	100

Based on the above information, answer the following questions.

Let x units and y units of the commodity be transported from factory P to the depots at A and B, respectively then

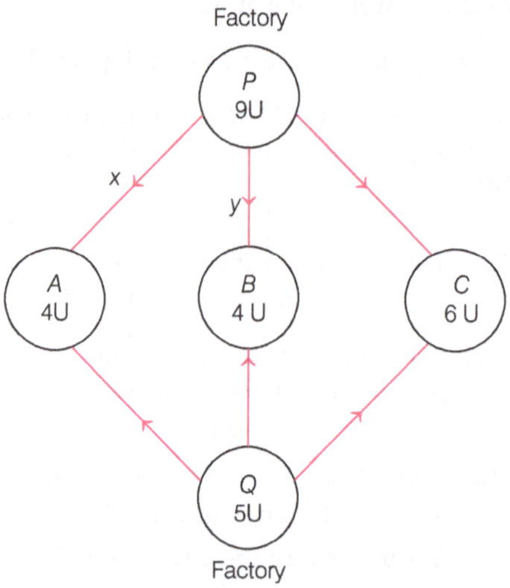

(i) Find (in terms of x and y) how many units of commodity be transported from factory P to depot C.

(ii) Find how many units of commodity be transported from factory Q to A, B and C, respectively.

(iii) Using (i) and (ii), find the total transportation cost Z.

OR

(iii) Using (i) and (ii), find the constraint inequalities for minimum cost Z.

38. Ramesh borrowed a home loan amount of ₹ 7,00,000 from a bank at an interest of 12% per annum for 30 years, to be paid in monthly installments.

Based on the above information, answer the following questions

(i) Write the formula for calculating EMI by reducing balance method.

(ii) Write the values of P, i and n respectively.

(iii) Find the EMI. [use $(1.01)^{-360} = 0.02781668$]

OR If the loan is to be returned in 20 years, find EMI. [use $(1.01)^{-240} = 0.09180584$]

Hints & Solutions

1. (a) We have,

$-41 \bmod 9$

First, divide -41 by 9

$-41 \div 9 \Rightarrow$ Remainder 5

Hence, $-41 \bmod 9 \equiv 5$

2. (d) Given, $a > b$ and $c < 0$

By option (a)

$$a + c < b + c$$

Since, $c < 0$, so adding c to both sides would decrease both values of a and b but since, $a > b$

So, $a + c$ cannot be less than $b + c$.

By option (b)

$$a - c < b - c$$

Since, $c < 0$, subtracting a negative number from a and b would increase both.

So, this would make $a - c > b - c$

$\therefore$ Option (b) is not correct.

By option (c)

$ac > bc$

Since, $a > b$ and $c < 0$, multiplying both sides of inequality by c (– ve) reverse the inequality.

So, ac cannot be greater than bc.

By option (d)

$a - c > b + c$

This hold $a > b$ and $c < 0$.

Hence, option (d) is correct.

3. (a) Given,

A and B are symmetric matrices

Then, $A' = A$

and $B' = B$

Now, $(AB' - BA') = AB - BA$

Hence, $(AB' - BA')$ is a symmetric matrix.

4. (c) We have, $A = \begin{bmatrix} 4 & -1 \\ 2 & 1 \end{bmatrix}$

Then, $|A| = \begin{vmatrix} 4 & -1 \\ 2 & 1 \end{vmatrix} = 4 + 2 = 6 \neq 0$

Therefore, A^{-1} exists.

Now, cofactor of each element of $|A|$ are

$$C_{11} = (-1)^{1+1}(1) = 1$$

$$C_{12} = (-1)^{1+2}(2) = -2$$

$$C_{21} = (-1)^{2+1}(-1) = 1$$

$$C_{22} = (-1)^{2+2}(4) = 4$$

Thus, matrix of cofactor $= \begin{bmatrix} C_{11} & C_{12} \\ C_{21} & C_{22} \end{bmatrix} = \begin{bmatrix} 1 & -2 \\ 1 & 4 \end{bmatrix}$

and $\text{adj}(A) = \begin{bmatrix} 1 & -2 \\ 1 & 4 \end{bmatrix}^T = \begin{bmatrix} 1 & 1 \\ -2 & 4 \end{bmatrix}$

Now, $A^{-1} = \dfrac{1}{|A|} \cdot \text{adj}(A)$

$$= \frac{1}{6}\begin{bmatrix} 1 & 1 \\ -2 & 4 \end{bmatrix} = \begin{bmatrix} 1/6 & 1/6 \\ -1/3 & 2/3 \end{bmatrix}$$

5. (d) We have, $\begin{vmatrix} 2x & 5 \\ 4 & x \end{vmatrix} = \begin{vmatrix} 3 & 5 \\ 4 & 6 \end{vmatrix}$

$\Rightarrow \quad 2x^2 - 20 = 18 - 20$ [expanding along R_1]

$\Rightarrow \quad 2x^2 - 20 + 2 = 0 \Rightarrow 2x^2 = 18$

$\Rightarrow \quad x^2 = 9 \Rightarrow x = \pm 3$

6. (b) Given curve, $y = \dfrac{x-3}{x-4}$

On differentiating both sides w.r.t. x, we get

$$\frac{dy}{dx} = \frac{(x-4)(1) - (x-3)1}{(x-4)^2}$$

$$\Rightarrow \quad \frac{dy}{dx} = \frac{x - 4 - x + 3}{(x-4)^2} = \frac{-1}{(x-4)^2}$$

Now, $\left(\dfrac{dy}{dx}\right)_{\text{at } x = 6} = \dfrac{-1}{(6-4)^2} = \dfrac{-1}{4}$

Hence, the slope of the normal to the given curve at $x = 6$ is $\dfrac{-1}{4}$.

7. (b) Rate of change of population $P(t)$ with respect to time is given by

$$\frac{dP}{dt} = (\text{Birth rate} - \text{Death rate}) \times P$$

Since, α and β are the constant birth and death rates, respectively.

$$\therefore \quad \frac{dP}{dt} = (\alpha - \beta)P$$

8. (c) Given,

a pair of dice is thrown two times.

$\therefore$ Total outcomes $= 6 \times 6 = 36$

Since, X represents the number of doublets obtained.

$\therefore$ Possible outcomes = (1, 1), (2, 2), (3, 3), (4, 4), (5, 5) and (6, 6)

Thus, there are 6 possible doublets.

$\therefore$ The probability of getting a doublet on a single throw of two dice $= \dfrac{6}{36} = \dfrac{1}{6}$

Since, X represents the number of doublets obtained.

Then, Expectation of X, $E(X) = 2 \times \dfrac{1}{6} = \dfrac{1}{3}$

9. (a) As, the mean of the t-distribution is always 0.

10. (c) As, the variation which occur due to change in climate, festivals or weather condition are known as seasonal variations.

11. (b) The intersection of $x + y = 40$ ...(i)

and $x + 2y = 60$ ...(ii)

On subtracting Eq. (i) from Eq. (ii), we get

$$x + 2y - x - y = 60 - 40$$

$$\Rightarrow \quad y = 20$$

Now, on substituting $y = 20$ in $x + y = 40$, we get

$$x + 20 = 40$$

$$\Rightarrow \quad x = 20$$

$\therefore$ Intersection point (20, 20)

The intersection of $x + y = 40$ and $x = 0$

On substituting $x = 0$ in $x + y = 40$, we get

$$\Rightarrow \quad 0 + y = 40$$

$$\Rightarrow \quad y = 40$$

Intersection point (0, 40)

The intersection of $x + 2y = 60$ and $y = 0$

On substituting $y = 0$ in $x + 2y = 60$, we get

$$\Rightarrow \quad x + 0 = 60$$

$$\Rightarrow \quad x = 60$$

$\therefore$ Intersection point (60, 0)

The corner points of the feasible region are (0, 0), (40, 0), (20, 20) and (0, 30).

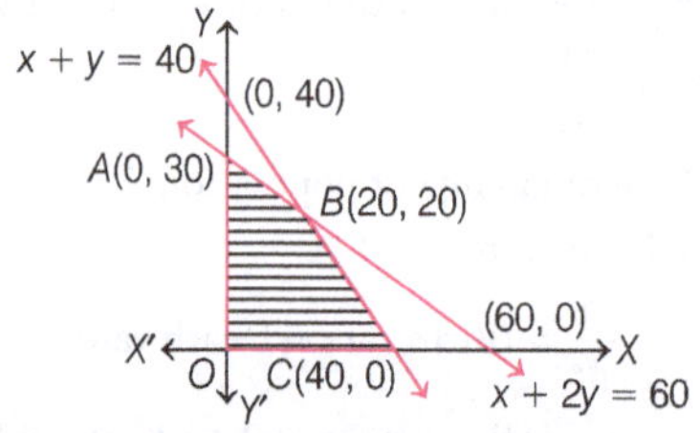

Evaluate $Z = 3x + 4y$ at each corner point

Corner Points (x, y)	$Z = 3x + 4y$
(0, 0)	$Z = 3\times 0 + 4\times 0 = 0$
(40, 0)	$Z = 3\times 40 + 4\times 0 = 120$
(20, 20)	$Z = 3\times 20 + 4\times 20 = 140$
(0, 30)	$Z = 3\times 0 + 4\times 30 = 120$

The maximum value of Z is 140.

12. (a) Given, $PMT =$ ₹ 100,

rate $i = 5\%$ i.e. 0.05

The present value of perpetuity is

$$PV = \frac{PMT}{i}$$

On substituting given values, we get

$$PV = \frac{100}{0.05} \quad [\because 5\% = 0.05]$$

$$\Rightarrow \quad PV = ₹\ 2000$$

13. (d) Revenue is $R = px$ and marginal revenue (MR) is the derivative of the total revenue with respect to quantity

$$MR = \frac{dR}{dx}$$

$$\therefore \quad R = p(x)$$
$$= (30 + 5x - 3x^2)\,x$$
$$= 30x + 5x^2 - 3x^3$$

Now, $MR = \dfrac{dR}{dx}$

$$= \frac{d}{dx}(30x + 5x^2 - 3x^3)$$
$$= 30 + 10x - 9x^2$$

Evaluate marginal revenue at $x = 2$,

$$MR(2) = 30 + 10\times 2 - 9(2)^2$$
$$= 30 + 20 - 9\times 4$$
$$= 30 + 20 - 36 = 14$$

The marginal revenue when 2 units are sold is ₹ 14.

14. (b) Profit function,

$$P(x) = R(x) - C(x)$$
$$\Rightarrow \quad P(x) = 3x - (100 + 0.015x^2)$$
$$\Rightarrow \quad P(x) = 3x - 100 - 0.015x^2$$

Now, $P'(x) = \dfrac{d}{dx}(3x - 100 - 0.015x^2) = 3 - 0.03x$

$$\because \quad P'(x) = 0$$
$$\therefore \quad 3 - 0.03x = 0$$
$$\Rightarrow \quad 0.03x = 3$$
$$\Rightarrow \quad x = \frac{3}{0.03}$$
$$\Rightarrow \quad x = 100$$

The value of x that maximize profit is 100.

15. (b) Set up the equation using the probability distribution.

$$P(X = 0) + P(X = 1) + P(X = 2) = 1$$
$$\Rightarrow \quad k + 2k + 2k = 1$$
$$\Rightarrow \quad 5k = 1$$
$$\therefore \quad k = \frac{1}{5}$$

16. (b) The correct formula is

$$t = \frac{\bar{x} - \bar{y}}{s\sqrt{\dfrac{1}{n_1} + \dfrac{1}{n_2}}}$$

17. (b) Effective interest rate formula, $r_{eff} = \left(1+\frac{r}{n}\right)^n - 1$

On substituting the given values into the formula, we get

$$r_{eff} = \left(1+\frac{0.04}{2}\right)^2 - 1$$

[$\because r = 4\% = 0.04, n = 2$ semi-annually]

$$= (1+0.02)^2 - 1 = (1.02)^2 - 1$$
$$= 1.0404 - 1 = 0.0404$$

Converting into percentage, $r_{eff} = 0.0404 \times \frac{100}{10000} = 4.04\%$

18. (a) We have, $PV = ₹\ 5{,}000$,

$FV = ₹\ 25{,}000$

and $n = 4$

Now, $\text{CAGR} = \left(\frac{FV}{PV}\right)^{\frac{1}{n}} - 1 = \left(\frac{25000}{5000}\right)^{1/4} - 1$

$$= (5)^{1/4} - 1 = (5)^{0.25} - 1$$
$$= 1.4953 - 1 = 0.4953$$

$\therefore$ $\text{CAGR}\% = \frac{0.4953 \times 100}{10000} = 49.53\%$

19. (a) See on pg 228.

20. (a) **Assertion**

Given, $y = mx$ ...(i)

On differentiating both sides w.r.t. x, we get

$$\frac{dy}{dx} = m$$

$\therefore$ From Eq. (i), $y = \left(\frac{dy}{dx}\right)x$

$$x\frac{dy}{dx} - y = 0$$

Assertion is true.

Reason correctly explains of the Assertion.

So, Assertion and Reason both are true and Reason is the correct explanation of Assertion.

21. (a) See on pg 11.

OR (b) See on pg 28.

22. Given, the speed of the current = 1 km/h

Let the speed of the boat be x km/h.

Speed upstream = $(x-1)$ km/h

Speed downstream = $(x+1)$ km/h

According to question,

$$\frac{3.5}{(x-1)} + \frac{3.5}{(x+1)} = 1.2$$

$$\Rightarrow \frac{3.5(x+1)+3.5(x-1)}{(x-1)(x+1)} = 1.2$$

$$\Rightarrow 3.5x + 3.5 + 3.5x - 3.5 = 1.2(x^2 - 1)$$

[$\because (a+b)(a-b) = a^2 - b^2$]

$$\Rightarrow 7x = 1.2x^2 - 1.2$$
$$\Rightarrow 1.2x^2 - 7x - 1.2 = 0$$
$$\Rightarrow 6x^2 - 35x - 6 = 0$$

[by multiplying 5 on both sides]

On comparing with $ax^2 + bc + c = 0$, we get

$a = 6, b = -35$ and $c = -6$

Now, by quadratic formula,

$$x = \frac{-b \pm \sqrt{b^2 - 4ac}}{2a}$$
$$= \frac{35 \pm \sqrt{(35)^2 - 4 \times 6 \times (-6)}}{2 \times 6}$$
$$= \frac{35 \pm \sqrt{1225 + 144}}{12} = \frac{35 \pm \sqrt{1369}}{12}$$
$$= \frac{35 \pm 37}{12}$$

We take the positive solution because speed cannot be negative.

$$x = \frac{35+37}{12} = \frac{72}{12} = 6$$

Hence, the speed of the boat in still water is 6 km/h.

23. Ratio of the speeds of A and $B = 3:2$

Let the speed of A and B be $3x$ and $2x$.

Let the distance covered by B be L.

Then, distance covered by $A = L + 40$

They both reach at the same time.

$$\therefore \frac{L}{2x} = \frac{L+40}{3x}$$
$$\Rightarrow L \cdot 3x = L \cdot 2x + 80x$$
$$\Rightarrow 3x \cdot L - 2x \cdot L = 80x$$
$$\Rightarrow x \cdot L = 80x$$
$$\Rightarrow L = 80$$

A will cover the total distance = $80 + 40 = 120$ m

Hence, the winning post will be 200 metres long from the starting point.

24. $A = \begin{bmatrix} 2 & 0 & 1 \\ 3 & 4 & 5 \\ 0 & 2 & 3 \end{bmatrix}$ and $B = \begin{bmatrix} 1 & 1 & -5 \\ -5 & 1 & -5 \\ 1 & -2 & 4 \end{bmatrix}$

$$\therefore BA = \begin{bmatrix} 1 & 1 & -5 \\ -5 & 1 & -5 \\ 1 & -2 & 4 \end{bmatrix} \begin{bmatrix} 2 & 0 & 1 \\ 3 & 4 & 5 \\ 0 & 2 & 3 \end{bmatrix}$$

$$= \begin{bmatrix} 2+3-0 & 0+4-10 & 1+5-15 \\ -10+3-0 & 0+4-10 & -5+5-15 \\ 2-6+0 & 0-8+8 & 1-10+12 \end{bmatrix}$$

$$= \begin{bmatrix} 5 & -6 & -9 \\ -7 & -6 & -15 \\ -4 & 0 & 3 \end{bmatrix}$$

25. (a) Calculate the probability of getting exactly 4 heads

$n = 6, x = 4$ and $p = \frac{1}{2}$

Binomial probability formula,

$$P(x) = {}^nC_x\, p^x(1-p)^{n-x}$$

$$\therefore \quad P(4) = {}^6C_4\left(\frac{1}{2}\right)^4\left(1-\frac{1}{2}\right)^{6-4}$$

$$= 15\left(\frac{1}{2}\right)^4\left(\frac{1}{2}\right)^2 = 15\left(\frac{1}{2}\right)^6 = \frac{15}{64}$$

Calculate the probability of a getting exactly 5 heads.

$$n = 6,\ x = 5,\ p = \frac{1}{2}$$

$$P(5) = {}^6C_5\left(\frac{1}{2}\right)^5\left(\frac{1}{2}\right)^{6-5} = 6\left(\frac{1}{2}\right)^6 = \frac{6}{64}$$

Calculate the probability of getting exactly 6 heads

$$n = 6,\ x = 6 \text{ and } p = \frac{1}{2}$$

$$P(6) = ({}^6C_6)\left(\frac{1}{2}\right)^6\left(\frac{1}{2}\right)^{6-6} = 1\left(\frac{1}{2}\right)^6 = \frac{1}{64}$$

P(atleast 4 heads) $= P(4) + P(5) + P(6)$

$$= \frac{15}{64} + \frac{6}{64} + \frac{1}{64} = \frac{22}{64} = \frac{11}{32}$$

OR

(b) Mean of normal variate $X: \mu = 9$

(i) Standard deviation of $X: \sigma = 3$

Data point for (i), $x_1 = 15$

z- score for (ii), $z_2 = 4$

Using the z-score formula,

$$z_1 = \frac{x_1 - \mu}{6} \Rightarrow z_1 = \frac{15-9}{3},\ z_1 = \frac{6}{3} = 2$$

(ii) $$z_2 = \frac{x_2 - \mu}{6}$$

$$\Rightarrow \quad x_2 = z_2 \cdot 6 + \mu$$

$$\Rightarrow \quad x_2 = 4 \times 3 + 9 \Rightarrow x_2 = 21$$

26. We have, $7^{295} = (7^4)^{73+3} = (7^4)^{73} \cdot 7^3$

$\because$ The unit digit of 7^4 is 1

and the unit digit of 7^3 is 3.

$\therefore$ The unit digit of $7^{295} = 1 \times 3 = 3$

27. Two numbers are selected randomly without replacement from the set {1, 2, 3, 4, 5, 6}.

The total number of ways to choose 2 numbers from 6 without replacement is ${}^6C_2$.

$$\therefore \quad {}^6C_2 = \frac{6!}{2! \times 4!} = 15 \qquad \left[\because {}^nC_r = \frac{n!}{r!(n-r)!}\right]$$

Let $P(X = x)$ be the probability that the smaller of the two numbers is x.

Probability distribution of X is given by

X	1	2	3	4	5
$P(X)$	$\frac{5}{15}$	$\frac{4}{15}$	$\frac{3}{15}$	$\frac{2}{15}$	$\frac{1}{15}$

Now, $E(X) = \sum_{x=1}^{5} x \cdot P(X = x)$

$$= 1 \times \frac{5}{15} + 2 \times \frac{4}{15} + 3 \times \frac{3}{15} + 4 \times \frac{2}{15} + 5 \times \frac{1}{15}$$

$$= \frac{5}{15} + \frac{8}{15} + \frac{9}{15} + \frac{8}{15} + \frac{5}{15}$$

$$= \frac{5+8+9+8+5}{15} = \frac{35}{15} = \frac{7}{3}$$

Hence, the expected value of the smaller number is $\frac{7}{3}$.

28. (a) We know that mean $= np$ and variance $= npq$

$\therefore np = \frac{4}{3}$ and $npq = \frac{8}{9}$

On dividing variance by mean, we get

$$\frac{npq}{np} = \frac{\frac{8}{9}}{\frac{4}{3}} = \frac{8 \times 3}{9 \times 4} = \frac{2}{3} \Rightarrow q = \frac{2}{3}$$

$$\Rightarrow p = 1 - q = 1 - \frac{2}{3} = \frac{1}{3}$$

Now, $np = \frac{4}{3} \Rightarrow n \times \frac{1}{3} = \frac{4}{3} \Rightarrow n = 4$

So, binomial distribution is given by

$$\therefore \quad P(x = r) = {}^nC_r p^r q^{n-r}$$

$$\Rightarrow \quad P(X = 1) = {}^4C_1\left(\frac{1}{3}\right)^1\left(\frac{2}{3}\right)^{4-1} = 4 \times \frac{1}{3} \times \left(\frac{2}{3}\right)^3$$

$$= 4 \times \frac{1}{3} \times \frac{8}{27} = \frac{32}{81}$$

Hence, the probability $P(x = 1)$ is $\frac{32}{81}$.

OR

(b) Given, Mortality rate = 0.007,

number of people = 400 and number of deaths = 2

We know that the average rate λ is the product of the mortality rate and the number of people.

$$\therefore \quad \lambda = 0.007 \times 400 \Rightarrow \lambda = 2.8$$

Now, by the poisson distribution formula,

$$P(x\,;\lambda) = \frac{e^{-\lambda}\lambda^x}{x!}$$

$$\Rightarrow \quad P(2\,;2.8) = \frac{e^{-2.8}(2.8)^2}{2!} = \frac{0.0608 \times 7.84}{2}$$

$$= \frac{0.476672}{2} = 0.238336$$

Hence, the probability of 2 deaths in a group of 400 people is approximately 0.2383.

29. (a) Let the farmer buy x kg of fertilizer F_1 and y kg of fertilizer F_2. Therefore, $x \geq 0$ and $y \geq 0$

	Nitrogen (%)	Phosphoric Acid (%)	Costs/kg
$F_1(x)$	10	6	6
$F_2(y)$	5	10	5
Requirement	14	14	

F_1 consists of 10% nitrogen and F_2 consists of 5% nitrogen. However, the farmer requires atleast 14 kg of nitrogen.

$\therefore$ 10% of x + 5% of $y \geq 14$

$$\frac{x}{10}+\frac{y}{20} \geq 14$$

$$2x + y \geq 280$$

F_1 consists of 6% phosphoric acid and F_2 consists of 10% phosphoric acid. However, the farmer requires atleast 14 kg of phosphoric acid

$\therefore$ 6% of x + 10% of $y \geq 14$

$$\frac{6x}{100}+\frac{10y}{100} \geq 14$$

$$3x+5y \geq 700$$

$\therefore$ Total cost of fertilizers, $Z = 6x+5y$

Then,

Minimise $Z = 6x+5y$ ... (i)

Subject to the constraints

$2x + y \geq 280$ ... (ii)

$3x + 5y \geq 700$ ... (iii)

$x, y \geq 0$ ... (iv)

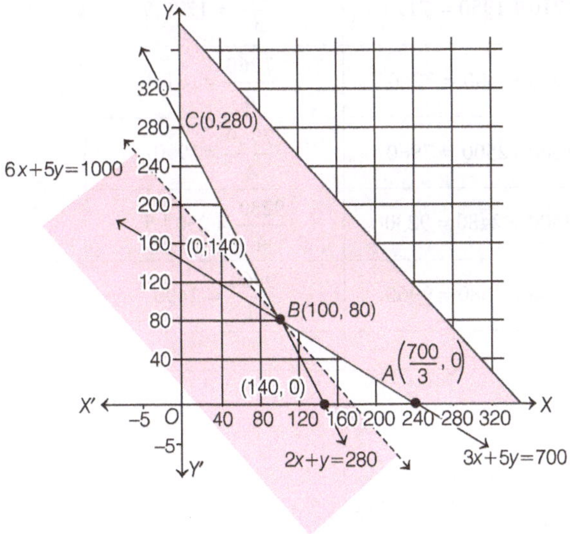

It can be seen that the feasible region is unbounded.

The corner points are $A\left(\frac{700}{3}\right)$, $B(100, 80)$ and $C(0, 280)$.

The values of Z at these points are as follows.

Corner point	$Z = 6x + 5y$
$A\left(\frac{700}{3}, 0\right)$	1400
$B(100, 80)$	1000 (minimum)
$C(0, 280)$	1400

As the feasible region is unbounded.

Therefore, 1000 may or may not be the minimum value of Z.

For this, we draw a graph of the inequality $6x+5y<1000$ and check whether the resulting half plane has points in common with the feasible region or not.

It can be seen that the feasible region has no common point with

$$6x+5y<1000$$

Therefore, 100 kg of fertilizer F_1 and 80 kg of fertilizer F_2 should be used to minimize the cost. The minimum cost is ₹ 1000.

OR

(b) See on pg 352.

30. The t-test statistics formula, $t = \frac{\bar{x}-\mu}{s/\sqrt{n}}$

$\left[\because \mu = 0.7,\ n = 10,\ \bar{x} = 0.742,\ s = 0.04\right]$

$$\therefore \quad t = \frac{0.742-0.7}{0.04/\sqrt{10}}$$

$$= \frac{0.042}{0.04/\sqrt{10}} = \frac{0.042\cdot\sqrt{10}}{0.04}$$

$$= 1.05\cdot\sqrt{10} \approx 3.316$$

The critical t-value is $t_9(0.05) = 2.262$

Since, $3.316 > 2.262$ then the calculated value of t is greater than the critical t-value.

$\because$ Reject the null hypothesis.

$\therefore$ The work is inferior.

31. Loan amount = ₹ 500000,

annual interest rate = 7.5% and loan term = 5 years

Total interest $= P \times r \times t = 500000 \times 0.075 \times 5 =$ ₹ 187500

Amount $= P + I = 500000 + 187500 = 687500$

Now, EMI $= \frac{\text{Total amount}}{t \times 12} = \frac{687500}{5\times 12} = \frac{687500}{60} = 11458.33$

Hence, the EMI for the loan is ₹ 11,458.33.

32. (a) See on pg 135.

OR

(b) This question is not in syllabus.

33. Given, the supply function $p_s = 4 - 5x + x^2$ when $x = 18$ i.e., $x_0 = 18$

Now, $P_0 = 4 - 5 \times 18 + (18)^2 = 4 - 90 + 324 = 238$

$$P_S = x_0 p_0 - \int_0^{x_0} P_s(x)dx$$

$$= 18(238) - \int_0^{18} (4 - 5x + x^2)\, dx$$

$$= 4284 - \left[4x - \frac{5x^2}{2} + \frac{x^3}{2}\right]_0^{18}$$

$$= 4284 - \left[4 \times 18 - 5 \times \frac{324}{2} + \frac{5832}{3}\right]$$

$$= 4284 - [72 - 810 + 1944]$$

$$= 4284 - 1206 = 3078$$

Hence, the producer's surplus is 3078 units.

34. A 4-year moving average is computed by taking the average of four consecutive years.

Formula is 4-year moving average $= \dfrac{\text{Sum of four consecutive years' production}}{4}$

Year	Production Index	Moving Sum (4 year)	4-Year Moving Average
2001	2450	-	-
2002	1470	-	-
2003	2150	$2450 + 1470 + 2150 + 1800 = 7870$	$\frac{7870}{4} = 1967.5$
2004	1800	$1470 + 2150 + 1800 + 1210 = 6630$	$\frac{6630}{4} = 1657.5$
2005	1210	$2150 + 1800 + 1210 + 1950 = 7110$	$\frac{7110}{4} = 1777.5$
2006	1950	$1800 + 1210 + 1950 + 2300 = 7260$	$\frac{7260}{4} = 1815$
2007	2300	$1210 + 1950 + 2300 + 2500 = 7960$	$\frac{7960}{4} = 1990$
2008	2500	$1950 + 2300 + 2500 + 2480 = 9230$	$\frac{9230}{4} = 2307.5$
2009	2480	$2300 + 2500 + 2480 + 2680 = 9960$	$\frac{9960}{4} = 2490$
2010	2680	-	-

Now, Seasonal Index = $\frac{\text{Production Index}}{\text{Moving Average}} \times 100$

Year	Production Index	4-Year Moving Average	Seasonal Index (%)
2001	2450	-	-
2002	1470	-	-
2003	2150	1967.5	$\frac{2150}{1967.5} \times 100 = 109.27$
2004	1800	1657.5	$\frac{1800}{1657.5} \times 100 = 108.6$
2005	1210	1777.5	$\frac{1210}{1777.5} \times 100 = 68.07$
2006	1950	1815	$\frac{1950}{1815} \times 100 = 107.44$
2007	2300	1990	$\frac{2300}{1990} \times 100 = 115.58$
2008	2500	2307.5	$\frac{2500}{2307.5} \times 100 = 108.34$
2009	2480	2490	$\frac{2480}{2540} \times 100 = 97.64$
2010	2680	-	-

OR

(b) Here, $n = 6$ (even). So, origin is mean of two middle years i.e. $\frac{2013 + 2014}{2} = 2013.5$

Year (t)	Production (Y)	$x = t_i - 2013.5$	x^2	xy	$y_t = a + bx$
2011	210	−2.5	6.25	−525	225.95
2012	225	−1.5	2.25	−337.5	229.24
2013	275	−0.5	0.25	−137.5	232.53
2014	220	0.5	0.25	110	235.82
2015	240	1.5	2.25	360	239.11
2016	235	2.5	6.25	587.5	242.40
	$\Sigma y = 1405$	$\Sigma x = 0$	$\Sigma x^2 = 17.5$	$\Sigma xy = 57.5$	

Here, $a = \frac{\Sigma y}{n} = \frac{1405}{6} = 234.17$ and $b = \frac{\Sigma xy}{\Sigma x^2} = \frac{57.5}{17.5} = 3.29$

$\therefore$ The required equation of the trend line is $y_t = 234.17 + 3.29x$

So, trend values

For year 2011, $x = -2.5$ $y_t = 234.17 + 3.29(-2.5) = 225.95$

For year 2012, $x = -1.5$ $y_t = 234.17 + 3.29(-1.5) = 229.24$

For year 2013, $x = -0.5$ $y_t = 234.17 + 3.29(-0.5) = 232.53$

For year 2014, $x = 0.5$ $y_t = 234.17 + 3.29(0.5) = 235.82$

For year 2015, $x = 1.5$ $y_t = 234.17 + 3.29(1.5) = 239.11$

For year 2016, $x = 2.5$ $y_t = 234.17 + 3.29(2.5) = 242.40$

35. Given, cost = ₹ 100000, $n = 12$

Scrap value = ₹ 5000, $i = 5\% = \frac{5}{100} = 0.05$

$\therefore$ Remaining amount,

$$S = 100000 - 5000 = ₹\ 95000$$

$$\therefore \quad R = \frac{S}{[(1+i)^n - 1]/i}$$

$$= \frac{95000}{\frac{[(1+0.05)^{12} - 1]}{0.05}}$$

$$= \frac{95000}{(1.05)^{12} - 1} \times 0.05$$

$$= \frac{4750}{1.7958 - 1}$$

$$= \frac{4750}{0.7958}$$

$$= 5968.84$$

So, the amount to be set aside at the end of each year is ₹ 5970.44.

36. The side of square piece which cut from each corner is x cm.

The new dimensions of the box will be $(36 - 2x)$ cm by $(36 - 2x)$ cm by x cm.

(i) The volume of the box is,

$$V = (36 - 2x)(36 - 2x)\,x$$
$$= x\,(36 - 2x)^2$$
$$= x\,(1296 - 144x + 4x^2)$$
$$= 4x^3 - 144x^2 + 1296x \quad \text{...(i)}$$

(ii) We have,

$$V = 4x^3 - 144x^2 + 1296x$$

On differentiating both sides w.r.t. x, we get

$$\frac{dV}{dx} = 12x^2 - 288x + 1296 \quad \text{...(ii)}$$

(iii) This question is not in syllabus.

OR

(iii) This question is not in syllabus.

37. (i) Let x units and y units of the commodity be transported from the factory at P to the depots at A and B, respectively.

Then, $(9 - x - y)$ units will be transported to depot at C.

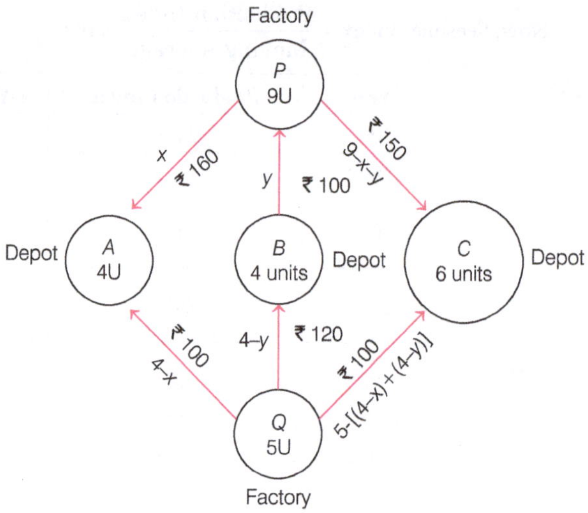

(ii) Hence, we have $x \geq 0$, $y \geq 0$ and $9 - x - y \geq 0$

i.e. $x \geq 0$, $y \geq 0$ and $x + y \leq 8$.

Now, the weekly requirement of the depot at A is 4 units of the commodity.

Since, x units are transported from the factory at P, the remaining $(4 - x)$ units need to be transported from the factory at Q.

Obviously, $4 - x \geq 0$ i.e. $x \leq 4$

Similarly, $(4 - y)$ and $5 - (4 - x + 4 - y) = x + y - 3$ units are to be transported from the factory at Q to the depots at B and C, respectively.

Thus, $4 - y \geq 0$, $x + y - 3 \geq 0$ i.e. $y \leq 0$, $x + y \geq 4$

(iii) Total transportation cost Z is given by

$$Z = 160 \cdot x + 100y + 100\,(4 - x) + 120\,(4 - y) + 100\,(x + y - 3) + 150\,(9 - x - y)$$
$$= 160x + 100y + 400 - 400x + 480 - 120y + 100x + 100y - 300 + 1350 - 150x - 150y$$
$$= 1930 - 290x - 70y$$
$$= 10(193 - 29x - 7y)$$

$\therefore$ The total cost of transportation,

$$Z = 10(193 - 29x - 7y)$$

OR

(iv) The constraint inequalities for minimum cost Z

$$x \geq 0,\ y \geq 0 \quad \text{...(i)}$$
$$x + y \leq 9 \quad \text{...(ii)}$$
$$x \leq 4 \quad \text{...(iii)}$$
$$y \leq 4 \quad \text{...(iv)}$$
and
$$x + y \geq 4 \quad \text{...(v)}$$

38. See on pg 342.

SAMPLE QUESTION PAPER 1

A Highly Simulated Sample Question Paper for CBSE Class XII Examination

APPLIED MATHEMATICS (Unsolved)

Time 3 Hours **Max. Marks 80**

General Instructions

Read the following instructions very carefully and strictly follow them.

(i) This question paper contains 38 questions. All questions are compulsory.
(ii) Question paper is divided into FIVE sections - Section A, B, C, D and E.
(iii) In Section A, Question number 1 to 18 are Multiple Choice Questions (MCQs) and Question number 19 and 20 are Assertion-Reason based questions carrying 1 mark each.
(iv) In Section B, Question number 21 to 25 are Very Short Answer (VSA) type questions carrying 2 marks each.
(v) In Section C, Question number 26 to 31 are Short Answer (SA) type questions carrying 3 marks each.
(vi) In Section D, Question number 32 to 35 are Long Answer (LA) type questions carrying 5 marks each.
(vii) In Section E, Question number 36 to 38 are Case Study Based question carrying 4 marks each.
(viii) There is no overall choice. However, an internal choice has been provided in 2 questions in Section B, 2 questions in Section C, 2 questions in Section D and 3 questions in Section E.
(ix) Use of calculator is NOT allowed.

SECTION A

Multiple Choice Questions

Each question carries 1 mark

Directions (Q. Nos. 1-18) *All questions are compulsory. No Internal Choice is provided in this section.*

1. In a 10 km race, P, Q and R, each running at uniform speed, get the gold, silver and bronze medals, respectively. If P beats Q by 1 km and Q beats R by 1 km, then by how many metres does P beats R?

(a) 1600 (b) 1500
(c) 1400 (d) 1900

2. The values of x satisfying $\frac{1}{2}\left(\frac{3}{5}x+4\right) \geq \frac{1}{3}(x-6)$ are

(a) $x \geq 120$ (b) $x \leq 120$
(c) $x \leq 12$ (d) None of these

3. If A is a square matrix, then $A - A'$ is a

(a) diagonal matrix
(b) skew-symmetric matrix
(c) symmetric matrix
(d) None of the above

4. If $A = \begin{bmatrix} 6 & x & 2 \\ 2 & -1 & 2 \\ -10 & 5 & 2 \end{bmatrix}$ is a singular matrix, then the value of x is

(a) -3 (b) 2 (c) 1 (d) -5

5. If $y = 3e^{2x} + 2e^{3x}$, then $\frac{d^2y}{dx^2} - 5\frac{dy}{dx} + 6y$ is equal to

(a) 0 (b) 1
(c) -1 (d) 2

6. The length of the longest interval, in which $f(x) = 3\sin x - 4\sin^3 x$ is increasing, is

(a) $\frac{\pi}{2}$ (b) $\frac{\pi}{3}$ (c) $\frac{3\pi}{2}$ (d) π

7. The order and degree of the differential equation $\frac{d^2y}{dx^2}+x\left(\frac{dy}{dx}\right)^2=2x^2\log\left(\frac{d^2y}{dx^2}\right)$ are respectively

(a) 1, 1 (b) 2, 1
(c) 1, 2 (d) 2, not defined

8. Consider the following hypothesis test

$H_0 : \mu \le 20$

$H_a : \mu > 20$

A sample of 40 provided a sample mean of 24.3 and population standard deviation is 5. The value of the test statistics is

(a) 4.24 (b) 5.63
(c) 6.84 (d) 2.36

9. The smallest non-negative integer congruent to 2796 (mod 7) is

(a) 1 (b) 2
(c) 5 (d) 3

10. If X is poisson variate such that $P(X=1)=2P(X=2)$, then the mean and variance are respectively

(a) 1, 1 (b) 1, 2
(c) 2, 1.2 (d) 1, 2.2

11. In hypothesis testing, the null hypothesis is typically

(a) the statement being test for significance
(b) the opposite of the research hypothesis
(c) always accepted as true
(d) always rejected

12. In a one-sample t-test, the degrees of freedom are calculated as

(a) $n-1$, where n is the sample size.
(b) n, where n is the sample size.
(c) $n+1$, where n is the sample size.
(d) $\frac{n}{2}$, where n is the sample size.

13. The number of letters, in hundreds, posted in a certain city on each day for a week is given as 3 5, 70, 36, 59, 62, 60, 71, the three day moving averages are

(a) 47, 55, 58
(b) 47, 55, 52.33
(c) 55, 47, 52.33
(d) 52.33, 47, 55

14. For his son's education, a man sets aside ₹ 4000 at the end of every year for 8 yr. If the rate of interest is 15% per annum, then the value of this sinking fund is [given $(1.15)^8 = 3.0590$]

(a) ₹ 52000 (b) ₹ 54900
(c) ₹ 54906.67 (d) ₹ 57906.67

15. The present value of a perpetuity of ₹ 5000 payable at the end of each year, if money is worth 5% compounded annually is

(a) ₹ 105000 (b) ₹ 100000
(c) ₹ 120500 (d) ₹ 101500

16. In what ratio must rice at ₹ 29.30 per kg be mixed with rice at ₹ 30.80 per kg, so that the mixture be worth ₹ 30 per kg

(a) 8 : 7 (b) 6 : 7 (c) 8 : 15 (d) 3 : 7

17. If $\frac{|x-2|}{x-2} \ge 0$, then

(a) $x \in [2, \infty)$ (b) $x \in (2, \infty)$
(c) $x \in (-\infty, 2)$ (d) $x \in (-\infty, 2]$

18. The maximum value of $Z = 4x + 2y$ subjected to the constraints $2x + 3y \le 18$, $x + y \ge 10$ $x, y \ge 0$ is

(a) 40 (b) 36
(c) 20 (d) None of these

Assertion-Reason Based Questions

Directions (Q. Nos. 19-20) *In the question number 19 and 20, a statement of Assertion (A) is followed by a statement of Reason (R). Choose the correct option.*

(a) Both (A) and (R) are true and (R) is the correct explanation of (A).
(b) Both (A) and (R) are true but (R) is not the correct explanation of (A).
(c) (A) is true but (R) is false.
(d) (A) is false but (R) is true.

19. **Assertion** (A) $f(x)=2x^3-9x^2+12x-3$ is increasing outside the interval (1, 2).

Reason (R) $f'(x) \le 0$ for $x \in (1,2)$.

20. **Assertion** (A) X is a binomial distribution with parameters $n=100$ and P.

If $p(X=50)=p(X=49)$, then $P=\frac{1}{2}$.

Reason (R) For the binomial distribution $(q+p)^n$, $p(x=k)={}^nC_k \cdot q^{n-k} \cdot p^k$.

SECTION B

[This section comprises of very short answer type questions (VSA) of 2 marks each]

21. (a) If $A=\begin{bmatrix}2 & 3\\5 & -2\end{bmatrix}$, show that $A^{-1}=\frac{1}{19}A$.

Or

(b) If $A=\begin{bmatrix}0 & 1 & 3\\1 & 2 & x\\2 & 3 & 1\end{bmatrix}$ and $A^{-1}=\begin{bmatrix}1/2 & -4 & 5/2\\-1/2 & 3 & -3/2\\1/2 & y & 1/2\end{bmatrix}$,

then find x and y.

22. Solve the following system of equations using Cramer's rule

$$2x-y=17$$
$$3x+5y=6$$

23. Find the solution to the following LPP (if it exists) graphically :

Maximize $Z=50x+30y$

Subject to the constraints

$2x+y\le 18$, $3x+2y\le 34$ and $x,y\ge 0$

24. A money lender charges interest at the rate of 5 paise per rupee per month, payable in advance. What effective rate of interest does he charge per month?

25. (a) The present value of a perpetual income of ₹ x at the end of each 6 months is ₹ 144000. Find the value of x if money is worth 6% compounded semi-annually.

Or

(b) The annual depreciation of a car is ₹ 30000, if the scrap value of the car after 15 yr is ₹ 50000, then find the original cost of the car, when depreciation is linear.

SECTION C

[This section comprises of short answer type questions (SA) of 3 marks each]

26. 80 L of milk is kept in a container. From this volume, 8 L of milk was taken out and replaced by water. This process was repeated two more time. How much milk (approximately) is now present in the container?

27. (a) Sketch the region bounded by $y=2x-x^2$ and X-axis and evaluate $\int_0^2 y\,dx$.

Or

(b) Evaluate $\int_1^2\left(\frac{x-1}{x^2}\right)e^x dx$.

28. Form the differential equation corresponding to $y^2=m(a^2-x^2)$ by eliminating parameters m and a.

29. In a meeting 70% of the numbers favour a certain proposal, 30% being opposed. A member is selected at random and let $X=0$, if he opposed, and $X=1$ if he is in favour, then find $E(X)$ and Var (X).

30. A random sample of size 16 has 53 as mean. The sum of the squares of the deviations taken from mean is 150. Can this sample be regarded as taken from the population having 56 as mean? (Given $t_{15}(0.01)=2.95$)

31. (a) Mr. Suraj took a loan of ₹ 3000. Find the effective rate of interest charged by the lender if while lending, the lender deducts in advance

(i) ₹ 200 as interest for 6 months

(ii) ₹ 100 as interest of 3 months

Or (b) Find the effective rate that is equivalent each of the following nominal rates :

(i) 6% compounded monthly

(ii) 5% compounded continuously

SECTION D

[This section comprises of long answer type questions (LA) of 5 marks each]

32. Three pipes A, B and C are connected to a cistern. Out of three A and B are the inlet pipes and C is the outlet pipe. If opened separately, A fills the tank in 10 hours and B fills the tank in 30 hours. If all the three pipes are opened together, if takes 30 min extra than if only A and B are opened. How much time does it take to empty the tank, if only pipe C is opened?

33. (a) Find the local maxima and local minima and the corresponding local maximum and local minimum values of the following functions :

(i) $f(x)=\frac{2}{x}+\frac{x}{2}, x>0$

(ii) $f(x)=x\sqrt{1-x^2}$, where $x\le 1$

Or

(b) Find the intervals in which the following function is strictly increasing or strictly decreasing

$$f(x)=\frac{3}{10}x^4-\frac{4}{5}x^3-3x^2+\frac{36x}{5}+11$$

34. (a) The probability distribution of a random variable X is given below :

$$X:0\ 1\ 2\ 3$$
$$p(X):k\ \frac{k}{2}\ \frac{k}{4}\ \frac{k}{8}$$

(i) Find the value of k

(ii) Determine $p(X\leq 2)$

(iii) Find $p(X\leq 2)+p(X>2)$

Or

(b) Between the hours 2 and 4 pm the average number of phone calls per minute coming into the switchboard of a company is 2.5. Find the probability that during one particular minute there will be no phone call at all. [Given, $e^{-2}=0.13435$ and $e^{-0.5}=0.60650$]

35. Shivangi purchased a house from a company for ₹ 700000 and made a down payment of ₹ 150000. She repays the balance in 25 years by monthly installments at 9% compound monthly

(i) What are monthly payments?

(ii) What is the total interest payments?

[Given $1.0075^{-300}=0.1062878338$]

SECTION E

[This section comprises 3 case-study/passage based questions of 4 marks each]

36. A manufacturer has three machines I, II and III installed in his factory. Machines I and II are capable of being operated for at most 12 h, whereas machine III must be operated for atleast 5 h a day.

She produces only two items M and N each requiring the use of all the three machines. The number of hours required for producing 1 unit of each of M and N on the three machines are given in the following table.

Items	Number of hours required on Machine		
	I	II	III
M	1	2	1
N	2	1	1.25

She makes a profit of ₹ 600 and ₹ 400 on items M and N, respectively.

Let x and y be the number of items M and N respectively and assume that she can sell all the items that she produced.

On the basis of above information, answer the following questions.

(i) What is the constraints on machine I?

(ii) (a) How many units of item M should she produce, so as to maximise her profit?

Or

(b) How many units of item N should she produce, so as to maximise her profit?

(iii) Find the all corner points of feasible region.

37. The following data shows the percentage rural, urban and suburban Indians who have a high speed internet connection at home.

Year	Rural	Urban	Suburban
2013	3	9	9
2014	6	18	17
2015	9	21	23
2016	16	29	29
2017	24	38	40

Based on above information, answer the following questions.

(i) Determine the equation of straight line trend by the method of least square for the rural Indians and suburban Indians.

(ii) (a) What is the forecast for the year 2018 for rural group using trend equation?

Or

(b) What is the forecast for the year 2018 for urban group using trend equation?

38. The order of a differential equation is the order of the highest derivative appearing in the equation and the power of the highest order derivative is a degree.

On the basis of the above information, solve the following questions.

(i) Find the order of the differential equation

$$\left(\frac{d^3y}{dx^3}\right)^3 + 5\left(\frac{d^2y}{dx^2}\right)^5 - 8y = 0.$$

(ii) (a) Find the degree of the differential equation

$$\left(\frac{d^2y}{dx^2}\right)^2 + \left(\frac{dy}{dx}\right)^3 = \log\left(\frac{dy}{dx}\right).$$

Or

(b) Find the sum of the order and degree of a differential equation $4\sqrt{\frac{d^2y}{dx^2}} = \sqrt{3\frac{dy}{dx}}$.

(iii) The solution of the differential equation $\frac{dy}{dx} = x^2y^2$.

SAMPLE QUESTION PAPER 2

A Highly Simulated Sample Question Paper for CBSE Class XII Examination

APPLIED MATHEMATICS (Unsolved)

Time 3 Hours **Max. Marks 80**

General Instructions

Read the following instructions very carefully and strictly follow them.

(i) This question paper contains 38 questions. All questions are compulsory.

(ii) Question paper is divided into FIVE sections - Section A, B, C, D and E.

(iii) In Section A, Question number 1 to 18 are Multiple Choice Questions (MCQs) and Question number 19 and 20 are Assertion-Reason based questions carrying 1 mark each.

(iv) In Section B, Question number 21 to 25 are Very Short Answer (VSA) type questions carrying 2 marks each.

(v) In Section C, Question number 26 to 31 are Short Answer (SA) type questions carrying 3 marks each.

(vi) In Section D, Question number 32 to 35 are Long Answer (LA) type questions carrying 5 marks each.

(vii) In Section E, Question number 36 to 38 are Case Study Based question carrying 4 marks each.

(viii) There is no overall choice. However, an internal choice has been provided in 2 questions in Section B, 2 questions in Section C, 2 questions in Section D and 3 questions in Section E.

(ix) Use of calculator is NOT allowed.

SECTION A

Multiple Choice Questions

Each question carries 1 mark

Directions (Q. Nos. 1-18) *All questions are compulsory. No Internal Choice is provided in this section.*

1. What time will it be after 800 hours, if the present time is 7:00 pm?

(a) 3 pm (b) 3 am
(c) 4 am (d) 4 pm

2. If the calculated value of $|t| > t_v(\alpha)$ (critical value of t), then the null hypothesis

(a) is accepted
(b) is rejected
(c) is neither accepted nor rejected
(d) cannot be determined

3. In a kilometer race, player X beats player Y by 40 m or by 5 sec. What is X's time to complete the race?

(a) 120 sec (b) 100 sec
(c) 60 sec (d) 130 sec

4. The order and the degree of the differential equation

$5\frac{d^2y}{dx^2} = \left(1 + \left(\frac{dy}{dx}\right)^2\right)^{1/4}$ are respectively

(a) 2, 2 (b) 1, 2
(c) 2, 1 (d) 2, 4

5. The value of $\Delta = \begin{vmatrix} 102 & 18 & 36 \\ 1 & 3 & 4 \\ 17 & 3 & 6 \end{vmatrix}$

(a) 40 (b) − 40
(c) 1 (d) 0

6. If $AB = A$ and $BA = B$, then B^2 equals

(a) 0 (b) I (c) A (d) B

7. Find the interval in which the function $f(x) = x^2 - 2x$ is strictly increasing.

(a) $[1, \infty)$ (b) $(1, \infty)$
(c) $(0, \infty)$ (d) $(-\infty, 1)$

8. If $y = e^{-3x}$, then $\frac{d^2y}{dx^2}$ is equal to

(a) $9e^{-3x}$ (b) $-3e^{-3x}$

(c) $-27e^{-3x}$ (d) $81e^{-3x}$

9. If $x \in R, |x| \geq -6$, then

(a) $x \in (-\infty, -6) \cup (6, \infty)$

(b) $x \in R$

(c) $x \in [-6, 6]$

(d) $x \in (-\infty, -6) \cup [6, \infty)$

10. Two dice are thrown simultaneously. If X denotes the number of sixes, then the mathematical expectation of X is

(a) $\frac{1}{2}$ (b) $\frac{1}{4}$ (c) $\frac{1}{6}$ (d) $\frac{1}{3}$

11. If m is the mean of a poisson distribution, then variance is given by

(a) m^2 (b) $m^{1/2}$

(c) m (d) $\frac{m}{2}$

12. When the researcher rejects a true null hypothesis, a .... error occurs.

(a) Type I (b) Type A

(c) Type II (d) Type B

13. For the given values 15, 24, 18, 33, 42, the 3 yearly moving averages are

(a) 19, 22, 33 (b) 19, 25, 31

(c) 19, 30, 31 (d) 19, 22, 30

14. A set of values of decision variables that satisfies the linear constraints and non-negativity conditions of on LPP is called its

(a) Unbounded solution

(b) Optimum solution

(c) Feasible solution

(d) Bounded solution

15. The point which does not lie in the half plane $2x + 3y - 12 < 0$ is

(a) (2, 1) (b) (1, 2)

(c) (−2, 3) (d) (2, 3)

16. A bond of face value ₹ 1000 matures in 5 yr, coupon rate is 6% paid semi-annually. If the discount rate is 6% p.a., then the present value of the bond is

(a) ₹ 952 (b) ₹ 1048

(c) ₹ 1000 (d) ₹ 1152

17. Using flat rate method, the EMI to repay a loan of ₹ 500000 by equal monthly payments in 10 yr at an interest rate of 7.5% p.a. compounded monthly is

(a) ₹ 5935 (b) ₹ 6380 (c) ₹ 7340 (d) ₹ 8520

18. A vehicle costing ₹ 125000 has scrap value of ₹ 25000. If annual depreciation charge is ₹ 12500, then useful life of the vehicle is

(a) 6 yr (b) 8 yr (c) 4 yr (d) 10 yr

Assertion-Reason Based Questions

Directions *In the question number 19 and 20, a statement of Assertion (A) is followed by a statement of Reason (R). Choose the correct option.*

(a) Both (A) and (R) are true and (R) is the correct explanation of (A).

(b) Both (A) and (R) are true, but (R) is not the correct explanation of (A).

(c) (A) is true, but (R) is false.

(d) (A) is false, but (R) is true.

19. **Assertion** (A) The function $f(x) = 6x - x^2, x > 0$ is increasing in (0, 3).

Reason (R) If $f(x)$ is continuous on $[a, b]$ and derivable on (a, b), then $f(x)$ is increasing on (a, b) if $f'(x) \geq 0$ for all $x \in (a, b)$.

20. In a binomial distribution, $n = 400$ and $p = 0.02$. Taking poisson distribution as an approximation to the binomial distribution

Assertion (A) Mean of poisson distribution = 8.

Reason (R) $P(X = 2) = \frac{64}{4e^8}$.

SECTION B

[This section comprises of very short answer type questions (VSA) of 2 marks each]

21. Using Cramer's rule, solve the following system of equations

$$3x + y = 5$$
$$x + 2y = 3$$

22. (a) If $A = \begin{bmatrix} 3 & -2 \\ 4 & -2 \end{bmatrix}$, find the value of k such that $A^2 - kA + 2I = 0$.

Or

(b) If $\begin{bmatrix} 2x & -7 \\ 5y & 3x + y \end{bmatrix} = \begin{bmatrix} 10 & -3 \\ -5 & 14 \end{bmatrix}$, find the value of $x + 5y$.

23. Find the solution to the following linear programming problem (if it exists) graphically

Maximise $Z = 2x + 5y$

Subject to the constraints

$$2x + 4y \le 8$$
$$3x + y \le 6$$
$$x + y \le 4$$
$$x, y \ge 0$$

24. At 5% p.a. compounded yearly, find the present value of a perpetuity of ₹ 900 payable at the end of each year.

25. (a) Vikas invested ₹ 20000 in a mutual fund in year 2012. The value of mutual fund increased to ₹ 36000 in year 2017. Calculate CAGR (Compounded Annual Growth Rate). [use : $(1.8)^{1/5} = 1.125$]

Or

(b) What nominal rate compounded quarterly will be equivalent to 12% compounded continuously? [given $e^{0.12} = 1.1274$]

SECTION C

[This section comprises of short answer type questions (SA) of 3 marks each]

26. (a) Evaluate $\int_{-1}^{1} (x+1)dx$ and hence show the region on the graph whose area it represents.

Or

(b) Evaluate $\int_{0}^{1} \frac{dx}{2e^x - 1}$

27. Find the differential equation of the family of ellipses having foci on the Y-axis and centre at the origin.

28. (a) The cost of a machine depreciating by ₹ 722 during the third year and by ₹ 685.90 during the fourth year. Calculate
   (i) the rate of depreciation per annum.
   (ii) the original cost of the machine.
   (iii) the scrap value of the machine, if the estimated useful life is 20 yr.

Or

(b) How many years will it take for money to double at the effective rate of 6%?

29. The weight of students of class XII follow normal distribution with mean 50 kg and standard deviation 2 kg. Find the probability that a student selected at random will have weight between 48 and 56 kg.

[given $P(Z < 3) = 0.9986$ and $P(Z < -1) = 0.8413$]

30. A container contains 100 L of milk. From the container, 10 L of milk was taken out and replaced by equal amount of water. This process was further repeated twice. Determine the quantity of milk left in the container.

31. A machinist is making engine parts with axle diameter of 0.7 inch. A random sample of 10 parts shows mean diameter 0.742 inch with a standard deviation of 0.04 inch. On the basis of this sample would you say that the work is inferior?
[given $t_g(0.05) = 2.262$]

SECTION D

[This section comprises of long answer type questions (LA) of 5 marks each]

32. (a) Find the intervals in which the following function f is strictly increasing or strictly decreasing

$$f(x) = 3x^4 - 4x^3 - 12x^2 + 5$$

Or

(b) Find all the points of local maxima and local minima of the function

$$f(x) = 2x^3 - 21x^2 + 36x - 20$$

33. (a) The probability distribution of a random variable X is given as under

$$P(X = x) = \begin{cases} kx^2, & \text{for } x = 1, 2, 3 \\ 2kx, & \text{for } x = 4, 5, 6 \\ 0, & \text{otherwise} \end{cases}$$

where k is a constant.
   (i) What is the value of k?
   (ii) Find the probability $P(X < 4)$.
   (iii) Find the probability $P(X \ge 4)$.

Or

(b) An airline accepts reservation for the seats on a particular flight of a 98 seater aircraft. It is known from past experience that 3% of the persons who reserve seats do not turn up and so the airline has a policy of a allowing 100 persons to book seats on the flight. What is the probability of more than 98 persons turning up for the flights?

34. Three pipes A, B and C connected to a tank. Out of the three A and B are inlet pipes and C is outlet pipe. If opened separately, A fills the tank in 10 hours, B fills the tank in 12 hours and C empties the tank in 30 hours. If all three are opened simultaneously, how much time does it take to fill the tank?

35. Aman buys a car for which he makes down payment of ₹ 150,000 and the balance is to be paid in 2 yr by monthly installment of ₹ 25448 each. If the financer charges interest at the rate of 20% p.a., find the actual price of the car.

$$\left(\text{Given} \left(\frac{61}{60}\right)^{-24} = 0.67253\right)$$

SECTION E

[This section comprises 3 case-study/passage based questions of 4 marks each]

36. Two schools M and N decided to award their selected students for the values of discipline and honesty in the form of prizes at the rate of ₹ x and ₹ y respectively. School M decided to award respectively 3, 2 students a total prize money of ₹ 2300 and school N decided to award respectively 5, 3 students a total prize money of ₹ 3700.

Based on the above information, answer the following questions.

(i) Write the system of linear equations in x and y formed of the given situation.

(ii) Write the system of linear equations, obtained in (i) above in matrix form $AX = B$.

(iii) (a) Find the inverse of matrix A.

Or

(b) Determine the values of x and y.

37. The feasible region for on LPP is shown in the figure given below :

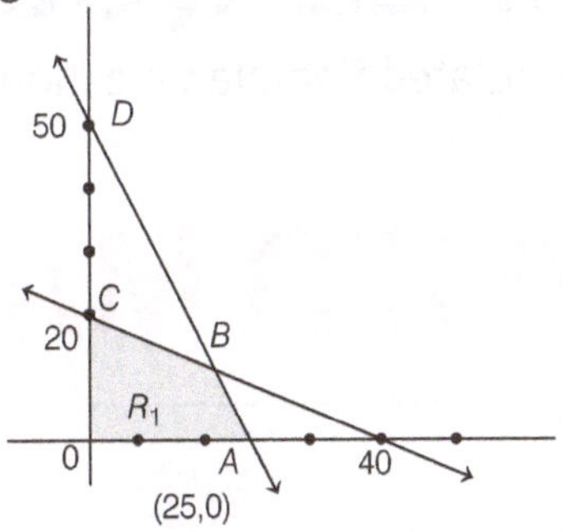

Based on the given information, answer the following questions.

(i) What are the two trivial constraints.

(ii) If R_1 is the feasible region, then find the maximum value of the objective function $Z = 3x + 4y$.

(iii) (a) If R_1 is the feasible region, then what are the other two non-trivial constraints?

Or

(b) If R_1 is the feasible region, then find the minimum value of the objective function $Z = 3x + 4y$.

38. The table given below shows the profit of a firm during 2004-2010.

Year	2004	2005	2006	2007	2008	2009	2010
Profit (₹ '000)	114	130	126	144	138	156	164

Based on the above information, answer the following questions :

(i) Determine the equation of the straight line trend.

(ii) (a) Tabulate the trend values of the years.

Or (b) Fit a straight line trend by the method of least squares and tabulate the trend values from the following data :

Year	2000	2001	2002	2003	2004	2005	2006
Productions (tonnes)	40	45	46	42	47	50	46

(iii) Determine the equation of the least square trend line for the profit of the firm from 2004 to 2010.

SAMPLE QUESTION PAPER 3

A Highly Simulated Sample Question Paper for CBSE Class XII Examination

APPLIED MATHEMATICS (Unsolved)

Time 3 Hours **Max. Marks 80**

General Instructions

Read the following instructions very carefully and strictly follow them.

(i) This question paper contains 38 questions. All questions are compulsory.
(ii) Question paper is divided into FIVE sections - Section A, B, C, D and E.
(iii) In Section A, Question number 1 to 18 are Multiple Choice Questions (MCQs) and Question number 19 and 20 are Assertion-Reason based questions carrying 1 mark each.
(iv) In Section B, Question number 21 to 25 are Very Short Answer (VSA) type questions carrying 2 marks each.
(v) In Section C, Question number 26 to 31 are Short Answer (SA) type questions carrying 3 marks each.
(vi) In Section D, Question number 32 to 35 are Long Answer (LA) type questions carrying 5 marks each.
(vii) In Section E, Question number 36 to 38 are Case Study Based question carrying 4 marks each.
(viii) There is no overall choice. However, an internal choice has been provided in 2 questions in Section B, 2 questions in Section C, 2 questions in Section D and 3 questions in Section E.
(ix) Use of calculator is NOT allowed.

SECTION A

Multiple Choice Questions

Each question carries 1 mark

Directions (Q. Nos. 1-18) *All questions are compulsory. No Internal Choice is provided in this section.*

1. $(09:30+16:40)$ in 24 h clock is
(a) 03 : 10 (b) 2 : 10
(c) 26 : 10 (d) 25 : 70

2. Consider the following hypothesis test
$$H_0 : \mu \le 20$$
$$H_a : \mu > 20$$
A sample of 40 provided a sample mean of 24.3 and population standard deviation is 5. The value of the test statistics is
(a) 5.63 (b) 6.84 (c) 2.36 (d) 4.24

3. If $x \le 8$, then
(a) $-x \le -8$ (b) $-x < -8$
(c) $-x \ge -8$ (d) $-x > -8$

4. What are the total degrees of freedom, if the number of species are 5, total streams are 2, stream temperature 2, stream pressure 2 and heat released 1?
(a) 1 (b) 12
(c) 5 (d) 6

5. In a 600 m race, player A beats player B by 37.5 m or 10 sec. What is time taken by B to complete the race?
(a) 512 sec
(b) 155 sec
(b) 125 sec
(d) 160 sec

6. A bag contains 2 white and 4 black balls. A ball is drawn 5 times with replacement. The probability that atleast 4 of the balls drawn are white is
(a) $\frac{8}{243}$ (b) $\frac{10}{243}$
(c) $\frac{11}{243}$ (d) $\frac{32}{243}$

7. If X has a poisson distribution such that $P(X=1)=P(X=2)$ and $e^{-2}=0.1353$, then $P(X=4)$ is

(a) 0.0213 (b) 0.9787

(c) 0.0902 (d) 0.9098

8. If A and B are square matrices of same order, then $(A+B)(A-B)$ is equal to

(a) $A^2-AB+BA-B^2$

(b) A^2-B^2

(c) $A^2-BA-AB+B^2$

(d) $A^2+AB-BA+B^2$

9. If $\begin{vmatrix} 2 & 3 & 2 \\ x & x & x \\ 4 & 9 & 1 \end{vmatrix}+3=0$, then the value of x is

(a) 3 (b) 0

(c) −1 (d) 1

10. The function $f(x)=x^2e^{-x}$ strictly increases on

(a) $[0, 2]$ (b) $[0, \infty)$

(c) $(-\infty, 0] \cup [2, \infty)$ (d) None of these

11. Integrating factor of the differential equation $(1-y^2)\frac{dx}{dy}+xy=ay$ is

(a) $\frac{1}{1-y^2}$ (b) $\frac{1}{\sqrt{1-y^2}}$

(c) $\frac{1}{\sqrt{y^2-1}}$ (d) $\frac{1}{y^2-1}$

12. The present value of a perpetuity of ₹ 750 payable at the beginning of each year, if money is worth 5% p.a., is

(a) ₹ 15000 (b) ₹ 15750

(c) ₹ 14250 (d) None of these

13. What sum of money is needed to invest now, as to get ₹ 10000 at the beginning of every month forever, if the money is worth 8% per annum compounded quarterly?

(a) ₹ 51000 (b) ₹ 15000

(c) ₹ 53456 (d) ₹ 61000

14. The demand of a product over 6 weeks is 180, 280, 250, 190, 240, 240. If 3 month moving averages is x and 5 month moving average is y, then $(x+y)$ is

(a) 245 (b) 563.34

(c) 463.34 (d) 444

15. The area of the region bounded by the curve $x=2y+3$ and the lines $y=1$ and $y=-1$ is

(a) 4 sq units

(b) $\frac{3}{2}$ sq units

(c) 6 sq units

(d) 8 sq units

16. If $y=e^x+e^{-x}$ and $\frac{d^2y}{dx^2}=\frac{y}{k}$, then k is equal to

(a) 1 (b) 3

(c) 4 (d) 2

17. The maximum value of Z for the problem maximise $Z=2x+y$ subject to constraints $x+y \le 2$, $x \ge 0$, $y \ge 0$ is

(a) 4 (b) 3

(c) 1 (d) 0

18. The annual depreciation of a car is ₹ 30000, if the scrap value of the car after 15 yr is ₹ 50000, then original cost of the car, when depreciation is linear.

(a) ₹ 600000 (b) ₹ 450000

(c) ₹ 495000 (d) ₹ 500000

Assertion-Reason Based Questions

Directions *In the question number 19 and 20, a statement of Assertion (A) is followed by a statement of Reason (R). Choose the correct option.*

(a) Both (A) and (R) are true and (R) is the correct explanation of (A).

(b) Both (A) and (R) are true but (R) is not the correct explanation of (A).

(c) (A) is true, but (R) is false.

(d) (A) is false, but (R) is true.

19. **Assertion** (A) If x is real, then the minimum value of $x^2-8x+17$ is 1.

Reason (R) If $f''(x)>0$ at critical point, then the value of the function at critical point will be the minimum value of the function.

20. **Assertion** (A) The experiment of tossing a coin three times is said to have binomial distribution.

Reason (R) A die is thrown 5 times, then the probability that an odd number will come up exactly three times is $\frac{5}{16}$.

SECTION B

[This section comprises of very short answer type questions (VSA) of 2 marks each]

21. (a) From the following matrix equation, find the value of x and y.

$$\begin{bmatrix} x+y & 4 \\ -5 & 3y \end{bmatrix} = \begin{bmatrix} 3 & 4 \\ -5 & 6 \end{bmatrix}$$

Or

(b) If $A = \begin{bmatrix} 2 & 0 & 1 \\ 2 & 1 & 3 \\ 1 & -1 & 0 \end{bmatrix}$, then find the values of $(A^2 - 5A)$.

22. Solve the following system of equations using Cramer's rule

$$5x - 7y + z = 11,$$
$$6x - 8y - z = 15$$
and $$3x + 2y - 6z = 7$$

23. Find the solution of the following linear programming problem (if it exists) graphically

Maximize $Z = 5x + 3y$

Subject to the constraints

$$3x + 5y \le 15$$
$$5x + 2y \le 10$$
$$x, y \ge 0$$

24. Find the present value of a sequence of payments of ₹ 8000 made at the end of each 6 months, continuing forever, if money is worth 5% compounded semi-annually.

25. (a) Mrs. Jyothsna invested ₹ 35000 in a mutual fund. In 2015, the value of mutual fund increased to ₹ 56000. In 2020, find the CAGR.

Or

(b) Assume an investment's starting value is ₹ 10000 and it grows to ₹ 22050 in 3 yr. Calculate CAGR (Compounded Annual Growth Rate).

(use : $(2.205)^{1/3} = 1.3016$)

SECTION C

[This section comprises of short answer type questions (SA) of 3 marks each]

26. A bottle is full of dettol. One third of it is taken out and then an equal amount of water is poured into the bottle to fill it. This operation is repeated four times. Find the final ratio of dettol and water in the bottle.

27. (a) Sketch the region bounded by $y = 2x - x^2$ and X-axis and find its area using integration.

Or

(b) Evaluate : $\int_0^1 x \log(1 + 2x)\, dx$

28. Find the differential equation of the family of circles having their centres on X-axis.

29. Find the probability distribution of the number of sixes in three throws of a die. Also, find the mean of the distribution.

30. The mean weekly sales of soap bars in departmental stores were 146.3 bars per store. After an advertising campaign the mean weekly sales in 400 stores for a typical week increased to 153.7 and showed a standard deviation of 17.2. Was the advertising campaign successful?

31. (a) Rajesh purchased a house from a company for ₹ 2500000 and made a down payment of ₹ 500000. He repays the balance in 25 yr by monthly installments at the rate of 9% per annum compounded monthly

(i) What are the monthly payment?

(ii) What is the total interest payment?

[given $(1.0075)^{-300} = 0.1062$]

Or

(b) The cost of a washing machine depreciates by ₹ 720 during the second year and by ₹ 648 during the third year. Calculate

(i) the rate of depreciation per annum.

(ii) the value of machine at the end of third year.

SECTION D

[This section comprises of long answer type questions (LA) of 5 marks each]

32. A cistern has three pipes A, B and C. Pipes A and B are inlet pipes whereas C is an outlet pipe. Pipes A and B can fill the cistern separately in 4 h and 5 h respectively, while pipe C can empty it in 2 h. If the pipes A, B and C are opened in order at 1, 2 and 3 am, respectively. When will the cistern be empty?

33. (a) Find the intervals in which the following function f is strictly increasing or strictly decreasing $f(x) = 3x^4 - 4x^3 - 12x^2 + 5$

Or

(b) Find the points of local maxima and minima of the function $f(x) = 3x^4 - 4x^3 + 5$ in $[-1, 2]$.

34. (a) Let X be a discrete random variable, whose probability distribution is defined as follows

$$P(X=x)=\begin{cases} k(x+1), & \text{for } x=1,2,3,4 \\ 2kx, & \text{for } x=5,6,7 \\ 0, & \text{otherwise} \end{cases}$$

where k is a constant.

Find

(i) k

(ii) $E(X)$

(iii) Standard deviation of X.

Or

(b) A manufacturer of cotter pins knows that 4% of his product is defective. If he sells pins in boxes of 100 and guarantees that not more than 3 pins will be defective, what is the approximate probability that a box will fail to meet the guaranteed quality?

[given $e^{-4}=0.01832$]

35. Ravi borrowed ₹ 1000000 from a bank to purchase a house and decided to repay by monthly equal installments in 10 yr. The bank charges interest at 9% compounded monthly. Find his EMI and total interest paid.

[given $(1.0075)^{-120}=(0.407937305)$]

SECTION E

[This section comprises 3 case-study/passage based questions of 4 marks each]

36. The following data shows the percentage of rural, urban and suburban Indians who have a high speed internet connection at home.

Year	Rural	Urban	Suburban
2001	3	9	9
2002	6	18	17
2003	9	21	23
2004	16	29	29
2005	24	38	40

Based on the above information, answer the following questions.

(i) Determine the equation of straight line trend for the rural Indians.

(ii) Determine the equation of straight line trend for the urban Indians.

(iii) (a) What is the forecast for the year 2006 for urban group using trend equation?

Or

(b) What is the forecast for the year 2006 for rural group using trend equation?

37. Deepa rides her car at 25 km/hr. She has to spend ₹ 2 per km on diesel and if she rides it at a faster speed of 40 km/hr, the diesel cost increases to ₹ 5 per km. She has ₹ 100 to spend on diesel. Let she travels x kms with speed 25 km/hr and y kms with speed 40 km/hr. The feasible region for the LPP is shown below.

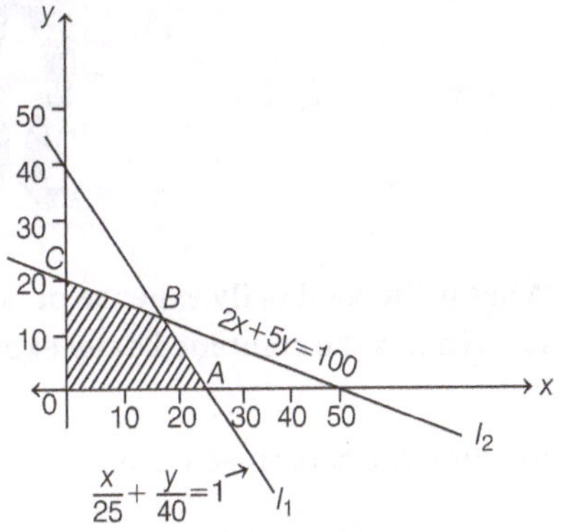

Based on the above information, answer the following questions.

(i) What is the point of intersection of line l_1 and l_2?

(ii) (a) If $Z=6x-9y$ be the objective function, then what is the maximum value of Z?

Or

(b) If $Z=6x+3y$ be the objective function, then what is the minimum value of Z?

(iii) Write all the corner points of the feasible region shown in the above graph.

38. There are three families A, B and C. The number of members in these families are given in the table below.

	Men	Women	Children
Family A	3	2	1
Family B	2	4	2
Family C	4	3	2

The daily expenses of each man, woman and child are respectively ₹ 200, ₹ 100 and ₹ 50.

(i) What is the total daily expense of family A?

(ii) (a) What is the combined daily expense of all women?

Or

(b) Find the combined expense of men in family A and children in family C.

Answers

Sample Paper 1

1. (d)	2. (b)	3. (b)	4. (a)
5. (a)	6. (b)	7. (d)	8. (a)
9. (d)	10. (a)	11. (b)	12. (a)
13. (b)	14. (c)	15. (b)	16. (a)
17. (b)	18. (d)	19. (b)	20. (d)

21. (b) $x = 1, \ y = -1$ 22. $x = 7, \ y = -3$
23. $x = 10, \ y = 2$ and $z = 560$
24. 8.5%
25. (a) ₹ 4320 (b) ₹ 500000
26. 58 L
27. (a) $\frac{4}{3}$ sq units (b) $\frac{e^2}{2} - e$
28. $x\left\{y\frac{d^2y}{dx^2} + \left(\frac{dy}{dx}\right)^2\right\} = y\frac{dy}{dx}$
29. $E(X) = \frac{7}{10}$, $\text{Var}(X) = \frac{21}{100}$
30. Sample is not taken from the population having 56 as mean
31. (a) (i) 14.8% pa (ii) 14.52% pa
    (b) (i) 6.16% (ii) 5.13%
32. 120 h
33. (a) (i) 2 (ii) $\frac{2}{3\sqrt{3}}$
    (b) $f(x)$ is strictly increasing in the interval $(-2, 1) \cup (3, \infty)$ and $f(x)$ is strictly decreasing in the interval $(-\infty, -2) \cup (1, 3)$
34. (a) (i) $\frac{8}{15}$ (ii) $\frac{14}{15}$ (iii) 1 (b) 0.0821
35. (i) ₹ 4615.58 (ii) ₹ 834 674
36. (i) $x + 2y \le 12$
    (ii) (a) 4 units (b) 4 units
    (iii) Corner points of the feasible region are (5, 0), (6, 0), (4, 4), (0, 6) and (0, 4)
37. (i) $y_t = 11.6 + 5.2x$ and $y_t = 23.6 + 7.4x$
    (ii) (a) 27.2% (b) 43.7%
38. (i) 3
    (ii) (a) Can not determine (b) 3
    (iii) $\frac{x^3}{3} + \frac{1}{y} + C = 0$

Sample Paper 2

1. (b)	2. (b)	3. (a)	4. (d)
5. (d)	6. (d)	7. (b)	8. (a)
9. (b)	10. (d)	11. (c)	12. (a)
13. (b)	14. (c)	15. (d)	16. (c)
17. (a)	18. (b)	19. (a)	20. (b)

21. $x = \frac{7}{5}, \ y = \frac{4}{5}$
22. (a) 1 (b) 0
23. 10, (0, 2)
24. ₹ 18000
25. (a) 12.5% (b) 12.4%
26. (a) 2 (b) $\log\left(\frac{2e-1}{e}\right)$
27. $x\left(\frac{dy}{dx}\right)^2 + xy\frac{d^2y}{dx^2} - y\frac{dy}{dx} = 0$
28. (a) (i) 5% p.a. (ii) ₹ 16000 (iii) ₹5729.60
    (b) 11.89 yr
29. 0.8399
30. 72.9 L
31. Yes
32. (a) $(-\infty, -1] \cup [0, 2]$
    (b) local maxima : (1, −3)
    local minima : (6, −128)
33. (a) (i) $\frac{1}{44}$ (ii) $\frac{7}{22}$
    (iii) $\frac{15}{22}$ (b) 0.2
34. 60 h
35. ₹ 650002
36. (i) $3x + 2y = 2300, \ 5x + 3y = 3700$
    (ii) $\begin{bmatrix} 3 & 2 \\ 5 & 3 \end{bmatrix}\begin{bmatrix} x \\ y \end{bmatrix} = \begin{bmatrix} 2300 \\ 3700 \end{bmatrix}$
    (ii) (a) $\begin{bmatrix} -3 & 2 \\ 5 & -3 \end{bmatrix}$
    (b) $x = 500, \ y = 400$
37. (i) $x \ge 0, \ y \ge 0$
    (ii) 100
    (iii) (a) $2x + y \le 50, \ x + 2y \le 40$
    (b) 75

38. (i) $y_t = 138.86 + 7.64x$

(ii) (a)

Year	2004	2005	2006	2007	2008	2009	2010
Trend values	115.94	123.58	131.22	138.86	146.50	154.14	161.78

(b) $y = 45.143 + 1.036x$

Year	2000	2001	2002	2003	2004	2005	2006
Trend values	42.03	43.07	44.11	45.14	46.18	47.21	48.25

Sample Paper 3

1. (b)	**2.** (d)	**3.** (c)	**4.** (b)
5. (d)	**6.** (c)	**7.** (c)	**8.** (a)
9. (c)	**10.** (a)	**11.** (b)	**12.** (b)
13. (a)	**14.** (c)	**15.** (c)	**16.** (a)
17. (a)	**18.** (d)	**19.** (a)	**20.** (b)

21. (a) $x = 1,\ y = 2$ *Or* (b) $\begin{bmatrix} -5 & -1 & -3 \\ -1 & -7 & -10 \\ -5 & 4 & -2 \end{bmatrix}$

22. $x = 1,\ y = -1,\ z = -1$

23. $x = \frac{20}{19},\ y = \frac{45}{19},\ z = \frac{235}{19}$

24. ₹ 320000

25. (a) 9.8% *Or* (b) 30.16%

26. 16 : 65

27. (a) $\frac{4}{3}$ sq units *Or* (b) $\frac{3}{8}\log 3$

28. $y\frac{d^2y}{dx^2} + \left(\frac{dy}{dx}\right)^2 + 1 = 0$

29.

X	0	1	2	3
$P(X)$	$\frac{125}{216}$	$\frac{75}{216}$	$\frac{15}{216}$	$\frac{1}{216}$

, $\frac{1}{2}$

30. Yes ($\because Z = 8.605$)

31. (a) (i) ₹ 16782.27 (ii) ₹ 3034681

Or

(b) (i) 10% pa (ii) ₹ 5832

32. 11 am

33. (a) $[-1, 0] \cup [2, \infty)$ and $(-\infty, -1] \cup [0, 2]$

Or

(b) Local minima at $x = 1$, local maxima at $x = -1, 2$

34. (a) (i) $\frac{1}{50}$ (ii) 5.2 (iii) 1.708

Or

(b) 0.56636

35. ₹ 12668, ₹ 520160

36. (i) $y_t = 11.6 + 5.2x$

(ii) $y_t = 23 + 6.9x$

(iii) (a) 43.7% *Or* (b) 27.2%

37. (i) $\left(\frac{50}{3}, \frac{40}{3}\right)$ (ii) (a) 150 *Or* (b) 0

(iii) $O(0, 0)$, $A(25, 0)$, $B\left(\frac{50}{3}, \frac{40}{3}\right)$, $C(0, 20)$

38. (i) ₹ 850 (ii) (a) ₹ 900 *Or* (b) ₹ 700